76530

D1557340

PEARL HARBOR AS HISTORY

Studies of the East Asian Institute
Columbia University

PEARL HARBOR
AS
HISTORY

Japanese-American Relations
1931-1941

Edited by

Dorothy Borg *and* Shumpei Okamoto
with the assistance of
Dale K. A. Finlayson

Columbia University Press

New York

Library of Congress Cataloging in Publication Data

Borg, Dorothy, 1902—
    Pearl Harbor as history.

    1. United States—Foreign relations—Japan. 2. Japan—Foreign relations—United States.
3. Pearl Harbor, Attack on, 1941. I. Okamoto, Shumpei, joint author.
II. Title.
E183.8.J3B67   327.73'052   72-10996
ISBN 0-231-03734-1   *Clothbound*
ISBN 0-231-03890-9   *Paperbound*
Second paperback and third cloth printing.
Copyright © 1973 Columbia University Press

Printed in the United States of America

To the memory of

JOHN M. H. LINDBECK
1915-1971

The best of men is like water;
*   Water benefits all things*
*   And does not compete with them.*
It dwells in (the lowly) places that all
*   disdain—*
Wherein it comes near to the Tao.

In his dwelling, (the Sage) loves the
*   (lowly) earth;*
In his heart, he loves what is profound;
In his relations with others, he loves
*   kindness;*
In his words, he loves sincerity;
In government, he loves peace;
In business affairs, he loves ability;
In his actions, he loves choosing the
*   right time.*
It is because he does not contend that
*   he is without reproach.*

—Lao Tzu

THE EAST ASIAN INSTITUTE OF COLUMBIA UNIVERSITY

The East Asian Institute of Columbia University was established in 1949 to prepare graduate students for careers dealing with East Asia, and to aid research and publication on East Asia during the modern period. The faculty of the Institute are grateful to the Ford Foundation and the Rockefeller Foundation for their financial assistance.

The Studies of the East Asian Institute were inaugurated in 1962 to bring to a wider public the results of significant new research on modern and contemporary East Asia.

CONTENTS

PREFACE

The essays published in this volume were presented at a binational conference held at Lake Kawaguchi, Japan, July 14-18, 1969.

The idea for the Kawaguchi project originated in late 1966 when, at the invitation of the American Historical Association, Professor Hosoya Chihiro of Hitotsubashi University came to the United States to deliver a paper on "Pearl Harbor: Twenty-Five Years After" at the Association's annual meeting. During the course of his visit, various meetings were held to consider the possibility of launching an enterprise in which Japanese and American scholars would cooperate in the study of some aspect of American-Japanese relations. As Richard W. Leopold indicates in his "Historiographical Reflections," which reviews the entire Kawaguchi project, plans for the papers and the conference soon took shape.

The East Asian Institute of Columbia University administered and financed the American side of the project. In Japan a committee was established to take charge of organizing the conference. The Japanese expenses were covered by the International House of Japan with assistance from the Science Research Fund of the Ministry of Education and the American Studies Foundation.

The staggering number of tasks that inevitably develop in connection with an undertaking of this magnitude were divided between the Japanese and the Americans. The Japanese assumed full responsibility for the running of the conference itself, which they did with an efficiency and thoughtfulness that can rarely have been equalled in the long annals of international meetings.

The Japanese edition of the Kawaguchi papers has been published in four volumes by the University of Tokyo Press. For its publication the press was the recipient in 1972 of one of Japan's most prestigious publishing awards, the Mainichi Special Book Prize (Mainichi Shuppan Bunka Tokubetsushō). The Japanese edition has also received the Yoshida Prize, awarded by the Yoshida Shigeru Commemoration Foundation for the best book in the field of Japanese history and diplomacy produced in the preceding year. It includes an edited version of the conference proceedings, which were compiled from the original tapes with singular ability and care by Michael K. Blaker and Dale K.A.

Finlayson. Because of lack of space it has not been possible to incorporate the proceedings here, but the English version has been issued separately by the East Asian Institute under the title "Proceedings of the Conference on Japanese-American Relations, 1931-1941."

Of all the positive memories that the participants carried away from the Kawaguchi Conference, one has become associated with deep sorrow. John M.H. Lindbeck, the director of the East Asian Institute, who was chairman of the American delegation to the conference, died suddenly on January 9, 1971. With an abiding awareness of the extraordinary qualities he brought to every task he performed, this volume is dedicated to him. The text of the poem by Lao Tzu was read at the memorial service at Columbia University.

Dorothy Borg
Shumpei Okamoto

INTRODUCTION

Pearl Harbor as History is part of the historiography of World War II. By now the literature on the causes of the war between the United States and Japan is far too voluminous to be discussed in anything short of a bibliographical essay, of which there are already several, some of very recent vintage, that are unusually good.* The following is therefore not an effort to review the literature but rather to isolate certain broad historiographical trends and to indicate how the Kawaguchi project related to them.

In the long, emotional aftermath of World War I a substantial number of American historians, reflecting the disillusionment of their country with the war, soon ceased to regard their former enemies as wholly or even largely responsible for the United States' intervention in 1917. Instead they attached a major share of the blame to America's allies and to individuals and groups within the United States. The ensuing debate, which throughout the interwar years dominated a large part of the writing on the foreign policy of the United States, often seemed to generate little more than revisionist rhetoric. But in retrospect it is apparent that it also stimulated some highly challenging criticism of the conduct of American foreign relations which was to have a far-reaching effect. Nevertheless, the intensity of feeling surrounding the controversy made it virtually impossible to achieve a balanced account of the developments that led to the United States' entry into World War I. Gradually, however, several outstanding historians emerged who were not concerned with either condemning or condoning the United States and its allies or its enemies but who sought to understand American intervention in terms of the many complex factors that affected both sides. As time and an even greater war obscured earlier events, historians came, as Ernest May has said, "to deal with World War I much as with the Punic and Napoleonic wars."

The aftermath of World War II was very different. In the late 1940s and the 1950s the great majority of American historians continued to believe that an overwhelming share of the guilt for the war rested with Hitler's Germany and that the United States had been compelled to do what it could to protect its

---

*The most recent is the essay by Louis Morton in *American-East Asian Relations: A Survey*, edited by Ernest R. May and James C. Thomson, Jr. (Cambridge: Harvard University Press, 1972).

own security. Since the anger and revulsion against the Nazis extended into the immediate postwar period, it might be presumed that this belief was largely a matter of emotions; yet, despite the passage of thirty years it remains widespread today. While it is true that a group of historians, consisting for the most part of men who had been revisionists after World War I, became revisionists after World War II, even they tended to narrow their criticisms to personal, although often virulent, attacks on President Roosevelt. For the large number of historians for whom revisionism had no appeal, the main question was and has remained, not why the United States entered the war against Germany, but why it did not do so earlier.

But even though American historians generally regarded the war between the United States and Germany as a clear-cut case of self-protection versus aggression, they might have viewed the war between the United States and Japan differently. Indeed, perhaps they would have done so if there had been in the United States a substantial number of specialists on American-Japanese relations to draw the necessary distinction between the relationship of the United States with Germany and with Japan. But such specialists were a rarity until well into the postwar era. In any event, the great majority of American historians probably shared the view of the public at large during the war and the succeeding years.

Throughout the course of the hostilities Americans by and large looked upon Japan primarily as the close and faithful partner of Germany. Since as a result of their many connections with Europe they had a considerable knowledge of Germany and since they lacked any comparable knowledge of Japan, they came, perhaps inevitably, to see the Japanese in the image of the Nazis. They therefore readily concluded that the Japanese were responsible for the war to the same extent and for largely the same reasons as the Germans.

In the emotional backwash of the war this attitude continued after the fighting in Europe and Asia was over. The war crimes trials conducted in Tokyo from 1946 to 1948 were little more than an echo of the far more famous proceedings held at Nuremberg. Applying the conspiracy thesis that had played a prominent part in the trials against the Nazi leaders, the International Military Tribunal for the Far East concluded that from 1928 to 1945 the Japanese defendants had been engaged in a conspiracy designed to secure Japanese domination of East Asia, the western and southwestern Pacific Ocean and the Indian Ocean, and certain islands in these areas. It rejected categorically all the charges of the Japanese against their former enemies, especially the United States, and contended that part of the Japanese conspiracy had been to wage aggressive war against the allied powers.

Some of the historians of the 1950s sought to achieve a more dispassionate view of the events leading to Pearl Harbor than that of the International Military Tribunal. In the introduction to *The Challenge to Isolation* and *The Undeclared War*, Langer and Gleason stated that their objective had been to present a "thorough analysis of all the circumstances and developments" related to the United States' entry into World War II in order to provide a basis for "understanding and evaluating" the historical forces at work. But despite the rare excellence of their study it is doubtful whether in dealing with Japanese-American relations the goal which they set for themselves could have been attained so near the end of the hostilities. Moreover, the difficulty was compounded as Langer and Gleason, like most of the leading historians of the 1950s who wrote about the coming of the war, were primarily specialists in European and American rather than Asian history.

Basically Langer and Gleason's thesis was that a small group of officials, mostly representative of the military, were in control of the Japanese government and pursued an expansionist policy that left the United States little choice but to defend its interests by fighting. A similar thesis ran through Herbert Feis' *The Road to Pearl Harbor*, also published in the 1950s. But such an interpretation overlooked many fundamental questions that have since been raised about American policy. And while it marked an advance over the International Military Tribunal's conspiracy theory, it still seemed to rest on the assumption that fundamentally the Japanese could be understood in the same terms as the Nazis. In sum, even the outstanding historians of the 1950s, inevitably influenced by the emotional legacy of the years of hostilities and lacking the kind of specialized knowledge of American-Japanese relations that might have had a moderating influence, were unable to see Pearl Harbor as though—like the Punic and Napoleonic wars—it had passed into history.

Langer and Gleason's two volumes and *The Road to Pearl Harbor* are still regarded as the foremost books on the coming of the war between Japan and the United States. In 1958 Paul W. Schroeder published a revisionist study, *The Axis Alliance and Japanese-American Relations, 1941*, a thoroughly scholarly work that has justly received considerable attention. Nevertheless, it too bears signs of having been written in the shadow of wartime attitudes. In essence, Schroeder contended that the war was "unnecessary and avoidable" and came about chiefly because of the obsessive moralism of United States foreign policy, especially as personified by Secretary of State Hull. While this argument served as a useful corrective to the conventional concept of Japanese war guilt, it presented a version of the causes of the war that was also oversimplified and one-sided, although it shifted the blame from Japan to the United States. In addition, as Schroeder too had no particular expertise in the Asian field, he dealt chiefly with events in America.

Beginning with the early 1960s an effort was made to reexamine the period before Pearl Harbor with attitudes that were free of the tensions generated by the war. The effort was limited largely to a few members of a new group of scholars, part of the post-Pearl Harbor generation, who had been trained as specialists in Japanese history. Their books on the whole were less concerned with the entire issue of responsibility for the war than with trying to obtain a fuller understanding of what happened in Japan. But just as proverbially a few swallows do not a summer make, a few historians are not necessarily harbingers of a new trend in the writing of history. Furthermore, while the specialists on European and American history had focused on developments in the United States, the specialists on Japanese history focused mainly on developments in Japan. This meant that historians were still not viewing American-Japanese relations equally from both sides.

Given this background, it was natural that at the outset of the Kawaguchi project the participants expected the papers and the discussions at the conference to be strongly influenced by the attitudes that had developed in the climate of the war and its immediate aftermath. The Japanese expected the American historians to hold what they regarded as the standard American opinion: that Japan's inordinate desire for power had made an all-out conflict with the United States inevitable. The Americans, on their part, felt that as a result of all that had happened between the two countries, the Japanese might be critical of the United States to an extent that would make it difficult to find any common ground.

It soon became apparent that these expectations were wide of the mark and that all the participants in the Kawaguchi project, whether American or Japanese, had much the same point of view. They believed the causes of the war had been far more numerous and difficult to discern than many of the earlier historians had recognized and that blame for the war could not be attributed primarily to either the United States or Japan. They felt that a deeper understanding was needed, not only of events just before the outbreak of hostilities, but more especially of the political, economic, and cultural factors in Japanese and American society that in the end made the war inescapable. They were also convinced that in the future historians would have to proceed on the assumption that formed the basis of the Kawaguchi project, namely, that American-Japanese relations were a two-way street that had constantly to be looked at from both ends.

These concepts dominated the whole of the Kawaguchi project, which therefore, in terms of the historiography of World War II, provided a further indication that a new trend in writing about the causes of the Japanese-American war had in fact set in. In other words, the Kawaguchi papers and the conference discussions served to demonstrate that the period of Pearl Harbor, like other important periods that gradually receded into the past, had come to be dealt with as history.

Because of the repeated references in the foregoing pages to the difficulty of seeing American-Japanese relations in American and Japanese terms alike, it seems pertinent to add a few comments about the current effort to improve American-East Asian studies and its connection with the Kawaguchi project.

In the past the study of American-East Asian relations might logically have been the particular concern of two groups of historians in the United States: those who specialized in American foreign policy and those who specialized in related aspects of East Asian history. But despite a number of outstanding exceptions, American diplomatic historians were generally reluctant to engage in any extensive research on American-East Asian relations because of their lack of training in the Asian field. Understanding the interaction of the United States with another Western country seemed hard enough without attempting to comprehend its relations with an Asian nation which in language, culture, and many other fundamental respects was profoundly different from anything in the American experience.

The reluctance of the American diplomatic historians was more than matched by the East Asian specialists. Latecomers to the family of professional historians in the United States, they tended to devote themselves to research on Japanese or Chinese history with a sense of commitment that precluded wandering into neighboring areas. Moreover, the expertise the American diplomatic historians lacked in regard to Asian history, the East Asian specialists lacked in regard to the history of United States foreign relations.

It was not until the latter part of the 1960s that an organized effort to develop American-East Asian studies got under way. A series of meetings was held in which both specialists on American diplomacy and on Japanese or Chinese history participated. As a result, the American Historical Association established the Committee on American-East Asian Relations, which has sought to define and to suggest solutions for some of the main problems in the field. Meanwhile, a growing number of universities have instituted Ph.D. programs in American-East Asian studies, following a precedent originally set by Harvard, Duke, and a few other graduate schools.

A large part of these activities has been directed toward encouraging the use of a variety of methods in studying American-East Asian relations. Much emphasis has been placed upon the value of training a new type of scholar with an expertise in both American and Japanese or Chinese history. From the beginning the Committee on American-East Asian Relations has been convinced of the vital importance of such training, and the increase in Ph.D. programs allowing for a dual specialization indicates a developing interest in the universities.

Another approach to the study of American-East Asian relations that has been stressed from the start is cooperation between historians who could present the American half and those who could present the Asian half of the American-East Asian equation. Such cooperation, it was recognized, could be between individual scholars or between groups of scholars; the scholars might all be Americans or they might be Americans and Asians.

It was in accordance with the latter idea that the Kawaguchi project was organized. The project was, in short, an experiment in pooling the expertise of a group of American and Japanese scholars with the objective of presenting a comprehensive picture of American-Japanese relations in the decade before Pearl Harbor. As Richard W. Leopold states in his "Historiographical Reflections," for a variety of reasons the experiment only partially realized its goal. While the Kawaguchi project may therefore seem just another of the ceaseless reminders that what is human is not likely to be perfect, it nevertheless showed that as a tool for the study of American-East Asian relations an undertaking of this nature can attain results that simply could not be achieved in any other way.

HISTORIOGRAPHICAL REFLECTIONS

Richard W. Leopold

Do the aims of this conference appear as sound in retrospect as they did in prospect? Three years ago it seemed desirable to explore new methods for enriching the study of Japanese-American relations, taking into account differences in culture, political process, and governmental structure. Scholarship in this area, it was felt, had been handicapped by the language barrier and a dearth of monographs. Encouragement must be given, it was asserted, to training more diplomatic historians who could read both Japanese and English and who could write with authority about the domestic scene in both countries. A more comprehensive and more comprehensible story might be told, it was believed, if a group of Japanese and a group of American specialists, working along parallel lines, examined through prepared papers and joint discussion the operations of their governments during a limited period of time.

The planners of the conference quickly settled on the years from 1931 to 1941. After discussing several alternatives—biographical, functional, and conceptual—they agreed that the institutional approach would yield the most novel information as well as open the door to the widest variety of questions. They envisaged paired essays on the corresponding institutions and organizations that took part in decision making in the two countries. Although each author would address himself generally to the entire decade, he would focus attention at three points within that ten year span. In analyzing the State, War, and Navy departments and their Japanese counterparts, for example, certain questions would be raised. How was the institution organized? What were the characteristics of the people who kept it functioning? Who were the key individuals and how did they relate to each other? How did they define the complex international issues? Did institutional weaknesses play a significant role in the Japanese-American confrontation?

Very early, then, the project was being described as one involving "the comparative study of the foreign policy decision making process" in which the

1

approach would be "institutional." Three rough sub-periods were chosen: September 1931 to March 1933 (the Mukden episode to Japan's withdrawal from the League of Nations), July 1937 to January 1940 (the outbreak of the Sino-Japanese War to the abrogation of the Japanese-American trade treaty), and September 1940 to December 1941 (the signing of the Tripartite Pact to the raid on Pearl Harbor). Participants were urged to analyze their institutions with particular reference to the organs responsible for handling Japanese-American problems. They were asked to examine the bureaucracy with respect to social origins and professional training, with respect to factionalism among its members, and with respect to the senses of value and internal norms within the group. Also to be dealt with was the question of images—the images each nation had of itself and of the other. It was hoped that something might be said about the manner in which each country conducted diplomacy, tried to maintain civilian supremacy, and kept open channels of information. Finally, each author was to appraise the place of Japanese-American relations in the totality of the foreign policies of the two governments.

Several criteria may be used to judge the success of the undertaking. Was the period chosen wisely? Did the papers conform to the original suggestions? What new methods were employed, what new data was unearthed, what new interpretations emerged? Which hypotheses and which conclusions merit further investigation? Was the discussion constructive? Has the foundation been laid for a comparative study of institutions in the decision making process?

At first glance the period appears to be well chosen. It is neither too long nor too short. It has a definable beginning and end. It witnessed change, and this change culminated in war. It is far enough back in time so that most of the American unpublished sources, private and governmental, are open for research. Studies of United States policy during the decade are numerous and, on some topics, of high quality. Not many American specialists concerned with the Washington side of the story have, however, drawn upon materials in Japanese, primary or secondary, and the records of the International Military Tribunal for the Far East have been shown to be an unreliable substitute. For the Japanese side of the story, there are a few excellent books in English based on Japanese manuscript collections and published works, but the language barrier makes those collections and works unusable to most Western scholars.

Given the nature of the studies in print, the focus of the conference made good sense. Institutional history has attracted all too few practitioners in the United States, and historians of its diplomacy have tended to concentrate on policymaking at the very highest level. Hence, an examination of how decisions were reached by the entire range of presidential advisers, at different levels within the State Department, in the several departments in Washington or at the embassy in Tokyo, or in the chambers on Capitol Hill, would not duplicate work already done. Even more important, the institutional approach would enlighten United States historians on the functioning of the Japanese government, a subject on which they have been greatly uninformed and, sometimes, misinformed. Admittedly, parallel endeavors on relatively short notice and by persons largely unknown to each other could not ensure a consistently comparative treatment, much less a true collaboration, but it might bring into clearer view than hitherto the manner in which both nations accepted the appeal to arms.

During the proceedings at Lake Kawaguchi each participant had an opportunity to make an opening statement, designed to pinpoint and (in some cases) to expand the main findings of his research and also to pose questions for his opposite number. These remarks, questions, and answers helped greatly in attaining some of the objectives of the conference. The historiographical reflections which follow will appraise the contribution of each American paper, draw comparisons with the Japanese counterpart, indicate the nature of the discussion that ensued, and offer observations on the larger meaning of the conference.

* * *

The difficulties inherent in the institutional and comparative approach appear at once in the first pair of essays. By its very title Norman A. Graebner's "Hoover, Roosevelt, and the Japanese" suggests a different emphasis from Imai Seiichi's "Cabinet, Emperor, and Senior Statesmen." Using with discrimination the best secondary works and printed sources as well as the Roosevelt papers at Hyde Park, Graebner has fashioned a clear, succinct, and balanced narrative on how two very different presidents responded to the challenge raised by Japan. Though both men wished to avoid armed conflict in Asia and though there was continuity in such policies as nonrecognition and the Nine Power Treaty, the situation changed greatly between 1931 and 1941. When diplomacy failed to halt the assaults on China and later on Indochina, the United States resorted gradually to economic pressure, confident that Japan was so vulnerable to embargoes and boycotts that its government would be compelled to abandon defiance of the status quo. Firmness in Washington, it was believed, would lead to irresolution and retreat in Tokyo. In the end, Graebner concludes, the Roosevelt administration accepted war not to defend China but to uphold the principle of peaceful change and to maintain a balance of power in East and Southeast Asia at a time when Germany threatened to dominate Europe for years to come.

Imai's essay represents a double assignment, his own dealing with the prime minister and cabinet and that of Yasui Tatsuya covering the emperor, the senior statesmen, and the Privy Council. In spite of the restrictions of space and the plethora of names—there were eleven cabinets during the decade—he provides a concise historical background and a satisfying general analysis of his enlarged topic based upon his extensive research and publication on the politics and diplomacy of the Shōwa era. Three points are emphasized. One was the decline of the cabinet after the Mukden Incident and the increase in the political influence of the court, the Privy Council, the lord keeper of the privy seal, and the last genro, Prince Saionji Kimmochi. A second was the gradual replacement of those moderates by pro-military leaders, such as Konoe Fumimaro and Hiranuma Kiichirō, after February 1936. The third was the rise of the armed forces and the shaping of governmental machinery to suit their purposes. Although Imai's treatment is inevitably brief, he has produced a report that is very helpful to the average American diplomatic historian who is usually unfamiliar with Japanese institutions and personages.

In his opening statement Graebner said that he could not have written a paper similar to Imai's because the decision making process in the United States was less formal than that in Japan and could not, except on a few issues, be accurately traced. In Japan, no single individual enjoyed the free hand in foreign affairs granted to Hoover and Roosevelt by the American constitution. In these remarks, as well as in the discussion that ensued, Graebner therefore dealt less with the operations of the presidency than with the kind of policy adopted by the presidents and its effect in bringing on the war. Was American policy, he asked, at least partly responsible for what seemed to be the irrational course pursued by Japan? The commitment of the United States to maintaining the status quo, because the existing order satisfied its needs, made eventual war with Japan inevitable unless American diplomacy could have brought about a shift in Japanese policies.

It was evident in the discussion that followed Graebner's and Imai's opening statements that most of the participants, and especially those from the United States, were more interested at this point in asking why war came than in comparing differences in institutions. In general, each side seemed to be more critical of its own government than of the future enemy's, since it appeared in retrospect that an unwillingness to modify positions and an inability to devise alternatives could lead only to armed conflict. Some delegates questioned whether the decision making process in Japan was more formal, as Graebner had maintained, than in the United States. Others suggested that in Japan there was a deliberate effort to build a consensus upward and horizontally, so that no choice was left by the time final action had to be taken, whereas in Washington Roosevelt made a deliberate effort to prevent consensus before an issue reached the White House, so that he might have the freedom to choose. The precise influence of the emperor also excited disagreement.

For the second pair of papers, James C. Thomson, Jr. drew heavily upon the hitherto unused personal manuscripts of Stanley K. Hornbeck and upon interviews with a couple of retired Foreign Service officers. His essay, entitled "The Role of the Department of State," offers, first, some brief but perceptive comments on Stimson, Hull, and their inner circle and, second, a fuller description of the thinking of the Division of Far Eastern Affairs and of Hornbeck after he left the division to become adviser on political relations (Far East). The second part is the more valuable, for the decision making process in the State Department is never easy to determine. Historians can speak with some confidence about the men who occupied the highest positions from 1931 to 1941–their attitude toward Japan, their negotiating skill, and their relations with other top policymakers within the government. But little is known about what was said or done at the divisional level or below. Departmental traditions of anonymity and departmental practices in record keeping have prevented scholars thus far from analyzing how the administrative machinery really functioned during this critical decade.

Thomson concentrates on four episodes. Two of these–the response to the Manchurian crisis and the Amō press statement of April 1934–serve to provide a clearer picture of Hornbeck's ideas. A third centers on the debate in July 1940, while Hull was in Havana, over the kind of economic sanctions to apply after the Japanese advance into northern Indochina. Here Hornbeck joined the "hard-liners," Treasury Secretary Morgenthau and Secretary of War Stimson, against Undersecretary of State Welles and Maxwell M. Hamilton, chief of the Division of Far Eastern Affairs. The fourth came in February 1937, when Roosevelt asked State's views on a vague plan he had devised to replace the nonfortification clause of the recently abrogated Five Power Treaty. A long memorandum, prepared by Hamilton and concurred in by Hornbeck, raised all sorts of valid objections. Annoyed by this response from below, the president charged the department with defeatism and said he wished to talk with Hamilton. Nothing came of this request, for Hull had a way of shielding his subordinates; and when Roosevelt failed to elicit support outside of State, even from Ambassador Grew, he dropped the scheme. This experience, Thomson suggests, may have reinforced Roosevelt's natural attraction to State's bureaucratic adversaries, the more daring and ambitious "pushers and doers at the Treasury."

Usui Katsumi's "The Role of the Foreign Ministry" is a superb essay that emphasizes institutions and personalities. Well organized and clearly written, reflecting a mastery of archival materials, it manages to mention a large number of persons and still make them intelligible to the reader. It poses a question at the outset and offers an answer at the end. Was it true, Usui asks, that Hirota Kōki, who was foreign minister from September 1933 to April 1936 and from June 1937 to May 1938 (as well as prime minister from March 1936 to February 1937), tried to restrain the military but was obliged to work covertly lest he be ousted or assassinated? The reply is no, but before reaching that verdict, the author describes the use of the imperial prerogative in external affairs and the structure of the Foreign Ministry. He excels in delineating factions within the bureaucracy and in summarizing the options available to the Japanese diplomats.

Three factions struggled to control Japanese foreign policy in this decade. One, identified with Shidehara Kijūrō, was willing to cooperate with the Occidental powers and refused to treat China as if it were the special domain of Japan. It sought to promote the nation's economic interests in all of Asia but without bellicosity or antagonism toward the West. Foreign Ministers Satō Naotake, Ugaki Kazushige, and Nomura Kichisaburō belonged to this so-called Europe-America group. At the other extreme stood Shiratori Toshio and his associates. Proclaiming the doctrine of the Imperial Way, they bitterly opposed Shidehara's diplomacy, symbolized by the Washington treaties of 1921-22, and supported the army in its demands for an advance on the mainland and an alliance with Germany and Italy. Although one of their number did not become foreign minister until Matsuoka Yōsuke took office in July 1940, they did much to undermine the policies of the Europe-America bloc. Somewhere in between, but certainly closer to Shiratori's followers, was the faction that contributed foreign ministers in the persons of Uchida Yasuya, Arita Hachirō, and Hirota. It, too, insisted that Japan's special position in East Asia be recognized by the Western governments, but it preferred to pursue an independent course, free from ties with Germany, Italy, or the Soviet Union.

In his opening statement Thomson made a good case for concentrating on Hornbeck but, at the same time, warned against exaggerating his importance. Hornbeck's influence stemmed from the fact that he "had been around" longer than anyone else. He never dominated Hull; and when the lengthy discussions with Ambassador Nomura began in April 1941, the secretary relied, not on Hornbeck, but on the less committed Hamilton and his assistant Joseph W. Ballantine. In his advocacy of a tough stand against Japan, Hornbeck was not always consistent; and although he spoke constantly of an inevitable conflict, he also believed that if the United States stood firm, the leaders in Tokyo would back down rather than risk war. After Pearl Harbor Hornbeck ruefully admitted that he had been guilty of wishful thinking. In 1941 he underestimated the striking power of Japan, just as in 1931 he exaggerated the damage sanctions would cause to Japanese life. Like all too many American leaders, Thomson concluded, Hornbeck knew relatively little about the working of the Japanese government, the psychology of the Japanese military, or the nuances of the Japanese economy.

In his opening statement, Usui again argued that the military's interference in external affairs has been exaggerated by earlier writers and that the Foreign Ministry must bear equal responsibility for the course Japan pursued after 1931. He then analyzed the major sources of Japanese-American tensions, emphasizing the lack of clarity, or so it seemed in Tokyo, in United States policy toward China. Comment on the Thomson and Usui papers was deferred until the two dealing with the embassies in Washington and Tokyo had been introduced.

In "The Role of the United States Embassy in Tokyo" Akira Iriye quite naturally concentrates on Joseph C. Grew. Drawing upon the Grew Papers, Grew's published writings, the *Foreign Relations* series, the best secondary works (especially Waldo H. Heinrichs' outstanding biography of the ambassador), and some Japanese-language materials, Iriye examines the Amō statement of April 1934, the outbreak of war in July 1937, and the *Panay* incident of December 1937 to answer the following questions: Did embassy officials play a significant role or were they passive observers of events over which they had no control? What understanding of the United States' policy did the Japanese gain through the embassy? How seriously did the State Department take the embassy's judgments and recommendations? Was the embassy simply a conveyor belt or ferryboat for messages between Washington and Tokyo?

Iriye concludes that the embassy's contribution was minimal. Although Grew's estimate of Japanese political and military thinking was more objective and sophisticated—though not always correct—than that of his superiors, his advice often went unheeded. All too frequently Hull and his associates acted upon data that substantiated their preconceptions. Both governments preferred to conduct negotiations in America. All too frequently decisions were reached in Washington without consulting Grew. Thus his opinion was not sought regarding the termination of the commercial treaty in July 1939, although he was home on leave at the time, or on the proposed modus vivendi in November 1941, although the views of Churchill and Chiang Kai-shek were carefully listened to.

In his opening statement Iriye drew a few comparisons before moving to more general issues of policy. He believed that the American embassy in Tokyo was more professional in character than the Japanese embassy in Washington and that it did a better job of reporting. He discounted the charge that the influence of the so-called "China hands" in the State Department put Grew and his colleagues at a disadvantage. In his opinion the department and the embassy shared common assumptions about Japan's foreign policy. Iriye discovered no examples of factionalism within the embassy staff, although his research on subordinate officials and military attachés was overshadowed by his attention to Grew.

Hosoya Chihiro's companion piece on the Japanese embassy in Washington could not be completed in time for the conference. Hosoya had wished to focus on the early part of the decade, believing that the years 1934-35 marked a turning point in Japanese-American relations that historians have tended to neglect. He had proposed, as he made clear in his opening statement, to discuss the steps taken in Washington to lower tensions with the incoming Roosevelt administration. One of these was Ishii Kikujirō's suggestion, while en route to the World Economic Conference in May 1933, to revive the bilateral arbitration treaty of 1908, a pact that had been renewed in 1913 and 1918 before lapsing in 1923. A second was Ambassador Saitō Hiroshi's efforts in 1934 to draft a new version of the Root-Takahira Agreement. A third was the visit by Konoe and a group of scholars that same spring. None of these endeavors bore fruit, partly because Hull preferred to handle most Far Eastern issues on a multilateral basis, but largely because they were offset by the Amō statement, the notice to terminate the naval treaties, and the trend toward violence in Japanese public life.

Hosoya's paper on the role of the Foreign Ministry and the Washington embassy contains useful observations on the defective communications between Ambassador Nomura and his superiors in Tokyo, as well as on the different attitudes of leaders in each country on the meaning of negotiations. He shows that the task of reaching a settlement was consequently hampered by a growing mutual distrust, a sort of diplomatic credibility gap. Nomura's disregard of instructions, of course, has been noted by earlier writers, but Hosoya is most helpful in detailing the steps taken by Matsuoka and his successors to make sure that they understood what Hull was saying and that Hull knew what they wanted.

The discussion following the papers by Thomson, Usui, Iriye, and Hosoya was wide-ranging and spirited. Almost every major diplomatic issue arose. China claimed close attention. What was the nature of America's concern? Did the United States really desire a modernized China, economic as well as political? Was the clash of interests there one of principle or power? How did the so-called Japanese Monroe Doctrine differ from the American version? Could the status quo in East Asia be changed by peaceful means? Indeed, was the very notion of peaceful change illusory? Several participants suggested broadening the angle of vision. The Japanese-American confrontation, it was argued, cannot be understood except in a triangular relationship with Britain. The Far Eastern configuration of power, it was contended, was part of a larger global configuration. To many American champions of collective security East Asia was subordinate to Europe and the Washington treaty system of less importance than the League of Nations covenant. The role of individuals was also appraised and note was taken of the greater continuity in the United States of personnel responsible for transpacific affairs. Yet it was also agreed that Hull, Grew, Hornbeck, Hamilton, and Ballantine often differed among themselves.

In "The Role of the War Department and the Army" Russell F. Weigley eagerly grasped the opportunity to break new ground. Historians have badly neglected the institutional development of the armed forces in the 1930s, and existing treatments of the military's impact upon foreign policy are woefully inadequate. The special merit of Weigley's essay is its careful delineation of the army's minimal role before 1941 in shaping most of the decisions affecting Japanese-American relations. In contrast to today, when the Pentagon is accused of overshadowing the State Department, the army before 1941 can be criticized for not fully warning the president of its inability to support the course upon which the nation was embarked in the Far East. Unlike the navy, which had come to regard a Pacific war as the supreme test of its planning and training, the army had long sought to cut its commitments in East Asia and to concentrate upon the defense of the hemisphere. Beginning early in 1939, however, the area to be protected was steadily expanded as war with the Axis powers became a possibility. Rainbow Plan 5, adopted in April 1941, contemplated coalition warfare with Germany as the primary target of an expeditionary force in Europe. The western Pacific was still to be, initially, a holding operation, but by midsummer the meaning of that phrase had changed. Elated by the performance of the Flying Fortresses, army strategists reversed a long-standing opinion and argued that the Philippines could be held against Japan without sacrificing interests elsewhere. These matters Weigley describes with accuracy and authority. He has used to advantage the records of the General Staff and of the adjutant general, including reports from Japan by attachés and itinerant officers. The only shortcoming in his most valuable contribution is the relatively slight attention paid to the civilian leaders and to the administrative organization of the War Department.

In his opening statement Weigley stressed two reasons for the army's limited attention to Japan during the 1930s. One was constitutional—a respect for civilian control of foreign policy. The other was internal—the problem of survival in a decade when available manpower and equipment ruled out transpacific campaigns. On the first topic Weigley offered a superb description of the army's traditional role in decision making. By education and training generals had learned not to intrude into the political arena, and in the early 1930s none of the civilian branches sought to involve the army in shaping foreign policy. In expanding on the second point, Weigley painted a depressing picture of unpreparedness. The one qualification he injected, and it came later in the discussion, was that Congress showed a growing solicitude for the air arm and the beginning of a faith in strategic bombing that became so important after 1941.

Fujiwara Akira's "The Role of the Japanese Army," presented orally, asserted that the key decisions leading to war in 1941 were made by middle-echelon officers (majors through colonels) in the Operations Section of the General Staff and the Military Affairs Bureau of the Army Ministry. In masterly fashion Fujiwara analyzed the origins, education, training, and assignments of those officers and the resulting cast of their minds. They tended to be absorbed in strategy and unconcerned with politico-economic forces. They were aggressive in character, often dogmatic and illogical, and better staff officers than field commanders. Fujiwara found that the army gave little serious thought, before 1939, to a possible war with the United States. Even in the next three years it made no adequate estimate of America's military capability, devised no effective collaboration with the navy, and drafted no workable plan to achieve victory by defeating the enemy in the field. Desperate to escape from the Chinese cul-de-sac and from the American embargoes, the army demanded a southward drive to Malaya and the Indies, knowing that it would bring war with the United States. In urging this step and in accepting confident statements from the navy that the admirals themselves did not believe, Fujiwara concludes, the middle-echelon officers displayed an irrational and unrealistic approach to problems of decision making.

The high quality of the papers on the two armies carried over into those on the navies. Like Weigley and Fujiwara, Waldo H. Heinrichs and Asada Sadao seized the opportunity to make major contributions to a field sorely in need of the scholarly touch. In "The Role of the U.S. Navy" Heinrichs draws upon an unusually wide array of manuscript collections, archival and personal, to provide an excellent portrait of the naval establishment in the decade before 1941. Understanding but not uncritical, he describes the dilemmas of a peacetime fleet. Avoiding the complaints about arms limitations and congressional penury that characterize most accounts on the subject, he argues that, except in a few fiscal years, the navy was not unduly starved for funds. Heinrichs also touches upon administrative conflicts, service traditions, and personal relations with a deftness that whets the reader's appetite for a fuller treatment. Along the way he sets straight the often distorted steps taken by the Hoover administration in the spring of 1932 when it tried to use the navy as a tool of diplomacy. As Heinrichs makes clear, the president did not order the entire fleet to remain in Hawaiian waters; he simply retained the Scouting Force on the west coast instead of allowing it to sail back to its customary station along the Atlantic seaboard.

Like Weigley, Heinrichs concentrates on issues that link the diplomat and the military. He traces the strategic thinking that produced important changes in basic war plans and relates those developments to building programs and fleet dispositions. In 1931, he contends, American naval leaders were introverted, bickering over secondary matters and looking upon Japan more in terms of budgetary needs for future construction than in terms of an opponent with whom battle was imminent. In 1940 Germany posed the more pressing challenge, and the world situation required a new set of war plans and a significant shift in ship deployment. The attempts of the naval hierarchy to abandon old ideas and to adjust to new conditions were not wholly successful.

In his opening statement Heinrichs suggested that of all the topics discussed at the conference, naval affairs best lent themselves to the comparative approach. Thus, he saw admirals on both sides of the Pacific worrying over budgetary restrictions, planning for a climactic Jutland-type battle, and facing the claims of airmen that the battleship was no longer the backbone of the fleet. But vital differences existed. The Japanese navy had only the Pacific to watch; it could not back away from a confrontation with the United States without losing face. The American navy had two oceans to guard; it might seek to avoid a clash with Japan by giving priority to the Atlantic, as its leaders tried to do in 1941. So far as Heinrichs could discover, within the inevitable limitations of his research, the American officer corps was not split into persistent and identifiable factions. The Japanese division between a command group and an administrative group seems not to have existed.

Asada's "The Japanese Navy and the United States" is one of the most ambitious and satisfying of the Japanese papers. Original in concept and rich in detail, it goes back to 1921 to trace the gradual erosion of the moderate leadership and its replacement by men given to a myopic strategic preoccupation and a highly emotional mode of thinking. The line of conflict over war plans and technology coincided roughly with divisions over ideological, political, and foreign orientations. One group—led by Katō Kanji, Suetsugu Nobumasa, and Nagano Osami—pinned their faith to heavily-gunned battleships, employed a spiritual vocabulary, and preferred German ties to American friendship. The other faction—followers of Katō Tomosaburō and headed by Yamamoto Isoroku, Yonai Mitsumasa, and Nomura Kichisaburō—urged greater use of carrier-based aircraft, argued in scientific terms, and favored the Anglo-American bloc over the Berlin-Rome axis. Like Fujiwara, Asada emphasizes the importance of middle-echelon officers (lieutenant commanders to captains); like Fujiwara, he is critical of the war planners.

Implicitly rather than explicitly, Asada suggests similarities and differences between the two navies. In budgetary matters and technological developments some of the same problems appear. But the tradition of civilian control in the United States and the absence of any doctrine of supreme command precluded further likenesses. The authority of the chief of naval operations did not rival that of the chief of the Japanese General Staff. In contrast to the Navy Ministry, the Navy Department had no uniformed head whose very appointment depended on the wishes of fellow officers and whose resignation could topple a cabinet. It would have been impossible for one faction in the United States navy to purge from high office all members of another, simply because they had supported the secretary and the president on an issue of foreign policy. Yet such was the fate of several Japanese admirals who had stood with Prime Minister Hamaguchi Osachi and Navy Minister Takarabe Takeshi after the London Treaty of 1930.

A lively discussion followed the papers by Weigley, Fujiwara, Heinrichs, and Asada. Participants stressed the institutional and educational differences between the armed forces in the two countries, especially the Japanese concept of the "independence of the supreme command." An attempt was made to explore problems of naval technology and weaponry, but most delegates preferred to speculate on broader questions, such as how war might have been avoided. It was argued that if the Japanese admirals had stated candidly their misgivings in November 1941, the generals might not have pushed for war at that time; but few were prepared to contend that hostilities would not ultimately have occurred. It was also asserted that the army would not have accepted any settlement of the China question which did not "secure the results" of previous sacrifices or ensure an "advantageous position" in the event of war with Russia.

Continuing at the governmental level, Lloyd C. Gardner's essay on "The Role of the Commerce and Treasury Departments" represents a welcome contribution to a somewhat neglected area. Diplomatic historians have not ignored Herbert Hoover's efforts to promote foreign trade while secretary of commerce from 1921 to 1928 or Henry Morgenthau's preoccupation with foreign affairs while secretary of the treasury after 1934, but no one has dealt systematically with the internal workings of the two departments and their impact upon American policy in East Asia. In his research Gardner examined the records of the departments of State and Commerce in the National Archives, as well as of the Bureau of Foreign and Domestic Commerce; but for the questions he raises, he found more useful the so-called Morgenthau diary and the personal papers of Roosevelt, Stimson, and Grew.

On the coming of the Pacific War Gardner's findings either confirm or correct in details earlier accounts. He feels that both departments viewed Japan's domestic and foreign policies in moral terms. Both criticized State for its vacillation, yet each, in its special area of responsibility, found it difficult to translate principles into practice. Gardner argues that personalities were more important than institutions. If Commerce played a smaller role than Treasury, it was partly because it faced problems unknown to Hoover in the 1920s and partly because it had no Morgenthau at the top. Morgenthau's consistently hard line reflected not only his desire to help China but also his identification of Japan with Nazi Germany.

Yamamura Katsurō's "The Role of the Finance Ministry" is an objective and workmanlike essay, solidly based on archival materials and oral interviews. Like most of the Japanese papers it starts well back of 1931 and describes the administrative structure. It carefully relates the policies of the interwar years to both internal and external events. The story is one of a steady decline in influence, especially after the assassination of Finance Minister Takahashi Korekiyo in 1936. His successors were unable or unwilling to challenge the military on budgetary matters; and although the ministry did oppose the Tripartite Pact, the Anglo-American faction lost ground as the United States instituted economic reprisals. In the final decision for war, Finance had no real voice.

In his opening statement Yamamura ascribed the moderate policy of the Finance Ministry to its knowledge that the Japanese economy could not withstand a long war with the United States and that Japanese capital could not alone develop Manchuria. He found no faction in the ministry desirous of a Pacific war. Gardner used his remarks to describe more fully the institutional set-up of Treasury and Commerce and to underscore the necessity of including the rest of the world, especially Britain, when analyzing Japanese-American financial relations. He contended that Morgenthau often thought Japan and Britain were collaborating when they were not and that the Tokyo government was equally mistaken as to the extent of joint Anglo-American action in the economic sphere. When questioned, Gardner asserted that the secretary of the treasury had less institutional power than the finance minister, since he had to share his authority with the Bureau of the Budget and other executive agencies. In the ensuing discussion some participants felt that Yamamura had exaggerated the declining influence of the finance minister, while others doubted that he was more powerful than the secretary of the treasury. Plans for economic mobilization in both countries were also explored.

To his assignment, "The Role of the United States Congress and Political Parties," Wayne S. Cole brings an expertise based on a long familiarity with legislative proceedings and years of intensive research in the private papers of American political leaders. Exploiting those manuscript collections—as well as printed sources, the unpublished files of the State Department, and the records of the Senate Foreign Relations and House Foreign Affairs committees—he has drawn a credible picture of the diverse congressional attitudes toward selected problems in Japanese-American relations from 1931 to 1941.

Since time did not permit an exhaustive investigation of his topic, Cole resorted to a sampling process. As a result of his findings he feels confident that the presidential and congressional elections from 1932 to 1940 would not have been very different even if there had been no tensions with Japan. He found few champions of Japan on Capitol Hill, yet almost no one advocated using force to check the trend of events on the Asian mainland. As the decade wore on, Cole believes, criticism of Japan mounted, sympathy for China increased, and impatience with executive timidity grew. Perhaps frustration is a better word than impatience. In any case, resistance to economic coercion dwindled, if indeed it did not disappear; well before Pearl Harbor most senators and representatives acquiesced in measures which, at an earlier date, they would have opposed as provocative. Cole argues that there was less legislative antagonism to military appropriations than is usually assumed and more presidential leeway in shaping policies toward Asia than in those affecting Europe.

At the conference Cole supplemented his paper by describing skillfully the prerogatives of Congress in foreign affairs and by offering tentative comparisons with the Diet. In neither country did the political parties and legislative bodies check the drift toward hard-line policies. In Japan, Cole thinks, they simply lacked the power. He seemed less certain about why there was approval or acquiescence in the United States but implied that by mid-1941 Congress may have been more willing than the president to take risks. Dislike of Japan in the Senate and House stemmed from moral, legal, and racial causes. It also reflected a concern for national security, economic well-being, and political advantage.

"The Role of the Diet and Political Parties" by Misawa Shigeo and Ninomiya Saburō describes the dwindling role of those bodies in the decision making process. The limits imposed on legislative power by the Meiji constitution were severe enough to begin with. The imperial prerogative and the right of supreme command ruled out any part in the declaration of war, the making of peace, the approval of treaties, or the control of the armed forces. That left, mostly, appeals to the Throne, representations to the government, questions to the cabinet, and action upon the budget. The concern for the budget, the development of party responsibility, and the search for new machinery (such as the Advisory Council on Foreign Relations or the Cabinet Advisory Group) gave rise to hopes that both legislature and parties might gain a real voice in diplomatic and military affairs, but those prospects disappeared in the 1930s as the generals prevailed over a timid civilian leadership.

In discussing the Cole and Misawa-Ninomiya papers, most delegates argued that the differences between the legislative bodies and political parties of the two countries were more significant than the similarities. The Congress, particularly the Senate, played an active role in determining foreign and military policy; the Diet did not. In the United States the legislature helped shape the economic aspects of diplomacy; in Japan such matters fell to the Finance and Foreign ministries. The Japanese had no equivalent of the Senate Foreign Relations Committee; its functions were discharged, in the opinion of some, by the Privy Council. Certainly the Senate and House wielded more control over the budget than did their counterparts. On the other hand, a few participants warned against the stereotype of a penurious Congress starving the armed forces and of a supine Diet yielding unwillingly to an aggressive military. But there was little disagreement with the conclusion that in Japan the legislators had criticized the generals more freely in 1918, and even in 1928, than they did after 1936.

Moving now to the private sector, we find "The Role of U.S. Business" by Mira Wilkins to be a model antidote to glib generalizations. Temperate, balanced, and lucid, her essay is a welcome contribution to a field more given to pontification than investigation. Drawing mainly on the best diplomatic histories, a wide array of printed sources, and two rich manuscript collections— the Thomas W. Lamont Papers at Harvard and the Ford Archives at Dearborn—she has systematically examined six kinds of United States business activity that were affected by, and perhaps affected, Japanese-American tensions from 1931 to 1941. These were: 1) exporters eager to sell in the Japanese market, 2) importers relying on Japanese goods for sales in the United States, 3) groups whose products competed with Japanese imports, 4) west coast fishing interests fearing competition from Japanese trawlers and canneries, 5) members of the banking community who dealt in Japanese securities, 6) enterprises of varying sizes that had direct investments in the Far East.

Wilkins' conclusions are carefully phrased. She found no single business policy or attitude toward East Asia but rather a spectrum of views. Diversity was the key. American businessmen shared only two common sentiments. One was a desire to survive and make profits in an increasingly hostile environment. The other was to preserve peace. Business leaders did not want war and did not urge measures that might result in war. Their thoughts and actions were more influenced by than influential upon the course of events. Wilkins makes clear that practical considerations prevented her exploring such subjects as the fur seal fisheries, the role of the Business Advisory Council in the Department of Commerce, the influence of mining companies upon the United States silver program, the potential conflict between cotton textile manufacturers and purchasers of raw cotton, and the possible divergence between corporation executives stationed overseas and those based at home. She might have added that she did not include either shipbuilders, airplane manufacturers, or other war-supporting industries.

In her opening statement Wilkins stressed the variety of business activities and the range of business attitudes with respect to Japan. She found American trade with that country more valuable than trade with China. Portfolio investments were also larger, although the reverse was true for direct investments. Wilkins mentioned methods by which businessmen sought to influence government, as well as the periodicals that articulated their opinions. She insisted, however, that such pressures were only a few among many that beat upon the Roosevelt administration, an administration not noted as a champion of Wall Street. Lamont, she felt, was a consistently important figure, but she received access only to those of his papers bearing upon East Asia. Lamont never lost interest in improving Japanese-American relations, but he did lose hope after the Tripartite Pact was signed in September 1940. Wilkins dissected with skill, at the end of the discussion period, the controversial question of Japan's desire to attract American capital to Manchuria after 1931.

By contrast, the Japanese papers dealt with the financial and business community in general terms. Nakamura Hideichirō's "The Activities of the Japan Economic Federation" describes the establishment, nature, and operations of a body designed to handle representatives of foreign enterprises. He concludes that large business interests in Japan desired harmony with the United States, did not fear rivalry at home or in China, but lacked sufficient popular support to restrain the military. Popular support, however, could be obtained only for a price the leaders were unwilling to pay—more liberal attitudes toward land reform, labor relations, and technological change. Chō Yukio's complementary essay, "An Inquiry into the Problem of Importing American Capital into Manchuria," surprised those United States delegates who had known about restrictions imposed on American oil companies after 1934 but not the repeated efforts to attract investors. In their papers neither author said much regarding individual industries or businesses, although Nakamura offered some evidence in his opening statement. Both men were readier than the American participants to accept the notion of economic harmony during the 1930s.

In "The Role of Private Groups in the United States" Warren I. Cohen appraises certain nonbusiness organizations that sought to influence Japanese-American relations. He draws upon a wide range of manuscripts—some used for the first time—including the unpublished files of the State Department and the Senate Foreign Relations Committee, the personal papers of individual citizens, and the records of such interest groups as the Committee to Defend America by Aiding the Allies and the American Committee for Non-Participation in Japanese Aggression. The rich Swarthmore College Peace Collection provided information on the Women's International League for Peace and Freedom, the National Council for the Prevention of War, the National Peace Conference, the Interorganization Council on Disarmament, and the Emergency Peace Committee.

Cohen believes that a chronological approach is revealing. In the 1930s the influence of the peace movement on United States policy was less significant than the impact of events abroad upon the pacifists at home. When the latter discovered that they could not control militarism overseas, they turned inward to concentrate on keeping the nation out of war. As time passed a desire for sanctions against the aggressor gave way to a demand for restrictions on the president. The anti-war leaders were often inconsistent and illogical. "In the quest for peace," Cohen observes, "a perverse moral relativism justified any provocative act by a potential enemy while condemning any American response as provocative." Nevertheless, no pacifist group could be said to have served Japan's ends, while the efforts of William Allen White's followers and of the American Committee for Non-Participation in Japanese Aggression aided China. But Roosevelt's course, Cohen insists, was a response to developments in Europe and to his own perception of Japan's intentions, not to any tide of public opinion.

Ogata Sadako's "The Role of Liberal Nongovernmental Organizations in Japan" and Itō Takashi's "The Role of Right-Wing Organizations in Japan" serve as companion pieces to Cohen's essay. Most helpfully, Ogata traces back to 1906 the history of the peace societies. Those liberals agreed with conservatives in believing that Japan had special interests in China and a need for additional territory on the mainland, but they differed in expecting its aims to be realized through cooperation with the West and within the framework of the League covenant and the Washington treaties. During the 1920s they saw American exclusionist policy as the chief problem; in 1931-32 they supported the army's operations in Manchuria as a proper defense against Chinese warlords and bandits. When Japan quit the League, its liberal leaders tried to find some regional security arrangement for the Pacific. In the end, however, they exerted minimal influence because they were elitists without a following and because, as nationalists, they wished to dominate China. Itō found that the reaction to the London Treaty of 1930 greatly stimulated the growth of the radical right, whose aims were to destroy the parliamentary system and existing political parties, to replace the capitalist economic order with a planned economy, and to overturn the white-dominated international regime in Asia. After 1935 these groups obtained vast sums from the military and from businessmen, large and small. Some contributions were voluntary; others may have resulted from blackmail.

In his opening statement Cohen declared that private groups in the United States had only slight influence on Roosevelt's policy in East Asia and that most members were more concerned with events in Europe. Many who supported China after 1937 did so in order to promote collective measures against Germany. Like other participants, Cohen felt the Tripartite Pact had a decisive effect in embittering Americans against Japan and created a link between Asia and Europe that the champions of China could never have forged by themselves. Cohen also offered some comparisons between private organizations in the two countries. In the ensuing discussion Rōyama Masamichi and Matsumoto Shigeharu—who had been active in the 1930s—recalled some developments of that decade. The session ended with the delegates asking why Japanese groups visiting the United States after 1931 had so few helpful contacts with government officials or their opposite numbers.

Ernest R. May's "U.S. Press Coverage of Japan, 1931-1941" offers a useful beginning to a meaningful study of public opinion. Without any pretense to completeness, it deals with the factual data about Japan supplied to American readers during three time periods. Four questions are posed by the author: Who were the individuals providing the United States public with information about Japan and Japanese policy? How competent were they to discharge their task? Did they make Japanese actions comprehensible to the American people who, without this background, might misjudge or misinterpret? To what extent did the public commentary in the United States mirror the pictures and judgments communicated by the reporters on the scene? May modestly leaves to someone better versed on Japan the difficult question of whether those reporters transmitted accurate descriptions and analyses.

Relying mainly on the reminiscent writings of journalists who had been assigned to Japan in the 1930s and on contemporary dispatches from a small number of influential newspapers, May easily explains why so little useful information emanated from Tokyo. The wire services were not willing to pay the cost of maintaining an effective bureau there. Only a handful of newspapers employed regular correspondents in the capital, and most of them worked part-time. These reporters rarely spoke or read Japanese; they were largely dependent on English-language newspapers, on official handouts, and on translations by local help. All three sources became increasingly unsatisfactory as the decade wore on, as tensions mounted, and as the government tightened controls. During the Manchurian crisis the messages to the United States were superficial and partook of Japanese propaganda. By 1937 the cables from China were much superior to those from Japan. As negotiations dragged out in 1941, press coverage from Japan actually misled the American public with respect to the genuine desire of some Japanese leaders for accommodation and to the frantic warning of others that war was a distinct possibility.

May makes no attempt to rear a thesis on this evidence. He suggests it might be fruitful to compare the quality of reportage by newspapermen with that of the embassy in Tokyo. Did Grew and his subordinates, including the military and naval attachés, paint a clearer picture of the turmoil in Japan? Did authorities in the government interpret the information at their disposal more wisely than the man in the street appraised his? May feels it can be argued that peace would have been better served if the divisions within the Japanese leadership had been more fully known in the United States. He wonders whether censorship in Tokyo did not deprive the American decision makers and public of essential data which, if available, might have made an armed clash less likely.

Kakegawa Tomiko's "The Press and Public Opinion in Japan, 1931-1941" examines the changes in the Japanese press and in the Japanese image of the United States after 1931, with particular attention to government controls. She describes the laws imposing curbs, the agencies entrusted with censorship, the growth of newspapers as a business enterprise, and the early years of broadcasting. She notes that journalism in Japan never enjoyed the freedom taken for granted in the United States. As to radio, the government first kept political issues off the air, prohibiting or discouraging ministerial speeches and legislative proceedings. Since, however, radio scripts could be checked in advance more easily than newspaper articles, broadcasting became after 1931 the official guide to how all patriotic citizens should think. Inasmuch as only half of Kakegawa's paper and none of May's were available before the conference met, the discussion of their topic was combined with that involving the last two essays.

Of these, Dorothy Borg's "Two Historians of the Far Eastern Policy of the United States: Tyler Dennett and A. Whitney Griswold" adds a new dimension to understanding the decade after 1931. Using for the first time the personal papers of both men and rescuing from neglect revealing articles appearing after their books, she effectively demonstrates the subjective and simplistic nature of their interpretations, interpretations which have greatly influenced writings on American diplomacy. Thus, although Dennett prided himself on belonging to the scientific school of history—with its concern for methodology, objectivity, and continuity—and while Griswold embraced the progressive school—with its emphasis on relativism, present-mindedness, and change—Borg clearly shows that a reaction to contemporary events, not a philosophy of history, shaped each man's thinking. *Americans in Eastern Asia* (1922) was based on extensive research in the State Department's archives and, ostensibly, was designed to stress the consistency of past practices; yet, in fact, Dennett had turned to history to find answers to questions that would arise at the forthcoming Washington Conference. In forgotten articles published from 1933 to 1938 he radically altered his earlier judgment of the Open Door and denied that the United States had any substantial stake in China. Here again he used history to bolster his opposition to any involvement in East Asia—armed or diplomatic, joint or unilateral.

In his *Far Eastern Policy of the United States* (1938) Griswold drew upon and expanded Dennett's ideas on the cyclical nature of American activity in Asia. Originally he intended to confine himself to Anglo-American rivalry in the Orient. In a preface never used he gave as his purpose the writing of an essay on American foreign policy, not a full-scale diplomatic history. The impact of current events on the development of his work is unmistakable, and his articles published after 1938 disclose a tendency to adjust his views to changing conditions. By 1941 he had even come to advocate support for Britain, a nation he had always cast in an unfavorable light. One of the special merits of the Borg essay is the information it provides on Griswold's thinking from 1939 to 1941 and the ammunition it gives to those who have long argued that his ever popular tour de force is badly dated.

Borg's opening statement again criticized Dennett and Griswold for using so simplistic an interpretation of history to buttress their contemporary attacks on American involvement in Asia. She noted their continuing influence on present-day scholars and attributed to Griswold some of the ideas contained in the writings of George F. Kennan and Tang Tsou. She then discussed two historians who might have been included if her paper had sampled a broader cross-section of books of the 1930s dealing with the Far East. They were Payson J. Treat and Paul H. Clyde, both of whom were regarded as pro-Japanese. As author of a widely used textbook Clyde is particularly interesting, and Borg sees in his *History of the Modern and Contemporary Far East* (1937) another example of a scholar contributing to the noninterventionist cause by indicting the policy pursued by the United States in Asia since 1898. Finally, Borg commented on the state of Oriental studies in the 1930s. Not one of the four—Dennett, Griswold, Treat, or Clyde—could read non-Western sources. In fact, few historians at the time had been trained to use Japanese materials, so that men such as Edwin O. Reischauer and Hugh Borton represented a new generation. At the conclusion of her remarks Asada spoke of the prewar translation into Japanese of Griswold's book and the high esteem in which it was held in Japan, a point also mentioned by the next speaker.

Mitani Taichirō's "Changes in Japan's International Position and the Response of Japanese Intellectuals: Trends in Japanese Studies of Japan's Foreign Relations, 1931-1941" differs markedly from the Borg essay. Instead of concentrating on two historians, he analyzes the ideas of typical personalities chosen from a broad spectrum of specialists in international relations. He concedes that these men were not completely free to say what they thought about the events of the decade, for they faced censorship in their published works and harassment in their academic life. Many had been imbued with the universal internationalism of the Wilson era and regretted the assault after 1931 upon the system symbolized by the League covenant and the Washington treaties. Resisting the extreme dogma of the military, they developed a concept of regionalism that reflected their concern for maintaining Japan's special position in Manchuria and for coping with China's burgeoning nationalism. This regionalism rested on their adaptation of the American Monroe Doctrine and their interpretation of two German authors, Carl Schmitt and Karl Haushofer. That is, these specialists condemned the existing international order as a front for Anglo-American domination and justified the war in

China as a means of destroying European imperialism and the old order in Asia.

The ensuing discussion ranged beyond the papers by Kakegawa, Borg, and Mitani. Attempts were made to analyze the nature and influence of public opinion in Japan. A letter was read from Takagi Yasaka, who had been unable to attend the conference, in which that distinguished professor emeritus of American history at Tokyo University commented on the shortcomings of prewar liberalism. The Monroe Doctrine was traced back to 1823 to discover what similarities, if any, the Japanese version contained and why American diplomats rejected the analogy so vigorously. Some delegates felt there was little difference between the United States' policy in the Caribbean from 1902 to 1929 and Japan's course in Manchuria and China after 1931. Carl Schmitt's denial of a universal international law and his argument for one that applied to limited areas of the world attracted further attention. The extent to which Japan felt diplomatically isolated, the reasons for that sentiment, and the time it became manifest occasioned disagreement. The Triple Intervention of 1895, the Siberian expedition of 1918, the Paris Peace Conference of 1919, the end of the British alliance in 1921, and the withdrawal from the League in 1933 were regarded as milestones along the path of isolation; racial consciousness and the status of a "have-not" nation were deemed the most significant reasons. "Iffy" questions were posed, such as what concessions would have been needed to ensure a successful meeting between Roosevelt and Konoe in 1941. Itō's treatment of right-wing organizations came in for renewed consideration. Those groups, it was agreed, did not want war with the United States. Their primary concern was Japan's relationship with China and the necessity of stemming the advance of communism on the mainland. Some Japanese participants argued that anti-American feeling did not seriously appear until late in 1941. In China, however, the Japanese-controlled press spoke out more bitterly at an earlier date.

The idea of a conflict of races over China provoked lively comments. People overseas, it was suggested, tend to become ethnocentric. On the mainland both the Japanese and the Americans had an exaggerated notion of themselves as saviors. The failure of the Greater East Asia Coprosperity Sphere, one delegate said, can be attributed to the opposition of not only the West but also the Chinese. Why was Japan unable to win over its fellow Asians? Was it the result of ignorance—a lack of understanding; or of pride—a sense of superiority? Undoubtedly the Japanese in China resented the penetration of an Asian nation by missionaries and merchants from the Occident and wanted to return the white intruder to his own land which, significantly, excluded the yellow race. As explanations for their country's failure to comprehend the strength of Chinese nationalism, the Japanese participants noted the confusion of the 1920s, the feeling of rivalry among siblings, the fear of communism, and the conviction that the movement toward unity was not indigenous but rather inspired by Anglo-American selfishness. Japan's treatment of the Koreans was also offered as evidence of this sense of racial superiority.

No papers were prepared for the final session, but Richard W. Leopold and Mushakōji Kinhide, with the aid of the steering committee, circulated in advance five questions to guide the discussion. In his opening statement Leopold spoke briefly about the benefits derived from a conference of this type. Mushakōji offered a chart showing concepts that can be used to illuminate the decision making process. Under constraints he listed culture and ideology, institutions, and personal character. Under images he gave role, interests, and appraisal of the situation. Under dynamics he mentioned communication, negotiation, situation, and decision. He then followed with examples affecting Japanese-American relations from 1931 to 1941, including the prerogative of the supreme command as an institutional restraint, the image that Americans cherished of their role in China, and the difficulty of communications in negotiations between people of different cultures.

The ensuing discussion centered first on the Japanese-American confrontation in China. Several delegates contended that this cause of tension during the decade 1931-41 could be understood only by going back to the aftermath of the Russo-Japanese War or even to the Boxer Rebellion. One participant suggested that during the turbulent 1920s individual Chinese warlords played one side against the other for their own advantage. Another noted a belief dating from 1913, perhaps earlier, in the democratic potential of the Chinese people and of the duty of the United States to speak for China on the international scene until it was strong enough to speak for itself. Wilson in 1919, Hughes in 1921, and Roosevelt after 1941 were cited as exemplars of this belief. It was obvious that the Japanese resented this presumption; as early as 1915 the Twenty-One Demands entered a counterclaim that was reasserted ever more strongly in the late 1930s. Not everyone in the United States shared this belief. The army took a dim view of China's future military vigor and consistently pleaded for a curtailment of American commitments in Asia. There were skeptics in the State Department, especially among the younger Foreign Service officers; their doubts about the Kuomintang's capacity to rule a truly democratic China increased during the war, at a time when Roosevelt and others suffered from an acute case of self-delusion. Even the supposedly pro-Chinese Hornbeck disapproved of steps to surrender extraterritorial rights because he felt China could not afford adequate protection to foreigners.

The conference turned next to determining whether this confrontation in China differed from the one both countries faced there with Britain and Russia. Why did the Japanese-American rivalry lead to armed conflict? The suggested reasons reflected, in part, the elements listed in the Mushakōji chart. One was divergent value systems, as seen in the education of the military or in the image of the enemy. Another was the difference in institutions. In Japan the decision making process was more diffuse and the voice of the middle-echelon officers and bureaucrats more effective. A third was the character and style of the leaders; the contrast between Roosevelt and Konoe or Hull and Matsuoka is obvious. A fourth involved communication. In Japan the language pattern is a silent one of tacit understanding; in the United States explicit articulation is the norm. The negotiations over the Tripartite Pact revealed these differences; for where Japan would go no further than to deny its obligations by an insinuated formula, the United States insisted upon an outright disavowal. To these generalizations one qualification was added. An important reason for the coming of war in 1941 was that both countries shared all too fully a Clausewitzian conviction that war is a continuation of political intercourse with an admixture of other means.

Finally, the conferees returned to the question of whether war could have been avoided. Was a permanent solution possible so long as Japan remained a "have-not" nation? Did the signing of the Tripartite Pact mark a point of no return? A consensus was conspicuously lacking on these issues. One American delegate asserted that the absence of machinery for peaceful change left Japan no recourse but to fight, for it could not accept the status quo indefinitely. A colleague denied that peaceful change was impossible. Roosevelt, he said, could have compromised, especially after his reelection, but he was overly cautious and needlessly fearful of public opinion. A third American dismissed the notion of a communication gap, arguing that the United States understood perfectly the Japanese negotiating position. Still a fourth attributed the administration's rigidity to pressure from Britain and China; he thought the memorandum prepared by Harry Dexter White on November 16, 1941 contained the basis for a reasonable settlement. At least one Japanese participant believed that American acceptance of Plan B at that time would have delayed the Imperial Headquarters timetable and thus might have changed the entire course of events.

In this last session, it became evident that the delegates had pierced the language barrier in a small way. The Japanese representatives spoke more frequently and more forcefully than they had in earlier sessions. Also, a difference could now be detected in the emphasis given by each side to the larger issues. The Americans tended to search for alternative courses or concrete proposals that might have halted the drift toward hostilities. The Japanese showed less interest in such specifics and more in the constraints, images, and dynamics that affected the decision making process. This difference, it was suggested, could be attributed to the fact that Americans look back on the Pacific War as a mistake, one that led to many of the intractable problems confronting the United States today, while the Japanese view that conflict somewhat fatalistically, as perhaps the only instrument by which the incubus of fascism and militarism could have been exorcised.

* * *

To decide whether the aims of the conference appear as sound to this American participant after the event as they did before, three final questions should be asked. Was attendance a rewarding experience? Were the primary objectives achieved? What lessons emerged that can influence future scholarship in this area?

The answer to the first question is emphatically in the affirmative. No American specialist could read the papers or listen to the discussion without deepening his understanding of the decade. From his colleagues he learned— depending on his own expertise—something new about the reasons Roosevelt acted as he did, the Division of Far Eastern Affairs in the State Department, the anomalous role of the embassy in Tokyo, the army's plans for mobilizing the nation's economy in wartime, the navy's use of war plans to secure larger appropriations in peacetime, the divergent responses of State, Treasury, and Commerce to the challenge from Japan, the lack of concern on Capitol Hill for an expanding program of economic reprisals in 1941, the distinction between portfolio investments and direct investments in East Asia, the dilemma of the peace groups during the decade, the identity and activity of newspaper correspondents in Tokyo, and the changing ideas of Tyler Dennett and A. Whitney Griswold. He saw used for the first time certain government archives—files of the armed forces and of congressional committees—and several manuscript collections—the personal papers of Stanley K. Hornbeck, Thomas W. Lamont, Tyler Dennett, and A. Whitney Griswold.

From the Japanese papers the American delegates learned even more. No matter how knowledgeable they may have been regarding Japan's governmental system—and all too many were all too uninformed—they were bound to profit from studies of the men surrounding the emperor, of the divisions within the Foreign Ministry, of the defective communications in 1941 between the Washington embassy and Tokyo, of the strength and the weakness of the army's training, of the factions within the naval establishment, of the declining influence of the finance minister after 1936, of the minor role played by the Diet and the political parties, of the limited achievements of spokesmen for economic groups, of the divergent goals of the right wing and liberal blocs, of the controls imposed on the mass media, and of the abandonment of universal internationalism by experts in international law. Thanks to probing in untapped sources and an emphasis on institutional operations, the prewar and wartime stereotype of an aggressive and monolithic Japan gave way to a more credible picture of a nation with sharp differences among the emperor's circle, the professional diplomats, the armed forces, and the business community.

Yet the most rewarding part of the conference for Americans was the personal contacts with their Japanese hosts. These relationships were of incalculable value. No amount of reading of books and articles, no amount of correspondence on common research could match this unique experience. In the ten discussion periods, spread over four days and interspersed with informal conversations, the passionate defense and the ethnocentric approach were conspicuously absent. Differences in value systems, perceptions, communication, and language—often neglected by diplomatic historians—became better understood because the visitors encountered these problems for themselves. Additional benefits were an opportunity to see, albeit briefly, sites associated with events of the decade: the conference room in the embassy where Grew deliberated with his staff, the Sanno Hotel where the mutineers of 1936 established their headquarters, the village of Okitsu where the last genro, Prince Saionji, lived, and the temple of Kiyomizu to which Tōjō Hideki alluded when he spoke of the need to take great risks in decision making.

To a large degree the aims of the conference were achieved, quite apart from enriching the lives of the visitors. The papers printed in this volume mark an advance in the parallel study of governmental institutions, interest groups, mass media, and scholarly writings. The Japanese essays are a boon to diplomatic historians, for they make available in English facts and interpretations drawn not only from current archival investigations but also from recently published primary sources and secondary accounts in a language that only two members of the United States delegation could read.

Not every paper at the conference fulfilled completely the intentions of the planners. In several, the institutional approach was insufficiently empha-sized—the Americans being the more frequent sinners. Possibly the instructions were too general. Probably some authors feared they might labor the obvious. Certainly all faced a dearth of monographs on which to rely. Yet the fact remains that the American contributors assumed more familiarity than was justified, even among their colleagues, with this aspect of their assignment. Happily, the Japanese avoided that assumption, while the Americans remedied the situation in their opening statements or in revisions made after the conference.

All of the papers slighted the comparative approach. Here the explanation may be both modesty and a lack of information. That modesty was a factor became apparent during the later sessions; once the ice was broken, the delegates did not hesitate to note transpacific similarities and differences. On the other hand, it is true that not many specialists in American foreign policy are trained to speak with confidence about the workings of the Meiji constitution, the imperial prerogative, or the right of supreme command. There are too few authoritative books in English on the organization of the Foreign, Army, and Navy ministries or on the general staffs of the armed forces. The uninitiated find it difficult to cope with the frequent cabinet changes and the unfamiliar names in the diplomatic and military hierarchy. For these reasons the essays of Usui, Imai, and Asada especially and the remarks of Fujiwara were particularly helpful.

As might have been predicted, two self-imposed restrictions proved to be a limiting factor. One was the focus on a single decade. Although the years from 1931 to 1941 remain the most appropriate for a study of this kind, all present agreed that the events of the decade became more intelligible by pushing back of 1931 and moving beyond 1941. Frequent allusions to the Triple Intervention of 1895, to the postwar reaction in Japan after 1905, to the memories of the Siberian venture of 1918, to the storm over the Exclusion Act of 1924, and to the civil-military conflict over the London Treaty of 1930—to cite a few examples—revealed the futility of trying to keep within the assigned dates. Secondly, the need to widen the angle of vision and to break out of the bilateral mold was repeatedly stressed. More particularly, it was argued that Britain was a constant element in the Japanese-American equation and that for most observers in the United States developments in Europe were more meaningful, at least after 1933, than those in Asia.

What are the chief lessons of the conference? What can be done to build upon this unique experience? Above all, the language barrier must be overcome. Thanks to simultaneous translation and an effective secretariat, it was possible to hold four days of stimulating discussion of prepared papers. But the time is long since passed, as the American Historical Association's Committee on American-East Asian Relations has maintained, when specialists on either side of the Pacific can do proper work in this field without a command of both languages. For those in the United States it is not only a matter of doing research in Japanese primary sources, archival and published, but also a question of reading the latest products of Japanese scholarship, many of which are unknown in America. The writing of recent Japanese history has come of age during the last fifteen years, but the pages of most American historical journals do not reflect that fact. To take a single example, neither the *American Historical Review* nor the *Journal of Modern History* reviewed the seven-volume *Taiheiyō sensō e no michi* (The Road to the Pacific War), edited by the Japan Association of International Relations Committee to Study the Origins of the Pacific War and published in 1962-63. In this major undertaking diplomatic history is broadly conceived. One part of the first volume covers naval affairs from 1921 to 1936. Two participants in the conference, Usui and Hosoya, were among the contributors. A partial English translation is, happily, being prepared under the general editorship of James W. Morley of the East Asian Institute, Columbia University, to be published by Columbia University Press. It is hoped that the growing number of younger scholars able to read Japanese, a few of whom attended the conference, will make such translations less necessary in the future.

In sum, there is still a need for further institutional and comparative studies of Japanese-American relations from 1931 to 1941. The papers printed here do not constitute the final word on the subjects they discuss, but they do take us well along the road to a complete understanding of that troubled decade.

HOOVER, ROOSEVELT, AND THE JAPANESE

Norman A. Graebner

I

For Herbert Hoover the issues raised by the Manchurian crisis of 1931 were clear and disturbing. Three times in the past—in 1894, 1904, and 1914—Japanese military forces had struck a neighboring region, with force and without warning, to alter the political status of East Asia. If on former occasions the United States had ignored the display of Japanese power, it could hardly do so in 1931. For Japan no less than the other major powers had supposedly underwritten the status quo in China by signing both the Nine Power Treaty of 1922 and the Kellogg-Briand Pact of 1928. At stake, therefore, was not only international morality but also the entire peace structure of the post-Versailles world.

Hoover's response to the Mukden Incident of September 1931 began with the assumption of Japanese aggression. Japanese militarists, he recalled in his memoirs, had taken advantage of a Western world wracked by depression and a China torn by warring factions to renew their slumbering policies of imperialism. While recognizing both Japan's need for raw materials and foreign markets as well as its special treaty privileges in Manchuria, the president rejected the Japanese rationale for the employment of force. The United States had no choice but to protest Japanese action, he wrote, "to uphold the moral foundations of international life."[1] Hoover's subsequent conceptualization of the Japanese challenge was a matter of profound significance. Not only as president of the United States did he carry the ultimate responsibility for the policies of his administration, but also, as the first national executive to confront a new phase of Japanese expansionism, he would establish the precedents which might determine the character of United States-Japanese relations through a still undetermined future.

Through practice if not through constitutional fiat, the executive branch of the United States government had gained almost unchallengeable primacy in foreign policy formulation long before Hoover reached the White House. Under the principle of separation of powers the Founding Fathers in 1787 had sought to compel any future president to share with Congress his control over external affairs. The constitution, it is true, granted the executive primacy in treaty-making and war-making decisions, as well as in matters of recognition and representation. But the House of Representatives gained control of the purse, while the Senate held the right to approve or reject treaties and presidential appointments. The constitution, moreover, ordered the president to secure the Senate's "advice and consent" on questions of foreign policy. Despite such constitutional limitations on presidential authority, however, the executive, as official spokesman of the nation, as commander-in-chief of the armed forces, and as head of the nation's entire bureaucratic structure, commanded from the beginning both the authority and the special knowledge required to dominate the decision making process in the entire field of foreign affairs. The State Department and the Foreign Service answered to the White House, not to Congress. Whether the president chose to accept advice from members of Congress or of his administration, or perhaps from personal friends, rested with him alone. Amid the increasing international complexities of the present century, the president's power to initiate policy became almost absolute.

Hoover, in facing the Manchurian crisis, reflected the concerns of a thoroughly satisfied nation which had long regarded war as a useless endeavor and a historic anachronism. Desiring both peace and the status quo, the United States in the 1920s had tied its dual purposes to two paper treaties—the Kellogg-Briand Pact and the Nine Power Treaty—which together guaranteed the end of armed aggression against the established treaty structure, not with threats of countering force but with the power of world opinion that would allegedly compel all signatories to honor their agreements. Every new Japanese advance in Manchuria, in defying the spirit and perhaps even the letter of the treaties, was terrifying primarily because it challenged the notion that world opinion alone would perpetuate the world which the Western democracies had created at Versailles.

Late in September 1931 Secretary of State Henry L. Stimson in a letter to Hugh R. Wilson, the American minister at Geneva, suggested three possible United States courses of action. First, he wrote, the United States favored direct negotiations between Japan and China. Second, if outside leadership was required, China and Japan should submit to the machinery of the League of Nations. If these two avenues to settlement proved impracticable, the United States would consider some resort to the Nine Power and Kellogg-Briand pacts.[2] At the same time Hoover instructed the American consul at Geneva, Prentiss Gilbert, to sit with the League Council. Gilbert's instructions, however, limited his participation to possible League action under the Kellogg Pact. On October 17 members of the Council, in secret session, agreed that the Council should urge all signatories of the Kellogg-Briand Pact to remind China and Japan of their obligations under the pact. Hoover and Stimson agreed that the United States should accept no responsibility for a Manchurian settlement and on October 19 ordered Gilbert to take no part in any League deliberations that involved action under League machinery rather than the Kellogg Pact.[3]

When the British and French governments argued that Gilbert's withdrawal from League deliberations would discredit the organization at a moment of great crisis, Stimson under direct pressure permitted Gilbert to remain at the table provided he act only as an observer. Thereafter the United States followed the League at a distance. Stimson held up his note to China and Japan under the Kellogg Pact for three days after Britain and France had sent theirs. When the League Council passed a resolution calling upon Japan to evacuate Chinese territory by November 16, Stimson hesitated to endorse it. He wanted no action which might commit the United States. With this Hoover agreed. Undersecretary of State William Castle recorded in his diary on November 4 that the president had stated at lunch that "he wants to get completely out of the League connection and thinks it might have been wise, politically, to make Stimson keep out."[4]

For Washington peace rested less on League action than on the willingness of nations to limit change in international life to mutual agreement. At a cabinet meeting on October 9 Stimson warned the president against getting into a humiliating position in case Japan refused to honor its own signatures on the paper treaties. But Stimson recorded in his diary the essential role of the Far Eastern treaty structure in United States policy:

> The question of the "scraps of paper" is a pretty crucial one. We have nothing but "scraps of paper." This fight has come on in the worst part of the world for peace treaties. The peace treaties of modern Europe made out by the western nations of the world no more fit the three great races of Russia, Japan, and China, who are meeting in Manchuria, than, as I put it to the Cabinet, a stovepipe hat would fit an African savage. Nevertheless they are parties to these treaties and the whole world looks on to see whether the treaties are good for anything or not, and if we lie down and treat them like scraps of paper nothing will happen, and in the future the peace movement will receive a blow that it will not recover from for a long time.[5]

Clearly what mattered for Stimson was an American response to the Manchurian challenge that would reestablish the credibility of the world's treaty structure. The time for decision had arrived. On October 8 the news reached Washington that the Japanese were bombing Chinchow in southern Manchuria. "I am afraid," Stimson recorded in his diary, "we have got to take a firm ground and aggressive stand toward Japan."[6]

Until that moment the views of Hoover and Stimson had coincided; thereafter they began to diverge. Stimson reminded Hoover in October that he had fundamentally two choices before him. He could either rely on collective economic sanctions against Japan or through diplomatic pressure attempt to secure "a vigorous judgment against Japan backed by the public opinion of the world, to save as much respect as possible for the great peace treaties. . . ."[7] To Hoover economic sanctions meant war, and a war against Japan, Hoover's military advisers informed him, would not produce a victory in less than four to six years. League interest in economic sanctions, moreover, was never more than spasmodic. When Stimson in November broached the subject of a blockade,

Hoover reminded him that the United States would limit its action to moral pressure. Patrick J. Hurley, the secretary of war, suggested to the cabinet that only force would stop Japan from seizing Manchuria. Stimson responded simply that "the policy of imposing sanctions of force" had been rejected when the United States made clear its refusal to support the League of Nations.[8] When the League Council reconvened at Paris in mid-November, Hoover sent Ambassador Charles G. Dawes from London to represent the United States as an observer and consultant. Stimson informed Dawes that the United States would not join any League embargo against Japan but would not interfere with such an embargo. Beyond that position Hoover would not go despite Stimson's argument for economic sanctions.

Hoover put forth the major ingredients of United States policy in a memorandum presented to his cabinet in mid-October 1931. He termed the Japanese behavior in Manchuria immoral and an outrageous affront to the United States but stated that the United States "had never set out to preserve peace among other nations by force. . . ." Both the Nine Power Treaty and the Kellogg Pact, he said, were "solely moral instruments based upon the hope that peace in the world can be held by the rectitude of nations and enforced solely by the moral reprobation of the world." Nor did the United States have any interests or obligations to China that would require the United States to go to war over Manchuria. "These acts," he asserted, "do not imperil the freedom of the American people, the economic and moral future of our people." Still the United States, he charged, had a "moral obligation to use every influence short of war to have the treaties upheld or limited by mutual agreement." Hoover discovered the means to prevent unwanted change in China in two sources. The first lay in world cooperation limited to moral pressures, organized largely under the League of Nations. The second comprised China's "transcendent cultural resistance," which had repeatedly demonstrated its power to absorb or expel foreign intruders.[9] Hoover approached the Manchurian problem with the dual purpose of making the United States' will effective in Japanese-Chinese relations but without any American commitment to economic or military sanctions. Within the context of China's weakness and Japan's tangible interests in Manchuria, Hoover's ambitions were prejudiced from the start.

Hoover defined his policy, and thereby the nation's dilemma, even further in his message to Congress on December 10, 1931. Again he acknowledged United States responsibility for the integrity of China under the Kellogg-Briand Pact and the Nine Power Treaty. The United States government, he said, had reminded both Japan and China of their responsibilities and had "indicated its unremitting solicitude that these treaty obligations be respected." Rather than take independent action, however, the United States, while still defending its complete freedom of action, would "aid and advise with the League and thus have unity of world effort to maintain peace. . . ."[10]

Having taken their stand on the treaties, Hoover and Stimson searched for the means of rendering them effective. To put the necessary moral teeth into the Kellogg Pact, Hoover suggested to his cabinet early in December that the United States consider proposing to the League that its members refuse to recognize any changes in Manchuria that resulted from violations of the pact. The United States could at least express its feeling of deep moral opposition to events in

Manchuria and satisfy public demands that the nation take a stand.[11] Stimson rationalized the nonrecognition doctrine as the best means available to the United States for reinforcing the treaty structure. "If the fruits of aggression should be recognized," he wrote, "the whole theory of the Kellogg Pact would be repudiated, and the world would be at once returned to the point of recognizing war as a legitimate instrument of national policy. Nonrecognition might not prevent aggression, but recognition would give it outright approval."[12]

II

From this rationale for nonrecognition Hoover and Stimson moved logically toward the note of January 7, 1932. When Hoover approved it three days earlier, the two men agreed that Britain and France should also publish statements of nonrecognition. The United States note, delivered to both China and Japan, declared that this nation could not "admit the legality of any situation *de facto* nor does it intend to recognize any treaty or agreement entered into between those Governments" which might impair either the treaty rights of the United States or the territorial and administrative integrity of the Republic of China.[13] Hoover was disturbed that the British communication did not refer to the territorial integrity of China, thus suggesting an absence of British interest in Manchuria's future.

Apparently the moral strictures of the January 7 note had no effect, for Japan continued to expand its pressure on China and finally, on January 28, seized Shanghai with a large naval and military force. Hoover ordered United States war vessels to Shanghai to protect American civilians. Early in February Stimson warned the Tokyo government that unless Japanese officers protected the International Settlement in Shanghai from destruction, the result would be a catastrophe. The secretary made it clear that the United States expected a settlement in China in conformity with the Far Eastern treaty structure.[14] In this burgeoning crisis Secretary of War Hurley argued that the administration should either prepare to fight or stop sending protests which Japan would ignore. Again the president rejected a showdown, declaring that he would fight for the continental United States but not for Asia.[15] United States intervention, he added, was rendered unnecessary by China's capacity to frustrate Japanese designs. Hoover argued finally that the Kellogg Pact was a great moral force against aggression and that the note of January 7 had been effective in mobilizing world opinion in favor of the pact. Indeed, predicted Hoover, that note would stand as one of the great state papers of this country.[16] For the president moral pressure was not only safe, it was the determining force in world affairs.

Stimson, barred by Hoover from any resort to sanctions, advocated during February a double course based on bluff and a restatement of American principles. Rejecting with Hoover any verbal threat to use force, Stimson believed nevertheless that "we had a right to rely upon the unconscious elements of our great size and military strength; that I knew Japan was afraid of that, and I was willing to let her be afraid of that without telling her that we were not going to use it against her."[17] Hoover opposed even an unspoken threat of war, although he agreed to retain the Scouting Force on the west coast following the fleet maneuvers at Hawaii in mid-February. Stimson, with Hoover's approval, then turned to his second recourse—a restatement and elaboration of the basic position of the United States in Asia. It seemed essential to him that he give official expression not only to American pro-Chinese opinion—much of it organized and demanding economic sanctions—but also to the historic evolution of United States policy in the Far East. "As I reflected upon it," he recalled later, "it seemed to me that in future years I should not like to face a verdict of history to the effect that a government to which I belonged had failed to express itself adequately upon such a situation."[18]

Stimson believed that he could, in another strong public statement, mobilize world opinion against Japan. Determined to concentrate on the injustice being done to China, he based his new statement on the Nine Power Treaty rather than the Kellogg Pact, inasmuch as the signatories of the former had agreed specifically to uphold the territorial and administrative integrity of China. Britain rejected Stimson's request for a joint reassertion of the Nine Power Treaty, but on February 16 the League Council supported the nonrecognition doctrine and called upon Japan to fulfill its obligations under the Nine Power Treaty. A new Japanese assault on February 20 helped Stimson over his inhibitions and prompted him to make a unilateral American declaration of principles in the form of an open letter to Senator William E. Borah. Castle approved the letter as "the kind of thing which the Secretary, a lawyer, can do admirably." But Hoover demanded the inclusion of a sentence "which would relate to the public opinion of the world as the sanction behind our note of January 7 and behind the action which the Borah letter proposes."[19] Stimson argued that it would be better to permit the Japanese to guess on the matter of sanctions and won his point. Through his letter to Borah, Stimson intended, he recalled, "to encourage China, enlighten the American public, exhort the League, stir up the British, and warn Japan."[20]

Stimson's letter, dated February 23, 1932, made clear the continued reliance of the United States on the Nine Power Pact and the expectation that Japan would abide by it. The United States, he wrote, stood for a strong China and for the protection of American interests in that country. For that reason it would not abandon the principles embodied in the Nine Power and Kellogg pacts. "We concur," he concluded, "with those statesmen, representing all the nations in the Washington Conference, who decided that China was entitled to the time necessary to accomplish her development. We are prepared to make that our policy for the future."[21] Stimson again attempted to emphasize the contrast between United States and Japanese purposes, with the United States insisting on Chinese independence and integrity and Japan determined, in defiance of the Nine Power Treaty, to impose a unilateral solution on the grounds of its special interests in China. For Stimson this moral judgment was still only a first step; for Hoover it was the maximum United States response.

Neither Stimson's strong historic defense of the Nine Power Treaty nor even his veiled threat of a naval race, if not war, stopped Japan or brought anyone to China's defense. Indeed, Ambassador Joseph C. Grew reported from Tokyo on June 13 that the Hoover policies, implying nonrecognition of any Japanese-imposed settlement, had aroused considerable interest as an abstract subject of conversation but were not regarded by Japanese leaders as a barrier to Japan's complete control of Manchuria. In May the Japanese withdrew from Shanghai but during the following summer gradually turned Manchuria into the puppet state of Manchukuo.[22]

Thereafter Stimson scarcely knew where to turn. Obviously the vast majority of the American people, the leading governments of Europe, and the president himself were opposed to sanctions. Still Stimson, no less than Hoover, placed great trust in the power of world opinion. When Stimson, in April, left for Geneva, the president announced that the secretary's mission would be limited to assisting the work of the disarmament conference. But Stimson recorded that he "set himself at Geneva and through the remainder of his service as Secretary of State to the purpose of obtaining and maintaining a world judgment against Japan." Such a policy might deter Japan. If not, "it would lay a firm foundation of principle upon which the Western nations and China could stand in a later reckoning."[23]

During the summer of 1932, with the Chinese position in Manchuria rapidly disintegrating, Stimson prepared his third public effort to strengthen the treaty structure. This time the secretary settled on a powerful plea to world sentiment, which he arranged to make in the form of a public address before the Council on Foreign Relations in New York. In this speech on August 8, 1932 Stimson returned to the Kellogg-Briand Pact as the bulwark of peace. By declaring war illegal, he admonished, the Kellogg Pact compelled the world to condemn aggressors as lawbreakers. The necessary exercise of this obligation to denounce war was in itself a powerful force for peace. "The Kellogg-Briand Pact," he added, ". . . rests upon the sanction of public opinion which can be made one of the most potent sanctions in the world. . . . Public opinion is the sanction which lies behind all international intercourse in time of peace. Its efficacy depends upon the will of the people of the world to make it effective. If they desire to make it effective, it will be irresistible."[24] Proud of his three public statements of 1932, Stimson insisted that the doctrine of nonrecognition was his own.

Three days later Hoover used the text of his speech accepting nomination for a second term to summarize the achievements of his administration in regard to Manchuria. "Above all," he said, "I have projected a new doctrine into international affairs, the doctrine that we do not and never will recognize title to possession of territory gained in violation of the peace pacts. That doctrine has been accepted by all nations of the world on a recent critical occasion. . . . That is public opinion made tangible and effective."[25] To Hoover nonrecognition promised success not only because it invoked world opinion but also because it "avoided precipitate action and allowed time to work out proper solutions."[26] Throughout his last months in office Hoover challenged Stimson by claiming full credit for the doctrine of nonrecognition as *his* major achievement in the realm of external affairs.

But public opinion had not stopped Japan and, as Lord Cecil had informed the British House of Commons in July 1919, "What we rely upon is public opinion . . . and if we are wrong about it, then the whole thing is wrong."[27] Clearly the Hoover administration had not laid the foundations of a realistic United States policy in the Far East. Actually through its doctrine of nonrecognition it had successfully avoided the obligation to create a policy. For to be effective an American response required more than time; it required nothing less than a clear definition of the irreducible interests of the United States in a changing Orient and a determination to defend those interests.

Undoubtedly the Hoover administration's response to Manchuria had created a formula which met the political, if not the diplomatic, requirements of national policy. Hoover had acknowledged the absence of any United States interests in China important enough to invite or risk war. But at the same time he had committed the nation to the moral and diplomatic rejection of change except that achieved through mutual agreement. For a democracy which had acquired the highly moralistic outlook of a status quo power, the doctrine of nonrecognition implied firmness, not appeasement. By promising to halt aggression through world opinion alone, nonrecognition assured many Americans that the nation could achieve its goal of peace with justice without war.

During January and February 1933 the doctrine of nonrecognition appeared even more promising when the Lytton Commission of the League of Nations, after conducting months of investigation in Manchuria, reported its findings to the League. The Lytton report was scarcely an indictment of Japan, but it recommended the nonrecognition of Manchukuo. When on February 24 the League Assembly adopted the Lytton report, Stimson was delighted, believing that his leadership had strengthened the League. Again Japan's complete rejection of the report and prompt withdrawal from the League demonstrated the limits of nonrecognition. "The military themselves, and the public through military propaganda," Grew warned from Tokyo, "are fully prepared to fight rather than to surrender to moral and other pressure from the West."[28] Similarly Hugh R. Wilson in Geneva reminded the administration that nonrecognition created a situation from which neither side could escape with dignity. "A declaration of nonrecognition," he wrote, "means that eventually one side or another will find itself in a position where it must 'eat crow.' "[29] Disturbed by such admonitions, Hoover again emphasized to Stimson that for the United States nonrecognition ruled out all sanctions other than moral. But Stimson believed that nonrecognition, even if it had not stopped Japan, had drawn a sharp line between United States and Japanese behavior and thus had laid the foundations for stronger action against Japan at some future time.

III

So completely did the Hoover-Stimson response to Japanese policy conform to the precepts of postwar American foreign relations that Franklin D. Roosevelt refused to question the decisions he inherited. Stimson himself served as the bridge between Hoover and Roosevelt on the matter of the Japanese challenge. Hoover agreed reluctantly to permit his secretary to confer with Roosevelt at Hyde Park. On January 9, 1933 Stimson spent several hours with Roosevelt to discuss such external issues as the world disarmament and economic conferences as well as the Hoover administration's Far Eastern policies.[30] On January 17 Roosevelt made clear his intention to rely on the international agreements when he declared that "American foreign policies must uphold the sanctity of international treaties. That is the cornerstone on which all relations between nations must rest."[31] To uphold those treaties, Roosevelt assured Stimson, he would continue the nonrecognition principle toward Manchuria.

After March 1933 Japan confronted Roosevelt less with an immediate crisis than with the clear intent of proceeding with its program of Far Eastern political and economic reorganization. For many American observers, officials, and editors Japan now loomed as a threat to the peaceful progress of the entire Orient. "This power since fifty years," ran the warning of one Roosevelt correspondent, "is working steadily toward the exclusion of . . . the white man from the Pacific. . . ."[32] Ambassador Grew told the new president in May 1933 that Japan was potentially so menacing because of its national spirit. "The force of a nation bound together with great moral determination, fired with national ambition, and peopled by a race with unbounded capacity for courageous self-sacrifice," he said, "is not easy to overcome."[33] Similarly Ambassador William E. Dodd reminded Roosevelt from Berlin that the Hoover-Stimson policies toward Japan had resolved nothing. "The failure of Stimson two years ago, perhaps inevitable," wrote Dodd, ". . . is going to be calamitous, I fear." In response Roosevelt acknowledged his own uneasiness: "I sometimes feel that the world problems are getting worse instead of better." Several weeks later Roosevelt informed another friend that he was not the only one who was "a bit shivery about the international situation, East and West."[34]

Even after the struggle within China ground to a temporary halt, Japanese officials made clear their refusal to stop with the absorption of Manchuria into the Japanese empire. On January 23, 1934 Foreign Minister Hirota Kōki declared before the Japanese Diet that "the path of a rising nation is always strewn with problems. . . . We should not forget that Japan, serving as only a cornerstone for the edifice of peace of East Asia, bears the entire burden of responsibilities." Then in April 1934, Amō (Amau) Eiji, a Japanese Foreign Ministry spokesman, elaborated on Japan's specific responsibilities for the peace and progress of East Asia. No country but China, he said, could share that responsibility. "We oppose, therefore," he warned, "any attempt on the part of China to avail herself of the influence of any other country to resist Japan. We do oppose any action taken by China calculated to play one Power against another."[35] Hirota informed Grew in September that before the end of the year the Japanese government would give notice of its intention to terminate the Washington Naval Treaty. Japan, Grew informed Washington, was developing its naval power to underwrite a new policy of expansion.[36]

Roosevelt faced the continuing Far Eastern crisis with limited policy choices. The United States could withdraw from that region, Grew wrote to the president, "gracefully and gradually perhaps, but not the less effectively in the long run, permitting our treaty rights to be nullified, the Open Door to be closed, our vested economic interests to be dissolved. . . ." Some Americans, including the noted journalist, Frank H. Simonds, advocated this course on the assumption that any other policy entailed the risk of war with Japan and that United States interests in China were not worth that price. Grew recommended as an alternative that the Roosevelt administration "insist, and continue to insist, not aggressively yet not the less firmly, on the maintenance of our legitimate rights and interests in this part of the world and, so far as practicable, to support the normal development of those interests constructively and progressively."[37]

Roosevelt and Secretary of State Cordell Hull adopted the latter course, hoping to limit Japanese expansion without war. War, they agreed, would serve no fundamental United States interests. During May 1933 the Chinese government, fearing a Japanese attack south of the Great Wall but unwilling to negotiate a settlement with Tokyo alone, pressed the United States to assume the role of mediator. Stanley K. Hornbeck, key spokesman of the State Department's Far Eastern Division, informed the Chinese minister in Washington that such initiative must come from the League, Britain, or France. The United States, he said, had already done what it could for China. This nation was on record, Hornbeck reminded the minister, that when the League took action it would be "predisposed favorably toward cooperation." Washington officials admitted freely that the United States had no vital interests at stake. United States trade and investment in China, Hornbeck observed in February 1934, was important but not essential. United States concern for the peace structure did not relate peculiarly to the Orient but to the entire world.[38]

Roosevelt and Hull, following Republican precedents, anchored their goal of peace to international law and the nonrecognition of imposed change. "The United States," declared an official State Department memorandum of April 26, 1934, ". . . cannot admit the legality of any unilateral action on the part of any other power calculated to restrict or otherwise to modify any right possessed by the United States by virtue of recognized principles of international law or by virtue of treaties to which the United States is party."[39] If this reliance on nonrecognition to uphold the treaty structure was designed to avoid war, it still, as the Japanese government complained in May 1934, encouraged a defiant Chinese attitude toward Japan and thereby obstructed Japan from working out its national aims in the Far East. Clearly Japan required an agreement with the United States which would terminate Washington's moral commitment to China's territorial and administrative integrity.[40] Hull, however, informed the Japanese ambassador that his nation, no less than the United States, had obligations to China under the Nine Power and Kellogg pacts. For the United States-Japanese confrontation in the Pacific, Hull's admonition was no answer.

Binding the ends of American policy to the perpetuation of the established treaty structure was simple enough; the means of achieving that purpose were far more elusive. No less than Hoover, Roosevelt rejected any reliance on force. Hornbeck in May 1933 asserted that the major responsibility for restricting hostilities in the Far East belonged to the League. But when League members, during a debate on an arms embargo against Japan, insisted that such action required the support of the United States, Hull promptly cabled Wilson in Geneva, "I desire absolutely to avoid being drawn into any discourse of this Government's attitude with regard to any proposed embargo on export of arms until the League shall have made its own decision. I do not intend that this Government shall assume the role of mentor to the League or accept a responsibility which initially lies with and belongs to the League. . . ."[41]

Some Americans believed that a larger navy alone would quell Japan without war. Ambassador William C. Bullitt assured Roosevelt in February 1934 that an American naval program would best guarantee peace in the Orient. "In the event that Japan begins to build above her present ratio," he said, "we should speak softly and build three ships to her one."[42] A military people such as the Japanese, declared one State Department memorandum of January 1935, respected military strength. The United States, it concluded, could prevent war by maintaining a greater force in the Pacific than that possessed by Japan. The Japanese might bluster and threaten, argued a Washington friend of the president, but they would ultimately back down in the face of the indomitable will of the United States.[43] From Tokyo Grew warned Roosevelt that unless the United States intended to accept a *pax Japonica* in the Far East, the United States delegation at the London Naval Conference must keep the Washington ratios intact in the face of Japanese intransigence. Roosevelt himself recognized the need for a larger navy when the Japanese, having been denied naval parity by the London Naval Conference, withdrew from the conference in January 1936 and brought an end to naval stability based on naval limitations.[44]

Limited United States interests in the Far East added to Roosevelt's determination to avoid compromise or war rendered China's alternatives disastrous—further military adversities or a dictated peace. Washington, in the interest of principle, preferred that China continue to fight, for any settlement, as Hornbeck admitted, would be "a capitulation on the part of China in terms of recognition of the new status quo in Manchuria and a pledge to refrain from any further efforts to upset that status quo." Better that China suffer, added Hornbeck, than recognize Japanese gains achieved in defiance of the Nine Power Treaty.[45] Nor would the United States gain anything from an agreement with Japan. Any settlement, declared Hull, would be as unsatisfactory as the Lansing-Ishii Agreement of 1917. The United States could afford to be deliberate. To scrap the Open Door in China would endanger United States policy everywhere. It would mean, in the words of a State Department memorandum of January 1935, that "we would go back on our treaties.... If we did this without making an announcement, we would produce all sorts of misunderstanding and confusion. If we did it with an announcement, such announcement would be tantamount to a declaration that, so far as we are concerned, Japan may do as she pleases in and with regard to China."[46] By such argumentation, compromise was an invitation to disaster.

Thus the immediate answer to Japanese ambition lay in Chinese nationalism and China's growing powers of resistance. Perhaps Japan's continuing assault on China would further dent and scratch the principles of United States policy, but it would not threaten any vital United States interests. Long run American purposes would be served by complete exposure of Japan's program and Japan's total involvement in problems of its own creation until the invasion of China reached its crest and then gradually ebbed. China carried the burden of sustaining the paper treaties by rendering any Japanese infringement of the status quo painful and finally hopeless.

IV

Roosevelt and his advisers entered the fateful year of 1937 in a mood of optimism. Their response to Japan appeared adequate to prevent further aggression, and in March the president proposed the formal neutralization of the Philippines to remove them as a source of United States-Japanese friction. Hull opposed the neutralization scheme from fear that it would create the appearance of a United States retreat from the Pacific and thus encourage Japanese ambition. Grew agreed. Hull was convinced, moreover, as Interior Secretary Harold Ickes recorded in his diary on January 24, that Japan "may break financially at an early date, which will render her impotent as to us ... that Japan had already discovered that she did not have the money to carry out her ambitious plans with respect to China."[47] Early in June Hull assured British Prime Minister Neville Chamberlain that the development of healthy trade relations in the Far East would create a state of mind "wherein those people will themselves be able to perceive that pathways of co-operation are the pathways of advantage."[48]

Roosevelt and Hull, by placing principle above expediency and thereby encouraging Chinese resistance, gave Japan the choice of capitulation to China's demands or the exertion of increased pressure on the treaty structure. Whatever the Japanese responsibility for the clash between Japanese and Chinese soldiers at the Marco Polo Bridge outside Peking on July 7, 1937, the Tokyo government seized upon the crisis and the subsequent failure of negotiations as an opportunity to renew its military assault on China. China responded with an appeal for American assistance. Dr. H. H. Kung, China's minister of finance, asserted that the United States itself would face Japanese aggression unless the Chinese were able to check it. Hornbeck again responded for the administration, declaring that United States interests and policies toward China coincided fortunately "with China's own desire to build up a stable and strong nation."[49] But Washington hoped to save China, or at least protect American citizens and property there, without direct assistance or sanctions in any form. Sanctions, Grew reminded Hull, would merely aggravate the situation without either serving any United States interest or stopping the Japanese.[50]

International crises in July 1937 stretched from Spain to China. Hull responded with a mighty effort to halt the use of force. On July 16 he released to the press a statement of principles that reaffirmed the nation's reliance on the treaty structure. "We advocate," said Hull, "adjustment of problems in international relations by processes of peaceful negotiation and agreement. We advocate faithful observance of international agreements. Upholding the principle of the sanctity of treaties, we believe in modification of provisions of treaties ... by orderly processes carried out in a spirit of mutual helpfulness and accommodation."[51] These principles, by reducing the area of legitimate change almost to the vanishing point, assigned a special morality to the rights of possession. The Chinese were not impressed. On August 20 Dr. C. T. Wang, the Chinese ambassador, admitted the rectitude of the principles, but what China required, he declared, was action. Three days later Chinese President Chiang Kai-shek criticized the Roosevelt administration for its refusal to take a firm stand in the Far East. "I do not want the United States to be dragged into the war," he admitted, "but I do look to her to maintain her position in the Pacific and to maintain peace there."[52] Hull that day reminded the press that his principles of July 16 had a direct bearing on the Sino-Japanese conflict and that the United States was "endeavoring to see kept active, strengthened, and revitalized in reference to the Pacific area and to all the world, these fundamental principles." Beyond his statement of principles Hull promised the Chinese nothing, not even United States cooperation with the League on possible sanctions against Japan.

Hull's principles had the effect of defining the Sino-Japanese conflict in sharply moral terms. Asking little of the American people, they created an illusion of positive national leadership and even the promise of ultimate peace. Still Hull's undefined objective of international cooperation lacked the support of a strong consensus at home and any collective tendencies abroad. Together with Norman Davis, the administration's key foreign policy adviser, Hull suggested to Roosevelt in September that he speak out for international cooperation during his forthcoming trip across the continent.[53] Roosevelt, conscious of the world role being thrust upon him by his own record of leadership at home and the strength of the country for which he spoke, had long searched for some program that would bring order out of the burgeoning chaos of Europe and the Far East without committing the United States to any specific course of action. On September 14 he proposed to Ickes a program whereby the peace-loving nations would deprive any future aggressor of trade and raw materials. Ickes responded favorably, for the plan promised to keep the United States out of war by preventing any future wars from occurring. Almost immediately, however, Roosevelt abandoned the plan.[54]

In accordance with the Hull-Davis recommendation, Roosevelt decided to confront the world situation with a speech in Chicago on October 5. To give pause to the totalitarian states, however, Roosevelt substituted for Davis' phraseology, which suggested that the United States would fight if pushed too far, his two famous "quarantine" sentences: "It would seem to be unfortunately true that the epidemic of world lawlessness is spreading. When an epidemic of physical disease starts to spread the community approves and joins in a quarantine of the patients in order to protect the health of the community against the spread of the disease." Roosevelt's speech was a halting effort to bring some solvency into American foreign policy, but no less than Hull, Roosevelt anchored United States purpose to the sanctity of treaties. He defined the nation's interests not in a specific world order defined by the Versailles system but in the concept of peaceful change then being challenged by aggression. A breakdown of the peace anywhere threatened the peace everywhere. Thus it was essential that the sanctity of international treaties be restored.[55]

Roosevelt's "quarantine" idea seemed to suggest common action among nations, perhaps economic sanctions against an aggressor, and a departure from the principle of neutrality. At a press conference in Washington on October 6 Roosevelt insisted that the term "quarantine" did not imply sanctions. While rejecting coercion, he argued that his decision did not limit United States action to the moral sphere alone. He favored, he said, a system of collaboration which could be made effective without any departure from the neutrality principle. Indeed, he told one newsman, his concept might create a stronger neutrality. "There are," said the president, "a lot of methods in the world that have never been tried."

Two weeks after the press conference Roosevelt handed Norman Davis some suggestions to guide him at the forthcoming Brussels Conference. The paper contained a statement, perhaps from a book or article, on "the principle of neutral cooperation, short of obligation to use force" and recommended "the possibility of a constructive program in which a group of neutrals, acting together, but without threat of force, might make their influence felt."[56] Whatever Roosevelt's conceptualization of "quarantine," he never formulated a program based on the idea. At Chicago he had recognized the forces disturbing the status quo and revealed his deep moral opposition to them. Summarizing the meaning of his Chicago speech, Roosevelt admitted that it comprised less a program than an attitude and a search for a program. What he sought, he told the nation in his fireside chat on October 12, was peace through peaceful means. "The common sense, the intelligence of America," he said, "agrees with my statement that 'America hates war . . . America hopes for peace, therefore America actively engages in the search for peace.' "

V

Roosevelt's Chicago speech scarcely touched the Far Eastern crisis. But on October 6, 1937 the League of Nations Assembly agreed to invite the League members who were also signatories of the Nine Power Treaty to call a meeting of nations with Far East interests "to seek a method of putting an end to the Sino-Japanese conflict by agreement."[57] The British, disturbed by their vulnerability in the Pacific region, urged another Washington Conference. Roosevelt, unwilling to accept any special responsibility for a conference, suggested Brussels and refused to permit the Belgian government to send out invitations in his name. The president selected Norman Davis to head the United States delegation to Brussels.

Brussels confronted the Roosevelt administration with a policy crisis, for the declared ends of American policy—the reestablishment of the treaty structure in the Far East—again raised the disturbing issue of means. Hornbeck had long questioned Washington's reliance on world opinion. "We think," he wrote on October 7, "that if there is developed a widespread public opinion adverse to . . . the course which Japan is pursuing, this public opinion will cause Japan to desist. . . . If we mean business and if we intend to be realistic, we must consider earnestly whether we are willing to do anything beyond and further than express opinions." Hornbeck envisioned a major conference which would not only adopt restrictive measures against Japan but also concentrate on finding solutions to the internal problems of Japan in order to eliminate the need for Japanese aggression. On October 12 Maxwell Hamilton, director of the State Department's Far Eastern Division, enlarged on Hornbeck's program with a long memorandum outlining specific proposals to guarantee Japan's economic and security requirements.[58] Ultimately Roosevelt rejected both the resort to sanctions and the possible infringement on Chinese integrity that any moderate Far Eastern settlement would require.

Roosevelt's objective at the Brussels Conference was clear enough. It was essential, he informed Davis, that the United States uphold the principle of the sanctity of treaties to prevent the spread of international anarchy. To that end the conference should seek a truce and, if possible, a constructive agreement between China and Japan. What, asked Davis, if the effort failed? Was he to come home or recommend coercion? On October 19 Davis traveled to Hyde Park for his final instructions. Roosevelt told him that he was to reject joint action with the League as well as a British-led quest for collective security in the Pacific. The United States, he said, must not be "pushed out in front as the leader in or suggestor of future action," nor was it essential that any nation take the lead.[59] Should Japan refuse to come to the conference, those nations attending should pose questions to Japan relative to its objectives "which would become increasingly embarrassing and which would continue to mobilize public opinion and moral force."

Roosevelt preferred that this effort be continued to the exclusion of sanctions in any form—the arming of China or the economic and diplomatic ostracism of Japan. No action short of war would be practical, said the president, unless it had the support of the overwhelming opinion of the world. What mattered at Brussels, therefore, was the success of the conference in gaining "the substantial unanimous opinion of the overwhelming majority of all nations, whether in or out of the League of Nations." As Davis departed for Brussels, Roosevelt expressed his hope that the conference would "at least serve to clarify intentions and perhaps to do even more than that."[60]

Long before Davis arrived at Brussels the Roosevelt administration had reduced the conference to a forum for the public condemnation of Japan. Hirota had made clear that since the League had already condemned Japan there was little value in Japan's attendance. Indeed, Hirota reminded Grew that the Nine Power Treaty no longer reflected the situation existing in the Far East.[61] The British delegation, led by Foreign Secretary Anthony Eden, was prepared to face the implications of sanctions but had no interest in passing mere condemnatory resolutions which it knew would be ineffective. What Eden wanted was active United States participation in international affairs. Davis argued, however, that the existence of large British interests in the Far East had convinced much of the American public that London was attempting to maneuver the United States into defending Britain's Asian interests largely at American expense. French Foreign Minister Yvon Delbos proposed that, in order to make possible the flow of aid to China through the Indochina gateway, the United States and Britain guarantee to protect Indochina in case of Japanese reprisals. Davis termed the question of reprisals too remote for discussion. Meanwhile Soviet delegate Maxim Litvinov, the commissar for foreign affairs, declared that "the Soviet Union was prepared to take a strong position . . . in cooperation with the United States, France, and England."[62]

When the conference opened on November 3, Jay Pierrepont Moffat, Davis' adviser on European matters, reported that eight persons out of ten were already seeking an excuse for terminating the talks.[63] Davis adhered to his instructions to avoid any agreement on sanctions, reminding the British, French, and Soviet delegates that "a large section of public opinion in America felt that there was nothing in the Far East worth fighting about." The real issue, he said, was much larger—the protection of the world against lawbreakers. It was not, he told Delbos, "a struggle between the haves and have-nots, but between the law-abiders and the law-breakers."[64] Davis' opening address had been altered in Washington so that it would, in the words of Undersecretary Sumner Welles, have the greatest possible impact on public opinion in the United States. Eden endorsed the speech with little comment, but Delbos and Litvinov warned the conference that it could not escape its responsibilities in the Far East by retreating to principles. Soon the Chinese delegation, under Wellington Koo, increased Davis' troubles by demanding either sanctions against Japan or direct military aid for his country.[65] The conference, unable to act, slowly disintegrated.

By mid-November the Brussels Conference revealed the full bankruptcy of the Roosevelt policy. On November 10 Davis reminded the president by cable that his purpose was to keep the conference in existence while successive approaches to Japan would "exert a united moral pressure of world opinion on Tokyo and enable public opinion at home and elsewhere to develop and crystallize." Japan, Davis complained, had refused to alter its actions and the other delegates resented the American tactics. Hull instructed Davis to prolong the talks and avoid any suggestion of failure either of United States leadership or of international principles.[66] What disturbed Roosevelt as well as Davis was the tendency of many leading newspapers in the United States to ridicule the conference. Roosevelt instructed the State Department to stop sending such press material to Davis, adding dryly, "It is well to remember newspaper opinion and prophesy in the summer and autumn of 1936."[67] On November 17 Hull informed Davis that American opinion was overwhelmingly against sanctions and that the longer he remained in Brussels the more the press would accuse him of advocating such policies. For Roosevelt and Hull there was no escape from censure. Whereas the press opposed sanctions, it blamed the conference's failure to find a Far Eastern solution on the absence of American leadership. Thereafter Davis faced the task of terminating the conference with a statement of principles. Despite British complaints that everything had already been said to no effect, Davis managed, when the conference recessed on November 24, to gain endorsement of his principles. But that was all.

For Stimson, now advising Roosevelt, the Brussels Conference comprised the gravest crisis of his experience. He reminded the president on November 15 that China was fighting the American battle for freedom. The United States, moreover, had a special relationship to China because that nation "had an historic faith in us which she has given to no other people." Thus it was essential, wrote Stimson, that the United States not surrender its principles at Brussels and that it find a long run solution of the Far Eastern problem, for with time running out the world crisis of freedom was trembling in the balance in China. Roosevelt and Hull accepted Stimson's definition of the challenge, but they agreed that they had no answer. "As for the answer," Roosevelt wrote to Stimson, "frankly, we have not found it." That the United States had failed at Brussels Roosevelt attributed to the reluctance of Congress and the American people to support a coercive policy. Only the future, he concluded, could determine what role the United States might play in shaping the final settlement.[68]

Scarcely a month after the close of the Brussels Conference, Roosevelt reaffirmed his noncompromising attitude toward Japan. Late in December 1937 Japan communicated peace terms to the Chinese government through the German ambassador in China. The terms, suggesting the minimum Japanese demands, included Chinese abandonment of all anti-Japanese activities and cooperation in combating communism in China; the establishment of demili-tarized zones; the granting of special economic concessions; and the indemnifica-tion of Japan for its losses in the war. When Chinese Ambassador Wang revealed these demands to Roosevelt, the president created the impression that he regarded them as being limited enough. Learning of the dissatisfaction of the Chinese government, Roosevelt penned a note to Hull on January 4, 1938 denying that he had ever believed the Japanese terms lenient. "So far as an independent Chinese republic goes," he wrote, "Japanese terms which we have seen are utterly impossible."[69] Thereupon the Chinese government rejected the Japanese proposals. Tokyo, convinced that it could never come to terms with Chiang Kai-shek, announced at last that it would make no further efforts to deal with the Nationalist government.

VI

Japan's expanding war in China confronted Roosevelt with increasingly limited and embarrassing choices. Japanese bombing of Chinese cities endan-gered American lives and property; advancing Japanese forces temporarily, but effectively, slammed shut the Open Door to further Western trade and investment. That Japan threatened all United States interests in China seemed clear enough. But Japanese ambition in the Far East appeared to respect no limitations whatever when, on November 3, 1938, the Japanese government announced its program for a "New Order in East Asia." That day Prime Minister Konoe Fumimaro explained the new concept in a radio broadcast: "Japan desires to build up a stabilized Far East by cooperating with the Chinese people who have awakened to the need of self-determination as an Oriental race. . . . History shows that Japan, Manchukuo and China are so related to each other that they must bind themselves closely together in a common mission for the establishment of peace and order in the Far East by displaying their own individuality. . . . Japan desires to establish a new peace fabric in the Far East on the basis of justice."[70]

However awesome the Japanese challenge to the entire Asian peace structure, Roosevelt still had no interest in formulating any United States response that might involve this nation in a Pacific war. Newspaper editorials that crossed his desk reminded him that United States trade with China was negligible—less than the cost of a week's war with Japan.[71] Still Roosevelt was under some obligation to act. As early as January 1938 he had penned a note to Hull: "I think we should start to lay the foundation for holding Japan accountable in dollars for the acts of her soldiers. . . . [I] t is a fact that there is a vast amount of Japanese owned property in the United States and that we have excellent precedent in the Alien Property Custodian Act for holding this property in escrow. Enough said!"[72]

Roosevelt's friends and advisers now urged him to consider some form of coercion to stop Japan. Few doubted that economic sanctions would compel a Japanese capitulation. "If America should take the lead in restraining Japan and saving China," wrote economist Irving Fisher, "we should have for generations, the 'goodwill' of China and no 'yellow peril'. . . ." In November 1938 Admiral William D. Leahy reminded the president that Japan depended on open sea lanes to acquire its necessary war materials. "Any threat against these lines of communication," Leahy predicted, "will have a profound effect on her attitude of mind regarding the settlement of the present controversy."[73] That month a regular Roosevelt correspondent, Major Evans F. Carlson of the Marine Corps, wrote from China, "If the flow of oil and munitions to Japan was stopped she could not continue this conflict for another six months." In July 1938 Hornbeck had already recommended to Hull that the United States prepare to exert economic pressure on Japan by terminating the 1911 Treaty of Commerce and Navigation. In December he declared that United States retaliatory measures against Japan would not only prevent a military conflict but also prompt revisions in Japan's recently announced "New Order."[74]

Throughout 1939 and 1940 the Roosevelt administration gradually adopted three distinct lines of action against Japan: increased economic pressure, direct aid to China, and an uncompromising adherence to the established treaty structure. Still Roosevelt's direct involvement in the Sino-Japanese war came slowly and haltingly. During January 1939 the United States initiated a "moral embargo" on airplanes and parts to Japan and in February ordered a cessation of credits. At this juncture the administration again preferred caution, for opposed to the hard-line faction in the State Department, led by Hornbeck, were such moderates as Grew, Assistant Secretary of State Francis Sayre, and Maxwell Hamilton, who warned that any abrogation of the 1911 treaty would strengthen the military within the Japanese government and increase the danger of war.[75] But in April Key Pittman, chairman of the Senate Foreign Relations Committee, submitted a resolution to the Senate empowering the president to effect an embargo and limit credits against any country which infringed on the Nine Power Treaty and ignored American lives and interests. Pittman's action suggested, as did the Gallup Poll, that the nation supported the hard liners within the administration. Then on July 18 Senator Arthur H. Vandenberg of Michigan, a powerful Republican spokesman, demanded the abrogation of the commercial treaty. Responding to this strong domestic pressure, the United States government on July 26, 1939 formally notified Tokyo that termination of the treaty would become effective six months later—on January 26, 1940.

That this warning of possible economic sanctions would stop Japan seemed evident to friends of the administration. "Warm congratulations on your notice to Japan terminating nineteen-eleven treaty of commerce and navigation," William G. McAdoo wired the president on July 27. "This ought to have a great and beneficial effect." Roosevelt expressed delight at this sentiment of approval. Admiral Richard E. Byrd commended the president on another successful step toward the prevention of war. "History will, without a doubt," asserted the admiral, "show the great effectiveness of the very firm stand you have taken in the direction of international law and order." Roosevelt agreed simply that his action was "the constructive thing to do at this time."

Many who favored Roosevelt's decision to terminate the Japanese treaty now pressed him for an embargo against Japan. The danger of war seemed negligible. As one Chicagoan assured the president, "War with us would ruin Japan without a shot being fired. A successful embargo on all war materials to Japan would in six months or a year weaken Japan severely." Evans Carlson was even more sanguine. The United States need only make clear to Japanese militarists that it would not be bribed or intimidated, he promised, to halt Japan without war. An embargo would not be necessary, for the mere granting of the authority "would serve notice on the Japanese militarists that the American people are not to be trifled with."[76] During January 1940 Stimson came out in favor of an embargo on war materials. This would entail no risk, he said, because Japan was determined to avoid war with the United States. Frank Knox, publisher of the *Chicago Daily News*, assured Roosevelt that Japan's position was weakening. "The tendency is a healthy one," he wrote, "which will continue if Uncle Sam stays tough and the Chinese remain uncooperative. The only hope for a return to peace and sanity in the Far East is the continuance of this trend."[77]

Grew and Sayre, among others, remained unconvinced. Grew warned Roosevelt in November 1939 that no government in Tokyo could survive that released the Japanese grip on China under United States economic or moral pressure. "If we declare an embargo against Japan which can be interpreted here as an economic sanction," he wrote, "we must expect to see American-Japanese relations go steadily downhill thereafter." In December Grew reacted favorably to a Japanese proposal for a new trade agreement based on the most-favored-nation principle. He again urged moderation in Washington: "The simple fact is that we are here dealing not with a unified Japan but with a Japanese Government which is endeavoring courageously, even with only gradual success, to fight against a recalcitrant Japanese Army, a battle which happens to be our own battle. The Government needs support in this fight."[78] Following his conversations with Foreign Ministry spokesmen in Tokyo in May 1940, Sayre informed the administration in Washington that a United States embargo would inflame Japanese opinion and render a settlement almost impossible. The violent reaction in Japan would compel the Tokyo government to pursue its objectives in China with more determination.[79] Roosevelt accepted this counsel of caution, and the lapsing of the commercial treaty in January 1940 produced no new restrictions or discrimination against trade with Japan.

Roosevelt revealed a similar reluctance to involve the United States in direct aid to China, although many of his advisers assured him that direct United States shipments to Chiang would sustain needed Chinese resistance without provoking any serious reaction in Japan. As early as August 1938 both Ambassador Bullitt and Treasury Secretary Henry Morgenthau pressed Roosevelt for a Chinese aid program, convinced that Japan was overcommitted in China and would collapse under increased pressure.[80] Chiang Kai-shek himself addressed an appeal to Roosevelt in October 1938, reminding him that a Chinese victory would reassert the principles of peaceful change among nations, while a Japanese victory would mean the loss of security throughout the Pacific. Thanking the president for past United States support, Chiang again asked for the financial and economic help required to assure ultimate Chinese success. Roosevelt in reply expressed hope for an acceptable Far Eastern settlement but refused to commit the United States to any specific program to achieve it. "I am sure," he wrote on November 10, "that you realize that, not withstanding the strong sympathies of this country and our desire that peace with justice shall prevail in the Far East, action by the American Government must conform to methods which are consistent with this country's laws, with the current opinion of our people, and with our estimate of what is practicable."[81] Hull and Roosevelt agreed that any effective financial arrangement with China would provoke Japanese charges that the United States had actively joined the Far Eastern conflict.

If the Roosevelt administration hesitated to commit United States power to the Chinese cause, it refused to compromise its principles. Washington rejected the notion of a Japanese "New Order" completely. "Fundamental principles such as that of equality of opportunity," ran the State Department's response, "are not subject to modification by a unilateral dictum."[82] Roosevelt informed Grew in December 1939 that the United States would not negotiate a new commercial treaty until Japanese behavior conformed to American demands. Hull had recommended to Roosevelt in November that Washington avoid any effort to end the Chinese conflict, for short of a Chinese victory any adjustment would have the effect of granting Japan legal title to political and territorial gains achieved through force. John Leighton Stuart, president of Yenching University in Peking, reported to Sayre in May 1940 that Chiang's terms were simple—complete independence for China south of the Great Wall with the question of Manchuria left undecided. Short of that, Chiang had informed Stuart, China would prefer to continue the struggle. Not desperate enough to negotiate with China on such terms, the Japanese government still looked to the United States for help in terminating the China Incident. Sayre reported to Roosevelt that the Japanese foreign minister had acknowledged Japan's difficulties in carrying on the war against China and admitted that Japan would prefer to retire gracefully, "provided of course that she were given certain compensations in North China." Again the Roosevelt administration refused to contribute to any imposition of Japanese will on China. Hornbeck that month warned that the Japanese would interpret any compromise as a sign of weakness and respond with a thrust toward the East Indies.[83] Roosevelt himself concluded that any effort of the United States to improve relations with Japan by modifying its principles would achieve nothing. Unable to move forward or backward, the cabinet of Abe Nobuyuki in Tokyo fell in January 1940. The succeeding cabinet of Yonai Mitsumasa gave way to a new Konoe cabinet in July. Pressed by extremists at home and barred from either diplomatic or military successes abroad, no Japanese government retained much chance of survival.

VII

By mid-1940 it was clear that Roosevelt's defense of principles in the Far East had failed to bring peace. Nevertheless United States officials still assumed that a combination of Chinese resistance and the mere threat of economic sanctions would stop Japan without any recognition of Japanese gains in China. They were wrong. The Japanese, unable to negotiate an acceptable agreement with China, now moved to consolidate their Asian position by controlling the southern approaches to China. At the same time the threat of an American embargo, especially on oil, focused Japanese attention on the oil resources of the Netherlands East Indies. The German offensive against Holland, Belgium, and

France in May-June 1940 rendered the Dutch and French empires in Asia vulnerable to Japanese expansion. During June the Japanese Foreign Ministry extorted the promise of a million tons of oil from the Dutch authorities in the Indies and pressed France for the right to blockade the Indochinese border with China.

For Washington the Japanese move into Southeast Asia shifted the issue from concern for the treaty structure in China to defense of the East Asian balance of power. Immediately United States policy began to harden as the Roosevelt administration began anew its search for the elusive deterrent. Admiral Harold Stark, chief of naval operations, explained that the continued presence of the fleet at Pearl Harbor "would serve as a deterrent, even if the U.S. were not in fact prepared to take action if the Japanese attacked the Dutch Indies. The mere uncertainty as to U.S. intentions would hold them back."[84] Then on July 2 the new National Defense Act gave the president authority to place under license arms, munitions, critical and strategic raw materials, airplane parts, optical instruments, and metal working machinery. But this new order omitted the two items Japan needed most urgently—oil and scrap iron. The moderates in the State Department, led by Hamilton, were still determined to avoid a showdown with Japan and the encouragement of a Japanese invasion of the East Indies. Grew warned the administration in July that the continuing hard line on negotiations would soon compel Japan to join the Axis.

Still convinced that Japan could be stopped without war, the hard-line faction around Roosevelt pressed for an embargo and no compromise. In July Roosevelt himself strengthened this group immeasurably by naming Stimson secretary of war and Knox secretary of the navy, two men who shared Hornbeck's long-standing opposition to Japanese policy. "The only way to treat Japan," declared Stimson shortly after taking office, "is not to give her anything."[85] On July 20 the president signed a bill to create a two-ocean navy. In time, the administration hoped, the United States would be able to confront Japan in the Pacific without deserting Britain in the Atlantic. At this point, under increased insistence from Stimson, Knox, and Morgenthau, Roosevelt ignored Sumner Welles' warning that further pressure would provoke a Japanese advance into Southeast Asia and on July 25, 1940 signed an order to include oil and scrap iron in the export license system. Subsequently, however, the State Department moderates forced a compromise that limited export restrictions to aviation motor fuel and lubricants and heavy iron and steel scrap. Japan countered with further thrusts into Indochina and increased demands for East Indian oil. The president responded to a Japanese ultimatum regarding Indochina in September by terminating the export of scrap iron and steel to Japan, but it seemed clear that further economic pressures on Japan would encourage not submission but a more rapid advance to the south and possibly war with the United States. Grew's prediction of July proved correct. On September 27, 1940 Japan signed the Tripartite Pact with Germany and Italy.

Still the illusion of Japanese vulnerability and momentary collapse did not die. Those who favored a stronger policy to restrain Japan—whether through economic sanctions, a show of naval might in the western Pacific, or aid to China—assumed that United States resistance would produce the desired result without direct United States military involvement in the Pacific. Early in

October 1940, in a letter which Roosevelt distributed to his key advisers, Enoch Walter Earle, a New York attorney, urged the administration to grant a large and immediate loan to China, reinforce the Asiatic squadron, impose an absolute embargo on Japan, and increase American aid to Britain. "Japan," he warned, "must be stopped sooner or later."[86] Later that month Ickes urged the president to impose an oil embargo on Japan. It would not stop Japanese expansion into Southeast Asia, he admitted, but shortages of oil would render an attack on the Dutch East Indies more difficult.[87] The more optimistic Stimson urged a display of United States military power in the East Indies to prevent a Japanese invasion. As Stimson declared in a memorandum of October 2, Japan "has also historically shown that when the United States indicates by clear language and bold actions that she intends to carry out a clear and affirmative policy in the Far East, Japan will yield to that policy even though it conflicts with her own Asiatic policy and conceived interest."[88] But Admirals Stark and James O. Richardson, commander of the United States Fleet, opposed any American naval presence in Southeast Asia. With this judgment Roosevelt and Hull agreed. During November a secret naval report made clear that the United States was not prepared for war in the Pacific. Whereas with Britian's collapse, ran the report, "we might not *lose everywhere,* we might, possibly, not *win anywhere.*" The United States, with its deep interest in the Far Eastern balance of power, the report warned, dared not reduce Japan to a second-class power.[89]

Roosevelt continued to move cautiously. On November 30 he placed another $100 million at Chiang's disposal and promised China fifty modern pursuit planes immediately. In December a State Department memorandum assured the president that China was inflicting heavy casualties on the Japanese and that further aid to China, including the establishment of a Chinese air force, would permit China to dispose of the Japanese invasion without further risk to the United States.[90] Roosevelt dispatched some ships and planes to the Philippines under the principle, as explained by Hull, of "letting them [the Japanese] guess as to when and in what set of circumstances we would fight. While Japan continued to guess, we continued to get ready for anything she might do." Unfortunately the vagueness of Roosevelt's policy kept the British guessing no less than the Japanese. As Harry Hopkins reported to Roosevelt from London in December 1940, "Eden asked me repeatedly what our country would do if Japan attacked Singapore or the Dutch East Indies, saying it was essential to their policy to know."[91] Roosevelt refused to answer. Three weeks later he explained his dilemma to Grew: "[T]he problems which we face are so vast and so interrelated that any attempt even to state them compels one to think of five continents and seven seas." The United States, he admitted, was on the defensive. It could not establish hard and fast plans; it could only determine its course as circumstances permitted.[92] If United States policy in the Pacific continued to perform on a "twenty-four hour" basis, the reason is clear. Roosevelt was never able to establish goals in the Far East which reflected the nation's limited interests, its lack of available strength, and its desire to avoid war. Nor could he, at any price, create a world which conformed to established American principles. No available policy, in short, could bridge the gulf between the nation's limited power and its unlimited objectives in the Orient.

VIII

Long before Admiral Nomura Kichisaburō reached Washington as Japanese ambassador in February 1941 to reopen conversations amid a crisis atmosphere, the character of United States-Japanese relations, as well as their diplomatic hopelessness, was well established. The Japanese challenge appeared obvious enough. As Hull reminded the House Foreign Affairs Committee in January: "It has been clear throughout that Japan has been actuated ... by broad and ambitious plans for establishing herself in a dominant position in the entire region of the Western Pacific. Her leaders have openly declared their determination to achieve and maintain that position by force of arms."[93] Still the administration, while rejecting any thought of compromise, hoped to counter Japan on all Asian fronts by exerting moral and, if necessary, economic pressure. At stake was less the defense of China than the nation's capacity to establish the principle of peaceful change. Hull spelled out United States purposes in a note to Roosevelt in March 1941: "We wish to be friends ... with any nation in the world—but in our concept real friendship and real cooperation can prevail only between and among nations each and all of which want peace, justice, and security for all."[94] Japan scarcely conformed to such standards.

Roosevelt greeted Nomura on February 14. Earlier the State Department had advised the president, in his conversations with the Japanese ambassador, to adopt the tactics of Theodore Roosevelt: to "speak softly" without any hint of compromise "while simultaneously giving by our acts in the Pacific new glimpses of diplomatic, economic, and naval 'big sticks.' "[95] Roosevelt addressed Nomura as an old friend but reminded him that the American people were troubled over Japanese aggression in the Far East. Because United States-Japanese relations were strained, Roosevelt suggested that Nomura "sit down with the Secretary of State and other State Department officials and review and reexamine the important phases of the relations between the two countries, ... to see if our relations could not be improved."[96]

Nomura awaited specific instructions from Tokyo. On March 8 he opened conversations with Hull which were to continue until December. From the beginning the disagreements were profound. Hull made it clear that the United States would accept no settlement until Japan abandoned its aggression and agreed to negotiate on the basis of the established treaty structure. Nomura responded that Japan's expansionism resulted not from a desire for conquest but to counter Western pressures and advantages in the Far East. He assured Hull as well as other Washington officials that his country did not want war with the United States but warned that embargoes would force Japan to take additional military steps. During subsequent meetings the two negotiators extended and embroidered their arguments; they never approached an agreement.

On April 16 Hull presented Nomura the four-point demands that became the final stand of the United States government:

(1) Respect for the territorial·integrity and the sovereignty of each and all nations; (2) support of the principle of noninterference in the internal affairs of other countries; (3) support of the principle of equality, including equality of commercial opportunity; (4) non-

disturbance of the *status quo* in the Pacific except as the *status quo* may be altered by peaceful means.

There could be no negotiation, Hull declared, until Japan agreed to these four principles. He suggested that Japan adopt the principle of the good neighbor and establish mutually beneficial relations with its Far Eastern neighbors as the United States had done in Latin America. Nomura replied that the United States enjoyed special privileges in South America and the Caribbean which the Western powers would never grant Japan in the Orient.[97] Nomura's dispatch to Tokyo scarcely revealed the full extent of Hull's demands, for he wanted the conversations to continue. Yet so bitter and pervasive were the disputes in Tokyo that the Japanese government did not respond for another month.

If Japan wanted peace, the Japanese reply of May 12 rejected totally the capitulation that Hull's principles demanded. It asked Roosevelt to compel Chiang to negotiate a peace with Japan (under threat of a cessation of all United States aid to China) in accordance with principles that would leave China independent but obligated to cooperate with Japan in the future. Hull distrusted the Japanese formula, for it failed to state precisely what terms Japan intended to impose. In exchange for peace in China, moreover, Japan demanded a resumption of normal trade relations with the United States. Hull found the proposal completely unacceptable.

To break this deadlock, both Japan and the United States began to escalate the means of policy available to them. To conserve shipping space in the Atlantic, Washington on June 20, 1941 terminated all shipments of oil from Atlantic ports except to the fighting British empire and the western hemisphere. But Ickes was not satisfied. He addressed Roosevelt on June 23: "There will never be so good a time to stop the shipment of oil to Japan as we now have. Japan is so occupied with what is happening in Russia and what may happen in Siberia that she won't venture a hostile move against the Dutch East Indies." An embargo on oil, wrote Ickes, would enjoy popular approval throughout the United States. Roosevelt asked Ickes if he would favor an embargo if this were "to tip the delicate scales and cause Japan to decide either to attack Russia or to attack the Dutch East Indies." To Ickes, who now tendered his resignation from the cabinet, such possible Japanese decisions were immaterial. "Foreign wars," he wrote on June 25, "cannot be fought without oil and gasoline, and we are furnishing Japan with this sine qua non in order to fight against what we are fighting for." Roosevelt reminded Ickes on July 1 that Japan was experiencing a deep internal struggle in its attempt to decide whether to invade Siberia, attack the Indies, or sit on the fence and be more friendly to the United States. "No one knows," he concluded, "what the decision will be but, as you know, it is terribly important for the control of the Atlantic for us to help to keep peace in the Pacific. I simply have not got enough Navy to go round—and every little episode in the Pacific means fewer ships in the Atlantic."[98]

Unable to reach agreement with either the United States or China, the Japanese government at an Imperial Conference on July 2 decided to establish the Greater East Asia Coprosperity Sphere and achieve a settlement of the China Incident with an invasion of Indochina, whatever the obstacles encountered.[99] Whereas the Konoe government still hoped to avoid war with the United States, it was now determined to choke off further Chinese resistance before the United States crippled Japan with economic sanctions. On July 10 Acting Secretary of State Welles notified the British ambassador of Roosevelt's decision to counter any Japanese thrust into Southeast Asia with economic and financial embargoes. Several days later General George C. Marshall informed Roosevelt that a decoded Japanese message contained an ultimatum to France for the Japanese occupation of naval and air bases in Indochina.[100] But in Washington the Japanese embassy denied any knowledge of an intended Japanese occupation of Indochina. On July 20 Nomura called on Admiral Richmond Kelly Turner, who reported the conversation to Admiral Stark. Turner warned that an embargo would drive Japan toward the East Indies and possibly into war with the United States. He recommended that existing trade with Japan continue. Stark on July 21 sent this report to Roosevelt with the notation, "I concur in general." For him the navy faced enough challenges in the Atlantic.[101]

On July 23 Nomura asked for a meeting with Welles. He admitted that the Japanese government had concluded an agreement with the French Vichy regime for the occupation of southern Indochina. Nothing less, he explained, would guarantee the flow of rice to Japan and terminate the overland flow of supplies to China. He warned again that an oil embargo would enflame Japanese opinion but assured Welles that his government wanted an agreement with the United States based on Hull's four principles. Welles retorted that the Japanese invasion of Indochina was a clear violation of the letter and spirit of those principles and rendered any further conversations pointless.[102] On July 24 Roosevelt received Nomura and warned him that any Japanese move against the Dutch East Indies would provoke Dutch-British resistance and bring a general war to the Far East. He then offered a proposal. If Japan refrained from occupying Indochina, he would "do everything within his power to obtain from the Governments of China, Great Britain, the Netherlands, and of course the United States itself a binding and solemn declaration, provided Japan would undertake the same commitment, to regard Indochina as a neutralized country."[103]

Finally on July 26 Roosevelt, having received no response from Tokyo, issued an executive order freezing Japanese assets in the United States and thus effectively terminating all United States commercial and financial relations with Japan. Roosevelt, unlike Stark, was convinced that Japan would not fight the United States and the British empire simultaneously. This judgment was fundamental to his decisions after July 1941.[104] But Roosevelt, in effect, had given the Japanese the immediate alternative of capitulating or committing more of their strength to the Far Eastern struggle. Again the warnings of the moderates in Washington proved accurate. The Japanese accelerated their move into Southeast Asia while they still had enough oil. The final crisis in United States-Japanese relations was but a matter of time.

IX

No Japanese effort at negotiation after July 1941, despite that nation's narrow choice between prolonged scrimping and expanded war, held any promise of success. Konoe's proposal of August 6 met with immediate rejection in Washington, for he sought to trade Japanese withdrawal from Indochina for restoration of normal trade relations with the United States. The United States, in addition, was to initiate direct Japanese-Chinese negotiations and recognize Japan's special status in Indochina even after the withdrawal of troops. Nor did Konoe's subsequent request for a personal meeting with Roosevelt assure any greater compliance with United States principles. Roosevelt reminded Nomura on August 17 that his administration was standing firmly on the principles laid down by Hull.[105] When Hull in September suggested how the president might explain his past refusal to meet Konoe, Roosevelt replied: "I wholly agree with your pencilled note—to recite the more liberal original attitude of the Japanese when they first sought the meeting, point out their narrowed position now, earnestly ask if they cannot go back to their original attitude, start discussions again on agreement in principle, and reemphasize my hope for a meeting."[106] Still Roosevelt's firmness appeared to Americans as a guarantee of peace. "Any sign of weakness, backing down, or palliation," wrote one Washington attorney in mid-August, "will certainly bring war. The Japanese military officers will consider it due to timidity. If they ever form that opinion, we will certainly have war.... There is a chance to avoid a conflict if the present policy is continued."[107]

Confronted by almost universal assumptions of invincibility within the United States, Japan's choices became desperate. Unless Japan returned to its position of 1937, it could never hope to come to terms with Washington. Such a retreat would require fundamental, gradual adjustments, but time was running out. Konoe could not sustain his own or his country's position any longer without an immediate settlement. On October 7 the prime minister's secretary informed the American embassy in Tokyo that private Konoe-Roosevelt negotiations comprised the last hope for peace. "Prince Konoe," he said, "was at a loss to know what further he could do.... When Prince Konoe had taken that responsibility [for starting the talks], the Army gave him full and unqualified support, and if his high hopes are not fulfilled he will have to 'assume responsibility,' and there would be no one who would have the courage to take the risks which the Prince has taken or with sufficient prestige and political position to gain the support of the Army."[108]

With the negotiations deadlocked and the two nations standing at the edge of war, the Konoe government fell on October 18. United States-Japanese relations had reached an impasse, not because Tokyo's demands had become greater—indeed, the Japanese, under intense economic pressure, would have accepted less after September than they would have earlier—but because the Roosevelt administration had made it increasingly clear that Tokyo could anticipate no compromise. Thus the final Japanese proposals of November 1941 sought only a modus vivendi—a temporary agreement—not a permanent settlement. That month an Imperial Conference made the fateful decision to fight beginning in December if the United States still refused to compromise on the tangential issues of Indochina and oil sanctions.

Standing firm on principle, the Roosevelt administration in November looked to the nation's defenses. Early that month Chiang warned the president and Churchill that Japan, if it succeeded in closing the Burma Road, would sever China's transportation with the outside world and perhaps force China out of the war. Hull and Roosevelt, reluctant to issue any further warnings unless the

United States were prepared to act, turned to the army and navy. Both Marshall and Stark said that the United States should avoid any immediate involvement in the Far East. Already the movement of Flying Fortresses and mechanized equipment to the Philippines was under way. These heavy bombers, with an operating radius of 1500 miles, could reach Japanese cities and hopefully the Japanese positions in Indochina. Stimson had reported to the president on October 21: "A strategic opportunity of the utmost importance has suddenly arisen in the southwestern Pacific. . . . From being impotent to influence events in that area, we suddenly find ourselves vested with the possibility of great effective power . . . even this imperfect threat, if not promptly called by the Japanese, bids fair to stop Japan's march to the south and secure the safety of Singapore."[109] Churchill was equally gratified at the growing United States military presence in the Pacific. He cabled Roosevelt on November 2: "The firmer your attitude and ours, the less chance of their taking the plunge."

No more than Japan did the United States want war. But Roosevelt and his advisers preferred war to recognition of any successful assault on the treaty structure of the Far East. They would fight, not for China, but for the principle of peaceful change and ultimately for the East Asian balance of power. In his press conference of November 28, 1941 Roosevelt declared that United States policy in the Pacific had been based on infinite patience. The situation was serious, he admitted, "because our one desire has been peace in the Pacific, and the taking of no steps to alter the prospects of peace, which of course has meant non-aggression. It really boils down to that." On both China and Indochina United States policy was set, he told the newsmen. There would be no compromise. Nor did Roosevelt's eleventh-hour message to the Japanese emperor on December 6 contain any suggestion of compromise. It was a moving appeal to reason and peace, but ultimately on American terms.[110]

Roosevelt's dilemma in confronting a clearly-definable Japanese challenge was understandable. Through two administrations he refused to alter, on the basis of independent advice and judgment, the Far Eastern policy that had been inherited from Hoover and perpetuated by the nation's dominant foreign policy elite. Unwilling to modify the ends of United States policy—the complete unraveling of the Japanese empire—Roosevelt moved cautiously but unerringly toward the acceptance of those judgments which promised victory in Asia without compromise or direct United States involvement. The result was a policy of escalation anchored to economic sanctions and a limited show of force. With each major increment of pressure, the administration sought and anticipated a Japanese capitulation.

Washington officials anchored their optimism to two assumptions. First, they believed Japan so vulnerable to United States economic policy that its government would ultimately be compelled to relent in its defiance of the Far Eastern status quo. Stimson himself informed a cabinet meeting on October 4 that "in the autumn of 1919 President Wilson got his dander up and put on an embargo on all cotton going to Japan and a boycott on her silk, with the result that she crawled down within two months and brought all of her troops out from Siberia like whipped puppies."[111] Whatever the truth of Stimson's observation, no Japanese government would submit to economic and moral sanctions in 1941.

Second, Hornbeck and others assured Roosevelt repeatedly that Japan would avoid war with the United States, especially if the nation remained resolute. In January 1941 Hornbeck developed the thesis that Japan always went to war suddenly and with a minimum of warning. Japan's open belligerence, he concluded, was evidence that Tokyo was engaged in a campaign of bluff. As late as November 27, 1941 Hornbeck declared that in his opinion "the Japanese Government does not intend or expect to have forthwith armed conflict with the United States. The Japanese Government, while launching new offensive operations at some point or points in the Far East will endeavor to avoid attacking or being attacked by the United States."[112] The disparity between Japanese and United States power was profound, but those who controlled Japanese policy, facing the simple choice between total capitulation or an interminable war in China, chose the most drastic solution available—a direct attack on the United States Asiatic Fleet. As Prime Minister Tōjō Hideki once phrased it, "sometimes a man has to jump with his eyes closed from the temple of Kiyomizu into the ravine below."[113] Roosevelt no less than Hoover had identified the American interest in the Pacific with the moral defense of existing treaties. Unfortunately, as Stimson observed so clearly ten years earlier, the old treaty structure no longer had much relationship to the political and military realities of the Far East.

CABINET, EMPEROR,
AND SENIOR STATESMEN

Imai Seiichi

Translated by
H. Paul Varley

I

During the fourteen-year period from the outbreak of the Manchurian Incident in September 1931 to the end of the Pacific War in August 1945, no fewer than fifteen cabinets followed one another in Japan. Their average duration was less than one year.

Under the Meiji constitution the authority of the legislative branch of the government, the Diet, was limited. While the administrative branch had great power, the cabinet itself was not in a strong position politically. The prime minister was literally only a "chief among equals" and possessed the right neither to direct nor to dismiss his ministers. When opposition arose within the cabinet, it led in a very great number of instances to the general resignation of its members.

The army and navy ministerships were restricted to military officers, and the active service provision, although abolished in 1912, was reinstated in 1936. Moreover, in accordance with the principle of the right of supreme command, supervision of both the army and the navy remained outside the purview of ministers of state as well as of cabinet deliberation.

The authority of the cabinet was further circumscribed by the fact that administrative positions within the ministries under the cabinet were filled exclusively by career bureaucrats who met specific qualifications. Appointment to the House of Peers or the Privy Council awaited particularly successful bureaucrats following their retirement from high-ranking posts. Inevitably, cabinet ministers with only political party backgrounds found it extremely difficult to exercise control over the bureaucracy, and in consequence the more important cabinet positions were often assigned to party politicians who had had bureaucratic careers. Foreign Ministry bureaucrats, like the professional army and navy personnel, constituted an exclusive group, and during the period of party cabinets no party man ever served as foreign minister.

The cabinet occupied an intermediate position between a powerful bureaucracy and the several privileged organs whose memberships were drawn largely from the ranks of former senior bureaucrats. One of these organs was the Privy Council which, functioning as an advisory body to the emperor, reviewed, in response to His Majesty's inquiries, matters such as those relating to constitutional law and to international treaties. Another was the indissoluble House of Peers, which was composed of former high-ranking bureaucrats and members of the nobility and possessed power equal to that of the House of Representatives.

Such privileged bodies narrowed the range of policy choices available to the cabinet. In addition, numerous checks had been placed upon political party cabinets in particular lest they attempt to transform Japan's traditionally despotic and aggressive foreign policy into a more liberal and cooperative one. The Meiji constitution required that the emperor personally designate the prime minister and order him to form a cabinet. In actuality, however, the imperial prerogative to form a cabinet was carried out by the genro, who customarily recommended the prime minister.

The genro, who were certified by imperial edict, were bureaucratic statesmen who had distinguished themselves in the building of the Meiji state. Until 1901 (with one exception) they uninterruptedly occupied the prime minister's chair; and even thereafter, although withdrawing from the center of the political stage, they manipulated the cabinet and exerted pressure on it as "kingmakers" and "guardians of the administration." After Saionji Kimmochi became the sole surviving genro in 1924, there came into being the so-called party cabinet system based on the principle of appointing as prime minister the leader of the majority party in the House of Representatives. Yet cabinets of this period were in actual practice not formed by holding general elections to determine majorityship among the parties. Invariably, when there was a change in administration, a new cabinet would first be appointed and *then* a general election would be held to make the party in office the majority party. Hence Saionji continued to play an important role in selecting the prime minister, and politicians did not neglect to make their "pilgrimages" to Saionji's residence in retirement at Okitsu.

From their experience of having molded the Meiji state into a great empire in the Far East through their skillful handling of international affairs, the genro were especially sensitive to the international setting and retained a strong interest in Japanese foreign policy. Indeed, they did not hesitate to offer the government advice and at times to interfere in the conduct of foreign affairs. Important diplomatic dispatches were circulated among the genro, who even held meetings on occasions of important foreign policy decision making, as, for example, when war was declared or peace was concluded. It is not known precisely how long the practice of circulating diplomatic dispatches among the genro was continued; but even after Saionji became the last of the genro, he paid great attention to foreign policy and considered it carefully when selecting a prime minister.

The Privy Council's importance in foreign affairs grew out of the powers accorded to it under the Meiji constitution. The constitution drafters had vested in the emperor supreme power over the conduct of foreign affairs and did not require Diet consent for concluding treaties, declaring war, or making peace. Instead, "treaties and agreements arising from negotiations with foreign powers" were to be referred to the Privy Council, and the government was thus obliged to secure Privy Council approval before signing or ratifying treaties.

After the death of Itō Hirobumi in 1909, the influential genro Yamagata Aritomo served as president of the Privy Council, whose membership was made up largely of retired bureaucrats. During the mid-Taishō period the most powerful councillors, who served also on the Advisory Council on Foreign Relations, a body directly answerable to the emperor, participated in the making of foreign policy and were able to exert pressure on the Foreign Ministry.

From about the time of the Hara cabinet the Privy Council, asserting the importance of national sovereignty, began to use its right of treaty review to curb the government's cooperative foreign policy. Saionji attempted to diminish the Council's power after 1924 by replacing its president and the bureaucrats who had theretofore served on it with scholars and lawyers who had no political ambitions. But Itō Miyoji, who had been a councillor since 1899, Hiranuma Kiichirō, and other powerful members of the Privy Council took an especially vigorous stand in opposition to Shidehara diplomacy and greatly hampered the actions of the Kenseikai-Minseitō cabinets of the 1920s and early 1930s. In 1927 these councillors attacked the government's laxity in dealing with the Northern Expedition of the Chinese Nationalist army and overthrew the Wakatsuki cabinet, which was already in difficulty because of the bank panic of that year. Moreover, these same councillors sought to use the London Naval Treaty to drive the Hamaguchi cabinet into a corner.

The character of the emperor at this time was, as Kuno Osamu has pointed out, a dual one. In "principle" he was an absolute monarch deriving his authority by divine right. By "understanding" among the ruling elite, however, he was a constitutional monarch, as described in the emperor-organ theory. Thus, while the ruling elite, in the interest of the rational conduct of state affairs, adopted the theory of constitutional monarchy, which more distinctly demarcated the distribution of powers among state organs advising the emperor,[1] the general masses were encouraged to worship him as a "living god." In this way the absolutist forces, spearheaded by the military, attempted to inculcate a strong sense of obedience and loyalty in the minds of the people. Liberal bureaucrats and party politicans, such as Saionji, disapproved of the absolutist approach, believing that it would only arouse popular resentment and bring harm to the state. The liberals therefore endeavored to emphasize the emperor's role as a constitutional monarch.

Shigemitsu Mamoru, who served as ambassador to Britain and as foreign minister in the Tōjō and Koiso cabinets, noted in his memoirs that Saionji expressed to the emperor his feeling that "emperorship" under constitutional government ought to consist of the sovereign's acting solely on the advice of responsible officials. And in fact, Shigemitsu observed, the Shōwa emperor did deal with political matters exclusively on the counsel of such officials. He might in the course of things occasionally point out errors to them, but he did not fail to accept their advice.[2]

This is not, however, a complete picture of the decision making process, which more often than not was hidden "behind a curtain." Only after a decision had been reached through conflict and compromise among the various organs advising the emperor was it presented to the people as the emperor's personal decision, a procedure that stifled almost all public criticism. This tendency became increasingly noticeable after the Manchurian Incident, when a imperial edict or an Imperial Conference frequently accompanied the announcement of a particularly significant foreign policy decision. Imperial edicts were promulgated at the time of Japan's withdrawal from the League of Nations in 1933, when the Tripartite Pact was concluded in 1940, and when war was declared the following year. Imperial Conferences were convened upon six occasions: November 30, 1938 (when the "Policies for Adjusting to New Japan-China Relations" were decided upon), September 19 and November 13, 1940, and July 2, September 6, and December 1, 1941. While such exploitation of the imperial authority effectively silenced public debate, it also meant that policy decisions were virtually unalterable and contributed to the inflexibility of Japanese diplomacy.

In addition, the role played by important court officials in the decision making process cannot be overlooked. Paramount among such advisers to the emperor were the lord privy seal and the grand chamberlain.

Decision making was also complicated by the fact that the Meiji constitution did not delimit clearly the respective spheres within which the various advisory bodies were to operate. In reality, their jurisdictions tended to vary according to the power relationships among the parties involved. To assert the principle of responsible party cabinets meant, in this context, to interpret as broadly as possible the advisory scope of the cabinet. The Meiji constitution invested supreme authority in the emperor, and it was intended that, in the event of jurisdictional disputes among the various governmental organs subordinate to him, His Majesty would decide those disputes with the advice of the Privy Council. Yet not only did this present the danger that, contrary to intent, the Privy Council might in practice severely limit the power of the cabinet, it even placed the Privy Council in a position to become a privileged body superior to the cabinet. The only course open to the cabinet was to broaden and make secure its sphere of authority by using its political power to revise laws and practices derived from the constitution. But party cabinets failed to do this to any significant degree. In particular, they never settled the issue of whether or not the right to determine the organization and personnel strength of the army and navy was a prerogative of the supreme command (Article 12 of the constitution).

II

The matter to which we must now turn is that of "working through the court." Decisions of the government and the military commands were finalized only after they had been submitted to and approved by the Throne. One area of dispute between the cabinet and the military commands was the question of how to handle appeals made by one of the latter directly to the Throne without consulting the cabinet. If the prime minister and one of the service heads happened to express differing views on the same matter to the Throne, the emperor would be faced with the problem of deciding between them. To make such a decision would simply have placed the responsible party whose authority was denied in the position of having to resign, leaving the basic issue unresolved. In order for the emperor to function as a constitutional monarch, it was mandatory that the procedure of "working through the court" operate in such a way as to avoid situations in which the emperor himself would be forced to make decisions.

The problem arose specifically at the time of the London Naval Conference in 1930, when the Hamaguchi cabinet clashed with the Navy General Staff over whether or not to accept the final compromise proposal put forward by the United States. The Hamaguchi cabinet—which through the mediation of Admiral Okada Keisuke and others of the moderate faction within the navy had obtained the reluctant agreement of Chief of the Navy General Staff Katō Kanji—formulated a directive for acceptance in principle of the American proposal and cabled it to the Japanese delegation after having obtained the emperor's approval. Katō, however, had the previous day attempted to petition the Throne about the directive through the office of the emperor's aide-de-camp and had been turned down. Grand Chamberlain Suzuki Kantarō, who was senior to Katō in the navy, persuaded him to withdraw his petition on the grounds that it would be improper for Katō to address the Throne concerning the issue before the prime minister had done so. The day after Hamaguchi received imperial approval of his directive, Katō advised the Throne that, inasmuch as the American proposal would severely handicap naval strategy, it should be carefully reviewed. Distorted reports later charged that Suzuki had obstructed the military's right of direct access to the Throne and even criticized him for having infringed on the autonomy of the supreme command.

As is apparent from the above incident, the effects of "working through the court" under the Meiji constitution were especially crucial in relations between the cabinet and the military commands. Accordingly, Saionji paid careful attention to the personnel at court, including the lord keeper of the privy seal, the imperial household minister, the grand chamberlain, and the aide-de-camp. From 1925 on the lord keeper of the privy seal was Makino Nobuaki, and the imperial household minister was Ichiki Kitokurō, both of whom enjoyed Saionji's confidence. Suzuki had resigned the key post of chief of the Navy General Staff in 1929 to become grand chamberlain.

The role of the last remaining genro, who was responsible for proposing candidates for prime minister, and of the various court officials, such as the lord keeper of the privy seal and the grand chamberlain, who were in constant attendance on the emperor, became increasingly important. Saionji's political significance is clearly attested to by the extraordinary number of prominent individuals who called on him at his Zagyosō residence in Okitsu while the naval disarmament talks were being held in London in 1930. Besides Wakatsuki Reijirō, who headed the Japanese delegation to the conference, and Navy Minister Takarabe Takeshi, his visitors included: Imperial Household Minister Ichiki Kitokurō, Lord Keeper of the Privy Seal Makino Nobuaki, Prince Konoe Fumimaro, Prime Minister Hamaguchi Osachi, Army Minister Ugaki Kazushige, Colonial Affairs Minister Matsuda Genji, Justice Minister Watanabe Chifuyu, and several Seiyūkai members such as former Finance Minister Mitsuchi Chūzō.[3] In addition, Saionji's personal secretary Harada Kumao would gather information from various sources, report it to Saionji, and pass the genro's views on to Prime Minister Hamaguchi.

After the Manchurian Incident Saionji found it exceedingly distasteful to be obliged to recommend military men to the prime ministership and went so far as to indicate his intention to relinquish his privileged status as genro and to hand over to the lord keeper of the privy seal responsibility for making such recommendations. But Saionji was dissuaded from doing this; rather, he contented himself with the procedure whereby he conferred, when he saw the need, with the senior statesmen and the lord keeper of the privy seal in making his recommendations.

The term senior statesmen (*jūshin*) at first signified the president of the Privy Council and certain especially honored former prime ministers, but eventually it came to include all previous holders of the office of prime minister. The practice finally evolved for the lord keeper of the privy seal, in consultation with the senior statesmen, to recommend successors to the prime ministership.

Beginning in 1931 there was a series of plots within the army and navy that aimed at establishing a military government through coup d'état, making Saionji's position even more difficult. The Minseitō cabinet of Wakatsuki Reijirō was overthrown in December of that year as a result of army pressure following the Manchurian Incident, and in the May 15 Incident the following year Prime Minister Inukai Tsuyoshi was gunned down by young navy officers. The political pressure of the military increased as it sought to ensure a cabinet amenable to it and to strengthen the voices of the service ministers in both foreign and domestic affairs. At the same time the army and navy high commands attempted to establish a superior position vis-à-vis the government by exercising direct influence on the emperor. There even appears to have been an attempt to change the emperor's personal staff by having Privy Council Vice President Hiranuma Kiichirō, who was friendly to the army and who headed the right wing organization Kokuhonsha (National Foundation Society), appointed lord keeper of the privy seal.

Following the May 15 Incident the selection of a prime minister was especially difficult. Saionji chose neither a party nor army cabinet but directed Saitō Makoto, an admiral in the navy and one of its moderates, to form an interim administration. Saionji's aim was, while avoiding a direct clash, to slow the army down. Where absolutely necessary he would grant concessions, but he hoped to await abatement of the storm of fascism by minimizing the dangers such concessions would create and playing for time. Admiral Okada Keisuke, who had mediated between the government and the navy at the London conference, became prime minister after Saitō.

The military and the right wing exerted various pressures and even made open attacks on these moderate cabinets, on Saionji (whom they saw to be backing them), and on influential court officials. Saionji reacted by devoting extraordinary attention to appointments at court and by constantly opposing the entry into it of such members of the right wing as Hiranuma. When Imperial Houshold Minister Ichiki resigned in 1933, Saionji put forward as his successor Yuasa Kurahei, who had risen through the bureaucracy of the Home Ministry and was known for his firmness of character. The following year, upon the resignation of Privy Council President Kuratomi Yūzaburō, the genro rejected the advancement of Hiranuma and designated Ichiki for the presidency. Makino's departure from the office of lord keeper of the privy seal in 1935, moreover, brought the appointment of former Prime Minister Saitō in his place. But the moderates, including Prime Minister Okada, Lord Keeper of the Privy Seal Saitō, and Grand Chamberlain Suzuki, became targets of assault in the mutiny of February 26, 1936.

III

In the years after 1931 Saionji continued his efforts to exert a moderating influence. To understand him, it is important to have some knowledge of his ideas.

Saionji had close personal relations with Saitō and Makino, also moderates, who had been associated with him since early 1906, when he had formed his first cabinet and named Makino as minister of education and Saitō as navy minister.[4] In 1919 Saionji and Makino were appointed by Prime Minister Hara Takashi to be Japan's chief delegates to the Versailles Conference. Before his departure, Makino addressed the Advisory Council on Foreign Relations, where he expressed the following sentiments:

> In its policy toward China, Japan has come to be viewed as a country of great duplicity and bad faith. We must henceforth strive, through the coordinated handling of foreign affairs, to revive and enhance international confidence in us. Moreover, in response to prevailing world sentiment, we must pursue a policy of strengthening the ties of friendship between Japan and China. It would be to our advantage to take the lead in proposing the abolition of extraterritoriality and the withdrawal of troops from China. Furthermore, in view of the development of humanitarian thinking in the countries of Europe and the United States, it is clear that there is nothing to be gained by assuming the passive attitude of simply going along with the times in regard to the League of Nations. We should go beyond this and positively affirm the establishment of this world organization.[5]

When the peace conference ran aground on the issue of Shantung and it was rumored that Japan would withdraw from the deliberations, Saionji likewise affirmed to the delegates the importance of establishing a League of Nations.[6]

While the Versailles Conference was in session, the March 1 Movement for Korean independence broke out and was temporarily suppressed. In August the Hara cabinet reinstated Saitō Makoto on active navy duty and appointed him governor-general of Korea. At Saitō's farewell banquet Saionji is said to have raised his sake cup and said, "To Your Excellency's enlightened administration!"[7] About this time Sakatani Yoshirō, who had served as finance minister in the first Saionji cabinet, wrote Saitō that the excessive severity employed in putting down the disturbances in Korea had aroused the indignation not only of the Koreans but also of the Western powers, particularly the United States. In light of this, Sakatani urged, it was essential to alter decisively such sentiments by punishing the officials responsible for the atrocities, providing funds to rebuild the homes and public buildings that had been destroyed, and granting a general amnesty. Sakatani argued that if the hearts of the Korean people could not be won, the peninsula would remain in a continual state of unrest and Japan's power vis-à-vis China and Siberia would be weakened.[8]

In using the phrase "enlightened administration" (*bunmei no seiji*) Saionji would seem to have been conveying views similar to those of Sakatani. As governor-general Saitō proclaimed an "enlightened administration" (*bunka seiji*) and not only abolished the military police but went out of his way to win over the American missionaries in Korea and to sway public opinion favorably in the United States.

Prince Saionji strongly supported the London naval talks of 1930 on the grounds that disarmament conferences were in keeping with the spirit of international cooperation and world peace that had prevailed since the Versailles Conference. Japan's international standing would be enhanced, he asserted, if it demonstrated to the other powers that it was striving for world peace by making a diligent effort to conclude a disarmament treaty. He felt it was not worth risking disruption of the London Conference by insisting upon a 70 percent ratio with the United States fleet. Japan, along with Britain and the United States, was in a position to determine the course of world affairs; hence, it was to Japan's benefit to cooperate with those countries. To join with France and Italy in order to secure acceptance of a 70 percent ratio, Saionji feared, would prove disadvantageous to Japan in the future. Furthermore, only when a country based its military preparations on its natural and financial resources could it maintain a durable fighting force.

Saionji not only expressed these views to his secretary Harada[9] but also declared to Wakatsuki, the head of Japan's delegation, that a disarmament treaty must be concluded at all costs. His conviction accorded with the attitude of the Hamaguchi cabinet, but Prime Minister Hamaguchi, faced with opposition from the navy, hesitated to accede to the American compromise proposal. Saionji urged him to conclude the treaty speedily and then deal with the navy. Hamaguchi accepted this advice and dispatched a directive to Wakatsuki ordering him to accept the American proposal.

In explaining his action to Chief of the Navy General Staff Katō Kanji and Admiral Okada, Hamaguchi's reasoning followed closely Saionji's views. From the standpoint of international relations, he said, cooperation among Japan, Britain, and the United States was essential for the maintenance of world peace. Should Japan, except in a situation of great crisis, withdraw from this triangular cooperation and cause a worsening of relations with Britain and the United States, it would place itself in an extremely precarious position internationally. Moreover, should the Anglo-American powers intervene in China, Japan would experience great difficulty in protecting Japanese interests there and in expanding its commercial and trading profits. Complications would also arise in regard to a large variety of other matters, including the American immigration issue and efforts to secure a loan from Great Britain. From a financial standpoint, Hamaguchi continued, Japan's resources definitely did not make feasible its entry into a naval race with the other powers. And finally, he was concerned that expansion of armaments in disregard of national resources at a time when demands were rife for implementation of social programs might actually be detrimental to national defense.[10]

IV

Let us now turn to the role of the cabinet in the making of foreign policy during the Manchurian crisis and its aftermath. At a cabinet conference on September 19, the day after military operations began at Mukden, Army Minister Minami Jirō supported the Kwantung Army's claims of having acted in self-defense, although Foreign Minister Shidehara had already received a telegram from the consul general at Mukden indicating that the incident had been an army scheme. Other ministers also suspected that the army had acted according to previous plan. The cabinet thereupon adopted a policy of "nonexpansion of military action," but Prime Minister Wakatsuki, fearing that the government would be unable to check the army now that hostilities had commenced, turned to Saionji and others for support. Saionji, the imperial household minister, and other officials at court, for their part, were distressed that Wakatsuki was casting about for outside help and hoped that the cabinet would unite and continue its deliberations in order to control the army.

On September 21 Hayashi Senjūrō, commander of the Japanese army in Korea, took it upon himself to dispatch troops to Manchuria. Although both the cabinet and the emperor rejected appeals by the army minister and the chief of the Army General Staff that Hayashi's action be approved, the army secured ex post facto imperial sanction when the cabinet agreed to defray the costs of the expedition. Foreign Minister Shidehara and Finance Minister Inoue Junnosuke took a firm stand against the army, but the comparative indifference of the party ministers apparently weakened cabinet unity and the army was able to secure government approval of actions it had undertaken autonomously.

The Japanese government sought desperately to avoid having the Manchurian Incident brought before the League of Nations and attempted to negotiate directly with China. As the fighting spread, however, the Chinese government on September 21 appealed to the League of Nations and at the same time sought to gain American support under the Kellogg-Briand Pact. On September 24 Japan announced that the Kwantung Army had acted in self-defense and that, as part of the government's policy of "nonexpansion of hostilities," Japanese troops were now being withdrawn to the South Manchuria Railway zone. But even as the Wakatsuki cabinet thus tried to avoid intervention by the League and the United States, the army continued to implement its plan to occupy Manchuria.

The position of the Wakatsuki cabinet grew rapidly more and more precarious. In October a group of middle-level army officers was discovered to be plotting to overthrow the government. The hand of the militarists was strengthened by the failure of Britain, the United States, and the Soviet Union to adopt positive measures to deal with the crisis in Manchuria. Faced with organized propaganda on the Manchurian and Mongolian issues and an overwhelming demand for a strong policy toward China, the Wakatsuki cabinet revised its plans for troop withdrawal and proclaimed its support for the establishment of a new regime in Manchuria, apparently fearing that any forceful attempt to suppress the army might have catastrophic results. Despite these measures, cabinet unity soon reached a point of total collapse, and in December 1931 the Wakatsuki government resigned.

Apprehensive that the antipathy of the military and the right wing might be turned against the emperor and the court, Saionji, in response to an imperial inquiry, suggested that Inukai Tsuyoshi, president of the Seiyūkai, be asked to form a new cabinet. Inukai appointed the elder statesman Takahashi Korekiyo as his finance minister in anticipation of a reimposition of the embargo on the export of gold. At the same time he gave the army minister's portfolio to Araki Sadao, a general who was popular with the young officers, and appointed Mori Kaku, who advocated a strong China policy and was allied with the radical faction in the military, to the post of chief cabinet secretary. Although Inukai headed a nominally "party government," his own authority as prime minister was weak and at cabinet meetings he found it extremely difficult to control the military.

Inukai attempted to deal with the Manchurian crisis by agreeing to the formation of an independent local regime in Manchuria while at the same time acknowledging the continuance of Chinese sovereignty over the country. In order to avoid a direct confrontation with the League of Nations, however, he withheld formal recognition of the state of Manchukuo, the founding of which was proclaimed in March 1932. Inukai's aim was to establish de facto Japanese control in Manchuria without violating the Washington Conference system, specifically the Nine Power Treaty. To achieve this aim, he employed the technique of personal diplomacy.

First, utilizing his long-standing ties with the Kuomintang, Inukai dispatched Kayano Nagatomo, an old acquaintance of Sun Yat-sen, as his personal emissary to Nanking. Next, he approached Field Marshal Uehara Yūsaku, an elder statesman of the army, and requested that he reassert control over the army. Finally, Inukai sought to restrain the army by invoking imperial authority. In particular, it is said, he attempted, with the approval of Prince Kan'in, chief of the Army General Staff, to request the emperor to dismiss some thirty young officers from their posts.[11]

All of Inukai's plans, however, ended in failure as they were opposed by both the military and its supporter, Chief Cabinet Secretary Mori Kaku. In addition, the army took strong exception to Inukai's efforts to suppress it by calling upon the authority of the emperor.

When the Shanghai Incident erupted at the end of January 1932, the attitude of the United States, Britain, and the League of Nations toward Japan stiffened. But although the Stimson Doctrine of nonrecognition of Japanese acquisitions in Manchuria, proclaimed on January 7, was later incorporated into a League resolution, the United States and Britain failed to come to any mutual agreement on how to deal with the Far Eastern crisis at this time.

The reaction to the Stimson Doctrine within the Inukai cabinet is not precisely known; but the Japanese government did try to assuage American opinion by supporting, so far as possible, the Open Door policy in Manchuria. At the same time, fearing that a setback in Shanghai would completely undermine Japan's aims in Manchuria and Mongolia,[12] the government attempted to find a quick solution to the Shanghai conflict by treating it as a matter separate from the Manchurian Incident. Even the emperor exerted himself to restrain the army's wild rampaging.

After Prime Minister Inukai was assassinated on May 15, 1932, the power of the military further increased. The succeeding cabinet of Saitō Makoto, a mixed assortment of party, bureaucratic, and military elements, was unable to assert strong leadership. As noted earlier, it attempted, while making such concessions as were unavoidable, to slow the army down and await a return to tranquil conditions.

Even before the report of the Lytton Commission was published, the Japanese government formally recognized Manchukuo on September 15, 1932. The Privy Council, moreover, unanimously approved this act after the government explained that, inasmuch as the establishment of the new state was in complete accord with the wishes of the people of Manchuria, it did not violate the Nine Power Treaty.[13]

Regarding the existence of Manchukuo as a fait accompli, Japan now assumed a posture of open defiance of the League and the United States. The Japanese government had already formulated a policy for dealing with the international situation.[14] While hoping to avoid provoking the League, it was prepared, in the event of a showdown over Japanese policies in Manchuria and Mongolia, to withdraw from the international body. To be ready for such an eventuality, it drafted a general plan that devoted attention both to completion of Japan's armament preparations and to national mobilization. In order to soften the anti-Japanese attitude of the United States, the plan called for Japan to pay appropriate deference to the principle of the Open Door in the Far East. It also proposed to restrain the United States through closer ties with Britain and France, which shared Japan's resistance to Chinese efforts to regain national sovereignty. Since Britain and France were also motivated by a desire to maintain their vested interests in East Asia, neither was likely to welcome a direct clash with Japan. Finally, the plan took note of the fact that even within the United States there was powerful opposition to the Stimson Doctrine of nonrecognition. "Once the United States is permitted a reasonable share of the commercial profits obtainable in Manchuria," it predicted, "American opinion will automatically soften."

Even after the Lytton report was issued, the Saitō cabinet tried to reach some kind of détente with the League. The Lytton report, while recognizing Chinese sovereignty, also acknowledged Japanese interests in Manchuria and recommended the establishment of broad spheres of regional self-government there. During the succeeding session of the League Council Britain took the lead in urging that a compromise be worked out with Japan. Both Prime Minister Saitō and Lord Keeper of the Privy Seal Makino placed their hopes in such a compromise, and even the navy opposed withdrawal from the League.

But the army remained in opposition and continued to defy the League by expanding its operations into Jehol province. Army Minister Araki hoped to gain freedom of action for the army by Japan's withdrawal from the League and consequent shedding of all League-imposed restraints. Although Araki was backed by Foreign Minister Uchida Yasuya, a number of other cabinet ministers advised greater caution. But when the League passed a resolution opposing recognition of Manchukuo, they too went along with the prevailing sentiment in Japan and accepted withdrawal as inevitable.

In the end the moderates, like the radicals, sought expansion and, if possible, international recognition of Japan's rights and interests. They soon concluded that the powers, while refusing to accord such recognition, would not exert any truly effective opposition. Before long they came to regard the results of military action as faits accomplis.

Saitō and Makino suggested that before making the final decision to withdraw, there should be a meeting of the senior statesmen to review the matter carefully. They had in mind that the senior statesmen for this occasion should include the president of the Privy Council, former prime ministers, and the heads of both the Seiyūkai and the Minseitō. Saionji at first agreed with the idea but later came to have doubts about it. He feared that far from producing worthwhile results, it might have an adverse effect. Specifically, he anticipated the danger that if the senior statesmen obligingly supported the hard-line attitude toward the League of Nations that was apparently in such great favor at the time, they might further restrict the Japanese government's power to act. Finally, as the movement to withdraw from the League of Nations gained momentum, the proposed meeting of senior statesmen was canceled.

As the Manchurian crisis deepened, maneuvering began among the Privy Council and other groups for leadership in the conduct of foreign relations. At the same time officials of the Foreign Ministry, which was hard-pressed by the military, called for the establishment of a deliberative bureau to function as a center for foreign policy planning. When the proposal for setting up this bureau was placed before the Privy Council, Kaneko Kentarō and other councillors urged that it be made into a body along the lines of the former Advisory Council on Foreign Relations and that it include prominent people from the military services, the Privy Council, and other groups. Saionji, however, had earlier opposed such a proposal on the grounds that it would violate the principle of ministerial responsibility, and Saitō's administration now rejected it.[15]

In expanding its influence in foreign affairs, the military had thus far, by means of threatened coups and the incitement of public opinion, succeeded in forcing the government to accept the army's attainments in Manchuria. After Japan's withdrawal from the League of Nations in March 1933 and the conclusion of the Tangku Truce the following May, the army paused temporarily. About this time the Nazis came to power in Germany, and the international sanctions that Japan feared would be imposed upon it did not materialize. On the contrary, there was even a brief respite for Japan from the pressures of world politics. During this period of respite, the military sought to strengthen its voice in foreign and domestic affairs by insisting that the government establish a "national policy." The service ministers joined in lobbying for such a policy and Army Minister Araki even completed a draft policy which he had begun in 1932 and discussed it with Finance Minister Takahashi and House of Peers Vice President Konoe.[16]

Not long after Hirota Kōki was appointed foreign minister in September 1933, the Five Ministers Conference—including the prime minister, foreign minister, army minister, navy minister, and finance minister—began to meet to coordinate policy on foreign relations, national defense, and finances. Although leadership of the Five Ministers Conference was assumed by Finance Minister Takahashi and other moderates, the very formation of such a body was undeniably tantamount to recognition of the military's great influence in foreign and domestic matters. It convened five times and at its last meeting on October 21 the five ministers agreed upon a policy with the following aims: to promote the development of Manchukuo; to complete preparations for national defense based on a consideration of financial resources; and to devise a policy for dealing with China, the Soviet Union, and the United States, countries with whom Japan's relations had deteriorated as a result of the Manchurian Incident. This policy was reported to the cabinet and received its endorsement.

The Saitō cabinet fell in July 1934 and was replaced by an administration headed by former Navy Minister Okada Keisuke. Okada formed his cabinet from the same moderate elements as his predecessor and retained the incumbent army, navy, and foreign ministers.

The military had begun at an early date to stir up talk about the coming "crisis of 1933-36"—when both the Washington and London naval treaties would expire—and the Okada cabinet now began to plan for conclusion of a new disarmament treaty. As the mediator between the government and the Navy General Staff at the time of the London Naval Conference in 1930, Okada now found himself and his cabinet the focus of attack from the navy.

As a precondition to his remaining in office, Navy Minister Ōsumi Mineo had stipulated that the new administration support the policy decisions of the Five Ministers Conference. Therefore, when he called for acceptance of a three-point demand concerning a proposed world disarmament conference to be held in London[17] and claimed that it accorded with the decisions of the Five Ministers Conference, Okada decided to reconvene the conference to consider Ōsumi's demand. Prince Fushimi Hiroyasu, the chief of the Navy General Staff, meanwhile attempted to block the proposal by appealing directly to the Throne. But the emperor rejected Fushimi's request, saying that he could not accept an appeal from a person not in an appropriate position of responsibility.

When the Five Ministers Conference met, the foreign and navy ministers undertook deliberations with a view to concluding a disarmament treaty. Even as they did so, middle-grade naval officers proclaimed their opposition to disarmament and harassed the navy minister for his support of it. Early in September the cabinet decided to abrogate the Washington Treaty before the end of 1934 and to insist upon parity with the United States at the forthcoming talks in London, a decision that virtually ensured the breakdown of the London Conference.

Meanwhile, the Army General Staff proposed that the army and navy supreme commands and personnel in both service ministries agree upon policies for abrogating the Washington Naval Treaty and dealing with the disarmament issue. They also urged that the army and navy ministers and the two chiefs of staff appeal directly to the Throne before the cabinet reached a decision. The Army Ministry, however, refused to go along with this suggestion. Nevertheless, once the cabinet's September decision was taken, the chiefs of staff presented their views to the Throne, which referred them to the Board of Field Marshals and Admirals of the Fleet. As a result, it was decided that the issues in question were not to be handled by the cabinet alone.[18]

The February 26 mutiny dramatically altered the political situation in Japan and greatly increased the power of the military. Although the moderates strengthened their hold on the court,[19] Hiranuma finally achieved the presidency of the Privy Council.

In the meantime, Saionji's influence declined. While he continued in his role as genro, reinstatement of the requirement that army and navy ministers be officers on active duty, coupled with generally changed conditions of government, made difficult the formation of cabinets on the basis of his decisions. This was clearly revealed in the abortive attempt to have General Ugaki Kazushige organize an administration in February 1937. Upon Saionji's recommendation, the emperor had duly directed Ugaki to make his ministerial appointments. Yet, as a result of army opposition, Ugaki was unable to obtain an army minister and was forced to abandon his efforts to form a cabinet. Saionji thereupon felt obliged to suggest Privy Council President Hiranuma Kiichirō or former Army Minister Hayashi Senjūrō. Hiranuma, taking into consideration the wishes of the military, declined and the prime ministership went to Hayashi. When the Hayashi cabinet fell a brief four months later, Saionji played his final trump card and recommended as head of the new government Prince Konoe Fumimaro, the president of the House of Peers.

Upon the resignation of the first Konoe cabinet in January 1939, Hiranuma organized a new government, while Konoe took his position as head of the Privy Council. But despite their seemingly powerful positions, they were unable to prevent the bewilderingly rapid turnover of cabinets that occurred between the time of the February 26 mutiny and the outbreak of the Pacific War. Only the first and second Konoe cabinets remained in power for any length of time or made any significant policy decisions. But with the beginning of the war in China and establishment of the Imperial Headquarters, Konoe himself was led around by the military, greatly betraying Saionji's earlier expectations of him.

As Saionji's influence waned, his functions were gradually assumed by the senior statesmen. After the miscarriage of the "Ugaki cabinet," Saionji moved even further to the sidelines as it became a practice for the lord keeper of the privy seal to consult Hiranuma and the senior statesmen whenever changes in administration became necessary. In January 1940, upon receipt of an imperial inquiry concerning a prime minister to replace Abe Nobuyuki, Yuasa Kurahei convened a meeting of the senior statesmen, including the president of the Privy Council and former prime ministers, which selected Yonai Mitsumasa. Yuasa then consulted Saionji and thereupon recommended Yonai to the emperor.

The same procedure was followed when army pressure brought about the collapse of the Yonai cabinet in July. Kido Kōichi, Konoe's intimate colleague who had replaced Yuasa in June, called together the senior statesmen, who selected Konoe to head a new government. On this occasion, however, Saionji refused to endorse their selection, but Konoe's name was presented to the emperor nevertheless and he proceeded to organize his second cabinet. In November Saionji died.

V

Prince Konoe was now at the height of his career. The nationalistic goals he espoused as prime minister were based on views he had long held and grew naturally out of his background as the scion of the Fujiwara line, whose father, Konoe Atsumaro, had served as president of the House of Peers from 1896 to 1903, and who, moreover, had close ties to the imperial family and to the Shōwa emperor himself.

In 1919 when Konoe accompanied the Japanese delegation to the Versailles Peace Conference, he announced in advance his opposition to a peace based on Anglo-American standards,[20] asserting the "legitimate right of survival" of the Japanese people and demanding both the emancipation of colonial territories by the great powers and the abolition of discrimination against Orientals. Thus Konoe, from Japan's standpoint as an Asian nation, early expressed his opposition to the world order that was to be established in the Versailles and Washington treaties. Yet there is reason to doubt how well he understood either the issue of Japan's position in Shantung or the Korean independence movement.

The opinions and measures that Konoe came to espouse after the Manchurian Incident differed from those of Saionji, Makino, and others among the senior statesmen. He urged the inclusion of the "have-not" nations in an impartial sharing of wealth on an international basis. In addition, although unable to accept certain of the more fanatical attitudes of the young military officers and members of the right wing, Konoe believed that "Japan must inevitably go in the direction" they had pursued since the Manchurian Incident. He argued that in order to regain political initiative from the military, the politicians would have to take the lead in acknowledging that Japan's destiny lay in this direction and would thereupon have to carry out various essential reforms.[21] He hoped for the establishment of a powerful "national unity cabinet" that would include both the military and the so-called reform forces allied with them.

In attempting to appoint rightists such as Hiranuma Kiichirō to influential positions in the court, which was being denounced at the time by the military and others as "liberal" and pro-Anglo-American, Konoe hoped to maintain and to strengthen the unity of the court viv-à-vis the military. In this, however, he met with Saionji's opposition. Konoe had also from an early date established ties with Mori Kaku of the Seiyūkai and was close to men like Obata Toshishirō and Suzuki Teiichi in the army and to others of the right wing. It is ironic that Konoe, who placed great faith in the so-called "Imperial Way faction" of the army, was himself expected by the moderates, as a new and informed leader close to the emperor, to restrain the army's reckless drive toward fascism.

In 1933, the year Konoe became president of the House of Peers, his old friend Gotō Ryūnosuke, along with Professor Rōyama Masamichi of Tokyo Imperial University and others, anticipating Konoe's appointment to the prime ministership, formed the Shōwa Kenkyūkai (Shōwa Research Society), which included scholars and journalists (ranging from liberals to converted leftists) as well as bureaucrats. The Shōwa Kenkyūkai engaged in the study of domestic and foreign policies and advanced a program of internal reform within the scope of the Meiji constitution, rejection of the political parties in their existing state of corruption, and opposition to fascism.[22]

In 1934 Konoe traveled to the United States with Rōyama and Ushiba
Tomohiko of the Institute of Pacific Relations. In recording his impressions of
the journey he wrote:

> Leading Americans whom I met criticized Japan's actions in
> Manchuria as having destroyed the international peace structure.
> Yet, in view of the demonstrated impotency of the League of
> Nations, they saw no likelihood that anyone would seek to place
> pressure upon or interfere with Japan. American public opinion is by
> and large more concerned with Japanese conduct in China proper
> than in Manchuria and hopes that Japan will set a limit to its
> aspirations there.
>
> It is significant to note that some Americans seem to doubt
> whether their principles for peace are truly applicable to existing
> conditions in the Far East. They say that if Japan were to set forth a
> new set of principles, it might be able to secure American
> recognition of them.
>
> In general, however, Americans are blinded by faith in the
> matchless superiority of their own brand of democracy. They believe
> that in Japan, as in prewar Germany, a dominant military clique has
> dispossessed the people of their liberty and that it would be difficult
> indeed to conclude a new diplomatic agreement with Japan.[23]

Like Konoe, Army Minister Araki Sadao was interested in enunciating a
new set of principles to replace the Nine Power Treaty as a basis for
international order in the Far East. In the draft policy proposal he completed in
1933, Araki suggested in regard to dealings with the United States that "both
the political and economic interests of the United States and Japan in the world
and particularly in the Far East must be made clear. We must, in addition, secure
American understanding of Japan's national policy and strive to establish
amicable relations between the two countries on a basis of true equality."[24] His
views appear to have been very close to Konoe's.

After the February 26 mutiny Konoe was directed by the emperor to form
a cabinet but declined. From this time on Sino-Japanese relations worsened and
the movement to "resist Japan and save the homeland" grew in China in
opposition to Japanese aggression. Konoe frequently observed during this
period: "There is division everywhere in Japan; it is urgent that we correct this
state of affairs and establish a firm foreign policy."[25]

Konoe formed his first cabinet in June 1937, amid overwhelming popular
support, replacing the discredited administration of General Hayashi Senjūrō. A
month later the Marco Polo Bridge Incident occurred and before long the
fighting evolved into full-scale warfare between China and Japan.

At that time it had become customary for a group known as the Three
Ministry Officials Conference—comprised of the chiefs of the East Asia Bureau
of the Foreign Ministry and of the Army and Navy ministries' Military and Naval
Affairs bureaus—to meet at the Foreign Ministry to discuss the "China
problem." On the morning of July 8, when the Marco Polo Bridge Incident was
reported to Tokyo, the three officials—Ishii Itarō, Ushiroku Jun, and Toyoda
Soemu—met and drew up a plan for the nonexpansion of hostilities, which was

approved by the cabinet that afternoon.[26] Yet, just three days later, when Army Minister Sugiyama Gen presented to the cabinet and the Five Ministers Conference a proposal to send troops into north China, only Navy Minister Yonai voiced opposition to it. Both Prime Minister Konoe and Foreign Minister Hirota approved the army's proposal, on the condition that the general principle of nonexpansion of hostilities be maintained, and announced that forces would be dispatched to China.

Later, representatives of the navy and the East Asia Bureau of the Foreign Ministry discussed with Ishiwara Kanji, chief of the Operations Division of the Army General Staff, and Shibayama Kaneshirō, chief of the Military Affairs Section of the Army Ministry, another effort to arrange truce negotiations. And a conference of the army, navy, and foreign ministers even agreed upon a proposal, lenient by the standards of the day, for a cease-fire and the adjustment of other differences between China and Japan.[27] Before these attempts to achieve a settlement could be pursued further, however, fighting broke out at Shanghai and the war was escalated to full-scale proportions.

At a meeting on August 14 the cabinet approved a declaration to take strong punitive measures against China. Minister of Railways Nakajima Chikuhei and Communications Minister Nagai Ryūtarō, both party politicians, spoke out so forcefully in favor of this declaration that even Army Minister Sugiyama was astonished.[28] As Foreign Minister Hirota, under strong pressure, lost all will to oppose the army, the other party ministers assumed an obsequious attitude toward it.

With the outbreak of total war the military claimed its right of autonomous command to push the fighting farther and farther without consulting the cabinet. In November the Imperial Headquarters was formed, and from that time on it was mandatory that all matters concerning the conduct of the war be handled by the Imperial Headquarters-Cabinet Liaison Conference, whose membership included: from Imperial Headquarters, the vice chiefs of the Army General Staff and the Navy General Staff (rather than the chiefs of staff, both of whom were members of the imperial family); and from the cabinet, the prime minister and the foreign, army, and navy ministers. In addition, the chief cabinet secretary and the chiefs of the Military Affairs and Naval Affairs bureaus of the Army and Navy ministries served as secretaries for the conference.[29]

At the time peace moves were undertaken between Japan and China through the good offices of Oskar Trautmann, the German ambassador to China, the Three Ministry Officials Conference submitted to the Liaison Conference a draft of a peace settlement with China. The only Liaison Conference officials who supported the original draft, however, were Navy Minister Yonai and Vice Chief of the Navy General Staff Koga Mineichi. One after another new conditions were added,[30] until in January 1938, when the peace negotiations became dead-locked, the Konoe cabinet announced that Japan would no longer deal with the Nationalist government but would seek to normalize relations with its continental neighbor through another Chinese regime. With this announcement all hope for a negotiated settlement of the war vanished.

Japanese aggression on the continent inevitably produced clashes with the interests of the various powers in China. Problems arose most frequently with the British, who had the greatest national stake there. The British, however, faced with the rise of Nazi Germany, sought to protect their position in China by compromising to some degree with Japan. The only country considered to have the power to curb Japanese aggression was the United States, which contented itself with issuing a statement of nonrecognition of Japan's actions and made no attempt to work in concert with the British. Under these circumstances there arose among Japanese leaders support for a proposal to terminate the China War by negotiations conducted through Great Britain.

In the spring of 1938, as the military situation in China worsened, Konoe undertook a radical reorganization of his cabinet, appointing Ugaki Kazushige as foreign minister, Ikeda Seihin as finance minister, and Itagaki Seishirō as army minister. On June 10 the cabinet decided to revive the Five Ministers Conference so that national policy might be deliberated at the highest level without the participation of the supreme command. The conference was directed to handle directly those minor pieces of business that were of no particular concern to the other ministries. More important matters were in principle to be presented to the cabinet, while issues of grave significance were either to be submitted directly to the Throne or transmitted privately to the emperor for his approval.[31]

The revival of the Five Ministers Conference was, in fact, suggested by the Shōwa Kenkyūkai as a means of controlling the military by having national policy decided by a small group of ranking officials.[32] In practice, however, since the ministers themselves were not appointed on the basis of common political views and, moreover, represented a variety of bureaucratic interests, it was difficult for them as a body to deal with national policy uniformly and smoothly. Moreover Konoe, while appointing prominent individuals to cabinet positions in the hope that they would be able to restrain the army, made no effort to provide them with the support they needed.

The Five Ministers Conference agreed to accept, under certain conditions, the "good offices of third countries" in the conduct of foreign relations. Thus Foreign Minister Ugaki initiated with British Ambassador Sir Robert Craigie discussions aimed at adjusting differences in Anglo-Japanese relations; at the same time he put out peace feelers to H. H. Kung, president of the Chinese Executive Yuan. Yet so long as Japan made no significant concessions in negotiations of this sort, they held little prospect for progress.

The army, meanwhile, intensified its demands for a strengthening of the Anti-Comintern Pact with Germany and Italy and for the elimination of British influence in the Far East. Under army pressure to terminate the Anglo-Japanese talks, the Five Ministers Conference created the Asia Development Board (Kōain) and sought to transfer to it the authority to handle diplomatic dealings with China. This infringement of the foreign minister's authority led to Ugaki's resignation in September.

Despite the occupation of Wuhan and Canton by Japanese forces in October, the Chinese refused to capitulate and the war entered a stage of protracted fighting with no end in sight. On November 3, following the defection of Wang Ching-wei from the Nationalist government, the Konoe cabinet announced the establishment of a New Order in East Asia based on a triple alliance for mutual assistance and cooperation among Japan, Manchukuo, and China. Arita Hachirō, the newly-appointed foreign minister, openly renounced the Nine Power Treaty and asserted that, in view of the formation of an economic bloc among these three countries, it was entirely fitting that severe restrictions be placed on the commercial activities of other powers in China. This assertion, needless to say, aroused the strong opposition of Britain and the United States.

In January 1939 the Konoe cabinet resigned and was replaced by a government headed by Hiranuma Kiichirō. About this time the situation in Europe became critical and Germany, anxious to have Japan's support in the war, sought to strengthen the Anti-Comintern Pact. The Five Ministers Conference, which became embroiled in the issue, convened more than seventy times in seemingly unending deliberation over what the newspapers at the time called the determination of "policy toward Europe." In the course of their discussions two opposing views emerged. Foreign Minister Arita, Navy Minister Yonai, and Finance Minister Ishiwata Sōtarō held that the pact was intended solely to deal with the Soviet Union and should not apply against either Britain or France. Army Minister Itagaki, on the other hand, insisted that although a revised pact should be aimed chiefly at the Soviet Union, its provisions should also bind the signatories to joint action against Britain and France. Under the vigorous prodding of middle-ranking army officers, Itagaki, even at the risk of losing his ministerial post, tried to force the other ministers to accept his demand. Only the persistent opposition of Yonai and Vice Navy Minister Yamamoto Isoroku prevented Itagaki from having his way.

The two groups also held diametrically divergent views as to whether a military pact directed against Britain and France would help to bring the war with China to a successful conclusion. The army believed that such a pact would divert Anglo-American aid away from China and thus undermine the Chinese war effort. In contrast, the navy held that it would have the reverse effect of causing Britain and the United States to provide even greater aid to China in order to check Japan. Navy Minister Yonai said to Itagaki:

> How can an alliance with Germany and Italy contribute to a solution of the China problem? We should instead seek to deal with this problem through cooperation with Britain.
>
> Moreover, continuation by the United States of its present policy of noninterference in Sino-Japanese hostilities is predicated on the maintenance of the principles of the Open Door and equal opportunity in China. In the event that certain countries recklessly undertake actions that appear to violate these principles, the United States will not stand idly by but will very likely ally itself with Great Britain.
>
> Thus, even if we achieve an understanding with Germany and Italy concerning the China problem, it will only serve to unite Britain and the United States in opposition to us. Not only would this greatly reduce our chances for success in China, it would place us in an incalculably dangerous position. Although Britain and the United States are for the time being unlikely to confront us militarily, the prospect of their imposing economic sanctions is cause for the greatest concern.

Yonai also urged caution in dealing with Germany and Italy. "Is it not true," he asked, "that Germany and Italy seek an alliance with Japan not from a feeling of good will but because they regard Japan as a country they can use to their own advantage? We must accordingly proceed with the utmost care in our relations with them."[33]

Even while the Anti-Comintern Pact was being debated by the Five Ministers Conference, the army blockaded the British concession at Tientsin with the twofold aim of forcing Britain to cooperate with Japanese management of the occupied areas and of dealing a blow to the Chinese resistance effort. On July 26 the United States retaliated by announcing that it intended to abrogate the U.S.-Japan Treaty of Commerce and Navigation. Events had developed just as Yonai had feared. In addition, in the summer of 1939 the Japanese army received a severe setback in a series of clashes with Soviet forces along the border between Manchukuo and Outer Mongolia. And when Germany and the Soviet Union concluded a nonaggression pact on August 23, the Hiranuma cabinet chose to resign. It did so not so much from a sense of its own responsibility for the reverses Japan had recently suffered, but to have the army feel the burden of that responsibility.

With the collapse of the Hiranuma government the line of foreign policy that Japan had pursued since the time of Konoe's prime ministership temporarily ended. The issue that arose in the attempt to select a successor to Hiranuma was whether Japan should make an immediate and radical shift in its foreign policy or, while appeasing the army and avoiding discord at home, should attempt to work out a new policy more gradually.

Lord Keeper of the Privy Seal Yuasa strongly urged the selection as prime minister of former Finance Minister Ikeda Seihin, the head of the Mitsui zaibatsu who had studied at Harvard and had close relations with American financial circles. Saionji concurred with the provision that Ikeda must have the support of Konoe. But Konoe, then president of the Privy Council, refused to back Ikeda on the grounds that his appointment as prime minister would bring a shift in foreign policy to a pro-British line, which would inevitably cause great unrest in Japan.[34] In the end General Abe Nobuyuki, who had the backing of the army, was instructed by the emperor to form a cabinet. His Majesty at the same time ordered Abe to cooperate with Britain and the United States and to appoint either Umezu Yoshijirō or Hata Shunroku as army minister.[35] Such a directive from the emperor was a most unusual event.

As it turned out, the foreign policies of the Abe cabinet were quite different from those it had been expected to adopt. Shortly after its formation World War II broke out in Europe and Japan was rendered more economically dependent than ever on the United States. The Abe government announced that, without getting involved in the war in Europe, it would work to find a solution to the China conflict. Yet in order to bring about a rapprochement with Britain and the United States, it would have been necessary for Japan not only to break away from the Axis alliance but also to alter its occupation policy in China—a course that would have been very difficult to pursue.

Abe appointed as foreign minister Admiral Nomura Kichisaburō, who had been naval attaché in Washington during World War I. Nomura was on cordial terms with President Roosevelt and now began negotiations for a new commercial treaty with the United States. Meanwhile the Foreign, Army, and Navy ministries drew up an "Outline for Foreign Policy"[36] which, while reaffirming the decisions already made in regard to the China conflict, expressed the intent to avoid a situation in which Japan and the United States would be left without treaty arrangements. It urged that Japan avoid in particular any infringement at this time of the Nine Power Treaty and refrain from placing unnecessary pressure on American activities in China. In contrast, the "Outline" called for curbing the British and forcing them to acquiesce in Japanese policy toward China.

American abrogation of the commercial treaty, however, had obliged Japan to acknowledge that relations with the United States and Britain could not be handled separately. "Britain has vast interests in China but not the power to protect them," the Japanese government noted. "The United States, on the other hand, with minimal interests there, possesses the greatest force to restrain Japan." It therefore proposed that, when an issue arose that concerned the interests of both Britain and the United States, negotiations be undertaken with Britain first in order to induce the Americans to take a more conciliatory attitude toward Japan.

Japan also hoped that relations with the Soviet Union could be normalized. In actual practice, however, Japan contented itself with the negative policy of declining to conclude a nonaggression pact with the Soviet Union so long as the Russians refused, among other things, to stop providing aid to China.

In talks with Ambassador Joseph Grew, Foreign Minister Nomura did make certain concessions to American wishes, such as agreeing to the opening of the Yangtze river tributaries. But he refused to abandon the New Order in East Asia. The United States government, for its part, insisted strongly upon maintenance of the principle of equal economic opportunity in China and refused to conclude a new treaty of commerce with Japan.

As economic difficulties mounted in Japan, the army abandoned the Abe cabinet, which resigned en masse in January 1940. Former Navy Minister Yonai Mitsumasa, with the strong recommendation of Lord Keeper of the Privy Seal Yuasa, was selected to form an administration. Arita Hachirō, who with Yonai had opposed strengthening the Anti-Comintern Pact at the time of the Hiranuma cabinet, was reappointed foreign minister, and Ishiwata Sōtarō, finance minister under Hiranuma, was made chief cabinet secretary. Foreign Minister Arita had two aims: to carry out the establishment of the New Order in East Asia and to improve relations with Britain and the United States. In pursuit of the first aim Japan set up the puppet regime of Wang Ching-wei in China and began to exert pressure on French Indochina and the Dutch East Indies. Even while taking these actions, however, the Yonai cabinet continued to hope that the United States would not resort to an embargo on exports to Japan.

The success of the German blitzkreig in May and June 1940 led to army demands for increasing cooperation with the Axis and a military drive southward on the continent even at the risk of war with Britain. The army used the resignation of Army Minister Hata Shunroku to bring down the whole Yonai government and set the stage for the formation of the second Konoe cabinet.

Before accepting the post of prime minister, Konoe first held a meeting at his villa at Ogikubo in Tokyo with Matsuoka Yōsuke, Tōjō Hideki, and Yoshida Zengo, his prospective foreign, army, and navy ministers. After securing their agreement on a policy memorandum in line with the demands of the military, he set about to form his cabinet. Thus cooperation between the cabinet and the military was assured.

Shortly after the Konoe cabinet assumed its duties, a new policy document was adopted after only one Liaison Conference between the cabinet and Imperial Headquarters. This document, entitled "Main Principles for Coping with the Changing World Situation," was virtually an invitation to war. The extraordinarily hasty agreement on policy, based on the expectation of a German victory over the British, was nothing other than an attempt not to "miss the bus."

From this time on foreign policy was determined chiefly by the Four Ministers Conference, with the army and navy ministers handling liaison with the supreme command. Even the finance minister was excluded from these meetings. Direction of the war, on the other hand, was managed by the Imperial Headquarters-Cabinet Liaison Conference (or the more easily convened "Liaison Conference talks"). Decisions relating to high national policy were submitted to the Imperial Conference.

Liaison Conferences had not been convened since 1938, when a split had developed between the government and the supreme command over the decision to discontinue the Trautmann peace moves. That they were now resumed is indicative of the fact that the government and the military had reached a mutual understanding on the question of military expansion.

Imperial Conferences were extremely formal affairs at which pronouncements were made in accordance with prearranged agenda. The only breaks in the staged formality of these gatherings were occasional exchanges between the president of the Privy Council on the one hand and the government or the supreme command on the other.[37] Such exchanges, it is said, were particularly lively when Hara Yoshimichi was council president.

In September 1940 Oikawa Koshirō replaced the ailing Yoshida Zengo as navy minister. Thereafter the government pursued a policy of strengthening ties with the Axis that led ultimately to the conclusion of the Tripartite Pact with Germany and Italy. Japan signed the pact on September 27, 1940 after it had been deliberated by the Four Ministers Conference, a preliminary meeting of the Liaison Conference, the cabinet, and the Imperial Conference and had been reviewed by the Privy Council.

Konoe and others stressed that the objectives of this military alliance were, first, to normalize relations with the Soviet Union through German mediation and, second, to place pressure on the United States sufficient to prevent it from entering the European war against Germany or interfering with Japan's southward drive in Asia. By linking the Far Eastern and European problems, however, the pact had the undesired effect of rendering more difficult than ever the adjustment of relations between the United States and Japan.

Several influential individuals within the government attempted to warn Konoe and his supporters of the possible adverse consequences of the pact. At an Imperial Conference, Privy Council President Hara predicted that conclusion of the Tripartite Pact would only spur the United States to increase its pressure on Japan and would further impede Japan's acquisition of needed raw materials. In addition, the entire Privy Council—with the exception of General Kawai Misao and Admiral Arima Ryōkitsu—expressed doubts about the advisability of signing the pact. Ishii Kikujirō and other councillors cautioned in particular that Germany and Italy were not trustworthy allies.

In response to these doubts and warnings Konoe and Matsuoka expressed the conviction that any indication of a willingness to compromise would simply lead to increased American arrogance. The only way to avert a conflict, they declared, was to take a firm stand. Nevertheless, in giving its approval to the pact the Privy Council added the stipulation that Japan should try, insofar as possible, to avoid antagonizing Britain and the United States.[38]

In April 1941 Japan concluded a neutrality pact with the Soviet Union. But by that time Russo-German relations had worsened and Konoe's and Matsuoka's expectations for the pact were soon dashed.

When the Tripartite Pact was concluded, Japan had looked forward to a German invasion of England and the opportunity to make a decisive military drive toward the South Pacific. In the process Japan had hoped to create an autonomous economic system that would enable it to procure critical military supplies and free itself from dependence on Britain and the United States. By April 1941 it was clear that Germany's plans to assault Britain had failed. Moreover the United States, in response to the Tripartite Pact, had increased its aid to Britain and China and tightened its embargo on the export of war matériel to Japan.

Meanwhile, in the same month talks between the United States and Japan, which had been conducted privately since the end of the previous year, were advanced to the stage of formal negotiations. A Catholic priest visiting Japan, Father James M. Drought, had in November 1940 met with Ikawa Tadao, director of the Central Bank of the Industrial Association, and proposed the opening of American-Japanese negotiations. When Father Drought returned home, he reported to President Roosevelt and talks had thereupon been arranged.

Ikawa had likewise informed Prime Minister Konoe of his meeting with Drought. In January 1941, together with Iwakuro Hideo, a section chief in the Army Ministry's Military Affairs Bureau, Ikawa was sent to the United States to begin discussions. Japan sought to achieve two objectives: by taking advantage of the split between the Nationalists and Communists in China, to enlist America's good offices to achieve a solution in the Sino-Japanese War; and to secure American guarantees for the supply of military matériel. But any negotiations with the United States (which had held fast to its policy of nonrecognition and continued to increase its aid to Britain) brought to the fore two major issues: the extent to which the United States and Japan could agree on conditions for settlement of the Sino-Japanese War, and the handling of the provisions of the Tripartite Pact dealing with Japanese participation in the war in Europe. Konoe stoutly maintained that the provisions of the Tripartite Pact were to be adhered to strictly and that there could be no reversion to the status quo ante in relations with China.[39]

While Japanese-American negotiations were stalled because of the opposition of Foreign Minister Matsuoka, who had just returned from Europe, war between Germany and the Soviet Union erupted on June 22. The Japanese military, which had been advancing its own preparations for war, looked for a quick German victory. On July 2 at an Imperial Conference a final decision was made on the issue of whether Japan should undertake a military drive to the north or to the south. In spite of Matsuoka's insistence that an attack be launched against the Soviet Union, plans were set in motion to invade southern Indochina.

Konoe reacted to the new developments by asserting his determination to come to some agreement with the United States, even though it might have a dampening effect on the Tripartite Pact.[40] Cooperation among Japan, Germany, and the Soviet Union, upon which the pact was predicated, had been shattered and communications between Japan and Germany were disrupted. In his distress, Konoe even considered abrogating the Tripartite Pact on the grounds that Germany had betrayed its promise to act as a mediator in fostering friendly relations between Japan and the Soviet Union. Although he did not actually press for abrogation, Konoe did vigorously promote negotiations with the United States in the hope of averting the danger of war that adherence to the pact presented.

Konoe was convinced that the United States, while attempting to extricate Britain from its predicament in Europe, would make every effort to avoid getting involved in any kind of conflict with Japan in the Pacific. He also appears to have felt that the United States might even seek to appease Japan for the sake of combating communism. In order to replace Matsuoka, who was opposed to Japanese-American negotiations, Konoe dissolved his cabinet on July 18 and promptly formed a new one—his third—with Admiral Toyoda Teijirō as foreign minister.

The subject of negotiations with the United States was now brought before the Liaison Conference, which at that time was meeting approximately twice a week. In attendance were the prime minister, the foreign, army, navy, and home ministers, the director of the Cabinet Planning Board, the chiefs and vice chiefs of the Army and Navy general staffs, the chief cabinet secretary, and the chiefs of the America and East Asia bureaus of the Foreign Ministry and of the Military Affairs and Naval Affairs bureaus of the Army and Navy ministries.[41]

In a short while, however, Japan completed the occupation of southern Indochina, and the United States, in retaliation, froze Japanese assets and placed a total embargo on the export of oil to Japan. Relations between the two countries were on the verge of collapse.

At this point Konoe proposed that he meet with President Roosevelt for personal talks, perhaps feeling that if he could secure an agreement adjusting Japanese-American differences and obtain imperial approval for it, he might then be able to restrain the military. Late in August the Liaison Conference approved a message from the prime minister to Roosevelt suggesting that such discussions be held, and on September 6 an Imperial Conference reached agreement on Japan's demands in the talks and set a time limit for the negotiations. Yet Konoe made no attempt to fashion the Japanese conditions into a workable basis for personal talks. Accordingly, when Secretary of State Cordell Hull notified the Japanese that there would have to be some understanding on general principles as a precondition to talks between the two chiefs of state, it became, for all practical purposes, impossible to hold the talks.

Even so, at the end of August Konoe met at Hakone with his private secretary Ushiba Tomohiko, cabinet adviser Saionji Kinkazu, and Matsumoto

Shigeharu to draft a document called the "Cabinet Plan." But at a meeting of the Liaison Conference on September 4 this plan was rejected in favor of a proposal drawn up by Terasaki Tarō, chief of the America Bureau of the Foreign Ministry.[42]

The tendency of the Konoe cabinet to work through private channels in its conduct of diplomacy is clearly illustrated by the negotiations with the United States. It resulted in part from the fact that, given the atmosphere in Japan at the time, the government found it impossible to acknowledge publicly that the country was in very difficult straits and thereupon to seek a solution to national problems through compromise with Japan's adversaries. Any admission of difficulty, it was feared, might adversely affect the prestige of the military. Moreover, so many policy decisions had been piled up that the formal organs of government had lost their capacity to function flexibly.

The approach to diplomacy that thus evolved was to undertake private negotiations first and, if these showed prospects of success, to shift them into official channels for handling by a small number of officials; once substantive progress had been made, Konoe, who was close to the military, would personally attempt to bring about an agreement. This approach was used following the outbreak of the Sino-Japanese War in 1937, when the government attempted to initiate discussions with Nanking through Funatsu Shin'ichirō, a businessman and former diplomat who had ties with high officials in the Nationalist government;[43] and again in December 1938, when arrangements were made to engineer Wang Ching-wei's escape from Chungking. Yet the dangers of failure were great. The Funatsu operation, for example, miscarried because of the insistence of Ambassador to China Kawagoe Shigeru that any talks be conducted through him; while in the case of Wang's flight, as planning moved from private to public channels a whole new series of demands were added that placed Wang and his followers in a very difficult situation. Finally, in the negotiations between Japan and the United States, the use of Nomura, a navy man, to handle the initial private phase caused friction with the Foreign Ministry that persisted until Pearl Harbor.

But Konoe's attempts at private diplomacy were destined to miscarry. On October 18, 1941 his cabinet fell after he and Foreign Minister Toyoda clashed with Army Minister Tōjō over the negotiations with the United States and the prospects that they would produce an agreement.

Voices were now raised in favor of appointing Prince Higashikuni Naruhiko as Konoe's successor in order to facilitate reconsideration of the September 6 decision of the Imperial Conference. Lord Keeper of the Privy Seal Kido, however, opposed the idea and convinced a meeting of the senior statesmen that the best course would be for Tōjō to form a cabinet, with instructions from the emperor that there must be cooperation between the army and the navy and that the Imperial Conference decision must be reconsidered. Any meaningful reconsideration of the decision, however, would have necessitated a more drastic change in the leadership of both the government—including Tōjō—and the supreme command, and therefore it was never actually undertaken. Kido's fundamental reason for proposing Tōjō to head a new government appears to have stemmed from a fear that reconsideration of the Imperial Conference decision would invite an outburst from the military. To

Kido, controlling the army was of far greater importance than such a reconsideration.[44]

In directing Tōjō to form a cabinet the emperor duly instructed him not to feel bound by the September 6 decision and, further, to formulate national policy with prudence. This imperial command is referred to as the "return to a clean slate," but it was destined to be a return in name only.

During the policy discussions of late 1941 the military was reluctant to provide the senior statesmen with an opportunity to express their views. As former prime ministers, it was feared, they were inclined to take a conservative stance in support of the status quo. When the emperor suggested that they be invited to attend the Imperial Conference of December 1, at which the decision was reached to make war against the United States and Britain, the Imperial Headquarters-Cabinet Liaison Conference opposed the idea. Instead, administration officials met informally with the senior statesmen on November 29 to explain the plans for war.[45] This was followed by a question-and-answer session and, finally, a banquet with the emperor.

On December 4 Prime Minister Tōjō and Foreign Minister Tōgō Shigenori discussed the course of Japanese-American negotiations with the Privy Council. At 7:30 a.m. on December 8 (December 7 in the United States), *after* the opening of hostilities, the emperor sought the Council's advice on the matter of issuing a declaration of war against the United States and Britain.

VI

In the course of the conference Professor Graebner asked whether it could be said that "formal" foreign policy decision making played a more important role in Japan than in the United States. When we recall the independent actions undertaken by local armies during the 1930s, we hesitate to respond affirmatively to his question. Nevertheless, from another point of view such a conclusion is justified. I should like, therefore, to explore the particular meaning of "formal" decision making in prewar Japan.

The basic aim of Japanese diplomacy was to expand Japan's influence over Korea, China, Siberia, and eventually Southeast Asia while avoiding a clash with British, American, and French interests in the Far East. This dual task was accepted by most of the prime ministers and foreign ministers in office during the decade, the men directly responsible for the execution of foreign policy. They frequently met with opposition from the military and expansionist politicians who, zealous to accomplish the first goal, rallied to advance Japan's continental policy. On these occasions the military and its political supporters attempted to elevate their so-called continental policy and the accompanying demand for arms expansion to the status of fixed national policy, thereby restricting freedom of action on the part of the prime and foreign ministers. Prior to the period under discussion we might point, for example, to the 1907 decision on national defense, which was based upon Field Marshal Yamagata Aritomo's memorial to the emperor; to the 1927 Eastern Conference resolution on China policy; and to the demand by members of both houses of the Diet that the government declare its determination to achieve a 70 percent ratio vis-à-vis the United States at the 1930 London Naval Disarmament Conference,[46] and their endeavors to mobilize nationwide public opinion in support of this demand.

After the Manchurian Incident foreign policy was "formally" established in "national policy" decisions adopted at Five Ministers Conferences, Imperial Headquarters-Cabinet Liaison Conferences, and Imperial Conferences, as well as in the course of Privy Council deliberations; in some cases foreign policy was determined by imperial edict. In consequence, the prime minister and his foreign minister were not free to conduct Japan's diplomacy as they believed best. Moreover, such decisions were often accompanied by declarations of "principles" that endorsed the military's forceful policy toward the Asian continent. In the nationalistic and militaristic atmosphere that predominated in political circles at the time, these decisions had the negative effect of restraining the agencies charged with the conduct of foreign relations under the control of the foreign minister. At the same time, there was no assurance that decisions would be fully executed. Fear of the grave consequences that might result not infrequently led to postponement of action or even to modification of a decision.

Saionji was opposed to a formal decision making process, believing that it could only hamper the flexibility required in the handling of foreign relations. Konoe, on the other hand, at another time and under different circumstances, made use of such a process in hopes thereby of unifying public opinion and controlling the radicals in the military. In the years following the Manchurian Incident, particularly after the February 26 Incident, each succeeding cabinet found itself increasingly restricted by the faits accomplis brought about through military action and by the "formal" decisions that sanctioned them, until, with the outbreak of the Sino-Japanese War and Konoe's declaration in January 1938 that he would "no longer deal with the Nationalist government," the combination of military action and formal declarations of policy amounted virtually to an official declaration of war. Thereafter it was practically impossible for a cabinet to alter the course of Japan's foreign policy, above all of policy toward China. An attempt might still have been made to improve relations with Britain and the United States, yet so long as China policy remained unchanged, such an attempt was doomed to failure. From the time of the second Konoe cabinet on, formal decisions served primarily to harmonize the conflicting demands of the army and navy.

THE ROLE OF THE
DEPARTMENT OF STATE

James C. Thomson, Jr.

"The Far Eastern policy of the United States will undergo neither a rapid nor a gradual 'reorientation' *unless and until* . . . the whole world becomes an *utterly different* world from that which it has been ever since the Pilgrims landed at Plymouth and the Cavaliers at Jamestown."

Stanley K. Hornbeck to Sumner Welles
May 18, 1940

In his eightieth year of life, Stanley Kuhl Hornbeck was asked by a friend on the Department of State's Policy Planning Council what America should "do" to meet the challenges of the 1960s in foreign affairs. "Well, I am sure about some things," the old man responded. "Our national concern for and regarding principles and practices of freedom, independence, justice and security is greater than is that of any other nation. . . . We should be prepared to go further and to make greater efforts in defense of those principles and practices than is to be expected of any other country."[1]

About the same time, Hornbeck filed a note to posterity in a box marked "Pearl Harbor": "Did I underestimate Japan's strength? The answer is: Yes, both in absolute terms and in comparative terms, and so did practically everyone else in the United States, both in the Government and out of the Government, in varying degrees. The strength of any country is relative."[2]

In these two separate reflections lies one central dilemma of Stanley Hornbeck and his department in the decade of the thirties: how to "go further" than other nations in defense of "principles and practices" when other nations are strong, perhaps stronger than we suspect—and perhaps zealous, one might add, to defend their own "principles and practices."

Stanley K. Hornbeck presided over the making of Far Eastern policy at the Department of State from 1928 to 1941, and beyond. The Hornbeck story is not the full story of State. But it is a good place to begin.

I

Hornbeck was the son of a Methodist minister who traced his roots back to the seventeenth century Hudson Valley and to Holland.[3] Stanley's father moved from theological training in Massachusetts to parish assignments in Illinois and finally in 1893, when the boy was ten, to Colorado. The household was "religiously minded," with Bible study and daily prayers. "There were instilled in me," Hornbeck stated in his later years, "principles of good behavior; but I was given to understand that choices and responsibility for them were to be mine."

Hornbeck's early education had a substantial classical component: "From my work in Latin and in Greek I acquired a habit of exactness and a breadth of vocabulary." He eventually acquired as well a B.A. from the University of Denver and, after teaching high school Latin for a year, became Colorado's first Rhodes scholar. At Christ Church he studied modern history and got a gentlemanly third in 1907. Back home, he entered a Ph.D. program in political science at the University of Wisconsin and came under the influence of Professor Paul S. Reinsch, who was eventually to become Wilson's minister to China.

Two years later Hornbeck and East Asia had come together: in 1909 he accepted a teaching job at Chekiang Provincial College in Hangchow. He stayed four years, absorbing China, and in 1913 went to Manchuria for a further year of teaching at Fengtien Law College in Mukden.

The returned Hornbeck, now a Far East specialist, joined the Wisconsin faculty, which had awarded him a doctorate in 1911, and in 1916 he published a book, *Contemporary Politics in the Far East*. With America's entry into the war came seven years of government service as a "technical expert" at the Paris Peace Conference, the Washington Conference, and on the staff of State's economic adviser. In 1924 Harvard appointed him lecturer on the history of the Far East. But in 1928 Washington produced a major job offer: chief of the Division of Far Eastern Affairs. President Lowell (in another day and age) "thought for a moment and then said: 'Of course, you should accept; we shall miss you here, but when the government asks for one of our number we cannot stand in the way.' "[4]

In February 1928 bachelor Hornbeck moved into a spacious third floor office in the State-War-Navy building, an office recently vacated by his friend Nelson T. Johnson who had recommended Hornbeck's appointment to Secretary Kellogg. There he reigned for nearly ten years until his promotion in August 1937 to the newly created post of adviser on political relations (Far East) to the secretary of state. From 1928 onward America's Far Eastern policy and "Dr. Hornbeck" were usually synonymous; at least, one could not tamper with the one without encountering the other, as many were to learn to their distress.

II

What was the nature of Hornbeck's bureaucratic domain in the decade under study? In 1931 the State Department's Division of Far Eastern Affairs

(FE) was manned by eight officers: the division chief, two assistant chiefs, and five "desk" men (three of them Foreign Service officers on home duty).[5] Political and economic reporting for China and Japan was divided among four desk officers, while one assistant chief handled problems of traffic in narcotics, an FE responsibility. Siam, the Pacific islands, and other trivia were assigned to the fifth desk man. The division also employed seven clerks and one messenger, bringing the grand total to sixteen employees, or roughly 2 percent of the department's 750-man work force.

Despite the Manchurian Incident and ensuing Asian troubles, FE's manpower remained virtually static over the next five years. The department as a whole was severely shaken by the depression. In 1933 its budget was reduced from $18 million to $13.5 million, bringing 50 percent salary cuts and a freeze on new appointments, and not until 1937 did appropriations exceed the levels of 1931-32.[6] Then manpower began to rise within the division. In 1938 FE had eleven officers, in 1940 twelve, and in the autumn of 1941 fifteen (plus eight clerks and three messengers, a total of twenty-six).

Within the division Foreign Service officers came and went. But continuity was present in the person of Stanley Hornbeck. It was also present in the two chief deputies he acquired over the years.[7]

In June 1930 Hornbeck had requested the appointment of an assistant chief, and by the following April his candidate, Maxwell M. Hamilton, was named to the job, a post Hamilton held until he himself became chief at the time of Hornbeck's promotion.[8] For the next ten years, under two secretaries of state, assorted undersecretaries, and others, Hornbeck and Hamilton worked in close tandem—indeed *were* the Far East Division in the eyes of those above.

Maxwell Hamilton was a Princetonian from Sioux City, a Chinese language officer who had served during the twenties as a vice consul in Canton and assessor on the Shanghai Mixed Court.[9] He had been in FE since the summer of 1927. Thirteen years younger than Hornbeck and milder of disposition, he was, as a colleague recalls, "a man essentially trained to point out why we should do nothing ever lest we rock the boat."[10] He is said to have chafed against his boss and judged the world less sternly. Others also chafed; the chief ran a "catankerous ship," one officer remembers, and required attendance at Saturday morning staff meetings at which he delivered extended public rebukes to those who had failed to meet his standards of diligence and precision during the previous seven days.[11] With his FE "family" (as another aide recalls) he was avuncular but fierce, evoking fear; yet his bluntness and rudeness "were directed at the idea, not the person."[12]

The second of Hornbeck's deputies was a later arrival. Joseph W. Ballantine, the son of missionaries to India, was an Amherst graduate and Japanese language officer.[13] From 1909 on he had served in Japan, as well as Formosa and Dairen. He worked under Hornbeck in 1928-30, then, after six more years abroad, spent in Canton, Mukden, and Tokyo, he returned to FE and became Hamilton's assistant chief a year later. Described by one who knew him as "frightfully timid, a broken-spirited clerk," Ballantine was nonetheless a man whose overseas experience made him a good deal more sympathetic to Japan's sensed needs and aspirations than Hornbeck or even Hamilton.[14]

As the decade wore on and the Far East crisis deepened, it was Hornbeck, Hamilton, and Ballantine who pressed the division's views, fended off the critics, and protected the evolving policy. If there were serious substantive divisions among them, they are hard to detect until late in the decade. Most likely they were usually submerged in the strength of Hornbeck's personality. The August 1937 reorganization—Hornbeck's shift to political adviser—only added another layer between FE and the secretary. Although the new structure was designed to release Hornbeck and his counterparts in the other regional divisions from day-to-day responsibilities and give them "time to think," this objective, according to Hornbeck, "was soon lost in the shuffle."[15] The former chief, now elevated, continued to preside; all significant FE documents required his clearance and/or comment.

The triumvirate, then, was not without cohesiveness. Nor was it without influence. When Cordell Hull chose to remember the names of "my principal associates" (some think the recurrent phrase suggests his misty distance from all who served under him),[16] he would invariably list "my three ranking Far Eastern experts," naming Hornbeck, Hamilton, and Ballantine as men who "had had long experience and training in oriental affairs and were especially equipped for the work they performed in the Department."[17] The threesome, Hull attests in his memoirs, were responsible for State's meticulous performance during the fateful talks with Nomura at the end of the decade: "This was owing to Dr. Hornbeck's precise draftsmanship and analysis of documents, Hamilton's infinite capacity for detail, and Ballantine's skillful industry in returning to the State Department after my night talks . . . and putting down on paper precisely what had been said."[18]

In style, however, the three men had their differences. As Herbert Feis reports the Hull-Nomura dialogues: "Hornbeck was seldom present. . . . A confirmed foe of compromise, inclined to lay down the law, he was little suited for this touchy and circuitous business. In the background his incisive analysis caused many vague Japanese proposals to crumble into dust. Any tendency to bypass some disputed point or to leave it in the mists of language was routed by him." By contrast, Hamilton, sometimes present, was "patient, gentle, and eagerly on the search for something in the Japanese proposals which might form the basis for a settlement. Within him the Japanese plight aroused worry, sympathy, rather than reproof—which led to a wish to give them all the chance possible to amend their course." As for Ballantine, Feis sees in him "the language scholar and the industrious draftsman. Behind the pale impassive face, a nimble mind kept account of every corner of the talk. His drafts were monotonous and exhaustive. They left no spaces in which the Japanese might hide their intentions. There was a dull evenness in his speech which made him a good interpreter."

With such a crew, Feis concludes, "the Secretary of State could have worn out even the voluble Matsuoka, had he been there."[19]

III

The State Department is not, however, its regional divisions alone, to the regret of some careerists. There are also those who come and go—the secretaries, undersecretaries, and assistant secretaries. In the period under discussion two figures loom largest, of course: Henry L. Stimson and Cordell Hull. Present but less clearly significant to the Far East crisis were their deputies—William R. Castle, Jr., William Phillips, and Sumner Welles successively as undersecretary, and R. Walton Moore as counselor.

Stimson and Hull were strikingly different men and by the end of the decade, when Stimson returned to government as secretary of war, their differences in approach to Far East policy were very evident. Yet there were similarities, or perhaps symmetries, in their Washington power positions. Each found himself estranged from—or at least uncomfortable with—his president; each served with undersecretaries who had closer ties to the president. Had the situations been reversed, Hull the Tennessee evangelist and Hoover the Quaker conciliator might have developed closer bonds, as would (and did) Stimson the warrior and Roosevelt the navalist, both East Coast patricians.

To the problems of East Asia each secretary brought a different cast of mind. Henry Stimson, recently governor general of the Philippines (or, as he put it, "an Oriental Potentate ... all I have to do is express a wish and it is taken as the law of the Medes and Persians"), was infused with a sense of America's western Pacific obligations. He also believed that he understood "the Oriental mind."[20] Worldwide, his high hopes for the Kellogg Pact were buttressed by his self-attributed "combat psychology." The important point was to enforce the law, to put teeth in the pacts. But how to do it in Asia? As he noted in his memorable diary entry of late 1931: "The peace treaties of modern Europe made out by the Western nations of the world no more fit the three great races of Russia, Japan, and China, who are meeting in Manchuria, than, as I put it to the Cabinet, a stovepipe hat would fit an African savage. Nevertheless they are parties to these treaties ... and if we lie down and treat them like scraps of paper nothing will happen, and in the future the peace movement will receive a blow that it will not recover from for a long time."[21]

One Stimson solution, an outgrowth of the "combat psychology," was to get his president to bluff Japan. (As he later put it, "To get on with Japan one had to treat her rough, unlike other countries."[22]) But Hoover would have none of this. Stimson complained that the president "has not got the slightest element of even the fairest kind of bluff." Hoover, of course, took a different view of the matter. Stimson, he declared "would have had us in a war with Japan before this if he had had his way."[23]

If the secretary's chair was occupied by a frustrated soldier prior to March 1933, it was possessed thereafter by an endlessly patient sermonizer. For the colonel, virtually any action was preferable to no action at all; for the senator, discourse was usually action enough. Cordell Hull came to office untutored in foreign affairs, though wedded to trade agreements as the key to peace. A Southern Democrat and Wilsonian, he revered high principles in personal and international conduct—moral abstractions, his critics would call them—and clung to them tenaciously throughout the turmoil of the thirties.

Hull not only clung to such principles, he reiterated them tirelessly, in public and private. He even insisted in July 1937 that a reformulation of his Eight Pillars of Peace, proclaimed at the Buenos Aires Conference a few months earlier, be circulated for comment to all the governments of the world (sixty obligingly subscribed, save for Portugal which raised some peevish doubts about the usefulness of "vague formulae"). As Hull later explained: "I never lost an opportunity, in fact, to state and restate these principles in public speeches, statements, diplomatic notes, and conversations with foreign diplomats and visiting statesmen. . . . To me these doctrines were as vital in international relations as the Ten Commandments in personal relations. One can argue that the Ten Commandments, too, are 'vague formulae.' But day after day millions of ministers of God throughout the world are preaching these formulae, and I believe there is untold value in this preaching."[24]

The crux of the problem was, of course, the appropriateness or efficacy of preachments by the American secretary of state, particularly when preachments seemed a cover for inaction—as frustrating to foreign diplomats as to some of Hull's cabinet colleagues. Carped Morgenthau to Roosevelt in September 1938: "You know Mr. Hull, as represented to the public, is about 100 percent different from the real Mr. Hull. . . . You know last June or July you put up to him the question of assisting the Chinese and he followed his usual policy by trying to wear all of us out and then do nothing." "That is right," responded Roosevelt.[25]

But inaction was not Hull's optimal objective. He attempted, rather, to keep all options open, less out of timidity than out of caution grounded in a shrewd understanding of political power. He also sought a central positive result: the transformation of the characters of men and nations. As Dorothy Borg has put it with great cogency: "The essence of the matter was that the Secretary believed, with a conviction too profound to be influenced by any external factors, that most of the basic problems of international relations could be solved by moral education."[26] It was a laudable if illusory faith.

Such, then, were the bosses, the "front office," with which State's Far East specialists had to contend in the shaping of policy. It remains to comment briefly on a few other pertinent figures in the departmental hierarchy.

Secretary Stimson, who had enjoyed a very close relationship with his hand-picked undersecretary, Joseph Cotton, found the situation much altered with Cotton's death in 1931. William R. Castle, Hoover's friend and choice (and, briefly, his ambassador to Japan), was a man of Hoover's conciliatory views. As the Stimson memoirs note, the secretary and Castle "were not fitted to make a team."[27] Stimson relied increasingly on advisers he had brought in from outside—Harvey H. Bundy, Allen T. Klots, and James Grafton Rogers. He relied, as well, on his former military aide from the Philippines, young Captain Eugene Regnier, who rode with him each morning from home to office with the nightly take of telegrams. As Stanley Hornbeck later commented, rather acidly, Stimson "was a man who instinctively believed (felt) that more important than what another man knows are the what and the where of his birth and upbringing. . . . He looked first of all for men who were Yale graduates and members of the bar. . . . Next in his choosing were his high evaluation of persons who had had experience in positions comparable to those in which he had served."[28] Bundy, Klots, and Rogers were the Yale men and lawyers, Frank McCoy a man whose army experience allegedly appealed to the secretary. It seems clear that Hornbeck, to whom some have attributed considerable influence on Stimson, felt nonetheless constrained by the role of the outsider. Captain Regnier, too, incurred Hornbeck's hostility; by the time Stimson had read through telegrams and newspapers and discussed them with his aide during the drive to the office, "he would have made up his mind, tentatively at least, with regard to action to be taken regarding some matters."[29] The colonel was a hard man to influence once his mind was made up.

The Far East Division's problems in the Hoover administration lay not alone with the secretary and his in-group. There are indications, at the time of the Manchurian Incident, that the undersecretary also posed a problem. However cool his relations with Stimson, Castle did occupy an office adjacent to the secretary; and in due course Hornbeck discovered that "several telegrams" had gone from Stimson and Castle to the embassy in Tokyo without the knowledge of FE. Hornbeck thereupon confronted Castle with "the evidence" and asked that the division henceforth "be excused from any participation in or responsibility for the handling of the Manchurian question." Castle was apparently chastened and from then on, says Hornbeck, FE was "invariably consulted."[30]

With the coming of Cordell Hull, the shape of bureaucratic and personal relations at State becomes much hazier. Gone was Stimson's incisiveness; gone, too, were the Stimson intimates, and Hull replaced them with none of his own. Aloof from most men and from his department associates, he practiced as well an aloofness from the White House, a stone's throw across West Executive Avenue. He early decided to permit his assistants "to see the President in my stead."[31] The secretary had a generous rationale for his procedure—he wanted to keep State's channels open and to reserve his own presidential visits for issues of great importance. Others, however, had less friendly explanations. James Dunn, one of the secretary's chief advisers, thought Hull "did not want the President to decide against him. Hence guards against going to him with any except major matters." Assistant Secretary of State Wilbur J. Carr, who resented the secretary's refusal to go to bat for higher departmental appropriations, thought the man was unforgivably timid on the big issues too.[32]

Whether through philosophy, generosity, or timidity, Hull avoided the White House but ran a department staffed by those who did not. His first undersecretary was Roosevelt's friend from Groton and Harvard, William Phillips, an experienced and proper diplomat who tried not to go to the White House "if he could prevail on Hull to do so because he regarded it as Hull's duty to go."[33] Others were less restrained from the very beginning. And Phillips' successor in 1937, Sumner Welles, also Groton-Harvard, made such full use of the secretary's diffidence and his own White House connections as to bring the long-simmering crisis to an eventual boil and produce his own resignation in 1943. There were those, Hull writes, who abused their White House privileges "by going over my head to see the President without instructions from me," who attempted "virtually to act as Secretary of State. Sumner Welles was the principal offender."[34] "I could not repose the same confidence in him that I did in my other associates."[35]

The White House problem aside, Hull's relations downward within the department are hard to fathom. By his account and those of others, he was methodically generous in the process of decision making. His daily regimen involved fully programmed consultation with the wide circle of "my principal associates." Even in a moment of extreme crisis—take, for instance, 3:30 a.m. on

September 1, 1939—"I asked that my principal assistants come to my office immediately. . . . There was much to do, but I called them in also because I knew they would not wish to be left out of this first conference after the outbreak of war in Europe."[36]

There are few indications of selectivity or favoritism in the Hull record; indeed, he even tolerated Sumner Welles for six years. Whether this should be diagnosed as an inability to judge men or a serene complacency with the given table of organization is another matter. The Tennessee preacher was not devoid of feelings and judgment. Nomura and Kurusu got something more personal from Hull on December 7. So—on a lesser occasion—did the junior officer from FE riding in State's elevator in 1936, to whom the secretary suddenly confided, "Now I don't dislike Stanley Hornbeck; but he just fusses at me all the time."[37]

Hull tells us nothing of his impatience with Hornbeck—or indeed with any others of his department colleagues save Welles. And if Hornbeck ever sensed the secretary's irritation, it left him quite undaunted, to judge by the record. Few other men in State's history can have contributed such an unending flow of policy memoranda to their superiors. Hornbeck's zest for the written word, his self-proclaimed "habit of exactness and breadth of vocabulary," was exercised indefatigably throughout the decade. What he might lack in grace or wit he made up in ponderously complex sentences and fine verbal distinctions, all done in pursuit of precision. The written barrage was supplemented, of course, by oral presentations. But it was the Hornbeck memorandum, usually addressed to the secretary and undersecretary, that was the chief internal carrier of policy continuity toward the Far East. The tactical advice might change as the external situation changed, but not the form of expression. And certainly not that other major childhood acquisition: a deep-seated attachment to "principles of good behavior." Although he might try the patience of Mr. Hull, Hornbeck could not but strike a responsive chord in the Tennesseean.

IV

Before moving to probe some moments of decision in the decade under study, it would be well to define more precisely the approach, the cast of mind that Stanley Hornbeck brought to the department and the problems of East Asia. By 1931 he had spent more than two decades as a student and occasional practitioner of American Far Eastern policy. He had also set down with clarity his view of the central components of that policy.

In 1916 scholar Hornbeck had written his major study of East Asia, *Contemporary Politics in the Far East*, a volume reissued without change in 1919, 1924, and 1928.[38] In it he had argued with some passion for the importance of the Far East to American foreign policy, the centrality and immense promise of China, the threat of Japanese imperialism, and the special responsibility of America toward China. "The question of the peace of the Far East," wrote Hornbeck, "lies with the fate of China. If China can develop strength to defend her own integrity, the peace of the Orient may be preserved. If the partition of China once seriously begins, nothing will save the Far East for the next several decades from being a theater of aggression, conflict, and political redistribution."[39]

In the shaping of China's future Hornbeck noted special "moral obligations" on the part of the United States, obligations rooted in the record of alleged American benevolence toward China—a record of "persistent good will," "international forbearance," and "straightforward methods." "Having assumed a position of informal guardianship it behooves us to realize that such a position creates an expectation of at least active sympathy when the ward has difficulties thrust upon him." Furthermore, to Hornbeck China's "disposition of good will" toward America was "both a moral and a business asset."[40]

Why a "business asset," when the disappointing reality was that "in commerce we have not made the most of our opportunities"? Hornbeck answered by quoting J. Selwin Tait, a prominent Washington banker: "China presents the greatest industrial and commercial opportunity not only of the world today, but the greatest which the world has ever seen." If China were to develop, the "volume of her business . . . would, it must be confessed, be unintelligible to the ordinary mind if placed in plain figures"—would be, in other words, mindboggling.[41]

Given moral obligations and business assets, Hornbeck argued that "any upsetting of the political status quo in the Far East becomes a menace to our interests, along with those of other nations." What was needed therefore from Washington was "something more than mere reiterated protestations of friendly interest." Rather, the situation required "most careful consideration and substantial, constructive political and economic effort."[42]

In 1916 the clear and present danger came from Japan. Hornbeck argued then—and repeated the argument in a subsequent article—that Japan's so-called "Monroe Doctrine for Asia" (i.e., the Twenty-One Demands) posed a serious threat not only to John Hay's Open Door doctrine but also to the Monroe Doctrine itself. The closing of the Far East to European traders, wrote Hornbeck, "will inevitably drive them to seek other markets . . . logically, in South America. Thus, inevitably, the two leading principles in the foreign policy of the United States, that of the Monroe Doctrine in application to the American continents, and that of the open door in application to China" were jeopardized by Japan's Asian moves.[43]

A year after the publication of *Contemporary Politics*, Hornbeck added to his previous message a call for the United States to "take the lead in a movement for the formulation of a co-operative policy" in East Asia, asserting that "co-operation of some sort must take the place of individualism, both in internal and international affairs." To Hornbeck, the Far East was one place "in which it is practicable to attempt the experiment of a league of forces, economic and political, for the preservation of the peace."[44]

Four years later came one major experiment along these very lines: the Washington Conference, which Hornbeck attended as a technical adviser. Its results made him jubilant. Here "co-operation" at last had triumphed—"a decisive turning point not only in the affairs of China, nor only in the annals of the Pacific and the Far East, but in the whole course of world politics." During the conference, he felt, the "principles" and the long continuity of America's Far Eastern policy had been both vindicated and enshrined in international law.[45]

In the aftermath of the Washington treaties, Hornbeck could respond with vigorous rebuttals to those who complained, during the decade of the twenties, that America had "no Far Eastern policy" or "no China policy." As he wrote in *Foreign Affairs* in 1922 and again in 1927, not only did America have such a policy, but it was a policy of consistency stretching back grandly through more than a century.[46] The policy had two central ingredients: one fundamental principle and one "corollary." The principle was "equality of commercial opportunity" in China; the corollary, "maintenance of the administrative and territorial integrity of China"—an "indispensable condition" for equality of commercial opportunity. Together, these elements composed the "Hay policy" of the Open Door—one which (unlike the Monroe Doctrine) had had from the outset "a quasi legal international status, in that both of its features were assented to and were positively affirmed not alone by the United States but by the other principal world powers" at the time of Hay's initiatives.[47]

But it was not merely the policy's "quasi legal status" that should commend it. The policy also stemmed, Hornbeck felt, from such deep-seated American values that policymakers would be powerless to change it even if they wanted to do so. The doctrine of commercial opportunity reflected "the average American's conception of justice and of his own and other countries' rights." And the corollary was "almost equally axiomatic" since "the average American believed, whether he could give reasons for his belief or not, that China's independence and integrity should be respected."[48] As he reiterated and elaborated these views in the turbulent spring of 1927, Hornbeck stressed anew the policy's roots in "public opinion"—"more and more an active and conclusive influence in the determining of policy and of action." How to account for the force and persistence of public opinion on this subject? The American people were possessed, he said, "of a peculiarly sympathetic attitude toward the Chinese people, an attitude which is somewhat sentimental and somewhat patronizing but genuinely benevolent. Warranted or not, Americans regard the Chinese as a nation of great potentialities, wish them well, believe that they will be better off and the world better off if they govern themselves, and believe them capable of self-government." Most notable of all, in view of what the thirties would bring, Hornbeck was convinced in 1927 that the American people "are opposed to any course of action which would constitute, in their opinion, 'aggression' against the Chinese people."[49]

Hay's diplomacy had made explicit and "quasi legal" the principles of America's Far Eastern policy. But to Hornbeck the crowning achievement of American diplomacy was the enactment of that policy into international law at the Washington Conference. The alternative would have been "a frank acceptance of the full implication of the spheres of interest idea and a resort without reservation to the principles of self-interest and self-help." But such an alternative was wisely rejected by the powers, under American leadership. (It must be noted that the euphoric Hornbeck of 1922 did prudently add that "during the next twenty years the value of [the Washington Conference] pledges will be tested.")[50]

Lest any still wonder if the principles of the Open Door really constituted a policy, Hornbeck patiently explained, both in 1922 and 1927, an important distinction that critics overlooked ("probably the most common error made by those who study foreign policy"). On the one hand, there was "policy," on the other hand, "plan of action." America always had the first, with extraordinary consistency, but it did not always have (or always need, one assumes) the second. Hornbeck offered, as well, some further necessary distinctions: between "plan of action" and "detail of action," and between "action which is *negative*—but nevertheless deliberate and consciously determined—and action which is *positive* and expressed in movement."[51]

What did Hornbeck mean by "cooperative action"? His intent is fairly clear from a small book he published in 1927. The "underlying principle" of the Washington treaties "was that there should be *cooperation* in a course of forbearance, self-denial and restraint" with regard to strife within China—a policy of nonintervention. But "cooperation" did not preclude "independence" in policy. Both concepts hark back to Hornbeck's views at a time of external threat to China ten years earlier. Then it was that cooperation implied to him the restraining of predator nations as well as the passivity of self-restraint. In words of later significance, Hornbeck had asked, "To prevent the establishing of inequalities, to insure against the partition of China, to save China herself from internal disturbances and to guard against some new form of anti-foreign agitation which may affect all foreign nations alike injuriously, should not every nation which is in a position to do so exert itself to restrain any other whose policies appear likely to induce some or all of these undesirable consequences?"

To the reader today—indeed to a reader in the decade of the thirties—it is remarkable how seldom and fleetingly Stanley Hornbeck made reference to that earlier predator, Japan, in his magazine writings of the twenties. It is also notable how lightly and quickly he passed over a significant question raised at the Washington Conference in the second meeting of the Committee on Pacific and Far Eastern Questions. Hornbeck himself reports that Briand had asked, in effect, "What is China?" To which Wellington Koo had responded by referring to the territories cited in the Chinese constitution.[52] That sufficed for Hornbeck. Nor did the question seem to bother the learned doctor later in the chaotic decade when central authority had altogether ceased to exist in China. The policy remained intact, the principles were right, continuity would be sustained. "The American Government has commitments," he wrote. The American government would "live up to its commitments."[53]

One further word should be said about Hornbeck's views as they had evolved by the end of the twenties. Although his earlier preoccupation with China clearly persists in his writings of the time, he had added to it an extra-regional or world view undoubtedly grounded in the peace structure of the decade, which was based upon the Paris and Washington conferences and, eventually, the Kellogg-Briand Pact. Within this framework, America's Far East and China policy became to him part of a larger American aspiration and conviction, rooted in the nation's history, "that free states should remain free—in the Orient as elsewhere—and should be encouraged to develop peacefully along their own lines without political interference."[54] In other words, the ideals that had infused the Monroe Doctrine and the Open Door—to Hornbeck so precious and interrelated—were now to be applied worldwide. As a corollary to that evolving conviction, threats to the peace structure in Asia were henceforth to be regarded as threats to the principles and structure of peace everywhere.

V

Against this backdrop of personal and bureaucratic relationships and of casts of mind within the Department of State, we turn now to a consideration of the role of the department—and of the Far East Division—at four junctures in the Japanese-American record: first, one phase of the Manchurian crisis, 1931-32; second, the challenge presented by the Amō (Amau) statement of April 1934; third, the Roosevelt scheme for the neutralization of the Pacific islands, 1936-37; and fourth, the "embargo" incident of July 1940. One of the episodes tests the department's response to a crisis situation—Manchuria. One tests its response to a Japanese initiative that fell short of crisis proportions—the negative initiative of Amō at a time of relative calm. One tests its approach to economic sanctions once the European war was under way—the July 1940 "embargo." And one tests its response to White House brain-storming—the neutralization scheme. In no case will a full chronicle be attempted; what is sought, rather, is some insight into the dynamics of decision making at State, and thereby an insight into the attitudes of the prevailing decision makers.

1.   *The Manchurian Crisis, September 1931-February 1932*

It seems fairly clear that the first weeks of the Manchurian crisis were Henry Stimson's show, pure and simple. Confident in his knowledge of "the Oriental mind," trusting of Japanese moderates, cautious and prudent himself, the secretary sought "to let the Japanese know we are watching them and at the same time to do it in a way which will help Shidehara, who is on the right side, and not play into the hands of any Nationalist agitators."[55] In so doing, Stimson sided with his undersecretary but ran counter to the initial instincts of his Far East chief. Hornbeck was appalled by the Japanese move. His first reaction was "to condemn Japan and brand her an outlaw," and he pushed both Stimson and Castle for a firm response. By the end of September, however, he had simmered down and found himself in closer agreement with his superiors.[56]

As noted earlier, the first stages of the crisis had found the Far East Division bypassed by the secretary and his deputy (indeed, there was eventually gossip of a Castle-Hornbeck feud).[57] Later in the autumn, however, FE was back in the picture. By now one recurrent question was the advisability of sanctions, on which views within the department fluctuated greatly as Stimson's own views remained unsettled.[58]

Meanwhile, on November 9, after the Japanese capture of Tsitsihar, with Shidehara still in office, Hoover had raised with his secretary of state the possibility of some procedure by which the United States might refuse to "recognize" or "avow" any Sino-Japanese treaty "made under military pressure," a revival of the Bryan formula. Stimson proceeded to broach the question with his advisers, including Undersecretary Allen Klots, James Grafton Rogers, and Hornbeck. Hornbeck was cool to the proposal, which seemed to him ineffectual, and the matter was put aside.[59]

A month later the Japanese cabinet was replaced by another that was more militant. A new stance seemed required to deal with the new situation. On the morning of December 6 Stimson discussed with Castle, Klots, Rogers, and Hornbeck the possibility of economic sanctions which he had mentioned in

November to the president. For sanctions Hornbeck had far greater enthusiasm; indeed, he defended a division appraisal that Japan could not stand a boycott "more than a very few days, or weeks." All apparently saw "the danger of an embargo going further and leading to . . . war," but except for the undersecretary, who vigorously dissented, all regarded Japan's collapse as a more probable outcome. The proposal, of course, came to an abrupt halt when Stimson talked to Hoover; the president had no interest in "sticking pins in tigers."[60]

By late December the secretary was once again intrigued with the idea of nonrecognition. A letter from Walter Lippmann in Geneva had strengthened his resolve, and on January 3 he produced a draft proposal for his advisers. By early evening, apparently, all seemed in agreement but Hornbeck, who argued that "the United States should go no further than to reserve the right to withhold recognition." The next afternoon Stimson met again with Klots and Hornbeck, and by the evening a document was ready for Hoover, who approved it. More refining followed, but at the end of two days Hornbeck was still trying "rather tenaciously" to soften the effect by reserving the right not to recognize. At this point the secretary, we are told, "got into one of his rages. He was exasperated both by the reservation and by the careful study Hornbeck concentrated on each word before accepting it." (Hornbeck later claimed that Stimson overinterpreted his degree of dissent, recalling that he had been "neither for nor against it.") The difficulties, however, were somehow resolved; and on the 7th the famous note was sent to China and Japan.[61]

What ensued is familiar—Britain's failure to follow suit as Stimson had hoped; Japan's attack at Shanghai; the Stimson-Simon telephonic negotiations; Stimson's bitter sense that Britain had "let us down"; and the secretary's new initiative, the letter to Senator Borah of February 24.

The Borah letter was the culmination of Stimson's efforts to bring collective pressure against Japan, a result soon undermined when Hoover, with Stimson abroad, instructed Castle to deny any U.S. willingness to resort to economic sanctions. In the production of the letter the Far East Division apparently played a significant role. Hornbeck claims to have written the first draft on the 22nd; then, "with that draft as a basis," Stimson, Rogers, Klots, McCoy, and Hornbeck put together the final document.[62]

What can be concluded about State's role in this brief portion of the Manchurian episode? First, of course, that State provided the initiators, pushers, and leaders. Stimson and his inner circle were the architects of policy, however much they groped and improvised. Aside from Hoover's November suggestion of a nonrecognition formula, the White House offered only reservations, doubts, and constraints. Second, that the secretary of state led his department and nation into a policy of rhetorical containment of Japanese expansionism on the basis of the Kellogg Pact and the Nine Power Treaty, a policy that was to outlast Stimson himself. And third, that the secretary found greater support within the Far East Division—specifically from Hornbeck—for the radical formula of economic sanctions than for the eventual fall-back of nonrecognition.

It may well be that Hornbeck was not only convinced of Japan's economic vulnerability; apparently he also believed that Japan's civilian leaders could better reestablish control if American pressure was manifested in ways that hurt the military. Such a view would account for his curious critique of Stimson, many years later, when he complained of the secretary's belief "that in Japan the 'government' exercised supreme control and the armed forces were agents, not makers, of policy. . . . He would not listen to what some of us in the Far Eastern Division said about the duality which prevailed, by inheritance from the feudal days and systems, in the set-up and functioning of the machinery of control, constitutional and conventional, in the Japanese state."[63]

In any event, the "role of State" at this juncture in the decade was predominantly the role of Henry Stimson, not Stanley Hornbeck, though the latter served, as usual, as a tireless analyst and critic. Yet Hornbeck's Stimsonian proclivity for firmness toward Japan, for the use of sanctions, if necessary, to induce Japan's collapse, was early suggested in this episode and would surface again as the decade progressed.

It should be noted that the proclivity was not immediately apparent, for the failure of collective security induced both disillusionment and caution. In late April 1932 Hornbeck presided at a session of the 26th annual meeting of the American Society of International Law. In his opening remarks he offered some comments on "principles and considerations" of American policy toward the "current situation" in the Far East. Despite the radical changes brought about in September 1931, his list of "general principles" remained substantially unchanged from those of 1927:

> (a) in general, respect for the legal and moral rights of other states and peoples—with expectation of respect by them for the legal and moral rights of the United States; (b) in regard to commerce, equality of opportunity and treatment—on the basis of most-favored-nation practice; (c) in regard to political methods, abstention from alliances and from aggression; (d) in the field of diplomatic approach, persuasion rather than coercion; (e) in regard to action, cooperation with other Powers wherever cooperation is found practicably possible.[64]

The usual explicit bow to China's territorial integrity was significantly absent, and those who were looking for teeth in the February Borah letter would look in vain in the Hornbeck presentation of April—a presentation which preceded by several days Castle's outright disavowal of sanctions. Clearly Hornbeck, though jolted by Japan's aggression, had swung back for the moment to the familiar security of his "principles."

2.   The Amō Challenge, April-May 1934

The Manchurian crisis left in its wake widespread disillusionment with the existing system of peace preservation, and the Department of State—and its Far Eastern Division in particular—was no exception to the rule. Stimson's efforts to marshal and lead the powers had failed, leaving Washington "out front," exposed to intense Japanese animosity. What ensued, out of disillusionment and a new administration with other preoccupations, was a drift toward a new posture. During the course of 1933, especially in the aftermath of the Tangku Truce, Washington moved toward a policy of noninterference in the north China situation and nonprovocation of Japan—a policy advocated by the men of FE, who rapidly achieved a greater influence within the Roosevelt administration than they had exercised under Stimson. (Hornbeck's memoranda following the Tangku Truce, for example, were sent to the president, who apparently was in agreement with them.)[65]

In the spring of 1934 the new approach underwent its first major test with the Amō press statement of April 17. Despite initial confusion about its wording and status, the Amō Doctrine was speedily recognized as a fundamental definition of Japan's East Asian role, of its responsibilities for peace and order in the region, and therefore of its activist aims.

Stanley Hornbeck later wrote of the Japanese leaders that "those men dreamed of an exercise of influence by Japan similar to what they mistakenly believed to be that which was exercised by the United States in the western hemisphere in application by this country of principles implicit in the Monroe Doctrine."[66] Whether or not the Japanese were actually mistaken in their view of the Monroe parallel is beside the point; Hornbeck and others at State understood the challenge and groped·for a proper response.

The groping took a number of forms. When the British government, deeply troubled over the Amō declaration, suggested Anglo-American cooperation, Hornbeck shied away, the Manchuria memories still fresh. The American government, he told the British ambassador, "did not intend to assume or be placed in a position of leadership in initiating proposals for joint or concurrent action."[67] Maxwell Hamilton, his deputy, urged deliberate inaction; Washington should take no notice of the Amō statement and should merely "carry on business as usual." America's stakes in China were no more important than those of other great powers, so why should the United States "stick out its neck?" Furthermore, words would be of little use against Japan unless those words could be backed by force and the determination to use force; neither force nor the determination was at hand. As with Hornbeck, the Manchurian episode was clearly on Hamilton's mind.[68]

It was Cordell Hull—at least so Hornbeck thought in retrospect—who finally made the decision that some response was necessary. The secretary asked FE for a draft of an aide-memoire. Hornbeck met with his officers and told them he wanted "a document which was effectively declarative and at no point vulnerable to a cavilling rejoinder by the Japanese government or from any quarter." That was no mean feat, apparently: "I vividly recall the many hours of intensive attention which we gave to every word, phrase, clause and sentence upon which we finally agreed."[69] Despite such fastidiousness, the division chief stressed at the time of drafting that the importance of the document should lie in the fact of its being issued at all rather than in the "vigor or lack of vigor, the completeness or lack of completeness of its content."[70]

The finished product, approved by Hull and delivered to the Japanese on April 29, contained the usual (although somewhat oblique) reference to the Nine Power Treaty, together with a restatement of respect for "the rights, the obligations and the legitimate interests" of others and the expectation of similar respect in return. Tossed into the message was one fresh but nonoperational thought: the application, by extension, of the "policy of the good neighbor" to the Far East. The assumption was that no one could be provoked by the message (much less "cavil"), and apparently no one was (or did), in part, perhaps, because of the secretary's background briefing to the press in which he urged newsmen to refrain from stories that might antagonize Tokyo.[71]

The chief result of the Amō episode was not, however, the aide-memoire. It was rather the internal memoranda that the Japanese challenge produced. Hull's message avoided provocation. The department's task now was to outline, at least for internal consumption, a "plan of action" (or inaction) to give meaning to the policy the secretary's message had implied. Indeed, the secretary specifically asked the Far East Division to undertake a review of ways in which friction with Japan might be minimized.

The division's response was a mid-May memorandum from Hornbeck and his colleagues. This document suggested first—with a gloomy eye to the recent Reconstruction Finance Corporation loan (which the division had opposed)—that "no further financial assistance be rendered to China by the U.S. Government or by agencies thereof" except through international action. Second, an attempt should be made to discourage American citizens from offering their services as military advisers to the Chinese government. (The State Department had already objected to the activities in China of an American air mission of private citizens who were reserve officers.) Third, Washington should continue to control rigidly the export to China of arms and munitions with "no attempt . . . to foster such trade." Fourth, the U.S. government should carefully scrutinize any new American "projects, or departure from the usual" in China "with a view to avoiding the creation of issues which may unnecessarily antagonize Japan." Fifth, China's best interests would be served by being treated "as an adult member of the family of nations" and being forced to "stand upon its own feet." Finally, the U.S. government should continue to help rehabilitate China, either alone or together with other powers, but should do so "along strictly practical lines and in such manner as to make it amply clear that it is the friendly action of a good neighbor, and . . . not in any way dictated or prescribed by Japan or by a desire to assist China to the detriment of any other nation."[72]

Some weeks later Hornbeck further reviewed the problem of foreign aid for China's reconstruction in a memorandum to the secretary and the president.[73] He suggested that the old Consortium, which was in danger of dissolution, be maintained so that multilateral aid might be provided with minimum provocation of Japan. As he subsequently told Thomas W. Lamont, the Consortium should be kept alive pending "more and clearer evidence with regard to what really are Japan's intention and plan of procedure with regard to China and the Far Eastern situation in general."[74]

Out of the Amō episode, the Far East Division seems to have emerged with good access to the secretary of state and even, by paper, to the president. But it reflected a post-Manchurian, post-Stimsonian (and depression-decreed) disinclination to respond with vigor—either rhetorical or economic—to the evolving shape of Japanese intentions. The Amō Doctrine was words, even dreams "of an exercise of influence," but it was not deeds. In the climate of America's preoccupation with internal economic conditions, its isolation, and its weakness, the division evidently deemed it prudent to await "more and clearer evidence"— and to hope for the best.

However devoted Stanley Hornbeck might be to the principles of the Open Door and the cause of China, he saw little in America in 1934—and, indeed, less in the fragile Nanking government—with which to advance those principles and that cause without excessive and unsupportable risks. Until the United States developed the requisite strength, in particular the naval strength, it should avoid such risks. In this conclusion Hornbeck and his division had the full support of Secretary Hull.

3. Pacific Island Neutralization, 1936-37

The year 1936 brought two developments of far-reaching significance for Japanese-American relations. On the one hand, the situation in China was profoundly altered by nationwide demonstrations against further appeasement of Japan, by the increasing effectiveness (and stiffened spine) of the Nanking government, and by the outcome of the Sian Incident in December. After years of chronic pessimism among officials in Washington and in "the field" over the prospects for Chinese unity and resistance to Japan, the climate was suddenly changed. On the other hand, and almost simultaneously with this transformation, came the news of Japan's adherence to the Anti-Comintern Pact.

Within the context of these broader developments, with their obvious impact on Washington policymakers, a small exchange took place between the White House and the State Department—an exchange that had little effect on the destinies of nations but serves to throw some light on bureaucratic relationships.

This was also the year in which the Washington Naval Treaty came to an end, leaving open (among other things) the question of future ground rules with regard to fortifications and bases in the Pacific islands under Article 19 of the treaty. In September a British proposal for a tripartite agreement to prolong the life of this article had been rejected. In general, the department was disinclined to negotiate any piecemeal renewal of the Washington Conference package lest the United States thereby indicate tacit approval of Japan's repudiation of other conference agreements.[75]

On November 16, out of the blue, Franklin D. Roosevelt proposed to his cabinet a different solution: a plan for the "neutralization" of the Pacific islands in order to help relieve international tensions. Roosevelt was on his way to the Buenos Aires Conference where he hoped to press for similar types of disarmament agreements. According to Harold Ickes, the president "did not go much into details, but he suggested a possible agreement for the disarmament of practically everything in the Pacific except Japan, Australia, New Zealand, and Singapore. This would leave the Philippines, Shanghai, Hong Kong, the Dutch East Indies, British North Borneo, and other important places neutralized." Hawaii would stay armed, but not "that portion of Alaska nearest Japan."[76] Although no action was taken on the November suggestion, Ickes reported in January that the president had again mentioned the "possibility of a neutralization policy of the Pacific" on a "couple of occasions."[77]

In February 1937 Franklin Roosevelt decided to press his point with State. He wanted the department to explore the prospects for "neutralization" and he wanted a memorandum on the subject. The task of research and, as it turned out, rejoinder fell to the cautious Maxwell Hamilton. The result, on February 16, was a thirty-six page memorandum entitled "Neutralization of the

Islands of the Pacific: Pros and Contras."[78] After noting the vagueness and hence nonusefulness of such terms as "neutralization" and even "Pacific Islands," Hamilton went to painstaking lengths to suggest four separate types of agreements—"A, B, C, and D"—that might conceivably be applied in the Pacific. He then presented the arguments "Pro" and "Contra." Overwhelmingly, as it turned out, the "Contras" had it. As Dorothy Borg summarized the document, "it was persistently asserted that the United States should not conclude a treaty in regard to any aspect of the Pacific area until the time arrived when conditions in the Far East had been stabilized and a comprehensive settlement could again be worked out involving concessions on both sides."[79] Central to the argument was the conviction that Japan could not be trusted to keep treaty pledges. The memorandum, bearing the concurring initials of Stanley K. Hornbeck, was sent to the White House via Hull.

Like many another president who has sought to implant ideas in the bureaucracy, Franklin Roosevelt was vexed by the rebuff from below. (As one undersecretary was to say to an underling twenty-five years later, "Don't tell me why it can't be done; tell me *how* to do it!") The president's response was a two page message to his secretary of state. Its first two sentences: "This discussion is interesting and inclusive of much information but may I suggest that it does not fire one's imagination in favor of neutralization of the islands of the Pacific. It is, for example, captious to object to the word 'neutralization' and suggest the word 'non-aggression' for the very simple reason that the laymen of all nations would understand what we were doing if we neutralize the islands of the Pacific against war being waged on them or from them by any of the powers owning them." After a further brief analysis of the "A-B-C-D" categories, the president closed with vexation at flood tide though controlled:

> The whole tenor of the argument is that this is not the time to do anything; that the proposal is merely idealistic and that an agreement would not be lived up to anyway.
> In other words, taking it by and large, this argument all the way through is an argument of defeatism.
> Being a realist, I wish you would let me have a talk with the author of this. Will you arrange it?[80]

Franklin Roosevelt's message to Hull may have been the only request for a White House command performance ever received by Maxwell Hamilton. There is no record, however, that the request was honored. Cordell Hull protected his young, even if he could not remember their names. Hamilton absorbed the White House salvo then dutifully sent it on to the Records Division marked "Confidential. Files. M. M. H." It should be added that FE, perhaps alarmed, sought support at once for its "Contras" and obtained such support from both Norman Davis and Ambassador Grew in Tokyo. The latter thought the Japanese would judge the Roosevelt proposal a confession of "defeatism" and "moral weakness." Despite one further effort by the president to interest Norman Davis, the end result of this interlude—besides presidential irritation—was the extension of what Dorothy Borg calls "the precept of inaction" to the problems presented by the Pacific islands.[81]

It is difficult to judge the "role of State" at this juncture, except to speculate that the president's innate distrust of the departmental bureaucracy and his distance from the secretary of state were very likely compounded by the Far East Division's nonresponsiveness to his personal initiative. One assumes that such experiences reinforced Roosevelt's natural attraction to State's bureaucratic adversaries, the pushers and doers at the Treasury who at least tried to "fire one's imagination."

4. *The July 1940 "Embargo"*

It was in 1938, Stanley Hornbeck recalled years later, that he first "ventured to express, orally, to Mr. Hull, an opinion that if Japan continued to pursue the course and to apply the methods to which her armed forces were more and more committing her, there would come sooner or later a collision, 'war,' between that country and the United States."[82] What had wrought the change in the post-Amō man of subdued caution is abundantly clear: the stiffening of China's spine before and after Sian, Japan's membership in the Anti-Comintern Pact, the renewal of Sino-Japanese hostilities, the failure of the Brussels Conference, and China's dogged survival power. Japan's "intention and plan of procedure," still misty after Amō, were now all too discernible. New U.S. moves toward naval preparedness complemented China's new unity. The wherewithal so long lacking might soon be at hand to protect that vital corollary of America's Far Eastern policy, the "territorial integrity of China"—and to protect as well the old central "principle," America's access to China.

As early as the naval talks of 1935 Hornbeck had been a fierce advocate of "preparedness" to deter the "psychology of adolescent imperialism" that had seized Japan. As early as 1935 he had decided, in addition, that "no conceivable concessions on the part of the Government and people of the United States would have any conclusive effect" on "the *politik* of force . . . upon which Japan relies."[83]

By the summer of 1940 Hornbeck's obsessions and Hornbeck's Far East Division (now managed by Hamilton) were part of the evolving American response to the larger European and global struggle. The effect was to make of the doctor a Stimsonian once again—a Stimsonian at last unleashed.

It was Henry Morgenthau, Jr., by now an old adversary of Hornbeck, who first noted the change. Long accustomed to Hornbeck's obstruction of Treasury's efforts to aid the Chinese government (lest Japan be prematurely provoked), Morgenthau visited State in December 1939 in an attempt to get Hull's backing for a voluntary embargo on the sales of molybdenum to Japan and the Soviet Union. Hull was negative, preferring not to "arouse the Japanese." But the secretary of state, holding to his customary routine, called in a "principal associate," Maxwell Hamilton who, much to Morgenthau's surprise (and perhaps to Hull's as well), favored the embargo. "He then sent for Dr. Hornbeck," Morgenthau recorded at the time, "and again I almost fell out of my chair when Hornbeck agreed that this ought to be done. He said, 'As a matter of fact, we are working on several other ways to put the screws on the Japanese and this is just what we ought to do.'"[84]

It was in the context of the Morgenthau-Hornbeck rapprochement that the July 1940 episode took place. In simplest terms, what happened was that on the 25th Franklin Roosevelt signed a proclamation placing *all* petroleum, petroleum products, and scrap metals on the list of valuable materials that were not to leave the country. The next day the signed proclamation was discarded and a new one substituted. The two-day turnabout gives some insight into the processes (and hazards) of decision making in 1940.[85]

In January 1940, at the urging of Stanley Hornbeck, the United States had abrogated its commercial treaty with Japan. Meanwhile, since June 1938 "moral embargoes" had been in operation. By June 1940, when Congress gave the president new licensing authority, mounting agitation in Japan prompted Maxwell Hamilton to urge caution on Hull. Hamilton believed that "restriction or prohibition of the exportation of petroleum products . . . would tend to impel Japan toward moving into the Dutch East Indies." He argued strongly against such restriction and was supported by Grew in Tokyo.[86]

A month later Hornbeck expressed a different concern regarding confusion over "embargoes" at home and abroad: "The embargoes should either be made more extensive or the 'moral embargoes' dropped altogether while placing the strictest construction upon the provision of the law with respect to certain limited embargoes."[87] At the same time Hornbeck was incensed over the imminent closing of the Burma Road and urged that in the event of its closing, as soon as there appeared evidence that American trade was "in fact being interfered with, . . . some form of retaliation" be applied to U.S. trade with Japan and perhaps even with Britain.[88] On June 25 Hornbeck had expressed himself even more bluntly in a private note to Sumner Welles in which he concluded that "nothing short of or less than the language of force, either military or economic or both, will exercise effectively restraining influence upon Japan's present leadership."[89]

In the midst of this concern and confusion, Cordell Hull's native caution reasserted itself; he refused to be pushed into any reduction of exports to Japan and on July 19 departed for a conference in Havana. On the very same day, with the Burma Road finally closed, Henry Morgenthau went to the president with a total embargo plan that he felt "might give us peace in three to six months."[90] The discussion was joined by Knox and Stimson and also by Acting Secretary of State Sumner Welles. Stimson sided firmly with Morgenthau, but Welles feared a total embargo would force Japan to go to war. The meeting ended without a decision. Morgenthau complained bitterly of "the beautiful Chamberlain talk that I listened to Sumner Welles give. . . . Thank heavens we have Stimson with us." Morgenthau also received the support of his old enemy and new-found ally Stanley K. Hornbeck. In the light of new Japanese bids to buy large amounts of petroleum, Hornbeck wrote to Welles, "if action is taken on our part which results in failure on Japan's part to receive these new supplies, such action and the resultant failure might retard or prevent such new adventuring and would certainly make it, if embarked upon, more difficult."[91]

Three days later, on July 22, Morgenthau pressed his case in writing to the president at Hyde Park. And when on the 24th word came of vast new Japanese purchases of oil, Morgenthau approached the president once again, this time citing a precedent from the allegedly successful imposition of U.S. trade restrictions during the Siberian episode of 1918. A day later Roosevelt acceded to his old friend and neighbor and signed the far-reaching proclamation prepared by Morgenthau's Treasury.[92]

So came about a fundamental policy decision by the White House—an order ending the export of all oil, steel, and scrap iron to Japan. The proclamation was passed across the street to the acting secretary of state for his countersignature and seal. Sumner Welles, of course, was appalled at what he read and argued, as had Hamilton, that such a move would drive the Japanese to invade the Dutch East Indies and perhaps declare war on Britain. Roosevelt's response to Welles was an announcement to the press that "at the request of the State Department another order would be issued to make clear what kind of oil and scrap were affected."[93]

The showdown came the next day at an afternoon cabinet meeting. Despite Morgenthau's angry assault on State and Welles, and despite strong support from Stimson and Ickes, "the President raised his hands in the air, refused to participate in it, and said that those two men [Morgenthau and Welles] must go off in a corner and settle their issue."[94] The resulting compromise was to limit the embargo to aviation fuel and No. 1 heavy melting iron and steel scrap, which made up but small percentages of Japanese purchases.

By 1940, it seems clear, worldwide conflict had bred tensions and divisions not only within the executive branch but within State itself on matters of Far Eastern policy. Secretary Hull remained instinctively wedded to "the precept of inaction," although willing to let others within the department have their say. Sumner Welles, a Europeanist by breeding, saw no good coming from conflict with Japan. Maxwell Hamilton shared the Hull and Welles view, still believing that collision could be averted by careful nonprovocation and a persistent search for areas of possible accommodation. Stanley Hornbeck, however, had a somewhat different opinion. To Hornbeck the central and nonnegotiable issue was Japan's failure to live up to agreements pertaining to China and American rights in the region. In his estimation, a policy of preparedness, firmness, and increasing pressure would eventually set the situation in East Asia aright by bringing Japanese misconduct and expansionism to a halt. He was to argue this view relentlessly from the summer of 1940 until December 1941.

VI

In early November 1941 a junior Foreign Service officer, just back from a tour of duty in Tokyo, paid a courtesy call on the Far East political adviser. Hornbeck asked the young man about the mood of the embassy staff. They were worried, was the answer, deeply worried about the imminence of war between Japan and the United States, a war that Japan might well initiate out of sheer desperation. Hornbeck was incredulous and disdainful. "Tell me," he said, "of one case in history when a nation went to war out of desperation." The flustered Foreign Service officer could think at the moment of none, and the interview was soon terminated.[95]

A year earlier a more senior colleague, Jay Pierrepont Moffat, who was Grew's son-in-law, had called on Hornbeck during a brief home leave from Ottawa. He found the political adviser convinced that America was "already at war" with Japan, "though if we adopted a firm and uncompromising stand we might yet avoid being dragged into a 'combat war.'" Moffat's wry comment was that "Stanley regarded Japan as the sun around which its satellites, Germany and Italy, were revolving."[96]

A further glimpse of Hornbeck comes from a memorandum he sent to Sumner Welles on July 23, 1941. "I submit," he wrote, "that under existing circumstances it is altogether improbable that Japan would deliberately take action in response to any action which the United States is likely to take in the Pacific which action if taken by Japan would mean war between that country and this country."[97]

How is one to understand the Hornbeck position during the critical months of 1941? He talked of war—indeed claimed to have predicted collision to Hull as early as 1938—and yet he seemed convinced that war could be avoided. He urged that increased pressure, increased force, be brought to bear on Japan; and yet he regarded a warlike response, whether out of despair or deliberation, as improbable.

The basis for the Hornbeck view seems threefold. In the first place, he was deeply convinced that the Japanese were bluffing or, at least, that they desperately wanted to avoid war with the United States and would back down under the threat of war. Second, he was haunted by the memory of the Anglo-American failure to stand up to Japan during the Manchurian episode, was convinced, in retrospect, that the weakness of Hoover and of Sir John Simon had sown the seeds of the present crisis.[98] And third, he was contemptuous of Japan's military strength, which, he judged, was severely reduced by the long China War.

If, in fact, Japan was bluffing, it was vital to call its bluff. If, in fact, the U.S. response to Manchuria had communicated a permissive signal, it was high time to communicate something tougher. As for Tokyo's capacity to fight a war, "Japan, whatever may have been four years ago her rightful rating, on the basis of military strength and capacity, as a major power, is today very tired and comparatively weak." Indeed, Hornbeck saw "more than a good chance" of Japan's collapse from overexertion before Germany's defeat, to be followed by "changes in Japanese leadership and Japanese psychology," after which the United States could "do business with Japan."[99]

Given such assumptions, and given Hornbeck's conviction as early as 1935 that "no conceivable concessions on the part of the Government and people of the United States would have any conclusive effect" on Japan, it is little wonder that the political adviser devoted his energies tirelessly during the months of 1941 to the propagation of the diplomacy of force and to the defeat of its bureaucratic opponents. Never had his sturdy pen been wielded more confidently or polemically.

It was Hornbeck within the department who pressed hardest for a freezing of Japanese assets in July 1941: "If we have any intention of freezing them and do not freeze them now, we should give ourselves pretty good reasons for not doing so."[100] It was Hornbeck who argued for additional pressures in a forceful July 16 memorandum and then again in a follow-up one month later in which he underlined in blue those things from his previous paper that had been done and in red those that had not. The latter included: "a new disposal of armed force . . . the only thing that really impresses and tends to restrain the Japanese at this point is evidence of armed capacity and intention; . . . keep open the line of communication into China at Rangoon; . . . make a new show of force in the western Pacific; . . . additional aid should be sent to China immediately; . . .

additional planes ... should be sent immediately to Manila" and "a cruiser squadron" to the Philippines, the Dutch East Indies, or Singapore.[101]

It was Hornbeck, as well, who fought hardest against the Konoe proposal for a summit meeting with Roosevelt. "Mr. Hull viewed it with suspicion," he recalled. "I viewed it from the outset with suspicion and disfavor. ... Mr. Grew was both disappointed and greatly vexed."[102] To Hornbeck, Grew was now advocating "appeasement."[103]

As for the Hull-Nomura conversations, the political adviser observed the long process with watchful distaste. He had no hope for the talks, and indeed they clearly posed some danger to his formula of pressures. Hornbeck did not attend but studied the transcripts and did what he could to keep the more conciliatory Maxwell Hamilton firmly in line. "Mr. Hull and I completely and expressly agreed that participation by me in the conversations would not be profitable ... and that I should play the role, in the background and off-stage, of observer, analyst and counselor."[104] Others recall a different Hornbeck, one who deeply resented his exclusion from the talks by a secretary of state who now distrusted him as a "firebrand."[105]

Hornbeck's rigidity, while more consistent than most, was not, of course, unique. Even the patient Cordell Hull felt his heart hardening as the MAGIC intercepts seemed to document Japanese duplicity. "Nothing will stop them except force," he told Welles on August 4. Stimson felt Hull had "made up his mind that we have reached the end of any possible appeasement with Japan and there is nothing further that can be done with that country except by a firm policy."[106]

As the autumn wore on and the crisis deepened, Maxwell Hamilton still hoped for a way out of the impasse. On November 17 Morgenthau passed on to State and the White House an extraordinary memorandum by Harry Dexter White proposing a "creative economic policy"—an imaginative regional settlement scheme—to arrest the drift toward war. Hamilton judged the memorandum a "most constructive one" and the services posed no objection. But the hour was very late and the document died in the bureaucracy.[107]

Ten days later Hull presented a proposal to the Japanese envoys that was "comprehensive, uncompromising, and entirely unresponsive to all Japanese drafts."[108] In this circumstance, on the 27th Hull met with Hornbeck, Hamilton, and Ballantine to plan for the president's meeting with the Japanese that afternoon. The talks had clearly failed. Hornbeck, reports A. A. Berle, "was urging determination to act by force of arms. The Secretary was pointing out that the Army felt it would not be ready for another three weeks, that the Navy wanted another three months. Hornbeck pointed out that the Navy had asked for six months last February and the Secretary, through his negotiations, had got them that six months. Now they wanted three more. Hornbeck's idea was that the President ought to stop asking the Navy, and tell it. The Secretary, rather wearily, passed it aside."[109]

Hornbeck's energy, his confidence, indeed his exhilaration that day were unbounded. He went so far as to write a memorandum whose opening sentence read, "In the opinion of the undersigned, the Japanese Government does not desire or intend or expect to have forthwith armed conflict with the United States." Not content with this assertion, he was in a wagering mood. His "bets," the memo continued, were five to one "that the United States and Japan will not be at 'war' on or before December 15," three to one against war by January 15, and "even money" against war by March 1. "Stated briefly," he concluded, "the undersigned does not believe that this country is now on the immediate verge of 'war' in the Pacific."[110]

Such uncustomary and ill-timed flamboyance requires some explanation, and Hornbeck has one for the student of history: "I made the mistake," he writes, "of yielding to an emotional urge and committing myself on the record in terms of wishful thinking and gratuitous predicting." But he was careful to add that "both my thinking and my predicting were, however, based on my scrutiny of materials which emanated from 'intelligence' services, some British and some American"—specifically, with regard to the strength of Singapore and the current position of the Japanese main fleet.[111]

Ten days after Hornbeck's confident predictions, the Japanese bombed Pearl Harbor. Did he foresee the attack? A candid answer to this very question may be found neatly typed in his private papers: "No, and so far as I am aware neither did any other American. The Secretary of State came nearer to it, in my opinion, than did any other American."[112] And did he underestimate the strength of Japan? Again the candid answer—with which we commenced this paper—is to be found in his files.

VII

This paper began as a study of the Department of State, yet became largely a study of one of its officers. Why? In part, the answer lies in convenience: Hornbeck persisted and survived, gathering to him the trappings of longevity in office as well as the actuality of accumulated bureaucratic power. He used both with skill and zest. "Stanley preferred power to what money could buy," one aide recalls. "He handled power as a draper handles bolts of cloth."[113] He personified the continuity of Far Eastern policy for more than a decade, despite tactical shifts, and deftly grafted that policy onto a century of previous history. He saw himself as the guardian of a grand tradition.

No one man "makes policy" in a pluralistic institution—as the previous pages have shown—and longevity in office is no automatic guarantee of influence. Yet Hornbeck's case is significant and his influence was real. For he represented more than himself: a resilient, deep-rooted constituency within the nation. It was a constituency of men with continuing material and professional interests in the Far East: traders, bankers, churchmen, military men, journalists, and academics. It was a group that shared a paramount interest in the promise of China and a belief in an activist American role in keeping open that promise. "We must consider," Hornbeck had written in 1917, "the disposition and temperament of our own people. We are a young, virile, self-confident, wealthy, idealistic, missionarily-inclined race. Our people never have stayed at home through fear of getting themselves into difficulties abroad. We are of pioneering stock."[114] Those he represented shared his national self-image.

The thirties, of course, were a dark time for the intellectual heirs of Captain Mahan. The nation was turned inward, disillusioned and self-absorbed, its economy at a standstill, its churches in a state of retrenchment, its military apparatus dismantled. In such a period the Far East Division and its wider constituency were realistic enough to know they must bide their time.

Nor were external conditions the only constraint. Simultaneous with these conditions there had also emerged within the Department of State another group of comparable power, though by no means as dominant within the Far East region. This was a "realist" school, with its roots in the Anglo-Japanese alliance, that had come to believe in "spheres of influence." Ambassador Grew came to be of this school; but it was doubtless his deputy in the Tokyo embassy, Eugene Dooman, who gave force to Grew's dispatches. In the uneven struggle between the advocates of universal principles and the advocates of spheres of influence, Hornbeck's chief adversary was Dooman.[115]

Hornbeck was well aware of these opposing forces, within the department as well as in Tokyo—forces that gained in strength as Washington's preoccupation with the European war gave new vigor to those who hoped for a Far Eastern modus vivendi. As early as the end of January 1940 he had discussed the matter in a very private memorandum to Sumner Welles. In response to an apparently cutting comment by the undersecretary, Hornbeck confessed that "certain newspaper writers who have affirmed that there is in the Department a division of thought or inclination" about Far Eastern policy must be right.[116]

Hornbeck then proceeded to describe two factions within the department. The first was composed of "officers several of whom have devoted the whole of their adult lives to study of and problems of action in relation to the Far East and several of whom, though junior, have specialized" in the field. "This group includes about a dozen officers. Within this group there is substantial unanimity of opinion in regard to practically all of the fundamental facts and the fundamental issues which underlie and which largely determine the character of the problems with which we have to deal." The second faction was "predisposed toward interest in and concern regarding situations eastward and southward from the United States as contrasted with situations and problems of the Pacific and the Far East (westward)." Among its members Hornbeck saw no unanimity but rather "a community of impression" that Far Eastern happenings were "relatively unimportant" in comparison with Latin America and Europe. "The cleavage in thought and in inclination between these two 'groups' " was illustrated, wrote Hornbeck, in the remark by a nameless member of the second faction who had said, "It is often good strategy to abandon some bastion in order the better to defend other bastions." Hornbeck tersely concluded that Welles seemed to share such views.[117]

So the guardianship of the grand tradition was no easy task. In the circumstances of the thirties it required more negation than innovation, more defense than creation. But it was, at least in the short run, a successful guardianship. Its effect, despite sharply lessened American interests and power in East Asia, was to offer no new avenues toward conciliation and adustment from the chief agency charged with foreign policy. All efforts at a modus vivendi that would have permitted Japan an enlarged sphere of influence were blocked; the principles of U.S. Far Eastern policy—and, by extension, its global policy—remained intact; and force was, in due course, brought to bear to subdue the aggressor.

But did Stanley K. Hornbeck understand *why* it all happened—the Japanese-American crisis and impasse, the Pearl Harbor attack, the war itself? His answer, twenty years later: "Japan's attack . . . came *not*, as is often affirmed, of our China policy but of (a.) the commitment of Japan's leaders to their program of conquest and (b.) American opposition to aggression in general and to Japan's and her Axis allies' aggressions in particular." And as a further elaboration he wrote that throughout the Far Eastern crisis in the decade of the thirties, Americans "were on the defensive. They were thinking and they argued in terms of principles. They were in effect saying to the Japanese that what had been, presumably, good for the United States, would be good for Japan and for each and all lands. To and for Japan's rulers that thinking, those principles and that contention had no meaning: they were committed to a program; they were engaged in and they intended to persevere in operations of conquest; as they saw it, what would be good for Japan would be good for Japan's neighbors."[118]

The struggle, then, was between America's "principles" and Japan's "program," the one universal and benevolent, the other particularist and self-serving. Principles were abstractions, perhaps—abstractions learned in the household of a Methodist minister, taught in college classrooms, applied to the people and promise of China, and practiced under the aegis of Stimson and Hull. But still potent abstractions, rooted, Hornbeck believed, in the American Experiment—and therefore abstractions to which all men must eventually pay homage, by persuasion if possible, by force if necessary.

THE ROLE OF THE
UNITED STATES EMBASSY
IN TOKYO

Akira Iriye

"American policy is formulated in Washington, not in Tokyo. All that we do, and what we aim to do, is to report and analyze and, occasionally, to recommend."

–Ambassador Joseph C. Grew[1]

Ambassador Grew's conception of the embassy's role was a modest one. A professional diplomat, he was never carried away by an undue sense of his importance but was constantly aware of the intricate decision making mechanism of which an embassy was merely a small segment. He also realized, from his experiences with the Turks and the Japanese, that relations with a non-Western country involved complexities that made traditional modes of diplomacy seem irrelevant. "In attempting to deal with such powers [as Japan]," he wrote, "the uses of diplomacy are in general bankrupt."[2]

These two points of reference–the role of professional diplomacy in American decision making and the functioning of a professional diplomat in a non-Western setting–defined the nature of the problems faced by Ambassador Grew and his staff in Tokyo in the 1930s. Despite his modest opinion of the embassy's influence, Grew never surrendered his faith in diplomacy to accept extra-diplomatic methods such as the use of force which, as he said, "can only constitute an admission of a lack, first of good will and, second, of resourceful, imaginative, constructive statesmanship."[3] He was committed to providing his small share of this statesmanship in the hope of preventing a violent rupture in Japanese-American relations. And as Japan presented a unique arena for conducting diplomacy, he had at least the satisfaction of endeavoring as best he could to "understand oriental psychology"[4] and of achieving some degree of success. He entertained frequently, played golf with Japanese, talked regularly with his colleagues and American correspondents about developments in Japan, constantly exchanged views with his subordinates, some of whom spoke

Japanese and had contacts of their own, and read Japanese newspapers (though not magazines) in translation.

A question presents itself. Did all this make any difference? Given the fact that Japanese-American relations deteriorated steadily throughout the 1930s, did the embassy in Tokyo play a significant role in the failure to prevent such deterioration? Or were embassy officials merely passive observers of the unfolding tragedy over which they had little control?

These questions are related to more specific problems concerning the functioning of the Tokyo embassy. An embassy should, of course, serve as a channel of communication between its home government and the host government. Official business between Japan and the United States would therefore normally be handled through the embassies in Tokyo and Washington. But how instrumental, in fact, was the American embassy in Tokyo in influencing the Japanese and American governments' views of and policies toward one another? Were the embassy's interpretations of events and proposals for policy taken seriously by decision makers in Washington? Did the Japanese gain an understanding of U.S. policy through the embassy in Tokyo? Was it an indispensable bridge to connect Japanese and Americans, or was it just a ferryboat carrying messages back and forth?

Such questions serve to analyze the Japanese-American crisis at one level of reference. For the purposes of the comparative institutional study of the 1930s in which we are engaged, the U.S. embassy in Tokyo constitutes a clearly defined and well documented subject for study. The American documentation is massive, as all users of the Grew papers, both published and unpublished, can testify. The Japanese sources are also valuable, for they reveal the impressions the embassy was making upon the Japanese as well as the gaps between the perception of events on each side. Waldo Heinrichs' study of Joseph C. Grew, *American Ambassador,* has skillfully traced Grew's ramblings in the tangle of Japanese-American relations. This essay will, therefore, draw on these sources and examine a few specific events with a view to clarifying the nature of the embassy's work as these relations deteriorated.

I

As a first example, the furor over the Amō (Amau) statement of April 17, 1934 may be cited. From Japanese and American sources it is clear that Amō Eiji, chief of the Foreign Ministry's Information Division, paraphrased in his statement an instruction Foreign Minister Hirota Kōki had sent to Minister Ariyoshi Akira in China on April 13. Hirota had referred to Japan's "mission" in East Asia and its determination to maintain peace and order in that part of the world "on its own responsibility, acting alone" and said that Japan would have to object to any military assistance or political loans to China provided by third powers. Asked by reporters about Japan's attitude toward Western financial schemes in China, Amō repeated the content of the instructions omitting only the last paragraph which referred to the need to "destroy" all foreign "schemes" in China.

Amō had not obtained the authorization of his superiors, and they, including Hirota, knew nothing about the statement until it was printed in newspapers on the morning of April 18. Since it had been given orally, foreign correspondents and newspapers, and to a lesser extent domestic newspapers, took the liberty of amplifying and dramatizing the message, giving the impression that here was an enunciation of an Asian Monroe Doctrine. The Chinese Foreign Ministry firmly denounced the statement, declaring that the maintenance of peace was not a responsibility devolving upon a single power. The upshot was a succession of queries from foreign governments, producing a clarification of Japanese policy by the Foreign Ministry toward the end of the month. By this time the original Amō statement had been watered down, and the episode ended with Japan reiterating its respect for the Open Door in China.[5]

To some officials such as Secretary of State Cordell Hull, the Amō statement was a clear revelation of Japan's ultimate intentions and had to be treated with the utmost seriousness.[6] Japanese-American relations, which had entered a brief period of lull after Japan's withdrawal from the League of Nations, were again threatening to deteriorate, and it became the task of the State Department to try to avoid friction across the Pacific while persuading Japan to abide by international agreements and the principle of the "good neighbor" that Hull had enunciated at the Montevideo Conference a few months earlier. As will be noted again later, Secretary Hull's perspective on international affairs was Latin America-oriented, and he saw no reason why the ideal of the good neighbor should not apply in Asia just as it did in United States relations with the American republics. The embassy in Tokyo had constantly to cope with this type of universalism and remind Washington that China was not exactly comparable to Nicaragua. Of necessity the embassy's perspective was Asia-oriented, and it continued to grope for principles of policy more practical and realistic than the good neighbor doctrine.

The Tokyo embassy, however, does not seem to have played a very substantial role in the Amō affair. It did not go beyond the conventional functions of gathering information and transmitting messages between the two governments. Moreover, the first function was not carried out to everyone's credit and even produced some feeling of uneasiness between the embassy and the Far Eastern Division of the State Department. Ambassador Grew was apparently first apprised of the seriousness of the Amō statement by Wilfrid Fleisher, managing editor of the *Japan Advertiser* and a correspondent for the *New York Herald Tribune*. Fleisher telegraphed to New York his translation of the statement as soon as it was made, but the embassy refrained from doing so, pending the release of an official translation by the Japanese Foreign Ministry. Instead, Grew telegraphed Hull on April 18 that Fleisher's translation was "substantially correct" and that the embassy would notify the department of any discrepancies between it and the official Japanese translation.[7] In reply, the department instructed the embassy to "follow up by mail all available pertinent material."[8]

These were perfectly routine exchanges. Trouble arose because the embassy failed to execute the self-imposed task contained in its telegram. It was only on April 26 that Grew could report to Washington that there was in fact no official translation of the Amō statement and that Amō refused to vouch for the accuracy of Fleisher's translation of the April 17 oral remarks.[9] As a result, the

State Department was, in the words of Stanley K. Hornbeck, chief of the Far Eastern Division, "groping about in something of a fog."[10] In the absence of substantial factual reports from Grew, the department had to turn to the Japanese embassy in Washington, which on April 25 supplied the department with the text of Hirota's instruction to Minister Ariyoshi on which the Amō statement was allegedly based.[11]

The Tokyo embassy was not proud of its performance, but it had its own complaints. As Grew related to Hornbeck in late June, "Reports were flying thick and fast around the capital, and whether or not Amau's statement could be considered as official, whether or not there was an official Japanese text, and whether or not there was an English translation which the Foreign Office would acknowledge as authentic, were questions which everyone was asking and to which answers could not be obtained until days later."[12] Moreover, the department had instructed the embassy to send "by mail" all pertinent information on the Amō statement, and this instruction was duly carried out on April 20. In a dispatch of that date, which did not arrive in Washington till May 5, Grew gave his well-considered interpretation of the origins, nature, and implications of the Amō statement, based upon the embassy's study of the Japanese press and its contacts with foreign and Japanese journalists and officials.[13] Since this report was not telegraphed, Washington continued to request a translation of the Japanese "text," much to the annoyance of the embassy.[14]

Grew did exercise initiative when, on the morning of April 25, he visited Foreign Minister Hirota at his residence, to avoid publicity, and provided him with an opportunity to explain the Amō episode. Grew had not been instructed to do so, and the department's April 24 telegram, directing him to inquire of Hirota whether the Fleisher version was an accurate translation of the Amō statement, had not yet arrived. The ambassador's call on Hirota was ostensibly to discuss the subject of the Open Door in Manchuria. But the foreign minister gladly seized the initiative and reiterated Japan's support of the Nine Power Treaty, the Amō statement notwithstanding.[15] The following day Grew again saw Hirota to carry out the department's instructions which had arrived in the meantime, and shortly thereafter the foreign minister sent the ambassador a watered-down version of the Amō Doctrine. In their talk Hirota again reassured Grew that Amō's original statement did not have the foreign minister's approval.[16] This pleased Grew, but he was irked by news stories from Washington that the State Department seemed to think the embassy was tardy in reporting how it had carried out instructions. The ambassador was so sensitive to such rumored criticism that he wrote a series of personal letters to Hornbeck, running well into July, trying to ascertain just when his telegraphic dispatches had reached the top government officials at home. As it happened, the April 26 interview between Grew and Hirota took place at 12:30 p.m. Had Grew telegraphed a report right away, it would have arrived in Washington and been decoded and distributed within the department by early morning of the same day. But Grew waited, as Hirota had told him that "only [Amō] could answer my inquiry as to whether Fleisher's telegram was a reasonably correct translation of [Amō's] statement." Amō, however, had a conference of his own with the foreign minister in the afternoon, and it was seven o'clock before a member of the embassy could see him and nine before a telegram could be sent. The telegram was received in the afternoon of April 26, by which time key department officials had met to discuss the next steps to be taken.[17]

Perhaps in the end such dilemmas and Ambassador Grew's efforts and agony did not matter much, for it appears that the State Department's response to the Amō statement was determined more by considerations of American public opinion and the attitudes of other nations, in particular Great Britain, than by factual reports emanating from Tokyo.[18] At any rate, on April 28 the State Department instructed Grew to present an aide-memoire to the Japanese government, reiterating America's adherence to the policy of the good neighbor and by implication rebutting Amō's argument for Japanese particularism. The message was taken to Hirota as soon as it was decoded, although the day happened to be the emperor's birthday. In Grew's opinion the aide-memoire was "wholly admirable, absolutely called for by the circumstances," and prevented Japan from issuing another pious statement on the China question.[19]

It seems obvious that in this instance the initiative for taking action was largely assumed by the State Department and that, on the whole, the embassy passively conveyed messages to and fro.

The episode did not cause Grew to change his evaluation of Japanese policy or of Foreign Minister Hirota. The Amō statement, whether labeled official or unofficial, merely confirmed the ambassador's view of Japanese continentalism. Grew described as "perfectly right" his Dutch colleague's observation that the affair marked but one more move toward Japan's eventual domination of East Asia.[20] In addition to the Japanese army's push for a continental empire, the ambassador had detected a psychological strain in the nation that revealed itself in anti-Western outbursts such as the Amō Doctrine. As Grew had written Hornbeck in February, "much of [Japanese] sensitiveness and bluster and truculence arises from an unacknowledged but subconscious inferiority complex (which manifests itself as a superiority complex) and an equally unacknowledged but subconscious realization of being in the wrong."[21] The Amō imbroglio, therefore, came as no surprise to Grew. It was a product of Japanese militarism and psychology.

For Foreign Minister Hirota, on the other hand, Grew had entertained kindlier thoughts, and they survived the incident. Shortly before the episode Grew wrote to Minister Nelson T. Johnson in China that "Hirota . . . is one of the strongest Foreign Ministers that Japan has had for some time."[22] His strength, it seemed to the ambassador, lay in his determination to improve relations with foreign countries, especially the United States, and in his ability to alter the tone of the Japanese press, which had tended to be hostile to America. Grew sympathized with the foreign minister during the Amō affair, as Hirota appeared to be placed "between the devil and the deep sea because of the chauvinists and the military on the one hand and the moderates on the other." The ambassador was convinced that Hirota was sincere in professing "complete support and observance in every respect of the provisions of the Nine Power Treaty," although whether this sincerity could be translated into action was another matter.[23] (Grew's accounts of Hirota, subsequently printed in *Ten Years in Japan*, were to be used by the latter's defense counsel during the war crimes trials after the war.)

In retrospect it would appear that Grew overestimated both the Japanese military's expansionism and Foreign Minister Hirota's ability to counter it. The army at this time was extremely sensitive to American policy and determined to avoid conflict with the United States. This was because the army was thinking in terms of successive stages and assumed that the next war would be with the Soviet Union. Consolidation of gains in Manchuria and China was, of course, crucial, but this was to be achieved piecemeal, not by wholesale denunciation of Western influence. Grew was entirely correct when he noted the prevailing sense of inferiority in Japan that manifested itself as a superiority complex toward the West. Hirota was an embodiment of this feeling, and Grew would appear to have given too much credit to the foreign minister's "strength" when in fact the latter shared the nativism and pan-Asianism of the right wing. There is evidence that Hirota did not wish to see Grew frequently, or rather to be seen visiting Grew frequently, for fear that it might arouse the chauvinists.[24] The foreign minister was desirous of improving Japanese-American relations, especially in view of the naval crisis expected to arise in 1935, but he seems to have counted on his new ambassador to the United States, Saitō Hiroshi, rather than on the American embassy in Tokyo, as the primary channel of communication.[25] (Grew had a rather negative opinion of Saitō, considering him too loquacious and insensitive to American feelings.)[26] Hirota shared with Shigemitsu Mamoru, the doctrinaire pan-Asianist vice foreign minister, the notion that Asian matters should be settled by Asians and that insofar as Japan had dealings with Western nations, they should be confined largely to endeavoring to avoid trouble.[27]

The Amō episode failed to shake Grew's confidence not only in Hirota but also in other civilian moderates in the Japanese government who were pictured as resisting the tide of militaristic expansionism. The State Department, on the other hand, had always been much more critical of the whole apparatus of Japanese decision making. Cordell Hull wrote in his memoirs that when he became secretary of state, he "had two points on the Far East firmly in mind." One was America's definite interest in maintaining the independence of China, and the other "was an equally definite conviction that Japan had no intention whatever of abiding by treaties but would regulate her conduct by the opportunities of the moment."[28] The Amō incident only confirmed him in such a low view of the Japanese government, and the Far Eastern Division under Hornbeck was in full agreement. The chief of the division himself discounted Hirota's assurances as transmitted through Grew and saw them as only a cover for sinister designs.[29] In other words, the embassy's reporting of the affair had not the slightest effect on the State Department's attitude toward Japan.

On the other hand, Ambassador Grew's generally conciliatory attitude may have convinced the Japanese that they could continue to count on the maintenance of pacific if not friendly relations with the United States. The Foreign Ministry went out of its way to praise the aide-memoire as "frank and friendly" and markedly different in tone from Secretary Henry L. Stimson's messages.[30] The Tokyo government's gaze, however, was set on Washington, and it was through the embassy there that, shortly after the Amō episode, Japan proposed a bilateral understanding on the Pacific. Hull flatly rejected any such scheme, a response that should have been foreseen by the Japanese if they had listened to Grew with care. He had done as much as he could to impress upon the Japanese that the United States was in no mood to agree to a division of the world into spheres of influence, but his counsel apparently had not registered.

Finally, it remains to be seen how the Tokyo embassy's activities were reported in the Japanese press at the time. The month of April 1934 coincided with a festival in Shimoda commemorating the coming of Townsend Harris eighty years earlier, and Grew duly attended and made speeches at the celebration. These were reported in full, with accompanying photographs. The ambassador's trip to Shimoda took place on April 22, during the height of the crisis over the Amō statement. Upon his return to Tokyo he visited the Ueno museum to view certain Japanese artifacts, a visit that also made news. It was, however, only in the evening edition of April 26 that the *Asahi,* which may be taken as typical, mentioned Ambassador Grew's doings in connection with the Amō affair. The headline said, "The American Ambassador Also Pays Visit." The British and Chinese ambassadors had already seen Hirota, who then "also" saw Grew to whom, it was reported, "Foreign Ministry officials have already given a detailed explanation, so that it is hoped the United States government will come to an understanding about the present problem." No other mention of the American embassy appeared in the *Asahi* between April 18 and 26 in connection with the Amō statement. But the affair itself was daily given prominent coverage, and reactions in Washington, London, and Tokyo made front-page news. On April 19, 21, 26, and 29 the newspaper printed editorials on the subject. It appears that the press was as surprised as the government by the intensity of the initial foreign reaction. Although in its editorial of April 19 the *Asahi* was complacent and saw nothing improper about the Amō statement, it soon changed its tone as reports filed by its correspondents in Washington and elsewhere revealed that the statement was "becoming a problem." The correspondent in New York, for instance, worked energetically, interviewing Americans and Japanese in the United States and phoning the embassy in Washington to ascertain facts and determine the depth of American feeling. The editorials of April 21 and 26 called on the Foreign Ministry to retract the statement that had given rise to such misunderstanding abroad and criticized the way it had been issued. After the matter was settled through the Hirota-Grew conversations, the *Asahi* wrote on April 29 that the whole incident had been magnified out of proportion by anti-Japanese elements in China and Western officials intimately connected with them, but that the storm should subside once the British and American governments understood Japan's "true intentions." Again, there was no reference to the United States embassy in Tokyo. It is difficult to escape the conclusion that the Amō affair revealed the very limited role played by the embassy in Japanese-American relations.

II

Heinrichs has written that the Amō episode "was a turning point in Grew's diplomacy. It began an important shift in his thinking about ways of dealing with Japan as well as in his understanding of Japanese expansionism."[31] The change would seem to have been more one of emphasis than of qualitative transformation. The incident confirmed what Grew had already formulated in his mind about the direction of Japanese militarism and the nature of the

Japanese government. After April 1934 he continued to see Japan's expansionism as a fixed policy. As he wrote later, he believed that "the military are too firmly in the saddle and will continue to remain there."[32] At the same time, he did not lose hope that open hostilities could be avoided in government-to-government relations. He believed that normal if strained relations could be maintained between Japan and the United States provided both refrained from mutual recriminations and conducted their day-to-day affairs in a spirit of pragmatism and moderation. Thus, despite the fundamental opposition in the foreign policies of the two nations, diplomacy had a role to play in sustaining a modicum of sanity in their relationship. Such a task, after all, was what an embassy was supposed to perform in all circumstances; so Grew stressed personal contacts with a few Japanese, official and nonofficial, to smooth the path.

A serious crisis nevertheless arose and the embassy was swept up by the rapidly evolving events following the outbreak of the Sino-Japanese War on July 7, 1937. The American embassy was caught by surprise, as were all embassies and governments, but it immediately went to work to obtain and telegraph available information to Washington. Purely quantitatively, the Tokyo embassy's role in this regard was not as impressive as that of the China posts. Between July 8 and July 16, when Secretary Hull made the first of his series of pronouncements on the war, some twenty telegrams were sent from Tokyo to Washington. During the same length of time, Ambassador Nelson T. Johnson in Peking sent over thirty telegrams, and the United States embassy in Nanking, under the charge of Counselor Willys Peck, another thirty. In addition, the State Department's Far Eastern Division obtained reports from occasional Japanese and Chinese visitors, the latter being far more numerous. Moreover, American embassies in Europe, especially in Britain, often conveyed data that the governments in London and elsewhere had obtained from their representatives in Asia and showed to the American ambassadors. In other words, the Tokyo embassy was only one of many sources of information, and certainly not the most important.

It would be difficult to judge precisely on whose information the State Department based its knowledge of the Sino-Japanese War. Hornbeck, the key official in Washington, was often evasive in putting down in writing what he thought of the conflict during its first stages. Nevertheless, the available documents seem to indicate that his views were quite close to those presented by American officials in China and by Chinese in the United States and elsewhere.

Hornbeck may indeed have had a preconceived notion of what happened and been influenced by data that conformed to his own judgments. For instance, in a long memorandum on the East Asian situation which he penned on July 14, Hornbeck stated categorically that the presence of the Japanese protocol forces in the Peking-Tientsin area, which had "made themselves a nuisance," had been the "provocative" element in the picture. The Japanese, he went on to say, "have been intent on cutting north China from the rest of China." The inference from these statements was that the Marco Polo Bridge Incident was far more than an accident and signified the beginning of a frontal assault on Chinese sovereignty. Military operations after July 7 conclusively indicated, according to Hornbeck, that the Japanese were aiming at driving the Chinese forces "out of and away from the (strictly Chinese) region involved."[33] While he stopped short of explicitly stating that the whole incident was a product of a carefully deliberated plot, his views virtually agreed with those of a Chinese Foreign Ministry spokesman who declared, only a few hours after the outbreak of the fighting, that it had been "clearly premeditated by the Japanese."[34] Although the Japanese repeatedly stressed their intention of localizing the conflict, Hornbeck did not put much trust in such professions. The simple facts were, he wrote in the July 14 memorandum, that "the Japanese have already moved in reinforcements from Manchuria" and that the "Japanese Government has either sent or assembled for sending, from Japan, two divisions." He reminded the reader of the memorandum that "all of the stationing of military reinforcements is taking place on Chinese soil."

Nobody would have disputed the last point. But Hornbeck's estimates of Japanese troop movements were wide of the mark. The Japanese government had considered dispatching three divisions from Japan to China but the final decision was not made until July 21, and this only after a series of serious debates and constant changes of views among top military and governmental leaders. Hornbeck's indictment of Japan could only have been derived from focusing upon reports that tended to agree with his preconceptions.

Another interesting example of Hornbeck's choice of information is his estimate of the number of Japanese soldiers in the Peking-Tientsin area during the first week after July 7. In the memorandum of July 14 he wrote that there were about 20,000 Japanese troops. Since he estimated that the Japanese protocol force numbered about 10,000, he accounted for this doubling by saying that the reinforcements must have been sent from Manchuria. The figure 20,000 had already cropped up in State Department memoranda and continued to do so rather consistently. It seems to have been derived from Chinese sources. On July 12 the counselor of the Chinese embassy telephoned to inform the department that the Japanese had 20,000 troops in the region around Peking. The same day the U.S. embassy in Nanking sent a similar report, adding that most of the 20,000 "had come from Manchuria via Tientsin."[35] Interestingly, a day or two later Colonel Joseph Stilwell, military attaché in Peking, reported that the Japanese forces in north China totalled only about 12,000, and on July 14 the attaché in the Tokyo embassy expressed the opinion that "only a small force, probably an infantry regiment, has reinforced the North China garrison."[36] Hornbeck nevertheless stuck to the figure of 20,000 for several more days. The facts, as now known, were that as of July 7 the protocol force numbered about 4,000 and that an additional two regiments from Manchuria and a division from Korea were being sent as reinforcements, making a total of 8,000 soldiers at most as of July 14.[37]

As the July crisis advanced, Hornbeck seems to have been increasingly inclined to dismiss anything that did not confirm his own evaluation. Thus on July 16, when the Japanese chargé d'affaires came to talk with Hull, Hornbeck recorded, "What Mr. Suma [the chargé] said was so little enlightening from point of view of specification and so completely enlightening from point of view of the general purport that Japan wished to establish Japanese influence more completely, that it is believed no useful purpose would be served in trying to set down the details."[38]

At the same time it should be stated that the embassy in Tokyo did little to assist officials in Washington in evaluating the situation. Although accurate information was conspicuously lacking, the quality of the embassy's factual reports was unimpressive; in fact they consisted largely of bits of information given out by Tokyo officials. Grew frankly expressed doubt that the actual origins of the incident could ever be known. "I don't know," he wrote in his diary. "It's all guesswork, and all we can do is to watch developments, gather facts, and try to the best of our ability to analyze them from day to day."

In the realm of policy, too, the Tokyo post's role was undistinguished. From the beginning Ambassador Grew was convinced that the United States should refrain from meddling in the conflict. He believed, as he stated on July 13, that "relations between the United States and Japan . . . are now better than they have been for a long time past."[39] This referred to the external calm in Japanese-American relations, in which he felt the self-conscious bitterness of the Stimson era was missing. It was the embassy's opinion that everything should be done to preserve this calm so as to maximize American influence should the time come to exercise it. So long as American rights were not openly violated by Japanese military action, there was no urgent reason why the United States should make itself a target of Japanese recrimination by inopportune intervention.

The State Department was in essential agreement with such an approach. Hornbeck expressed the belief on July 12 that "any step that might be taken by this Government toward action 'in a mediatory capacity' would (at this moment) be premature and ill-advised; would be likely to aggravate rather than to ameliorate the situation."[40] The effect of such a view, which formed the basis of Secretary Hull's policy for the remainder of the decade, was to discourage Chinese attempts to obtain American mediation. As he had done so often in the past, Hull would simply refer the combatants to the principles enunciated at the Montevideo and Buenos Aires conferences and stress noninterventionism (the good neighbor policy) as the cornerstone of world peace. This meant that, just as the United States had renounced the right of intervention in the Caribbean, it would expect Japan to do likewise in Asia, and that America would not intervene to mediate between China and Japan. The United States and Japan, moreover, were neighbors across the Pacific, and they ought to remain good neighbors. As Hull wrote to Grew in a private letter in October: "We are, and we will have to continue to be, their neighbors. That fact this Government will at no time overlook. And, we will persevere in the effort to be a good neighbor."[41] American interventionism had not worked in the past, and there seemed no assurance that it would fare better this time.

Since noninterventionism had become an article of faith with Cordell Hull, and since the disillusionment with the Stimson approach to Asian crises was pervasive within the U.S. government, the State Department undoubtedly would have adopted a policy of passivity even without Grew's endorsement of such a stand. There is, for example, no direct evidence that Hull's famous July 16 statement, defining the basic American attitude, was in any way influenced by Grew's reports and recommendations. Rather it was derived from Hull's convictions of many years' standing, and the ambassador's views were not solicited prior to the issuing of the statement.

Grew himself seems to have felt at the time that the embassy was but a minor cog in a vast machinery of decision making in the United States. "Lately I have been rather reluctant to make recommendations to Washington," he noted in October, "having felt that my recommendations fell on somewhat stony ground."[42] His attitude was apparently shared by his staff, for the morale of the embassy as a whole was far from high during the first months of the war.

While, therefore, policy was formulated in Washington with little regard for the views of the Tokyo embassy, the latter did continue to play its conventional role as a channel of communication between the two governments. The embassy, to be sure, was not supplied with all essential information by the State Department. As Hull wrote to Grew, "we realize that it is not possible for us to keep you completely informed of all of the many developments which affect our attitude and influence our course."[43] Often Grew obtained from his British colleague pertinent information not only on British policy but also on American policy, communicated by Washington to London and then forwarded to Tokyo. Still, the U.S. embassy in Tokyo was a crucial arm of the home government as a transmitter of messages. Its staff met with Japanese officials more often than the staff of the Japanese embassy in Washington did with State Department officials. Ambassador Saitō, for all his efforts to be frank and fraternize with Americans, was mistrusted by Washington officials, and the State Department "felt not at all certain that the Japanese Embassy in Washington was reporting fully to its Government."[44] Whatever the accuracy of such an observation, the department tended to rely more on its embassy in Tokyo to communicate important messages to the Japanese government. For instance, during the crisis in Shanghai in August 1937 the State Department took care to instruct Grew to communicate to Hirota what Hull had already told Ambassador Saitō—that he emphatically urged the Japanese forces to exercise restraint.[45]

Irrespective of the role or non-role of the Tokyo embassy in Japanese-American relations during the initial stages of the war in China, how accurate were its evaluations of the situation? For instance, how sound were its estimates of Japanese army thinking especially as it related to policy toward the United States? Army memoranda and policy papers in the first several months of the war were filled with references to Japanese-American "friendship" and intimate relations. The army believed that so long as American rights were not openly tampered with, normal relations could be maintained between the two countries and that normal relations were imperative in view of the likelihood of war with the Soviet Union. "Our diplomatic efforts," said a Supreme Headquarters memorandum of December 15, "should focus on maintaining friendly relations with the United States."[46] Similar expressions of opinion were to be found in almost every army paper discussing the international aspect of the Sino-Japanese War. Friendly relations, the army believed, could be maintained by such means as increasing economic cooperation between the two countries, protecting American rights and interests in Asia, securing a bilateral pact on the Pacific, and in particular soliciting America's good offices to mediate a settlement.

Japanese policy on this last point was ambiguous, as the history of the Trautmann and Dirksen mediation efforts revealed. But the point is that the army was interested in utilizing America's good offices whenever the occasion arose. Judging from numerous memoranda, it can be stated that some army officers preferred the United States to other countries as a potential mediator. There is no evidence, however, that the army's interest was made concrete through approaches to the American embassy. Any inclination it had toward American mediation was confined to its inner circles and was not communicated to the embassy, either directly or indirectly. It is not surprising, therefore, that Ambassador Grew remained generally pessimistic about the prospects for peace through American good offices or, for that matter, through the mediation of any third power.

Just once, in mid-November, Grew took the initiative and broached the subject to the Japanese. On November 1 he recorded, "No Japanese official has approached me with any indication that the Government wants to discuss ... the terminating of the warfare."[47] Five days later he still "did not think that the time is ripe for any move towards peace discussions."[48] This was just at the time when Japan was beginning secret negotiations with Chiang Kai-shek through the German ambassadors in Tokyo and Nanking, and when the Washington Conference powers, plus the Soviet Union and minus Japan, were meeting in Brussels to consider some sort of intervention. Quite suddenly, Grew decided to approach the Japanese informally to sound out their interest in seeking America's good offices just as they had done during the Russo-Japanese War. One reason was apparently that he had received a slight signal indicating that Japan might welcome a United States initiative at that juncture. The venerable journalist Tokutomi Sohō had visited him on November 4 and talked of the prevailing anti-British feeling in Japan, with the implication that the United States was viewed in a more favorable light.[49] Since Grew was strongly opposed to the idea of collective action such as the Brussels Conference represented, he may have decided to try to bring about peace through bilateral talks between Japan and the United States. Moreover, he wanted such talks to take place in Tokyo, not in Washington, since "Saitō does not enjoy the complete confidence of the American Government." The Far Eastern Division did not enjoy the complete confidence of the ambassador either, and Grew may have sought through his approaches to forestall any strong action by his home government.

The State Department, as expected, was unresponsive. On November 15 Grew suggested to Hirota, through intermediaries, that if the foreign minister wanted to talk with him in secret concerning peace overtures, the best way would be for Grew to see him at his residence to avoid publicity. Less than an hour after this message was conveyed to Hirota, he got in touch with Grew and arranged for a private meeting at Hirota's residence. The meeting took place on November 16. Although the foreign minister did not give the impression that Japan was seeking America's good offices at that juncture, the tone of his remarks caused the ambassador to hope that he might be "exploring the ground for possible consultation with the United States."[50] Encouraged, he wired the gist of the talk to Washington, but no immediate response came from the State Department. The department still adhered to the Nine Power Treaty as the only valid framework for an East Asian peace, an attitude more inflexible than that of Grew, who candidly recorded his feeling that "it would be deplorable if we were to insist upon a peace by collective action to a point where any prospect of peace outside of the machinery of the Nine Power Treaty would be rendered impossible."[51]

A few days later Grew was visited by John V. A. MacMurray, who had served as minister to China in the 1920s. They reminisced nostalgically about their experiences in those earlier days when the diplomat in the field (MacMurray) had an understanding undersecretary of state (Grew) and a basic rapport existed between them. This was no longer the case in 1937, when the ambassador found no one in the top hierarchy of the State Department with whom he felt an identity of views. Grew had nothing but praise for MacMurray's celebrated 1935 memorandum, of which he wrote that it "would serve to relieve many of our fellow countrymen of the generally accepted theory that Japan has always been the big bully and China the downtrodden innocent." Grew went on to remark that the memorandum "bears out completely the soundness of the policy which we in Tokyo have been recommending ever since the present hostilities began."[52] The pity was that Tokyo's recommendations did not carry much weight. It was at least consoling that for what it lacked in influence the embassy seemed to be compensating with insightful analyses.

III

An opportunity came sooner than expected for the embassy to put an end to its feeling of insignificance. Its finest hour, in the sense of playing a distinctive and constructive role in Japanese-American relations, came at the time of the *Panay* crisis. At 11:30 on the morning of December 13, literally minutes after he learned what had happened by reading telegrams from China, Grew called on Hirota and impressed upon him the seriousness of the situation. In less than four hours the foreign minister returned the call, expressing his genuine dismay and regret over the incident. This speedy action on the part of both Grew and Hirota contributed much to keeping the situation from heating up further. Grew's initiative, taken without any instruction, was timely as well as successful. The first contact between Secretary Hull and Ambassador Saitō in Washington did not take place until 1:00 p.m. on December 13, fifteen and a half hours after Grew's first visit to Hirota. And Hull's instruction to Grew, sent from Washington at 11:45 p.m. on December 12 (1:45 p.m. on December 13, Tokyo time) had been fully anticipated by the ambassador. By the time the instruction arrived in Tokyo, Grew and Hirota had met twice and taken steps toward solving the crisis.

December 14 was an extremely busy day. Grew had appointments with three reporters, his British colleague, and two Japanese officials, all in connection with the incident. Between noon and eleven o'clock at night he sent eight telegrams to the State Department. Instructions that he convey a list of demands to the foreign minister arrived late in the afternoon, and an appointment with Hirota was set for 8:30 p.m. Grew had difficulty getting to the Foreign Ministry as the streets were jammed with people carrying lanterns to celebrate the fall of Nanking. On his arrival Hirota said, "I wish to do everything in my power to maintain good relations with the United States." A report of this conversation was dispatched at nine o'clock, and only after sending two more telegrams to Washington was Grew able to conclude his busy day.[53]

Cordell Hull in his memoirs gives no credit to Grew for settling the incident, but it is clear that the speedy action of the ambassador, taken before any instructions were received, did a great deal to lubricate an otherwise sticky situation. The quick and satisfactory settlement of the *Panay* crisis was admittedly possible only because the Japanese were unwilling to invite a rupture with the United States, and because of the position of the State Department and the president toward the event—to make stern demands for an apology and reparations but desist from taking forceful countermeasures—a position that happened to agree with Grew's own views. Nevertheless, here was one instance in which the American embassy in Tokyo could and did play a key role in preventing a deterioration in Japanese-American relations.

The Japanese press, usually reticent, acclaimed the embassy's contribution to calming the crisis. Newspapers, of course, were under censorship and printed only those items supplied them by the government and the military establishment or by other officially approved sources. Announcements by army and navy spokesmen, reiterating that the sinking of the *Panay* was a regrettable accident, covered front pages almost daily, as did statements by the Foreign Ministry. But information was spotty, and readers of newspapers were in the dark as to what role the American embassy was playing. For instance, Grew's first call on Hirota, on December 13, which should have been reported in the evening editions, was not mentioned until December 15 and even then, as a result of the State Department's announcement of the Grew-Hirota talks, it appeared with a Washington dateline. On the 16th the press printed the full text of the American note of protest that had been delivered by Grew two days earlier. The *Asahi* covered its pages with excerpts from editorials in the United States showing the depth of concern over the developing crisis. On the 14th the influential newspaper had already editorially expressed its "heart-felt regrets" over the "lamentable affair" and urged the Japanese government to take every necessary step to bring about a speedy solution.[54]

The final stages of the settlement of the *Panay* incident—consisting of Japan's formal reply, on Christmas eve, to the American note of protest and the United States' acceptance of it on Christmas day—were closely followed by the press. In fact, even before Washington's acceptance arrived, the *Asahi* described the American ambassador as expressing "general satisfaction" with the Japanese note. In the evening editions on December 26 the Japanese learned that the incident had just been concluded with Grew having communicated to Hirota Hull's statement of satisfaction. The foreign minister had actually been so moved that he said, "I heartily thank your Government and you yourself for this decision. I am very, very happy."[55] This exchange was made public by the Foreign Ministry, which announced on December 27 that the foreign minister had expressed deep appreciation of the efforts exerted by the American ambassador in the settlement of the crisis. The press followed suit. The *Asahi* declared, "The peoples of Japan and America have been extremely fortunate to have Mr. Grew as American ambassador in Japan" during the period of crisis. His efforts, plus Japan's unanimous and frank expressions of regret, were considered the crucial factors behind the successful termination of the incident.[56] For once the embassy had vindicated its role.

IV

This, unfortunately, was an exceptional case that proved the rule. There was in fact little real rapport between the Japanese people, the embassy, and the

U.S. government. During the height of the *Panay* crisis the *Asahi* had talked of "the recent intimate relations" between the two countries and written that "the Japanese people are truly impressed with the American government's attitude of fairness, justice, and neutrality" during the war.[57] Such expressions were indicative of a sentiment that persisted in Japan long after the United States had ceased to regard as practical any possibility for a rapprochement short of drastic changes in Japanese policy. Far from effecting such changes, Japan was to take further steps to undermine Western interests in China and go on to proclaim the coming of a new era in East Asian international relations. And yet, as some of the essays in this volume reveal, there did not really develop in Japan a sense that the two nations were on a fatal march toward collision. The Tokyo government, the press, and even the army continued to view Japanese-American relations with complacency and even equanimity. Somehow it did not seem possible, at least not until 1941, that Japan's action on the Asian continent had made war with its neighbor across the Pacific inevitable. Antagonism was expressed much more openly toward the Soviet Union and, after 1939-40, toward Great Britain.[58]

Without doubt there was a serious gap between Japanese views of Japanese-American relations and the official American view of them. From Washington's standpoint, it was futile to talk of improving relations with Japan while the latter was ceaselessly imposing its power upon China and violating the principles of the peace structure. The effect of American policy was increasingly to remind the Japanese that their image of Japanese-American relations was illusory and that they would have to amend their ways if they seriously entertained any thought of amity and peace between the two countries. After 1938, when the East Asian crisis became part of the global crisis and as universalism reemerged in the United States, linking Japan to Germany in a Manichean conception of world politics, such tendencies became even more pronounced.

Under the circumstances, the field of action open to the embassy's initiative and imagination became even more restricted. As the East Asian conflict was globalized and as the military variable in the policymaking equation became more significant, the importance of the State Department in the United States government and of the Far Eastern Division in the overall apparatus of decision making shrank proportionately. The embassy in Japan had to compete with an ever increasing number of organs and individuals to attract the attention of the top leaders. This is not to say that Japanese-American relations themselves grew less critical, for as U.S. policy focused upon preventing Nazi control of western Europe and as Japan sought to settle the China Incident in order to advance southward, the two nations across the Pacific found it crucial to evolve a well-considered strategy toward each other. The story of how Japanese military leaders tried to utilize America's good offices to terminate the hostilities in China; how they resisted Nazi pressures for a more explicitly anti-American alliance; how the military in the United States developed alternative Rainbow plans and prepared for a two-ocean war; and how, throughout 1941, the unresolved problem of Japan made the risks of an outright declaration of war against Germany far greater for the United States—this story is beyond the scope of the essay. But it shows the fundamental significance of the relationship between Japan and the United States in their respective world strategies.

The trouble was that the gap between the Japanese and American definitions of this relationship continued to widen. All that the embassy in Tokyo could do in trying to bridge the gap was to adhere to the official American interpretation and seek somehow to make the Japanese definition approximate it. There was little room for maneuver. Japan went ahead with negotiations for a German pact while professing friendly sentiments toward the United States, which continued nevertheless to stiffen its attitude toward Japan.

Throughout 1938-39 the Tokyo embassy sought to prevent an alliance between Japan and Germany which, Ambassador Grew was certain, would bring about harsh American retaliation and make war inevitable. He attempted to convey this message through private talks with his Japanese friends and journalists. He deplored the fact that the press was thoroughly anti-British and took every occasion to remind the Japanese of the basically pro-British orientation of America's foreign policy. As of the spring of 1939, when he left for an extended leave in the United States, no Axis alliance had been concluded and Grew assigned considerable credit to himself. In a personal memorandum dated April 1939, Grew wrote: "My efforts to keep Japan out of a general alliance with the totalitarian states were constant and, so far as we can see at this writing, effective. . . . My Japanese friends in high positions still tell me that I need have no further worry."[59] Again, as he sailed for America he jotted down in his diary: "The high light of the first half of May until we sailed on leave of absence was the effort to keep Japan from tying up in a general alliance with Germany and Italy. Up to our departure this effort was successful."[60]

The facts were, of course, far otherwise. Until the very eve of the Nazi-Soviet pact the Japanese army had pressed for a treaty with Germany, directed primarily against the Soviet Union but also applicable to France and Britain. The government was willing to go along and carried on its negotiations through the spring and summer of 1939. When Grew penned the above observations, the Japanese were engaged in a serious debate not on the advisability of a German pact but on its application. He was utterly misinformed when Baron Harada Kumao told him, in April, that he "need have no further anxiety on that score."[61] Those Japanese who gave him these assurances were themselves ignorant of army and navy deliberations, and therefore it is not surprising that the American ambassador should have congratulated himself for having squelched the alliance. When he came back from his furlough in October, the Japanese had shelved the project in view of the signing of the Nazi-Soviet pact, and the army had begun talking of "cooperation with all the powers" rather than a German alliance in order to settle the China War. This shift was obviously brought about by changes in German-Soviet relations, not by Grew's efforts.

The remaining months of 1939 and the beginning of 1940 found the Japanese keenly interested in improving relations with the United States, but little progress was made in that direction. Grew's return to America for the first time in three years had made him realize that there had been "an unmistakable hardening of the Administration's attitude toward Japan."[62] He must have felt the insignificance of his embassy's role when in July the State Department announced its intention to terminate the commercial treaty with Japan without soliciting his views even though he was in the United States. Grew had repeatedly warned the State Department against embarking upon sanctions unless the government was prepared to see them "through to the end which, in the last analysis, might mean war." His thesis, he wrote just before departing for his country, "has been one of cold academic fact and unassailable truths, but never an implication of threat."[63] The decision to terminate the commercial treaty must have run counter to all his cherished thoughts about the conduct of international affairs. A Japanese ambassador in a comparable situation might have tendered his resignation then and there. But there is no evidence that Grew felt himself either slighted by the official decision or influential enough to argue against it. Instead he went back to his post deeply impressed with what the administration apparently desired of his job, namely to convey America's determination to protect its interests in East Asia and never to compromise with the faits accomplis of Japanese militarism.

Under the circumstances there was an unbridgeable gap between Japanese and American attitudes as Japan sought to mollify the United States so as to prevent the abrogation of the treaty and then, after the abrogation went into effect in January 1940, to negotiate a new one. Grew was under strict orders not to diverge from official policy, and his freedom to maneuver between the two governments was curtailed as he opened talks successively with Foreign Ministers Nomura Kichisaburō and Arita Hachirō. Should Grew be approached by the Japanese government, Hull told him, "the Department relies upon your judgment and your knowledge of the general attitude of this Government in regard to questions underlying American-Japanese relations as to what you should say in the presence of such an approach. . . . Should the Minister for Foreign Affairs bring up the question of a new commercial agreement, it might be advantageous for you to be in a position to say that you are without instructions, and the department suggests that you may wish to indicate to the Foreign Minister that you must refer that matter to your Government for consideration." The Japanese army generally supported the talks with the American ambassador, hopeful and confident that there was no really insoluble problem between the two countries in regard to China. American policy was based on the opposite assumption, and the embassy's function in effect was to discourage such hopes and make the Japanese realize the futility of settling the China War through American "cooperation." More than ever before, Grew became an instrument through which the U.S. government sought to influence Japanese behavior. Washington was at least aware of his high standing among Japanese; he was told to ensure "the preservation and strengthening of your wholesome influence with the Japanese Government."[64] The influence was to be unidirectional.

It would be interesting to speculate whether Grew might have been more effective if he had been given more leeway by his government or, contrariwise, if he had not been such an experienced diplomat well respected by the Japanese people. His task was to tell them that they were deluding themselves in thinking that Japanese-American friendship and understanding were possible on their terms. This, for instance, was the message he conveyed in the "horse's mouth" speech at the America-Japan Society upon his return from the United States.

But Grew does not seem to have succeeded in shaking Japan's general complacency. Typical of the Japanese response to the speech was an article in the *Gaikō jihō* (Revue Diplomatique), written by Okabe Saburō. He noted that Grew's speech "was a frank expression of the views of the American government and leading classes toward Japan" and thus merited Japan's serious and careful attention. But the writer went on to say that American policy as represented by the ambassador applied abstract principles, good in themselves, to specific situations and ignored the reality of these situations. Any workable policy should recognize, for instance, that China was not a unified country and that Japan was a country seeking an outlet. Restrictions on foreign rights in China were unavoidable while a new order was being constructed. Once the transitory phase was over, there could be lasting and realistic amity between Japan and the United States in East Asia. The article concluded, "we greatly welcome Ambassador Grew's frank expression of the viewpoint of the American people. It is incumbent upon the two peoples to remove all misunderstanding between them." In other words, Grew's effort to convey the sense of American-Japanese differences was appreciated, but it did not necessitate reorientation of Japanese thinking.[65] There was a reservoir of good will left in Japan for the ambassador, but his pleas were dismissed as reiterations of official American policy. The Japanese saw that there was little that Grew himself could do. When they discussed American policy or Japanese-American relations, they usually referred to the officials in Washington, not to those in the Tokyo embassy. Every issue of the *Gaikō jihō*, for example, had several articles on these subjects, but the above was the only one in this period that talked specifically about the embassy and the ambassador.

After the blitzkrieg commenced in the spring of 1940, the United States became once more aware of the danger of a German-Japanese pact, and Ambassador Grew resumed his efforts to persuade the Japanese that America rather than Germany should be Japan's best friend. "He is certainly trying hard to make adjustments in diplomatic relations between Japan and the United States," reported a speaker at a confidential talk given to Japanese Diet members, businessmen, journalists, and others who gathered together periodically to listen to off-the-record reports on sensitive international issues. But, the speaker went on, Grew could not be expected to go beyond limits prescribed by his government.[66] Lacking sufficient inducements to offer Japan to stay out of an Axis alliance, Grew was helpless to reverse the massive trend toward it. His "green-light message" was a bitter confession of the failure of his endeavor.

After the formation of the Axis alliance, however, Japanese sentiment did not immediately turn against the United States. If anything an innocent attempt to get the United States interested in mediating the Chinese conflict was renewed with some genuine seriousness. This was basically because the army had become convinced that America presented the major obstacle to the successful termination of the war, a precondition deemed essential before a southern advance was undertaken to take advantage of the Axis pact. It was considered imperative to prevent further American interference by encouraging the United States to mediate between Japan and China. The series of talks in Washington in 1941 were designed, from the Japanese point of view, to achieve this end. When they produced little tangible result, the Japanese finally accepted the possibility that they might have to choose between hegemony over China and eventually the rest of Asia and friendly relations with the United States in Southeast Asia and on the Asian continent as well as in the Pacific. They had sought to have both, to predominate over Asia while remaining friendly with America. When they discovered that they could not do so, they substituted one image of the United States for another.

The Tokyo embassy was generally bypassed in the crucial though unreal talks conducted in Washington in 1941. This was unfortunate, since the Japanese embassy in the American capital operated haphazardly under a nonprofessional ambassador. The Tokyo government would have preferred that talks be held in Japan, through the U.S. embassy in Tokyo, but the president and the secretary of state thought otherwise. The result, as Heinrichs points out, was that "while Washington spoke through Nomura, Tokyo continued to speak through Grew, and the two governments never seemed to be talking to each other."[67] Ambassador Grew and his staff were not given a chance to distinguish themselves as diplomats in a moment of crisis. Conflict could be avoided, so it seemed to them, only through a will to conciliation on both sides producing a climate for understanding. But it never occurred to them that they might plead their case directly with the officials in Washington. "Airplane diplomacy" was still in the future, and Grew confined himself to written communication with his superiors. He was not even consulted on the modus vivendi proposals of November, a belated though rejected alternative considered by Washington.[68]

V

In the final analysis the U.S. embassy in Tokyo played a minimal role in the deteriorating relations between Japan and the United States. "Sad as it is to contemplate over the perspective of the intervening years," writes John K. Emmerson, who started his foreign service career in a minor post in the Tokyo embassy in 1937, "the Embassy did not play a crucial role in the unfolding Japanese-American drama."[69] It occupied but a small part in the scenario leading to the denouement of December 8. The Japanese knew it, and their view of the embassy's functions was essentially in agreement with the reality. They discussed American foreign policy almost always in terms of forces and ideas operating within the United States. In the series of confidential talks and reports on Japanese-American relations given before the Nihōn Gaikō Kyōkai (Japan Council on Foreign Affairs), for instance, an increasing number of sessions were devoted to interpretations of trends in American policy, but few of them bothered to refer to Ambassador Grew and his embassy.

Could the embassy have played a more significant role? No one could say that it did not try to exercise more influence in order to prevent a rupture in Japanese-American relations. In retrospect, embassy estimates of Japanese politics and military thinking seem to have been more sophisticated and accurate than those in the State Department on which the latter based its policies. The embassy had long maintained that the Japanese might fight "in desperation," but the State Department remained supremely confident that its policy would not bring about a war in the Pacific. Had the embassy been given more leeway, especially after Grew's return to his post in October 1939, it is not inconceivable that the Japanese military might have retained some hope that the China War could be settled without inviting open conflict with the United States. This does not mean that the embassy's reporting and recommendations were all that could be desired. Ambassador Grew and his staff tended to dwell on the side of the Japanese mentality that might drive the nation to commit irrational acts out of a sense of isolation, frustration, and desperation. They might better have emphasized to their superiors that there existed no strong current of anti-Americanism in Japanese public opinion. Had they done so, the administration in Washington might have been forced to reexamine its assumption that there was an unreconcilable gap between the two countries' policies in East Asia.

This, however, would have been tantamount to challenging the basic tenet of American universalism. Once the conflict in East Asia had been defined in terms of good and evil, it was impossible for the United States to maintain friendly relations with both. To talk of an understanding with Japan was to desert China, and so long as the policy was to help the latter there could be no easy compromise with the former while there was conflict between the two. From the Japanese point of view, China and America were separate problems and could remain so unless the United States chose to link them together in a universalistic view of Asian politics.

Grew and his embassy stood between these two worlds, these two diametrically opposed definitions of the Asian crisis. Unlike his superiors he retained a sense of relativism, derived from his awareness that Asia was not the same thing as Latin America or Europe. But his image of Asia was very different from that entertained by the Japanese. They visualized an Asia for Asians under the imperial predominance of Japan, an alternative both to Western imperialist power and to the nationalism of weaker peoples. World peace would be erected upon harmony and cooperation between such an Asia and two or three other regional blocs. Grew, on the other hand, conceived of an Asia in which the legitimate interests of the Japanese empire could be reconciled with those of China, America, and the British empire without necessitating any armed conflict. All three—the State Department, the embassy, and the Japanese—had different images of China and different notions of how to fit China into the scheme of international relations in Asia. Perhaps the Tokyo embassy's role should be evaluated in the larger framework of this collective attempt to find a place for China in the contemporary world. If the embassy had ceased to count, long before Pearl Harbor, within the American decision making mechanism, it was to leave a more enduring mark upon history by its effort to comprehend the meaning of fast-changing events in East Asia.

THE ROLE OF THE
FOREIGN MINISTRY

Usui Katsumi

I

In 1966 a biography of Hirota Kōki, the only civilian to be condemned to death by the International Military Tribunal for the Far East, was published. In a postscript to this work Morishima Gorō, chief of the First Section of the East Asia Bureau of the Foreign Ministry from 1934 to the spring of 1936, made a number of significant comments. The period when Hirota was foreign minister, he said, coincided with a time when the military was in complete control. Their blind and ill-considered actions eventually destroyed Japan. Although the Foreign Ministry did its utmost to restrain them, in the end its efforts were of no avail. Hirota Kōki was representative of those responsible for the "difficult task" of opposing the military. In Morishima's words:

His task was not to oppose openly the actions of the militarists, for this could in no way serve the objective of controlling them. Had he opposed them openly, he either would have been obliged to resign or, at worst, would have been assassinated. Hirota was the kind of man who would have accepted either alternative, but where would this have led? It would only have meant that someone willing to comply with the demands of the military would have assumed the post of foreign minister or prime minister. The "difficult task" that confronted Hirota was, therefore, to remain in his position, irrespective of the cost to himself, and, while making some concessions, attempt to restrain and guide the military. It has been the tradition since Meiji times for members of the Foreign Ministry to devote themselves to "difficult tasks" such as this.[1]

Two particular features of Morishima's theory should be noted. One is the black and white division he makes between the evil, jingoistic, adventuresome

127

military and the good, peace-oriented, moderate Foreign Ministry. The other is his suggestion that the Foreign Ministry's resistance to the military was extremely ambiguous in that it did not attempt to oppose or restrain the military outright but rather made compromises in an effort to guide them in a better direction. Admittedly, Japanese diplomacy was from time to time characterized by a certain dualism created by conflict between the Foreign Ministry and the military, especially the army. The basic cause of this dualism lay in the provision of the Meiji constitution concerning the prerogative of the supreme command. In reality, however, did the Foreign Ministry make a consistent effort to restrain the military as Morishima claims? Did those responsible for foreign relations actually oppose military meddling in foreign affairs after the failure of Shidehara diplomacy in 1931? How did the Foreign Ministry respond to questions such as that posed by a contemporary critic who said, "If the Foreign Ministry's failure to fulfill its responsibilities stems from military interference, those in charge of foreign affairs should risk their positions to preserve their prerogatives"?[2]

II

In the Meiji constitution foreign affairs came under the articles related to the imperial prerogatives. It has been commonly said that Article 11 of the constitution, which stated, "The emperor has supreme command over the army and navy," established the imperial prerogative of the supreme command. But it could equally well be asserted that Article 13—"The emperor declares war, makes peace, and concludes treaties"—fixed the imperial prerogative over the conduct of foreign relations. Throughout modern Japanese history, just as the question of the supreme command has caused controversy, so the question of the prerogative relative to foreign affairs was bound to raise problems.

Take for example the issue of strengthening the Anti-Comintern Pact in 1939. Ambassadors Ōshima Hiroshi in Germany and Shiratori Toshio in Italy made statements that virtually committed Japan to enter into a war in which either European power was engaged. Their actions created a critical situation in Tokyo, leading the emperor on April 8 to ask Foreign Minister Arita Hachirō, "Does not the conduct of these ambassadors violate the imperial prerogative?" Similarly, when Army Minister Itagaki Seishirō had an audience with the emperor two days later, the emperor inquired, "Are not the commitments, which the two ambassadors have made without my approval in regard to Japan's participation in the war, a defiance of the imperial prerogative?" And when Itagaki appeared to support the ambassadors, the emperor expressed his extreme displeasure.[3] In addition, early in April Lord Keeper of the Privy Seal Yuasa Kurahei personally reproved Vice Chief of the Army General Staff Nakajima Tetsuzō, saying, "The conduct of Ambassador Ōshima is utterly inexcusable; it could well be regarded as a violation of the imperial prerogative over foreign affairs." Nakajima replied that the prerogative over foreign affairs clearly belonged to the emperor and the army "had never intended to violate it." In short, it is apparent that in crises such as that which developed in 1939, the question of the imperial prerogative over foreign relations aroused such serious controversy that the emperor himself became involved.

Article 55 of the constitution provided, "The respective ministers of state shall give advice to the emperor and be responsible for it." Thus the foreign minister, as a minister of state, could advise on foreign affairs. Moreover, the Privy Council existed as a special body to participate in foreign policy deliberations, its authority resting upon Article 56 which read, "The Privy Council shall, in accordance with the provisions for the organization of the Privy Council, deliberate upon matters of state, when it has been consulted by the emperor."

Article 1 of the provisions for the organization of the Privy Council stipulated that "the Privy Council shall be the organ to deliberate important matters of state in the presence of the emperor." The enumeration of subjects to be deliberated was twice revised. The law of 1890 stated that the Privy Council could discuss "treaties and agreements with foreign countries" (Article 6, item 4). In 1938 this phrase was altered slightly to include all matters pertaining to the conclusion of international treaties prior to their ultimate ratification by the emperor (Article 6, item 6). At the same time it was provided that, in addition to the items specifically enumerated, the Privy Council might deliberate any question on which the emperor chose to consult it (Article 6, item 11). In practice this meant issues pertaining to the declaration of war, the termination of major international treaties, and the establishment and abolition of Japanese embassies and legations abroad.

As far as the Privy Council's functions were concerned, Article 8 of the provisions stated, "Although the Privy Council is the emperor's highest resort of council, it shall not interfere with the executive." This clearly meant that the council was merely to advise the emperor and had no right to interfere in the executive functions of the government. In actuality, however, the Privy Council often interfered, gradually enlarging the scope of its deliberations. In 1919, for example, when the Privy Council was considering the question of Chinese tariff revision, Prime Minister Hara Takashi pledged that "whenever we reach agreement with a foreign nation on a matter of importance, we shall consult the Privy Council before making a final decision—that is to say, before entering into any binding agreement."[4]

Another example of the expanded power of the Privy Council can be seen in Japan's handling of the requirements laid down in the agreement establishing the International Labor Organization, which formed part of the Versailles Treaty. The agreement provided that the recommendations and draft conventions passed by the ILO should be submitted to the appropriate national deliberative body by each of the contracting parties within a year. For most of the nations concerned, the appropriate national deliberative body meant an assembly or congress. For Japan, however, it meant the Privy Council. Consequently, we must conclude that under the Meiji constitution the Privy Council certainly participated in the foreign affairs decision making process.

III

In 1894, the year the first Sino-Japanese War broke out, the Japanese Foreign Ministry began the special training of officials for the diplomatic and consular services. At first the number of those who passed the qualifying examinations and thus formed the elite core of the diplomatic service was extremely small: in the first class, three; in the second, five; in the third, two; in the fourth, four. Shidehara Kijūrō and Koike Chōzō were among those who successfully took the examinations for the fourth class in 1896. Of those who qualified for the first four classes, Shidehara was the first to become vice minister and then foreign minister, attaining these positions in the years 1915 and 1929 respectively. From the point of view of career advancement alone, Shidehara was the outstanding example of the new career diplomat.

Between 1894 and 1903, 53 persons passed the examinations; in the succeeding fourteen years 74 passed. During the period covered by the present study (1931-41) individuals from the latter group occupied the most important positions in the Foreign Ministry, their posts ranging from foreign minister to head of a division or bureau. These men included (with the year that they qualified): Matsuoka Yōsuke (1904), Satō Naotake (1905), Hirota Kōki (1906), Arita Hachirō (1909), Saitō Hiroshi (1910), Shigemitsu Mamoru, Ashida Hitoshi, and Horinouchi Kensuke (all in 1911), Tōgō Shigenori (1912), and Shiratori Toshio (1913).

In 1918 the examinations for the diplomatic and consular services were reorganized so that a candidate for the foreign service took the general higher civil service examinations, supplemented by specialized tests. Thereafter the number who qualified for the foreign service increased markedly. This conformed with the official decision that Japan should train more foreign service officers to meet the needs imposed by its enhanced international status after World War I. Under the new system 121 men passed the examinations successfully between 1918 and 1921 (23 in 1918, 24 in 1919, 37 in 1920, and 37 in 1921). In other words, during these four years the Foreign Ministry appointed almost as many officials as it had in the preceding twenty-four.

As just noted, this trend reflected Japan's rising international position. The sudden increase in the number of foreign service officers, however, created difficulties in regard to promotions. During the period from the outbreak of the second Sino-Japanese War to Pearl Harbor, most section chiefs in the Foreign Ministry had entered the foreign service between 1918 and 1921. They became—as will be more fully discussed later—an influential group in the ministry.

The core of the Foreign Ministry bureaucracy consisted of Tokyo Imperial University graduates and a small number (less than 20 percent of the total) of graduates of the Tokyo College of Commerce, now known as Hitotsubashi University. This elite was assisted by lower-echelon officials who had passed examinations, established as early as 1894, qualifying them for special language training abroad (necessary for such posts as interpreter) or for clerkships. A majority of the personnel in the lower ranks were graduates of the Tokyo College of Foreign Languages, the East Asia Common Culture Academy in Shanghai, and other special foreign language schools.

In sum, the Foreign Ministry bureaucracy constituted an exclusive group of specialists within the structure of the Japanese government. Precisely because of the specialized nature of their work, Foreign Ministry officials with long experience had little opportunity to obtain employment outside the government, compared to their counterparts in other ministries such as Finance or

Commerce and Industry. Officials of the Ministry of Communications, for example, could easily find employment in the government broadcasting agency after a successful career in the ministry. Similarly, officials of the Ministry of Railways might secure positions with a private railway company. Successful members of the Ministry of Commerce and Industry had even better opportunities. In comparison, Foreign Ministry officials were at a great disadvantage—some even went so far as to say that "no government official was as useless as a retiring member of the Foreign Ministry."[5]

On the other hand, bureaucrats in the Foreign Ministry as a whole were reluctant to accept outsiders appointed to high positions in the ministry. This is well illustrated by their attitude when General Ugaki Kazushige and Nomura Kichisaburō assumed the post of foreign minister. Arita Hachirō, the dominant figure in the Foreign Ministry in the early Shōwa period, remarked that the appointment of Ugaki, his predecessor as foreign minister, was a major disaster for he had "failed to drive the nails where the nails were needed. He had let matters get out of hand. After all, unless a person has been brought up in Foreign Ministry circles, he cannot grasp the situation and is likely to commit some quite irreparable mistake." Such a statement reflects, in essence, the astonishing narrowmindedness of the Foreign Ministry bureaucrat.

Just as there was a marked increase in the number of officials in the Foreign Ministry, drastic alterations were made in the organization of the ministry, especially after World War I. Briefly summarized, the changes were as follows. In 1919 a Treaties Bureau was added to the Political Affairs Bureau and the International Trade Bureau. In October 1920 the Political Affairs Bureau was abolished and its functions divided between the Asia Bureau and the Europe-America Bureau. In April of the same year a Public Information Division was established. As a result of further changes, in the early Shōwa period the Foreign Ministry was made up of the Asia, Europe-America, International Trade, and Treaties bureaus, the Public Information and Cultural Affairs divisions, and the Secretariat. In December 1933 a Research Division was created. In June 1934 the Europe-America Bureau was divided into a Europe-Asia and an America Bureau, and at the same time the Asia Bureau became the East Asia Bureau. Later important changes included the establishment of the South Seas Bureau in 1940 and the absorption in the same year of the Public Information Division by the Cabinet Information Bureau and the Cultural Affairs Division by the East Asia Bureau.

In terms of distribution of officials within the ministry, the number of officials in the East Asia and America bureaus remained more or less constant from 1924 to 1941, amounting to about 40 to 60 in each agency. However, a comparison of the number of officials serving in the United States and China shows that the number in the United States increased only from 70 in 1934 to 82 in 1941, while the number in China—excluding Manchukuo—rose from 232 to 640 during the same period. It was, therefore, only natural that the influence of officials whose careers were or had been associated with China predominated in the ministry.

IV

During the Shōwa period, a powerful group was formed in the Foreign Ministry under the leadership of Arita Hachirō. Its numbers included such influential officials as Shigemitsu Mamoru, Tani Masayuki, and Shiratori Toshio. After September 1927, when Arita was appointed head of the Asia Bureau, it became known as the Asia faction. At times it was also referred to as the Renovationist faction because Arita had once led a movement for the renovation of the Foreign Ministry. Initiated by Foreign Ministry officials who were then serving as aides to the Japanese delegation at the Paris Peace Conference, it had called for the expansion and strengthening of the organization of the Foreign Ministry, more extensive training of ministry officials, and other reforms. To promote their cause, they had organized the Association for the Renovation of the Foreign Ministry.

Important ministry officials who did not support the Asia faction gradually came to be regarded as members of the so-called Europe-America faction. This group included Shidehara Kijūrō, Debuchi Katsuji, Saitō Hiroshi, and Hirota Koki. For various reasons, however, Hirota's position was quite ambiguous. When, for example, Arita issued his call for the formation of the Association for the Renovation of the Foreign Ministry, Hirota, then a secretary at the Japanese embassy in Washington, was among the first to express his support. Moreover, friction between Shidehara and Hirota contributed to coolness toward the Europe-America faction on the latter's part. Although Shidehara and Hirota ostensibly belonged to the same faction, when Shidehara was ambassador to Washington, he slighted Hirota and relied more heavily on Saburi Sadao, Hirota's senior by one class. In addition, Hirota was drawn to the Asia faction because of his long-standing connection with the ultranationalistic Genyōsha (Dark Ocean Society).

In 1930 Asia Bureau Chief Arita was appointed minister to Austria and thus was out of the country when the Manchurian Incident occurred. However, in May 1932 he returned as vice foreign minister in the short-lived Inukai cabinet. Under Arita's leadership the Renovationist faction increased its influence in the ministry despite a divisive rivalry between two of its important members, Chief of the Asia Bureau Tani and Chief of the Public Information Division Shiratori.

When the Inukai cabinet collapsed following the incident of May 15, 1932, Admiral Saitō Makoto organized a cabinet under the slogan of "national unity." For the position of foreign minister Saitō wanted Uchida Yasuya, who had twice served in that post and at the time was president of the South Manchuria Railway Company. On May 25 Vice Minister Arita, expressing the unanimous feeling of the Foreign Ministry, on his own initiative entreated Uchida to assume the post.

In view of this strong sentiment in favor of Uchida, it is important to examine his response to the Manchurian Incident. In an earlier telegram to Arita, Uchida had stated, "Ever since the outbreak of the Manchurian Incident, I have cooperated closely with the Kwantung Army and have done everything I possibly can to assist them." In October, after the outbreak of the incident, Uchida met with Commander-in-Chief of the Kwantung Army Honjō Shigeru, and the two men agreed that it was essential for Japan to "resolutely push forward." They also agreed that they should try to persuade the authorities in Japan to settle the Manchurian dispute once and for all and establish a new regime in the area. They further concluded that it was essential to enlighten genro Saionji Kimmochi and Lord Keeper of the Privy Seal Makino Nobuaki concerning the actual situation in Manchuria and Mongolia so that the attitude of the people surrounding the emperor, which was regarded as the real reason for the government's cautious policy, would be altered.

Uchida returned to Japan in October 1931 and on the 13th called on Saionji in Kyoto. The following day he reached Tokyo and reported to Prime Minister Wakatsuki Reijirō and Foreign Minister Shidehara on the situation in Manchuria and Mongolia. Uchida's vigorous advocacy of a strong policy shocked Shidehara. In fact, he was so incensed by Uchida's open support of the Kwantung Army's actions that he said bluntly: "Why, if you are so convinced of the necessity of such an aggressive policy, don't you carry it out yourself? Please take my place and do what you can to achieve your ends." In contrast to Shidehara's reaction, military leaders such as Army Minister Minami Jirō and Chief of the Army General Staff Kanaya Hanzō met with Uchida on October 15 and urged him to accept the post of foreign minister.

Meanwhile, a critical situation was developing with the Kwantung Army on the rampage abroad and with right wing activists on the rise at home, as seen in the October Incident. Shidehara diplomacy seemed on the verge of collapse. At the same time, Uchida's anti-Shidehara views were receiving the full support of the Kwantung Army as well as of the authorities in Tokyo. The attitude of the Foreign Ministry toward the Manchurian Incident was shown in its unanimous desire to have Uchida become foreign minister.

In memoranda dated May 11 and 28, 1932, before he assumed office as foreign minister on July 6, Uchida wrote that, as far as Japan was concerned, the Manchurian Incident was over and the only pending issue was recognition of Manchukuo.[6] After he became foreign minister Uchida consistently maintained, whether in talks with the Lytton Commission or addresses before the Imperial Diet, that the only possible solution to the Manchurian crisis was recognition of Manchukuo. Rejecting every proposal for a compromise, he defiantly proceeded to bring about Japan's recognition of Manchukuo in September 1932.

On December 27, when the League of Nations was still discussing the Lytton report, Uchida informed the Japanese embassies abroad that Japan would make no compromises. He declared that the cause of the Manchurian Incident was China's disregard of the covenant of the League of Nations and the Kellogg-Briand Pact and its anti-Japanese activities that aimed at undermining Japan's position in Manchuria and therefore threatened its national existence. Moreover, as China was the aggressor, Uchida asserted, should the League of Nations condemn Japan, the Japanese government would not hesitate to withdraw from the League. Basically, his view was that foreign countries should recognize that Japan, as the sole stabilizing force in East Asia, constituted the only check to the spread of communism in that area.

Furthermore, Uchida believed that the Japanese social structure had unique positive attributes. Japan's agricultural production was almost sufficient to provide the nation with the food it needed. In case of an economic depression the unemployed in commerce and industry could always return to the agricultural communities they had come from with the assurance that they would be taken care of by the family system. Also medium and small enterprises in Japan had certain exceptional features that ensured the security of their workers. His overall idea was that "capitalism, which has come to a standstill in

Europe and America, is in the process of bearing new fruit in the special environment of Japan." Thus he proceeded on the mistaken assumption that the anti-modern and feudalistic vestiges in Japanese society were, in fact, positive factors of which the nation should be justifiably proud.

It was out of such unrealistic notions that Uchida fashioned his plans for solving the Manchurian Incident, eventually leading to Japan's withdrawal from the League. His policies drew considerable criticism in the ruling circles of Japan. General Ugaki Kazushige, then governor-general of Korea, stated harshly: "Uchida has been greatly influenced by those in the military who are exceedingly short-sighted, and he is advocating policies such as only a bunch of young officers would try to promote. His actions are not the result of careful consideration. He knows only how to plunge forward blindly. He is indeed an extreme example of reckless diplomacy."

On the other hand, Araki Sadao spoke highly of Uchida and asserted that during the period he was foreign minister, relations between the Foreign Ministry and the army were the best within memory. It seems obvious, therefore, that what Morishima referred to as the "difficult task" which the Foreign Ministry had to perform, namely, exercising restraint over the military, was not a task that the Foreign Ministry assumed.

V

Vice Minister Arita's resignation in May 1933, following Japan's withdrawal from the League of Nations, stemmed from opposition within the Renovationist faction. Shiratori, then head of the Public Information Division, was a nephew of Privy Councillor Ishii Kikujirō and was close to Hiranuma Kiichirō. He was also on very good terms with Lieutenant Colonel Suzuki Teiichi of the Army Ministry's Military Affairs Bureau, who came from the same prefecture. Politically, Shiratori represented an extreme element in the Renovationist faction.

In the spring of 1932 Shiratori met with Konoe Fumimaro in what was clearly a political attempt to force Foreign Minister Yoshizawa Kenkichi to resign. Earlier Shiratori had had a dispute with Asia Bureau Chief Tani. This had been followed by a controversy with Vice Minister Arita which had considerable repercussions within the ministry. In order to avoid any further difficulties, immediately after taking up his post Foreign Minister Uchida decided to send all three men abroad. He appointed Shiratori minister to Sweden and offered Arita the position of ambassador to Great Britain. Arita, however, did not believe he merited the same treatment as Shiratori and refused the offer. A few months later, when Hirota became foreign minister, he appointed Shiratori ambassador to Belgium. Tani likewise was sent outside the country, being assigned as counselor to Manchukuo. As a consequence, the rift within the ministry was temporarily healed.

Shiratori worked to strengthen his position within the ministry. Soon Kurihara Tadashi, who was Shiratori's junior by two years and belonged to the class of 1915, and Matsumiya Jun, three years Shiratori's junior and of the 1916 class, emerged as leaders of the Shiratori faction. The faction also gained the support of many of the younger secretaries of the 1932-33 class and, as a consequence, became a powerful pressure group within the ministry. From this point on the Shiratori group was referred to as the Renovationist faction, while the older group, which included Arita, Shigemitsu, and Tani and was formerly called the Association for the Renovation of the Foreign Ministry, now became known as the Traditionalist faction.

In September 1933, after Arita, Tani, and Shiratori had been given appointments abroad, Foreign Minister Uchida announced his intention of resigning. Meanwhile Hirota Kōki, whose ambiguous position in the factional strife has already been noted, had served as ambassador to Russia until November 1932 and was waiting reassignment. He was appointed foreign minister to replace Uchida.

In January 1934 Foreign Minister Hirota in a speech in the Imperial Diet declared that Japan bore complete responsibility for the maintenance of peace in East Asia and that foreign countries must recognize that fact. Through this and similar statements that followed, the outline of his policy gradually became clear. On April 17 Chief of the Public Information Division Amō Eiji made a statement embodying what has come to be known as the Amō (Amau) Doctrine. Asserting that joint action by Eurqpean nations and the United States on behalf of China, even if it took the form of financial and technical assistance, could not but be regarded as having political implications, he declared that Japan would oppose such aid as a matter of principle. In addition, it would oppose any action by an individual nation that would disturb the peace and order of East Asia. Amō's declaration was in keeping with the policy of former Minister Uchida, who had taken the position that aid from Western nations to China must be funneled through Japan or at least be undertaken in cooperation with Japan.

After the collapse of the Saitō cabinet in July 1934, the Okada cabinet was formed with Hirota retaining his post as foreign minister. In 1935 Hirota, making full use of the army's desire to advance into north China, exerted further pressure on the Chinese Nationalist government. At the end of May, when the Japanese garrison at Tientsin presented the Chinese with a number of severe political demands, the Nationalist government asked for a settlement by diplomatic negotiation. Hirota, however, rejected the request, and in the end China was forced to accede to a local settlement reached by the military commanders on the spot, who signed the Ho-Umezu Agreement. Furthermore, late in the same year, when the army was applying military pressures against the Chinese in an attempt to put into effect its plans for the division of north China, Hirota tried to take advantage of the situation to force the Nanking government to conclude an agreement on the basis of "Hirota's three principles." In short, Hirota's method of dealing with the Chinese was to try a variety of tactics, always with the threat of military action in the background. This, in truth, was a union of the military and the diplomatic, and it is hard to see any serious division between the two.

Within the Foreign Ministry it was Shigemitsu Mamoru who, as vice foreign minister for almost three years (May 1933-April 1936) under Uchida and Hirota, was in a key position to vigorously promote Hirota diplomacy. Having entered the Foreign Ministry in 1911, Shigemitsu was junior to Hirota by five years and to Arita by two, but senior to Tōgō by one year and to Shiratori by two.

In September 1933, in discussions of Japan's policies toward the Washington and London disarmament conferences, Shigemitsu took the position that Japan must avoid the kind of wide-ranging political discussion that had characterized disarmament conferences in the past. As a neighbor of "uncontrolled" China and of the Soviet Union "whose ideology and political system are totally different," he asserted, Japan could not commit itself to a general "peace security system and the idealistic abrogation of war as an instrument of national policy." Japan's action at the time of the Manchurian Incident had been legitimate and justifiable in terms of self-defense, yet Japan had been criticized by the League and denounced under the provisions of the Kellogg-Briand Pact. Furthermore, Shigemitsu indicated, he was determined not to repeat the bitter experience of the Washington Conference which, in his view, had limited Japan's means of self-defense through conclusion of a general treaty concerning China. He maintained that just as the United States sought to exempt the Americas and the Monroe Doctrine from the stipulations of the League covenant, which it regarded as applicable only to European international relations and not to international relations in an underdeveloped area, "international relations in the Far East, which is even more underdeveloped, cannot be properly controlled by an idealistic peace treaty or organization that might be suited to Europe."

Shigemitsu summarized his basic conviction, which might be termed an East Asian Monroe Doctrine, as follows:

> In short, Japan is responsible for guaranteeing peace and security in the Far East. Japan must fulfill this role even if it requires the use of force. Other nations should, explicitly or implicitly, recognize Japan's special position in the Far East. Should any nation attempt to interfere with this position, Japan must resolutely take any measures necessary for its defense. Japan has no aggressive intentions, territorial or political, toward the United States or other powers. Japan is, however, determined to defend at any cost its position of responsibility in the Far East.

The Amō statement was a concrete expression of Shigemitsu's approach to Japan's East Asia policy, which thereafter became increasingly clear. On October 20, 1934, six months after the Amō statement, he asserted that to thoroughly execute its policy toward China, Japan must pursue two aims concurrently: (1) the elimination of foreign political influence from China and (2) the devising of a means to bring about reconciliation and cooperation between China and Japan. These goals were to be realized by expelling from China the United States and the European powers whose semi-colonial political and economic policies dominated East Asia, and by Sino-Japanese cooperation in sharing the resulting benefits. Shigemitsu pointed to the maritime customs service and the European and American garrison forces and naval squadrons as examples of the Western dominance that had to be overthrown. Japan, he declared, should take from Britain and restore to China the administration of the maritime customs service, even though a less efficient customs system might result. In order to achieve his objective of a withdrawal of the Western military presence in China, Shigemitsu proposed to elevate the Japanese legation to embassy status and transfer it to Nanking, inviting the other powers to move their representatives to Nanking as well and at the same time recommending the withdrawal of garrison troops in north China. Such a withdrawal Shigemitsu considered to be "the basic step for the full execution of our north China policy." Japan would still be able to defend its interests in China by military force, for it would maintain troops in the area of the Great Wall and in Manchuria. Essentially Shigemitsu's plan was to drive foreign political influence out of China, leaving Japan with the task of guaranteeing the security of all foreign interests in China. The Western powers were to be content with an equal opportunity to engage in commercial and economic activities.

Shigemitsu's scheme constituted the basis of Hirota diplomacy. Moreover, it was remarkably similar to that of the military, which also desired the destruction of the maritime customs service and the withdrawal of foreign troops from China. In fact, the army later did abolish the customs service. Unlike Uchida, however, who practically became a puppet of the military, Shigemitsu promoted his plan independently through the Foreign Ministry.

Another expression of Shigemitsu's ideas is found in a statement he made at a meeting on China policy held at the Foreign Ministry on June 27, 1935. In addition to Shigemitsu the participants included Kuwashima Kazue, chief of the Asia Bureau, counselor Tani Masayuki, and Morishima Gorō, chief of the First Section of the Asia Bureau. Shigemitsu argued that rather than forcing China to accept several demands at once, as in the Twenty-One Demands, Japan's strategy should be to solve pending issues one by one, but always with the threat of military force in the background. For instance, China should be induced to accept Japanese demands in Chahar by warnings that should it fail to give Japan complete freedom of action in the region, China's future could not be guaranteed. In holding this meeting on the day the Ch'in-Doihara Agreement was concluded, Shigemitsu was expressing personal approval of the methods adopted by the military. We have already noted that prior to the conclusion of the Ho-Umezu Agreement, Foreign Minister Hirota refused to work for a diplomatic solution and compelled China to accept a military agreement. Both Shigemitsu's and Hirota's views, although conceived independently, supplemented the actions of the military.

It will be remembered that the leaders of the Renovationist faction, Arita and Shiratori, had been transferred to Belgium and Sweden respectively. In the fall of 1935 they began an exchange of letters[7] that clearly reveals the differences between the views of these two men who from this time on were to have such an important influence on the making of Japanese foreign policy.

Shiratori's ideas grew out of the theory that the Slavic and Yamato races were destined to fight it out on the Asian continent. Therefore he called for a strong policy toward the Soviet Union and, while advocating negotiations with Russia with a view to stopping its advance into East Asia, believed that the Japanese government must recognize that war with Russia was inevitable. Japan should demand the complete cessation of all communist activity throughout East Asia, the removal of all armaments from Vladivostok and other specified locations, and the withdrawal of all troops stationed east of Lake Baikal and in Outer Mongolia and Sinkiang. Shiratori also envisioned the future purchase of the Maritime Provinces and was in favor of concluding an anti-Soviet alliance with China. He declared that "a Sino-Japanese alliance against communism, the enemy of all races of the world today," would win universal sympathy. Even the United States would understand the good intentions of Imperial Japan toward China, and one by-product would be a widespread reappraisal of the Manchurian Incident. Seen in the light of the negotiations currently being conducted on the basis of "Hirota's three principles," Shiratori's ideas were obviously wholly unrealistic. Furthermore, his views were based on the wishful assumption that if Japan and Russia did engage in a war, Germany and Poland would support Japan and that as soon as the Soviet Union became involved in hostilities, it would collapse internally.

Arita did not share Shiratori's ideas about the likelihood of a Soviet collapse and was opposed to Japan's embarking upon an adventure as hazardous as war with Russia. He was personally convinced that Japanese foreign policy should be directed toward gaining exclusive control in China. "We should proceed at once," he said, "to drive Communist Russia out of China and then gradually exclude Britain, the United States, and other nations. It is essential to establish a close relationship between Japan, Manchukuo, and China in political and economic matters, to secure full control of the natural resources of China, and to strengthen our position generally so that we can effectively deal with such world powers as Britain, the United States, and France." In short, Arita urged the establishment of a sphere of influence in China that would render Japan self-sufficient in terms of markets and resources. While he believed that communism in China must be eradicated, he also thought Japan should make a genuine attempt to cooperate with China and toward this end should prevent encroachments upon China by the Western powers. Shiratori, on his part, envisioned a policy toward China that would in some measure appease Britain and America and make it possible for Japan to concentrate upon the Soviet Union. Arita, on the other hand, saw no need to adopt a conciliatory policy toward Britain and the United States, either by making concessions or by reaching a mutual agreement on spheres of influence in China, and he therefore advocated the complete elimination of their influence in China. Arita's ideas, in fact, represented the policy of the Foreign Ministry as implemented by both Uchida and Hirota.

Shiratori's chief differences with Arita concerned Japan's policy toward the Soviet Union. He was prepared to agree with Arita about the inadvisability of war with the Soviet Union in the event that Japan had complete freedom of choice but, as he himself stated the matter: "The problem is whether or not the army will want to move in the direction of war with the Soviet Union in the near future, for if it does, given the existing circumstances, nothing can stop it. So if we are in agreement that neither the diplomats nor the political parties can restrain the army, is it not better for the Foreign Ministry to go along with the army in order to be ready for any eventuality?" In other words, for Shiratori everything hinged upon the military, which in his estimation was heading toward war with the Soviet Union. He therefore believed that the Foreign Ministry must be prepared to cope with events as they developed. It is evident that Shiratori had already fully accepted the fact that Japanese foreign policy was being determined by the military. In contrast, Arita adhered to beliefs that were in line with the policy the Foreign Ministry had been pursuing ever since Uchida had served as foreign minister following the collapse of Shidehara diplomacy.

In February 1936, shortly after this exchange of letters with Shiratori, Arita went to China as ambassador. But soon thereafter, following the February 26 Incident, he became foreign minister in the Hirota cabinet and finally assumed the heavy responsibility of carrying on Japan's foreign relations. Placing their faith in the Imperial Way as the ideal that must guide Japan's overseas expansion, Hirota and Arita, in accordance with Arita's concepts, strove to strengthen Japan's control over China. At the same time, their nationalistic philosophy caused them to promote economic expansion not only into China but into the South Seas as well.

In little less than a year (February 1937) the Hirota cabinet was replaced by that of Hayashi Senjūrō. Four months later, with the formation of the Konoe cabinet, Hirota assumed the post of foreign minister for the third time. At this point the second Sino-Japanese War began.

VI

With the outbreak of hostilities following the Marco Polo Bridge Incident, the Konoe cabinet embarked upon extensive military operations in China. As the area occupied by the Japanese armies in China increased, the Japanese government expanded its economic activities, using monopolistic methods that excluded other nations. In January 1938 the uncompromising attitude of the Konoe cabinet reached the point where it severed relations with the Nationalists, declaring, "The Japanese government will henceforth cease to deal with the Nationalist government of China." Throughout this period Foreign Minister Hirota continued to support the aggressive policy propounded by the military and Prince Konoe. He favored extension of the war and refused to respond to the appeals of such Foreign Ministry officials as Ishii Itarō, chief of the East Asia Bureau, who was opposed to any further escalation and advocated limiting the shipment of troops to China. Meanwhile other Foreign Ministry officials, contrary to Ishii, urged the settlement of the China Incident by military means. One of these was Kawai Tatsuo, a "renovationist" diplomat who in April 1937 had replaced Amō as chief of the Public Information Division. His remarks in response to President Roosevelt's October 5 "quarantine" speech attracted attention both in Japan and abroad when he stated:

> The essence of good politics is not to assume that the dissatisfied should simply be left in the condition that causes their dissatisfaction. This principle applies to international as well as to domestic politics. The population of Japan has doubled in the last fifty years, yet Japan's attempts to find outlets for its expanding population have been rebuffed. The United States, for example, has persistently violated all humane precepts by barring Japanese immigrants. This is a source of utmost regret to Japan. Today's world is divided into have and have-not nations. Voices are raised in protest against the unequal distribution of resources and raw materials. Should this inequality remain uncorrected and the have nations continue to refuse to yield some of their vested interests to the have-not nations, what solution is there except war?

Kawai's speech implied that action by the "have-not" nations to overthrow the established world order was justified and that the Sino-Japanese War itself was this kind of action. Such a position, needless to say, totally contradicted the Japanese government's public stance that it was a defensive war fought solely against the evil influence of communism and China's determination to defy Japan.

In April 1937 Shiratori was relieved of his position as minister to Sweden. Returning to Tokyo without assignment, he proceeded to express his views vigorously in speeches and in writing. In a special issue of the magazine *Kaizō* (Reconstruction) devoted to the China Incident, he published an article entitled "The Significance of Japan's Continental Policy from a Cultural and Historical Viewpoint." Elaborating on the thesis that civilization based on individualism or materialism had come to a standstill, he asserted:

> In today's world such ideologies as liberalism and democracy, which place high value on the individual, are rapidly becoming obsolete. Nothing can arrest the trend toward statism and nationalism. Surely totalitarianism will be the political philosophy of the future.

To Shiratori, Japan's policy on the continent represented the fulfillment of a cultural and historical mission.

British Ambassador Sir Robert Craigie, aware of Shiratori's views, requested a special interview with him, which took place on December 13. In the course of their discussion Shiratori stated that Japan was the original home of fascism. "In the final analysis," he declared, "the so-called democratic countries and Communist Russia have much in common." Both, in his view, were founded on historical materialism, whereas such nations as Germany and Italy had adopted a political philosophy based upon a complete rejection of Marxism. Clearly Shiratori was filled with admiration for the fascist states, which he believed were attempting to eradicate individualism and class differences. Thereafter Shiratori became more and more closely associated with the Japanese right wing. According to his own statement, for example, he regarded Amano Tatsuo, a member of the Aikoku Kinrōtō (Patriotic Labor Party) who was involved in the Heaven-Sent Soldiers Unit Incident (*shinpeitai jiken*), as a "god-like fellow."

In February 1938 Foreign Minister Hirota indicated that if, as anticipated, a China Affairs Bureau were established as an external bureau of the ministry, he would designate Shiratori its chief.[8] With the reorganization of the Konoe cabinet on May 26, however, Hirota resigned and Ugaki was made foreign minister. People both inside and outside the ministry immediately did their utmost to persuade him to appoint Shiratori vice minister. Within the ministry some young officials, in particular, urged Ugaki to replace Vice Minister Horinouchi Kensuke with Shiratori, while at the cabinet level Army Minister Itagaki Seishirō strongly recommended Shiratori's appointment. Prime Minister Konoe himself was greatly influenced by the attitude of middle-echelon army officers toward Ugaki and therefore was inclined to endorse Shiratori. But Ugaki decided to postpone the issue until after the summer and retain Horinouchi for the time being. The essential point, however, is that Shiratori enjoyed the firm support of Prime Minister Konoe, Army Minister Itagaki, and former Foreign Minister Hirota.

The core of the young Foreign Ministry group that so ardently backed Shiratori was composed of men who had passed the qualifying examinations in 1932-33. Being radicals, they were dissatisfied with Ugaki who, supported by financial and business circles, was inclined to follow a friendly policy toward Great Britain and the United States. On July 30, 1938 eight of these young officials (including Nakagawa Toru, Ushiba Nobuhiko, Aoki Morio, and Kai Fumihiko) went to see Ugaki at Ōiso and demanded a reshuffling of Foreign Ministry personnel. While the question of Shiratori's appointment was not specifically raised, this was certainly what the young officials had in mind. Moreover, they wanted a termination of the talks Ugaki was currently conducting with Craigie. Such diplomatic exchanges, they felt, could only be regarded by the rest of the world as a sign of Japan's weakness, for Craigie represented a country in which, as was being evidenced in parliamentary debates, there was widespread insistence upon a pro-China policy. A record kept by the young officials of their meeting with Ugaki indicates that they spoke as follows:

> [We] members of the Foreign Ministry have primary responsibility for the spread of the Imperial Way throughout the world. We have, therefore, been trying to formulate a program which we feel should be carried out under the name of "Imperial Way diplomacy." We have in the past discussed with Foreign Minister Hirota our ideas of what such a program should entail and we have been waiting for the opportunity to present them to you. In essence our view is that we should adhere to "Imperial Way diplomacy" and should not attempt to reach a compromise with the Anglo-Saxon nations in East Asia, for any such policy will not solve our basic problems.[9]

In September Foreign Minister Ugaki finally undertook to make some personnel changes. Vice Minister Horinouchi was appointed ambassador to the United States; Shigemitsu, ambassador to Great Britain; and Tōgō, ambassador to the Soviet Union. Shiratori, the focus of our concern here, was given the post of ambassador to Italy. A military attaché in Berlin, Ōshima Hiroshi, was promoted to replace Tōgō as ambassador to Germany. On September 30, however, Ugaki resigned over the issue of the Asia Development Board (Kōain), whereupon Konoe assumed his post concurrently with that of prime minister.

Taking advantage of the situation created by these changes, Ishiba Nobuhiko and other young officials in the Foreign Ministry submitted to Konoe a letter signed by about fifty of their colleagues demanding Shiratori's appointment as foreign minister. Shiratori had been assigned to the embassy at Rome, but he delayed assuming his post while awaiting further developments. In the end Konoe summoned Shiratori to tell him that for the present various circumstances stood in the way of his appointment as foreign minister and ask whom he would recommend for the office. Shiratori suggested Arita, who subsequently became foreign minister on October 29. As chief of the East Asia Bureau, Kurihara Tadashi was appointed to replace Ishii Itarō, who had been greatly trusted by Ugaki. Since Kurihara was one of the principal members of the Shiratori group, the East Asia Bureau increasingly became a stronghold of the Renovationist faction and the young officials began to dream of the day when Shiratori and Kurihara would dominate the Foreign Ministry as foreign minister and vice minister respectively.

VII

On November 18 Foreign Minister Arita replied to an American note of October 6 protesting Japanese activities in China as violations of the Open Door. Arita stated that to invoke principles that might have been applicable prior to the outbreak of the China Incident but had no relation to the new situation emerging in East Asia did not contribute to the establishment of a permanent peace in that area. He thereby, in effect, announced that Japan had rejected the Nine Power Treaty and the so-called "Washington Conference system." Furthermore, at a press conference on December 19 Arita emphasized that the cooperative arrangement among Japan, Manchukuo, and China, known as the New Order in East Asia, was only a defensive mechanism designed politically to serve as a protection against communism and economically to provide safeguards against tariff barriers. "Japan," Arita said, "has few resources and no domestic market and China is economically weak. As a matter of national survival, therefore, they must cooperate to ensure that they have the goods and markets that will enable them to meet any crisis that may develop. Insofar as the economic activities of Western nations conflict with these basic requirements, we must restrict them."[10] Arita's remarks were a public expression of the views he had advanced in his letter to Shiratori and corresponded closely to the controversial speech made more than a year earlier by Kawai demanding justice for the "have-not" nations.

Within the Foreign Ministry Arita had the complete backing of officials at or above the level of bureau chief; even those who were not members of the Renovationist faction gradually banded together in his support and formed a "Traditionalist" faction. A contemporary commentator wrote:

> Arita's prestige and influence within the ministry were tremendously high. The Renovationist faction could not help feeling insignificant in comparison. An increasing number of officials defected from the Renovationist faction. Its leader, Shiratori, had been sent to Italy and Kurihara, who had been left to guard the fort alone, was spending his days in discontent, awaiting an opportunity to regain power.[11]

Nevertheless, even during this period the Renovationist faction was far from inactive. East Asia Bureau Chief Kurihara, Research Division Chief Matsumiya Jun, and other young officials kept in close touch with Ambassador Shiratori in Italy and Ambassador Ōshima in Germany. Together they attempted to strengthen the ties among Japan, Germany, and Italy. In April 1939, for example, the young officials submitted a proposal to Foreign Minister Arita urging him to try to transform the Anti-Comintern Pact into a military alliance, for they believed that if Japan, Germany, and Italy were fully allied, no nation or group of nations would dare to challenge them. Moreover, they feared that if the pact were not strengthened, Germany and the Soviet Union might effect a rapprochement or the Western powers—Germany, Italy, Britain, the United States, France, and Russia—might revive their struggle for concessions in China, with even more serious consequences. Should such a situation actually develop, they said:

> Japan will be subjected to so much concentrated economic and military pressure from the Western nations that it will be virtually helpless and have no alternative but to retreat from China, and indeed from the entire continent. This will in turn create nationwide dissatisfaction that may well result in the most serious domestic turmoil. If these eventualities actually materialize, Japan may, in our view, be placed in a position from which it can never recover, either externally or internally. For this reason we regard the issue of whether or not Japan concludes a military alliance with Germany and Italy as being of major importance and are convinced that the fate of the nation depends upon the outcome.[12]

The young officials hoped through this statement to overcome the foreign minister's hesitancy to fully ally Japan with Germany and Italy.

Those within the cabinet and the Foreign Ministry who were especially concerned over the problem of strengthening the Anti-Comintern agreement reacted with dismay to the sudden announcement of the German-Soviet Nonaggression Pact. The Hiranuma cabinet fell, to be replaced on August 30, 1939 by the Abe cabinet. At the outset Abe Nobuyuki served as both prime minister and foreign minister. In light of the changed situation East Asia Bureau Chief Kurihara, in cooperation with the army, once more renewed his efforts to secure the appointment of Shiratori as foreign minister. Kurihara's activities led the prime minister to exclaim on September 16: "The so-called Shiratori faction is certainly creating a lot of trouble! They have even dared to resort to such incredible tactics as presenting me with a jointly signed letter in which they demand the appointment of Shiratori as foreign minister." The friction within the Foreign Ministry finally reached the point where the emperor himself became concerned and told the prime minister that he "must replace the chief of the East Asia Bureau."

On September 25th Prime Minister Abe finally appointed Admiral Nomura Kichisaburō as foreign minister and Tani Masayuki as vice minister. At the same time Kurihara was replaced by Horiuchi Kanjō, and both Ōshima and Shiratori were recalled from Europe. Upon returning to Japan Shiratori advised Prime Minister Abe to conclude an alliance with Germany and the Soviet Union as a means of exerting pressure against Great Britain and the United States. Abe flatly rejected this suggestion, saying, "It would be highly unwise for Japan to rely upon the Soviet Union for any such purpose, as Russia would not, in any event, be of any help to Japan either materially or morally." Nevertheless the Shiratori faction continued its activities until Vice Minister Tani, reaching the end of his patience, declared: "These young people of the Shiratori group, who belong to something they refer to as the Renovationist faction, are now being transferred abroad so that, by the end of the year, almost all of those who are causing so much disturbance will be out of the country. Having assumed the responsibilities of vice minister, I will see to it that they are dealt with appropriately."

As was inevitable, the young bureaucrats in the Renovationist faction resisted such efforts to control them. Their resistance was reflected in Japan's handling of the abrogation of the Japanese-American commercial treaty—the most important diplomatic event of Nomura's term as foreign minister.

Several months earlier, on July 26, 1939, while the Hiranuma cabinet was still in office, Secretary of State Cordell Hull requested Ambassador Horinouchi to call on him and abruptly informed him that the United States had decided to terminate the Treaty of Commerce with Japan after the six months delay required by the treaty was over. The United States' purpose in making this move was partly to encourage the British not to concede to Japan's demands in the Anglo-Japanese talks currently being held in Tokyo concerning the Japanese blockade of the British and French concessions in Tientsin. The prospect that Japan's relations with its most important trading partner, the United States, would soon be conducted without treaty protection caused considerable consternation in Japan. At a top-level meeting on August 3 the Foreign Ministry therefore decided to establish a Committee to Deliberate Policies toward the United States (Tai-Bei Seisaku Shingi Iinkai). The committee was headed by Matsumiya Jun, chief of the Research Division, and included East Asia Bureau Chief Kurihara Tadashi, International Trade Bureau Chief Matsushima Shikao, America Bureau Chief Yoshizawa Seijirō, and Public Information Division Chief Kawai Tatsuo. A subcommittee was also established consisting of five section chiefs, one of whom, Takase Shin'ichi of the First Section of the Research Division, served as chairman. The Renovationist faction was well represented in the new organization. On the general committee were Matsumiya, Kurihara, and Kawai; on the subcommittee were Takase, Tsuchida Yutaka, chief of the First Section of the East Asia Bureau, and Fujimura Nobuo, chief of the First Section of the America Bureau. The committee as a whole, therefore, and in particular the subcommittee were vehement in their criticism of Foreign Minister Nomura and Vice Minister Tani and proceeded to plan their downfall.

Foreign Minister Nomura believed that, in view of its economic and financial needs, Japan should maintain good relations with the United States. Any further deterioration of these relations, he feared, would "certainly make impossible the execution of existing plans for national defense, the management of the national economy during wartime, as well as the settlement of the China Incident." What made Nomura realize that normalization of relations with the United States was indispensable were the actual conditions resulting from the Sino-Japanese War, especially the situation in the occupied areas of China. In north China, and even more in central China, serious delays had occurred in the recovery of vital sectors of the economy, such as the communications system and mining industries, owing to lack of mechanical equipment. Under these circumstances, Nomura concluded, it was absolutely essential to secure foreign capital. In short, if only for the sake of ensuring the revival of the economy in the occupied areas, he was convinced that Japan must remain on friendly terms with the United States and strengthen economic cooperation between the two countries.

Nomura believed, therefore, that the policy his predecessor Arita had adopted toward the United States and Great Britain and expressed in his note to Washington of November 1938 must be modified. Arita had, in effect, stated that Japan was justified in placing certain restrictions on the rights, interests, and economic activities of foreigners in China for the sake of establishing the New Order in East Asia. Nomura feared that Arita had created the impression that Japan intended to impose many varied and far-reaching restrictions on foreign activities in China and that, as a result, the United States and Great Britain had become decidedly apprehensive and more determined than ever to take a noncooperative attitude toward Japan's efforts to achieve a settlement of the China Incident.

On October 24, 1939 Foreign Minister Nomura met with Prime Minister Abe and other cabinet members. Stressing the need to modify Arita's policy, he said:

> In order to improve our relations with Britain and the United States and induce them to cooperate with us to settle the China Incident, we must first clarify the scope of the restrictions that we intend to place on foreign rights and interests in China for the sake of establishing the New Order. We must further convince the United States and Great Britain that the restrictions will be extremely limited. In view of our need for capital for the revitalization of industries basic to our economy and national defense, I am sure that we [members of the cabinet] will all agree that we cannot impose extensive restraints.

The concrete measures Nomura advocated for modifying the Arita policy included complete cessation of anti-British activities in China, appropriate compensation for the damages Japan had inflicted upon British and American rights and interests to date, appropriate limitations on the aerial bombing operations that were presently being conducted, and a partial opening of the Yangtze to foreign navigation. In essence, Nomura's policy was designed to ensure respect for foreign rights and interests in China and for the principle of the Open Door.

As was inevitable, some of the young Foreign Ministry officials found Nomura's policy toward Great Britain and the United States completely unacceptable. The Renovationist faction believed that the conflict between Japan and the United States hinged upon one question: whether to maintain or destroy the Washington Conference system. They were convinced that the establishment of the New Order in East Asia required the abolition of that system and that since the United States desired its preservation, conflict was inevitable. The young officials who had enthusiastically accepted Arita's statement in the autumn of 1938 as establishing the guidelines for a positive and independent Japanese foreign policy watched Nomura's activities with suspicion. The subcommittee of the Committee to Deliberate Policies toward the United States regarded Secretary Hull's announcement of the abrogation of the Treaty of Commerce as an insult to Japan and advocated the immediate recall of Ambassador Horinouchi.

Fujimura Nobuo, chief of the First Section of the America Bureau, submitted an exceptionally strongly-worded opinion opposing Nomura's proposal to open part of the Yangtze to American and British merchant ships, a proposal intended as a concession to the United States that might help pave the

way for the conclusion of a new commercial agreement. Fujimura argued that
the ultimate objective of the United States in abrogating the commercial treaty
was to nullify all the gains Japan had made in the war against China and,
furthermore, that the United States would not be satisfied with a partial
concession such as the opening of the Yangtze river. Fujimura's more
fundamental criticism, however, was directed against his superiors for adopting a
conciliatory attitude toward the United States. Fujimura denounced Nomura,
stating:

> In this time of crisis the man in charge of our foreign affairs seems to
> have forgotten the great expression of national feeling of a year ago
> and to have abandoned the high ideal of establishing the New Order
> in East Asia. . . . He does not have the courage to stand firm and
> take the resolute action essential at this critical moment. Instead,
> out of an excessive desire to settle the China Incident, he is devoting
> himself to trying to promote friendly relations with other countries
> even, I fear, at the sacrifice of the vital mission of our imperial
> nation in this war. I must conclude, therefore, that he has mistaken
> the means for the end.

In short, the Renovationist faction feared that with a foreign minister like
Nomura Japan was heading into a dark future and that, through a breakdown in
diplomacy, the nation's efforts to establish the New Order in East Asia would
terminate in disaster.

As Fujimura predicted, the United States persistently maintained that it
would not conclude a new commercial treaty unless Japan's policy toward China
underwent a fundamental change. As a consequence Nomura's attempts to
improve relations with the United States ended in failure, and from January
1940 on no treaty governed these relations. In that same month the Abe cabinet
was replaced by the Yonai cabinet and Arita assumed the post of foreign
minister for the third time.

VIII

In this brief account of the activities of the Foreign Ministry from the time
Foreign Minister Uchida took office in 1932 until the retirement of Foreign
Minister Nomura at the end of 1939, it is evident that three different lines of
policy more or less coexisted during this period. The first was that advocated by
the Europe-America faction. This policy is hard to define precisely but its
outstanding characteristics included: (1) a willingness to recognize the power of
the advanced nations, the European countries and the United States; (2) the
formulation of a rational and objective foreign policy; (3) the conduct of foreign
affairs with economic considerations constantly in mind; (4) the maintenance of
a consistent policy, whether dealing with the United States, Europe, or
China—which meant in China's case refusing to treat it as a special, colonial area.

The foreign ministers who adhered to this line were Shidehara Kijūrō, who
was forced to resign at the end of 1931; Satō Naotake, who served for only a
brief period, from February to June 1937; and Ugaki and Nomura. Foreign
Minister Satō was in office just prior to the Sino-Japanese War and devoted his

efforts to normalizing diplomatic relations with China. It is, however, a matter of particular interest that, other than Satō, the two foreign ministers who adhered to Shidehara diplomacy—Ugaki and Nomura—had military backgrounds and, therefore, were not part of the Foreign Ministry bureaucracy. The result was in part that they were attacked not only from outside the ministry but also from within, the severe criticism of the Renovationist faction being one of the major causes of their failure.

The second line of policy was the radical course advocated by Shiratori and his associates. The members of the Shiratori faction, proclaiming the doctrine of Imperial Way diplomacy, formed a closely knit group that exercised a powerful influence. Demanding a change in diplomacy and personnel policies and believing in the army's foreign policy aims (continental advance and alliance with the totalitarian states), they were vehement in their opposition to the Europe-America faction. They repeatedly initiated movements to have Shiratori appointed foreign minister or vice minister. They did not realize their major objectives, however, until the appointment in July 1940 of Matsuoka Yōsuke as foreign minister in the Konoe cabinet. This, for once, seemed to satisfy them. At the time of Matsuoka's appointment, moreover, Shiratori became an adviser to the Foreign Ministry and Matsumiya, chief of the Research Division, became an influential member of Matsuoka's "brain trust." The Shiratori faction, while in conflict with the Arita faction, actually paved the way for the latter's reemergence by its attempts to undermine the Europe-America faction.

The third policy line was, needless to say, that followed by the Arita faction. Among its advocates were Uchida Yasuya and Hirota Kōki. It represented the main line of thought within the ministry and differed from the Europe-America faction in that it strongly supported the idea of Japan's special position in East Asia. Its main tenet was that the European nations and the United States must abandon their entrenched positions in East Asia and recognize Japan's leadership in that area. In line with this conviction they believed that Japan should adopt strong measures toward China.

Like the Shiratori faction, the Arita faction was critical of the Europe-America group. But it differed from the Shiratori faction in that it was opposed to any radical action either for or against Germany and Italy or Russia. In other words, it did not favor the pursuit, under any circumstances, of a reckless course. As the policy that predominated from the time of the Manchurian Incident on, it opened the way to Pearl Harbor.

This paper began with a reference to Morishima's thesis that a persistent rift existed between the army and the Foreign Ministry and that the latter continuously undertook the "difficult task" of attempting to restrain the military. But the facts in relation to the three lines of action just mentioned do not support Morishima's contention. The only policy that was really unacceptable to the army was that of Shidehara. The military did not oppose the views of the Shiratori faction for the simple reason that they took much the same position. The third line of policy, that of the Arita faction, was less clear-cut. Its advocacy of the establishment of the New Order in East Asia and the destruction of the existing world order did not conflict with the aspirations of the military. On the contrary, those foreign ministers who followed the third course often did not hesitate to threaten or actually resort to the use of military power. It is true that they criticized the army in one respect: they believed that, like the Shiratori faction, it was following an unrealistic and dangerous foreign policy. Yet, in the last analysis, were there not more similarities than differences between the outlook of the Arita faction and the military?

More precisely, we might say that it was the Renovationist faction, comprising elements of both the second and third groups, that dominated the Foreign Ministry from 1931 to 1941. Arita was its central figure; Hirota and Shigemitsu were its leading members. The Shiratori faction was the vanguard of the Renovationist faction. While at times criticizing and restraining the independent action of the Shiratori group, the Renovationist faction fully utilized the group as a vanguard and came to dominate the Foreign Ministry.

THE ROLE OF JAPAN'S FOREIGN MINISTRY AND ITS EMBASSY IN WASHINGTON, 1940-1941

Hosoya Chihiro

The final attempt through diplomatic negotiations to avert a war between Japan and the United States began early in the spring of 1941 and ended in total failure with the outbreak of the Pacific War. Today there is a widely held belief that the conflicts between Japan and the United States were too deep-rooted to allow for any negotiated settlement. Tracing the history of their clashes of interest and struggle for power in the Far East during the period after the Russo-Japanese War, the proponents of this view argue that a military confrontation was inevitable and that the efforts in 1941 to avoid such a conflict were like those of a frail craft attempting to navigate a raging current and of only minor historical significance.

Yet, as I have argued elsewhere,[1] I do not believe that the Pacific War was inevitable. Rather, the negotiations represented the last opportunity, however small, to avoid war. In this essay I wish to consider certain factors that hindered the negotiations, in particular the breakdown in effective communication between the Japanese government and its embassy in Washington and between the governments of Japan and the United States.

I

On January 23, 1941 Admiral Nomura Kichisaburō, the newly appointed ambassador to the United States, boarded the *Kamakura-maru* for Washington. Entrusted with the extraordinarily difficult task of improving relations with the United States, which were already seriously strained, Nomura was personally convinced that, in his own words, "there was still some slight chance of success in the negotiations and if I conducted them on the basis of instructions from the government, I might be able to avoid a war in the Pacific."[2] Two memoranda written by Nomura on December 16, 1940 and January 13, 1941[3] indicate how he intended to carry out his mission. Japan, he believed, should "try anything, however insignificant, that might contribute to the easing of existing tensions, while seeking at the same time some compromise with Britain and the United States." He felt that a compromise meant that Japan must make certain concessions on the most serious issues: China, Japan's southward advance, and the Tripartite Pact. Japan should guarantee equal commercial opportunity for other countries in China; its advance into Southeast Asia should be limited to economic activities; and an understanding should be reached with the United States on the Tripartite Pact to the effect that "Japan is not obliged to go to war automatically, even should the United States enter the European war."

Nomura, who had served briefly as foreign minister in the fall of 1940, was known in Japanese naval circles to favor closer ties with Britain and the United States. During World War I he had spent several years in Washington as a military attaché at the Japanese embassy and had become acquainted with Franklin D. Roosevelt, then undersecretary of the navy. His personal friendship with Roosevelt was considered an asset that might be useful in the negotiations with the United States. It was for this reason that Matsuoka Yōsuke, shortly after he was named foreign minister, strongly urged Nomura to accept the trying job of overcoming the impasse in Japanese-American relations.

With his own ideas in mind for resolving U.S.-Japanese differences, Nomura arrived in Washington on February 11, 1941. By that time nonofficial efforts to improve relations had also been set in motion by Ikawa Tadao, a trustee of the Central Bank of the Industrial Association, and two Americans, Bishop James E. Walsh and Father James M. Drought. The Catholic priests had initiated private discussions in Japan in November of the previous year, when they had talked with various Japanese leaders both in and out of the government regarding the question of reaching an accommodation between the two nations. After the priests' return to the United States and Ikawa's arrival in February, the talks shifted to Washington, where Postmaster General Frank C. Walker also became involved. According to Ikawa's memoirs, he had been asked by Prime Minister Konoe Fumimaro to sound out the United States government on the subject of negotiations and to report to Tokyo.[4] Moreover, there is evidence that other Japanese leaders, including Arima Yoriyasu, a former minister of agriculture, had endorsed Ikawa's visit to the United States. Early in April, when Ikawa was joined by Colonel Iwakuro Hideo, a former section chief of the Army Ministry's Military Affairs Bureau, the "private discussions" entered a new phase.

Ikawa withheld information on the private discussions from the Japanese embassy in Washington and reported directly to Konoe, avoiding the official channels of communication through the embassy and the Foreign Ministry.[5] This procedure evoked a hostile reaction from the embassy. Indeed, the Foreign Ministry itself began to look upon the "private discussions" with suspicion. On March 6 Matsuoka instructed Nomura to watch Ikawa's activities closely and on March 17 stated in another cable:

> Ikawa has been sending cables asking Konoe's help. This is preposterous, for it is against our policy interests to lead Roosevelt and other American leaders to believe that Japan is trying through

certain channels to approach the U.S. government with the idea of offering joint mediation in the European war. This would also be a breach of faith on the part of Japan toward its allies, Germany and Italy. You are requested to persuade him not to go too far.[6]

Unlike the professional diplomats, however, Nomura seemed to view the private discussions favorably, perhaps because he was convinced that every available opportunity to improve relations had to be explored and because he had no objections to "nonofficial negotiations." He therefore established liaison with Ikawa, and it was through the good offices of Ikawa, Walker, and others that Nomura and Secretary of State Hull were able to hold their first meeting at the Carlton Hotel in Washington on March 8 without attracting public attention. In early April, after Colonel Iwakuro joined in the private discussions as special assistant to the ambassador, the embassy became indirectly involved in the talks. Thereafter it received reports on progress in the negotiations, and plans for adjusting U.S.-Japanese differences were examined at the embassy, a process in which Iwakuro played a leading role.

On the other hand, the United States government was much better informed than Tokyo of developments in the private meetings. Walker acted as intermediary between the priests and the president or secretary of state, and the State Department became involved to the extent that it went over and even suggested revisions in a draft proposal prepared by Iwakuro and Drought on April 9.[7]

This collaboration led to the formulation of the document known as the "Draft Understanding of April 16," originally drawn up by Iwakuro and Ikawa on the Japanese side and by the two Catholic priests and Walker on the American side, and then discussed by Hull and Nomura on April 14 and 16. An agreement was reached at the latter meeting that the draft would be considered as the "basis for discussion" once unofficial talks were opened on a governmental level.[8]

Japanese leaders in Tokyo were quite surprised when they received a cable from Washington concerning the Draft Understanding, for they had been told little about the progress of the private meetings.[9] Moreover, some of the telegrams sent from Washington deliberately misled them into thinking that the Draft Understanding was actually a United States proposal. And since the terms of the document, as translated into Japanese, appeared very favorable to Japan, officials in Tokyo became optimistic about the prospects for the negotiations.[10]

On the night of April 18 a Liaison Conference was held to discuss the "American proposal." Konoe strongly emphasized that "acceptance of the American proposal would be the best way to deal with the China War," and a majority at the conference agreed that "Japan should accept it [the proposal] in essence."[11] Indeed, the emperor himself was encouraged to hope that the crisis in U.S.-Japanese relations might be surmounted. On April 21 he observed to Lord Keeper of the Privy Seal Kido Kōichi: "It is rather surprising that the American president went this far, although it would seem that the reason for the shift in the American attitude was our alliance with Germany and Italy. All that is needed is patience and forbearance, isn't it?"[12]

Foreign Minister Matsuoka was then returning from Europe on the Trans-Siberian Railway, triumphant over his successful conclusion of the Neutrality Pact with the Soviet Union. Since he was unaware of the progress that had been made in the private discussions in Washington, he had no inkling that Hull and Nomura had reached an "agreement" on the Draft Understanding.

Matsuoka had his own ideas on how to deal with the United States, developed over a period of nine years in America when, from the age of 13 to 22, he had worked his way through high school and college in the west. His experiences had convinced him that firmness, not weakness, was the best way to deal with Americans. Japan had to take a forceful stand vis-à-vis the United States and strengthen its military and political ties with other nations in order to impress America with its power.[13] In keeping with these views, at the Imperial Conference held on September 19, 1940 to sanction the conclusion of the Tripartite Pact, Matsuoka had argued as follows:

> Not only does it seem that there is little likelihood of improving U.S.-Japanese relations through mere courtesy or a desire for friendship, but such an attitude will simply make matters worse. If there is any hope of improving the situation, or at least preventing it from deteriorating further, it may be achieved only if we take a firm stand.[14]

Leaving Tokyo on March 12, Matsuoka had visited Germany and Italy, where he attended lavish parties given by leaders of the two countries to display their friendship toward Japan. On his way back to Japan Matsuoka had staged a diplomatic coup by signing the Neutrality Pact with the Soviet Union on April 13. These moves were designed to strengthen Japan's position vis-à-vis the United States and might be looked upon as stepping-stones to later negotiations. Matsuoka hoped to talk personally with Roosevelt in order to improve relations and, to that end, tried through Minister Wakasugi Kaname in Washington to contact Roy Howard, a longtime friend and well-known journalist. He also asked Drought and Walsh to relay a message to Roosevelt[15] and, when he stopped in Moscow on his way through Europe, met three times with American Ambassador Laurence A. Steinhardt to communicate his desire to meet with the president. He remarked to Steinhardt that, since Roosevelt was in a position to influence Chiang Kai-shek, he should act decisively on "the big things, not the little things" to "clear up the entire Far Eastern situation."[16] Matsuoka was encouraged when he received a message from Howard through Nomura, asking him to come to the United States.[17] There was also a message from Steinhardt indicating that Roosevelt was favorably disposed toward the idea of a meeting.[18]

As he returned home on the Trans-Siberian Railway, Matsuoka considered his next moves toward the United States. On January 22 he had given Nomura "top secret instructions"[19] that ordered him to take a "firm position" in the negotiations, in accord with Matsuoka's own thinking. Nomura was to make the United States understand that any settlement was to be based upon maintenance of the Tripartite Pact as the foundation of Japanese policy and upon recognition by the United States of Japan's Greater East Asia Coprosperity Sphere. There had been no mention of terms for U.S.-Japanese negotiations.

For Matsuoka the Draft Understanding was a setback to the "firm" approach he had been developing in preparation for official negotiations with the United States. Furthermore, he was disturbed that informal discussions had been pursued without his knowledge and, undoubtedly, that a strategy in accordance with his own policies had been frustrated by a subordinate's failure to follow instructions.

On the night of April 22, immediately after Matsuoka's return, a second Liaison Conference was called to decide upon a reply to the Draft Understanding. Contrary to expectations, Matsuoka pressed strongly for postponement of a decision on the grounds that the document needed to be examined more carefully.[20] His position made it difficult for the government to reach any conclusion concerning this urgent question, particularly when, despite the impatience of governmental and military leaders in Tokyo and the Japanese negotiators in Washington, he remained at home on the pretext of being ill and refused to participate in Liaison Conference discussions.

On May 3 Matsuoka finally abandoned these tactics and appeared at a Liaison Conference with his own plan for negotiations with the United States. He suggested that Japan offer to conclude with the United States a neutrality pact similar to the one signed with the Soviet Union. In addition, the government should issue an "Oral Statement" indicating that the German and Italian leaders were strongly opposed to a negotiated settlement since they were clearly winning the struggle in Europe and any American intervention would merely prolong the conflict and be the cause of great suffering. The statement should further stress that responsibility for averting another world war and the possible destruction of modern civilization rested with President Roosevelt. Both the proposal for a neutrality agreement and the oral statement, Matsuoka insisted, should be presented to the United States government before any reply was made to the Draft Understanding. Despite opposition, the conference endorsed Matsuoka's approach.[21]

Upon receiving instructions to this effect, Nomura met with Hull on May 7 and introduced the idea of a neutrality pact. However, he mentioned only briefly the oral statement that Matsuoka was counting on to alter the impression created by the Draft Understanding that Japan was willing to make concessions. In fact, Nomura did not show the text of the statement to Hull but attempted to soften the provocative nature of the note by saying that it contained "many erroneous matters."[22] Noting Hull's cool response to the proposal, Nomura cabled Tokyo the following day that the best way to adjust the complicated relations between the two countries was not to try to solve everything at once but, through a series of gradual steps, to create mutual feelings of friendship.[23]

In accordance with further instructions from Tokyo, Nomura submitted the official Japanese reply to the Draft Understanding on May 12. Basically a new proposal, the reply reflected Matsuoka's main ideas and departed significantly from the Draft Understanding. With regard to the Tripartite Pact, whereas the Draft Understanding had sought to define as narrowly as possible and even to nullify Japan's responsibility for providing military assistance under the pact, the new draft made the pact the cornerstone of Japanese policy and avoided any language that might be interpreted as weakening Japan's ties with Germany and Italy. The two documents also differed with regard to the China

War. While the Draft Understanding viewed the United States as a mediator in the conflict and listed eight conditions for peace, the new draft provided for no such American role, merely taking the arbitrary position that the United States ought to have faith in "Japanese policies of friendship with neighboring countries" and should "recommend peace to Chiang Kai-shek." There were other differences as well. For example, the Matsuoka draft omitted the pledge made in the Draft Understanding that Japan would act only through peaceful means in the South Pacific; furthermore, there was no mention of the agreement for a summit conference, such as there had been in the earlier document.[24]

In order to convey Japan's "firm attitude" more forcefully, Matsuoka instructed Nomura on May 13 to submit a new memorandum stating that any understanding with the United States would have to be based on an American commitment not to become involved in the European conflict and a promise to recommend peace talks with Japan to China.[25] The following day, in yet another move to convince the United States of his resolve, Matsuoka met with Ambassador Joseph C. Grew and threatened that if, as a result of initiating the convoy system, the American and German navies exchanged fire, Japan would fulfill its Tripartite Pact obligation to aid Germany militarily.[26]

Receiving the foreign minister's cable on the 13th, Nomura protested that presentation of the document would impede discussions and reduce the chances of reaching an agreement; therefore, he said, it was best not to submit it. Matsuoka disagreed and on May 15 ordered Nomura to follow his earlier instructions.[27] Whether Nomura ever gave the memorandum to the U.S. government is not clear; the evidence, however, suggests that he did not, for there is no reference to such a document in the American diplomatic records.

Nomura disagreed with Matsuoka over the most effective diplomatic approach to the United States. In Nomura's view relations between the two nations might best be adjusted through a psychological approach—that is, through attempting to bring about a change in attitudes by reaching a compromise based on mutual concessions. In his recommendations of May 8 he noted:

> It is extraordinarily difficult to clear up all at once the serious and complicated situation that has been growing for many years between Japan and the United States. However, once we begin to move toward an understanding, problems can be eliminated and friendly feelings can develop. Therefore, if we bring this about as quickly as possible, we can induce a gradual shift in the American position on the European war.[28]

Feeling that Matsuoka's tough approach was so out of line with the actual situation in the United States as to cause unnecessary harm to relations between the two nations, Nomura thought it best when transmitting messages to soften any phraseology that might anger the American side, or even not to deliver at all a communication that might interfere with the smooth progress of the negotiations. Nomura, it would seem, pictured himself as a "mediator."

Nomura sought to play a similar role in delivering messages from Washington to Tokyo. On May 16 Hull called Nomura to his office and handed him an oral statement prepared after consultation with the Far Eastern Division of the State Department. Although Hull explained that it did not constitute an official reply but merely represented the informal views of the United States government, it was nevertheless significant in being the first American reaction to the Matsuoka draft and his proposed oral statement. Hull's comments and the oral statement indicated that the United States maintained the position it had taken in the Draft Understanding with regard to Japanese assistance to Germany under the Tripartite Pact. The oral statement made several other points clear. First, the United States remained firmly committed to carrying out its program of defensive aid to Britain. Second, Roosevelt was willing in advance to "make known in confidence to Chiang Kai-shek the fundamental terms . . . within the framework of which China and Japan might agree to negotiate a peace settlement." Finally, the principle of equal opportunity should be applied to both Japanese and American economic activities in the South Pacific.[29] Despite the obvious importance of this statement, Nomura failed to deliver the message to Tokyo.

To clarify further the American position, on May 31 Joseph W. Ballantine, one of Hull's chief advisers on the Far East, gave Nomura an American draft proposal marked "Unofficial, Exploratory and Without Commitment." On the subject of the Tripartite Pact it stated: "Obviously the provisions of the Pact do not apply to involvement through acts of self-defense. The Government of the United States maintains that its attitude toward the European hostilities is and will continue to be determined solely and exclusively by considerations of protection and self-defense."[30] In short, Washington's position was that the pact would not apply if the United States became involved militarily in the European war. Once again Nomura withheld the American message from Tokyo.

When Matsuoka learned of the document through the Army General Staff, he ordered Nomura on June 9 to forward the full text. "An important matter of this sort should be dispatched without delay," he declared. ". . . This kind of message would be most helpful in understanding the thinking of the president, the secretary of state, and others and therefore is indispensable for Japan in considering and formulating its policy toward the United States. I hope you will bear this in mind."[31]

Without Matsuoka's knowledge, Nomura told Hull on June 2 that "he thought that he and his associates were in agreement with the document which Mr. Ballantine had handed to him, with the exception of some of the phraseology."[32] Thereupon a drafting committee was organized to work out the details of an agreement. On the Japanese side Ikawa, Iwakuro, and Matsudaira Kōtō, second secretary of the Japanese embassy, participated and on the American side, Ballantine and Maxwell M. Hamilton, chief of the Far Eastern Division of the State Department. In the course of several meetings of the committee and parallel private talks among Ikawa, Iwakuro, Drought, and Walker, a Japanese draft dated June 8 was given to Hull through Walker on June 9.[33] On the 15th Nomura forwarded to Hull, who was ill at the time, a new Japanese draft aimed at reconciling the views of both sides.[34] Nomura did not report the details of these discussions to Matsuoka, who thus was unaware that the ambassador had actually presented proposals to Washington without instructions from Tokyo.

The famous American draft proposal that Hull gave to Nomura on June 21 therefore came as a surprise to the Japanese leaders when they received it on the

24th. The product of the negotiations just described, incorporating the points expressed in the American notes of May 16 and May 31, diverged from the earlier Matsuoka draft in several respects. On the Tripartite Pact issue, it called upon Japan to state clearly that it was under no obligation to provide military assistance to Germany in the event of U.S. participation in the European war. Concerning the China problem, it provided that, when the Japanese government had indicated its general terms for peace, the president would suggest to the government of China that it undertake negotiations with Japan. In addition, it stipulated that both countries should pledge to carry on their activities in the Pacific area by peaceful means alone and in accordance with the principle of nondiscrimination in international commercial relations.[35] To Japanese officials in Tokyo, poorly informed of developments in Washington and therefore optimistic concerning Japan's prospects in the negotiations, the American proposal was both a shock and a disappointment.

The outbreak of the German-Soviet war on June 22 diverted the attention of the Japanese government, and it was not until July 10 and 12 that the question of a reply to the American proposal was finally brought up at two Liaison Conferences. Matsuoka expressed his indignation at the oral statement that had accompanied the American proposal, which had declared:

> Some Japanese leaders in influential official positions are definitely committed to a course that calls for support of Nazi Germany and its policies of conquest. . . . So long as these leaders maintain such an attitude in their official capacity, . . . it is illusory to expect that a proposal such as the one under consideration can offer a basis for achieving substantial results along desired lines.[36]

The conference accepted Matsuoka's emphatic demand for rejection of the oral statement, which he claimed treated Japan as a "weak and inferior nation." At the same time it decided to continue the negotiations and to present a new proposal that would contain some concessions to the American position.[37] On July 18, however, the Konoe cabinet was dissolved, and although Nomura received instructions concerning the new Japanese proposal, he did not submit it to the United States negotiators.

Following his resignation as foreign minister, Matsuoka penned a lengthy note to Konoe to express his outrage at Nomura's behavior in the negotiations. The letter reveals how profoundly Matsuoka had come to distrust Nomura's handling of communications between Washington and Tokyo:

> Nomura's weak and obsequious attitude in the negotiations has made American leaders contemptuous of us. . . . He concealed from us information unfavorable to Japan and kept information unfavorable to the United States from them. In his desire to reach an agreement on the basis of the Draft Understanding, he tried to stand in the middle and curry favor with both sides. I believe you are aware of this without my pointing it out.
> It is perhaps not inaccurate to say that Nomura failed to deliver to Hull even half the instructions I sent to him. Under these circumstances no important negotiations could ever have succeeded.[38]

It was tragic for Japanese diplomacy that a breakdown in communication occurred at such a critical moment. An ambassador must perform the function of a "communicator" as well as a "negotiator." In his intense desire to reach an accommodation with the United States, Nomura became so conscious of his role as a negotiator that he neglected to fulfill adequately his duties as a communicator. Indeed, although Matsuoka exaggerated in describing Nomura as trying to "curry favor with both sides," Nomura frequently did attempt to function as a mediator between the United States and Japan.

Nomura's neglect of his task as "communicator" may have been due in part to the presence and influence of Colonel Iwakuro. Iwakuro, who played a major role in the negotiations from April to June, had formerly been involved in a number of plots and subversive activities in the Japanese army. More generally, Nomura's negotiating style resembled that of Ambassador Ōshima Hiroshi in Germany. A lieutenant general and former military attaché in Berlin, Ōshima was a fervent supporter of the Tripartite Pact, to the point where his obsession with securing an alliance with Germany led him to bypass his responsibility to follow instructions from Tokyo. Moreover, when the conclusion of the Tripartite Pact emerged as the most crucial foreign policy issue for Japan in 1938-39, he gave Tokyo a distorted image of the situation in Germany. This pattern of diplomatic behavior might be termed "military diplomacy."

In "military diplomacy" goals are absolute while means are flexible. A "military diplomat" is like a military leader who must often make arbitrary decisions on the battlefield and carry them out resolutely in order to win. If victorious, his behavior is justified even though he may have ignored instructions from above. Even subversive actions in another country pursued without the knowledge of central authorities could be allowed in some cases. That the 1938-39 negotiations with Germany and those with the United States in 1941 were conducted in this way is not unrelated to the fact that both sets of negotiations were handled by military men.

In any event, Nomura was a poor "communicator," and as a result the views and expectations of the Japanese government, lacking essential and accurate information on American thinking, were unrealistic. Foreign Minister Matsuoka was especially hampered in carrying out his brand of "hard-line diplomacy" toward the United States, for he was unable to judge correctly the effectiveness of a particular course of action.

From the American point of view, information Nomura transmitted concerning the Japanese position conflicted sharply with the reports received from Ambassador Grew in Tokyo and with Matsuoka's uncompromising remarks as reported in the mass media. Even though MAGIC had enabled the American negotiators to learn Japan's intentions, the discrepancy must have generated distrust and made them question whether the Japanese government was negotiating with the United States sincerely.

II

Admiral Toyoda Teijirō succeeded Matsuoka as foreign minister in the third Konoe cabinet. Toyoda had long known Nomura in the navy and as vice navy minister had persuaded Nomura to accept the ambassadorship. Their close personal relationship, it was expected, would help improve communications between the Foreign Ministry and the Washington embassy. Toyoda shared Nomura's basic approach to negotiations with the United States in that he recognized the need to make concessions and work toward goals gradually.

U.S.-Japanese relations entered a critical phase early in August 1941 when Japan's military advance into southern Indochina led to a freezing of Japanese assets and an oil embargo by the United States. As a fresh approach to averting a crisis and improving relations, the new foreign minister supported the idea of a summit conference between Konoe and Roosevelt. On August 7 Toyoda sent Nomura instructions on a possible summit meeting and for nearly two months after that the Japanese government pinned its hopes for improved U.S. relations upon such a meeting.

While he was pressing hard for the summit conference, Toyoda did not overlook the need to eliminate the defects in communications between Tokyo and Washington that had earlier blocked progress in the negotiations. Both Iwakuro and Ikawa were summoned back to Tokyo in mid-August, and in the subsequent negotiations Nomura was assisted mainly by Minister Wakasugi Kaname and other subordinates. Toyoda also made use of the existing channels of communication between Ambassador Grew and the State Department. In order to ensure that Washington correctly interpreted Japanese intentions, Toyoda furnished Grew with copies of all important messages that Nomura was to submit to the U.S. government.

The American government, on its part, endeavored to improve communications between the two countries. Ballantine, who was fluent in Japanese, was asked to sit in regularly on the Hull-Nomura talks, and minutes of certain discussions, such as the Nomura-Roosevelt meeting of August 28, were transmitted to the Japanese government through Grew. Thus, to some extent deficiencies in the communications system between Tokyo and Washington were remedied.

But in spite of these efforts, Nomura's exaggerated notions of his mission as a negotiator continued to create difficulties. He took it upon himself to make several changes in wording before delivering the so-called "Konoe message" of August 27 proposing a summit conference between Konoe and Roosevelt. And on September 4, without any instructions from Tokyo, he presented his personal proposal to Hull, indicating Japan's willingness to accept the substance of the June 21 "American proposal" except for the part dealing with the Sino-Japanese conflict. Moreover, on the most sensitive aspect of this issue—withdrawal of Japanese troops from China—he promised that Japanese forces would be evacuated "as promptly as possible with the restoration of peace, within a period of two years and in accordance with an agreement to be concluded between Japan and China."[39] There was no reference whatever to the possibility that Japanese forces might thereafter be stationed in China.

The Japanese government itself made some concessions in a new draft presented to the United States government on September 6. On the issue of the Tripartite Pact it stated: "Should the United States participate in the European war, the interpretation and execution of the Tripartite Pact by Japan shall be *independently* decided." Regarding American economic interests in China, the proposal provided that "the economic activities of the United States in China will not be restricted so long as they are pursued on an equitable basis." The document did not go so far as to specify a time period for Japanese evacuation from China, merely stating that "Japan is prepared to withdraw its armed forces from China as soon as possible in accordance with agreements between Japan and China."[40] With the arrival of this formal Japanese proposal, Nomura was naturally obliged to rescind his own offer.[41]

As he became aware of Nomura's arbitrary actions, Foreign Minister Toyoda grew increasingly doubtful of the ambassador's performance as "communicator." On September 25 he finally sent a cable in which he attempted to bring Nomura back into line:

> I can imagine that, as ambassador, you have your own views on the negotiations. . . . However, you are again reminded that you are to refrain from adding to or deleting from any message on your own without consulting us first.[42]

On October 18 a new government headed by General Tōjō Hideki replaced the Konoe cabinet and Tōgō Shigenori, former ambassador to the Soviet Union, was appointed foreign minister. When he took up his post, Tōgō recalled in his memoirs, "It was my judgment, based on a cable from Nomura dated October 3, that an understanding had almost been reached on the Tripartite Pact and on nondiscriminatory trade treatment, leaving only the question of stationing forces in China unresolved."[43] Nomura's report had specifically stated that "of the three pending issues, two are nearly resolved; what remains is perhaps only the question of armed forces being stationed in China."[44] Tōgō therefore had expected that if agreement could be reached on this final point, a peaceful settlement with the United States was possible.

On November 1 a Liaison Conference was held to discuss the issue of war with the United States and to decide whether or not the negotiations should be continued. The focus of concern was the question of Japanese troops in China. Foreign Minister Tōgō felt that a compromise might be reached if a definite time limit were set for the withdrawal of Japanese forces—a position to which the Army General Staff was sharply opposed. At last an agreement emerged: all Japanese forces were to be withdrawn from China within twenty-five years after a peace settlement. It was also decided to make a final attempt to reach an understanding with the United States on the basis of two draft proposals labeled "A" and "B."[45]

In an attempt to improve communications between Washington and Tokyo and inform the embassy in Washington of the urgent situation in Japan,[46] Tōgō sent Kurusu Saburō, an experienced career diplomat, to assist Nomura in the final negotiations. Kurusu flew to Washington in mid-November. His presence, however, did not induce Nomura to follow instructions more closely. When, for instance, Nomura saw no prospect for coming to terms with the United States on the basis of draft proposal A, he presented another plan to Hull on November 18 without informing Tokyo. This proposal, which was along the lines of draft proposal B but less general, aimed at achieving a modus vivendi through a Japanese pledge to withdraw its forces from southern French Indochina in exchange for an American promise to rescind the order freezing Japanese funds and to export a certain quantity of oil to Japan.[47]

There was no chance that the Japanese army would accept the proposal, and Tōgō openly expressed his disapproval of Nomura's action. In a cable ordering Nomura to submit draft proposal B immediately, Tōgō admonished the ambassador as follows:

The situation is so serious that it is impossible for us to continue negotiations on the basis of the proposal you have presented in an effort to relax tensions. Furthermore, it is regrettable, given the delicate situation here, that you offered your own personal plan without prior consultation with us. This can lead only to a delay in or breakdown of the negotiations.[48]

The most dramatic event underlining Nomura's failure to act as a "communicator" occurred when he handed the December 7 ultimatum to the United States government. Japan's leaders had reached a decision for war at an Imperial Conference on December 1, fully aware as a result of the famous Hull note of November 26 that no compromise was possible unless Japan liquidated the possessions it had acquired on the Chinese continent during the preceding decade. But the foreign minister and the navy supreme command had been unable to agree on when the ultimatum should be delivered to the United States. In the end the government decided to present the note at 1:00 p.m. Washington time on December 7. The navy command estimated that if notice were given at that time, fifty minutes would still remain before the start of the Hawaii attack, thus conforming to international legal procedure regarding a declaration of war. As is well known, however, the two Japanese ambassadors did not arrive at Secretary Hull's office to deliver the ultimatum until 2:20 p.m., nearly an hour after the Pearl Harbor attack had begun. This incident left an ugly blemish upon Japan's diplomatic record and led after the war to the Tokyo Tribunal's assertion that Japan had violated international law.

The delay was not intentional, as Tōgō noted with regret in his memoirs:

The staff of the Washington embassy was negligent to some extent. They should have decoded the final part of the telegram immediately after they arrived early on the morning of the 7th and should also have finished typing those parts of the telegram that had come in on the 6th.

Due to their negligence, they were unable to make available a cleanly typed document by the time we had instructed them to notify the U.S. government. . . . I wonder whether the two ambassadors had read the telegrams of the 6th that had been decoded that night and why, if they had read them, they were unable to comprehend the gravity of the situation.

I fail to see why the embassy personnel were so careless that they began to process such an important cable only on the morning of the 7th, after the naval attaché, who had just come to the embassy office, called their attention to a number of undecoded cables.[49]

This incident, occurring at the very end of the negotiations, was the most obvious symptom of a defect in communications that persisted throughout the discussions preceding the Pacific War and, it might be argued, one of the reasons the negotiations ultimately failed.

III

Thus far we have focused primarily upon the difficulties in communication that developed between the Japanese government and its embassy in Washington, impeding the negotiations between Japan and the United States. It remains to consider the equally serious communications problem that arose between the Japanese and American governments.

One of the most persistent obstacles to progress in the negotiations was, of course, Japan's obligation under the Tripartite Pact. Foriegn Minister Matsuoka wanted to make use of Japan's close ties with Germany and Italy to prevent the United States from entering the European war. Secretary Hull, on the other hand, sought to weaken the Axis alliance so that Japan would not provide military assistance to Germany if America should become a belligerent. Thus their positions were diametrically opposed.

Following Konoe's suggestion of a summit conference in August 1941, however, there was an unmistakable shift in the Japanese position. Konoe seemed to want to avoid war with the United States at any cost, even if it meant virtually nullifying the pact. Thus, the Japanese proposal of September 6 declared that "the attitudes of Japan and the United States toward the European war will be decided in accordance with the concepts of protection and self-defense, and should the United States participate in the European war, the interpretation and execution of the Tripartite Pact shall be *independently* decided."[50] This was a significant concession that met in large part the American demands concerning the Tripartite Pact. Ambassador Grew took note of the change in the Japanese government's attitude in a report dated September 29: "The Japanese Government, while consistently refusing to give an undertaking overtly to renounce membership in the alliance, has in actual fact shown itself ready to reduce to a dead letter Japan's adherence to the alliance by indicating readiness to enter into formal negotiation with the United States."[51] Paul W. Schroeder has commented that the proposal "would largely have met the American requirements as put forward in the spring of 1941."[52] Furthermore, Schroeder states, "there was no longer any real need to fear that the Tripartite Pact would at present be invoked against the United States. The Axis Alliance was in fact rapidly becoming a dead issue."[53]

One can assume that, given the domestic situation in Japan and the need to avoid any drastic change in Japan's relations with the Axis, it would have been extremely difficult for Konoe and the other Japanese leaders to state unambiguously to the United States that they expected virtually to abrogate the pact, even had they wished to do so. Still, the government did try in the September 6 proposal to convey its intention to change its earlier position on the pact and made a similar, though more guarded, effort in a second message on September 25.[54] As Schroeder has written:

> More specific evidence that the Tripartite Pact was not to be enforced by Japan began to accumulate rapidly. First, because of the

tight secrecy imposed by Foreign Minister Toyoda, the Germans
were unable to find out what was going on in the Japanese-American
negotiations. Next, the Japanese witnessed the extension of American patrols all the way to Iceland without a qualm and, when
informed by the United States of the move, had no comment to
make on it. . . .

The Konoe government thus gave ample evidence that the
Tripartite Pact was to be treated as a dead letter.[55]

Japanese leaders seem to have taken for granted that their real purpose had
been made clear to the United States by the two messages they had sent and by
their failure to supply aid to Germany. Therefore Foreign Minister Tōgō was
surprised when Hull insisted in a talk with Nomura on November 15 that Japan
must clearly indicate that if it entered into an agreement with the United States,
"the Tripartite Pact would automatically become a dead letter."[56] It was
evident that the Japanese leaders had failed to communicate their position to the
American officials.

The incident points to one of the grave problems in communication that
had grown up between the two governments. Mutual trust is an essential factor
in communication, and Japan's expansionist policies in China had, over a
number of years, aroused in American leaders a strong suspicion of Japanese
objectives. This distrust was especially marked among certain high officials,
notably Secretary of War Henry L. Stimson and Stanley K. Hornbeck, the
political adviser on Far Eastern affairs in the State Department. Hornbeck, as the
most experienced specialist on Far Eastern matters, played a major role in the
negotiations by offering advice to and preparing memoranda for Hull.

American suspicions reached a peak when Japan advanced into southern
Indochina in the midst of the negotiations. A psychological atmosphere was
thereby created that made it exceedingly difficult for American officials to
interpret Japan's intentions accurately, especially when, as in the messages
concerning Japan's withdrawal from the Axis, those intentions were only
implied.

Yet another factor hampered the ability of the two governments to
communicate: the different patterns of negotiation the Japanese and American
governments had traditionally followed. Secretary Hull once criticized Japan's
negotiating behavior, observing that when he attempted to work out "an agreement in clear-cut and unequivocal terms" that would "speak for itself," the
Japanese negotiators "manifested an ever greater reluctance to agree to clean-
cut provisions, capable of no equivocation, that would guarantee peace in the
Pacific. What they had in mind when they said they could agree to our proposals
'with the exception of some of the phraseology' was soon apparent. They wanted
provision after provision changed to such indefinite wording that it would be
capable of various interpretations . . . ."[57]

Hull's statement was made while Matsuoka was foreign minister, but the
Japanese endeavored throughout the negotiations to avoid precise language.
Instead they tended to use flexible, all-inclusive expressions that would
accommodate as many claims as possible on both sides and would permit a
number of interpretations. Such phraseology could also accord with the position

of the army and other groups in Japan. This approach, which may be termed *sakubun shugi* or "emphasis on literary style," is a characteristic pattern in Japan and may be observed in most documents setting forth Japan's basic policy and future plans,[58] as well as in private contracts.[59]

The Japanese also tended to stress the very existence or the form of an agreement, while the Americans emphasized the substance. To the Japanese way of thinking, the conclusion of an agreement is considered to have some positive effect on a relationship, whether interpersonal or international, even though the agreement may be only a formal one and may not represent a true convergence of opinion. It might be argued that Nomura's poor performance as a communicator—his ignoring of instructions from Tokyo, his failure to deliver important messages and distortion of others—was due in part to his judgment that, as long as some kind of "understanding" was reached, it would significantly aid in "changing the psychology of the people of the two countries from war to peace."

On the other hand, from Hull's rational approach, an agreement had to be fixed and definite. To Hull, an agreement in form not only would not help to improve relations but would merely be a source of future trouble. American leaders recalled concluding agreements with Japan in the past which, from their point of view, the Japanese government subsequently interpreted arbitrarily and in effect distorted. Instances such as the Lansing-Ishii Agreement of 1917 and the agreement for a joint Siberian expedition the following year made American negotiators wary of concluding any agreement with Japan.[60]

The aborting of the proposed Konoe-Roosevelt meeting was also related to fundamental differences in the negotiating attitudes of the two countries. On the one hand, the Japanese government felt that "the two heads of state should first meet to discuss broadly all important problems between Japan and America covering the entire Pacific area and to explore possibilities of improving the situation," while "adjustments of minor issues were to be left to negotiations among the competent officials of the two countries after the summit meeting."[61] The United States government, on the other hand, insisted "that it would seem highly desirable that we take precautions toward ensuring that our proposed meeting shall prove a success by endeavoring to enter immediately upon preliminary discussion of the fundamental and essential questions on which we seek agreement."[62]

Japanese leaders placed great value on face-to-face communication, thinking that if the two heads of state met and talked over outstanding issues "from a broad standpoint" and in a statesmanlike manner, a breakthrough might be achieved. Konoe was prepared to make significant concessions at the time, despite army opposition, if Roosevelt would meet Japan's demands to some extent.[63] But this emphasis on direct, personal communication between the two leaders was not understood by the Americans, who continued to maintain that a top level meeting was in and of itself meaningless. They felt that the problems had first to be clearly defined and an agreement nearly concluded in preliminary discussions, whereupon the remaining issues could be settled by top level discussions.[64]

In summary, although the failure of the 1941 negotiations was due preeminently to the clash of vital Japanese and American interests, the breakdown in communications within the Japanese government, the distrust that was so frequently a barrier to understanding, and the differences in negotiating techniques are important factors that must also be considered.

THE ROLE OF THE WAR
DEPARTMENT AND THE ARMY

Russell F. Weigley

"These questions are matters for the State Department and the Peking Legation to settle, so I will not attempt to discuss them, except to say that even morally correct decisions might lead to more serious consequences than we would care to contemplate."

United States military attaché,
Tokyo, commenting on American
responses to Japanese policy, 1933[1]

I

To understand the attitudes of the U.S. army in the 1930s toward Japan or, indeed, toward anything else, the immense American military machine of the present must be erased from the mind. The American army of the 1930s, hovering about 145,000 officers and men in the early years of the decade, rising slowly to some 190,000 when World War II began, and lacking a large force of trained reserves, was small even by the standards of medium-sized powers. Its equipment consisted mostly of hand-me-downs from World War I, matériel which not only was obsolescent but was wearing out. Its preoccupation was with its own mere survival in the face of congressional economies.

Reduced in the 1920s to a skeleton of the 280,000-man peacetime force envisioned by the National Defense Act of 1920, the army found its appropriations still further stunted by the fiscal exigencies of the early depression years. During the depression too it felt itself beleaguered in yet another way: the officers who shaped its attitudes were generally conservative members of the white, Protestant, Anglo-Saxon middle class who felt their kind of America to be slipping away under the batterings of the depression and the policies of the New Deal. Indeed, the officer corps was a sort of Anglo-Saxon gentlemen's club, small enough that its members generally knew each other and found their paths crossing frequently—but a gentlemen's club that was on the defensive, as all such institutions were in the 1930s.

These circumstances, plus an exaggerated estimate of the strength of pacifist and anti-militarist sentiment among civilian Americans, caused the officer corps and the army to draw into themselves, to set themselves apart from the rest of America. This they did perhaps even more than in the past, although the historic tradition of the American officer corps already was one of isolated military professionalism that carefully abstained from involvement in the turmoils of civilian life and the vicissitudes of national policymaking. During most of the 1930s the army played no large role in the making of American foreign policy. Nor did it seek to do so. To its officers, it seemed enough to preserve their institution's existence in an apparently hostile society.[2]

The constitutional position of the U.S. army of course contributed much, as it always had, to the army's drawing inward upon itself. The U.S. constitution had been written by men mindful and fearful of the possibility of military domination over civil governments and societies. They were heirs to a long Anglo-Saxon tradition of suspicion of the military, a tradition sharpened for them by the example of Oliver Cromwell's military dictatorship in the then recent past and, more importantly, by their own experience with the British regular army in America, whose presence had been a direct and major cause of the American revolution.

The American constitution therefore sought carefully to subordinate the military to the civil government and to assure the isolation of the military from national policymaking except within its own distinctive sphere. Financially, the army was made dependent upon Congress, specifically upon appropriations that could run no longer than two years. For purposes of command, the army was subordinated to the civilian chief executive, the president, in his role of commander-in-chief. It became the custom for the president to exercise this role through the instrument of his civilian secretary of war, a cabinet officer responsible not to the army but to him. For times of peace at least, the constitution even went so far as to preserve a division of military power between the federal government and the states, each of which retained its own army in the militia system. To be sure, such constitutional prescriptions and safeguards were subject to modification and even distortion in interpretation; but after a brief interval in the 1790s when it appeared that the army might become an active political force despite the constitution, the army subsided into the political passivity the constitution had designed for it. By the 1930s this passivity had come to seem an unbreakable tradition. The events of the 1940s and later, which were indeed to modify the constitutional arrangements, were not yet foreseen or imagined.

Despite the army's constitutional position and its straitened circumstances and defensive frame of mind in the 1930s, the larger demands of U.S. policy did compel it to give some thought to such issues as the military defense of U.S. interests in Asia and the Pacific and the possibility of war with Japan. For one thing, what seemed to many officers an inordinately large proportion of the army's limited manpower lay exposed to Japan in the Philippines and China. Thinking about Japan was an activity that caused considerable uneasiness. The historic interests of the U.S. army lay mainly in the western hemisphere and in Europe; it did not desire Asian and Pacific entanglements. To the extent that it was already bound by such entanglements in the Philippines and in China, the army generally regarded them as misfortunes, if only because they placed its troops in positions sure to be untenable in the event of a Pacific war.

As for the Japanese army as a possible adversary, the U.S. army in part affected a condescension toward the Japanese as it did toward all Orientals. However impressive the Japanese army might have been in fighting the Chinese, most American soldiers seem to have thought it not up to Western standards in tactics or military technology. In this view lay the implication that the Japanese army would be an adversary not quite worthy of American mettle, so that a contest with it would be an unfortunate distraction from greater military concerns.

Yet at the same time the Japanese army could seem especially dangerous because it was mysterious. It was not only that anything Oriental might seem so. Military attachés in Tokyo habitually complained of the unusual secrecy that surrounded Japanese military affairs, of their uncommon problems in acquiring information. When Japanese troops clashed with Chinese at Shanghai in 1932 within sight of American observers, the Americans eagerly snatched at the rare opportunity to watch Japanese soldiers in action and tried to draw large conclusions from small battles. What they could see on that and other occasions in China in the thirties suggested a tough, aggressive Japanese army that should not be condescended to after all. Meanwhile, what American military attachés saw in Japan itself suggested a growing military ascendancy over the Japanese government and a consequent dangerous aggressiveness in Japanese national policy that made the possibility of war less and less remote.[3]

By 1940 the likelihood of conflict with Japan had become much more than a matter of vague foreboding. By that time also, the rise of Hitler had confirmed the American army in its greater concern for European than for Asian interests. General George C. Marshall, the chief of staff of the army, remarked that "a serious commitment in the Pacific is just what Germany would like to see us undertake."[4] From first to last, the leaders of the U.S. army hoped to avoid a Pacific war. Yet the war came. It came in part because the civil departments of the U.S. government formulated policy toward Japan with little regard for the military capacities and limitations of the United States in the western Pacific.

The principal policy question raised by the role of the U.S. army in American-Japanese relations from 1931 to 1941 is the currently much-debated issue of the proper influence of the nation's armed forces in its foreign affairs. But the familiar issue arises here in an unfamiliar form, at least for Americans accustomed to the circumstances of their country since 1945. The problem in the 1930s was not the one so commonly thought to have reached alarming proportions in America after World War II, namely, excessive military influence upon foreign policy; it was more nearly one of insufficient military influence. The American army's own traditions, combined with those of the nation at large, permitted the foreign policy of the United States to become inconsistent with its military capacities, and the army felt itself bound to do no more than acquiesce.

Throughout most of the period leading to the American confrontation with Japan, not even the most rudimentary machinery existed for the weighing of military considerations in establishing foreign policy. The Standing Liaison

Committee of the State, War, and Navy Departments was created belatedly in 1938 and was not notably effective. It confined its interests largely to Latin America and to hemisphere defense; it met irregularly, and with its three departments unaccustomed to working together, the exchanges were by no means completely trustful.[5] As for the army's attitude on such matters, as late as 1940 the War Plans Division of the Army General Staff stated that the concern of the army was simply with the "how" of national policy, that is, with the means of carrying out policy; the "what" of national policy, its formulation, was exclusively the concern of the civil government.[6] The navy was somewhat more involved in foreign policy, both because of a different tradition that lacked the army's severe insistence on political abnegation, and because under President Franklin Roosevelt there prevailed a rapport between the president and the navy, the service he regarded as peculiarly his own, which did not exist between him and the army. Almost to the eve of Pearl Harbor, the U.S. army remained largely separated from the men and institutions that made foreign policy. The concerns and fears of the army barely touched American policy toward Japan.

It is true that in 1940 and 1941, at long last, events mainly outside the Far East impelled the chief of staff of the army to the president's side and obliged him to speak out on foreign policy and specifically on the army's misgivings about possible war with Japan. The concerns of the army also began to receive a larger hearing in the State Department. By then, however, it was extremely late. By then the fateful direction of U.S. Pacific policy had been set; and the army at last alternated between belated iteration of misgivings concerning a Pacific war and an effort, pathetic in retrospect, to wish the misgivings away.

II

The difference between the army's and the navy's position in American-Japanese relations was not limited to the navy's willingness to seek (even though it did not always receive) a larger role in foreign policy matters. The navy did not display quite the same revulsion as the army at every prospect of a Pacific war. Whatever problems a war against Japan might pose for the navy—and the distances of the western Pacific assured, of course, that the problems would be large ones—the navy could hardly help feeling a kind of fascination in and even an attraction to the idea of a war that was sure to be mainly naval, a contest across the greatest ocean in the world against the fleet that had established its stature when Admiral Tōgō crossed the Russians' "T" in the battle of the Straits of Tsushima.

For the U.S. army, in contrast to the navy, thoughts of a Pacific war suggested first of all a picture of sacrifice: the sacrifice of the army's Far Eastern garrisons in China (until 1938) and in the Philippines to initial Japanese advances that the army could not hope to contain. The small size and the defensive mood of the army in the 1930s made it all the more sensitive to such a prospect. With the officer corps still a sort of gentlemen's club, the loss of the Philippine garrison would mean the loss by death or capture of personal friends—worse than that, of brothers in the fraternity of American officers. Preoccupied already with problems of survival, the small army of the 1930s could all the more readily become preoccupied with the perils facing that part of it which lay isolated and exposed in the Far East, until the fate awaiting the Philippine garrison overshadowed everything else in army thinking about Japan. While in 1940 and 1941 issues much larger than the fate of the Philippines came to govern American-Japanese relations, still for the army the problem of the defense of those islands remained the symbol and epitome of all the larger problems.

The 7,000 or so Philippine islands lie 7,000 miles from the west coast of the United States but only about one-seventh that distance from Japan and about 200 miles from what was then Japanese-controlled Formosa. As soon as the euphoria of America's 1898 victory over Spain faded away, and especially after Japan defeated Russia in 1904-05, American strategic planners began to awaken to the harsh realities of the imperial position awarded their country by the 1898 Treaty of Paris, most notably in the Philippines. Theodore Roosevelt's disillusioned reference to the Philippines as the Achilles heel of American defense is proverbial.[7] Within the armed forces the Joint Army and Navy Board began in 1903 to grapple with the problem of creating a viable national strategic policy that included defense of the Philippines. At the instigation of Lieutenant General Adna R. Chaffee, chief of staff of the army, the Joint Board commenced in 1904, soon after Japan's attack on Russia, to prepare a series of plans for joint army-navy action against possible enemies. This evolved into the so-called color plans, each known by the color that served as a code reference to the country to which the plan referred. The Orange plans for Japan were among the most prominent of the color plans from the inception of the strategic planning idea and placed the services, especially the army, in a quandary over the Philippines.[8]

Early in the planning process, for example, the General Board of the navy proposed the Philippines as the site for a major naval base, to be located at Olongapo on Subic Bay. The army responded that it could not assure the defense of Olongapo against attack by land. By 1909, in consequence, the Navy General Board gave up on the Philippines and moved its suggested site for a Pacific base to Pearl Harbor in Hawaii.[9]

By 1914 the Joint Board had completed a version of War Plan Orange that envisioned, realistically, the arrival in the Philippines of a Japanese fleet with troop transports eight days after leaving Japanese ports, which in all likelihood would be no more than eight days after the outbreak of war. There was no prospect of the army's having a garrison in the Philippines strong enough to hold the islands against the kind of force Japan would land, and the navy calculated that at best sixty-eight days would be required for the first section of the U.S. fleet to fight its way to the islands bringing assistance to the garrison. So the army settled for a plan—or a hope—to hold on to Corregidor island in Manila Bay for at least sixty days, until the fleet arrived. Unfortunately, the navy conceded that reaching the Philippines even within sixty-eight days was the best it could hope for and beyond the capacity of the existing fleet if opposed by the Japanese.[10]

These gloomy prospects grew more gloomy during the 1920s. Possession of the former German islands in the central Pacific under League of Nations mandate placed Japan across the American line of communications between Hawaii and the Philippines. The Washington Naval Treaty combined a 5:5:3 ratio in capital ships with a nonfortification agreement by which the United

States bound itself to abstain from improving its Pacific fortifications west of Pearl Harbor; the effect was to guarantee Japanese naval superiority in the western Pacific. The rise of air power increased American strategic problems. Aircraft adequate to defend the Philippines represented another expense the United States was not likely to undertake, when already it had been unwilling to devote enough resources to the defense of the islands in the pre-air power age. Japanese air power therefore became one more threat to the land defense of the Philippines and to the passage of the U.S. fleet westward to the islands' relief.[11]

As a result War Plan Orange had to be revised. But the joint army-navy planners did not consider themselves free to draw the reasonable conclusion that in a war with Japan the Philippines simply could not be held—and that the civil authorities should be urged to formulate American commitments in the Far East accordingly. Instead, the 1924 revision of the Orange plan contemplated the army's defending Manila Bay until the navy could fight its way there with reinforcements and thenceforth base itself upon Manila Bay for the final contest to win naval supremacy in the western Pacific. These projections were offered despite the fact that the army defenders of the Philippines against Japanese invasion would number only 15,000; that the largest initial reinforcement that could be contemplated totaled only 50,000 men, which, however small, represented one-third of the existing army; and that even assuming Manila Bay could somehow be held, its limited facilities, fixed by the Washington Treaty, could not possibly support a battle fleet strong enough to overcome the Japanese in their home waters.[12]

For all its quality of fantasy, this outline of War Plan Orange persisted through various modifications into the 1930s. The 1928 version, in force when the Manchurian Incident erupted in 1931, predicted that Japan could mobilize and transport to the Philippine islands a force of 300,000 men within thirty days; 50,000 to 60,000 Japanese might be secretly mobilized to appear off Luzon seven days after the beginning of war, 100,000 within fifteen days. To oppose such forces, the U.S. army had 11,000 troops in the Philippines, 7,000 of them Filipinos, plus 6,000 Filipinos in the islands' constabulary. The army air component consisted of 56 officers and 652 enlisted men with eleven pursuit, forty-nine observation, and nine bombardment planes—though only nine pursuit, six observation, and five bombardment planes could be flown initially because there were not enough men for the rest. Still, the plan called for the forces in the Philippines to hold the Manila Bay area as long as possible and to deny this area to Japan as a naval base if it could not actually be held. The hope persisted that holding the area as long as possible would mean until the arrival of enough American naval strength to turn the tide.[13]

At the beginning of the 1930s, when the Japanese penetration of Manchuria produced the decade's first crisis in American-Japanese relations, the chiefs of the armed forces on at least one occasion did call these facts about the weakness of the Philippines to the attention of President Herbert Hoover. The Manchurian crisis led Hoover to inquire about American preparedness in the Far East, and the service chiefs told him that war with Japan would mean the temporary loss of the Philippines. In the long run, they believed, the United States would win such a war, but they estimated the long run to mean four to six years.

Mainly, however, the U.S. response to the Manchurian crisis was characterized by Secretary of State Henry L. Stimson's efforts to rebuff the Japanese by means of the force of public opinion, not only without recourse to America's dubious military power in the Far East, but without the cooperation of the military. In fact, the State Department did not even avail itself of army and navy intelligence reports from the area. In this phase of his career Stimson seems to have regarded the State Department as possessing absolute primacy among the executive departments to the point that in foreign policy matters the military were expected simply to do as they were told. Since the army itself did not view things much differently, the Manchurian crisis is an especially noteworthy illustration of the failure to formulate a coordinated diplomatic and military policy.[14]

When the Japanese moved against Shanghai in 1932, there occurred a brief flurry of military-diplomatic discussions, and the army's 31st Infantry Regiment was sent to the city as an earnest of American concern. But Stimson's implied threat to fortify Guam and the Philippines, expressed in his famous letter to Senator William E. Borah, was apparently conceived without consultation with the military and marked a return to his customary independence of action.[15]

In part because Manchuria and Shanghai raised increasing fears that the Orange plan might not remain a mere abstraction, the joint army-navy planners developed another revision that injected additional modesty into the role of the Philippine defenders. Under the revised plan, the primary task of the forces in the archipelago was to hold the *entrance* to Manila Bay; holding the Manila Bay *area* became only a secondary mission, to be pursued as long as it did not endanger the first. This modification meant that the planners no longer affected much of a pretense that the bay area could be defended until the U.S. fleet arrived, although holding the bay area would be necessary if the fleet was to have a base. The planners hoped at best to deny a Manila Bay naval base to the Japanese; this much could be accomplished by retaining only the entrance to the bay—specifically the Bataan peninsula—as long as possible and then fighting a last-ditch action to hold Corregidor and its satellite islands at the mouth of the bay.[16]

This scheme was to persist through the final revision of War Plan Orange at the close of the decade, in 1938. To follow the plans of this decade from the joint war plans of both army and navy to the army's own plans is not only to pursue in increasing detail the methods contemplated for effecting the major scheme, but also to meet still deeper forebodings that not even a small part of the Philippines could be defended until help arrived. Despite the pessimism of the joint plans, those products of army-navy cooperation remained illuminated by the navy's persistent conviction that sooner or later the Battle Fleet would fight its way across the Pacific and triumph over the Japanese navy in the home waters of Japan. But the army's plans, those of the Philippine Department most of all, are permeated by the different theme of impending loss. For example, although the defense of the entire Manila Bay area persists as a secondary mission in the joint Orange plans, as early as 1934 the army's Philippine Department plan included the decision "to forego attempts to perform the secondary mission and to effect such evacuation as to be independent of the Manila Bay area for both supply and personnel within fifteen days."[17]

Because many of the troops defending the archipelago would be Filipino, the army felt qualms not only about the small numbers but also about the fighting qualities of the defenders. Of Filipino soldiers the department command wrote:

They have not been tested in modern battles. They are not inspired by the degree of loyalty to the United States which characterizes the attitude of ORANGE [Japanese] soldiers to their country. Moreover, it cannot be assumed that Filipino political leaders will remain zealously steadfast in view of probable ORANGE inducements and the uncertainty of the final outcome. Therefore, it appears proper to ascribe a greater combat value to the ORANGE mobile troops in comparison with equal forces of Filipino troops.[18]

The Philippine Department anticipated that a Japanese attack would fall upon the islands with little or no warning and would feature multiple landings. To try to oppose multiple landings would spread forces that were already too thin still thinner and thus might ultimately make a stubborn defense of Bataan and Corregidor no longer possible. But not to oppose multiple landings would yield the population centers of the islands to the Japanese so quickly that the Filipinos might become permanently estranged from a United States that did so little to protect them. It would also cause the loss of supplies that might with time be shifted to the final centers of resistance. It would sacrifice airfields, when the army hoped by "conservative employment" of its small Philippine air arm from scattered fields to prolong the utility of that arm. It would sacrifice what the army considered to be the "aggressive action and high morale incident to meeting the enemy at the beach where he is most vulnerable, and where telling losses can be administered by a comparatively small force." So the Philippine Department planned to meet the enemy on the beaches with the forces of small sector commands.[19]

Yet Chief of Staff General Malin Craig felt obliged to respond to this plan by warning: "The forces immediately available to you are . . . so small that in the event of an attack of which there is little warning, there will be danger of an over extension which will jeopardize the accomplishment of the joint mission" to protect at least the entrance to Manila Bay. Thinking about how to make the best possible fight for the Philippines posed nothing but dilemmas. General Craig had to concede that the department plan to which he objected might nevertheless be about as good as any, that it "appears to conform literally and in spirit to the mission assigned your forces."[20]

The "spirit" of the army's mission was the lugubrious one embodied in the "guiding principles" of the Philippine Department plan:

a. The fortifications at the entrance to Manila Bay must deny entrance to any enemy to Manila Bay.

b. Every preparation will be made in these fortifications to withstand a protracted siege, and Corregidor particularly must hold out to the last extremity.[21]

An officer forthright enough to cut through all delusions found excessive optimism even in such phrases about fighting to the last extremity. Brigadier

General Stanley D. Embick had been involved in Philippine defense planning since Theodore Roosevelt's time and by 1933 was commander on Corregidor. He reported that his island fortress might hold out against the Japanese for as much as a year, but that even a year's defense would not be enough. Corregidor alone could not give the navy the base it would need in Philippine waters, so that when the fleet appeared it would still be necessary to seize and develop a base. But the fleet could never fight so far westward without seizing and developing intermediate bases on the way, and ⸱that could never be done in the time Corregidor might conceivably hold out. "To carry out the present Orange Plan," said Embick, "—with its provisions for the early dispatch of our fleet to Philippine waters—would be literally an act of madness." He recommended that the United States arrange for the neutralization of the Philippines and roll back its Pacific defenses to Alaska, Oahu, and Panama. The commanding officer of the Philippine Department concurred.[22]

The movement to grant independence to the Philippines gave further impetus to such disillusioned thinking. The Tydings-McDuffie Act of 1934 set the islands upon a road that was to lead through gradual enlargement of self-government to independence after ten years. As a result the navy commander in the Philippines joined with his army counterpart to request that Washington make a fundamental reevaluation of the military future of the archipelago. In their view, if the United States expected to retain a military presence even after Philippine independence, there must be large reinforcements and strengthening of the defense, including abrogation of the nonfortification agreement of 1922. Without such reinforcement, the United States should abandon responsibility for Philippine defense.[23]

But the high commands of both services in Washington were unwilling to second these voices of realism from the islands. At the highest echelons of the navy all thought was still dominated by the vision of the Battle Fleet's final triumphant thrust across the Pacific, along with a vaguer notion of the Philippines' indispensability to the Mahanian grandeur of American sea power. The army's position remained simpler. In the army questions of policy raised in the islands collided with the fixed belief that the service had no business meddling with national policy. The decision to neutralize or to go on attempting to defend the Philippines was a decision for Congress and the executive to make; the duty of the army was not to question the wisdom of such decisions but to attempt without protest to implement them.

III

That a base which cannot be held against a prospective enemy is indispensable in war against that enemy is a proposition difficult to sustain under even the most Fabian theories of strategy. Yet out of the differing motives of the army and navy, the Joint Board continued through the late 1930s to reiterate precisely that conclusion about the Philippines in a war against Japan. The islands were indispensable to American Pacific strategy, and planning to defend them had to continue.[24]

General Embick remained unable to overcome such reasoning even when he became chief of the War Plans Division of the Army General Staff in 1935. In that post he asserted again that a base which cannot be defended is not indispensable to strategy but an invitation to disaster and that the American strategic frontier in the Pacific should therefore be pushed back to Alaska, Hawaii, and Panama. But the navy planners again rejected such argument, and in the discussions of the Joint Board the army's aversion to involvement in policy must have weakened any defense of Embick's opinion. Subsequently the Orange plans did give greater attention to the defense of Hawaii, but Embick could not change the fundamentals of the plans.[25]

In 1936, meanwhile, Japan joined Germany and Italy in the Anti-Comintern Pact. Obviously the pact added a new complication to Orange planning—the possibility that war against Japan might not be only a Far Eastern war. Such a contingency was, however, not altogether novel to the war planners' thinking. At the beginning of the 1920s, when it had been necessary to revise the color plans to fit post-World War I conditions, the Joint Board had considered a similar possibility in its Red-Orange plans, which envisaged a war against Great Britain and Japan simultaneously. The growing unlikelihood of any such confrontation had caused a gradual neglect of the Red-Orange plans, but those exercises had included an assumption that now suggested itself again in light of the German-Italian-Japanese partnership: that if the United States had to fight across both oceans, the concentration of American cities and industries upon the Atlantic coast, much closer to Europe than the Pacific coast was to Japan, decreed that America should deal with the transatlantic enemy first. The transatlantic enemy was likely to be the more threatening in other ways as well. Therefore in a two-ocean war the United States should content itself with a defensive stand against Japan until the transatlantic threat had been eliminated and American armed forces could freely concentrate upon the Pacific. After 1936 this line of reasoning seemed to the army to apply to a war against Germany and Japan as much as it had to a war against Great Britain and Japan.[26]

Such reasoning must also have strengthened the arguments of General Embick and others who thought as he did about the delusions in the Orange plans. In any event, when in 1937 the "China Incident" was added to the Anti-Comintern Pact, the Joint Board was shaken enough to pronounce the Orange plans "unsound in general" and to call for their reappraisal. The board proposed "a position of readiness" in the "strategic triangle" of Alaska, Hawaii, and Panama, but when the planners moved to translate these ideas into further specifics, the old obstacles reappeared. Facing the Philippine problem candidly would carry the planners beyond the strategic into the policy realm. Furthermore, the navy still insisted that even with the prospect of a two-ocean war, planning for the Pacific could not be essentially defensive because only offensive action could produce victory. In the end the joint planners reached a compromise that emphasized both the army's defensive mission to protect the United States and its possessions in the Pacific and the navy's offensive commitment to an eventual advance across the ocean.[27]

The army had to be thankful for small blessings. The imperial ambitions and international good intentions of the earlier part of the century had created a detachment called the United States Army Forces in China, consisting of one understrength infantry regiment, the 15th (minus a battalion which was in the

Philippines), plus auxiliary troops stationed mainly in the American settlement in Tientsin. If the army did not worry as much about these troops as about its forces in the Philippines, it was only because the garrison in China was smaller and because the implication of American policy commitment to a distant people did not run as deep in China as in the islands. But the China garrison was surely a pawn offered to the Japanese, and after the Japanese invasion of China acquired new momentum in 1937, the American army's presence was more than ever an anomaly as well as a sacrificial offering. The army had wanted to withdraw at least since the time of the Manchurian Incident, and it had been more than customarily assertive in quarreling with the contrary wishes of the State Department. Now the anxieties produced by Japan's latest advances permitted it to have its way. In 1938 its China garrison departed. Reflecting the still differing conceptions of the Navy Department, for the time being the Marine Corps garrison remained.[28]

IV

In the Philippines the U.S. government was encouraging a new variation on the theme of self-delusion about the defense of the islands. Under the gradual development of Philippine autonomy provided for by the Tydings-McDuffie Act, the Philippine government was to undertake construction of its own defense force. In 1935 General Douglas MacArthur approached the end of a one-year extension of his term as chief of staff of the army. No American soldier had closer ties to the Philippines, through family inheritance as well as through personal service there. Manuel Quezon, the president-elect of the Philippine Commonwealth, had come to know MacArthur well, and Quezon now approached him with an offer of appointment to a six-year term as Quezon's military adviser to supervise the building of the Philippine defense force. MacArthur accepted the task.

To many Americans Douglas MacArthur has come to seem the preeminent embodiment of American militarism. It is often forgotten that he was not the very model of a soldier but a headstrong individualist and throughout his army career a persistent maverick. Among his differences with prevailing army opinion in the period of World War I was his belief in the merits of a citizen soldiery, of part-time military training for citizens in time of peace to prepare them to take up arms in time of war; most army officers in those years preferred as thoroughly professional an army as they could get. The disagreement between MacArthur and most of his colleagues reached into fundamental issues that had shaped the whole history of the U.S. army and of American military thought, such as the appropriate organization of an army in a democracy. Such issues cannot be our concern here, but they were an important element in the background of MacArthur's new mission in the Philippines, where he believed he would be able to build an army according to his own lights. He proposed to give the islands the means to provide their own defense through a citizens army modeled on the military system of Switzerland.

MacArthur divided the Philippines into ten military areas, each of which was to give about 4,000 men five and a half months of basic military training annually. The training was to take place in 128 camps, each staffed by a training cadre of four officers and twelve enlisted men, initially chosen from the Philippine constabulary. A military academy modeled on West Point was to provide a permanent supply of officers. At first the citizens training camps were to produce units only of platoon size, but MacArthur expected to create regimental units within four or five years and to establish a citizens army of about 400,000 trained men organized in forty divisions by 1946, the year of independence. He hoped by that time also to have created a navy built around light, fast torpedo boats, a type of vessel whose development he now stimulated, and an air force of 250 planes. All this was to be accomplished within a budget of eight million dollars a year. Meanwhile the military training plan was to enhance immeasurably the literacy, health, and economic standards of the islands.[29]

MacArthur's confidence in his ability to do whatever he set out to do soon created a widespread impression in the United States that his Philippine citizens army was rapidly approaching reality. Some American pacifists seem to have feared that MacArthur was successfully militarizing the islands. The U.S. government itself tended to take an optimistic view of what MacArthur was achieving, for its own inability to defend the Philippines was a strong motivation for wishful thinking. President Quezon was impressed enough and hopeful enough to appoint MacArthur a field marshal in the Philippine Commonwealth army.

Unfortunately for the experiment in transplanting a Swiss-style popular army to the Orient, however, much depended on procuring American equipment for the Philippine army. MacArthur knew he would have to settle for obsolete stuff; mostly he did not get even that. With military budgets low and equipment short in the United States itself, MacArthur never received enough to form more than a shadow of the army planned.

Furthermore, the financial and other problems of the Philippine Commonwealth kept MacArthur from recruiting more than a shadow army. In late 1940 the regular Filipino army had only 468 officers and 3,697 men. The largest single unit, the 1st Infantry Regiment, had 286 enlisted men. Of the 6,416 officers and 120,000 enlisted men in the reserves, 50 percent of the officers had received no training at all; another 15 percent had received no field training; none had led a unit larger than a company; only some 17,000 enlisted men had received as much as five months' training in the preceding three years; and no unit as large as a battalion had ever assembled for training. After MacArthur reached the Philippines, relations between the United States and Japan moved rapidly toward their final crisis, but the Philippines remained undefended.[30]

V

When the European phase of World War II erupted in September 1939, the total strength of the U.S. army was slightly under 190,000 officers and men. This figure was up from the 165,000 of the years immediately preceding because of alarm over both Europe and the Pacific; but it was far below even the theoretical peacetime strength of 280,000 authorized by the National Defense Act of 1920. Supposedly the army was organized into four field armies and eleven divisions. But the field army commands hardly existed except in theory, corps headquarters were essentially administrative rather than tactical organizations, and only three of the nine infantry divisions possessed even a skeleton of divisional organization. Armament still remained mostly that of the First World War.

After the European war began, the most the army could hope for from initial administration proposals was an increase to 227,000 regulars, together with complete equipment for that force, for a strengthened National Guard of 235,000, and, in stockpiles, for 500,000 additional men who might be called in an emergency. Meanwhile fewer than 140,000 of the army's personnel were serving in the United States as a possible nucleus for a larger mobile force; the rest were scattered through the overseas possessions. Such an army had nowhere near the capacity to challenge either the German or the Japanese army separately, let alone simultaneously. The war in Europe convinced army leaders that they must husband their limited resources for the possibility of a German challenge first. The prospects for the Philippine garrison thus became even dimmer than before; an army draft of new joint war plans went so far as to deny that the Philippines and Guam any longer involved interests that the United States should acknowledge as vital.[31]

In January 1939 the Joint Planning Committee of the Joint Army-Navy Board had stated as an official basis for planning that the war in which the United States was now most likely to find itself engaged was one against an alliance of Germany, Italy, and Japan. Therefore during 1939 the joint planners initiated a new series of war plans to supplement Orange and the other color plans with projections for a war against not one enemy but a hostile coalition. The result was the preparation of five Rainbow plans contemplating various coalition war situations. Rainbow 1 prepared for a defensive struggle to guard the western hemisphere, while the other plans were concerned with several kinds of wars overseas.

Rainbow 2 and 3 both emphasized the Pacific front in a two-ocean war. Rainbow 2 called for the armed forces to "sustain the interests of the democratic powers in the Pacific, and defeat enemy forces in the Pacific." Rainbow 3 envisioned a vigorous offensive in the Pacific to "insure the protection of United States vital interests in the western Pacific by securing control there." Initially, Rainbow 2 and 3 were to have priority in preparation just after the defensive Rainbow 1, as their numerical designations imply. When the sequence was assigned, however, the planners were assuming that France and Great Britain would stand firm against the European Axis powers. The next year produced instead the collapse of France. Thereupon the joint planners shifted their attention from Rainbow 2 and 3, concentrating first on Rainbow 4, which provided for western hemisphere defense plus the dispatch of American forces wherever they might be needed in South America or the eastern Atlantic, and then on Rainbow 5, which emphasized transatlantic operations to defeat Germany and Italy in Europe. Rainbow 5 eventually became the basis of American operations in World War II; eventually also, on August 6, 1941, Rainbow 2 and 3 were explicitly cancelled by the Joint Board. Thus a vigorous war in the Pacific was specifically ruled out as long as Hitler survived in Europe. Even with rearmament, American forces in the Pacific might continue to have to subsist on thin gruel.[32]

The fall of France in June 1940 caused a shock that produced the first peacetime federal draft in the history of the United States and the mobilization of the National Guard. But during the remainder of 1940 and throughout 1941, the strengthening of the army proceeded much less rapidly than the alarm immediately following France's capitulation would have suggested. As Great Britain and China continued to resist Germany and Japan despite the French disaster, alarm subsided; and the president feared he might outrun public opinion if he pushed mobilization forward anything but cautiously. The army with some reluctance had to share the output of a gradual industrial mobilization with the British, to a limited extent with the Chinese, and after June 1941 with the Russians. In the fall of 1941 army equipment was still in such short supply that President Roosevelt suggested the remedy might be to reduce the army's size.

But at the same time the enlargement of American commitments around the world led the Army General Staff to prepare an estimate of the total strength that would be needed to defeat both the European Axis and Japan, based on the assumption that the country's commitments eventually would take the United States into a two-ocean war. The resulting "Victory Program" suggested requirements for an American army of 8,795,658, an estimate remarkably close to the total strength the army was in fact destined to achieve by 1945. Meanwhile, however, the existing army in December 1941 mustered only 1,638,086 men. Its thirty-six divisions included no more infantry divisions than had existed at least in outline as either regular army or National Guard divisions in peacetime; and only one division had yet achieved a full war footing, with eight expected to attain that status by February 1942. In view of these limitations, the army felt no more enthusiasm than before at the prospect of a Pacific war and still favored caution in U.S. dealings with the Japanese.[33]

In the months following September 1939 and again after the fall of France, the army at last articulated its attitude clearly and sought to impress it upon the civil government. The outbreak of the European war led President Roosevelt to establish direct and regular personal communication with his military chiefs, and regular meetings with the president demanded that the new chief of staff, General Marshall, move gradually away from the army's previous self-denial in policymaking.[34]

When Marshall took the oath of office as chief of staff on the day Germany invaded Poland, one of the first items of business he found waiting on his desk was a memorandum from the War Plans Division reminding him of the problem of the Philippines. Marshall evidently saw nothing useful to be done about the problem; he simply held the memorandum until the following spring. Similarly, when before the end of 1939 the president raised the Philippine issue with the new chief of staff, Marshall responded that reinforcement of the islands would remove from the United States the army's "few grains of seed corn." In February 1940 the navy suggested to Marshall an increase in the air garrison in the Philippines; but even had there been sufficient planes to make it worthwhile, which Marshall thought there were not, the chief of staff believed that reinforcement should be by a balanced force of all arms. He rejected the navy's proposal.

Meanwhile the president placed before the military chiefs the larger issue of British representations urging the United States, while Britain was busy in the

Atlantic, to take up the general burden of resisting Axis expansion in the Pacific. Once more Marshall pointed to the lack of weapons and equipment. Without matériel, he said, one could not fight, therefore there was nothing practical to do in a military way in the Far East. He urged restraint toward Japan.[35]

In response to the British representations as in everything else that concerned the Far East, the Philippines governed the army's reaction; if it could not defend the American islands, the army had little hope of doing larger things. But British pleas for a strong American policy in the Pacific continued, and the president was sufficiently receptive for the army to feel obliged to initiate a new comprehensive survey of the American military position around the world. The result was the Strong Memorandum of September 1940, which emerged first from the office of Brigadier General George V. Strong, Embick's successor as chief of the War Plans Division, but to which many pens eventually contributed, in the State and Navy departments as well as the War Department.

Still, the Strong Memorandum remained basically an army statement. It stressed the strategic perils that the collapse of France and possible Axis occupation of French North Africa posed for the western hemisphere, by way of the westward bulge of Africa and the eastward bulge of South America. As long as Britain held out, the perils did not seem immediate; but how long Britain would continue to fight appeared questionable. Relative safety, and continued time for American defense preparation, might persist even for a year after a British surrender. But the memorandum examined America's defenses and found them woefully inadequate. It indicated that the country would need all the time it could hope to get to strengthen those defenses, and it warned that all calculations about the time remaining, and thus about the United States' military safety, could be upset by a war with Japan. Such a war would compel the bulk of the U.S. fleet to fight in the Pacific, and an Axis assault in the Atlantic would thereby become a direct possibility. By 1940, therefore, the army not only feared its inability to defend the Philippines; it saw a war with Japan, allied with the European Axis, as a danger to the western hemisphere itself.[36]

In these circumstances the chief of naval operations, Admiral Harold R. Stark, suggested military consultations with the British, Canadians, and Dutch to explore coordinated action that might ease the perils. General Marshall acquiesced, but he did so with no enthusiasm because the army's strength was still so small that he preferred to build it further before running any risk of still more commitments. Stark went ahead anyway, and his preparations for consultations included his Plan Dog Memorandum. In this he urged that of four possible military courses—one of which was to direct American attention primarily toward Japan and only secondarily toward the Atlantic—the United States adopt course "D" (in military code language "dog"), to concentrate upon the Atlantic in cooperation with Britain; activity in the Pacific was to extend to additional consultations with the British and Dutch concerning the defense of Malaya and the East Indies. For the army this was still too much. The army read Stark's plan as still reflecting, despite its apparent turn toward the Atlantic, a navy bias for the Pacific, a suggestion that the United States go on seeking "diminution of the military power of Japan, with a view to retention of American economic and political interests in the Far East." Perhaps the army was now showing excessive caution; perhaps in its reaction to Plan Dog it was shying away from chimeras. But nothing could demonstrate more clearly its extreme distrust of Pacific entanglements and its emphatic aversion to provoking the Japanese.[37]

It was at this juncture that Marshall stated, "A serious commitment in the Pacific is just what Germany would like to see us undertake." Stark, disturbed that the army appeared to have read into Plan Dog the opposite of what its words said, insisted that if the United States became involved in the war described in Rainbow 3—the war for control of the western Pacific—it would not be because the American navy willed it so; nevertheless such a war might come. Marshall replied that every effort must be made to avoid that war; he insisted on a clear restatement of military priorities that would place transatlantic interests first. In the upshot, this novel advocacy of the army's views on policy secured what Marshall wanted. A joint memorandum of the secretaries of state, war, and navy affirmed the army's basic principle for the Pacific: "A decision not willingly to engage in any war against Japan."[38]

VI

But it was too late for that sort of army intervention in policymaking to mean much. President Roosevelt went his own way, and his way was one of increasingly tough resistance to Japanese aims in Asia and the Pacific, by means of economic sanctions as well as words, whatever the dangers of war. The War Department itself was divided, for despite the caution of the military men, Henry L. Stimson, the new civilian secretary of the department since July 1940, could fairly be called a hard-liner in his opinions on Japanese policy. Since his days as Hoover's secretary of state during the Manchurian crisis, he had believed in doing whatever must be done to thwart Japanese ambitions, and he no longer felt the confidence in the mere force of public opinion that had tempered his policies then.

Thus the army could find no escape from its eternal problem with the Philippines. As 1940 turned into 1941 and the strains in American-Japanese relations visibly approached the point of rupture, the army planners naturally thought about Hawaii too. Yet, although they still preferred to base Pacific strategy upon the Alaska-Hawaii-Panama triangle, they did not worry much over Hawaii. In April 1940 the president had insisted that the Pacific Fleet, normally operating from San Diego, should remain at Pearl Harbor, where he thought it would be a deterrent to the Japanese. The army too saw the fleet as a deterrent, and specifically as a guarantor that the Japanese could not attack, let alone seize, this apex of the strategic triangle.

The Philippines, in contrast, not only remained obviously vulnerable, but they lay close to the paths which, it was becoming increasingly clear, the Japanese wanted to take—southward through French Indochina to the Netherlands East Indies on the one hand and to British Malaya and Burma on the other. As the United States grew more hostile, Japan seemed likely to decide it could not maintain its southward course while leaving the Philippines untouched; for from the Japanese viewpoint, while at present the islands were militarily weak, if they remained in U.S. possession eventually they might well be turned into a springboard for attack. Especially after the Japanese occupation of Tonkin in the late summer of 1940 and the subsequent American embargo on iron and steel scrap, the Philippine Department commander, Major General George Grunert, kept up a steady flow of communications to the War Department warning that MacArthur's Philippine defense force was not the weapon that optimists hoped it was and pleading for reinforcements.[39]

At the beginning of this paper I said that after the direction of U.S. Pacific policy had been fatally set toward collision with Japan, the army at the last alternated between belated assertion of its misgivings and an effort, pathetic in retrospect, to wish the misgivings away. We have reached that penultimate stage of the army's role in U.S. relations with Japan.

In response to the pleas of General Grunert and others in the Philippines, the army did what it could for the islands. At the beginning of 1941 it moved to increase the Philippine Scouts, the Filipino detachment of the regular army, from 6,000 to 12,000; to increase the American infantry regiment in the islands from 1,100 to 1,653 and the two coast artillery regiments from 1,489 to a total of 2,954; to ship more artillery and seek more funds for defense construction. This was not much, and once decided upon it was slow in coming; but it was an earnest of intentions toward the Philippines that were beginning to change.[40]

Another possible step of at least moral significance would be to recall that magnificent and inspiring soldier, General Douglas MacArthur, into the active service of the United States as commanding officer of American army forces in the islands. At least as early as May 1941, and probably before, General Marshall suggested this notion to Secretary Stimson. In June MacArthur was informed of the idea; indeed he seems to have received hints of it well before Marshall's suggestion in May. On July 26, after Japan's occupation of southern Indochina and simultaneously with President Roosevelt's freezing of Japanese assets in the United States, Marshall named MacArthur commanding general, United States Army Forces in the Far East, and the War Department announced the calling of the Philippine Commonwealth armed forces into the service of the United States.[41]

The Philippine Department command passed into eclipse, and General Grunert, relieved of his post as head of it, returned to the United States in October. MacArthur meanwhile used his reappearance in U.S. service to lead the War Department toward consequences it had not altogether foreseen. He had no intention of pinning on his stars as an American general merely to lend glory to defeat. He regarded himself as a man of destiny, and never would he willingly submit to any military role other than that of victor. MacArthur believed the Philippines must be saved. He pronounced them "the Key that unlocks the door to the Pacific." He renewed Grunert's pleas for reinforcements with a power of persuasion and an influence in the War Department immensely greater than Grunert's. More than that, as several occasions in his career demonstrate, he was a man capable of believing what he wanted to believe however solid the evidence to the contrary, and he now chose to believe that if he defended them, the Philippines must be defensible.

MacArthur grew enthusiastic as he reviewed the Filipino regiments that he mobilized; he reported that his total force would soon be equivalent to an army of 200,000 men. Under both the timeworn Orange plans and Rainbow 5, caches of supplies for six months had been stored in Bataan, ready for a prolonged siege of the peninsula to deny Manila Bay to the Japanese. MacArthur now redistributed those supplies throughout Luzon and to the invasion beaches. He intended to hold the whole island—or at the very least, he said, to make the conquest of the Philippines a more expensive task than an invader would be willing to undertake. Ten days before Pearl Harbor he reported to Marshall in terms so confident that Marshall congratulated him on having his force "ready for any eventuality."[42]

Consistent with these developments but surprising in light of all previous army planning, on July 31, 1941 General Marshall had already announced to his immediate staff in Washington that "it was the policy of the United States to defend the Philippines." To say this within the secrecy of the General Staff, and apparently to mean it, did not reverse formal policy, to be sure; but it did reverse the conclusions of more than twenty years of strategic planning. And Marshall soon showed that he did mean it, to the extent at least of doing all he could to give MacArthur whatever he required to defend the islands. Presiding over what his biographer calls "the hungry table," where the armies of the United States, Great Britain, the Soviet Union, China, and lesser powers all sought to nourish themselves with supplies that were never adequate, Marshall nevertheless strained to divert resources to the Philippines. Soon he, like MacArthur, was saying that if Japan did not strike before mid-December, the Philippines might be held. We have few more dramatic instances of Douglas MacArthur's renowned ability to mesmerize both himself and others.[43]

Even MacArthur's hypnotic talents, however, probably could not have reversed the Orange plans had not the army and the government desperately wanted to escape their pessimistic conclusions about the Philippines. Although the U.S. government believed that Japan might consider the conquest of the Philippines a necessity to protect the flank of a southward advance, it desired to halt such an advance and therefore hoped that the Philippines might in fact be made to menace the Japanese flank. The islands obviously could not do so if they fell an easy conquest to the Japanese. But with all the potential might of the United States, could not a way be found, despite the lateness of the hour, to rescue the Philippines from easy conquest? Beyond that, could not a way be found to make the islands after all a dagger pointing toward the Japanese flank? Might not such an arming of the islands even deter new Japanese advances, hold the Japanese where they already stood, and permit the United States to turn its major energies to Europe without a war in the Pacific?

Not for the last time, American military planners now dared to believe that in air power they possessed an almost magical solvent for such otherwise impossible problems. Probably even more persuasive than MacArthur in urging Marshall that the Philippines could and should be held was Marshall's deputy chief of staff for air and chief of the Air Corps, Major General Henry H. Arnold. Arnold had been one of the army's first aviators and an associate and disciple of Billy Mitchell. He had helped concentrate the energies of the Army Air Corps in the 1930s upon the development above all else of a long-range heavy bomber, designed to realize the theories of Mitchell and the Italian Giulio Douhet that bombing the enemy's industrial and population centers would be decisive in future wars. In the twenties Mitchell had argued that the way to solve the strategic problem of the Philippines was to hold over Japan the threat of using air power against the crowded Japanese islands. By 1940 the efforts of the Army Air Corps to create an instrument to fulfill the Douhet-Mitchell theories had produced the B-17 Flying Fortress. In that year the War Plans Division of the General Staff proposed that henceforth "principal reliance would be placed on air power, not only to deter an attack on Luzon, but to defeat one if made." Arnold recommended that the Philippines be supplied with B-17s, which in moderate numbers he believed could destroy the convoys and landing ships of a Japanese attack and carry destruction to Japanese expeditions against other friendly territories, to Formosa, and perhaps to Japan itself.[44]

Marshall had become chief of staff determined to remedy what seemed to him the army's previous undue neglect of the air arm. Certainly in the past the army had tended to dismiss the air arm. But in 1940 and 1941, when dependable military aircraft were still new, it was apparently easy to go to excess in the opposite direction and place too much confidence in air power. To bear up under his heavy burdens Marshall probably had to grasp at hope somewhere, and in 1941 air power was still mysterious enough, and the long-range heavy bomber untested enough, to give color to hope.

Marshall scheduled the Philippines for heavy reinforcement in air strength. In August General Arnold informed the Far East Air Force, based in the Philippines, that it could expect four heavy bomber groups with a total of 272 planes, with 68 additional planes in reserve plus two pursuit groups of 130 planes each. Of 220 heavy bombers scheduled for production by February 1942, the General Staff allotted 165 to the Philippines. The B-17s would reach the islands under their own power. In September nine of them showed the way by flying from Hawaii to Manila via Midway, Wake, Guam, Port Moresby, and Port Darwin. Marshall instructed MacArthur to make arrangements for regular use of British airfields along this route.[45]

Secretary Stimson asserted that the bombers gave the United States the opportunity to "get back into [the] Islands in a way it hadn't been able to for twenty years." Major General Leonard T. Gerow, current chief of the War Plans Division, announced in October that the air and ground forces scheduled for quick delivery to the Philippines had changed "the entire picture in the Asiatic area." A Japanese movement toward Malaya and the Indies west of the Philippines would now expose itself to American air attack from the islands, and American air strength provided new abilities to counter Japanese movements in any other direction as well. Gerow hoped that reinforcement of the Philippines might "have a vital bearing on the course of the war as a whole." The War Plans Division suggested that the Rainbow plans might be revised to provide for army—that is, mainly air—support of the navy in raiding Japanese sea communications, destroying Japanese expeditionary forces, and assaulting the very bases and installations from which the Japanese might mount attacks.[46]

On November 15, 1941 General Marshall repeated similar conclusions in a press briefing for seven Washington correspondents. He now believed war with Japan was imminent, but his attitude was no longer one of resigned acquiescence in the consequent loss of American possessions. The United States was not only preparing to defend the Philippine islands; it anticipated using them as bases for an air offensive against the Japanese and against Japan itself. Already the build-up begun in the early fall had placed thirty-five B-17s in the Philippines. This was the largest concentration of heavy bomber strength anywhere in the world and many more planes were scheduled to go to the islands. If Japan chose war, the B-17s would bomb Japanese bases and destroy the "paper" cities of the Japanese home islands. This latter feat would be accomplished, despite the limited range of the B-17, by flying the Philippine-based bombers on to Vladivostok, whence the aircraft could shuttle back and forth to the Philippines by way of Japan. Soon the new B-24 Liberators would be available, able to fly higher than any Japanese interceptors; Marshall optimistically called them "super-Flying Fortresses." The army's air power might well be able to defeat Japan singlehandedly, without much need for the navy.[47]

MacArthur responded to the reinforcements with similar and predictable enthusiasm. "They are going to give us everything we have asked for," he told his chief of staff. He was not far from the truth. In November MacArthur had one-half of all heavy bombers (35) and one-sixth of all pursuit planes (175) stationed overseas. Marshall shifted troops and supplies from all over the United States to west coast ports as he gave the reinforcement of the Philippines top priority. He promised a National Guard division. He fretted that he lacked the necessary shipping to dispatch the men and matériel he had collected. He pleaded for ships so forcefully that the reinforcements scheduled for January were expected to arrive by mid-December instead.[48]

Major General Lewis H. Brereton, assigned to be MacArthur's air commander, feared the Philippine build-up was so impressive that the Japanese might decide they must strike before it could be completed, to nip it in the bud.[49] As events turned out, the Japanese did strike while many of the last supply increments which Marshall had strained to procure were still crated in their ships at sea. But it was not the Philippine build-up that determined Japan's timing.

Unlike the U.S. army, the Japanese at this juncture did not need to grasp at straws. They knew, as any rational observer not blinded by fears and hopes must have known, that the Philippine build-up was too little and too late. Although the B-17 was a good airplane and perhaps a better heavy bomber than any other then in service anywhere in the world, its capacities were not so far beyond those of aircraft tested elsewhere in combat to justify the hope that a nucleus of thirty-five could begin to halt Japan's southward advance and turn the war back upon the Japanese empire. On the ground General Grunert's estimates had always been more realistic than MacArthur's, and it was a pity that Grunert went home unheeded, for MacArthur's dispersal of supplies for a general defense of Luzon in the end handicapped the defenders of Bataan when the army had to revert to that old bastion of the Orange plans after all. When war came, MacArthur had some 29,000 U.S. troops and some 80,000 Filipinos, far from the 200,000 he had hoped to have by the end of the year and had pronounced adequate for his needs.[50]

VII

Yet the impression is difficult to escape that General Marshall, the War Department, and the General Staff knew at heart, even while they uttered them, that statements like those of Marshall's November 15 press briefing were far more wish than substance. At the last, such determinedly optimistic pronouncements alternated with army warnings that the United States should do all it could to avoid fighting Japan, because unpreparedness persisted and commitments elsewhere were more vital to the security of the United States.

On November 1, 1941 Secretary of State Cordell Hull, though he was an old man impatient with the Japanese, said he saw no use in further warnings to them "if we can't back them up," which the army and navy were disinclined to do. By this time Marshall of the army and Stark of the navy appeared to see eye to eye. Marshall said that both he and Stark were trying "to do all in our power here at home, with the State Department or otherwise, to try to delay this break to the last moment, because of our state of unpreparedness and because of our involvements in other parts of the world." On November 3 the chief of the War Plans Division reasserted that "the principal objective in the Far East is to keep Japan out of the war." On November 5 Marshall and Stark restated to the President that Germany was more dangerous than Japan and must be defeated first, that the United States should avoid war with Japan if possible, and that if war with Japan came it should be fought defensively until security across the Atlantic could be assured.[51]

By November 1941, of course, the chiefs of the army in Washington knew that war with Japan was almost certainly imminent no matter how much they might now urge upon the president and the State Department a Pacific Ocean policy of restraint. After all, it had been Lieutenant Colonel William F. Friedman, chief cryptanalyst of the War Department, who in August 1940 had broken the principal Japanese diplomatic code to make possible the MAGIC intercepts, and in November those intercepts bristled with the Japanese conviction that the time for negotiating with the United States had run out and a warlike crisis was at hand.[52]

To be sure, the army chiefs in Washington can with a degree of justice be accused of not sharing their knowledge of the MAGIC intercepts with their Pacific deputies as fully as they should have. But if their messages to the Pacific fudged the details, they did state categorically the central fact that war was imminent. The oft-repeated story of the intelligence failures preceding the Pearl Harbor attack does not belong properly in an account of the army's larger role in Japanese-American relations. Nevertheless, one close connection exists between the lapses that contributed to the surprise at Pearl Harbor and the thread of the present narrative. Although theoretical studies of a possible war in the Pacific had long suggested that Japan might open with a surprise attack on Hawaii, one important reason for the failure to see any indication of such an attack in the MAGIC intercepts of late 1941 seems to have been the military preoccupation with the Philippines which we have here surveyed. The army was confident that Hawaii was safe because of the presence of the Pacific Fleet—despite the army's tendency to play down the value of sea power as opposed to air power in other situations. But nobody in the army, except possibly Douglas MacArthur, felt any real confidence about the Philippines, and so it was where the army chiefs felt weakness—in the Philippines, not Hawaii—that they expected the blow to fall.

All in all, the record of the U.S. army in American-Japanese relations during the period 1931-41 must be counted a record of failure to perform adequately its duty to advise the government concerning the military limitations and other factors relevant to decisions regarding national policy. Perhaps, more precisely, the failure was one of the U.S. governmental system as it was constituted in the 1930s. Throughout the thirties, strategic studies of the Pacific increasingly confirmed the army and the Joint Board in their conviction that America's commitments to defend the Philippines could not be kept. The army, however, interpreted its obligation to remain apolitical so narrowly that it felt constrained to try to fulfill national policy, no matter how wide the gap between what it could actually do and what it was committed to do. It made no attempt to carry its misgivings effectively and systematically to the civil councils of government. The civil officers for their part did not feel obliged to confer regularly with the army. Through most of the 1930s the army was therefore a by-stander barely involved in the formulation of national policy toward the Far East.

While the army's apolitical tradition was the official and surely the principal reason for its willing acquiescence in a passive role, other army attitudes doubtless contributed to that result. Despite all the forebodings, through much of the 1930s the army displayed a kind of indifference to the Japanese, a tendency both to emphasize Japan's remoteness and to not take Japan quite seriously as a military power. The army certainly bore no active hostility to the Japanese; if the Japanese were willing to be friends with America, the army was prepared to reciprocate. Army emissaries who visited Japan and found themselves welcomed there before relations approached a crisis responded with gratification. As the head of one such mission wrote:

> I was *not* prepared for the warm cordiality shown by the high officials of the Japanese Army toward the mission and their ready and unreserved acceptance of my statement of the principal [friendly] purpose of the visit. This attitude was too real and hearty to have been a pose, and the impression gained on the early part of our visit was only more and more forcibly sustained as the inspection proceeded . . . without exception, the earlier impressions of true cordiality and friendliness became more and more accentuated as the inspections progressed.[53]

Even such friendly reports, however, tended to be colored by condescension toward the Japanese. American army officers seemingly could not escape a tendency to regard them as rather amusing little people, as in a further passage of the report just quoted: "The Japanese enthusiasm for group photographs was in frequent display and hardly any school or center visited is not now in possession of many photographs or snap shots of the mission."[54] This attitude of condescension permeated—and in part vitiated—more serious efforts to analyze Japanese military skills.

Too often American observers of the Japanese army saw only the stereotypes they had carried in their heads from the United States, not the real Japanese army. Japanese bayonet training, for example, was reported to be merely an adaptation of traditional Japanese techniques of the sword and therefore surely unsuited for combat against Western armies. As late as 1933, after the Japanese army had been blooded in Manchuria and at Shanghai, an American observer reported that "the fighting capacity of these troops appeared to be well below that of occidental troops. The staff work appeared to be fair, but the tactical handling of company and battalion commanders left much to be desired."[55] In 1934 an Army Air Corps observer of the Japanese air arm consigned it to perpetual inferiority: "The probabilities are that they will remain several years behind in many items of equipment because of their 'copyist' proclivities and their apparent lack of creative ability."[56] Military attachés in Tokyo were men whom the army tried to select for their knowledge of Japan and its language, and these informed, long-term observers tended to regard Japanese military qualities with greater apprehension; but their opinions did not penetrate throughout the American army.[57]

As relations between the two countries worsened, attitudes of condescension and amusement gradually became mixed with yet more grotesque fears that every Japanese encountered might be a person of sinister intent, specifically a spy. Extravagant alarms in the American popular press were echoed in the files of the Adjutant General's Office, where today the student can read the requests of army base commanders for advice about how to restrict the activities of Japanese visitors or exclude them altogether. The suspicion of Japanese nationals was, however, closely linked with and even somewhat undermined by the amusing-little-people stereotype. It is hard to take altogether seriously a staff report warning of spies in such terms as: "The Philippines are overrun with Japanese political spies—businessmen, sidewalk photographers and bicycle salesmen in every small town and hamlet. One is sure to see them."[58]

On a more reasoned level, still another element in the army's attitudes toward Japan in the 1930s was doubt whether the policies of distant Japan would carry the Japanese into an area where their interests and those of the United States would directly collide. The reports of the army's military attachés in Tokyo emphasized in more and more somber terms the domination of the military over the Japanese government and the consequent aggressive ambitions of that government. Through most of the 1930s, however, Japan's ambitions seemed to army observers to be focused upon China; and whatever the rhetoric of American policy might be, through most of the decade the army did not believe that the United States would be likely to go to war with Japan over China. To the extent that Japan's ambitions were perceived as running beyond China, the military attachés in Tokyo and the General Staff in Washington both persisted until very late in believing that Japan was more likely to attack the Soviet Union than territories over which the United States might go to war. This conviction, or hope, did not altogether die until the very eve of Pearl Harbor. Meanwhile a report dated November 1936 was characteristic of judgments maintained in the military attaché's office in Tokyo well into the late thirties. It stated that "the southward expansion project probably exists as an ill defined 'policy' of the Japanese government" but that Japanese ambitions to the south would not provide cause for much alarm in the foreseeable future. Here was yet another crosscurrent to dilute fears over the weakness of the army's Pacific defenses.[59]

A persistence of prejudices, assumptions, and mistaken judgments such as the ones coloring these intelligence estimates of the 1930s probably helps to account for the army's spasms of optimism as late as 1941—in particular for the readiness of otherwise reasonable officers such as General Marshall to profess the belief that a handful of B-17s could turn back the military might of Japan without much help from the navy. Through such professions of belief the army badly weakened its warnings when at last the circumstances of global war obliged it to inform the civil government of its fears about the distance between the commitments of national policy and the limits of American military power.

Professor Samuel P. Huntington, writing in *The Soldier and the State* of the functions of the military in advising the civil government about the relationship between policy and power, states that "before the United States entered the [Second World] War, the military did play their proper role in warning of the need for greater military force and urging a delay of conflict until that force could be achieved."[60] Would that it were so clearly thus; but the statement at best is only partially true of the army and the developing crisis with Japan. The U.S. army contributed to the tragedy of the war, not through the bellicose militarism of which popular opinion is so quick to accuse the professional soldier, but through failing to perform consistently its proper duty to acquaint the civil government with the military dimensions of national policy.

Of course, we have dealt here with relatively narrow matters. One issue this paper has ignored—for it is an issue the army itself was clearly right in ignoring—is whether the United States, regardless of its military weakness in the Pacific, was right in challenging Japan because it was strong enough to win a war with Japan in the long run and because there were larger principles involved. It is an issue different from those with which this paper has been concerned. To make sure that the civil government recognizes the relationship between its policy and its military power is the duty of the armed forces. To advise whether policy should nevertheless boldly overreach its military limits is not the province of the armed services. Nevertheless, narrow and even technical though the concerns of matching policy with power may sometimes be—as with the army's preoccupation with Philippine defense—it may well be wiser to base a nation's course of international action upon such grounds than upon bold risks for the sake of apparently lofty moral goals. When the limits of military power are neglected, "even morally correct decisions," to quote again the military attaché with whom we began, "might lead to more serious consequences than we would care to contemplate."

THE ROLE OF THE JAPANESE ARMY

Fujiwara Akira

Translated by Shumpei Okamoto

I

Ever since its establishment as a modern military force, the Japanese army had looked upon Russia as its primary potential enemy. It is true that the 1907 Imperial National Defense Policy, drawn up jointly by the chiefs of the Army and Navy General Staffs and accorded the imperial sanction, had designated Russia, the United States, and France, in that order, as potential enemies. This, however, was largely in response to the navy's aspirations to rival the sea power of the United States. As far as the army was concerned, its major interest was to prepare for another war with Russia and an advance on the Asian continent. Consequently, the army paid no serious attention to strategic planning vis-à-vis the United States. In 1918, when the Imperial National Defense Policy was amended to take into account the post-World War I international situation, Russia, the United States, and China, respectively, were designated as Japan's potential enemies. Meanwhile, the navy stepped up its operational preparations with a view to meeting the competition in naval armaments that was developing between Japan and the United States. The army followed suit to the extent of incorporating into its annual operations plans a stipulation that in the event of war with the United States, it would immediately attack Luzon in the Philippines in collaboration with the navy. In actuality, any cooperation was on paper only, for the army made no concrete preparations for an attack on the Philippines.

In 1923 the National Defense Policy was again revised and the order of Japan's potential enemies now became the United States, the Soviet Union, China.[1] The new Tactical Plan stated that the army, in cooperation with the navy, would occupy Guam as well as the Philippines. The following year the Army General Staff set up a Committee to Study Preparations for War against the United States.[2] And from 1925 on the army's annual operations plans incorporated increasingly detailed strategic programs for use in a conflict with America. The 1925 plan, for example, stipulated that immediately upon the outbreak of war an emergency force of one and a half divisions would invade Luzon from Lingayen and Lamon Bays and seize Manila with a view to occupying the Philippines before the United States main fleet could reach the islands.

Both the National Defense Policy and the Tactical Plan underwent further revision in 1936, though along the same lines. Great Britain was added to the list of potential enemies, following the United States, the Soviet Union, and China. The strategy in case of war with the United States was reaffirmed, and the following year it was decided that any attack on the Philippines would be undertaken by the 5th and 11th Divisions, which were also to prepare for operations against the Soviet Union.[3]

Despite this seeming concern with the United States, the army's primary focus remained on the Asian continent. It had reached the stage of formally adopting plans for war with the United States as one of Japan's potential enemies, but it continued to make no serious effort to implement them.

This peculiar situation was a result of the duality that existed in the formulation of Japanese defense policy. During the first Sino-Japanese War and the Russo-Japanese War the political control of the Satsuma-Chōshū leadership was still sufficiently strong to facilitate cooperation between the two services and give definite direction to Japan's war plans. After the Russo-Japanese War, however, as the genro began to play a less significant role on the political scene and the military became an increasingly important and relatively independent factor, interservice rivalry grew, producing a split in basic defense planning.

The rivalry was expressed annually in the process of budget formulation, when the army and navy would compete with one another for ever larger appropriations to assure a greater degree of preparedness vis-à-vis other nations. In assessing its needs, the navy early came to envisage the United States as Japan's rival for power and primary potential enemy in contrast to the army's casting Russia in that role. Since there existed no governmental machinery to coordinate and establish priorities between the demands of the two services, the decision makers attempted to accommodate both, without, however, coordinating their policies. Consequently, although in view of the limitations of Japan's naval power it was clearly irrational even to consider a policy based upon waging war simultaneously against a great land power, Russia, and a great naval power, the United States, such a policy was adopted. Nevertheless, as has been indicated, naval planning continued to concentrate on the United States, army planning on Russia, with each service paying only formal attention to the other's focus of concern. It was not until after 1939 that the army initiated somewhat more purposeful war plans in respect to the United States, and even these contemplated attacks only on the Philippines and Guam and contained no overall program for a conflict with the United States.

Yet even though the army gave little consideration to the United States, it played the decisive role in Japan's involvement in war with America. On the surface this seems hard to explain, the more so as the navy had always regarded the United States as its particular responsibility and as custom in Japan prohibited one of the armed services from meddling in the other's business.

The key to an understanding of the army's conduct would appear to lie in the situation in which it found itself in China. The army had been bogged down in a full-scale war in China for four years and had finally come to the conclusion that a way out might be found by occupying Southeast Asia. It knew that if it advanced far to the south, a clash with Great Britain was inevitable. But as late as 1940, when Japan moved into northern Indochina, the army, unlike the navy, believed that even if Japan occupied the Netherlands East Indies it could separate Great Britain and the United States and avoid fighting the latter. In the end, its calculations proved wrong and its southward advance led to war with America. While the army's actions were therefore crucial in bringing on a conflict with the United States, they were not so intended. From its point of view, Japan's southward advance was no more than a desperate effort to terminate the stalemate in China, and war with the United States, contrary to its plans, became an inevitable by-product of that effort.

II

From the beginning of its campaign in China, the army made serious mistakes. Although it continued to prepare for a conflict with the Soviet Union, it became deeply involved in the fighting in China so that it ran the risk of being engaged in a war on two fronts. Moreover, it compounded its difficulties by initiating the advance to the south. Such errors were in part the result of the army's tendency to react to each new situation as it developed instead of formulating an overall policy. But in addition, as one event followed another, the army's decisions were progressively influenced by men who advocated an aggressive policy. To appreciate this point more fully it is necessary to consider certain characteristics of the decision making process in the army and the outlook of the men who held key posts.

Every important decision made in the years before the outbreak of war in 1941 was reached through the same procedure. Plans were initiated and drafted in the middle echelons of the army. The initiators and drafters were field grade staff officers of major, lieutenant colonel, and colonel rank who occupied critical positions in the army central command—chief or staff member in the Operations Section (a branch of the Operations Division) of the Army General Staff and in the Military Affairs Section (a branch of the Military Affairs Bureau) of the Army Ministry. The plans were coordinated by the Army Ministry and the Army General Staff. Subsequently the opinions of the Navy Ministry and Navy General Staff were sought and, if necessary, adjustments were made. In the final step the document was presented to the Imperial Headquarters-Cabinet Liaison Conference to be sanctioned as supreme national policy.[4]

It was, therefore, the middle-echelon staff officers in important positions in the army central command who played the key role in the policymaking process. These men were part of the army elite. Some 25 to 30 percent of them had attended official military preparatory schools *(rikugun yōnen gakkō)*, where from the age of twelve or thirteen they had received a special professional and spiritual education designed to mold them for an army career. From school they had gone to the Army Academy, which up to about 1930 without exception produced all the regular army officers, graduating approximately five hundred annually.[5] After graduating from the academy, receiving their commissions, and undergoing several years' experience in regimental duties, about fifty officers each year passed the examination to enter the Army War College. It was these men who, after completing their course at the War College, were appointed to the important positions in the Army General Staff and the Army Ministry. Particularly vital posts, such as those in the Operations Division of the Army General Staff and the Military Affairs Bureau of the Army Ministry, were always assigned to the top graduates, who were then promoted within these agencies, serving briefly from time to time as staff officers in important field armies and regiments. Some of this group were also sent to Germany as students or military attachés, assignments which, for reasons that will become apparent later, served to enhance their prestige when they returned to take up their positions as staff officers at home.[6]

The type of education received by the staff officers played a vital part in determining their attitudes. A large proportion of them were men who had had seven years of specialized training, three in a military preparatory school and four in the Army Academy. Immersed in preparing for a military career, they had from a young age lived in surroundings totally isolated from ordinary society. As a consequence they had become peculiarly ingrown and narrow-minded, aware largely of their own point of view. Moreover their schooling had stressed the mission of the army officer and his special position in society, which bred in them the conviction that they were members of a chosen group. They had therefore developed a dogmatic self-confidence that also led them to disregard the views of outsiders and, indeed, the realities of a life other than their own.

Another important element in the education of army officers was a tendency to emphasize the importance of spiritual factors and neglect training in logical thinking. In part this was an outgrowth of the army's experience in the Sino-Japanese and Russo-Japanese wars, when it had been victorious despite its often inferior numerical and material position. Attributing these triumphs to the loyalty, unfailing belief in victory, and fighting spirit of the Japanese soldier, it concluded that the power of the spirit, not the rational calculation of relative strengths in troops and matériel, led to victory in war.

Yet spiritual factors alone had not determined Japan's success against the Chinese and Russian forces. In 1894 China was ruled by a feudalistic, foreign regime, whereas Japan had successfully transformed itself into a modern state. The Chinese army was not a national army but the private military organization of Li Hung-chang. It was only natural that there were great differences in the quality and morale of the armies of the two nations at such different stages of historical development. The same was true in the Russo-Japanese War. Russia was ruled by a despot whose government was threatened by revolutionary activities. Most of its forces at the Manchurian front were Siberian frontier guardsmen whose spirit and fighting condition were extremely low; furthermore, they too had been influenced by the tide of revolution at home.

Clearly, therefore, Japan's experience in these earlier wars could not apply directly to a struggle against a nation at an equal or higher level of modernization, whose armed forces differed little from those of Japan in the quality of their arms and training. In educating its officers, however, the Japanese army overlooked this obvious fact and continued to stress spiritual qualities rather than the element of rationality as the decisive factor in victory. The product was an officer who frequently manifested an irrational spiritualism along with his limited intellectual vision.

The army system of education also demanded that officers develop a fierce fighting spirit and the ability to act quickly and resolutely. Harking back once again to the Sino-Japanese and Russo-Japanese wars, when opponents often beat a hasty retreat despite a superior firing capacity and fewer casualties, the Japanese army instructed its cadets that offense was the best tactic under any circumstances without regard for the cost.[7]

A further aspect of military training that had a strong effect upon the staff officers in particular stemmed from the reorganization of the Japanese army in the nineteenth century. In the 1880s, partly under the influence of Major Klemens Wilhelm Jakob Meckel of the Prussian army,[8] Japan decided to build its army in accordance with the German system rather than the French, which had served as an earlier model. One of the concepts underlying the German system was the unusual importance attached to the role of staff officers, an idea that Japan applied to its training program. The Japanese Army Academy therefore instructed its cadets primarily in highly sophisticated strategies that might be useful to them as division commanders twenty or thirty years later rather than in the more immediately practical tactics needed to command a platoon or company. Similarly the War College placed its emphasis upon how to direct an army instead of upon things officers would need to know in the day-to-day command of a small military unit. Thus, the army's methods of education consistently prepared cadets to undertake responsibilities far greater than they would assume upon graduation and to plan operations far beyond their experience and abilities. Such methods were bound to reinforce their tendency to be excessively self-confident and to live in a world that seemed to have lost many of its connections with reality.

The increased importance attached to staff officers was, moreover, a direct cause of the phenomenon known as *gekokujō*—dominated by lower-echelon officers. In contrast to the British and American tradition, a Japanese commander rarely issued orders on the basis of his own independent judgment. Instead, his staff officers reached decisions for him and prepared directives for his signature. Indeed, it was considered a virtue for an army commander to entrust everything to staff officers and assume responsibility for the consequences of their action. The high reputation enjoyed by Ōyama Iwao, the commander of the Manchuria Army during the Russo-Japanese War, stemmed from his total dependence upon staff officers.

Such a tradition naturally fostered a sense of self-reliance among the staff officers and resulted frequently in an appeal for positive independent action. At such times staff officers of a stronger and more aggressive character tended to dominate. At the outbreak of the Manchurian Incident, for example, Kwantung Army staff officers Itagaki Seishirō and Ishiwara Kanji wielded more power than Army Commander Honjō Shigeru. In the Nomonhan Incident of 1939 Hattori Takushirō and Tsuji Masanobu, on the operations staff of the Kwantung Army, actually assumed positions of greater responsibility than that of Commander

Ueda Kenkichi. Yet those who took responsibility for the defeat and resigned were Ueda and his chief of staff, Isogai Rensuke. Hattori and Tsuji soon resumed their posts in the Army General Staff, which they still occupied at the beginning of the Pacific War.

The situation was, therefore, that from the end of the nineteenth century onward the influence of staff officers in the army constantly increased, until by the late 1930s they occupied the controlling positions in its decision making process. Consequently, the sense of superiority and the dogmatism, irrationality, and recklessness bred in them by their military training came to dominate policymaking within the army.

III

By 1941 the army had come to recognize that the United States and Great Britain could not be dealt with separately and that hostilities against one would inevitably involve the other. Thereafter, under the influence of the army elite, with staff officers continuing to play a pivotal role, the army became a stronger advocate of war with the United States than either the navy or the civilians in the government.

Nevertheless the army's attitude toward planning and preparing for such a war altered little. It made no real effort to evaluate the strength of the United States as an enemy. It was, in fact, poorly equipped to do so. It had concentrated its intelligence activities upon the Soviet Union, stationing the majority of its military attachés in Russia or in border states such as Poland that provided a vantage point for gathering information about the USSR. Those within the Army General Staff primarily concerned with the United States and Great Britain wielded relatively little influence, so that their judgments were seldom heeded. As a result the army's views of the United States tended to be highly superficial, in contrast to those of the navy, which had a number of officers with a discerning knowledge of the United States. Army attitudes were often permeated by wishful thinking. For example, it was believed that the American people, because of their liberalism and individualism, would not be able to endure a protracted war and that American soldiers could not withstand hardship and privation as well as Japanese soldiers.

The army's overriding idea was that the navy would bear the burden of the war in the Pacific. "Operations against the United States," it said, were "primarily the responsibility of the navy" and victory or defeat was to be determined "in an all-out battle between the main naval forces of the two nations; therefore operations involving the army would be limited."[9]

Indeed, the army frequently acted as though, as far as it was concerned, the question of how the war in the Pacific developed was a matter of little consequence. Far from giving any serious consideration to assisting the navy, the army entered into a competition with it for war supplies, attempting in particular to surpass the navy in obtaining such essentials as iron and oil. Moreover, in planning operations in the southern area the army insisted that its sphere of influence, in respect to both military operations and administration, should be in the region nearest the Asian mainland while the navy's should extend into the Pacific. After considerable dispute, a line of demarcation was drawn with the understanding that the army would be responsible for the territories to the west of it—the Philippines, North Borneo, Malaya, Sumatra, and Java—and the navy for those to the east—South Borneo, the Celebes, the Moluccas, the Lesser Sundas, New Guinea, and the Bismarcks.[10] Subsequently the army made limited preparations to take the offensive, but it never drew up any plans for the defense of the areas under its occupation or for the type of amphibious operations that took place later in the Pacific theater.

Basically the army's concept of the war was that it would attack the Philippines at the outset. At the same time it would occupy Southeast Asia and exploit the resources of the region, thereby enabling it to extricate itself from the morass in China. The army was so committed to the idea of leaving to the navy the conduct of the fighting against the United States and Great Britain that it even planned, after establishing control over Southeast Asia, to withdraw its forces there to Manchuria in anticipation of a conflict with the Soviet Union. The army hoped that the war in the Pacific could be brought to an end when Germany achieved its expected victory over Great Britain, as it believed that at that point the United States would lose its will to fight.

Beyond such vague considerations the army never made any attempt to estimate the outcome of a war with the United States. Like all else related to such a war, it regarded this as the navy's responsibility. So long as the navy failed to declare unequivocally that there was no chance of victory, the army saw no reason to concern itself with the problem. Ignoring everything but its own interests, it continued to implement its policies. Despite the persistent appeals of the navy and the highest civilian officials, the army stubbornly refused to give ground on the China issue, although its unwillingness to do so obviously made the chances of a conflict with the United States far more likely. The army argued that to consent to the American demands concerning the withdrawal of Japanese troops from China would mean a reversal of the policy Japan had been pursuing since 1931 and would totally nullify the sacrifices the nation had made. The army's attitude was perhaps best represented by Tōjō Hideki when he served as army minister in the last days of the Konoe cabinet in October 1941. In view of the enormous human and material sacrifices Japan had made on the Asian continent and in view of their dreams of establishing a Greater East Asia Coprosperity Sphere, the navy and civilian officials could not withstand the army's arguments for long. Thus the views of the army officers, unaccustomed to consider the needs of others or to calculate in realistic terms, prevailed in the end and the die was cast for war.

THE ROLE OF THE
UNITED STATES NAVY

Waldo H. Heinrichs, Jr.

The model navy in time of war is a solidary, purposeful organization. Cut loose from civilian impedimenta and constraints, it keeps at sea, lean, limber, prowling in search of the enemy. Commanders are proven leaders and skilled fighters. They serve a monolithic, strictly hierarchical organization. The chain of command is clear, orders are seldom questioned, and discussion is minimal. Civilian and technical support services ashore are deferential: what the fleet requires it must have, at once and at any cost. Command is flexible: units are shuffled, disbanded, or created according to need with scarce thought to parochial interests and sensitivities. Everything is subordinate to the higher purpose of achieving the most effective fighting force.

A peacetime navy is different. It is moored to civilian life. Doctrine, precedent, routine, and habit take hold. Money is scarce and cruising is costly. The navy may contend with a hypothetical enemy in annual maneuvers but its most pressing engagement is the battle of the budget. To get its share it must deal effectively with other elements of government and with influential public groups through the political process. The more it engages itself, the more it is bound by other institutions. Within the peacetime navy power is diffuse. Decision is a matter of reconciliation and coordination among diverse groups of specialists. Like a Machiavellian state each bureaucratic sub-unit maneuvers to enlarge its sphere or resist encroachment. Running the navy calls less for the qualities of a fighter than those of a politician and diplomat. Of course the navy plans, builds, and trains for war, but when it will come, with whom, and how it will be fought are matters of prediction and speculation. The impulse at the top is to play safe and rely exclusively neither on the weapons of the last war nor on new, untried ones. Always there is value in maintaining a common front and preserving and imparting traditions. Peacetime navies are conservative, complex institutions.

These peace and war characterizations represent the polarities of naval organization. In actuality navies stand somewhere in between. Given a stabilizing world situation they tend to become conservative, complex, and political; in a darkening world unitary, decisive, and adaptable. Needless to say, the character of government, the relative size of the nation, and the level of hostilities contemplated or experienced influence the range of movement between the polar concepts. Something of a wartime footing is conceivable in peacetime and something of a peacetime footing in war. But these considerations are irrelevant; the utility of this way of looking at navies lies not in describing how far a navy approximates one condition or the other but what happens as it moves from one to the other. In the case of movement from peace toward war, which is pertinent here, the expectation is that adjustment will be awkward and disjointed because inertia is great and control weak. The navy will change raggedly, some sub-units faster than others. Outdated weapons and doctrines will exist side-by-side with new ones. Movement to a war footing will be incremental.

Consideration of the United States navy and Japan, 1931-41, must take into account this process of piecemeal readjustment. The navy covered a good deal of the distance between a peacetime and a wartime footing in the decade but, as Pearl Harbor showed, still had further to go. Preparation for war was conducted in the midst of rapid expansion and an international situation that became more bewildering as it grew more menacing. In this light, changes in strategic thinking, building programs, fleet dispositions, and war plans—the relevant aspects here—should be viewed not as adaptations to new realities but as efforts to encompass new realities within an existing framework of compromise and consensus.

I

World War I provided the United States navy with neither an opportunity like Jutland nor a victory like Manila Bay to nourish its traditions, but only the dreary if vital duty of convoy protection. Then came postwar contraction and the Washington Conference, blasting hopes for naval supremacy. After this inauspicious start, the twenties improved. Once the reductions had been accomplished, Congress proved reliable: appropriations stayed in the three hundred millions, better than twice the figure of 1916. The navy learned to live with treaty limitations, however much it disapproved of them. In 1930 one officer conceded that the 5:3 ratio with Japan at least provided a "sporting chance" in case of a main fleet action in the western Pacific. Treaty limits allowed the building of two large aircraft carriers and the start of a third, with over fifty thousand tons to spare. Funds were sufficient to modernize most of the battleships and complete eighteen cruisers. Three hundred World War I destroyers provided an abundance of that type. Naval aviation enjoyed the period of its most rapid technological development. The navy of the twenties may not have prospered but it certainly did not starve.

In 1930-32 the navy's fortunes took a sharp dip. The London Treaty of 1930 undermined the 5:3 ratio and in 1932 President Hoover proposed reductions of one-fourth to one-third in most ship categories. Neither relatively nor absolutely did there appear any stopping point in disarmament; under the pressure of "pacifists" and budget cutters navies seemed to be shrinking virtually to the point of extinction. Furthermore, the London Naval Conference resulted in bitter disagreement among naval officers on the relative merits of 6-inch and 8-inch cruisers and testimony on the treaty showed the navy in professional disarray. So bitter was the feeling against those officers who supported the treaty that Admiral Charles F. Hughes refused to shake hands with his successor as chief of naval operations, Admiral William V. Pratt, at the transfer of command ceremony.[1] The depression brought further economy moves and Hoover dealt severely with the navy, even canceling the building of six destroyers for which funds had already been appropriated.[2] This cut was of particular concern because the fleet was aging. The World War I destroyers would soon be obsolete and were in any case too small for distant cruising. After the naval holiday the battleships would quickly reach replacement age and Congress did not seem likely to provide the large sums necessary to build these mastodons of the fleet. For all these reasons the navy entered the thirties in a bleak and sour mood.

Paradoxically, this interlude of pessimism and dissension was accompanied by rapid innovation. Admiral Pratt proved to be a strong chief of naval operations. His tenure and that of the commander Aircraft, Battle Force, Rear Admiral J. M. Reevès, witnessed rapid development of carrier tactics and the concept of the long-range carrier task force. The explanation is perhaps that when finances pinch hardest, pressure is strongest to assign priorities and anticipate and prepare for new realities in warfare.

With Franklin D. Roosevelt the budgetary outlook brightened. Within his first hundred days as president he allocated $238 million in supplementary emergency relief funds for the construction of thirty-two vessels over a three-year period, including two aircraft carriers, four light cruisers, and twenty destroyers. These were in addition to seventeen vessels already under construction. Appropriations thereafter rose virtually every year, doubling by 1937, and by the end of the decade not budgets but procurement and shipyard facilities were the limiting factors. The navy of the Roosevelt years grew at an accelerating rate. In this prospering condition, pressure to assign priorities was less; each year a little more money was available for each sub-unit. We might hypothesize that a starving bureaucracy is innovative, a fattening one complacent.

The navy of the thirties dispersed rather than centralized authority. Who should run it had long been an issue. On the one hand stood the military side of the navy, those whose professionalism revolved around the science of warfare and the exercise of command, who contended for increasing the power of the chief of naval operations. On the other hand was the civilian side, represented in the secretary of the navy, suspicious of militarism and determined not to place too much power in the hands of the uniformed head of the navy. With the secretary stood the bureaus responsible for building, maintaining, and manning the fleet, which were anxious to preserve their autonomy. In this everlasting quarrel President Roosevelt, who had been assistant secretary of the navy under Woodrow Wilson, decided against the professionals, allowing the chief of naval operations only a coordinating role over the bureaus.[3] This solution was entirely characteristic of Roosevelt, who preferred divided authority because it allowed him closer control of the bureaucracy and opened up options in his decision making.

The result was to leave the bureaus relatively autonomous. They were under the supervision of the secretary of the navy, but the incumbent from 1933 to 1939 was the elderly, failing Claude Swanson. His successor, Charles Edison, began bureau reorganization but suffered ill health and served only briefly. The president lacked time for detailed supervision. Not until the regime of Colonel Frank Knox and Undersecretary James Forrestal, beginning in the summer of 1940, did civilian leadership of the Navy Department exert itself vigorously. Meanwhile each bureau–Navigation (personnel), Engineering, Construction and Repair, Yards and Docks, Ordnance, and Aeronautics–jealously guarded its special "cognizance," controlled its share of the budget, and maintained its own relationship with Congress.[4] No central authority existed to rationalize their separate technical competencies or enforce priorities. Each bureau in effect had a veto on change.

Initiative for change would most likely come from the chief of naval operations. He had the responsibility for war readiness, access to decision makers, and the means of finding out what was happening in the world and planning against it. The War Plans Division and Office of Naval Intelligence were under his direct control. He and his war plans director were members of the national strategic planning agency of the time, the Joint Army-Navy Board. Subject to higher direction, he disposed the fleet, controlled ship movements, and planned maneuvers. He could set problems for the game board at the Naval War College and request special studies from the General Board. He maintained liaison with the State Department through his Central Division and represented the navy at high-level conferences involving military aspects of foreign policy. With Roosevelt the chiefs of naval operations had a friend in the White House. They often found him mysterious and ambivalent on policy and a busybody in matters they regarded as properly within their own sphere of competence. But having access to the president, they were not slow to put forward ideas they wanted to bring to his attention.

To suggest that the military side of the navy, headed up by the chief of naval operations, was the logical vehicle for change is not to imply that it was bristling for change. It was not receptive enough to new problems and ideas. War Plans found it hard to conceive of war except according to the Orange plan. Naval Intelligence played a minor role. It lacked prestige compared to command afloat and suffered a rapid turnover of directors.[5] Relations with "Mrs. Hull's" State Department were formal and distant. The course at the Naval War College was traditionalist, "a mixture of Clausewitz and salt water" served with an annual gaming of the Battle of Jutland, according to one critic.[6] The General Board had a limited scope of activity and operated under the predominant influence of senior officers on the verge of retirement who were out of touch with new weapons and tactics.[7]

Selection for high command under Roosevelt depended on qualities other than forceful leadership and innovative disposition. It followed from exposure to the technical, civilian, political side of the naval establishment. Admirals William D. Leahy and Harold R. Stark were selections for chief of naval operations whom the president knew personally. The latter had been captain of the naval yacht *Dolphin* which cruised congressmen on the Potomac when Roosevelt was assistant secretary of the navy. Exposure to the civilian leadership of the department and to congressmen came by way of tours of duty under the secretary of the navy, in positions a line officer might hold without becoming trapped in a technical specialty. Thus Admirals Leahy, Richardson, Bloch, Kimmel, and Stark served as budget officer, judge advocate general, or chief or assistant chief of ordnance or navigation. The successful products of these experiences had smoothness and political savoir faire. Leahy, for example, was regarded in the navy as a "shrewd operator." Admiral Ernest J. King, on the other hand, represented an assertive branch of the service, aviation, and took no pains to please anyone. After a tour as commander Aircraft, Battle Force he was shunted aside to the General Board, to be rescued therefrom only by the imminence of war. Chiefs of Naval Operations Standley, Leahy, and Stark had in common the virtue of being widely acceptable in the naval establishment and skilled at coordination and mediation. They were not inclined to "rock the boat."[8]

The Roosevelt navy was a growth enterprise. It felt it required managers and policy that would avoid costly errors, keep naval opinion together, prevent public brawls, and make the most of favoring winds in the executive and legislative branches.

II

Occupational grouping and world view are not necessarily related but often in subtle ways influence each other. It may well be the case that an external policy conception governs a bureaucracy's definition of its mission, as bureaucracy will always claim. But it may also be the case that bureaucratic needs influence the definition of policy, especially where the situation is complex and policy hazy. Thus with the navy and American foreign policy. The world of the twenties and early thirties from the naval point of view presented some areas of interest and some of indifference. To consider the western hemisphere as a region of paramount naval interest would have been to claim little of active importance. War with Britain was virtually inconceivable. So long as the British fleet guarded the Channel, the North Sea, and the Atlantic, no European power posed a menace. Japan's very insistence on an Asian Monroe Doctrine implied acceptance of American supremacy in the eastern Pacific. Protecting the citadel, American home territory, might be accomplished by light forces and aircraft and not require a great battle line. Just as the Japanese navy needed a "blue water" mission to the south to justify a larger allocation of the nation's resources, so the United States navy needed a mission outside the hemisphere to remain a big navy. Thus world powerhood required a first-class navy and a first-class navy required world powerhood. The American navy conceived its mission to lie in the defense of American Far Eastern interests.

The basic question in American Far Eastern policy was whether the United States had sufficiently important interests to justify the use of force. The president was not prepared to answer that question and Secretary Hull's resonant generalities offered little guidance. The navy accepted that government set policy but, lacking direction, felt impelled itself to search for "inherent" interests and assign values.[9] The result was a medley of turn-of-the-century themes, which is not surprising in view of the fact that the leaders of the navy in the thirties were Annapolis graduates of that era. Hart, Leahy, Yarnell, and Bloch, for example, had served in the Spanish-American War. Imperial visions of their junior years inspired by Alfred T. Mahan and Theodore Roosevelt hardened into axioms of their senior years.

The most obvious interest was the protection of the Philippines. That responsibility would not necessarily end with the islands' independence, and neither would the need for a base there to support other interests. One of these was the China trade. No naval officer needed to be taught Mahan's equation of seaborne commerce, sea power, and national greatness. The myth of the China market still lived: on the eve of the Sino-Japanese War this vast potential seemed almost ready to be tapped as Chiang Kai-shek stabilized China.[10] In any case, the United States had a historic duty to uphold the Open Door. Furthermore, with the integrity of China now a treaty obligation, it had a stake in maintaining the sanctity of treaties. The United States also shared the white man's civilizing mission. It had "removed the Filipinos from the jungle"[11] and set them on the road to independence, but Britain, France, and the Netherlands retained responsibilities and the United States should avoid weakening their efforts at "restraining radical social and political changes in the lesser developed races."[12] At Manila in 1941 Admiral Thomas Hart wrote that "the white man should continue his hold and his influence in this area."[13]

Overarching particular interests was the idea of the United States as a Far Eastern power. Indeed, to some that role was the outstanding manifestation of America's status as a world power. The United States exerted a stabilizing influence on the Far East: "her voice is heard and her counsels heeded."[14] Like it or not, the nation could not divest itself of the "dangers and responsibilities of a first class power," Admiral H.E. Yarnell warned.[15] Withdrawal from the Far East would upset the balance of power there, creating another Balkan situation, and weaken American prestige in Oriental eyes, with detriment to commerce and investments. The particular mix of interests perceived varied from officer to officer and from one period of time to another, but the idea of the United States as a Far Eastern power remained constant.

There were dissenters, it is true. Admiral Montgomery Taylor, commander of the Asiatic Fleet during the Manchurian crisis, doubted the ability of the Chinese to create a viable nation and the willingness of the United States to assist them. China was "up to her old tricks trying to get someone, preferably the U.S., to fight her battles for her."[16] Taylor's successor, Admiral F. B. Upham, questioned the importance of the China market and the ability of Americans to compete successfully in it. Any gain in the Far East hardly justified the cost of maintaining a remote and vulnerable position there. The nation should avoid such "futile dissipation of effort" and concentrate on its zone of paramount importance, the western hemisphere.[17] Taylor and Upham were exceptions, however. Generally naval officers assigned a high value to the interests and role of the United States in the Far East, higher it seems than did American diplomats. The difference was one of bureaucratic perspective: the navy needed to find the Far East important.

Lying athwart American interests lay the shadow of Japan, the navy's chief hypothetical enemy of the interwar period. Hypothetical is the wrong word if taken to mean "conceivable": the navy regarded war with Japan as practically inevitable some day. The enemy on the game board at the Naval War College was almost always Orange (Japan). Red (Britain) was substituted every now and then, one graduate recalled, "just to be able to say that we weren't always fighting the Orange Fleet."[18] The navy's image was of an enemy poor in resources, overpopulated, historically expansionist, imbued with a warrior tradition, and, in the thirties, ruled by a fanatical military clique. The direction, timing, and nature of Japanese expansion would depend on circumstances, but the plan was ultimate domination of eastern Asia and the western Pacific. This image attributed to the Japanese confidence not insecurity, calculation not indecision, consensus not factionalism. The United States confronted a monolithic, aggressive Japan, and each event of the thirties—Manchuria, Shanghai, Jehol, Hopei, Marco Polo Bridge, and the southward advance— reinforced that image. For the United States the navy had the reverse image, that of peaceful guardian of the status quo.

Of course not every officer shared this simplistic view. Admiral Pratt, who was brought out of retirement in 1941 as an adviser and had several talks with his old friend Ambassador Nomura Kichisaburō, pictured Japan in that year as torn with dissension and anxious to avoid an Axis commitment to war. The Japanese, he said, were a strange people: "Intensely loyal to their friends—they conciliate like an elephant. Forced too far they would bang their heads against the wall."[19] Furthermore, naval intelligence presented a more complicated picture. The naval attachés in Tokyo and Peking and the staff of the Asiatic Fleet shared the information and analyses available in the American embassies and consulates and in the colonies of foreign diplomats, correspondents, and businessmen in the capitals and port cities, and their reports reflected some of the dualities and contradictions in Japanese decision making. One finds depicted, for example, the moderate-radical dichotomy that framed the analysis of Ambassador Grew and army-navy contention over routes of advance and the Axis commitment. But forces inhibiting expansion—industrialists, elder statesmen, the financial strain of the China War, fear of American retaliation—always seemed to be overtaken by events. The view from the Whangpoo in 1932 or 1937, with shells whizzing overhead, was bound to contradict that from the quiet embassy compound in Tokyo. The constant reshuffling of high command in the American navy made it difficult for any single officer to devise a pattern of events, and the consistently low value attached to intelligence work by navy "generalists" did not incline them to try. The result was a lack of any alternative framework for viewing Japan to that of monolithic expansionism.

Information respecting the Japanese navy was scarce because of stringent Japanese security precautions. Unthinkable in the thirties would have been the experience of one naval attaché in the twenties who talked freely with pilots at Kasumigaura, rode in their planes, and watched a bombing demonstration.[20] Visits of the Asiatic Fleet commander to Tokyo involved exchange of formal amenities followed by more relaxed occasions plentifully supplied with hot sake, but the cordiality was evanescent. Relations between American commanders and their Japanese opposites at Shanghai were correct and businesslike but, in the circumstances, distinctly official. During the war in China Japanese light forces were much in evidence and were closely scrutinized. The crews seemed hardy and proficient and the newer vessels formidable.[21] From the Asiatic command

Yarnell wrote enviously of the rigorous training Japanese seamen received in rough northern waters.[22] Popular stereotypes of the Japanese as dissimulating, imitative, and lacking initiative had some currency. Intense pride in American naval aviation perhaps accounts for a tendency to belittle the Japanese counterpart. On the whole, however, the American navy had professional respect for its most probable enemy, conceiving him a well-trained, forehanded, determined, and disciplined foe.

These conceptions of the American role in the Far East and the threat of Japan firmly established the sequence and locus of events in case of war between the two nations. War would arise from a clash of interests in the Far East and open with a Japanese attack on the American strategic outpost, the Philippines. Unless reinforced, capture of the islands was only a matter of time. Once they had been captured, Japan would not be likely to press its challenge into America's own sphere, the eastern Pacific. Having secured its objective of dominating the Far East and western Pacific, it would hold fast. Such an outcome the United States would not accept. Rather, it would thrust sufficient strength into the western Pacific to relieve the Philippines or recapture them and then move on to bring Japan to terms by blockade. Thus in the opening round Japan was cast in the offensive role and the United States in the defensive, but thereafter the roles would be reversed. These had been the basic assumptions of army-navy strategic thinking since before World War I, as embodied in the Orange plan and its various modifications.

The war would be primarily a naval one. As the plan stood in 1931, the fleet would concentrate at the main outlying bastion of Hawaii for a "steamroller"[23] advance across the central Pacific, taking and making such bases in the Japanese Mandates as needed. In grand array it would march through the Marshalls and Carolines until the Japanese were forced to commit their main fleet to a decisive engagement. The rest would be anticlimactic. The plan flowed smoothly from its premises and the geographical determinants of the Pacific. Much of it found its way into the real war after the Battle of Midway. In the thirties, however, it simply would not work, given the existing strengths of the two fleets and the great distance that had to be covered under constant attritional attack. In 1940 Admiral James O. Richardson, confronted with the disturbing prospect of having to put the Orange plan in motion at any moment as commander-in-chief of the fleet, explained the navy's devotion to it:

> It is the general conception that the Plan had its inception primarily in the desirability of having a guiding directive for the development of the Naval Establishment to meet any international situation that might be thrust upon it. It is my belief that the impracticalities of the ORANGE Plan, in the absence of a better one, have been overlooked in order that the Department might have for budget purposes and presentation to Congress the maximum justification for the necessary enlargement of the Navy.[24]

Richardson had been budget officer of the navy in 1934-35. The War Plan Orange of the thirties was not a sailing plan; it was a building plan.

III

Three interrelated principles governed the development of the United States navy in the first half of the decade under consideration. The first of these was War Plan Orange, which provided the rationale for a big navy. The second was the concept of the "balanced fleet," which served as the best available compromise of competing perspectives and interests within the navy. The third was the concept of the "treaty navy," which provided public justification for naval growth.

At its most practical the "balanced fleet" was a device to secure orderly growth by rationing funds among the various categories of ships. Thus submariners, aviators, battleship enthusiasts, and all those who attached themselves for one reason or another to a particular kind of ship or weapon could be assured of a share in the navy's future. Striking a balance was made easier by the model national navy prescribed in the Washington-London treaty system. The Orange plan laid down further guidelines. It set forth scouting, raiding, and commerce destruction missions that provided justification for development of several ship types, among them the heavy cruiser, a vessel with the speed to escape a battleship, guns to destroy anything smaller than a battleship, and endurance to cruise to the China Sea and back. Foreign ship characteristics established a third criterion. The Japanese met American light cruisers of the *Omaha* class with their *Mogami* class, to which the Americans replied with the *Brooklyn* class. Altogether, the "balanced fleet" idea provided the navy a measure of internal harmony at the cost of flexibility in restructuring the fleet.

However the balance was struck, the battleship remained the weightiest element. It had so many built-in advantages over other fleet types. Battleships were still the main index of naval power and the backbone of foreign navies. Naval doctrine always dictated that fleets concentrate upon the most powerful element, which delivered the decisive punch in the inevitable main fleet engagement. Pictures of the battle line appeared regularly in movie halls and Sunday picture supplements, and the sight of those burly ships stretching to the horizon gave Americans a lively sense of security which the navy was pleased to cultivate. They provided "tangible" evidence of national strength, according to Representative Carl Vinson, chairman of the House Naval Affairs Committee.[25] Battleships also represented great and continuing investments. Admiral Pratt urged that they be modernized so that Congress would not have to face replacing them wholesale, a wise strategy perhaps, but one that increased the navy's stake in the vessels.[26] High command in the navy generally went to officers who had been closely connected with battleships and gunnery, such as Admirals Leahy and Stark. Indeed, command of a battleship was regarded as critical in attaining flag rank. Those who reached the top were not inclined to disparage their specialty. The battleship had a secure place in the heart of the American navy.

The aircraft carrier would not come into its own as the main striking force of the fleet until well into World War II. In the thirties naval aviation remained a distinctly auxiliary service, charged with scouting, long-range patrol, raiding, and protection of the battle line.[27] Given the variety of assignments, the number of aircraft available for attack carrier duty was a small proportion of the total. A proposal to place all planes under one admiral reporting directly to the commander-in-chief of the fleet was rejected, so they remained divided among the Battle and Scouting Force commanders.[28] The fast carrier task force had emerged but it involved only one or two units with screen.[29] In 1939 Admiral King gathered four carriers and evolved tactics for a multi-carrier group and a multi-group task force but the idea did not take hold; the Battle Force commander refused to assign cruisers and destroyers long enough for them to learn the complex maneuvers.[30] In 1933 naval aviation lost its brilliant salesman, Rear Admiral W. A. Moffett, who was killed in a dirigible crash. But the very confidence aviation zealots displayed in their weapon tended to defeat the argument for a large number of carriers, while at the same time their admission of the vulnerability of carriers encouraged the spending of available sums on more light, battle-line carriers rather than fewer large attack carriers.[31] Having made a strong case for the small carrier before Congress, Admiral Moffett pointed out, it would be embarrassing for the navy to reverse itself and ask for money for a large one.[32]

Naval aviation was an exceedingly costly initial investment, requiring extensive training, technical, and support facilities, as well as inevitable wastage in the development of a variety of new airplanes. To place it in the central position before the war would have required a radical restructuring of the navy that leading admirals were not disposed to attempt. Rear Admiral Leahy put the case within the framework of the "balanced fleet" in 1934 when he said:

> It would seem to me that in view of the necessity for economy in total naval expenditures that an aviation branch of the size indicated will bring about an unbalanced situation in the entire Navy and will result in an expenditure for naval aviation out of proportion in view of the need for funds to support the other branches. . . .[33]

The "treaty navy" concept in the thirties proved to be a magic formula for securing appropriations, attesting to the wisdom of Admiral Pratt in cooperating with the administration to secure an agreement at London in 1930 in spite of the unfavorable ratio. The climate of opinion in America was profoundly distrustful of war machines and foreign entanglements, making it difficult to justify requests for naval increases. The Washington and London treaties, by outlawing building above certain limits, cast an aura of legitimacy over building within limits as well as building for replacement. Since the navy was short of its upper limits in most categories, it had the best possible justification for budget requests founded on a "treaty navy." At the same time, it felt a strong sense of urgency to keep up to treaty limits because it anticipated on the basis of painful past experience that existing ships, not those on the ways or in blueprints, would provide the basis for negotiation at the next naval conference.

These three mutually dependent concepts—the Orange plan, the "balanced fleet," and the "treaty navy"—provided a satisfactory bureaucratic strategy for resolving internal differences and securing external support. In the 1931-37 period world conditions, though disturbing, did not seem to require a reappraisal. The strategy was therefore governing in the events bearing on Japanese-American relations in which the navy played a significant role. These were the fleet concentration in the Pacific in 1932, the 1933 and 1934 naval building programs, the decision for Philippine independence, and the London Naval Conference of 1935.

The significance of the navy as a deterrent in the Manchurian crisis should not be exaggerated. On January 31, 1932 the president dispatched the Asiatic Fleet from Manila to Shanghai to protect American nationals during the fighting in that city. The Asiatic Fleet had fleet status and a four-star admiral only to keep up appearances among foreign navies on the China station. The only ship in the fleet that made "face" for the Americans was the heavy cruiser *Houston*, and consideration was being given to replacing her with the ancient, coal-burning *Rochester*.[34] Admiral Taylor, the fleet commander, saw his role as that of "innocent bystander."[35] Admiral Pratt, the chief of naval operations, urged the Japanese to appoint his friend Admiral Nomura to the Shanghai command.[36] Nomura was appointed and he and Taylor cooperated well. The following year, on a visit to Japan, Taylor received gift swords from General Araki Sadao and Admirals Shimada Shigetarō and Nomura.[37] Insofar as "signals" were exchanged in this episode, the message would seem to have been that both navies were determined not to let the Shanghai Incident embroil them with each other.

The famous fleet concentration in 1932 should be kept in proportion as well. It was not, as Secretary of State Stimson later recalled, a concentration at Hawaii, the Orange plan jumping-off point. The fleet was not ready to jump anywhere. It did visit Hawaii, as scheduled, for a critique after maneuvers, but then returned to the west coast. The concentration lay in then retaining the Scouting Force, much the lesser half of the fleet, on the west coast instead of sending it home to the east coast. This occurred after the May 15 Incident in Japan, presumably as a warning to Japanese army and navy fanatics. It undoubtedly demonstrated that the United States felt sufficiently confident about Atlantic security to keep the entire fleet together in the Pacific for an extended period.[38] But it served other purposes as well, having little immediate relation to Japan. By cooperating fully with Stimson, Pratt showed the value of the navy as the strong right arm of American diplomacy, just at the moment when the navy was agonizing over its finances. Furthermore, according to Admiral Leahy, who was commander Destroyers, Scouting Force at the time, the concentration enabled Pratt to pry the Scouting Force loose from the east coast shipyards for extended training with the main fleet.[39] For Japan there was a hint, not a demonstration, of force; for the navy, some satisfying bureaucratic rewards.

Legislation of 1933 and 1934 funded or authorized new tonnage for the navy not far from doubling that in existence, a sharp increase that could not fail to have an impact on Japanese-American relations. Undoubtedly the favorable attitude of the congressional leadership contributed to the result. Representative Carl Vinson exerted powerful influence as chairman of the House Naval Affairs Committee. Dedicated to building up the navy, he was chiefly responsible for the Vinson-Trammell Act of 1934 that provided blanket authorization for ship construction and replacement up to treaty limits. Congressional agreement on the necessary size of the navy made the task of securing money to build the ships much easier, a task efficiently managed by another friend of the navy, Representative William Umstead, chairman of the Navy Subcommittee of the

House Appropriations Committee. Also, Manchuria, Jehol, and Japan's withdrawal from the League of Nations created anxiety about Japan's course that undoubtedly contributed to favorable action on naval increases. But these factors do not adequately explain the timing of the increases. Legislation similar to the Vinson-Trammell Act failed to secure executive approval in 1932; the passage of the act in March 1934 came at a moment of relative quiescence in the Far East.

The new element in 1933-34 was President Roosevelt, whose attitudes on government spending and military power differed from those of his predecessor. On becoming president he was somewhat dismayed to learn that the American navy "was and probably is actually inferior to the Japanese Navy."[40] This was true in light cruisers, destroyers, and submarines. By steady, yearly increments Japan had built these categories almost to treaty limits, while the American navy still depended on World War I vintage ships. Though by no means set on a course of opposition to Japan, the president did not wish to be placed in a position where such a program would be impossible for want of strength. Accordingly, he offered no opposition to pressures for navy increases.

The navy moved energetically to take advantage of the opportunity. In 1933 Rear Admiral Emory S. Land, chief of the Bureau of Construction and Repair, lobbied to include ships and planes among public works projects designated for emergency relief funds and then flew to Hyde Park with Admiral Pratt, chief of naval operations, to win an allocation of $238 million from the president.[41] It was easier to get money for new ships from relief funds than directly from Congress, as Secretary of the Navy Swanson noted in a letter to Roosevelt: "Perhaps it would be better to obtain these funds from PWA [Public Works Administration] (thus giving quick employment) because it is possible . . . that a larger sum will be desirable than could be obtained in the appropriation bill. . . ."[42] In appealing for relief allocations the navy was ready with figures showing how ship construction was a particularly valuable recovery measure because so much of the cost went into labor. It could also point out that spending would spread over shipyards in many states since most of the planned construction was in light ships. A year earlier the navy had been the right arm of American diplomacy; now it was the instrument of industrial recovery.

The decision for eventual independence of the Philippines occurred while the military was awakening to somber new realities about the American position in the Far East, among them the fact that air power laid open the Philippines to attack from Formosa. In January 1933 the army, whose garrison had steadily dwindled, decided it could not hold Manila longer than fifteen days after war began and would withdraw to Bataan and Corregidor. The navy, which had reluctantly come to accept Cavite, near Manila, as its Philippine base rather than Subic Bay, now had lost its perch again and would have to seek shelter under army guns at Mariveles at the tip of Bataan peninsula. The best American forces could do would be to hold the entrance of Manila Bay until relief arrived.[43] But now the progress of the main fleet westward was measured in years not weeks or months. First it would have to seize a base at Wotje in the Marshalls, still over a thousand miles from its goal.[44] Meanwhile the Philippines were bound to fall. In March 1934 the army and navy commanders at Manila wrote a joint letter to their superiors saying that they considered their Orange plan missions impossible. The United States would have to build up militarily in the Philippines or get out.[45]

The perspective from Washington was different. In all discussions of the 1933-36 period in the War Plans Division, the General Board, and the Joint Board, the navy invariably reaffirmed its traditional position. The battle of the Philippines, it was held, should not be thought of in isolation. Evident determination to hold fast in the islands would force Japan to undertake a major invasion in case of war, diverting its forces from defense against the American main thrust, the fleet's westward advance. Thus a stand in the Philippines, regardless of outcome, would be a contribution to eventual victory. Within this framework, the navy was prepared to grant some latitude to the Asiatic Fleet commander. Though disapproving his proposal to dispatch Asiatic surface forces eastward to join the main fleet, in effect to escape destruction, the navy enlarged the scope of his mission to include, besides the preferable task of defending Luzon, diversionary operations against Japanese commerce elsewhere. In other words, he might contemplate some other outcome than going down with his ship in Lingayen Gulf. However, the army thesis that the United States should withdraw to the eastern Pacific was unacceptable. The navy insisted on retaining the original Orange plan concept of war in the western Pacific in defense of American Far Eastern interests and by way of its veto in the Joint Board was able to prevail.[46]

Lying behind these strategic disputes was the basic question of the future United States position in the Far East in the light of prospective Philippine independence. In April 1935 the secretary of the navy urged the president to set aside naval base sites for American use after independence, as authorized in the Tydings-McDuffie Act. The navy, he wrote, maintained that the United States must continue to hold a fortified base in the islands unless "it is definitely and finally determined not to support, under any circumstances, now or in the future, the existing Far Eastern policies or to be a factor in Western Pacific developments." The president was not prepared to accept such unequivocal options. He was dubious about the defensibility of any site and determined to retain no military commitment after independence. In case independence did not eventuate (presumably he had in mind continuation of commonwealth status by mutual consent), it was impossible to foresee what defense arrangements might be advisable. Reservation of base sites now, before conclusion of the London Naval Conference, would suggest lack of support for the naval treaty system. In any case, he did not construe the act to require an immediate decision and called on the navy for further study of possible sites.[47]

The navy refused to be discouraged by the president's doubts and indecision. The lack of national policy on the question did not preclude consideration of what might happen. Rear Admiral J. W. Greenslade of the General Board drew up two sets of variables, the first consisting of all possible future relationships between the Philippines and the United States, from independence to retention of American sovereignty, and the second all possible postures of the United States in relation to the Far East, from abandonment to maintenance of existing policies. He concluded that only one combination between variables in the two sets, the case of Philippine independence and American withdrawal from the Far East, would rule out the need for a naval base. Having thus established the probability of retention, he turned to the question of location.[48] That problem occupied naval thinking throughout the thirties; study after study compared possible sites in terms of their relationship to the local population, strategic location, and suitability for protection and anchorage. The search seems academic: the navy did not force itself to pick a site and it knew Congress was not disposed to provide funds. However, the object of the navy was not to choose a site but to keep alive the possibility of choice. It had to prevent a decision not to have a naval base in the Philippines if it were to maintain the Orange plan concept and thereby its basic strategy for growth.

Meanwhile the navy worried about a broader challenge, this one posed by the London naval talks of 1934 and the Naval Conference of 1935. As the navy treaty system came up for renewal, the Japanese made their position abundantly clear. According to the naval attaché in Tokyo, they would insist on parity, demand an end to limitation by category so as to allow each nation to fashion the navy best suited to its requirements, and seek the abolition of "offensive" types—the heavy cruiser, the battleship, and especially the aircraft carrier.[49] The British, though generally satisfied with the 5:5:3 ratio, wanted qualitative (tonnage and gun size) reductions for larger vessels balanced by a quantitative increase for light cruisers, their handiest ship.[50] Were the United States to grant Japan parity or agree to reduction in "offensive" types, long-range operations in the Pacific would be impossible. The "balanced fleet" would constantly have to be rebalanced to meet the changing composition of the opponent fleet. Yet if the United States stood fast on the old treaty, Britain and Japan, which had a common interest in qualitative limitation, might come to an understanding, especially in view of Britain's new concern for European peace and its large, vulnerable Far Eastern interests. At the very least the onus for breakdown in the treaty system might be thrown on the United States. In a treatyless situation or under qualitative limitations only, the United States could always outbuild Japan, but the navy would lack its public justification for building appropriations. As one member of the General Board noted, "without quantitative limitation the magic phrase 'Treaty Navy' will be lost and history indicates that we will have a greatly reduced Navy falling behind other large naval powers."[51]

In this maze of dilemmas the navy took what it considered the only safe course, that of holding fast to the Washington-London treaty system. In September 1934 at a policy conference in the State Department, Admiral W. H. Standley, chief of naval operations, insisted that the current ratio between the American and Japanese fleets must be maintained "at all costs." If the United States was "prepared to stand up for the Open Door, for the 9-Power Treaty, for the Kellogg Pact, et cetera," it must have a strong enough fleet. A few days later at the White House, Standley, Cordell Hull, Norman Davis, who was to be the chief U.S. representative at the London talks, and the president agreed to that principle. Further they agreed "that in no circumstances should we indicate any intention either to weaken ourselves in the Orient, to indicate an unwillingness to join issue under certain circumstances or a willingness to allow Japan to continue pressing forward without protest on our part."[52] At the London talks American naval officers made every effort to establish cordial relations at the Admiralty and explain American naval needs. As it turned out, the Japanese position was so adamant as to offer no encouragement to an Anglo-Japanese understanding and the American position was so adamant as to make any modification of the treaty system impossible. The Japanese gave notice of abrogation and bore the stigma of destroying naval limitation. Giving up the treaty system was costly to the American navy, but less costly than giving up the freedom to maintain a substantial superiority over the Japanese navy. In the circumstances, to accept anything less than the current differential would have implied retreat from the overseas mission that established its quality as a first class navy.

It cannot be denied that American national policy relating to Japan in this period was one of noncondonation and yet nonprovocation: the United States did not take steps actively to oppose Japan and continued to search for ways of resolving differences consistent with its principles, traditional policies, and interests. Considering policy less in terms of decisions than options, however, and concentrating on a unit of government rather than government as a whole does perhaps enlarge this picture. The United States navy was by no means inclined to encourage immediate, active opposition to Japan, but it was determined to develop its capacity to oppose. In the national policy deliberations and decisions in which it played a part, it had a firming influence on the underside of American policy, making traditional Far Eastern policies somewhat more dogmatic and absolute. It influenced not so much the course of policy as the range of choice, weakening options involving settlement with concession and reinforcing those implying resistance. The result was to shift the spectrum of alternatives toward confrontation while the base course remained the same for the time being. The explanation for the navy's position is to be found not in imminent danger to American national interests but rather in long-term danger as conceived within the framework of bureaucratic needs and interests.

IV

The navy of 1931-37 was a relatively static organization. War with Japan seemed inevitable but not imminent. Strategy of the Potomac was realistic but strategy of the Pacific was not. Thinking about the Far East was circular: the navy saw what it wanted to see. No impelling need arose to revise preconceptions until the Sino-Japanese War. Then suddenly hostilities lay just beyond a mishandled incident. Thenceforth the international situation steadily deteriorated and the navy moved toward a war footing. The difficulty was that reality presented itself in a most complex form, not as one probable war but as a shifting set of probable wars. The navy constantly had to adapt and readapt.

One of the first to sound a new note was the commander of the Asiatic Fleet, Admiral Yarnell. Perhaps the most articulate American admiral of the period, he was unorthodox after the fashion of Admiral Sims, on whose staff he served in World War I, and accustomed to thinking of strategy in a broad international political and economic context. His hopes set on a high command in the "Big Fleet," he had been bitter about his assignment to the small fleet.[53] But hostilities in China made him the center of attention. He repeatedly affirmed the rights of American nationals and shipping in the war zone against Japanese infringement. On September 22, 1937 he ordered his ships to protect

American nationals in Chinese ports, even under risk, as long as these citizens felt it necessary to remain, although they had been warned. This was more extensive protection than the administration was prepared to provide, and Admiral Leahy, chief of naval operations, though not countermanding the order, warned Yarnell to clear such policy declarations through Washington in the future.[54] This was not Yarnell's last brush with his superiors. He continued his policy of firmness in dealing with the Japanese and sought to provide a strategic justification for it.

Yarnell recommended rejection of the traditional conception of war with Japan, a conception he himself had played a part in developing after World War I.[55] Then as now he portrayed Japan as a menace to American Far Eastern interests, only then he had stressed the importance of the China market and now he saw China more as one of a number of democratic powers in the Far East drawing together to oppose "an international gun man."[56] Now a slow, costly advance of the fleet westward no longer seemed necessary. A more effective plan, he advised Admiral Leahy, was to take advantage of the economic vulnerability of Japan, its dependence on external sources of raw materials. If China, together with the United States, Britain, France, the Netherlands, and Russia, countries naturally opposed to Japan, would form a common front, they could encircle this aggressor and cut off all its trade except in China from the Yangtze northward. From the American point of view such a war of "strangulation" could be waged economically, without huge, expensive armies or dubious main fleet encounters. China would provide troops to tie Japan down. The other nations would attack Japanese commerce from a string of bases running from Dutch Harbor, Alaska, through Hawaii, Guam, the Philippines, and Java to Singapore. The United States would employ naval aviation, submarines, and light forces.[57] Yarnell failed to explain how his base line could be held without great sea and land battles when Guam and the Philippines, as he admitted, were virtually defenseless. But his idea of a long-range blockade by a concert of powers represented a new departure in naval thinking.

Leahy had been thinking along somewhat the same lines. In August, at the time the fighting spread to Shanghai, he wrote in his diary:

> If it were possible to obtain an equitable agreement with Great Britain to share the effort and expense, this appears to be a wonderful opportunity to force Japan to observe her treaty agreements, and to depart from the mainland of Asia, which would ensure Western trade supremacy for another century. The cost of accomplishing this purpose at a later date will be enormously increased and it still does appear inevitable that a major war between the Occident and the Orient must be faced at some time now or in the future.[58]

Therefore he was interested in Yarnell's ideas and passed them on to the president, who replied:

> Yarnell talks a lot of sense. . . . It follows what I wrote in an article in *Asia* . . . back in the early 20's—and it goes along with the word "quarantine" which I used in the Chicago speech last month.

>Yarnell forgets to mention an example of successful strangulation—when the United States, without declaring war, strangled Tripoli.

The president went on to suggest that Leahy look into the possibility of developing a vessel that was part picket ship, part armed cruiser, and part seaplane tender, the idea being, presumably, to station such vessels at intervals across the ocean to intercept Japanese commerce.[59]

In the *Asia* article, devoted to bettering relations with Japan, Roosevelt had written of the strategic deadlock that existed between the two countries, neither being able to invade the home territories of the other, leading to the result that "war would, in all probability, have been decided on economic issues. And in these the United States had, and has, a vast superiority."[60] It was this brief warning the president apparently alluded to. Obviously he displayed a marked interest in Yarnell's ideas, though by no means committing himself to them. Conversely, it is possible that Yarnell, writing on October 15, 1937, was influenced by the internationalist approach of the president's quarantine speech and that Leahy, in passing on Yarnell's letter, was probing for the concrete meaning of it. In any event, Roosevelt was willing to allow the navy to interpret "quarantine" to embrace the concept of economic war, without implying that such an interpretation exhausted all possible meanings of that puzzling word. Most importantly, he seems to have been encouraging the navy to think along different lines of strategy than the outworn Orange concept.

The *Panay* crisis brought these speculations to the forefront of decision making. The sinking had a powerful psychological impact. For some months the navy had suffered the collapse of Western prestige and influence in China and the infringement of American rights with a sense of helpless outrage. Yarnell's firmness had been the only consolation.[61] Now the destruction of an American naval vessel placed naval leadership under strong pressure not to let this most serious indignity pass without some response. Furthermore, there was an indication that this might not be the last incident. Hallett Abend's dispatch in the *New York Times* of December 20, 1937 revealed that Colonel Hashimoto Kingorō, identified as one of the Young Officer fanatics involved in the February 26, 1936 Incident, had been responsible for the attack order. Yarnell informed Leahy that this information came by special plane from the headquarters of General Matsui Iwane, commander of the Central China Expeditionary Forces.[62] Here was most authoritative evidence that discipline had broken down in the Japanese army. Leahy commented that Abend's revelations gave "the first understandable reason for the attack . . . and point to difficulties in the way of preventing a similar incident which would have serious repercussions."[63] So in spite of Japanese explanations at Tokyo and the settlement of the incident, the *Panay* had a continuing effect on naval thinking.

There was little the administration could do by way of immediate response to the attack on the *Panay*. The president talked of blockade, picking up Yarnell's idea of a line of bases but bestowing responsibility for the line west of Guam on the British.[64] Leahy felt it was "time to get the fleet ready for sea, to make an agreement with the British navy for joint action, and to inform the Japanese that we expect to protect our nations."[65] Nevertheless, display of force seemed too dangerous. Roosevelt went so far as to order three cruisers to Singapore in February for opening ceremonies at the British naval base, but this was a mere gesture since the ships he sent, old, light cruisers, would hardly make the Japanese shiver. A new heavy cruiser visited Australia at the time but did not go on to Singapore. Of greater significance was the London mission of Captain Royal E. Ingersoll, director of the War Plans Division. The idea of naval staff conversations had been in the air for several weeks. On December 23, when the import of the *Panay* affair was clear, Ingersoll received instructions from the president and departed.

Ingersoll had two assignments in London. The first, a subsidiary mission, was to find out British post-treaty building plans in advance of a final decision on American plans with a view to freeing the navy from restrictions on the size of battleships. His principal task was to explore with the Admiralty joint action by the two navies in the event of further incidents in the Far East. On January 13, 1938 Ingersoll signed an agreed record of conversations with his British opposite, Captain Tom Phillips, which envisaged far-reaching Anglo-American naval cooperation in the Pacific. The plan contemplated a massive, synchronized display of force against Japan, the American fleet moving to Hawaii as the British main fleet moved to Singapore. The plan did not specify strategy thenceforward in the event of war, aside from a gradual American westward advance, but it provided for exchange of codes and signals and other communications coordination and for use of each other's territorial waters. It also provided for establishment of a joint "distant blockade or 'quarantine' ": the United States would interdict Japanese commerce with the western hemisphere and around Cape Horn, and the British would block it along the line Singapore-Dutch East Indies-New Guinea and east of New Zealand and Australia. Together the two navies would sever Japan's vital trade lines with the world outside East Asia.[66]

The Ingersoll-Phillips agreement was a plan not a commitment to action. It required for implementation the decision of both governments and on the American side the proclamation of a national emergency. Furthermore, Germany was an increasing concern and Britain could not be sure when and in what strength its fleet would appear in the Far East.[67] The agreement accepted that war in Europe would necessitate reconsideration of the project. Ultimately the Ingersoll mission was less important in establishing a program for dealing with Japan than in forming the core of a progressively broadening common defense. Implicit in the agreement was a division of world responsibility between the two navies: the British would maintain control of the Atlantic, Mediterranean, and Indian oceans while the Americans concentrated on the Pacific.[68] At the same time, the agreement reflected the new departures in American naval thinking, namely the idea of concerted action in the Pacific and long-range blockade.

These new perspectives as well as old ones were reflected in the latest version of the Orange plan, completed in February 1938. Revision started early in November 1937 and proceeded through prolonged disagreement and deadlock between the army and navy sides of the Joint Board to a final compromise. The latest version of Orange was in effect three plans. From the army point of view it set forth a holding operation in the eastern Pacific. The plan dropped explicit reference to offensive war in the western Pacific and was silent about reinforcement of the Philippines. It called for a period of concentration and preparation, a time of watchful waiting when the army, its eye more and more on European developments, might ensure that no threat existed from across the Atlantic before committing forces to operations against Japan. The navy consequent to the Ingersoll mission was less concerned about the Atlantic. From the naval point of view the Orange plan embraced two courses of action in the Pacific. It now included the idea of economic warfare by blockade and it retained the traditional concept of a progressive advance westward across the Pacific to engage the main forces of the enemy. However, the timing of the advance was more flexible since it was no longer tied to relief of the Philippines. While the fleet prepared, the blockade would squeeze Japan.[69]

A third development, besides the new Orange plan and the Ingersoll mission, was the introduction of the second Vinson building program. New danger in the Far East was obviously a factor in the president's decision to enlarge naval defense, which he announced to congressional leaders on January 5, 1938. But a further consideration was the fact that construction authorized by the Vinson-Trammell Act had been virtually completed and a new program was necessary if the momentum of shipyard activity were to be sustained. Now the president sought authority to raise the size of the navy 20 percent above treaty limits, an additional four hundred thousand tons in sixty-nine ships. After bitter debate the bill became law on May 17, 1938.

It was a rather conventional program. The notion of a "treaty navy" persisted in spite of the demise of the treaty system. The United States with Britain and France had recognized the value of some form of international naval agreement, however innocuous, by negotiating a treaty in London in 1936 that bound the signatories only to qualitative limitations and exchange of information on construction plans. The new program suggested an enlargement of the treaty base rather than what in fact it was, an American entry in the naval race of a treatyless period.

As before, the fleet would balance on the battleship. The authorization enlarged the air arm of the navy considerably, it is true, adding two carriers and ten seaplane tenders and doubling the number of planes. Yet Leahy believed the navy had carrier superiority and had advised against constructing more.[70] Instead he pressed for more battleships. Before the building holiday ended at London, the navy had been working on plans for battleship replacements and began two 35,000-tonners right afterward.[71] Now it gained authority for three more and, soon after, a fourth for a total of six, as well as clearance to plan 45,000-tonners as soon as Britain and France agreed to the larger sizes. A heated race in battleships was on: the Japanese were understood to be constructing two ships larger than 35,000 tons and planning a third and possibly a fourth.[72] Naval rivalry tended to perpetuate the existing composition of fleets.

The administration presented the program as a means of defending both the Atlantic and Pacific coasts in a time of fascist as well as Japanese aggression. The argument failed to convince military columnist Hanson Baldwin, who pointed out that the force contemplated would be insufficient to defend both coasts and more than sufficient to defend either coast. He estimated that it provided a 50 to 75 percent superiority over the Japanese navy, not enough margin for operations in the western Pacific but enough to remain in contention for that margin.[73] Thus traditional Orange strategy could persist within the broader popular conception of the navy's mission.

The idea of long-range blockade and common defense with Western powers in the Far East roused American interest in the paths to Asia by way of the South Pacific. Particularly important were the islands between Hawaii and Samoa—the Gilbert, Ellice, Phoenix, Palmyra, Cook, and Union groups—some of which seemed suitable for airfields and others as anchorages and seaplane bases.[74] The United States had already taken steps to perfect its claims to Howland, Baker, and Jarvis islands. In February 1938 the president ordered occupation of the disputed Canton and Enderbury islands and held fast to them, in spite of British protests, while negotiations for joint occupation continued.[75] The navy investigated the route but remained dubious. It was subject throughout to flank attack from the Japanese Mandates and culminated in a dangerous bottleneck in the Mindanao-Morotai-New Guinea area or in risky navigation through the Torres Strait.[76] The Hepburn report of December 1938 on expansion of naval air bases recommended development of several islands along the route but assigned priority to Palmyra and Johnston, which also served for reconnaissance of the Marshalls and screening of Hawaii, and to Wake, Midway, and especially Guam, along the classic central Pacific route.[77] South Pacific base construction did not become a matter of urgency until 1941.

The Sino-Japanese War had an important influence on the development of the navy. The outbreak of hostilities coincided with a pause in programming the growth of the fleet and encouraged pressing on to the next stage. It aroused some new thinking about weapons, strategy, and communications, encouraging the idea of economic war, movement toward naval entente with Britain, enlargement of air power, and base development. In some respects the navy was moving toward a more complex and flexible approach to war in the Pacific, but it was not yet abandoning its customary precepts.

The Munich crisis in the fall of 1938 led to a fundamental reappraisal of American military strategy and a new framework for planning. Of course the Ingersoll mission had established a connection between Europe and Far Eastern problems, but so long as Britain and France confined the German threat to Europe, the navy could view the Pacific in isolation. However, Munich raised the possibility that the European democracies might look the other way in the event of fascist infiltration and subversion in Latin America.[78] Furthermore, negotiations for a German-Japanese alliance were under way, so far without open accord but possibly with secret understandings. The United States might be involved in war alone or in concert, in either direction, Atlantic or Pacific, or in both directions. Rather than pile new contingencies on old, it seemed wiser to undertake a global reassessment. In April 1939, after months of study, the Joint Board produced a set of broad strategies for five conceivable situations known as the Rainbow plans.

Of the numerous contingencies, one engaged the attention of the navy more than the rest. Rainbow 1 and 4, strategies concentrating on protection of the western hemisphere, aroused little enthusiasm. Members of the Joint Board (presumably naval members particularly) rejected the argument that the United States lacked strength to undertake offensive operations in the Pacific while ensuring defense in the Atlantic and therefore should draw in its forces. They insisted that hemispheric security was not enough; to maintain its position as a world power the United States must adopt a "dynamic" attitude and be prepared to project its strength beyond the seas in one direction or the other. Rainbow 5, which assumed concentration against Germany with Britain and France, seemed a remote contingency in 1939. There remained the strategies for the Pacific, Rainbow 2 and 3. Rainbow 3 was essentially the old Orange plan of single-handed war on Japan. That strategy might be necessary of course, but it was slow and costly and objectionable to the army. Rainbow 2, reflecting the new thinking of 1937-38, was more and more appealing. With allies, the United States might maintain a position in the Far East instead of having to fight its way back atoll by atoll.[79]

Rainbow 2 dominated naval thinking from May 1939 to May 1940. In case of a Japanese attack on the Dutch East Indies, the United States might send a naval force south from Hawaii to the Fijis then westward north of New Guinea through the Moluccas to the Java Sea, there to join the Asiatic Fleet and allied forces in defending the Malay Barrier (Singapore to Timor).[80] The object, as explained by Chief of Naval Operations Stark, was to defeat Japan by economic strangulation. To accomplish it, he said, Japan must be prevented from securing the resources of the East Indies, especially oil.[81] The route would require bases. Admiral Leahy encouraged Pan American Airlines to develop Canton, halfway to Fiji.[82] Manus and Rabaul seemed suitable locations along the New Guinea coast. In the Philippines the southern base sites gained attention. Previously the choice spots had been Manila or islands near Luzon.[83] Now Tawitawi or Jolo in the Sulu chain running between Mindanao and Borneo seemed best, and President Quezon of the Philippines encouraged the navy to believe it might have any site it wanted there after independence.[84] Ships of the Asiatic Fleet cruised to Borneo and the southern Philippines more frequently while students at the Naval War College poured over maps of the East Indies.[85]

The idea of a concerted defense of the Malay Barrier remained a speculative proposition nonetheless. It depended greatly on what the main fleet could accomplish moving due west from Pearl Harbor. If conditions warranted, the fleet would pounce on Truk in the Carolines, setting up a "guardian buffer" for movement of forces southward.[86] A leap that far seemed increasingly doubtful, however. Lacking access to the Mandates, the navy had always suspected illegal fortification and base development there. In fact construction in the islands by Japan, though convertible to war purposes, remained within a reasonable interpretation of its international obligations until 1940 when, among other projects, it began developing airfields and seaplane ramps in the Marshalls.[87] The American navy was aware of the development at least of Jaluit,[88] and the less inclined to contemplate a long, quick movement westward. Consequently, the South Pacific voyage remained an exceedingly hazardous prospect. Furthermore, Congress having denied funds for minimal development of Guam, the navy had no hope of securing money for a base in the Sulus.

Supposing the South Pacific force arrived unscathed in the Java Sea, how much help could it expect? In the spring of 1939 the American fleet moved to the Caribbean for maneuvers and a visit to New York for the opening of the World's Fair. But after the German takeover of Czechoslovakia and the Italian invasion of Albania, the president canceled the visit and ordered the fleet back to San Diego as a precaution in case Japan took advantage of the European crisis to move southward. The British were unable to do their part by sending a fleet to Singapore, however. Their naval attaché informed Leahy that the Admiralty did not contemplate employment of any naval force on the coast of Asia until the situation in Europe was clarified. Then, with the outbreak of World War II, Britain began withdrawing vessels from the China Squadron for convoy duty.[89]

The Sino-Japanese War forced the navy to take a hard look at its war plans and accept the practical difficulties of conducting a transpacific campaign in the traditional way. The idea of concerted defense in the Far East and economic war offered an alternative solution that implied no contraction in the role of the United States as a Far Eastern power. The means of effecting such a strategy remained elusive, however. Rainbow 2 was still a concept, not a national policy decision or international undertaking. But it had a life of its own. In November 1940, under drastically altered circumstances, Secretary of the Navy Frank Knox still believed that the navy in combination with the British and Dutch could "contain the Japanese fleet" and prevent the transport of Japanese troops to the Dutch East Indies.[90] The idea of containment, of halting Japanese expansion by encirclement, had a diplomatic version in the increasingly popular notion of a program of economic pressure short of war. The navy contributed a military version and thereafter would find it difficult to disown the containment thesis.

V

The shock effect of the fall of France greatly accelerated the process of change in the navy. It radically altered the security picture and ushered in a period of rapid flux in the navy's planning and preparation for war. One result was an immediate, gigantic increase in the projected size of the navy. The third Vinson program, authorizing an 11 percent increase, was already out of date when it became law in June 1940. The following month a fourth program called for an expansion of 70 percent. Now the cliché was not "treaty navy" but "two-ocean navy."

The projected composition of the fleet reflected the new waves of change. In November 1939 Admiral Stark pleaded with a reluctant president for two more 45,000-ton battleships and gained approval.[91] These with the ones authorized or building made a total of twelve new battleships. The General Board expressed its concern over reports that Japan was building eight battleships and urged faster construction.[92] Intelligence estimated eight as a conservative figure.[93] Meanwhile carrier building lagged: only one keel was laid between April 1936 and April 1941. The trend was reversed under the impact of air war in Europe. Eleven *Essex*-type attack carriers were ordered in July and September 1940. At the same time, the navy added no more battleships and ultimately canceled two.

The fall of France also hastened a gradual reorientation of naval strategy and dispositions from the Pacific to the Atlantic. The first trace of this shift is detectable early in 1938 when the administration presented the second Vinson bill as a measure for the defense of both coasts. According to a naval officer closely involved in the legislation, the worsening situation in Europe during debate on the bill gave it a boost toward passage.[94] In July 1938 the president decided to send the fleet to the opening of the New York World's Fair in 1939.[95] This visit to the east coast after a long absence was to provide tangible evidence of the fleet's covering role in the Atlantic, but in fact a real European crisis forced the fleet back to its usual position in the Pacific. Nevertheless, the Atlantic could not be left bare. The Atlantic Squadron, United States Fleet, was formed in October 1938 in part as a "politico-diplomatic gesture aimed at the totalitarian powers on the eve of the Munich Crisis."[96] By September 1939 it consisted of four old battleships, four new heavy cruisers, an aircraft carrier, and a destroyer squadron.[97] Atlantic responsibilities continued to assist naval growth: Admiral Stark noted in September 1939 that the European war gave him "leverage" in securing additional appropriations.[98] These responsibilities steadily expanded. In February 1941 the Atlantic force attained fleet status and its commander, Ernest J. King, the rank of vice admiral. The president had desired a higher rank for the Atlantic commander for over a year.[99] Thenceforth the Atlantic Fleet never had enough ships and the aggressive King regarded any warship on either coast not otherwise attached as "legitimate prey."[100]

The Pacific tugged at American naval strength too. After German victory in the west, Japan joined the Axis alliance and moved into northern Indochina. Events pointed toward a climax as Roosevelt responded with a scrap iron embargo and the British by opening the Burma Road. Since May 1939 Britain had repeatedly urged the sending of an American naval force to Singapore to stand in for the fleet Britain itself was unable to send. Predominant opinion within the administration regarded the Singapore venture as wholly impractical, but in October 1940 the president seriously considered reinforcing the Asiatic Fleet. The navy was dubious and finally reduced the allotment to ten submarines, vessels able to do their damage and escape. Meanwhile the president reverted to the containment thesis in contemplating moves in case of a further Japanese advance southward. In that case he would place a total embargo on Japanese trade and set up a long-range blockade. He toyed with the idea of setting up two lines of patrol vessels, one from Samoa to the Dutch East Indies and another from Hawaii to the Philippines, to intercept Japanese commerce, along the lines of Yarnell's recommendation of 1937. The thought of war measures with the fleet still unprepared and of such a blithe dispersion of naval forces in dangerous waters horrified Admiral Richardson, who managed to dissuade the president. But U.S. policy was now drifting steadily toward active opposition to Japan in the Far East and the navy, the traditional exponent of a firm Far Eastern policy, found itself the voice of caution and restraint.[101]

In the middle, pulled both ways, was the United States Fleet. It had been conducting maneuvers in Hawaiian waters at the time of the German invasion of France and the president ordered it to remain at Pearl Harbor indefinitely as a deterrent to Japan. At the moment some in the navy would have preferred to withdraw it to the Atlantic to guard against loss of the British and French fleets.[102] Richardson argued for return to the west coast on the ground that congestion in Hawaii made training difficult. But the president, strongly supported by the State Department, refused, saying he would first need a statement convincing to the American people and the Japanese government that such a move would not be a step backward.[103] During the summer of 1940 the governing condition was Rainbow 4, hemispheric defense, which precluded westward movement of the fleet in case of war; but in October, with fears for Britain easing slightly and American policy toward Japan hardening, the door to Pacific strategies reopened.[104] Richardson, perhaps for no other reason than to save himself from the president's strategic notions, drew up a plan that was a hybrid of Rainbow 2, 3, and 4. In the event of an American embargo, the fleet would move west, but not beyond recall to the Atlantic. This was a convenient restriction since venturing as far as Truk was regarded as too hazardous in any event. Instead Richardson proposed to attack the nearby Marshalls and "if possible" to send a single-carrier task force to join the Asiatic Fleet, which would retire southward to assist in the defense of the Malay Barrier.[105] This was less a plan than a recognition of the failure of planning.

This was a painful moment for the American navy and no one expressed the mood of uncertainty and frustration better than the commander-in-chief of the fleet. In communications to Knox and Stark, Richardson bitterly reflected on the awkward position of his fleet, posed as a deterrent, yet inadequately manned and trained, lacking sufficient superiority in ships, and consequently unready to fight if deterrence failed. He wondered whether the navy had presented its views forcibly and frankly to the rest of the government so that there could be no misunderstanding about what it could and could not do, and whether coordination between the State, War, and Navy departments was adequate. Above all he pointed out the anachronism of naval thinking. Waging transpacific war had been a budgetary strategy that was unrealistic now. There was always a danger of overemphasizing the point of view of staff corps officers whose long removal from sea duty distorted their priorities. He inveighed against the public image the navy cultivated of a fleet ready to fight, big enough to keep America out of war, to impose the nation's will on others, or, if war came, to provide a "mobile Maginot line" behind which the citizenry could reside in peace. Such publicity lulled the public into believing the United States could "risk war without danger or wage war without risk." The time had come for the nation to decide what the objectives of a Pacific war might be and to compare its costs and value. And the navy must formulate "sound plans" based on "present realities."[106]

Richardson's views arrived in time for a major reassessment of American naval strategy directed by Admiral Stark that culminated on November 4, 1940 in the well-known Stark Memorandum, otherwise known as the Plan D or, in military parlance, Plan Dog Memorandum, a document that played a vital part in crystallizing American strategy in favor of prosecution of war on Germany first.[107] The awkward position of the fleet in the Pacific was one of a number of factors contributing to the reassessment and the result, another being the obvious threats in and across the Atlantic. Other factors were the passing of Hitler's opportunity to invade Britain until spring, making long-term plans for assisting the British worthwhile, and the passing of the election season in America, promising undivided presidential attention to problems of national defense. The memorandum reflected the growing influence of the professional side of the navy as war approached. Prominent on the Stark planning team was Captain Richmond Kelly Turner, director of War Plans, who had been in charge of the advanced course at the Naval War College in 1938-39. The revamped course dealt with war in a broad social, political, and economic context.[108] An estimate prepared by the staff in 1939, for example, had deliberately ignored the Orange plan and concluded that the correct employment of the fleet at the beginning of war was in protection of the assembly and preparation of the nation's forces for maximum effort.[109] The correct location of the fleet, according to a study of April 1940, was the Caribbean.[110] Other factors contributing to Plan Dog can be surmised. One was certainly the fact that it would be several years before completion of the "two-ocean navy" and realization of the nation's full potential naval strength. Also, an Atlantic war was a familiar war. The staff could proceed according to precedents of World War I, when Stark had been flag secretary to Admiral Sims at London. At the same time, with reentry to Europe necessary now, the navy could anticipate a more significant role.

The main premise of the Plan Dog Memorandum was that the vital interest of the United States lay in the continued existence of Britain and the British empire. To defend that interest the United States should direct its concentrated effort toward Europe, even to the point of waging war on the continent for the defeat of Germany. The memorandum measured alternative strategies against the imperative of European concentration and rejected them. Plan A, hemispheric defense, and Plan B, the Orange or Rainbow 3 war, ruled out American influence on the outcome in Europe. Plan C, the Rainbow 2 concept of limited war in the Pacific presented similar difficulties. The memorandum raised the question whether Japan was necessarily committed to military action against British and Dutch territories. Given the hope of long-term economic influence in those territories and assurance of trade with Britain and the United States, Japan might bide its time. If it did attack, a Plan C war might be waged in two ways, both involving an economic blockade. The first involved dispatching forces to assist the British and Dutch in defense of the Malay Barrier, and the second operations against the Marshall Islands to divert the Japanese from pursuing the southward advance. The memorandum raised the question of the extent to which the British and Dutch were willing or able to resist Japan and ruled out the possibility of sending the battle fleet to Singapore. But even sending a smaller force or raiding the Marshalls would drain American strength from Europe. Limited war in the Far East in cooperation with Britain would probably mean war against Germany as well. Reverses in the Pacific might lead to popular clamor for escalation, to the detriment of the European theater. Thus limited war could develop an irreversible dynamic of its own.[111]

A strategy of Europe first meant a strict defensive in the Pacific. The memorandum did not entirely reject the possibility of a limited war with Japan. Rather it insisted that any decision on joint defense with the British and Dutch must depend on a clear understanding of the strength and extent of their commitment to the defense of the Malay Barrier, keeping in mind the priority of Europe. For the moment the fleet should remain at Hawaii. Meanwhile "positive efforts" should be made to prevent war with Japan and between Japan and the British and Dutch. The memorandum was obscure about the cost of avoiding war, but its acceptance of the necessity of paying some cost illustrates how naval thinking had changed.

The containment thesis survived despite the severe doubts of the naval planners. The Plan Dog concept gained broad acceptance in the government but strong opinion, particularly in the State Department, still favored some sort of assistance to the British and Dutch in the Far East. A note in the margin of the Stark Memorandum illustrates the persistence of the idea. The text at that point read: "Under Plan (D) we would be unable to exert strong pressure against Japan, and would necessarily gradually reorient our policy in the Far East." Next to that statement Secretary Knox, who approved Plan Dog, scribbled: "In combination with Dutch and British could contain Jap. fleet + prevent army transport to Dutch E. Indies."[112] Stark himself continued to hope some force might be sent. He wrote the commander of the Asiatic Fleet that a reinforcement, probably to Soerabaja or Singapore, could be counted on, but he warned that its size and composition would be influenced by the necessity of holding the fleet at mid-Pacific for possible recall to the Atlantic.[113]

The hope lingered on into 1941. On seeing the Stark Memorandum the British urged, without success, the sending of nine American battleships to Singapore.[114] A British naval representative saw Stark in December and explained in great detail the importance of Singapore to the defense of Britain and the British empire as well as to the interests of the United States, thereby seeking to redirect the Plan D assumption of defense of the British empire toward a Plan C limited-war solution.[115] In January 1941, as reports circulated of an imminent Japanese move southward, the question arose of sending four heavy cruisers to Singapore and Secretary Knox called a meeting to discuss it, attended by Eugene Dooman, counselor of embassy in Tokyo, who was home on furlough. Dooman pointed out that the Japanese would not tolerate the presence of major American fleet units in the South China Sea and that sending lesser ships would be a futile gesture. Knox disagreed, Stark agreed, and, according to Dooman, the discussion became heated.[116] Ultimately the president, who was never enthusiastic about the Singapore project, sent four cruisers to New Zealand and Australia instead.[117] With no better success, the British continued to press the issue at the staff conversations in Washington early in 1941 that led to the basic British-American strategic agreement known as ABC-1.

Specific decisions succeeding the Stark Memorandum hardened theoretical misgivings into final rejection of the Singapore reinforcement project. An important consideration was the unsatisfactory state of British defenses. As the chairman of the British staff delegation in Washington admitted:

> On the one hand we shall say to the Americans that the whole safety of the Far East depends on the arrival of their battle fleet at Singapore. On the other hand we shall also have to say that we have not placed a garrison in Malaya sufficiently powerful to ensure that the base at Singapore will be intact when the United States fleet arrives. . . .[118]

At a crucial point in the staff discussions the British admitted that Singapore could not repair capital ships.[119] Other factors contributed too: the political awkwardness of defending a British imperial bastion, the great distance of the supply route, the violation of the naval maxim of concentration, and the fear of losing the ships sent. By 1941 the United States had virtually conceded control of the western Pacific to Japan. The ABC-1 staff agreement assigned the United States defense responsibility to the international date line north of the equator and to the line of the Solomons south of it, still one thousand miles short of the Malay Barrier.[120] Henceforth Barrier defense and Pacific defense would be considered as distinct problems.

The final moves to resolve the Singapore problem were like chess: American warships would move from the Pacific to the Atlantic and an equivalent force of British warships would move to the Far East. Atlantic needs alone argued for the transfer. Admiral King was beginning escort of convoys and planning landings at strategic points in the Atlantic to forestall the Germans.[121] The move had the added virtue of getting at least part of the fleet at Pearl Harbor unstuck without seeming to step backward. At first the idea was to switch roughly half the fleet including six battleships. Both service secretaries and both service chiefs supported the move, but the State Department strongly objected to losing its deterrent and the commander-in-chief of the Pacific Fleet to losing half his command. According to Secretary of War Stimson, Admiral Stark wavered under these contradictory pressures and the president finally decided to move no more than about one-quarter of the fleet.[122] This was still a major force, consisting of three battleships, an aircraft carrier, four new cruisers, sixteen new destroyers, and auxiliaries.[123] The British may have doubted the equivalent value of nonbelligerent battleships but in the end ordered three capital ships to Singapore. The carrier went aground and did not go: the fate of the two vessels that did arrive, the *Repulse* and *Prince of Wales,* is well known.[124]

By June 1941 the navy had moved about as far in planning and dispositions as it would go before December 7. It was operating under Rainbow 5, a forward policy in the Atlantic and strict defense in the Pacific. It was also somewhat reluctantly operating under a limited containment strategy, maintaining the Pacific Fleet as a deterrent against a Japanese southward advance. No early decisive action was expected of that fleet in the event of war. The president talked of hit-and-run raids, interdicting enemy commerce, and protecting American commerce and home territory. He doubted any seizure of the Marshalls or Carolines until the second or third year of war.[125] Interallied arrangements for the defense of the Malay Barrier were the responsibility of the commander of the Asiatic Fleet. He would have to make do with light forces.

The events of July 1941 changed the situation in the Pacific, but the navy stayed on course. Admiral Stark opposed the application of an embargo on the ground that it would probably result in an early Japanese attack on Malaya and the Dutch East Indies.[126] The navy's build-up in the Philippines—more patrol planes and submarines—was relatively modest compared with the army's, particularly the army's deployment of a long-range bomber force. The two services in fact switched roles on containment of Japan, the navy hanging back and the army pressing forward. With the embargo economic war began in the Pacific. For the navy real war was beginning in the Atlantic.

THE JAPANESE NAVY
AND THE UNITED STATES

Asada Sadao

In the course of the 1930s the Japanese navy underwent momentous transformations that go far to explain its role in the coming of the war with the United States. The process may be viewed as a gradual breakdown, under mounting challenges from within, of the Japanese naval tradition and the "moderate" leadership that inherited it.

Several salient strains defined that tradition. Originally patterned after the British model and subsequently influenced by American technology and strategic doctrine, the Japanese navy long retained traces of an "Anglo-American" orientation. More generally, its officers prided themselves on their "cosmopolitan" outlook, fostered by tours of duty at sea and overseas, that distinguished them from the more provincial army officers. And their professional life aboard a ship put a premium on technical—therefore "scientific" and "rational"—mental habits. Institutionally, the traditional navy was a relatively well-ordered, solidary organization. While operational and tactical problems fell within the jurisdiction of the chief of the Navy General Staff, policymaking power was centralized in the hands of the navy minister. Through a clearly defined line of authority he exercised firm control over the naval establishment in peacetime, an arrangement that assured a measure of internal harmony and a fraternal spirit among its officers and men.

All this changed in the turbulent, crisis-ridden thirties. Beginning with the domestic strife engendered by the London Naval Conference, that decade witnessed the aggravation of internal splits within the navy and a steady erosion of the top ministry leadership by the high command and middle-echelon officers (commanders or captains of section chief rank). As in other branches of the Japanese government, so in the navy the policymaking process came to be marked by diffusion, dispersion, and decentralization of authority and power. With the rise of violently anti-British, anti-American, and pro-German elements, the navy's policy was increasingly dominated by highly emotional modes of thinking and myopic strategic preoccupations. By the mid-1930s the "moderate" naval leadership had been reduced to a decided minority.

In order to analyze this process, the first part of this paper briefly surveys: (1) the various groupings of officers in the naval leadership; (2) their respective influence on naval policymaking[1] and its institutional framework; and (3) the conflicting images, values, and strategic concepts that conditioned their attitudes and policies toward the United States.

I

It would be misleading to speak of "factions" and "cliques" within the navy of the 1930s if these words are taken to mean formal, fixed, or institutionalized subgroups. The former monopoly of naval leadership by the Satsuma clan had long since been broken by Admiral Yamamoto Gonnohyōe, navy minister from 1898 to 1906. By the First World War one had to look hard for commanders-in-chief of Satsuma origin on the flag list. Instead, a new type of "clique" (if it can be called that) had emerged: the elite officer corps recruited from high-ranking graduates of the Naval Academy. To a greater extent than was the case in the army, the record an individual made at the academy determined his promotion as a naval officer—a tendency that did not slacken before or during the 1930s. To be sure, ambitious young officers on attaining lieutenancy usually applied for the Navy War College, but its graduates did not enjoy anything like the privileged position of their army counterparts and hardly constituted a "clique."[2]

It should be noted that the navy's entire system of education and promotion had certain baneful consequences. Starting about the time of the First World War, the Naval Academy placed increasing emphasis on a Spartan regimentation and memory work at the expense of the student's originality. And the Navy War College, though designed to train high-ranking commanders, actually functioned as the nursery of staff officers. Its curriculum was heavily oriented toward narrowly strategic and tactical subjects to the neglect of a comprehensive "science of war." In time, such training became a factor in causing a dearth of creative leadership.[3] The navy's system of "semi-automatic" promotion also tended to accentuate a rigid bureaucracy in which seniority often placed and kept in positions of authority older officers who had been left behind in the march of technological innovation. Another feature of the navy's personnel administration was the rapid turnover and constant reshuffling of its officers, especially the abler ones, which was bound to militate against consistent and well-thought-out policies.[4]

The most readily apparent grouping of naval officers was along functional or organizational lines—the "administrative group" in the Navy Ministry and the "command group" in the Navy General Staff. (The latter were charged with "high command" matters relating to operational and tactical problems.) Officers were generally classed in either of the two groups, according to their relative length of service in each branch during the early stage of their careers. Since important posts in the Navy General Staff—head of the Operations Division or the Operations Section—required previous experience as a staff officer in that organization, appointments to these "command" posts tended to be separate from those to "administrative" positions. There were a few admirals like Toyoda Soemu who urged more active interchange of personnel between the two branches of the service, warning that otherwise officers would become one-sided in their outlook. But their advice seems to have had little effect.[5]

Traditionally the key policymaking posts in the Navy Ministry went to an elite corps who excelled in politico-administrative ability, while the pivotal positions in the Navy General Staff were occupied by officers of the "warrior type." Until the early 1930s the former group constituted the "establishment" in the navy; its members were commonly regarded as "prima donnas" and figured prominently in the public press as spokesmen for the imperial navy. The smoldering frustration and discontent of the "command group" at having what it regarded as an inferior position and being denied a place in the sun finally erupted after the London Naval Conference of 1930.

The differences between the two groups in their views and attitudes toward the United States were brought out in full relief by the issue of naval limitation. The ministry leadership decided to accept the compromise formula of the London Naval Treaty on the basis of broad political considerations—a belief in the need to cooperate with the Anglo-American powers and to avoid a ruinously expensive naval race. On the other hand, the Navy General Staff, led by the impetuous Admiral Katō Kanji and the scheming Vice Chief Suetsugu Nobumasa, adopted a predominantly military-strategic viewpoint. They adamantly insisted on a 70 percent ratio for heavy cruisers and retention of Japan's existing submarine strength as absolutely indispensable to successful operations against the United States navy.[6] Although the Katō-Suetsugu team was overruled at this time, the turbulent aftermath of the London Naval Conference (as will be explained presently) actually enhanced the power of militant elements not only in the Navy General Staff but also in the Navy Ministry. Thenceforth the differences between the two branches in their posture toward the United States became blurred and began to cut across neat organizational lines.

According to the conventional view, the navy's factionalism during the 1930s is defined in terms of antithetical stands on the London Naval Treaty. Thus its supporters are labeled the "treaty faction" and its opponents the "fleet faction." One difficulty with this classification is that not all commanders and officers of the Combined Fleet had opposed the treaty. When viewed in a larger perspective, the basic split may be seen to revolve around the "Washington treaty system." What occurred during the early thirties was an intensified challenge to the moderate naval leadership that was committed to that system.

Already at the time of the Washington Conference of 1921-22, the issue had been dramatically symbolized in the "battle between the two Katōs." Admiral Katō Tomosaburō, head of the Japanese delegation and navy minister, had chosen to avoid a dangerous naval race with the United States by accepting a 60 percent ratio in capital ships, because he recognized the limits of Japan's national power. Viewing the problems of national defense in terms of the realities of modern total war, he had ruled out a conflict with the United States and concentrated his efforts on diplomatic adjustment. For him, the Japanese navy was an instrument of deterrence, not of war. On the other hand, Vice Admiral Katō Kanji, his chief naval aide, clamored for a 70 percent ratio as a strategic imperative; but his spirited opposition was squelched by the elder Katō.[7]

Katō Tomosaburō's philosophy defined what subsequently came to be known as "navy orthodoxy." A figure of towering prestige and unquestioned leadership, he defied any challenge from his subordinates.[8] But with his untimely death in 1923, effective control over the insurgent elements within the navy began to collapse. Viewed in this context, the dissension over the London Naval Treaty in 1930 was a culmination of the revolt against the "mainstream" personified in the elder Katō; in other words, it merely brought into the open the antagonisms and discontents that had been building in the course of the 1920s. As Prime Minister Saitō Makoto (a former navy minister and retired admiral) succinctly put it in 1933, "The present commotions have their roots in Katō Kanji's antipathy to Plenipotentiary Katō Tomosaburō at the time of the Washington Conference."[9]

Thus the origins of the two opposing groups during the 1930s can be traced back to the two Katōs, in terms of both the direct personal patronage they dispensed and the more indirect influence they exercised. The naval leaders who steered the London Treaty safely to its final ratification—Vice Minister Yamanashi Katsunoshin, head of the Naval Affairs Bureau Hori Teikichi, and former Navy Minister Okada Keisuke—were all protégés or self-conscious heirs of Katō Tomosaburō. Among later inheritors of his legacy one may count Admiral Yonai Mitsumasa, navy minister from February 1937 to August 1939, and a handful of senior officers who loyally supported him—Admirals Yamamoto Isoroku, Inoue Shigemi, Koga Mineichi, Nomura Kichisaburō, and (with some qualifications) Yoshida Zengo.[10]

Turning to the opposite side, Katō Kanji remained an ever powerful force as a vocal member of the Supreme War Council after his resignation as chief of the Navy General Staff. In February 1932 he managed to have his protégé Takahashi Sankichi appointed vice chief of the Navy General Staff, and in November 1933 Admiral Suetsugu became commander-in-chief of the Combined Fleet, to be succeeded by Takahashi the following year. Also Admiral Ōsumi Mineo (navy minister in 1931-32 and again in 1933-36) and his successor Nagano Osami (who was to return in April 1941 as chief of the Navy General Staff) came close to the Katō-Suetsugu group in terms of the policies they pursued. But it was among the spirited young officers that Katō and Suetsugu wielded their greatest influence. Some of them had fallen under Katō's powerful sway as students when he was vice president of the Naval Academy (1911-13) and president of the Navy War College (1920-21). They acclaimed Katō to the point of idolizing him when he boasted that Japan could lick the combined Anglo-American fleet with no trouble, and similarly extolled Suetsugu when he harangued "Down with America and Britain!"[11]

A third grouping of naval officers took shape in the mid-1930s on the basis of differences in foreign orientation: an "American (or Anglo-American) faction" and a "German (later, Axis) faction." This division was dictated by the experiences of the individual members abroad, as language officers, attachés, or assistant attachés.

It had long been traditional for the Japanese navy to send its most promising junior officers—the top graduates of the Naval Academy—to Washington as attachés, and its naval architects to Greenwich, England to be trained at the Royal Naval College. But in the course of the 1930s Germany became the preferred nation. The origins of this significant shift go back to the years immediately after the First World War, when many Japanese naval officers bitterly resented Great Britain's sudden "abandonment" of Japan after having fully exploited it as a "watchdog of the British empire" during the war. Young officers, who were particularly susceptible to such resentment, had risen to the rank of captain or commander with considerable influence by the outbreak of the Second World War.[12]

As Great Britain ceased to extend special privileges and favors to the Japanese navy after the termination of the Anglo-Japanese Alliance,[13] Japan turned increasingly to Germany for technical know-how. Already in 1920, during his inspection tour of Europe, Admiral Katō Kanji was greatly impressed with defeated Germany's technology, especially as applied to the submarine and its optical equipment, and his reports stressed that the Japanese navy would have much to gain by introducing German weaponry. (His reports are also noteworthy for the strongly pro-German sentiments permeating them.)[14] During the latter half of the 1920s the Japanese navy sent more naval architects to Germany than to England or the United States. And after 1936—the year the Anti-Comintern Pact was concluded—the total number of Japanese naval officers stationed in Berlin (as attachés, assistant attachés, and members of their staff) generally surpassed those in Washington or London.[15]

Upon their return from Berlin these junior officers formed the influential "nucleus group" of the pro-German and anti-American elements in the navy. With their fanatic enthusiasm for Nazi Germany,[16] they stood out in sharp contrast to the elder generation of officers with similar experience. (For example, Admiral Yonai, who had spent two and a half years in Berlin shortly after the First World War, had become firmly convinced of the danger of lining up with Germany—a conviction that was later reinforced by his perusal of *Mein Kampf*.)[17] Apparently the Nazis were quite successful in "indoctrinating" Japanese naval attachés. In March 1936 an assistant naval attaché in Berlin talked a visiting commander, Ishikawa Shingo, into believing that "Germany would rise in arms around 1940 and this would be Japan's golden chance to break through the encirclement against it."[18] By 1940 the "German faction" had come to occupy some of the key middle-echelon posts that provided the driving force in the navy's policymaking.

The personal and ideological antagonisms that existed between these overlapping groups—the "administrative group" versus the "command group," the supporters of the Washington system versus its enemies, the "Anglo-American faction" versus the "German faction"—were deep-rooted. Admirals Yonai and Suetsugu, as leaders of opposing groups, reportedly refused even to speak to each other. Nevertheless, the factionalism within the navy never approached in intensity the strife within the army that at times erupted into fratricidal incidents. The difference may be partly accounted for by conditions peculiar to sea duty and by the comparatively small scale of the naval establishment.

II

Traditionally, the navy's political influence on the national scene was overshadowed by that of the army. There were several reasons for this. The size of the navy's officer corps had always been less than a fifth of the army's. In addition, the naval limitations imposed by the Washington Treaty had prompted a drastic cut in enrollment at the Naval Academy. The entering class of 1923 numbered only about one-sixth of its counterpart during the heyday of the "eight-eight fleet" program, and it was not until 1937 that the enrollment climbed back to the pre-Washington Conference level.[19] Furthermore, the navy contained a higher proportion of volunteers than the army. These factors tended to isolate the navy from national life, while sea duty bred a degree of indifference to and innnocence about political and social problems at home. Above all, the tradition of the "silent navy"—noninvolvement in politics—lay at the base of its passive attitude toward state affairs in general.

As has been indicated, the upshot of the domestic fight over the London Naval Treaty was a badly divided navy. According to an educated estimate by the "naval intellectual" Rear Admiral Takagi Sōkichi, the relative weight of the navy's political power, which in normal circumstances amounted at most to about one-third that of the army, was further reduced by the internal split to a fourth or a fifth.[20] This situation gave the Katō-Suetsugu group a chance to expand its own influence, with the strong backing of young officers who had been prematurely retired under the program of naval reduction. These men, fired by a dual sense of rivalry, desired both to wrest control from the "administrative group" in the Navy Ministry and to assert the navy's equality with the army.

The navy's first step in this direction was to install a member of the imperial family, Prince Fushimi Hiroyasu, as chief of the Navy General Staff. This was partly a move to emulate the army, which had recently secured the appointment of General Prince Kan'in as chief of its General Staff. More importantly, it would serve to restrain the voice of the "treaty faction," for Prince Fushimi had revealed himself to be quite susceptible to suggestions from his entourage, particularly Katō Kanji and Suetsugu, at the time of the London Naval Conference.

Admiral Okada, the senior naval leader, and the genro Saionji Kimmochi were indeed worried that Prince Fushimi might be used as a "robot" by his subordinates. Their fears were amply vindicated.[21] During Prince Fushimi's long and undistinguished career as chief of the Navy General Staff, which lasted from January 1932 to March 1941, his vice chiefs usurped and abused his authority, often to enhance the power of the "command group." Worse, the august name of the imperial prince was often invoked to intimidate and pressure the navy minister and even the prime minister into acquiescing in the demands of the General Staff. Whenever the vice chiefs happened to be weak leaders, the initiative was assumed by middle-echelon officers. Things were not much better even when Prince Fushimi was actually in command, for as a member of the imperial family, he could not be held accountable for any error or misjudgment. This could not but impede the responsible policymaking functions of the navy.

The second important move to strengthen the "command group" was to restructure the Navy General Staff after the army pattern. Traditionally, its power had been far more limited than that of the Army General Staff. It had not been directly involved in the administrative aspects of naval policy, such as budget formulation and institutional reorganization. Even regarding high command matters, it had been customary for the chief of the Navy General Staff to seek the consent of the navy minister before making a presentation to the Throne; moreover, after imperial sanction had been obtained for the proposed measure, the navy minister was charged with its implementation.[22] In 1922 Katō Kanji (then vice chief) had made an abortive attempt to modify this system. He had ordered his confidant Takahashi to draft a plan to expand the authority of the Navy General Staff. In the end the project was shelved, as he did not dare submit it to the elder Katō. But it was revived when Takahashi became vice chief in February 1932.[23]

This time circumstances were far more favorable. The London Treaty controversy had given rise to powerful demands, both inside and outside the navy, to establish the "right of supreme command." After the Mukden Incident the Navy General Staff came to view with increasing envy the army structure which enabled its service chief to direct the Manchurian campaigns without restraint. In contrast, the naval action in the Shanghai Incident of 1932 was fettered by instructions from the navy minister, whose prerogative it was to command the naval forces in peacetime. Fearing the eventual escalation of the Shanghai Incident into war with the United States, Takahashi advocated enhancing the authority of the Navy General Staff partly as a preparatory measure for such a contingency.[24] The May 15 Incident (in which a group of young naval officers played a leading role in the assassination of Prime Minister Inukai Tsuyoshi) had a stunning impact upon the navy and provided Takahashi with additional leverage to push his project by dramatizing the necessity of placating the young malcontents.[25]

Taking advantage of these events, Takahashi presented to the Navy Ministry a series of high-handed demands designed (in his own words) to "reduce the navy minister's authority to a minimum." The demands met with the staunch resistance of Captain Inoue Shigemi, chief of the First Section of the Naval Affairs Bureau. Takahashi then forced a personal confrontation with Navy Minister Ōsumi and threatened that Prince Fushimi would resign as chief of the Navy General Staff unless the proposed revisions were effected at once. Soon thereafter the prince himself brought direct pressure to bear on Ōsumi, who hastily complied.[26]

In addition to the revision of the "Rules of the Navy General Staff," Takahashi made demands for far-reaching changes in the "Regulations Concerning the Mutual Jurisdiction of the Navy Ministry and the Navy General Staff." The very procedure of drafting and pressing these demands constituted, in itself, a flagrant violation of the existing rule which invested such authority in the Navy Ministry. Moreover, the demands themselves amounted to such a total negation of the navy's tradition that Captain Inoue considered them "tantamount to raising the standard of revolt against the [navy] minister."

The revisions Takahashi had pressed went into effect in September 1933 and established the supremacy of the General Staff over the Navy Ministry. With the right of command over naval forces *in peacetime* transferred to the chief of the Navy General Staff, the navy minister's control over the navy was sharply reduced. Addressing his subordinates, Prince Fushimi celebrated the new revisions as "a great reform for the rebirth of our imperial navy."[27] But at about the same time Captain Iwamura Seiichi, senior aide to the navy minister, confided to his friend Inoue that he feared the danger of war had been increased

by weakening the ability of the navy minister to apply the "brake" to the Navy
General Staff.[28]

Senior officers of moderate persuasion—the leaders of the "treaty
faction"—who shared Iwamura's misgivings were systematically retired or placed
on the reserve list during 1933-34. The mastermind behind this so-called "Ōsumi
purge" was, again, Katō Kanji. One of its victims was Vice Admiral Hori
Teikichi, known as "the most brilliant mind ever produced by the navy." To
Inoue, the loss of such a man as Hori was more costly for the Japanese navy than
a 10 or 20 percent reduction of its fleet ratio. Another naval leader who was
greatly distressed by this development was Rear Admiral Yamamoto Isoroku,
then in London attending the naval talks. He remarked bitterly, "Perhaps there
is no way left to rebuild the navy until it has wrought its own ruin by such an
outrage."[29]

The far-reaching consequences of the "Ōsumi purge" cannot be overemphasized.[30] It decimated the finest segment of the navy's upper leadership
and fatally weakened the moderate forces that might conceivably have exercised
a measure of rational restraint over the Katō-Suetsugu group and, later, over
fire-eaters in the middle echelons. The "command group," which had for years
chafed under the tight control of the navy minister and the domination of the
"administrative group," could at long last hope to have their day.

One indication of the active interest the Navy General Staff had begun to
take in the "guidance" of foreign policy was the creation in May 1933 of a
peculiar post designated "staff officer A" (kō buin). Directly linked to the head
of the Operations Division and holding section chief rank, "staff officer A" was
specifically charged with formulating national policy and maintaining close
liaison with the officials of the Army General Staff, the Army Ministry, and to a
lesser extent the Foreign Ministry.[31] This was something of a new departure for
the Navy General Staff, which in the past had possessed no formal organ for
maintaining direct and independent contact with other branches of the
government over the head of the navy minister.

Within the Navy Ministry the locus of political functions was the
Naval Affairs Bureau; the head of the bureau joined the vice minister in
assisting the navy minister. Until the reorganization of the bureau in the fall
of 1940, the officer formally in charge of "national policy" matters was the
chief of its First Section. For the most part he was handicapped by an
understaffed office, although in the late 1930s he could call on some
assistance from one or two subordinates who specialized in foreign affairs.
There was also a Research Section—attached to the secretariat of the navy
minister and officially incorporated as a permanent office in 1939—which
was charged with the collection and analysis of data bearing on naval
policy. Captain Takagi Sōkichi, who intermittently headed the Research
Section after 1937, however, went beyond its stipulated functions and
served as the navy's "political antenna," using his personal connections with
such personages as Prince Konoe Fumimaro, Marquis Kido Kōichi, and
Saionji (through his private secretary Baron Harada Kumao). In 1940 the
scholarly Takagi was instrumental in setting up the navy's "brain trust,"
composed of a galaxy of professors and intellectuals, in part to improve the
navy's public image vis-à-vis the army's.[32]

Starting in 1936 the navy created several ad hoc committees staffed with key section chiefs (and some bureau or division heads) of the ministry and the Navy General Staff. Apparently their main aim was to bolster the policymaking machinery of the navy so that it could better compete with the army which had a much larger staff charged with "national policy" matters. Three committees were organized in the spring of 1936 to carry out certain specified functions: the First Committee to formulate "the empire's national policy and the concrete naval policies required for its implementation"; the Second Committee to recommend organizational reforms of the navy; and the Third Committee to study problems of the naval budget.[33] Suffice it here to note that an increasing reliance on these committees tended to enhance the influence and power of the middle-echelon officers who dominated them.

It was on the basis of the Second Committee's recommendations that the Naval Affairs Bureau was restructured in November 1940. Many of its manifold duties were transferred to the newly established Naval Ordnance Bureau. Moreover a Second Section was created within the Naval Affairs Bureau to specialize in foreign and defense policy and to take over liaison with the army. By the very nature of its assigned tasks, the Second Section came to be infected with the army's biases and so was strongly inclined to assume a bellicose posture toward the United States and Great Britain. Its chief, Captain Ishikawa Shingo (already mentioned in connection with the "German faction") was generally known as "the direct heir to the Katō-Suetsugu line." A brilliant but somewhat unbalanced man with a touch of fanaticism, Ishikawa took the toughest stand of all the middle-echelon officers. Maintaining extensive contacts not only with "radical" army officers but also with men prominent in political and right-wing circles (Foreign Minister Matsuoka Yōsuke, for example), he was perhaps the most active of the junior officers during the crises of 1940-41.[34]

Another institutional factor that added to the influence of middle-echelon planners was the establishment in late 1940 of a new First Committee (not to be confused with the earlier committee bearing the same name). This machinery, designed to provide strong "collective leadership," was an outgrowth of the mounting impatience of energetic junior-grade officers with the "vacillation" and "inaction" of upper-echelon leaders. Their aims were to create a consensus of views among the key section chiefs in both the ministry and the General Staff, draft policy recommendations, and press them upon their superiors. Recent studies[35] have thrown light on the catalytic role played by this committee in crystallizing the navy's "determination" to go to war with the United States.

The central figures on the committee were Captains Ishikawa and Tomioka Sadatoshi, chief of the Operations Section; the other two members were "staff officer A" and the chief of the First Section of the Naval Affairs Bureau.[36]

These men naturally tended to view Japanese-American relations from the parochial perspective of their professional or sectional concerns—war planning and preparations—rather than in the broader context of national policy. (None of them, incidentally, had any close firsthand knowledge of the United States.) Yet, in the pervasive atmosphere of *gekokujō* (rule from below) their recommendations met with little resistance from their superiors, so that for all practical purposes the navy's policymaking came, in the words of one of its members, to "revolve around the First Committee." Moreover, within the Navy

General Staff the Section Chiefs Conference, which met on an informal basis from November 1940 on, had also come to serve as an instrument for pressing the demands of junior staff officers.[37] The views of these officials, whether voiced collectively or individually, carried all the more weight because the "Ōsumi purge" had by then effectively crippled the navy's upper-echelon leadership.

III

The almost fatalistic belief in the inevitability of war with the United States which pervaded the ranks of the middle-echelon officers can best be understood by turning once more to Admiral Katō Kanji and the total negation of the "Washington system" which he personified.

At the heart of Katō's naval doctrine lay the Mahanian dictum that "the rise and fall of sea power determines the destiny of nations."[38] He maintained that the "irresistible lure of the Pacific" spelled an eventual naval showdown between Japan and the United States in which each side would contend for its economic stake in China. As a "capitalistic-imperialistic nation," the United States was bound to find the outlet for its expansive energies where it would meet the least resistance—the Pacific Ocean. Naval limitation was merely a thin humanitarian veil to hide America's desire for economic domination over East Asia, and the Washington and London conferences were simply steps in this direction. The resulting treaty system was an instrument for perpetuating America's naval supremacy and preserving a status quo that benefited the United States.

These ideas were, of course, not original with or peculiar to Katō Kanji, but the way in which he related them to his world view brought out certain ideological strains alien to the Japanese naval tradition. According to his reading of history, the westward advance of American civilization across the Pacific, with all its "poisonous" effects on Japan, was the grand culmination of four centuries of steady expansion of "materialistic Western civilization." In this overall framework, his anti-Americanism merged into a general revulsion against Westernism, capitalism, and materialism—"isms" which he identified externally with the Washington treaty system and domestically with the established political and social order. And so his doctrine came to be associated with a sort of right-wing "spiritualism" or "Japanism." His speeches during the 1920s and 1930s abound in semi-mystical exhortations of the "unparalleled Yamato spirit," "bushido," "Japan's great mission to purify world thought." It was no coincidence that he was an influential member of Baron Hiranuma's ultrana-tionalist Kokuhonsha (National Foundation Society).[39]

Viewed in another way, however, Katō's brand of "spiritualism" may also be regarded as a psychological compensation for the inferior ratio of 60 percent accorded Japan in the Washington Treaty—a ratio which he calculated was insufficient to meet Japan's security needs. One way to overcome such handicaps, he believed, was to pit Japan's "will power" against America's physical superiority, thus "turning an impossibility into a possiblity." In order to attain maximum fighting efficiency, he immediately ordered the Combined Fleet to engage in relentless drills and maneuvers whose target was the United

States.[40] In time his obsession bred a mental habit of slighting the material basis of national power so crucial in modern total war. And his idée fixe that Japan must have a ratio amounting to 70 percent of the American fleet strength fostered the belief that once this ratio was attained Japan would prevail in war.

Katō's ideas were reflected in the significant changes that had taken place in the meaning of the term "hypothetical enemy." Beginning with the Imperial National Defense Policy of 1907 it had simply stood for a "budgetary" enemy—in other words, the United States had conveniently served as the target for the navy's building plans and was utilized as such in contests with the army over budgetary appropriations.[41] For Katō, however, the United States was far more than a "hypothetical enemy" in this limited sense: it was an arch-antagonist with whom hostilities were unavoidable. At the time of the Washington Conference he is said to have asserted that, as far as he was concerned, war with the United States started on the day the inferior ratio was "imposed" on Japan.[42] In accord with such a conviction the 1923 version of the Imperial National Defense Policy singled out the United States as the power "most likely to collide with Japan in the near future." It was a supreme irony of naval limitation that the idea of inevitable war with the United States began to take root in the Japanese navy just when the Washington Treaty had made it seemingly impossible for either side to wage offensive naval warfare across the Pacific.

The Japanese navy's answer to the strategic deadlock it faced was to devise submarine tactics that would offset the "deficiencies" of the 60 percent ratio in capital ships. Developed by Admiral Suetsugu Nobumasa in 1923-25 when he commanded the First Submarine Squadron, the plan was perfected in the "strategy of interceptive operations" (*yōgeki sakusen*) after he became commander-in-chief of the Combined Fleet in 1933. Simply stated, this strategy sought: (1) through repeated submarine attacks to "gradually reduce" by about 30 percent the actual fighting capabilities of the U.S. fleet on its transpacific passage; and (2) to seek an all-out "decisive encounter" with the main fleet after it had advanced to the western Pacific. The combat mission assigned to the submarine—a major role in the early stage of interceptive operations and an important auxiliary role in the main fleet engagement—was a unique feature of Japanese strategy.[43] For this purpose large, high-speed submarines were built in great numbers. Supremely confident that his strategy would overcome the U.S. navy, Admiral Suetsugu freely indulged in warlike talk. However, the Japanese navy vastly underestimated the capability of American submarines. Assuming that Americans were inherently unsuited to strenuous submarine duty, Japanese naval strategists commonly regarded two weeks as being the limit of American endurance.[44]

In the course of the 1930s the anticipated theater of the main fleet encounter moved steadily eastward as the range of ships and planes increased. Originally situated in Japan's home waters, it was relocated in 1934 on the line linking the Bonins and the Mariana Islands and by 1940 had been further advanced to the line of the Marshalls. But the basic conception remained intact throughout the decade. Despite the modern flavor added by the submarine (and later by aircraft), the concept of interceptive operations essentially embodied the traditional "principle of huge battleships and big guns" (*taikan kyohō shugi*). It was based on the "lesson of history" derived from the legendary Battle of the

Japan Sea in 1905, when Admiral Tōgō's Combined Fleet annihilated the Russian Baltic Fleet which was already exhausted by the long cruise from Europe. The "lesson" was reinforced by the Battle of Jutland during the First World War. This classic pattern had hardened into a dogma that continued to govern conservative naval strategic thinking throughout the 1930s and even beyond. The building programs, fleet organization, education, and maneuvers of the Japanese navy were all based upon this precept.[45]

The strategy of "interceptive operations" raised some questions that disturbed Japan's naval planners. Would the United States navy choose to throw its main force into a decisive fleet encounter early in the war? Would it not be more likely to refrain from advancing into the western Pacific until it had built up an overwhelming strength? One would also expect Japanese naval planners to prepare for another contingency: should a quick and decisive engagement fail to materialize and the conflict instead turn into a drawn-out war of attrition, would not Japan be placed at a mounting disadvantage by America's industrial superiority? Yet, strangely enough, such a prospect does not seem to have been squarely faced until hostilities loomed immediately ahead. To cite one notable example, the Tactical Plan adopted in 1936 provided only for the initial stages of operations—the annihilation of the U.S. fleet in Far Eastern waters and the capture of the Philippines and Guam. The subsequent phases of a possibly protracted war were dismissed with the simple statement that "such expedient measures as the occasion may demand shall be taken."[46]

The fact was that even if a successful main fleet engagement should take place early in the war, the chances of ultimate victory still remained questionable. The expectation widely shared among Japanese naval officers in the mid-thirties was that a smashing victory in the main encounter would cause such heavy damage to U.S. battleships (which could not be speedily replaced) as to cripple America's will to fight on. As an additional measure to shake the enemy's morale, the Japanese navy from time to time apparently toyed with the rather unrealistic idea of submarine raids to disrupt the sea communications of the United States in its home waters.[47] Behind this underestimation of the enemy's fighting morale lay an image of the United States as a composite nation of immigrants lacking in national solidarity. Be that as it may, the fixation with a main fleet encounter tended to blind conservative naval officers to the extent to which technological innovations were rapidly transforming the conventional methods of naval warfare and necessitating a fundamental reassessment of their strategic concepts.

In sharp contrast to the conservative majority stood men like Admirals Yamamoto and Inoue, who had successfully readjusted their strategic thinking and had radically different images of the United States. Yamamoto's views were informed with a realism derived from firsthand observations and experience in the United States. He had attended Harvard as a language officer during 1919-21, revisited the country on an inspection tour in 1923-24, and served as naval attaché in Washington from 1925 to 1927. He often warned against the mistake of dismissing the American people as "weak-willed and spoiled by material luxuries"; on the contrary, he asserted, they were infused with "a fierce fighting spirit and an adventurous temperament." As historical evidence he cited the legendary frontier spirit, the daring exploits of Admiral Farragut of "Damn the torpedoes!" fame, and the blockading of Santiago and the advance through a minefield in Manila Bay during the Spanish-American War.[48] Contrasting the "Yamato spirit" and the "Yankee spirit," he pointed out that the former too often verged on blind daredevilry, whereas the latter was soundly grounded on science and technology—a case in point being Lindbergh's transatlantic solo flight. America's industrial might and matchless resources convinced him of the manifest impossibility of waging naval war against the United States. "Anyone who has seen the auto factories in Detroit and the oil fields in Texas," he observed on one occasion, "knows that Japan lacks the national power for a naval race with America." Concerning the existing naval situation he declared: "The 5:5:3 ratio works just fine for us; it [the Washington Naval Treaty] is a treaty to restrict the *other* parties [the United States and Britain]."

In his days as an attaché in Washington Yamamoto had come under the powerful influence of the new school of strategic thought, vociferously advocated by that champion of air power Brigadier General William (Billy) Mitchell. As early as 1928 he had predicted that in the near future air power would become the mainstay of the navy. The keen interest he took in building air armaments and a modern flying corps is attested to by the fact that upon his return from the London Naval Conference of 1930 he asked to be appointed chief of the Technical Division of Naval Aviation, and in 1935-36 he headed the Naval Aviation Headquarters. Sharply critical of "hardheaded gunners" and Admiral Suetsugu's strategy of a main fleet encounter, Yamamoto argued that a frontal engagement of battleships á la grand naval review was a thing of the past. By 1940 he was convinced that the air-power age he had foreseen in 1928 had become a reality. He expressed these views forcefully to the navy minister.[49]

An even more thoroughgoing and outspoken advocate of air power was Vice Admiral Inoue, head of Naval Aviation Headquarters in 1940-41: he envisaged nothing less than a virtual conversion of the navy into an air force. In a closely argued memorandum to the navy minister he pointed out with alarm how obsolete Japan's armaments had been rendered by the "great revolution" in technology. He derided the Japanese navy's fixation with naval ratios, aptly terming it a "ratio neurosis," and insisted that it was simply a waste of money to build battleships that were no match for land-based planes. Asserting that "who commands the air commands the sea," he declared that American naval leaders would not be "so stupid or reckless" as to mount offensive operations in the western Pacific if Japan controlled the air. And, he added, mastery of the air would in turn require adequately fortified air bases on the islands of the South Pacific. With a prophetic note, Inoue stated that any future war with the United States would revolve around a contest for those islands. In conclusion, he again urged the vital necessity of rational armaments plans based on a redefinition of the nature, the form, and the strategic objectives of a possible war with the United States.[50]

While they did not always possess the broad outlook of men like Inoue and Yamamoto, Japanese naval aviators since about 1934 had become increasingly convinced that the battleship was "superfluous" and must give way to the aircraft as the decisive weapon of naval warfare. Some in aviation circles adopted the concept of an air offensive against the United States as early as 1936. In November of that year the Navy War College produced a "Study of

Strategy and Tactics in Operations against the United States," which contained
this striking passage: "In case the enemy's main fleet is berthed at Pearl Harbor,
the idea should be to open hostilities by surprise attacks from the air."[51] In July
1937 Naval Aviation Headquarters asserted in a notable study that since control
of the western Pacific would be decided by land-based planes, "the ratio of fleet
strength between Japan and the United States would hardly come into the
picture." In fact, the study went on to suggest a *reduction* of the navy on the
grounds that a large part of its conventional tasks could now be performed by an
air force with greater effectiveness and at less cost.[52]

   In view of the fact that both in the United States and in Britain the
battleship was still commonly regarded as the backbone of the navy, the
aviation-oriented Yamamoto-Inoue group must be credited with unusual
far-sightedness. But this group was in a decided minority, and its ideas were far
too advanced to find acceptance among the leaders of the Navy General Staff
and the fleets. Having built their careers on battleships and gunnery, the
conservative "mainstream" remained committed to these weapons.[53]

   From the above analysis, it would appear that the many diverse views that
existed within the Japanese navy of the 1930s fell into a recognizable pattern in
that the line of conflict over strategy and the related question of types of
weapons roughly coincided with divisions over concepts of foreign policy and
ideological orientation. Thus, on the one hand, the Katō-Suetsugu group adhered
to the traditional precept of "huge battleships and big guns," introduced a
"spiritualistic" mode of thinking into the navy, and professed jingoistic,
anti-American, and pro-German sentiments. On the other hand, men like
Yamamoto and Inoue adjusted their strategic ideas to the realities of air power
and, in doing so, upheld the "scientific-technical" or "rational" mentality
traditional in the navy; moreover, politically they championed the anti-Axis line
and the policy of avoiding war with the Anglo-American powers.

   These, then, were the leadership groupings and the interrelated sets of
assumptions, images, and values that shaped the navy's policymaking. The
second part of this paper will focus on several key issues to examine the
development of naval policy during the 1930s.

IV

   The central concern of the Japanese navy during the first half of the
decade was the "problem of naval limitation," that is, the problem of how to
remove the "fetters" of the "humiliating treaties" of Washington and London.
The bitter memories of past naval conferences had so conditioned the majority
of Japanese naval officers that the words "disarmament" or "naval limitation"
automatically conjured up the image of American "oppression" of Japan.[54]

   Efforts to offset the "deficiencies" of Japan's "treaty navy" had begun
early—in fact, even before the London Naval Treaty was signed. As a quid pro
quo for accepting the treaty's compromise formula, Japanese naval leaders had
won the government's consent to a supplemental naval budget and certain
practical measures designed to minimize the anticipated shortcomings in naval
defense.[55] The navy's "secret" aim, as Vice Navy Minister Kobayashi Seizō later
disclosed, was "to avail ourselves of the seeming concessions [of the London

Treaty] as a golden opportunity to fill deficiencies that had theretofore plagued the navy and to effect a substantial increase in our naval strength."[56] The navy's budgetary demands were concretely spelled out when on July 23, 1930 the Supreme War Council presented the "official reply to the Throne"—again with Prime Minister Hamaguchi's concurrence. Significantly, this document stated that upon the expiration of the London Treaty at the end of 1936, "the empire should complete its naval defense by whatever means it deems best." Thus the navy clearly indicated that the treaty was not to be renewed in its existing form.[57]

In early October, soon after official ratification of the treaty by the Privy Council, Navy Minister Abo Kiyokazu began to press the government for approval of a supplemental naval budget, holding the prime minister to his earlier promises. Abo was under strong pressure from Admirals Katō Kanji and Suetsugu, who threatened to overthrow the cabinet unless the navy's demands were granted.[58] After considerable wrangling with the Finance Ministry, the navy finally obtained budgetary support for a "first supplemental building program," to span the years 1931-36.[59] Under this program Japan proceeded steadily to enhance its naval strength. Toward the end of 1933 its overall fleet strength was approaching 80 percent of that of the United States, which had failed to build up to treaty limits. But by this time the Manchurian Incident had so aggravated relations with the United States that the navy was rapidly coming to the conclusion that Japan's security required the removal of all restrictions on naval armament.

During the summer of 1932, when a crisis was anticipated over the submission of the Lytton report, the Japanese naval attaché in Washington wired Tokyo a series of overly alarmist forecasts of an impending armed clash between Japan and the United States over the Manchurian question. His reports also noted "warlike preparations" on the part of the U.S. navy. The decision to retain the American Scouting Force on the Pacific coast (instead of sending it home to the east coast) after the annual naval maneuvers, coupled with subsequent rumors that the Scouting Force might even be advanced to Hawaii, caused further anxiety, which in turn strengthened the hands of Japan's naval expansionists.[60] A deepening sense of isolation in the aftermath of Japan's withdrawal from the League of Nations in March 1933, the prospect of a continuing crisis in its relations with the United States, the fear of active American (or Anglo-American) intervention in Far Eastern affairs, and an uneasiness about the predicted U.S. naval build-up—all these factors had combined by the fall of 1933 to crystallize a resolution among Japanese naval planners to terminate the "unequal" treaties and demand parity at the forthcoming London parley.[61]

This was the course vigorously advocated by Commander Ishikawa Shingo of the Navy General Staff. In a lengthy memorandum submitted to Katō Kanji in October he argued that parity was indispensable to Japan's security since nothing less would suffice to prevent the United States from mounting a transpacific offensive. On the achievement of parity, he said, depended the fate of Japan's Manchurian venture and its claims regarding the "Asian Monroe Doctrine."

Similarly, Admiral Suetsugu asserted that the naval and Manchurian questions were inseparable. Was it not, he asked, the forbidding presence of the imperial navy that had enabled Japan to defy the protests of the League of Nations and beat off American efforts at intimidation by covering the ocean flanks while the army completed the conquest of Manchuria?[62] Admiral Katō also shared these views, but he denounced the inferior naval ratio particularly for its pernicious effects on the navy's morale. If only, he asserted, the "cancer" of the Washington Naval Treaty could be excised, "the morale and self-confidence of our navy would be so bolstered that we could count on certain victory over our hypothetical enemy, no matter how overwhelming the physical odds against us."[63]

Katō's sweeping assertion, made in total disregard of the limits of national power, typified the highly emotional, all-or-nothing psychology that was seizing naval circles. Furthermore, Germany's concurrent bid for rearmament, followed by its withdrawal from the European disarmament conference, gave a powerful stimulus to Japan's naval planners who were clamoring for "the sovereign right of free armament."[64] Indeed, naval spokesmen from Admiral Suetsugu on down became so shrill in their inflammatory talk of "the coming crisis of 1935-36" (when the Washington and London naval treaties were to expire) that Vice Foreign Minister Shigemitsu Mamoru seriously feared the navy wanted to "fight with the United States around 1936."[65]

That the agitation within the navy led the ranking ministry leaders to adopt a stiffer attitude is clear from Navy Minister Ōsumi's statements at a Five Ministers Conference in October 1933. "If the United States should take a strong stand in opposition to our fundamental policy," he declared, "we must resolutely repel it, and with this in view we must proceed to complete our [naval] preparedness." To do so required "freeing ourselves of the disadvantageous restrictions imposed by the existing naval treaties."[66]

Interestingly, the initiative in restraining the navy came from Army Ministry leaders, ever sensitive to any diversion of military appropriations to a large-scale naval race. In a series of army-navy parleys beginning in the spring of 1934, the representatives of the two services vainly tried to iron out their differences. By early summer the Navy Ministry was demanding nothing less than out-and-out parity, although it admitted that there was not the slightest chance that this demand would be accepted at the forthcoming London talks.

On July 20 Army Minister Hayashi Senjūrō entreated Ōsumi to reconsider the inflexible policy which, he felt, was bound to cause the rupture of negotiations. But the navy minister refused to budge. In reply to the objection that prior announcement of Japan's intention to abrogate the Washington Naval Treaty would provoke a joint Anglo-American front at the coming London talks, he retorted: Would not America team up with Britain in any event? Had it not been the practice of the United States to browbeat Japan with the specter of a naval race? Harboring a deep distrust of the United States, he was prepared to force a showdown.[67]

Meanwhile Ōsumi had been applying pressure on the new Prime Minister Okada Keisuke by threatening to resign unless the navy's demands regarding parity were accepted. These demands, Ōsumi declared ominously, had already been privately presented to the emperor by Chief of the Navy General Staff Prince Fushimi and had won his approval. Ōsumi appeared to be resorting to the familiar device of abusing Prince Fushimi's authority—this time to intimidate the prime minister, a naval genro squarely in the "orthodox" tradition,[68] who had been chosen in the expectation that he would be able to check the Katō-Suetsugu group, control the navy, and conclude a new naval treaty. However, Prince Fushimi had in fact submitted to the Throne a sealed letter containing the "wishes" of the navy, which had been drafted—as might be surmised—by his vice chief. The document stated: "There is no other choice but to discard the existing system of [discriminatory] ratios and vigorously pursue a policy of equality [of armaments]; *otherwise, the navy will not be able to control its officers.*" As it turned out, the emperor had indignantly rejected the document, commenting with unusual severity on Prince Fushimi's highly irregular procedure in submitting it.[69]

At the Five Ministers Conference of July 24 Prime Minister Okada maintained that the notice to abrogate the Washington Treaty should be delayed at least pending the preliminary London talks. He received the solid support of the army, foreign, and finance ministers. Uppermost in the ministers' minds, of course, were the financial consequences of an unlimited armaments race. They believed that while Japan might be able to hold out for a year or two, it would eventually face bankruptcy. They also feared a possible Anglo-American coalition which, if it eventuated, was bound to have serious repercussions on Japan's policy toward China. Their arguments, however, failed to move Ōsumi, who objected that naval circles could "hardly be pacified by such explanations."[70]

Ōsumi's response was an allusion to the backstage maneuverings of Katō and Suetsugu, then at the peak of their influence. The two senior admirals had been making a round of visits to the commanders of the Combined Fleet to line them up firmly behind the demand for parity. Katō had even induced some sixty of them to draft a joint memorial which was submitted to Ōsumi and Prince Fushimi through Suetsugu.[71] Moreover both Katō and Suetsugu spoke up forcibly at a conference of senior naval leaders. Katō asserted that the demand for parity was "absolute" and that the entire navy had "burned its bridges behind it." Unless the cabinet at once decided for parity, he warned, the navy would no longer be able to maintain control over its restive young officers.[72]

Notoriously vulnerable to such pressures, Ōsumi became frantic. Any attempt by the government to "suppress the general wishes of the navy," he nervously told Saionji's secretary Harada, would be an "utter disaster." Prime Minister Okada had earlier considered the possibility of replacing Ōsumi with the moderate Admiral Kobayashi Seizō, but he apparently concluded that it was too risky, for he was fully cognizant of the activities of the Katō-Suetsugu team. Finally, on September 7 Okada admitted defeat when the cabinet decided that before the end of the year it would issue the required two years' notice of the abrogation of the Washington Naval Treaty.[73] Since the navy remained utterly irreconcilable, there was no alternative that would not have produced an internal political crisis.

General conditions and the climate of opinion in 1934 were essentially different from those which had prevailed at the time of the London Naval Conference of 1930. The deterioration of Japan's international situation has already been noted. At home, party government had come to an end. Within the navy the "Ōsumi purge" had made such a clean sweep of the "treaty faction" that there remained few voices of caution and restraint in the upper echelons. The emperor was deeply worried that the navy was "jeopardizing vital diplomatic problems for the sake of placating subordinate officers." Clamoring for the "right of supreme command" and fortified by its recently revised rules, the Navy General Staff asserted its exclusive right to determine fleet strength and flatly rejected any outside interference. Suetsugu even insisted on appealing directly to the Throne in order to circumvent the cabinet, although in the end such a procedure proved unnecessary.[74]

Above all, the nightmarish memory of the May 15 Incident practically immobilized the government leaders. They were haunted by the fear that another controversy over naval limitation would rekindle domestic violence which would surpass in scale the earlier "incidents." In that event jingoists and right-wing malcontents might well exploit insurgent young naval officers—and vice versa—to upset the existing social order. Admiral Suetsugu had been warning that such would be the consequences of any concession that might be made at the coming naval talks. His and Katō's known connections with "radical" right-wing forces within and without the navy lent sinister color to such a threat. The Finance Ministry, although hypersensitive to the economic consequences of a naval race, felt compelled to remind the ruling circles of the importance of handling the navy with great care and of assuring it that the government would rather break up the London talks than go against its wishes. Even moderate admirals like Nomura Kichisaburō and Kobayashi Seizō admitted that emotions in the navy had been allowed to go too far for the government to reverse the tide.[75]

How did the navy expect its aim of security to be served by withdrawing from the existing system of naval limitation? Deeply disturbed by this question, the emperor queried Prince Fushimi about the self-defeating nature of the navy's demand for parity: Would it not result only in wrecking the naval conference and reopening the armaments race, and in that event would Japan not inevitably be outbuilt by the United States? Prince Fushimi merely repeated the navy's stock answer: There was nothing to fear from an arms race since it would entail no substantial increase in naval expenditures. Going further, the Navy General Staff contended that unrestrained naval construction would actually be *more economical,* for Japan would be free to concentrate on ship categories "best suited to its peculiar national requirements."[76]

The key to the navy's seemingly paradoxical position was the "unsinkable" monster battleship of the *Yamato-Musashi* type carrying 18-inch guns. With a rough plan for the construction of such ships ready in the fall of 1934, the navy counted on getting a head start of at least five years on the United States. Even if the latter should in due course attempt to catch up, the mobility of any comparable ships it built would be curtailed by the Panama Canal bottleneck. Commander Ishikawa, one of the early enthusiasts of the plan, calculated that the mammoth battleships would "at one bound raise our [capital ship] strength from the present ratio of 60 percent of U.S. strength to a position of absolute supremacy."[77] Here was an inverted expression of the "ratio neurosis" discussed earlier. Japanese strategists designed these mighty battleships (which were to operate under an "air umbrella") as the navy's decisive weapon to deliver the fatal blow in the main fleet encounter. Despite some technical innovations,[78] the *Yamato-Musashi* plan essentially rested on—in fact improved on—the conventional precept of "huge battleships and big guns." From the very moment of its inception, such air power advocates as Yamamoto mercilessly derided the plan as anachronistic, but he was unable to dissuade its devotees led by Admiral Suetsugu.

As had been anticipated, the preliminary talks in London were ship-wrecked on the rock of the Japanese demand for parity. Yamamoto, who represented Japan, subtly registered his disagreement with his superiors when he stated in his report to the Throne that "there was no appearance whatsoever of two powers [the United States and Great Britain] combining to oppress the third [Japan] at these talks." But his remarks met with a frigid reception from the navy minister.[79] In January 1936 Admiral Nagano walked out of the main conference, thus signaling the resumption of the armaments race. Under the impetus of the Vinson-Trammell bill passed in March 1934, the Japanese navy had already embarked on its "second building program" (to span the years 1934-37) and by the end of 1935 had exceeded the quota set by the Washington and London treaties.

V

In the mid-thirties Japanese officers generally tended to regard the U.S. naval build-up as a hostile move aimed at checking Japan while furthering America's own "ambition to dominate the Far East." Their suspicions were intensified by what they took to be provocative statements by American admirals, made publicly or in the Senate Committee on Naval Affairs. They carefully noted the remarks of Admiral Harry E. Yarnell and other "hard-liners," especially when such comments referred to an eventual collision over China or to the need for a 40 percent naval superiority so that the United States could defeat Japan in its home waters. Furthermore, the large-scale American naval maneuvers of 1935, held west of Hawaii near Midway, were a major irritant to the Japanese navy.[80] In addition, by the mid-1930s the Navy General Staff had fairly accurate information about America's War Plan Orange; it therefore knew that the plan envisaged a steady advance of the U.S. fleet from Hawaii to the Marshalls, the Carolines, and westward for the eventual main encounter.[81]

The total effect was to reinforce Japanese naval officers in their mental habit of viewing themselves in a defensive role vis-à-vis the United States, whereas in reality their war plans were predicated on Japan's taking the offensive at the outset. In any event, they entertained a growing conviction that the United States had embarked on a course of containing Japan—by gradually tightening the ring of bases that menaced the Japanese islands from the west (Hawaii), the south (the Philippines), and the north (the Aleutians); by extending assistance to China, especially with regard to aviation; and by restoring diplomatic relations with the Soviet Union. Moreover they believed that Great Britain, acting in concert with the United States, was strengthening the defense of Singapore. In 1936 Commander Ishikawa returned from an inspection tour of Southeast Asia with the vivid impression that a "military-political-economic ABCD encirclement" of Japan was in the making. In the spring of the same year the Operations Section of the Navy General Staff reached the point of fearing that the United States might decide to move the advanced base of its fleet from Hawaii to the Philippines, thereby totally undermining Japan's operational plans.[82]

These fears and anxieties, greatly exaggerated and premature as they were, seem to have been cultivated by Japanese naval planners as a pretext for naval expansion. Nevertheless the fact remains that the geographical advantages the Japanese navy had hitherto enjoyed in Far Eastern waters were beginning to disappear as a result of rapid advances in weaponry—the increased range of ships and planes—and the consequent lessening of strategic distance. That elusive goal of naval security, which Japan had sought to attain by withdrawing from the existing treaty system, was farther away than ever.

The search for a rationale for fleet expansion in the treatyless situation eventually led to the articulation of the navy's aim of "southward advance" in the now famous "Fundamentals of National Policy" adopted by the Five Ministers Conference on August 7, 1936. The navy's aims, resting on the premise "defend the north, advance to the south," can best be seen in a policy paper it had produced in April. In this it was stated that in expanding into the South Seas Japan must "as a matter of course anticipate obstruction and coercion by the United States, Britain, and the Netherlands, etc. and must therefore provide for the worst by completing preparations for a resort to force." Thus the "hypothetical enemy" character of the United States was further accentuated, and Great Britain was included for the first time among Japan's potential enemies.[83]

As to the naval officers and attachés stationed in China, they were comparatively free of the intense preoccupation with the problem of operations against the United States that prevailed in naval circles in Tokyo, and took a more cautious attitude toward a "southward advance." The commander-in-chief of the Third Fleet recommended that for the moment the strategic target be confined to the Soviet Union and the danger of a showdown with the United States avoided. The Navy General Staff, however, rejected this counsel as a negation of Japan's destiny as a sea power and as a virtual surrender to the army's desire for priority in armaments.[84]

Repudiating the army's demand for concentration on the Soviet Union, the navy remained adamant in its insistence on having priority in arming against the United States. In support of its position Navy Minister Nagano argued that "at the time of the Shanghai Incident it was our naval strength which caused Chief of Naval Operations Pratt to oppose the coercive policy Secretary Stimson suggested."[85] After tortuous interservice negotiations, the "Fundamentals of National Policy" merely registered the competitive claims of the army and the navy—expansion toward both the north and the south. In pursuance of the latter aim the document stressed the need to "strengthen naval armaments in order to ensure the command of the western Pacific against the American navy." On the basis of this decision Nagano demanded and obtained appropriations of up to one billion yen for a huge "third building program" involving sixty-six new ships and fourteen flying corps.[86]

The navy's characteristic mode of policymaking stands out clearly in the process described above. Instead of formulating strategic plans in accordance with national policy, the navy started with its defense needs and the necessary budgetary support and proceeded to define a national policy. A typical product of interservice compromise, the policy decision of 1936 failed utterly to establish any system of strategic priorities and to coordinate military planning with foreign policy. Nor was the newly revised Imperial National Defense Policy adopted in 1936 ever to come up for review in subsequent years; bureaucratic rivalry between the army and the navy simply precluded any such attempt. Thus it was destined to become too antiquated by 1940-41 to provide any useful guidelines whatsoever.

With the adoption of the "Fundamentals of National Policy" the navy's program of southward advance entered a new stage significantly different from the earlier phases that had emphasized commercial expansion. After 1936 the governing factor was a strategic consideration—the need to secure in the South China Sea advance bases for operations or springboards en route to the South Seas. A perfect pretext for acquiring such territories seemed to be presented by the Pakhoi Incident of early September 1936, which involved the murder of a Japanese merchant in a city bordering on the Gulf of Tonkin. The Navy General Staff meditated a forcible occupation of the Chinese island of Hainan with the full expectation that this would lead to a confrontation with Great Britain. In fact, the Operations Section went so far as to draft a plan for preliminary fleet mobilization aimed not only against China but also against the Anglo-American powers. Although the coercive, even belligerent measures advocated by the Navy General Staff did not materialize at this time, they foreshadowed the firm stand it was to take after the outbreak of the China War.[87]

The navy, which had remained a censorious bystander to the army's "positive policy" as long as it was confined to north China, began to outdo the army once the fighting threatened to spread to central and south China, traditionally the navy's "spheres of defense." Thereafter it pursued a highly opportunistic policy, taking advantage of the China War, whenever possible, to push its program of southward advance. Thus on July 11, 1937—barely four days after the Marco Polo Bridge Incident—the Navy General Staff wrung from the reluctant army an agreement to send expeditionary forces to Shanghai and Tsingtao to protect Japanese residents. Navy Minister Yonai opposed a Shanghai expedition for fear of provoking Britain and the United States, but on August 12 he finally yielded to the demand of the Navy General Staff. At the same time the navy decided to step up its preparedness with a view to repulsing possible "interference by third powers."[88] As a result of the China War the navy now had at its disposal a large emergency fund, so that thenceforth its demands centered on the allocation of war matériel rather than on budgetary appropriations.[89]

The China War had revived the navy's hopes of acquiring Hainan, rich in iron ore and strategically located for further moves southward. Again the views of the Navy General Staff prevailed. In February 1939 Hainan was brought under Japanese occupation, and the Spratley Islands a month later.

One reason why the moderate naval leaders from Yonai on down were unable to restrain the southward drive of the Navy General Staff was that they had their hands full trying to block the military alliance with Germany. As Admiral Inoue later stated: "A large part of our time and energy was spent, not in positive and constructive endeavors, but in negative efforts at naysaying."[90]

VI

The first and foremost task that Navy Minister Yonai had set for himself upon assuming office in February 1937 was to restore order and control within the navy, which had been allowed to all but disintegrate during the Ōsumi-Nagano era. For this purpose, he strictly forbade naval officers to meddle in politics. He was determined to assume full responsibility for handling the question of an Axis alliance. In this endeavor he had the loyal support of Vice Minister Yamamoto and head of the Naval Affairs Bureau Inoue. For Yamamoto, whose political shrewdness made him Yonai's right-hand man, here was the opportunity he had long dreamed of: to "rebuild" the navy along "orthodox" lines. In fact, he was prepared to have Katō Kanji and Suetsugu cashiered if they stood in the way. And Inoue, who styled himself a "radical liberalist," was a man of determination, if at times dogmatic and somewhat eccentric.[91]

From the outset, however, this celebrated "trio" was beset with handicaps; they had to contend not only with the army but also with active Axis sympathizers within the navy. Among the middle-echelon officers who were "spearheads" of the pro-German forces were Captain Oka Takasumi, the chief of the First Section of the Naval Affairs Bureau; Oka's subordinates Commanders Kami Shigenori, Shiba Katsuo, and Fujii Shigeru; and "Staff Officer A" Yokoi Tadao. (Kami, Shiba, and Yokoi had recently returned from the attaché's office in Berlin.) The Yonai-Yamamoto-Inoue triumvirate therefore represented an isolated minority. One method of controlling their unruly subordinates was to keep them ignorant of the policy deliberations being conducted at higher levels. But this had the drawback of causing deep resentment among section chiefs, who were all the more distressed because their army counterparts seemed fully apprised of the course of discussions at Five Ministers Conferences.[92] Moreover, this lack of communication between the upper and middle echelons of the navy hampered, confused, and misled the latter in their tasks of policy formulation and staff coordination with the army.

When in August 1938 the navy's subordinate officers began seriously to study Ribbentrop's proposal for a military alliance, they proceeded on the mistaken assumption that the navy minister approved of a pact aimed not only against the Soviet Union but also against Britain and France.[93] Their support for a broad military alliance with Germany drew its emotional force from the violent anti-British feelings that were rapidly permeating naval circles, especially in the staff corps.

An idea of the intensity of the hostility toward Britain and its causes can be obtained from a revealing memorandum drafted by the Navy General Staff about this time. The memorandum not only revived the old image of Great Britain as a haughty, selfish ingrate who had abandoned the Anglo-Japanese Alliance, but indicated that the old animosity was exacerbated by new frictions, incidents, and mutual recriminations arising out of the China War. In another memorandum Oka asserted that the China Incident had resolved itself into "diplomatic warfare" with Britain and that Japan's hand would be materially strengthened by a military alliance with Germany and Italy. Unlike his superiors, Oka was not deterred by fear of an Anglo-American coalition. Banking on the strength of isolationism in the United States, he was certain that America would never be persuaded to join Britain against the Axis bloc. The leaders in Washington, he asserted, had learned a bitter lesson from the First World War, during which they had poured out sixty billion dollars without reaping any benefits; moreover, they had not forgotten the postwar controversy over war debts. "It is only by maintaining its neutrality," Oka declared, "that the United States can hold the 'casting vote' in the world and fish in troubled waters."

Oka revealed the navy's inner motive for an anti-British alliance when he went on to argue that if the pact were to be directed against the Soviet Union alone, it could not "be used for the pursuit of national policy (*expanding to the South Seas*, etc.)." In other words, a strictly anti-Russian alliance would concede the army's priority in armaments, whereas a broader pact aimed against Britain as well would serve to direct national policy to a southward course, thereby strengthening the navy's case for increased armaments against the Anglo-American powers.[94] The budget-minded advocacy of an Axis alliance found a more explicit—if somewhat inverted—expression in a memorandum Captain Takagi handed to Baron Harada:

> To confine the target of the proposed pact to the Soviet Union alone would be inconsistent with the [navy's] reasons for reinforcing naval armaments. . . . We have set Britain and America as the targets of our fleet expansion program . . . and have not hesitated to demand naval appropriations amounting to a billion and a half yen. By reversing this stand and agreeing to confine our target to the Soviet Union, we would not only expose contradictions and inconsistencies in our naval policy, but also cause the army to draw the erroneous conclusion that the navy, though ready to use Britain and America as "pretexts" for securing a [large] budget, does not really intend to confront these powers.[95]

Such, then, were the motives of the navy's subordinate officers as they pursued their discussions with the army representatives. However, in mid-December 1938 they suddenly found themselves in a most awkward position vis-à-vis the army when they learned that Navy Minister Yonai had all along been absolutely opposed to an unconditional military alliance with Germany that included Britain, France, or the United States among its targets.[96]

As is well known, Admiral Yonai's objection was that such an alliance would most likely cause the United States to join hands with Great Britain, that together they would apply crushing economic pressure against Japan, and that eventually Japan would be dragged into war. At a Five Ministers Conference Yonai flatly declared that there was no chance of Japan's winning a conflict of this nature—the Japanese navy was "simply not designed to fight a war with America and Britain."[97]

As heir to Admiral Katō Tomosaburō's legacy, Yonai and his associates held fast to navy "orthodoxy": the Japanese fleet was an instrument of deterrence, not of war. Their anxiety to avoid provoking the United States was apparent during the crisis over the *Panay* incident of December 1937, when Yamamoto hastened to the American embassy to offer explanations in person. Also symbolic of their attitude toward the United States was the lavish hospitality extended to the officers and crew of the visiting *Astoria* in April 1939. During a dinner in honor of the *Astoria*'s Captain Richmond Kelly Turner, Yonai whispered to a highly receptive Ambassador Grew that the navy had no thought of ever fighting the United States.[98] The Germans, on their part, sought desperately through Ambassador Eugen Ott to dispel the senior naval leaders' awe of the U.S. and British fleets. In May Admiral Richard Foerster, former commander-in-chief of the German fleet, was dispatched to Tokyo to attempt to allay Japanese fears, but he was given the cold shoulder.[99]

In the course of some seventy-five sessions of the Five Ministers Conference Yonai, staking his office on his opposition to the Axis alliance, fought verbal duals with Army Minister Itagaki Seishirō. Yamamoto ably supported his chief at the risk of assassination, while Inoue restrained the dissident junior officers. But their efforts were destined to be no more than a holding action. They never managed—perhaps never really tried—to persuade their subordinates and, by simply ignoring the strongly held convictions of middle-echelon officers, succeeded only in inflaming further their antipathy. The Yonai-Yamamoto-Inoue leadership was of a highly personal type, resting on sheer force of "character"—therein lay its main weakness. Control over pro-German elements began to falter as soon as the three men left their posts when the Hiranuma cabinet fell in the bewildering aftermath of the Nazi-Soviet pact of August 1939.

Doubt remains as to how much Yonai and his associates were actually aware of this precarious situation. For example, when he recommended his soft-spoken classmate Yoshida Zengo as navy minister and an equally mild-mannered man as vice minister, Yamamoto said, "No matter who becomes navy minister or vice minister, it is absolutely impossible for the navy ever to be taken in by any such scheme as an offensive-defensive Axis alliance." Such comments certainly suggest over-confidence. On the other hand, when informed of the consummation of the Tripartite alliance, Yonai remarked: "Our opposition to the alliance was like paddling against the rapids only a few hundred yards upstream from Niagara Falls."[100]

Shortly after Navy Minister Yoshida took office, middle-echelon officers presented to him a policy paper ("Outline of Policy toward America") which indicated that their attitude was stiffening. In view of "the inseparable connection between Britain and America," it stated, an anti-British policy would inevitably lead to a deterioration of relations with the United States; therefore, the program of naval preparedness must be stepped up to guard against "a sudden unpredictable turn in American diplomacy."[101]

The German blitzkrieg in the spring of 1940 dazzled the Navy General Staff and further enhanced its admiration for Germany and its disdain for Britain and the United States. Those who urged a cautious policy toward the United States were branded "cowards" or "weaklings." No longer confined to middle-echelon ranks, the rekindled pro-Axis fervor came to infect bureau and division chiefs.[102] Though increasingly isolated, Navy Minister Yoshida continued to resist the trend of events despite mounting pressures from the Army and Foreign ministries. But in early September, as the result of severe mental strain, he suffered a physical collapse. His resignation was followed by a reshuffling of officials in the upper echelons of the

Navy Ministry and in consequence its leadership lacked coherence at this crucial juncture.

The appointment of Admiral Oikawa Koshirō as the new navy minister tipped the balance in favor of the Tripartite alliance. A scholarly type and a man of few words, Oikawa was not a very powerful leader. The only reservation he demanded in the treaty provisions was that Japan retain the right to determine the time and circumstances under which it would extend military assistance; once this condition was met, he promptly gave his formal consent at the Liaison Conference of September 14.

But why did the navy, which had so staunchly blocked the alliance for over two years, finally reverse its position? The major consideration, according to a version later given by Oikawa and his aggressive Vice Minister Toyoda Teijirō, was "political": they feared a frontal clash with the army might precipitate a serious domestic crisis. Indeed, the interservice antagonism had reached such a critical state that naval leaders are said to have considered an army coup d'état a distinct possibility.[103] Even if their fears were justified, however, this explanation hardly tells the whole story. For one thing, Oikawa did not dare admit openly (as Yonai had done earlier) that the navy was not capable of fighting the United States and Britain, because he felt that such a confession of weakness would seriously jeopardize the morale of naval officers and call into question the raison d'etre of the imperial navy itself. He may also have been partially persuaded by Foreign Minister Matsuoka's logic of "brinkmanship"—that the alliance was an instrument calculated to avert war with the United States. Furthermore, the pressures from naval subordinates could not be ignored.

The navy's perennial concern to obtain a larger share of the budget and war matériel was another unstated but important factor. The navy desired to reverse the priority given the army since the outbreak of the China War. This purpose could be served by an emphasis on a southward advance and a military alliance aimed at Britain and the United States. It was precisely with this in mind that Oikawa carefully coupled his consent to the Tripartite alliance with an insistence that the navy be given special consideration in the allocation of matériel.[104]

Vice Minister Toyoda years later described the navy's basic position as follows: "The navy accepted the Tripartite Pact, but it desired so far as possible to avoid war with the United States and to reserve Japan's freedom of action should hostilities break out between Germany and the United States. As regards the United States, however, we had to be adequately prepared to meet the worst contingency; we therefore demanded further reinforcements of naval armaments." The underlying ambivalence—the desire to avoid war coupled with a demand for preparations for war with the United States—was to prove the undoing of the Japanese navy.[105]

One additional factor in the navy's policymaking was its assessment of the war situation in Europe. From early summer into the fall of 1940 naval planners, especially at middle-echelon levels, tended to exaggerate the prospect of an imminent German victory, believing that German air strength ensured the favorable outcome of cross-channel operations against Britain. On the other hand, senior naval leaders attached greater value to the staying power of the royal navy and were skeptical of the chances for a quick German success.

Nevertheless the report submitted by the Intelligence Division of the Navy General Staff (headed by Oka Takasumi) on September 7, 1940 took a pessimistic view of Britain's chances. On the basis of this assessment the navy apparently came to look upon the Tripartite alliance in part as an instrument to restrain the United States from going to war with Germany before the end of 1940, by which time Britain would hopefully have been disposed of and the war in Europe ended. Despite repeated indications to the contrary, this kind of wishful thinking persisted long afterward and was later reinforced by the reports of Vice Admiral Nomura Naokuni, head of a naval inspection mission to Germany in 1941. As late as April of that year he was still predicting that a German invasion of the British Isles would be successful.[106]

VII

As noted previously, one of the navy's major motives for agreeing to the Tripartite alliance was a desire for southward expansion. In the end it was the question of the southward advance—or rather the American reaction to it—that precipitated what the navy termed its "determination" to go to war with the United States. Yet it is difficult to pinpoint exactly when this "determination" was reached. Lacking firm leadership and racked with confusion and dissension, the navy simply drifted into it. What can be said for certain is that the Navy General Staff conclusively decided on an armed conflict with the United States before the Navy Ministry leaders, and that middle-echelon leaders did so before their superiors.

After September 1939 the navy's program of southward advance had shifted to a frankly opportunistic policy of taking advantage of the European war to realize longstanding goals. Carried away by the succession of German victories in the west, the Navy General Staff lost all sense of balance about the world situation and the policy became a consuming obsession. Thus in April 1940 a conference of section chiefs concluded that now was "the finest chance to occupy the Dutch East Indies." After the fall of France in June, French Indochina also seemed to be rapidly becoming a "ripe persimmon." Almost single-handedly Navy Minister Yoshida resisted these pressures. He was all the more convinced of the need for caution because the war games conducted in June had shown conclusively that a surprise attack on the East Indies would inevitably involve Japan in a war with the Netherlands, Great Britain, and the United States simultaneously. Henceforth, America rather than Britain was to loom large athwart Japan's southward path.[107]

Yet the rising tide of impatience summed up in the slogan "don't miss the bus" could not be contained and in July 1940 found official expression in a national policy paper bearing the ponderous title, "Main Principles for Coping with the Changing World Situation." While it was the army that took the initiative in drafting this paper, the navy assumed a tougher stand on one provision: that Japan would "not shrink from [the possible consequences of] the inevitable deterioration of relations with the United States" that would result from a southward march.

Behind the navy's special emphasis on the prospect of war with the United States one can detect, as usual, its desire for a larger share of the nation's resources. The Japanese navy was greatly alarmed by the huge building plans the United States had recently announced. The second Vinson plan of 1938 would have resulted in an American fleet four times the size of that envisioned by Japan's "third building program." When Japan responded with the "fourth building program" of 1939, which involved the construction of eighty ships and the doubling of its naval air force in a five-year period, the United States countered in June 1940 with the third Vinson plan and the decision to create a two-ocean navy. Thus caught in the straits of an ever-escalating arms race, the Japanese navy needed a rationale that would establish its priority in national defense. Viewed in this context, the "Main Principles" may be said to have been a mere verbal show of strength, more budget-minded than war-minded.[108]

On July 26, the day before this document was officially approved by the Liaison Conference, President Roosevelt signed an executive order placing aviation gasoline, high-grade iron, and steel scrap under an export licensing system. The Japanese navy immediately seized the occasion to step up its program of southward expansion. On August 1 the Operations Section of the Navy General Staff produced a policy paper concerning an armed advance into French Indochina. This document contains a peculiar style of circular reasoning based on the premise that war with the United States was inevitable: In order to prepare for hostilities with the Anglo-American powers, Japan would have to march into Indochina and obtain raw materials and strategic vantage points. The United States would retaliate by imposing a total trade embargo upon Japanese goods. This in turn would compel Japan to seize the Dutch East Indies and secure the vital oil resources there, a step that would essentially involve a "determination to initiate hostilities" against the United States. By the end of August the Navy General Staff had apparently reached a consensus on this line of reasoning.[109]

At the same time the General Staff pressed Navy Minister Yoshida to place the fleets on an emergency semi-wartime footing and won his agreement to commence "preparatory mobilization" in November.[110] This, it will be noted, was a significant departure from Yonai's previous policy of eschewing any measure that anticipated hostilities with the United States. A further point worthy of attention is that throughout this period the navy avoided any full discussion in the highest councils of state of the grave implications of its contemplated southward course. Instead, the navy independently and secretly committed itself to a logic of mutual escalation pointing to war and set in motion programs of mobilization in preparation for that eventuality.

As a result of the informal agreement by which the navy had consented to the Tripartite Alliance in return for priority in the allocation of war resources, the navy gained precedence over the army in the materials mobilization program. Thenceforth the navy could take a more confident view of its preparedness against the United States. But instead of calming the clamor for a hard-line policy, which had been tied to the need for naval appropriations and matériel, the improvement in the navy's position, ironically enough, encouraged the advocates of war in the middle echelons. In October 1940 a staff officer of the Operations Section (Kami Shigenori) told the Army General Staff that by April of the following year—when Japan would have attained 75 percent of the U.S. fleet strength—a war should be initiated in the south, adding that otherwise it would be difficult to control restless officers. Such a view was by no means confined to the ranks of junior staff officers. Vice Chief of the Navy General Staff Kondō Nobutake also argued that as war preparations would be completed by the following April, it would be to Japan's advantage to strike at the United States before it had time to outbuild Japan.[111] Reflecting these views, from late 1940 on the navy began to seize the initiative in drafting programs for the southward advance, whereas earlier it had been content to respond passively to the army's proposals with counterdrafts and verbal changes.

VIII

In retrospect, the replacement in April 1941 of Prince Fushimi as chief of the Navy General Staff with Admiral Nagano, who was already inclined to regard war with the United States as inevitable, was a milestone in the drift toward the final catastrophe. In a desperate effort to stem this drift Commander-in-Chief of the Combined Fleet Yamamoto had earlier urged Navy Minister Oikawa to strengthen the naval leadership by appointing Yonai as chief of the Navy General Staff, with Yoshida Zengo or Koga Mineichi as vice chief and Inoue Shigemi as vice minister. But this appeal was ignored.[112]

Despite his stately appearance, Admiral Nagano was an impulsive and ineffective man lacking in settled convictions. He forfeited his own claim to being a "genius of Tosa prefecture" when he nonchalantly remarked that he turned to his section chiefs as the most reliable guides on policy matters. Rather than restraining them, he often acted more like their mouthpiece. His vice chief, Kondō Nobutake, was equally pliant. Moreover, neither the vacillating Navy Minister Oikawa, his soft-spoken Vice Minister Sawamoto Yorio, nor head of the Naval Affairs Bureau Oka Takasumi could exert effective control. It was hardly surprising, therefore, that the middle-echelon "nucleus group"—now asserting a sort of "collective leadership" through the First Committee—became the virtual locus of the navy's policymaking. As part of their assigned duties, these officers formulated naval policy from a strategic standpoint—that of war planning. There was nothing irregular about this, but as their recommendations were almost automatically approved by their superiors, strategic requirements came to have excessive influence in the making of national policy. Their demands for "war preparations" were to drive the ranking naval leaders into an impasse that finally forced their "determination" for war.[113] The decision to march into southern Indochina was a case in point.

April 1941 marked a crucial turning point for the navy. Rear Admiral Fukudome Shigeru, upon being recalled that month from the Combined Fleet to head the Operations Division, was surprised to note that naval attitudes in Tokyo had grown even more bellicose than those in the fleet. By then the Section Chiefs Conference had come out in favor of opening hostilities with the United States. Captains Tomioka and Ishikawa were heard to say, "Now is the time to strike; we won't be defeated."[114] In such an atmosphere the plan to occupy strategic areas to the south took concrete shape. In late April the head of the Intelligence Division, Rear Admiral Maeda Minoru, was dispatched to

Thailand and Indochina to estimate the probable consequences of an invasion of southern Indochina. He concluded: "Britain will not choose to repulse our move by force of arms because of the insufficient state of its armaments in Singapore. Nor, of course, will America rise in opposition—although it might conceivably resort to an oil embargo." On June 5 he reported to Prime Minister Konoe that "the navy deems it quite safe to move into southern Indochina."[115]

That same day the First Committee produced a notable policy paper, drafted chiefly by Ishikawa and entitled "The Attitude to Be Adopted by the Imperial Navy under Present Circumstances." This document was pervaded with a fatalistic belief that a war with the United States was "unavoidable." Its authors demanded an end to the nagging uncertainty and vacillation of their superiors, which had made it impossible to push war preparations to the final stage, and expressed the fear that, as long as the issue of war or peace hung in the balance, Japan might lose the most favorable moment to strike quickly and decisively. They therefore urged that the navy immediately "make clear its *determination for war*" with the United States, "lead" the government and the army to commit themselves to this stand, and carry out an armed advance into Indochina and Thailand "without a day's delay."[116]

The First Committee justified these moves as "preemptive" measures against the Anglo-American "military offensive." It maintained that inasmuch as the United States was rapidly reinforcing its forces in the Philippines and, in collusion with Britain, steadily consolidating its strategic, political, and economic position in Southeast Asia, Japan would find itself forestalled unless it moved quickly into Indochina. Admittedly there was no evidence that such a danger existed in reality. But the subjective notion of being oppressed by an "ABCD encirclement" undoubtedly cast a powerful spell on Japan's naval planners who therefore argued the case for breaking through it in terms of self-defense.[117]

The visible stiffening of Admiral Nagano's attitude in mid-June was apparently influenced by the recommendations of the First Committee as well as those of his subordinates in the Navy General Staff. As he put his stamp of approval on the navy's draft policy for the drive to southern Indochina, he is said to have muttered, "This will mean war with America." At the Liaison Conference of June 11 and 12 he declared in a belligerent tone which surprised even army leaders that if the United States and Great Britain should stand in the way, "we must attack them." At the meeting of July 21 he went so far as to argue for the early commencement of hostilities.[118]

All this time Navy Minister Oikawa maintained silence, but apparently he had acquiesced in the southward drive, still hoping that somehow it could be accomplished without inviting war with the United States. Chief of the Naval Affairs Bureau Oka, recalling these events years later, stated: "We did not think America would impose a total embargo, although we did recognize the risk. But under the existing circumstances there was no other alternative but to accede to the demands of the high command."[119]

Whatever the inner thoughts of the navy minister may have been, there is little doubt that Nagano and his subordinates fully anticipated a sharp American reprisal in the form of a total embargo when it was decided to send forty thousand Japanese troops marching into southern Indochina. On July 25—the day *before* the United States issued the order freezing Japanese assets in America—Nagano was heard to say that there was "no choice left but to break the iron fetters strangling Japan."[120] The total embargo on Japanese trade that went into effect on August 1 completed this "strangulation" by confronting Japan with an oil shortage. The logic of events, foreseen for a year, was now becoming a reality, and a policy predicated on the necessity for war preparations had thus trapped the Japanese navy in a predicament that would before long force its leaders to make up their minds for war.

As far as the navy was concerned, the Rubicon had been crossed, the point of no return reached when Japan marched into southern Indochina. Yet the decision for this fateful step had been made without thorough discussion of its probable consequences. There is no evidence that the Liaison Conference studied fully the risks and ramifications of a total embargo. A partial explanation for this may be found in the lack of coordination and communication between the two armed services and between the Navy General Staff and the ministry leaders.

More difficult to account for is the fact that some members of the First Committee were apparently "stunned" by the severity of the American reaction. As Captain Ōno Takeji later stated, he and some of his colleagues underestimated the risk of an embargo because they did not expect Washington to resort to such a drastic measure. America must surely realize, Ōno judged, that Japan would be compelled to strike in return, and the United States was hardly ready to face the two-ocean war that would be the inevitable consequence.[121] He and his colleagues had obviously paid scant attention to warnings from Captain Yokoyama Ichirō, the naval attaché in Washington, that the United States, while pursuing a Europe-first strategy, was also girding itself for possible two-ocean operations and might very well impose an all-out embargo. When the embargo actually materialized, Japanese naval planners took it as unmistakable proof that the United States was prepared to go to war.[122]

Whatever may have been the reasons for their miscalculation, it was too late for the navy minister and ranking ministry officials to assert their influence for peace. They had long since abnegated their leadership, and in any case they could hardly have overruled the chief of the Navy General Staff, which joined the army in pressing for an early decision for war. With the lifeblood of the fleet—fuel oil stocks—being drained at the rate of 12,000 tons daily, time was fast running out. Thus it was the navy that took the initiative to produce a draft policy to the effect that a resort to force would become unavoidable should diplomacy fail to bring about a settlement by mid-October. Somewhat toned down and sanctioned by the Imperial Conference of September 6, this amounted to a decision for war—with a time limit.

Admiral Nagano's statements at this historic Imperial Conference sounded like an echo of Katō Kanji as, driven to "the last extremity," he reverted to a brand of "spiritualism" instead of rationally calculating Japan's chances of victory. Nagano maintained that if Japan faced national ruin whether it decided to fight the United States or to submit to America's demands, it must choose to fight. He would rather go down fighting than surrender without a struggle, for surrender would spell "spiritual as well as physical destruction for the nation." On another occasion he resorted to the metaphor of a drastic surgical operation which, although very risky, gave the only hope of "finding a way to life out of a seemingly fatal situation."[123]

However, Nagano by no means despaired of Japan's chance of victory. By "chance" he apparently meant the advantages the nation could count on at the initial stage of hostilities. Obviously affected by the "ratio neurosis," he based his hopes on Japan's current fleet strength of slightly over 70 percent (75 percent in terms of actual operational capabilities) of that of the United States. When queried about Japan's prospects in a drawn-out war, he equivocated: he could say "nothing for certain" beyond the first two years. Perhaps the fullest exposition Admiral Nagano ever gave of his war plan is found in his statements at the same Imperial Conference of September 6. He did admit that in all likelihood the war would turn into a protracted conflict in which Japan would be progressively handicapped by its paucity of resources. But he contended that it would be able to overcome this difficulty by speedily establishing an "impregnable sphere" in the south to control strategic raw materials there.

In reality this plan was scarcely feasible. For one thing, little had been accomplished in the way of adequately fortifying the islands of the South Pacific, despite Vice Admiral Inoue's urgent request in January. Secondly, the air power sufficient to defend the "impregnable sphere" was not provided by the "fourth building program," and a "fifth program," hurriedly drawn up at the eleventh hour, involved huge figures clearly beyond the nation's economic capacity. Thirdly, there was a serious shortage of vessels to transport the essential oil resources from the south and of ships to convoy them.[124] In sum, there was little to substantiate Nagano's plan from an operational standpoint.[125]

Perceiving the fatal flaws in Nagano's plan, Commander-in-Chief of the Combined Fleet Yamamoto sought a personal interview with him in late September. But Nagano could not be dissuaded from his "determination" for war. The results of war games had convinced Yamamoto that Japan could never hope for a decisive victory in interceptive operations. To be sure, his strategy of an attack on Pearl Harbor was a supreme gamble, but it remained the only viable substitute for a successful main fleet encounter, which was not expected to materialize at an early stage of the war. The Navy General Staff, deeply committed to conventional strategy, was finally but reluctantly brought to accept Yamamoto's bold plan on October 19.[126]

The last chance to register opposition to war was lost when at the Ogikubo conference of October 12 Navy Minister Oikawa failed to state clearly the navy's lack of confidence in its ability to wage a war against the United States. Instead, he reverted to the tradition of "the silent navy," saying merely that he would leave to the prime minister the decision on war or peace. As Oikawa later explained, he felt that the navy, "after so many years of clamoring about its 'invisible fleet,' was hardly in a position to say it could not fight the United States," for it would then have had "no ground to stand on" in dealing with its officers or with the army and the public.[127] This, it will be recalled, was precisely the same logic that had guided his support of the Axis alliance: in both instances he identified the navy's bureaucratic interests with Japan's national interest.

Another explanation of Oikawa's failure to speak out was subsequently offered by naval leaders who emphasized the fear of a domestic upheaval. They claim to have believed that if Japan surrendered to the American demands, army diehards would stage a coup d'état and plunge a badly divided nation into war under the worst possible circumstances.[128] But this explanation smacks strongly of an ex post facto rationalization. Perhaps Admiral Toyoda Soemu, whose prospects for succeeding Oikawa as navy minister were frustrated by his pronounced anti-army bias, described the situation accurately when he attributed Oikawa's behavior to "pressures being exerted by hard-line elements in the upper and middle echelons of the navy acting in concert with 'radical' army officers."[129]

At any rate, from this time on strategic imperatives and operational requirements governed naval (and national) policy. On October 30 the new navy minister Shimada Shigetarō gathered together the ranking naval leaders and informed them of his "determination" in favor of war.[130]

IX

In an age of total war the Japanese navy conceived of the coming conflict essentially in terms of a limited war. Banking heavily on eventual German victory, it expected that the collapse of Great Britain would so cripple America's fighting morale that it would agree to terminate hostilities on the basis of some compromise settlement rather than continue to pay heavy sacrifices in the South Pacific. Beyond this, the Japanese navy had no concrete idea of how the war could be brought to an end.[131] Moreover, its operational plans could hardly be said to constitute a grand strategy. The traditional strategy was based on the premise of a single "hypothetical enemy"—the United States—and not until June 1941 did the Operations Division begin to draft a plan for simultaneous operations against a coalition of enemies—the United States, Great Britain, and the Netherlands. Completed in rough form in late August, this plan merely added to the conventional strategy for war with the United States operations to seize the "southern resource areas."[132]

A further point to be noted is that there existed nowhere in Japan a master plan for the conduct of war based on an overall estimate of national power. To be sure, the government, with the backing of the high command, had established the Total War Research Institute in October 1940. But the institute served mainly for research and training and contributed little to the making of national policy.[133] Nor could reliable data on the nation's war resources be obtained from the Cabinet Planning Board. While this board also provided an institutional structure for coordination, it failed to function properly because of bureaucratic rivalry. For example, the army and the navy were so suspicious of one another that they refused to pool information on their respective oil holdings, hence the board did not possess even rough figures on the nation's stockpiles until late October 1941.[134]

Within the Navy Ministry the problem of mobilizing and allocating war matériel was handled by the Naval Ordnance Bureau, but its assessments were sometimes vitiated by pressures from middle-echelon officers in charge of war planning. In one instance its head, Rear Admiral Hoshina Zenshirō, stated at a Bureau Chiefs Conference that it was impossible to prepare adequately for war with the United States, yet subsequently Captain Ishikawa was able to pressure him into reversing his conclusions. On occasion Ishikawa would come up with his own optimistic estimates of oil stockpiles to support his advocacy of war. Again, when the chief of the Mobilization Section confessed that the shortage of matériel precluded a long drawn-out war with the United States, Captain Tomioka of the Operations Section called him to task for voicing a "counsel of defeatism" and told him that his duty was to devise ways of fighting with the limited resources at hand.[135] Assuring the government that control over the resources in the south would enable Japan to wage a protracted war, staff officers tended to make light of the difficult task of transporting crude oil under convoy protection. One is almost led to wonder whether the Navy General Staff tended to slight these problems because more careful consideration would have made any viable plan of operations impossible.

If the navy's estimates of Japan's national power were faulty, its calculations regarding the United States were even more so. The Navy General Staff tended to vastly underestimate American war potential while overestimating that of Germany. It was not that naval planners lacked adequate information; the reports of the naval attaché in Washington (after October 1940 Captain Yokoyama Ichirō) were generally of a high caliber. Until the breakdown of the Japanese-American negotiations in October 1941 he maintained close contact with Rear Admiral Richmond Kelly Turner, director of war plans of the U.S. navy, with whom he had been on friendly terms since Turner's visit to Japan in 1939 as captain of the *Astoria*. In March 1941 Yokoyama had a "violent altercation" with the chief of the Fifth (America) Section of the Navy General Staff, who visited Washington. Shocked to learn about the warlike attitudes of the Navy General Staff, Yokoyama urged caution, emphasizing the formidable industrial power of the United States. His warnings went largely unheeded in Tokyo, however.[136]

The Operations Division tended to slight attaché reports because it maintained independent sources of information—including, among others, intelligence reports from the scout forces, intercepted messages of foreign navies and chancelleries, and, of course, contacts with the army.[137] Thus, as tension with the United States mounted, the really crucial information reached the Operations Division first, bypassing the Intelligence Division.

Perhaps what misled junior naval planners was their overconfident assumption that the Japanese navy was best informed about its traditional "hypothetical enemy number one." The leading war advocate, Captain Ishikawa, boasted, on the basis of his intensive study at the Navy War College, that he was better versed in the history of American Far Eastern policy "than any specialist in the Foreign Ministry." In 1936 he had visited the United States on the last leg of an inspection tour of Southeast Asia (where he became alarmed at the "encirclement of Japan" led by the United States) and Europe (where he busied himself gathering data on Germany's rising strength). How much he learned in the United States may be gathered from his own nonchalant statement: "I passed through America in a relaxed tourist mood, because the Japanese navy was constantly in possession of detailed information about that country." As Admiral Inoue later observed, the truth of the matter was that the middle-echelon officers "neglected to inform themselves adequately about the United States."[138] There is no denying that a lack of expertise about American affairs among junior officers affected their advocacy of hard-line policies.

Army-navy rivalry as a bureaucratic factor in Japan's drift toward war is an important topic that deserves fuller treatment than is possible here. As far as the First Committee and junior-rank staff officers were concerned, they urged a "determination for war" so that the navy could speedily complete its war preparations regardless of the final outcome of the Hull-Nomura conversations. The more cautious leaders of the Navy Ministry did try to draw a line between "preparations" and "determination," although in the end the line virtually disappeared. For the army, however, the two terms were synonymous, since "preparations" involved the large-scale mobilization of manpower and its concentration toward the south—a process which, once set in motion, could not easily be stopped. On the other hand, the navy could proceed with "preparations" without having to make any real "determination" for war, expecting that they could be canceled should a diplomatic settlement be reached. This basic difference lay at the heart of the interservice bickering that always accompanied the formulation of national policy. Indeed, until November 1941 the navy's advocacy of "preparations without determination" seemed to army planners a "political trick" to secure war materiel at the army's expense. A disgusted army staff officer scrawled in the Imperial Headquarters "Secret War Diary": "The navy's whole attitude and preparations to date have been directed toward the single aim of expanding itself." "The navy is as unprincipled as a woman!"[139]

While admittedly the army's self-righteous indignation at the navy's "irresponsibility" was motivated largely by its own bureaucratic concerns, it contained a grain of truth. The all-too-frequent invocation of such slogans as "war with America" and "U.S. the enemy" to fortify the navy's claim to building appropriations had so vulgarized these terms that many of its officers—especially in the middle and lower echelons—had grown insensitive to their grave import.

In June 1936, when Admiral Nagano as navy minister was pushing for the adoption of the "Basic Principles of National Policy," he made a significant statement in confidence: "It is for the sake of the morale and training of our forces [and, he might have added, for budget purposes] that we make an outward pretense of some day conducting operations against America and Britain. But in reality I wish to guide the navy toward friendly relations with these powers."[140] A former officer put in a nutshell the central dilemma that faced naval leaders: "Although the navy demands priority to complete its armaments against the United States in order to prepare for the worst, it does not desire to go to war with that country. But it cannot say it is absolutely opposed to war either, for others will retort that in that event armaments against the United States are unnecessary."[141] Such an ambivalent policy became bankrupt as soon as it was confronted with a real crisis. Middle- and lower-echelon officers, long trained by intensive drills to regard America as *the* enemy," had become obsessed with the idea of war with the United States. In the end, concern for the "morale of our fleet" became a matter of overriding importance that immobilized Navy Minister Oikawa and overcame his inner reservations about the Tripartite alliance and a decision for war.

Looking back on the "road to Pearl Harbor" after the imperial navy had been vanquished, many of its former leaders came to the conclusion that it had all been the work of fate. Yet, in December 1940 Admiral Yamamoto remarked bitterly in a letter to Admiral Shimada:

> As I see the circumstances surrounding the conclusion of the Tripartite alliance and the subsequent course of the materials mobilization program, the government is putting the cart before the horse in all these matters. To be stunned, enraged, and discomfited by America's economic pressure at this belated hour is like a schoolboy who unthinkingly acts on the impulse of the moment.[142]

When the government finally reached the decision for war, Admiral Yonai wrote sadly that Japan had only itself to thank for the impasse in which it found itself.[143] And the day before the Pearl Harbor attack, Chief of Staff of the Combined Fleet Ugaki Matome (who had served as head of the Operations Division during the critical months of 1940-41) made the following entry in his diary: "When we concluded the Tripartite alliance and moved into [southern] Indochina, we had already burned the bridges behind us on our march toward the anticipated war with the United States and Great Britain." These men attributed the train of catastrophic events squarely to "man-made circumstances."[144]

The above is, of course, not intended to make villains of Admirals Nagano, Oikawa, and Shimada and the "nucleus group" of middle-echelon officers. The accumulated weight of the recent past—especially after the London Naval Conference of 1930—had perhaps grown too heavy by 1940-41 for them to manage a sudden volte-face, especially at a time when the United States was tightening the economic screws on Japan. A recent writer has suggested, with much plausibility, that "the ghost of Katō Kanji" (and, we might add, the ghost of Alfred T. Mahan as it found a pale reflection in Katō) hung over these leaders.[145] As this paper has shown, the eclipse of Japan's naval leadership, the supremacy of the naval high command, the idée fixe of the inevitability of war with the United States, the demise of the Washington-London treaty system and the reopening of the armaments race, the beginnings of southward expansion—all these had their roots in decisions made at the zenith of Katō Kanji's influence by men like Admirals Suetsugu, Takahashi, Ōsumi, Nagano, and Prince Fushimi.

THE ROLE OF THE COMMERCE AND TREASURY DEPARTMENTS

Lloyd Gardner

I

Japan's forward movement into Manchuria signaled the end of the Washington Treaty era in the Pacific. For a decade Japanese-American relations had been stable—and mutually profitable, both politically and economically. During those years the United States Commerce Department, under Herbert Hoover's leadership, had become the primary government instrument for the promotion of foreign trade and investment. Commercial attachés and trade commissioners were sent out from the department's Bureau of Foreign and Domestic Commerce to "practically every foreign country."[1] Hoover's system and the Bureau of Foreign and Domestic Commerce were, however, programmed to function effectively only under conditions of world financial and economic stability. Without confidence in the integrity and safety of international relations, peaceful and profitable commerce between nations under this system was impossible.

The destruction of the Washington Treaty structure, therefore, could not be separated from a more general challenge to American interests on a worldwide scale. In a candid admission that the United States had inherited Britain's economic position, even if it still refused political responsibility in Europe, an officer of the bureau wrote to the commercial attaché in China on August 6, 1931: "Truth is, all of the world is trying to adjust itself to the industrial revolution as it has expressed itself in the area east of the Mississippi and north of the Ohio and Potomac rivers in this country. . . . Even on this side of the world, and at this late date, we appear not to have realized what it is that machinery does for civilization. The industrial revolution has released forces of greater strength and more serious import than we appear to have recognized."[2]

Although the Commerce Department exerted itself to come to grips both with the specific Japanese challenge in Asia and the larger social upheavals of the

1930s, it always regarded the decade as abnormal even as it devised temporary methods to meet the state-controlled foreign economic policies of Tokyo, Berlin, and London. In 1936, for example, Secretary of Commerce Daniel C. Roper came back from a European tour still convinced that the foreign policy of the United States should be to exchange commodities and stand clear of European political squabbles.[3] This commitment to the "world order" of the 1920s—an order most conducive to American economic expansion—was fundamental to the Commerce Department's outlook on all questions. "We do not like to visualize a world of economic blocs," Undersecretary Wayne C. Taylor said, affirming the obvious in an address to the Chicago World Trade Conference in 1941. "Such a world is quite apart from our tradition; quite contrary to our basic beliefs about free enterprise and trade."[4]

Far more was at stake in Manchuria in 1931 (and after) than any direct losses to American foreign trade. Indeed, the New York Post criticized the Commerce Department in 1938 for bragging about the "hefty amount" of American business there and in the war zones in China. The Post's criticism brought a terse reply from Commerce that the paper wanted to show up alleged differences between it and the State Department. But these differences did not exist, Commerce insisted; the policy was the same.[5] Regardless of trade figures in Manchuria, which American officials assumed were only temporary anyway, the Commerce Department was in full agreement with the statement of American long-range interests made by Cordell Hull in his instructions to Ambassador Joseph Grew on November 20, 1938: "In our opinion an endeavor by any country in any part of the world to establish in favor of itself a preferred position in another country is incompatible with the maintenance of our own and the establishment of world prosperity."[6]

What concerned the Commerce Department, therefore, was not simply the question of Japan's military adventure in Manchuria as a threat to American trade in Asia, but how the Japanese planned to shape their industrial activities at home and integrate Manchurian enterprises and resources into their state-trading system. This is a crucial point in understanding American reactions to Japanese expansion throughout the prewar decade. Even before the forward movement into Manchuria, for example, Commerce Department experts had been worried about economic trends in this direction. In 1930 Charles K. Moser, director of the Far Eastern Section of the Bureau of Foreign and Domestic Commerce, temporarily vacated his post to author a report for the Pepperell Manufacturing Company on the outlook for American textile exports to Asia. Moser concluded that the future seemed bleak indeed unless American textile manufacturers were willing to establish their own mills in Far Eastern countries to meet Indian and Japanese competition. If the Japanese, therefore, established mills in Manchuria and elsewhere, the situation would be just that much worse. As Moser put it: "Foremost among the factors underlying Japan's success in the cotton industry is the innate Japanese capacity for organization and unity of action, developed by their conception of the family, the clan, the state—never the individual—as the unit which is to benefit. Second in importance is the coordination between all branches of the industry not only between themselves but with practically every principal industry in the empire."[7] In other words, the extension of that system by whatever means, military or political, meant the extension of an alien economic system and a greater threat to American interests.

Hence the Commerce Department's attention to domestic developments in Japan at the time of the Manchurian Incident and its interest in the commercial attaché's reports on the progress of the "Industrial Investigation Committees" that had been charged with developing a plan for rationalizing the entire Japanese economy through forced mergers and direct subsidies. And in 1933 the Bureau of Foreign and Domestic Commerce instructed the commercial attaché in Tokyo: "There is probably more interest here in Japan's industrial activities than in those of any other foreign nation."[8] Quite plainly it was more important to know whether Japan planned to establish monopolies in Manchuria and organize them "under a perfect single unit," thus paralleling in a way German autarchy and foreign trade practices and the British Ottawa Imperial Preference System, than it was to be informed about possible trade opportunities arising from Japan's "New Order" in the area Tokyo now called Manchukuo. There was something of a parallel between Japanese economic policies and those of the United States government in the creation of the National Recovery Administration and the Agricultural Adjustment Administration, which depended upon import restrictions and government subsidies to producers, but both Commerce and State expected these to be temporary expedients and made policy upon the assumption that the commitment to reestablishment of the predepression world economy remained unchanged. Thus Secretary Roper explained to a west coast businessman concerning the State Department's Reciprocal Trade Agreements program: "I have never felt more optimistic about this phase of our economic future than I do at the present time."[9]

But Japan's commitment to a permanent forward policy in Asia, carried on in the economic sphere by the spread of monopolies, darkened the future and, as we shall see, changed Roper's mood to one of pessimism by late 1937. Tokyo's policies and statements about future policies raised the question of what effect a "surrender" of apparently nonvital economic interests by the United States might ultimately have on the protection of its essential markets and investment opportunities not only in Asia but throughout the world. If Japan finally did manage to create a fairly stable "bloc" in Manchuria and north China, even though the closing of the Open Door there involved relatively small losses, would not America's political and economic interests be endangered in Europe or even in Latin America? While the Commerce Department had no final answer to that question, at least when considered solely in terms of Japanese-American relations, there was general agreement that the struggle between closed economies and open economies could not be permanently resolved on a basis of coexistence in the world as it was developing in the 1930s.

II

In all branches of the government there were a few who felt that it was a mistake to cling to the Stimson Doctrine, especially since Secretary Hull apparently intended to confine his support of Stimson's pronouncement to "preaching" and an ineffective "trade treaty" policy. Perhaps, they argued, if Japanese-American relations could be put on a different basis, if the Stimson

Doctrine could be pushed off in a dark corner and forgotten, new vistas would open for relations between Tokyo and Washington. Treasury Secretary Henry Morgenthau, Jr., however, had not the slightest hope that anything would be made better through bypassing the Stimson Doctrine. To his mind Japanese-American relations were inextricably bound up with the totalitarian challenge to democracy—or, it might be more accurate to say, with the fascist challenge, as subsequently Morgenthau proposed working with the Soviet Union to check both Germany and Japan. Several State Department officers regarded Morgenthau's views as "rash and rigid" when it came to Japan and believed the man "possessed of a romantic notion of rescuing the Chinese."[10]

Unlike the secretary of commerce, Morgenthau's relationship with President Franklin Delano Roosevelt was an intensely personal one. He used every opportunity he had in White House tête-à-têtes with the president to advance his ideas about Far Eastern policy but more often than not came away disappointed at Roosevelt's reluctance to challenge the State Department's supremacy in deciding policy toward East Asia. It was only because of an unexpected development stemming from the 1934 Silver Purchase Act that Morgenthau was able to exploit fully his personal relationship with the president to influence him toward his world view. Under the requirements of the act, which had been passed by Congress under pressure from the "silver bloc" in alliance with "inflationist" sentiment, the United States Treasury was required to purchase silver on the world market at high prices. This caused a serious drain on China's reserves, for although China was a "silver standard" nation, it did not produce the metal and American silver purchases, in combination with other adverse factors, finally forced it to adopt a managed currency. As we shall see, Secretary Morgenthau seized this unanticipated consequence of the Silver Purchase Act to convert American policy to a prewar foreign aid program.[11]

Believing that democracy was already besieged by expanding fascism, Morgenthau was concerned with the counterexpansion of liberal capitalist democracy. But his view of Far Eastern relations was far more traditional than popular postwar interpretations of the 1930s would suggest. He defined Far Eastern politics in that decade as a three-way contest between currency "blocs"—the emerging yen bloc, the established sterling bloc, and an energetic dollar bloc. In speaking of the dollar bloc, he pointedly informed State Department officers on several occasions, the president meant to include "North and South America and China."[12] In the context of the 1930s the Treasury described its policies as defensive; but had there been no Japanese invasion of Manchuria, no Anti-Comintern Pact, and no Axis Tripartite Alliance, the secretary's efforts would have been seen (as the Japanese did see them) as a continuation of earlier plans for developing Asian markets. The war itself has obscured this aspect of Treasury policy, even though State Department representatives well understood the traditional reasoning behind the desire to link Chinese currency to the dollar and unsuccessfully tried to dissuade Morgenthau from trying to bring it off by citing past difficulties. The secretary himself explained to a Democratic leader in the Senate, "This thing is awfully big—it's an international battle between Great Britain, Japan and ourselves and China is the bone in the middle, see?"[13]

III

Representatives from both Treasury and Commerce sat on the advisory board of the second Export-Import Bank of the United States, a specialized agency originally chartered under the Reconstruction Finance Corporation. The first Export-Import Bank had been created in 1933 for the specific purpose of facilitating exports to the Soviet Union by meeting German and British competition evidenced in government-backed credit offers to the Soviets. The Russian plan failed but the general principle appeared sound, hence a "second" bank was created which was designed to support the Reciprocal Trade Agreements program, so that it would not flounder in a sea of blocked currencies and bilateral barter agreements. By 1937 it was clear that the bank would have to do even more; within a year it was engaged in making the first American development loans in Latin America. As in other countries the foreign trader (and his problems) was being nationalized, first to find markets and then to create them. The president of the Export-Import Bank, Warren Lee Pierson, made an extensive tour of China in 1937, which convinced him that the United States had to meet British and Japanese policies with countermeasures or see itself excluded from all China. As a result of this tour arrangements were nearly completed for the extension of a $50 million credit for Chinese purchases in the United States when on July 7, 1937 Japan launched its attack on north China.[14] Following the outbreak of the Sino-Japanese War the bank was used to handle the paper work for American economic aid to Nationalist China. The Japanese had charged that Pierson's activities in China were unfriendly, an interpretation they then tested by asking for Export-Import Bank credits to purchase 500,000 bales of American cotton. Pierson's response left little doubt in their minds, but it was an honest statement of Japanese-American differences. He told the Japanese that "the activities of Japan in China were very disturbing and bewildering to Americans generally, and that in my opinion it was out of the question for us to consider granting such credits at the present time."[15] By 1938 diplomatic and economic definitions of the world, subtleties of offense and defense, stimulus and response, cause and effect, were collapsing into a flat military view of international relations.

IV

Near the end of 1930 the Department of Commerce received reports from its commercial attachés in China regarding various private American proposals for a so-called silver bullion loan to that country. Over the next half-decade both the Commerce Department and the Treasury Department as well as the State Department were to be involved in vigorous debates over some form of this proposal.

When one looks beyond the government debates to find the deeper sources of support for silver bullion loans, there were usually special interest groups busily working for their own ends—either the silver mining associations themselves or some overblown silver politician still trumpeting the inflationist tune. Both often used the specious argument that America's trade in China and the Far East could be increased manyfold by some silver tonic or inflationist panacea.[16]

The Commerce Department, despite Commercial Attaché Julean Arnold's numerous statements and appeals, thought very little of such proposals. An attempt to stabilize the price of silver, argued Moser, would become an attempt to stabilize Chinese exchange. Stabilization of world silver prices could, perhaps, eventually lead to China's adopting a "gold-exchange" standard, but the necessary prerequisites for such a development were not present either in the world as a whole or in China as the depression deepened. There were certain tendencies, however, that the Commerce Department thought might some day improve the chances for such sweeping changes. The civil war in China had come to an end and hopes for the leadership of the Kuomintang were rising. "If you promise not to pull off any more civil wars for a year or two," Moser wrote Arnold, "I feel that we can promise, for our part, a considerably revived interest in Chinese development, which may even take a practical form."[17]

But equally important to the success of such "revived interest" was China's relationship to other powers, especially Japan and Great Britain. Japan wanted to see a settlement of China's foreign debts, believing that conditions for its trade and investment in that country could not improve without such an arrangement. Politically, Japan's interests were more complex and ambitious, a factor that decreased the willingness of other interested powers to force China to come to terms with its creditors. Consequently, it was the Japanese who put pressure upon the Chinese government to call a creditors' conference; moreover, they objected to any independent activity, such as an American silver bullion loan, as harmful to their interests. Noncommittal at first, the British eventually refused to cooperate with the Japanese to pressure China into calling a creditors' conference. Efforts to enlist American support were likewise frustrated. Akira Iriye suggests that this was the result of the activities of domestic silver interests that had been urging an independent silver bullion loan to China. Although the Commerce Department never encouraged Chinese leaders to anticipate such a loan, certain prominent figures in Nanking looked upon it as a way to "rehabilitate the country without first settling the issue of debts."

The Commerce Department's representative Julean Arnold had little desire for three-power cooperation in China. When it appeared that Washington had no interest in the silver bullion loan, he proposed that Great Britain and the United States together take the lead in calling an international conference to explore whether other silver remedies might be applied to Chinese ills, without including or consulting Japan. Like other "old China hands," Arnold considered Japanese-American rivalry inevitable and Japanese proposals for debt settlements directed at excluding all American economic interests.[18]

Though Commerce officials in Washington had a somewhat cooler assessment of Japanese policies than Commercial Attaché Arnold, their basic interest was also in improving American trade in China. Their discussions, however, centered on various kinds of independent actions to achieve this aim. Nevertheless, the breakdown of international cooperation was not the result of pressures beyond any single nation's control. In the United States demands for silver inflation were bolstered by newly conjured visions of the Great China Market—the myth that would not die. Occasionally, however, serious consideration was given to the whole problem of Chinese economic reforms. The *Wall Street Journal,* for example, noted approvingly that the Senate Foreign Relations Committee was about to unfold a plan for a large loan to China to assist in currency stabilization. But memories of past failures by bankers on "the Street" to bring off such a gigantic endeavor prompted the editor to add: "If we can learn from experience with some other loans we will realize that unless the money is applied under competent American supervision it would be as useless as pouring water through a sieve. Wisely spent, it would result in developing a great customer for the surplus goods that now embarrass us."[19]

From a Japanese point of view, past American efforts toward this end had been a disruptive element in their own long-range policy in China. Even when the Japanese had been invited to cooperate with American plans, mutual suspicions negated all hope of permanent achievement. The first attempt by America to supervise Chinese economic reform had been in 1903-04 when Professor Jeremiah Jenks made a world tour to enlist the support of the major powers for a plan to put China on a gold-exchange standard. With full State Department backing, Jenks tried to persuade the Japanese to cooperate by "dividing the international responsibility so that the chief control of the projected Chinese monetary system should be vested in an American, the head of the mint should be a Japanese; and the head of the bank should be an Englishman."[20] Jenks found Tokyo unenthusiastic, but within the next decade Washington proposed far more grandiose plans for putting China under an international economic trusteeship. An International Banking Consortium for China was formed before World War I and re-formed in 1920. Its total record, however, boasted only one achievement—the negative claim that its existence had prevented independent action in China. Besides the inhibiting mutual suspicions among the Consortium powers, the Chinese themselves opposed foreign control of their finances.[21]

In the early 1930s the principal Japanese objection to the Consortium was that it had been used by Great Britain and the United States to check the independent activity of the Japanese and, in effect, to put them in an inferior position among the holders of options on China's future. At the time of the Consortium agreement in 1920 Tokyo had very reluctantly agreed to include certain Manchurian and Mongolian projects, even some it had already begun. If Americans regarded Japan's forward movement in Manchuria as a breach of contract, political and economic, Tokyo's position was that American inattention to big power economic cooperation in China had already invalidated the agreement. Yet some sentiment existed in both countries for renegotiating the contract as the Far Eastern crisis worsened.

V

However faint such hopes were, they provided the Far Eastern Division of the State Department with an additional reason for opposing in 1933 a $50 million credit to China for wheat and cotton purchases. On his way to the London Economic Conference, Chinese Finance Minister T. V. Soong had stopped in Washington long enough to negotiate the credit with the Farm Credit Administration, then headed by Henry Morgenthau, Jr. As the Far Eastern

Division suspected, Soong privately invisioned a more elaborate program for China's internal reconstruction than a mere $50 million credit from the United States. He hoped to bury the Consortium once and for all and begin again with a consultative committee made up only of British, French, Italian, and American financiers and businessmen. The chairman-designate of this committee was Jean Monnet, who approached Sir Charles Addis and Thomas Lamont, the British and American Consortium representatives, about the idea. Long experienced in Chinese finance puzzles and their unexpected solutions, Lamont was as wary of the scheme as the State Department and insisted upon speaking first to the Japanese representative in the Consortium, who reacted as negatively as might have been expected.[22]

But Morgenthau was unimpressed with State Department objections that the $50 million credit would further anger the Japanese. With the "smell of revolution in the air," writes John Blum, the farm credit administrator insisted that even if the loan were never repaid it might boost the value of American agricultural stocks as much as $100 million, forestalling Agriculture Secretary Henry Wallace's repugnant proposal to plow under standing crops to create scarcity pressures upon the law of supply and demand. Roosevelt agreed and the loan was made. But the Chinese never made full use of the credit and it became a sore point within the administration. Nevertheless it was at least potentially a good vaccination against the "China loans" malady, though it never took with most American officials and even in Morgenthau's case did not begin having a real effect until 1941, too late for a Japanese-American reconciliation.[23]

At the time, however, the Japanese were pleased by Lamont's unwillingness to join the Monnet committee, and the Japanese ambassador told Secretary of State Cordell Hull that his government still hoped there would be consultation among the Consortium powers looking to some plan to aid China.[24] What prevented serious progress toward that goal was the Japanese Foreign Ministry's insistence that the United States negotiate a new Lansing-Ishii agreement or its equivalent so that Chiang Kai-shek's government could not solicit political, economic, and moral support from the United States when it wanted to disregard Japan's demands for closer Sino-Japanese relations.[25] No one in the State Department desired collaboration on such terms, but several officers in the Far Eastern Division were willing to try to resurrect the Consortium in preference to unabated competition. And, perhaps somewhat surprisingly, they made a remarkably fair presentation of the Japanese case in this regard to those who opposed any efforts at Japanese-American cooperation. But they could never close the gap between the two powers over the Stimson Doctrine. All Japanese proposals began with insistence that "Manchukuo" be recognized; all American notes on the subject began with a reaffirmation of the Open Door policy.

Morgenthau, now secretary of the treasury, had little inclination to engage in a study of the diplomatic documents or, more importantly, to seek a way to bridge the gap. On February 26, 1934 he convinced Roosevelt that he should be permitted to send a special representative to Japan and China to study trade conditions in the two countries and the impact of the American silver purchase policy. Japan, he advised the president, "was the most important focal point in world politics." Roosevelt agreed, adding that American information about

China was "largely inspired by Japan and British interests."[26] Morgenthau's expert, Professor James Harvey Rogers, either stumbled or was pulled into Chinese political affairs by Finance Minister H. H. Kung on board a Chinese customs yacht. Kung appealed for an American "rehabilitation" loan to back highway construction, flood control, currency reorganization, and other national projects. "I have agreed to receive from him detailed proposals," cabled Rogers to the Treasury Department.[27]

As the message passed through the State Department on its way to Treasury, the head of the Far Eastern Division, Stanley K. Hornbeck, read it and immediately dictated a memorandum to Secretary Hull opposing any further activity by Rogers or the Treasury in connection with Kung's proposal. Reemphasizing State Department arguments of the previous summer against the $50 million agricultural credit, Hornbeck concluded: "Irrespective of the fact that the primary purposes of the American Government in granting the credit under reference were to aid the domestic price situation and to remove from the American market surplus stores of cotton, wheat and flour, objectives that were attained in only a small degree, it would appear that in concluding the Consortium Agreement in 1920 the international banking groups ... were assured of the full support of their respective governments and that they did not contemplate encountering competition from the concerned governments in the granting of loans to China." Although, as later events would demonstrate, he did not accept State Department reasoning on this matter, Morgenthau deferred temporarily to Secretary Hull.[28]

This brief episode was the beginning of a full-scale State-Treasury confrontation on Far Eastern policy, which climaxed within a very few years. Bolstering his position with additional memoranda on the 1933 Chinese credit and the Rogers mission, Hornbeck soon secured Hull's and Roosevelt's permission to encourage the American bankers in the International Consortium not to pull out of the four-power agreement. The bankers had long been weary of Consortium politics; the depression, Japan's forward movement, and New Deal laws restricting certain of their former operations in the foreign field all contributed to a general lack of enthusiasm for putting any more time or energy into its operation. Moreover, Hornbeck himself was not sure what should be done next. But he was convinced that no plan for China could succeed if the Japanese refused to cooperate. In a telephone conversation with Thomas Lamont he suggested that the three-power naval talks then in progress might produce a break in the overcast military picture; yet even if such discussions indicated a changed atmosphere, the matter would have to be handled so that neither the Chinese nor the Japanese felt that the United States was behind the move to bring the Consortium out of its comatose state. Both men realized that the odds were against any such fortuitous sequence of events. As it turned out, Treasury pressure for independent action soon forced Hornbeck to decide whether to take a chance without all the preconditions having been fulfilled.[29]

Though prohibited from further dealings with H. H. Kung, Professor Rogers continued to advocate to both Morgenthau and Roper that independent aid be extended to China. The American silver purchase program, he insisted, only aided the Japanese by encouraging them to smuggle the metal out of China. This opinion was confirmed by other monetary experts abroad who warned the

Treasury that Tokyo was carefully managing the yen so as to keep it in line with the Chinese dollar. Increasingly alarmed by these reports, which he always sent on to the White House, the treasury secretary was not surprised when China asked directly that the United States either lower its silver price on the world market or provide a large credit so that the Chinese Finance Ministry might carry out a currency reform and go off the silver standard.[30]

The American Treasury was thus put at the very center of the Far Eastern crisis, while the State Department had seemingly been pushed aside in this as in other instances in which domestic considerations dominated the actions of the early New Deal. Domestic politics had forced the New Deal to adopt the Silver Purchase Act but, thought Morgenthau and his aides, here was a chance to turn those politics to national advantage. Since the 1890s silver politicians and inflationists had argued that their ideas, if put into effect, would increase American trade with all silver standard countries. Now they had been proved wrong. Nevertheless, by adjusting the workings of the Silver Purchase Act, contended Morgenthau, something very big might come out of a misguided policy. "To sum up my feelings," he told a very sympathetic listener, William C. Bullitt, Roosevelt's first ambassador to the Soviet Union, "I've . . . [felt] that I was on the pay of the Japanese." He urged Bullitt to help him secure better employment by seconding a Treasury suggestion to Roosevelt that the Chinese Central Bank be invited and encouraged to send a representative to Washington to talk over possibilities of an American loan for Chinese currency reform.[31]

The Treasury needed all the help it could get at that moment, for not only was Secretary Hull glowering at this interference in foreign policy matters of such consequence, but Roosevelt had surprisingly turned a cold shoulder to all plans for aiding China—at least for the time being. As part of the campaign for an independent Asian policy, Morgenthau's aides had prepared a memorandum stressing the importance of the China trade, present and future, to American economic well-being. Roosevelt had fired back with a blistering attack on the international money changers in the temples. To the Treasury's consternation, the president had gone on to state that he was personally inclined to hasten the crisis in China rather than try to prop up an unsound foundation: "China has been the Mecca of the people whom I have called the 'money changers in the Temple.' They are still in absolute control. It will take many years and possibly several revolutions to eliminate them because the new China cannot be built up in a day."[32]

There was little in the president's response to encourage the Treasury in its approach to Far Eastern questions or, for that matter, the State Department in its belief that the right way to deal with the China issue was by reinvigorating international cooperation to provide aid. In any event the matter could not end there because Roosevelt himself was not prepared to accept the consequences of his prophecy. The Chinese soon began hinting darkly that they would have to seek financial aid from Japan, which would mean that for a long time to come the Chinese currency would be secured to the yen. Exasperated by the Chinese legation's arguments and maneuverings with the Treasury, Hornbeck warned his superiors: "The United States cannot embark upon a project for financial assistance by itself alone to China without flying in the face of all the experience of the past twenty years and turning our backs upon the principles of which we have been the most consistent advocates and for which, as developed in Washington and insisted upon by this Government since 1921, we have the greatest responsibility."[33] In fact, Hornbeck had already written in an earlier memorandum that a U.S. loan "would be absolutely inconsistent with our commitments (contractual and moral) in regard to the China (Banking) Consortium." It could not work, he asserted, unless China gave the United States full control of its finances and unless the United States was "willing and prepared to make, toward overcoming Japan's definite opposition and efforts of obstruction, threat or use of force."[34] To such arguments Morgenthau replied simply that the State Department's position seemed to be, "If you do nothing you will insult nobody, will not hurt anybody's feelings and you take no risks."[35] On January 6, 1935 Morgenthau's persistence was rewarded when the president himself suggested that Treasury ask China to send over T. V. Soong or H. H. Kung.[36]

With this reversal in the White House, Hornbeck and the rest of the Far Eastern Division had the choice of accepting Treasury supremacy in Asian economic affairs or rushing their own slowly developing Consortium ideas to completion. Hornbeck's earlier conversation with Lamont had given him one small suggestion that might expand to something positive if nurtured carefully or, at the very least, might open up the situation and permit the White House to choose between two clearly defined alternatives. Jean Monnet had mentioned to Lamont in passing some months earlier that a key British official had hinted that Chinese currency reform should be handled by the Consortium.[37] On February 14, 1935 Hornbeck went to Morgenthau's office to discuss their differences. After going over the "past four decades" of Chinese currency reform failures, he read to the treasury secretary the State Department's proposed reply to the Chinese appeal for aid. Without mentioning the word "Consortium," it recommended that China "simultaneously" request financial aid from the powers that in the past had shown themselves interested in this problem. Openly irritated at what he thought was a namby-pamby response to a once-in-fifty-years opportunity, Morgenthau remarked curtly that such a reply would "get us nowhere." Why not treat the matter as purely monetary? Let the Treasury handle it "aggressively." "We ought to go it alone." There was little point, he concluded, in pursuing the discussion further.[38]

That is, thought Morgenthau, there was little point in continuing the discussion with any of Hull's men. He therefore appealed to the president, who held a White House luncheon four days later at which Morgenthau and Hull each presented his case. Each came away believing he had a presidential mandate. This confusing situation resulted from the following sequence of events: On February 17 Ambassador Bullitt took to the president a cable the Chinese ambassador had entrusted to him for delivery to Roosevelt in order to circumvent Hornbeck and his cohorts in "FE." In the message the Chinese government implied once again that if China was left to Japan's designs, control of the country north of the Yellow River would be the price of Tokyo's economic aid.

The next day Hull and Morgenthau had their luncheon with Roosevelt. According to Morgenthau's diary notes, the president instructed the secretary of state to reply to the Chinese politely—and then step aside so that Treasury could handle the matter as a purely monetary question. Roosevelt repeated this three times, Morgenthau recorded, but no matter how he put it, Hull stubbornly failed to understand. After a time Hull left the meeting, allowing Morgenthau to answer the State Department's arguments unimpeded. Morgenthau said that should the United States do as State wanted and take up the problem through the "nine power consortium," there was a good chance the other eight powers would protest the American silver policy. "The President felt that it was important that we should avoid at this time sitting down with the eight powers."[39]

Whether or not the treasury secretary was really so confused about the China Consortium of 1920 and the Nine Power Treaty of 1921, his aim was to make the best possible use of domestic political considerations to discourage the president from deciding in favor of the State Department. But despite Morgenthau's record of the luncheon meeting, Roosevelt's formal instructions to Secretary Hull merely told the State Department to avoid any reference to cooperation with other powers in any specific plan.[40] Apparently the president had not been convinced by either secretary, because he withdrew from the argument for the time being, leaving the two to their own devices.

About this time the State Department thought it detected stronger signals from London that the British were ready to take the lead in revitalizing the Consortium. If that were so, the chances of four power cooperation seemed on the rise. The department suggested to the British Foreign Office that the Manchurian question would have to be considered separately, as under no circumstances could the United States be expected to recognize Manchukuo. In early March 1935 a report from Tokyo indicated some interest in cooperative action. On the basis of this slim information, Secretary Hull personally discussed the subject with the Japanese ambassador.[41] Before this trial balloon got more than a few feet off the ground, however, press reports emanating from Washington described the still half-formulated plan as a way to "checkmate" a Sino-Japanese entente. The result was a quick reply from the Foreign Ministry in Tokyo that it was not considering any international loan to China. A few weeks later London announced its own plan to send a technical adviser to the British legation in Nanking. He was to be a consultant on monetary affairs and was to be available to the Chinese Central Bank. The British announcement was coupled with private suggestions to Washington, Paris, and Tokyo (the Consortium powers) that they should follow suit.[42] Did the British have in mind four-power negotiations inside China itself as a means of avoiding the kind of adverse publicity that had punctuated the State Department's timid endeavors? The State Department did not know, but it very much wanted preliminary talks in Washington to find out.

Public opposition in Tokyo grew in the weeks that followed, as did Morgenthau's private determination to keep out of any entanglements with the British. The State Department was caught in the middle, especially since there was still lingering uncertainty about which department Roosevelt wanted to have handle the affair. Seeking to free itself from this bind, the State Department urged Morgenthau to invite the British "technical adviser," Sir Frederick Leith-Ross, to Washington or at least agree to talk with him in Canada between legs of his journey to the Orient. But having sensitized Roosevelt to reports of unilateral British plans in China, Morgenthau obtained the president's full backing for a flat refusal to see Leith-Ross anywhere, anytime. What he wanted, and what the president wanted, he told the State Department, was to be left alone to work on the "American Dollar bloc including North and South America and China."[43]

VI

In July 1935 the Treasury Department received a message from an unofficial representative it had appointed to observe economic conditions in China—and the progress of the Leith-Ross mission. The report stated that Chiang Kai-shek now thought that some form of "gold exchange standard" was best for his country. The transition could only be accomplished if China could sell its silver stocks to the United States for enough gold to provide a reserve for a managed currency linked to the dollar.[44] It was almost more than Morgenthau had dared hope for. On the crest of this excitement he telephoned Senator Joseph Robinson and exclaimed—as already quoted—that "this thing" was "awfully big," a battle between the three nations over China's future.[45]

After several additional soundings of likely American reaction, the Chinese announced publicly in early November that they were going off the silver standard. The Chinese ambassador had in fact called upon Morgenthau at ten o'clock in the evening on October 28 to offer the Treasury 200 million ounces of silver and to ask for an American loan. Without consulting with anyone in the administration, Morgenthau laid down his conditions on the spot, conditions that amounted to nothing less than American supervision of the currency reform. The next morning he called the president: "This is our chance, if they are down low enough, to hook them up to the dollar instead of the pound sterling."[46] As for the loan request, Morgenthau explained to Roosevelt, he had replied that American silver purchases alone would provide the Chinese with profit enough if the plan were well managed. In this particular, however, Morgenthau found the Chinese balky. They even seemed unwilling to talk about linking the yuan to the dollar. For the next several days, as Morgenthau himself put it, he played two-handed poker with the Chinese ambassador. "You are bluffing," he finally told the Chinese emissary. "You have not enough to back up your bets." Tying the two currencies together would be good for both countries, the secretary insisted. In the economic world there was "the Sterling bloc and the dollar bloc. We are not going to invest $65,000,000 and have you tie your money to sterling. We are dealing with today."[47]

For the moment Morgenthau had forgotten that the third hand was held by Tokyo. Assuming that Leith-Ross, probably in connivance with Washington, had encouraged the Chinese to go off silver, the Japanese acted to obstruct the plan. They were wrong about Anglo-American cooperation, but the Yokohama Specie Bank "raided" Chinese currency exchange reserves in an effort (at least so the Treasury thought) to stop an American-Chinese agreement. Whatever motivated the Japanese raid, Morgenthau assumed the worst and gave up his stand-pat position. The world situation made it impossible to play out the hand, he advised a somewhat hesitant Roosevelt, who finally agreed that the Treasury would just have to go ahead with arrangements to purchase large quantities of

Chinese silver without all the guarantees Morgenthau had originally demanded.[48]

One of the most revealing aspects of this episode was that American leaders were also suspicious of British maneuvers. An internal memorandum in the Treasury Department argued that Leith-Ross might well have been the culprit behind the Chinese move for any one or all three of the following reasons:

> (a) She [Great Britain] believed her economic interests in China and her trade with China were being harmed by China's attempt to cling to the silver standard.
> (b) She hoped to be able to get the yuan tied to sterling and thereby enhance the prestige of sterling, increase the area of sterling's influence, and profit by the economic and political consequences of the tieup.
> (c) The Treasury authorities in England were probably not adverse to promoting a turn of events which would make it appear that the American silver policy was getting what they would be inclined to regard as its just deserts.[49]

These suspicions concerning British and Japanese plans suggest that it might be well to look at the Far Eastern crisis of the 1930s as Morgenthau did—as a triangular affair, with each party suspicious not only of what the other two might do independently, but of collusion against its aims. This would help to explain, for example, why Morgenthau was anxious to cooperate in Europe with Britain and France against Germany yet much less enthusiastic about joining with the British to check Japan in Asia. But the State Department, at least in November 1935, was eager to see if Great Britain and the United States could not reach some kind of an agreement on how to go about aiding Chinese currency reform, perhaps by means of a joint loan. Brief talks in Washington produced nothing, in part because Morgenthau stood aloof. Finally, Undersecretary of State William Phillips tried to force the issue by asking the treasury secretary if the two departments could not agree to inform the British that the United States wished to participate in any loan to China by Great Britain, per the 1920 Consortium agreement. Angered at having the State Department put words in his mouth, Morgenthau spat them back at Phillips: "I told Phillips he could not do any such thing, the Consortium had expired in 1920."[50]

In any event, it was clear Morgenthau wanted to see the question of cooperation with the British buried. In a few months, by May 1936, final details had been arranged for a monthly silver purchase program under which the United States agreed to take 75 million ounces of Chinese silver. Despite initial skepticism and continuing Japanese obstructionism, the plan seemed to be succeeding as the months went by. China's economy was making gains and things looked good from Morgenthau's office. "I honestly believe," he told H. H. Kung, "that when all this thing blows over—that ten years from now, maybe the most important thing that I did when I was here was to save China ... that over a period of fifty years that may be the most important thing ... the fact that China was not gobbled up by Japan and again becomes a strong nation."[51]

Almost every report confirmed Morgenthau's optimism. From China the Treasury observer, Professor J. Lossing Buck, cabled: "It is evident that China's increased strength is having its effect on Japanese policy in China and a stiff attitude on part of other nations at right moment should help curtail Japan."[52] The undersecretary of the treasury, reporting on a conversation with the Japanese ambassador and financial attaché, said: "I got a distinct impression, which is that the Japanese are adjusting their policies and at least temporarily have decided to be less aggressive in the Far East and to attempt to cooperate with occidental countries."[53] Morgenthau actually became worried about the stability of the yen, and he and Secretary Hull both speculated on the "final breakdown" of Japan in cabinet meetings.[54] The presumption that Japan could be broken economically grew steadily with Morgenthau and took root in the State Department as well.

VII

Although there was no great blossoming of business interest in China during what was to be a short season of sunny optimism, some economic strategists had already begun to cultivate that country even before the currency reform was well under way. In 1935 the National Foreign Trade council had sponsored an American trade mission to both China and Japan. It was an open secret that the members of the mission took for granted Japan's economic dependence upon the United States and that the group's imagination, as well as its practical work, focused upon improving trade conditions in China. The mission concluded that the basic problem was how to get the government involved in improving credit conditions in China. At the same time the Department of Commerce was being urged by other businessmen to look into the possibility of using Boxer indemnity funds as a basis for a revolving credit to facilitate heavy machinery sales. Among those pressing this idea was the president's son-in-law John Boettiger. In addition, Commerce officials on their own were surveying business opinion on revitalizing the Webb-Pomerene and Edge Act corporations. Both schemes presumed a close alliance between business and government, in line with the steady growth of extreme nationalism in international affairs. Hornbeck, on the other hand, had little hope that much could be done by the United States alone. To him as to others it seemed that past experience had demonstrated that whether operating under laisser-faire conditions, as when Elihu Root was secretary of state, or under close business-state cooperation, as when Philander Knox was secretary of state, the United States had been unable to sustain the Open Door policy in China; unless something was done to reestablish Consortium cooperation, the open door would close and Japan would take the cream of the China market.[55]

But the Consortium never regained consciousness. Proper burial rites were performed by the British in 1937 in order to be free to extend to Nanking a new railway loan. The Chinese had insisted that this be done as a precondition to negotiating a loan agreement. Even if the Chinese had not taken this stand, there was no denying that the Foreign Office in London had two very good arguments in support of its position: first, there was no way to prevent powers outside the Consortium, such as Germany, from taking advantage of the moribund to advance their own interests; second, the Consortium had defeated its own stated purpose, the rational development of China.[56]

The Consortium's demise, however, speeded up efforts in the United States to meet Japanese competition. Secretary of Commerce Roper replied to John Boettiger's letter that his aides thought it would be better to use the Export-Import Bank than the Boxer Indemnity Fund. The trouble was, said Roper, that American exporters wanted full and absolute guarantees; it was not likely that even the Export-Import Bank could go so far with its promises, even if that was the practice in other nations.[57] But the bank's president, Warren Lee Pierson, gave the Chinese minister of railways somewhat more encouragement, promising to go to China to see in what ways his agency could be useful, not only for supplying credits to American exporters doing business there but even more in coordinating government-business cooperation in Asia.[58] Pierson's trip to China was immediately attacked by the Japanese as another Anglo-American scheme to deprive them of a voice in China's economic development. Although Pierson insisted that he was only surveying the field, newspaper reports of the bank's $1.5 million credit for the purchase of forty locomotives from the United States, the inauguration of regular transpacific commercial air routes to China, and the improvement of other Sino-American communications facilities indicated more than a nonchalant interest in the economic development of the "new" China. The principal instigator of the press reports was the Commerce Department's commercial attaché, the always enthusiastic Julean Arnold.

"Probably never in its history," began a spokesman for the Bureau of Foreign and Domestic Commerce at the National Foreign Trade Convention in 1937, "has China offered greater promise for its future trade, industry, and general economic progress than it evidenced at the end of the first six months' period of the current year. . . . We had built up in China organizations capable of those measures of expansion which are characteristic of American enterprise where very favorable trade conditions permit."[59] This statement could have been interpreted by others to read: the Chinese currency reform and other steps we have taken have laid the groundwork at last for the realization of the great China market.

But however the Japanese interpreted American policy, Pierson's very vocal British counterpart, W.M. Kirkpatrick of the Export Credits Guarantee Department, was also touring China at this time. An American diplomatic official in Peking overheard a heated conversation between Kirkpatrick and the first secretary of the Japanese embassy. After complaining that Japan talked about "cooperation" in north China only as a cover for pushing everyone else out, Kirkpatrick added in his best Victorian demeanor that Great Britain looked upon smuggling from that area "not only as theft from China but also from England." American commercial attachés reported several such instances in which Kirkpatrick or other British officials delivered public and private scoldings to the Japanese over their behavior in China.[60]

The American ambassador to China, Nelson T. Johnson, doubted that either Pierson or Kirkpatrick would turn up very much new business. Nevertheless, he agreed with Julean Arnold that foreign competition and China's development of state capitalism called for a stronger and more coordinated American policy.[61] Pierson's inquiries produced uncomfortable news about Sino-British plans. The minister of railways, for example, told him bluntly that railroad loans set up spheres of influence throughout areas traversed by the new lines. From this he drew the conclusion that some kind of showdown among the powers was likely in the near future.[62] Pierson's meagre $1.5 million bid was completely overshadowed by rumors of a British loan of £10-20 million to be consummated in the near future. The American Chamber of Commerce in Shanghai asked that Washington meet all such antes and include stipulations in American loans that all purchases of materials and employment of foreign technical advisers must be from the United States.[63] Pierson, meanwhile, had returned to the United States and was trying to stir up interest on the west coast for cooperation among private bankers and the government to establish a large credit pool for new China business. The newspaper headline reporting these meetings read: CHINA BEING MADE OVER, SAYS L.A. MAN.[64]

VIII

Arrangements for continuing the silver purchase program and for a new Export-Import Bank credit to China of $50 million were ready to be signed as first reports of the Japanese invasion of north China reached Washington.[65] "We are certainly living in a dramatic era," Secretary Roper wrote an aide, "when one cannot prepare and distribute a report on world affairs without finding it out of date before doing so."[66] He had just finished reading Pierson's Far Eastern report which concluded that while the main responsibility for developing the China trade would ultimately have to rest in private hands with only "modest governmental assistance," for the present such aid was essential to erase the impression that "we are prepared to abandon our proper share in the commerce of the Far East."[67]

A South Carolinian whose world had always centered in the problems of cotton growing and marketing, Roper had great admiration for Secretary Hull's Reciprocal Trade Agreements program. The Japanese issue had a very special and direct meaning for him. Throughout the 1930s Japan's economic policies were a source of conflict between American cotton and textile interests. Although the world market had shrunk, Japan continued to purchase about 25 percent of America's raw cotton. On the other hand, its textile exports to the Philippines and even to the United States posed a threat to the American textile industry. One company wrote to the Commerce Department: "Until the Government makes up its mind to help the manufacturers of cotton textiles and the exporters of cotton textiles, there is no hope left; we are simply licked—we have no markets today for our cotton goods—why? ask any other exporter and you will be told. The Japs; the ever-increasing textile industries in Latin American countries...."[68]

The Commerce Department had taken the lead in the mid-1930s in an attempt to work out with the Japanese voluntary textile quotas on exports to the Philippines and the United States, but it could do little about Japanese penetration of other world markets previously dominated by Americans.[69] The invasion of north China perturbed Roper for several reasons. Quite clearly it was a direct challenge to his department's efforts in China. More importantly, it raised the question of whether the "gentlemen's agreements," while they might curb Japanese competition in the American market, would be of any value at all. For if Julean Arnold was correct in his analysis of the economic impact of the invasion of north China and its conversion into a Japanese monopoly, the United States would have to reconsider its economic outlook in that area and ultimately throughout the world. Arnold warned that the Japanese would find alternate supplies of raw cotton, tobacco, petroleum, and other raw materials, convert them to finished goods in state-owned monopolies, and usurp American outlets in Asia. "It can only be expected," he declared, "that should other sections of China fall under Japan's control, our trade will suffer accordingly."[70]

The sharp downturn in the American economy in the winter of 1937 raised very serious questions about the New Deal's ability to meet the continuing domestic crisis. Only a few weeks earlier Roper had written in a personal letter: "The whole world is more or less nationally minded, and, in my opinion, we must expect to sell to foreign countries during the next few years less cotton and probably less manufactured cotton."[71] He was in a much darker mood after the recession began, when he advised Roosevelt that if the Japanese succeeded in conquering China, American cotton exports to Japan as well would be endangered—a loss of $100 million annually. "This possibility and other factors," he went on, "would thus combine to reduce our raw cotton exports in the next five years to probably as low as four million bales. In the absence of new domestic outlets, our domestic consumption would not likely exceed eight million bales. This would call for drastic readjustments on the part of our cotton growers, in fact, a recharting of the economy of the South and definite Federal production control procedure."[72]

Like Morgenthau, Roper was fast racing to the conclusion that Secretary Hull's policy was likely to be impotent in the face of these developments, that the State Department's "trade treaty" policies could not even contain the surge of world events threatening to overwhelm American institutions, let alone reverse their course. The choices before the administration seemed to come down to two starkly drawn alternatives: drastic readjustments at home or a far more aggressive foreign economic policy. For a time, indeed, it was likely that both would have to be undertaken. Hence Roper asked the Bureau of Foreign and Domestic Commerce to prepare full memoranda on German, Italian, and Japanese tactics for his use in press conferences, paying special attention to the question of whether or not the Reciprocal Trade Agreements program could resolve "all difficulties" in competing with these nations.[73] Ironically, American trade with Japan itself increased during 1937 by more than $30 million.

IX

When the Japanese sank the American gunboat *Panay* in December 1937 while it was protecting Standard Oil Company tankers in Chinese waters, Morgenthau brought forward a proposal based on his conviction that Japan could be defeated economically without a war. He had first suggested it in September as a way to prevent a Japanese victory in China; now, he argued, it would also solve the question of what to do about the *Panay*. If the United

States, Great Britain, and France refused to buy foreign exchange or gold from Japan, he declared, "overnight those people can't buy their raw materials. It is effective at once. At once! And we can do it! We've got the power, we've got the instruments, we've got the agreement, we can do it.... What the hell is Japan going to do?"[74] To a State Department official Morgenthau said, "Now, if you people get to the point that you want to stop this god-damned thing, I believe—and if the President and Mr. Hull want me to do it—that in one week I can have it for them."[75]

Roosevelt was under a good deal of pressure to "do" something about the Far Eastern crisis and the spread of war and chaos. Morgenthau talked of his proposal in this context as a means of "expanding" American neutrality policy to that end. The president's own ideas, the quarantine speech, and the Brussels Nine Power Conference had led nowhere. The League powers had made it quite clear that they would only follow the United States at a great distance if it went around tacking up "quarantine" signs. Congress and public opinion had indicated they would never support such risky adventures.[76]

The *Panay* crisis, therefore, offered the secretary of the treasury an opportunity to try his hand at a solution. Delighted by Roosevelt's interest in a means of "expanding" American neutrality, Morgenthau supplied him with a memorandum on how the president could use the World War I Trading with the Enemy Act to declare a "national emergency" and proceed to prohibit all transactions in foreign exchange, withdrawal of bank credits, or export of gold or its proceeds. The declaration would, of course, be limited to the "Oriental situation."[77] Roosevelt pulled the Treasury document from his pocket during a cabinet meeting and, without explaining its source, read it aloud. When he finished, he declared that if Japan and Italy had been able to find a way to fight without declaring war, the United States must also be able to find a way. "We want these powers to be used to prevent war," the president insisted. There was such a thing as using economic "sanctions" without going to war. "We don't call them economic sanctions, but call them quarantines. We want to develop a technique which will not lead to war. We want to be as smart as Japan and Italy. We want to do it in a modern way."[78] Morgenthau promised that he would see if Great Britain could be lined up behind such a proposal, but by the time he reported back that the British were unprepared to do any such thing, Roosevelt's own resolve had fled with the coming of nightfall.[79]

The *Panay* episode was brought to an end in the weeks that followed with a Japanese apology. For the next several months Morgenthau devoted his time to devising projects to aid China economically. Taking Agriculture Secretary Henry Wallace along for support, he went to Hull's office on June 1, 1938 to urge that China be granted a loan to purchase cotton, wheat, and grey goods. What he had in mind was that Chiang's government could then sell the goods on the world market and make whatever use it wanted of the proceeds. Well, countered Hull, if the government did that it would have to offer similar credits to Japan, and that would destroy the State Department's "moral embargo" on private credits to the Japanese.[80] From one point of view, said the State Department logicians, it could even be argued that such activity would run directly counter to the half-developed quarantine idea; Roosevelt had urged that outbreaks should be localized and isolated, while this plan would extend the area, economically if not geographically.

To Morgenthau, State Department officers seemed to be going around in circles while the world went up in flames. One man in the department had, however, broken out of the centrifugal inertia—Stanley Hornbeck, who was now urging that the Export-Import Bank make credits available to China to buy American trucks. But Roosevelt still seemed unwilling to force a showdown between Hull and Morgenthau on Asian questions.[81] By mid-September 1938 Morgenthau had all but despaired of the stalemate. Roosevelt, he wrote in his diary, had practically asked *him* to try to persuade Hull! "He said, I will go as far as Hull will go." Here was perhaps the last chance to save world democracy, and Hull was spending his time on speeches before management people, extolling the splendid results of the trade treaties in the cause of world peace, "and while he was discussing it one country after another goes under."[82]

"Let us *while we can peacefully do so* try to check the aggressors," Morgenthau pleaded with Roosevelt. "Let us not be placed in a position of having to compound with them. Let it not be necessary for the President of the United States to fly to Tokyo and in humble manner plead with the Mikado that he be content with half the Philippines rather than wage war for the whole." Whether the Munich analogy alone did it or a combination of factors including the secretary's warning that the only nation extending significant aid to China was the Soviet Union, which would extract "plenty" in the end for coming to the rescue, the president finally acted on a plan to aid China in mid-December 1938.[83] But even then Morgenthau may have been right in claiming that his new idea survived only because Hull was on the high seas heading for the Lima inter-American conference.

What the Treasury proposed at this juncture had originated in several conversations between the Chinese ambassador and Morgenthau. It called for a large Export-Import Bank credit to a Chinese-owned American corporation for the importation of tung (wood) oil into the United States. Hornbeck and Hull both opposed the scheme, albeit for different reasons. The former argued that it was a gesture, an act of defiance, but hardly a policy. A coherent policy would have to begin with the abrogation of the 1911 Japanese commercial treaty and proceed from that point in logical steps to the center of the problem. Hull opposed the plan because he believed it to be, in fact if not in name, a war policy requiring congressional approval.[84]

In July 1939 the United States formally notified Japan that it was terminating the 1911 Japanese-American commercial treaty, effective in February of the following year. When the European war broke out in September 1939, many policymakers saw Japan as a co-conspirator, but Morgenthau was still dissatisfied with the pace of American policy and called for an oil embargo. Welles and Hull objected that such a giant step would only precipitate a crisis with Japan while the nation was not psychologically or physically prepared for war. The State Department, believing that at some point Tokyo would retreat rather than force an unwanted war, desired a carefully balanced holding policy in China combined with gradually increasing economic pressure on Japan. This was Morgenthau's expectation too, but he thought it unlikely that a measured policy such as State was proposing would produce satisfactory results.

The Treasury point of view gained a powerful supporting voice in the cabinet when Roosevelt appointed Henry L. Stimson as secretary of war. His presence even seemed to have a salutary effect on Hull. Stimson's repeated statements that the Japanese always backed down when confronted by a clear and definite stand were listened to with respect, with renewed conviction that the former secretary of state had been right in 1931, and perhaps even with some embarrassment that at that time the nation had not made the nonrecognition doctrine the first step in a strong policy.[85] Morgenthau was immensely pleased.

As part of its balanced policy the State Department now reversed its 1934-35 attitude on a Chinese currency loan and tried to stimulate the Treasury's interest. But it had crossed paths with Morgenthau, who was off in a different direction altogether. He had come to the conclusion that such a loan would be unwise and inefficient.[86] Moreover, he had come to distrust T. V. Soong, and the Kuomintang as well, fearing there were powerful factions in that party which wanted a negotiated peace with Japan. This led him to warn Roosevelt about Soong's financial slipperiness and his dubious American connections. To Chinese importunities Morgenthau came up with two alternatives which he thought would bring more immediate and more effective results: (1) a three-way loan, whereby the United States would purchase strategic commodities from the Soviet Union, which would in turn extend equivalent credits to China; and (2) a dramatic plan, suggested first by the British ambassador at a private dinner, for shutting off all oil supplies to Japan by means of an Anglo-American embargo on aviation gasoline followed by British destruction of oil wells in the Dutch East Indies. Part of the second alternative actually materialized in presidential directives of July 25, 1940, but even that step was too small for Morgenthau, who wanted a total embargo on oil shipments.[87]

Japan's threatened move southward to counter American economic pressures supplied a fresh issue for cabinet debate. Hull wanted another $20-25 million loan to China and an embargo on scrap iron; Morgenthau reargued the case for a three-way loan and a total embargo on oil. The secretary of state remarked that if Morgenthau's plan were adopted, Japan would simply get oil from the Dutch East Indies. Roosevelt turned to the treasury secretary with a query of his own in the same vein: Why indeed take such a risk if the Japanese could get the oil so close by? Morgenthau was afraid to bring out the plan for destruction of the wells but went out on a different limb and, without further explanation, flatly asserted, "The answer is, she can't." After the cabinet meeting ended, Morgenthau briefed his aides on what had taken place. Hull had agreed with him, he told them. Harry Dexter White was the first to catch on: Japan could not get the oil because the wells would be destroyed. "I threw a little bluff," admitted the secretary, and Stimson had supported him. Hull had apparently agreed after deciding that the Treasury had in reserve charts that proved Japan could not get oil even with the wells intact.[88]

By itself Morgenthau's minor triumph in this game of wits did not lead to anything. Hull won on the question both of the loan and of the embargo. It was only one of several incidents that finally prompted the president to call in both Morgenthau and Stimson on October 4, 1940 and advise them rather sharply that the Department of State was still in charge of American foreign policy.[89] What it did indicate was that the secretary of the treasury would use unorthodox

means when he felt others did not understand or were evading their
responsibilities. Some weeks later Roosevelt demanded that the Treasury quit
delaying implementation of the currency stabilization loan. "My own opinion
is," complained Morgenthau to his aides, "that the time to put the pressure on
Japan was before she went into Indochina and not after and I think it is too late
and I think that the Japanese and the rest of the dictators are just going to laugh
at us. The time to have done it was months ago and then maybe Japan would
have stopped, looked and listened."[90]

Morgenthau deeply resented Chinese tactics in bringing pressure to bear on
him. "We have to do something for the Chinese in order to save their face," said
Roosevelt on April 21, 1941. "I want you to make that $50 million loan right
away." "Well, Mr. President," replied Morgenthau glumly, "that is just like
throwing it away."[91] Even back in 1935 he had doubted the wisdom of a big
currency loan, especially one without supervision. Had he been just a bit more
introspective, he might now have pondered whether his estimate of State
Department behavior then was quite so justified.

X

Morgenthau's discovery of the "mad inextricability," as Blum puts it, of
relations with the Chinese came just as the "informal" talks between
Ambassador Nomura and Secretary Hull were beginning in Hull's suite at the
Wardman-Park Hotel. The secretary of the treasury had been unable to gain
control over economic relations with Japan, though his constant pressure for a
stronger policy over the years had indeed helped to bring the situation down to
this final attempt to settle things without a war. Shut off from the talks almost
completely, Morgenthau approved a remarkable memorandum by his aide, Harry
Dexter White, which closes this part of the story with an unusual twist—or
perhaps several, depending upon one's point of view.

Since 1934 Hull had countered all Japanese suggestions for a bilateral
understanding with highly moralistic restatements of the Open Door policy.
However unsatisfactory the State Department's tactics appeared to Morgenthau,
they were equally unsatisfactory to the Japanese, who contended that
reaffirmations of principle could not substitute for an understanding by which
each side agreed to specific measures aimed at containing the spread of
bolshevism and preventing the Chinese from playing one nation off against
another. Of course the United States disagreed that Japanese foreign policy
would realize these ends or that it was primarily motivated by them. This basic
disagreement was symbolized above all by the Stimson nonrecognition doctrine,
which in 1941 was newly rephrased in Hull's insistence that the Japanese accept
his famous "Four Principles" before serious negotiations ever began.

Of all the attempts to find a meeting place for renegotiating Asian
"contracts," the Far Eastern Division of the Department of State believed that
the only one with a real chance of success came in the middle of the decade
when Great Britain seemed ready to take the lead in reviving the Consortium.
Whether or not this was an accurate reading of the situation, to American
policymakers the Consortium represented the only compromise possible
between an Open Door policy and spheres of influence. In the view of the

division, Morgenthau's refusal to cooperate blocked the most constructive effort which had developed since 1931 toward an economic understanding among the powers.

It was ironic, then, that White's memorandum turned Treasury criticism inside out; but its full measure is realized only when one is aware that Morgenthau, uninformed of American positions in the Hull-Nomura talks and consistently linear in his historical interpretations and equations, failed to see any difference between the memorandum and past Treasury statements. The only explanation that comes at all close to satisfying the desire for an answer to his seemingly disjointed behavior—but one that may not stand up under close examination—is that Morgenthau's vision was blocked by the European situation.

The secretary of the treasury certainly was not alone in feeling that in 1941 the greater immediate danger to American interests was across the narrow Atlantic, and probably he did not read White's memoranda of June 6 and November 17 on Japanese-American relations as anything other than a way of holding on to the slippery status quo in the Far East until prospects were brighter elsewhere.

White's June 6 memorandum began with a condemnation of Anglo-French appeasement for producing a situation in which the United States was likely to be drawn into a long and costly war. It went on to call for "diplomatic preparedness," suggesting that a rich nation like the United States could do things a poor one could not. The whole introduction stressed the United States' greater options in its foreign relations, options that it had paid insufficient attention to developing. The United States, it said for example, should recognize that Japan needed increased foreign trade and investment opportunities, that American immigration laws had done serious damage to Japanese-American relations, and that the United States could help to reconstruct Japan's economy. It then proposed that Washington offer to withdraw the bulk of the American naval forces from the Pacific, sign a twenty-year nonaggression pact with Japan, "recognize Manchuria as a part of the Japanese Empire," impose a four-power trusteeship over Indochina, give up all extraterritorial rights in China, persuade Great Britain to cede Hong Kong back to China, negotiate a fair trade agreement with Japan (including most-favored-nation treatment), stabilize the dollar-yen rate, and extend a $3 billion thirty-year credit to Japan. For its part, Japan would be expected to withdraw from China, give up its extraterritorial rights there, extend to China a one billion yen loan, lease naval vessels to the United States up to 50 percent of its current strength, sell to the United States one-half of its current output of war materials, and negotiate a ten-year nonaggression pact with the United States and its Asian allies.[92] The memorandum also included proposals for economic aid to Russia should that nation give up its alliance with Hitler.

Nothing came of this dramatic effort to reverse the tide of events in the summer of 1941. White's second memorandum of November 17 was swallowed up in the days before Pearl Harbor, not to emerge until long after the war in the Pacific came to an end as a historical curiosity.[93] Many of the specific proposals were virtually the same as in the earlier memorandum, although in one key instance he modified his position—on recognition of Manchuria. This second plan, while not granting immediate recognition, would have set in motion negotiations for a final settlement of that issue, allowing the Japanese government—in White's words—to devote its energies to "reconstructing Japan, building up Manchuria, and developing new trade possibilities."[94]

Whether or not Morgenthau had examined carefully these aspects of the White plan, he sent copies to Roosevelt and Hull with the brief comment that it might be "helpful." When the president asked for Hull's opinion, the secretary jotted a handwritten note across Roosevelt's covering letter: "There are several good points within—I am using some of them—C.H."[95] But the only use he made of the "good points" was within the old framework of American policy since 1931, and he was by no means prepared to talk about a Manchurian settlement of the kind White suggested even had all other issues between the two countries been settled. He and Stimson had agreed that the first step, which had to be taken unilaterally by Japan, must be an evacuation of China south of the Great Wall. "He said he wanted to discuss Manchuria afterwards," noted the secretary of war in his diary. White's memorandum, on the other hand, set forth a process to be undertaken by the United States for its resolution. As the White memorandum went through various redrafts in the Far Eastern Division, almost every proposal he had put forth was changed into abstract multilateral undertakings, more in conformity with traditional American Far Eastern policy. The suggested nonaggression pact with Japan, for example, became in the first redraft a proposal for a nonaggression pact with China, the British empire, the Netherlands, Thailand, and the Soviet Union. A proposal to withdraw the bulk of the American fleet from the Pacific was changed in the second redraft into a far less definite promise to effect a "normal" disposition of the navy. Meanwhile the Manchurian concession was reduced to nothing more than a promise to "suggest" to the Chinese that they should enter into negotiations (a remarkable comparison to the 1945 Yalta agreement on the Far East), and the nonaggression pact was further transfigured into one of the Department's sacred Four Principles, the territorial integrity of Indochina.[96]

Nothing was left but the shell, comments William L. Neumann. Hull's note to Roosevelt was only nominally true; none of White's spirit survived the change and very little else of his proposals made up even the outside rim of a modus vivendi the department considered for a time. Perhaps the most difficult of all the turnabouts of the episode to explain—unless one assumes that Morgenthau simply did not understand what his aide had put in the memorandum—took place now. Hearing rumors that the State Department planned some kind of "deal" with the Japanese, Secretary Morgenthau drafted a letter to the president which was never sent because there was no need to do so. "No matter what explanation is offered to the public of a truce with Japan," he warned, "the American people, the Chinese people, and the oppressed peoples of Europe, as well as those forces in Britain and in Russia who are with us in this fight, will regard it as a confession of American weakness, and vacillation."[97]

The White memorandum continues to be something of a puzzle for the historian, but Henry Morgenthau's views on Japanese-American relations remained perfectly clear throughout the decade. For that matter both departments, Commerce and Treasury, had fixed views about Japan's foreign and domestic policies and their relationship to the world situation. White's last-minute effort to break through the "temper of the times" was foredoomed not only because of the Japanese-American impasse, but also because of the European war and the existence of the Axis Tripartite Pact. The world seemed to be closing in around American policymakers and their institutions. The Japanese challenge was inextricably bound up in their minds with the worldwide threat to liberal democracy.

THE ROLE OF THE FINANCE MINISTRY

Yamamura Katsurō

Translated by Mitsuko Iriye

The Ministry of Finance played an interesting role in Japanese decision making. Because it had ultimate power over compilation of the budget, at least theoretically, it functioned as a regulatory agency coordinating policies pursued by different organs within the government. Domestically it had authority over the computing and collecting of taxes, the floating of government bonds, the administering of public property and funds, and the supervising of local finances. Because of these functions the Finance Ministry was far more influential than the Ministry of Commerce and Industry or the Ministry of Agriculture and Forestry. But what gave the Finance Ministry a prominent role in regard to Japanese foreign policy was its control over such matters as the flotation of foreign bonds, capital investments from abroad, colonial finances, and Japanese investments and loans overseas. The finance minister, as head of an organization with such powers, occupied a crucial position in the inner circles of the policymaking elite.

I

The growth of the Finance Ministry's influence was, however, a slow process. Under the Meiji constitution its powers were restricted because compilation of the budget was not considered a legitimate legislative act. Theoretically the budget was decreed by the emperor as a command to the administrative branch of the government. Article 67 of the Meiji constitution provided that the Diet could not veto or reduce appropriations for purposes connected with the imperial prerogative, such as the organization of the army or the conclusion of treaties. This provision limited the authority of the finance minister over budgetary matters. Especially with respect to military affairs, he was obliged always to defer to the supreme command, since the organization of the army and the size of the reserve forces were part of the imperial prerogative.

Furthermore, the Accounts Law allowed the military services wide latitude in disposing of funds allocated for military expenditures in the budget. In the realm of foreign policy, therefore, the finance minister had to draw up his financial and economic plans in accordance with guidelines over which he had little control.

Not until the 1920s did the Finance Ministry's role in decision making become significant. Due to its phenomenal industrial growth during and after World War I, Japan managed to attain a position of equality with other advanced countries as an industrial nation. It started to export industrial goods and to import raw materials and foodstuffs. Private capital was invested in China and governmental loans extended to the Chinese government. Since the home market was easily saturated, even a modest increase in surplus capital or products had to seek an overseas outlet. Japan's foreign policy therefore became closely linked both to internal economic conditions and to possibilities for expansion abroad. The political parties gained more power and began to play a coordinating role between Japan's foreign and economic policies. Finally, the general tendency toward armament reduction restricted the autonomy of the military in Japan. Because of all these factors, the authority of the finance minister within the cabinet, as well as his position in the entire governmental structure, was strengthened. More specifically, the Finance Ministry's influence in the realm of foreign affairs grew as such matters as foreign loans and foreign exchange became more and more important. The ministry was directly involved in international gatherings such as the Genoa Conference and the Young Committee, in which its officials participated. One may cite Inoue Junnosuke (finance minister in the Hamaguchi cabinet, 1929-31) as the most prominent example of the increasing power of the Finance Ministry.

Another change took place in the Japanese governmental structure with the advent of the 1930s. Japan's policy of rationalization and retrenchment failed to overcome the panic of the late 1920s, and as a result policies of inflation and exchange manipulation were adopted. At the same time, the army's invasion of Manchuria in 1931 became an important factor in the recovery of the national economy, for it led to the expansion of domestic war industries and the creation of new markets in China and Manchuria. These developments affected Japanese foreign policy and should have brought about greater coordination between economic foreign policy and military action, but the outcome proved otherwise. The power of the Finance Ministry, although augmented in the 1920s, had never been clearly legalized or institutionalized, hence the military, through the imperial prerogative and the right of supreme command, easily seized the initiative in foreign policymaking. Still, at least until 1936 the Finance Ministry was able through its power over the budget to check the military's interference in Japanese foreign policymaking, although this resulted in frequent and violent clashes between the army and the Finance Ministry over foreign and economic policies. With the assassination of Finance Minister Takahashi Korekiyo on February 26, 1936, however, the position of the finance minister in the government and in foreign policymaking declined sharply, until he no longer served as the coordinator of economic and foreign policies. To make matters worse, in October 1937 the Cabinet Planning Board was established as a policymaking institution and took over from the Finance

Ministry the task of coordinating budgetary matters. Army and navy officers occupied important positions on the board and drew up basic policies for each ministry. After the outbreak of the Sino-Japanese War, the finance minister became less and less a policymaker and more and more a mere administrator. Finance ministers in this period were either Finance Ministry bureaucrats or businessmen such as Yūki Toyotarō (February to June 1937), Ikeda Seihin (May 1938 to January 1939), and Ogura Masatsune (July to October 1941). Although Ikeda and Ogura were in office when important decisions were made, as representatives of the financial community they served not to check the army but chiefly to preserve the financial community's control over the functioning of the wartime economy. In 1940, when Japan decided upon a policy of southward expansion and preparation for war with the United States, the finance minister was not present at the crucial meetings of the Imperial Headquarters-Cabinet Liaison Conference. The Finance Ministry received no formal communication from the army concerning the ministry's attitude toward a possible war with the United States. Only with the inception of the Tōjō cabinet did the finance minister start to attend Liaison Conferences. Consequently, the Finance Ministry was simply incapable of undertaking the function it should have performed—namely, to assess the economic cost of the military's policy of expansion into China and the rest of Asia, frequently undertaken without regard for Japan's economic capacities.

Historically, capitalism in Japan developed under the protection of the government, enabling Finance Ministry bureaucrats to play an important role. They exercised leadership as economic administrators and, after retirement, became important figures in the business community, occupying crucial posts in various financial organizations, government-financed concerns, and big enterprises. To become a member of this powerful elite was not an easy matter. Most Finance Ministry bureaucrats were graduates of Tokyo Imperial University who had received the best grades in the higher civil service examinations. The number of new recruits was limited to five to ten a year until the ministry was enlarged after 1937. As their role was to promote the development of a capitalistic economy, they tended to be more rational and to have a more international outlook than officials of the Ministry of Home Affairs or the service ministries. They can be said to have represented modernity in an otherwise "premodern" government. However, their modernity was confined to their functions as administrators; in politics they were conservative and passive. They expressed their political opinions only occasionally and did not form groups based on particular political ideologies. Their status depended on a strict hierarchical and seniority system, and while conflicts among various cliques and bureaus became conspicuous in other government agencies (e.g., the Foreign, Army, and Navy ministries) in the latter half of the 1930s, strict discipline was characteristic of the Finance Ministry.

Typical of the bureaucrats who held key positions in the Finance Ministry during the 1930s and the war years were Tsushima Juichi, Kaya Okinori, Aoki Kazuo, Ishiwata Sōtarō, Hirose Hōsaku, Kawada Isao, and Sakomizu Hisatsune. Under Takahashi these men began drafting plans for a war economy. Since Takahashi left the task entirely in the hands of the bureaucrats and merely acted as spokesman for their proposals at cabinet meetings or Five Ministers

Conferences, they even came to take the initiative in policymaking. After the outbreak of the Sino-Japanese War these officials one by one succeeded to the post of finance minister. Unfortunately, they turned out to be administrative technicians lacking in political skill and unable to win the confidence of political and financial circles. Consequently, whenever an important change of policy was to be made, a representative of the financial community had to be chosen to occupy the post of finance minister. This lack of political ability on the part of Finance Ministry bureaucrats accounts in part for the decline of the ministry's position in the decision making process.

II

With this structural survey as background we can proceed to discuss specific instances of decision making within the Finance Ministry during the interwar years. In the 1920s Japanese economic policy was based upon the idea that in diplomacy Japan would follow a cooperative rather than an independent policy. As Finance Ministry officials viewed the world situation, America's postwar policy in East Asia at first posed a serious threat to Japan. After the Washington Conference, however, they saw indications of a desire for international cooperation. They assumed that the concern of the powers over the problems of East Asia would shift to the urgent question of how to restore the capitalist economies after the devastation of the war and that such issues as the gold standard, reparations, war debts, and the reconstruction of Europe would become the focus of attention. From the current of opinion manifest at various international conferences in the 1920s, the Japanese judged that world economic trends were in the direction of stabilization and a return to the gold standard, and they therefore decided to do their utmost to improve Japan's economic position with these considerations in mind.

As a result Japan adopted as one of its main objectives the removal of the gold embargo. Each successive finance minister concentrated upon preparing the economy for a return to the gold standard, until finally, on January 11, 1930, the gold embargo was lifted by Finance Minister Inoue Junnosuke. The rationale for this action was that it would lead to a thorough readjustment of Japan's economy, which had expanded abnormally during and after the war, and would make Japanese commodities more competitive in the world market. Its success, however, depended upon obtaining American capital and credit, which meant that the policy of the Finance Ministry was in conflict with that of the military. For the latter were prepared to use forceful methods to suppress the Chinese revolution in order to maintain and extend Japan's rights and interests in China, and in doing so they inevitably impeded all efforts at international cooperation. These difficulties caused a growing rift between those directing Japan's economic course and those who favored a hard line toward China.

Finance Minister Inoue instituted a policy of retrenchment, based upon the return to the gold standard, that coincided with the world economic crisis. The crisis itself had a far greater impact upon Japan than he had anticipated. As a consequence, the Japanese public became increasingly dissatisfied and army radicals, seeking a way out of the depression, demanded the abolition of the Washington Conference system, which they generally regarded as having determined Japan's postwar economic policy. The net result was that their power in the army increased.

On September 18, 1931 Prime Minister Wakatsuki Reijirō was informed by the army minister that the Kwantung Army had been engaged in a military incident in the vicinity of Mukden. Apprehensive that its activities might jeopardize Japan's international position, the Wakatsuki cabinet decided against any extension of hostilities. But the Kwantung Army ignored this decision and, disobeying the supreme command, extended its sphere of action. The United States repeatedly expressed its objections and Wakatsuki feared the possible effect on Japanese-American relations when the Kwantung Army pushed on to occupy Chinchow, which bordered on north China. But although some members of his cabinet objected to appropriating funds for further military operations in Manchuria, on the grounds that the Kwantung Army had disregarded the government's decision, Wakatsuki recorded in his memoirs that he took a different position. He felt that once Japanese troops had been dispatched to Manchuria, not only they but also the Japanese living in the area would suffer unless the home government accorded them financial support.[1] This placed Finance Minister Inoue, who had hoped to continue his retrenchment policy even to the extent of checking the spread of the war, in an extremely difficult position.

Britain's departure from the gold standard, announced three days after the outbreak of the Manchurian Incident, was a great blow to Japan's economy, especially to the new gold standard. Expecting the imposition of a gold embargo by the Japanese government, big banks, both at home and abroad, started large-scale speculative purchases of American dollars, precipitating anew the drain on Japanese gold reserves that had begun after the lifting of the gold embargo. At the end of 1931 the Seiyūkai came to power under the leadership of Inukai Tsuyoshi, and on December 13 Finance Minister Takahashi Korekiyo abolished the gold standard. Takahashi had never placed much faith in the apparent trend toward trade liberalization and industrial rationalization during the 1920s and had favored instead the establishment of an autarchy. He had, moreover, always emphasized the importance of preventing a gold drain and as finance minister in 1920, when the United States lifted its gold embargo, had refused to let Japan follow America's example. He later explained his action by saying:

> Japan's attitude toward China had been aggressive and I was against any forceful measures. But I believed that our country should expand into China by economic means. Since it was obvious that China would soon be asking for large foreign loans, I felt Japan should be ready to lend China 500 or 600 million yen at once. Otherwise Britain or the United States would monopolize the loan market and be in a position to dominate China financially. It is much harder to nullify the results of an economic than of a military conquest. If Japan decided to organize a consortium loan with other powers, it would not mean anything unless Japan itself occupied the leading position. That is why I thought it imperative for Japan to have a gold reserve of at least 500 to 600 million yen.[2]

Although such ideas were not popular among financial bureaucrats in the 1920s, Takahashi did not change his mind and insisted that Japan maintain a strong gold reserve in case the Washington Conference system collapsed. It was therefore only natural that as soon as he regained power as finance minister, Takahashi reinstituted the gold embargo, anticipating that the system of international economic cooperation would soon break down.

Takahashi's financial policy had various implications. Domestically, he sought to expand aggregate demand through vast military expenditures, deficit financing, and aid to the agricultural sector. Externally, he approved of military action in order to establish Japanese control over the Manchurian market. Moreover, he attempted, by means of exchange devaluation and by lowering the prices of Japanese commodities, to penetrate overseas markets hitherto dominated by Western nations. Thus the Finance Ministry became involved in Japan's foreign affairs on two different levels: in Manchuria (and China) and in Western and West-dominated markets.

The Finance Ministry's participation in Japanese policymaking on China had never been great. After the failure of the Nishihara loans, Japan's activities in China were for a time limited to military involvement in the Chinese revolution, and as a result, the influence of the Finance Ministry declined. After the war the ministry's concern was with the consolidation of governmental loans to China, and the government itself regarded policy toward China as a much less serious problem than policy toward the United States and Europe. All this contributed to the further weakening of the Finance Ministry's standing in Japanese-Chinese relations. The ministry stationed in London a financial attaché with the rank of bureau chief, charged with gathering information on economic trends in the West. But the officers it dispatched to China were assigned only on a temporary basis and, moreover, were of relatively low rank with limited authority. Information concerning China was acquired indirectly from such sources as the Foreign Ministry, the Yokohama Specie Bank, the South Manchuria Railway, and the Bank of Korea. No office within the Finance Ministry dealt exclusively with China, and the appointment of personnel in charge of affairs relating to China and Manchuria was considered of little importance. Small wonder that the Finance Ministry failed to produce any competent China specialists!

While the Finance Ministry neglected its task of adjusting such factors as the Four Power Consortium, the Nine Power Treaty, and the growing interests of Japanese capital in China, the military steadily undermined the Washington treaty system and carried out its own policy in China. In time the military began to interfere in matters that should have devolved exclusively upon the Finance Ministry. Under such conditions the Manchurian crisis broke out, drawing the Finance Ministry more directly into Japan's China policy. After Japan recognized Manchukuo, the Finance Ministry acquiesced in the government's policy of distinguishing between Manchuria and China proper and proceeded to assist in the development of the former. Thus, when the Manchukuo government requested that a Japanese financial expert be sent to advise the new state on economic development, the Finance Ministry, attaching much more importance to the selection of personnel than it had earlier, decided to send some senior officials. Among these was Hoshino Naoki, who was appointed vice minister of Manchukuo's Finance Ministry and actually functioned as its head. (Following his service in Manchuria, Hoshino was to become president of the Cabinet Planning Board and chief cabinet secretary in the Tōjō cabinet.) Quite characteristically, immediately after his arrival in Manchuria Hoshino asked the Japanese government to subscribe to 30 million yen worth of Manchukuo's "national construction bonds." Initially this posed a problem for the foreign and finance ministers in Tokyo, who felt bound by a provision of the Four Power Consortium which specified that, should one of the four countries issue a loan in the form of public subscription to either the central or a local government in China, it must consult with the other three. But Finance Minister Takahashi decided that since Manchukuo was not a local government of China but an independent nation, Japan need not consult the United States and Great Britain. Foreign Minister Uchida agreed.[3] From this time on the Finance Ministry regarded Manchukuo as an independent country to which the provisions of the Consortium would not apply.

The first serious project the Finance Ministry undertook in Manchuria was the unification of its monetary system. Many currencies with varying names, standards, and values were in circulation in Manchuria. The resulting confusion in the monetary system hindered the growth of commercial transactions and encouraged the issuance of numerous paper currencies. Thus reform of the monetary system was an essential precondition for the unification of Manchuria. To cope with the situation the Japanese government granted the Central Bank of Manchukuo a loan of 20 million yen, furnished by the Mitsui and Mitsubishi companies, as the basis for a new unified currency system based on silver. This decision was a victory for the Finance Ministry, since the Kwantung Army and the Bank of Korea had insisted upon linking the Manchurian currency to the yen. Takahashi successfully argued that the silver standard was more suitable for Manchuria, for its economic relations would be not only with Japan but also with China. It is evident that Takahashi was willing to adopt an open door policy in Manchuria in order to avoid giving the impression to other countries that Japan was intent upon colonizing Manchuria. The silver standard, however, did not last long. After the summer of 1934 American purchases of silver had serious repercussions in Manchuria, and the Finance Ministry feared a sharp increase in the price of silver. As a result, in November 1935 the Manchurian currency system was shifted from the silver standard to the yen.

Concerning other aspects of the Manchurian economy, the Finance Ministry at first took a passive stand. It did not oppose the efforts of the Kwantung Army and Japanese financial circles in Manchuria (both of which were hostile to the big financial cliques in Japan) to restrict severely private capital investment and to subordinate all such activities to the needs of the military. However, it soon became apparent that governmental control of private capital investment could discourage the much-needed flow of funds to Manchuria, and the Finance Ministry began to interest itself in the question of providing sufficient financial assistance to ensure the development of Manchukuo. According to Hoshino Naoki, the Finance Ministry was extremely anxious to obtain American capital for this purpose, and he took special note of a cabinet decision to the effect that American capital should be introduced into Manchuria for the development of that region.[4] It has not been possible to ascertain to which cabinet decision Hoshino referred, but the episode demonstrates the general trend of thought within the Finance Ministry at the time. Again, when Ayukawa Gisuke considered establishing a monopoly dealing with heavy industry and mining in Manchuria and thought seriously of admitting American technology and capital, the Finance Ministry showed decided interest. Nothing came of this plan, however, as strong opposition, headed by Matsuoka Yōsuke, developed within the government and the Sino-Japanese War broke out before any decision could be reached. Yet the possibility of introducing American capital into Manchuria was revived from time to time in Japanese financial circles in the hope that the nation's balance of payments crisis, aggravated by the increase of Japanese investments in Manchuria after 1935, might be alleviated by attracting foreign capital to Manchuria.

The second area of Finance Ministry involvement in economic foreign policy was in Western and West-dominated markets. After 1932 the focus was shifted from the reduction of imports to the expansion of exports and the ministry allowed a devaluation in the exchange rate. The yen, which had been valued at $49.375, depreciated rapidly and fell below $20 by the end of 1932. Finally a foreign exchange control law was enacted, reversing Japan's exchange policy in order to prevent further depreciation. As it happened, the American gold embargo, instituted in March 1933, caused the value of the dollar to fluctuate drastically, producing great instability in the yen-dollar ratio. Japan sought instead to stabilize the yen at one shilling two pence sterling. All in all, the policy of exchange devaluation provided a turning point in Japanese foreign trade. Along with the various measures undertaken by the Ministry of Commerce and Industry for the promotion of export trade, such as an export subsidy system and the organization of export unions, devaluation enabled Japan's foreign trade to recover much more quickly than that of other advanced nations who were still suffering from the impact of the world economic depression.

The remarkable growth of its export trade was one factor behind Japan's prompt recovery from the economic crisis. At the same time, the vigorous penetration of the world market by Japanese goods aroused fear among other countries, who responded with a general move to restrict Japanese imports. The British empire's economic regionalism was consolidated after the Ottawa Conference of 1932, and in India the tariff on cotton goods was raised, followed by the abrogation of the Indo-Japanese commercial treaty. Japanese goods were boycotted in Canada, Egypt, Australia, and the Dutch East Indies. Many Japanese items were almost totally excluded from the United States, coming under the anti-dumping law. Driven from these markets, Japan sought new outlets in Latin America. The Foreign Ministry dispatched commercial attachés to this region, while the Ministry of Commerce and Industry established export unions and increased the number of trade correspondents in Latin American countries. Japan succeeded in exchanging ministers with Colombia and concluded a most-favored-nation treaty with Uruguay. The consequent flood of Japanese goods to Latin America caused such a great sensation in the United States that the United States official trade report for 1933 addressed itself to the problem. It indicated the importance of concluding reciprocal commercial treaties with Latin American countries as soon as possible and negotiations were actually started. Thus everywhere in the world Japanese goods began to encounter obstacles that placed Japanese trade in a difficult situation.

The ministries of Finance, Foreign Affairs, and Commerce and Industry were obliged to reappraise their trade policies in order to cope with the new circumstances. The fundamental question of how to preserve the existing markets for Japanese goods against the competition of rival countries became the new concern of the Japanese government at a time when, especially after the failure of the London Economic Conference, the free trade system based upon international cooperation had collapsed and reciprocity, bilateralism, and retaliatory measures were becoming the order of the day. It seemed evident that the only way left was for the Japanese government to negotiate reciprocal trade agreements under which it would control export prices, impose quantitative restrictions upon exports, and admit an increasing amount of imports from countries that agreed to abrogate or soften various anti-Japanese regulations.

Developments in Japanese-American relations are of particular interest. Although there was no quantitative decrease in Japanese exports to the United States, their dollar value declined tremendously after 1932, Japanese goods accounting for only 18 percent of the total value of American imports in 1934. The primary reason for this was a sharp fall in the price of silk, which comprised 80 percent of Japanese exports to America. Moreover, higher tariffs and import controls authorized under the Agricultural Adjustment Act and the Industrial Reconstruction Act of 1933 and the power granted the president in 1934 to alter tariff rates by as much as 50 percent were considered a serious menace to Japanese-American trade. The Tokyo government, accordingly, commenced negotiations with the Tariff Commission and succeeded in obtaining a trade agreement stipulating that the United States would not raise its duties on Japanese pencils and cotton rugs if Japan restricted the quantity of these commodities exported to America. No agreement was reached, however, on commodities such as tuna fish and matches. The distinctive feature of these negotiations was that the initiative on the Japanese side was taken by the business community. Negotiations with India, the Dutch East Indies, and Great Britain were usually carried out by government representatives, but in the case of the United States a Japanese-American Trade Council was organized, consisting chiefly of businessmen, and this council undertook the negotiations for the two governments.

In contrast to exports, imports from the United States grew steadily after 1932 and consistently exceeded exports. This was due to a marked increase in the importation of raw cotton, necessitated by the growth of Japan's textile industry, of iron, steel, machines, oil, automobiles, and nonferrous metals needed for Japan's heavy industry, and of raw materials such as timber and pulp for light industry. The development of war industries in Japan soon made the United States and Great Britain indispensable sources of crucial raw materials, and the Finance Ministry attached great importance to this fact.

Another aspect of Japanese-American economic relations was the competition between the two countries in China. The Japanese government was particularly concerned over American loans to China. In July 1933 the Foreign Ministry declared: "A program of massive assistance to China will not only contribute to the civil war in China and the movement against Japan and Manchukuo, but will also present serious obstacles to the maintenance of permanent peace in Asia. . . . We must express our resolute opposition to such action." Japanese trade with China had dwindled after the Manchurian Incident, as a result of the widespread boycott against Japanese goods, and the government feared that American and British loans to the Nanking government would further accelerate the anti-Japanese movement in China. At the same time, with the mounting obstacles to the sale of Japanese goods abroad, Japanese financial circles became increasingly interested in the China market. The upshot of these developments was the emergence of a policy of Japan-Manchukuo-China "cooperation" designed to regain the lost market in China. The Amō (Amau) statement of April 1934 was an enunciation of that policy.

The Finance Ministry's attitude was somewhat different. It feared that Britain and the United States might provide China with arms and financial assistance in order to keep China and Japan divided. But it was also convinced that the raw materials supplied by Manchuria and China, such as coal, iron, and raw cotton, were not sufficient to enable Japan to do without imports from the United States and Great Britain, even if Japan were further to develop China and Manchuria by investing its own capital. Therefore the Finance Ministry considered it imperative to maintain trade relations with the United States and Great Britain and opposed any attempt by Japan to gain monopolistic control over the China market by expelling American and British capital, a move that would obviously create much antagonism. Moreover, when Sir Frederick Leith-Ross, Britain's foremost economic adviser, came to Japan in the summer of 1935 and indicated that Britain desired to cooperate with Japan in reforming the Chinese monetary system (and might even be willing to provide Japan with funds to cover its share of the expense), Finance Minister Takahashi concurred in principle. But the military rejected the idea of Anglo-Japanese cooperation, despite the assurance of Leith-Ross that Britain was prepared to recognize Manchukuo if Japan agreed to the proposal. The Foreign Ministry was unable to overcome the army's opposition,[5] showing that the Finance Ministry was denied a decisive voice even with respect to a matter clearly within its purview.

III

The attitude of the Finance Ministry toward the army changed drastically after the February 26, 1936 Incident. Departing from Finance Minister Takahashi's practice of challenging the military's excessive demands for money, his successor Baba Eiichi gave priority to defense requirements and resorted to increasing revenues by means of higher taxes and a larger national debt. This change in financial policy had the effect of sanctioning the army's military expansionism and giving it a free hand to carry out a policy based on armed strength. In August important foreign policy questions were discussed by the Five Ministers Conference, and a plan entitled "Fundamentals of National Policy" was adopted. The ideas that formed the basis of the plan had been advanced by the Army Ministry's Military Affairs Bureau, the Navy Ministry's Naval Affairs Bureau, and the East Asia Bureau of the Foreign Ministry. The fundamental principles involved were to preserve Japan's predominant position on the Asian continent, to plan for southward expansion, and to undertake military preparedness against the Soviet Union in the north and the United States in the western Pacific. The army at this time was concerned to remedy the relative inferiority of the Kwantung Army's resources and equipment vis-à-vis those of Russia's military forces in the Far East, a concern shared by the Foreign Ministry, which sought to cope with the situation by promoting Sino-Japanese cooperation and maintaining friendly relations with the United States and Britain. The Anti-Comintern Pact of November 1936 was likewise designed as part of a strategy to counteract the threat of Soviet communism.

These basic principles provided a framework within which the Finance Ministry had to define its sphere of action. Regarding military support as essential to the expansion of Japan's overseas trade, Finance Minister Baba accepted almost in toto army and navy estimates of the defense budget for the fiscal year 1937 and planned to finance enlarged armaments programs by means of increased taxation and the issuance of bonds. Obviously, this was essentially a fiscal policy, unrelated to any real increase in production. As a result, the money market fluctuated abruptly and events did not work out as he had expected. Baba's successor, Yūki Toyotarō, was obliged to moderate this policy, but even so arms expansion remained a basic principle that could not be altered. The only solution lay in restructuring the Japanese industrial system so as to develop a heavy industry that could supply the needed war matériel. Thus expansion of production became the slogan of the Finance Ministry. The big question was where to turn to obtain the necessary raw materials. Even though the Finance Ministry placed great hope in the economic development of Manchuria, it knew the raw materials provided by Manchuria as well as Korea would be quite inadequate to meet the nation's enormous military demands. It was for this reason that Kaya Okinori, finance minister in the first Konoe cabinet, saw no alternative to continued dependence on the United States and Great Britain. Shortly before the outbreak of the Sino-Japanese War he stated that an increase in productivity, balance of payments equilibrium, and supply-demand stability were the three fundamentals of his economic policy. Although the picture changed after the war broke out, he still considered it desirable, if difficult, to obtain American resources. For instance, while he did not think it possible for the Japanese government to obtain loans from America,[6] when Kubo Hisaji, a lawyer, offered to undertake private negotiations for a cotton loan, Kaya assented believing it would help Japan maintain a stable balance of payments.[7] Unfortunately, these negotiations came to nothing.

In October 1937 the Cabinet Planning Board was established as the culmination of developments begun in 1935, when a coordinating organ was created within the cabinet to adjust conflicting policies. After the outbreak of the Sino-Japanese War systematic planning to regulate the supply and demand for goods became important, and the Cabinet Planning Board was organized as a central agency to draft plans for mobilizing goods, funds, and manpower. The Second Committee of this board undertook to compare the relative strengths, in terms of resources, of Japan, the United States, and Great Britain, in anticipation of worsening relations with those countries. At the beginning of 1938 Aoki Kazuo, chairman of the Second Committee, concluded that even if the army and navy were to carry out their strategy successfully and occupy China and Southeast Asia, they would still not be able to wage a prolonged war because of Japan's dependence on American and British resources.[8] The vice army minister objected to his estimate of the situation, but the vice navy minister as well as the entire cabinet concurred. Meanwhile the First Committee drew up plans for mobilization of raw materials that provided for the full-scale development of the resources of Japan, Manchuria, and China in order to make Japan self-sufficient in light metals, ammonium sulfate, pulp, and the production of automobiles.

At the same time the Finance Ministry did what it could to prevent further deterioration in Japanese-American relations. The story of the gradual hardening of the United States' attitude toward Japan need not be recounted here. Suffice it to say that the Japanese business community as well as the Finance Ministry were greatly concerned about the inevitable involvement of the powers in the Sino-Japanese War as it spread to central and south China. They tried desperately to seek a way out but were unable to do anything; the war dragged on and American opinion continued to stiffen throughout 1938. The only significant role played by the Finance Ministry in these developments was its opposition to an Axis alliance directed against Britain and France. At the Five Ministers Conference of July 19, 1938 that approved an alliance with Germany directed against the Soviet Union, Finance Minister Ikeda Seihin strongly opposed Army Minister Itagaki Seishirō's proposal for extending the target of the alliance to Britain and France. Ikeda, unlike his predecessor Kaya, was a representative of the financial community, being head of the Mitsui zaibatsu, and was expected to be more forceful than Kaya, a Finance Ministry bureaucrat, in checking the trend toward neglect of business interests. Ikeda believed that economic control could be established under the aegis of the business community in order to avoid antagonizing Britain and the United States and repeatedly harped upon this theme in his talks with cabinet members and senior statesmen.[9] The Konoe cabinet fell before a decision was made on the Axis alliance. Ikeda recommended Ishiwata Sōtarō as his successor in the Hiranuma cabinet, with the understanding that the latter would carry on his views. Loyal to his predecessor, the new finance minister continued to oppose the army's plan for an Axis alliance on the grounds that it would be dangerous to exacerbate Japanese-American tensions when the country had to concentrate on expanding production.[10] His position was supported by the foreign and navy ministers, and no decision was reached on the question even after some seventy meetings of the Five Ministers Conference. When Germany concluded a nonaggression pact with the Soviet Union on August 23, 1939, the Five Ministers Conference met once again and agreed that this had in effect put an end to the negotiations for an Axis pact.

IV

On July 26, 1939 the United States notified the Japanese government of its intention to terminate the Japanese-American commercial treaty in six months. Although this did not mean an immediate embargo on trade with Japan, it was nevertheless a great blow to the so-called "Anglo-American faction" who in their planning for war mobilization had taken for granted that Japan would continue to depend upon Britain and the United States for raw materials. At the same time, the conclusion of the Nazi-Soviet pact necessitated a reorientation of Japanese policy away from infatuation with the idea of a German alliance. Thus

Foreign Minister Nomura Kichisaburō of the new Abe cabinet tried to negotiate either a new or an interim agreement with the United States to replace the old commercial treaty. However, the United States government remained unresponsive. Nor was this the only blow to Japan's wartime economy. The outbreak of war in Europe made trade with the sterling bloc extremely difficult. The Finance Ministry, the Ministry of Commerce and Industry, and the Cabinet Planning Board became seriously concerned that Japan's productive capacity might cease to expand. This concern was obviously felt outside these agencies as well, as revealed, for instance, in a Diet interpellation in February 1940, when government officials were asked whether Japan had a sufficient quantity of goods to carry out the production plans envisaged in the budget for the fiscal year 1940-41.

Under these circumstances, it was natural that members of the Cabinet Planning Board began more and more vociferously to demand that Japan cease to rely on the United States for war matériel and instead try to establish a self-sufficient economy. Their idea was that Japan should push ahead with the economic development of Manchuria and China and at the same time seek strategic resources in Southeast Asia. The discovery of iron ore on Hainan Island in February 1939 following the Japanese invasion seemed to them a promising omen.[11] During 1940 the Yonai cabinet concentrated its efforts on southward expansion and in February asked the Netherlands to sign a reciprocal treaty covering the Dutch East Indies which was to include the relaxation of trade restrictions, the offer of special privileges to Japanese enterprises, and the easing of entry regulations for those employed by such enterprises. When Germany invaded Denmark and Norway in April, Foreign Minister Arita Hachirō issued a statement calling for maintenance of the status quo in the Dutch East Indies but also demanding special treatment for Japan on the grounds that "Japan has close economic relations with the South Seas, in particular with the Dutch East Indies." In June Japan concluded a treaty of friendship with Thailand and demanded that the French government of Indochina prohibit the transmission of arms and munitions to Chungking and permit the stationing of Japanese forces in Indochina to supervise the carrying out of this injunction. The government of Indochina consented to these demands. Finally, on June 29 Arita made a radio broadcast declaring that the "New Order in East Asia" now extended to Southeast Asia. However, since his message did not refer specifically to the strengthening of ties among Japan, Germany, and Italy but instead hinted at an entente with the United States and Great Britain, the army, which had already made plans for a southward advance, forced the resignation of the Yonai cabinet.

On July 17 Konoe Fumimaro was given a mandate to organize a new cabinet. Two days later he met with his prospective army, navy, and foreign ministers, who reached agreement on a policy program that was approved by the Imperial Headquarters-Cabinet Liaison Conference on the 27th and adopted as the "Main Principles for Coping with the Changing World Situation." This document called for a speedy termination of the China War, solution of Southeast Asian problems through the use of force, the strengthening of political ties with Germany and Italy, and adjustment of Japan's relations with the Soviet Union. Regarding the United States, it stated that unnecessary friction was to be avoided, but at the same time Japan should not fear the deterioration in Japanese-American relations that would naturally result from the execution of its other policies. Military action was to be considered primarily against Great Britain, but thorough preparations should also be made for war with the United States. This did not mean that the Konoe cabinet had decided in favor of an Axis military alliance or war with the United States.[12] Nevertheless, the phenomenal successes of the German army in Europe in the spring of 1940 had impressed the Japanese, and public opinion was turning more and more toward Germany and Italy, partly because of the sense of international isolation that resulted from Japan's deteriorating relations with the United States and Great Britain. Gradually, the pro-Axis groups within the government regained influence. Moreover, the Japanese were attracted to the rich resources in the Southeast Asian colonies of the European countries now occupied by Germany. At the Four Ministers Conference of September 4, attended by Konoe and the foreign, army, and navy ministers, Foreign Minister Matsuoka brought up the issue of strengthening Axis ties, and steps were taken that led to the signing of the Tripartite Pact on September 27.

By this time the influence of the Finance Ministry in foreign policy decision making had declined substantially and there was little Finance Minister Kawada Isao could do, even though he feared the adverse effects of the alliance on Japan's wartime economy. No Finance Ministry bureaucrats participated in the crucial decisions made by the Konoe cabinet, and the finance minister did not attend any Liaison Conferences until shortly before the outbreak of the Pacific War. Nor was the Finance Ministry kept informed on military planning. At the beginning of 1941 it learned through private sources that the imperial army had already started preparations for war against the United States. The ministry was also ordered to consider an emergency plan in the event of air raids. But when Vice Minister Hirose Hōsaku asked Vice Army Minister Anami Korechika if the army intended to start a war with America, in which case the Finance Ministry would have to make contingency plans, the latter answered in the negative. According to Hirose, the Finance Ministry chose to believe Anami's assurances and made no preparations for a possible war with the United States until July 1941.[13]

The situation in the Finance Ministry, however, differed from that existing in the Cabinet Planning Board. By late 1940 the board had given up the idea of seeking resources and matériel from the United States and Great Britain and under the leadership of Hoshino Naoki was concentrating on obtaining them in Manchuria, China, and Southeast Asia. Many military officers came to work for the board, and the distribution of war matériel was carried out under their direction.

The Finance Ministry was only indirectly involved in the Japanese-American talks in Washington prior to the war. Formal negotiations were conducted by Ambassador Nomura Kichisaburō, but private exchanges took place behind the scenes. Ikawa Tadao, who started informal conversations with Bishop James E. Walsh through the intercession of Lewis Strauss of Kuhn, Loeb and Company, was a former Finance Ministry bureaucrat who had been stationed in the United States as secretary to the financial attaché and knew Strauss personally. However, the Foreign Ministry looked askance at these conversations, and the Japanese embassy in Washington was reluctant to transmit Ikawa's telegrams to Tokyo. Konoe thereupon asked Finance Minister Kawada to have the ministry act as a channel of communication, and the prime minister and Ikawa exchanged messages through Nishiyama Tsutomu, financial attaché in New York.[14] But the Finance Ministry itself had little to do with the actual negotiations.

About the same time certain, members of the financial community advanced a proposal for obtaining loans from the United States. They suggested that the Japanese government invite Wendell Willkie to Japan and seek his good offices to procure an American loan by explaining to him the seriousness of Japan's financial condition. Sakomizu Hisatsune, chief of the Finance Section of the Finance Ministry, transmitted the plan to Finance Minister Kawada, suggesting that a loan would help to improve Japanese-American relations. Kawada approved of the idea and agreed to make available $100,000 from the budget to cover Willkie's trip to Japan. Unfortunately, Foreign Minister Matsuoka vehemently objected to the scheme and nothing came of it.[15]

Officials of the Finance Ministry were seriously disturbed by the deterioration of Japan's relations with the United States, Great Britain, and other nations. They feared in particular that one or more of the powers might freeze Japanese overseas assets and that, since such action would make it difficult to obtain funds, all export trade would cease. To prepare for this contingency, the ministry decided to enter into separate bilateral negotiations with a few countries in order to facilitate foreign financial transactions and lessen Japan's dependence on the American and British currencies as a means of settling accounts by making it possible to carry out trade transactions in yen. Agreements were concluded with the Dutch East Indies in December 1940 and with French Indochina in July 1941. Negotiations with Thailand were carried out through former Vice Finance Minister Ōno Ryūta, who was sent as an adviser of the Japanese Foreign Ministry. A boundary dispute between Thailand and Indochina was settled through Japanese mediation. This enabled Japan to expedite the conclusion of an agreement with Thailand under which Japan was to purchase rubber and tin from the latter on credit.[16] Then on July 25, following Japan's decision to occupy southern Indochina, the United States and Great Britain froze Japanese assets, and the Dutch East Indies immediately followed suit, annulling its financial agreement with Japan. The Finance Ministry decided to take retaliatory measures, and the freezing of American, British, and Dutch funds was announced on the 28th. On August 1 the United States issued a general embargo that excepted cotton and foodstuffs but included oil. The reaction of the Japanese navy was that it might be preferable to start a war rather than suffer an inevitable depletion of oil reserves.

On September 6 the Imperial Conference decided to declare war against the United States if Japan's terms for a modus vivendi were not accepted by the end of October. On October 18 the army caused the collapse of the Konoe cabinet, which was succeeded by the Tōjō cabinet. The director of the Cabinet Planning Board as well as the army, navy, foreign, and finance ministers attended the meetings of the Liaison Conference continually after November 1. At one of these meetings Finance Minister Kaya stated that since commodity prices, foreign exchange, and the currency system were relatively stable, a runaway inflation would not occur even if Japan became involved in a war with the United States. Nevertheless, he asserted, the crucial question of whether the necessary goods could be procured remained unresolved. To this the director of the Cabinet Planning Board answered that in one way or another the government would be able to supply the materials essential for the conduct of war.[17] In the end the conference decided to start military action at the beginning of December, and Finance Minister Kaya agreed to an emergency disbursement of 193 million yen. This was a fitting finale to a decade of uneasy relations between the Finance Ministry and the military over basic questions of policy.

THE ROLE OF THE
UNITED STATES CONGRESS
AND POLITICAL PARTIES

Wayne S. Cole

From 1931 to 1941 American congressmen and political party leaders were virtually unanimous in their denunciations of Japanese military conquests in Manchuria, China, and Indochina. At the same time, however, they generally gave less priority to relations with Japan and East Asia than to relations with European states and considered Nazi Germany and fascist Italy more dangerous than Japan. Though shocked by Japanese actions, most of them regarded Japan as a less formidable potential adversary than Germany; most treated the possibility of war with Japan less fearfully than they did the possibility of involvement in a European war.

The foreign policy debates in the United States between so-called "isolationists" and "internationalists," between "noninterventionists" and "interventionists," emerged primarily from considerations of America's relation to developments in Europe. The isolationist-interventionist divisions extended in modified forms to considerations of policies toward Japan and East Asia, but the lines blurred a bit. Despite individual exceptions, they did not differ with each other quite so sharply when considering developments in Asia in the 1930s as they did when looking toward Europe.

Though opponents worried that President Franklin D. Roosevelt's Far Eastern policies might provoke a war with Japan, they worried less about that possibility than they did about the dangers of entanglement in a European war. Secretary of State Cordell Hull and others feared the strength of isolationist opposition to the administration's foreign policies. Nevertheless, congressional attitudes allowed both the Hoover and the Roosevelt administrations more freedom of action in dealings with Japan in East Asia than they had in coping with Germany and Italy in Europe. Congressmen and party leaders did not want war with Japan, but that possibility disturbed them less than involvement in Europe. The administration's actions short of war against Japan won widespread approval from legislators in both parties. Indeed, many were impatient with the administration for its failure to block the flow of goods to Japan sooner and more completely.

Those congressmen, senators, and party leaders who were particularly outspoken on East Asian matters often reflected special sectional and economic considerations. Support for economic restrictions in relations with Japan were rooted in chauvinism, moralistic feelings, and economic interests at least as much as in any calculations of national security.

With the possible exception of the presidential election of 1940, foreign policy issues did not substantially affect the outcome of any national election from 1931 to 1941. Domestic and local issues were far more powerful in determining election results than foreign affairs. And Far Eastern policies won even less attention in political campaigns than policies toward Europe.

I

Both major American political parties were heterogeneous alliances of dissimilar groups with diverse views that were drawn together for the purpose of getting into public office and controlling the government. Neither the Republican Party nor the Democratic Party presented a united front on most domestic or foreign policy issues. Normally government policies, domestic and foreign, required support from some in both parties. The parties may have had slightly different tendencies in foreign affairs. For example, the Republican Party may have represented a relatively greater interest in Asia, while the Democratic Party had somewhat more of a "Europe first" focus. There may have been more internationalism in Democratic circles, while Republicans perhaps were a bit more nationalistic and determined to maintain American sovereignty and freedom of action. Insofar as those tendencies prevailed, however, the differences were only matters of degree.

Domestic issues, local matters, personalities, and party politics determined the nomination and election of United States senators and representatives; foreign affairs did not. Even those who served on the Senate Foreign Relations Committee and on the House Foreign Affairs Committee won election to office on grounds other than foreign affairs for the most part.

Similarly, foreign policy issues generally were not decisive in the nomination and election of the president every four years. Though contenders for the party presidential nominations and later the presidential nominees addressed themselves to such questions, neither the nominating conventions nor the presidential elections turned primarily on foreign policy considerations. The platforms outlining the party views and goals always included foreign affairs, but the foreign policy planks in those platforms were phrased in broad generalities designed to please many and displease as few as possible. And most voters did not study the platforms or their foreign policy planks anyway.

In 1932 the Democratic nominee for president, Governor Franklin D. Roosevelt of New York, defeated the incumbent Republican nominee, Herbert Hoover of California, because voters identified Hoover and his party with the stock market crash of 1929 and with the depression that followed. Most were not certain what Roosevelt would do about the depression if elected, but they proposed to find out. The domestic issue of how to end the depression and restore prosperity determined the election of Roosevelt as president in 1932. The Republican platform defended the Hoover-Stimson policies toward Japan and East Asia; the Democratic platform did not even mention Japan explicitly. Despite the continuing Manchurian crisis, Far Eastern foreign policy issues had no significant influence on the outcome of the election.[1]

In 1936 the Democratic Party renominated Roosevelt for president and John Nance Garner of Texas for vice president. The Republican Party turned to Governor Alfred M. Landon of Kansas and Frank Knox of Illinois. With the possible exception of Garner, none of the four was an isolationist on foreign affairs. Neither party platform explicitly mentioned Japan or East Asia; both treated foreign affairs in terms of peace, neutrality, nonentanglement, and nonintervention. Isolationist sentiment was strong in American public opinion, and none of the candidates seriously challenged that view during the campaign. Indeed, none of the candidates said much about foreign affairs. Roosevelt and Garner won an overwhelming election victory on the grounds that the Democratic New Deal program had alleviated the intensity of the depression and on the hope that the chances for full economic recovery might be greater if Roosevelt were continued in office four more years. Personalities and domestic issues determined the election results; foreign policy issues had no significant direct influence. The party leaders, candidates, and voters gave little thought to Japan in the presidential campaign and election of 1936.[2]

In 1940 war raged in Asia, Europe, and Africa. Hitler's forces overran much of Europe. France fell. Britain survived the Battle of Britain, but few were confident that Hitler had abandoned all plans for an invasion of the British Isles. And Japanese military forces successfully swept over much of China and even expanded into French Indochina. Within the United States the "great debate" between isolationists and internationalists, between noninterventionists and interventionists, increased its tempo. The critical international situation led Roosevelt to accept the Democratic nomination for an unprecedented third term as president. The Republican nomination of Wendell Willkie of Indiana and New York City for president was a victory for the urban internationalist wing of the party and a defeat for the isolationists. The fact that both parties nominated internationalists for president left the isolationists with no really acceptable candidate so far as foreign affairs were concerned. Both party platforms opposed American intervention in foreign wars, both urged building American military forces, and neither explicitly mentioned Japan.[3]

Leaders of both parties in 1940 feared that isolationist voting strength might be great enough to determine the outcome of the election. It was not great enough to control the nominations, but in a close contest the isolationists could swing the election one way or the other. Consequently both parties and their candidates felt compelled to talk like noninterventionists as the campaign progressed. As Willkie and his supporters increasingly denounced Roosevelt as a "warmonger," Democratic leaders urged the president to talk peace. Near the close of the campaign he did so, particularly in an address in Boston, Massachusetts on October 30, when he promised, "Your boys are not going to be sent into any foreign wars." Foreign policy issues were very prominent in the 1940 campaign, but voters did not have clear alternatives to choose from. The reelection of Roosevelt for a third term did not provide a clear indication of popular views on foreign affairs in general or on American policies toward Japan in particular.[4] If Japan and East Asia had not existed from 1931 to 1941, the congressional and presidential nominations and elections in the United States would have turned out much as they did anyway.

II

The powers of Congress in foreign affairs were largely negative, but its approval was required for taxes, appropriations, neutrality legislation, tariffs, a declaration of war, and (in the case of the Senate) diplomatic appointments and treaties. Congressional hearings and investigations affected legislation and could influence an administration's conduct of foreign affairs. Congress also served as a vehicle for public opinion and special interest groups; it was a sounding board on foreign policy issues. Though both houses of Congress were concerned, the Senate had greater interest, authority, and power in foreign affairs than the House of Representatives. Theoretically each of the 96 senators and 435 representatives shared congressional responsibilities in foreign affairs; in practice most members of both houses were preoccupied with domestic matters.

Most of the work in both houses fell to committees. Various committees treated aspects of foreign affairs, including the Naval Affairs and the Military Affairs committees in both houses of Congress. Primary responsibility, however, went to the Senate Foreign Relations Committee and to the House Foreign Affairs Committee. Occasionally a congressman who was not a member of either of those committees played a conspicuous role in foreign policy matters (Senator Gerald P. Nye of North Dakota was a prominent example in the 1930s), but that was the exception to the general pattern. The Foreign Relations Committee was far more powerful than its counterpart in the House. Assignment to the Foreign Relations Committee was a much sought-after honor. The political party that commanded the majority in each house also filled a comparable majority of the standing committee seats. Assignment to committees and choice of the committee chairman normally was determined by seniority. The member of the majority party who had served on the committee longest usually was its chairman. Knowledge and ability in foreign affairs were not irrelevant, however, and through many years of service senators often became highly knowledgeable. Nevertheless, seniority (not knowledge or ability) determined the chairmanship. Though the chairman of the House Foreign Affairs Committee played a relatively minor role in foreign affairs, the chairman of the Senate Foreign Relations Committee generally was the most powerful legislator on foreign policy matters.[5]

Four men served as chairman of the Senate Foreign Relations Committee from 1931 through 1941. William E. Borah, a Republican from the western wool-producing state of Idaho, presided until 1933. Key Pittman, a Democrat from the western mining state of Nevada, served from 1933 until his death late in 1940. Walter George, a Democrat from Georgia, succeeded Pittman briefly in 1941, before Tom Connally, a Democrat from Texas, assumed the responsibilities in July 1941.

William E. Borah was a powerful orator and an independent, progressive senator who, as an "irreconcilable," had opposed U.S. membership in the League of Nations after World War I. He became chairman of the Foreign Relations Committee in 1924, after the death of Henry Cabot Lodge, and served until the Republican Party lost control of the Senate with the election of 1932. An "isolationist" or "noninterventionist" toward U.S. involvement in Europe, he was also a nationalist who was not prepared to abandon the United States' defense of its "rights" as he understood them. Proudly independent, he could not be depended upon to conform to any particular party line on either domestic or foreign issues. Because of his great personal power and prestige as chairman of the Foreign Relations Committee, Republican presidents and secretaries of state often deferred to his wishes on important foreign policy matters. As ranking minority member of the committee after the election of 1932, he continued to play a powerful negative role during the Roosevelt administration until his death in February 1940.[6]

Key Pittman from the sparsely populated state of Nevada was chairman during Roosevelt's first two terms as president. Tall, lean, blue-eyed, and hard-drinking, Pittman was primarily interested in the economic welfare of the silver mining interests of his beloved Nevada. Neither scholarly nor colorful, Pittman was a shrewd politician. Often pessimistic in his analyses, he tended to emphasize the strength of the political opposition and the weakness of his own forces. In politics he preferred maneuver and manipulation to frontal assaults. Except on the silver issue, he generally did not engage in political crusades. As an early admirer of Franklin D. Roosevelt and as a Democrat, Pittman usually supported the Roosevelt administration, though his enthusiasm for it gradually cooled. For the most part he cooperated with President Roosevelt, Secretary of State Hull, and the internationalists on his committee. He voiced opposition to "isolationism" and urged U.S. military preparedness. As a chauvinist Pittman opposed appeasing aggressor states. Like others from the western part of the United States, he favored more vigorous opposition to Japanese expansion in the Pacific and East Asia than the administration was prepared to endorse. Though alarmed by the Axis powers, he was no Anglophile and tended to distrust foreigners in general. He was a militant nationalist in foreign affairs rather than a doctrinaire internationalist. He was sensitive about any executive efforts to bypass him or his committee. Cautious about the strength of congressional opposition, he often warned the administration against over-ambitious steps in foreign policy and encouraged more cautious and compromising approaches in its drive for internationalism and more executive discretion than many of the internationalists preferred. That caution was evident in his attitudes toward Europe, but not toward Japan and the Far East. He favored a hard line in dealing with Japan and won warm gratitude from official Chinese spokesmen.[7]

When Pittman died in November 1940, his successor as chairman was Walter George, a conservative southern Democrat from Georgia. Though sharing the south's interventionist sentiments, he guided the committee with an even hand that gave all sides a fair hearing. Tom Connally of Texas, however, took over the chairmanship of the committee at the end of July 1941, when George became chairman of the Finance Committee. A militant nationalist and interventionist, Connally vehemently opposed the isolationists and supported the administration's increasingly interventionist foreign policies.[8]

The membership of the Senate Foreign Relations Committee changed a bit from time to time, but some members served throughout the decade before Pearl

Harbor. The membership included some able spokesmen for internationalism—particularly from southern and eastern states. Among them were Joseph T. Robinson of Arkansas, Robert F. Wagner of New York, and later Theodore F. Green of Rhode Island and Claude Pepper of Florida. But the isolationist opposition in the committee—particularly from western and middle western states—was even more powerful. It included, among others, Hiram Johnson of California, Arthur H. Vandenberg of Michigan, Arthur Capper of Kansas, Robert M. LaFollette, Jr. of Wisconsin, and Henrik Shipstead of Minnesota. That opposition was strengthened in 1939-40 by the addition of Bennett Champ Clark of Missouri, Robert R. Reynolds of North Carolina, and Gerald P. Nye of North Dakota.[9] Senator Nye's role in foreign affairs was due not so much to his membership on the Foreign Relations Committee as to his performance as chairman of the Senate Special Committee Investigating the Munitions Industry from 1934 to 1936. In that capacity, in nationwide speaking tours, and in legislative maneuvers on neutrality proposals, the agrarian radical Republican senator from the Great Plains was a powerful leader of U.S. isolationism in the 1930s.[10]

III

Even the Great Depression could not wholly divert U.S. attention away from the military and diplomatic aftermath of the Mukden Incident in Manchuria in 1931 and the later hostilities near Shanghai. In Congress sympathies were overwhelmingly with China as opposed to Japan. The economic interests of Pittman's silver producers and Nye's wheat farmers probably reinforced sympathy for China. Some were impatient with the seemingly timid and hesitant initial responses of the Hoover-Stimson administration to the Manchurian crisis. Senator George W. Norris, an independent Republican progressive isolationist from the Great Plains state of Nebraska, complained that the "public and the country at large are in ignorance as to just what our State Department has done." Others criticized British and French inaction in the face of Japan's moves.[11]

Like the Hoover administration, like the European powers, like the League of Nations, and like the American people in general, however, congressmen and senators were uncertain how best to respond to the crisis. Most agreed that Japan had violated the Nine Power Pact of 1922 and the Kellogg-Briand Pact of 1928. In their view Japan was guilty of aggressive warfare and endangered the Open Door in East Asia. "Someone ought to do something." But congressmen did not want "to do something" that might involve the United States in an Asian war. Most approved the Hoover-Stimson nonrecognition policy announced in early 1932.[12] Many favored a boycott or embargo, but they disagreed whether it should apply only to aggressor states or to all belligerents. They also disagreed whether such an embargo should apply only to munitions or also to raw materials useful for war. President Hoover, some in the State Department, and many in Congress feared that meaningful economic coercion would involve the United States in war abroad. Senator Borah, chairman of the Foreign Relations Committee, opposed a boycott of Japanese products because he believed it would be "the first step toward war." He considered a boycott "an instrument of war, estrangement and bitterness." Many agreed with him. Congressman Hamilton Fish, an isolationist Republican from New York who served on the House Foreign Affairs Committee, proposed an embargo on shipment of munitions to all belligerents, but he feared that an embargo aimed at Japan alone would lead to war with that country. Congress did not adopt any embargo affecting Japan so long as Hoover was president of the United States.[13]

In 1933 when the Roosevelt administration pushed for discretionary legislation authorizing the president 'to embargo shipment of munitions to aggressor states, the proposal won approval in the House of Representatives. The Senate Foreign Relations Committee under Pittman, however, attached an amendment that would have applied the embargo to all belligerents alike. Believing such a measure would hurt China more than Japan, the administration dropped the matter and the resolution never became law.[14]

For several years Senator Borah had urged the United States government to extend diplomatic recognition to the Soviet Union. In 1932 he renewed that proposal in a letter to Secretary Stimson. Borah hoped recognition might help prevent an accord between Russia and Japan that could make the situation in Asia even more dangerous. Through recognition he believed the United States "could have the friendly cooperation of Russia" that "would greatly mollify the situation in the Orient." Hoover's secretary of state disagreed. Stimson feared that recognition of the Soviet Union despite its "very bad reputation respecting international obligations" would cause the United States to "lose the moral standing" it had "theretofore held in the controversy with Japan." He doubted that Japan and Russia could reach anything more than a "transitory" understanding because the "rivalry between those two nations in respect to Manchuria is so keen and the lack of confidence of each in the promises of the other so real" and because their interests were "too antagonistic for that."[15] The United States did not recognize the Soviet Union until November 1933, several months after Roosevelt became president. That was too late to affect Japan's actions in Manchuria, and it did not prevent subsequent Japanese expansion in East Asia.

During the Manchurian crisis American congressmen sympathized with China, felt moral indignation against Japan, and groped for effective expression of those attitudes. But all came to nothing in the face of American preoccupation with the depression and the fear of involvement in war abroad.

IV

U.S. relations with Japan were central to congressional attitudes and actions on naval construction. Congressmen divided sharply on the subject. Most Republican congressmen from inland parts of the United States doubted Japan's military intention or capacity to endanger U.S. security. They insisted that U.S. naval construction strengthened the militarists in Japan, encouraged Japanese naval construction, and further strained relations between the two nations. Senator Nye spoke vigorously and repeatedly along those lines. In more restrained terms Senator Borah and others shared his general views. The more militant and "realistic" congressmen contended that Japan was responsible for preventing naval limitations agreements and for ending earlier accords. They saw in Japanese armaments and aggression alarming justification for U.S. naval preparedness. An ever more powerful navy was essential, they believed, to guard American security against Japanese power in the Pacific and to deter Japan's aggressive ambitions. Such reasoning seemed particularly convincing to senators and congressmen from coastal states, including David I. Walsh of Massachusetts and William Gibbs McAdoo of California, and to Key Pittman of Nevada. By 1938 even the former isolationist Senator Norris followed President Roosevelt's lead on the issue.

Senator Nye illustrated an isolationist continentalist view common to the middle west in the 1930s. For example, in an address opposing the naval appropriations bill of 1936 Nye regretted the "wild, mad armament race" between the United States and Japan. He contended "that the military dominance in Japan would have died of its own weight long ago except for the fact that at least once a year the United States gives the Japanese military some ground or other upon which to stand when they say, 'We have to be better prepared for the trouble that the United States is getting ready to make for us.'" Nye insisted that the naval armaments race between the United States and Japan would not "get us anywhere except into the very thing we are trying to prevent." In opposing U.S. naval appropriations in 1938 Senator Nye contended that "Japan would not be prepared with the armaments she has today if it had not been for the year after year challenge which the United States has laid down to Japan in the form of increased armament programs." He thought that the United States could not successfully defend the Philippine islands even if the U.S. navy were five times as large as it was in 1936. But he also believed that even if the Japanese navy were twenty times larger than it was, it "could not get within hundreds of miles of our shores." The independence of the Philippines would be wiser, in his judgment, than unending military expenditures to defend them and Guam and other islands in the western Pacific. In a similar vein Senator Borah, in opposing the naval appropriation of 1938, wrote: "Ever since I have been in the Senate, we have been building navies allegedly to fight Japan, and now they are again citing Japan as a menace. However much we may disapprove of what is going on in the Orient, there is, to my mind, no probability of Japan attacking the United States. She would have to have a navy three times the size she now has if she were going, or coming, seven thousand miles to engage this country in war. It is sheer folly, in my opinion, to talk about it."[16]

Others sharply disagreed. Frank Knox, the Republican vice presidential nominee in 1936 and President Roosevelt's secretary of the navy beginning in 1940, insisted in 1933 that "it is only the counsels of safety alone that dictate, despite our financial situation, a swift building of our naval strength to the maximum allowed under the London treaty." In December 1937 he urged sending the fleet to Hawaii. "Conversation will not convince the Japanese militarists that we mean business. But the presence in Asiatic waters of a fleet more powerful than their own, would be most eloquent." During his six years as Democratic senator from California, William Gibbs McAdoo consistently supported U.S. naval preparedness. After leaving the Senate in 1939 he lauded President Roosevelt for urging the fortification of Guam. In his view an impregnable Guam would be "a standing exhibit of our organized might" that would deter Japan "from committing any future aggressions which would inevitably lead ultimately to war." He urged more adequate preparations for a possible attack on Pearl Harbor. In 1940 he urged the president to obtain naval bases for the United States at Singapore and Hong Kong to "give Japan serious pause." Senator Pittman similarly urged massive U.S. military preparedness to deal with Japan. Pointing to the failure of the Washington Conference treaties of 1922 and the Kellogg-Briand Pact, Pittman in 1939 saw no alternative for the protection of American security than "preparation for defense with force."[17]

Even Senator Norris turned to that alternative by 1938. He wrote:

> Recent events have shown that some countries, particularly Japan, have no respect for anything except force. She has disregarded her solemn treaties and has violated every sense of honor. . . . It simply means, if there is any country which Japan believes she can conquer, she will proceed to invade it. Her methods of warfare are disgraceful, ignoble, barbarous, and cruel, even beyond the power of language to describe. . . . If we were unarmed, or nearly so, or if our navy in the course of time were to become inferior to that of Japan, there is no doubt in my mind but what, some bright morning, we would awake to find ourselves at war with Japan. Right or wrong, I am impressed with the idea that it is imperative for us to make some preparation, at least for our own protection, against any such unreasonable and unwarranted attack as may come from Japan, or from a combination of nations similar to Japan.

In May 1941 Norris warned that the danger of a surprise Japanese attack "without warning" on the United States was "greater than people realize" and urged maintaining a strong "protective force" in the Pacific.[18]

Senator Hiram W. Johnson was an old progressive Republican isolationist from California. His early affection for Roosevelt faded and he came to hate the president. He opposed any U.S. intervention in Europe or cooperation with Britain. At the same time, however, he was a nationalist with anti-Japanese prejudices. In a letter to his son in 1938 he emphasized his misgivings about Roosevelt and Britain, but he endorsed "a big Navy" and conceded that the United States "may need it to whip the Japs."[19]

In practice President Roosevelt began to build the navy to authorized treaty levels very soon after taking office in 1933. And the administration never failed to win from Congress the funds and authorizations it sought for naval construction, generally winning them by overwhelming majority votes.

V

With the beginning of the undeclared Sino-Japanese War in July 1937, the vast majority of congressmen in both political parties were anti-Japanese and sympathetic to China. Most believed that a Japanese victory over China would be contrary to American interests, security, and peace. None approved of Japan's military conquest of China. In a few instances legislators who were noninterventionists toward Europe favored a hard line toward Japan. Nevertheless, despite individual exceptions and variations, the divisions in congressional attitudes toward the Sino-Japanese War generally paralleled attitudes toward Europe.

An early and continuing focal point for congressional controversy concerned the application of the Neutrality Act of 1937 to the war in East Asia. Drafted largely with the possibility of a European war in mind, the neutrality laws adopted in the 1930s represented compromises between diverse foreign policy views and interests. Internationalists led by Roosevelt and Hull wanted discretionary authority for the president to discriminate against aggressor states in support of the victims of aggression. Traditionalists led by Senators Borah and Johnson wanted to defend conventional neutral rights, including the right to trade with belligerents in noncontraband goods. Isolationists led by Senators Nye, Vandenberg, and Clark wanted mandatory legislation to restrict both the president and urban business groups. They thought the discretionary authority sought by internationalists would put the United States on one side in a war and inevitably bring the country into that war. They wanted to abandon neutral rights on the high seas and bind the president to treat all belligerents alike in the interest of noninvolvement. The neutrality laws actually enacted fell short of the desires of isolationists, but they were closer to their views than to those of the internationalists or the traditionalists.[20]

The so-called permanent Neutrality Act of 1937 (like its predecessors in 1935 and 1936) included a mandatory arms embargo that prohibited the sale of munitions to all belligerents. The president could not discriminate against an aggressor in applying the embargo. It also included a ban on private loans to all belligerents, prohibited U.S. citizens from traveling on belligerent ships, and until May 1, 1939 included cash-and-carry provisions that required belligerents buying nonembargoed goods in the United States to pay cash and transport those products in non-American ships. The president had the authority to determine when a state of war existed abroad requiring application of the act.[21]

Since Great Britain and France presumably would control the seas, cash-and-carry would work to their advantage in any war against the Axis powers in Europe. The reverse was true in the Pacific, however, where in effect it would open American ports and production to Japan but close them to China. As President Roosevelt phrased it in 1939, "while the cash and carry plan works all right in the Atlantic, it works all wrong in the Pacific." Roosevelt, Hull, Pittman, and their followers opposed applying the Neutrality Act to the Sino-Japanese conflict primarily because they believed it would operate in favor of Japan against China.[22]

In his capacity as chairman of the Foreign Relations Committee, Senator Pittman took the lead in defending the administration's refusal to apply the Neutrality Act to the Sino-Japanese conflict. Party loyalty, personal conviction, and a strong pro-Chinese bias influenced his course. In a major radio address in August 1937, Pittman defended the administration's policies and lauded the president for "performing a most difficult duty in an able and patriotic manner." He saw nothing that the United States could gain by invoking the Neutrality Act. In an interview in May 1938 he contended that so far as he was concerned personally, if the Chinese government were "driven back to a cave in the mountains 3,000 miles from the coast and the government consists only of

Chiang Kai-shek," he "would continue to recognize that government as the government of all China."[23]

Others were more torn by conflicting desires on the issue. They favored policies that would help China against Japan but opposed policies that might draw the United States into the Asian war as a belligerent. Senator Norris was one of those honestly and deeply troubled by the dilemma. Even Senator Borah had mixed feelings on the subject.[24]

Senator Nye, however, felt no such mixed emotions. He repeatedly criticized the Roosevelt administration for failing to invoke the Neutrality Act in the Sino-Japanese War and saw the administration's refusal as evidence of the need for more mandatory neutrality legislation. He urged evacuation of Shanghai and withdrawal of all U.S. troops and ships. In a joint statement with Senators Clark of Missouri and Homer T. Bone of Washington in August 1937, Nye insisted that the main purpose of the Neutrality Act was to keep the United States out of foreign wars, not to treat both sides alike. In contrast to the administration's view, these isolationist senators insisted that invoking the law would hurt Japan more than China. Japan blocked China's access to American products; the Neutrality Act would, in effect, partially block Japan's access as well. They doubted "that any action—short of economic, which could finally become military, war on the part of the United States—would hold Japan back."[25]

At the same time Nye denounced the shipment of scrap iron and steel by American firms to Japan. In a short speech in the Senate on August 10, 1937 he predicted that "the only return we may expect from a continuation of this exportation, aside from the munificent return in dollars to the several exporting companies, is the probability that one day we may receive this scrap back home here in the form of shrapnel in the flesh and in the bodies of our sons." He warned that it was "quite conceivable that our exports may one day be used for war against our own country."[26] Repeated by the senator in countless speeches all over the country, that theme aroused enthusiastic approval from his audiences.

The more moderate Charles L. McNary of Oregon, Republican minority leader in the Senate and his party's vice presidential nominee in 1940, also urged Roosevelt and Hull to invoke the Neutrality Act in the Asian war,[27] but the administration never yielded to that advice.

President Roosevelt's quarantine address in Chicago on October 5, 1937 aroused mixed responses among party and congressional leaders. Governor Landon objected to excessive presidential power and urged greater congressional control of foreign policy. At the same time, however, he was less critical of the address than he might otherwise have been because he was convinced that "a considerable section of opinion in the Republican Party" supported the president's position.[28] Frank Knox, Landon's running mate on the Republican ticket in 1936, was less equivocal on the matter; he enthusiastically lauded the president's address.[29] Senator Pittman urged "an economic quarantine of Japan" by all the "civilized governments" of the world. He predicted that such a quarantine "would be successful in itself in stopping the Japanese invasion of China in thirty days" without "a single shot fired." Such a course in his opinion would be "more powerful than the army and the navy of the United States."[30]

There was much favorable response from members of both parties in Congress to the president's address.

At the same time, however, isolationists vehemently denounced the speech. In Senator Nye's view, "However resentful we might be against Japan's moves at present, there was absolutely no reason for us to take the initiative as we did." He feared "that we are once again being caused to feel that the call is upon the United States to police a world that chooses to follow insane leaders. Once again we are baited to thrill to a call to save the world. We reach a condition on all fours with that prevailing just before our plunge into the European war in 1917."[31] Senator Johnson of California said that his "sympathy for China" was so great that he "would do anything short of war and our people will not have war." But he believed the president's address was designed to divert attention away from the administration's domestic political difficulties and feared it could lead to sanctions that would in turn lead to war.[32] Senator Borah considered the quarantine idea "just as impracticable" as the idea of "a war to end war."[33]

The Nine Power Brussels Conference in November 1937 aroused no optimism among congressional leaders; many warned against agreements that might commit the United States to joint action against Japan. Fear of isolationist opposition inhibited Roosevelt, Hull, and the chief U.S. delegate Norman H. Davis. Senator Pittman did not expect success for the conference, but he did not object to keeping U.S. representatives there so long as other governments wanted to confer.[34]

The *Panay* incident on December 12, 1937 further inflamed anti-Japanese emotions in Congress. Most supported the administration's handling of the crisis. Frank Knox in a letter to Secretary Hull hoped "that the strong position taken by the American government will be maintained, and I hope further strengthened by the early dispatch of the fleet to Hawaii or some further point east."[35] Nevertheless, neither Congress nor the American people wanted to go to war over the incident. Senator Nye blamed the Roosevelt administration, insisting that if the president had invoked the Neutrality Act it would not have happened.[36] Senator Borah wrote that he was "not prepared to vote to send our boys into the Orient because a boat was sunk which was traveling in a dangerous zone. That which happened might be expected to happen under such circumstances." He believed that the United States government had "done all that a government could do, and that is, to demand satisfactory apology and reparations, and an assurance that such things will not happen in the future."[37] Senator Henrik Shipstead of Minnesota said that so long as neutrals remained in the war zones they "can be sure they will get injured or even killed!" He did not believe the nation should "lose its head over an incident or accident due to the fortunes of war." He urged Americans "to keep cool and try to muddle through and get some business done here at home. We have plenty to do."[38] U.S. congressmen and senators railed at the Japanese action; most approved the administration's course in the crisis, many believed the United States and its citizens should withdraw from the troubled areas of East Asia, but none favored an American declaration of war against Japan over the incident.

The *Panay* episode did, however, enable Louis M. Ludlow, a Democratic congressman from Indiana, to force a decision on his so-called Ludlow

Amendment, a proposed constitutional amendment that would have required that any declaration of war be approved by a direct vote of the U.S. people, except in case of armed attack on the United States, its territories, or the western hemisphere. Though introduced in various forms in both houses of Congress, it won greater support in the House of Representatives than in the Senate. Ludlow and various peace groups had been urging adoption of the amendment for some time. He persistently tried to get enough signatures on a petition to force the House to vote on a motion to discharge the amendment from the Judiciary Committee. Early in December 1937 he had 205 signatures, thirteen less than the required 218. The Japanese attack on the *Panay* enabled the determined congressman to get the necessary signatures within twenty-four hours after the incident.[39]

Leaders of both politial parties in and out of Congress threw their weight against the Ludlow Amendment. On the Democratic side President Roosevelt, Secretary Hull, Senator Pittman, Speaker of the House William B. Bankhead, and Sam D. McReynolds, chairman of the House Foreign Affairs Committee, all opposed the proposal. In a letter to the speaker of the House President Roosevelt warned that the proposed amendment "would cripple any President in his conduct of our foreign relations; and it would encourage other nations to believe that they could violate American rights with impunity." Both "Alf" Landon and Frank Knox in the Republican Party supported the president in opposing the amendment. Indeed, Knox believed that "action of that sort right now in the face of our crisis with Japan is little short of treason." Even Senator Norris followed the president and opposed the amendment.[40]

In the formal vote on January 10, 1938 the House of Representatives rejected by a vote of 209 to 188 the motion to discharge the Ludlow Amendment from committee. A majority of the Democratic congressmen voted against the motion to discharge, but a very large minority of the Democrats voted for it. A majority of the Republicans voted for the motion, but they were nearly as divided as the Democrats. The motion won its greatest support from representatives of middle western and Great Plains states; it encountered its greatest opposition among congressmen from the south and the urban northeast. The vote on the motion to discharge the Ludlow Amendment from committee was not a clear and unequivocal indication of congressional attitudes on U.S. policies toward Japan in 1938. Party, patronage, European, and many other considerations entered into the vote on a proposal that in any event only partially and indirectly concerned Japanese-American relations. Neither the Senate nor the House ever voted directly on the Ludlow Amendment itself.[41]

VI

Throughout the decade before Pearl Harbor Americans in both parties in and out of Congress considered various economic policies of one sort or another in dealing with Japan. Their economic proposals varied widely, were inspired by diverse motives, and aimed at different (even conflicting) goals or objectives. Some advanced proposals designed to protect the interests of specific U.S. economic groups against Japanese competition; others supported measures they hoped would protect or expand the foreign markets of U.S. producers, exporters, or investors. Some of the radical isolationist persuasion wanted to eliminate or prevent economic involvement abroad that might draw the United States into a war with Japan; others in the internationalist pattern hoped to use aid to China and economic sanctions against Japan to check Japanese aggression and to protect and preserve U.S. peace and security. Some warned that economic sanctions would lead to war; others warned that if Japan were not checked by China (and perhaps partly by U.S. steps short of war), U.S. involvement was virtually inevitable. Millions of Americans (both isolationists and internationalists, Republicans as well as Democrats) objected on moral grounds to the sale of munitions and war materials for use by Japan in its aggressive military conquest of China. The moral and noninterventionist objections by isolationists and pacifists to certain exports to Japan inadvertently weakened the effectiveness of their opposition to certain essentially coercive and interventionist economic restrictions urged by internationalists in their efforts to aid China against Japan with methods short of war. Whatever the motives and intentions, the Roosevelt administration gradually tightened the United States' economic screws on Japan. One consequence of that increasing economic pressure was the Japanese attack on Pearl Harbor and the Philippines.

Various groups within the United States had economic interests directly related to one or another of the areas or countries in the western Pacific or East Asia, and those groups made their wishes known to Congress. Some had economic reasons for wanting good relations with Japan; they opposed embargoes or boycotts that would have reduced trade with Japan. Some southern cotton producers and exporters considered Japan one of the most valuable foreign markets for their raw cotton. They opposed increased U.S. tariffs on cotton textile imports, cancellation of the trade treaty of 1911, and export embargoes that might endanger the Japanese market for their raw cotton. They made their views known to the White House and to Tom Connally, as the senator from a cotton producing and exporting state and a powerful member of the Foreign Relations Committee. In deference to their wishes, in 1939 Senator Pittman excluded raw cotton from the list of commodities that would have been embargoed under legislation he introduced against Japan.[42] In 1937 the National Association of Hosiery Manufacturers objected to a boycott of hosiery manufactured in the United States out of raw silk imported from Japan.[43]

Some Americans, particularly farmers, had economic reasons for favoring independence for the Philippines, an action that could have reduced U.S. interests in the western Pacific. Rope and twine manufacturers were eager to reduce competition by placing the Philippines outside the tariff wall. In 1934 Senator Norris pointed out that it would be easy to provide tariff protection for producers of copra and coconut oil in the United States if "we gave the Philippines Islands their freedom." In 1939 Senator Nye neatly tied together defense, economic, and ideological arguments for granting immediate independence to the Philippines: "A first consideration with me on this point is the fact that continued connection with the Philippines is placing a tremendous military burden upon our country. If we can remove from the Philippines we can anticipate a much smaller requirement in the way of National Defense. In the second instance, Philippine products are entering severely into competition with the products of American farmers who I have always felt were the first ones entitled to the American market. A third consideration which moves me grows out of a desire to see America divest herself of anything and everything which would make her appear to be at all imperialistic." Nye's North Dakota got little economic benefit from defense expenditures and was largely a farming state; it was easy for that particular senator to see the soundness of ideological arguments against imperialism![44]

Despite the importance of U.S. trade and investments in Japan, certain groups had economic reasons (actual, potential, or imaginary) for urging discrimination against Japan and for wanting policies favorable to China. U.S. farmers suffered hard times during the two decades between World War I and World War II and most proposals designed to restore agricultural prosperity related to foreign affairs directly or indirectly. For example, in the early 1930s Senator Nye from the wheat producing Great Plains region urged congressional authorization for the sale of 100 million bushels of wheat to the Chinese government on long-term easy credit—essentially government financing of foreign purchases of U.S. wheat. Even Senator Borah from Idaho supported the proposal. If the United States government could not sell wheat to the Chinese, he would give it to them ("anything to be rid of its depressing effect upon the American market"). Nye, Borah, and their constituents were not so concerned about the welfare of the Chinese people as they were about farm prosperity in the United States.[45]

Senator Pittman was even more interested in the importance of China to the prosperity of the silver mining industry in his state of Nevada. One partial explanation for Pittman's pro-Chinese and anti-Japanese attitudes in the 1930s lay in the significance of China's silver monetary system for the world silver market. In 1931 Pittman wrote that the "general silver question is of world-wide import and the China question is the most important that we have to consider relative to our surplus production." U.S. steps to increase the price of silver (a policy vigorously urged by Pittman) contributed to China's acute financial difficulties in 1935. In 1940 Pittman wrote Secretary Henry Morgenthau, Jr. objecting to Treasury Department purchases of silver from Japan.[46]

Spokesmen for the Alaskan fishing industry urged Pittman to do what he could to stop Japanese fishing in Alaskan territorial waters. Textile manufacturers urged tariff increases and quotas to protect their domestic market against Japanese competition. And independent iron and steel producers in the United States in 1937 wanted to preserve domestic supplies of scrap for their own use by seeking enactment of legislation to limit the export of iron and steel scrap to Japan.[47]

Depending upon the particular interests involved, economic self-interest affected the attitudes of some individuals and groups toward Japanese-American relations. Economic groups sought congressional assistance, and many legislators did not hesitate to serve those constituents against Japan. Economic interests reinforced other considerations in encouraging the United States' increasingly hard line toward Japan.

Moralistic outrage at Japanese military aggression, legalistic opposition to Japanese violation of the Nine Power Pact and the Pact of Paris, isolationist determination to avoid involvement in foreign wars, internationalist desire to guard peace and security through measures short of war, and special interests of specific economic groups all encouraged the Roosevelt administration, organized pressure groups, members of Congress, and millions of individual citizens to favor various economic restrictions against Japan. But each of the several alternatives considered, proposed, or implemented hurt or alarmed some Americans. And while each alternative could conceivably serve one or another of the considerations involved in U.S. policies toward Japan, each conceivably (or at least all combined) could lead eventually to war with Japan. Individual awareness of the possibilities, limitations, and risks involved in each proposal varied widely over time.

One proposal that did not require government action was for Americans individually to boycott Japanese products. Senator Norris urged the idea in 1938. He believed that "if for a reasonable time the American people would cease to buy products of Japan, it would be impossible for Japan to continue her program of conquest." Pittman expressed the view that, "If all of the churches and the peace societies in the country would condemn the brutality and the aggression of Japan and would bring about a cessation of the purchase of Japanese goods—chiefly silk stockings—it would have a far greater repressive effect on Japan than anything else." But Senator Borah considered such a boycott as "fooling with dynamite" and advised the United States to "move cautiously and with patience." The American hosiery industry that used Japanese raw silk in their manufacturing processes did not like the idea at all.[48]

Others favored an export embargo in one form or another. An arms and loan embargo with a cash-and-carry arrangement for non-munitions goods could have been implemented against both Japan and China if President Roosevelt had invoked the Neutrality Act in the Sino-Japanese War—a course he rejected. Various isolationist senators and congressmen (including Senators Nye, Borah, and Capper and Congressman Hamilton Fish) urged banning sale of munitions and war materials to both Japan and China. If Nye had had his way there would have been "no exportation of war materials to any land in peace time or in war time." But he could not win congressional adoption of such a sweeping trade ban.[49]

Still others led particularly by Pittman and Senator Lewis B. Schwellenbach of Washington favored special legislation aimed against Japan alone. That proposal won the eager endorsement of collective security spokesmen and various foreign policy pressure groups. Particularly important in working with Pittman in the effort was the American Committee for Non-Participation in Japanese Aggression led by Harry B. Price in New York City.[50]

Pittman introduced his bill in April 1939. It would have authorized the president to impose restrictions on trade with any party to the Nine Power Pact of 1922 that violated that treaty. The trade restrictions would not, however, extend to the export of agricultural products from the United States or its possessions. Later Senator Schwellenbach introduced a similar resolution, and others were introduced in the House of Representatives. In July 1939, however, the Foreign Relations Committee postponed action on the Pittman and Schwellenbach resolutions pending information from the State Department as to their possible effects on the commercial treaty of 1911 between the United States and Japan.[51]

On July 18, 1939 Senator Arthur H. Vandenberg, an isolationist Republican from Michigan, introduced a resolution urging the administration to give notice of the abrogation of the treaty of 1911 "so that the Government of the United States may be free to deal with Japan in the formulation of a new treaty and in the protection of American interests as new necessities may require." Eight days later, before the Senate had acted on Vandenberg's resolution, Secretary Hull gave Japan the required six months notice that the United States would terminate the treaty on January 26, 1940. Despite the threatening connotations of that action, Vandenberg insisted that he had introduced his resolution to avoid an anti-Japanese embargo by facilitating negotiation of "a new treaty of commerce and amity between the United States and Japan for the purpose of resolving—if possible—any controversy between us affecting American interests." In a letter to Hull, Vandenberg emphasized that his "theory of abrogation" was "definitely predicated upon earnest efforts to agree upon a new engagement." He insisted that he did not want "a mere arbitrary prelude to a one-sided embargo." In responding to Vandenberg's letter, however, the State Department deliberately kept the Japanese uncertain as to the intentions of the United States.[52]

With the outbreak of the European war in September 1939, the Roosevelt administration, Congress, and most Americans focused their attention on the Atlantic. President Roosevelt called a special session of Congress to repeal the arms embargo and reenact cash-and-carry. In a letter to Pittman, Harry Price wrote: "Following your advice, we have purposely refrained from pressing the Far Eastern issue during the present special session." But Price, Pittman, and others were planning their future moves after Congress revised the Neutrality Act and after the commercial treaty with Japan expired. With the ending of the treaty in January 1940, Pittman and his associates renewed their efforts to enact the Pittman resolution that would have imposed a sweeping embargo on exports to Japan. In doing so, however, they had to reassure cotton producers and exporters in the South that it would not affect the export of cotton to Japan. Both Pittman and Schwellenbach denied that their embargo resolutions would lead to war with Japan.[53]

The alarming military successes of Nazi Germany in the Low Countries and western Europe in the spring of 1940 led those seeking restrictions on U.S. trade with Japan to change tactics. With Hull, Pittman, Price's group, and others cooperating, Congress adopted the National Defense Act that Roosevelt signed into law on July 2, 1940. It included a provision authorizing the president to prohibit or limit the export of any materials he considered essential for national defense. Broader and more flexible than the resolutions introduced by either Pittman or Schwellenbach, both these anti-Japanese western senators were content with the new law. Appropriately, Price of the American Committee for Non-Participation in Japanese Aggression warmly thanked Pittman for his role in winning adoption of the legislation. With the passage of the National Defense Act the Roosevelt administration had the authority to control or end exports to Japan virtually at will. When the president licensed the export of scrap iron and steel, he was conserving supplies for the United States' defense production, denying those supplies to Japan's war machine, and incidentally following a course that independent iron and steel producers in the United States had been urging for more than three years.[54]

By the fall of 1940 petroleum exports had become the principal subject of controversy in the application of the law. President Roosevelt understood the dangers involved in turning the economic screws on Japan too quickly and too tightly. In a personal and confidential memorandum to his wife on November 13, 1940 Roosevelt wrote that "if we forbid oil shipments to Japan, Japan will increase her purchases of Mexican oil and furthermore, may be driven by actual necessity to a descent on the Dutch East Indies. At this writing, we all regard such action on our part as an encouragement to the spread of war in the Far East." Nevertheless, on July 26, 1941 the Roosevelt administration froze all Japanese assets in the United States. So far as Japan was concerned, the freeze particularly hurt with regard to oil. That drastic action aroused very little criticism from congressmen. Even Burton K. Wheeler of Montana, the leading Democratic isolationist in the Senate, approved the decision, reasoning that it would "slow up Japan from an economic standpoint and call their bluff so they will not start anything." Long before Japan and the United States went to war against each other, Congress ceased to provide significant opposition to the economic coercion that many had earlier predicted would lead to war.[55]

VII

As Japanese-American relations neared the breaking point, some congressmen continued to criticize the administration's policies, but they were only a small minority. In August 1941 Senator Wheeler contended that if the United States went to war with Japan it would be "undertaking to preserve the British domination of Asia." He labeled Japan one of America's "best customers" and saw "no reason why we should not live in peace with her." Late in November Senator Nye said he believed the United States could end the Asian war satisfactorily if it would help Japan "save her face" by making relatively minor concessions in China. He was convinced, however, that the Roosevelt administration really did not want to settle the Far Eastern crisis peacefully.[56]

In Pittsburgh, on Sunday afternoon, December 7, 1941, Senator Nye addressed the last major isolationist meeting. As he was commenting on the role of British propaganda in U.S. relations with Japan, a reporter gave him a note informing him of the Japanese attack. Uncertain whether to believe it or not, he finished the point he was making at the moment by citing an English authority to the effect that the only way the United States might be brought into another British war would be through war with Japan. He then told his audience of the Japanese attack and quickly closed the meeting—still somewhat doubtful about the truth of the report. His was the last gasp of noninterventionist opposition to the Roosevelt administration's policies toward Japan before war was declared. But the strength of that opposition among congressmen and party leaders had faded substantially long before that final address in Pittsburgh. The next day Nye joined with his Senate colleagues in voting for the declaration of war against Japan. With only a single dissenting vote in the House, Congress (like the American people in general) united behind President Roosevelt in the determination to defeat the enemy.[57]

THE ROLE OF THE DIET
AND POLITICAL PARTIES

Misawa Shigeo and Ninomiya Saburō

Translated by Michael K. Blaker

The ten-year period from the Manchurian Incident to the Pacific War marked the decline of party politics in Japan. Since the popular rights movement began in the early Meiji period, the influence of political parties had grown, reaching a peak in the 1920s. The rise of fascism touched off by the Manchurian Incident, however, led to a deterioration of their political power until, just prior to the outbreak of the Pacific War, they ceased entirely to exist. The Diet was also gradually deprived of its orginal functions and became by 1940 a hollow institutional shell known as the Imperial Rule Assistance Diet. Thus, the Diet and the political parties did not play any significant role in Japanese policymaking after the Manchurian Incident.

This paper is concerned, first, with the reasons for the exclusion of the Diet and parties from the process of national policy formation as viewed from an institutional and historical perspective and, secondly, with their actual functions and activities during the period.

I

As provided in the Meiji constitution, the role and functions of the Imperial Diet were extremely limited. Final legislative authority rested with the emperor. The Diet gave its consent to the budget and to laws promulgated by the Throne, but its authority was circumscribed in various important ways by the imperial prerogative.[1] It did not participate in declaring war, making peace, concluding treaties, or other diplomatic matters that belonged to the "diplomatic prerogative" and were, therefore, part of the imperial prerogative. Moreover, in military affairs the Diet was limited additionally by the "right of supreme command," which lay outside the sphere of both Diet and cabinet authority. As a consequence, no standing committees on foreign relations or special committees to deliberate treaties were established in the Diet.[2]

The powers held by both houses of the Diet fell within the area of general affairs of state (*kokumu*) and included the right of appeal to the Throne, the right to make representations to the government, and the right of interpellation and questioning. The right of appeal to the Throne was unlimited in scope and consisted of opinions and appeals presented in written form to the emperor. This right had been employed by the Diet during the early constitutional period as a device to pressure the government; but as it was thought the emperor should be kept out of politics, it came to be used less frequently and gradually lost its political significance. Ultimately it became the practice to use the right exclusively for replies to imperial rescripts opening Diet sessions and for ceremonial expressions of condolence to the imperial household.

Representations (*kengi*) were submitted to ministers of state but were restricted to constitutionally defined areas of ministerial authority. Resolutions (*ketsugi*) were only hortatory and were not presented formally to ministers of state, for the Diet lacked the power to force the cabinet to comply with its wishes. On the other hand, unlike representations, resolutions were not limited to areas of ministerial competence and were, therefore, widely employed as a means of exerting pressure upon the cabinet or individual ministers of state. They were often so effective as to determine the fate of a particular cabinet.

Interpellations (*shitsumon*) and questions (*shitsugi*) differed in that the former were written representations to the government by thirty or more concurring Diet members, while the latter normally consisted of oral statements directed to ministers of state by individual members on the floor of the Diet. The more important of the two were the questions. It was accepted practice in both houses of the Diet for representatives of the various political parties to raise questions in response to policy speeches made by the prime minister, foreign minister, and finance minister at the plenary sessions opening the Diet and at meetings of the Budget Committee. The Diet was able to use these opportunities to criticize government policy and to question the competence of cabinet ministers.

Thus, under the Meiji constitution the Diet originally occupied an extremely inferior position with decidedly limited authority.[3] As is well known, however, after the inception of the Diet in 1890, the political parties launched an intensive campaign to overthrow oligarchic and autocratic government and establish party cabinets. Eventually the parties and the Diet went beyond their constitutional limitations and came to occupy an important and even decisive role in the Japanese political system.

In this process the right to decide the budget emerged as the most effective means of Diet control over the government. Diet reduction of the budget—especially in the area of appropriations for the expansion of military armaments—often placed the government in an untenable position. The Diet influenced government policy both directly and indirectly by such means as motions censuring the government and by severe and critical interpellations in Diet plenary sessions and the Budget Committee.

During the 1930s, however, these applications of Diet authority became increasingly infrequent, especially in relation to questions of war and diplomacy.

Following the Manchurian Incident interpellations attacking the cabinet's foreign policy were rare and resolutions criticizing policy nonexistent. Even with reference to the budget, despite distressing financial conditions, the Diet never rejected or reduced the vastly expanded military allocations.

The reason that severe limits had been imposed on the powers of the Imperial Diet under the Meiji constitution was to guarantee the superior position of clan government over the Diet. The Diet and political parties were not intended to occupy a central role in national politics; in fact, the Imperial Diet was fated by the constitution itself to become an organ of imperial rule to legitimize and secure popular support for government and military leadership in national affairs.

Apart from the role and functions of the Diet and parties in national politics, there was the question of the connections between the government on the one hand and the Diet and parties on the other. One link was the participation of party representatives in decision making bodies such as special committees.

A typical example was the Advisory Council on Foreign Relations, created under the Terauchi cabinet in 1917. This organization was under imperial jurisdiction and was designed to deliberate important matters relating to foreign relations. The prime minister served as chairman and its membership included the foreign minister, home minister, army minister, navy minister, certain privy councillors, and party heads. Representing the political parties were Hara Takashi of the Seiyūkai and Inukai Tsuyoshi of the Kokumintō. Katō Takaaki, president of the Kenseikai, was invited to join the group but declined on the grounds that it was only a tactical political ploy by Terauchi. Moreover, he felt that an organ like the council, under the emperor's direct control and beyond cabinet authority, would impose restraints on the ministers of state and interfere with their constitutionally guaranteed right to advise the Throne.

The Advisory Council on Foreign Relations was a rare example of party participation in foreign policy formulation. After its dissolution in 1922 no precisely analogous organization was found. In 1935, however, a somewhat comparable group was established known as the Cabinet Deliberative Council. This council, in which representatives of the parties participated, was designed to investigate and discuss important matters of national policy at the request of the cabinet, but it was abolished a year later without having produced a single policy position paper.

During the first Konoe cabinet (1937) the Cabinet Advisory Group was set up to assist in the formulation of government policy regarding the China Incident. Military, financial, and diplomatic leaders as well as party representatives were appointed to the group, but it too was ineffective and was abandoned without achieving any concrete results.

A second link between the government and the parties were the parliamentary vice ministers and party members appointed to serve as counselors within each ministry. Set up in 1924 under Katō Takaaki's three-party coalition cabinet following the Second Movement for Constitutional Government, this *sanyokan* system was a revival of the *sanseikan* arrangement established under the second Ōkuma cabinet in 1914 as a result of the First Movement for

Constitutional Government. These individuals advised the ministers of state on national affairs and performed functions of liaison and negotiation between the government and the Diet. Officials were appointed to these posts from both houses of the Diet.

Mori Kaku, parliamentary vice minister for foreign affairs under the Tanaka cabinet, used this system most effectively. In collaboration with Councillor Uehara Etsujirō and Vice Foreign Minister Yoshida Shigeru, Mori actually performed the duties of the foreign minister, a position held concurrently by Prime Minister Tanaka Giichi. This was unusual, however, for generally the system was strictly formal and was seen by party politicians as a gateway to ministerial position or by office seekers as an opportunity to acquire status. Even so it had its positive aspects, as party men appointed to these positions acquired practical experience with administrative responsibilities that produced more realistic party politicians. This was demonstrated, for example, in the case of Uchida Shinya, longtime parliamentary vice minister for the navy who was known as the Seiyūkai's "naval expert."

As far as military matters were concerned, special measures were taken to exclude Diet interference. It was specifically stipulated that "the duties of the parliamentary vice minister and councillor shall not extend to military secrets or military command."

II

In considering the role of the Diet and political parties during the decade, we have examined their legal position and powers from an institutional viewpoint. Our next concern is the historical situation that produced their decline. We do not intend to analyze the domestic political process itself but only those factors that contributed to the loss of Diet and party influence.

1. *The challenge of military and right-wing activities.* The worldwide depression of 1929 worsened considerably the already poor economic situation in Japan, and the resulting decline in agricultural prices aggravated the chronically distressed state of rural life. The government, however, failed to take any effective countermeasures. At the same time, Japanese public opinion became incensed over the inability of the government to contain rising Chinese nationalism and called for the protection of Japanese interests threatened by the growth of the rights recovery movement in China. The political parties might have seized this opportunity to assert their leadership, but they merely fought for power among themselves. As a result, public disaffection with party politics increased. Particularly toward the end of the Tanaka administration the repeated exposure of party scandals and free-for-alls in the Diet convinced the public of the rottenness and corruption of their parliamentary representatives.

Against this background of popular disenchantment with the political parties, the military and the right wing moved rapidly onto the political stage. The conclusion of the London Naval Disarmament Treaty provided them with a perfect occasion for an assault on party cabinets. They accelerated their campaign for political renovation, focusing on the issues of national defense and the military's right of supreme command.

The military leadership did not try to stop this interference in politics. For example, in January 1931 Army Minister Ugaki Kazushige declared in a communication to army and divisional commanders:

> It is true that we military men should not be influenced by public opinion and should not participate in politics. On the other hand, we bear the responsibility for national defense. If national defense policy is imperfect, our nation will be in danger. This being so, our discussion of national defense issues should not be regarded as meddling in politics.[4]

This message is said to have led many middle-echelon army officers to attend meetings and lectures on national defense questions and thus contributed to the military's increasing involvement in politics.[5]

Radical groups of young officers seeking to change the existing order and to effect a fundamental renovation of the political system coalesced around Major Hashimoto Kingorō of the Army General Staff. In the fall of 1930 they formed the Cherry Blossom Society (Sakurakai), the wellspring of fascism in the army. Hashimoto conspired with Colonel Itagaki Seishirō, a staff officer of the Kwantung Army, and with Major Ishiwara Kanji to bring about the Manchurian Incident.

Within Japan these officers, joined by the civilian rightist Ōkawa Shūmei, plotted an abortive military takeover of the government in what are called the March Incident and the October Incident of 1931. The motivation for the March Incident was the idea that "the deadlock in domestic politics and diplomacy has resulted from the greediness of party politicians and from a lack of great patriotic plans." "Eradication of the Diet" was seen as an essential first step.[6] The October Incident, a reaction against the government's policy of nonexpansion of hostilities in Manchuria, was aimed at "the destruction of the governmental process overnight."[7]

While unsuccessful, these incidents—in which the assassination of Prince Saionji, certain cabinet ministers, party leaders, and industrialists was planned—had a serious impact upon political circles. However, political leaders did not act to control the reckless and high-handed military or to protect parliamentary government. They ignored the March and October incidents and failed to conduct a rigorous investigation of those responsible.

With the tacit endorsement of the government for the reformist activities of the military and with the escalation of the Manchurian Incident, the political parties attempted to forge closer ties with the military. Just after the October Incident Adachi Kenzō, home minister in the Wakatsuki cabinet, and Kuhara Fusanosuke of the pro-army faction in the Seiyūkai demonstrated their conciliatory attitude toward the military by advocating an agreement with the army to form a joint Minseitō-Seiyūkai cabinet.[8] The disunity within the Wakatsuki cabinet caused by this attempt to create a coalition government led to its collapse. Earlier, Yamamoto Teijirō and other Seiyūkai leaders had visited Army General Staff headquarters shortly after the Manchurian Incident and, in talks with Imamura Hitoshi, chief of the Second Section, had tried to secure army cooperation to bring down the Wakatsuki cabinet.[9] Additionally, Mori Kaku, who was to be appointed chief cabinet secretary in the Inukai cabinet, secretly gained the support of Koiso Kuniaki, Military Affairs Bureau chief in the Army Ministry, for a plan to create a cabinet under the rightist Hiranuma Kiichirō. They intended to dissolve the Diet repeatedly until a one-party dictatorship was established.[10]

In February 1932 Inoue Junnosuke, chief director of the Minseitō and former finance minister, was assassinated. This was followed by the so-called Blood Brotherhood Incident, in which Dan Takuma, managing director of the Mitsui company, was fatally stabbed. These events clearly revealed the risk of a complete collapse of parliamentary government.

On May 8, 1932 Prime Minister Inukai spoke at a Seiyūkai meeting in the Kantō area, where he stated: "Lately certain people have lost confidence in the Diet because they feel it is something remote and beyond reform. On the contrary, I believe firmly in the beneficial effects of parliamentary government and in our ability to improve it."[11] Two days later, at a ceremony opening a party branch in Kanagawa prefecture, Minseitō president Wakatsuki Reijirō criticized the trend toward fascist politics in Japan, citing the experiences of certain foreign nations and asserting: "To adopt one-party politics means that Japan will follow the path of Russia, China, and Italy.... Political leaders in Russia and China suppress their countrymen by a rule of terror and eliminate anyone who opposes their leadership."[12] Thus the Minseitō and the Seiyūkai attempted, albeit belatedly, to unite for the preservation of constitutional government. But just then the May 15 Incident occurred and Prime Minister Inukai, who had attempted to lead a movement in support of parliamentary government, was assassinated. With his death the era of party cabinets founded upon the idea of normal constitutional government ended.

While there were attempts to extend party cabinets, the parties, and particularly the government party, the Seiyūkai, submitted to military pressure without a fight. The position of the military had been strengthened by the very unusual situation in which active-duty officers had participated in the uprisings. Instead of resisting the military, the parties agreed to the idea of "national unity" cabinets and voluntarily relinquished their political positions. Thereafter, as the parties sought to prolong their existence by working with the military, their influence continued to decline until, with the February 26 Incident four years later, they had become nothing more than "government agencies" for advancing militarism.[13]

2. Decline of party influence within the cabinet. A product of the May 15 Incident and the strong military opposition to party cabinets was the Saitō cabinet, a national unity cabinet controlled neither by the military nor by the parties. It was succeeded by a series of similar cabinets in which a few party men participated but which were dominated by the military and the bureaucracy. Moreover, the wishes of the military were strongly reflected in the selection of cabinet ministers.

The shift toward national unity cabinets signalled the loss of a party voice in the government. The seven cabinets during the period of party cabinets were headed by prime ministers from either the Kenseikai (later the Minseitō) or the Seiyūkai. The average number of cabinet ministers, including prime ministers, with party affiliations was 8.7 per cabinet (average number of cabinet posts = 12). However, after the initiation of national unity cabinets, no party men served as prime minister and the number of cabinet ministers from the parties dropped sharply. In the eight cabinets from the Saitō cabinet to the Yonai cabinet (the last before the political parties were disbanded), the average number of party ministers fell to 3.1 (average number of cabinet ministers = 13).

An especially extreme case was the Hayashi cabinet, in which thirteen ministerial posts were filled by eight ministers. The only party men asked to join the cabinet were Nagai Ryūtarō, a member of the pro-army faction in the Minseitō, and Nakajima Chikuhei of the Seiyūkai, who were required first to resign from their respective parties. When they refused, Yamazaki Tatsunosuke of the Shōwakai alone entered the cabinet. Moreover, the Hayashi cabinet faced the Diet without having named a parliamentary vice minister. With this, the exclusion of parties from the cabinet was complete.

This marked decline in the number of party-affiliated ministers during the period of national unity cabinets underlines how great was the reduction in party influence. Moreover, the appointment of party ministers to cabinet posts in the first place stemmed either from a desire to preserve party cooperation with the cabinet or from the fact that ·those who were appointed held strongly pro-military views. Party representatives who joined the cabinet gradually compromised their principles and, as noted above, their withdrawal from the party at times became a condition for cabinet appointment. In the first Konoe cabinet, although "resignation from the party was not a condition, party-affiliated ministers could not represent their parties in the cabinet."

3. *Exclusion of the parties from policymaking organs.* Not only were the parties thus forced out of the cabinet, but they were also excluded from other important national decision making organs. One was the Five Ministers Conference (composed of the prime minister, foreign minister, finance minister, army minister, and navy minister) set up by Prime Minister Saitō Makoto in 1933 to deliberate and establish basic policy in diplomatic, fiscal, and national defense matters.

At first Saitō was deferential toward the political parties and, in an effort to secure their support, held talks with Suzuki Kisaburō of the Seiyūkai, Wakatsuki Reijirō of the Minseitō, and Adachi Kenzō of the Kokumin Dōmei. The military and the bureaucracy, however, opposed this effort to encourage cooperation between the government and the parties. Saitō therefore decided he had gone far enough and, while expressing his satisfaction at having achieved a degree of understanding with the parties, proceeded to establish the Five Ministers Conference which excluded them entirely.

The military especially opposed the parties' playing any leading role in policy formulation. Army Minister Araki Sadao advised Finance Minister Takahashi Korekiyo that "the government will take the initiative in formulating a firm national policy" with respect to the Manchurian Incident and questions of national defense.[14] The Five Ministers Conference decided to assist in the development of Manchukuo, to strengthen national defense, to promote a cooperative foreign policy, to carry out various administrative reforms, and to arouse the national spirit.

The major organ for top-level domestic policymaking was the Domestic Policy Council (Naisei Kaigi), which particularly emphasized the problem of rural distress. Representatives of both the Seiyūkai and the Minseitō participated in council discussions. The dominant member of the council, in addition to Army Minister Araki, was Agriculture and Forestry Minister Gotō Fumio, a Minseitō bureaucrat who had first entered the cabinet as personal adviser to Home Minister Yamamoto Tatsuo. By this time, however, he was no longer associated with Yamamoto and had the strong backing of Araki. The bureaucracy led by Gotō, in collusion with the army under Araki, seized the reins of political leadership and moved in the direction of a controlled economy.[15]

Saitō's exclusion of the parties from the national policy deliberations of the Five Ministers Conference stimulated a joint Seiyūkai-Minseitō movement to preserve parliamentary government. Due to dissension between and within the parties, however, nothing resulted from their efforts.

Subsequent policymaking bodies were the Cabinet Deliberative Council (Naikaku Shingikai) and the Cabinet Research Bureau (Naikaku Chōsakyoku) formed under the Okada cabinet in May 1935. They represented the fruits of repeated military demands for high-level advisory organs directly under the cabinet. The Cabinet Deliberative Council was designed to study critical areas of national policy at the request of the cabinet. The Cabinet Research Bureau was its secretariat. Both were intended in part to strengthen the cabinet by winning over the Seiyūkai, the opposition party that held an absolute majority in the Diet.[16]

As questions of national defense and diplomacy had been placed outside the jurisdiction of the Cabinet Deliberative Council,[17] its membership did not include diplomatic or military officials. Fifteen political and financial leaders were originally appointed to the group, including Prime Minister Okada as chairman and Finance Minister Takahashi as vice chairman. Former Minseitō president Wakatsuki Reijirō declined to join the council, feeling that it was a duplication of the Privy Council and therefore a violation of constitutional government. The Minseitō itself, however, was closely allied with the government and decided to send four representatives, including Yamamoto Tatsuo, to participate in council discussions. The opposition Seiyūkai, on the other hand, even after formal negotiations between Okada and party president Suzuki Kisaburō, held to its original decision not to join the group. The prime minister approached three members of the anti-Suzuki faction in the Seiyūkai—Mizuno Rentarō, Mochizuki Keisuke, and Akita Kiyoshi—to join the council. Akita had previously left the party but now Mizuno and Mochizuki as well bolted the Seiyūkai and the three entered the council together.

The Cabinet Deliberative Council was criticized as a device to expand Minseitō power. It dealt only with two relatively minor matters, one dealing with local finance, and was abolished by the Hirota cabinet before it had accomplished anything substantial. Creation of the council, however, had an adverse effect upon the political parties in that it widened the divisions between the Seiyūkai and the Minseitō, dissolved their cooperative efforts, and caused dissension within the Seiyūkai. It is significant that even though the council lasted only a year and proved ineffective, the Cabinet Research Bureau was quite active under Suzuki Teiichi, later chief of its offshoot, the Cabinet Planning Board.

In October 1937, during the first Konoe administration, the post of cabinet councillor was established to "carry out cabinet planning on important matters relating to the China Incident." Ten individuals were named from military, political, financial, and diplomatic circles; four additional members were appointed during the Abe cabinet. Three senior party leaders participated: Machida Chūji (Minseitō), Maeda Yonezō (Seiyūkai), and Akita Kiyoshi (Shōkaiha). Machida has described the cabinet councillor system as follows: "The councillors' meetings were nothing extraordinary and councillors had no decision making power. Being appointed simply to hear reports, their participation in policy planning was perfunctory."[18]

These, then, were the major decision making organs of the 1930s. The parties, of course, were excluded from the Five Ministers Conference. Moreover, those organs that did include party representatives wholly lacked real policymaking authority. In every case the parties were unable to influence national decisions.

4. *Failure to secure reforms in the parliamentary system.* In response to general popular disaffection with parliamentary government and the resulting violent actions aimed at its destruction, the Diet and the political parties made some feeble attempts to regain public confidence by removing two main sources of criticism: widespread election corruption and the inefficient procedural system within the Diet.

Efforts began to be made to change the organization of the Diet in July 1932 when the All-Party Committee to Renovate the Diet (Gikai Shinshuku Kakuha Iinkai) approved an "Outline of Disciplinary Policy for the Diet" containing thirty provisions.[19] This Outline was designed to improve Diet efficiency, strengthen the maintenance of order, and achieve greater discipline among party and Diet members. Its contents were incorporated into a later draft bill presented to the 64th Diet in 1933. Neither document, however, suggested a radical overhaul of the election system or of Diet operations but merely indicated a desire to tighten discipline in the Diet because of widespread popular criticism. The draft bill passed the House of Representatives but was pigeonholed by the House of Peers, which had already displayed a negative attitude toward the Outline.[20] As a result, although it was again passed by the House of Representatives during the 65th and 67th Diet sessions, in both cases it failed to become law.

In the 69th Diet session, convened in May 1936, a Diet organizational reform measure was approved by both houses of the Diet. On the basis of the resolution the cabinet created under its jurisdiction three research committees to deal with Diet organization, elections, and the House of Peers.

A much more radical approach to Diet organizational reform was incorporated in a draft proposal given to Prime Minister Hirota Kōki by the military on September 21, 1936. It called for the "renovation of all aspects of government" through the reform of Diet, local, and central administrative organization. In those provisions dealing with Diet organizational reform the proposal stated, "Considering the advancement of our national fortunes and the present condition of the Diet, the Diet law and the election law shall be revised and the Diet shall be reformed." The draft came as a tremendous shock to leaders within the government.

When on October 30 the entire contents of the proposal appeared in the press, which had obtained them through important army sources, it clearly revealed the army's intention to destroy parliamentary government. The major points of the draft proposal were as follows:

> 1. Rejection of the party cabinet system and its transformation into one with separate legislative, executive, and judicial powers.
> 2. Passage of a law restricting party activities in the Diet.
> 3. Complete dissolution of the present system based on confrontation between the government and the Diet, taking as our standard the cooperation of all in the Japanese spirit; revocation of the Diet's right to pass no-confidence resolutions.
> 4. Reorganization of the House of Peers and the addition of an "economic general staff office" to the House of Representatives.
> 5. Restriction of the franchise to heads of households and to those who have completed their military obligation.[21]

The military's draft proposal met with united opposition from the parties and brought to an immediate halt the work of the three Diet research committees. In the Research Committee on Diet Organization and in the cabinet Army Minister Terauchi Hisaichi felt compelled to apologize for the army, claiming that it did not actually intend to oppose parliamentary government. Nor, he maintained, did the draft represent the views of the entire army. Thus, army efforts toward Diet organizational "reform" failed.

The three research committees began to meet again after accepting Terauchi's excuses and even prepared several revised drafts. In the end, however, no organizational reforms were undertaken.

A final reform effort was made by the Deliberative Council on Diet Organization (Gikai Seido Shingikai) created in June 1938 under the first Konoe cabinet. It did not hold discussions until after the Konoe cabinet had fallen and nothing substantial resulted. In sum, no noteworthy reforms of the Japanese Imperial Diet were achieved during the 1930s to check the rapid decline of parliamentary government.

5. *Clarification of the meaning of the national polity.* Behind the degeneration of the Diet into a mere legitimizing organ for military action was the so-called "issue of the clarification of national polity" (*kokutai meichō mondai*), which developed during the administration of Okada Keisuke out of a theory of Minobe Tatsukichi, a professor of law at Tokyo Imperial University. In the 67th Diet session both houses by unanimous resolution rejected Minobe's thesis—that sovereignty rested with the state, not the emperor, who was merely the highest organ of the state—and demanded clarification of the *kokutai* and renovation of political education. A "Resolution on the National Polity" passed on March 23, 1935 by the House of Representatives declared:

> Clarification of the cardinal principles of the national polity and elucidation of the proper direction for public sentiment to follow is of prime importance at the present time. The government must take firm steps at once with regard to any statements that are incompatible with the sublime and incomparable *kokutai.*

Such a position was suicidal for the Diet and the parties. Rejection of Minobe's theory, when carried to its logical conclusion, meant preservation without qualification of the imperial prerogative and destruction of the theoretical foundations of parliamentary democracy and the party cabinet system. Moreover, clarification of the *kokutai* had the effect of returning the Diet and parties to the limited position and authority provided under the Meiji constitution. In unanimously passing the resolution on *kokutai*, the Diet proclaimed its intention to withdraw from politics, to back the government, and to support "national unity."

6. *Voluntary Diet and party restraint in criticizing the government and the military.* In addition to external restraints upon party policy statements, the controls voluntarily imposed by Diet and party members upon their own speeches and statements critical of the government and the military further contributed to the deterioration of parliamentary politics. We shall see later that the Diet and parties under the national unity cabinets feared a decisive confrontation with the military and the government. Of course, attacks on the military by some party politicians did occur, and there was some criticism of governmental policy based on the idea of the "supremacy of the national livelihood." But most Diet members, more than anything else, hesitated to provoke the military for fear of direct retaliatory action. In addition, the threat of Diet dissolution by the government and their desire for governmental positions and power made them acquiesce in the cabinet's policies.

These concerns led to voluntary restrictions on speeches attacking the military and to the imposition of punishments for improper statements. During the 64th Diet session, under the Saitō cabinet, the Seiyūkai, hoping for its unhampered assumption of power, prohibited interpellations and statements by party members on certain political issues. Moreover, speeches on other subjects were checked and toned down in advance by party leaders. Ashida Hitoshi, for example, was ordered to "modify" a speech denouncing dual diplomacy. At the 70th Diet session, during the Hirota cabinet, the Minseitō leaders, from President Machida on down, restrained younger party members from attacking the military. Another case arose when the 70th Diet reconvened under the Hayashi cabinet. Hamada Kunimatsu, the Seiyūkai member previously involved in the famous confrontation known as the "hara-kiri exchange" with Army Minister Terauchi on the floor of the Diet, asked for permission to speak in order to defend his earlier statements. The Seiyūkai and the Interparty Council (Kakuha Kōshōkai), however, after some deliberation refused to grant his request.

Punishments for improper statements were occasionally imposed upon Diet members. One can mention the case of Tsumura Jūsha, a member of the House of Peers who was referred to the Discipline Committee and forced to resign because of "inappropriate" statements he had made attacking the military during the 69th Diet session. Saitō Takao was expelled from the House of Representatives at the 75th Diet session for the same reason. At the 73rd session Nishio Suehiro was excluded from the lower house for his comments during deliberation of the national mobilization law.

Thus, actions by the Diet and the parties to control their own statements, potentially their most effective tool for influencing policy, merely demonstrates the suicidal nature of their final surrender.

7. *Party dissolution.* The ultimate downfall of the Diet and the political parties was brought about by the "new party problem" which for some time had

been smoldering in political circles. The idea of concentrating political power by the formation of a new "national unity" party and by the construction of an "advanced national defense state" (*kōdo kokubō kokka*) based on cooperation with the military was transformed into a concrete plan of action following the Ogikubo conference at the end of 1936. A brief delay occurred when Konoe refused to head the organization, but plans for the party moved ahead swiftly after June 1940 when he decided to accept the post after all.

The new party movement was not simply an effort to reorganize the established parties nor to wrest political power from them. It was labeled the "new political structure movement" (*shin taisei undō*) to publicize the objective of building a political system based upon national unity, and in October 1940 the Imperial Rule Assistance Association was organized as the nucleus of a movement to promote this goal. All the parties had decided to join in this popular expression of national unity and voluntarily dissolved during July and August 1940. Following the breakup of the Minseitō on August 15, parties ceased to exist and when the 76th Diet convened in December, a Diet under military control and without political parties—the Imperial Rule Assistance Diet—emerged bearing none of the characteristics of the original institution.

III

The net effect of the factors discussed above was the loss of that unprecedented level of influence the parties and the Diet had attained during the 1920s. Nevertheless, as the Diet continued to exist at least in name—as did the parties until their voluntary dissolution in 1940—the military was unable to disregard it completely. The military had to secure Diet acceptance of huge military budgets as well as help in passing domestic legislation, including economic control measures essential to the national economy. Further, in order to formulate and maintain "national unity," the military was forced to seek popular support and legitimization of its authority through the Diet.

What role did the Diet and parties play after the Saitō cabinet? A well-known political critic, Abe Shinnosuke, attended the 69th Diet session during Hirota's administration and recorded his impressions:

> When a large number of monkeys are put in a cage, a fierce battle first breaks out among them. The stronger dominate the weaker and when the latters' defeat becomes inevitable, there is finally peace. Observing from outside the cage, we can tell that the weak ones haven't really given up because they still try to rebel whenever the opportunity arises.
>
> What strikes me about the Diet is its resemblance to a cageful of monkeys. Excluding those who are too few to count, the rest all support the government. Yet one can clearly see that beneath the surface they go along with the idea of "national unity" reluctantly, contrary to their true feelings.[22]

Abe made some additional observations on the 70th Diet session (Hayashi cabinet):

I notice that there are many Diet members who enthusiastically back the cabinet ministers as if to say, "Look how loyal we are!" while exchanging insults with their fellow Diet members. . . .

Raising his clenched fist above his head, Kawakami [Jōtarō, a member of one of the proletarian parties] asked, "What does the military think about rural distress?" This question made the supporters (*yaji*) of the established parties roar with laughter. When a member of the cabinet retorted to Kawakami's query, the mood became pro-government and there was great applause. The proletarian parties must be regarded as bitter enemies indeed if they are hated even more than a cabinet that refuses to respect the parties at all.[23]

This typical scene clearly depicts the situation in the Diet under the national unity cabinets. Excluding a small number of pro-military elements and those party politicians who were consistently anti-military, the vast majority of Diet members ultimately felt obliged to acclaim the cabinet and the military while inwardly resenting their contempt for parliamentary government. As Abe's observations indicate, this resentment was then transformed into antagonism and ill-will toward their traditional rivals within the Diet.

While it is true that party representatives on occasion launched strong, concerted attacks on military and government policies, in general they lacked the courage for any such action. Each successive change in government after the Saitō cabinet created divisions between and within the parties over whether or not to back the new administration. As a result, neither the parties collectively nor any one party by itself was ever able to adopt an uncompromising stand toward the government. Moreover, even if they had succeeded in toppling a cabinet, rejecting a budget, or defeating a major piece of legislation, they most likely would not have been able to agree upon a successor cabinet and would have lacked the confidence necessary for national leadership. Under these circumstances, the parties had little choice but to approve the policies of the government and the military.

The requirement under the Meiji constitution that the government's annual budget be approved by both houses of the Diet might have provided a means to limit the actions of the government and the military. But in practice this authority was never exercised during the 1930s, despite the rapid increase in the size and proportion of military expenditures after the Manchurian Incident in 1931. Under the 1931 budget military spending totaled 450 million yen, a sum that swelled to 940 million yen in 1934, 1.05 billion yen in 1936, and 1.4 billion yen in 1937. In 1935 military expenditures comprised fully 50 percent of the total annual budget.

Such a tremendous increase in military spending naturally created pressures on other parts of the budget, caused financial instability due to the flotation of deficit-covering bonds, and increased the risk of inflation. The effect of military spending on the funds available to relieve rural distress was especially acute. Nevertheless, the parties lacked the courage to put the people's livelihood ahead of military armaments in order to alleviate rural hardship and stabilize the economy.

In fact, a general survey of the budgetary process in Japan from 1933 to 1941 reveals that the government's budget was never once rejected or revised by either house. Furthermore, neither the Seiyūkai nor the Minseitō, although they strenuously opposed budget bills during questioning of the finance minister in Diet plenary sessions and the Budget Committee, ever voted against a bill. In the mid-1930s the only groups that opposed the budget or abstained from voting on it were those without power to affect its passage decisively, such as the Kokumin Dōmei, the Daiichi Hikaeshitsu (First Chamber Faction), and independents. After the 70th Diet in 1937 the budget was always passed by unanimous vote.

The only time the budget faced possible rejection, or at least major revision, was in October 1933. Opposing Saitō's creation of the Five Ministers Conference, the Seiyūkai and Minseitō united to attack fascism, preserve parliamentary government, restore trust in the political parties, and establish a common domestic and foreign policy. On October 25, at a joint meeting of party leaders, they pledged to work together to maintain constitutional government. During the 65th Diet both parties denounced the military's interference in politics and assailed the 1934 budget, charging that it overemphasized military spending and neglected to provide sufficient funds to relieve rural distress. Holding 450 of the 466 seats in the Diet, they could have forced a repudiation or a fundamental alteration of the budget. Instead, it was accepted without change and passed through the House of Representatives because of disagreement over the question of taking a hard line on the budget and thus overthrowing the government. The resulting impasse ended any hope for united party action.[24]

As a consequence, budget debate in the Diet became irresponsible and perfunctory. Although Hirota's 1937 budget represented a radical 700 million yen increase over the 1936 budget of 2.3 billion yen, the cabinet is said to have accepted it after only an hour and twenty minutes' deliberation despite the fact that ministers of state customarily worked for three or four days without rest or sleep when considering a budget bill.[25] Moreover, the 70th Diet passed it without any revisions whatsoever. Abe Shinnosuke reacted sharply against this lack of responsibility, remarking:

> The sense of irresponsibility on the floor of the Diet was demonstrated by the fact that when Finance Minister Yūki Toyotarō frankly admitted that he had no clear view of what to do regarding future financial policy, his confession was met with applause. Is there any justification for a confession like this from a minister of state who should be certain of his opinions about such matters? Can Diet members who applaud his lack of confidence in financial policy really fulfill their own responsibility to the people?[26]

The outbreak of the China Incident led to demands for "national unity" and therefore only served to accelerate the deterioration of the Diet into a body that merely formalized government decisions. During the 72nd Diet session the Diet approved in just four days a special military budget exceeding 2 billion yen and in the 73rd session unanimously passed a budget containing military appropriations of 3.51 billion yen. Thereafter the Diet consented to every bill submitted by the government without a single dissenting vote. In the end the budgetary power, the most direct and substantial means by which the Diet and the parties might have controlled the government, became nothing but a sham.

The Diet might also have exercised some influence over government policy through questions directed at ministers of state and in its deliberation of draft legislation submitted to it by the government. As with the budget, there was some criticism of policy, but in the end the Diet and the parties fell into line.

The disinclination of the parties to resist the military directly was symbolized by their approach to the issue of reviving the active-duty requirement for service ministers that arose during Hirota's administration. Restricting potential army ministers to generals and lieutenant generals on active duty would have meant that the military, by refusing to name a candidate for the position, could apply extra pressure on the government. During the controversy in 1913 over "increasing army strength by two divisions," the parties had been instrumental in abolishing the active-duty requirement on the grounds that it was a violation of constitutional government. Consequently, revival of the earlier system, which would have guaranteed military dominance over the government, was of vital concern to the parties and the Diet. Nevertheless, when the military presented to the cabinet a draft for revisions in the organization law of the army and the navy, the four Seiyūkai and Minseitō ministers quietly assented. Moreover, even though the Diet was in session while the measure was being considered by the Privy Council, it took no action.[27]

Had the Japanese public known of such a crucial revision of the government system, there probably would have been a popular outcry. But the party ministers in the cabinet cooperated with the government in keeping the public in the dark. Lacking any concrete policies of their own, the parties were unable to resist governmental pressures and allowed themselves to be carried along by the strong current of developments.

The impotence of the parties was especially clear in foreign relations. During the era of party cabinets, for example, the Minseitō opposed the Tanaka cabinet's dispatch of troops to Shantung. Charging in a party resolution that the government's China policy lacked farsightedness and merely created difficulties, it asserted, "We have no confidence in this policy." Moreover, when Tanaka sought to cover up the circumstances of Chang Tso-lin's murder by declaring in the Diet that the situation was "under investigation," the Minseitō publicly denounced the government's action in a resolution demanding to know what had taken place.

Conditions following the Manchurian Incident, however, were very different. The parties never again displayed such an independent approach to critical foreign policy issues. Indeed, the Seiyūkai and Minseitō approved the policies of the government and the military almost in toto. Matsuoka Yōsuke, for example, was applauded by the Diet when on June 3, 1932 he asserted in his customary grandiloquent manner that the Manchurian Incident was "fortunate," for "luck works in strange ways in the world . . . and has unified the public behind a positive policy toward Manchuria and Mongolia such as our party has been advocating for years."

Showing a similarly submissive attitude toward the government, the Diet on June 14, fully three months before the government actually took action, passed a resolution demanding the immediate recognition of Manchukuo. In the following session, on August 25, Mori Kaku of the Seiyūkai stated that the true purpose in recognizing Manchukuo was to proclaim to the world that Japanese foreign policy had become "autonomous and independent" and, in effect, to issue a "diplomatic declaration of war" against those who believed in international peace and cooperation. Mori thus encouraged Foreign Minister Uchida Yasuya to take a strong stand. In response, Uchida delivered an address considerably more forceful than Mori's which became known as the "scorched earth speech."

Most cabinet ministers, however, including Prime Minister Saitō and the genro Saionji, disagreed with Uchida and the army, fearing that if Japan were to withdraw from the League of Nations over the Manchurian issue it would become isolated. The differences within the government were so serious that Saitō even suggested a conference of the senior statesmen (*jūshin*), including party presidents, to settle the issue. But in the end Japan's decision to leave the League was reached without such a meeting. Although as far as can be ascertained from the parliamentary record the parties and the Diet took no final stand, their position in favor of withdrawal had already been made clear.

Most Diet members favored Japan's resignation from the League on the grounds that it unlawfully interfered in Japan's affairs and that participation in League activities was contrary to Japan's national interests. On January 23, 1934, at the first Diet session held after Japan's departure from the League, Tokonami Takejirō of the Seiyūkai declared: "I think the recognition of Manchukuo's independence and withdrawal from the League are the most decisive acts of the present cabinet. They represent the will of the people and will prove the best course in the long run." Other Diet members shared Tokonami's views. Deeply shocked by the May 15 Incident and caught up in the current wave of militarism, they supported the army's hard-line policy. Even the Minseitō, once the advocate of a conciliatory foreign policy, only perfunctorily exercised its right of interpellation on diplomatic questions.

On the rare occasions when a member of the Diet made critical statements, whether in support of a stronger or a more conciliatory policy than the government was pursuing, he was quickly taken to task. For example, at a lower house plenary session on January 23, 1933, Seiyūkai Diet member Ashida Hitoshi took a hard-line position, declaring:

> The essence of the Manchurian question is the development of Manchukuo, but the government acts as though running Manchukuo is someone else's affair. It does nothing regarding the issue of withdrawal from the League. If our interests are incompatible with those of the League, we should resolutely withdraw.

Ashida supplemented these comments by questioning:

> The view is prevalent abroad that Japan has a military diplomacy and a Foreign Ministry diplomacy, but not a diplomacy based on the will of the people. It is a disgrace to constitutional government that foreign countries have been given the impression that our policy is still being controlled by the military. Are we in fact prepared to establish a people's diplomacy?

In reply, Foreign Minister Uchida maintained that it was "not yet the proper time to speak of withdrawal from the League." There was, he contended, "no dual diplomacy." Army Minister Araki supported Uchida. "I have been in the army for thirty years," he asserted, "and during that time I have never seen a period in which there has been so much cooperation and joint activity, so many frank exchanges of opinion, and so much discussion between the army and the Foreign Ministry as is the case today."

Matsumoto Tadao of the Minseitō was not prepared to let the case rest there. In a question he expressed the opinion that the recent negotiations with Manchukuo had, contrary to the government's claim, reflected a dual diplomacy. Addressing himself to Foreign Minister Uchida, Matsumoto said: "At one time during the Hara cabinet you took the position that we must not follow a hard-line policy toward China. Now you are adopting just such a policy. Will this not create serious tensions in relations between China and Japan?" In reply, Uchida drew a distinction between Japan's policy toward China and toward Manchukuo. "We cannot give an inch on the Manchurian question," he declared, "but we are ready to cooperate insofar as possible in regard to China proper."

Ashida's comments became a source of controversy when they were cabled abroad and reported in the press two days later in a manner that played up a "Seiyūkai attack" on the foreign minister in the Diet and suggested that his response implied that Japan intended to be conciliatory. As a result of this publicity, a motion introduced by Katō Taiichi of the Minseitō was passed declaring that "to discuss matters in the Diet contrary to our national interests violates the will of the people." This meant, in essence, that both Ashida and Matsumoto were ordered to "modify" their statements.

This trend to restrict Diet discussion of foreign policy issues only worsened with time as Diet members increasingly rallied in support of the government's forward policy. Yamamoto Teijirō of the Seiyūkai, for example, urged the government to abrogate the Washington Naval Treaty on the grounds that to do so would concur with the "steadfast and unalterable desire of the people." Yamamoto's comments were endorsed by Minseitō Diet member Tomita Tsunejirō, who on November 30, 1934 advocated that the government adopt a stronger policy because "Japan's demands on the disarmament question" were "proper and reasonable" and in complete harmony with the views of the public.

A noteworthy exception to these requests for a more vigorous policy, however, was Representative Saitō Takao of the Minseitō, who on January 24, 1935 appealed to the public to be aware of the threat of war, saying:

> It is the first requirement of national defense that diplomacy take precedence over military matters. If this axiom is forgotten and military affairs take precedence, it will lead to misunderstanding abroad, the flash of lightning will appear in the thunderclouds of East Asia, and the nation will face a grave crisis.

While it is true that when the Anti-Comintern Pact was concluded late in the following year, both the Seiyūkai and the Minseitō protested the government's foreign policy, their concern was not so much with the contents of the treaty itself but rather that the cabinet had made such an important policy decision in secret. After the outbreak of the Sino-Japanese War foreign policy discussions within the Diet continued to become less and less frequent, until the attitude of the parties and the Diet toward the military degenerated almost to total servility. A striking case in point is that of Saitō Takao, who in February 1940 made certain adverse comments concerning the New Order in East Asia, charging that Konoe's statement could only be detrimental to a solution of the Sino-Japanese conflict. Fearful of the military, who felt that his remarks constituted "blasphemy against the holy war," the Diet by majority resolution at its plenary session voted to expel Saitō from the House of Representatives.

Thus, the right to criticize policy by questioning ministers of state in the Diet fell into disuse. At the 76th Diet session, following the formal dissolution of the parties, the Diet cancelled all questions directed at cabinet ministers. Nor were interpellations allowed in either house during the 77th session, with one exception. In the following session, because of the outbreak of the Pacific War, both houses refused to pose questions to the ministers. They had thus, of their own accord, relinquished the Diet's role as critic in the formulation of national policy.

The parties in the Diet even had to follow the government's lead in their consideration of domestic legislation. This is evident from the fact that of all government bills presented to the Diet from its 62nd session in 1932 to the 78th session under the Tōjō cabinet in 1941, excluding those withdrawn by the government itself, nearly 90 percent were passed. In the 66th, 72nd to 74th, and 76th to 78th sessions every piece of government legislation was endorsed. Moreover, the great bulk of significant legislation was accepted precisely as presented in the original government proposals.

An example is the General National Mobilization Law, which gave the government sweeping authority to impose wartime economic controls, presented to the 73rd Diet in 1938. Enactment of the law would have imposed extraordinary limits upon the Diet's legislative authority, and strong opposition inevitably arose. In the plenary session of the House of Representatives Saitō Takao (Minseitō) and Makino Ryōzō (Seiyūkai) attacked the bill vehemently, charging that it was unconstitutional. Nevertheless, it was finally passed unanimously and without revision in a manner reminiscent of the Reichstag's Authorization Law. Party resistance to the measure was limited, taking the form of a supplementary resolution, jointly sponsored by the Seiyūkai and the Minseitō, which was to be appended to the mobilization law. It stated:

> Far-reaching authorization such as this is quite exceptional. The government shall in the future seriously consider obtaining legislative authorization for any measures taken [under the mobilization law] ... and in the application of the law shall not, of course, violate the spirit of the constitution.... The government shall strictly guard against any abuse whatsoever of the law.

The parties were unable to present any genuine opposition to the mobilization law, in part because of the split within the two major parties between supporters of Konoe's "new party movement" who wanted to cooperate with the military and those who wished to maintain constitutional government. Home Minister Suetsugu Nobumasa and others were willing to dissolve the Diet if necessary to force passage of the law. The final passage of the General National Mobilization Law signaled the end of Diet authority in legislative matters; the role of the parties and the Diet in Japanese policymaking had reached its lowest ebb.

As we have seen, the Diet and political parties could not substantially affect government policy during the 1930s. This was true in the areas of Diet authority—budget deliberations, questions and interpellations to ministers of state, and legislative action. Moreover, no representations or resolutions were ever passed directly repudiating the policy of the government; on the contrary, the Diet generally supported and even encouraged it. Several resolutions might be named that underline this point.

> Resolution of Gratitude to the Officers and Men of the Army and Navy (passed a number of times after the 60th Diet)
> Resolution Concerning the Recognition of Manchukuo (62nd Diet, July 1-15, 1932)
> Resolution of Appreciation to the Japanese Representative to the League of Nations (64th Diet, December 26, 1932-March 25, 1933)
> Resolution of Congratulations to Manchukuo (65th Diet, December 26, 1933-March 26, 1934)
> Resolution of Appreciation to the Members of the Japanese Delegation to the London Naval Disarmament Conference (68th Diet, December 26, 1935-January 21, 1936)
> Resolution of National Cooperation and Government Support in the North China Incident (71st Diet, July 26-August 8, 1937)
> Resolution of Obedience to the Imperial Will and on Stability in East Asia (72nd Diet, September 4-9, 1937)
> Resolution on the Execution of the Holy War (75th Diet, December 26, 1939-March 27, 1940)
> Resolution on Dealing Successfully with the Crisis (76th Diet, December 26, 1940-March 26, 1941)
> Resolution on Strengthening the Wartime System (76th Diet)

Clearly the Diet and the parties, within the limits of their own authority, were unable effectively to resist governmental and military policies. Could they, however, have checked these policies by overthrowing the cabinet? This question must be answered in the negative for, while they were successful in toppling the Hirota, Hayashi, and Abe cabinets by their attacks on the military and the government, once a cabinet had fallen, the Diet and the parties were unable to formulate a clear policy toward its successor and the demands to be presented to it.

Iwabuchi Tatsuo discusses three features of cabinet change in Japan during the prewar period:

> One characteristic was that while cabinets were changed as a result of political crises, there were no policy differences between one cabinet and the next. Rather, the successor cabinet would merely follow the same policies at those formulated by its predecessor. No one even regarded this as strange.

A second point is that the parties, after assailing the previous cabinet's policies and charging it with misgovernment, abandoned both their denunciations and attacks once a cabinet change and a shift in personnel occurred. They submissively, even obsequiously, approved the programs of the new cabinet, even though they were the same as those of its predecessor.

A third feature relates to the tendency of certain political leaders, who were aware of the nature of power relations among the cabinet, Diet, and political parties and the ineptness of the last, to force a cabinet to accept a particular program. When criticism by the Diet and the parties became severe and problems arose, they would switch cabinets and use the new cabinet to force the same program upon the Diet, the parties, and the public.[28]

In sum, party attacks on the government occasionally resulted in cabinet shifts, giving the impression that traces of political power remained. But this was not the case. Changes in administration were not the result of party influence; rather, party opposition to the government was a tool used by powerful segments of the military to manipulate the nominal holders of governmental authority, the ministers of state. An example is the overthrow of the Hirota cabinet. The military, wishing for a new government that would support a strengthened Anti-Comintern Pact, used party opposition as a means of undermining the cabinet. The fact is that despite the bewildering succession of cabinets in the 1931-41 period, the military steadily advanced toward its goal. As the drama unfolded, the political parties seemed cast almost in the role of a court fool whose antics were at the service of those in power.

THE ROLE OF U.S. BUSINESS

Mira Wilkins

The American business community is not, and never has been, monolithic. This becomes readily apparent in the study of American businessmen's thoughts and actions apropos Japanese-American relations, 1931-1941. At least six general types of U.S. businesses seem to have been involved in U.S.-Japanese relations in the 1930s: (1) those that met competition from Japanese imports into the United States and to some extent also competed with Japanese goods in export markets; (2) Pacific coast fisheries, which not only were alarmed about competition from Japanese canned fish but feared that Japanese fishermen were stealing their fish; (3) enterprises that thrived on imports from Japan—importers, chain stores, silk manufacturers (especially makers of hosiery); (4) companies that wished to extend their sales to Japan and elsewhere in the Far East (and the shippers that carried the exports); (5) financial houses that handled Far Eastern securities; and (6) commercial banks and corporations with direct investments in the Pacific area (many of these were exporters but, unlike the enterprises in the fourth group, they had a direct stake in the Orient). Each of these six general types faced diverse difficulties. Each group exhibited different points of view; moreover, within each group there were also some pluralistic attitudes. Let us look at each group in turn.

I

American business in a variety of industries met competition from Japanese imports in the 1930s. Table 1 shows the course of Japanese imports to the United States during the decade. During the 1920s the United States had been Japan's best customer for raw silk and silk fabrics. In 1929 U.S. imports from Japan totaled $431,873,000, of which 83 percent was raw silk.* That year

---

*This represented 96.7 percent of Japanese exports of raw silk.

341

the American silk market "collapsed." Silk, a luxury product, was not in demand in depression time; moreover, rayon provided competition. From June 1929 to June 1931 the price of Japanese silk dropped by 60 percent. Nonetheless, in 1930—still based on silk exports—Japanese imports into the United States were the highest for the decade. In December 1931 Japan reimposed the gold embargo.* This devaluation of the yen aided Japanese exports. But while silk sales abroad persisted, during most of the 1930s the price of silk continued to slump, leading the Japanese to diversify their exports, selling in the United States and elsewhere pottery and porcelain, toys, canned crab and tuna, straw hats, and cotton goods. Despite these new exports, total Japanese imports into the United States declined steadily between 1930 and 1934. The drop was due to the lessening of demand for silk, the depression, new U.S. tariff restrictions, plus American antagonism to Japan after the Manchurian Incident. The nadir was reached in 1934; thereafter Japanese low-priced articles began to appear in growing quantities on American five-and-dime store counters. U.S. manufacturers of similar products felt threatened by these cheap goods made by low-cost labor and to varying extents also worried about their sales abroad. They saw Japanese cotton goods competing with U.S. textile exports to the Philippines. For the most part, however, U.S. producers were alarmed about their largest market, the United States, and through their trade associations they appealed to the U.S. government for protection against Japanese imports.[1]

The Hawley-Smoot Tariff of 1930, which hiked duties on all foreign products, had adverse effects on Japanese imports but it was not discriminatory. As the depression worsened, the United States imposed restrictions specifically against Japanese goods under the so-called "flexible provision" in the Hawley-Smoot Tariff and the Anti-Dumping Act of 1921. As costs and prices rose under the industry codes of the National Industrial Recovery Act (1933), U.S. producers appealed for aid under Title I, Section 3e (a section designed to be used in emergencies to protect American industries operating under the codes—the majority of the applications being for relief from Japanese goods. But administrative processing of the demands proved slow, and the section became inoperative when the Supreme Court in 1935 ruled the National Recovery Administration unconstitutional.[2]

Meanwhile, in 1934 the Reciprocal Trade Agreements Act came before the U.S. Congress. This was a special cause of Secretary of State Cordell Hull, who hoped it would aid in enlarging international trade. It authorized the president to enter into reciprocal trade agreements with other governments for reduction of specific duties by as much as 50 percent.[3] In accord with plans for extending trade, the State Department was prepared to negotiate with the Japanese means by which tariff increases recommended by the U.S. Tariff Commission "might be avoided."[4]

American businessmen who faced Japanese competition found such policies abhorrent. One by one they had gone to Washington to testify against the reciprocal trade measure, or at least to ask for amendments to it, and most

---

*Japan had gone off the gold basis in 1917 and had only resumed free gold payments in January 1930.

important, to call attention to "Asiatic competition." Representatives of the National Federation of Textiles, the Cotton Rug Association, the U.S. Potters Association, the American Match Institute, the toy industry, and the lead pencil industry all indicated in 1934 that their industries were meeting "unfair competition" from cheap Japanese products. They appealed to patriotism. "What a brand of Americanism it is to advocate turning our markets over to the foreign manufacturers because American manufacturers cannot compete with pauper labor, governmental subsidies, depreciated currencies," declared the representative of the pottery industry. "Is our industry to be sacrificed on the altar of international trade, because we have a 40-hour per week schedule of work, against the 60-hour week prevalent in Japan?" asked Frank X. A. Eble of the American Match Institute. He also complained that the State Department wanted to suppress the agitation against Japanese competition for fear it "might be objectionable to our friendly neighbor in the Orient." J. H. Schermerhorn of the lead pencil industry had a similar complaint against the State Department. He reported that the Tariff Commission had recommended "that a minimum price of $1.50 a gross be placed on imported pencils, Japanese, as a protection to the domestic wage scale, but this was waived by the State Department and not included in the agreement."[5]

Such parochial demands were bypassed. Congress passed the Trade Agreements Act, which became law on June 12, 1934. The American nation became committed to freer trade. Nonetheless, when the Japanese ambassador to the United States complained of restrictions on Japanese imports in February 1935, Secretary of State Hull told him that "until we can proceed further with the general program of a more liberal commercial policy . . . and also educate and organize sufficient public sentiment . . . to support and sustain it, we naturally would not be supported by public sentiment if we should allow an unreasonable and excessive amount of imports." Hull asked the Japanese to cooperate in "gentlemen's agreements." Such evidence of flexibility notwithstanding, Hull had not veered from his overall policy of removing restrictions on trade.[6]

In the spring of 1935 representatives of the textile industry launched a new campaign in Washington. "This is no time for kid gloves in diplomacy, a real fight and raising a certain amount of 'hell' are the only things which will cause the administration to do anything to retard the flow of Japanese goods," declared the *Textile Bulletin* of March 1935. Republican members of Congress took up the cudgel. The cotton textile industry wanted two things: an end to the processing tax on cotton (so they could produce cotton goods at lower cost) and added restrictions on imports. Investigations were conducted under Section 3e of the NIRA and Section 336 of the Tariff Act of 1930. A cabinet committee looked into the woes of the industry. State Department officials undertook negotiations with the Japanese. In the fall of 1935 the Japanese agreed to limit voluntarily their export of textiles to the Philippines, and finally, in December 1935 the State Department announced that they had also consented to restrict their cotton textile exports to the United States.[7]

After 1935 the United States placed "here and there" restraints on imports of Japanese textiles, wool-knit gloves, zippers, rubber shoes, electric bulbs, toys, matches, brushes, carpets, pottery and porcelain, imitation pears, canned fish, and pencils. In each case the restrictions were imposed only after pleas by the particular industries. As explained in 1935 by Charles K. Moser of the Far Eastern Section of the Department of Commerce, the policy of the Roosevelt administration involved "a method of adjustment." "It is that of the substitution of voluntary and reciprocal trade agreements . . . for the old arbitrary, and oftentimes retaliatory, imposition of direct trade restrictions."[8]

The policy met with problems. When the Japanese did not hold to their agreement on cotton textile exports to the United States, the industry in March 1936 appealed to the Tariff Commission, the Department of Agriculture, and members of Congress for new protective action. On behalf of their business constituents, members of Congress put pressure on the State Department, which undertook further prolonged but fruitless negotiations with Japanese officials. On May 21, 1936 Roosevelt—on the recommendation of the Tariff Commission —raised duties an average of 42 percent on imports of yarn and of bleached, printed, and dyed cotton cloth.[9] The entire reciprocal trade program seemed in jeopardy.[10] The U.S. government continued to try—with the assistance of American textile makers—to reach an agreement relating to the industry. A five-man team of U.S. cotton textile industry representatives, headed by C. T. Murchison, traveled to Japan, returning early in 1937 with a new agreement.[11] Other pacts negotiated individually with the Japanese proved successful—cotton rugs and pencils, for example—but no general U.S.-Japanese trade agreement under the Reciprocal Trade Act was ever concluded.

During 1935-37, despite sporadic restraints, Japanese imports increased (see Table 1). When the Trade Agreements Act came before Congress for renewal in 1937, opposition was articulated by the pottery and rubber footwear industries, which continued to fear Japanese competition.[12] But the attackers could not muster sufficient strength to defeat or amend the act.

After Roosevelt's quarantine speech of October 5, 1937 a group of American manufacturers who suffered from Japanese competition formed the League for the Protection of American Standards. As of October 9, 1937 its membership included producers of toys, glassware, pottery, and cotton goods. It urged a boycott on Japanese goods. At first, its efforts produced negligible results, but with the *Panay* incident on December 12 its activities met with more success.[13]

In 1938 Japanese imports into the United States declined dramatically—38 percent. This was, however, a year in which total U.S. imports fell by 36 percent, for with the recession in the United States Americans had less money to buy imports and reduced prices made homemade goods more competitive. The greater downturn in imports of Japanese goods appears to have been due to rising costs in Japan and to antagonism toward Japan in the United States.[14] But the 2 percent difference is hardly substantial, and I find no evidence that any new restrictions were imposed on Japanese imports. The next year U.S. imports from Japan turned upward, then dropped in 1940 as relations with Japan worsened. When in 1940 the Reciprocal Trade Act again came before the House Ways and Means Committee for extension, the only U.S. industry that testified against imports from Japan were the potters.[15] In 1941 imports from Japan sank.

Thus during the years 1931-33, with declining imports, U.S. businessmen who met competition from Japanese products were not sufficiently alarmed to participate in boycotts of Japanese goods, although then and especially after 1934 they desired tariff protection. After 1937 these businessmen engaged actively in boycott movements. In 1940-41, with imports dropping, such pressure group activities lapsed. Throughout the decade most of these men were strongly anti-Japanese in their rhetoric, with complaints specific to their economic needs.* Washington listened to their pleas and the State Department tried to abate the ardor of their demands. Did they represent the majority of American businessmen? The answer, as we will see, is "no."

II

The second group of American businessmen involved in U.S.-Japanese relations, the Pacific coast fisheries, shared with the first a concern over competition from Japan, in this case from Japanese canned fish. In the mid-1930s and especially in 1937 they protested to President Roosevelt and their senators and congressmen the Japanese invasion of their salmon fishing areas, threatening boycotts of Japanese goods and shipping. Washington became concerned. Hull took up their cause and even Roosevelt was interested because of the question of conserving American food supplies. At a cabinet meeting early in 1938 Roosevelt indicated that the Japanese had been making huge catches of salmon from ten to twenty miles off the Alaskan coast; the salmon was processed on shipboard and then sold in the American market. The president was determined "to raise an issue with Japan with respect to the salmon fisheries" and prepared to declare the Pacific coast closed to all alien fishing. Yet, when his associates indicated the international implications of such a measure, the president abandoned the project.[16]

In short, the Pacific fisheries interests represented a second business group that felt threatened by Japanese business activity. Especially in the years 1937-39 they helped create anti-Japanese sentiment in the United States, but while they met with sympathy in Washington, they received little aid.

III

The two groups of businessmen considered thus far had economic reasons to be articulate in their antagonism to Japan. A third group dealt with imports from Japan and found themselves involved in a profitable activity. Large American wholesale and retail chain stores sent buyers to Japan for cheap products; silk knitters and weavers desired Japanese raw materials. These businessmen looked askance at suggestions for boycotts, tariffs, or embargoes.

When after the Manchurian Incident talk prevailed in the United States of boycotts and embargoes against Japanese goods, Paulino Gerli of E. Gerli and Co., one of America's largest importers of Japanese silk, told a reporter that while silk traders would of course comply with an embargo imposed by the U.S. government, he felt that private boycotts would harm American industry and

---

*C. T. Murchison, president of the Cotton Textile Institute, was a notable exception in his reasoned comments.

disrupt international relations.[17] Similarly, as American antagonism toward Japan mounted with the Japanese invasion of China in July 1937, U.S. manufacturers of silk products and distributors of Japanese goods were described by *Business Week* as "watching such developments nervously." After the *Panay* affair *Business Week* noted that "in the last two months 55 hosiery manufacturers in the United States have turned to the production of lisle hose." Four of the nation's largest chain stores—F. W. Woolworth, S. S. Kresge, S. H. Kress and Co., and McCrory Stores Corp., outlets for Japanese cheap glass, pottery, cotton textiles, and novelty items—announced they were discontinuing "for the present" the purchase of Japanese goods. The manufacturers that turned to lisle hose did not, however, represent the bulk of the industry, which continued to depend on silk from Japan* and insisted that American labor was being injured by the boycott far more than the Japanese economy.[18] In 1939 the chain stores apparently resumed—albeit on a modest level—imports from Japan. When Japanese assets in the United States were frozen on July 26, 1941, bringing imports to an abrupt halt, Paulino Gerli sought to calm the "hysteria" the event seems to have produced in the silk industry.[19]

In sum, American importers, chain stores, and purchasers of raw silk desired good relations with Japan because they thrived on Japanese imports. They asked no special concessions from the U.S. government, although many favored lower duties.** Their voices were rarely heard in Washington. They seem to have been more influenced by popular sentiment—especially after 1938—than influencers of public opinion. Only in mid-1941, when the silk trade ended, did Washington show profound concern for the manufacturers of silk products (although not enough concern to alter U.S. foreign policy).

IV

U.S. exporters were far more articulate on questions of U.S.-Japanese relations (see Table 2 for U.S. exports to Japan). Because of the large volume of silk exports, Japan had a favorable balance of trade with the United States prior to 1931, but during the succeeding decade American exports to Japan exceeded imports from Japan.[20] Japan's efforts to increase its exports, as we have seen, met with obstacles in the United States, and as a result Japan felt impelled to restrict U.S. imports. The American embassy in Tokyo sought to avoid this,[21] but with no success. Increasingly throughout the decade Japan tried to purchase and manufacture within its empire, thus curtailing certain imports.

For U.S. traders Japan was an excellent market—by far the largest in the Far East. From 1932 to 1936 U.S. exports to Japan exceeded U.S. exports to all of South America.[22] In the eight years 1932-39 Japan ranked as America's third largest export market, being surpassed only by Britain and Canada (see Table 2 for a comparison of U.S. exports to Japan and China and Table 3 for Japan's importance in total U.S. exports). During the 1930s the most important U.S. export to Japan was raw cotton. Japan was America's largest foreign customer,

---

*Nylon stockings were first put on the market on May 15, 1940.
**Raw silk carried no duty, since it was not competitive with American products.

but after 1934 Japan annually curtailed its imports of U.S. cotton. At the same time, however, it enlarged its purchases of the raw materials and machinery needed for its expanding armaments and heavy industries. While oil and oil products, metal goods, and machinery comprised less than one-third of U.S. exports to Japan in 1936, by 1940 they constituted more than two-thirds of such exports.[23]

American exporters sought to improve U.S.-Japanese relations. In the early 1930s they advocated reconsideration of legislation that excluded Japanese immigrants from the United States.[24] In 1932 a representative of U.S. exporters indicated understanding of Japan's need to balance its trade: "Only deepest sympathy is felt for Japan and her financial situation and hope is everywhere expressed for Japan's economic recovery and development." At the same time the spokesman looked forward to liberalization of trade by both America and Japan.[25]

The official proceedings of the National Foreign Trade Council, meeting in Honolulu in May 1932, took note of "the recent disturbances in Manchuria and Shanghai" and "the unfortunate situation now existing between Japan and China." One speaker declared: "It is not for us at this Foreign Trade Conference to take sides in this controversy.... We look upon both China and Japan as friends, desiring with whole-hearted sincerity an early and amicable settlement of the differences and misunderstandings which have precipitated the clash." No U.S. exporter wanted boycotts of Japanese goods in response to the Manchurian Incident.[26] For an economist of the New York Cotton Exchange in 1934, "the one vividly bright spot in the cotton trade picture" was the Orient, especially Japan. A speaker at the 1934 National Foreign Trade Convention pointed out to an applauding audience that U.S. cotton exports were much more important to the economic life of America than the braid and lead pencil industries that met Japanese competition. Likewise, Japan offered a vital market for American capital goods industries, which had suffered during the depression. U.S. exporters in 1934 protested New Deal measures designed to raise prices, attacking in particular the production curtailment program under the Agricultural Adjustment Act, which would have made American cotton less competitive in Japan. On the other hand, they warmly endorsed Hull's reciprocal trade program.[27]

The 1934 declaration of the National Foreign Trade Convention read: "As the future of our world is indissolubly bound up with the maintenance of a full measure of reciprocal trade in that area [the Far East], no obstacles or discriminations should be imposed by legislation of embargoes, discriminative duties, or other trade barriers, which would affect the natural flow of reciprocal trade."[28] By 1935, with the antagonism of small businessmen to Japanese imports rising, that same organization reiterated its position with the following modification: "The Convention approves the procedure adopted by our Government in attempting to solve the difficulties which have arisen in regard to certain competitive commodities of importance to our domestic economy, by agreement upon a formula in respect to such imports."[29] In short, the U.S. policy of seeking individually negotiated trade agreements, which was discussed earlier in this paper, was appreciated more by exporters than by manufacturers of goods that met competition from Japanese imports.

Until 1936 the State Department took no action to curtail U.S. exports. Then on April 4, 1936 Cordell Hull announced an embargo on the export of tin scrap (April 15-July 1), stating that after July 1 it could be exported only with a special license from the National Munitions Control Board. Hull took this step under authority granted by legislation (February 15, 1936) designed to conserve vital domestic resources. Japan had been America's largest buyer of tin scrap; Japan would now have to look elsewhere. But among exporters the measure provoked no protest, for the United States provided an alternative market.[30]

Exporters were far more alarmed when in May 1936 President Roosevelt raised *import* duties on cotton cloth. *Business Week*, in an article entitled "Slapping a Big Customer," reported that exporters considered the move "unfortunate" and hoped negotiations would soon be opened for a reciprocal trade agreement with Japan. In November 1936 the National Foreign Trade Council urged U.S. governmental and private bodies to seek "friendly cooperation with Japan in the solution of questions of commercial economic competition."[31]

When the Japanese in January 1937 imposed governmental controls on all foreign exchange transactions, exporters feared for their sales. After July 1937 exporters expressed concern over their markets in China (markets far smaller than those in Japan), but on September 18 *Business Week* reported that exporters were "not altogether pessimistic." The magazine noted that trade with Manchukuo had increased since the region came under Japanese control. "A similar commercial acceleration might occur in other parts of China if Japan takes over the region and sets up puppet states." It pointed out, however, that if this happened, Japan more than anyone else would be the key beneficiary.[32] Nevertheless, care should be taken in interpreting these comments, for in general exporters spoke bitterly of the Japanese entry into China.

With the outbreak of the Sino-Japanese War, the question arose as to whether the United States should invoke the Neutrality Act.* Exporters were divided, as it became evident that implementation of the act would probably benefit Japan more than China.** The *Commercial and Financial Chronicle* and the *Journal of Commerce*, both advocates of free trade, opposed application of the Neutrality Act. The *Wall Street Journal*, on the other hand, cognizant of America's important stakes in Japan, declared that it should be invoked as a matter of law and principle. The administration did not invoke the Neutrality Act, although American sympathy for China remained strong.

Some American exporters now reappraised their marketing plans. "After long discussion" and "wide divergence of opinion," the executive committee of DuPont decided in September 1937 not to negotiate new contracts for the sale of arms to China. When Mitsubishi and Co. asked Du Pont to sell it a license to construct a nitric acid plant in Japan, DuPont, desiring to avoid being "crucified by publicity," "refused to consider the proposal." The corporation had

---

*Under the Neutrality Act the president could declare that a state of war existed between Japan and China, whereupon it would become unlawful to sell munitions or grant loans (except for ordinary commercial transactions) to either belligerent.

**Japan in 1937 did not depend upon munitions from the United States, whereas China required both munitions and loans.

developed its own "private neutrality policy."[33] But such an attitude seems to have been exceptional. By contrast, other companies, less in the limelight, sought to enlarge their trade with both Japan and China, politics notwithstanding. Exporters of iron and steel scrap felt no hesitancy about supplying the Japanese, and such exports reached a new peak in 1937 (see Table 4). Most exporters condemned restrictions on trade and boycotts of Japanese goods continued to meet their staunch disapproval, for they knew Japan would have to sell in order to buy. The *Commercial and Financial Chronicle* called boycotts a sign of "temporary resentment rather than mature reflection" and warned that such action might mean the loss of the Japanese market for cotton, scrap iron and steel, and war materials which "the world [read America] could not so easily forego."[34]

Roosevelt's quarantine speech of October 5, 1937 seems to have outraged most U.S. exporters. Cotton growers saw their markets in Japan, which were already dwindling, even more curtailed. *Business Week*, sympathetic to the views of exporters, argued that a quarantine would only "inflame the Japanese people ... sanctions, in all probability either would prove ineffective ... or would drive the Japanese people to military retaliation ... kWARantine means war." The president should keep the United States out of war. Other business journals joined in condemning the address for similar reasons.[35] The *Commercial and Financial Chronicle*, for example, thought the speech aggravated the difficulties of maintaining friendly relations with Japan. Two months later the same journal praised Roosevelt and Hull for refusing to be "stampeded" by the *Panay* incident.[36]

U.S. exports to Japan peaked for the decade in 1937 (see Table 2). Thereafter they declined annually as the Japanese imposed restraints and the United States introduced embargoes. In 1938 Japan also began to place controls on U.S. exports to China. Until early 1941, U.S. measures (see Table 5) notwithstanding, Japanese restrictions proved most instrumental in curbing U.S. commerce; then U.S. embargoes began to have serious consequences, and after Autust 1, 1941 U.S. exports to Japan sank to practically nothing.[37]

While U.S. exporters consistently deplored Japanese restraints and condemned aggression, their attitudes toward American policy after 1938 were at variance and subject to change. In response to the moral embargo on aircraft exports in June 1938, the *Commercial and Financial Chronicle* stated, "Our foreign policy is dictated not by principle, but by dangerous whimsicalities of particular reactions to special situations."[38] In the same vein *Business Week*, while never attacking U.S. policy in sharp terms, expressed concern over Japanese restraints on U.S. trade with China and Japan and fretted lest the newly-developing Japanese industries threaten American exports in world markets. It asked policymakers the following rhetorical questions: ". . . should diplomats and executives . . . spend all their energies trying to brake the growing power of the new rival in the Orient? Or will they profit more if they work toward a plan, acceptable to them and to Japan for mutually profitable cooperation?"[39]

Taking a different view, on May 2, 1939 C. H. French, vice president of the Chinese-American Foreign Trade Council, told a dinner group of the U.S. Chamber of Commerce that with Japanese industrialization American exports to

Japan had peaked; China would be the large American market in the future. A strong, independent China, he insisted, was in America's interest. But most U.S. exporters remembered that Japan was still an excellent customer; most believed with *Business Week* that it was wise to accept Japanese action in China as a fait accompli.[40]

The opinions of exporters were divided when in July 1939 the United States gave notice it would terminate the U.S.-Japanese trade treaty of 1911 in six months. The *Commercial and Financial Chronicle* saw in the action "seeds of warfare." *Business Week*, on the other hand, found "general satisfaction in the U.S." over the step but added that southern cotton exporters and California oil producers were not "completely happy." The *Wall Street Journal* advocated cancellation of the treaty, commenting that "Secretary Hull clearly puts his trust in the resources of diplomatic interchanges rather than in the possibilities of retaliatory legislation. At the present stage of our relations with Japan, at least, we had better follow his lead."[41]

With the end of the treaty on January 26, 1940 the State Department could place actual—not only moral—embargoes on sales to Japan. *Business Week* noted, "We have the advantage ... if we play this advantage too hard we are likely to create a martyr complex among the Japanese which will drive them to extremes rather than help their conservative leadership capture the helm." The views of the *Wall Street Journal* are reflected in the following excerpts:

> 1) "We regard the Japanese armed invasion of that country [China] as a wanton aggression." The "demand is heard here that we prohibit export of war material to Japan, which demand is likely to become more insistent." (The journal did not commit itself on whether it approved or not.)
>
> 2) "This newspaper cannot accept Senator Pittman's declaration that Japan's 'new order in east Asia' policy must be abandoned. ... We do not, and may never, recognize Japanese sovereignty over any part of China, but we know very well that we are not going to war with Japan to preserve China's territorial or political integrity."
>
> 3) The abrogation of the treaty is "not for the purpose of dictating Japan's policy in Asia but only in order to bring pressure to bear on Tokyo for recognition of the rights of our nationals in China."[42]

As late as mid-1940 the majority of U.S. businessmen were still hopeful of resuming normal trade relations with Japan. *Fortune* formed a Forum of Executive Opinion including 15,000 businessmen (the presidents of all businesses rated AA-1 by Dun and Bradstreet, directors of the 750 largest corporations in the United States, and executives "qualified to speak for business") and asked the panel:*

---

*Unfortunately, *Fortune* published the results in its September issue without indicating the month in which the poll was taken. I would speculate that it was taken in early July.

In dealing with Japan do you think we should:
a. appease them
   (if so) with a new trade treaty
      with a recognition of their claim to a sphere of influence
b. attack them
   (if so) with an embargo
      with a meaningful threat of force
c. Let nature take its course

Seventy-five percent of the respondents chose to "appease them" (40.1 percent) or "let nature take its course" (35 percent). Of those advocating appeasement, 50.6 percent replied "with a new trade treaty," while 40.8 percent favored recognizing Japanese spheres of influence. Of the 19.1 percent who endorsed "attack them," 71.6 percent checked "with an embargo" and only 20.9 percent indicated "with a meaningful threat of force." Clearly this sample of American businessmen did not want to "upset the boat"; they desired continued trade with Japan.[43]

Along the same line, on July 13, 1940 a *Business Week* editorial read: "It looks now as though American business is going to be forced to accept a new deal in the Orient." (The reader is free to use his imagination as to whether the phrase "new deal" instead of "new order" was intentional or unintentional usage and, if intentional, what it implied.)[44]

On the other hand, on July 6 the *Wall Street Journal* agreed that the new export controls were required for America's defense; the National Foreign Trade Convention's official declaration (at the close of July) commended the manner in which the U.S. government "had handled and is handling" Far Eastern problems. By October 19—after the Tripartite Pact had been signed on September 27—*Business Week* too had come to accept the new U.S. embargoes as necessary. Its approach was philosophical: "If Japan refuses to be cowed and strikes at our trade interests and supply bases in the East, our business must be prepared to withstand the loss of markets."[45]

The *Commercial and Financial Chronicle* was not convinced. The Tripartite Pact notwithstanding, the *Chronicle* on October 5, 1940 was still calling American embargoes "unrealistic" and "extraordinarily naive." To induce Japan to change its policies, the journal endorsed economic aid to Japan in the form of credits, a new trade agreement, and lower tariff rates on Japanese goods together with changes in the law barring Japanese immigration.[46]

A reading of the business press—and the comments of exporters—seems to indicate that most exporters by the end of 1940 were reconciled to the new controls (the *Commercial and Financial Chronicle* was exceptional in its continued denunciation of embargoes). According to Herbert Feis the Iron and Steel Institute by the end of 1940 was prepared to accept embargoes on its products. The National Foreign Trade Council had representatives in Washington giving advice on necessary government controls over foreign trade and shipping.[47] By 1941 business sentiment was being propelled along a course from which there was no return. The National Foreign Trade Convention's official declaration of October 1941 stated, "The defeat of the Axis ambition for world domination is essential to the peace and prosperity of all nations." The National

Foreign Trade Council saw its role as one of "watchfulness, and consultation with government and with businessmen, in order that the inevitable dislocation of foreign trade be no greater than is necessary for attainment of the defense objectives of the government."[48]

How much effect did U.S. exporters have on government policy? Between 1931 and 1933 they may have influenced attempts to reduce U.S.-Japanese tensions. After 1933 the Roosevelt administration—especially Cordell Hull—clearly felt strongly that U.S. export trade should be encouraged. Here the goals of the exporters and the U.S. government coincided. In the development of the reciprocal trade program, the formation of the Export-Import Bank, and the recognition of the need to subsidize cotton,* the administration took into account exporters' needs. Furthermore, U.S. government officials were always invited to and always participated in the conventions of the National Foreign Trade Council. After 1937, as U.S. public sentiment was appalled by Japanese bombings of civilians in China, exporters were still seeking to ameliorate U.S.-Japanese relations. The strong opposition of the business press to Roosevelt's quarantine speech must have added to the administration's awareness that public opinion in the United States was not ready to accept sanctions. The extreme opposition of the *Commercial and Financial Chronicle* to all embargoes and its support of aid to Japan between 1938 and 1941 had little influence in Washington. On the other hand, the views of the National Foreign Trade Council, the *Wall Street Journal*, and *Business Week*—views which variously moderated and approved U.S. policies—may have had an impact. During the late 1930s, however, Washington turned away from the policy of appeasement that had so many advocates in the business community. Hull insisted the American interest in the Far East was "that orderly processes in international relations must be maintained ... this interest far transcends in importance the value of American trade with China or American interests in China, it transcends even the question of safeguarding the immediate welfare of American citizens in China."[49] He could have added, "It is more important than American trade with Japan." Washington was *not* willing—as were many exporters—to accept Japanese hegemony in China and work toward "mutually profitable cooperation." After the Tripartite Pact and in 1941 most exporters were less influencers of than influenced by the march of events and administration policy, even though representatives of the National Foreign Trade Council worked with Washington officials "in relation to necessary government controls."

In short, American exporters desired good relations with Japan and China—but especially with Japan—because they wanted to continue and expand their trade. Their voices were heard in Washington; they found much support there; but after 1937 the pleas for appeasement of some members of this group more often fell on deaf ears.

---

*When embargoes were discussed in Washington, the cabinet was conscious that if cotton were embargoed "the southern farmers should be compensated for what they would be unable to sell as a result of such action." But raw cotton was never embargoed. Nonetheless, with reduction of cotton exports Henry Wallace in 1939 introduced export subsidies for cotton growers.

V

The fifth group of American businessmen concerned with U.S.-Japanese relations were those associated with large financial interests. They sought portfolio* investments abroad; they issued and dealt in foreign securities. Of all individuals in this group, probably the one most familiar with conditions in the Far East was the sage, thoughtful Thomas W. Lamont, a partner in J. P. Morgan and Co. and head of the American group in the China Consortium. As will be evident, Lamont's role in U.S.-Japanese relations was through his firm's involvement in Japanese financing, through his activities in connection with the China Consortium, and through his extensive personal friendships.

J. P. Morgan and Co. in 1931 was the fiscal agent for the Japanese government in the United States. In the giant international reconstruction loan of 1924 to Japan and in loans to Yokohama and Tokyo, to the Toho Electric Company (1930), and to the Taiwan Electric Company (1931), J. P. Morgan and Co. between 1924 and 1931 had been important in Japanese financing. A U.S. government estimate at the end of 1930 put U.S. long-term portfolio investments in Japan at $383,189,000—a sum larger than in any other Asian country.[50]

When the Manchurian Incident occurred, Lamont readily accepted the Japanese explanations. He penned a long memorandum to Walter Lippmann indicating that the Chinese had "piled Pelion upon Ossa by withholding payments on Japanese government loans and in effect taking the amounts due thereon and applying them to building the railways [in Manchuria] in contravention of the existing treaties [between China and Japan]." Lamont concluded: "China has conducted the most lawless and aggravating course possible. Yet they have an extraordinary knack of making an effective yell to the public when anything happens."[51] Lamont agreed to arrange publicity for a statement by Japanese Finance Minister Inoue Junnosuke defending Japanese actions in Manchuria.[52]

Early in 1932 Lamont rejected suggestions that J. P. Morgan and Co. become involved in a relief loan to China. He explained his reasons: "With China already in default upon her outstanding foreign obligation it would be quite impossible at this time to interest investors in the purchase of Chinese bonds."[53] But the Japanese action in Shanghai in 1932 perturbed Lamont. He could no longer accept the Japanese explanations; he condemned the aggressor.[54] As for business considerations, he wrote the head of the New York agency of the Yokohama Specie Bank: "Fortunately for Japan, her government requires no present foreign credit. If it did, of course, it would be quite impossible to arrange any credit, either through investment or banking circles. The effect which the Shanghai disturbance has had upon outstanding Japanese obligations here is only too obvious."[55] In short, the bankers would lend neither to China nor to Japan.

Lamont's concern about Japanese action in Shanghai notwithstanding, when Harvard president A. Lawrence Lowell wrote to urge him to join the

---

*Investments in foreign-controlled corporations or in the issues of foreign governments (local or national).

advocates of a boycott of Japanese goods, Lamont declined and added (March 10, 1932), "It seems to me that every effort should be made to encourage the Chinese and Japanese to settle the difficulties themselves." Interestingly, Lamont sent his correspondence with Lowell to Secretary of State Stimson; he also discussed his views with the secretary and reported to his banking partners that, judging from Stimson's comments, he (Lamont) was taking a position the administration would approve.[56]

In 1933 Lamont's views on loans to China had not altered. He told Chinese Finance Minister T. V. Soong that because of earlier defaults there was little chance that Westerners would furnish new capital to China; moreover, so long as warfare between China and Japan continued, investors would be wary.[57] As for Japan, Lamont condemned the trend toward militarism in that country: "The old and prudent element made up of your Count Makinos, Baron Dans, Inouyes, Shideharas, Uchidas, et al, are either killed off or blanketed," he wrote his close friend, Nelson T. Johnson, the U.S. minister to China.[58] At the same time, he saw himself as sympathetic to Japan. Lamont had known the new Japanese ambassador to the United States, Saitō Hiroshi (appointed in December 1933), "a good many years" and looked upon him as a friend.[59] Lamont hoped for a reversal of existing trends.

Meanwhile, Lamont acted as representative of the American group in the China Consortium. On the urging of the U.S. State Department the American group had been reestablished and in 1920 became a partner in the new Consortium, which consisted of American, British, French, and Japanese banking groups.* The American group involved almost forty of the leading banking enterprises. The Consortium was to handle loans for "important constructive purposes that were required by the Chinese government." But the "noble experiment," as Lamont later described the venture, failed and the Consortium never made any loans.[60] In 1934 the American bankers expressed a desire to withdraw, for several reasons. First, the Banking Act of 1933 prohibited American bankers of deposit from issuing or dealing in securities, and the American group had been made up almost entirely of banks of deposit, which after 1933 could no longer issue Chinese securities. Second, the possibilities for good investments were not present; because of defaults there was no American market for Chinese securities. Third, the Chinese were hostile to the Consortium, seeing in it strong Japanese influence. Fourth, the inactive Consortium was incurring high administrative expenses. The State Department, however, advised that the time was not opportune for the U.S. bankers to leave the Consortium. In the Amō (Amau) declaration the Japanese had made it clear that they did not like the idea of U.S. aid to China and withdrawal of the American bankers might be misinterpreted. The bankers agreed to remain in the Consortium.[61]

Throughout 1934 Lamont maintained cordial relations with Japanese officials. When Prince Konoe Fumimaro—later prime minister of Japan—visited

---

*President Taft had convinced American bankers to participate in the Consortium for railroad construction in China before World War I, but they withdrew in 1913 when President Wilson refused to support them. The new Consortium agreement—promoted by President Wilson—was signed October 15, 1920.

the United States, Lamont arranged his entertainment.[62] At the same time Lamont watched occurrences in China, where he thought U.S. silver policy had been harmful.[63] In March 1935 former governor of the Philippines and former U.S. ambassador to Japan W. Cameron Forbes headed an American economic mission that went to China with the aim of developing business there. Upon his return Forbes was optimistic, but he failed to obtain support for his plans. As Dorothy Borg has put it, he found "apathy" in the U.S. business community and "pessimism" in the State Department.[64] Lamont correctly diagnosed the situation: Americans were not interested in undertaking new investments in China.

Lamont remained concerned about Japan's military activities. In September 1935 he expressed to Fukai Eigo, president of the Bank of Japan, the hope that the Japanese government would lower its military expenditures.[65] In anticipation of future events Lamont in May 1936 wrote Nelson Johnson: "I am sorry to see China under the control of Japan . . . but if she lacks the strength to protect herself from aggression and exploitation, she cannot reasonably expect the other nations to do the job for her. Certainly, America is not going to court trouble by any quixotic attempt to checkmate Japan in Asia."[66] That year Lamont again proposed dissolving the inactive China Consortium, not to avoid involvement but for the same reasons he had put forth in 1934. But Stanley K. Hornbeck, head of the Far Eastern Division of the State Department, countered: "If the principle of cooperative action passes into discard, it is going to be increasingly difficult for American commercial interests to hold their own, to say nothing of making progress in China. The break-up of the China Consortium would be a step in that direction . . . the way for Japan for establishing hegemony in the Far East will have been made easier." Hornbeck records that Lamont indicated his agreement. Hornbeck wrote Lamont in April 1937 of his strong feeling that—in a negative fashion—the Consortium served as a "distinct benefit to China"; by not giving loans the Consortium had encouraged China "to adopt an attitude of self-reliance."[67]

By the spring and early summer of 1937 there was, as the National City Bank *Monthly Letter* later reported, a sense that "growing political unity, currency stabilization, improving finances, industrial expansion and a remarkable highway and railroad construction activity, made the economic situation of China more promising . . . than at any other time in the past twenty years."[68] In June 1937 Lamont met with H. H. Kung, the new Chinese finance minister, and reached agreement upon a new (renegotiated) loan to China. Lamont's views toward China were undergoing modification.

The hopeful outlook was suddenly shattered by the events following the Marco Polo Bridge Incident of July 1937. In September Lamont wrote Ambassador Saitō, "We must all be very distressed over the recent developments in the Far East. . . . Japan certainly is gaining no new friends." From this point on Lamont reiterated to Japanese friends his opinion that the Far Eastern situation was dreadful and tried to inform them of the antagonism to Japan developing in America. He spared no words in declaring that the "whole civilized world is aghast at these bombings by the Japanese military of innocent non-combatants."[69] By September, J. P. Morgan and Co. was replying to correspondents, "We are lending no money to any phase of Japanese activity nor have we done so for some years past." With the exception of two or three American banks which had active Japanese banking customers, American banks were not providing funds for the Japanese.[70]

Early in 1938 Lamont wrote Johnson:

All the Japanese in this country whom I see are simply sick abed over the whole affair [Japanese aggression in China], and although some of them have to give lip service to their Government, they have no heart in it. A considerable number of them have been over here lately, men like Tsurumi, Kasai, Matsukata, Hatoyama, and Kobayashi.* They have all been trying to get us to urge the American Government to start a mediation. But you know as well as I do that the [State] Department has no disposition to get its fingers burned in such a situation. Each of these Japanese has been very careful to explain that he didn't represent the views of his Government, and I actually don't think he did. I think each one has been so upset about the state of affairs that he has been seeking every possible way out.

Lamont had talked to C. T. Wang, the Chinese ambassador to the United States, and others who "scouted any idea of mediation." He also consulted Ambassador Saitō, who "voiced the same opinion, namely, that neither side had reached a point where mediation would be welcome to it." Although "these Liberal Japanese all claim that it [Japanese action in China] was a horrible mistake," Lamont did not see it as simply a "mistake." "To tell the truth, I am pretty blue about it." Yet as for a boycott of Japanese goods, Lamont learned from Hull that "while of course the [State] Department would desire to take no strong action on this point, it would not look with particular favor upon such private means of warfare." He fully agreed.[71]

By this time Lamont was beginning to express admiration for Chinese leaders, especially H. H. Kung, who was "actually carrying out" the agreements Lamont had made with him in the spring and summer of 1937. Nonetheless, in the fall of 1938 when Kung sought a loan for China, Lamont responded that while U.S. public opinion was with China, "a popular loan cannot be floated in this market in behalf of China ... nobody can ask a private American investor to put up his money in this Far Eastern struggle."[72] In fact, nobody did. All Chinese financing from the United States came from the public rather than the private sector.

In 1939 American bankers continued to want to withdraw from the China Consortium. Lamont explained to State Department officials in January 1939 that "he personally would not wish to hurt the Chinese or help the Japanese at this time; he had told the Japanese repeatedly and emphatically that American finance would do nothing to help them." He felt dissolution of the Consortium would aid China more than Japan and that "politically it would be a good thing for the Japanese Group and the Japanese Government to realize that under prevailing circumstances the Western banking groups prefer no formal association with them." The State Department once more disagreed, fearing dissolution

---

*Tsurumi Yūsuke, Kasai Jūji, and Matsukata Kōjirō were Japanese Diet members; Hatoyama Ichirō was a leader of the Seiyūkai and former minister of education; Kobayashi Shōichirō would become the U.S. representative of the Bank of Japan.

would be seen as a sign of abandonment of aid to China by the United States. Thus the Consortium remained in inactive existence.[73]

In the summer of 1940, under the sponsorship of the Japan Economic Federation (an organization of Japanese big business leaders), General John F. O'Ryan traveled to Japan, Manchuria, and China to view economic and political conditions; involved in his study was the American investment firm Eastman, Dillon and Co. There is no indication that other banking houses participated. But here was one enterprise that still was ready to *survey* the opportunities.[74]

After the Tripartite Pact was signed, as world tensions rose, Americans began to sell Japanese securities. *Business Week* estimated on October 26, 1940 that "wary [U.S.] investors in Japanese national, municipal, and corporate bonds (totalling about $500,000,000 last April 1st) have recently unloaded to Japanese buyers."[75] That fall Thomas Lamont told a meeting of the Academy of Political Science that "for years I was personally active, with many others, in carrying through plans for friendship for, and material aid to, Japan." Yet he had no sympathy for Japanese plans for "Asia's New Order." The U.S. government, he urged, must give China "more material aid in her heroic struggle for independence."[76] Before making the speech Lamont checked with Hull, telling the secretary that he wanted to bring out that "business interests would not oppose but would cooperate with economic measures that our Government saw fit to lay down." He reported to one of his colleagues that Hull seemed pleased. In addition, Hornbeck in the State Department went over the speech before it was delivered.[77]

After the address U.S. Ambassador to Japan Joseph Grew congratulated Lamont—"the best thing of its kind that I have seen." He passed the speech around in Japan, hoping that the strong statements of Lamont, who had been well known as "fundamentally friendly to Japan," would have an impact. Lamont sent copies of the speech to Japanese Prime Minister Konoe and Foreign Minister Matsuoka Yōsuke. Both replied. Konoe stated: "Notwithstanding the difference in political philosophy or in form of government, there should be a final agreement concerning the fundamentals of lasting international peace and welfare." Matsuoka wrote that Japan wanted friendly relations with the United States and had "never attempted to subjugate China by force." Lamont forwarded both letters to Washington, noting when he sent the Matsuoka letter that "if the situation were not so tragic, the latter [Matsuoka's letter] would appear comic." Replying to Matsuoka in early 1941, Lamont recalled his longtime friendship with Japan and predicted that "disaster is the only thing ahead of her [Japan] if she continues to pursue her present course."[78]

Early in 1941 Ikawa Tadao, a former Japanese Finance Ministry official who knew Lewis Strauss of Kuhn, Loeb and Company, initiated informal conversations designed to lead toward better U.S.-Japanese relations. Strauss introduced Ikawa to James Edward Walsh, a Maryknoll bishop with experience in China. Bishop Walsh and Father James M. Drought, who had recently returned from Japan, obtained an interview with Roosevelt. They argued that the moderates in Japan would triumph over the militarists—if the United States would offer "security" to Japan. Their efforts came to naught. There is no indication in the Lamont Papers that Lamont had any role in these negotiations. What is interesting is that clearly some Japanese still saw at least one representative (namely Lewis Strauss) of the American financial community as a possible intermediary on their behalf. But this was a straw in the wind.[79]

In June Lamont prepared a memorandum on the Far Eastern situation, indicating he felt "more severe economic sanctions could be imposed upon Japan without due risk." He sent the memorandum to Hornbeck, who agreed. Hornbeck wrote Lamont on June 25 that "Japan's bark is much bigger than Japan's potential bite," to which Lamont replied, "In what you say in regard to Japan's real capacity in raising cain, I am in hearty accord. I myself think that they would curl up."[80] Less than a month later the stiffest sanctions yet were imposed (see Table 5).

By the end of 1940 the National City Bank estimated that U.S. holdings of Japanese bonds totalled $100 million. In August 1941, after the freezing of Japanese assets in the United States and U.S. assets in Japan, Japan still stated officially that it was determined to continue interest payments on all Japanese government direct and guaranteed bonds outstanding in the United States. But Lamont failed to be impressed with Japan's conscientious financial behavior. On November 13 he expressed the belief that the United States ought "to tighten her blockade" and that Japan would not take any action that would get it into war.[81]

In short, the financial community, while associated with plans to aid China, felt no inclination to make loans or grant long-term credits to the Chinese. With the exception of one renegotiated loan, no private capital went to China. On the other hand, Japan had "an unblemished record" in fulfilling its financial obligations. Japan did tempt the foreign investor. Nonetheless, from 1932 on leaders in the banking community such as Lamont could not countenance Japan's aggressive activities. After 1937 especially, Lamont recognized that America's *political* interests lay with China and not Japan. Yet Eastman, Dillon and Co. in the summer of 1940 was still open to the study of investment possibilities in Japan, and in early 1941 Lewis Strauss was ready to be an intermediary in trying to better Japanese-American relations. Did the financial community influence U.S. government policy? It is hard to answer. Clearly, Lamont's voice was heard by those who formulated U.S. policy, but his point of view was simply one of many considered in Washington. His desire to have the American group leave the China Consortium was vetoed regularly and he accepted the government's position. Otherwise his views seem to have been in accord with most of the administration's policies on the Far East. One wonders, however, whether it was complete coincidence that the strongest measures taken in Washington along the lines of an economic embargo were endorsed after Lamont declared the business community's warm support. Lamont must have provided evidence to Washington that after the Tripartite Pact "businessmen" who had been associated with Japan and who had been most reluctant about economic pressures were—following general public opinion—fully in accord with vigorous U.S. government action in imposing sanctions on Japan and supporting China.[82]

VI

The sixth group of American businessmen involved in Japanese-American relations were those with direct investments in the Far East.* The group

---

*Direct investments involve a *management* interest in a business abroad.

included trading companies (handling U.S. exports and imports and some internal commerce), small businesses with varying stakes, certain large banks, a few utilities, and more than a dozen major industrial corporations. Table 6 indicates the size of U.S. direct investment in East Asia. Although U.S. trade with Japan far exceeded that with China and although U.S. portfolio investments in Japan were far greater than those in China, U.S. direct investments in Japan were less than in China. The reason lies in the large direct investments in China made by U.S. oil companies and utilities.* Table 7 indicates some of the large U.S. utilities and industrial corporations with stakes in Japan and China. Because of space limitations, I shall consider only a few key enterprises.

National City Bank—the largest U.S. bank in the Far East—had branches throughout Japan, China, Malaya, and the Philippines. When in 1931 the Japanese moved into Manchuria, the bank's management feared substantial losses. In Japan the bank encountered anti-American hostility because of U.S. sympathy for China. The bank tried to come to terms with Japanese antagonism, and by the close of 1932 it found Japanese opinion more friendly. In appointing a single manager (John L. Curtis) for its Japanese and Manchurian branches, the bank indicated acceptance of the Japanese role in Manchuria. By the fall of 1933 Curtis spoke in favor of U.S. recognition of Manchukuo.[83]

When in 1934 the baneful effects of the U.S. Silver Purchase Act were being felt in China, the National City Bank's *Monthly Letter* reported the situation in a detached fashion. The Chinese finance minister wanted the U.S. Treasury Department to urge the National City Bank "to encourage silver to return to Shanghai," but the Treasury Department (March 1, 1935) thought such a step outside "its province." Without the department's prompting the National City Bank did nothing.[84] Apparently, after 1932 the Chinese government concluded that the National City Bank was pro-Japanese.[85] Actually, the bank was just trying to operate successfully, although bank officials seem to have had more admiration for the Japanese than the Chinese. When, for example, Japan imposed new exchange controls in early 1937, the bank's *Monthly Letter* noted that American businessmen would view the restrictions "with sympathetic understanding of Japan's difficulties. As between the alternatives of exchange control and an unstable and depreciating yen it is certain that the former is less disturbing to orderly trade."[86]

When the Japanese moved into north China in 1937, National City Bank officials were dismayed. Nonetheless, the bank continued to function in both occupied and unoccupied China as well as in Japan. In March 1939 Chinese authorities complained to the U.S. State Department that the bank was "bearing down on Chinese currency," a charge the bank denied. On March 10, 1939 Guy Holman, assistant vice president of the National City Bank in New York, called at the State Department in Washington to discuss U.S. policies in China. State Department officials recorded that Holman thought "vigorous official efforts in defense of foreign—'open door'—

---

*Total U.S. investment (portfolio plus direct investment) was greater in Japan than in China throughout the 1930s.

interests in China *should be suspended and opposing of the Japanese should be avoided"* (italics added). Hornbeck suggested that such a policy might "prove disastrous," to which Holman retorted that the National City Bank "was inclined to favor in various international situations, the principle of proceeding with business when and where available, without being inhibited by too much consideration or 'theorizing.' "[87]

Nonetheless, the National City Bank apparently complied when State Department officials urged it to resist "trade and exchange restrictions imposed by Japanese authorities" in north and central China, although the evidence is not entirely clear.[88] While the bank maintained branches in Tientsin and Shanghai until American entry into the war, in early 1941 it closed its last branch in Manchuria (at Harbin) and on July 31, 1941 shut its branches at Canton and Peking. When U.S. assets in Japan were frozen on July 27, 1941 (Tokyo time) in response to U.S. action freezing Japanese assets in the United States, the National City Bank could no longer do business in Japan. The bank's *Monthly Letter* in the United States declared that the freezing of Japanese assets "has widened the area of economic disturbance." Nonetheless, National City Bank kept its Tokyo office staff intact, hoping for better times. A spokesman for the bank indicated that by the end of July the enterprise "had pretty well balanced up its position, save for physical assets in Japan, which have been written down to practically nothing."[89] Not until December 7, 1941 did its business come to a complete halt.

U.S. industrial corporations with stakes in Japan and China were in much the same position as the National City Bank—seeking survival in both countries, eager to do "business when and where available." After the Japanese invasion of Manchuria, U.S. industrial corporations in Japan encountered the same hostility that existed toward the National City Bank, and they too sought not to reciprocate with hostility but to try to assuage the situation. The few companies with operations in Manchuria desired to continue business, but the U.S. consul in Mukden reported in December 1933 that American businessmen there (with the exception of the National City Bank representative) were generally "apathetic" on the question of recognizing Manchukuo.[90] Local managers of U.S. businesses in China in 1931-33 deplored Japanese actions. In the case of international businesses, most home offices in the United States saw their largest market in Japan but sought good relations with both China and Japan.

After 1933, as Japan's industry expanded, the Japanese tried to take advantage of American businesses with stakes in their country. They did so (1) by watching the American methods, developing parallel Japanese enterprises, and then choking off the American companies when the techniques had been mastered; (2) by arranging the transfer from American into Japanese hands of U.S. stakes in Japan; and (3) by seeking to use American business in Japan for national purposes. These not necessarily distinct actions meant that the Japanese molded American enterprises to meet the ends of Japanese industrialization.

This happened to the U.S. automobile companies (Ford and General Motors) that had built assembly plants in Japan in the 1920s. The companies exported from the United States so-called "knocked-down" vehicles which they assembled in Yokohama and Kobe. In the early 1930s U.S. car sales in Japan rose, meeting virtually no Japanese competition. In March 1935 the general manager of the Ford operations in Japan wrote his home office that in the last two or three years, "when the country seriously felt that it might become embroiled in warfare with one or more of the largest Western powers. . .desperate efforts are being made to bring forth a complete, self-sufficient motor industry, almost regardless of cost; but it is intended that this industry shall be in the hands of the Japanese exclusively." As soon as automobile manufacturing was established by the Japanese, he continued, "restrictive measures of diverse kinds will be enforced against foreign (imported) vehicles, and the only way for us to retain this important market is to take timely steps to manufacture locally before we are shut out of the market." The manager felt Ford would not be able to manufacture as cheaply as it could export, but he expected the Japanese government to protect local industry.[91] Accordingly, the company acquired a large waterfront property in Yokohama.[92] Late in 1935 General Motors also began to negotiate with Japanese interests about future manufacturing in Japan.[93]

On July 11, 1936 the Japanese passed an Automobile Industry Law, under which licenses to manufacture in Japan went only to firms whose shareholders were more than 50 percent Japanese. Ford accepted the terms of this act and began negotiations, but no arrangements were made and the Yokohama site was never used. General Motors, likewise, never started to manufacture. In 1937 Ford and G.M. did excellent business in Japan, still as importers of "knocked-down" vehicles. In November of that year Ford was approached by the Nihon Industrial Company about the possibilities of a joint automobile manufacturing enterprise in Manchukuo; Ford's local manager thought that with "blocked" yen (yen that could not be converted into dollars), participation might be considered. "State guarantees of dividends, monopoly rights, etc., makes such an investment not unattractive," he wrote his superiors. But his home office vetoed the plan. To a Japanese visitor Detroit officials explained on February 24, 1938, "recent events in the Far East were resented by the American public, and . . . we must take no steps as a company which cause a loss of good will in America."[94]

The U.S. automobile companies did far less business in China than in Japan. When in 1937 the Japanese moved into China proper, U.S. truck exports to China rose sharply; by 1939 they were almost four times the 1936 figure.[95] Late in 1938 G.M.'s regional director in the Far East indicated in a private appraisal that "from the automotive point of view it is possible that complete domination of China by Japan would mean an upturn in business." He added that the China market was important, whether dominated by Japan or independent.[96]

American companies in the electrical, glass, and rubber tire industries contributed technical know-how to Japan as that nation developed its industrial strength. They operated with Japanese partners—Mitsui, Mitsubishi, Sumitomo, or other interests—and as the decade proceeded, the Japanese increased their control over the U.S. businesses. Japanese partners politely suggested to their American colleagues that in corporate capital increases the latter not take up their share. Americans were given to understand that they had no choice but to comply. In some instances the Japanese encouraged Americans to repatriate their capital investments.[97] As a result there was in the 1930s a striking reduction in the percentage of equity held by American companies in Japanese enterprises (see Table 8). The Japanese continued to use American technology, but they obtained control. The situation was accepted reluctantly by American businessmen, who had no alternative. A few U.S. companies just gave up in Japan. Unable to get import permits, Eastman Kodak, for example, in 1938 was "completely forced out of business in Japan."[98] U.S. direct investment in Japan dropped.

After 1937 U.S. international businesses faced innumerable difficulties in pursuing their operations in China. A U.S. government report explained the decline in U.S. direct investments in China from 1936 to 1940 (see Table 6) as due to the effects of the Japanese invasion and to "a currency exchange depreciation of 81 percent during the four year period."[99] U.S. businessmen rejected their government's efforts to get all American citizens to withdraw from China and remained to watch over their properties. The U.S. Chamber of Commerce passed a resolution urging Washington to protect American lives and interests.[100] One observer in November 1938 found "incomprehensible" the attitudes of other foreign businesses which, he reported, regarded the Sino-Japanese War as just another war, comparable to past warlord activity, which "will pass away and conditions will eventually return to normal." In March 1940 a visitor noted booming business in the International Settlement at Shanghai.[101]

What then of the U.S. oil companies in the Far East? How were they affected by the changing situation? In 1933 only two American oil companies had direct investments in Japan—Standard-Vacuum Oil Company (Stanvac)* and the Associated Oil (later Tidewater Oil) Company. The latter owned 50 percent of the Mitsubishi Oil Company and because of its joint venture with Mitsubishi was not considered by the Japanese to be a "foreign company."** Stanvac and the British/Dutch Royal Dutch Shell complex with its subsidiary in Japan, Rising Sun Petroleum Company, were the two most important oil companies in Japan. Stanvac had only a marketing network and no refineries in Japan. In China (including Manchuria) Stanvac, Texaco (an American company),*** and a Shell subsidiary sold petroleum products and had giant investments in distribution networks.

In 1933-34 Stanvac**** found itself in considerable difficulty in Japan and Manchuria. In the first place, the Japanese wanted an indigenous refining industry. While the Japanese stated that they did not intend "to deprive the foreign oil companies [Stanvac and Shell] of their business," the latter were uncertain. Japanese imports of U.S. refined oil had declined annually between 1930 and 1933.[102] Secondly, rumors had spread that the Japanese would

---

*Stanvac was jointly owned by two American corporations, Standard Oil of New Jersey and Socony-Vacuum Oil Company (now known as Mobil Oil).

**The problems that "foreign oil companies" had were those of Stanvac and the Shell company, not those of Associated Oil, which was considered a Japanese company and conformed to all Japanese rules and regulations. *Foreign Relations of the United States*, which has long sections on the difficulties of the "foreign oil companies," never mentions Associated Oil.

***Texaco had once sold in Japan, but after the 1923 earthquake it stopped operations there.

****This paper will focus its attention on Stanvac, the most important American company in the Far East.

initiate an oil monopoly in Japan. Although this did not prove to be the case, on March 27, 1934 a Petroleum Industry Law was passed. Stanvac found the law and subsequent interpretations of it unsatisfactory. The possibility that the Japanese government would unpredictably alter import quotas, the six-month stockpiling provisions, and the price-fixing rules were untenable to the American firm's management.[103] Meanwhile, in Manchuria Stanvac and Texaco met discrimination against their products in 1933, and on November 13, 1934 a Petroleum Monopoly Law was approved by the cabinet and Privy Council of Manchukuo.[104] Increasingly, Stanvac officials feared that if the Japanese accomplished their objectives in Japan and Manchuria—i.e., built up local refining and pushed Stanvac out—"Japan will feel free to proceed without fear of opposition by re-export of refined [oil] products and other means to dominate the petroleum situation in China as well."[105]

At first Stanvac was prepared to sell crude oil to the new Manchurian oil company, which had a refinery under construction,[106] but then a new idea took form. On August 20, 1934 Stanvac officials in Japan told Ambassador Grew that perhaps Japanese authorities could be influenced to treat the company better by even an indication that the American and British governments were considering restrictions on or stoppage of sales of crude oil to Japanese and future Manchurian refineries. Grew wrote Washington endorsing the oil company's suggestion. Two days later American representatives of Stanvac and Shell talked with U.S. Undersecretary of State William Phillips and the next day with Secretary of the Interior Ickes. They asked the U.S. government to consider an embargo on crude oil shipments.[107] If the Japanese had no crude oil for their refineries, they would have to continue buying U.S. *refined* oil, in which case they would be compelled to treat the foreign oil companies better. In accord with this plan, on August 31, after consultation with the Shell company and Texaco, Stanvac decided not to submit bids for the sale of crude oil to the Manchuria Petroleum Company; the other foreign companies agreed. The agreement, however, proved futile, because Standard Oil of California and Union Oil were ready to sell crude oil to the Manchurian company.[108]

By October 1934 the oil companies regarded the situation in Japan as critical. The Japanese were pressing them to conform to the stockpiling provisions of the March 27 Petroleum Industry Law, which they did not want to do. E. L. Neville, counselor of the embassy, recommended that the U.S. government make "every effort . . . to protect as far as possible the large interests of our nationals in the oil trade" of Japan and Manchuria, "*even at the risk that such efforts may bring added irritation to the relations between Japan and the United States*" (italics added). Neville pointed out that the "oil problem in Japan and Manchuria . . . is more than a mere matter of the protection of commercial interests; it is a matter which directly concerns international policy and international amity." Japan had inadequate oil resources. "By controlling the supply of crude oil at the sources, . . . the interested countries [the United States, Britain, Holland] may be able to induce a more reasonable attitude on the part of the [Japanese] government." Neville noted that if the U.S. government could regulate U.S. crude oil exports, the foreign oil companies (Shell and Stanvac) believed that Japan's entire crude oil supply could be curtailed. What it came down to was that Stanvac could not control the independent U.S. oil companies, but that Stanvac and Shell together could control the rest of the world's crude oil and would do so—*if* the U.S. government would take care of the independent American companies. Neville approved the Stanvac position, although he realized that an embargo on crude oil might impose some hardships on the small companies in California.[109]

These then were the views of Stanvac and the embassy. What was happening in Washington? When the bill to control the Japanese oil industry was before the Diet, Hull instructed Ambassador Grew to discuss it with the Japanese government and to add:

> I assume that the Japanese government in regulating the oil industry will accord to American oil dealers and refineries* in Japan the same rights and privileges as are or may be granted to Japanese oil dealers and refineries and that it will give the same considerations to the interests of the American oil concerns that it may give to the interests of Japanese oil concerns.

The U.S. government protested discriminatory duties against American kerosene in Manchuria and tried to get the British to join in the protests.[110]

After the Japanese oil bill became law on March 27, 1934, the State Department continued to protest on behalf of American oil companies in Japan. When on August 8 a Stanvac representative told the State Department that the company would, if requested, submit crude oil bids to the Manchuria Petroleum Company, Hornbeck replied that the State Department would try to persuade the Japanese to honor the treaty provisions under which American interests in Manchuria were established. He noted that "the Department realized that you [Stanvac] and the other American oil companies established in Manchuria [MW: only Texaco] are faced with a practical situation . . . and the Department is not inclined to advise against any practical steps you might decide to take to meet an emergency thus involving your interests. It would appreciate, however, being kept informed of any such steps that you may take."[111]

On September 21 Hull instructed Ambassador Grew to communicate to the Japanese foreign minister the State Department's concern about the "disabilities" which the new Japanese petroleum law "threatens to impose upon American petroleum interests in Japan."[112] He likewise protested the oil monopoly in Manchuria. Thus far Hull would go, but no farther. When Stanvac and Shell proposed a U.S. government embargo on crude oil shipments to Japan, Hull drew back. Despite the endorsement of the Tokyo embassy, despite pressure from Stanvac officials in the United States and Japan, Hull in 1934 was not inclined to disturb the delicate relations between Japan and the United States. In October-December, with naval negotiations being conducted with the Japanese, Hull desired to do his best to "avoid any controversy with Japan." The State Department did not want to mix naval conference matters and the oil

---

*With the exception of Associated Oil's joint venture with Mitsubishi (commonly thought of as a "Japanese oil company"), there were no American refineries in Japan. Either Hull wrote in ignorance or he was thinking about the possibility of future U.S. refineries; perhaps he was just repeating the phrase used in the Japanese legislation.

business.[113] The State Department, in short, refused to take the punitive step of imposing a crude oil embargo. The policy that evolved was that the oil companies should arrive at a definite understanding among themselves with regard to the course they would follow, a course not contingent on further U.S. government action.[114]

From late 1934 to mid-1937 it became evident that the Japanese did not want Stanvac to leave Japan. Japanese refined oil imports rose. "You know we are absolutely dependent on American oil," Hirota told Grew early in March 1935. The Japanese desired Stanvac and Shell to stockpile six-month supplies of oil for Japanese military needs, which the companies refused to do.[115] Years later, when the petroleum adviser to the State Department, Charles Rayner, was explaining to a U.S. Senate committee how the State Department aided the oil companies, he pointed to the success of the embassy in prewar Japan in seeing to it that Stanvac did not have to undertake the expensive stockpiling required under the Petroleum Industry Law. Rayner reported:

> We did not succeed in inducing the Japanese Government to abrogate or modify the law . . . but we did succeed in inducing that Government to postpone indefinitely the application to the two foreign companies [Shell and Stanvac] of the stock-holding provisions of the law. As a result the Standard-Vacuum Oil Co. was relieved of the necessity of expending the large sum of money (estimated at ten to twenty millions of dollars) which would have been needed to fulfill the requirements of the law.[116]

Rayner did not tell the whole story. In order to maintain their position in Japan Stanvac and Shell offered in December 1935 to trade research on the hydrogenation process for developing oil from coal resources. Clearly the Japanese would use the information for military purposes. But although the State Department knew of this, it raised no obstacles to the proposal. Hull's only comment to the embassy in Japan was, "You should guard against the Japanese authorities gaining the impression that the American government is in any way associated with the proposal."[117]

As for the Manchurian oil monopoly which became effective April 10, 1935, Texaco soon agreed to sell out and retreated from doing business in Manchuria. Stanvac and Shell also made an effort to liquidate, but their demands were stiffer than those of Texaco. Stanvac officials were in regular contact with the U.S. State Department on the oil situation in Manchuria. Grew protested to Hirota the imposition of the monopoly. The State Department felt the Japanese government should take responsibility for the Manchurian legislation; the Japanese maintained that Manchukuo was a sovereign state and refused to be accountable.[118] Hull, however, had no objection to the companies' dealing directly with the oil monopoly and/or with the authorities in Manchuria, although the American government did not recognize Manchukuo.[119]

During 1935 the State Department continued to refuse to embargo crude oil shipments to Japan or Manchuria, but it offered no objection should Stanvac desire to reach a common policy with the California oil companies. A. H. Defriest, representing Stanvac, however, had no success when he tried "to cause . . . California companies to refuse to make shipments of crude oil to

Manchuria." Stanvac then sought to get the California companies to agree to sell to the Manchurian monopoly only at a premium. A Stanvac executive told a State Department official that his company "desired to make clear to all that the Monopoly will encounter many obstacles and that it will have to 'pay through the nose' for its supplies." But Stanvac failed to control the other American companies. Early in 1936 Texaco and Standard Oil of California were selling crude oil to the monopoly and apparently were not charging exorbitant prices.[120] Strong U.S. government action on behalf of Stanvac might have blocked the oil monopoly in Manchuria. But Hull and Hornbeck, while ready to protest vigorously on behalf of U.S. companies, were not willing to cut off U.S. crude oil exports to Manchuria. The oil monopoly remained.

In 1937, when the Japanese moved into China proper, Stanvac and Texaco continued to do business in China. The *Panay* crisis, involving as it did three Stanvac vessels, was smoothed over by rapid compensation from the Japanese. The oil companies, however, encountered other difficulties in China. For example, when the Japanese went into Nanking, they removed stock from Stanvac and Texaco installations. Company personnel were not permitted to travel freely in occupied China. In May 1938 Chinese authorities refused to issue foreign exchange to the U.S. oil companies because the latter were selling to the Japanese.[121] In north China the American companies feared a repetition of the Manchurian oil monopoly. Secretary of State Hull expressed "grave concern" and in September 1938 the companies learned that no Japanese oil monopoly was planned for north China.[122] Under steadily worsening conditions—from bombings of their installations to a depreciating currency—the oil companies tried to operate. Regularly they wrote down their giant investments, but until the U.S. entry into the war in December 1941, Stanvac and Texaco continued to sell refined oil in occupied and unoccupied China.[123] Stanvac was in the curious position of having larger investments in China than in Japan but a larger trade with Japan than with China. It wanted help from Washington in defending its position in both countries.

From 1937 to 1941 Stanvac continued to supply refined oil to its marketing network in Japan. It is something of a surprise to find U.S. refined oil exports to Japan in 1940 reaching a peak for the decade (see Table 4). Apparently Stanvac never agreed to stockpile oil, and the Japanese, hoping to gain knowledge of hydrogenation and needing massive supplies of refined oil, did not push the American company out. Instead they kept purchasing. While the U.S. embargo of July 26, 1940 stopped aviation gasoline and lubricant exports to Japan, neither regular gasoline nor crude oil was placed on the list until August 1941.[124] This was not to aid the oil companies. Rather, as Roosevelt explained on July 25, 1941, "if we [had] cut the oil off, they [the Japanese] probably would have gone down to the Dutch East Indies [to get oil] a year ago, and you [the American people] probably would have had war."[125]

At least as early as January 1937 oilmen became conscious that Japan in time might seize the Netherlands East Indies to assure itself of oil supplies. Royal Dutch Shell held the key oil stakes in the Netherlands East Indies, but Stanvac also had substantial properties and a company jointly owned by Standard Oil of California and Texas Oil Co. had started operations there. Late in 1939 and in 1940 the Dutch government issued to the companies plans to blow up the oil wells and refineries should Japan invade. On July 28, 1941 the Netherlands East Indies government put restrictions on oil exports to Japan.[126] With the U.S. restraints, Japan's main sources of oil were cut off. The oil companies accepted the new restrictions.

Meanwhile, the U.S. government was obtaining from the oil companies information on Japanese resources—in case a war occurred. Oil company officials cooperated in supplying data that could be used to appraise Japan's economic strength.[127]

In short, American banks, manufacturers, and oil companies that operated in Japan had to adapt to changing conditions. The Japanese skillfully mobilized practically all these businesses to meet Japan's industrial needs. The National City Bank—except at the urging of the U.S. government in China in the late 1930s—did nothing to antagonize the Japanese, and Japan dealt with the bank respectfully. The Japanese fondled the U.S. automobile companies *until* Japan developed its own industry. They encouraged other U.S. manufacturing companies to give them technical knowledge and hoped the oil companies would continue to provide them vital products and knowledge. American business in Japan took no righteous stand. Rather, it sought to survive—and in doing so aided the development of the Japanese industrial complex. When the Japanese froze U.S. assets in Japan, the result was "an almost complete cessation of financial and business activities on the part of American individuals and firms in Japan."[128]

While some companies—Ford, General Motors, and General Electric, for example—had larger investments in Japan than in China, the oil companies had far larger investments in China.* In general, the policies of American corporations were oriented toward preserving their business in *both* Japan and China.

How much influence did these large companies have on U.S. policy? In Japan they may have had considerable influence on Ambassador Grew. Reading Grew's dispatches to Washington, the impression emerges that he often stood up for U.S. business interests in Japan. When the National City Bank, however, favored recognition of Manchukuo, it had no influence whatsoever. Likewise in 1934-35, when the oil companies wanted crude oil exports from the United States barred, Hull was not ready to comply.

State Department policy before 1937 that sought not to enflame Japanese-American relations met with general approval and may even have been influenced to some extent by the large businesses (Stanvac representing the exception to this generalization). After 1937, while the oil companies and other businesses with large stakes in China looked to the State Department for defense of their properties, other key enterprises sought improved relations with Japan. In fact, the continual protests made by the State Department on behalf of U.S. businesses *in China* may well have made the situation more difficult for U.S. business interests in Japan. When after 1937 the State Department moved steadily away from a policy of appeasement, it was defining for itself America's interests rather than accepting definitions endorsed by National City Bank representatives or General Motors managers. For Stanvac, with large stakes in both nations, keeping its Far Eastern enterprises functioning took priority over trying to influence broad U.S. government policies.

---

*Although, as indicated, Stanvac's *trade* with Japan in the 1930s was far larger than with China.

VII

In this paper I have sought to isolate the key business groups involved in
U.S.-Japanese relations in the years 1931-41. Not all business groups have been
considered. Negotiations on fur seal fisheries, for example, have been excluded
because they were tangential. Areas for further research might include: (1) the
specific influences of U.S. businessmen on their congressmen and on congressional committees; (2) the role of U.S. mining companies in formulating the U.S.
silver program; (3) the conflict and convergence in interests between the raw
cotton and cotton textile industries and their relative impact on U.S. policy; (4)
the regional aspects of U.S. business and Japanese-American relations: eastern
manufacturing and financial interests, southern cotton growers, midwestern
automobile makers, western mining groups, and west coast exporters, shippers,
and fisheries; (5) the divergence and/or agreement in opinion between overseas
executives of large corporations and their officials at home. Some of these
questions have been barely touched upon and others have been excluded
altogether because of the limitations of space.

In trying to determine the U.S. businesses most concerned with Japanese-
American relations, I have examined six groups. I found that American
companies that met competition from Japanese goods generally had a hostile
attitude toward Japan, and their rhetoric served to intensify anti-Japanese
sentiment in the United States. While they tried to influence U.S. tariff and
certain other New Deal policies, while they sought aid in Washington, they had
only a minimum of impact on the U.S. government. They met with the most
friendliness from the U.S. Tariff Commission. They occasionally obtained
sympathy from Roosevelt himself. But in general, as W. W. Lockwood has
written:

> The Roosevelt Administration ... sought to allay the hue and cry
> over Japanese competition. ... In the realm of diplomacy, agitation
> over Japanese competition was an unwelcome complication of
> diplomatic relations already strained; in economic policy, higher
> protection against Japanese goods was directly counter to Secretary
> Hull's tariff reduction program and, in addition, ran the risk of
> retaliation. The State Department did its best to limit import
> restrictions.[129]

The second group—the west coast fisheries—were also hostile to Japan. In
appealing to Roosevelt's commitment to conservation they got attention, but
they achieved little in the way of altering the foreign policy of the United States.

By contrast, the third group of businessmen—the importers, chain store
owners, and silk weavers and knitters—looked for expanded imports from Japan.
They shared with Hull his desire for freer trade. They were not, however,
articulate in their pro-Japanese point of view and seem to have had relatively
little impact on U.S. policy.

Businessmen who exported to Japan were most vocal in their desire for
better relations with Japan, at least before 1937. They viewed Japan as an
important market. They agreed with the third group in seeking freer trade and in
supporting government policies that encouraged trade. They looked on both

Japan and China as "friends," but their markets were larger in Japan and therefore they did not want to antagonize the Japanese. Their words promoted "friendly cooperation" with the nations of the Far East. Most exporters were vehement against Roosevelt's quarantine speech. As late as the mid-1930s fully three-quarters of the American big business community (which included a large number of companies that exported) opposed measures that might antagonize Japan. Did this group have influence in Washington? More work needs to be done to document the answer. Here I will tentatively note only that in the early years of the New Deal there seems to have been a coincidence between the needs of this group and the policies of the administration apropos Japanese-American relations. Later, after 1937, the policies of the administration came to be less in accord with the needs of the exporters as seen by the latter. Washington became unwilling to accept appeasement of Japan as advocated by many exporters. In 1940-41, acting as Americans rather than for business reasons, most exporters became reconciled to U.S. policy.

The banking community—like the foreign traders—were more involved with business interests in Japan than in China. They too looked to greater trade expansion and worldwide cooperation, and their sympathies lay with Japan and with the liberal element in Japan. The banker Thomas W. Lamont had close communications with Washington. He often took a stand on Japanese-American relations only after consultation with Stimson (in 1932), Hornbeck, and occasionally Hull (after 1934). Japanese aggression in China alienated him; whereas in 1937 he did not favor sanctions against Japan, after the Tripartite Pact he—and others in the financial community—believed strongly that America must stand up for an independent China and take vigorous measures against Japan. He did not expect such action to lead to war. The coincidence between the policies of the State Department and the views of Lamont (on all issues except the China Consortium) is very evident.

The last group—Americans with direct investment in the Far East—sought to protect their foreign stakes. These men favored expanded world trade, peace and order, and the opportunity to do business unfettered by foreign government restrictions. While in general they aimed to improve both Japanese-American and Chinese-American relations, one corporation—the Standard-Vacuum Oil Company—was prepared to ask the government to risk increasing tension to take strong measures on its behalf. Grew at the Tokyo embassy seemed more sympathetic to this group's needs in Japan than did the administration in Washington. When the State Department wanted American businessmen to get out of China in 1937 in order to calm the situation in the Far East, the latter looked narrowly at their stakes in China and preferred to remain and protect their properties. No one made them leave. While the State Department's insistence on an "open door" in China appears to have been appreciated (if not influenced) by executives of the U.S. oil companies and some other U.S. corporations in China, many American enterprises simply wanted to continue profitable operations, whether in an independent or an occupied China. Within this sixth group business opinion was thus divided. After 1938 U.S. businesses in Japan found themselves in an increasingly precarious position and watched with a sense of futility and resignation the trends in Japanese attitudes.

In sum, there was no single U.S. business policy toward the Far East, but rather a spectrum of views. Businessmen shared only one sentiment: they did not want America to become involved in a Far Eastern war. For the most part, their thoughts and actions were more influenced by than influencers of the course of events. Their efforts to survive and to make profits in a hostile environment met difficulties even before the events following December 7, 1941 put all U.S. business "out of business" in the Far East for the duration of the war.

TABLE 1

JAPANESE IMPORTS TO THE UNITED STATES, 1930-1941
(in 000s of U.S. dollars)

1930	$279,040*
1931	206,349
1932	134,011
1933	128,418
1934	119,251#
1935	152,902
1936	171,744
1937	204,201
1938	126,757
1939	161,212
1940	158,376
1941	78,271

      *Peak   #Nadir for 1930s

Source: Statistical Abstract of the United States, 1934, p. 429; *1938,* p. 465; *1943,* p. 539.

TABLE 2

U.S. EXPORTS TO JAPAN AND CHINA, 1930-1941 (includes reexports)
(in 000s of U.S. dollars)

Year	Japan	China
1930	$164,570	$89,605
1931	155,715	97,923*
1932	134,921#	56,171
1933	143,435	51,942
1934	210,480	68,667
1935	203,283	38,153
1936	204,348	46,819
1937	288,558*	49,703
1938	239,662	34,719#
1939	232,184	55,614
1940	227,200	77,968
1941	59,901	95,349

     *Peak   #Nadir for the 1930s

Source: Statistical Abstract of the United States, 1934, p. 428; *1938,* p. 464; *1943,* p. 538.

TABLE 3

JAPAN'S RANK IN U.S. EXPORT TRADE, 1930-1941

| 1930–5 | 1932–3 | 1934–3 | 1936–3 | 1938–3 | 1940–4 |
| 1931–4 | 1933–3 | 1935–3 | 1937–3 | 1939–3 | 1941–18 |

Source: Statistical Abstract of the United States, 1934, pp. 424ff; *1938,* pp. 460ff; *1943,* pp. 534ff.

TABLE 4

SELECTED U.S. DOMESTIC EXPORTS TO JAPAN, 1930-1941
(in 000s of U.S. dollars)

Year	Raw Cotton	Crude Oil	Refined Oil	Scrap Iron + Steel
1930	$ 65,910	$ 3,223	$15,290	$ 2,946*
1931	79,843	3,518	12,821	843*
1932	85,821	4,895	10,292	1,325*
1933	86,699	5,505	8,476	4,739*
1934	112,178	7,944	12,811	12,428*
1935	98,587	11,781	13,519	10,844
1936	88,338	14,194	14,164	11,897
1937	61,724	22,103	20,644	37,418
1938	52,850	29,858	19,779	21,685
1939	42,498	20,924	23,833	32,526
1940	29,608	15,875	35,303	16,971
1941	6,566	6,939	21,113	0

*including tin plate scrap

Source: U.S., Department of Commerce, Bureau of the Census, *Foreign Commerce and Navigation of the United States, 1930,* pp. 64, 102, 115; *1931,* pp. 736-37, 102; *1932,* pp. 63, 98-99, 110; *1933,* pp. 52, 89, 100; *1934,* pp. 398, 51, 87; *1935,* pp. 403, 440, 452; *1936,* pp. 56, 94-95, 109; *1937,* pp. 447, 486, 502; *1938,* pp. 867, 518-21; *1939,* pp. 381, 383, 484, 499; *1940,* pp. 368, 371, 467-70, 483; *1941,* pp. 293, 295, 380-81.

TABLE 5

U.S. ECONOMIC ACTIONS AFFECTING JAPAN, 1938-1941

1938:	June 11	"Moral embargo" placed on export of aircraft, armaments, engine parts, accessories, aerial bombs, and torpedoes (Japan not specifically mentioned).
		Department of Commerce advised U.S. exporters to have a "confirmed irrevocable letter of credit in their hands before accepting orders for shipment to Japan."
1939:	July 26	Washington announced, it would terminate the 1911 U.S.-Japan Treaty of Commerce and Navigation, effective January 26, 1940.
	Dec. 15	Moral embargo list expanded to include molybdenum and aluminum.
	Dec. 20	Equipment and information not in general circulation relating to the production of high quality aviation gasoline added to moral embargo list.
1940:	Jan. 26	U.S.-Japan Treaty abrogated, opening the way to mandatory rather than merely moral-embargoes.
	July 2	Congress gave the president authority to subject U.S. exports to a licensing system.
		Licensing system for U.S. exports established, requiring permits for a large number of items exported to Japan.
	July 26	Restrictions placed on the issuance of export licenses for aviation motor fuel and lubricating oil, tetraethyl lead, and heavy melting scrap (which equaled about 20 percent of scrap exports to Japan).
	Oct. 16	All exports of iron and steel scrap to Japan barred.
	Dec. 10	Restrictions placed on export of iron and steel products, effective December 30.
1941:	Jan. 10	Export of copper, brass and bronze, zinc, nickel, potash, and many semi-manufactured products made from these materials required an export license, effective February 3.
	July 26	President froze Japanese assets in U.S.; all financial and import-export transactions involving Japanese interests came under U.S. government control.
	Aug. 1	Sharp restrictions placed on flow of oil and gasoline to Japan (to the extent of 75 percent of U.S. shipments). Japanese silk imports to U.S. ended.

TABLE 6

U.S. DIRECT INVESTMENT IN EAST ASIA—1930, 1936, 1940
(in 000s of U.S. dollars)

Country	1930	1936	1940
China	129,768	90,593*	46,136
Japan	61,450	46,694	37,671
Philippines	81,435	92,150	90,695
Netherlands East Indies	66,212	69,759	71,275
British Malaya	27,103	23,740	21,403

*Part of this drop from the 1930 level was due to changes in valuation by compliers; part was due to currency depreciations.

Source: U.S., Department of Commerce, Bureau of Foreign and Domestic Commerce, *A New Estimate of American Investments Abroad* (*Trade Information Bulletin*, No. 767) (Washington, D.C., 1931), p. 20; U.S., Department of Commerce, Bureau of Foreign and Domestic Commerce, *American Direct Investments in Foreign Countries—1936, Economic Series, No. 1* (Washington, D.C., 1938), pp. 16-17; U.S., Department of Commerce, Bureau of Foreign and Domestic Commerce, *American Direct Investments in Foreign Countries—1940, Economic Series, No. 20* (Washington, D.C., 1942), p. 16.

TABLE 7

KEY U.S. INDUSTRIAL CORPORATIONS AND UTILITIES WITH DIRECT INVESTMENTS IN JAPAN AND CHINA—1931

Corporation	Location	Activity	Percentage U.S. Ownership in Japanese & Chinese Enterprises
			majority interest
American & Foreign Power Co.	China	Power plant in Shanghai	
Associated Oil Co. (see Tidewater)			
Carrier Corp.	Japan	Manufactured air conditioners	50%
Columbia Co.	Japan	Manufactured records	67
Eastman Kodak	Japan and China	Sales outlets	100
Ford Motor Company	Japan	Assembly of automobiles	100
	China	Sales branch	100
General Electric	Japan	Manufactured electrical products	57 - 32 (2 cos.)
	China	Manufactured lamps; trading activities	100 (1 co.), ? (other cos.)
General Motors	Japan	Assembly of automobiles	100
	China	Sales branch	100
Goodrich (B.F.)		Manufactured tires	57
International General Electric Co. (see General Electric)			
International Standard Electric Co. (see International Telephone & Telegraph Corp.)			
International Telephone & Telegraph Corp.	Japan	Manufactured telephone equipment	59
	China	Manufactured telephone equipment and operated telephone system in Shanghai	
			majority interests
Libbey-Owens Glass	Japan	Manufactured glass	30
Singer Sewing Machine	Japan and China	Sales outlets	100
Radio Corporation of America	Japan and China	Radio connections	100
Socony-Vacuum (as of 1933 Standard-Vacuum Oil Co.)	Japan and China	Oil distribution	100
	China	Oil distribution	100
Texas Oil Co.	Japan	Establishing oil refining	50
Tidewater	Japan and China	Sales outlets	100
U.S. Steel	Japan	Manufacturing	68
Victor Talking Machine	Japan	Manufacturing	9
Westinghouse			

Source: Information from Record Group 151, National Archives, Washington, D.C.; Ministry of International Trade and Industry, Tokyo; and records of the companies involved.

TABLE 8

EQUITY HELD BY AMERICAN COMPANIES IN JAPANESE ENTERPRISES

U.S. Corporation	Equity in Japanese Enterprise	
	1931	1941
Carrier Corp.	50%	46%
Columbia Co.	67	3
General Electric	57 - 32 (2 cos.)	15
Goodrich (B.F.)	57	9
International Telegraph & Telephone Co.	59	20
Libbey-Owens Glass	30	17
Tidewater	50	25
Victor Talking Machine	68	0
Westinghouse Electric	9	4

Source: Data from Ministry of International Trade and Industry, Tokyo.

AN INQUIRY INTO THE PROBLEM
OF IMPORTING AMERICAN CAPITAL INTO
MANCHURIA: A NOTE ON JAPANESE-
AMERICAN RELATIONS, 1931-1941

Chō Yukio

Translated by Edgar C. Harrell

I

An important aspect of Japan's efforts to improve relations with the United States was its attempt to attract American capital for investment in Manchuria. In making such an attempt Japan had two ends in view: (1) to secure American recognition of Japan's vested interests—acquired through aggression—in Manchuria and China, and (2) to meet the critical need for funds for Manchuria's development in part by securing supplementary investments. On the assumption that the participation of American capital in the economic growth of Manchukuo would create a bond of mutual interest between the United States and Japan, efforts, both official and unofficial, were initiated to obtain American funds for investment. These efforts, however, were unsuccessful and could not prevent the deterioration in Japanese-American relations and the catastrophe of December 1941.

The endeavors of the Japan Economic Federation (Nihon Keizai Renmeikai) to attract American investment began with the establishment of its External Relations Committee (Taigai Iinkai) in April 1939.[1] The federation had been working through the Japanese-American Trade Council to ease tensions in Japanese-American economic relations. In March of 1939 it had invited the journalist William O. Inglis to visit Japan in order "to dispel misunderstandings in the United States about Japan and to bring about Japanese-American amity."[2] Inglis arrived in Japan on March 16 and stayed in Tokyo for about two weeks studying the effect of the Sino-Japanese War on industrial, economic, and social conditions in Japan. Thereafter he undertook a tour of inspection in Manchuria and north China.

With the occupation of the Wuhan cities in late 1938 and the creation of special territories in north China and the lower Yangtze, the nature of the Japanese advance into central and south China became obvious. Direct conflict with American interests in the region appeared likely, and from this time on United States protests to Japan grew increasingly strong. In light of these events, the leaders of the Japan Economic Federation felt keenly that a more positive policy of cooperation with the United States was essential, and they therefore put forward a plan to bring American private capital into Manchuria and the occupied territories of China. The External Relations Committee was organized to promote this end.

Because political and social conditions at the time demanded that such an organization exercise judicious care in its activities, the only public record of the External Relations Committee consists of the following statement in the 18th report of the Japan Economic Federation (April 1, 1939-March 31, 1940):

> The External Relations Committee, established within the federation in April 1939, has as its objective the dissemination of information abroad and the carrying out of research in order to promote understanding and cooperation with various foreign countries concerning the long-term industrial and economic construction of Japan, Manchuria, and China.
>
> The committee is presided over by Baron Gō Seinosuke, and the membership includes former Ambassador Sawada Setsuzō and several influential businessmen.
>
> The Executive Office for External Relations of the Japan Economic Federation functions under this committee. With Takashima Seiichi as managing director and Ayusawa Iwao as assistant director, the Executive Office consists of three sections and one division, known as the Administrative, Research, and Business sections and the Editorial Division. The Executive Office is attempting to achieve the following goals: (1) monthly publication in English of a magazine called *East Asia Economic News* and an "East Asia Intelligence Series"; (2) foreign broadcasting; (3) initiation of discussions between influential Japanese businessmen on the one hand and foreign newspaper reporters in Tokyo and members of the Overseas Japanese Newspaper Association (Kaigai Hōji Shinbun Kyōkai) on the other; (4) holding receptions for influential foreigners visiting Japan; (5) providing support for their inspection tours; and (6) collection and circulation of English language materials.

According to this statement, the committee's primary responsibility was to disseminate information abroad and undertake related research projects. While activities were in fact carried out along these lines, behind all of them lay a plan to promote cooperation with the United States that involved efforts to attract private American capital. According to Takashima Seiichi, the committee hoped to borrow $1 billion from American sources and use it for the development of Manchuria. To this end, despite "harassment from the die-hard militarists," he was able to secure from the Manchukuo government an annual 100,000 yen subsidy through Hoshino Naoki and Kishi Nobusuke, then chief and vice chief, respectively, of the General Affairs Bureau of the Manchukuo Ministry of State Affairs.

As the first step in its endeavors, the committee invited General John F. O'Ryan to tour Japan, Manchukuo, and China. General O'Ryan, a New York lawyer who was believed to have considerable influence in American financial circles, arrived in Japan in June 1940 with a number of aides. On the 29th the Japan Economic Federation held a luncheon reception for the group at the Imperial Hotel. Several leaders of the Japanese financial world attended, most notably Ayukawa Gisuke, president of the Manchuria Heavy Industries Development Corporation, suggesting that such circles viewed the plan with considerable optimism.[3] O'Ryan's tour lasted for about a month. Prior to his departure, the federation feted him once again, at a farewell dinner held at the Japan Industrialists Club on August 14.

These efforts to promote cooperation with the United States, however, were already too late. One month after O'Ryan returned to the United States, Japan signed the Tripartite Pact with Germany and Italy, and its relations with the United States and Great Britain came one step closer to a final rupture. On October 16 the United States placed an embargo on exports of scrap iron to Japan. In light of these developments, the plan for the importation of American capital was no more than a dream.

There is reason to suppose that the arrangements with O'Ryan were made through the New York office of the Japan National Committee of the International Chambers of Commerce and the Japanese-American Trade Council. But if so, what kind of support did his trip have in the United States? What were his relations with industrial groups such as the National Trade Council and with financial concerns such as Kuhn, Loeb and Company that in the past had had close connections with Japan? Available sources do not provide answers to such questions, nor is there any indication of what kind of report O'Ryan gave after his return. The details needed to clarify developments on the American side are therefore lacking, although it would appear that O'Ryan's influence in American financial circles was extremely limited. On the Japanese side, however, it is possible to deduce the general intent behind the attempt to import American capital, and it is with this subject that the following section is concerned.[4]

II

C. F. Remer wrote of American investments in China in 1930 that while Manchuria was the center of United States political and financial concern, Shanghai was the center of American business investment. Of the total of $150,227,978 of American investment in China, $97,495,917 or 64.9 percent was concentrated in Shanghai. In addition, of 213 American firms in China, 146 or 68.5 percent had Shanghai offices. Although American capital was invested in various business activities, the most important was the import-export business, the major portion of which was also concentrated in Shanghai. The second most important field of investment was public utilities, and more than 20 percent of all American business investment in China was in the two public utilities of Shanghai's International Settlement.[5]

Thus, almost all of American investments in China were either in China proper, centering in Shanghai, or in Hong Kong. Investment in China, moreover, constituted only a fraction of total American overseas investments and, compared to those of Great Britain or Japan, were relatively insignificant. This was especially true of investments in Manchuria, which were almost nonexistent (see Table 1, Appendix I). Therefore, we may assume that United States interest in Manchuria was more political than economic. Furthermore, of the total American investment in the Far East, investment in Japan was greater than in China. (It might be pointed out that it was American investment in Japan that made possible Japanese investment in China.)

In short, United States vested interests in China were relatively minor. It is possible that their very lack of importance encouraged Japanese political and financial circles to embrace a policy of continuing to negotiate with the United States regarding investments in Manchuria while at the same time seeking to broaden their own sphere of control in China proper. Before turning to this problem, however, let us look more closely at the background of American investments in China.

The United States developed an interest in Manchuria at the beginning of the twentieth century, when foreign ambitions in Manchuria made that area the focal point of Far Eastern international politics. The United States made clear its attitude toward the political and economic problems of China on September 6, 1899 when John Hay, in his notes to the powers, asserted the principle of the Open Door in China. Subsequently, three areas of tension in the Far East served to heighten American interest in Manchuria: the expansion of Russia's political and economic role in China after the Boxer Rebellion, the conclusion of the Anglo-Japanese Alliance in 1902, and the outbreak of hostilities between Russia and Japan in February 1904. Theodore Roosevelt's role in bringing about a settlement of the Russo-Japanese War also indicated that the United States and Great Britain were attempting, in cooperation with Japan, to arrest Russia's imperialist expansion in the Far East. The reader will recall the part played by Jacob H. Schiff of Kuhn, Loeb and Company in regard to Japan's wartime loans.

The first proposal pointing to the possibility of American investment in Manchuria was E. H. Harriman's plan to acquire the south Manchurian railway as one link in his projected round-the-world transportation system. At the invitation of Lloyd C. Griscom, the United States minister to Japan, Harriman arrived in Japan in August 1905. That October he reached a preliminary understanding with the Japanese government regarding joint management of the southern branch of the Chinese Eastern Railway, and on October 12 the Katsura-Harriman agreement was drawn up, providing for the organization of a Japanese-American syndicate to manage the southern line. Other enterprises in Manchuria, such as coal mining, were also included in the agreement. In principle, both Japan and the United States were to have common and equal rights of ownership and management and a share of the profits.

Two plans concerning the postwar administration of assets in Manchuria had aroused considerable debate in Japanese financial circles. One called for joint Japanese-American management, the other for administration by the

Japanese government alone. The Katsura-Harriman agreement followed along the lines of the former. The character of the joint management plan was clearly indicated by the genro Inoue Kaoru, when he said in a speech:

> Regarding the management of the Chinese Eastern Railway and the Fushun Coal Mine, we should encourage the participation of business leaders from both China and the United States, promote the organization of a syndicate of private businessmen, and transfer to the syndicate the management of the railway and mines. A certain percentage of the profits should be remitted to the government. The advantage of such a course is that with the participation of American business leaders, our future policy toward China will be in complete accord with that of the United States.[6]

When Foreign Minister Komura Jutarō returned from the negotiations at Portsmouth, however, he sharply opposed the Katsura-Harriman agreement on the grounds that the Sino-Russian agreement of August 1896, which had stipulated that ownership of Chinese Eastern Railway stock be limited to Chinese and Russian nationals, was intended to apply as well to the south Manchurian railway, transferred to Japan by the Portsmouth Treaty. Hence, stock ownership was to be restricted to Japanese and Chinese nationals. On October 23 the Katsura-Harriman agreement was canceled and the idea of joint Japanese-American management was abandoned. In its stead a policy advocated by Gōto Shinpei and others for administration of the railways by the Japanese government alone was adopted.[7]

Next to appear was a plan put forth by Willard Straight for joint British-American construction of a railroad from Hsinmintun to Aigun. Japan, however, obstructed its implementation, citing a certain "secret protocol" appended to the 1905 Sino-Japanese treaty in which the Chinese government had recognized the rights and interests in China that Japan had obtained by the Portsmouth accord. It is clear, therefore, that in the period following the Russo-Japanese War imperialistic antagonisms had deepened in the Far East between Japan on the one hand and the United States and Great Britain on the other.

On November 6, 1909 the American secretary of state proposed to Great Britain the well-known "Knox Plan" providing for pooling or "neutralizing" all of the railroads in Manchuria. The plan envisaged lending capital to the Chinese government for the redemption of all these railroads, including the Chinese Eastern Railway and the South Manchuria Railway. Russia and Japan, regarding it as an encroachment on their political and economic interests, opposed the scheme and it fell through. The two countries informed the Chinese government that they were to be consulted in advance should it become necessary to raise capital for Manchurian railroad development. China had already signed a loan agreement with Japan concerning the Kirin-Changchun railway and the Hsinmintun-Mukden railway (August 18, 1909). In addition, two Sino-Japanese conventions had been concluded, one regarding Chientao and another dealing with railroads and coal mining in Manchuria (September 4, 1909). The failure of the United States to realize plans such as the Knox proposal was due not to a lack of capital but to the resistance of Japan and Russia, whose ambitions in Manchuria the United States was challenging.

United States maneuvers in China next took the form of participation in a consortium for loans to China. After the United States entered into the Three Power Consortium of Great Britain, Germany, and France (thereby transforming it into the Four Power Consortium), which held interests in the Hukuang railway, loans were offered to China for currency reform and industrial enterprises. On April 15, 1911 a loan agreement for currency reform was concluded by the new Consortium in the amount of £10 million sterling. In the area of industrial development, the Consortium negotiated a loan agreement providing for £6 million for repair and construction of the Hankow-Canton and Hankow-Szechwan rail lines. The prospects these transactions opened up for the international banking group stimulated Russia and Japan to take part as, with the fall of the Ch'ing dynasty and the establishment of a republic under Yuan Shih-k'ai, the Chinese government was in need of loans. Russia and Japan therefore joined the Consortium in June 1912, with the Yokohama Specie Bank representing Japanese investment groups. On April 27, 1913 the Reorganization Loan Agreement was signed, providing a loan to China of £25 million at 5 percent interest, to be repayed in installments over a period of fifty years. Each of the five signatories (Woodrow Wilson had taken the United States out of the negotiations on March 18) assumed responsibility for £5 million. Japan, unable to supply its share from its own resources, sold debentures in France and Britain to cover the deficit. Thus, it was in the peculiar position of being able to invest in China only by relying upon the importation of foreign capital—in other words, its ability to import capital permitted Japan to assume the role of a capital-exporting nation.

With the changes in the international situation after World War I—specifically, Japan's strengthened position in the Far East and the increasing influence of the United States as a leader in global politics and finance—the United States took the initiative in forming a new consortium, created by an agreement signed on October 15, 1920 and composed of Japan, the United States, Great Britain, and France. Evidence of Japan's new position of power was supplied in the political realm by the Twenty-One Demands and in the economic sphere by the Nishihara Loans. To oppose these aggressive imperialistic advances, the United States felt compelled to offer supplementary loans to the Chinese government. In addition, enhanced American prestige, demonstrated at several international conferences on postwar reconstruction, induced the United States to take the lead in forming a new consortium. However, the Chinese government refused to recognize it on the grounds that it was nothing more than a scheme by the four powers to monopolize China's foreign loans, and in the end the consortium served only to obstruct loans that in other circumstances might have been extended to China separately by some countries. In like manner, until the 1930s American investment in Manchuria failed to achieve any notable success, as it became enmeshed in the complexities of the imperialist interests of the powers. Japan, which had taken the lead in expanding its rights and interests in China following World War I, now faced the need to import foreign capital for its investments in Manchuria.

In June 1921 the management of the South Manchuria Railway's Anshan Iron Works invited to Manchuria a seven-member mining and excavation research team headed by Dr. William Ramser Appleby, dean of the Metallurgical College of the University of Minnesota. The Anshan Iron Works had been founded in May 1918 to compensate for inadequate supplies of steel during World War I. The war was already over and the Paris Peace Conference had begun, however, before the factory commenced operations on April 29, 1919 with the formal firing of the first blast furnace. Soon thereafter steel prices collapsed, and at the end of 1919 the Iron Works were forced to cut back production. The mission of the research team was to study the possibility of raising the efficiency of Anshan through technical rationalization and to assess the feasibility of a joint Japanese-American operation. According to the team's findings, lowering production costs to one yen or less per ton was possible by strip mining iron ore and increasing its purity to over 55 percent through a magnetic selection process. It was thought that in this way the operation could be placed on a profitable basis.

What might be termed a "plan for cooperative management" was devised. This was, in essence, a grandiose design calling for separation of the Anshan Iron Works and Fushun Mines from the South Manchuria Railway and the establishment of a joint Japanese-American venture capital corporation—specifically, a company operated jointly by the South Manchuria Railway and United States Steel.[8] Domestic politics in Japan, however, intervened when the purchase of the Talien Coal Mines bordering Fushun became a pretext for an attack on the Seiyūkai, the party then in power in Japan. The management of the South Manchuria Railway was indicted in what became known as the South Manchuria Railway Scandal of 1921, and following the assassination of Prime Minister Hara Takashi, the entire management of the railway resigned; in addition, Dr. Inoue Kyōshirō, head of the Anshan Iron Works and Fushun Mines, who had been a party to the joint venture plan, retired. As a result, the ambitious joint management scheme was buried in oblivion.

On January 17, 1922 a branch office of the South Manchuria Railway was established in New York primarily for the purpose of obtaining $50 million in the United States. Through the efforts of Thomas W. Lamont of J. P. Morgan and Co., direct negotiations with Dillon, Read and Company were very nearly successful before opposition from the Japanese government, and particularly from the Finance Ministry, brought about their failure.

The above is a rough sketch of American investment in Manchuria up to the 1930s. Now let us examine Japanese efforts to import American capital during the 1930s.

III

Japan's overseas investments were concentrated in China. According to H. G. Moulton's *Japan: An Economic and Financial Appraisal* (1931), Japanese private investment and foreign loans at the end of 1929 amounted to 1.657 billion yen, of which 1.527 billion yen, or 92 percent, was in China. Of Japan's total investment overseas of 2.262 billion yen, that in China totaled over 1.891 billion yen, or 84 percent.

From about 1936 on Japan's economy was placed on a semi-wartime footing that aimed at the formation of the Greater East Asia Coprosperity Sphere. Earlier, when Japan had faced severe economic hardship as a result of the worldwide depression, the development of Manchuria had served as an important means of ameliorating the situation. Japan had also adopted an inflationary policy, involving mostly military expenditures, which had created new demands for goods in Japanese industry, and expansion of exports to Manchuria meant a new area of activity for idle Japanese capital.

The funds that made possible this additional demand for goods came from Manchukuo's exports to Japan and from Japanese investments in Manchukuo. Capital for the latter was derived from the excess that had accumulated in the Japanese money market during the depression, when demands for investments were low. Once the money market tightened as a result of inflationary trends in the semi-wartime economy, however, these unused funds were quickly depleted and by 1936 the improving economic situation had led to the complete absorption of existing productive capacity and stimulated a demand for funds for its further expansion. The problem was, therefore, one of Japan's ability to supply the capital necessary for investments in Manchuria.

Funds invested in Manchuria immediately flowed back to Japan via the purchase of goods in Japan. Although in the beginning this was beneficial in that it absorbed idle production capacity, once this capacity was fully utilized, investment in Manchuria—similar in effect to exports to Manchuria—led to an inflationary spiral in Japan in much the same way as did military expenditures based on deficit financing. The goods exported to Manchuria represented for the Japanese economy a demand for goods outside the normal production-consumption cycle. "Reexamination of Manchurian investment" and "problems associated with supplying funds to the South Manchuria Railway" soon became important topics of discussion.

An additional factor upon which any successful investment in Manchuria depended was Manchukuo's ability to supply goods to Japan. The "General Outline of a Program for the Economic Construction of Manchukuo," drawn up in March 1933, offered a unique plan for the economic build-up of Manchukuo. It proposed to terminate the agriculturally-based, single commodity economy and set up a new heavy chemical industry in order to utilize untapped natural resources. In 1936, however, the plan was still in the preparatory stages, and consequently it was unreasonable to anticipate a significant expansion of Manchukuo's export capacity in the near future. Furthermore, exports of mining and manufactured products from Manchukuo to Japan competed with the consumption of these goods in Manchukuo itself. Although in terms of nominal prices total imports from Manchukuo to Japan increased, the proportion decreased considerably in relation to total Japanese imports into Manchukuo. This situation created problems in regard to the effective use of funds (whether to invest in Manchuria or in Japan) that became increasingly serious as Japan's balance of payments situation deteriorated. Throughout 1935-36 the merits of investing in Manchuria were debated. One policy designed to resolve this dilemma was urged in the slogan "expand production capacity by uniting Japan and Manchukuo into a single economic bloc."[9] When Ishibashi Tanzan, editor-in-chief of the *Tōyō keizai shinpō* (Oriental Economist) commented that Finance Minister Takahashi Korekiyo in January 1935 had "created quite a stir by reportedly saying something about restricting investments in Manchukuo," Takahashi replied to his implied questions by saying:

It is quite possible that the effort in Manchukuo might, after all, prove fruitless. . . . We have issued a warning because of the unfortunate practice of blindly setting up companies without adequate investigation. Nevertheless, since Manchukuo has not yet been recognized by other nations as an independent nation, Japan must of course render it as much assistance as possible. We must supply funds. Yet for all that we will be in trouble if operations are begun haphazardly and if domestic industries conflict with industries in Manchukuo. Because the Japanese are impatient, there is danger that they will rush forward without such thought.[10]

We would probably do well to regard Takahashi's statement as expressing not only his own viewpoint but also the apprehensions that prevailed in financial circles concerning investment in Manchuria.

Let us look at actual investments in Manchuria. Manchukuo, which was "founded" in March 1932, had by 1935 barely begun to take steps to promote economic construction and the maintenance of public peace and order. In its early years the new nation was administered on the basis of an "anti-capitalist" ideology. Few new enterprises other than the South Manchuria Railway and its affiliates were in operation. There was no large-scale public investment. Investment in Manchukuo was conducted principally through the South Manchuria Railway (see Table 2, Appendix I). Out of a total investment in Manchukuo of 1,160 billion yen during the 1932-36 period, the South Manchuria Railway and its affiliated companies absorbed 68 percent. If we consider only industrial capital, their share totals 80 percent. The reason for this was that the South Manchuria Railway had long enjoyed public confidence as a quasi-governmental enterprise (part government, part private) and was not entirely bound by the regulations by which Manchukuo controlled most corporations. The South Manchuria Railway Company soon expanded into heavy industry, notably the Fushun Mines and the Anshan Iron Works. The affiliates indicated in Table 3, Appendix I were established in this process of expansion.

In 1933 the South Manchuria Railway Company was entrusted with the management of all the railroads in southern Manchuria and two years later with management of the North Manchuria Railway. It was also given the responsibility of constructing lines which, while financially unprofitable, were intended to advance national policy goals. For this reason, most of the company's funds were tied up in railroad undertakings, and its ability to channel investment into heavy chemical industries was reduced. This was one reason the company encountered difficulties when it attempted to secure capital funds after 1933. The problem was resolved, however, with the transfer of the Nihon Industrial Company (Nissan) to Manchukuo, where it was incorporated as the Manchuria Heavy Industries Development Corporation.

As a result of the government's policy of rejecting zaibatsu funds for investment in Manchukuo, these large conglomerates made few economic gains there during the first two or three years after Manchukuo was founded. But from about 1934 on zaibatsu investments gradually increased, after a change in economic conditions led to a relaxation of government policy (see Table 4, Appendix I).

With the outbreak of the Sino-Japanese War in the summer of 1937, the plan for developing Manchuria as a "self-sufficient continental base of operations" and the idea of "one major industry under one company" was abandoned. In their place guidelines were adopted for linking the Japanese and Manchurian economies so as to promote expansion of industrial capacity and increase investment in Manchuria. The new policy was designed to expand Japan's war capability by attempting virtually to incorporate Manchukuo's economy into Japan's, as one link in the chain.

The Five Year Plan for the Industrialization of Manchuria, promulgated by cabinet decision in June 1936 and revised in 1937 and 1938, was incorporated into the Four Year Plan for the Expansion of the Industrial Capacity of Japan, announced on January 1, 1939. Active importation of capital from Japan into Manchukuo was now formalized, giving further impetus to the construction of heavy industry there by Nissan. As noted earlier, problems in raising funds for investment in Manchuria—except during the first year of Manchukuo's existence—accompanied the inflationary advance of the Japanese semi-wartime economy. Beginning in 1933 a domestic debate broke out over the question of providing funds for the South Manchuria Railway, and steps were taken to encourage the importation of American capital. The issue was first reflected in the plans of the military for the economic construction of Manchuria, although at first even the army in its invasion of Manchuria sought to avoid world criticism as much as possible, as an army document entitled "Evaluation of Conditions in Late Autumn 1931 and Some Remedial Policies" indicates:

> . Since it is generally unprofitable for us to show marked hostility toward the United States and to make it our enemy, we should adopt a pragmatic policy that will lead to actual gains for the empire. As long as there is no fundamental interference with our policies in China, Manchuria, and Mongolia, we should go along with the principle of the Open Door and equality of opportunity. Even in the establishment and consolidation of a new regime in Manchuria, we should avoid antagonizing the United States by refraining, insofar as possible, from unnecessary provocation.[11]

Far from wishing to confront the United States in the Far East, the army seemed to have hoped to keep the way clear for Japanese-American cooperation in the development of Manchuria by respecting, to some degree, the traditional American Far Eastern policy of the Open Door.

In a memorandum entitled "An Evaluation of the Situation" drawn up by staff officer Itagaki Seishirō and dated April-May 1932, a passage evaluating conditions in the United States asserted:

> As a measure to counter the depression and with a view toward future economic development, the United States plans to expand its markets in South America and to open new markets as well as increase those already secured in the Orient. A reexamination of present United States economic relations in the Far East shows that the major element is its relations with Japan. United States trade with China amounts to no more than 40 percent of that with Japan, while its investment in China amounts to no more than 20 percent

of that in Japan and is insignificant in relation to United States trade and investment as a whole. Nevertheless, it is no doubt true that the United States has its sights on China as a good future market. In fact, even such principles as the "Open Door" and "equality of opportunity," which the United States has been advocating for a substantial period of time, are nothing more than slogans in a drive by the United States, a latecomer in the struggle for the China market, to force itself into that market.

Itagaki scrutinized American motives with the realism of a military man viewing the imperialistic competition of the powers in the Far East. Nevertheless, he came to the wishful conclusion that because American interests in the Far East, particularly in China, had little weight relative to the total American economy, the United States would take a somewhat tolerant attitude toward the expansion of Japan's special interests in China. In proposing a policy toward the United States Itagaki wrote:

> In the administration of the new states in Manchuria and Mongolia we must acknowledge the spirit of the Open Door and equality of opportunity, import American capital, and force a close relationship with the United States based on common interests. Nevertheless, because unlimited direct American investment will foster competitive investment between the United States and Japan and may place pressures on the industries of the empire, thus sowing the seeds of discord, we must impose an adequate system of controls.[12]

Recurring in Itagaki's writing is the theme of Japanese-American cooperation once intoned by Inoue Kaoru when, following the Russo-Japanese War, Japan was just beginning to lay the foundations for its advance into Manchuria. This theme, as suggested in the opening paragraphs of the present essay, was repeated in the plan of the Japan Economic Federation and its External Relations Committee.

As a result of its concern over the lack of funds for the South Manchuria Railway, the army appears to have taken great pains to formulate a remedial policy. In a document of August 28, 1935 the chief of the Army Ministry's Military Affairs Bureau urged:

> As to the essential guidelines for the South Manchuria Railway, one major concern is that a year or two from now the company will lose its ability to procure funds. Quite apart from whether or not we build the new rail lines, in order to cover the expenses of repairing the North Manchuria Railway, of advancing into north China, and of constructing the harbor at Hulutao—expenses completely unforeseen at the time of the 800 million yen increase in capitalization—the South Manchuria Railway still will need quite a large amount of capital. Even a segment of the Japanese public feels uneasy about the railway's prospects. In view of this situation, we ask that you use your discretion to gain the consent of the appropriate parties so that we can quickly carry out thorough and adequate research and formulate a sound plan for post-reorganization management of the company.[13]

In a draft policy proposal of June 10, 1937 the army anticipated the importation of foreign capital, particularly from the United States but from Great Britain and Germany as well, through the acquisition of some 500 million yen in long-term credits.[14] The attempt to import foreign capital became official cabinet policy on October 22, 1937 when a "General Plan for the Establishment of Heavy Industries in Manchuria" was adopted. The plan declared:

> In regard to the management and development of the above-mentioned enterprises [that is, iron and steel, heavy industries such as automobile and aircraft manufacture, light metal refining, and the mining of coal and mineral products except by the Anshan Coal Mines and the South Manchuria Railway], we wish to attract foreign capital as well as foreign technology and equipment. In fact, the securing of foreign capital must be regarded as a prerequisite for the plan.[15]

The evident intention of the plan was to entrust to Ayukawa Gisuke in particular the management of Manchurian heavy industries. Ayukawa himself repeatedly advocated in the strongest terms the "introduction of foreign capital" which the plan had stressed.

Prior to assuming his responsibilities as head of the Manchuria Heavy Industries Development Corporation, Ayukawa made a month-long inspection tour of Manchuria, following an itinerary drawn up by Matsuoka Yōsuke, then president of the South Manchuria Railway Company. At the conclusion of the tour, in discussing the question of importing foreign capital with Kwantung Army Chief of Staff Itagaki and a staff officer, Ayukawa stated:

> To build up the Manchuria Heavy Industries Development Corporation in five years (truthfully, I think it will take ten) will require 3 billion yen. We should depend for at least one-third and preferably one-half of this sum upon foreign capital (principally American dollars). As for the means of importing foreign capital, I would hope that it would be in the form of stockholding, not loans. The probable result of pooling our interests with those of other countries will be to reduce the danger of a future war.[16]

Ayukawa sought to visit the United States himself in order to procure resources but was prevented from doing so by strong opposition from the Foreign Ministry. On December 27, 1937 the Nihon Industrial Company was reorganized as the Manchuria Heavy Industries Development Corporation and incorporated in Manchukuo with a capitalization of 450 million yen. Ayukawa became president of the company. Just at that time, however, relations with the United States took a serious turn for the worse as a result of the sinking of the *Panay* and the attack on the British *H.M.S. Ladybird* on December 12, and the occupation of Nanking by the Japanese army the following day. Ayukawa's plans for the importation of American capital had to be set aside.

Yet the desire to involve American capital in Manchurian development remained alive. On August 27, 1938 Yūki Toyotarō, president of the Bank of

Japan, remarked at a dinner given at the villa of Yamashita Kamesaburō, president of the Yamashita Shipping Company, and attended by Konoe Fumimaro, Harada Kumao, and others:

> The public bond issue of 3 billion yen was so well subscribed that it was almost completely absorbed. The financial situation is not as bad as had been anticipated and I believe that we can still feel confident of public support. Nevertheless, in my judgment we should try to end the war as soon as possible. In any event, since Japanese abroad are not aware of the fact that financial conditions have taken an unexpectedly favorable turn, they are naturally anxious. It is unfortunate that when finally we were about to conclude an agreement with the United States involving American interests in Manchuria, the right wing and the military smashed the negotiations to pieces and obstructed the import of foreign capital without any understanding of the significance of their actions.[17]

It is apparent that Yūki, a pivotal figure in the making of financial and monetary policy and having a keen understanding of Japan's economic capacity, hoped to bring the hostilities with China to a quick end. Although his reference to negotiations that were smashed to pieces is not clear, they obviously involved imports of American capital. It is unfortunate that, given the fact that senior military officers such as Itagaki were not opposed to the idea, financial and military leaders failed to coordinate their activities. The reason for this failure appears to have been that an increase of anti-British and anti-American propaganda, which was designed to further the war effort, affected not only the general public but also officers in the middle and lower ranks of the military who, lacking the responsibility for making policy decisions or even the information upon which decisions were based, were strongly inclined to object to the importation of American capital "without any understanding of the significance of their actions." Their attitude, supported by public opinion, served to constrain the senior statesmen and higher-echelon officers.[18]

On June 2, 1938 a new development took place when Ayukawa, in response to Japan's advances in the war with China, made an about-face, abandoned the idea of securing American capital, and indicated his determination to expand production principally through cooperation between Japan and Manchuria. In all probability he was reacting to pressures from a section of the military and the right wing who were insisting upon such cooperation. Under the changed circumstances negotiations with the United States would indeed have been difficult.

The final effort to introduce American capital into Manchuria was that of the External Relations Committee of the Japan Economic Federation, described in the opening paragraphs of this paper. Ayukawa's testimony concerning an annual 100,000 yen subsidy from the Manchukuo government suggests that this effort was carried on with the understanding of leading Japanese officials in Manchukuo and the military—at least those in the army who had drafted the policy of June 1937. Some of the evidence presented to the International Military Tribunal for the Far East also indicates that Kishi Nobusuke and Hoshino Naoki, as well as Obata Tadayoshi, Hoshino's immediate subordinate when he was president of the Cabinet Planning Board, had supported the efforts of the External Relations Committee to import foreign capital.[19]

The conclusion seems justified, therefore, that the efforts of the External Relations Committee to introduce American capital into Manchuria were endorsed by the military as well as by businessmen. Even the army, which favored an aggressive policy in China and the establishment of Manchukuo, in the beginning, far from planning war with the United States, sought to create common interests through joint investments and industrial enterprises in Manchuria. Among businessmen a similar position was taken both by members of the old school (*kyūtaisei-teki,* to use a contemporary term) such as Gō Seinosuke, who was strongly opposed to the increasing military control of the economy, and by others such as Ikeda Seihin and Yūki Toyotarō who were relatively tolerant of such controls.

Nevertheless, there was a difference between the attitudes of the military and businessmen. The former remained tied to the old imperialist concept of the importance of military and political controls in the conduct of relations with other countries and semi-colonial areas. In addition, the notion that certain territories had to be secured because of their strategic value (the so-called "lifeline of national defense") was a view peculiar to professional soldiers. The introduction of capital from the United States was acceptable to them, since it was a means of attaining the traditional imperialistic goal of expansion.

In contrast, businessmen, the representatives of "cosmopolitan" capital, thought first and foremost of the need to augment and stabilize foreign investments and to increase profits. This purpose, they believed, would be furthered by collaboration with American capital. They therefore approved of military and political expansion only insofar as it was a means of fulfilling their investment objectives and reacted negatively to military adventures that threatened in the long run to reduce rather than enhance their economic interests. In sum, while both the military and the business world believed in Japan's advance on the Asian continent, to the military this advance was an end in itself, while to the financiers it was simply a means to an end.[20]

Nevertheless, the military and businessmen came to much the same conclusion regarding the importance of obtaining American capital. Their belief that American capital might be available for the construction of Manchukuo was, as has been suggested, based in part on the view that as United States investments in China were exceedingly small, a clash between the United States and Japan was unlikely. (It might, however, be argued that precisely because American investments in China were so small, the United States government had greater latitude for action.) Moreover, they thought that because of the limited nature of American investments in China, American businessmen would welcome the new opportunities opened to them in Manchuria. Presumably it was considerations of this kind that moved Japanese business leaders to return repeatedly to the idea of economic cooperation with the United States in Manchuria, despite the deepening hostility between the United States and Japan that resulted from the Sino-Japanese War.

When Japan signed the Tripartite Pact, however, and thereby posed a direct challenge to Anglo-Saxon domination of world markets, any possibility of a compromise between Japan and the United States concerning their interests in

China was destroyed. Even so, Japanese-American cooperation in China would have meant only the exploitation of a semi-colonial area and, in the last analysis, the greatest obstacle to such cooperation was the growth of Chinese nationalism, given impetus by the Manchurian Incident and the Sino-Japanese War. China's resistance brought about the isolation of Japan internationally and changed the world situation so that a Japanese conflict with Great Britain and the United States became virtually inevitable.

Furthermore, at the time the question of American capital arose in Japan, the decision making process in governmental, military, and financial circles was in a state of extreme chaos. This situation had an adverse effect not only on the issue of using American capital but on all important decision making in wartime Japan. On the surface the Japanese political structure appeared unified and strong, but in reality it was constantly subjected to a variety of internal stresses that weakened its capacity for decision making. Japanese politics of the prewar period leaves the observer with a painful awareness that, as a rule, errors in setting goals and in selecting means to achieve those goals inevitably undermine the decision making process.

IV

In 1936 the second "General Outline of a Program for the Economic Construction of Manchukuo" was adopted and blueprints were drawn up for the first five year industrial plan, to begin in 1937 with an initial funding of about 2.5 billion yen. With the outbreak of war between China and Japan the following year, the plan was completely revised to stress mining and manufacturing industries, and total funding was increased to 4.8 billion yen. As military requirements made necessary further expansion of production, the plan was again revised upward, until the total reached 6.06 billion yen, of which Japan was to supply 3.04 billion and Manchukuo 1.69 billion, with the remaining 1.33 billion yen to be met with foreign capital. At the time of this second revision it was estimated that, based on the Japan-Manchukuo-Italy Trade Agreement of August 1938 and the revised Japan-Manchukuo-Germany Trade Agreement of September, Manchuria's annual foreign exchange earnings would total about 150 million yen; an American capital inflow of 600 million yen into the Manchuria Heavy Industries Development Corporation was also anticipated. But in the end, as we have noted, Manchukuo's industrial plans had to depend solely upon investment from Japan.

In November 1940 the "General Outline of a Program for the Economic Construction of Japan, Manchukuo, and China" was promulgated. This ambitious program projected the creation within ten years of a self-supporting, self-sufficient, integrated Japan-Manchukuo-China bloc. With the outbreak of the war in the Pacific, however, the plan ended in complete fiasco.

Actual investments in Manchuria during the 1937-41 period were divided among the government of Manchukuo, the Manchuria Heavy Industries Development Corporation and the South Manchuria Railway Company, and a number of "national policy" companies (see Table 5, Appendix I).

At the beginning of the period government securities, denominated in Japanese yen and issued through the Industrial Bank of Manchukuo (established in December 1936) and the Central Bank of Manchukuo, were an increasingly important means of acquiring investment funds. Nevertheless, these securities amounted to slightly less than 20 percent of all funds invested during the period and represented government investment in various industrial development programs that did not take business profits as the major investment criterion.

Soon after Nissan transferred its head office to Hsinking in the South Manchuria Railway zone in November 1937 and began operations anew as the Manchukuo-registered Manchuria Heavy Industries Development Corporation, it doubled its capitalization to 450 million yen, with the entire amount guaranteed by the Manchukuo government. When the revised Five Year Industrial Plan was implemented, the corporation planned to raise 6 billion yen from various sources, with 300 million yen being supplied by foreign capital. Escalation of the war prevented the introduction of American capital, however, and Manchukuo proved to be an uncertain source of supply for another projected 900 million yen. From 1939 on the corporation was forced to rely principally on the Japanese money market, and that year a syndicate was formed to underwrite the debentures issued by the South Manchuria Railway Company and the Manchuria Heavy Industries Development Corporation.

In this way the Manchuria Heavy Industries Development Corporation became the most important route for investment in Manchuria. In the process of fund raising, one of its most notable methods involved the transfer to the corporation of Nissan equity investments in Japan proper. During 1939 and 1940 55.8 million yen was raised in this way. For the purpose of selling its stocks, valued at 400 million yen in June 1941, the corporation set up the Manchukuo Investment Securities Company to capitalize these stocks over a four year period.

The funds invested by the corporation as of the end of November 1941 totaled 1.498 billion yen, according to the figures of the Closed Institutions Liquidation Commission (see Table 6, Appendix I), and extended to thirty-two affiliated companies. The corporation's direct investment in these companies is shown in Table 7.

With the establishment of the corporation, the South Manchuria Railway Company focused its attention upon railroads and ancillary industries. New investment during the period is outlined in Table 8.

Other so-called "national policy companies" in Manchukuo raised capital funds by issuing debentures in financial markets in Japan. These included the Manchuria Telegraph and Telephone Company (established in 1933), the Manchuria Electric Industries Company (November 1934), the Manchuria Colonial Development Company (August 1937), and the Manchuria-Yalu River Hydroelectric Power Plant (September 1939). In addition, influential businessmen in Japan proper invested in Manchuria through equity participation in local corporations (see Table 9).[21]

APPENDIX I
TABLES

TABLE 1

INVESTMENT IN CHINA BY THE GREAT POWERS
AT THE END OF 1930
(in 000s of U.S. dollars)

Country	Business Investment	Loans to the Government	Advances to Chinese Companies	Total	Percent
Great Britain	963,400	225,800	––	1,189,200	36.7
Japan	874,100	224,100	38,700	1,136,900	35.1
Soviet Union	273,200	––	––	273,200	8.4
United States	155,100	41,700	––	196,800	6.1
France	95,000	97,400	––	192,400	5.9
Belgium	41,000	48,000	––	89,000	2.7
Germany	75,000	12,000	––	87,000	2.7
Netherlands	10,000	18,700	––	28,700	0.9
Italy	4,400	42,000	––	46,400	1.4
Scandinavia (three countries)	2,000	800	––	2,800	0.1
TOTAL:	2,493,200	710,500	38,700	3,242,400	100.0

Source: Higuchi Hiroshi, *Nihon no tai-Shi tōshi kenkyū* (A Study of Japanese Investment in China) (Tokyo, 1939), p. 602.

TABLE 2

NET INCREASE IN INVESTMENT IN MANCHURIA

	1932 (¥1000) (%)	1933 (¥1000) (%)	1934 (¥1000) (%)	1935 (¥1000) (%)	1936 (¥1000) (%)	Total (¥1000) (%)
Capital by Source						
South Manchuria Railway	65,000 66.9%	81,200 53.7%	166,000 61.1%	246,340 65.1%	133,205 50.6%	691,745 59.5%
South Manchuria Railway including affiliated companies	(65,000) (66.9%)	(81,200) (53.7%)	(188,000) (69.2%)	(266,350) (70.3%)	(191,705) (72.9%)	(792,255) (68.2%)
Others	12,203 12.5%	40,045 26.5%	95,675 35.2%	60,858 16.1%	91,190 34.7%	299,971 25.9%
Government of Manchukuo	20,000 20.6%	30,000 19.8%	10,000 3.7%	71,400 18.8%	38,600 14.7%	170,000 14.6%
TOTAL	97,203 100.0%	151.245 100.0%	271,675 100.0%	378,598 100.0%	262,995 100.0%	1,161,716 100.0%

Capital by Method	1932 (¥1000) (%)	1933 (¥1000) (%)	1934 (¥1000) (%)	1935 (¥1000) (%)	1936 (¥1000) (%)	Total (¥1000) (%)
Public Debentures	20,000 20.6%	30,000 19.8%	10,000 3.7%	71,400 18.9%	38,600 14.7%	170,000 14.6%
Company Debentures	20,000 20.6%	21,900 14.5%	148,450 54.6%	160,475 42.4%	205,400 78.1%	556,225 47.9%
Paid-in Capital (Equity stock)	37,203 38.3%	99,345 65.7%	101,225 37.3%	57,983 15.3%	95,440 36.3%	391,196 33.7%
Public Subscription	–– ––	–– ––	–– ––	340 0.1%	17,205 6.5%	17,545 1.5%
Loans	20,000 20.6%	–– ––	12,000 4.4%	88,400 23.3%	-93,650 -35.6%	26,750 2.3%
Industrial Capital as part of Total Capital above	77,203 79.4%	121,245 80.2%	261,675 96.3%	307,198 81.1%	224,395 85.3%	991,716 85.4%

Source: Report of the Research Department, Manchurian Affairs Office, quoted in Nihon Kōgyō Ginkō Rinji Shiryō Shitsu (Industrial Bank of Japan, Special Historical Documents Section), ed., Nihon Kōgyō Ginkō goiūnenshi (A Fifty Year History of the Industrial Bank of Japan) (Tokyo, 1957), pp. 292-93.

TABLE 3

AFFILIATED COMPANIES OF THE SOUTH
MANCHURIA RAILWAY COMPANY

1933: Shōwa Steel Works takes over management of Anshan Iron Works (May)

Manchuria Chemical Industries Co. (established in May)

Japan-Manchuria Magnesium Co. (October)

1934: Manchuria Petroleum Co. (February)

Manchuria Gold Mining Co. (May)

Fushun Cement Co. (July)

Dōwa Automobile Industries (March)

Manchuria Electric Industries Co. (November)

1935: Manchuria Lead Mining Co. (June)

Manchuria Mining Development Co. (August)

1936: Manchuria Soda Co. (May)

Manchuria Light Metals Manufacturing Co. (November)

TABLE 4

ZAIBATSU INVESTMENT IN MANCHUKUO

Year	Company	Date Established	Subscription (yen)	Investors
1932	Manchuria Aviation	Sept. 1932	30,000,000	Government of Manchukuo, Mitsubishi, Sumitomo
1933	Ta-t'ung Colliery	Dec. 1933	authorized capital 12,000,000	Asano
1934	Manchuria Petroleum	Feb. 1934	40,000,000	Mitsubishi Mines, Mitsui Trading Co., Nihon Oil
	Dōwa Automobile Industries	March 1934		South Manchuria Railway, Mitsubishi Heavy Industries
	Manchuria Arsenal	May 1934	20,000,000	Nihon Life Insurance
	Manchuria Cement	May 1934	10,000,000	Iwaki Cement, Asano Cement
	Japan-Manchuria Flour Mill	June 1934	10,000,000	Japan Flour, Mitsui Trading Co.
	Manchuria Sumitomo Steel Tubing	Sept. 1934	30,000,000	Sumitomo Metal

Year	Company	Date Established	Subscription (yen)	Investors
1935	Manchuria Onoda Cement	May 1935	5,000,000	Onoda Cement
	Japan-Manchuria Steel Tubing	June 1935	50,000,000	Nihon Steel Tubing
	Manchuria Mitsubishi Machinery	Nov. 1935	20,000,000	Mitsubishi Heavy Industries, Mitsubishi Electrical Machinery
	Manchuria Kubota Cast Steel Tubing	Dec. 1935	5,000,000	Kubota Iron Works
	Manchuria Sugar Manufacturing	Dec. 1935	20,000,000	Dai Nihon Sugar Manufacturing, Taiwan Sugar Manufacturing, and others
1936	Harbin Cement	Feb. 1936	10,000,000	Onoda Cement
	Manchuria Cast Steel Works	March 1936	10,000,000	Kobe Steel Manufacture
	Manchuria Salt Industry	April 1936	25,000,000	Dai Nihon Salt Industry, Asahi Glass
	Manchuria Pulp Manufacturing	May 1936	10,000,000	Mitsubishi Paper Manufacturing
	Mukden Arsenal	July 1936	25,000,000	Ōkura, Mitsui Trading Co.
	Japan-Manchuria Pulp Manufacturing	Sept. 1936	10,000,000	Ōji Paper Manufacturing
	Manchuria Light Metals Manufacturing	Nov. 1936	80,000,000	South Manchuria Railway, Sumitomo Metals, Shōwa Electric Works, Nihon Sōda, and others
	Manchuria Communications Machinery	Dec. 1936	6,000,000	Japan Electric

TABLE 5

NET INCREASE IN INVESTMENT IN MANCHURIA

	1932-36 Total (¥1,000,000) (%)	1937	1938	1939	1940	1941[1]	1937-41 Total
Government of Manchukuo [channels][2]	170	75	111	117	262	230	(565)[3] 795
	14.6	21.6	25.3	10.7	25.9	16.2	(19.5) 18.4
South Manchuria Railway Company	692	167	79	290	343	377	(879) 1,256
	59.6	48.1	18.0	26.3	34.0	26.5	(30.3) 29.0
Manchuria Heavy Industries Development Corp.[4]	— —	10	58	316	145	816	(529) 1,345
	— —	2.9	13.3	28.6	14.4	57.3	(18.3) — —
Others	299	95	190	379	259	— —	(923) 923
	25.8	27.4	43.4	34.4	25.7	— —	(31.9) — —
TOTAL	1,161	347	438	1,102	1,009	1,423	(2,896) 4,319
	100.0	100.0	100.0	100.0	100.0	100.0	100.0
Total Japanese overseas investment[5] (¥1,000,000)		844	1,190	1,176	1,408	1,628	
Percentage of total overseas investment		41%	37%	94%	72%	87%	

[1]Source: Manchurian Affairs Office release.

[2]Government of Manchukuo [channels] means the Central Bank of Manchukuo and the Industrial Bank of Manchukuo.

[3]Figures in parentheses indicate the totals for 1937-40.

[4]In 1941 "Others" are included in Manchuria Heavy Industries Development Corporation.

[5]Source: Ōkurashō-Nihon Ginkō (Finance Ministry and Bank of Japan), comps., *Zaisei keizai tokei nenpō* (Yearbook of Financial and Economic Statistics) (Tokyo, 1948).

Source: Report of the Research Department, Manchurian Affairs Office, quoted in *Nihon Kōgyō Ginkō gojūnenshi*, pp. 408-09.

TABLE 6

INVESTMENTS OF THE MANCHURIA HEAVY INDUSTRIES
DEVELOPMENT CORPORATION

Year ending	Amount (in ¥1000)
November 1938	250,236
November 1939	638,471
November 1940	1,123,303
November 1941	1,498,039
November 1942	1,781,639
November 1943	2,363,770
November 1944	3,258,502
November 1945	4,174,711

TABLE 7

COMPANIES CONNECTED WITH THE MANCHURIA HEAVY INDUSTRIES
DEVELOPMENT CORPORATION (May 1945)
(¥1000)

Company	Est.	Authorized Capital	Paid-up Capital	Direct Investment by MHID Corp.	Other Principal Stock Holders
Manchuria Iron Works	April 1944	740,000	640,000	475,000	Ōkuragumi, South Manchuria Railway, Government of Manchukuo*
Fuhsin Coal Mine	Feb. 1943	220,000	220,000	220,000	
Manchuria Aircraft Manufacturing	June 1938	200,000	175,000	175,000	
Hao-kang Coal Mine	Feb. 1943	170,000	170,000	170,000	
Manchuria Mining	Feb. 1938	150,000	150,000	150,000	
Manchuria Light Metals Manufacturing	Nov. 1936	200,000	140,000	138,100	Sumitomo Metal, Shōwa Electric Works, Nihon Soda, South Manchuria Railway
Mishan Coal Mine	July 1941	200,000	100,000	100,000	
Manchuria Coal Mine	May 1934	100,000	100,000	100,000	

Company	Est.	Authorized Capital	Paid-up Capital	Direct Investment by MHID Corp.	Other Principal Stock Holders
Manchuria Automobile Manufacturing	May 1939	100,000	75,000	75,000	
Sian Coal Mine	Feb. 1943	70,000	70,000	70,000	
Manchuria Heavy Machinery	May 1940	50,000	50,000	45,000	
Pen-chi Region Coal Mine	Nov. 1942	50,000	50,000	44,031	
Lungyen Iron Ore Mine	July 1939	180,000	108,000	36,000	
Antung Light Metals	April 1944	200,000	100,000	25,000	North China Development, Manchuria Light Metal, Sumitomo Chemical, Sumitomo Co. (head office)
Chalai Coal Mine	Nov. 1941	50,000	25,000	25,000	
Others (twenty companies)		278,000	218,000	131,658	
TOTALS (35 companies)		2,958,000	2,391,000	1,979,789	

*Manchuria Iron Works was a joint venture company managed by three companies: Shōwa Steel Works, Pen-chi-lu Coal and Iron Co., and Tung-pien-tao Development.

Source: Report by the Closed Institutions Liquidation Commission, in *Nihōn Kōgyō Ginkō gojūnenshi*, p. 42.

TABLE 8

NEW INVESTMENT BY THE SOUTH MANCHURIA RAILWAY

The Fuchow Mining Company	August 1937
The Manchuria Colonial Development Company	August 1937
The Dairen Shipbuilding Company	August 1937
The Manchuria Bean Stalk Pulp Company	September 1937
The North China Transportation Company	April 1939
The Manchuria Special Paper Manufacturing Company	March 1939
The Ta-t'ung Coal Mine	January 1940

TABLE 9

INVESTMENT IN MANCHURIA BY BUSINESS FIRMS OF JAPAN PROPER

Year	Company	Date	Subscription (¥ 1 million)	Investors
1937	Manchuria Synthetic Fuels	August	50	Government of Manchukuo, Mitsui Mining, Mitsui Trading
	Kang-te Mining	October	10	Kanebō Spinning
	Manchuria Foundry	October	10	Nihon Life Insurance, Manchuria Arsenal
	Mukden Manufacturing	October	5	Tokyo Shibaura Electric
	Kyōwa Industries	November	10	Fujikoshi Steel Materials
1938	Manchuria Hitachi Manufacturing	March	10	Hitachi Manufacturing
	Manchuria Bearing Industries	March	8	Tōyō Bearing
	Eastern Manchuria Industries	March	50	Dai Nihon Cotton Spinning
	Manchuria Vehicle	May	20	Nihon Vehicles, Mitsubishi Heavy Industries, Hitachi Manufacturing, Sumitomo Metals
	Manchuria Oils and Fats	June	6	Nihon Oil and Fats
	Manchuria Electric Chemicals Industries	October	100	Government of Manchukuo, Manchuria Electric Chemicals Industries
	Pen-chi-lu Special Steel	October	10	Ōkura
1939	Chinchou Pulp	February	30	Ōji Paper Manufacturing
	Manchuria Coal Liquefaction Research Institute	August	10	Kobe Steel
	Kirin Synthetic Oil	September	200	Government of Manchukuo, Teikoku Fuel, Nihon Nitrogen
	Tōyō Synthetic Fiber	September	10	Tōyō Cotton Spinning
1940	Shōtoku Mining	February	6	Mitsubishi Mines
	Antung Cement	March	8	Onoda Cement
	Manchuria Soybean Chemical Industries	June	30	Nihon Oil and Fats, Shinkō Rayon, Tōyō Cotton Spinning, Kureha Cotton Spinning
1941	Manchuria Powder Industries	February	8	Nihon Powder Manufacturing, Mukden Arsenal

APPENDIX II

BIOGRAPHIES OF MEMBERS OF THE JAPAN ECONOMIC FEDERATION ATTENDING LUNCHEON FOR JOHN F. O'RYAN, JUNE 29, 1940
(major positions only are cited)

Akashi Teruo
President, Daiichi Bank
Director, Tokyo Savings Bank
Shibusawa Affiliated Concern
Tokyo Commercial Inquiry Association
Auditor, South Seas Colonization Co.
Bank of Japan
Executive, Tōyō Colonization Co.
Chief executive, Tokyo Clearing House
Executive, Tokyo Bankers Association
Vice president, Economic Association League

Aoki Kamatarō
Adviser, Nagoya Chamber of Commerce and Industry
President, Aichi Watch and Electric Machine Co.
Tōhō Chemical Industry Co.
Chūbu Trade Promotion Co.
Nagoya Sightseeing Hotel Co.
Director, Chūō Trust Co.
Hokkaido Development Co.
Fukuju Life Insurance Co.
Nihon Group Life Insurance Co.

Ayukawa Gisuke
President, Manchuria Heavy Industries Development Corp.
Former president, Nihon Industrial Co.

Fujiyama Aiichirō
President, Japan Chamber of Commerce and Industry
Tokyo Chamber of Commerce and Industry
Nittō Chemical Industry Co.
Fujiyama Affiliated Concern
Dai Nihon Sugar Manufacturing Co.
Hokkaido Sugar Manufacturing Co.
Director, Shinkō Nitrogen Industry Co.
Mitsukoshi Co.

Tōhō Metal Smelting Co.
Manchuria Sugar Manufacturing Co.
Kokka Conscription Insurance Co.
Taiwan Pulp Industry Co.
Chōsen Chemical Industry Co.
Eastern Manchuria Industry Co.
Nihon Kyōdō Securities Co.
Japan-China Life Insurance Co.
Chūō Sugar Manufacturing Co.
Nihon Special Steel Pipe Co.
Chief director, Nihon Sugar Manufacturers Association
Chairman, Nihon Trade National Service League
Vice chairman, South Seas Association
Japan-Manchukuo Business Council

Gō Seinosuke (Baron)
Cabinet consultant
Member, House of Peers
Adviser, Finance Ministry
Japan Chamber of Commerce and Industry
Tokyo Chamber of Commerce and Industry
Chairman, Board of Directors, Nihon Group Life Insurance Co.
Adviser, China-Japan Corporation
Nihon Yūsen
Kokusai Transportation Co.
Tōyō Hemp Spinning Co.
Kawasaki Ship Building Co.
Executive director, Japan Industrialists Club
Chairman, Japan-Manchukuo Business Council
Japan Association of Industrial Organizations
Nihon Trade Promotion Council
Japan Economic Federation

Haraguchi Hatsutarō (Lieutenant General)
Member of House of Representatives and former aide to the Japanese
plenipotentiary to the Washington Conference

Hatsuta Yoshiaki
Member, House of Peers
President, Tokyo Export Promotion Co.
Chairman, Board of Directors, Tōbu Railway Co.
Head, Japan Division, East Asia Economic Council
Chairman, Japan-Manchukuo Business Council
Director, Imperial Rule Assistance Association

President, Japan Chamber of Commerce and Industry
   Tokyo Chamber of Commerce and Industry
Former vice president, South Manchuria Railway Co.
Former colonial affairs minister
Former minister of commerce and industry

Ichinomiya Reitarō
   Former director, Yokohama Specie Bank

Izaka Takashi
   Adviser, Yokohama Chamber of Commerce and Industry
   President, Yokohama Fire and Marine Insurance Co.
      Taisei Co.
      Nihon Aluminum Co.
      Tokyo Gas Co.
      Kagaku Kōgyō Chemical Co.
      Yokohama Kōshin Bank
   Chairman, Board of Directors, Tokyo Bay Electric Power Co.
      Fujisawa Golf Co.
   Managing director, Japan Industrialists Club

Kabayama Aisuke (Count)
   Member, House of Peers
   President, Chiyoda Fire Insurance Co.
   Chairman, Board of Directors, Nihon Steel Manufacturing Co.
   President, America-Japan Society
   Director, International Council for the Promotion of Culture
      Mitsui Hōon Foundation
   Former aide to Japanese plenipotentiary to London Naval Conference

Kadono Jūkurō
   Member, Tokyo Chamber of Commerce and Industry
   President, Tokyo High Speed Railway Co.
      Tōyō Spinning Co.
   Chairman, Board of Directors, Nihon Kyōritsu Fire Insurance Co.
      Nihon Telephone and Telegraph Co.
      Tachikawa Airplane Manufacturing Co.
      Keihin Electric Railway Co.
   Vice president, Ōkura Gumi
   Adviser, Manchuria Ōkura Trading Co.
   Director, Japan Economic Federation
      Japan Industrialists Club

Kashiwagi Hideshige
  Consultant to Foreign Exchange Bureau, Finance Ministry
  Vice president, Yokohama Specie Bank
  Director, Japan-France Bank
    Nihon Silk Yarn Control Co.

Matsumoto Kenjirō
  Adviser, Tobata Chamber of Commerce and Industry
  President, Kurosaki Ceramic Industry
    Kyushu Electric Industry Co.
    Ryuhō Railway Co.
  Chairman, Board of Directors, Kyushu Corporation
    Kyushu Steel Manufacturing Co.
    Kyushu Hydroelectric Co.
    Kasui Mining Co.
    Shōwa Coal Co.
    Wakamatsu Harbor Works Co.
  Director, Mitsui Trust Co.
    Nihon Iron Manufacturing Co.
    Nihon Group Life Insurance Co.
    Japan Industrialists Club

Miyoshi Shigemichi
  President, Mitsubishi Oil Co.
  Director, Ōgimachi Tanker Co.
    Mitsubishi Trust Co.
    Nihon Yūsen Co.
    Mitsubishi Steel Materials Co.
    Asahi Glass Co.
  Auditor, Central China Development Co.
  Executive director, Japan Industrialists Club
  Former president, Mitsubishi Iron Manufacturing Co.
  Former director, Mitsubishi Shipbuilding Co.

Mori Kōzō
  Executive director, Yasuda Family Corporation
  Chairman, Board of Directors, Yasuda Building Co.
  Director, Yasuda Trust Co.
    Mitsui Trust Co.
    Kyushu Electric Power Co.
    Kumamoto Electric Co.
    Asano Cement Co.
  Auditor, Kokusai Electric Communications Co.
    Hokkaido Synthetic Oil Co.

South Manchuria Railway Co.
Former president, Bank of Taiwan
Former vice president, Yasuda Bank
Former vice president, Economic Association League

Morimura Ichizaemon (Baron)
 President, Morimura Industry Co.
  Morimura Gumi
 Chairman, Board of Directors, Fuji Electric Power Co.
 Director, Yokohama Specie Bank
  Tokyo Shibaura Electric Co.
  Tokyo Golf Co.
  Tōyō Ceramics Co.
  Nihon Insulator Co.
  Shōwa Rubber Co.
  Daiichi Life Insurance Co.
 Auditor, Mitsubishi Bank
  Meiji Sugar Manufacturing Co.
  Hodogaya Golf Co.
  Tōa Dōbunkai (East Asia Common Culture Association)
 Vice chairman, Board of Trustees, Japan Industrialists Club

Nagai Matsuzō
 Chief director, International Council for the Promotion of Culture
 Director, Dai Nihon Athletic Association
 Former vice foreign minister
 Former member of Japanese delegation to London Naval Conference

Nanjō Kaneo
 Adviser to president, Tokyo Chamber of Commerce and Industry
 Director, Central China Development Co.
 Consultant, Tōyō Carrier Industry Co.
  Tōyō-Otis Elevator Co.
  Mitsui Combine
 Former chairman, Board of Directors, Taishō Marine Fire Insurance Co.
 Former director, Tōyō Rayon Co.
  Tōyō Cotton Co.

Sawada Setsuzō
 Executive director, World Economy Research Institute
 Former envoy extraordinary to the United States
 Former head, Japan Office, League of Nations

Shimada Katsunosuke
Chairman, Board of Directors, Hokkaido Coal Mining and Steamship Co.
Nihon Iron Manufacturing Co.
Nihon Colonial Agriculture and Forestry Co.
Tropical Industry Co.
Former director, Mitsui Trading Co.
Former executive director, Mitsui General Partnership Co.

Takashima Seiichi
Managing director, Japan Economic Federation
Auditor, Yanagi Manufacturing Co.
Manchuria Lead Mining Co.

Tsushima Juichi
Vice president, Bank of Japan
Former vice minister of finance

Yamamuro Sōbun
Chairman, Board of Directors, Mitsubishi Trust Co.
Mitsubishi Realty Co.
Director, Mitsubishi Bank
Auditor, Mitsubishi Heavy Industry Co.
Mitsubishi Electric Co.
Nihon Kasei Chemical Industry Co.
Tokyo Marine Fire Insurance Co.
Mitsubishi Mining Co.
President, Trust Association

Yūki Toyotarō
Member, House of Peers
President, Bank of Japan
Director, Imperial Rule Assistance Association
Former finance minister
Adviser, Finance Ministry
Executive, Japan Industrialists Club
Former executive director, Yasuda Family Corp.
Former president, Nihon Industrial Bank
Former vice president, Japan-France Bank
Former executive, China Exchange Bank

THE ACTIVITIES OF THE JAPAN ECONOMIC FEDERATION

Nakamura Hideichirō

Translated by Teruko Craig

I

The Japan Economic Federation (Nihon Keizai Renmeikai) was instrumental in shaping the views of important figures in the Japanese financial world on matters pertaining to Japanese-American economic relations and exerted great influence on the government's economic policies toward the United States.[1] It was established in 1921 by leaders of the Japanese business community who felt a need for Japan, as a rapidly industrializing nation, to be represented in the International Chambers of Commerce. Its founders hoped that the federation, as spokesman for their views on domestic and foreign economic problems, would have a significant effect on the government's economic policies. Article 3 of the federation's statutes describe its purposes as follows:

> ... in order to promote the progress of the nation and the development of its industries, [the federation will] investigate and discuss matters pertaining to finance and economics; study opinions presented by its members, formulate thereby the views of the federation, and, when necessary, work toward their implementation; and in regard to international economic problems, arrive at harmonious solutions through cooperation with business groups in various countries.[2]

The leadership of the federation was drawn largely from the major corporations in Japan, the zaibatsu. Its president from April 1928 was Dan

Takuma, chairman of the board of directors of Mitsui Gōmei, and its membership, which numbered 660 in 1930, included many influential businessmen.

It would be wrong, however, to regard the Japan Economic Federation as representing all the various economic interests in Japan. There were a number of other organizations that performed a similar function, the most influential of which were the regionally-based chambers of commerce (shōgyō kaigisho, later shōkō kaigisho) established in 1878, which by the 1920s had expanded into a nationwide federated organization. In contrast to European and American chambers of commerce, which are private federations established to protect regional commercial and industrial interests and to communicate their views to the government and the nation as a whole, the Japan Chamber of Commerce was organized to mold opinions within private business circles for the purposes of the state, and the central government accordingly had a strong voice in its affairs.[3] It was a legally constituted body which exacted compulsory membership and compulsory dues and whose operations were centered on medium and small businesses. There also existed many industry-based trade associations, linked together in a national federation. This was composed largely of middle and small businesses, however, and its primary function was to prevent the proliferation of poor quality goods.

In contrast to these were the Textile Federation (Bōseki Rengōkai) and other autonomous industrial organizations dominated by big business. Somewhat in the nature of cartels or employers associations, they served mainly to represent the interests of large companies in their respective industries and seem never to have expanded into comprehensive economic organizations.[4] The fact that large industries had economic organizations separate from those of medium and small businesses reflects the dual structure of Japan's prewar economy. In addition, employers associations never developed to the same degree as labor unions, and not until 1931 was an organization of this kind—the National Federation of Industrial Organizations (Zenkoku Sangyō Dantai Rengō-kai)—formed.

In short, the Japan Economic Federation was merely one among many similar groups. Nevertheless, since together with the Chamber of Commerce it composed the domestic committee of the International Chambers of Commerce and in actuality was the dominant force on the committee, it came to be the major spokesman for economic organizations in Japan.[5]

Yet it would be difficult to say that the Japan Economic Federation functioned democratically to represent the wishes of a majority of its members. Leadership theoretically reposed in an executive board (jōmu rijikai), but in practice decision making seems to have been controlled by Inoue Junnosuke, president of the Bank of Japan and later finance minister. Takashima Seiichi, the director of the Executive Office, once commented that Inoue "had the power of chairman without the title."[6]

In 1928 the federation was reorganized. Although the executive board was retained, it soon became merely a formalistic entity with the actual administrative tasks being performed by a standing committee (jōnin iinkai) whose members were selected from the ranks of the executive board by the committee chairman. Thus, important decisions tended to be made by a tiny minority within the federation.[7] And at times even the director of the Executive Office was not present at their meetings.

On the other hand, decisions of highest consequence to Japanese business were not usually made within the federation itself but in gatherings of business leaders such as the Yōkakai (Eighth Day Club),[8] the Banchōkai (Banchō Club), and later the Hoshigaoka Kondankai (Hoshigaoka Forum). Takashima has written that the Yōkakai "had no connection whatever with the Economic Federation, but in practice it exerted a considerable amount of influence." Nakajima Kumakichi, a member of the federation's standing committee, has described the founding of the Yōkakai as follows:

> After the Economic Federation came into being, contacts between the business and political worlds became more frequent. . . . People like Wada Toyoji and Inoue Junnosuke started saying that close understanding with the political world on a day to day basis was essential, and so, with Wada as its guiding spirit, a special "detached column" (*betsudō-tai*) of the federation was formed. . . . The first meeting was held on the eighth of the month, so the group was called the Yōkakai. Membership was to be limited to ten, and on no account was it to be increased. Subsequently nine men were chosen—Inoue Junnosuke, Ikeda Seihin, Wada Toyoji, Naitō Hisahiro, Kushida Manzō, Fujiyama Raita, Fukui Kikusaburō, Gō Seinosuke, Shimura Gentarō, and myself.

The group met on the eighth day of each month at the Tokiwaya restaurant in Hamachō. Cabinet ministers and other important individuals were invited to join in their frank discussions, which Hara Takashi is said to have attended frequently. Prior to the Washington Conference Katō Tomosaburō met with them to discuss their hopes for the conference. One might say that the Yōkakai, in effect, promoted the aims of the Economic Federation and guided its ideas. The federation itself functioned not as a body for making important decisions but as a channel for expressing the desires of those at the highest levels of the financial world. Thus, it was only natural that Takashima Seiichi, who as director of the Executive Office was responsible for the actual administration of the federation, should have remarked: "The public often said that the Economic Federation was the spokesman for the zaibatsu. In my memory there is nothing whatever to support such a statement, and so whenever I heard this sort of thing, I used to have a curious feeling. . . . There were times when the zaibatsu would head the list of contributors [to the federation], but there was never a time when priority was given to them in discussing policy issues."

During the prewar period the zaibatsu possessed, especially through the activities of their foreign trade companies, an international information network that enabled them, it was said, to obtain information in advance of the press. Furthermore, they had excellent research institutes and thus required little help from other organizations. In contrast, the Economic Federation was dependent upon zaibatsu and government funds to fulfill its investigatory functions. Its staff (which in 1930 numbered twelve) frequently called together the heads of the research divisions of six major companies—the Bank of Japan, Mitsui Gōmei, Mitsubishi Gōshi, Nihon Yūsen, the Yokohama Specie Bank, and the South

Manchuria Railway Company. The federation's activities were disclosed only to its members and to the government, never to the newspapers, and not until about 1940 did articles discussing its operations begin to appear in the press.

II

Before discussing in greater detail the activities of the Japan Economic Federation, let us look at the major sources of conflict between Japanese and American industry.

The volume of Japanese cotton textile exports to the United States remained insignificant up until 1931 but grew rapidly thereafter, totaling 17,730,000 yards in 1934 and 48,330,000 yards in 1935. The resulting demands from American cotton manufacturers that limitations be placed on Japanese imports led in May 1935 to a series of public hearings held by the United States Tariff Commission, which appointed an investigating committee composed of the secretaries of state, agriculture, commerce, and labor. The committee concluded that, while restrictions on Japanese cotton textile imports were necessary, it would be best if Japan voluntarily adopted appropriate measures.

In 1936, however, Japanese imports rocketed to 73,440,000 yards, and American producers became more vociferous in their demands for thorough-going restrictions. Thereupon the American government opened negotiations with Japan, and in May Roosevelt raised the tariff on Japanese cotton textiles. But the improving economic situation and a general price rise in the United States enabled Japanese textile imports to increase despite the higher tariff, and the grievances of American producers remained unassuaged.

Fearful that the textile problem might develop into a serious domestic political issue, the administration urged producers from both countries to enter into direct talks. In January 1937 an American commission headed by C. T. Murchison, president of the American Cotton Textile Institute, went to Japan to consult with Japanese producers. A settlement was reached under which Japan agreed to restrict cotton textile exports to the United States over the next two years (until the end of 1938) to 225 million yards, and in return the American side agreed to cease calling for higher import tariffs and other restrictions on Japanese cotton goods.[9] The discussions were hailed as proof that international negotiations could be conducted through nongovernmental channels, and their successful conclusion aroused great interest in other industries.[10]

Exports to the United States of Japanese "sundry" items also faced growing opposition from American producers at this time. Purchases of cheap articles such as tablecloths, accessories, toys, and chinaware had increased drastically during the 1920s as the operators of retail chain stores in the United States expanded their business.

A third area of conflict was in the automobile industry. During the 1920s and 1930s the automobile industry in Japan was dominated by Ford and General Motors, which produced automobiles with imported assembly parts through the "knocked-down" method. In 1929, when Japan-Ford produced 10,674 cars and Japan-General Motors 15,745 cars, Japanese automobile production totaled a mere 437 cars. After the Manchurian Incident expansion of domestic production came to be regarded as a necessity in order to improve

Japan's international balance of payments and provide for national defense, and the Army Ministry and the Ministry of Commerce and Industry began to study ways of increasing domestic production. About the same time the Nissan Automobile Company planned in cooperation with General Motors to produce Chevrolets in quantity in Japan, including the manufacturing of parts. Meanwhile, Japan-Ford made public a plan for a factory to handle the entire process, from the production of steel to the output of parts and the assembling of automobiles.

These activities on the part of American corporations led to the promulgation in 1936 of an Automobile Industry Law drafted by the Army Ministry and the Ministry of Commerce and Industry, which aimed at the development of the automobile industry in Japan. Classifying the automobile industry as one requiring governmental authorization, the law stipulated that such authorization could be obtained only by joint-stock corporations in which a majority of the stockholders and directors were Japanese citizens and more than half of the capital and voting rights were held by Japanese citizens. The Toyoda Automatic Loom Manufacturing Company (now the Toyota Automobile Company) and the Nissan Automobile Company were designated as authorized corporations under the law, and as a result Nissan dropped the plans for its venture with General Motors. Japan-Ford and Japan-General Motors were placed under rigid operating controls that restricted their annual production, based on their average outputs during the three years prior to August 9, 1935, to 12,360 and 9,470 cars respectively. In December 1936 tariffs were raised on imports of finished and knocked-down vehicles.[11]

Nevertheless, even after the Automobile Industry Law was passed, individual Japanese companies continued their efforts to strengthen relations with American firms. For example, as late as 1938 Nissan's parent company, the Manchuria Heavy Industries Development Corporation, drew up a plan for Nissan-Ford cooperation to supply the capital needed to import machinery for automobile production in Manchuria. The plan did not materialize, however, because it failed to obtain governmental authorization.[12]

In the oil industry, the Japanese market was dominated by Royal Dutch Shell's subsidiary, the Rising Sun Petroleum Company, and Stanvac (Standard-Vacuum Oil). Other oil refining companies, including Associated Oil (later Tidewater Oil), which owned 50 percent of Mitsubishi Oil, had to adapt to the marketing policies of these two giant firms.

About the time of the Manchurian Incident severe competition among Japanese and foreign oil companies forced down prices in the Japanese oil market. Price stability was temporarily restored when the Ministry of Commerce and Industry mediated an agreement on prices and quantities. In 1933, however, Matsukata Nisso Oil began to import oil from the Soviet Union, and the agreement fell apart.

This crisis made the Japanese government increasingly conscious of the military importance of oil reserves. In May 1933 Minister of Commerce and Industry Nakajima Kumakichi, an influential business leader, drafted two plans for control of the oil industry. The first called for a state monopoly on oil production and sales and for the buying up of foreign shares in the oil industry. The second plan was a proposal for a licensing system under which all oil imports and construction of oil refineries would require governmental authorization. In order to ensure a constant supply of crude oil, the plan also required authorized companies to maintain fixed stockpiles of oil.

The first plan proved impractical, since it would have excluded from Japan all foreign oil, then Japan's only source of supply. Consequently, in March 1934 a Petroleum Industry Law was passed providing for the licensing of refiners and importers of oil, setting quotas for oil refining, imports, and sales, and requiring that both importers and refiners maintain stockpiles amounting to one-half of their annual imports.

Under the new law Japanese oil companies enjoyed preferential treatment and by the second half of 1939 came to control 50 percent of the domestic market. The foreign firms protested the quota system and the stockpile requirements, and the American government lodged an official protest, but in the end they were forced to operate under the quota system. However, they never maintained the stipulated oil stockpiles, although they agreed to maintain supplies up to the "three months need" then considered optimum.[13] In short, despite passage of the law, foreign control of the Japanese oil market did not completely disappear.

Economic relations between Japan and the United States, therefore, presented a complex picture. And although there were many sources of tension, business leaders had no reason to fear they might lead to war with the United States. As we shall see, most business leaders were optimistic concerning the future of economic relations between the two nations. Nevertheless, as the situation in the automobile and oil industries indicated, Japanese industrialization could only increase the contradictions between Japanese and American industry. Continuing cooperation could have been ensured only if drastic solutions to these contradictions could have been found, but the major business leaders in Japan failed to work vigorously for such solutions.

III

The Japan Economic Federation first gave signs of coming to grips with the problems that existed in Japan's economic relations with the United States when it organized in 1934 the Japanese-American Trade Council (Nichi-Bei Tsūshō Hyōgikai) as a result of the growing awareness among leaders in the financial world that positive measures would have to be adopted to deal with the problems they increasingly faced in conducting foreign trade. The federation responded to the worldwide tendency to form economic blocs through such organizations as the Japanese-American Trade Council and the Japanese-British Trade Committee.

The immediate occasion for organizing the Japanese-American Trade Council was the establishment in New York in January 1934 of the American-Japanese Trade Council to facilitate liaison and consultation between Japanese businessmen in New York (mainly the branch managers of Japanese companies and banks) and the National Foreign Trade Council, which represented the major export industries in America. The Japanese-American Trade Council was set up in Tokyo by the Japan Economic Federation to perform parallel functions.

What the federation expected of the Japanese-American Trade Council is clearly set forth in the statement issued at the council's inaugural session on June 19, 1934.[14] Looking back upon some eighty years of peaceful relations between Japan and the United States and anticipating the continuation and development of these relations, the council saw little sign "of the sort of economic competition that so often is the root of international friction." It was the duty of businessmen in both countries, the statement continued, to "strengthen these relations and ... thereby ward off the evils of economic nationalism sweeping the world and wreaking damage on nations. Precisely for this reason, it is fitting and appropriate to the demands of the times that representative businessmen of Japan and America work together for the expansion of trade and economic relations."[15]

According to the *Keizai Dantai Rengōkai zenshi*, the council not only concerned itself with issues of all kinds that arose in U.S.-Japanese trade, which were discussed at its monthly meetings, but also with such social functions as "welcoming and sending off businessmen of both countries or entertaining visiting members of American organizations." It further promoted personal contacts between Japanese and American businessmen, and as a result, "whenever tense situations involving tariffs and restrictions on imports arose, businesslike opinions on these issues were exchanged in the friendly atmosphere of council meetings, and American businessmen living in Japan did their best to convey the true intentions of Japan to their own country." Communication between the economic representatives of both governments was facilitated by the presence at monthly meetings of the chief of the Japanese Foreign Ministry's International Trade Bureau and of the American consul general, commercial attaché, and other consular representatives.

In the period prior to the Marco Polo Bridge Incident in 1937, the most important problems to which the council addressed itself were the issue of telegraph fees, the movement in the United States to prevent the import of Japanese goods, the controversy over Japan textile exports to the United States, and the petition to lower import duties on vegetable and fruit produce from California. Although the council could not solve "problems that struck at the very root of the policies of the respective governments," the *Keizai Dantai Rengōkai zenshi* acknowledged, in many instances when unnecessary problems arose, as for example over procedural questions, the council "was able to be 100 percent effective in communicating ideas and seeking solutions."[16]

In 1935 the federation and the council joined with the Japan Trade Association (Nihon Bōeki Kyōkai) and the Tokyo and Yokohama chambers of commerce to welcome the American Economic Mission to China and Japan, an event the *Keizai Dantai Rengōkai zenshi* viewed as one of the federation's most important activities. The significance that both the government and financial circles in Japan attached to the visit is brought out by the careful preparations that were made at the highest levels of government and industry. The mission, which arrived in Japan on April 4, was headed by former Ambassador to Japan W. Cameron Forbes, with Charles J. Carroll, an engineer who had spent many years in China, as vice chief of the mission.[17] In addition to calling on various Japanese officials, including the prime minister, and attending official meetings, the members of the mission inspected factories that produced export goods and held talks with many Japanese businessmen.

The most important exchange of views took place over a period of three days in a series of discussions moderated by three committees: the Committee on Products, Imports and Exports, chaired by Kadono Jūkurō on the Japanese side and by Thomas Y. Wickham on the American side, discussed such matters as discriminatory Japanese duties on wheat and flour, the impact of the Japanese petroleum industry law, and the anti-Japanese immigration laws; the Committee on Exchange, Investments, and Finance, chaired by Kushida Manzō, dealt with the declining value of the yen, the effectiveness of the exchange control law, American investments in Japan, the reasons why the yen was linked to the pound rather than to the dollar, the effects of America's silver policy on China, and other related issues; the Committee on Transportation and Communications, chaired by Izaka Takashi, exchanged opinions on issues such as the American immigration laws, Japanese-American telegraph rates, America's policy on air traffic to the Far East, and the impact on the Japanese shipping industry of American shipping policies.[18]

How did Japanese financial leaders evaluate Japanese-American relations at this juncture, and what was their outlook for the future? The remarks made by Gō Seinosuke, the chairman of the Economic Federation, are very revealing:

> The goods that are traded between the two countries are on the whole complementary; very few of them compete with the domestic products of the other country. For this reason I sincerely hope that both Japan and America will take a long-range view of their interests and that neither will embark upon such self-strangulating policies as arbitrarily raising customs duties or imposing import restrictions, which are so prevalent in other parts of the world.[19]

We find here the same idea as was expressed in the statement of the Japanese-American Trade Council—that trade relations between Japan and the United States were essentially complementary and harmonious—a view that seemed to dominate the thinking of most businessmen concerned with Japanese-American economic relations. In addition, they saw little reason for conflict over American exports to China, which consisted primarily of oil, cotton, wheat, flour, and tobacco,[20] or over American investments in China, which they hoped would increase. This desire for an expansion of American investments in China was indicated by the federation and council's request that the mission also visit Manchuria.

A similarly optimistic assessment was made the previous year by the federation's adviser Fujiyama Raita in *Keizai renmei* (Economic Federation), the bulletin of the Economic Federation:

> International relations are by nature very complex and subtle. For example, at one time it was reported that Japanese-American relations were extremely strained. But when one thinks about it calmly, Japan and America have been on friendly terms for a long time and there is no reason why their economic interests should clash. The goods each sells to common markets—China, Central

America, and South America—are completely different. Japan sells textiles and sundries, while America sells mostly machinery and the like, and so there is no fear of competition. In regard to investments in China, America and Japan admittedly have overlapping interests, but there is still no reason to compete. Nevertheless, it seemed for a time as though darkening clouds were gathering in both countries, but this too was merely an illusion bred by policy differences and emotionalism. In such cases, trying to avoid needless clashes through diplomatic and economic negotiations is never difficult. Indeed, it is the wisest course.[21]

As he departed from Tokyo, Forbes declared, "There is no doubt that this visit has produced excellent results and that friendly relations will continue between influential people in both countries." But he made it clear that the mission would also take Sino-American relations into account and would deal with America's relations with both China and Japan as an inseparable whole.[22]

Although the mission's report was not available to me,[23] an account written by Hayashi Kaoru, the acting consul in Chicago, of the 23rd annual conference of the National Trade Council on November 18-21, 1936 contains an interesting statement by W. Cameron Forbes. Replying to a comment by Yoshizawa Seijirō, the counselor of the Japanese embassy, who had stressed the basically complementary nature of Japanese-American trade relations and had set forth the opinion that differences could be solved through mutual cooperation, Forbes pointed to the growing strains in Japanese-American relations and predicted that Japanese goods would begin to encounter protective tariff barriers if Japan did not voluntarily raise the prices of its commercial products. "America cannot abandon its domestic production in favor of the products of any other country," he asserted, and "unless some sort of restriction [on cheap goods] is imposed through an agreement, sooner or later Americans will be put into the position of having to prohibit imports or having to impose prohibitive duties." He also warned against Japanese violations of the Open Door in Manchuria, where American banks and oil companies had been forced to close down. "If such instances are repeated all over China where Japan's power is felt, . . . they will destroy freedom of trade and will inevitably provoke the nations of the world."[24]

Evidence of the mission's assessment of Sino-American relations was given in another statement by Forbes at a meeting of the American-Chinese Trade Council soon thereafter. Concluding that China's unification and restoration of order was "truly amazing," he expressed the conviction of the economic mission that the United States should participate actively in China's reconstruction by facilitating trade, investments, and loans. The American government, he suggested, "is in a position to carry out truly constructive plans. For instance, the enormous amounts of purchased silver could certainly be used in ways beneficial to both China and America." Another member of the mission, Professor C. F. Remer of the University of Michigan, similarly argued that "it is precisely in opening the way for making available long-term credits that a fundamental change in the economic life of the Chinese people will be effected."

In contrast, the leaders of the Japanese financial world did not look at the problem of China as having any bearing upon Japanese-American relations, and in consequence, they tended to overemphasize the complementary nature of Japanese-American trade. In dealing with the export of capital to China they saw only the common interests of Japanese and American capital. The American economic mission, on the other hand, judged that the pro-American policies advocated in financial circles did not have wide support in Japan and would not be sufficient to restrain the actions of the military in China. Its members therefore emphasized the sources of conflict between Japanese and American capital. At the same time, however, they seem to have concluded that Japan, because of its immediate economic problems, was not likely to pose a challenge to America's Far Eastern policy.[25]

Prior to 1937 leaders of the Japanese financial world did not actively support the military's policies in China, and they urged cooperation in Japan's relations with the United States and Great Britain. As a result, the activities of the Economic Federation and the Japanese-American Trade Council were said to have been "viewed with a jaundiced eye" by the military and right-wing groups.[26] The financial world hoped that China would achieve the political and social stability that would facilitate trade and investment. Yet its leaders made little attempt to oppose the militaristic policies that had contributed to the disorder, perhaps because they viewed territorial aggrandizement as ultimately beneficial to Japan's economic expansion.[27] They apparently did not see that the prerequisite for harmonious relations with Great Britain and the United States was a China policy premised on respect for the rights of China, including Manchuria, a policy that would have meant Japanese military withdrawal from China. Had Japanese business leaders advocated such a policy, confrontation with the military would have been inevitable, and strong popular support alone could have enabled it to prevail. But public antagonism toward the zaibatsu was very deep-rooted, and only thorough-going reforms in agriculture, industry, and commerce could have countered this sentiment. At this stage, it would have been impossible to obtain unified support in the financial world for such reforms.

THE ROLE OF PRIVATE GROUPS IN THE UNITED STATES

Warren I. Cohen

The role of private groups in Japanese-American relations, 1931-1941, is examined most easily in accordance with the following periodization: (1) 1931-32, the initial crisis: Manchuria and Shanghai; (2) 1933-37, the lull: preparations for and against war; (3) 1937-39, focus on Asia: the Sino-Japanese War; (4) 1939-41, shift to Europe: World War II. In all four periods the most active organizations, with one exception, came from within the loosely defined American peace movement. Only from 1938 to 1940 did an organization peripheral to the peace movement, the American Committee for Non-Participation in Japanese Aggression (Price Committee) wage an important campaign to influence the course of American policy toward the Far East. The Price Committee was unusual not only in its focus on the Far Eastern crisis, but also in that it received financial support from and may have been inspired by the Chinese government.

As a result of this configuration, two generalizations are readily apparent. First, the study of private organizations attempting to influence the policy of the United States toward Japan, 1931-41, is largely a study of the splintering of the American peace movement. Second, because the dominant groups on both sides of most relevant issues were peace groups, the future of either China or Japan or of the Far East generally was incidental to their particularistic programs for peace. In other words, all but one of the major organizations that addressed themselves to relations between the United States and Japan in this decade were concerned primarily with issues of war and peace. They focused on the Far East only until a war came in Europe, after which China and Japan might have been forgotten but for the Tripartite Pact and the efforts of a small group of China's friends.

I

The principal group pressure in response to the incident at Mukden on September 18, 1931 was a demand from the peace movement that the United

States call upon Japan to stop its military operations. Support for this position came from individual missionaries in China and, obliquely, from missionary organizations in the United States. There was no important organized opposition to this demand for action for peace. Despite agreement on ends, once it became apparent that words would not stop Japan, the groups concerned with events in Manchuria failed to agree upon the next step. Within the peace movement there was satisfaction with American cooperation with the League of Nations and hope that this cooperation would lead to a strengthening of the peace machinery—a hope that out of Japanese aggression would come a greater American commitment to international cooperation for peace.

There remained, however, the question of how much collaboration with the League was advisable. What should the United States do if the League invoked Article 16 of the covenant calling for economic and possibly military sanctions? On the issue of sanctions, the peace movement fragmented. The division was not over what method would be most effective, but rather over how far men and women whose ultimate concern was peace could go toward the use of coercion or toward risking American involvement in war.

During the crisis over Manchuria there existed in the United States two groupings, perhaps most easily viewed as "meetings," through which elements of the peace movement attempted to coordinate activities. The largest of these, the "nonsectarian" Interorganization Council on Disarmament (ICD), contained representatives of all of the major organizations, and its offices and executive committee were filled by men and women from the Federal Council of Churches of Christ, Foreign Policy Association, League of Nations Association, National Council for the Prevention of War, Women's International League for Peace and Freedom, and several similar groups. The Interorganization Council on Disarmament served as the broadest level at which the peace movement debated and sought to take a stand on American policy during the crisis. The second "meeting" was the Emergency Peace Committee, a "board of strategy" for the self-styled "left-wing" peace societies. Membership in this group was extremely fluid, embracing sympathetic members of organizations not affiliated with the "left," but generally including representatives of the American Friends Service Committee, Fellowship of Reconciliation, Methodist Peace Commission, People's Lobby, Socialist Party, Women's International League for Peace and Freedom, and World Tomorrow.[1]

The Interorganization Council on Disarmament began discussions of the Manchurian question in September, with parallel discussions under way at Emergency Peace Committee meetings. On October 14 a boycott resolution originating at a meeting of the Emergency Peace Committee was presented to the ICD. The resolution referred to Japan's violations of the Kellogg and Nine Power pacts and called upon the president to warn Japan that the United States was prepared to cooperate with the League of Nations in an economic boycott unless Japan withdrew its troops from Manchuria. It further called upon the League to present the problem to the World Court and to investigate Japan's needs toward the end of satisfying these and those of China in a peaceful way. Although the resolution received strong support within the ICD, a motion to table it succeeded.[2]

On October 26 a similar resolution was introduced. Modified to avoid prejudging the situation, this resolution declared that if the Council of the

League of Nations should determine that the Kellogg-Briand Pact and the covenant of the League had been violated, the government of the United States should join League members in breaking off economic relations with the aggressor. The step toward a boycott was regretted but viewed as preferable to war: "to keep peace we will support such a boycott or any other plan short of military intervention." Again concern over the proposed boycott caused the resolution to be tabled. Finally it was decided to approve the boycott in principle, but to have the resolution rewritten.[3]

The basic dilemma indicated by discussions within the ICD derived from the effort to present the government with a substantive program for action in the Manchurian crisis—action which would strengthen the peace system by discouraging aggression. How was this to be done without risk of widening the war, without forcing pacifists to compromise their beliefs? Early in November the ICD considered a different approach: a call for an international commission to investigate the Manchurian crisis with a threat that the United States and members of the League would withdraw their ambassadors from any capital that refused to accept the proposal. If peace were still not restored, the United States would assure the League that it would not obstruct economic sanctions. A motion to delete the sentence on sanctions was defeated by only one vote, 23-22, and a subsequent attempt to table the sentence on sanctions lost 16-17. Clearly the division was too close for the ICD to take a stand on sanctions.[4]

By the end of November it became increasingly apparent that the ICD was not going to be able to receive a clear mandate from its membership in support of any form of sanctions. At the meeting of November 23 a resolution calling for the president to withdraw the American ambassador from Tokyo unless Japan removed its troops from Manchuria passed by a vote of 20-18, "which was not called decisive." The resolution that was adopted at this meeting indicated concern over secret diplomacy, requested that Charles G. Dawes, the American ambassador to Great Britain, be instructed to sit with the League, asked that arms shipments to both Japan and China be stopped, and opposed loans to either country as contrary to public policy. Here then, for better or worse, was the maximum program upon which men of good will could agree as the Kwantung Army rolled on in Manchuria.[5]

At the ICD meetings organizations affiliated with the Emergency Peace Committee had supplied much of the pressure for sanctions, eliciting from the chair a plea for patience from the "left-wing" groups. But the division over coercive measures had not been between "right" and "left." Certainly the "right-wing" League of Nations Association had been at least as aggressive as any other organization in advocating sanctions. Moreover, discussions within the Emergency Peace Committee indicated that the left could not unite on a program stronger than that of the ICD. In January 1932 the committee prepared a program which, for the most part, stood behind Secretary of State Henry L. Stimson's nonrecognition policy. The "radical" part of the statement was the demand that the United States end *its* intervention in Nicaragua, Haiti, and the Philippines.[6]

Perhaps most instructive was the debate inside the American section of the Women's International League for Peace and Freedom (WILPF), traditionally under the influence of the Society of Friends. In Dorothy Detzer, the executive secretary, the organization had the queen of the hotspurs, pressing incessantly for sharp action against Japan and convinced of a Japanese-American plot when Stimson chose to wait watchfully. But Miss Detzer was responsible to her national chairman, Hannah Clothier Hull, a staunch and unyielding pacifist, and to the national president, Emily Balch, who, though less rigid than Mrs. Hull, was also considerably less apocalyptic than Miss Detzer. Privately, Miss Detzer tried to convince Mrs. Hull of the acceptability of an economic boycott which, unaccompanied by a naval blockade, she contended was akin to the methods used by Gandhi. Mrs. Hull remained unmoved by the analogy but was unnerved by Miss Detzer's support of sanctions. At the National Board meeting in mid-December, Miss Detzer tried several different approaches focused around the idea of recalling the American ambassador from Japan, but she failed to convince the board.[7]

Miss Detzer's officemate Mildred Olmsted, the organization secretary, found it "intolerable" to be still and "watch our hardly wrought peace machinery crumbling under our eyes, while the State Department counsels patience and the peace leaders urge us to do nothing to hurt the feelings of the Japanese." She warned Miss Balch that Miss Detzer was discouraged and depressed: "She feels that the situation is critical and vital—the cornerstone of all our work—and yet that she can take no action because of the lack of the support of our National Board. . . ." Mrs. Olmsted drew a parallel with the American Peace Society during the World War—when that group called for vigorous prosecution of the war as the best peace measure because it would mean the end of German militarism—and advocated the same approach to Japan. Mrs. Olmsted and Miss Detzer felt that "without waiting any longer for dear old souls like Dr. Gulick [Sidney Gulick of the Federal Council of Churches, a former missionary to Japan] who think that all is well because peace sentiment in this country is growing, the Women's International League should take the lead" in demanding that the president take "vigorous and unqualified measures against Japan."[8]

Miss Balch attempted a compromise between Miss Detzer and Mrs. Hull at the January 1932 board meeting, but Miss Detzer was not pacified, voting against the successful compromise because it did not contain a condemnation of Japanese aggression, although it provided for an arms embargo and moratorium on loans to Japan. The official Women's International League position was stated in a letter from Hull and Balch to President Hoover, in which they urged action under the Kellogg and Nine Power treaties, declaring: "Critical as is the Manchurian situation, we are inclined to believe that preserving faith in the usefulness of treaties is of more far-reaching and fundamental significance."[9]

Miss Detzer took her defeat gracelessly. Within two weeks, she triumphantly informed Miss Balch that she had discussed the WILPF letter with Senator William Borah, who had agreed that Japan should have been condemned as Miss Detzer had demanded. But Borah did not satisfy her either. She tried to convince him that the time had come to break relations with Japan, refuse it loans, and institute an economic boycott so as to "isolate the conflict." On these points Borah could not be interested and Detzer announced: "He is wrong. I believe we have to have some way to deal with 19th Century Militarism."[10]

Up to this point, the eve of the Japanese navy's operations against Shanghai, of those who stood fast against sanctions the man who had expressed his position most clearly was Frederick Libby, executive secretary of the National Council for the Prevention of War. In the 1920s Libby was generally acknowledged to be the most important of the radical peace leaders; but when Miss Balch suggested that Miss Detzer discuss the Manchurian situation with him, Miss Detzer replied that "Mr. Libby has been so slow and so 'unseeing' that I personally can get no light from him."[11]

Libby's position was very carefully thought through. He was pleased that the Manchurian crisis had advanced American cooperation with the League, and in conversations, letters, and telegrams to Assistant Secretary of State James Grafton Rogers, he encouraged closer cooperation and criticized Dawes' aloofness. On the other hand, he was very concerned about the effect the emergency in Manchuria might have on other, perhaps more important parts of his program for peace. What would happen to efforts to repeal the laws providing for the exclusion of Japanese immigrants? How would the crisis affect his efforts for disarmament, which he believed to be the most crucial step toward world peace? In searching for a suitable policy, he looked favorably upon the idea of nondiscriminatory arms embargoes against belligerents, the discouraging of loans to all sides. The Japanese government had to be condemned for violating the Kellogg Pact, yet it was important to avoid the rise of anti-Japanese sentiment, for an atmosphere of hate was more conducive to an arms race than to arms limitation. Libby feared William Randolph Hearst, feared that the Hearst papers would pick up this anti-Japanese mood and inflame it into a call for war—and so he was slow to respond to Miss Detzer.[12]

At the onset of the Japanese move against Shanghai, Libby prepared a detailed and characteristic statement on Japanese policy and the program appropriate to the United States. He opened by suggesting that Japan was following "unfortunate precedents created by our own Government" and others in the dark days before the Kellogg Pact but noted that for making a mockery of treaty obligations the Japanese had been condemned by the forces of peace throughout the world. The problem was to find a policy which would "reestablish faith in the sanctity of the Peace Pact" and like agreements. But everything that Miss Detzer argued for he opposed, contending that to urge an economic boycott or to seek the withdrawal of diplomatic representatives was a move toward war. He warned that the munitions makers, shipbuilders, and airplane manufacturers were whispering of the danger of war between the United States and Japan and the consequent need for more armaments. He considered it essential that the peace groups avoid giving aid to warmongers.[13]

Libby could endorse Stimson's nonrecognition policy, for it contained no threats. Beyond that, his solution for the Manchurian situation was another dose of the cure he prescribed generally: have the United States adhere to the protocol of the World Court and join the League; bring the Soviet Union into the League; reduce armaments.[14]

Before the Japanese left Shanghai, Libby wavered once, ever so slightly. The Japanese attack on Shanghai, coming weeks after Stimson enunciated his nonrecognition policy, served to underscore the dilemma of the peace movement: words, even condemnation, did not stop armies bent upon conquest any more than appeals to world public opinion could enforce the Kellogg Pact. For the most part those in the movement were opposed to meeting force with force, and yet Japan could not be allowed to destroy the peace machinery "so hardly wrought." Some means short of force had to be found. In the autumn, as the peace societies debated and shied away from economic sanctions, Japanese troops had occupied Manchuria and there seemed no way to make them withdraw. Now, by attacking Shanghai, Japan seemed bent on conquering China proper. To many pacifists there was no choice between finding a nonviolent means to check Japan and conceding that superior force alone determined the course of relations among nations. As a result, the boycott idea was revived and for a moment seemed destined to carry the entire peace movement.

Out of the angry reaction to Japanese aggression in Shanghai came two ad hoc committees, the American Committee on the Far East Crisis and the Committee on Economic Sanctions, both identified with the right wing of the peace movement and both financed by the Twentieth Century Fund. The American Committee, aided by Clark Eichelberger of the League of Nations Association and Raymond Rich of the World Peace Foundation, attempted to arouse mass support for a consumers' boycott. They were successful in getting A. Lawrence Lowell and Newton D. Baker to spearhead a drive for signatures to a petition that called for the United States to join with the League in sanctions, and they obtained thousands of signatures but not the endorsement of the peace movement. Although Stimson denied the claim, it was generally believed that the American Committee had his encouragement. But with President Hoover unmoved and the League of Nations showing no desire to risk sanctions, the American Committee effort faded away.[15]

The Committee on Economic Sanctions followed a different mandate, seeking not to mobilize public opinion but rather for some way to make economic sanctions palatable to those who feared they would lead to war. Counting on support for the Kellogg Pact, Nicholas Murray Butler, the chairman of the committee, announced that the pact had outmoded neutrality: any nation that resorted to force in violation of its commitment under the treaty had committed an offense against all signatories. He urged that the United States call for a conference of signatories to arrange for joint economic sanctions against any nation guilty of aggression. An arms embargo against the aggressor would be effective immediately. Here was the formula that tempted even Frederick Libby.[16]

In February Libby's *Newsletter,* issued by the National Council for the Prevention of War, suggested that mild economic sanctions without naval support "might conceivably be employed" but hastened to add that the threat of using them would probably do more harm than good. After a breakfast meeting with Eichelberger, he informed his staff that he had not been converted: "Please note that I still regard the plan of getting the US to put an official economic boycott on Japanese goods as chimerical and probably an unwise attempt." On March 10, in a press release, Libby announced that Butler's plan was superior to Lowell's and worthy of serious consideration—although he suggested that Stimson's nonrecognition note was a preferable form of protest. Finally he raised the crucial question: would any of these plans stop the Japanese army? His answer was evasive, but clearly Libby did not think so. In fact, Libby had given up on getting Japan out of Manchuria or Shanghai and was verging onto a new course revealed to him by the helplessness of the American peace movement in the face of militarism abroad.[17]

Where Libby was tempted, Ray Newton, secretary of the Peace Section of the American Friends Service Committee, could not resist. In letters to Hoover and Rogers he guardedly endorsed the economic boycott. At a meeting of the Emergency Peace Committee at which he was present, that group determined to go beyond its previous stand and endorse "progressive sanctions," to be used only in cooperation with other governments and not to involve a blockade of Japan or the stoppage of food supplies. The decisive argument, offered by the Emergency Peace Committee's chairman Tucker Smith, focused again on the importance of peace groups offering practical alternatives to military action—and the group agreed that a boycott seemed less likely to lead to war than the recall of the American ambassador. Early in March Smith, accompanied by Newton and Emily Balch, went to Washington where they spoke with Allen T. Klots, Stimson's assistant. They called attention not only to their letter urging Hoover to avoid involvement in war under all circumstances, but also to the letter to Stimson in which they called for strengthening their program for peace by joining the League or the Kellogg or Washington treaty signatories in measures of economic "noncooperation" with Japan. Klots suggested that the economic measures they envisaged might lead to war, but they were adamant. Although they appreciated the dangers, they found nonrecognition wanting and suggested that economic pressure might be essential at this point.[18]

Ten days later the Emergency Peace Committee's determination dissolved. John Nevin Sayre of the Fellowship of Reconciliation, who had earlier pressed for the recall of the American ambassador and treatment of Japan as an outlaw, announced that he could not work out a series of "progressive" sanctions he could support and that "it is unwise and useless for the Emergency Peace Committee to advocate an economic boycott." For months thereafter, the committee "studied" economic sanctions. One day in January 1933, however, Smith explained that the study had been dropped in favor of a campaign for arms traffic control.[19]

At the Women's International League for Peace and Freedom, the attack on Shanghai came while Mrs. Hull was in Geneva representing the organization at the World Disarmament Conference. In her absence a majority of the National Board endorsed the Emergency Peace Committee's concept of "progressive" sanctions. Miss Balch announced that boycott had been the accepted Quaker method against slavery and was a characteristic tactic of Gandhi, so she could accept it. Mrs. Hull, however, was unmoved, writing: "as for a boycott in the good old safe (?) USA, *well* if it doesn't stir up a war, I shall be thankful."[20]

By May all was quiet in Manchukuo, the Japanese were extricating themselves from Shanghai—and the American peace movement turned to other problems. A little more than a year later Emily Balch summed it up in a letter "To Our Friends in China," an apology for the failure of the United States and the League to prevent the Japanese conquest. Mostly she apologized for the peace movement, explaining that "the peace people differ among themselves as to the use of non-violent coercioning boycotts, economic sanctions, etc., and are less influential than they might be if they had a united front." For her, if not for the Chinese, "the bitterest part of it all is that the course of events has furnished such plausible arguments to those who believe that force alone is respected or effective."[21]

For the American peace movement the Far Eastern crisis meant the end of innocence; the euphoria which followed the signing of the Kellogg Pact had dissipated; the hope of a world without war had gone. For all of the peace people there was a need to devise new programs for a world in which the existing peace machinery was inadequate. Some insisted that sanctions had not been tried and that in cooperation with the League there was still the possibility of preventing war. Others drew a very different lesson. They had learned that they were powerless to control militarism in other parts of the world, that they could do nothing to prevent or stop aggression in Asia or elsewhere. As a result, they determined to concentrate their efforts within the United States. If war could not be kept out of the world, at least the United States could be kept out of war. In 1931 and 1932 the American peace movement had been united in opposition to Japanese policy and had generated considerable support for policies to stop Japanese aggression. Subsequently, the lessons of Manchuria split the peace movement into two clearly discernable wings, one of which provided much of the support for anti-Japanese policies while the other provided almost all the opposition to such policies.

Outside of the peace movement, events in the Far East interested missionary organizations and the Institute of Pacific Relations (IPR), but neither the missionaries nor the IPR proved important at this time. The Chinese credited Edward C. Carter, secretary general of the IPR's International Secretariat, with enabling Americans to understand what was happening in Manchuria, but Americans seemed to understand without him. As an individual Carter was unquestionably sympathetic to the Chinese cause and appears to have worked for it, but the IPR as an organization with Japanese and Chinese councils kept its apolitical appearance. Similarly, the missionary organizations, with workers in both China and Japan, avoided partisanship while forwarding to the Department of State and the president descriptions from the field of Japanese aggression. A. L. Warnshuis, principal liaison between the Department of State and both the International Missionary Council and the Foreign Missions Conference of North America, wrote frequently to Stanley K. Hornbeck, chief of the Division of Far Eastern Affairs, to indicate the urgency felt by missionaries in China, but without committing the organizations he represented.[22]

Patriotic groups exhibited virtually no interest in events in the Far East, although before the close of 1932 there was evidence of discontent with Hoover's and Stimson's limited cooperation with the League. The American Legion held its annual convention September 21-24, 1931, and although the headlines carried news of the events in Manchuria and of Stimson's pleas for peace, the legionnaires were far too concerned with their demands for bonuses and the repeal of prohibition to notice. When they met again in September 1932, their principal interests had not changed, but the convention voted down a motion to support the World Court and resolved against joining the League. Other patriotic organizations were more explicit, as the Veterans of Foreign Wars and Spanish Veterans opposed American interference in the Sino-Japanese conflict.[23]

From September 1931 to April 1932, the critical months of the crisis, the peace societies worked without notable opposition from patriotic groups—or from any other organizations. Evidence of their influence is offered by the testimonial of an American propagandist for Japan, but it would be impossible to demonstrate that the administration would have acted differently in the absence of the pressure by the peace organizations.[24] Moreover, on the essential question of sanctions the American peace movement reflected the same uncertainty that troubled Stimson, Hoover, and responsible statesmen throughout the world. Looking back, it seems clear that the influence of the peace movement on American policy was less significant than the influence of the crisis on the peace movement.

II

The years 1933 to 1937 were years of relative quiet in which the course of Japanese-American relations was disturbed by nothing comparable to the storms unleashed at Mukden and Shanghai or by the later incident at the Marco Polo Bridge. Just as the government of the United States acquiesced in the continued but undramatic Japanese encroachments in China, so private organizations in the United States failed to respond to Japanese actions. Nonetheless, in the pursuit of their general programs, several organizations pressed for legislation or other government measures which could not but influence American policy toward Japan. Once again the peace movement provided the groups most deeply involved, but with a difference. In 1931 and 1932 a deep commitment to the peace machinery provided by the League of Nations and the Nine Power and Kellogg-Briand treaties led the American peace movement to be highly critical of Japan and, in some instances, to endorse policies hostile to Japan. From 1933 to 1937 faith in the world's peace machinery and hopes for world peace diminished, and the dominant peace groups focused on keeping the United States out of war. Fear of a Japanese-American conflict led to the muting of complaints against Japanese imperialism or treaty violations and to sympathetic explanations of Japanese behavior as part of the effort to alleviate tension between the two countries. Some elements within the peace movement, most notably those close to the Carnegie Endowment for International Peace, retained their conviction of the importance of collective action for peace, but in the mid-1930s they were no match for the forces headed by Libby and his erstwhile critic Dorothy Detzer.

Until 1935 the peace organizations managed to work reasonably well together. The Interorganization Council on Disarmament and the Emergency Peace Committee had withered away, but in their place had been created the National Peace Conference, which held together twenty-eight to forty peace groups, including all the most prominent. Walter Van Kirk of the Federal Council of Churches served as director, John Nevin Sayre of the Fellowship of Reconciliation as president. The steering committee was positively ecumenical, including Detzer, Libby, Eichelberger, Newton, and James T. Shotwell. As with the Interorganization Council, this effort to harness all the energies of the peace movement resulted in an organization that could reach agreement on few specifics. Still, on two issues of importance to Japanese-American relations the forces of peace united. They opposed military spending in general and naval spending in particular, and they favored an end to discrimination against Orientals in American immigration policy. On these issues, men of good will could take a stand to distinguish themselves from the members of patriotic societies like the American Legion who pressed for "preparedness" and regularly recorded their opposition to Oriental immigration.[25]

Beyond clear stands on these important issues, the National Peace Conference indicated interest in Japanese-American relations by its approval of Roosevelt's "good neighbor and nonintervention" policies and the hope that they would be applied everywhere, "particularly to the Far East."[26] The participating organizations continued to proclaim their own positions, but there were few deviations from the Peace Conference line. Of interest for the future, however, were developments in the thinking of Libby and Miss Detzer.

Libby's panacea for tensions leading to war had long been disarmament. To this end he had created the National Council for the Prevention of War in 1921 as a clearing house for groups concerned with the Washington Naval Conference. After that conference he had suffered disappointments, but his success within the United States, particularly against lobbyists for naval building, had been impressive. However, Roosevelt's reputation as a big-navy man worried him—and Roosevelt's naval building program provided no opportunity for rest. Aware of Japan's desire for naval parity, fearful that a continued refusal by the United States to grant that parity would lead to a new arms race—and ultimately to war—Libby took up Japan's case. He was able to do so by assuming that the Japanese were willing to attain parity by having the other powers reduce their navies. Apparently accepting as valid reports that Japan wanted to abolish battleships, aircraft carriers, and big cruisers while cutting other tonnage drastically, he believed that Japan sought "reductions so tremendous that navies would become police forces and a war between the United States and Japan would be literally impossible for years to come." He contended that American opposition to granting Japan naval parity, presumably in these idyllic terms, was based on unwillingness to give Japan a free hand in East Asia.[27]

Libby's argument against the American position indicated the extent to which fear of war with Japan had altered the moral stand he had taken against Japanese aggression in 1931. In the first place, he explained, Japan already had a free hand in Asia. The Japanese could seize slices of Chinese territory at will, and if they chose to take the Philippines, even an American navy twice its present size would require years to regain the islands. He argued that the American people were not willing to fight in the Far East, that a war there would be essentially a war on behalf of American investments in China, and that these were not worth an armed struggle. But Libby had never endorsed any simplistic notion of economic determinism and understood that many of his antagonists were concerned with questions of international justice, particularly justice for China, concerning which he exhibited the most uneasiness. There had to be better ways of deterring Japan than with navies, perhaps through utilizing the fact that the United States was Japan's best customer. In any event, China had long defended itself in its "own oriental way," and no injustice the Chinese might suffer would be comparable to the injustice of the United States embarking on another world war.[28]

The Manchurian crisis had shown that force or economic pressures that might lead to the use of force were necessary to obtain justice for China. Libby never stopped wanting justice for China, never advocated recognition of

Manchukuo, but as a pacifist he could not accept a resort to force or to sanctions that might lead to war. The ends for which he worked therefore had to be limited to those attainable by means he could countenance—and justice for China now seemed out of reach. He did not cease to see himself as a believer in international cooperation for peace, but he sensed that any cooperation against Japan might lead to war. From this point it was a natural step to join the campaign for legislation to keep the United States out of war at the cost of sacrificing the international cooperation he preferred. With events in Europe presaging war in 1935, Libby placed the influence of the National Council for the Prevention of War behind the Nye-Clark efforts for mandatory and inflexible "neutrality" legislation.[29]

The Women's International League for Peace and Freedom followed the general peace movement line, expressing concern over plans for naval building and maneuvers in the Pacific. But of greater significance was the fascinating metamorphosis of Dorothy Detzer, probably the most vocal sanctionist of the 1931-32 period. By 1935 Miss Detzer was probably the peace movement's most vocal opponent of sanctions and most convinced supporter of mandatory, impartial neutrality legislation. Two converging currents in her thought appear to account for the change. The first was a fear that Stanley Hornbeck, chief of the Division of Far Eastern Affairs of the Department of State, was hell-bent on war with Japan. In February 1932 Miss Detzer had visited Hornbeck to instruct him on the need for an economic boycott, precisely the policy Hornbeck had been advocating for months within the Department of State. But she chose to open by lecturing Hornbeck on the virtues of pacifism and Hornbeck took this poorly. He responded with a tirade on the dangers of pacifism and then suggested that the Women's International League agitate for an economic boycott. He explained to Miss Detzer that this course, followed by a show of force at Shanghai, would put an end to Japanese foolishness. Always quick to jump to conclusions, always suspicious of the Department of State, she became convinced that Hornbeck was leading a war party within the department and that this war party was seeking to manipulate the peace movement. For years afterward, her correspondence reflected this fear, accompanied by a general mistrust of the executive branch of the government.[30]

The second current in Miss Detzer's thought, an elemental form of economic determinism, may have derived from her persistent desire to be "radical" or may have merely reflected the popularity of such thinking in reform circles during most of the 1930s. Whatever the source, she explained to Emily Balch that the Pacific question could only be understood in terms of markets and particularly of the unwillingness of American capitalists to jeopardize the last great market, China. Her new method of analysis also provided an easy way to transcend her earlier concern for Japan's violation of the Nine Power Treaty. In July of 1934 she reported that the treaty was imperialistic and that the United States ought to renounce it immediately. As in the past when she thought Miss Detzer's judgment hasty, Miss Balch suggested that Libby be consulted, but Detzer, though she had changed her own position, still found Libby unreliable: "He is utterly blind to the economic forces and present world trends."[31]

Nonetheless, Libby and Detzer came together in their belief that mandatory neutrality provided the best hope for keeping the United States out of war, and their organizations provided the principal support that the "new neutrality" received from the peace movement. Failing to carry the National Peace Conference, where Eichelberger and others held out for legislation that would allow the president some discretion in dealing with aggressors, in 1936 the Women's International League for Peace and Freedom and the National Council for the Prevention of War joined with the Fellowship of Reconciliation, elements of the American Friends Service Committee, and other pacifist groups to launch the Emergency Peace Campaign. The Emergency Peace Campaign, like the earlier Emergency Peace Committee, was less a campaign than a board of strategy for those within the peace movement driven by the greatest sense of urgency. All these organizations continued to participate in the National Peace Conference. Thus, while the conference continued to meet and lines of communication remained open between the advocates of collective security and the pacifists, the peace movement had in fact been split by the debate over the appropriate form for neutrality legislation and by the larger question of the role of the United States in the event of aggression in Europe or Asia. When full-scale war erupted in China in 1937, the lines were already drawn and the groups associated with the Emergency Peace Campaign, predictably, led the fight for application of the neutrality laws and the disengagement of the United States from East Asia.[32]

III

From July 7, 1937 to September 1, 1939 the crisis in East Asia was able to compete for American attention with occasional success. The outbreak of hostilities in north China and the battle at Shanghai briefly drew attention away from the civil war in Spain and the rapidly mounting tensions in Europe. Sporadic reports of Japanese atrocities, the bombing of cities, the rape of Nanking, and incidents like the sinking of the *Panay* served to distract a people increasingly apprehensive of the impending disaster across the Atlantic. By the summer of 1939, however, Hitler had established Europe's claim to the center ring from which it was dislodged only on December 7, 1941—and then but briefly.

For private groups concerned with American policy toward Japan, the debate focused initially on the question of whether Roosevelt should apply the provisions of the neutrality law to the undeclared Sino-Japanese War. Subsequently, as the administration withstood attacks on its decision not to invoke the law, pressures mounted for sanctions against Japan. During the first year of the Sino-Japanese War Roosevelt and Hull defended themselves against organizations that charged them with risking involvement in war by pursuing a pro-Chinese policy. In the second year the administration faced organizations that called for sanctions against the Japanese aggressors and contended that existing American policy actually favored Japan.

In the months immediately following the Marco Polo Bridge Incident, the dominant voices still came from within the peace movement, from those groups participating in the Emergency Peace Campaign led by the National Council for the Prevention of War and the Women's International League for Peace and Freedom. They received support from patriotic societies which, despite their pressures for policies pointing toward confrontation with Japan, opposed any

American involvement in the Far Eastern crisis. The opposition was still very much the same: those within the peace movement who had consistently advocated discrimination between the aggressor and his victim and now called for sanctions against Japan.

The most striking feature of group activities in the period 1937-39, however, was the proliferation of organizations concerned solely with American policy in Asia. All of these organizations were pro-Chinese and all worked for aid to China or for policies intended to obstruct Japanese militarism. Most prominent was the American Committee for Non-Participation in Japanese Aggression (Price Committee), which succeeded in getting Henry Stimson to serve as its honorary chairman. Although the Price Committee received support from several leaders of the collective security or sanctionist wing of the peace movement, of perhaps greater interest was the support it received from missionaries, members of the American Council of the Institute of Pacific Relations, and the Chinese government. On the eve of Germany's invasion of Poland, the Price Committee and like organizations appeared to have at least neutralized the efforts of the pacifist groups and to have generated significant pressure for an end to American appeasement of Japan.

When the fighting started, the groups that generally followed the leadership of Libby and Detzer campaigned vigorously for the withdrawal of American nationals and protective forces from China. In August they spearheaded a successful drive to prevent the transport of bombers to China on a government-owned vessel. Although the peace movement as a whole did not take up the question, there was no opposition from other peace societies. The divisive issue emerged clearly in a closed meeting of the National Peace Conference on which Libby reported at the end of August. Thirty-five members attended the meeting, including Libby, Eichelberger, and Sayre. Ray Newton was present for the Emergency Peace Campaign, Mrs. Hull and Mrs. Olmsted for the Women's International League for Peace and Freedom, and Oswald Garrison Villard for the Committee on Militarism in Education. William Stone of the Foreign Policy Association spoke first, reporting on two days of interviews at the Department of State, where he had found Hornbeck in the saddle, responsible only to Roosevelt. Stone concluded his report with a call for an immediate declaration of neutrality. He received support from Maxwell S. Stewart of the *Nation*, a member of the conference's Committee on the Far East, and from Max Weis of World Peaceways. Eichelberger provided the opposition, deploring American retreats before the pressures of fascist nations and seeking a new means for collective action, perhaps under the Nine Power Treaty. Libby reported that Eichelberger was willing to resort to military sanctions, if collective, and "in any case, he wanted application of the Neutrality Law postponed as long as possible in the interest of China." In rebuttal Libby spoke for neutrality and the evacuation of American nationals from China, receiving Villard's endorsement. A vote indicated that application of the neutrality law was favored, 21-7.[33]

Although a large majority of the National Peace Conference organizations sought to have the neutrality law invoked, the methods of the National Council for the Prevention of War, the Women's International League for Peace and Freedom, the Emergency Peace Campaign, the Fellowship of Reconciliation, World Peaceways, and the Committee on Militarism in Education, which had announced their cooperation in a joint strategy board, attracted the most attention. Flooding the newspapers with press releases and the airwaves with broadcasts, their pressures for invoking the neutrality law and for the evacuation of Americans worried the administration. That Roosevelt's vacillation on questions involving the protection of American citizens in China was attributable to these pressures does not seem open to question, nor was it doubted by his subordinates. The American community in China, missionaries and businessmen, believed that the efforts of the peace movement endangered the work to which they had devoted their lives. The influence of the six groups on the decision to stop the bombers destined for China was still more apparent.[34]

Dorothy Borg has provided an excellent summary of the general line that prevailed among peace radicals who combined moral relativism with an economic interpretation of world affairs and a fundamentalist anti-imperialism. They argued that the Treaty of Versailles had been unjust, imposing upon the world conditions unfavorable to those nations which had achieved power late or were yet to achieve power and denying these "have-not" countries a reasonable opportunity to acquire needed resources by peaceful means, thus sowing the seeds of war. So long as the United States and other "have" nations failed to alleviate the distress of the "have-nots," the latter would use force to improve their lot. To oppose them in their struggle for development was equivalent to playing the role of a new Holy Alliance in maintaining an unholy status quo. The only just policy for the United States would begin with the immediate and unilateral cessation of American imperialism and be characterized by cooperation with other powers to alleviate the legitimate grievances of the "have-nots."[35]

Sharing few of the assumptions of the radical analysis, the American Legion and the Veterans of Foreign Wars nonetheless agreed on the importance of isolating the United States from alien quarrels. While the American Legion's annual convention met in September 1937, newspapers headlined the bombing of Chinese cities by the Japanese, but the matter was never raised during the sessions. Without reference to the conflict in the Far East, the legionnaires called for strict neutrality, taking the profits out of war, and investigation of organizations alleged to be serving foreign powers. The veterans, however, specifically protested Roosevelt's failure to apply the neutrality laws to the Sino-Japanese War, called for the evacuation of American nationals from China, and went on record as opposed to the United States' playing the role of peacemaker in quarrels that did not threaten it.[36]

Libby's argument for applying the neutrality legislation was not without substance. Aware that Roosevelt and his supporters sought to favor China, he insisted that they were mistaken in their means. Japanese naval power could easily deny supplies to China and the theoretical availability of supplies to both sides would in fact mean that Japan alone could purchase American munitions. Libby had heard the argument that Japan, the aggressor, was not in need of munitions but he also knew that Japan needed other materials such as scrap iron and steel not covered by the provisions of the neutrality legislation. To meet this problem, he called for amendment of the neutrality law to provide for the control of other war materials. He contended that given the needs of the belligerents and their very different capabilities for satisfying those needs, an extended neutrality law, denying China nothing since China could obtain nothing, would serve as an equalizer, to the ultimate benefit of China.[37]

Given the fact that Libby was less concerned with China's fate than with precluding American involvement in an Asian war, his argument was disingenuous and left China's friends as well as those who sought sanctions against aggressors unmoved. Only action or inaction which appeared to discriminate against Japan provided hope for such as these. Within a year, however, the complaint that American policy limited to nonapplication of the neutrality law was beneficial to Japan was being echoed by Libby's antagonists.

Although the administration's course had from the first received support from within the peace movement, most notably from Eichelberger and the League of Nations Association, it was Roosevelt himself, in his "quarantine" speech, who appears to have stirred interest in the idea of a consumer boycott and renewed hope among those who advocated American participation in collective action for peace. Predictably, the six radical peace groups condemned the speech and opposed the boycott idea, thereby intimidating Hull. Equally as predictable was the response of the World Peace Foundation in praise of the speech and in support of the administration's Far Eastern policy. Less predictable and apparently unknown to Roosevelt and Hull was the support for the speech and for administration policy *within* the radical six. Villard of the Committee on Militarism in Education still wanted the neutrality law applied but "heartily" approved of the "quarantine" idea. He believed that the United States could remain neutral "and still take part in a complete boycott of Japan." Within the Women's International League for Peace and Freedom a serious split emerged at the National Board meeting, where Dorothy Detzer's policies came under sharp attack. Emily Balch, honorary international president, and Mildred Scott Olmsted, national organization chairman, both insisted upon the need to condemn aggression and several other members of the board were disturbed by Miss Detzer's cooperation with the "isolationists." Privately, Miss Balch had been depressed by the challenge posed to her faith in nonviolence by the results of Chinese pacifism, writing: "Those who believe in force grow the more dangerous when they are led to believe that everyone is too much afraid of them to oppose them, and pacifists who avoid war by mere yielding are likely to be more overwhelmed by it later." Gradually Miss Balch and Mrs. Olmsted found themselves repelled by Miss Detzer's ideas and increasingly in sympathy with Eichelberger. Miss Detzer remained able to muster a narrow majority of the National Board, but her trumpet was muted.[38]

In the months that followed, though Roosevelt offered no plan to implement the "quarantine" idea, evidence of support for this approach mounted as several peace groups resolved to work for revision of the neutrality legislation to allow for discrimination against aggressors. Toward this end Eichelberger, who may have inspired the "quarantine" speech, organized the American Union for Concerted Peace Efforts. Additionally, numerous groups emerged determined to aid China and seeking relief funds or economic sanctions against Japan. Although members of the peace movement joined some of these groups, the efforts of missionaries and others more directly concerned with Asia were apparent.[39]

The origins of the so-called Price Committee indicate the frustration of missionaries in China in the face of inaction by the American government. Many had sought the endorsement of their boards for a consumer boycott, but the boards, concerned about mission work in Japan, took no official stand. On the other hand, they did not accept the demand of radical peace groups for the evacuation of American nationals from China, preferring to allow the missionaries to decide for themselves when and if they would leave. Indeed, Paul Varg suggests that one reason the mission boards abstained from anti-Japanese activity was the fear that Americans would react to revelations of Japanese atrocities by demanding the recall of all missionaries lest an incident occur that would provoke war.[40]

Unable to work through the mission boards, the missionaries did what they could as individuals. They wrote letters to newspapers, to congressmen, to the president, and to the secretary of state. Home on leave, they toured the country, considering propaganda activity on behalf of China as part of their mission. The affluent few contributed to organizations seeking aid for China and sanctions against Japan. Examples of these activities are easy to provide, but the total impact remains impossible to measure. The men who created the Price Committee, however, left a record of activities that can be compared to those of other private groups seeking to influence American policy toward Japan.[41]

The Price Committee was not a missionary organization, but Frank and Harry Price, the brothers responsible for its creation, were themselves missionaries and the sons of a famous missionary to China. Appalled by the extent to which American supplies appeared to be fueling the Japanese war machine, they called together a small group of men, including two others associated with mission work in China, two students of Asian affairs, and Earl Leaf, an American employed as a propagandist for the Chinese government. After several meetings these men decided that no existing organization provided a vehicle suitable for a campaign to stop American "assistance" to Japan and that a new committee was needed. Financial support was soon forthcoming from the Chinese government. There is no evidence to prove that the formation of the committee was inspired by Chinese authorities, but given the relations between the two, especially during the early stages, this possibility cannot be ignored. Moreover, the Chinese government considered itself entitled to reports.[42]

Despite the initial role of the Chinese, as the Price Committee's campaign got under way, efforts were made to restrict contributors to Americans and to sever potentially embarrassing ties with the Chinese. Roger S. Greene, who joined the national board in July, urged that money received from Chinese officials be returned, warning that the organization might otherwise be viewed as an instrument of foreign propagandists and its influence greatly reduced. Harry Price, who as executive secretary directed the committee, never seemed to share Greene's concern, but when he received a letter from the Department of State enclosing a copy of regulations for the registration of agents of foreign principals, he chose to follow Greene's advice. Leaf, who had no recourse but to register, submitted a letter resigning from the committee, but the resignation appears to have been formal rather than real. The committee never registered.[43]

Greene ultimately became chairman of the committee and for the next three years may have been the most important private influence on the course of Japanese-American relations. The son of a famous missionary, Daniel Crosby Greene, he was born and raised in Japan and had served as a consular official in

Japan, Siberia, Manchuria, and China. Subsequently, he had worked with the Rockefeller Foundation in China for approximately fifteen years before returning to the United States in 1936. Greene had been at Harvard with Franklin Roosevelt and Joseph Grew, Nelson Johnson had been his protégé in China, and his brother Jerome, once head of both the IPR and the American Asiatic Association, was in 1938 secretary of the Harvard Corporation. In short, Greene had valuable connections among missionary, business, diplomatic, academic, and government figures interested in East Asia.

Closely associated with the Price Committee were the Eichelberger-led elements of the peace movement. Eichelberger appeared as a sponsor on the committee's letterhead. Josephine Schain of the National Committee on the Cause and Cure of War served as vice chairman and Chase Kimball of the League of Nations Association as a member of the national board. Harry Price joined the board of the American Union for Concerted Peace Efforts and Frederick C. McKee, a businessman from Pittsburgh, held positions of leadership in both the Price Committee and the American Union. Other friends of the organization were Edward C. Carter and Frederick V. Field of the IPR. Because the staff of the IPR had chosen to refrain from activities with partisan groups, both Carter and Field cooperated privately, helping with contacts and offering advice and financial assistance.[44]

Organizing the Price Committee, from the initial discussions to the naming of Stimson as honorary national chairman, required seven months, from May to December 1938. Decisions on the committee's program were easier to reach. Carefully and deliberately the founding group avoided involvement in the broader issues dividing the peace movement and the American people and asked only that the United States cease "cooperating" with Japan in its war with China—cease serving as Japan's "partner." European affairs, the League, the World Court, disarmament, collective security, and like matters were left to others as the committee sought the broadest possible support. If pacifists like Villard could support the boycott movement, other pacifists could be attracted to a movement to embargo the sale of war supplies to an aggressor, could say "we will not underwrite Japan's cruel war."[45]

On August 1, 1938 the Price Committee began its campaign by mailing 22,000 copies of a booklet entitled "America's Share in Japan's War Guilt." The addressees included every congressman, selected officials of the Department of State, and key people in a variety of academic, civic, and church organizations. The booklet contained materials selected to label Japan as an aggressor, demonstrate the importance of the American sale of war supplies to Japan, and indicate widespread support for economic sanctions among congressmen, church leaders, union members, and youth groups. In the foreword not only China's suffering but the problems helping to build the Japanese war machine posed for the United States were underscored.[46]

Paralleling the efforts being made in New York, two Methodist missionaries in Shanghai reprinted "America's Share in Japan's War Guilt" for distribution to Americans in China. They attached form letters to be sent to the United States and instructions for stimulating friends and relatives to take action. Americans in China were also asked to support the Price Committee by providing mailing lists and like information.[47]

Within the committee Roger Greene's focus on American rather than Chinese ends and his tendency to view problems in a global rather than Asian setting created occasional friction, most notably with Geraldine (Mrs. George) Fitch but sometimes with Harry Price as well. Before Greene became chairman, Price had written to him expressing fear that Greene's idea of seeking arbitration of the Sino-Japanese War would result in the betrayal of China's interests as those of Czechoslovakia had been betrayed a few days earlier at Munich. In reply Greene suggested that Price was "unduly anxious about the possibility of injustice to China." To further ease Price's concern, he mentioned a discussion with Roosevelt, whom he had found "surprisingly well informed on the Far Eastern situation and keenly interested in it." In the work of the committee this difference in focus appeared as a dispute over how to relate to Roosevelt and the Department of State. When he accepted the chairmanship, Greene expressed the desire to work with and be guided by the Department of State and was particularly anxious for the committee to maintain its good relationship with Hornbeck. Mrs. Fitch and a few others sought to condemn American policy and to fight the American government on behalf of the Chinese—with funds supplied by the latter. As a result, Price occasionally found himself in a cross fire between Greene and what may be called the "China first" group. Though he was sometimes lax and accepted suspect financial contributions, Price realized the wisdom of Greene's course, especially if establishment figures like Stimson were to play a role in the organization's campaign.[48]

By the end of December 1938 Stimson and Greene had accepted their positions and discussions with Hornbeck had helped to give the committee direction. It would not work for specific legislation but would seek instead to increase public and congressional opposition to the sale of war materials to Japan. Price and Greene found the administration friendly to their objectives—as well it should have been. Any organization that served to neutralize opposition to the idea of discriminating against aggressors might help Roosevelt to obtain the discretionary power he sought. At a minimum, by adding new sounds to the voice of the people the Price Committee's campaign would leave the administration free to do—or not to do—as it pleased. For Hornbeck in particular it provided public support for a stiffening of American policy toward Japan, a course for which he was the principal advocate within the Department of State.[49]

Early in 1939 Roosevelt, seeking revision of the neutrality law, accepted Senator Key Pittman's offer to press for the administration's program. Roosevelt's desire for repeal of the arms embargo and extension of the cash-and-carry concept to all commerce with belligerents indicated that he was responding to the post-Munich crisis in Europe. If this program succeeded, arms and munitions could be sold to the European democracies but, still lacking authority to discriminate against aggressors, Roosevelt would be able to do nothing against Japan—or for China. Though China's friends were helping to create a climate in which neutrality revision was conceivable, the administration was unwilling to jeopardize its European policy by a blatant admission that it would put aid to the victims of aggression ahead of neutrality.[50]

But before Pittman acted, Clark Eichelberger decided to try to go beyond Roosevelt's limited plan. In February 1939 Eichelberger succeeded in having

Senator Elbert D. Thomas (D-Utah) sponsor a bill to grant the president the authority to prohibit the export of all war supplies to belligerents and, with congressional approval, to lift the embargo against victims of aggression. The Price Committee did not support the Thomas bill, nor did the Senate act on it.[51]

In March, apparently in response to the German seizure of Czechoslovakia, Pittman introduced his own bill to repeal the arms embargo and extend to arms the cash-and-carry provision of the 1937 law. It also required the president to apply the neutrality law to undeclared wars but contained no provision for discrimination against aggressors. Whatever Pittman's intentions, such legislation could not have been less satisfying to China—as witnessed by the barrage of criticism from Chungking. H. H. Kung, president of the Executive Yuan of the Republic of China, sent Pittman the clearest statement of the problem. Kung declared that he appreciated the fact that Pittman had acted "for the best interest of the United States and to help the democratic cause in Europe," but he was pained to note that the bill did not distinguish between aggressor and victim, "thereby tending to penalize China in face of Japan's aggression."[52]

Predictably, the Price Committee opposed Pittman's efforts toward revision of the neutrality legislation. Price wrote to Pittman, Hull, and Undersecretary Sumner Welles to spell out the difficulties Pittman's proposal created in the Far East, noting that the cash-and-carry stipulation presented no obstacle to Japan while China, dependent upon credit and other nations' carriers, would be affected adversely. He insisted that Pittman's bill would have harmful effects on the United States as well, undermining Chinese friendship for America and affecting the world situation in a way detrimental to American security. Unlike those whose ultimate concern was collective security or those concerned primarily with the war in Europe, China's friends could take no solace from compromise measures that would aid France and Britain in a war against Hitler without a promise of commensurate support for China. The threat of a schism between the Price Committee and the Europe-oriented peace movement had emerged.[53]

With Hornbeck prodding from the State Department and with the advice and assistance of members of the Price Committee, in April 1939 Pittman introduced a separate resolution authorizing the president to place restrictions on trade between the United States and any nation that violated the Nine Power Treaty. Since the administration was unwilling to fight for legislation that would openly discriminate against aggressors, this method of discriminating against Japan could supplement the assistance the cash-and-carry concept would provide Britain and France across the Atlantic. China would be satisfied with nothing less and the Price Committee could not otherwise be quieted. Mrs. Price informed Pittman that the organization would oppose his neutrality bill "unless the Far East is excluded from its provisions and unless special legislation is also provided to check Japan's extensive purchases of war materials from the United States." Pittman replied that he knew of no way to spare China the effect of his bill and, in the absence of agreement, feared that no neutrality legislation would be passed before Congress adjourned.[54]

Other bills providing for economic sanctions were introduced in both the House and the Senate, but despite intensive lobbying by the Price Committee and similar groups, these efforts came to naught. Harriet Welling, whose Stop

Arming Japan! functioned in Chicago, interviewed the Illinois delegation and other congressmen but reported that "everyone seems much more concerned with the Neutrality Bills and Europe than the Embargo on goods to Japan." Concerned by Hull's temporizing, Price spoke to him on July 25.[55]

Then suddenly, on July 26, the administration served the required six months' notice of intent to abrogate the Treaty of Commerce and Navigation between the United States and Japan. Often cited as an obstacle to economic sanctions, the treaty could no longer be used as an excuse. Interestingly enough, the administration appeared to be responding to a resolution by Senator Arthur H. Vandenberg (R-Michigan), who was in fact opposed to sanctions against Japan. Moreover, the termination of the treaty had been under consideration since April because of complications created by domestic cotton policy. Nonetheless, most scholars are agreed that Hull's action had been prompted by congressional pressures and evidence of public support for an embargo on the sale of war supplies to Japan. Afraid that such sharp measures might lead to a crisis with Japan at a time when the European situation appeared ominous, Hull chose Vandenberg's proposal as the safest way to encourage the Chinese government and relieve the pressures generated by the Price Committee and other friends of China.[56]

Shortly after the administration took this step, seemingly in the direction sought by the Price Committee, Roger Greene suggested that the group merge with Eichelberger's American Union for Concerted Peace Efforts. Greene expressed fear that the Price Committee's program would collide with revision of the neutrality legislation. He personally believed that if the administration wanted to be cautious, it should back the embargo against Japan first, but there was always the danger that it would opt for the cash-and-carry plan offered by Pittman in the spring. To forestall this possibility, with the attendant frustration of the Price Committee's program, Greene felt they should work with Eichelberger to give Roosevelt what he really wanted: approval for discriminating against aggressors.[57]

In response to Greene Price indicated the narrower concern of many members of the committee. Opposing the merger, he informed Greene of a general unwillingness to dilute the focus on the Far East. Earlier Mrs. Fitch had argued that the Pittman bill approached the problem backward in that it failed to recognize that "the Far East is the crux of the whole world situation." Price, who was never so extreme, conceded that the neutrality revision and the embargo against Japan were complementary, but he was unwilling to risk the success of the latter to work for the former. He found the quest for neutrality revision full of complications, ethnic and political, which the clear-cut issue of nonparticipation in Japanese aggression did not possess. Price feared that the committee would lose the support of people who were not prepared to urge revision of the neutrality legislation, and he reminded Greene that their work was not yet done, that no sanctions had been imposed on Japan. With the Price Committee unwilling to work for neutrality revision, the merger idea was dropped for the moment, a fortnight before Hitler's invasion of Poland.[58]

For those whose principal interest in world affairs focused on China, there was indeed reason for concern. Eichelberger had consistently favored sanctions against Japan, but he would never sacrifice to a "China first" appeal his larger program for revision of the neutrality legislation and sanctions against all aggressors. Similarly, the World Peace Foundation had resolved that the continued supply of war materials to Japan was "intolerable and contrary to the fundamental interests of the American people," but this organization also sought revision of the neutrality legislation. The American League for Peace and Democracy, generally considered well to the left of the organizations affiliated with the National Peace Conference, continued to call for an embargo against Japan, but it too was responding primarily to events in Europe. Moreover, the prominence of the American Communist Party in the American League left its policies dependent upon the vagaries of the Soviet line. In the fall of 1938 the Committee for a Boycott against Japanese Aggression had extended its efforts to Germany and Italy and in 1939 renamed itself the American Boycott against Aggressor Nations. Of the major private groups attempting to influence American foreign policy, only the Price Committee remained focused on the war in East Asia—and many of its most active members were increasingly distracted by the threat of war in Europe.[59]

The principal organized opposition to any stiffening of American policy toward Japan came from the radical peace societies, but they too were concerned with European affairs and with the larger problem of neutrality revision which they opposed. Nonetheless, in February 1939 Libby and Miss Detzer helped congressional opponents of Roosevelt's policy to defeat plans for the fortification of Guam, viewing the proposal as provocative. In July Libby declared himself as much opposed to the embargo against Japan as to "any other proposal to abandon our neutrality policy." But a few weeks later, when he sought to have the radical peace groups attack the administraton for giving notice of its intent to terminate the commercial treaty with Japan, he found himself isolated. Not only did Miss Detzer desert him on this issue, but key members of his own organization opposed him. Miss Detzer explained to Emily Balch that she had "never been one who thought we should never take any kind of action" and regarded abrogation of the treaty as a useful means of expressing disapproval of Japanese actions in China. Miss Detzer may also have been reflecting the increasing pressure from the international branch of her organization, which had been calling for a boycott against Japan, or the apparent growth of opposition to her policies within the American section. As war threatened to engulf Europe, the men and women who sought to isolate the United States from war through mandatory neutrality legislation found themselves on the defensive, their successes of the mid-1930s threatened, and the battle in which they were engaged the most important they had ever fought.[60]

In sum, during the first few months of the Sino-Japanese War the clamor of the radical peace societies had contributed to the vacillating and timid course pursued by the Roosevelt administration. But these tiny groups suffered a major defeat when the president defied their demand that he invoke the neutrality law. Still, this defiance, though pleasing to the Chinese and their American friends, brought China no tangible benefits. Nor was the rhetoric of Roosevelt's "quarantine" speech accompanied by any shift in American policy, even though that modicum of presidential leadership did seem to inspire new efforts by China's friends and by those who sought sanctions against aggressors.

In mid-1938 mounting evidence of the value of American trade to Japan's war effort had evoked a popular demand for an embargo against Japan and led to the formation of the American Committee for Non-Participation in Japanese Aggression. Less than a year after the Price brothers began to organize the committee, the polls indicated overwhelming support for an embargo on the sale of war materials to Japan. The influence of the organization on the public was apparent in letters to Washington demanding "nonparticipation in Japanese aggression," enclosing committee leaflets or parts of pamphlets, and referring to Dr. Walter Judd, the committee's most effective speaker. But the only action by the administration for which the Price group might be credited was the notice given Japan of the intent of the United States to terminate the commercial treaty. By the summer of 1939, however, despite the continued strength of pacifist sentiment, American opinion had been brought to the point where economic sanctions against Japan were possible—had the administration desired to impose them.[61]

IV

From September 1, 1939 to December 7, 1941 the war in Europe captured the attention of the American people, the American government, and most of the private groups attempting to influence the foreign policy of the United States. In the autumn of 1941 many of these groups became aware of a crisis in Japanese-American relations but only one, the Committee to Defend America by Aiding the Allies (White Committee), made a major effort to affect American policy. By then the Price Committee had disappeared, many of its members frustrated by Roosevelt's indifference toward China. The major radical peace groups continued to exist, but pacifism could not thrive in the atmosphere Hitler had created. Hurt also by internal dissension and defections, these organizations ceased to be of significance. Their efforts to keep the United States out of war through a policy of "strict" or "real" or "absolute" neutrality were taken over by new organizations, most notably America First, whose appeal extended well beyond the peace movement. America First, however, virtually ignored the Far East. Not until September 1941 was an organization created which was devoted to reducing American pressure on Japan: the Committee on Pacific Relations.

The coming of war in Europe reaffirmed Roosevelt's belief in the need to revise the neutrality law to enable Great Britain and France to purchase arms in the United States. Though he remained cautious, even devious, insisting that he sought a return to traditional American neutrality rather than admitting that he wanted to aid Hitler's enemies, Roosevelt openly called for repeal of the arms embargo. There was loud, immediate, and substantial opposition to neutrality revision, but none of the existing pressure groups played an important role in organizing this dissent. Its leadership came from the ranks of Congress, from Senators William E. Borah, Bennett Champ Clark, Robert M. LaFollette, and Gerald P. Nye and from Representative Hamilton Fish. In addition prominent men like Herbert Hoover, Charles A. Lindbergh, Norman Thomas, and Father Coughlin appealed to a wide spectrum of Americans who feared the United States would be drawn into the war.[62]

To counter this opposition, Roosevelt sought help from Clark Eichelberger and the American Union for Concerted Peace Efforts. Eichelberger formed a new group, the Non-Partisan Committee for Peace through Revision of the Neutrality Act, and succeeded in getting William Allen White to head it. Stimson, "Al" Smith, Henry Luce, and Frederick McKee also played prominent parts in this campaign to win support for repeal of the arms embargo. Although the proposed changes did nothing to alter American policy toward China and Japan, it is worth noting that all of these men, except Smith, were involved with the Price Committee.[63]

Within the committee Price was not easily persuaded to suspend efforts to obtain an embargo against Japan. On September 15, 1939 he circulated a memorandum, "War in Europe—What About Asia?" in which he argued that the Nazi-Soviet Nonaggression Pact had isolated Japan, forcing the Japanese to be more receptive to American pressures. But Greene remained adamant in his conviction that the campaign would have to be reined in until the neutrality law was revised, and he was apparently supported by Stimson. Meanwhile Greene wrote to "Dear Joe" Grew, attempting to win him over to support of the embargo program and questioning his earlier estimate of the danger of war. Similarly, Eichelberger's League of Nations Association endeavored to keep the Far Eastern war in the public consciousness. In September, while the association focused its efforts on neutrality revision, its journal *New World* contained an article entitled "Don't Forget Japan." The writer conceded that the European crisis was more serious but compared Japanese aggression to a cancer of the leg which, if left alone, could be as deadly as cancer of the stomach. Nonetheless, until repeal of the arms embargo was accomplished, Price could evoke no more than a willingness to continue preparations for a future campaign. On October 30 he made a virtue of necessity, informing Pittman that "we have purposely refrained from pressing the Far Eastern issue during the present special session."[64]

Once the neutrality law was revised, the Price Committee wasted little time before returning to action. Two days after Roosevelt signed the new law, Greene wrote to congratulate White for his work on behalf of revision and to enlist his aid in the forthcoming campaign for an embargo against Japan. Five days after the law was signed, Stimson held a lunch meeting in New York at which the Price Committee and friends were to work out a legislative program with Pittman. As he was wont to do, Pittman missed the meeting but a telegram sent in his name requested that the group advise him on the course he was to follow. Price prepared a synopsis of the talks, participated in by Carter of the IPR, the executive secretary of the Federal Council of Churches, Luce and several other businessmen, as well as the usual committee stalwarts. In brief, it was agreed that the committee would keep its program separate from neutrality revision and, following Pittman's advice, concentrate on a legislative program to be passed at the end of January 1940, when the treaty between Japan and the United States would lapse.[65]

To facilitate the committee's lobbying efforts, Greene opened an office in Washington early in January 1940. But the optimism with which the members of the organization had looked to the end of the treaty soon evaporated. By mid-January it was apparent that there would be no embargo, no sanctions against Japan. Thwarting the organization was not any other private group nor any bloc in Congress but rather Roosevelt, Hull, and the Department of State. The administration had concluded that the danger of a conflict with Japan resulting from the imposition of sanctions was too great to risk, given the war in Europe. As a result, pressures mounted within the committee for a break with the administration.

Price argued that piecemeal measures short of an embargo would do nothing for Chinese morale and would probably not deter Japan. The public, he contended, had long indicated support for a more aggressive anti-Japanese policy, and Pittman was prepared to work for an embargo. Price wanted immediate action, fearing that if the Department of State succeeded in getting the committee to surrender its demand for a mandatory embargo, the department might then obstruct even discretionary embargo legislation. He contended that if the committee continued its campaign, putting pressure on the administration, they might at least be able to get legislation authorizing the president to impose sanctions on Japan. Still not grasping Roosevelt's evaluation of the relative importance of the European and Asian wars, Price professed himself unable to understand why the courage shown by the administration in the fight for neutrality revision was not demonstrated on the embargo issue, where public support was overwhelming.[66]

At the outset Greene was relatively sanguine, convinced that Roosevelt and Hull would make no concessions to Japan although he recognized their lack of enthusiasm for the embargo proposal. Within the administration he found support for a program of gradual pressure by tariff manipulation and direct financial aid to China, but he came to fear that Hull would not push either of these measures. Ultimately Greene reached the same conclusion as Price: the committee had to go ahead with its campaign in the hope that the administration would then work toward the same end by some other means.[67]

By mid-February Price seemed on the verge of panic, fearful that time was running against the committee. With noteworthy prescience he warned that spring might bring intensified fighting in Europe, diverting public attention and interest from events in the Far East. He worried about the pressures on the Chinese economy; about the possibility that the party conventions in the spring and summer and the subsequent election campaign would focus attention on domestic politics; about the difficulty of sustaining interest in the organization. Price also argued that it was possible to "act decisively" in the Far East without resort to war, contending that the United States could enforce a just peace in Asia and then be in a better position to deal with the situation in Europe.[68]

In April, after the German offensive had swept through Denmark and Norway, Hull talked with Price for forty-five minutes, praising the work of the committee and its impressive accomplishments. But Price was not easily put off by flattery and warned the secretary that, despite his own desire to continue a constructive relationship with the administration, there were pressures which he could not resist unless effective action were taken against Japan. Hull indicated his fear that embargo bills, if voted upon, might fail and the problem be further complicated by election year politics. Price concluded that Hull would block any attempt to obtain mandatory embargo legislation but would like to have the authority to impose economic sanctions if it could be obtained without the administration having to face warmongering charges.[69]

In May the Germans invaded Belgium, Holland, and France, and Price's prediction about public loss of interest in the Far East was fulfilled. Ironically, the Nazi onslaught also resulted in the National Defense Act, one section of which authorized the president to prohibit the export of materials necessary for the defense of the United States—authority that could be used to embargo the sale of war supplies to Japan. Although this section had been inserted at the request of the army, the Price Committee may have played a part in its formulation and acceptance by Congress and the administration. Almost from the moment news reached the United States of the invasion of the Low Countries, Greene and Price had campaigned for export restrictions as a means of conserving critical resources. This new tack, stressing national defense rather than discrimination against aggressors and treaty violations or the territorial integrity of China, interested Pittman, Hull, and Hornbeck. While Price pressed the case with these three men, Greene, unable to see Roosevelt, tried to persuade him with letters. Approximately a month after Greene had suggested this course, the National Defense Act, with the support of the administration, was passed by both houses of Congress. On June 17, 1940 Price and Greene informed their supporters that "our legislative hurdle is passed."[70]

During the months of the "phony war" the Price Committee had encountered little in the way of organized opposition, partly because little opposition to an embargo against Japan existed and partly because the opposition had become complacent. At the Women's International League for Peace and Freedom Emily Balch, now honorary international president, favored the embargo; and while at the National Council for the Prevention of War Libby did not, he was satisfied that the Department of State opposed any embargo legislation. Both organizations focused their attention on the war in Europe, though Libby did take cognizance of the Price Committee's campaign. While conceding that Judd and other missionaries had won the support of distinguished church leaders and recognizing the "sincerity" of the men involved, he stated his emphatic opposition on the grounds that discrimination against Japan would lead to war. To those concerned about China he suggested that Roosevelt should mediate to bring an end to the war. But in brushing aside any brief for American intervention, he went a step further than any of his earlier arguments, contending that the Open Door policy "be replaced by a policy that recognizes, as Secretary Lansing recognized twenty years ago, that Japan has 'special interests' in China." To avoid war, Libby was apparently willing to condone Japanese imperialism, but this was probably the inevitable result of a practice among the peace radicals of apologizing for the actions of any country with which the United States might run the risk of armed conflict. In the quest for peace a perverse moral relativism justified any provocative act by a potential enemy while condemning any American response as provocative. But as of April 22, 1940 Libby saw little likelihood of Congress or the administration putting pressure on Japan "while the war in Europe is active."[71]

In the summer of 1940, however, after passage of the National Defense Act, Price and Greene concluded that coercion of Japan was forthcoming and that their energies might best be utilized elsewhere. Greene had returned to his previous suggestion of a merger between the committee and Eichelberger's American Union for Concerted Peace Efforts in May 1940, a few days after the German sweep into France. Greene had developed an excellent relationship with

Eichelberger, but Price had not been enthusiastic about the proposed merger, apparently because of personality differences with Eichelberger. Price had also been reluctant to surrender his focus on the Far East, but a talk with Stimson in June aroused his interest in working with an organization that dealt with broader issues of foreign policy. Greene, who had joined the Committee to Defend America by Aiding the Allies, continued to press Price, contending that more could be accomplished by working for action in the Far East within a general rather than a regional organization. He became especially insistent late in the summer, arguing that the country faced urgent questions outside the Far East and that it would be difficult for the committee to raise funds for another campaign. Disagreements over liquidation kept the Price group in existence until February 1941, but it had ceased to be of significance by July 1940.[72]

Coercion of Japan was indeed forthcoming, although not on the scale for which Greene and Price had hoped. In July, after Stimson joined the cabinet, aviation gasoline and high-grade scrap iron were added to the list of articles for which export licenses were required and such licenses were then denied to Japan. This was a far more limited version of the embargo than that advocated by the Price Committee, but it was an important step—the first meaningful victory for those who demanded the use of economic pressure against Japan. The committee's desire for a complete embargo on war supplies was not realized during the years of its existence, and Japan continued to buy huge quantities of oil until after the freezing of Japanese assets in July 1941. Greene was intensely disappointed but not entirely surprised. Recognizing the administration's preoccupation with the grave crisis in Europe, he hoped through his work with the Committee to Defend America by Aiding the Allies to alert authorities to the necessity of countering aggression across the Pacific as well. In August 1940 he believed the European and Asian problems were about to merge and hoped that if Britain could be sustained, it would be easier to get "the necessary action taken for China."[73]

Within the Committee to Defend America by Aiding the Allies there was, however, little inclination to include China among the "Allies." The committee had been organized by the ubiquitous Eichelberger in May 1940 in response to the blitzkrieg, and that summer, with William Allen White as chairman, it focused its campaign entirely on aid to Great Britain as the "first and vital duty" of the United States. For the most part, its efforts were channeled toward obtaining old American destroyers for the British navy, a campaign that ultimately culminated in the destroyer-bases deal. On those occasions when the Japanese were mentioned in committee literature, their activities were conjured up as further justification for rushing aid to Britain. In July 1940, in a letter to local chapters, Eichelberger discussed Japanese politics and the desire in some Japanese circles for an alliance with Germany and Italy to point up the danger to the United States if the British fleet fell and the United States were left isolated. China was not even mentioned in the letter, which called for the speeding up of all possible aid to Britain.[74]

Indifference to China in particular and Asia generally persisted even after the destroyers-for-bases arrangement was announced. On September 8 Greene was invited to attend a meeting of the executive committee, at which he "was asked and agreed to continue the study" he had been making of the situation in the Far East.

The following day he appeared at a meeting of the advisory committee, only to have the problems of China and Japan brushed aside again. An outline of policy for that date declared that the subject of the Pacific "is now too complicated for much attention by this committee . . . it would distract attention from the need of rushing all material to Britain instantly." Later in the month Greene was allowed to send out a newsletter calling for an American initiative in the Far East in which he focused his argument on the relevance of the Far Eastern situation to Britain's position. This was the surest way, and perhaps at this point in time the only way, to interest the White Committee leadership in anti-Japanese activities.[75]

In September 1940 the formation of the America First Committee, the most vigorous and responsible opposition to the White Committee, was announced. Like the White Committee, America First directed its efforts toward the war in Europe, seeking to prevent the involvement of the United States by demanding impartial treatment of the belligerents. The leaders of this organization were equally opposed to war with Japan but gave little attention to the affairs of the Pacific. Not until the summer of 1941 did America First seriously consider the danger of a Japanese-American war. Wayne Cole in *America First* has noted that plans for opposing war with Japan "never got beyond the talking stage in America First national headquarters." A concerted campaign was never launched.[76]

Clearly the problem faced by Greene, Price, and other friends of China during the summer of 1940 was not organized opposition to sanctions against Japan or aid to China. Whether they supported or opposed Roosevelt's policy for aid short of war to Great Britain, the groups attempting to shape America's role in world affairs were preoccupied with Europe and indifferent to the Far East. While those who prevailed in the Department of State doubted that the outcome of the Sino-Japanese War would be of sufficient importance to risk the provocation of anti-Japanese sanctions, private groups like America First or the White Committee simply viewed the war in Asia as an abstraction, a relatively unimportant war being fought by relatively unimportant people over relatively unimportant issues. There was no shortage of sympathy for China in either group, nor lack of condemnation of Japanese militarism—simply doubt as to the relevance of the Far East at this point in time. For Greene to win support for further sanctions against Japan or assistance to China, he had to find a way to demonstrate a relationship between the European and Asian wars, to convince men whose attention was focused on Great Britain's battle for survival that Japan too threatened Britain, that China too was fighting America's battle. It was, of course, the Japanese who made the fulfillment of Greene's task possible when, on September 27, they signed the Tripartite Pact.

Despite tremendous American sympathy for China, nothing the Chinese or their friends in the United States had done convinced Americans of their stake in the outcome of the Sino-Japanese War as effectively as the Japanese decision to ally with Nazi Germany. For the leaders of the White Committee the Tripartite Alliance had made two wars into one: "it would now seem that China is unmistakably an ally," worthy of the committee's support. White wrote of the need to enable the American people to understand that "the menace in the Atlantic and the danger in the Pacific is all just one danger," all one "totalitarian war cloud." Livingston Hartley, a former Foreign Service officer who served as the committee's principal liaison with the Department of State, reported that Hornbeck had urged the committee to stress the unity of the world situation. Hornbeck had said that assistance to the Allies affected all fronts and could be provided by aid to China as well as to Great Britain. He had therefore recommended that the committee work for aid to all powers resisting the Axis and the restriction of aid to the Axis.[77]

White, however, troubled by the possibility that the Tripartite Alliance might achieve its purpose of reducing American aid to Britain, sought to avoid any commitment to the Far East that might hurt the British cause. Eichelberger stated the official position in mid-October 1940, announcing that the Axis alliance and increased tension in the Pacific had not changed the committee's program but rather required an intensification of its efforts. He noted that the alliance had been directed against the United States and declared that "Britain and China in the Pacific, with Britain in the Atlantic must now constitute our first lines of defense." But, Eichelberger added, "the key to our entire future is the survival of Great Britain." If Britain won, the Pacific would pose no problem, but "if Britain loses the aggressors will be victorious all over the world." It followed, therefore, that "under no circumstances" should there be a change in the policy of all aid to Britain as quickly as possible. China, the other "ally," should be given as much assistance as possible "without lessening the tempo of our aid to Britain." To supplement this assistance, which might well be nonexistent, Eichelberger called for a complete embargo on all products needed for the Japanese war machine.[78]

China was now to be viewed as an ally, but alas, a second-class ally. Greene, however, was encouraged by this start and undeterred by the continued focus on Britain. He prepared a memorandum, "How a Strong American Policy in the Far East Could Help Britain," and persuaded the committee to circulate it as confidential background material prepared by an unidentified "eminent authority on the Far East." It was accompanied by the disclaimer that "not all of the views expressed herein represent the official policy of the Committee to Defend America by Aiding the Allies." This was manifestly a less than complete vote of confidence, especially in view of Greene's deliberate appeal to the Europe-oriented. But it was indicative of the difficulty of obtaining serious consideration for the problems of the Pacific. In his analysis Greene contended that Britain had shown it could stave off invasion, thus postponing the threat to the security of the United States from across the Atlantic "so long as Britain can continue to get men and supplies from other parts of the empire and from neutral states." Unfortunately a grave new danger had arisen in the Middle East where the Suez, the lifeline of the British Commonwealth, was being threatened. British forces in the area had, therefore, to be reinforced immediately, and the reinforcements would have to come from Australia, New Zealand, and Canada through the Indian Ocean. But if Japan were left unchecked in Southeast Asia, the dominions would need these forces for home defense and Japan could cut off the flow of supplies from India. If Japan were checked, however, there would be no problem. And Japan could be checked by economic aid to China and an embargo on war materials to Japan; a boycott might even be imposed on Japanese imports into the United States. Naval "precautions" might also be taken by sending units of the U.S. navy into the western Pacific. With Britain strengthened in the Middle East, there was a possibility that Turkey and the Soviet Union would be deterred from aiding Germany. But the heart of Greene's message was that economic pressures against Japan would preserve the British position at Suez, ultimately saving Britain—and the United States.[79]

There were other ways in which Greene was able to work within the White Committee to further his hopes for a firmer American policy toward the Far East. On one occasion a member of the Boston chapter of the committee contacted the Washington office to inquire whether a Price Committee appeal for telegrams to Roosevelt urging planes and money for China would be in harmony with the overall program. Greene replied affirmatively, triggering a New England-wide campaign. On November 23, 1940 Greene became associate director of the White Committee, serving under Eichelberger, providing assurance to China's friends that the Orient would not be neglected. Indeed, the appointment may have been made for the purpose of stilling agitation for a more active campaign on Far Eastern issues. The day after he took over his new post Greene had to inform McKee that proposals for a boycott against Japanese products were going to be omitted from the committee's press releases. In order to hold a position from which he could hope to influence the White Committee's program, Greene acquired responsibility for pacifying his former associates in the Price Committee.[80]

As the months passed, Greene had reason to despair of his influence. The White Committee persisted in its basic strategy of advocating aid to China only after Britain's needs were satisfied. The administration had extended credits to the Chinese government and several new items were added to the list of materials excluded from export, but oil still flowed from the United States to Japan in enormous quantities. Meanwhile, during the winter of 1940-41 the committee focused its attention on mustering support for Roosevelt's lend-lease program, with continued emphasis on aid to Great Britain. In February 1941 Greene wrote to Admiral Harry E. Yarnell, with whom he had worked during the active days of the Price Committee, and indicated that he was troubled by the apparent failure of the United States to meet the Japanese menace and by the continued export of critical materials to Japan. In reply Yarnell indicated his own sense of failure: "I have often wondered why all the pressure that was brought to bear by the Non-Participation in Japanese Aggression was so ineffective, and why we continued to arm Japan when every indication pointed to eventual war."[81]

While the Lend-Lease Act was pending, the White Committee reflected the administration's caution and avoided new initiatives that might be construed as warmongering. But once the lend-lease program became law, Eichelberger gave Greene his full support and Greene's entire program for the Far East became part of the official program of the committee. At a meeting of the national board on March 15, 1941 Eichelberger announced that the local chapters were unanimous in advocating a strong policy toward Japan. With the help of Chester Rowell, a prominent California newspaperman, Greene's statement was adopted. The committee thereby called for an increase in American naval strength in the western Pacific, more aid to China, extension of the embargoes on war materials to Japan, and naval cooperation between the United States and Great Britain in the Pacific. In addition it warned of America's determination to prevent the conquest of Singapore and the Dutch East Indies. There was opposition to the clause referring to naval strength in the Far East, but the dissenters failed. Greene later admitted that this was a technical matter, beyond the concern of the committee, but "since we cannot always depend on the administration to take far-seeing and energetic action in time, it does not seem inappropriate to interest ourselves in such details." Faith in the wisdom of the administration had ceased to be a part of Greene's intellectual baggage.[82]

At Greene's request Hartley visited the Department of State, where he obtained confidential information indicating that the navy had already been reinforced and that through a variety of clever devices the government was preventing Japan from obtaining oil and other materials required for the Japanese war effort. Hartley liked these methods, which he believed would accomplish the ends Greene sought without arousing hostile feelings in Japan. He warned Greene not to pass this information on to his anti-Japanese friends or even to the local chapters of the White Committee because of the importance of moving quietly. Greene, however, had heard these lines before and refused to be put off with less than an end to the sale of petroleum products to Japan. For the next several months, with the assistance of Price and the approval of Eichelberger and Hornbeck, Greene criticized the Department of State and pressed for an embargo on the sale of oil. In June the executive committee issued a sharp statement demanding that the department "immediately lay down a rule that no more licenses for export of petroleum or petroleum products to Japan shall be issued."[83]

Although he had won in the battle over the White Committee's Far Eastern program, Greene became deeply concerned over the sentiment for appeasement of Japan that seemed to exist among people who could countenance forceful action against Germany. He reported his fears to Admiral Yarnell, explaining that he had gained the impression from his colleagues that "there are some who are extremely anxious to mollify Japan on the ground that we should do one thing at a time." Greene doubted that appeasement would provide security from an attack by Japan should the United States become heavily involved in the Atlantic. He suspected that appeasement would be too transparent to the Japanese, who would expect to be next in line after the defeat of Germany and therefore would not wait until the United States had eliminated their allies. Greene's apprehensions were not alleviated by letters from Hartley and Donald Blaisdell, both working out of the committee's Washington office. With incredible gaucherie, given Greene's known views, Hartley assured him of the wisdom of the administration's gentle tactics with Japan and their effectiveness in deterring Japan in Southeast Asia and stated that, as a result of these tactics, "we will obviously be freer to carry out our policy in the Atlantic."[84]

In late July 1941 the Japanese appeared in Camranh Bay on the coast of southern Indochina. Appeasement had not deterred the Japanese advance. On the very day the Japanese were sighted, Roosevelt called the Japanese ambassador's attention to "the bitter criticism that had been leveled against the administration" for allowing oil to be shipped to Japan. Two days later, on July 26, the White Committee added to that criticism, responding to news of the Japanese advance in Indochina. The committee insisted that there was no longer any reason to hope the continued flow of supplies would limit Japanese expansion and that an embargo against Japan, long urged as a moral duty and an obligation to China, had now become essential to the national defense and America's security in the Pacific. Finally, the committee urged "the immediate adoption of direct embargoes of all shipments of essential war materials to Japan and a freezing of Japanese assets in the United States." And lo, on the same morning the order to freeze Japanese assets was signed by the president.[85]

But to Greene and others who were aware of the strength within the administration of those who opposed a policy of pressure, the "freezing" order was no guarantee of victory. From Lauchlin Currie, a presidential secretary concerned with lend-lease for China, Greene learned that a complete embargo on oil would not be imposed immediately but that some licenses to use frozen funds and export oil would continue to be granted. Indeed, on August 1 the president approved such a program. Throughout August Greene fretted and worked with Eichelberger to launch a new campaign for an oil embargo. In an article for the committee's Washington Office Information Letter he warned that the United States might wait too long before doing anything and expressed fear "that for the moment the influence of appeasers in Washington will prevail against really decisive action." In the same letter, however, Hartley bracketed Greene's article with two of his own stressing the need to avoid war in the Pacific and insisting that "the Atlantic remains the vital area in which America's destiny will be decided." Hartley maintained that no matter what happened in the Pacific, victory in the Atlantic would permit "repair." The task of handling Japan at this juncture was extremely delicate, he concluded, and day-to-day planning should be left to the authorities. A week later Hartley replied indirectly to Greene's argument, conceding that "the Chinese" might see the oil policy of the United States as appeasement but contending that a larger view suggested this policy was in China's interest. He explained that the liberation of China depended upon "our victory," which might not have been possible if Japan had been provoked into attacking Singapore in 1940.[86]

Eichelberger, however, gave constant support to Greene's position, particularly in his regular letters to the committee's various chapters. Finally, on September 2 Greene was satisfied that Japan would get no more oil and indicated a willingness to relent in his attack on the administration. He had been watching a number of Japanese oilers in west coast ports and learned that although the Department of State and the administrator for export control had approved licensing for the sale of oil, the Treasury Department had come to the rescue, successfully resisting the attempt to license funds. Now Greene was willing to admit the possibility that the pressure on Japan was so strong that an occasional easing might be in order.[87]

As the summer drew to a close with intensified American pressure on Japan and continued resolve in Tokyo, the possibility of war between the two nations became very real to Americans struggling to keep their nation at peace. Two weeks after Roosevelt ordered the freezing of Japanese assets in the United States, the executive committee of America First expressed unanimous opposition to war in the Pacific but without further action returned its attention to the Atlantic. Although Emily Balch had written to Harold Ickes, secretary of the interior, calling for an oil embargo, Dorothy Detzer and the National Board of the Women's International League for Peace and Freedom urged the continuation of negotiations with Japan and called for a generous gesture by the United States. Miss Detzer told Undersecretary of State Sumner Welles that as a matter of justice Japan was entitled to an adequate trade agreement, repeal of the Oriental exclusion acts, and an agreement by the United States and Britain surrendering concessions and privileges in China. Perhaps these actions could be offered in exchange for an agreement by Japan to get out of China. She found Welles "rigid and unresponsive."[88]

At the National Council for the Prevention of War Frederick Libby kept up his efforts, adopting a new "Peace in the Pacific" program for the fall of 1941. He called for all possible efforts to keep the diplomats in Washington talking and, if the negotiations broke down, for an American delegation to resume conversations in Japan. But like Miss Detzer he could only reiterate the ideas of justice in the Orient the peace movement had been advocating at least since 1931. However valuable this plan might have been earlier, in the autumn of 1941 the Japanese-American crisis had gone too far to be halted by a wiser immigration policy and the end of American privileges in China.[89]

However, one further effort was made by a private organization to stave off war between the United States and Japan. In September a new group, the Committee on Pacific Relations, was organized for the purpose of improving Japanese-American relations. The central figure in the new committee was O. K. Armstrong, a sometime member of the Missouri legislature, journalist, prominent legionnaire, and committed opponent of American involvement in war. In 1940 Armstrong had been a member of the American Legion's three-man Foreign Relations Committee which had attempted to have the national convention demand that Roosevelt pursue a course of "absolute" neutrality in the European war. The convention, however, called for aid to Great Britain. Armstrong then joined America First, where from the start he was unhappy about that organization's emphasis on preparedness and the defense of the United States. He proved to be an unusual type of legionnaire who wanted the major effort of America First to be placed upon a constructive program for peace. On the other hand, he was not a pacifist but rather a man who saw his role as one of uniting the pacifist and fortress-America wings of the anti-war movement, linking the internationalists of the peace movement with the nationalists of the veterans organization. To that end he worked to organize the No Foreign Wars Campaign, for which he initially was acting chairman. He was quickly moved out of his position of authority by colleagues contemptuous of his sympathy for pacifists and ultimately resigned when the organization appeared to be taking a pro-Nazi, anti-Semitic course. In the spring of 1941 Armstrong found himself without a satisfactory organization within which to work for peace and decided to form a new one focused on the Far East.[90]

By the end of the summer an increasing sense of urgency led to a meeting of a number of men and women interested in working to prevent hostilities with Japan. Armstrong believed that his major problem would be finding a way to present the project so that it would not be open to attack as a pro-Japanese attempt to betray China. To Libby he insisted that "no one connected with this would countenance that, of course." Joining Armstrong were, in addition to Libby, several former missionaries to Japan, three authorities on Far Eastern affairs (including Payson Treat of Stanford University), Paul Hutchinson of the

Christian Century, William Henry Chamberlin, a noted journalist, and Ralph Townsend of *Scribners-Commentator*. Mark Shaw, a missionary affiliated with America First and the National Council for the Prevention of War, served as acting chairman and plans were made to hold a conference in October. On September 30 Armstrong visited the Department of State, where he declared that the United States had no interests "worth the candle" in the Far East and should "make a deal" with Japan rather than go to war. In listing the members of his committee he included two noted scholars, A. Whitney Griswold and Paul Clyde, but the State Department made special note of Townsend's membership.[91]

Armstrong, pleased with the interest shown in his idea and the publicity the meeting received, acquiesced readily in the decision to delay the conference so as to plan it carefully and ensure its success. Then lightning struck—Townsend was charged with being a foreign agent, receiving foreign money, and Libby warned Shaw that "we hear that there is another member of the Committee liable to the same charge." Armstrong tried to clear the committee and apparently succeeded, but the damage was done. Shaw resigned, but not before joining Armstrong in a letter to Hull. The letter presented a remarkably tame program, calling for continuation of negotiations provided Japan refrained from aggravating the situation; efforts toward the resumption of normal trade contingent upon Japanese willingness to cooperate in "reasonable" measures toward peace in China, such as a token withdrawal of troops and recognition of China's territorial integrity; a gesture by the United States, such as the export of some materials essential to normal Japanese industrial activity; an effort by the United States to encourage the Soviet Union to observe its nonaggression pact with Japan; and a conference of all nations with interests in the Pacific. A week after the letter was sent, Armstrong made one last sally to the Department of State, accompanied by E. Stanley Jones, a famous missionary. Jones had been an early advocate of an economic boycott against Japan and had served as a sponsor of the Price Committee, but in the fall he became fearful of war. He argued that Japan was prepared to give up its course of aggression, break with the Germans, and be reconciled with China and the United States. The Japanese embassy, he said, had advised him that if the United States lifted the oil embargo, the forces of peace in Japan would be strengthened and Japan could leave China voluntarily. But by November 1941 most Americans and their government had grown weary of waiting for the forces of peace in Japan, and the terms proposed by Armstrong and Shaw were nowhere near sufficient to stave off the forces of war.[92]

Nonetheless, China's friends took no risks. McKee had organized his own group—Don't Arm Japan—in Pittsburgh, and Mrs. Fitch, having harassed the White Committee staff perhaps more than she had her friends in the Price Committee, had launched the Emergency Committee for Complete Embargo. But the most effective campaign to prevent the administration from seeking a modus vivendi with Japan was the one fought by Greene, Eichelberger, and Price, largely through the White Committee but also through the journal of the League of Nations Association and in personal letters and appearances. The final battle against appeasement started when it became increasingly clear that the freezing of Japanese assets would end the flow of oil to Japan. From that point on every effort was made to prevent backsliding by appeals to American ideals and to America's self-interest. Eichelberger began in August by referring to China's remarkable resistance and the need to reevaluate China, to view it as one of the four "great powers" resisting aggression. A letter from the Washington office of the White Committee conceded that temptation existed to reach agreement with Japan so that the United States could concentrate on the war in Europe; but it warned of the danger of a compromise that would undermine the common front, sacrifice China, and leave the United States to fight Japan under less favorable circumstances. Price exploited the idea that appeasement of Japan might eliminate China as an ally. In September he wrote to Hull enclosing a telegram from his brother Frank and other Americans in China warning that appeasement would strengthen pro-fascist elements in China. A month later another letter to Hull and to Hamilton contained Frank Price's warning that Chinese morale was being endangered by the continuation of the Japanese-American talks.[93]

Another tack was taken by Roger Greene in appealing to American principles. On September 16, 1941 the White Committee prepared a new statement of policy calling for rejection of any agreement with Japan that sacrificed American principles respecting China. Greene was pleased by the strong support for the statement, which included a tip from Washington, probably from Hornbeck, that a letter and telegram campaign to Hull and Roosevelt would be valuable. Using the statement he had already drafted, Greene sent out a special appeal under Price Committee auspices, with the organization presumably resurrected for the occasion.[94]

Two further points of significance were raised in this last battle against appeasement. One appeared in a letter written by a friend of Greene, Julian Randolph. The letter interested Hornbeck, who promised to bring it to the attention of certain of his associates. Randolph claimed in particular (a point that among others was underscored by Hornbeck) that altogether too much consideration was being given to preserving Japanese "face," overlooking the fact that the Japanese were excellent bluffers and very capable of backing down. For those who feared that the Oriental psychology would not permit the Japanese to yield to American pressure, this may have been a comforting argument. The second new point was made by Emmett Corrigan, a member of the White Committee's executive committee. In a long statement charging the organization with having obscured the menace of Japan and with following Roosevelt instead of pushing him, he warned of public suspicion that "interventionists" were concerned merely with the preservation of the British empire. Corrigan insisted that this suspicion could not be overcome so long as the "rape of China" was condoned.[95]

Toward the end of November Hartley and Herbert Bayard Swope, who was active in the New York chapter, attempted to dilute the committee's stand on China. Swope wanted all reference to China deleted from the new policy statement to avoid interference with the Japanese-American negotiations in progress. Eichelberger, however, had already indicated he would not retreat again. The United States, he insisted, had to atone for supplying the materials for Japan's aggression in China. There could be no further appeasement and there was a good chance that Japan would yield if America stood firm. Despite his dedication to peace, Eichelberger took the position that if Japan would not yield, better war than appeasement. On November 28, 1941, after the renewal at Berlin of the Anti-Comintern Pact, the committee demanded an end to Japanese-American negotiations, charging that the talks were a Japanese stall designed to delay American action in the Pacific while Japan built more battleships and the Germans sought to regain the initiative in Europe. In the twilight hours of peace the White Committee proved unrelenting in its attitude toward Japan.[96]

And so, as Nomura talked with Hull, there was but one feeble effort by a private organization, that led by O. K. Armstrong, to bring about a relaxation of the pressures on Japan as a means of avoiding war. Most of the groups working in opposition to administration policy sought to avoid involvement in war by keeping the United States impartial, feared being drawn into the war in Europe, but virtually ignored the mounting crisis in the Pacific. Similarly, those groups that viewed Britain's battle as America's and either supported the administration's course or, like the influential Fight For Freedom group, demanded intervention concentrated their. efforts on events across the Atlantic.[97] But those individuals—like Roger Greene and Harry Price—whose efforts with the Price Committee were largely frustrated by the administration's Europe-first orientation, were able, with an assist from the Japanese, to use mounting American opposition to Germany against Japan. Japan's decision to ally with Germany and Italy had provided them with a means of linking the two wars far better than any they might have devised themselves. Greene, by disassociating himself from members of the group who seemed more interested in China than in the United States, by his close relationship with Eichelberger, and by his ability to recognize the primacy of the European theater, had been able to win for his program the support of the influential White Committee and to gain for the Asian theater the attention of the vastly larger audience to which that organization appealed. Given the inability of other Price Committee regulars to win comparable respect from the advocates of collective security, it is not inconceivable that, without Greene's presence in a position of authority in the White Committee, the elements in that organization that favored concentration on the Atlantic community, to the point of willingness to appease Japan, would have prevailed.

In the period 1939-41, however, private groups appear to have had little influence on American policy toward Japan. Most organizations shared the attitude of the administration in that they were preoccupied with the war in Europe, and those like the Price Committee that looked toward the Far East were thwarted by that preoccupation. The persistent demands for an embargo on the sale of war supplies to Japan, which first the Price Committee and later the White Committee stimulated, did not succeed in moving Roosevelt to act until he believed that events in Europe and Japanese policy warranted action. These demands, when called to the attention of the Japanese, enabled Roosevelt to point to his own more moderate policies, but the Japanese did not reciprocate with moderation of their own.

In one sense, however, the campaign of the White Committee after the signing of the Tripartite Pact may have been important. In addition to arguing that the pact made one war of two, the committee elevated China to the status of ally. Once China became an ally, its distress was no longer a matter for mere sympathy. The further appeasement of Japan was no longer simply a matter of sacrificing limited American interests to buy time, but of betraying an ally. Once having stopped the sale of war supplies to Japan, a resumption of the sale of oil in even the most limited quantities would not only have outraged China's friends and evoked a cry of appeasement from the White Committee, but it might well have touched a public nerve, left raw by the committee and by earlier Price organization campaigns. To the extent that fear of public reaction prevented the administration from reaching a modus vivendi with Japan in the autumn of 1941, to that extent the work of the Price and White committees was not in vain.

V

The activities of private organizations seeking to influence American policy toward Japan did not become important until the Sino-Japanese War began in 1937. During the Manchurian crisis the peace societies had been unable to agree on any program that went beyond the policies the administration chose to adopt. In the absence of unity, whatever slim chance they may have had of convincing Hoover of the wisdom of economic or other pressure was lost. In the early years of the Roosevelt administration relative quiet in the Far East allowed the peace movement to focus on other problems, especially the divisive issue of neutrality legislation. Before full-scale war began in 1937, the American peace movement had split into pacifist and collective security wings. Until this time no organizations other than peace groups had been of any importance.

In 1937 six tiny pacifist societies, representing perhaps less than ten thousand members but employing every known means of mobilizing public opinion, succeeded in terrorizing the administration. Roosevelt vacillated on questions of American rights in China and refrained from extending any aid to China, apparently in response to the campaigns of the groups led by Frederick Libby of the National Council for the Prevention of War and Dorothy Detzer of the Women's International League for Peace and Freedom. For Hull the experience seems to have been traumatic, but Roosevelt recovered sufficiently to refuse to apply the neutrality law to the undeclared Sino-Japanese War and to defy the radical pacifists with the rhetoric of his "quarantine" speech. The episode suggests that in the absence of either organized opposition or presidential leadership, Libby and Miss Detzer were able to seize the initiative, give the appearance of expressing the public will, and send the administration scurrying. That their power was limited was evident when Roosevelt defied them successfully. In the years that followed, the influence of the pacifists diminished as men of lesser faith sought other formulae with which to live in the world of Japanese militarism and Nazi brutality.

Nonetheless, the American people remained overwhelmingly opposed to involvement in the Far Eastern conflict or in any war. Roosevelt's power was limited by this anti-war sentiment, to which the pacifists could appeal. In 1937 he dared go no further than refuse to invoke the neutrality law. Before he could do more—if he wanted to do more—public attitudes had to change. Missionaries, the Chinese government, and the collective security wing of the peace movement helped Roosevelt effect that change.

The advocates of collective security within the peace movement had been outmaneuvered consistently during the mid-1930s, but in 1938 they joined with a number of men and women responsive to China's plight in the Price Committee's campaign for economic sanctions against Japan. Although the Chinese government helped the committee financially, it exercised no control over Harry Price and Roger Greene, the two men who provided the committee's leadership. The Price Committee served as the principal vehicle for the efforts of American missionaries to China, many of whom saw their anti-Japanese activities in the United States as part of their mission. By the summer of 1939 the organization had helped to focus American sympathy for China on a demand for an embargo on the sale of war supplies to Japan. At this point the committee came into conflict with the administration, which had earlier encouraged its campaign. Roosevelt and Hull were pleased to have the committee neutralize pacifist sentiment in the United States, largely because of the greater freedom this provided the administration. But though they appreciated the rising demand for sanctions, to which they could direct the attention of the Japanese, they did not desire mandatory embargo legislation that would limit their flexibility in dealing with Japan. The Price Committee had helped to shape public opinion along the lines desired by the administration, but it had not won Roosevelt and Hull over to its program.

In July 1939 the administration sensed that pressures for anti-Japanese action were intensifying to the point where a fierce debate over embargo legislation was likely in the Senate. To relieve these pressures at a time when Roosevelt and Hull were too full of forebodings over the crisis in Europe to risk provoking Japan, the American government notified Japan of its wish to terminate the Treaty of Commerce and Navigation between the two countries. No sanctions were applied against Japan in the following months or in January 1940, when the treaty lapsed. Given the administration's preeminent concern with European affairs and the unwillingness of Roosevelt and Hull to stir the Far Eastern pot, the Price Committee found itself in de facto opposition to government policy.

With the coming of war in Europe and the intensification of that war in the spring of 1940, the advocates of collective security were drawn away from the Price Committee into campaigns that had little relevance to the Far East. The organization ceased to be of importance, but several of its members, particularly Roger Greene, worked within the Europe-oriented White Committee to win support for the Price group's program.

Before the Price Committee ended its campaign, Congress passed the National Defense Act giving the president authority to control the export of items he considered essential to the defense of the United States. Roosevelt's use of this authority did not satisfy China's friends, but in July 1940 control of the flow of scrap iron and oil to Japan began. Greene and Price had worked to obtain the authority for the president, and their campaign had left no doubt of public receptivity to such economic pressure against Japan. Nonetheless, it is unlikely that the committee's efforts would have met with even this limited success without the German spring offensive and subsequent Japanese pressures in Southeast Asia.

The intensification of economic pressure on Japan and aid to China in the year that followed was related less to the activities of private groups than to

Roosevelt's estimate of the responses necessary to a policy of encouraging China, checking Japan, and keeping the United States out of war in the Pacific. Roosevelt was aware of continued demands for an embargo on all war supplies to Japan and of a mounting dissatisfaction among men who feared for China, but his policy toward Japan does not seem to have been influenced by the activities of private organizations. On the contrary, the administration had used the Price Committee to neutralize organizations critical of administration policy and then abandoned the committee well short of its goals. Similarly, the White group accomplished only those parts of its program that it held in common with the administration. Both organizations were important in that they mobilized public support for Roosevelt's policies, but they had little influence on Roosevelt, the shape of his policy, or his timetable.

The question that remains is perhaps the most difficult of all to answer: did the work of private organizations prevent Roosevelt from seeking an accommodation with Japan in the autumn of 1941? The efforts of Roger Greene within the White Committee had prevented that organization from ignoring China's cause and focusing exclusively on the war in Europe. Without denying the greater importance of Britain and the European war to the security of the United States, he maintained that the United States had a stake in the outcome of the war across the Pacific, that China was an ally and could not be sacrificed. Clark Eichelberger, always the driving force within the White Committee, agreed with Greene, and in the autumn of 1941 the advocates of collective security and the friends of China again joined forces in a final campaign against Japan. The White Committee would not countenance appeasement in the Far East, nor would the American people, long sympathetic to China and conditioned by three and a half years of Price and White Committee campaigns. If concern for public opinion dictated the American response in the negotiations with Japan, then private organizations, specifically the Price Committee and the White Committee, helped to determine that response. But again, the evidence suggests that Roosevelt acted in accordance with his perception of Japanese intent, that Japan rather than any private organization was responsible for Roosevelt's decision.

THE ROLE OF
LIBERAL NONGOVERNMENTAL
ORGANIZATIONS IN JAPAN

Ogata Sadako

The decade that began in 1931 was characterized by the rapid growth of right-wing nationalist groups and the subsequent decline of liberal power. In evaluating liberal nongovernmental organizations and their role in Japanese decision making vis-à-vis the United States, this paper will first study them in the 1920s when their objectives and activities were relatively distinct. It will then proceed to observe their reactions to the Manchurian affair and to Japan's withdrawal from the League of Nations, events that marked the turning point from liberal leadership to nationalist domination. The third part will discuss the declining influence of liberal groups as a whole. At the same time it will inquire into the limited ways in which some of them tried to maintain their identities.

In selecting the organizations two criteria have been applied: The organization must have been liberal and its primary interest must have been to maintain peaceful relations with the United States. Christian groups have been examined only to the extent that they were involved in problems of war and peace.

I

The origin of nongovernmental organizations with interest in the problem of peace may be traced to the period immediately following the Russo-Japanese War of 1904-05. Victory over Russia gave a tremendous boost to Japanese national self-confidence. Some began to think in terms of Japan's contribution to the preservation of world peace. Convinced of the importance of nongovernmental circles in ensuring good relations with the United States, Foreign Minister Komura Jutarō, when he returned from Portsmouth, called upon Shibusawa Eiichi to solicit his support. Shibusawa, founder and president of the Daiichi Bank, was the outstanding business leader of modern Japan. He came to take great personal interest in Japanese-American relations, and it was through him that many organizations dedicated to the preservation of peace were founded.[1]

The Japan Peace Society, formed in April 1906, was the first peace organization in Japan. Gilbert Bowles of the Friends Mission is said to have been responsible for encouraging Ebara Soroku, a member of the House of Representatives and founder of the Azabu Middle School, to form such an organization.[2] Ōkuma Shigenobu became its first president. The Japan Peace Society expanded its leadership and activities in 1922 when Shibusawa became chairman of its council and former Finance Minister Sakatani Yoshirō became vice chairman; its board of directors included outstanding parliamentarians such as Ozaki Yukio and Shimada Saburō, professors such as Nitobe Inazō and Anesaki Masaharu of Tokyo Imperial University, as well as university presidents and business leaders. A few American missionaries and businessmen were active members, including Bowles who became one of the three non-Japanese directors. The regular membership of the society in February 1912 totaled 562, of which 11 were women. In terms of nationality, there were 478 Japanese and 84 foreign nationals. While 119 sustaining members paid annual dues of 5 yen, over 400 regular members paid 1 yen yearly. Some business leaders, including Shibusawa, made lump sum contributions.

The activities of the Japan Peace Society were largely educational and directed toward domestic as well as overseas groups. It published a magazine called *Peace* between 1912 and 1917 and sponsored many lectures on international affairs. For its overseas audiences it issued in 1917 an English-language magazine called *The Japan Peace Movement.*

The Japan Peace Society took the initiative in coordinating the activities of various peace groups. The years just after World War I were the heyday of the peace movement in Japan. The Japan Peace Society, League of Nations Association, Fellowship for the Limitation of Armaments (Gunbi Shukushō Dōshikai), International Education Association (Kokusai Kyōiku Kyōkai), Women's Peace Association (Fujin Heiwa Kyōkai), Women's Christian Temperance Union, YWCA, YMCA, and World Christian League (Kirisutokyō Sekai Renmei) formed the Japan League of Peace Movements (Heiwa Undō Nihon Renmei) and held meetings once a month until the great earthquake of 1923. Tagawa Daikichirō, Christian educator and member of the House of Representatives, served as chairman.

Although the primary concern of the Japan Peace Society was the general question of preserving peace, the issue that constantly harassed the society was anti-Japanese sentiment in the United States. On December 11, 1920 it sponsored a joint meeting with more than twenty nongovernmental organizations. This meeting adopted a resolution demanding the abrogation of anti-Japanese legislation passed by the state of California and opposing any negotiations that might lead to the complete shutting off of Japanese immigration to the United States.[3]

Growing concern over Japanese-American relations occasioned the founding of several organizations devoted primarily to the promotion of friendly relations between the two countries. In 1915 Gilbert Bowles representing the American Peace Society, composed of American residents in Japan, proposed to the Japan Peace Society the organization of a joint investigating committee to study questions of mutual interest. Fifteen were chosen from each society, the Japanese members including Ebara Soroku, Shibusawa Eiichi, Nitobe Inazō, Sakatani Yoshirō, and Soeda Juichi. The committee continued to meet periodically until the functions of the Japan Peace Society were largely taken over by the League of Nations Association of Japan, which was formed in 1920. The American Peace Society together with the Japan Peace Society in 1917 set up the International Service Bureau with Kawakami Isamu as executive director. The main activities of the bureau were to correspond with peace organizations abroad, to exchange publications with overseas organizations, and to undertake translation of materials that might benefit the members of the two societies.[4]

In October 1915 Shibusawa visited the United States and met Wallace M. Alexander, president of Alexander and Baldwin, Ltd. of San Francisco, who had already organized the Japanese Relations Committee consisting of twenty-three members of the San Francisco Chamber of Commerce. Upon his return to Japan Shibusawa organized the counterpart Japanese-American Relations Committee whose sole purpose was to promote friendship through mutual understanding and to attempt to settle any disputes that might arise between the two countries.[5] Like the American group, its membership was theoretically limited to twenty-four but in fact numbered a few more. It represented the "cream" of the internationally minded Japanese business leadership as well as a few individuals from academic circles, such as Professors Nitobe and Anesaki and President Harada Tasuku of Doshisha University. Takagi Yasaka, the first professor of American constitutional history and diplomacy at Tokyo Imperial University, also became a member several years later.[6]

When the anti-Japanese movement in California aroused the concern of the Carnegie Endowment for International Peace, it turned to the Japanese Relations Committee and the Japanese-American Relations Committee. Since the Berne Conference of 1911 the Carnegie Endowment had been in close contact with Sakatani Yoshirō and sponsored the founding of the Japanese Research Committee. With regard to the California issue, it proposed to undertake joint American and Japanese studies on such topics as "labor conditions in California and Japan" or "the opportunities for using American capital jointly with Japanese capital in Asiatic investments." Apparently the Carnegie Endowment itself was handicapped in its efforts to finance "a Commission for directly influencing the action of the state of California" because of the antagonism it would create among "the demagogues of the Pacific Coast."[7]

The Japanese-American Relations Committee entertained and conferred with many Americans visiting Japan. It also exerted pressure on business leaders and government officials in both countries to bring about the repeal of discriminatory legislation in America. In March and April of 1920 it invited to Japan two business groups headed by Wallace M. Alexander and Frank A. Vanderlip, chairman of the board of American International Corporation and president of the Japan Society of New York. The Vanderlip group included, among others, former Treasury Secretary Lyman J. Gage, Henry W. Taft, a lawyer and brother of President Taft, and Jacob Gould Schurman, then president of Cornell University; Julian Street, editor of the *Saturday Evening Post*, was to report on his observations and conclusions drawn from the conference trip.[8]

Another product of the anti-Japanese movement in California was the founding of the America-Japan Society on April 13, 1917. It was initiated by B. W. Fleisher of the *Japan Advertiser*, Kaneko Kentarō, the America-educated privy councillor and member of both the Japan Peace Society and the Japanese-American Relations Committee, and Dr. Takamine Jōkichi, a well-known pharmacologist. Its purpose was largely social—to attain friendly relations through "promoting and facilitating the intermingling of Japanese and Americans."[9] The United States ambassador was to be honorary president, while Kaneko became the first president and Fleisher and Hioki Eki, former minister to China, served as vice presidents. The inaugural meeting was attended by 173 members, of whom 112 were Japanese. They were largely from business circles but included also diplomats and scholars.[10]

When Japanese-American relations took a sharp downturn in 1920 over the question of anti-Japanese land legislation in California, E. W. Frazer and J. R. Geary went to the United States as representatives of the American members of the society to warn the authorities in Washington and California of the intense feelings aroused in Japan. Associations of Americans residing in Yokohama, Tokyo, and Kobe as well as American members of the America-Japan Society cabled to the secretary of state resolutions calling for "patience and careful deliberation" and warning that the action in California was "threatening the destruction of the traditional friendship and the future estrangement of the two peoples."[11] When Frazer and Geary returned, they recommended setting up a Japanese publicity center in the United States. Thereupon, the America-Japan Society, in cooperation with the Japanese-American Relations Committee, formed a special committee to examine the possibility of opening such a center.[12]

Although most organizations devoted to improving relations with the United States were experiencing difficulties, on April 23, 1920 the League of Nations Association of Japan was formed with a good deal of popular approval. The idea of establishing such a body was conceived by a group of scholars and diplomats who had been in Paris at the time of the Versailles Conference and had become convinced that world peace could be advanced only through the cooperation of nongovernmental organizations. Their plan received the ready support of Shibusawa, Sakatani, Soeda, Anesaki, Tagawa, and Date Gen' ichirō and Miyaoka Tsunejirō of the Foreign Ministry. Shibusawa himself became president and Sakatani and Soeda served as vice presidents. Six of the twelve directors were university professors, the rest were businessmen and diplomats.[13]

In September of the same year Prime Minister Hara Takashi called in a group of leading businessmen to explain to them the importance of the League of Nations Association and to seek their financial and moral support.[14] The post-Versailles enthusiasm for the League of Nations helped the association to develop rapidly. From the original 683 members in 1920, the association claimed 11,771 in 1932, of whom 5,652 were students and 556 were women. Student members were organized into forty-eight campus-based groups that sponsored debates and lectures. In 1930 the women members formed a separate group headed by such educators and leaders of women's organizations as Yoshioka Yayoi, founder and president of Tokyo Women's Medical College, Inoue Hideko, founder and president of Nihon Women's College, and Tsuneko

Gauntlett, president of the Women's Christian Temperance Union. The association also set up sixteen prefectural associations led by local political and business leaders.[15]

From the beginning the association relied for its financial support not on membership dues but on business contributions and government subsidies. Largely through Shibusawa's efforts, contributions from heads of zaibatsu families and the presidents of major industries and banks totaled 164,080 yen between 1920 and 1923.[16] Although in 1931 contributions from business groups decreased to 31,000 yen, due largely to the depression, government subsidies seem to have increased gradually from 10,000 yen in 1920 to 50,000 yen in 1931.[17] In 1924-25 the Foreign Ministry is said to have provided as much as 100,000 yen.[18]

Being thus well endowed, the association was able to sponsor lectures and publications that aroused public interest in the League of Nations. Many of its directors made speaking tours throughout the country, while some of the prefectural associations sponsored three-day summer schools to which lecturers were invited from Tokyo. It issued two monthly magazines in Japanese—*Sekai to warera* (The World and Ourselves) and *Kokusai chishiki* (International Knowledge)—and an English-language monthly called *International Gleanings from Japan* which was distributed throughout the world. It also published books on the League and other aspects of international affairs, averaging a book a month during its most active period.[19] Representatives of the association regularly attended the annual meetings of the World Confederation of the League of Nations.

The last nongovernmental organization of concern here is the Institute of Pacific Relations (IPR). It was organized following a conference convened in Honolulu in July 1925 as a result of the feeling among many groups and individuals concerned with international affairs that the Pacific nations had entered "a period of disillusionment and readjustment of [their] ideas of one another" and that the exchange and discussion of accurate information might promote peace in the area.[20] Delegates to the conference decided to establish a permanent organization in various countries of the Pacific area and a central office in Honolulu. The Japanese delegation was headed by Sawayanagi Masatarō, a member of the House of Peers and president of the Imperial Education Association, Professors Takagi and Takayanagi Kenzō of Tokyo Imperial University, Saitō Sōichi, general secretary of the Tokyo YMCA, and several representatives of Christian and youth organizations. To cover the expenses Shibusawa Eiichi raised 10,000 yen through members of the Japanese-American Relations Committee and the Foreign Ministry provided 20,000 yen.[21]

On April 6, 1926 the Japanese Council of the IPR was organized with Shibusawa as chairman and Inoue Junnosuke, governor of the Bank of Japan and a leading member of both the Japanese-American Relations Committee and the League of Nations Association, as chairman of the board of directors; Sakatani Yoshirō, Sawayanagi Masatarō, Tsurumi Yūsuke, Takayanagi Kenzō, Takagi Yasaka, and Saitō Sōichi served as directors. Fifty-five members were named to the council, including all the members of the Japanese-American Relations Committee.[22] The IPR was strongly supported by businessmen and scholars actively concerned to improve relations with the United States. They saw in the institute an important channel through which to voice Japanese views on immigration and racial problems, trade relations, and other issues likely to become sources of tension in the Pacific area.[23] The IPR played a major role in Japanese-American relations until it merged with the League of Nations Association in 1935.

A brief survey of the attitudes of Christian organizations is appropriate, although their main focus was not on international relations. Generally speaking, Japanese Christian churches concentrated on the task of individual spiritual salvation and tended to regard as "dangerous" those who became involved in social problems. In 1919, however, the Union Church of Japan became the first to set up a social section to deal with labor conditions, social policy, and the Christian approach to social unrest. By then Christian socialists such as Suzuki Bunji, Matsuoka Komakichi, and Kagawa Toyohiko were actively participating in socialist movements. When the Japan Christian League (Nihon Kirisutokyō Renmei) was formed in 1923 to promote cooperation among Christian groups, it also established a social section to formulate a Christian position on moral and social problems. Other churches followed suit.

The Japan Christian League took a positive step to examine social problems in Japan in a report presented to the World Missionary Conference at Jerusalem in the spring of 1928. This conference greatly stimulated the social consciousness of Japanese Christians, and the league adopted a declaration that resolved to draft a social creed for Japanese Christians. The creed was to emphasize two principles: to assure that industries served human purposes, and to uphold the spirit of the League of Nations, the Pact of Paris, and peaceful international cooperation.[24] Tagawa Daikichirō headed the special committee that was to draw up the social creed.

The creed marked the high point of Christian liberalism in confronting the mounting social, economic, and political problems of postwar Japan. Its fourteen articles enumerated the social goals for which Japanese Christians were to strive. The more political and international articles, which Tagawa himself was in charge of drafting, included:

   1. human rights and equal opportunity;
   2. nondiscriminatory treatment of various races and nationalities;
   11. establishment of organs to mediate disputes between labor and management;
   14. arms limitation, a system of courts of arbitration, and a world without war.[25]

The other articles dealt with labor conditions—protection of women and minors, working hours, holidays, wages, social security, etc.

In stressing social involvement, however, the creed distinguished the Christian approach from that of the "right" or the "left." It was especially careful to state its opposition to "materialistic education, materialistic ideology, class struggle, and social reform through revolutionary means."[26] This concern is not surprising in view of the fact that rising communist influence in Japan had led to mass arrests of communists and radicals on March 15, 1928 and the official banning of the far left Rōdō Nōmintō (Labor-Farmer Party) on April 10. Taking advantage of the Christians' anxiety, the Ministry of Education repeatedly urged the Japan Christian League to act as a brake on the radicalization of Christians, lest Christianity itself be counted, together with socialism and communism, as "dangerous thought."[27]

Two other Christian groups should be mentioned because of their strong commitment to liberalism and peace: the Mukyōkai (Non-Church) movement, founded by Uchimura Kanzō, and the Society of Friends. The Mukyōkai movement involved a considerable number of individuals who resisted official pressure during the 1930s, but it is difficult to treat it as an organization because its very raison d'etre was a protest against sectarian division and formal church organization. It stressed direct contact between God and the individual and centered its activities on small Bible-reading groups. It won the support of many leading Christian intellectuals, notably Yanaihara Tadao, professor of colonial policy at Tokyo Imperial University.

The Friends' strong pacifist tradition gave them a special interest in the question of peace. Gilbert Bowles in particular was a leading figure in many peace organizations, including the Japan Peace Society, the American Peace Society, and the Japan Fellowship of Reconciliation. The Friends also claimed among their members Nitobe Inazō, who was to make great personal efforts for peace between Japan and the United States.

II

It is clear from the preceding brief survey that nongovernmental organizations in Japan were interrelated in their objectives and leadership. Aside from the Christians, they can be divided into two broad categories: those interested in the general problem of peace and those primarily concerned with Japanese-American relations. The two were closely aligned and eventually merged into a single organization. The Japan Peace Society dissolved into the League of Nations Association of Japan in 1925. The Japanese-American Relations Committee joined the Institute of Pacific Relations, which in turn united with the League of Nations Association in 1935.

As to their leadership, we find a very high correlation especially at the top level. At least two persons, Shibusawa Eiichi and his son-in-law Sakatani Yoshirō, served as president, vice president, or board member of all five organizations. Shibusawa's importance in the development of nongovernmental organizations cannot be overemphasized. He was the most influential figure in the business world and the one man through whom funds could be raised for practically any purpose. Around him developed a network of personal relationships drawn in part from business but also from academic and other circles. Government authorities turned to him whenever they needed public support. As time went by, his own involvement seemed to strengthen his sense of personal mission, which was directed in particular at promoting friendship with Japan's neighbors, especially the United States.[28] At the top administrative level were also Professors Nitobe Inazō and Anesaki Masaharu, Kaneko Kentarō, Soeda Juichi, and Inoue Junnosuke, who were each on the boards of four organizations. Many members of the Japanese-American Relations Committee played important roles in two or three groups.

Although nongovernmental, these organizations had ties to the government in two respects: personnel and contacts. Many of their leaders were members of the Diet and some were former high government officials. The Foreign Ministry was especially well represented in the League of Nations Association and the America-Japan Society. In addition, the League of Nations Association received substantial subsidies from the government, while the Institute of Pacific Relations conferred frequently with the Foreign Ministry and, at least in the earlier period, received financial assistance to send delegates to conferences.

The general political outlook of the leadership was that of the post-Versailles liberal movement in Japan. Externally they supported the international system embodied in the League of Nations; internally they favored parliamentary government and universal manhood suffrage. This position was in clear contrast to right-wing demands for continental expansion and the establishment of a national socialist government at home. Needless to say, it was also distinct from that of Marxist groups that advocated revolutionary reform of the existing social order.

The first foreign policy issue that drastically divided the liberals from the right wing was the Washington Conference. While the latter regarded the conference as the "lost rights" conference[29] that had clamped "fetters and shackles" on Japanese expansion,[30] the liberals were ready to give it their full endorsement. During the conference the Japan Peace Society sent its executive director, Kawakami Isamu, to the United States to cultivate close relations with peace societies and religious groups there.[31]

Two leading parliamentary members of the Japan Peace Society, Ozaki Yukio and Shimada Saburō, together with Tagawa Daikichirō and Ishibashi Tanzan of the *Tōyō keizai shinpō* (Oriental Economist), organized the Fellowship for the Limitation of Armaments at the time of the Washington Conference. It included such controversial figures as Mizuno Hironori, a navy captain with literary talents who was put into the reserves as punishment for his pacifist writings during World War I. The fellowship made great efforts to arouse public support for disarmament and world peace. Tagawa himself went to the United States to appeal to the American authorities and the public. The *Tōyō keizai shinpō* sponsored a disarmament conference and forwarded its resolutions to President Harding.[32]

The League of Nations Association also favored disarmament and appointed committees to study naval disarmament as well as disarmament in general. When the League of Nations held a disarmament conference in Geneva in February 1932, the association embarked on a signature campaign to mobilize public support. At the same time it tried to show how disarmament could alleviate the economic burdens caused by the depression.[33] To the liberals the disarmament issue was important from two standpoints. Domestically it meant providing funds for public welfare. Internationally it represented one of the two pillars of the League security system, the other being the strengthening of mechanisms for the pacific settlement of international disputes. The League of Nations Association insisted that Japan sign Article 36 of the statutes of the Permanent Court of International Justice, thereby placing itself under the compulsory jurisdiction of the court. The opening statement of the November 1,

1931 issue of *Kokusai chishiki* pressed for the immediate signing of Article 36; Japan, it declared, might stipulate conditions and reservations if necessary, but at least such an act would make its peaceful intentions clear to the world.[34]

Did the liberals then expect that Japan's foreign policy demands could be met within the framework of the League of Nations and the Washington Conference system? Apparently they did. The liberals were no different from their rightist opponents in their belief that Japan possessed special interests in China and that expansion onto the continent was just and necessary. What distinguished them, however, was the fact that they envisaged expansion largely in economic terms and felt that conflict with the principles of the Open Door and the territorial integrity of China could be avoided.[35] For example, in 1926 the Japanese Research Committee proposed that the Carnegie Endowment for International Peace undertake a study of the economic importance of Manchuria and Mongolia. In making the recommendation Sakatani wrote to Professor James T. Shotwell, director of the Division of History and Economics of the Carnegie Endowment, that the topic had been selected because of the "economic significance of these Chinese dominions in molding the destiny of" and maintaining peace in the Far East. "They are destined to play such a part in the future history of the world that well informed persons, as I deem, cannot afford to overlook them."[36]

Some went even further, expecting to gain American recognition of Manchuria and China as an area for Japanese economic expansion and immigration. In September 1924 Sakatani himself had handed a memorandum to Anesaki Masaharu, who was then leaving for the United States, in which he suggested that Japan restrict emigration to the United States and make no military demands respecting any part of North or South America; in exchange, the United States might agree not to make military demands, interfere politically, or extend political loans to China.[37] Although such a deal was clearly out of the question, Japanese expansion in China continued to be linked to the American exclusion acts. Both Kaneko Kentarō and Ishii Kikujirō, former ambassador to the United States, privy councillor, and president of the League of Nations Association after Shibusawa, argued that Japanese expansion on the continent had received the blessing of Theodore Roosevelt. Kaneko stated that the president had personally declared to him that he intended to divert the direction of Japanese immigration from the United States to Manchuria.[38]

Up until the eve of the Manchurian Incident in 1931 the liberals regarded the immigration question rather than the China issue as the main cause of conflict between Japan and the United States. We have already noted the great stress the nongovernmental organizations with which we are concerned here placed on the immigration problem. Their motives appear to have been mixed. To some it was the most pressing threat to peace in Japan's foreign relations. To others it endangered business relations with the United States. To still others it was an affront to Japan's national pride. Underlying all these reasons, however, was a sense of affinity with the United States that strengthened their desire to maintain good relations.

Shibusawa's study of Townsend Harris is said to have prompted his great respect for the United States as a country of "just and humanitarian" principles. Harris' approach to Japan appeared in marked contrast to the pressures Great

Britain had employed in China, especially at the time of the Opium War.[39] Through his personal contacts with Americans, however, Shibusawa had perceived a certain arrogance in their dealings with Japanese, and he was not without fear that the two peoples might clash someday.[40] When the immigration law was enacted in 1924, he was "deeply hurt" and probably felt it "more keenly than any other high-minded Japanese."[41] Shibusawa's indignation was never erased, and in a message to the Kyoto Conference of the IPR in 1929 he made clear that "the dispute caused by the immigration law in 1924 has not been solved, and the scar left on Japanese national honor will remain until it is justly solved."[42] According to the *Japan Advertiser* of November 2, 1929, Shibusawa's reference to the immigration law aroused "a rather pained surprise in Washington, which long [has] been accustomed to regard the incident as diplomatically closed."[43]

The image of the United States as a champion of equality and justice was indeed shattered by the passage of the immigration law, which came like a "bombshell" to the liberals.[44] Nitobe Inazō, who had studied in America, was married to an American, and aspired to be a "bridge across the Pacific," was so incensed by the law that he resolved never to visit the United States until it was revised.[45] Perhaps the most dramatic protest was the resignation of Kaneko Kentarō as president of the America-Japan Society on July 22, 1924. His letter of resignation stated that ever since his student days at Harvard fifty years earlier he had devoted himself to improving Japan's relations with the United States. Passage of the immigration law, however, had terminated all his hopes and in consequence he could no longer continue as president of the society.[46] Kaneko was particularly aroused because he regarded the act as racially discriminatory and therefore a great insult to Japanese national honor.[47]

In vigorously protesting the passage of the immigration laws, the liberals were not acting merely out of a sense of national pride; many of their leaders were clearly defending universal principles of racial equality and minority rights. Although nationalistic sentiments operated strongly, we cannot disregard the fact that many advocated better treatment of Koreans, Taiwanese, and Chinese in Japan. The Japan Peace Society entertained and provided many advisory services to Korean, Taiwanese, and Chinese students.[48] Shibusawa was one of the organizers of the Japan-China Academic Society (Nikka Gakkai), which was formed in May 1918 to provide educational and housing facilities for Chinese students. The concern for Asian students was based upon the realization that negligence if not mistreatment had often made them discontented and eventually had driven many to take part in anti-Japanese movements.[49] When the Korean independence movement broke out in 1919, Japan resorted to strong repressive measures that evoked a violent reaction from American missionaries in Korea. Sakatani Yoshirō, who was president of the Central Korean Association (Chūō Chōsen Kyōkai) and the Asian Students Association (Ajia Gakuseikai), promptly requested that Gilbert Bowles of the Friends Mission in Japan and Kawakami Isamu, executive director of the Japan Peace Society, proceed to Korea to pacify the missionaries. When Saitō Makoto was appointed governor-general of Korea, Sakatani reminded him in a long letter of the importance of winning the support of the Korean people. He advised Saitō to undertake major reforms of the Korean administration in order to show respect for the Korean language and culture, as well as for fundamental rights of speech and assembly. He emphasized that Koreans should be accorded equal status with Japanese, that the instigators of the independence movement should be treated leniently, and that Japanese officials who had resorted to unlawful suppressive action should be punished.[50]

How should liberal groups be characterized prior to their period of trial in the 1930s? Within Japan they were increasingly challenged by the right wing. Externally they were sorely disillusioned by the discriminatory action of the United States, with which they were closely associated. Sawayanagi Masatarō has described the position of the Japanese liberals when faced with the passage of the immigration laws as follows: the right-wing militarists said that such an act served the liberals right; the left-wing Marxists said they could not expect anything else from the largest capitalist country in the world.[51]

The liberals were indeed a group caught in the middle, and their position was to become more and more precarious as domestic as well as foreign pressures increased. Their travail began with the outbreak of the Manchurian affair.

III

In 1929 an anti-Japanese nationalist movement spread rapidly throughout Manchuria and Japan began to think seriously of measures to safeguard its rights and interests in the area. At home nationalist groups, both civilian and military, were organized to exert pressure on the government, which to them appeared too weak in asserting Japan's rights in Manchuria, a weakness they ascribed to its deference to the League of Nations and the Washington Conference treaties.

When the Institute of Pacific Relations met in Kyoto in the fall of 1929, the Japanese Council decided to give Manchurian problems a major place on the agenda. It was "a bold decision" to deal with a topic that was generally regarded as involving Japan's vital interests, and to expose it to critics of Japan's Manchurian policy.[52] In so doing, the Japanese Council hoped to use the occasion to reach some understanding with the participants from China, as well as to present the Japanese case to interested members from other countries. Rōyama Masamichi, professor of public administration at Tokyo Imperial University, prepared a lengthy paper on Japan's position in Manchuria, and Matsuoka Yōsuke, former vice president of the South Manchuria Railway Company, delivered a speech on the economic development of Manchuria. Nitobe Inazō served as conference chairman. A powerful delegation of forty-eight members was appointed, including many prominent businessmen, journalists, and scholars. The following spring a group of the younger participants in the Kyoto Conference organized the Tokyo Institute of Politics and Economics (Tōkyō Seiji Keizai Kenkyūjo) to follow up any issues raised at the conference. They were Rōyama Masamichi, Matsukata Saburō, Matsumoto Shigeharu, Uramatsu Samitarō, Kaji Ryūichi of the Tokyo *Asahi*, Ichimura Kesazō of Waseda University, and Ushiba Tomohiko, who was soon to become an official of the Japanese Council of the IPR. The institute published a series of political and economic yearbooks, and its members later served on Konoe's brain trust.

From the outlook of the Japanese participants at the Kyoto Conference we can discern three basic attitudes that might be regarded as typical of the liberal approach to Manchurian problems. First of all, there was virtual unanimity in recognizing Japan's contribution to the economic development of Manchuria and in supporting "the present *status quo*, in regard both to treaty rights and to economic organization." At the same time there was equally strong agreement "in disclaiming any further developments which might be construed as aggressive interference with Chinese political rights of sovereignty."[53] Secondly, there was apprehension at growing revolutionary nationalism in China. This fear had two aspects: that China might demand total exclusion of Japanese interests from Manchuria, and that the Chinese authorities might not be able to carry out the functions of government in times of unrest.[54] Japanese willingness to accept the withdrawal of political rights was necessarily related to the ability of the Chinese government to maintain its authority in the region. Thirdly, there was strong suspicion that the existing peace machinery might prove inadequate to meet the problems of China, particularly of Manchuria.[55] This feeling was shared by all the participants in the conference and was held particularly strongly by the Chinese. Suggestions were made to set up regional organizations in the Pacific, to decentralize the League organization, or even to have the League Council meet occasionally in the Far East.[56] One Japanese participant proposed the formation of a permanent nongovernmental conciliation board, consisting exclusively of Chinese and Japanese representatives, which would meet regularly and hold emergency sessions whenever urgent issues arose.[57] In general, the Japanese representatives at the conference were anxious to devise means through which "China and Japan could come to agreement between themselves."[58]

When conflict broke out between Japanese and Chinese troops in Manchuria on September 18, 1931, no liberals came out in strong opposition to Japanese actions, despite fears that the government might lose control over the forces in the field.[59] For so long as liberals regarded Japanese interests in Manchuria as sacrosanct and believed that the Chinese nationalist movement endangered those interests, they had to acquiesce in the army's use of military force.

At its board of directors meeting on October 30 the League of Nations Association of Japan adopted a resolution that attributed the conflict to ten years of anti-Japanese education and nationalistic activities in China. Defending Japanese treaty rights in Manchuria, it charged that "the basic condition for the improvement of Sino-Japanese relations lay in making China control and reform the psychology of its people toward Japan as well as their actions, which disregarded Japanese interests throughout China and particularly in Manchuria."[60] Thereafter the association concentrated on preparing materials to publicize to the world Chinese anti-Japanese activities. When Lord Cecil and six leading members of the League of Nations Association of Great Britain in a letter to *The Times* of London on February 18, 1932 declared that the Japanese action in Manchuria was the first step toward military conquest of China and called for British cooperation with the United States and the League of Nations to exert diplomatic pressure on Japan, President Ishii and five representatives of the League of Nations Association of Japan immediately drafted a justification of Japanese policy. In a reply to *The Times* they argued that the conflict at Mukden had been a defensive response by legally stationed Japanese troops to the actions of Chinese warlord bandits and warned that "generous but undiscerning sympathy toward an illusionary China was the greatest danger to world peace."[61]

Christian organizations reacted to the Manchurian affair with a sincere wish for peace but without censuring Japanese military actions. When Chinese Christian organizations called upon the Japan Christian League "to oppose Japanese aggression in China in the name of Christ," it cabled a reply promising to work for a peaceful settlement and asked Japanese Christians to pray for a "peaceful settlement of the present dispute for the sake of the happiness of the peoples of China and Japan."[62] The annual meeting of the Society of Friends issued a resolution expressing deep regret at the outbreak of hostilities and pledging "to pray and strive for the speedy realization of permanent peace not only between China and Japan but for the whole world."[63] But there was no attempt to oppose Japanese military action nor to engage in any organized protest.

Individual Christians, however, did initiate peace movements and published critical articles in minor publications. One of these was Takahashi Gen'ichirō, a follower of Kagawa Toyohiko, who regarded the Manchurian affair as the inevitable outcome of Japanese militarism and imperialism. He tried to mobilize Christian groups to form a Christian Peace League, with Kagawa as chairman and Ozaki Yukio, Nitobe Inazō, Tagawa Daikichirō, Abe Isoo, and Yoshino Sakuzō as advisers,[64] but he failed to win sufficient support. Other individuals who strongly protested Japanese militarism were Fujisawa Takeyoshi and Morimoto Keizō of the Mukyōkai, who called in their publication *Kyūdō* (Search for the Way) for the withdrawal of the army from Manchuria. Their criticism grew more and more intense, until in October 1933 they condemned the Japanese public for accepting the army's action in Manchuria as "inevitable" or the exercise of "lawful rights" and declared that it had been "a clear case of plunder to Christian eyes fixed upon the Bible." *Kyūdō* was banned for this article and was proscribed repeatedly thereafter. Kashiwagi Gien, a journalist and minister of the Union Church of Japan, perhaps the most liberal of the formal churches, also advocated the immediate withdrawal of Japanese troops from Manchuria. He went even further and attacked Japanese special rights in Manchuria as the heritage of Russian imperialism, arguing that such spoils did not justify military action.[65]

In the course of the Manchurian crisis the political pendulum swung very far to the "right." Liberals—both as individuals and as groups—became increasingly conscious of the dangers involved in expressing views critical of current events. Moreover, in the winter of 1931-32 they lost several of their outstanding leaders. Shibusawa Eiichi died on November 11 at the age of ninety-two, and the group of businessmen, scholars, and others that had formed around him disintegrated. The assassination of Inoue Junnosuke on February 9 and of Dan Takuma on March 5 deprived the liberals of two powerful business leaders and in addition made them far more aware of the threat from the radical right.

At about the same time Nitobe Inazō drew the fire of nationalist groups. Early in February 1932 he went to Ehime at the invitation of the prefectural government to deliver a series of public lectures. At an informal press interview in Matsuyama on February 4 he "spoke in broad terms of international conditions and said that he saw the world menaced by two forces, communism and militarism. Of the two, he feared militarism might do the more harm."[66] This statement was publicized in the local press as a direct attack on the Japanese army, and the repercussions were great. The Imperial Reservists Association issued a pamphlet assuring the public that while they themselves did not favor military disturbances or oppose Nitobe's peaceful ideals, nevertheless they felt that he had misled the people at a time when the entire country was devoting its energies to bringing about a successful conclusion of the Manchurian affair. The pamphlet further quoted many angry reactions that branded Nitobe as "disloyal," "unpatriotic," and "traitorous."[67] Thereafter he was subjected to such abusive threats from the right that he decided to appear before the Reservists Council to explain that his statements at Matsuyama had been "misconstrued."[68] American journalists, however, reported the incident as a compromise on Nitobe's part, arousing criticism in the United States.[69] Soon after this Nitobe reversed his decision not to go to the United States so long as the immigration laws were in effect and in April left on a speaking tour of that country, where in one year he gave more than a hundred lectures on Japan. It was his conviction that just as it was primarily the task of Americans to provide an explanation of the immigration laws in order to assuage Japanese feelings, similarly, it was the responsibility of Japanese to explain the problem of Manchuria to Americans.[70]

IV

With the military occupation of south Manchuria, the controversy turned into a conflict between Japan and the League of Nations. League debates often aroused the Japanese public, which regarded Council recommendations as interference with Japanese rights, and even as a recurrence of the Triple Intervention of 1895. When the Council voted thirteen to one in favor of U.S. participation in its debates, a sense of national humiliation was felt in Japan. And as time passed, although the liberals continued to support the League, they found themselves in an increasingly difficult position.

Liberals were hopeful, therefore, that a favorable report by the Lytton Commission might prevent a complete rupture with the League. Nitobe Inazō, who was hospitalized when the commission came to Japan in March 1932, arranged for a few of its leading members to meet privately with Iwanaga Yūkichi, managing director of the Shinbun Rengōsha, and Maeda Tamon, editorial writer of the Tokyo *Asahi*, both of whom were active in the IPR.[71] Rōyama Masamichi and five journalists of the Tokyo Institute of Politics and Economics drew up a "Plan for the Settlement of Manchurian Problems" in which they proposed to recognize the existence of an independent, self-governing unit in Manchuria that would assure public order and prosperity in the area.[72] They further emphasized that the League, in acknowledgment of the peculiar nature of the dispute, should leave a settlement to be worked out through direct negotiations between Japan and China. In such an event, Japan would not be forced to withdraw from the League and could continue to work for disarmament and the strengthening of the peace machinery.[73]

Indeed, reforming the structure of the League became a central concern among liberal groups, the means most often proposed being to set up a regional organization in the Pacific. The lead article of the December issue of *Kokusai chishiki* called for the establishment of a permanent committee of the League of Nations in the Far East. Criticizing the League for its lack of understanding of the "peculiar and complicated situation in the Far East," the article proposed that "a permanent committee be established consisting of representatives only from countries with direct interests in the Far East. Local incidents should be dealt with by this committee first, with the Assembly and Council giving only their final approval or disapproval."[74]

At the Shanghai Conference of the Institute of Pacific Relations in the fall of 1931 Takayanagi Kenzō, professor of law at Tokyo Imperial University, described the Manchurian crisis as a test of the existing diplomatic machinery. Referring first to the Chinese attitude toward the League as expressed at the Kyoto Conference—that the League was "too far away, that the League could not know the actual situation in China"—he then proceeded to argue:

> It seems to me that the conception of universalism—the League as a universal organ, to deal with all disputes arising throughout the world—is a very valuable one. There should not be too many competing organs. There is much justification for that argument. But that conception may well be reconciled with an attempt to set up here in the Pacific an organ to investigate in a realistic way the conditions in China and Japan, and ultimately to solve the international difficulties in the Pacific area. Arrangements may be made in such a way that such an organ will not do away with the idea of the universality of the League. And in such arrangements the United States and Soviet Russia should be invited to take part in some capacity or other.[75]

Following up Takayanagi's presentation at Shanghai, a security pact for the Pacific area was proposed at the Banff Conference of the IPR in 1933 by Takagi Yasaka and Yokota Kisaburō, professor of international law at Tokyo Imperial University. The proposal carried a poignant note, for by then Japan had already given notice of its withdrawal from the League, leaving the three major Pacific nations—Japan, the United States, and the Soviet Union—outside the scope of the League. The proposed treaty was based upon the following considerations:

> 1. Existing peace machinery (especially in the Pacific) does not provide for constructive examination and revision of international conditions likely to disturb peace. A prerequisite of international justice is that there should be some means for the redress or alleviation of economic inequalities among different peoples of the world.
> 2. There is a lack of order and unity within certain nations. There does not exist in the Pacific area an international society of nations at similar stages of development. For such a society a prerequisite is that individual states should fulfill the conditions of civilized society and adhere to their international obligations. This lack makes necessary a special regional organization.

3. There are special problems arising from vigorous and uncontrolled nationalism in the world. There is thus an urgent need for a revived internationalism and a re-establishment of some basis for international cooperation.[76]

The Japanese participants at Banff stressed that the great need was not for "treaties guaranteeing a fixed condition in political or economic relations, but for new machinery permitting a periodic review and adjustment of existing conditions to national economic needs and opportunities." Their argument was prompted by a conviction that "as long as there is a class of 'have-nots' in the community of nations, the mere maintenance of the *status quo* will never be a workable principle for diplomatic machinery."[77] This question of "haves" and "have-nots" in international relations was to gain increasing importance in Japanese foreign policy debates.

The proposers of a regional security pact further stated that "the convocation, periodically if possible, of a conference of the Pacific Powers along somewhat similar lines to the Pan-American conferences" was of paramount importance in order "to remove the causes of disputes before they arise."[78] Should such preventive measures fail, however, the security pact was to come into effect. Consultation among the contracting parties was to follow "in order to arrive at an understanding as to the most efficient measures to be taken jointly or separately to meet the exigencies of the particular situation."[79] Should consultation fail in turn, the parties were to settle their differences by other pacific procedures, either by conciliation or by arbitration or judicial settlement. For purposes of conciliation permanent conciliation commissions were to be established through bilateral agreements. Every commission was to have five members, consisting of a representative of each of the two disputants and of three other states. Where adjudication was needed, cases were to be sent to the Permanent Court of International Justice, the Permanent Court of Arbitration at The Hague, or an ad hoc arbitration tribunal.[80] The doctrines of nonaggression and nonrecognition were accepted as fundamental principles of the security pact. Its promoters did not foresee any difficulty in winning Japanese approval for the nonrecognition doctrine, for although Japan had abstained from voting on the Assembly resolution based on this principle, its representative had stated at the time that Japan did not oppose the principle itself. In a recent statement to the writer Takagi Yasaka said that the proposal for a security pact was drawn up with the encouragement and advice of the Foreign Ministry. Sugimura Yōtarō, former assistant secretary general of the League of Nations, was most sympathetic to the plan.[81] The proposed security pact can be regarded as one of the few concrete efforts for peace by a liberal organization. Unfortunately, it did not materialize because many delegates to the conference found in it too many practical problems to overcome.

Most members of the League of Nations Association probably shared with the Institute of Pacific Relations members their basic support for the League. But they made no open attempt either to prevent Japan's withdrawal from the League or to propose alternative plans for international cooperation. President Ishii Kikujirō was hopeful that the League and Japan could somehow reach agreement on the Manchurian question,[82] and Vice President Yamakawa Tadao opposed Japan's withdrawal.[83] Both Tagawa Daikichirō and Hayashi Kiroku wrote and spoke in support of international cooperation and of the League.[84] These four, together with three other directors, formed a special committee on Manchurian problems, but it took no action on behalf of the association to protest Japan's departure from the League. Honorary President Sakatani Yoshirō issued a statement expressing his profound grief at Japan's decision and emphasized that it had not been Japan's choice but was the result of inevitable circumstances. He also conveyed the hope that the League of Nations would review the Manchurian problem once more before Japan's withdrawal became effective and that it would check its inclination to act as a supra-national organization and become more conciliatory.[85]

After Japan's withdrawal from the League became definite, the League of Nations Association faced the critical issue of whether and how to change its articles of incorporation. A special committee to study the issue was set up on March 17, consisting of Ishii, Yamakawa, and six directors. The committee's decision was presented to the board of directors, then to the board of advisers, then to the presidents of the local associations, and finally to a general meeting on May 12. Apparently heated discussion occurred at each stage, as many members strongly insisted upon retaining the name of the organization as well as its objectives.[86] Two local associations proposed to reestablish the Japan Peace Society, a plan Tagawa favored because he did not find the League of Nations Association sufficiently committed to peace or unified in its ideas.[87] Available materials do not indicate how the different opinions were adjusted. Yamakawa later declared that he chose to take a practical course and adapt the objectives of the association to the new circumstances.[88] Since Yamakawa was the most powerful figure in the association, it is not surprising that his opinions prevailed in the end. The League of Nations Association formally changed its name to the International Association of Japan. Its primary objective was no longer to be "the fulfillment of the spirit of the League of Nations" but "the promotion of friendship and cooperation with various nations, the establishment of international justice, and the realization of international peace."[89] The International Association, however, retained its predecessor's membership in the World Confederation of the League of Nations.

The organization was saved. The League of Nations Association of Japan survived Japan's withdrawal from the League. After its transformation into the International Association it continued its activities as before, making studies of international affairs and sponsoring lectures and essay contests. The support of some members may have diminished, but none of the directors resigned. At least one person, however, left the association—Reserve Captain Mizuno Hironori, who had been active in the Fellowship for the Limitation of Armaments with Tagawa Daikichirō, resigned from the association during the Manchurian crisis primarily because he was disillusioned by the League's powerlessness to prevent Japan's action in Manchuria. The League, he felt, was nothing but a "live corpse." In despair he wrote to a friend: "The League was a failure; disarmament was a failure. Perhaps the world should revert to the old days of militarism and engage in an armaments race. The Japanese people should fight wars against America and Britain, for unless they are baptized once more by modern warfare, they will not be awakened to the importance of peace!"[90]

Thereafter Mizuno turned to the socialists and helped to organize the Friends for Peace in the Far East (Kyokutō Heiwa no Tomo no Kai) in response to the Amsterdam anti-war appeal of 1932 issued by Henri Barbusse with the support of Romain Rolland.[91] Some seventy progressive intellectuals active in the proletarian literary movement and noncommunist left-wing politics are said to have pledged their support, their objective being to start an anti-fascist movement in line with the popular front movement that was being organized in Europe at that time. The Friends for Peace was never actually launched, however, because right-wing gangsters caused trouble at the founding meeting, inviting police suppression of the organization.[92] Through Mizuno a slender but significant link can be traced between liberal groups and noncommunist left-wing socialists such as Suzuki Mosaburō, Arahata Kanson, and Katō Kanjū, who remained unconverted to national socialism throughout the Manchurian affair. Their main efforts were directed toward maintaining their identity as an anti-fascist proletarian group. The only instance of pacifist activities on their part appears to have been the distribution of Suzuki Mosaburō's anti-war pamphlets.[93]

Kiyosawa Kiyoshi, a journalist who frequently contributed articles to *Kokusai chishiki*, was perhaps the only person who publicly challenged the League policy of Foreign Minister Uchida Yasuya and Matsuoka Yōsuke, Japan's delegate to the League of Nations. Kiyosawa was an uncompromising liberal to whom peace and freedom of speech were of utmost importance. In two *Chūō kōron* articles—"Question to Foreign Minister Uchida" (March 1933) and "Advice to Representative Matsuoka" (May 1933)—Kiyosawa criticized their diplomacy as having prematurely committed them to a fixed position that would not allow for any compromise. To Kiyosawa the art of "give and take" was the essence of diplomacy, making it by nature a strategy of restraint and therefore at times an object of popular outrage. He blamed Uchida and Matsuoka for "not having the will to turn their backs on public opinion in order to save Japan at this critical juncture."[94]

About the same time, Tagawa Daikichirō wrote in *Kokusai chishiki* that although he wished it were true that Japan's difficulties with the League were due to some defect in the League machinery as generally assumed, the real problem was that the purpose of the League—"to pursue and maintain peace"—was not understood. To achieve such a purpose there were two prerequisites: arms had to be reduced, if not totally abolished, and the authority of the Permanent Court of International Justice had to be recognized. Tagawa felt that these conditions might be met, but he was doubtful about realizing a third which, in his mind, was even more important—the establishment of parliamentary government in all the states that were members of the League. Tagawa was convinced that parliamentary government alone could transmit to the League free and undistorted public opinion that would enable it to devise solutions which were fair and acceptable to all involved. "The heart of the matter," in his opinion, was "to create a new spirit that attempts to realize prosperity for the nation and people without resorting to military power. . . . Without such a spirit, the League of Nations cannot be maintained."[95] He further believed that it was the responsibility of Japanese supporters of the League to understand the relationship between the development of liberal political principles at home and the maintenance of international peace.

Not much credit can be given to the performance of the organized churches at the time of Japan's withdrawal from the League. The Japan Christian League in its *Renmei jihō* (Current News of the League) of April 15, 1933 stated that despite its hopes that a peaceful settlement would be achieved through the League, it found the League merely a Europe-created organization that could not understand the actual situation in the Far East. It therefore supported Japan's withdrawal as having been forced upon it by defects in the League system.[96] From that time on the Christian League moved slowly toward support for Japanese expansion in China. Kashiwagi Gien, however, perceiving the danger inherent in Japan's withdrawal from the League, wrote that Japan had taken the first step on the road to war.[97]

V

A short lull set in after the vicissitudes of 1931-33. In 1935 the Japanese Council of the Institute of Pacific Relations merged with the International Association of Japan, thus uniting the two major offspring of liberal organizations that had been active since the 1920s. Available materials give no indication that outside pressure was applied to effect this union. Iwanaga Yūkichi, a prominent leader of the IPR since its founding and also a director of the International Association, personally promoted the move. Iwanaga played a pivotal role not only among liberals but also between liberals and influential persons in the governments of both Japan and the United States. His close connections with Konoe and Ambassador Grew are well known. He apparently judged that the time had come to unify existing resources to strengthen the position of liberal groups. For the IPR, the merger would provide wider domestic support; for the International Association, it would bring about direct contact with an international forum now that the League of Nations was no longer available.[98] As of December 1, 1935 the Japanese IPR became a section of the International Association, although it continued to conduct its research and publication activities in the name of the Japanese Council of the Institute of Pacific Relations.

The Japanese delegation to the IPR conference held at Yosemite, California in August 1936 was headed by Yamakawa Tadao, the long-time leader of the League of Nations Association of Japan. Although the views expressed by the Japanese Council at Yosemite generally echoed those of delegations to previous conferences, two changes seem important. First, the denial of any intent to interfere in Chinese political rights of sovereignty was replaced by a strong assertion that "it was essential to have in China not only a stable government but one that was not hostile to Japan."[99] One member of the Japanese Council even admitted that "military measures might be necessary if a hostile government should develop in China."[100] North China, due to its geographic propinquity to Manchuria, was especially earmarked as an area in which Japan could not be unconcerned politically.[101] Japan's interest in China was characterized as analogous to that of the United States in Latin America which had given rise to the Monroe Doctrine.[102]

Secondly, the Japanese delegates no longer advocated a regional organization for the Pacific area. To a British proposal that a collective security system be established on a regional basis, they "steadfastly maintained their preference for a bilateral settlement of outstanding issues and doubted the feasibility of a collective agreement until such bilateral settlements had been achieved."[103] Their principal objection to a system of collective security, they explained, was based on their experience with the League of Nations, which did not properly understand Japan's position and which permitted decisions to be made on the basis of inadequate information according to majority vote. Furthermore, they stated, the Japanese felt that the League imposed the status quo upon Japan and was unable to provide for peaceful change. Emphasizing the last point in particular, they said that the capacity to effect peaceful change was becoming the most important criterion in determining the attitude of the Japanese people toward a collective security system, for most Japanese believed that Japan had "a legitimate desire to expand" and therefore wanted to know by what means a nation could expand "legitimately."[104]

By 1936 a definite tendency was manifest in Japan to affirm with pride the nation's need and ability to expand. This was reinforced when both Germany and Italy withdrew from the League of Nations because of dissatisfaction with the status quo. Thereafter Japan no longer felt isolated in its challenge to the world order created at Versailles and Washington, and international relations were increasingly looked upon as a power struggle between two groups—Britain, France, and the United States striving to maintain the status quo, and Germany, Italy, and Japan attempting to overthrow it. The former represented the "have" nations of the world, the latter the "have-nots."

Tagawa Daikichirō attempted to warn of the dangers involved in identifying Japan's goals with those of Germany and Italy. An important difference between Japan and the two European states, he wrote, lay in the fact that whereas Germany and Italy had already abandoned parliamentary government in favor of fascism, there was still hope that through reform parliamentary government might be upheld in Japan. Insisting that only a parliamentary system could assure freedom of speech and thought and of the individual, and that it alone could bring about change through evolutionary rather than revolutionary measures, he called upon Japan to part company with Germany and Italy and join with Britain, France, and the United States.[105] Most liberals, although not as articulate or as outspoken as Tagawa, shared his desire to detach Japan from Germany and Italy and narrow the growing gap with Britain and the United States.[106] The Anti-Comintern Pact of November 25, 1936, however, placed Japan firmly in the fascist bloc.

The outbreak of war with China on July 7, 1937 seriously strained Japan's relations with the world. In Geneva the World Confederation of the League of Nations, at the behest of the League of Nations Association of China, called an extraordinary meeting of its council on September 12. The council adopted a resolution stating that Japan's military action was a further step in the imperialistic conquest begun in Manchuria in 1931 and was the outcome of the League's failure to take appropriate measures at that time. The resolution urged member states to consider means to take common action against Japan should it refuse to abide by the League covenant. In response, the council of the International Association of Japan warned the World Confederation that the association might be forced to terminate its relations with the World

Confederation if the latter continued to censure Japan. On February 21 of the following year the International Association sent formal notice of its decision to withdraw from the World Confederation after two further resolutions condemning Japan were adopted.[107]

Meanwhile, within Japan the war brought suppression of the right of freedom of speech. The Home Ministry banned publications containing objectionable articles and issued to publishers lists of undesirable writers, thereby depriving them of any forum in which to express their views. From this time on, articles criticizing Japan's action in China or its policy toward the United States disappeared from the International Association's *Kokusai chishiki*.

Relations with the United States further deteriorated after the United States on October 6 and December 31, 1938 protested the closing of the Open Door in China. Inahara Katsuji, in his column in *Kokusai chishiki*, took exception to the two American notes on the grounds that the United States was not qualified to complain about Japanese violations. Recalling the mistreatment of and discrimination against Japanese nationals in the United States, he argued that America was audacious even to raise the question of treatment of its nationals under circumstances of war. Nothing could make the Japanese angrier, he concluded, than a protest against their treatment of Americans.[108] He revived the old theme linking the U.S. exclusion policy with Japanese expansion in China and defended Japanese expansion by pointing to U.S. practices of racial, economic, and commercial exclusion in the past.[109] How, he asked rhetorically, can the United States object to Japan's control over China so long as it espouses the Monroe Doctrine for the Americas?

On October 19, 1939 Ambassador Grew gave a speech at the America-Japan Society that produced a strong reaction. Grew had intended this address to be "historical" and had hoped to impress upon the Japanese public that the government and people of the United States, once started on a policy of sanctions, would feel that they must persist, and that such a policy might conceivably terminate in war.[110] The America-Japan Society was chosen because Grew felt that it was "about the only forum that we possess" and would bring his speech "to the attention of a considerable element of influential Japanese both in the government and out of it."[111] He had already reached the conclusion that "the time for exclusive reliance on the good will and efforts of the Japanese Government, as contrasted with the Japanese military, is past."[112]

The December 1939 issue of *Kokusai chishiki* carried two articles in answer to the Grew speech. One, signed "Anonymous," violently attacked the United States government on the assumption that it had been responsible for the address. The author argued that in warning the Japanese public that once aroused the American people would not turn back, the United States had attempted to create division between the public and the military, which was tantamount to interference in Japanese domestic affairs. He suggested that the United States government might be exceeding the demands of its people in exerting pressure on Japan or might be neglecting its responsibility to provide them with accurate information on East Asia. He blamed Western imperialism for the existing chaos in China and denied that Japan had any imperialistic intentions in that area. The United States, he said, should reconsider its attitude toward the "new order" that Japan was developing in China and should leave

Asia to the Asians. The author also stated that Grew was making a mistake in relying on his contacts in the higher echelons of government and business in the belief that Japanese policy could be influenced through them. He advised Grew to cultivate a better understanding of the radical reform groups that were becoming powerful in Japan and stressed the importance of his comprehending the causes of their rise to prominence and reporting them accurately to his government.[113] It is interesting to note that, even before preparing his speech, Grew's thinking had been moving in a similar direction.

The conclusion of the Tripartite Pact on September 27, 1940 resulted in a sudden worsening of Japan's relations with the United States. News of the pact, however, did not produce any sense of fear or shock among Japanese liberals. The "Commentary" column of *Kokusai chishiki* took it as "a very natural" outcome of the developments of the past few years,[114] and there is little indication that liberals were at all apprehensive that the pact might have a provocative effect. Kajima Morinosuke emphasized that it was fundamentally defensive in character, merely applying the Monroe Doctrine to the respective areas of the Tripartite powers. He believed that it was up to the United States to decide whether to challenge the pact or to back out.[115]

At a meeting of the Privy Council on September 26 Ishii Kikujirō criticized the conclusion of the Tripartite Pact. He did not object to the pact itself, for he thought Japan, Germany, and Italy had common interests as the "have-nots" of the world. But he expressed grave concern over its possible disastrous effects and attacked Germany as a most undesirable partner in any alliance. He referred to history to prove that Germany had repeatedly forced its allies to act in accordance with its demands. Furthermore, he found Hitler extremely dangerous and warned Japan against following his lead.[116] This was Ishii's last expression of protest, and perhaps the most he could do under the circumstances.

Under increasingly severe restrictions on freedom of speech, what activities might individual liberals or liberal organizations engage in? What resistance did they carry out, and what efforts for peace did they make? As far as the International Association was concerned, its formal activities remained much the same as in its heyday. There were luncheons, speeches, and continued interest in international affairs. There was compliance with the new ritual of observing a minute's silence in honor of the soldiers and of bowing in the direction of the imperial palace at the beginning of each meeting. The International Association held weekly luncheons at which speeches were frequently given by individuals, especially members of the Foreign Ministry, who had recently returned from abroad. *Kokusai chishiki* carried translations from Western publications every month. Members of this organization must have been much better informed than most of the Japanese public on the situation in Europe and the United States as well as in Asia. At the general meeting of the association on May 3, 1940, 150 persons were present. Prizes were given to members of the board and to those on the staffs of four local student associations who had served continuously for over ten years. The activities of the Japanese Council of the Institute of Pacific Relations in its new role as a section of the International Association dwindled somewhat after the Yosemite Conference. In fact, Yosemite proved the last occasion on which the Japanese Council made a concerted effort to address an international audience. While it continued to maintain some contact with the other national councils and the International Secretariat, it limited its activities for the most part to publishing the results of research on Far Eastern international relations.

Positive efforts for peace were made by a few individuals. Both the International Association of Japan and the Japanese branch of the IPR included members who worked to prevent a war with the United States. When Konoe Fumimaro became prime minister in June 1937, Ushiba Tomohiko, an official of the IPR, was appointed one of his personal secretaries, the other being Kishi Michizō, a consultant to the South Manchuria Railway. Ushiba had met Konoe when he and Rōyama Masamichi, upon the recommendation of Iwanaga Yūkichi, had accompanied the prince on a trip to the United States in 1934. Iwanaga felt that their IPR contacts and participation in its conferences had equipped them to advise Konoe on Japan's foreign relations.[117] When Konoe formed his government, Ushiba and Kishi arranged a series of informal meetings to discuss policy alternatives. These meetings gradually turned into breakfast gatherings that were held regularly—bimonthly in the latter half of 1938 and every Wednesday morning in 1939. Some of the IPR-trained Tokyo Institute of Politics and Economics group joined this Asameshikai, or Breakfast Club, as it became known, including Rōyama Masamichi, Watanabe Sahei, professor of economics at Hōsei University, Matsumoto Shigeharu, and Matsukata Saburō. Other participants were from the Shōwa Kenkyūkai (Shōwa Research Society)—Ozaki Hotsumi of the *Asahi* and later of the South Manchuria Railway, Sassa Hiroo and Ryū Shintarō of the *Asahi*, and Taira Teizō of the South Manchuria Railway. The Shōwa Kenkyūkai was founded in November 1936 through the efforts of Gotō Ryūnosuke, a personal friend of Konoe, to bring together leading intellectuals to serve as a brain trust in high-level policy planning. With a membership of three hundred in the peak year of 1940, it presented a curious mixture of liberals as well as reform-minded intellectuals both of the left and of the right.[118] The Breakfast Club was influential because it had direct access to Konoe. In the summer and fall of 1941 this group drew up plans to serve as a basis for Konoe's negotiations with the United States.

Takagi Yasaka should be singled out for his attempts to lessen tensions between Japan and the United States. As a professor of American constitutional history and diplomacy at Tokyo Imperial University and in his long association with organizations such as the Japanese-American Relations Committee and the Institute of Pacific Relations, Takagi personified Japanese efforts to improve relations with the United States. According to his recollections of this period, after 1936 he shifted the focus of his activities from discussions with Americans to attempts to persuade politically powerful groups within Japan. He approached the navy, in which he had had close friends since the time of the Washington Conference, and in 1940 held a series of informal talks with a group of officers that included Takagi Sōkichi and Ōgi Kazuto.[119] He tried to convince them that the United States valued China highly as a potential market and believed the principle of orderly process must be upheld in recognizing any kind of change in international relations. He insisted that there must be a partial withdrawal of Japanese troops from China and concentration on the economic aspect of the Greater East Asia Coprosperity Sphere. In addition he warned strongly against any military advance to the south that might arouse the fear and suspicion of the outside world.[120]

Takagi argued similarly to Konoe, whom he had known since his school days at Gakushūin. In the summer of 1941, when Konoe resolved to make a last effort to reach an understanding with the United States, Takagi was actively engaged in advising Konoe and conferring with Grew. After Konoe's proposal for a meeting with President Roosevelt was rejected and all further effort seemed fruitless, Takagi wrote two letters to Grew on September 26 and October 7 pleading, "with all due respect" for the arguments against any policy of appeasement, that the U.S. government adopt "a more understanding attitude" and "a more conciliatory policy that would in effect strengthen Konoe's position in his desperate fight to control the internal turmoil."[121] While admitting, in regard to Japan's contentions on the nature of the New Order and Japanese military activities, that "the burden of proof, by action and facts instead of repeated assurances," lay with Japan, Takagi argued that "the so-called Democratic Powers should regard the situation with no preconceptions."[122] He defended the New Order in East Asia as providing Japan with a new goal based upon neighborly friendship and economic cooperation and justified Japanese military actions in China as an effort to force China to abandon its anti-Japanese policies. Takagi tried to impress upon Grew that unless some sign of understanding was shown by the United States on these questions, the Japanese would interpret American policy as "one of intervention or decidedly unfriendly interposition."[123] In the second letter Takagi spoke of his great concern over the increasingly strong policy of the U.S. government.

> I am convinced that uncompromising demand, under the present circumstances, arising out of such a strong policy is capable of precipitating the greatest disaster imaginable in our relations. . . .
>
> In this connection, I think I can say that the apparently prevalent American attitude, expressed in such phrases as "Squeeze Japan Now," or "Firmness backed up by the power of force is the only language Japan understands," is based on fundamental misconceptions of Japanese psychology, conducive to the gravest consequences rather than to settlement. If such misconceptions are the result of misrepresentations, they may be called almost criminal.
>
> The danger of war is by far the greatest not when Japan thinks that she can wage safely a war of aggression, as some people argue, but when she feels, rightly or wrongly, that she is driven into a corner, and therefore, desperately strikes back defying consequences.
>
> Allow me to stress once again the urgency of the situation. The irresistible force of fate driving the two nations along the road toward destruction seems so strong that, unless some colossal efforts are made in time, it may be impossible to prevent abysmal catastrophe. . . .[124]

Apart from those who tried to prevent or delay the approaching war by assisting politically influential groups, many were forced into inaction because they no longer enjoyed freedom of speech. By the end of 1937 the left-wing activists of the Nihon Musantō (Japan Proletarian Party) and the Nihon Rōdō

Kumiai Zenkoku Hyōgikai (National Council of Japanese Labor Unions),[125] including Suzuki Mosaburō, Arahata Kanson, and Katō Kanjū, had been imprisoned as a result of the December 15 Popular Front Incident (*jinmin sensen jiken*). The following spring liberal academicians such as Wakimura Yoshitarō, Ōuchi Hyōe, Minobe Ryōkichi, Arisawa Hiromi, Abe Isamu, and Takahashi Masao were arrested for having allegedly directed the formation of the popular front.

The liberals were no safer from attack than the socialists. For example, in the period from 1925 to 1938 Kiyosawa Kiyoshi had written one to three books a year, which consisted of commentaries on social, political, and diplomatic problems. But by 1939 he had been deprived of his audience. In that year he produced no books at all; between 1940 and 1942 he published four, which were, however, diplomatic histories; thereafter he wrote nothing until his death in 1945. This is testimony to the restrictions placed upon liberal publicists such as Kiyosawa. At the same time, it should be noted that his turning to history was not a form of escape, for he attempted to convey his criticism of his own day through his presentation of historical events.[126]

Kiyosawa also helped organize small groups of liberal journalists and academicians. Although they could not express their views openly and had no influence on policy, they represented the liberal layer in wartime Japanese society. The Nishichikai (Twenty-Seventh Day Club), which was formed on August 27, 1929 and continued until war broke out, met monthly under the leadership of Shimanaka Yūsaku of the *Chūō kōron*. Among its members were Obama Toshie of the *Chūgai shōgyō*, Suzuki Bunshirō of the *Asahi*, Baba Tsunego of the *Hōchi*, Ishibashi Tanzan of the *Tōyō keizai shinpō*, Mizuno Hironori, Ito Masanori of the *Jiji shinpō*, Diet member Ashida Hitoshi, Rōyama Masamichi, and Hasegawa Nyozekan. There was also the Nirokukai that met on the 26th of each month. This group was organized in 1937 by a businessman, Kobayashi Ichizō, and was in existence until the beginning of 1944. The membership of the two organizations overlapped to a considerable extent, with Ashida Hitoshi, Baba Tsunego, Shimanaka Yūsaku, *Bungei shunjū* publisher Sasaki Mosaku, the critic Miyake Haruteru, the writer Kunieda Kanji, Itō Masanori, and Kiyosawa Kiyoshi attending both regularly. In May 1939 the National Society for Learning (Kokumin Gakujutsu Kyōkai) was organized by Shimanaka Yūsaku, with an office at the *Chūō kōron*. Its aim was to bring together scholars of all schools of thought to work out a basis upon which to build a new Japanese culture. Among those who joined were Ashida Hitoshi; Yanagida Kunio of the *Asahi shinbun* and a specialist on folklore; Matsumoto Jōji, professor of commercial law at Tokyo Imperial University; Koizumi Shinzō, professor of economic thought at Keio University; Nishida Kitarō, professor of philosophy at Kyoto Imperial University; Watsuji Tetsurō, professor of ethics at Tokyo Imperial University; Tōhata Seiichi, professor of agricultural economics at Tokyo Imperial University; Ryū Shintarō of the *Asahi shinbun*; Suehiro Izutarō, professor of civil law at Tokyo Imperial University; and Ueda Teijirō, professor of economic history at Tokyo Commercial University; Kiyosawa and the critic Miki Kiyoshi served as secretaries. Perhaps the single most important contact for Kiyosawa was the *Tōyō keizai shinpō*, which in 1938 set up an advisory group consisting of Kiyosawa together with Diet member Ōguchi

Kiroku, Tagawa Daikichirō, Itō Masanori, Hasegawa Nyozekan, and a few others. During the war the regular members of the group were Ishibashi, Kiyosawa, Itō, and Rōyama Masamichi. Here Kiyosawa found "just about the only place where they could discuss" national problems freely and confirm each others' liberal positions.[127] *Tōyō keizai shinpō* was the only magazine that did not change its liberal policy, although its size shrank from the original seventy-eight pages to four in 1945.

Another liberal who continued to show great courage was Tagawa Daikichirō. He was closely associated with Kiyosawa, especially through the *Tōyō keizai shinpō*. In August 1938 Tagawa published *Kokka to shūkyō* (State and Religion), in which he attacked the authority of the thought police to question Christian ministers and educators on matters of belief, such as their position on the Japanese ancestral gods, on the relationship between the Christian God and the emperor, or on the relationship between the Bible and imperial edicts. Arguing that the police should have sought answers to these questions at the Religious Bureau of the Ministry of Education, he invited Christians and government officials to express their views on the proper function of the thought police. He himself feared, he wrote, that before long freedom of religion would not exist for Christians.[128] In 1938 the police still hesitated to arrest a leading Christian and Diet member for challenging their authority. They waited until February 1940, when Tagawa gave a speech in Osaka, and arrested him on the grounds that he had made false statements concerning military matters. Tagawa's case had the effect of silencing critics and of deterring Christians from involvement in public affairs.

Among Christian groups, members of the Non-Church movement continued to attack war and militarism. Fujisawa Takeyoshi's *Kyūdō* was repeatedly banned and Fujisawa himself spent three months in prison in 1937. Yanaihara Tadao also came under fire on account of the pacifist views he expressed in *Minzoku to heiwa* (The Nation and Peace) and in "Kokka no risō" (The Ideal of a Nation) in the September 1937 issue of *Chūō kōron*. Yanaihara resigned from Tokyo Imperial University on December 2, 1937, his publications were banned, and he was placed on the list of undesirables that the thought police handed to publishers in February 1941. Hirakawa Masatoshi, secretary of the yearly meeting of the Society of Friends, relinquished his post in 1938 after the police interrogated him concerning his pacifist views. Hirakawa was formerly president of the Friends High School and an outstanding leader of the Christian pacifist organization, the Fellowship of Reconciliation.[129]

There were others who suffered official suppression for their opposition to war and militarism. As a group, however, the main preoccupation of Christians lay elsewhere. Their target was the power of the state symbolized in the forms of the state religion. Worship of shrines, loyalty to the emperor, affiliation with an international church organization—these were the problems that harassed Christians. Their desire to defend and strengthen their position developed into a movement to unite all Protestant sects, but it was the pressure of the religious organization bill enacted on May 23, 1939 that finally led to the founding of the Japan Christian Association (Nihon Kirisuto Kyōdan) two years later. At its inaugural meeting members of the association vowed "to regard loyalty to the state as their primary obligation both as Christians and as Japanese subjects of the emperor."[130] Once unified and having pledged their loyalty to the state, the Christian churches rapidly began to promote the national cause.

VI

As was suggested at the outset, the role of liberal nongovernmental organizations in the foreign policy decision making process of Japan was minimal. The period between 1930 'and 1940 marked only the decline of the liberals in terms both of the views and programs they propounded and of the impact they had on policymaking. Obviously, historical circumstances were the decisive factor in this decline. Growing nationalism and militarism in the late 1920s hardened American policy toward Japan, which in turn strengthened Japanese opposition to the United States. Caught in the chain reaction, the liberals had little scope for action. This was the fundamental difference between the 1930s and the 1920s, when the liberals could exercise some initiative in Japanese-American relations strained over the immigration problem.

There is no doubt that there existed a group of liberals who remained faithful to their liberal convictions and who tried, within the narrow range left, to prevent the final breach between Japan and the United States. But two attributes of the liberals reduced the impact of their efforts. First, those we have considered were all nationalists. They reacted strongly to the immigration issue in part because their nationalist sensitivities were aroused by such evidence of racial discrimination. Similarly, they responded as nationalists to Japan's military expansion in China and supported it. Granted they believed in economic rather than military expansion and in the Open Door and the territorial integrity of China, but once the Chinese began to threaten Japanese rights and interests in China, these beliefs no longer seemed satisfactory, and when the military successfully brought Manchuria under Japan's direct control, they were virtually abandoned. The liberals adjusted to the changed situation by accepting the view that the purpose of Japanese military action was to defend Japanese rights against Chinese attack. Thus, having upheld the sanctity of Japanese interests in China, they ended up by acquiescing in the means adopted to maintain those rights. In addressing the United States, liberals stressed the chaos in China and compared Japanese claims to hegemony in Asia with America's Monroe Doctrine. In so doing, they could not but give the impression that they were defending Japanese expansion.

The second attribute of the liberals which contributed to their weakness was their tendency to act individually and not as a group. Liberal organizations certainly included many dedicated people, but they did not look to the organizations as a base from which to arouse public opinion or affect legislation. Fundamentally these organizations were elitist. A handful of leaders made all the decisions with at best the passive approval of the other members. Individual liberals, therefore, could not turn to the rank and file for active support; nor could they expect assistance from other organized groups, such as existed in journalistic, business, and academic circles, for the main objective of such groups was to ride with the times. For example, when Japan's withdrawal from the League of Nations became definite, the League of Nations Association was confronted with a crisis by the differences of opinion that resulted among its members. However, when the association chose the expedient course of changing its articles of incorporation to conform to the new circumstances, not only did it survive, but hardly anyone resigned in protest. From the viewpoint of the organization's existence such a compromise was an advantage; the League of Nations Association was not suppressed. But from the standpoint of effective action, compromise only brought weakness.

In evaluating the power of liberals in Japan, Ambassador Grew wrote on December 7, 1940 that Japanese liberals

> ... continually maintain that just beneath the surface there exists a great body of moderate opinion in Japan ready to emerge and to wrest control from the extremists if supported by some practical gesture of friendship from the United States, and they find it hard to understand why the American people feel that it is now up to Japan to take the initiative in any such gesture.
>
> It is true that a large element of such moderate opinion exists in Japan, but unfortunately that element is just as powerless and inarticulate now as ever.[131]

There seems to have been much truth in what the liberals told Grew as well as in what Grew thought of them. The liberals craved some sign that U.S. policy was softening, so that they might assert the validity of their position. But had the liberals, instead of working as individuals behind the scenes or through private channels, utilized their organizational base to publicize their views and proposals, at least Grew might have had more concrete evidence with which to convince the American government and public of liberal power. The weakness of liberal organizations was a failure both of liberalism and of organized action.

THE ROLE OF RIGHT-WING ORGANIZATIONS IN JAPAN

Itô Takashi

Translated by Shumpei Okamoto

I

The term "right wing" calls to mind a small number of fanatical and mysterious Japanese secret organizations. Of these perhaps the most typical is the Kokuryūkai (Amur River Society, often incorrectly translated as the Black Dragon Society), whose activities were revealed by the International Military Tribunal for the Far East. However, if the "right wing" is defined as those individuals and groups imbued with the ideology of "ultra-nationalism,"[1] practically all political organizations in Japan after the out-break of the Sino-Japanese War in 1937 will fall into this classification.

Let us therefore try first to determine the position and role of the right wing in the changing course of Japanese politics after the Manchurian Incident. The diagram below may be of use to indicate the position in the Japanese political spectrum of individuals and groups that were politically active during the period between the ends of the two World Wars. It is based on two factors that influenced the fundamental attitudes of individual political activists and groups. One is their idea of their own place in history and that of other groups and individuals. The other is their conception of the nature of the political tasks with which they were confronted.[2]

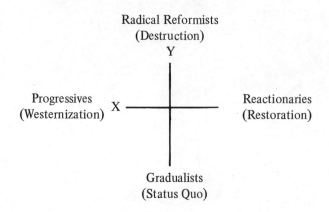

Axis X represents two sets of contrasts, namely, "Progressives vs. Reactionaries" and "Westernization vs. Restoration." Those who regarded themselves as Progressives saw Japan after the Meiji Restoration as a nation that had cast off the fetters of "barbaric" Tokugawa "feudal" society and was developing toward a "civilized" society with constitutional government. To them the achievements of the advanced European nations and the United States usually constituted the essence of "civilization." In particular, the Progressives regarded Britain as the mirror for Japan. In their view Japan was to follow Britain in adopting such political practices as universal suffrage, renovation of the House of Lords (Peers), popularization of the crown (the emperor), political party reforms, promotion of social policies, and a two-party (conservative vs. labor) system in parliament. The Progressive believed the rise of political liberalism was historically inevitable and that Japan, like it or not, must be prepared to respond properly. The Progressive regarded as his antithesis the stubborn and closed-minded Reactionary who failed to perceive progress in history.

In the second set of contrasts, "Westernization vs. Restoration," the Restorationists viewed Japan after the Meiji Restoration as a decaying nation which, as a result of the importation of Western civilization, had lost the essence of national existence, the *kokutai* (national polity) rooted in Oriental civilization. The Restorationists advocated spiritualism and a martial spirit as opposed to materialism and culturalism, which they thought were the basic tenets of Western civilization. In regard to international relations, the Restorationists asserted that the world was dominated by the Anglo-Saxon nations led by Great Britain and that the basic cause of the deadlock in Japanese diplomacy was Japan's having forgotten its East Asian heritage and followed in the wake of the Anglo-Saxons. Japan, they argued, must put an end to westernization and, under the leadership of the Restorationists, return to the traditional spirit of Japan.

Axis Y represents two further sets of contrasts: "Radical Reformists vs. Gradualists" and "Destruction vs. the Status Quo." The Radical Reformists viewed the course of world history as follows: World War I had produced frustration and decay in the Western democracies and introduced an era of reform. The fascist victory in Italy and the establishment of "socialism in one country" following the Russian revolution marked the beginning of an age of "nationalism." To respond to these changes, a radically transformed Japan must be constructed on the ruins of the corrupt and decadent political system dominated by the zaibatsu and their cohorts, the political parties and the government bureaucracy. As the standard bearers of the reform movement, the Radical Reformists saw their immediate political task to be to wage an all-out struggle against the forces of the status quo, which were aided by the "special privilege class." With regard to the international situation, the Radical Reformists believed the new Japan would lead the oppressed peoples of the world in a struggle for national emancipation from the Anglo-Saxon imperialism that dominated the world from behind a mask of "democracy" and "peace."

In diametrical contrast to the Radical Reformists, the Gradualists attached the greatest value to the maintenance and gradual extension of Japan's achievements since the Meiji Restoration. They branded all who opposed them as "Reds" (politically dangerous elements).

Both the Progressives and the Radical Reformists regarded themselves as the vanguard of historical development. The Restorationists and the Gradualists, on the other hand, considered themselves the "protectors" of "good tradition." However, both the Progressives and the Gradualists adopted a more or less positive attitude toward the contemporary situation, whereas the Radical Reformists and the Restorationists shared a more negative view. Because of these similarities it was possible for individuals and groups to shift their self-images from one group to another, and in actual practice such fluctuations did occur.

Where then is the "right wing" to be located in the diagram? Assuming that the diagram faithfully reflects the dynamics among various political groupings, we may state that during the interwar period the "right-wing" sector (shaded area) shifted A to B, indicating a drastic increase in the combined forces of the Restorationists and the Radical Reformists. For the purpose of this paper, the "right wing" is defined as that sector of the diagram between the Restorationists and the Radical Reformists and its immediate periphery.

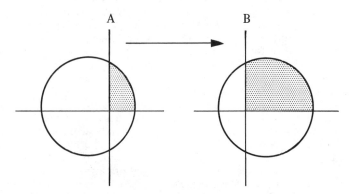

What were the characteristics of the Restorationists-Radical Reformists? I have already mentioned one common feature of the two groups—their essentially negative outlook on the contemporary situation, which led them to demand the destruction of the existing political-economic system based on the principles of "liberalism" and "individualism" and dominated by the zaibatsu, the military, bureaucratic cliques, and political parties. At the same time, however, their concepts of their target differed. The Restorationists were opposed to the results of westernization, which they regarded as fundamentally irreconcilable with the traditional Japanese political system characterized by the personal rule of the emperor. In contrast, the Radical Reformists attacked the forces of the "establishment" for resisting the laws of historical development—the progression from "liberalism" and "individualism" to "totalitarianism" that promised the rapid advance of the Japanese nation. Thus, while both the Restorationists, who labeled themselves the "Nipponist" or "patriotic" camp, and the Radical Reformists, who referred to themselves as the "reformist" camp, called for the destruction of the existing order, these differing viewpoints produced an element of conflict between them. The Police Bureau of the Ministry of Home Affairs designated these two factions more or less accurately as "nationalists" and "national socialists" respectively.

The term "right wing" (*uyoku*), first used in contrast to "left wing" (*sayoku*) by those outside the right-wing movement, included both the Restorationists and the Radical Reformists. Within the right-wing camp, however, the Radical Reformists frequently referred to the Restorationists as the "right wing." Nevertheless, it is practically impossible to divide the right wing into two such distinct groups. The Police Bureau of the Ministry of Home Affairs tried repeatedly to differentiate among the various right-wing groups but failed to find a satisfactory classification system. Their difficulty is illustrated in the following quotation:

> Although [these right-wing groups] all proclaim Nipponism and nationalism as their slogans, when we examine their ideological bases we find great differences among them. For example, Nipponism has been used variously to mean:
> 1) The simplistic ideal held by every Japanese that the imperial family is the pivot of the Japanese nation.
> 2) The idea that it is essential for every Japanese subject to equip himself with a deep understanding of the so-called ancient Japanese spirit. This concept advocates no change in the status quo.
> 3) A call for total and comprehensive reform which, with the traditional spirit of the Japanese race as its core and with a thorough knowledge of the merits and shortcomings of liberalism and communism, attempts to transcend such foreign ideologies.
> In addition, the right wing contains such diverse groups as the national socialists, who uphold national socialism as the ultimate form of modern socialism, and the agrarians, who demand reform of the current system, which they see as dominated by bureaucratic-industrial forces and thus advocate the construction of a new Japan based on the principles of agrarianism and rural autonomy.
> The activities of right-wing groups also vary, as follows:
> 1) Those confining their activities to the areas of education and nationalistic indoctrination.
> 2) Those devoting themselves to conventional political activities with such immediate objectives as cabinet overthrow.

3) Those seeking domestic political reforms and the eradication of communism and liberalism through legal activities alone.

4) Those advocating reform through illegal means.

5) Those engaging in criminal profit-making activities in the name of "patriotic organizations."[3]

Although the term "right wing" covered all Restorationist-Radical Reformist groups, not all members of the right wing were formally affiliated with these groups. For example, many high- and middle-ranking military officers and the so-called "renovationist bureaucrats" in various government agencies such as the Ministry of Home Affairs and the Cabinet Planning Board might be labeled Restorationists-Radical Reformists. Such individuals usually did not openly join right-wing organizations even though they often had close but secret ties with them. The same was true of some business leaders and members of political parties. In this paper, the "right wing" refers to those nongovernmental organizations whose membership did not normally include persons holding positions in established institutions. The right wing thus defined is virtually identical with the "nationalist and national socialist organizations" kept under surveillance by the Police Bureau of the Ministry of Home Affairs.[4]

II

In examining the activities of right-wing movements in Japan from the Manchurian Incident until the outbreak of the Pacific War, I have relied primarily upon two important sources: *Shakai undō no jōkyō* (The Current State of Social Movements), published annually from 1929 on by the Police Bureau of the Ministry of Home Affairs; and *Kokkashugi dantai no dōkō ni kansuru chōsa* (Report on an Investigation of Trends in the Activities of Nationalist Organizations), a special supplementary issue of the *Shisō shiryō panfuretto* (Materials on Thought Studies) series, published quarterly after April 1939 by the Criminal Affairs Bureau of the Justice Ministry.

The 1932 volume of *The Current State of Social Movements* contained a report that traced the rise of right-wing groups in Japan[5] beginning with nationalist movements during the Meiji period, whose activities it characterized as "either attempts to preserve the national essence in opposition to westernization or various acts of patriotism performed in a period of national emergency such as war." With the upsurge of socialism around 1918, the nationalists came to regard socialism as their primary target. Many became involved in disputes between capital and labor and, according to the report, invariably sided with management against the workers. They often resorted to violence against "leftists" and were wont to employ appeals to patriotism. That they did not always win the full support of the public is indicated by the "unflattering names" they were sometimes given—"company gangs," "reactionaries," and "gangsters."[6]

The report described their aims during the Taishō period as being "generally confined to preserving the national essence and opposing communism," although some—such as the Yūzonsha, the Kōchisha, and the

Kenkokukai—"demanded the construction of a new and restored Japan governed in accordance with the doctrine of the Imperial Way" and "advocated vigorous internal reforms and positive diplomacy." Their activities, however, were limited and were not characteristic of the nationalist movement as a whole.

In the view of the Police Bureau, nationalist groups began to exert a significant degree of influence only when the signing of the London Naval Disarmament Treaty in 1930 touched off a nationwide controversy. Soon afterward "the nationalist movement took a new and drastic turn as right-wing radicals began calling for the overthrow of the financial capitalists and 'special privilege class,' who were accused of manipulating the system of party politics for their own selfish purposes." Over the next two years the movement expanded rapidly, given impetus by "continuous unrest among the intellectuals and the ever-deepening economic crisis," by the Manchurian Incident in 1931 and radical assassination plots that led in 1932 to the Blood Brotherhood (Ketsumeidan) and May 15 incidents, and by the secret distribution of "pamphlets inciting to violence."[7] A chart indicated the rapid growth of nationalist organizations after 1922, until by 1932 almost five hundred such groups had been established. The report acknowledged, however, that "some functioned for only a short time or existed in name alone."

1880 -	1	1922 -	5
1894 -	1	1923 -	10
1896 -	1	1924 -	17
1901 -	1	1925 -	16
1912 -	1	1926 -	23
1914 -	2	1927 -	25
1916 -	1	1928 -	29
1917 -	1	1929 -	32
1918 -	1	1930 -	40
1919 -	2	1931 -	87
1920 -	1	1932 -	196
1921 -	1	*Total*:	494

As the Police Bureau noted, the controversy over the 1930 London Naval Disarmament Treaty was a major cause of the rise of the Restorationist-Radical Reformist groups as an influential political force in Japan.[8] In opposing the treaty they employed two major arguments. The first was that the treaty, like the Washington Conference system, was part of an American scheme to weaken Japan and prevent it from expanding onto the Asian continent where it might interfere with American ambitions to establish hegemony over Asia. A "peace" based upon the Washington Conference system, the right wing charged, was nothing but a cover-up for eventual Anglo-American domination of the world. Their second argument was a racial one: that Japanese expansion onto the continent was necessary in order to unify the nonwhite peoples of Asia and inspire them to resist domination by the white race, whose attitude was symbolized by the United States' treatment of Japanese immigrants.[9] It was Japan's mission, they believed, to provide this inspiration by universalizing the principle of Japan's national polity.

In the end, the Japanese government overrode the fierce opposition of the military and the radical nationalists and signed the treaty. In the course of the dispute, however, the right wing identified as the "enemies within" those who had sided with "Anglo-American imperialism": the genro, senior statesmen, party politicians, zaibatsu, military cliques, the bureaucracy, and the system of party politics in general. Because of their faith in the tenets of "liberalism" and "individualism," the radical nationalists asserted, these traditional forces had misguided the Throne. As a result, the government was led astray and the progress Japan had made in the years following the Meiji Restoration was blocked. As long as these enemies continued to dominate Japanese politics, they concluded, the nation would be led down the road to destruction. The only course was to replace "liberalism" and "individualism" with the principles of "Nipponism." Thus, although their goals differed, the Restorationists and Radical Reformists waged a united struggle, externally against white imperialism (including "Soviet Red imperialism") and internally against the liberal and capitalist ideologies upon which party politics were based. Under the banner of reform, radicals with a wide variety of programs and orientations flocked together. They included members of the venerable Kokuryūkai, radical national-socialists such as Kita Ikki, some Restorationists in the Privy Council and the Seiyūkai, as well as Restorationists-Radical Reformists in the military. The activists received money and information from high-ranking supporters in political circles and the military, whom they endeavored to unite and coerce into supporting the nationalist cause.

Following the signing of the treaty, a growing number of socialists switched their allegiance to the rightist cause. Thereafter, the number and membership of nongovernmental right-wing groups grew rapidly, as the table on page 494 indicates.

The increase in the membership of nationalist groups from around 300,000 in 1932 to over 660,000 in 1936 reflects the rapid growth of both right-wing organizations and Restorationist-Radical Reformist groups. After 1936 the latter apparently continued to grow, while the size of the right-wing organizations remained about the same.[10] *The Current State of Social Movements* also indicated that no one group ever became significantly larger than the rest, and none of the repeated attempts to unite those nationalist groups with similar aims ever succeeded.

The year 1936 is a watershed in the history of Japanese right-wing movements. The earlier period was one of rapid growth, whereas after 1936 the size of the right wing remained more or less constant. A more important difference was that during the later period the ideas of the Restorationists-Radical Reformists came to be regarded as the orthodox ideology of the state. The "emperor organ" theory controversy of 1935, the February 26 Incident in 1936, and the establishment of wartime controls after the outbreak of the Sino-Japanese War in 1937 supplied the necessary momentum for this development. In the following sections we shall observe more closely the characteristics of nationalist movements in the two periods.

III

The series of assassinations and attempted coups d'état that marked the years before 1936 began in the wake of the controversy over the London Treaty

MEMBERSHIP IN NATIONALIST AND AGRARIAN GROUPS

Classification	1932	1933	1934[a]	1935[b]	1936	1937	1938	1939	1940	1941
Nationalist Groups	330	501	572	692	688	733	820	839	988	896
Membership	306,857	280,912	297,428	325,309	614,983	562,705	497,555	687,576	587,028	537,387
Agrarian Groups	31	49	57	49	59	67	60	79	63	37
Membership	12,240	8,261	26,951	55,751	53,804	64,933	82,051	15,367	46,951	16,262
Total Number of Groups	361	550	629	741	747	800	880	918	1,051	933
Membership	319,097	289,173	324,379	381,060	668,787	627,638	579,606	702,943	633,979	553,649

[a]In addition, there were 307,922 right-wing political party members and local political party members (15,341, including members of the Shakai Taishūtō) in 1934.

[b]In addition, there were 258,202 right-wing political party members and local political party members (18,745, including members of the Shakai Taishūtō) in 1935.

Source: Naimushō Keiho Kyoku (Ministry of Home Affairs, Police Bureau), comp., *Shakai undō no jōkyō* (The Current State of Social Movements), 1932-41.

with an abortive attack on Prime Minister Hamaguchi Osachi by Sagōya Tomeo, a member of the Aikokusha, at the end of 1930. The ensuing March and October incidents in 1931[11] clearly aimed at the overthrow of the cabinet. Both incidents were planned by reform-minded "young officers" in central army headquarters who were members of the Cherry Blossom Society (Sakurakai), a secret organization led by Hashimoto Kingorō, and by various right-wing groups under the leadership of Ōkawa Shūmei. From February 1932 on there were several attempts to assassinate political and business leaders. The twenty-two targets of these plots, collectively referred to as the Blood Brotherhood (Ketsumeidan) Incident, included the genro Saionji Kimmochi, Lord Keeper of the Privy Seal Makino Nobuaki, Seiyūkai President Inukai Tsuyoshi, Minseitō President Wakatsuki Reijirō, the chief executive of the Mitsui combine Dan Takuma, and the head of the Mitsubishi family Iwasaki Koyata. However, only Dan and former Finance Minister Inoue Junnosuke, then secretary-general of the Minseitō, were actually assassinated before the conspiracy was discovered and all the Ketsumeidan members arrested. The core of the assassination group consisted of twelve men, among whom were several students from Tokyo, Kyoto, and Kokugakuin universities who had been greatly influenced by the old China activist and Nichiren monk Inoue Nisshō, as well as several members of the Nippon Kokumintō (Japan Nationalist Party) and a leader of the agrarian organization Aikyōjuku (Institute for Rural Patriotism). The incident began as a coup planned jointly by reformist "young officers" in the army who were led by Kita Ikki's disciple Nishida Mitsugu, by a group of young naval officers under the leadership of Fujii Hitoshi, and by the followers of Inoue Nisshō. But the army officers lost their enthusiasm for the plot when Araki Sadao was appointed army minister in the Inukai cabinet; and when Fujii was transferred to China upon the outbreak of the Shanghai Incident, the naval officers too fell away. In the end the assaults were carried out by the Inoue group alone.

On May 15 some thirty reformist army and navy officers and some members of the Aikyōjuku took up where the Ketsumeidan had left off. The Japanese public was horrified when the official residences of the prime minister and the lord keeper of the privy seal were attacked and Prime Minister Inukai was killed. In addition, assaults were made on the headquarters of the Seiyūkai, the Metropolitan Police Board, the Bank of Japan, the Mitsubishi Bank, and several power stations in the Tokyo area. Weapons used in the foray had been supplied by Jinmukai head Tōyama Hidezō. Later that year several more assassination plots were exposed: one against Prime Minister Saitō Makoto by Imamaki Yoshio, an adviser to the Jinmukai; one against Baron Wakatsuki by members of the Kokusui Taishūtō (National Essence Mass Party); and another by the Tenkōkai (Society for Heavenly Action) against several high-ranking officials including Lord Keeper of the Privy Seal Makino.

Two further plots were averted in 1933—an attempted coup, commonly known as the Heaven-Sent Soldiers Unit (Shinpeitai) Incident, in July and in November the Saitama Young Patriotic Volunteers conspiracy. The volunteers were a group of students, reservists, and army cadets who had been strongly influenced by Lieutenant Kurihara Yasuhide, later one of the leaders in the February 26 Incident. Their plans to establish a military government in accordance with Kita Ikki's *Nihon kaizō hōan taikō* (General Outline of

Measures for the Reconstruction of Japan) were frustrated by Kurihara's constant opposition, whereupon a small number schemed independently to assassinate Seiyūkai President Suzuki Kisaburō. But this plot was uncovered before it could be carried out. A similar conspiracy was revealed that year when members of the Tōtenjuku (Institute for Controlling Heaven's Way) were captured in a raid on a post office in an attempt to secure funds for their operations. Radical factions of such right-wing groups as the Jinmukai, Dai Nihon Gokokugun (Great Japan Defense Corps), Dai Nihon Seisantō (Great Japan Production Party), and Jikishin Dōjō (Pure Heart Seminary) were also involved.

During the succeeding year the Ministry of Home Affairs tightened its controls. Although a large number of people were arrested for involvement in minor sporadic plots, none were on the scale of the earlier conspiracies. Then the February 26 Incident of 1936 occurred.[12] Carried out by troops under the command of young army officers influenced by Kita Ikki, several political leaders were assassinated and the central part of Tokyo occupied for four days. Some members of right-wing groups that accepted Kita's ideas participated in the uprising, but they played only a secondary role to the Radical Reformist young officers, who had been unimpressed by the performance of right-wing organizations in the past. On the other hand, any collaboration with the military, which after the Manchurian Incident had rapidly taken over leadership of the Radical Reformist forces, was particularly difficult at the time of the February 26 Incident, when the Radical Reformist camp of the army was split by a factional struggle between the Imperial Way faction (Kōdōha) and the Control faction (Tōseiha). The Control faction, which then constituted a majority within the army central command, was attempting to unify not only right-wing groups outside the government but also Restorationist-Radical Reformist elements at the top echelons of political circles with a view to winning control over the policymaking process. They were identified by the Imperial Way faction, which was made up largely of radical young officers, as "advocates of the status quo" to be eradicated by force. The young officers of the Imperial Way faction who carried out the incident feared that if the right-wing groups were intimately involved, their plans might leak out. The rivalry within the army was further intensified in 1934, when the Control faction disclosed the so-called November 20 Incident, an alleged coup d'état plotted by the Imperial Way group. In 1935 more oil was added to the burning factional strife when Lieutenant Colonel Aizawa Saburō of the Imperial Way faction was placed on trial for murdering Military Affairs Bureau Chief Nagata Tetsuzan in retaliation for the dismissal of Mazaki Jinzaburō, an Imperial Way leader, from his post as inspector general of military education. Many right-wing groups now became involved in the dispute, most notably certain ones under the influence of Kita and Nishida that published what the Police Bureau termed "slanderous documents" in support of the Imperial Way faction.

The failure of the coup dealt a serious blow to the hopes of right-wing groups. Thereafter, despite repeated rumors of another "February 26 Incident," no large-scale armed uprising was planned either by the military alone or by right-wing forces in collaboration with it.

Another aspect of the activities of right-wing groups was the attempt to unify the Restorationist-Radical Reformist forces in order to bring about change by legal means. According to *The Current State of Social Movements, 1932*, these efforts were repeatedly frustrated by leadership conflicts and personal rivalries, particularly among groups that were unable to agree on matters of program and principle.[13] Following the signing of the London Naval Treaty in 1930, however, nationalist groups found common cause in attacking the government for not adopting a stronger foreign policy stand on such issues as Japanese rights and interests in Manchuria and Mongolia. "Their common action against the government," the report stated, "gradually fostered a mood for union among traditionally contentious nationalist groups." As early as February 1930 sixteen right-wing groups established the Aikoku Kinrōtō (Patriotic Labor Party). In March 1931 ten right-wing groups set up the Zen Nihon Aikokusha Kyōdōtōsō Kyōgikai (All-Japan Patriots Joint Struggle Council), and the following June more than ten influential groups of the Nippon Kokumintō and Kokuryūkai line combined to form the Dai Nihon Seisantō. The reporter added, however, that the first two "gradually lost the spirit of unity primarily as a result of differences over issues of leadership and ideology" and ultimately were reduced to "collections of groups under the influence of various individuals."

The outbreak of the Manchurian Incident in September 1931 created a national crisis that again aroused the nationalists' enthusiasm for a united front. The Police Bureau reported that "beginning with the founding of the Nihon Kokka Shakaishugi Gakumei (Japan National Socialist Student League) on April 16, increasingly intensive movements for establishing nationalist and national socialist political parties have been going on." It listed several other "central organizations for joint struggle" founded that year: the Kokumin Nihontō (Japan Nationalist Party) on May 29 (which immediately split into the Nihon Kokka Shakaitō and the Shin Nihon Kokumin Dōmei), the Kokunan Dakai Rengō Kyōgikai (Joint Council to Solve the National Crisis) in June, the Daidō Kurabu (Great Unity Club) in November, and the Kokutai Yōgo Rengōkai (Joint Association to Defend the National Polity) in December. Similar groups also began to appear in major cities such as Osaka, Kyoto, Aichi, and Toyama. But while the bureau expected this tendency toward a united front to "continue to make progress in the future," it anticipated that "the reality of amalgamation" would inevitably lead to ideological dissension. It therefore concluded that "it will take some time and many ups and downs before the nationalist movement realizes a united front."

On March 20, 1932 the Zen Nihon Aikokusha Kyōdōtōsō Kyōgikai held a "Smash the Unpatriotic Diet Rally" to air grievances against the actions of the Diet. The platform called for: (1) the overthrow of "unpatriotic parliamentary politics" and establishment of a government under the personal rule of the emperor; (2) extension of the imperial prerogative to industry and the destruction of capitalism; and (3) putting an end to internal class conflict and enhancing Japan's international prestige.

The Kokunan Dakai Rengō Kyōgikai held a rally on June 14 to demand that the government and the Diet immediately recognize Manchukuo and conclude a military and economic alliance with the new state, and that several measures be adopted "to alleviate the impoverished livelihood of the nation." They proposed that the government (1) encourage new industry and open up farm lands in Manchuria to 350,000 emigrants annually "in order to achieve immediate full employment"; (2) order local governments to provide the poor "without charge with such daily necessities as food, clothing, and fertilizer" for a full year; (3) allow a three-year moratorium on debts of less than 1,000 yen; and (4) liquidate all national, local, and village bonds and other public debts, the costs to be defrayed by a public loan. They also asked the government to institute controls on interest rates, prices, and foreign exchange, to introduce a managed currency based upon commodity prices, and to establish state controls over all industrial enterprises.

A wide range of nationalist groups came together in agrarian societies that called for replacing "the present social system which gives undue importance to urban areas under bureaucratic administration" with "an autonomous agrarian society centered around the Imperial Household." In 1932 these groups formed the San-ka-jō Seigan Kisei Dōmeikai (Alliance to Achieve Our Three Demands), which called for a debt moratorium, fertilizer subsidies, and funds to facilitate emigration to Manchuria and Mongolia. The San-ka-jō Dōmeikai was soon reorganized as the Go-ka-jō Seigan Kisei Dōmeikai (Alliance to Achieve Our Five Demands), which collected over 42,500 signatures on a petition to the Diet in support of Dōmeikai policies.

Another important collection of right-wing groups was the Kokutai Yōgo Rengōkai, which had a strong Restorationist tinge. Originally demanding the reform of the Justice Ministry and the resignation of the prime minister and the justice minister, it capitalized upon an incident in November 1932 in which two judges were charged with being communists and indicted for violating the peace preservation law.

On October 18, 1933 the Kokutai Yōgo Rengōkai held a forum on current problems attended by some 250 members of various right-wing groups. A resolution was passed condemning the "senile and ineffectual" Saitō cabinet for its lack of accomplishment and demanding that it "strive to be equal to today's extraordinary situation" and become transformed into "a cabinet of true national unity." Thereafter, the Rengōkai continued to sponsor rallies and distribute bills and posters.

The leaders of the Kokunan Dakai Rengō Kyōgikai and the Daidō Kurabu in the meantime concentrated their efforts more openly upon overthrowing the cabinet and working for "cooperation and unity among various right-wing groups scattered all over the nation." The Police Bureau reported that from November 1933 on these efforts "enjoyed growing support from many local groups." Right-wing rallies served to "strengthen both nationalistic consciousness among the general public and the mood for a united front of nationalist movements," until on December 11, just before the Diet reconvened, the Aikoku Undō Itchi Kyōgikai (Council for a Union of Patriotic Movements) was founded at a Shōwa Restoration National Conference in Tokyo. At a rally the previous day a resolution was passed demanding the "immediate execution" of steps to bring about an "Imperial Way Shōwa Restoration."[14] These included the resignation of the Saitō cabinet, the appointment of a "national restoration cabinet," and the dissolution of all political factions within the House of Peers. In foreign policy they demanded that a "diplomacy of justice and pan-Asian alliance" replace the "traditional humiliating diplomacy submissive to the dictates of European powers and the United States," and that "a state of kingly rule" (*ōdō*) be established in Manchuria. Japan, it was resolved, "must maintain the right of equality in armaments and must complete preparations for a broad national defense (*kōgi kokubō*) based upon total national mobilization." In order to accomplish this, the Kyōgikai called for economic controls that included nationalization of banks and major industries, price stabilization, assistance to medium- and small-scale commercial and industrial enterprises, a monetary system based on "actual national resources rather than gold," promotion of industry and colonization to eliminate unemployment, as well as tax exemptions and debt moratoriums for the poor and higher taxes on the rich. The statement further called for educational reforms to promote a "pure Japanese culture movement" that would eradicate "the poisonous and corrupt education characterized by formalism, liberalism, and materialism" and asked that "in accordance with the principle of unified imperial prerogative in judicial matters," all distinctions between civilian and soldier in legal proceedings be erased.

The opposition of nationalist groups to the Saitō cabinet continued into 1934 and was transferred to the Okada cabinet, which replaced it on July 8. Although during 1934 no issue arose that mobilized the right wing on a large scale, there was considerable support for a pamphlet on national defense distributed by the army,[15] for the army's efforts to reform and control the Japanese administration of Manchuria, and for the navy's opposition to arms reduction. Moreover, the right wing at this time came increasingly to rely on the military for support and inspiration. According to *The Current State of Social Movements, 1934* there was a trend away from "the traditional methods of arousing public opinion—speech meetings and lecture forums" and a growing expectation that their dreams of "national renovation" would soon be realized by an uprising of "certain powerful forces"—i.e. the military.[16]

During this first period, the coalition of right-wing forces won an important political victory in the controversy over "clarification of national polity" (*kokutai meichō*). The debate began[17] when Minoda Kyōki, a professor at Kokushikan, and other right-wing activitists charged that the writings of Minobe Tatsukichi, a professor of law at Tokyo Imperial University and a member of the House of Peers, and of Suehiro Izutarō, the dean of the university's law faculty, contained statements of lese-majesty. Their efforts to arouse public opinion through the publication of accusatory books and pamphlets eventuated on June 6, 1934 in Minoda's filing a complaint against Suehiro for having in his writings committed lese-majesty and violated the peace preservation laws and the constitution. On November 28, however, the case was dropped.

The succeeding year the Kokutai Yōgo Rengōkai embarked on an intensive campaign against Minobe's theory of "the emperor as an organ of the state" and "as if responding to the right-wing campaign," the Diet soon took up the issue. On February 18 in the House of Peers Baron Kikuchi Takeo, Viscount Mimurodo Yukimitsu, and Baron Inoue Kiyosumi attacked Minobe's theory in the course of an interpellation of the home and education ministers. A week later, on February 25, Minobe spoke for an hour in explanation and defense of his theory. Then, on February 28 and again on March 7 charges of lese-majesty were filed in the Tokyo District Court by Reserve Major General Etō Genkurō, a member of the lower house who was closely allied with Minoda. The controversy intensified on March 20 when the House of Peers passed a resolution calling for "a reform of political education." Meanwhile, the question of *kokutai* and its relationship to the organ theory was raised in the House of Representatives by Yamamoto Teijirō, followed on March 23 by passage of a resolution, introduced by Seiyūkai President Suzuki, urging the "clarification of national polity."

Diet support of their campaign encouraged right-wing groups to intensify their attack upon the emperor-organ theory. The Police Bureau summarized their demands as follows:

> 1) The government should at once prohibit the sale and distribution of works on the emperor-organ theory and at the same time ban dissemination and propagation of the doctrine.
> 2) Professors and government officials who uphold the emperor-organ theory should be immediately dismissed.
> 3) The government should openly declare that the emperor-organ theory is erroneous.
> 4) Dr. Minobe should resign from all his public posts and commit suicide.
> 5) Prime Minister Okada Keisuke and Privy Council President Ichiki Kitokurō should assume responsibility for the incident and resign.

The Seiyūkai, which then constituted a majority in the Diet, was quick to seize this opportunity to attack the government with the aim of overthrowing the Okada cabinet. They were joined in the assault by all the Restorationist-Radical Reformist forces in the upper echelons of the political parties and the bureaucracy, and the government was forced to bow to their pressures. On April 7 Minobe was interrogated at the Tokyo district procurator's office, and two days later the Ministry of Home Affairs banned three of his works—*Chikujō kenpō seigi* (Commentary on the Constitution), *Kenpō satsuyō* (Essentials of the Constitution), and *Nihon kenpō no kihonshugi* (Basic Principles of the Japanese Constitution)—and ordered him to revise his *Gendai kensei hyōron* (Critique of Modern Constitutional Government) and *Gikai seiji no kentō* (Examination of Parliamentary Government) before their next printing.

The right wing received support also from Inspector General of Military Education Mazaki Jinzaburō, who spoke against the emperor-organ theory on April 13. Similar addresses were given by Education Minister Matsuda Genji on April 10 and by Kwantung Army Commander Minami Jirō on April 13. As the campaign grew more intense, new groups were organized to spearhead the attack. On April 17 right-wing activists formed the Seikyō Ishin Renmei (League for Restoration of Political Education), and on June 1 the Kokutai Meichō Tassei Renmei (League for the Clarification of National Polity) was founded by the Kokutai Yōgo Rengōkai and Restorationist elements in both houses of the Diet. On August 3 the government publicly denounced the emperor-organ theory in an official statement and a speech by the prime minister. This action, however, did not satisfy right-wing groups that had been demanding that the cabinet assume responsibility, and the pressure from the right wing continued to mount. On August 27 the Imperial Reservists Association at its national convention issued a declaration charging that the government's statement had lacked "sincerity." The contention was supported by the army and navy ministers at a cabinet meeting on September 25. As a result, on October 15 the government issued a second statement, whereupon the army and navy declined to press the matter any further. Although the right wing was not fully mollified, the movement gradually subsided by the end of October.

In the view of the Police Bureau the movement for "clarification" and the attack on Minobe were important in having focused public attention on the radical reform movements which had theretofore been "more or less ignored and despised" by the general public. The bureau's 1935 report stated:

> The campaign for the clarification of national polity spread all over the country like wildfire and developed into a political and social issue that had a profound impact on all areas of life. Even though the campaign originated in an attack upon the emperor-organ theory and an effort to chastise the liberal legal school, the true intent of the movement was to attack liberalism in general. Its ultimate aim was the thorough eradication of all liberal elements in the nation. The movement was truly epoch-making in that it destroyed in a day the constitutional theory that had been widely accepted for some thirty years, forced an influential liberal scholar into social oblivion, and thus destroyed a segment of the liberal camp.

The bureau further saw the campaign as having brought into the realm of political controversy what had previously been no more than an academic debate, and as advancing efforts to achieve a united front of right-wing groups, for it "provided not only a perfect cause which no one could openly oppose but one in which every right-wing group might participate." And its success brought renewed hope for the eventual triumph of the right wing.[18]

Strengthened by their success in branding liberalism as heretical to Japan's national polity, the Restorationist-Radical Reformist forces suddenly found their ranks swelled by former members of the Restorationist-Gradualist and Progressive-Radical Reformist camps, although such conversions had taken place on a smaller scale previously. Serious debate now commenced on the possibility of establishing a united right-wing political party. But in the end the discussions came to nothing and, in contrast to the Nazis, the Japanese right wing never secured a foothold in the Diet. The table on page 502 shows the number of local assembly members in 1934 and 1935 who belonged to right-wing groups.

In the nationwide elections for prefectural assemblymen in 1935, the third held after universal manhood suffrage went into effect, considerable success was predicted for nationalist candidates. However, out of 127 who ran, only 37 were elected.[19] Furthermore, right-wing candidates polled a total of 227,087 votes—fewer than the estimated membership of the right-wing groups in 1935. The Police Bureau saw three reasons for their failure. First, many members of the right wing tended to underplay the importance of elections, believing that their goals were to be achieved through extra-parliamentary means. Second, nationalist organizations, being relatively new to the political scene, had not had time to consolidate their power and build up a large voting constituency. Finally, the bureau observed that "their policy proclamations have generally

	Assemblies		Seats held by members of the Shakai Taishūtō	
	1934	1935	1934	1935
Prefecture	38	57	21	28
City	105	103	62	59
Town	210	97	87	89
Ward	16	3	3	23
Village	671	356	280	275
Agricultural Association Representatives	383	949	380	386

Note: Figures on "local political parties" have been omitted, for they do not distinguish between the "right wing" and the Shakai Taishūtō.

been infused with a high-sounding spiritualism" and ignored "practical programs that would appeal to the general public."[20] The right wing met similar frustration in the general election of 1936, when only 9 out of 39 right-wing candidates were elected. In addition, several of the successful candidates had previously been elected to the Diet as members of the Seiyūkai, the Minseitō, or the Shakai Taishūtō and thus had already built up their own constituencies.

IV

The failure of the February 26 uprising had made it clear that the right wing would not be able to bring about a "restoration" through a military coup d'état, and the hope that political power might be achieved through a grand right-wing political party in accordance with parliamentary tactics was banished to a distant future. By 1937, moreover, as a result of the 1935 campaign for the clarification of national polity and the outbreak of the second Sino-Japanese War, many of the Restorationist-Radical Reformist demands had been accepted by both the government and the public and almost every political group had joined the Restorationist-Radical Reformist bandwagon. Thus, right-wing groups ceased to constitute a peculiar minority in society and their passion for action was concomitantly reduced. In fact, as renovationist bureaucrats, in order to meet the pressing needs created by the war with China, put into practice the controlled economy the right wing had been demanding, Restorationist voices began to be raised in protest against "bureaucratic controls."

Under such changed circumstances, the right wing increasingly turned its attention to foreign policy issues, on which it gave full support to the actions of the military. Imperialism, of both the Soviet and the Western variety, came under renewed attack from the right wing. Whereas in the first period opposition to imperialism had been expressed largely in theoretical terms, after 1936 more concrete programs of action were devised. These activities were aided by the growing feeling of crisis that had arisen among the general public as a result of the tension between Japan and the powers, which had led to more and more frequent attacks on the government for its "weak" diplomacy.

Meanwhile, efforts to bring about a right-wing political coalition continued. The Police Bureau reported several such attempts in 1936: the formation of the Nigatsukai (February Society) in the Kantō region on March 11; a movement led by the Hachigatsukai (August Society) in the Kansai region to form a "restorationist political party"; organization of the Aikoku Rōdōkumiai Zenkoku Konwakai (National Council of Patriotic Labor Unions) by labor unions throughout the country on April 19; and in Osaka the calling of a "meeting to prepare for the formation of a restorationist political party" (*ishin seitō kessei junbikai*) on June 20. Chaired by Yoshida Masuzō, this meeting expressed strong interest in joining forces with the Nigatsukai in the Kantō region.[21] The trend was observed the following year, when a united front movement was initiated by the Seiji Kakushin Kyōgikai (Political Reform Council); and a group supported by the Jikyoku Kyōgikai (Society for the Discussion of Current Affairs), the Aikoku Rōdō Nōmin Dōshikai (Patriotic Labor-Farmer Comrades Society), and other organizations called upon all associations upholding "Nipponism" to coalesce. During this year were formed the Nihon Kakushintō (Japan Reform Party, an amalgamation of the Shin Nihon Kokumin Dōmei, Kokumin Kyōkai [Nationalist Association], Aikoku Seiji Dōmei [Patriotic Political Alliance], and Aikoku Kakushin Renmei [Patriotic Renovation League]), the Nipponshugi Bunka Dōmei (Alliance for a Nipponist Culture), and the Tai-Ei Dōshikai (Anti-British Comrades Society).[22]

By the end of 1937 calls for the formation of a national unity party had become increasingly insistent, fueled by the national crisis that had followed in the wake of the China Incident. Internal dissent, many believed, could be eradicated only by abolishing all the existing political parties and establishing in their place "a national unity party, squarely based upon the principle of personal rule by the emperor." In early December such individuals as the publisher Akiyama Teisuke, Diet member Akita Kiyoshi, and several right-wing China activists including Miyazaki Ryūsuke, Sanekawa Tokijirō, and Yamamoto Kamejirō solicited support for this goal from a wide range of individuals, among them Tōyama Mitsuru, Prince Ichijō Sanetaka, Admirals Yamamoto Hidesuke, Arima Ryōkitsu, and Suetsugu Nobumasa, General Honjō Shigeru, and newspaper publishers Tokutomi Sohō and Ogata Taketora. On December 16 several Tokyo newspapers printed a statement signed by Ichijō, Tōyama, and Yamamoto Hidesuke which read: "AN APPEAL TO THE ENTIRE NATION. A powerful political party amalgamating all existing political parties into one is fervently desired." According to the Police Bureau, this event "suddenly reinvigorated the debate over abolishing the political parties . . . and had considerable impact upon the general public and the political parties, which, in keeping with the general mood of national unity in the face of the incident in China, had deliberately avoided interparty conflicts. Reformist groups and like-minded volunteers in particular seem to have been greatly encouraged by the fact that individuals whom they held in deep esteem had expressed precisely the idea that the reformists had been advocating." In closing the report cautioned: "They are now about to embark on a vigorous movement. Their activities must be closely watched."[23]

Despite the agreement of the right wing on its slogan—"Smash the existing political parties"—the response to the call varied. Testimony to this fact may be found in the reaction to the Hayashi cabinet's dissolution of the Diet in March 1937, when Reformist groups "expressed their satisfaction with the government's resolute action and energetically embarked on a campaign in the belief that the golden opportunity had arrived to abolish the existing political parties and eradicate liberal elements." The subsequent activities of some groups were aimed at expanding their representation in the Diet. The Shin Nihon Kokumin Dōmei, Dai Nihon Seisantō, Kokumin Kyōkai, Aikoku Seiji Dōmei, and others operated under the umbrella of the Seiji Kakushin Kyōgikai, while other groups—such as the Rikken Yōseikai (Society for the Cultivation of Constitutional Justice), Meirinkai (Society of Enlightened Ethics), Kōdōkai (Imperial Way Society), Kinrō Nihontō (Laboring Japan Party), Kōkoku Jichikai (Autonomous Council for Reviving the Nation), and Kōkoku Nōmin Dōmei (Imperial Farmers Alliance)—nominated their own independent candidates and conducted energetic campaigns, each under the banner of "Destroy the existing political parties and establish a Diet to assist the Imperial Way." Such efforts were directly opposed by a coalition of youth groups under the leadership of the Junsei Ishin Kyōdō Seinentai (Pure Restoration Youth Corps) on the grounds that "it is meaningless to advance in the present Diet, which fails to perform its duty to assist the emperor's rule. Rejection of such a Diet is the only way to assist His Majesty's rule." Their campaign to "return suffrage to the emperor" drew wide attention. They received indirect support from the Jikyoku Kyōgikai, Aikoku Rōdō Nōmin Dōshikai, Dai Nihon Seisantō, and other groups that viewed electoral campaigns as a trap set by democracy and therefore endeavored to arouse public opinion through speeches and literature urging the "prohibition of political groups and parties, fundamental reform of the election laws, and repeated dissolution of the Diet."[24]

Closely related to these nationalist activities was the plan then being formulated by Restorationist-Radical Reformist groups to replace all the political parties with a powerful national party headed by Prime Minister Konoe Fumimaro. This party was to amalgamate all the right-wing groups, the Renovationist bureaucrats, and that part of the Shakai Taishūtō led by Asō Hisashi and Kamei Kan'ichirō, who were in sympathy with the Restorationist-Radical Reformist forces. As early as September 1937 the government had been considering ways of mobilizing nationwide public support for its China policy. Its discussions soon resulted in the organization of the Kokumin Seishin Sōdōin Chūō Renmei (Alliance to Mobilize the National Spirit), which brought together associations from such diverse fields as labor, agriculture, religion, education, youth, and industry, as well as right-wing groups including the Kokutai Yōgo Rengōkai, Jikyoku Kyōgikai, Junsei Nipponshugi Seinen Undō Zenkoku Kyōgikai (Nationwide Council of Pure Nipponist Youth Movements), and Aikoku Nōmin Dantai Kyōgikai (Patriotic Farmers Association Council). In the fall of 1937 Konoe ordered several of his cabinet members to draft a concrete program for a national unity party.[25]

To the right wing, which had been frustrated in its efforts to win control of the Diet through a united political party, Konoe's idea had a strong appeal. The Police Bureau reported in 1938 a swelling chorus of demands for "one nation, one party" and the establishment of organizations such as the Kyokoku

Itchi Renmei (National Unity League) and the Bōkyō Gokokudan (Anti-Communist National Defense Corps), which campaigned for "eradication of internal dissension and establishment of a one nation-one party system." These organizations also launched direct attacks against the political parties. On February 17 members of the Bōkyō Gokokudan occupied the Seiyūkai and Minseitō headquarters, and on March 3 a group of Kōfūjuku (Imperial Way Institute) members led by Chichiba Keitarō assaulted the head of the Shakai Taishūtō, Abe Isoo. Such activities, however, lost them public support and provoked Diet debate. And in the end public criticism and internal conflict forced both the Bōkyō Gokokudan and the Kyokoku Itchi Renmei to disband.[26]

The governmental discussions likewise bore little fruit. In part this was because the limited proposal to found a new political party gradually expanded, in the course of cabinet debate, into a grandiose program for a new structure around which the entire political, economic, and social life of the nation would be organized. This inevitably led to Restorationist accusations that the new political party would become another bakufu and encroach upon the authority of the emperor. Meanwhile, more radical elements of the right wing charged that Konoe's design was merely an effort at reorganization proposed by the "advocates of the status quo." A similar process occurred in 1940, when Konoe's second attempt to found a new party led to the establishment of the Imperial Rule Assistance Association.

With the formation of the Hiranuma cabinet in January 1939 the new party issue was temporarily set aside, and the right wing turned its attention to the internal split that had developed in the course of the controversy. The immediate cause of conflict was the question of the right wing's attitude toward the Hiranuma cabinet. The debate became public on February 11, when Iwata Ainosuke of the Aikokusha, Kuzū Yoshihisa of the Kokuryūkai, Irie Tanenori and Ikeda Hiroshi of the Kokutai Yōgo Rengōkai, and Homma Ken'ichirō of the Shizanjuku (Purple Mountain Institute) openly declared their support of Hiranuma's government in a statement, published in a number of Tokyo newspapers under the title "Our Faith in the Hiranuma Cabinet," which pointed out the necessity of eradicating "various elements in society that erroneously uphold socialistic reform ideologies." The breach was widened on July 19, when the Kōa Dōshikai (Asian Development Comrades Society) put up posters all over Tokyo that called upon the public to "Destroy pseudo-patriotic socialist groups!"—by which it meant the Dai Nihon Seisantō, Aikoku Rōdō Nōmin Dōshikai, Nihon Kakushintō, and Shakai Taishūtō.[27]

The split within the nationalist camp continued in 1940 during Konoe's second attempt to found a new party—his "new structure movement" that eventuated in the formation of the Imperial Rule Assistance Association. According to *The Current State of Social Movements, 1940*, some Reformist groups immediately indicated their cooperation with the movement by voluntarily dissolving. Others formed new organizations to promote a "grand alliance" in support of the new structure movement. However, it became increasingly clear, the Police Bureau reported, that certain reformist factions were actually utilizing the movement to preserve their organizations, and the exhortations for a grand alliance, although they generated a "great amount of noise," failed to produce any substantive results.

Meanwhile, official encouragement of the new structure movement continued. In August a preparatory committee was selected, including from the Reformist camp several members of the Tōa Kensetsu Kokumin Renmei (National Alliance for the Reconstruction of East Asia): Suetsugu Nobumasa (who was also chariman of the Kokumin Kyōryoku Kaigi [Council for National Cooperation]), Hashimoto Kingorō, Nakano Seigō, Ida Iwakusu, Kuzū Yoshihisa, and Ōta Kōzō. When in October the Imperial Rule Assistance Association (IRAA) was initiated as the nucleus of the Imperial Rule Assistance Movement, these individuals and their associates were appointed to key posts—Ida, Hashimoto, and Nakano as permanent directors; Kuzū and Kobayashi Jun'ichirō as directors; and Suetsugu, Amaya Kikuo, and Honryō Shinjirō as assistant directors.

Not surprisingly, this aroused great resentment in the ranks of other Reformist groups. At first their discontent was expressed in an ideological attack upon Arima Yoriyasu, Gotō Ryūnosuke, and other top leaders of the IRAA. Their criticism gradually intensified to the point where they began to question the constitutionality of the association and to press a public attack upon it. On December 18 the Nipponshugi Seinen Kaigi (Nipponist Youth Council), headed by Matsuki Yoshikatsu, Saigō Takahide, and Ōmori Issei, called an emergency meeting at which a resolution was passed demanding Arima's immediate resignation as IRAA secretary. On the 25th Arima's ouster was demanded by the Taisei Yokusankai Junka Yūshi Kondankai (Volunteers Council to Purify the IRAA), whose members included Iwata Ainosuke, Ikeda Hiroshi, Tanabe Sōei, and Terada Inejirō. The IRAA was also vigorously opposed by the "rōnin" faction of various "pure Nipponist" (junsei Nipponshugi) groups. In contrast, the Tōa Kensetsu Kokumin Renmei struggled to maintain its dominant position in the IRAA, and members of the Dai Nihon Sekiseikai (Great Japan True-Hearted Society) and the Shintōsha (Society to Arouse the East), while proclaiming their radicalism, endeavored to expand their influence in the association.[28]

During 1941 the "pure Nipponist" groups (which the Police Bureau described as being divided into rival kokutai meichō [clarification of national polity] and zentaishugi [totalitarianist] factions) continued to challenge the IRAA, charging that its one nation-one party slogan was merely a cover-up for what was actually a bakufu and, therefore, unconstitutional. They further accused the association of "employing numerous socialists" and promoting "reform policies that are increasingly national socialistic or communistic."[29]

Ultimately the IRAA was forced to bow under the attack of the "restorationist" forces. In March both Nakano Seigō and Hashimoto Kingorō resigned their positions in the association. Sweeping organizational and personnel changes in April revealed the official nature and close governmental ties of the IRAA, and in the end it was changed from a political association to an official business association.[30]

We have noted that after the failure of the February 26 Incident and the outbreak of the China War, foreign policy issues increasingly became a focus of right-wing concern. Let us therefore examine in greater detail the attitudes toward foreign policy of nationalist groups.

Immediately upon the outbreak of the China Incident, the Criminal Affairs Bureau's Report on an Investigation of Trends in the Activities of

Nationalist Organizations stated in 1940, right-wing groups encouraged the government to "thoroughly chastise" China. At first their activities were limited to urging the government to pursue a strong diplomatic policy and fully implement the national mobilization law. But as the war dragged on, concern became centered on the nations that were supplying aid to the Nationalist forces—Britain, the United States, France, and the Soviet Union—and a campaign was begun in support of a military alliance with Germany and Italy.[31]

Right-wing groups were also at the forefront of an anti-British movement that began in the fall of 1937. On October 30 influential members of various Nipponist groups—including Yamamoto Teijirō, Tatekawa Yoshitsugu, and Tōyama Mitsuru—founded the Tai-Ei Dōshikai, which called a public rally on November 20 to denounce British anti-Japanese activities and call for a national campaign against Britain. Another group prominent in the anti-British movement was the Seinen Ajia Renmei (Asian Youth League), founded about this time by Shimonaka Yasaburō and Nakatani Takeyo. Their propaganda activities resulted in a nationwide outburst of rallies to denounce Britain.[32]

In 1938 the Police Bureau reported that rumors of peace overtures and mediation by a third power, prompted by the Ugaki-Craigie talks, had raised sentiments against Britain and China to a new pitch. Right-wing assemblies that summer called upon the government to energetically prosecute the "holy war" against China by attacking Canton and Hainan island and to reject any "meddling by third powers." When the Changkufeng Incident broke out in mid-July, public opinion turned also against the Soviet Union. Some right-wing groups, including the Kenkokukai, Dai Nihon Seisantō, and Jikyoku Kyōgikai, clamored for war against Russia which, they argued, had been aiding China and therefore must be destroyed before Japan's objectives in China could be achieved. On August 18 at Kyōgikai headquarters Akao Bin, Maeda Torao, Nakazawa Benjirō, and others held a meeting to plan the establishment of the Tai-So Dōshikai (Anti-Soviet Comrades Society).[33]

Concurrently with the anti-British and anti-Soviet movements the right wing led a campaign to strengthen the Anti-Comintern Pact, some calling for the conclusion of a military alliance with Germany and Italy which, the Police Bureau noted, "have maintained a very friendly posture toward Japan since the outbreak of the China Incident ... [and] are diametrically opposed to the powers that are assisting Chiang Kai-shek." A number of rallies in support of a tripartite alliance were held, most notably one in Tokyo on November 25, 1938, the second anniversary of the signing of the Anti-Comintern Pact. Sponsored by the Kokusai Hankyō Renmei (International Anti-Communist League), the Kokumin Seishin Sōdōin Chūō Renmei, and the Tokyo government, the 80,000 persons who attended included such dignitaries as Chief of the Army General Staff Prince Kan'in, Foreign Minister Arita Hachirō, Welfare Minister Kido Kōichi, Vice Army Minister Tōjō Hideki, and the ambassadors from Germany, Italy, and Manchukuo.[34]

These campaigns reached a climax in 1939, under the auspices of the Nichi-Doku-I Gunji Dōmei Yōsei Zenkoku Seinen Renmei (Nationwide Youth League to Demand a Military Alliance with Germany and Italy), which had been formed in late April 1939 by some thirty right-wing groups led by the Dai Nihon Seisantō, Kakumeisō (Society of the Cry of the Crane), Seisen Kantetsu Dōmei

(Alliance for Total Victory in the Holy War), and Kenkokukai. The Criminal Affairs Bureau described their activities as follows: "They called upon governmental authorities and at the legations and embassies of various foreign countries and carried out a high-powered public campaign through literature and speeches. Soon numerous small, local right-wing groups joined them, and the campaign spread all over the country." When the government remained undecided on the question of a military alliance, however, their actions took on a more radical cast and rumors began to circulate that imminent terrorist acts were planned against pro-British elements among the senior statesmen and zaibatsu. Fortunately, the Police Bureau noted, their plots were exposed through "swift and proper investigative and detective activities by the police," and no one was killed, although several arrests were made on charges of plotting assassination.[35]

As the preceding has made clear, the right wing concentrated its attack upon Great Britain. France, Russia, and the United States were often secondary targets of their wrath, but it is worth noting that even after the United States abrogated the Treaty of Commerce and Navigation, it did not replace Britain as a primary target. In July 1939 alone 387 anti-British rallies were attended by some 850,000 people and over 400,000 participated in street demonstrations.[36] Such campaigns served to arouse public opinion, strengthen those within the military who espoused hard-line policies, and threaten the position of the moderates and advocates of the status quo within the government.

The onslaught abated somewhat with the conclusion in August 1939 of the German-Soviet Nonaggression Pact. But the anti-British campaign was rekindled once more when the *Asama-maru* incident occurred in January 1940. On April 29 Adachi Kenzō, Nakano Seigō, Suetsugu Nobumasa, Matsui Iwane, Hashimoto Kingorō, and others formed the Tōa Kensetsu Kokumin Renmei, declaring that "in close collaboration with newly rising nations such as Germany and Italy, Japan should readjust its relations with the Soviet Union and concentrate its energies on the anti-British campaign." When Holland fell the following month, many right-wing groups, in opposition to Foreign Minister Arita's expressed hope that there would occur "no change in the status quo in the Dutch East Indies," urged that Japan occupy the region in order to forestall an Anglo-American advance.

Only in late 1940, said the Police Bureau, did right-wing groups begin to express strong anti-American sentiments, in response to growing Anglo-American pressure on Japan after the conclusion of the Tripartite Pact. Increasingly, the report noted, "the nationalist camp seemed to be dominated by those demanding resolute action against the United States and the execution of a southern advance policy."[37] Even then, a number of right-wing groups continued to argue for an attack upon the Soviet Union, even at the cost of compromise with Britain and the United States. According to the Police Bureau, the most vocal proponents of a northern advance were the members of the *kokutai meichō* faction among the Nipponist groups, who were elated by the German attack upon the Soviet Union in June 1941, seeing it as Japan's "golden opportunity to chastise the old enemy." To the *zentaishugi* faction, however, this was rather the golden opportunity to launch the southern advance, to strengthen ties with the Axis, and finally to establish the Greater East Asia

Coprosperity Sphere.[38] Nevertheless, both sides were by this time in agreement that a decisive policy must be followed in the negotiations with the United States and, in fact, had come to advocate war against America. Thus, when war finally broke out in December, it was with the full endorsement of the entire right wing.

Throughout the 1931-41 period the goal of the right wing in Japan was to drive out of Asia Western capitalist imperialism and communist imperialism alike and to construct an Asia for Asians under the leadership of Japan. The establishment of Manchukuo, based on the myth of harmonious coexistence among the five races and rejection of zaibatsu capitalism, served to harmonize these incongruent aspirations, as did the belief that the China War was a crusade to destroy the "semi-feudalistic" warlords of China and promote a united East Asia. As the war progressed, ideas such as an "East Asia League" (Tōa Renmei) and an "East Asia Cooperative Community" (Tōa Kyōdōtai), which were among the slogans used in the anti-British movement, came to be accepted as official ideology. Yet, the right wing and its supporters could not hide the facts that the war in China was being waged against the Chinese people and that the Japanese-created puppet regimes in the occupied areas obviously promoted Japan's economic exploitation of the region. Declaration of war against the United States and Great Britain served in some measure to assuage any feelings of guilt members of the right wing may have felt. And once war had come, even those who had not previously advocated it became enthusiastic supporters of the cause.

U.S. PRESS COVERAGE OF JAPAN, 1931-1941

Ernest R. May

Public opinion is an aggregate of individual opinions, and individual opinions have many sources. Self-interest affects them. So do cultural norms and accepted myths. So do personality, temperament, life history, beliefs about what are right and proper opinions to be held by people of certain economic, educational, or social standing, and estimates of other people and the opinions they hold. These and other factors influence the ways in which individuals perceive and react to information about political events.[1] But the information itself also exerts an influence. Factual data received or not received can induce a verdict by jurymen, for example, almost regardless of the prejudices they bring into the box.

This paper concerns the factual data about Japan supplied to interested Americans in the decade 1931-1941. More specifically, it concerns reportage transmitted from Japan to American newspapers and periodicals. Focusing on three critical points—the months between the Mukden Incident of September 1931 and the Shanghai Incident of January 1932, the interval between the opening of the Sino-Japanese War and the conclusion of the *Panay* crisis, and the period in 1941 between the Japanese move into northern Indochina and the aborting of Prince Konoe Fumimaro's proposed conference with Roosevelt—the paper addresses itself to four questions. Who were the individuals who provided the American public with information about Japanese policy? How well-informed were they? How well did they perform for the public the function that diplomats and attachés performed for the Washington bureaucracy—that of making understandable actions which, without knowledge of the context, observers at home might misjudge, misinterpret, or see in the wrong light? Finally, to what extent did public commentary in the United States mirror the pictures and judgments communicated by reporters on the scene? The further question of whether these reporters communicated accurate pictures can be attacked only by someone with a better sense than mine of Japanese realities. Responses to the other questions posed should, however, make some contribution to closer comprehension of the tragic conflict in which the decade of the 1930s culminated.

I

As of 1931-32 relatively few reporters covered Japanese affairs for the American public. The principal American wire service, the Associated Press, maintained a small bureau in Tokyo. At the time, however, a network of alliances between the AP head office in New York and other press agencies limited the ability of the Japan bureau to act as an independent newsgatherer. A treaty dating back to 1893 linked the AP with Reuters Agency of Britain, France's Agence Havas, and lesser services. Though repeatedly modified over the years, this treaty still provided that the AP should have exclusive rights in the western hemisphere but that, in return, the other signatories should have jurisdiction elsewhere. And Japan belonged to Reuters.[2]

This arrangement had most effect on news provided to the Japanese press. The Reuters office in London culled reports from its own correspondents and from the AP, Havas, and other allies and cabled a budget of international news via Aden, Singapore, and Shanghai. This news went to the Japanese partner in the alliance, Shinbun Rengōsha (the Associated Press of Japan), a cooperative, nonprofit organization like the American AP, which in turn distributed the service to member papers, *Hōchi, Chūgai shōgyō, Tōkyō nichi nichi*, Tokyo and Osaka *Mainichi, Kokumin,* and *Asahi,* and others.[3]

In addition to paying Reuters a substantial annual fee, Shinbun Rengōsha reciprocated by providing both the Reuters and AP bureaus in Tokyo with news about Japan. Probably the political news thus supplied was slanted to reflect the Japanese government's wishes and attitudes, for Rengō's predecessor, the Kokusai Tsūshinsha, had received government subsidies; Rengō had taken over intact the Kokusai staff; and Rengō's general manager, Iwanaga Yūkichi, had formerly managed Kokusai and, prior to that, served the South Manchuria Railway and headed the Imperial Railway Secret Service.[4] Even if the government had no hand in Rengō releases, however, Iwanaga and the Rengō directors concerned themselves with Japan's image and admitted to "clarifying and filtering" information given Reuters and the AP.[5]

Some AP officers in the United States believed that these arrangements did not detract from the quality of AP coverage of Japanese affairs. Kent Cooper, the general manager of the AP, favored dissolving the treaty with Reuters, but largely so that the AP could provide direct service to Japanese newspapers. Addressing the AP directors in 1930, he declared that reportage in Japan from the AP's Tokyo bureau was superior to that of Reuters. "Its coverage of China and Japan," he said, "once sufficient for our purposes, in no way compares with the efficiency that we have through our own staff correspondents in the Western Pacific. We could without any embarrassment cease relying at all upon Reuters for any news of that part of the world."[6] Subsequently, when negotiating for freedom of action in East Asia, Cooper pointed out that Reuters frequently felt obliged to send "from New York to London a protective service on what the

Associated Press has obtained from its own correspondents in the Western Pacific, including Japan."[7]

Nevertheless, the impression prevailed in Tokyo that the AP was a subsidiary of Reuters. Rengō provided the AP with nothing that did not also go to the Reuters bureau, and government officials and others with news to release often supplied it to the Reuters agent, assuming that he would arrange for transmission to the United States. To an extent, therefore, the regular system of AP dispatches—the principal news about Japan received by most American newspapers—was "clarified and filtered" not only by Rengō or issuers of handouts but by a Reuters agent who had in mind primarily the interests of British, not American, readers. Not surprisingly, American editors found less of interest in AP traffic from Japan than their counterparts in the United Kingdom found in Reuters traffic. Prior to the Mukden Incident American papers exclusively dependent on the AP were publishing little or nothing about Japanese politics or foreign policy.

The second major American wire service, the United Press, had somewhat fewer customers. The AP was a cooperative, serving a thousand papers, mostly in the United States. The UP, a profit-making corporation, served twelve hundred subscribers, including a number of European, Latin American, and Asian dailies.[8]

From Japan these subscribers received news from sources not available to the Tokyo staff and not filtered through a Reuters agent. It obtained some information from the Nihon Denpō Tsūshinsha (Japan Telegraph News Agency), a profit-making newsgathering organization and Rengō's principal competitor in Japan. In addition, its correspondents, unlike those of the AP, received news directly from officials and others interested in reaching American audiences. Even the president of the AP conceded that AP representatives "repeatedly found themselves at a disadvantage in official and public favour, in status, and in the measure of help and opportunity afforded them, compared with the correspondents of the United Press. . . ."[9]

Heading the UP in Tokyo in 1931 was Miles Vaughn. A Kansan, he had joined the UP in 1916, shortly after graduating from the University of Kansas. After working in various UP bureaus in the midwest, he had been transferred to South America. Two years in Rio were followed by one in Buenos Aires, a year of service as head of the important New York bureau, and in 1925 appointment as manager of the newly-organized Far Eastern division.[10]

With headquarters in Tokyo, Vaughn had responsibility not only for the Tokyo bureau but also for bureaus in Peking, Shanghai, and Manila. For routine gathering of Japanese news he depended on Nihon Denpō and on Japanese staff housed in a large office in the Nihon Denpō building. But he made it a practice, he asserts in his memoirs, "to cover in person all news which had American or foreign angles."[11]

The one other major American wire service, William Randolph Hearst's International News Service, did not maintain a full-time correspondent in Japan. Special coverage of Japanese affairs was provided INS by James R. Young, who functioned also as advertising manager of the English-language Tokyo daily, the *Japan Advertiser*, as correspondent of the Sydney, Australia *Sun*, and as sales representative for the King Features syndicate. Twenty-eight years old in 1931,

Young had studied at the University of Illinois and Johns Hopkins, left school to become a police reporter for the *Baltimore Sun*, and spent a fabulous year sailing the Atlantic on a yacht with the tempestuous old publisher E. W. Scripps. Stranded after Scripps' sudden death, Young had come to New York and worked for the UP and the *New York World.* After a year there he had signed on as a seaman with the Hugo Stinnes line, crossed the Pacific in the *Emil Kirdorff*, and jumped ship in Yokohama after finding a job with the *Advertiser*. Ambitious and energetic, Young did his best to turn up stories worth cabling to INS at the going rate of fifty cents a word. As of 1931-32, however, he was spending most of his time selling space in the *Advertiser* and persuading Japanese editors to buy such King Features products as "Bringing Up Father," "Popeye," and Ripley's "Believe It or Not!"[12]

A few leading American dailies employed part-time correspondents much as INS employed Young.

The *New York Times* received special correspondence from Hugh Byas. A Scot with a pronounced burr, Byas had come to Japan before World War I. From 1914 to 1922, with one brief interruption, he edited the *Japan Advertiser*. For a time during the mid-1920s he returned to the U.K., serving there partly as an *Advertiser* correspondent. Back in Tokyo by 1926, he made arrangements to act as Tokyo correspondent for both the *New York Times* and the London *Times*.[13]

The *New York Herald Tribune* shared with the *Japan Advertiser* the services of Wilfrid Fleisher. The son of B. W. Fleisher, who owned the *Advertiser*, Fleisher had been educated in England, attended the Columbia School of Journalism, covered American intervention in Siberia for the *New York World*, and subsequently worked in the Paris bureau of the UP. In 1925, at the age of twenty-eight, he had joined his father's paper as business manager, working on the side for the *New York Times*. When Byas left the *Advertiser*, Fleisher took over as managing editor, relinquishing his *Times* connection to Byas but signing on soon afterward with the *Herald Tribune*.[14]

The principal dailies in America's second city, Chicago, used special correspondence from newspapermen who worked for the *Advertiser*. R. O. Matheson sent occasional dispatches to the *Chicago Tribune*, and James Butts to the *Chicago Daily News*.

During the 1920s the *New York World*, the *New York Evening Post-Philadelphia Public Ledger* syndicate, and the *St. Louis Globe-Democrat* employed "stringers," that is, newspapermen not on salaries but paid by the word for any copy filed and used. Given the Great Depression and the shaky financial condition of these once-great newspapers, the relationship between these stringers and their newspapers had become tenuous by 1931.[15]

Aside from the *New York Times*, the *New York Herald Tribune*, the *Chicago Tribune*, and the *Chicago Daily News*, the only American daily receiving much special correspondence from Japan in 1931 was the Boston-based *Christian Science Monitor*. It employed Frank H. Hedges, who had served as managing editor of the *Advertiser* during part of Byas' four years in London.[16] Emphasizing commentary more that spot news, the *Monitor* accepted stories sent by mail rather than cable and printed a good deal of what Hedges filed.

When the Mukden Incident erupted, the interested American public depended for the Japanese side of the story largely on Reuters-AP dispatches, supplemental bulletins sent in by Vaughn of the UP and Young of INS, stories cabled by Byas, Fleisher, Matheson, and a few other special correspondents, and more extensive "mailers" arriving three weeks after the event from these correspondents and from Hedges of the *Monitor*.

None of these reporters possessed real expertise. None had made any special study of Japanese history or culture. Few had even finished college. Though some had friends in the Japanese government—Vaughn for example, was on good terms with Shiratori Toshio of the Foreign Ministry Public Information Division[17]—none could even speak, let alone read, the Japanese language. They thus had access to oral information only if passed on by English-speaking Japanese, and they could extract from Japanese newspapers, periodicals, and other publications only what Rengō, Nihon Denpō, or their own Japanese employees elected to translate. Except for Byas and Hedges, none of these reporters had experience or knowledge of Japan that extended back to pre-Washington Conference events, such as the Japanese intervention in Siberia which, if remembered, supplied a clearer context for events of 1931-32. In consequence, reportage from Tokyo about the Mukden Incident and subsequent events had a superficial character.

The first news of the September incident from Tokyo took the form of an AP dispatch summarizing Army Ministry communiqués and Rengō bulletins from Manchuria. It indicated that "three or four companies" of Chinese troops had staged an attack against the South Manchuria Railway, that Japanese forces had taken defensive action, disarming Chinese police in Mukden, and that other Japanese units were adopting precautions "in event it was deemed necessary to protect Japanese subjects."[18]

The Foreign Ministry promptly convened a press conference. Ever since 1920 the ministry had included a Public Information Division (Jōhōbu) modeled after the Press Bureau of the German Foreign Ministry. In addition to collecting data about foreign countries and arranging lectures and exhibits in Japan, it provided information to foreign press representatives. Shiratori Toshio, a career diplomat with experience in China and the United States and an excellent command of English, served as its spokesman. He conducted not only the press conference called on September 19 but also those held almost daily thereafter.[19] On the basis of what Shiratori said at the first conference, Vaughn, Young, Byas, Fleisher, and others cabled to the United States interpretive dispatches.

Vaughn and Young called attention to recent incidents of friction in Manchuria, particularly those stemming from the killing by Chinese of Captain Nakamura Shintarō. Byas and Fleisher likewise commented on how strained had become the tempers of Japanese in Manchuria. Perceptively, however, both observed that the Japanese army might be overreacting and that, as Byas put it, "the actual question now is whether the Foreign Office or the army is in charge of Japan's policy."[20]

In subsequent weeks and months the correspondents in Tokyo remained largely dependent on Shiratori. Though the Army Ministry and Navy Ministry also held press conferences, their spokesmen confined themselves to describing operational details. On questions of policy they referred correspondents to the Foreign Ministry. And Shiratori, despite a deserved reputation for blunt candor, would only say over and over that Foreign Minister Shidehara Kijūrō and the cabinet were doing their utmost to reestablish peace.

In general, the American correspondents in Tokyo sympathized at least with the civilians in the Japanese government. "Most foreigners in the Orient who were at all familiar with the Manchurian problem had a great deal of sympathy for Japan," comments Vaughn. Byas had reported to the *New York Times* shortly before the Mukden Incident a "widespread . . . feeling that China's policy deliberately aims at squeezing Japan out of Manchuria and must be checked." Though his subsequent dispatches implied criticism of the army for not obeying the central government, he took occasion to question whether Manchuria could properly be considered Chinese territory. Matheson of the *Chicago Tribune*, who had earlier spoken to friends of the inevitability of Japanese expansion into Manchuria, included similar remarks in his dispatches.[21]

The correspondents in Tokyo, however, found themselves at a double disadvantage. In the first place, their sources provided them with somewhat distorted information. Not only Shiratori but also officials of Rengō and Nihon Denpō supplied principally facts and commentary designed to make it appear that civilian authorities and the army were acting in harmony and were taking only such measures as conditions in Manchuria made necessary. In the second place, foreign correspondents in Tokyo were denied the kind of information that would have allowed them to claim front page space at home. Since the Army and Navy ministries censored all communications coming to Japan from battlefronts, reporters in Tokyo could send home only bland, laconic, and somewhat out-of-date news about the war.

As a result, Tokyo dispatches to U.S. newspapers resembled Japanese government press releases. AP wires, for example, repeatedly affirmed that Japanese troops were withdrawing to the railway lines. In December and early January they described the march on Chinchow as necessitated by the activity of Chinese bandits. When U.S. Secretary of State Stimson filed a protest note embodying the "Stimson Doctrine"—nonrecognition of political or territorial changes effected by force—AP dispatches reported Japanese officials as concerned primarily lest it prevent the Chinese from following up their "serious overtures" for a negotiated settlement. Before and during the bloody Japanese punitive expedition against Shanghai in January-February 1932, AP cables from Tokyo told merely of the provocations that Japanese had encountered and of official assurances that the Japanese government meant neither to annex Manchuria nor to remain at Shanghai.[22]

Communications from Vaughn, Byas, Fleisher, Matheson, and Hedges stated more clearly that the army command in Manchuria did not necessarily act according to dictates from Tokyo. Nevertheless, they copied Shiratori in attempting to explain and justify faits accomplis. After the Wakatsuki cabinet resigned because of its inability to restrain the army, Vaughn's dispatches represented the new prime minister, Inukai Tsuyoshi, as a strong man on whose discretion and judgment the Western powers should rely. Byas cabled the *New*

York Times following the Japanese march on Chinchow, "Japan's main objective is to have Manchuria under a non-militarist Chinese government which can maintain order and will not obstruct Japanese economic enterprises."[23]

It is not clear to what extent news dispatches from Japan reflected the actual opinions of American correspondents. Drawing on a diary that he kept at the time, Vaughn comments in his autobiography, "The daily press conference at the Foreign Office was little better than a joke, for the 'Gaimusho' ... had far less information than did the correspondents."[24] He and other reporters may have echoed Shiratori primarily because of recognition that, if they failed to do so, they might be cut off from the only sources of information accessible to them. Hedges had told Harry Emerson Wildes some years earlier that he felt compelled to cooperate with the Jōhōbu because, without the ability to read or speak Japanese, he depended so heavily on official handouts. And though outgoing reports were not censored, they were read, with Japanese officers of the International Press Association reserving the right to take accreditation away "from unscrupulous newspapermen who misrepresent Japan."[25] Correspondents in Tokyo may have been protecting their livelihood rather than reporting the news as they saw it. In any event, reports from American newspapermen in Tokyo resembled Japanese official propaganda.

Meanwhile, correspondents elsewhere in Asia sent to the United States dispatches which not only contradicted those coming from Tokyo but which contained the kind of hard eyewitness news that editors inevitably preferred to feature. Thus, when Vaughn was filing cables describing Inukai as resolutely opposed to annexation of any territory, U.S. papers served by the UP were running ahead of his reports dispatches from Frederick Kuh in Mukden, labeled as "uncensored," declaring that Japanese authorities had systematically seized control of all political, financial, and business organizations in Manchuria. Hearst's newspapers headlined Edward Hunter's reports from Manchuria instead of Young's from Tokyo and, as the *Literary Digest* observed, Hunter's cables reflected "ill-concealed resentment and indignation against Nipponese arrogance."[26] From September 1931 through January 1932 the *New York Times* usually placed in parallel columns Tokyo cables from Byas and Nanking or Shanghai cables from Hallett Abend, the latter attributing aggressive and imperialistic aims to the Japanese.

After Japanese forces landed at Shanghai in January 1932, American correspondents in the Japanese capital became even less able to claim attention at home. Their cables repeated monotonously reassurances from official spokesmen that Japan had no annexationist designs. Reporters on the scene meanwhile sent back cables describing in detail what seemed to them a ruthless and determined Japanese effort to conquer the city. The *New York Herald Tribune*, which had until then featured Fleisher's reports from Tokyo, gave front page columns to Shanghai dispatches from Victor Keen, picturing Japanese troops as deliberately shooting and bayoneting Chinese women. Papers served by the AP and by INS featured similar stories from special correspondents Christine Diemer and Karl von Wiegand.[27] Reporters based in Tokyo did not serve up information or interpretive commentary that could claim comparable attention or space.

II

By 1937 the American press corps in Japan had grown in numbers. The successful detachment of Manchuria from China, Japan's withdrawal from the League of Nations, recurring border incidents involving Japanese, Chinese, and Soviet troops, the wave of assassinations in Tokyo in 1936, the seeming turn of Japan toward totalitarianism, and the Anti-Comintern Pact of 1936 linking Japan with Nazi Germany—all these events made Japan more interesting to American newsmen. Meanwhile, the economic depression in the United States left a number of college-educated Americans footloose, and some gambled savings on steerage tickets or worked their way to the Orient, hoping to eke out livings as journalists and enjoy some adventure in the process. One, Howard Norton, wrote:

> I was only 22 years old when I went to Japan. I was broke and had borrowed money to get over there, and spent my first two years paying off that debt and my college debts. The majority of the American correspondents in Japan at that time were in somewhat the same situation. We were all young adventurers. We were in Japan mainly because it was impossible to get a meaningful job in the United States. Our main purpose was to pile up experience that we could "sell" later in life. Most of us were the rawest of beginners.[28]

As Norton also comments, most American correspondents in Japan served a number of newspapers:

> At one time I held down *SIX jobs* all at once; I was part-time (string) correspondent for the Philadelphia Inquirer, the Kansas City Star, Los Angeles Times, San Francisco Chronicle and Portland Oregonian; also I was on a part-time retainer for the Whaley-Eaton Service of Washington, D.C., writing their Far Eastern letter every other week, and I worked several hours a day on the copy desk of various Japanese (English language) newspapers.[29]

Such conditions were not peculiar to American newsmen. Richard Sorge—later exposed as head of a Soviet spy ring—acted as Tokyo correspondent for the *Frankfurter Zeitung*, the *Berliner Tägliche Rundschau*, the *Berliner Börsen Zeitung*, and the *Amsterdam Handelsblad*.[30]

As in 1931-32, only the major wire services retained full-time reporters. And by 1937 the AP had preempted a position not only as agent for the majority of American dailies but as the principal gatherer of Japanese news. Kent Cooper of the AP and Iwanaga Yūkichi of Rengō had compacted as early as 1930 to seize the earliest opportunity to revise their separate understandings with Reuters and establish instead a bilateral relationship. At the end of that year Cooper notified Sir Roderick Jones of Reuters that the AP-Reuters treaty would have to be revised. In 1932 Iwanaga served notice that Rengō would not renew the contract making Reuters its exclusive source for foreign news. Either in pique or as a result of overestimating his leverage, Jones reacted by denouncing the entire AP-Reuters treaty and threatening to offer an agreement instead to the UP. Convinced that the AP would profit from being able to compete freely with Reuters not only in Asia but also in Europe, Cooper and the AP directors agreed readily to dissolution of the Reuters tie. The UP did not take up Jones' offer. Instead the UP and AP signed a pact providing that neither would enter into any agreement with a European news agency "for availability of such European agency's news to the exclusion of availability to the same extent to the other party and upon the same terms."[31] The AP's longstanding treaty with Reuters terminated on February 12, 1934.

Since the AP-UP pact did not immediately extend to Japan, the AP took over from Reuters exclusive rights to Rengō news. The UP continued to have similar rights to news originating with Nihon Denpō Tsūshinsha. In 1936 the two Japanese organizations merged as the Dōmei Tsūshinsha. With a substantial annual subsidy from the government and subject to some degree of government supervision, Dōmei monopolized the distribution of Japanese news, and the AP and UP both received its service.

Since the AP had many more subscribers at home and since the UP no longer had a unique source of Japanese news, the AP became the principal vehicle for transmitting to the United States reportage on Japan.

Heading the AP Tokyo staff in 1937 was Relman ("Pat") Morin. A graduate of Pomona College in California, Morin had worked for the *Los Angeles Times* while an undergraduate. In 1930 he went to China. Studying briefly at Lingnan University in Canton, Shanghai College, and Yenching University in Peking and working on the *Shanghai Evening Post*, he acquired a smattering of Chinese. After less than two years he returned to Los Angeles. Then in 1934, at the age of twenty-seven, he went back to the Orient for the AP and by 1937 had his base in Tokyo. He added to his knowledge of Chinese some ability to speak and understand conversational Japanese. (Later, Morin scored a scoop by overhearing, through paper-thin partitions in a Javanese restaurant, some unguarded conversation among Japanese diplomats charged with demanding trade concessions from the government of the Netherlands East Indies.)[32]

The UP's Tokyo bureau, now less busy than in 1931-32, no longer served as headquarters for UP newsgathering in East Asia. Vaughn's successor, Ray Marshall, presided over all UP Pacific services from a base in San Francisco.[33]

James R. Young continued to represent Hearst's INS in Tokyo. Hugh Byas and Wilfrid Fleisher remained the chief correspondents for the *New York Times* and *New York Herald Tribune*. Byas by now had a full-time Japanese assistant but still represented both the *New York Times* and the London *Times*.[34]. Fleisher continued to spend most of his days as managing editor of the *Japan Advertiser*.

Though Frank Hedges remained in Tokyo, he no longer served the *Christian Science Monitor*. Perhaps irregularities in his life had led to his being dropped by the *Monitor*, for an entry in Ambassador Joseph C. Grew's diary suggests that Hedges was a toper. "When sober," wrote Grew of Hedges, "he is an excellent analyst of Japanese affairs."[35] Perhaps, on the other hand, the *Monitor* dispensed with Hedges because of pro-Japanese leanings, which the editor of the *Monitor* did not share.[36] In any event, Hedges now filed occasional dispatches and "mailers" with the North American Newspaper Alliance.

Chief correspondent for the *Monitor* in 1937 was William Henry Chamberlin. A Haverford graduate and one-time Philadelphia newspaperman, Chamberlin had covered the Soviet Union for the *Monitor* from 1922 to 1934. During these years he published three books, each betraying diminishing enthusiasm for the Soviet economic system. Meanwhile, he worked on a detached history of the Russian revolution. It was to appear in 1935, and he judged it prudent to be in another country when it came out. Also, as he says in his autobiography, he wanted "to write an uninhibited book about contemporary Russia" (*Collectivism—A False Utopia*, it emerged in 1937). Hence his move to Japan.[37]

An occasional contributor to the *Monitor* was Gunther Stein. Formerly a reporter for the *Berliner Tageblatt*, Stein had fled Nazi Germany. In Tokyo he served not only the *Monitor* but also the *London Financial News*, the *London News Chronicle*, and the *London Daily Telegraph*. In addition, he worked with Sorge's spy ring.[38]

Some correspondents had, of course, left Tokyo. Vaughn had returned to the New York office of the UP in 1933. Matheson no longer represented the *Chicago Tribune*. Nor did John Powell, who had moved to Shanghai. Instead the *Tribune* relied on Shiba Kinpei and other Japanese nationals. Nevertheless, with Byas, Fleisher, and Hedges remaining and Morin, Chamberlin, and Stein having arrived, the quality of the American press corps in Tokyo stood at a somewhat higher level than in 1931-32. And there were able and enterprising reporters among the young adventurers washed in by the depression: Norton, who would later win a Pulitzer Prize while on the *Baltimore Sun* and become an associate editor of *U.S. News and World Report*; Reginald Sweetland of the *Chicago Daily News*, who evaded police barriers to report first-hand on a famine in northern Hokkaido; and Percy Noel of the *Philadelphia Public Ledger* and the *Paris Intransigeant*, who in his spare time composed an opera about the love life of Townsend Harris, the first American consul in Japan and a figure with whom many American newsmen, similarly isolated in an alien culture, tended to identify.[39]

Intelligent and energetic though these reporters may have been, however, they still lacked adequate resources for deciphering Japanese politics. Chamberlin comments, "I never met a correspondent of a well known foreign newspaper or news agency who could casually pick up and read a Japanese newspaper, magazine, or book."[40] It was rare for any to be able to converse even haltingly in the Japanese language. Morin and Stein were exceptions.

American correspondents remained dependent therefore on official handouts, on translations supplied by Dōmei or English-language Japanese newspapers or, as in Byas' case, Japanese assistants, and on conversation with English-speaking Japanese or figures from the foreign diplomatic or business community. And all such sources had become more restricted by 1937 than in 1932.

Infrequent press conferences held by the Army and Navy ministries yielded very little news. To learn the government's position, correspondents were more dependent than ever on the now thrice-weekly conferences with the Foreign Ministry spokesman. And Kawai Tatsuo, who succeeded to this post in the summer of 1937, provided much less information than had his predecessors, Shiratori and Amō Eiji. Fleisher recalls:

Kawai spoke poor English and was extremely slow in speech and manner. Often when a foreign correspondent would question him, he would sit motionless for several minutes, pondering his reply, while the inquirer wondered whether his question had been heard. The answer would then come slowly word by word with an evident effort, and the labored construction of his phrases often led to misunderstandings.[41]

Kawai compensated to some extent by enlarging his staff and making its members readily available to answer questions from foreign correspondents.[42] By and large, however, neither he nor his aides supplied much in the way of hard news.

Likewise, the Dōmei agency provided foreigners with less information than Rengō and Nihon Denpō had supplied earlier. Dōmei releases to Japanese newspapers as well as to foreign correspondents received careful censorship. Much news about events in China and developments in Japanese policy was withheld by Dōmei, and all dailies, including those in the English language, received frequent directives from the Home Ministry, the Metropolitan Police Board, and procurators of district courts forbidding stories on certain subjects. Fleisher cites one such directive received during the abortive military uprising of February 1936. It ran, "You are hereby advised not to print any news pertaining to a rumor in circulation that Army men in Kagoshima prefecture 'did something.' "[43] At the very outset of the "China Incident" all newspapers received a comprehensive order prohibiting publication of:

a) All items calculated to oppose war or abuse the Army or bring about alienation of the people from the Army.

b) Any item liable to give the impression that the Japanese are a bellicose people or that Japanese foreign policy is aggressive.

c) In reproducing articles from foreign newspapers, especially editorials appearing in Chinese newspapers, any item abusive to Japan or contrary to Japanese interests, or likely to cause the people in general to exercise mistaken judgment of the incident.

d) Besides the foregoing, any item liable to stir the public mind and to disturb peace and good order.[44]

With such a regulation in effect, foreign correspondents could not hope to learn much from the press about Japanese foreign policy.

Correspondents also experienced some restrictions in obtaining information through conversation. Both the Kenpei (the military police) and the Tokkō (the special higher police or "thought police") had intensified and extended their activities during the mid-thirties. Members of the Kenpei displayed special suspiciousness of foreign correspondents, finding little to distinguish newsgathering from intelligence collection. During the disturbances of 1936 Tokkō officers gave some foreigners—Young of INS, for example—friendly warnings to hide from the Kenpei.[45] The Tokkō, however, had a special department for keeping watch on foreign nationals, and few newspapermen failed to find some evidence that their belongings or files had been searched or that their movements were spied upon. And Japanese, aware that Kenpei or Tokkō agents might be near, sometimes showed hesitancy about conversing with correspondents.[46]

American or other diplomats sometimes shared information with American newsmen. Grew or his deputy, Eugene Dooman, or Cabot Coville, the counselor of the embassy, would discuss current issues with them. Grew and Coville both attempted to speak frankly to those whose discretion they trusted.[47] None of the correspondents felt, however, that he gained much from these conversations, and several resented what they interpreted as efforts by Dooman to encourage slanting of their reportage. Morin and Chamberlin testify that they obtained better information from British or European diplomats, particularly the great Japanologist, Sir George Sansom, the commercial counselor of the British embassy.[48]

At best, American newspapermen in Tokyo received slim fare. They had to patch together bland statements from Kawai and other official spokesmen, censored Dōmei releases, such stories as official directives permitted Japanese newspapers to publish, testimony from relatively brave or relatively foolish Japanese friends, and information supplied by other resident foreigners.

Not surprisingly, the summer and autumn of 1937 saw a repetition of the pattern of 1931-32. At the outset of the "China Incident" dispatches from Tokyo could command lead space at home. The Japanese government was the principal source concerning the clash at the Marco Polo Bridge and its possible consequences. No wire service or newspaper appeared to have a regular correspondent in the Peking area, where the clash occurred. At any rate, no cables with Peking datelines appeared in U.S. dailies until more than a week later.

As cables from Tokyo developed the story, moreover, the issues seemed to be two. Would local Chinese authorities in Peking agree to Japanese terms? Would the Chinese Nationalist government based in Nanking send troops northward to engage the Japanese? To the first question no one in China seemed able to supply an answer, for no American reporter won access to Sung Che-yuan, the Chinese general with whom the Japanese appeared to be negotiating. Moreover, no one on the scene knew what demands the Japanese had made.

In regard to the second question, reporters in Tokyo and in Shanghai united in stating that Chiang Kai-shek had dispatched thirty to fifty thousand men to the Peking area. The former took their information from the Japanese Army Ministry. The AP correspondent in Nanking, on the other hand, denied that Nationalist troops were moving.[49]

Tokyo dispatches had the flavor of Japanese government communiqués. Thus, for example, an AP cable of July 14 described Japanese officials in China as "making strenuous efforts to solve the Sino-Japanese crisis amicably"; and cables of July 16 and 18 portrayed the Japanese government as holding that the situation in China "does not permit further procrastination" and described it as Japan's view that Chinese troop movements constituted "a direct act of aggression against Japan."[50]

After July 27, when Japanese-Chinese negotiations reached an impasse and Japanese forces opened coordinated ground, artillery, and air attacks on Chinese positions, Tokyo reports lost their prime news value. The dispatches that claimed feature space in American newspapers came instead from Peking, Tientsin, Shanghai, or Nanking. Even reports on Japanese operations bore such datelines, for Japanese field commands answered questions much more freely than did ministries or spokesmen in Tokyo.[51]

The principal American reporters working in China sympathized with the Chinese. This was true of Haldore Hansen, Yates McDaniel, and James Mills of the AP; E. R. Ekins, Weldon James, and John Morris of the UP; M. C. ("Hank") Ford and John Goette of INS; Hallett Abend, Tillman Durdin, Douglas Robertson, and Norman Soong of the *New York Times*; Victor Keen of the *New York Herald Tribune*; John Powell of the *Chicago Tribune*; A. T. Steele of the *Chicago Daily News*; and Randall Gould of the *Christian Science Monitor*.

Since the majority of dispatches with news value came from these reporters, it was inevitable that coverage of the war by American newspapers should have some pro-Chinese slant. The *Chicago Tribune* provides an example. During the last week in September, when the Japanese command yielded to proponents of strategic bombing and authorized air raids on Chinese cities, almost all reportage in the *Tribune* came out of China. On September 20 page one included a Shanghai dispatch saying that Japanese spokesmen described raids on Nanking as hugely successful but that "trustworthy foreign observers" denied this claim. On September 21 and 22 the front page carried AP reports from Nanking on the bombing. That printed on September 22 opened: "Japan ignored an American and British protest against the threatened devastation of the Chinese capital today and bombed the teeming city from the air for an hour and a half. The lives of twenty American refugees—including seven women—... were endangered by the bombardment." Sharing first page space was a story from a *Tribune* stringer in Hong Kong dealing with a Japanese air attack on Canton. "Daring Chinese aviators drove off two fleets of Japanese bombing planes," it declared. On September 24 the *Tribune* ran headlines summarizing AP dispatches from Tientsin, Shanghai, and Peking: "20 CITIES HIT BY JAP AIR RAIDS/2,000 CIVILIANS STRUCK DOWN IN CANTON ATTACK/CHILDREN HUNT KIN IN CHINESE RUINS." During this period only three useable reports were received from Tokyo by the *Tribune*. Two were AP stories saying that Emperor Hirohito was celebrating the festival of the autumnal equinox and that the *Tōkyō nichi nichi* had printed an editorial criticizing the U.S. government for recommending that Japan not bomb Chinese cities. The third was a report from the *Tribune's* Tokyo correspondent, Shiba Kinpei, saying simply that Japan would promise every effort to avoid injury to foreign noncombatants.[52]

In December 1937 newspapermen in Tokyo gained an opportunity once again to seize leading space in American papers. On December 8 Japanese troops entered Nanking. On December 12 Japanese aircraft and naval units on the Yangtze bombed, machine-gunned, and sank the U.S. gunboat *Panay*. Both occurrences brought reportage from China to feature places on American front pages. Reporters such as Mills of the AP, Goette of INS, and Durdin of the *New York Times* began cabling eyewitness accounts of indiscriminate killing, burning, and looting by Japanese soldiers in Nanking. Their accounts were to make "the rape of Nanking" a household phrase. Firsthand stories of the *Panay* sinking, including those of the AP's Weldon James, who had been aboard the boat, told in detail of how deliberate and systematic had been the attack on a vessel whose markings as a U.S. naval craft were unmistakable.[53]

But if the colorful news necessarily came from Nanking and Shanghai, the major questions raised by these episodes were ones that could only be answered from Tokyo. What did the Japanese government plan after the capture of Nanking? And, more important for American editors and newspaper readers, what position would Japan adopt with regard to the *Panay*? Would it strike an attitude which would or could spell war with the United States?

Owing to their own limitations, the strict censorship that Japanese authorities had instituted, and the suspiciousness with which Japanese officials treated all newsmen, American reporters in Tokyo proved able to make little use of their opportunity. They could not obtain much information about Japanese intentions in China. They could transmit even less. An AP dispatch quoted Kawai's statement that "all Japan desired was China's abandonment of anti-Japanism." A UP cable predicted on the basis of other comments by Kawai that a Chinese government "friendly to Japan" would soon be established. The *Chicago Tribune's* Shiba Kinpei forecast that Prime Minister Konoe would announce "that Japan had come into the position of shouldering responsibility for . . . the welfare and happiness of the Chinese masses not only in north China but in virtually all China."[54]

Only the *New York Times'* Hugh Byas and the *Herald Tribune's* Wilfrid Fleisher detected and reported division and confusion within the Japanese government over whether to seek some negotiated settlement or to proceed with an all-out campaign for conquest of the mainland. For the most part news suggesting either the possibility of negotiations or the outlines of new Japanese campaigns in China came from reporters picking up gossip in Shanghai, and they took it as a foregone conclusion that, as one AP cable put it, "Japan's army would push on into the heart of beleaguered China."[55]

In regard to the *Panay* case reporters in Tokyo were able to send back somewhat more news. Morin of the AP described officials in the Navy Ministry as upset and dejected, implying thus that they probably had not ordered or even had advance knowledge of the attack. Marshall of the UP added to his report of the Japanese note of apology the interpretive comment that such an apology for misconduct by Japanese military personnel was "unparalleled in history." He cabled subsequently that Emperor Hirohito had taken personal control of the *Panay* investigation and was "determined to make full amends no matter how humiliating they may be to the nation's armed forces."[56] Though ascribing to the emperor more initiative than he actually exercised, this report, like Morin's, conveyed an accurate impression of the Japanese government's mood. These AP and UP cables helped to answer for American editors and readers the question of whether war was likely or not, and together with dispatches from Young, Byas, Fleisher, Chamberlin, and others, they became lead stories in U.S. dailies.

Even so, some significant news relevant to the Japanese position on the *Panay* case had to be taken by American editors from reporters outside of Japan. Thus, for example, the important information that Colonel Hashimoto Kingorō had been relieved at Shanghai and that Japanese commanders in China had received strict orders to prevent future incidents involving U.S. vessels or citizens reached the United States via UP wires from China.[57]

During two periods in 1937—the first few weeks of the "China Incident" and the weeks surrounding the capture of Nanking and the *Panay* sinking—

American newsmen in Japan commanded front page space at home. In neither period, however, were they able to supply much intelligence enabling American readers to understand the checkerwork of perspectives, attitudes, ambitions, and motives that underlay the actions of Japanese officials and Japanese agents in China.

III

By the summer of 1941 the American press corps in Tokyo consisted mostly of new faces.[58] In December 1940 Morin had sailed for Southeast Asia, assuming that the major stories of the near future would break in Indochina, the Netherlands East Indies, and adjoining areas. He left in charge of the AP bureau in Tokyo Max Hill and Joseph Dynan. With Ray Marshall working primarily in San Francisco, the UP bureau fell under Robert Bellaire. James Young had returned to the United States. Al Downs and Percy Whiteing covered Japan for INS. Hugh Byas departed early in 1941 after Otto Tolischus came to take his place as correspondent for both the *New York Times* and the London *Times*. Wilfrid Fleisher had joined the *Herald Tribune* staff in New York. Joseph Newman succeeded him in Tokyo. Both William Henry Chamberlin and Gunther Stein had left Japan, the former going to the United States and the latter to China. Frank Hedges had died in 1940.

The new group was larger than that of 1937 or 1931-32. It included Raymond Cromley, representing the *Wall Street Journal*, and correspondents for the major American radio networks—Richard Tennelly of the National Broadcasting Company and W. R. Wills of the Columbia Broadcasting System. Not all were newcomers. Downs, Newman, Cromley, and Tennelly had each worked for a year or more on the *Advertiser*. Only Whiteing of INS, with thirty years of experience as Japan correspondent for Canadian and Australian newspapers, rated as an "old Japan hand."[59] Some were experienced senior reporters. Tolischus had had a key assignment as a *New York Times* correspondent in Nazi Germany. Nevertheless, they were mostly men with little background on Japan or Japanese politics and with few special contacts in Tokyo.

These correspondents worked, moreover, under even more severe handicaps than those experienced by reporters in 1937. Not only the Army and Navy ministries but the Foreign Ministry as well had ceased to hold press conferences for foreign correspondents. All releases now came from a Cabinet Information Bureau modeled on Joseph Goebbel's Propaganda Ministry in Berlin.[60]

To a much greater extent than in 1937 Dōmei releases consisted of official propaganda. The Japanese press was more tightly controlled. The independent English-language press had disappeared. Pressure of various kinds had compelled the Fleisher family to sell the *Japan Advertiser*. It was taken over by and merged with the *Japan Times*, published with government subsidies and under government control.[61] Foreign correspondents thus received no printed material in English other than emissions from the government. Those, like Tolischus, who employed Japanese nationals to make translations from the Japanese press, obtained little besides a sense of varying editorial expressions, for the news columns of Japanese papers likewise contained primarily information given out by the government.

American correspondents of 1941 also encountered more difficulty than their predecessors in sending news out of Japan. Although Japanese authorities denied censoring outgoing cables, reporters had the experience in 1937 of discovering that whole sections of their dispatches would sometimes not be transmitted. With Wilfrid Fleisher taking the lead, some began using the telephone to relay important stories. After 1938, however, telephone communications came under overt censorship. Correspondents had to disclose in advance the messages they intended to relay; they would speak only the approved lines; if they departed from these lines, the circuit would be closed. Often correspondents experienced long delays in getting cables out or in obtaining a telephone connection with the United States, Manila, or Shanghai.[62]

Police surveillance of foreign correspondents had tightened. In the thirties it had seemed a joking matter. Everyone had his anecdote concerning thefts of cryptic documents or photographs that the Japanese police would discover, after much labor, to be bridge scores or stock market quotations or bone X-rays. By 1941 attitudes had changed. In the previous year James Young of INS had been jailed for sixty-one days, subjected to third-degree questioning, and prosecuted in secret on trumped-up charges of espionage. Joseph Dynan of the AP had also experienced jailing. Worst of all, Reuters correspondent Melville James Cox, a veteran of the Japanese scene, had been arrested and, while in police hands, had fallen to his death from a fifth floor window in the Tokyo military prison. The police alleged suicide and produced in support a note written by Cox. Most foreigners doubted the official story, regarding the note as a fake, and they received independent testimony that Cox's arms and legs had shown many hypodermic perforations. Cox's fate had influenced the decisions by Morin and Byas to quit Japan. The new men were all familiar with the Cox case. They feared for their own lives.[63]

Thus few American reporters in Tokyo in 1941 had any background for interpreting Japanese affairs. The sources of information open to them were minimal. The Japanese government discouraged them, to say the least, from making efforts to obtain and relay any news other than that which officials handed out. At the same time, however, editors at home had a greater demand for reportage on Japan than at any time in the past. The war in China had lost most of its news value. By 1941 American papers seldom printed dispatches relating to it. On the other hand, the Tripartite Pact of 1940, the movement of Japanese forces into Indochina, pressure by Tokyo on Bangkok and on the government of the Netherlands East Indies, the possibility after June 22, 1941 that Japan would join Germany in attacking the USSR, and the further possibility that if the United States entered the European war, Japan would come to the aid of its Axis allies provoked interest in Japanese politics and policy. Editors in the United States were prepared therefore to give front page or near front page space to any interesting and relevant dispatches.

Reporters in Tokyo responded by sending whatever news they could glean. It is not unfair to observe, however, that their communications contributed relatively little to the understanding of American readers.

During August, September, and early October 1941, for example, Prime Minister Konoe was engaged in a desperate effort to arrange a summit conference with President Roosevelt. Konoe, other civilians in the government and the bureaucracy, and certain senior officers in the Japanese navy regarded such a conference, and some resultant exchange of concessions, as the only possible means of preventing the army leadership, together with hotheads in the navy, from forcing war.

American reporters picked up and relayed to the United States some of the signals that Konoe and his collaborators urgently wanted to send. The AP bureau in Tokyo reported on August 26 a statement by Ishii Kō, the spokesman for the Cabinet Information Bureau, that Japan would welcome negotiations with the United States to ease tension in the Pacific. After Wilfrid Fleisher, now in Washington for the *Herald Tribune,* broke the story that Konoe had proposed a mid-Pacific meeting with Roosevelt, the UP bureau in Tokyo noted that *Japan News-Week*, an organ reflecting Foreign Ministry opinion, had questioned editorially whether German success in the war was as certain as had previously been assumed. Both AP and UP dispatches commented on lessening criticism of the United States in the government-controlled press.[64]

On September 15 Joseph Newman of the *Herald Tribune* reported that a number of Japanese officials serving in China had returned to Tokyo for a conference. Without citing a source, he observed that this conference could be interpreted as a sign that Japan might consider some accommodation with the United States concerning China. On September 21 Tolischus cabled the *New York Times* that the *Japan Times-Advertiser,* "the organ of the Foreign Office," had characterized Japan as too preoccupied with China to consider war on another front. Subsequently, Tolischus reported statements commemorating the anniversary of the Tripartite Pact by Itō Nobufumi, the head of the Cabinet Information Bureau, and Foreign Minister Toyoda Teijirō. He noted that both described the pact as designed primarily to preserve peace and thus by implication minimized the likelihood of Japan's joining Germany and Italy in war. On October 12 Newman cabled the *Tribune* that unidentified Japanese had taken occasion to speak to him of Japan's strong desire for resumption of trade with both the United States and Britain.[65]

Indications of Japanese interest in a détente with the United States were more than offset, however, by reports suggesting that most Japanese were intransigent, unrealistic, and determined to pursue aggressive courses of action.

Correspondents in Tokyo distrusted Information Bureau spokesmen. Newman had the impression that these spokesmen "were kept almost as much in the dark about the intentions of the Japanese leaders as were representatives of the press."[66] Nor did correspondents trust Japanese who approached them. Assuming that these Japanese expected to be observed by the police, reporters suspected—usually rightly, of course—attempts to "plant" a story. In reaction, correspondents paid more attention to information they obtained on their own, and, in the circumstances, such information came largely from the Japanese press.

On August 16, when cabling about a conciliatory statement by Ishii Kō, Tolischus emphasized that Dōmei releases and Japanese editorials had an entirely different tone. Two days later he quoted Captain Hiraide Hideo, whom he characterized as "the Navy spokesman," as saying that the United States and Britain sought to encircle Japan and declaring, "One step farther and Japan will be driven to make a decision involving life or death." AP dispatches pictured the

Japanese press in late August as expressing determination that Japan should accomplish its destiny not only in China but also in Southeast Asia. A UP cable quoted a fiery editorial appearing in the consistently militant *Yomiuri*.[67]

In September and October Tolischus devoted most of his dispatches to warlike utterances by military figures or journals associated with them. He reported Colonel Mabuchi Itsuo as having broadcast that American-British-Chinese-Dutch "encirclement . . . is strangling Japan economically and therefore Japan must break it without delay" and as accusing the United States and Britain of "unpardonable crimes." Tolischus reproduced from *Kokumin* a statement by Major Nakajima Shōzō to the effect that the United States and Britain should be driven out of Asia. He reported equally bellicose declarations by Nakano Seigō, head of the extreme nationalist Tōhōkai (Eastern Society).[68]

Joseph Newman sent similar dispatches to the *New York Herald Tribune*, including a report on September 20 of an uncompromising speech by Army Minister Tōjō. And on the eve of Konoe's fall from power Bellaire of the UP quoted a further statement by Captain Hiraide. "Despite our government's most strenuous efforts," the captain said, "the situation now seems to have reached a final parting of the ways. The fate of our empire depends upon how we act at this moment. It certainly is at such a moment as this that our navy should set about its primary mission." As Bellaire commented, the navy's "primary mission" was to engage the battle fleets of Britain and the United States. He added that Hiraide further described the Japanese navy as "itching for action."[69]

Rarely did dispatches from Tokyo suggest that a fateful contest, of uncertain outcome, might be in progress in Tokyo. One INS cable, dated September 12, commented on the emperor's assumption of personal control over the armed services and Konoe's substitution of Gotō Fumio for Admiral Suetsugu Nobumasa as chief of the Imperial Rule Assistance Association, Japan's copy of a political party for a one-party state. Together these two moves could be interpreted, said the INS correspondent, "as a drastic step to keep the empire out of a new war—especially war with the United States." An earlier report from the AP's Max Hill (noted as "delayed" and probably therefore smuggled out of Japan) described Konoe, Toyoda, Minister of State Hiranuma Kiichirō, and Finance Minister Ogura Masatsune as leaders of a group profoundly concerned about Japan's economic situation and eager, above all, for arrangements regaining for Japan petroleum imports. If Konoe could not soon achieve such arrangements, said Hill, his cabinet would resign. Hill implied that its successor would be one determined to solve the problem by military means.[70]

For practical purposes, the INS cable and Hill's dispatch were the only reports sent to the United States that dealt explicitly with the factional line-up inside the Japanese government and the stakes for which these factions were playing. All other incoming news cables concerning Japanese internal politics emanated from Shanghai or Southeast Asia.

Sensitive and deeply informed editors and columnists in the United States might, of course, have pieced together a more-or-less accurate picture. To do so, however, required bringing to the fragmentary news dispatches much understanding of Japanese politics and much ability to read between lines, calibrating the relative knowledgeability and reliability of various U.S. correspondents and inferring a great deal of news not reported.

Only one man regularly writing commentary for U.S. newspapers possessed these attributes—Wilfrid Fleisher of the *Herald Tribune*. From July onward he published columns pointing out the terrible dilemma faced by the Japanese government. The imposition of economic sanctions by the American government meant, said Fleisher, that "Japan must move quickly to consummate her conquests in Asia or face economic ruin and defeat."[71] He warned repeatedly that if the United States could find no means of helping the Konoe cabinet discover some escape, Japan would inevitably choose a violent solution.

Other commentators with experience in East Asia lacked Fleisher's comprehension of the Japanese scene. Miles Vaughn occasionally distributed columns to UP subscribers, but his knowledge of Japan was seven years out of date. He assured his readers that "most observers believe that Japan under no condition will declare war on either Britain or the United States."[72] Glenn Babb, an AP staff writer who had served in Tokyo, suggested that Konoe's various moves could be seen either as preparation for a reorientation of Japanese policy or as a means of buying delay so that Japan could avoid acting against the USSR until it was more sure of German prospects for victory.[73] Other alleged experts, such as free-lance columnist Mark Gayn, George Sokolsky of the Hearst syndicate, and radio commentator Upton Close (Josef Washington Hall), were old China hands, little acquainted with Japan.

Columnists without special knowledge of Asia had little or no means of judging Japan other than through dispatches from the correspondents in Tokyo. And what they thought they saw was a government blustering through mouthpieces such as Colonel Mabuchi, Captain Hiraide, and General Tōjō but actually seeking to weasel out of a potentially dangerous situation. "The one certainty," observed Ernest K. Lindley of *Newsweek*, "is that Japan's bargaining position is weakening." Barnet Nover of the *Washington Post* predicted that Japan would have no choice but to repudiate the Tripartite Pact. Kenneth G. Crawford wrote of Japan in the left-wing *PM*, "For a time it may bluster. . . , but in the end it can only whimper and capitulate."[74] The sage Walter Lippmann declared in a syndicated column of August 28:

> Whereas a year ago we felt constrained to buy time by a policy of concessions and retreats, we are now in a position to insure our security in the Pacific by positive and, if need be, by decisive action.
>
> We are able now to talk with Tokyo on the basis of a new situation. . . . It is so much better that the opportunity now exists to make sure that Japan will not, because she cannot, stab us in the back. . . .
>
> Our conversations with Japan will, let us hope, continue. But if they do continue, it will be because we are now able to speak the language which the Japanese militarists understand. They will understand us in China, that we intend not only to continue supporting free China but that our military mission will determine how airplanes and other weapons can most effectively be made available and then used. . . .

> The Japanese diplomats and militarists will understand also
> that two can play at the game they have been playing this last year,
> and that now our turn has come . . .—it is our turn to say that Japan
> shall advance no further and that this constant menace must be
> reduced.[75]

On the basis of such commentary, one is entitled to conclude that American
reporters and American "experts" on Japan conveyed to the public a profound
misunderstanding of the genuineness of Japanese appeals for negotiation and the
genuineness of the warnings which Japanese military figures were uttering.

IV

To assert that American reportage on Japan was superficial, fragmentary,
insensitive, and, in the end, misleading is not to argue that reportage of a
different character would have checked the post-1931 deterioration in American-Japanese relations or prevented war. It is not even to argue necessarily that
better reportage would have modified significantly the opinions ultimately held
by commentators such as Lindley and Lippmann. Through Grew and attachés of
the U.S. embassy in Tokyo, American officials received not only a great deal of
additional information but also much thoughtful analysis of the Japanese
political scene. By 1941 the president and his inner circle of advisers possessed,
in addition, decipherments of the most important Japanese diplomatic cables.
Yet their estimates of the Japanese situation, their appraisals of decisions that
the Japanese government would probably reach, and their judgments as to how
the United States might influence those decisions were not markedly more
subtle than those of the major newspaper columnists.[76] As was remarked
earlier, the opinions of individuals are not necessarily direct functions of the
information they receive.

Yet one cannot discard altogether the hypothesis that better reportage on
Japan might have altered the course of events. If interested Americans had had a
clearer understanding in 1932 or in 1937 of the actual dynamics of Japanese
policy, public opinion might have exerted a somewhat different influence on
U.S. policy. If writers for and readers of American newspapers had perceived
more accurately the ordeal of Japanese statesmen in 1941, they might not so
zestfully have urged on the administration an uncompromising attitude toward
Konoe. Probably, of course, history would have run in the same track. Probably
war would have come when and as it did. But one cannot be absolutely sure. For
that reason the mind looks back with regret at American reportage on Japan and
speculates on what mistakes were made, whose they were, and how, in other
times and places, their repetition might be avoided.

Clearly some of the fault lay with the reporters themselves. They went to
Japan ignorant of the country's history, culture, and language. For the most part
they remained ignorant. Relman Morin and Gunther Stein stood out as
exceptions because they learned to speak some Japanese. Frank Hedges was
another exception in that he religiously devoted time to reading in Western
languages about Japan.[77] Most reporters spent short tours in Japan. Most,
during those tours, made little effort to expand their acquaintance beyond the

circle of journalists, students, businessmen, and diplomats who frequented the Silver Bell bar, the Tokyo Club, and embassy parties.

Of course, the wire service managers and the publishers and editors of U.S. newspapers were as much at fault as their employees. They paid depression wages. They made do in their Tokyo bureaus with young reporters whom they should have recognized as ill-equipped. And they provided their agents with little direction or guidance. Howard Norton observes that he "never received any comment or suggestion" from most of the numerous editors for whom he filed stories.[78] The Far Eastern desks of the wire services and the city desks of major dailies were no better equipped than the bureaus in Tokyo to decide what questions really needed investigation and how they might be explored.

Even with relatively uneducated reporters serving parsimonious and comparatively ignorant employers, Japanese affairs might still have been more accurately and sensitively reported to the American public had Japanese officials not systematically created difficulties for foreign newsmen. In explaining defects in American press coverage of Japan, one cannot avoid placing the heaviest blame on Japanese politicians and bureaucrats.

By channeling news through agency spokesmen, censoring releases to the Japanese press, imposing ever tighter controls on what journalists could investigate or publish, and eventually terrorizing the foreign press corps, Japanese officials attempted to conceal all information except that which they chose to reveal. The impulse to do this is shared by all bureaucrats. In the Japanese case it had special strength, for Japanese officials feared embarrassment and loss of face if foreigners, or Japanese themselves, should discover how divided were the emperor's ministers or how difficult they found it to impose decisions on their presumed agents in the field.

It is not clear in retrospect, however, that censorship, concealment, and obfuscation served Japan's national interests—no matter whether those interests were as perceived by a left-wing moderate or by a right-wing militarist. It was—and is—an illusion common to men in public life that evidence of governmental disunity weakens the nation in its relations with other nations. Frequently the reverse can be the case. The Wakatsuki cabinet enjoyed some freedom from foreign pressure in the immediate aftermath of the Mukden Incident because statesmen and interested citizens in the United States and elsewhere recognized that Shidehara was struggling to master dissident groups at home and in Manchuria. The Inukai cabinet, on the other hand, witnessed immediate and adverse foreign reaction to the landings at Shanghai in part because it had created a false impression of purposeful unity. In 1941 the Americans most disposed toward conciliatory policies were those, like Grew and Dooman and the well-connected private negotiator Father James M. Drought, who understood how variously and deeply divided was the Konoe regime.[79] At all points in the decade 1931-41 more knowledge abroad about internal crosscurrents would probably have produced for Japanese governments greater sympathy, or at least tolerance. Almost all Japanese should have seen such a result as advantageous.

A price would, of course, have been paid. Inukai in 1932, Konoe in 1937, or Konoe in 1941 could reasonably fear losing support domestically by allowing news to leak out of divisions or controversy within the government. Rivals of these prime ministers might have wanted foreign powers to refrain from protesting or otherwise reproaching the government. On the other hand, they could reasonably fear that the prime ministers would be strengthened if they seemed to win concessions abroad. Both holders of power and aspirants for power probably judged rightly in calculating that, however Japan's interests might be served, their own individual interests would not necessarily prosper as a result of allowing political news to be more freely gathered by foreign correspondents.

Though one could argue from the example of American reportage on Japan that government officials should not conceal information about governmental divisions, it would be frivolous to end with such a moral. Nowhere are ministers and major bureaucrats likely to put it into practice. The example should, however, encourage those with no personal stakes in play—or those, such as scholars, publishers, and legislators, who have something to gain—to be more skeptical about decrees, rules, and practices that restrict access to information. American-Japanese relations could conceivably have followed a different pattern had there been more such skepticism in Japan after 1931. There could be fewer tragic episodes for historians of the future to analyze if such skepticism were stronger today among elite groups in all major nations.

THE PRESS AND PUBLIC OPINION IN JAPAN, 1931-1941

Kakegawa Tomiko

Translated by Shumpei Okamoto

I

This paper will discuss the changing views and images of the United States during the period 1931-1941 as expressed in the Japanese press. As a background to this discussion it is essential to review briefly the reaction of the Japanese press to one of the most serious issues in Japanese-American relations during the 1920s, the so-called "Japanese Exclusion Act" of 1924. This issue was of crucial importance in the prewar relations of the two countries, and American attitudes on Japanese immigration were regarded by the Japanese public as a measure of the degree of cordiality between the two nations.

The news that the Japanese Exclusion Act had been passed on April 15, 1924 by an overwhelming majority of the U.S. Senate shocked the Japanese people. Five days earlier Ambassador Hanihara Masanao had sent a note to Secretary of State Hughes, stressing that the Japanese government had faithfully carried out the 1907 Gentleman's Agreement and requesting that the proposed immigration bill be reconsidered. Secretary Hughes had concurred with the ambassador's argument and forwarded the note to the Senate Committee on Immigration, where debate on the bill was in progress, in hopes that it might convince the committee to block passage of the legislation. But Hughes was to be sadly disappointed. In the final paragraph of his note Hanihara had warned that passage of the bill would have "grave consequences" for Japanese-American relations, a phrase certain senators chose to interpret as a "veiled threat" to the United States.[1] Their interpretation led to the passage of the bill by a large majority who believed that "no foreign nation has the right to influence the legislative action of the United States by a veiled threat."[2]

The passage of the Japanese Exclusion Act received sensational headlines in the Japanese press. The liberal Tokyo *Asahi*,[3] for example, proclaimed: "SENATE PASSES JAPANESE EXCLUSION ACT. PRESIDENT'S APPROVAL LIKELY. SURGING ANTI-JAPANESE SENTIMENT MAKES REPUDIATION OF ACT HOPELESS." Its lead article traced the development of the Japanese immigration issue from the San Francisco school board incident of 1906 to the events of 1924 and closed with strong criticism of the U.S. Senate for having purposefully misinterpreted the Hanihara note.

On April 21 fifteen Tokyo newspapers, including the *Asahi* and the *Mainichi*, sponsored a joint declaration against the Japanese Exclusion Act. Should the bill become law, it warned, it would "not only have an adverse effect on the long-standing friendship between Japan and the United States but seriously impede potential cooperation between the two countries that might be highly beneficial to both sides." It is noteworthy that the declaration placed great faith in the possibility that a movement against the immigration bill would arise among responsible Americans and urged the Japanese public to "watch closely the results that the fighting American people will achieve!"

In the days following passage of the bill many public protest meetings were held in Japan. The political parties as well as many other groups—the Federation of Japanese Chambers of Commerce, Tokyo Chamber of Commerce, America-Japan Society, Japanese Immigrants Association, Japan Christian League, Japanese Bar Association, and a number of women's organizations—declared their opposition to the bill. Many of these groups even sent protest telegrams to the American Congress. But on May 16 the Japanese public was informed that the president of the United States had signed the bill.

On June 8 angry Tokyo movie theatre owners resolved to suspend the showing of American movies as of July 1, the date on which the Exclusion Act was to take effect.[4] While protests of this type were partly due to the press campaign, they reflected the genuine sentiments of many Japanese.

The July 1 issue of the Tokyo *Asahi* was filled with articles relating to the bill. There was a report that a resolution against the act would be presented to both houses of the Diet. Another item listed the schedule of anti-American demonstrations sponsored by major civic organizations. Several cartoons dealing with the immigration issue also appeared, among them an anti-Japanese cartoon that had originally been published in a number of papers on the American west coast. Another cartoon displayed a soiled American flag and a defaced Statue of Liberty with the caption, "Insult to Japan. Insult to America." In addition, the paper carried a picture of a huge billboard in a large California town advocating Japanese exclusion. An editorial "On Enforcement of the Japanese Exclusion Act" labeled the event a "tragic incident in Japanese history" and an "infamous turning point in international relations" and lamented the fact that the burden would be borne by the next generation. Declaring July 1 a "Day of National Humiliation," it went on, was merely superficial anti-Americanism, for "the concern of the Japanese people over the immigration issue is so deeply rooted that it cannot be erased by mere demonstrations." From this humiliating experience the Japanese should learn that in the world of "realpolitik" national boundaries were more important than humanitarian idealism, that friendship between civilized nations was subject to the whims of willful politicians, and that international cooperation among members of the laboring class was an ideal impossible of achievement. Therefore, the editorial concluded, the Japanese people could achieve happiness in this world only "by the promotion of mutual aid and relief activities among their fellow countrymen in a patriotic spirit" and "by adopting a spirit of tolerance toward the peoples of neighboring countries."[5]

The following day the Tokyo *Asahi* reported an anti-American demonstration at a large temple in Tokyo with the headline: "CRIES OF INDIGNATION. UNFORGETTABLE DAY OF HUMILIATION INFLICTED ON US BY THE UNITED STATES. 10,000 ANGRY PEOPLE ATTEND RALLY." The paper reported that similar meetings had been held at Shinto shrines throughout Japan. Tōyama Mitsuru, a leader of the right wing, quickly took the initiative in the national protest movement, seeing in it a golden opportunity for political agitation. Truly the *Asahi* had analyzed the situation accurately when it had editorially condemned emotional anti-Americanism, fearing that right-wing activists would turn public animosity toward the Exclusion Act into fanatic anti-Americanism.[6]

Realization that Americans feared Japanese immigration as a "Yellow Peril"[7] came as a traumatic shock to many Japanese, and their reaction was expressed in a number of war scare books published in the years that followed: nonfiction works such as "The Inevitability of a Japanese-American War and Our Nation's Resolve" and "Japan in Crisis: America Is the Cause of Japan's Trouble"; fiction works such as "The Coming War with America"; and numerous magazine articles on the possibility of war with the United States.

During the 1931-41 period the emotional attitude of the public, which began as a direct response to personal experience and gradually developed into a frenzied nationalism, significantly affected Japanese foreign policy. In particular, the sense of shame and humiliation created by the passage of the Exclusion Act promoted the formation of a negative image of the United States that had fatal consequences for Japanese-American relations in the 1930s.

II

Newspaper publishing began in Japan in 1862. Serving largely as political forums, newspapers at first had limited circulation and did not become successful commercial enterprises until the turn of the century, when they began to place increasing emphasis on news reporting. By the time of the Manchurian Incident newspapers had become highly commercialized, competitive undertakings that stressed speed over accuracy of reporting. Despite, or perhaps because of, the general deterioration in quality that resulted, newspapers in Japan prospered. The Manchurian Incident produced a boom in the newspaper business as the public avidly followed the fighting in Manchuria. As speed and scope of coverage became more and more important, large newspapers with nationwide and international newsgathering networks came to dominate the field, pushing aside the minor, local papers. In this way the *Asahi*, the *Mainichi*, and the sensational *Yomiuri* became the giants of the industry. In January 1932 the Osaka *Mainichi* boasted a circulation of two million.

As the press of Japan grew increasingly commercialized, certain tendencies became apparent. To expand their circulation, newspapers blatantly appealed to popular desires and emotions and, as a result, the press came to be characterized by a high degree of uniformity. Secondly, they began to cultivate an emotional style of writing that catered to public sentiments. Circulation increased rapidly, reaching ten million in 1934. By 1931, the beginning of our period, Japan had developed a "mass" press.

Radio broadcasting began in 1925. Controlled at first by private corporations under the supervision of the Ministry of Communications, the industry was taken over in 1926 by the Japan Broadcasting Association (Nihon Hōsōkyōkai or NHK), a semi-government monopoly. Because of its swift and direct impact, radio broadcasting was placed under particularly rigid censorship. Whereas newspaper and magazine articles were inspected after publication, radio programs and scripts had to be submitted for official approval prior to broadcasting.[8]

By late 1931 over one million radio sets kept the Japanese people entertained. In the early days of broadcasting the government had kept politics off the air by prohibiting or discouraging broadcasts of Diet sessions or speeches by cabinet ministers. With the Manchurian Incident, as we shall observe, this situation changed and radio broadcasts rapidly became the official source of information for the Japanese people through such devices as special newscasts, broadcasts of important speeches, and patriotic programs.

Before trying to determine the attitude of the mass media toward Japan itself, the United States, and the international scene, it is necessary first to define the particular circumstances in which the media functioned. The salient trend in Japanese society during the decade of the 1930s was the development, and ultimate attainment, of a fascist state. Beginning in the wake of the Manchurian Incident, the tendency was given new impetus by the outbreak of the Sino-Japanese War in 1937. During these years the nation marched inevitably toward the establishment of a "government by conformity" under an "emperor-system fascism" that was intensified by the Pacific War and finally led the nation to defeat and destruction.

From the beginning the mass media of Japan were subject to powerful state control.[9] Even so, the system of government surveillance imposed upon the mass media between 1931 and 1941 was extraordinarily rigid and far-reaching. During the initial stage of "fascization" the mass media criticized while at the same time they conformed to government policies. As national and international tensions mounted, however, their criticisms were silenced, and in the end they became merely tools to propagate, both consciously and unconsciously, the ideology of "emperor-system fascism."

The evolution of state control of the mass media was parallelled by the enhanced status of the agencies of control. The Cabinet Information Committee, formed in July 1936, became the Cabinet Information Division in September 1937 and finally, in December 1940, the Cabinet Information Bureau, which assumed the function of controlling and manipulating the mass media for official propaganda purposes. In this process of increasing state control two developments are particularly significant: first, the mass media were gradually institutionalized to fulfill the propaganda needs of the state; and secondly, control of the mass media fell increasingly into the hands of the military. In addition, government intervention induced the news agencies to accept the role of censors of the news they reported, until in June 1936 the Dōmei Tsūshinsha (Dōmei News Agency) was established as a "national policy company" under the jurisdiction of the Cabinet Information Committee.

Control of the mass media meant indoctrination of the Japanese public in the official ideology of the state—in a belief in the unique national polity of Japan (*kokutai*) and its governance under the direct rule of the emperor.[10] Ever since the Meiji Restoration the leaders of Japan had expounded this idea of *kokutai*, and in periods of national crisis it had served to heal deep internal splits. The ideology was codified in 1925 in the Peace Preservation Law, which effectively curtailed freedom of thought and speech. As revised in 1928 by an emergency imperial ordinance, Article 1 of the law decreed, "Anyone who initiates or occupies the position of executive member or leader of an organization whose aim is to change the *kokutai* shall be sentenced to not less than five years imprisonment, life imprisonment, or death."

In 1936, under the Law for Protection against and Surveillance of the Holders of Dangerous Thoughts, the secret police were empowered to interfere freely in the realm of individual conscience and to prosecute "dangerous thoughts" as well as actions contrary to the *kokutai*. Thereafter, also under the guise of "peace preservation" and in the belief that "liberalism is the seedbed of communism," the state began to place heavy restrictions on liberal scholars and thinkers.

III

When the Mukden Incident occurred in September 1931, the Japanese press could not have known it was to be the beginning of an ever-expanding war, and only after fifteen bitter years of fighting did the Japanese people learn that the incident had been provoked by the Kwantung Army. Although the press and radio paid close attention to developments at the battle front, the origins of the incident were never discussed. The pattern of reporting is illustrated by the September 20 issue of the Tokyo *Asahi*,[11] whose editorial, entitled "Strict Defense of Our Rights and Interests," simply accepted the government's explanation of the clash at Mukden as a "response to the blasting of the South Manchuria Railway by Chinese troops." The cause of the trouble is "as clear as fire," the editorial judged, and China "must bear the entire responsibility for the incident. . . . In the face of this clear violation of our vital rights and interests in Manchuria and Mongolia, the 'stern reality' is that Japan must defend its rights even at great sacrifice." The editorial expressed the hope that the incident would be regarded as a "local issue" and settled through diplomatic negotiations before the situation deteriorated further. Neither then nor in the days that followed did the *Asahi* question the official account or attempt to conduct an independent investigation.

Following the government's proclamation of a policy of nonescalation, the *Asahi* of September 25 carried the headline: "OUR IMPERIAL NATION'S PROCLAMATION TO THE WORLD. DEFENSE OF OUR RIGHTS IS GOVERNMENT'S RESPONSIBILITY. JAPAN HAS NO TERRITORIAL AM-

BITIONS IN MANCHURIA." The editorial page supported the policy and again defended the action of the Kwantung Army as having been "totally and exclusively for the defense of one million Japanese residents and for the protection of an investment in that region of 2 billion yen." Its only criticism was directed against the "government's delay in issuing the proclamation," which had allowed the foreign press to indulge in insulting speculations.

The next day, in an editorial entitled "Anglo-American Press Views of Incident," the *Asahi* reproached the League of Nations and the U.S. State Department for having called for the immediate withdrawal of Japanese troops. The editorial stated:

> These recommendations are erroneous and unjust, for they attempt to apply abstract concepts of war and peace to a concrete, current crisis. Further, the background of this affair can be understood only in the light of a thorough knowledge of the extremely complex relations between China and Japan in this region of the world.
> Japan's national survival is dependent on the defense of our rights and interests in Manchuria. . . . Our military action was a legitimate action guaranteed by various treaties concluded since the Russo-Japanese War in which two hundred thousand lives were sacrificed and the fate of the entire nation was at stake.

The London *Sunday Times* and the *New York World Telegram*, it charged, had reported "as if Japan were the aggressor, without knowledge of Japan's historical rights in the area." To illustrate this kind of reporting the *Asahi* reprinted an editorial from the *World Telegram* that called "if necessary" for economic sanctions, and a statement by California Senator Hiram Johnson which it branded as "the wild remarks of a demagogic politician."[12] In contrast, the *Asahi* praised as an example of positive reporting a September 23 editorial in the *New York Herald Tribune*, which had "accurately grasped the total reality of the Manchurian question." The *Tribune* editorial had condemned China for having "completely disregarded justice" in encouraging the growth of a strong anti-Japanese movement and for having "openly approved of the murders of Japanese soldiers." In view of the "irresponsible action of the Chinese nation," the editorial went on, it would be "unjust" to Japan, "a powerful and responsible nation" that had been forced to protect its interests, to respond to China's "cries for assistance from the League of Nations" by invoking the Nine Power Treaty or the Kellogg Pact. The *Asahi* concurred fully, its headline declaring, "INTERVENTION OF LEAGUE, OR MAJOR POWERS NOT NECESSARY!"

A few Japanese writers did charge that Japan's action had been a blatant violation of international law. One of these was Yokota Kisaburō, professor of international law at Tokyo Imperial University, who pointed out that in response to the blowing up of "a few meters of railway track," Japanese troops had "immediately occupied every key area in south Manchuria" and "in their great haste," had "crossed the Korean border without waiting for imperial sanction." Was the action taken by the League really beyond its power, he asked, and did it constitute unjustified intervention? This was a question, he admonished, to be examined "not from the narrow viewpoint of selfish national interest but rather in the broad terms of objective scholarship." Yokota judged that the League's recommendation had been "entirely legitimate." Had Chinese soldiers indeed blown up the railway track, counteraction was justified. "But the Japanese troops occupied K'uan-ch'eng-tzu (400 kilometers north of Mukden) and Ying-k'ou (200 kilometers south of Mukden) a mere six hours after the initial clash occurred. In occupying these areas, the Japanese met no Chinese resistance. Can this also be justified?" In conclusion he declared: "Both theoretical and practical considerations lead me to believe that the League's recommendation constitutes no improper intervention. Japan must therefore carry out the recommendation quickly and faithfully."[13]

Yokota's views, however, were published only in the *Tokyo Imperial University News*, whose distribution was limited largely to faculty and students of the university, and thus his criticisms failed to reach the general public in Japan.[14]

In its response to the government's recognition of the puppet regime of Manchukuo, which preceded publication of the Lytton Commission's report, the Japanese press continued its pattern of uncritically accepting the situation as a fait accompli. The activities of the commission were followed closely by the Japanese press, which early predicted a report unfavorable to Japan. On August 19, 1932 the Tokyo *Asahi* reported, "Government Contemplates Counter-measures in Anticipation of Adverse Report." Given the fact that the League's attitude toward Japan was not likely to soften, the paper recommended that Japan "take a resolute stand concerning Manchukuo without waiting for the League's report."

On August 25 Japan's readiness to recognize Manchukuo was announced and Foreign Minister Uchida Yasuya declared that the government would make no concession on recognition even if Japan should as a result become "a scorched earth." The Tokyo *Asahi* praised Uchida for having "frankly and succinctly expressed Japan's determination to recognize Manchukuo" and applauded him "for having discarded traditional diplomatic talk in making our nation's intentions known to the world." The *Asahi* generally subscribed to the view that Japanese recognition of Manchukuo, in that it would lead to the constructive development of Manchuria, was a necessary first step toward guaranteeing peace in East Asia. Once again its editorial expressed acceptance of the new situation brought about by the Manchurian Incident and the creation of Manchukuo. Under other circumstances, it acknowledged, there might have been a different solution, but given the "facts" of the situation, the Lytton report, whatever its conclusions, could have "no power to alter the reality of the situation."

This naive acceptance of "reality," without taking into account the possibility that "facts" might be created,[15] characterized the Japanese mass media right up until the end of the Pacific War. What such a view failed to perceive was that "reality" is never of a piece but is rather a complex set of diverse elements that allow for various options and interpretations. Furthermore, the media tended to look to the ruling authorities as the sole source of "political reality" and to dismiss conflicting information as untrue. As "reality" changed and developed, moreover, the mass media found it necessary to revise their judgments in order to achieve "harmony" with the new "reality." Thus, rather than attempting to influence the actions of the government, the Japanese mass media merely rationalized each change in the political situation as it occurred.

One practice common in the Japanese press, however, was to quote views critical of Japan's foreign policy from the foreign press. American press opinions in particular received close attention. On August 28, for example, under the headline *"TIMES* CHARGES UCHIDA SPEECH DIRECT CHALLENGE TO LEAGUE,"* the *Asahi* reported that a *New York Times* editorial had rejected Japan's self-defense justification and strongly criticized Uchida's "scorched earth" speech as "a direct challenge to the authority of the League of Nations." There is good evidence that this practice of quoting foreign views, most of which were from the American press, was a deliberate attempt on the part of the Japanese press to avoid direct association with anti-government statements.

When the government extended formal recognition to the new state of Manchukuo in September 1932, Japanese newspapers attempted to reassure the public as to the reaction of the United States. On September 9 the *Asahi* reported that Ambassador Debuchi Katsuji, who had just returned from the United States, considered any positive action by the United States unlikely and "very unwise." The evening edition of September 16 was filled with news of the recognition of Manchukuo, including photographs of the signing ceremony in Manchuria, the celebration of Tokyo citizens at the palace plaza, a lantern march in front of the Yasukuni Shrine, and numerous parades. Its editorial predicted that the "prejudiced international powers who have tried to solve the Manchurian question on unreasonable and unrealistic grounds will eventually recognize Manchukuo when they observe its steady progress under the new regime." An editorial of September 22 on Japanese-American relations asserted that American opposition to the recognition of Manchukuo was "simply the arbitrary action of Secretary Stimson" and did not represent the "true feelings" of the American public. In any case, it added, "the opposition of the United States will not affect Japan's determination." Moreover, it was "ironic" that America should criticize the way in which Manchukuo had been established, given the fact that it had "set the precedent by its actions in Cuba and Panama." In the view of the *Asahi*, "Manchukuo's qualifications for statehood are not to be determined by the process used to establish the new regime. An ethical or moral standard is not required for the establishment of a state." The Japanese people, it concluded, were overly sensitive about the attitude of other powers, particularly the United States, a sensitivity that it blamed upon the ignorant reactions of the United States and the League of Nations.

It was to be expected that the press would wax indignant against the Lytton report when it was published on October 3, 1932. "COMMISSION FORGETS ORIGINAL MISSION. REPORT SHOULD BE THOROUGHLY REPUDIATED," the *Asahi* contended in an article that quoted Shiratori Toshio, chief of the Foreign Ministry's Public Information Division, who had charged that the report was "completely biased" and pointed to Chapter 6 as "a fine example of distortion of the facts. The basic rule followed in the report is that every statement from Japan or Manchukuo is unreliable, while all statements against the new regime must be accepted verbatim." The commission had spent only two weeks in Manchuria, Shiratori stressed, and would certainly retract its "erroneous conclusions" once Japan had brought about the development of Manchukuo.

The *Asahi's* summary of the Lytton report bore the headline, "FULL OF STATEMENTS TOTALLY UNACCEPTABLE TO JAPAN. COMPLETELY REJECTS OUR MANCHURIAN POLICY." An article on the "unrealistic, distorted, ignorant commission report" charged that the League's idea of unconditional troop withdrawal had dominated the commission's thinking from the start and had led it to "completely disregard the reality of the situation. For the sake of world peace we hope the League will not repeat the commission's mistake."

On October 4 the *Asahi* editorially attacked the commission once again, claiming that its proposals were "no longer applicable" since Japan's recognition of Manchukuo was "now a fact." The report only proved that the commission had "learned nothing" from its investigations.

A foreign report favorable to the commission was occasionally printed. On October 4, for example, the *Asahi* quoted the *New York Herald Tribune* of the previous day, which had called the report "fair, objective, and highly knowledgeable" and "inclined to be more sympathetic toward Japan than China." A similar opinion from the *New York Times* was also quoted. In general, however, such comments from the foreign press were carried primarily as "fillers."

Given the strong criticism of the Lytton report, it is not surprising that the Japanese mass media supported the government's decision to withdraw from the League of Nations. On March 28, 1933, the day after the imperial edict was issued, the *Asahi* praised Japan's earnest attempts to cooperate with the League, whose "obstinate attitude" and "complete ignorance of the Far East" had led it to contend that Japan's actions had exceeded the limits of self-defense, thereby forcing Japan's final decision. Pointedly offering no explanation for Japan's use of brute force, diametrically opposed to the basic spirit of the League covenant, the *Asahi* expressed the hope that "Japan's decisive action will stimulate the League to reflect and repent and learn an important lesson."

The press further proclaimed Matsuoka Yōsuke, Japan's plenipotentiary to the League of Nations, a national hero. Huge cheering crowds, including grade school children waving Japanese flags, sent him off to the fateful League session of February 21 and greeted him enthusiastically at Tokyo station upon his return.[16] Matsuoka later said that only a handful of the tens of thousands of letters he received prior to his departure had urged him to avoid a rupture with the League.[17] Few influential Japanese—Yokota and the well-known international relations expert Kiyosawa Kiyoshi were notable exceptions—publicly opposed Japan's withdrawal from the League,[18] and their numbers were far too small to have had much influence on public opinion in Japan. According to Kiyosawa, "The overwhelming majority of the Japanese people were genuinely relieved when the government decided to cast off the restrictions of the League covenant and other international treaties."[19]

The Manchurian Incident had a significant impact on radio broadcasting in Japan. Nakayama Ryūji, who played an important role in its development, later recalled:

When the Manchurian Incident occurred, the general public in Japan, unable to understand the nature of the incident, failed to take a common stand toward it. ... Even the press and others who were ordinarily better informed failed to grasp the truth about the incident and held divergent opinions. Worse yet, many were so confused as actually to believe that Japan had initiated an attack against China.[20]

His concern led Nakayama to approach Hatakeyama Toshiyuki, chief of the Telegraph and Telephone Bureau of the Communications Ministry, Lieutenant General Hata Hikosaburō, chief of the Army Ministry's Research Office, and Shiratori Toshio, chief of the Foreign Ministry's Public Information Bureau. The result was a decision to alter the traditional approach to radio broadcasting and to embark on a program of "political broadcasting," employing soldiers in active service whenever necessary.

Since November 1, 1930 nationwide NHK networks had carried regular news broadcasts. On the morning of September 19, 1931 NHK inaugurated the practice of "special bulletins" with news of the incident at Mukden. During the remainder of the month news concerning the incident was broadcast on seventeen occasions, totaling an hour and five minutes. The public was greatly impressed by the radio's capacity for instant reporting. Radio bulletins even began to replace "extra" newspaper issues, to the point where several representatives of Tokyo newspapers are said to have requested that the bulletins be suspended. Newspapers vied with radio for speed of reporting. The Tokyo and Osaka *Asahi*, for example, in the period between the outbreak of the Manchurian Incident and the establishment of Manchukuo the following February, jointly flew the airplane "Asahi" to Manchuria as many as 295 times—a total of 826 flying hours over a distance of 142,000 kilometers.

During the Manchurian campaign the radio contributed to the mounting bellicosity of the Japanese public through its broadcasting of special bulletins and of speeches made by ministers of state (more than thirty times in 1931 alone). "Prayer meetings for greater national glory" held at the Yasukuni Shrine were relayed to the battlefront, an hour-long evening program was begun "to encourage and console the soldiers in Manchuria and Mongolia," and stories told by soldiers in Manchuria were broadcast to the public on the home front.

Movies were also an important factor in creating public support for the war, and the outbreak of the Manchurian Incident, it is said, ushered in an "era of war movies."[21] Thus the press, radio, and motion pictures all worked to create a fervent war spirit in Japan. During the period of the Manchurian crisis government information controls, aimed at regulating the content of news available to the people, resulted in an abundance of slanted information that was directly, if not totally, responsible for the rise of fanaticism among the Japanese public.

IV

With the beginning of the Sino-Japanese War in July 1937 the fascist tendency in Japanese politics became more pronounced, and controls over speech and writing were tightened further. The incident of February 26, 1936 proved to be a watershed in this process, for as political leadership in Japan fell into the hands of the military, all aspects of life became subject to regulation by the government. In addition, the raid on the offices of the Tokyo *Asahi* by a group of the rebels opposed to its "liberal" tendencies marked the first occasion on which the military employed tactics of violence against the mass media. Although little damage was done, the raid apparently served its purpose, for the *Asahi* thereafter retreated from its traditional liberal line.[22] At the time of the May 15, 1932 Incident, the *Asahi* had strongly criticized the rebels who assassinated Prime Minister Inukai Tsuyoshi, refusing to "condone actions that destroy the foundations of constitutional government"–a position that was echoed by newspapers throughout the country. In contrast, the *Asahi*'s editorial of February 29, 1936 merely addressed itself to "The Duty of His Majesty's 100 Million Subjects," namely to dedicate themselves to the "firmer establishment of our national polity and the renovation of politics."

Clearly recognizing the role of the mass media, the military determined to tighten its controls through the establishment of a state information agency. On June 19, 1936 the cabinet declared:

> . . . both domestic and international reporting have entered a new era. Domestically the radio transmits news directly to the nation; internationally cables spread news of one country throughout the world. Today we can no longer be satisfied with passive measures to maintain public security by means of the supervisory powers of the ministries of Home Affairs and Communications. To serve the interests of the state we must take positive action and provide state control and scrutiny over the dissemination of news.

On July 1 the Cabinet Information Committee was organized. Its function was to coordinate the dissemination of information essential to the execution of national policy, domestic and international news, and educational and propaganda activities.

Even earlier, in October 1934, a pamphlet published by the Army Ministry's Press Office entitled "The Essense of National Defense and Proposals to Strengthen It" (Kokubō no hongi to sono kyōka no teishō) had argued the importance of manipulating public opinion at home and abroad through active use of the instruments of mass communication. "War is the father of creation and the mother of culture," the pamphlet began, and communication, information, and propaganda "the components of national power." In order to strengthen national defense and to meet the needs of ideological warfare, it urged that some government agency, such as a ministry of propaganda or an information bureau, be established. With the inauguration of the Cabinet Information Committee, the military was provided with a legitimate institutional basis for control of propaganda and the mass media. The committee was chaired by the chief cabinet secretary, with its standing committee members being the chiefs of the Information Division of the Foreign Ministry, the Ministry of Home Affairs' Police Bureau, the Army Ministry's Military Affairs Bureau (which supervised the Press Office), the Information Division of the Navy Ministry's Naval Affairs Bureau, and the Telegraph and Telephone Bureau of the Communications Ministry, plus seven other officials from these five ministries. Vice ministerial level officials from each were also appointed to the committee. The daily business of the committee was handled by ten full-time appointees, among whom were two army lieutenant colonels and one navy commander.

Preceding the establishment of the Cabinet Information Committee, a state-controlled press agency, the Dōmei Tsūshinsha, was founded. Japan had long relied upon Reuters for its international news and for some time, particularly after World War I, there was a keenly felt need for a Japanese news agency. Following the outbreak of the Manchurian Incident Iwanaga Yūkichi, the executive director of the Shinbun Rengōsha, and others had suggested that the government set up a national news agency. In December 1931 Iwanaga had submitted to the Kwantung Army a proposal for a "Manchuria-Mongolia news agency" that would be accorded special privileges and operate under governmental supervision. Accordingly, the Kwantung Army in December 1932 inaugurated the Manchukuo News Agency, whereupon Rengō and Nihon Denpō Tsūshinsha both suspended their activities.

Meanwhile, a liaison committee had been formed in September 1931 by the Foreign, Army, and Navy ministries to promote the idea of a national news agency. After some delay due to conflicts among the existing news agencies and various governmental agencies, in June 1936 the Shinbun Rengōsha and the Denpō Tsūshinsha were merged to form a government news agency known as the Dōmei Tsūshinsha.[23] The Dōmei Tsūshinsha became inseparably connected with the Cabinet Information Committee, whose regulations stipulated that the committee should, "in collaboration with other governmental agencies concerned, promote the sound development of the Dōmei in line with the national interest in order that it shall function to its fullest capacity." The committee was further charged with supervising the activities of the Dōmei and with overseeing its use of government subsidies.[24] Committee directives regulated in detail the Dōmei's activities, specifying the kind of news it was to emphasize, which networks were to be strengthened, and so forth. "The Dōmei transmits to the world the voice of Japan and to Japan the events of the world," the Dōmei slogan proclaimed. Its monopoly of the news not only allowed the agency to manipulate the Japanese public's understanding of the outside world but enabled it to present to the world at large the image of a unified Japanese public opinion.

Systematic control of the communications media was heightened following the outbreak of the Sino-Japanese War in July 1937 and soon developed into full-scale wartime controls. Immediately after the war began, the foreign, army, and navy ministers exercised the powers given to them under Article 27 of the newspaper law and Article 18 of the publications law to prohibit the publication of stories dealing with diplomatic and military issues. At first the newspapers supported somewhat equivocally the government's policy of trying to solve the incident locally without escalating the fighting and placed major reponsibility for a solution upon the Chinese authorities.

On July 13 the Tokyo *Asahi* abandoned even a pretense of reportorial objectivity, declaring it was "no longer able to bear our unpleasant relations with China. We wish we could somehow find a way to dissipate this ominous air of suspicion and misunderstanding and escape from this depressing atmosphere. Frankly, we feel like a person gazing at a corner of the sky in hope that a refreshing rain will fall." The day before the *Asahi* had reported an unusual meeting called by Prime Minister Konoe Fumimaro, at which representatives of both houses of the Diet, financial circles, and the mass media were asked by the prime minister and the army and home affairs ministers to aid the government in securing the unanimous support of the nation. The meeting had been attended by Iwanaga Yūkichi, now president of the Dōmei Tsūshinsha, Ogata Taketora, editor-in-chief of the Tokyo *Asahi*, an executive director of NHK, and some forty other important press figures.

On July 13 the Publications Section of the Home Affairs Ministry's Police Bureau issued to the chiefs of the prefectural police sections a directive on the "handling of current affairs news" that stated: "Some mass media agencies at times carelessly engage in reporting and discussion that are contrary to the interests of the state. . . . You should therefore conduct thorough talks with those responsible for the publication of major daily newspapers and periodicals in the areas under your jurisdiction."[25] Such talks, although they lacked any legal basis, proved an extremely effective means of controlling the mass media by encouraging a kind of self-censorship. In addition, the authorities resorted to a "directive method" of control that listed news items not to be published, and a "warning method" by which they suggested the withholding of certain news from publication. However, the "talk method" appears to have served the purpose as well as the more rigid "directive" and "warning" methods.

In September 1937, with the war in China continuing to escalate, the Cabinet Information Committee was reorganized and expanded into a Cabinet Information Division. Slogans such as "the total mobilization of national spirit" and "the establishment of a higher national defense state" began to resound throughout the nation, and in April 1938 the Konoe cabinet promulgated a national mobilization law. Article 20 provided the legal foundation for wartime newspaper controls, giving the government power to "restrict or prohibit publication of newspapers and other printed matter whenever it deems such action necessary for the execution of the war and total national mobilization." In July 1938, under the auspices of the Cabinet Information Division, representatives of the Home Affairs, Foreign, Army, and Navy ministries agreed upon "principles of newspaper guidance" under which the authorities would give "internal guidance" in such matters as editorial policy. For this purpose, the "talk method" was extensively utilized, and increasingly coercion from above was met with voluntary cooperation from below. Direct pressure upon the mass media increased after the autumn of 1938, when the Ministry of Home Affairs tightened its controls through a system of special prefectural police sections. The situation further deteriorated as a shortage of newsprint brought about the rapid liquidation or amalgamation of many newspapers and periodicals. The process was carried out by the government in three stages: (1) "liquidation of the yellow press," 1938-40, (2) "liquidation of minor newspapers," 1940-41, and (3) establishment of a "one newspaper in one prefecture system" after September 1941. Whereas at the beginning of the process there were 739 daily papers, by 1942 the number had dropped to 108, and in the end there existed only 54 newspapers in the nation.[26] The liquidations were carried out on a "voluntary" basis through various pseudo-voluntary associations established to facilitate the process.

Under these circumstances, soon after the outbreak of the Sino-Japanese War the press had virtually ceased to express any independent opinions and devoted itself to reporting "reality" as handed down by the authorities. On September 5, 1937 the Tokyo *Asahi* reported that both houses of the Diet had unanimously passed a resolution "to express gratitude to the imperial army." The major portion of the news was devoted to reports of the actions and achievements of the army, and many pages were filled with articles on battle results and victories. The letters to the editor likewise expressed this wartime mood, such as one on July 31, 1937 that urged "Let's compose military songs!"

Support for the actions of the military had been widespread ever since the Manchurian Incident, and the Sino-Japanese War served to raise the public to a new pitch of nationalistic fervor that encouraged the press in its role as champion of the government. And as total war brought full employment and an end to labor disputes, both the people and the media willingly cooperated with the government's policies for "domestic peace and overseas expansion."

As the war expanded in China, Japanese-American relations became increasingly tense, reaching a critical point on October 6, 1938 when the United States lodged with the Japanese government an unusually comprehensive and sharp protest against its conduct of the war. Japan responded by announcing the establishment of a "New Order in East Asia," thus for the first time frankly declaring its intention to abrogate the Nine Power Treaty. The Tokyo *Asahi* gave the New Order its full support on November 19 in a full page article under the six-column head, "CONCEPTS AND PRINCIPLES OF PRE-INCIDENT DAYS NO LONGER APPLICABLE." Its editorial argued:

> Any declaration or treaty that may have international applicability represents a codification of the balance of power relations existent at the time of its formulation. What is implied by the diplomatic term "existing situation" changes constantly with the passage of time and alterations in other factors. No doctrine or treaty can ever be absolute and permanent. . . . We earnestly hope that not only the United States but other nations as well will refrain from making the present situation more complex by arguing exclusively on the basis of principles . . . that they will frankly recognize the new situation . . . and that as soon as possible they will willingly join in the great task of reconstructing East Asia in such fields as industry and trade.

Immediately after Konoe's announcement of the New Order on November 3, the Tokyo *Asahi*'s Washington correspondent reported general American public acceptance of the new policy as a "natural and reasonable demand." But as American official opposition continued, the *Asahi* began to depict the United States as clinging to traditional principles "with eyes closed to reality" and upholding an "excessive idealism." No direct animosity was expressed until the United States announced the abrogation of the commercial treaty in July 1939, an action the press at first interpreted as an effort to bolster Great Britain's position in the talks with Japan that had been under way since July 15 and were to rupture on August 21. The Anglo-Japanese talks, the press reported, had aroused widespread opposition to British policy in China, expressed in huge anti-British rallies, demonstrations, and resolutions. On July 18 the *Asahi* published an editorial bitterly critical of British interference with Japanese military actions in China and describing the united sense of outrage as a "national excitement tinged with desperate heroism and supported by an unshakable determination from within." Far from attempting to influence public opinion in a more rational direction, the *Asahi* and other newspapers encouraged the heightening frenzy and irrationality of the Japanese public.[27]

The Tokyo *Asahi*'s immediate reaction to the American abrogation notice was that it provided a "golden opportunity to renovate relations between Japan and the United States." Its editorial of July 28, which completely lacked the aggressively hostile tone of its reporting on Great Britain, expressed the hope that within six months Japan would conclude a new and more advantageous treaty with the United States. Before long this attitude began to change, however, and America came to be linked with Great Britain in an Anglo-American bloc antagonistic to Japan. During November 1939 the *Asahi* contained five editorials on U.S.-Japanese relations, none of which exhibited the least criticism of Japanese policy. The United States alone, they argued, was responsible for whether or not a thaw would occur in relations between the two countries, the key to which lay in American recognition of the realities of the situation in China.

V

The conclusion of the Tripartite Pact on September 27, 1940 effectively terminated all internal debate on foreign policy and caused a further decisive deterioration in Japanese-American relations. The day the pact was signed, in an editorial on the Sino-American loan agreement, the *Asahi* declared that the ill will demonstrated by American aid to Britain and Chiang Kai-shek forced Japan "to prepare with a total resolution for the worst to come" and made a clash between Japan and the United States inevitable. The editorial concluded, "We invite the United States, which has been engaging in hostilities in a creeping manner, to embark instead on immediate and decisive action." Defending the Tripartite Pact in an editorial of October 12 on "United States Oppressive Tactics Against Japan," the *Asahi* charged the United States with "groundless suspicion" in its unfriendly policy toward Japan. Despite the demands of "some frantic anti-Japanese advocates" of a strong stand against Japan, the paper looked hopefully toward those more cautious individuals, "who point out that the oppressive policy of the United States has been one major cause of the course of action that Japan has thus far followed," to help effect some improvement. It concluded by assuring its readers that the United States would not "escalate to the use of force."

Meanwhile, within Japan dissolution of the political parties and labor unions soon after the second Konoe cabinet was formed in July 1940 and the establishment of the Imperial Rule Assistance Association in October and the Greater Japan Association for Service to the State through Industry in November systematically closed off the few remaining avenues for organized dissent to the policies of the government. Without exposure to moderating influences, Japanese public opinion became more and more emotional and more fervently anti-American.

In December 1940 the Cabinet Information Division was elevated to the status of a bureau responsible for the dissemination of "information and propaganda" and overall control of the mass media. The core of the Information Bureau was its Second Division, which was charged with comprehensive guidance and supervision of news reporting and with the allocation of newsprint among the various publications. Within the division its First and Second sections were particularly important, for both the army and the navy attached full-time information officers to them and thereby came to have great influence over the bureau.

In January 1941 government press controls were extended by an imperial edict giving the prime minister (and therefore the Information Bureau) the power to restrict or prohibit, by issuance of directives, publication of any article that had significant bearing upon the execution of national policies, whether financial, economic, diplomatic, etc. In March 1941 the national defense security law stipulated extremely severe punishments for anyone found guilty of violating the restrictions on speech and publication: death for revealing secret information on diplomacy, public finance, and the economy; life imprisonment for publishing such information or even for discussing issues in a manner deemed by the authorities to serve the interests of foreign countries or to be harmful to public security. These restrictions relegated newspaper reporters to serving merely as messengers for the military and governmental authorities.

On October 16, 1941 the Tokyo *Asahi* published a noteworthy article reviewing Japanese-American relations since the beginning of the Sino-Japanese War. Ever since the outbreak of the China Incident, it charged, no matter what measures Japan had adopted in an attempt to find a solution, the United States had persisted in its misunderstanding and denounced every effort as an act of aggression and a violation of international agreements. Yet the United States itself had often violated international treaties, in proof of which the article pointed to what America regarded as its territorial limits, its dispatching of troops to Greenland and Iceland, and its arbitrary drawing of oceanic defense boundaries. "In real politics the United States worries about nothing but its own interest," the article accused, despite its "proclaimed faith in the welfare of the world." Although it acknowledged that responsibility for saving the world from global war belonged to both Japan and the United States, the article clearly placed the burden on the latter. The "daily tightening of the anti-Japanese encirclement" caused it to regard with great pessimism the prospect that a solution might be found in the Washington negotiations. Japan's "strategic requirements are absolute," it concluded, and the nation "must endure whatever difficulties it may meet in pursuit of our national policies."

A similar emotionalism characterized most articles on the Japanese-American negotiations. For example, on February 13, 1941 the *Asahi* printed a Dōmei dispatch stating that "American papers are indifferent to Ambassador Nomura," but "the serene ambassador continues his utmost efforts." In fact, in comparison with the attention paid to the eye-catching activities of Foreign Minister Matsuoka Yōsuke in Germany, Italy, and the Soviet Union, the negotiations received relatively little coverage in the Japanese press.

The outbreak of the war in the Pacific united the Japanese press in an all-out campaign in support of the war. On December 10 they organized a "national rally to smash the Anglo-American forces," at which leaders of every major newspaper and press agency shouted for victory and sang the Patriotic

March. In this manner the spokesmen of the mass media mobilized and led the Japanese common people into their wartime hysteria.[28]

New controls were clamped on speech, writing, and association with promulgation of a special law on December 19. The next day the Ministry of Home Affairs issued an order stipulating that under the new law it would be necessary to obtain permits in advance for any publication or meeting. Furthermore, it extended the power of suspension to future issues of publications, not merely to single issues containing objectionable items, and threatened with imprisonment anyone spreading "harmful rumors concerning current affairs." Thus, freedom of opinion was clearly impossible under the circumstances in wartime Japan, and with objective reporting nonexistent, all information available was nothing but conjecture and rumor.[29]

TWO HISTORIES OF THE
FAR EASTERN POLICY OF THE
UNITED STATES: TYLER DENNETT
AND A. WHITNEY GRISWOLD

Dorothy Borg

I

Much has been said over the years about the writing of history by American historians. Ever since the latter part of the nineteenth century, when the study of history was professionalized in the United States, American historians have repeatedly reviewed the state of historical scholarship in this country. Following World War II historiography became especially popular and many excellent studies have been published in the last decades.

Unfortunately most of the work that has been done deals with American historians' treatment of the internal history of the United States to the exclusion or near-exclusion of its foreign policy. As a consequence it has not seemed feasible in this paper to go beyond a consideration of the writings of the two historians who have had the greatest influence upon the study of American diplomacy in the Far East, Tyler Dennett and A. Whitney Griswold.[1]

As Dennett and Griswold undertook their research in the interwar period, it is necessary to review some of the previous developments. Around the turn of the century two trends emerged that had a strong influence on the writing of history in the United States up to the outbreak of World War II. One was represented by the scientific, the other by the progressive school of historical scholarship. The line between the two was frequently thin as their tenets were often loosely defined; nevertheless each had a few outstanding characteristics.

The scientific school arose toward the end of the nineteenth century, when most professional historians in the United States had received their training in Germany. There they had learned certain techniques that reflected the strong influence the natural sciences were exercising in many areas of research. As a result they regarded the historian as a "laboratory technician par excellence" whose job it was to collect all the documents and other pieces of primary evidence available and to study them with meticulous care.

Closely linked with their methodology was the scientific historians' emphasis upon objectivity, an emphasis that stemmed in part from the natural sciences but even more directly from the famous Rankean thesis that history must be writtten *wie es eigentlich gewesen*. In essence the scientific historian believed that he must divest himself of "bias of any kind," search for the facts, and present his findings with a minimum of analysis and interpretation.

Given their faith in absolute objectivity, the scientific historians quite naturally tended toward what is termed "historical-mindedness" in contrast to "present-mindedness." In other words, while they hoped that their research would provide further insights into contemporary problems, they felt that a historian was obligated to try to see the past in its own terms and that to study it primarily as a means of understanding the present was bound to result in distortion.

The scientific school attached great importance to its concept of historical continuity. According to its philosophy, human experience was a unified whole and history was a continuous chain of events. It was, therefore, the task of the historian to trace developments to their origins and show the elements of consistency that bound the various links of the chain together.

In general the scientific school was also characterized by a tendency to narrow the scope of historical study. Many of its members were primarily interested in the growth of political institutions and paid relatively little attention to the influence of economic, social, and intellectual forces on the shaping of history.

The progressive school came to the fore gradually in the early part of the twentieth century. During the first decade James Harvey Robinson and Charles Beard, building on ideas that had already gained substantial support, began to urge the adoption of a new approach to the study of history. In 1910 Carl Becker launched the first of his attacks on some of the fundamental beliefs of the scientific school, and two years later Robinson issued his collection of essays entitled *The New History*. Meanwhile the progressive historians were publishing books in which the new theories of historical scholarship were applied, so that their colleagues of the scientific tradition, although remaining in the majority, felt increasingly on the defensive.

The progressive historians challenged most of the ideas upon which the doctrine of scientific history was based. They were especially critical of the scientific school's claims to objectivity and insisted that no amount of effort would enable the historian to present the past *wie es eigentlich gewesen*. As the historian worked with a large body of documentation, they said, he was compelled to select certain "facts" and to arrange them in accordance with his judgment. To assume that his judgment could be neutral was wholly unrealistic.

The progressive historians were also strongly opposed to the concept of historical-mindedness. As part of the progressive movement, they were dedicated to effecting reforms and felt that historians should enter into the past for the purpose, not simply of observing whatever existed there, but of discovering that which was relevant to the present. Moreover, as reformers they were interested in studying change rather than continuity and in enlarging the scope of historical research so as to include sociological as well as political factors.

The movement to professionalize the study of history in the United States did not achieve real momentum until the turn of the century. In the 1870s there were less than a dozen full-time professors of history in American universities. By the 1890s, however, graduate schools had been established that were granting about twenty Ph.D. degrees in history annually. One of the most prominent of these was Johns Hopkins University where Herbert Baxter Adams conducted a famous seminar, attended by a galaxy of promising scholars, that was a classic example of the scientific approach to historical scholarship.[2]

In the first two decades of the twentieth century a number of histories of American diplomacy were written by well-known historians including Albert Bushnell Hart, John Bassett Moore, John Holladay Latané, and Archibald Cary Coolidge.[3] Their works were not based upon extensive research and fell far short of meeting the need for academic studies of the history of American foreign policy. Nevertheless they were pioneer efforts that attracted considerable attention at the time. Hart and Moore, who were firm believers in the scientific school of historical scholarship, wrote surveys covering the entire history of American diplomacy in which they emphasized its continuity. In contrast, Latané and Coolidge, who were progressive historians, dealt with recent and current events and stressed the frequent shifts in American policy instead of its consistencies.

The study of American diplomacy was, therefore, still in its beginnings in the early 1920s. While there were a few monographs on various aspects of United States relations with East Asia, the only general account was John W. Foster's *American Diplomacy in the Orient*, published in 1903.[4] A former secretary of state and veteran diplomat, Foster had not, however, attempted to write a scholarly history based upon extensive research. Moreover his assessment of the Far Eastern policy of the United States had been more that of a statesman anxious to extol his country's record than of a scholar trying to appraise it critically.

II

Tyler Dennett, who in the 1920s was to attempt to do what Foster had left undone, originally had no intention of engaging in an academic career. Graduated from Union Theological Seminary in 1908, he held a pastorate for several years but soon left the ministry, convinced that his own advanced religious beliefs were not in harmony with the views of his congregation. Making the first of a number of abrupt changes that were to punctuate his professional life, Dennett became a journalist, working mostly for religious publications. In that capacity he made two trips to the Far East, visiting Japan, China, and India, and attended the Versailles Conference. As a result of these experiences, Dennett wrote many articles and two small books, *The Democratic Movement in Asia* and *A Better World*, published respectively in 1918 and 1920. Both volumes were devoted to the thesis that, in order to realize the Wilsonian ideal of world organization, the peoples of all nations—especially the "backward races" of Asia—would have to be educated in the Christian principles of democracy and brotherhood upon which alone internationalism could be founded.[5]

In 1920 Dennett decided to give up journalism and turn to the study of history. He undertook an extensive survey of documentary and manuscript

materials with the intention of issuing a source book on the relations of the
United States and China up to 1870. In the end, however, the source book did
not materialize as Dennett was persuaded by the State Department to prepare a
detailed paper on the history of American Far Eastern policy for the
information of the United States delegation to the Washington Conference on
the limitation of armaments and the problems of the Pacific area. This paper
formed the basis of *Americans in Eastern Asia*, which was published in 1922.[6]

   Americans in Eastern Asia was written in the tradition of the scientific
historians. Always a prodigious worker, Dennett immersed himself in primary
sources, devoting special attention to the State Department archives to which he
had privileged access. As a result, he accumulated an astonishing amount of
information out of which he constructed a history of American relations with
East Asia from the end of the eighteenth century to the beginning of the
twentieth. He refused to carry the story beyond the McKinley administration on
the grounds that the primary materials were not yet available and that he would,
therefore, have to substitute "speculation and hearsay evidence" for "documentary facts."[7]

   Like others who believed in the scientific approach, Dennett felt that strict
adherence to an orthodox methodology would in large measure guarantee the
attainment of complete objectivity. He never seems to have doubted that
complete objectivity could be achieved and that to do so was the essence of
historical scholarship. In the preface to *Americans in Eastern Asia* Dennett said,
in effect, that he had conducted his research without any preconceptions and
had reconstructed the past faithfully from the record. In an article written some
years later he declared that for a historian to take sides concerning the "rightness
or wrongness" of historical developments was, in his opinion, "indecent."[8]

   Besides his concern for objectivity, Dennett shared the scientific historians' preoccupation with the idea of the continuity of history. Indeed it would
be difficult to exaggerate the extent to which he emphasized the element of
continuity, not only in *Americans in Eastern Asia* but also in the articles he
wrote in the early 1920s. Dennett's main argument was that American Far
Eastern policy was as "old as the Declaration of Independence" and that, while
it had passed through a period of experimentation and innovation between the
1840s and 1860s, it had not undergone any significant changes since nor was it
likely to do so in the twentieth century.[9] In an article published in the *American
Historical Review* in the autumn of 1922, Dennett made the characteristic
statement that "absolutely no new principles" had been added to United States
policy in eastern Asia since 1870.[10]

   In *Americans in Eastern Asia* Dennett maintained that American Far
Eastern policy had always had a single aim—the expansion of American trade
with the countries of East Asia, especially China. Successive administrations in
Washington, he held, had regarded this aim as vital to the national interest, a
view that Dennett himself frankly endorsed.[11]

   Dennett's chief emphasis, however, was on the means rather than the ends
of policy. He was convinced that American officials had consistently proceeded
on the assumption that the promotion of American trade in the Far East
required the realization of two conditions: the maintenance of the principle of
the Open Door and the development of strong Asian states capable of enforcing

that principle within their boundaries. The "real issue" had been one of strategy, the question being whether the United States should act independently or in cooperation with the other powers with interests in the Far East.

Dennett believed that in what he regarded as the formative period of American Far Eastern policy in the mid-nineteenth century, American officials had alternated between an isolated and a cooperative policy and that by 1870 both possibilities had been fully explored so that nothing remained but to apply one or the other. Among the outstanding advocates of independent action, in his view, were men such as Humphrey Marshall, Commodore Perry, and Dr. Peter Parker. Marshall had wanted to use American military forces to shore up a China that he felt was on the verge of disintegration and of falling prey to the European nations. Perry and Parker, on their part, had favored the acquisition by the United States of territory in the Far East as the best means of safeguarding America's economic stake in that area. Among the exponents of cooperation was, first and foremost, Anson Burlingame whose "cooperative policy" was based on the idea of a voluntary agreement among the powers to respect the integrity of China and the principle of the Open Door.

After the formative period, Dennett thought, the United States allowed its interest in the Far East to lapse for almost three decades. At the end of the century, however, a new crisis developed when the European powers seemed about to partition China and close the Open Door permanently. McKinley met this situation by returning to the isolated policy conceived by his predecessors almost half a century earlier. In order to counter European aggression he established a foothold in the Pacific and annexed the Philippines. Hay, on the other hand, revived Burlingame's concept of cooperation and attempted to get the powers to agree to respect the independence of China and the Open Door. Hay therefore issued his Open Door notes of 1899 and his circular of 1900. While Dennett conceded that the Open Door notes had fallen short of their objective, as they had not secured complete equality of economic opportunity for all nations, he asserted that Hay had prevented the partition of China and established a "base line" for all subsequent American policy in the Far East. In his "dream" of perpetuating a cooperative policy founded upon voluntary agreement rather than coercion, Dennett said, Hay had been a "statesman fifty years, perhaps, ahead of his time."[12]

Dennett therefore took the position that historically American Far Eastern policy had a fixed pattern. The pattern, as he saw it, was a simple one. The aim of American policy, commercial expansion, had been static and its importance had never been open to question. Only the means were subject to change. The United States had "oscillated" between an independent policy which was "essentially belligerent" and bound to lead to conflict with other nations, and a cooperative policy based upon voluntary compliance. The cooperative policy alone had stood the "test of time."

Following the publication of *Americans in Eastern Asia*, Dennett went to Johns Hopkins where he taught and at the same time fulfilled the requirements for a Ph.D. degree. His dissertation, *Roosevelt and the Russo-Japanese War*, was accepted with acclaim in 1924 and published the following year. Dennett's experience at Hopkins, where memories of Herbert Baxter Adams' seminar were still very much alive, seems to have confirmed his faith in the tenets of the scientific school of scholarship. In the lecture courses he gave subsequently, he admonished his students to adhere to sound scientific methods in their historical research, to remember that a consideration of current events had no place in the study of history, and to recognize that every development was the result of a long, continuous process which must be traced to its source.[13]

In *Roosevelt and the Russo-Japanese War*, in contrast to *Americans in Eastern Asia*, Dennett covered a very brief period, 1902 to 1905. He may thereby have helped to establish a tradition of limiting studies of American Far Eastern policy to monographs, a tradition that has dominated the field to the present. Otherwise Dennett did not alter his methodology. *Roosevelt and the Russo-Japanese War* was based largely on primary sources, mainly parts of the hitherto unused papers of Theodore Roosevelt.

At the beginning of *Roosevelt and the Russo-Japanese War* Dennett stated that Roosevelt had not been concerned with the expansion of American trade in eastern Asia.[14] Dennett himself, therefore, departed from the thesis that the goal of United States Far Eastern policy had been exclusively economic and from this time on asserted that the United States had had two objectives in the Far East, the maintenance of both the Open Door and the integrity of China.

Dennett's main interest, however, continued to be in the method of conducting policy rather than in its ultimate purpose. In his view, Roosevelt regarded the Russo-Japanese War as fundamentally instigated by the kaiser who, in his attempts to secure world supremacy, was ready to support the efforts of the Russians to seize Manchuria and as much of China as possible. Dennett believed Roosevelt had warned Germany at the outset of the war that if it went to the aid of Russia militarily, the United States would go to the aid of Japan. By this action, he declared, to all intents and purposes the president transformed the United States into a member—though an "unsigned member"—of the Anglo-Japanese alliance. He thereby prevented Germany from entering the war and turning it into a worldwide conflict and averted, probably for all time, the partition of China.[15]

At the end of *Roosevelt and the Russo-Japanese War* Dennett compared the policy of Hay with that of Roosevelt. Both policies, he asserted, had rested upon the concept of cooperation. However, in a complete reversal of his previous position, Dennett stated that as Hay had relied solely on voluntary compliance, he had scored some "verbal victories" but otherwise accomplished "nothing." Roosevelt, on the other hand, had threatened the use of force, an action which was worth a "thousand diplomatic notes" and, as a precedent, might prove the "largest contribution" ever made to the conduct of American Far Eastern policy.[16]

Apparently the explanation for the shift in Dennett's position lies in the changes that occurred in his views about contemporary developments. At the time of the Washington Conference the controversy over international coopera-tion, which had achieved such dramatic proportions in the fight concerning the League of Nations, continued to dominate all discussion of American foreign policy. Dennett was among those who remained convinced that some form of international cooperation would have to be developed if peace were to be maintained. He moreover shared the view, which prevailed in the State Department, that cooperation by voluntary agreement, such as was to form the basis of the Nine Power Treaty, would provide the best means of preserving peace in the Far East. As indicated earlier, *Americans in Eastern Asia* was originally planned as a historical survey for the use of the United States delegation at the Washington Conference and Dennett, as was almost inevitable under the circumstances, seems to have looked for material which might have a bearing upon the problem that was bound to be uppermost in everyone's mind. Subsequently he sought to apply his findings to the contemporary situation. In a memorandum on the "Policy of Cooperation of the Foreign Powers in the Far East," evidently prepared for official use, he summarized the relevant parts of *Americans in Eastern Asia* and stated that they were "to be studied in the light of [the] present proposals for a Cooperative Policy." In *Americans in Eastern Asia* he went further and asserted that, in view of the vital necessity of preserving "the peace of the East and of the world," it was essential to examine the record of the cooperative policy in eastern Asia, a record which showed that the maintenance of that policy was imperative.[17]

In short, despite his determination to be objective and historical-minded, Dennett had turned to the past to find answers to the compelling problems of his own day. In so doing he reduced a large segment of history to a strikingly simple formula that supported his belief that, in the existing situation, cooperation that relied on voluntary agreement furnished the best solution to the problems of the Far East.

Almost immediately after the completion of *Americans in Eastern Asia*, Dennett's ideas began to change. The bitter rejection of any form of internationalism, which characterized certain groups of American intellectuals after the Versailles Conference, became more widespread as the 1920s advanced. Clearly affected by the rising mood of disillusionment, Dennett lost faith in the Nine Power Treaty and the cooperative principle that it embodied. As early as 1923 he wrote that the Nine Power Treaty only committed the United States to consult and that the policy of cooperation upon which it was founded was, therefore, no more than a "policy of courtesy," a position which he maintained thereafter.[18]

At the same time Dennett continued to believe that some sort of international cooperation was essential and increasingly advocated a cooperation backed by coercive measures, including the use of force if necessary. Furthermore, he became convinced that the effectiveness of any form of international cooperation would depend on the closest possible relationship between Great Britain and the United States. In an article, also written in 1923, that dealt primarily with American policy in the Far East, Dennett urged the American people to disregard the "nonsense" traditionally mouthed by "demagogues" about "entangling alliances" and to enter into a formal alliance with the British. It was apparently these ideas that led Dennett to reverse himself concerning Hay's policy and to take such a positive stand about what he regarded as Roosevelt's readiness to join the Anglo-Japanese alliance and to resort to coercive tactics.[19]

In the early 1930s Dennett's views underwent a further transformation. As the situation in both the Far East and Europe began to give rise to alarm for the future, Dennett joined the many intellectuals whose disillusionment led them to declare their opposition to any intervention by the United States in other parts of the world. While he continued to assume that the aims of American Far Eastern policy were static, in marked contrast to his previous attitude Dennett denied that the United States had any important stake in East Asia and opposed its involvement in that area whether by independent action or by cooperation based on either agreement or coercion. At the time of the Manchurian crisis he vehemently denounced Stimson's declaration of the nonrecognition doctrine, asserting that the United States should not interfere in the Far East. In addition, while he regarded nonrecognition as in itself a coercive measure, he was convinced that, to be effective, it would have to be implemented by the use of force and he did not believe that the United States would fight in East Asia. With the advent of the Roosevelt administration, Dennett predicted that America would quickly withdraw from the position Stimson had taken.[20]

In 1933 and 1934 Dennett published a number of articles in which he reviewed the history of United States relations with East Asia. Returning to the idea that American policy had revolved in a continuous pattern, he asserted that the United States had vacillated between coercion and noncoercion. Over a long period of time, with "almost mathematical regularity," one administration had moved forward aggressively while the next, convinced that a further advance was not worth the cost, had beaten a "quiet retreat." Dennett stated that currently American policy was going through another such cycle which, as in the past, was bound to prove futile if not dangerously provocative.[21]

Dennett had, therefore, constructed another formula similar to that which he had evolved in the 1920s. Like the earlier version it seemed to reflect his own strong reactions to the increasingly pressing problems of the world around him. Also like the earlier version it sought to compress a long stretch of history into an unusually simple pattern. Yet the complexity of the material with which he was dealing ran counter to such a limited analysis. As is evident from Dennett's own writings, as well as those of others, more often than not a course of action was the result of so many different considerations that it could not be categorically defined as coercive or noncoercive. Indeed, a comparison of Dennett's articles shows that he himself classified various policies, including that of John Hay, differently at different times. Moreover, while Dennett continued to adhere to the theory that the objectives of the United States in East Asia were the maintenance of the Open Door and the integrity of China, in dealing with specific situations he repeatedly indicated that other goals—such as the strengthening of the United States position as a great power and the establishment of world order—predominated.[22]

Dennett's career as a historian reached its peak in 1933 when he published his life of John Hay, a biography of rare sensitivity that received the Pulitzer Prize. In 1934 he was appointed president of Williams College and, although he resigned over a controversy with the trustees three years later, did little writing thereafter. In his outlook on contemporary events Dennett became an extreme anti-New Dealer and his great distrust of Roosevelt, whom he regarded as an interventionist, strengthened his own isolationist views. By 1940, however, his abhorrence of nazism convinced him that the United States should join the war. While he therefore regarded the defeat of Germany as essential, he believed that, in fact, the war was only a prelude to a worldwide revolution that could not be forestalled whatever the outcome of the existing hostilities.[23]

It is generally recognized that Dennett's books have had an extensive influence. *Americans in Eastern Asia*, which was long considered a classic in its field, has been reprinted as recently as 1963. *Roosevelt and the Russo-Japanese War*, although admittedly outdated, remains a standard reference. Dennett's *John Hay* is still regarded as one of the best biographies by an American historian. Some of Dennett's shorter studies, based on solid research, have also become a permanent part of the literature of the history of American diplomacy in the Far East. But the articles written in 1933 and 1934 have received relatively little attention. Nevertheless they seem to have had considerable influence upon other historians at the time and, through them, upon the later study of American Far Eastern policy. In the subsequent discussion an attempt has been made to show their affect on Griswold's writings in particular.

III

The controversy between the scientific and the progressive schools of historical scholarship reached its climax in the 1930s when the former lost much of its original influence and the latter gained the ascendancy. For the most part the scientific historians adhered to the views they had maintained from the beginning; but in some respects the progressives went considerably beyond their earlier thinking.

Carl Becker led the attack against his scientific colleagues in his presidential address, "Everyman His Own Historian," before the American Historical Association in December 1931. The most dramatic feature of his presentation was his discussion of the relationship between the study of history and the needs of the moment. Becker suggested not just that historians should search the past for that which was relevant to the present, but that they should adapt history to the requirements of their own day. In essence, he embroidered upon an idea that appears in one of his early essays: that "facts" are not objective realities but mental images which, if "useful and necessary" to a given generation, should be accepted by it as "true."[24]

Beard in his presidential address, "Written History as an Act of Faith," given two years later, added to Becker's somewhat abstract comments a characteristic note of activism. He did not deny that historians could in a measure reconstruct previous developments, although he emphasized that their perception was severely conditioned by the bias of their own times. But he increasingly adopted the position that a historian should try not so much to understand the past as to shape the future, that through his own subjective interpretation of history he should participate in attempting to change the course of events.[25]

It seems unlikely that even among the progressive historians of the 1930s many wanted to go as far as Becker in denying the possibility of recreating history or as far as Beard in wanting to influence it. Nevertheless it is evident from the positive response to Becker and Beard that an insistence upon present-mindedness, in the broad sense that a study of the past should be undertaken primarily for its bearing upon the present, had a great appeal at a time when the urgency of contemporary problems, both domestic and foreign, could scarcely be overlooked.

The situation that prevailed among the small group of specialists in American diplomatic history differed somewhat from that in the field at large. While beginning with the 1920s some progressive historians produced excellent studies of American diplomacy, the scientific tradition still dominated in the 1930s. Among diplomatic historians Samuel Flagg Bemis emerged as perhaps the foremost representative of the scientific school. Bemis joined the Yale faculty in 1934 and two years later published the first important textbook on the history of American diplomacy which rapidly became a mainstay of the profession and remains so today. Bemis shared many of Tyler Dennett's views not only on historical questions but on the contemporary scene, for he was an impassioned opponent of the New Deal and of America's involvement abroad.[26]

There were, however, factors other than those ordinarily emphasized in discussions of the progressive and scientific historians that had an important effect in the 1930s on the writing of the history of American diplomacy. While there was a trend toward the study of international relations after World War I, it was not until the mid-1930s that political scientists started to try to analyze and assess the way in which states functioned in respect to foreign affairs. Among the issues that they stressed throughout the next years was the need for the United States to have a "realistic" foreign policy designed to serve its national interests. The same note was struck by some historians, most especially Charles Beard, who in 1934 published *The Idea of National Interest* and its sequel *The Open Door at Home*. As the 1930s advanced, historians and political scientists worked together on problems of American foreign policy in research centers such as the Institute for Advanced Study at Princeton and the Yale Institute of International Studies established in 1935.[27]

Another important influence upon the writing of the 1930s was the disillusionment about the international situation that gripped so many American historians in the interwar years. Reference has already been made to some of the phases through which the reaction against the war and the internationalist movement passed, but it may be useful to recall a few of the details that form an essential background to the story that follows.

It has frequently been said that the disillusionment of American historians after World War I arose from their participation in official wartime activities such as the propaganda efforts of the so-called Creel Committee.[28] Many of the leading historians in the United States, who had originally been skeptical about the war, supported President Wilson after 1917 in the belief that he would succeed in establishing a world based on democracy and international coopera-tion. When the results of the war fell disastrously short of their expectations, they felt that their idealism had been ill-founded and that they had furthered a cause which, but for their own short-sightedness, they would have opposed.

This feeling, though characteristic of some groups in the early 1920s, as suggested earlier, gradually became more widespread. After the mid-1920s it was fed by the first phase of the revisionist movement, the controversy over the war guilt question. The more extreme revisionists claimed that it was not the central European powers that had started the war but America's allies, Britain and France. They thereby paved the way for an outpouring of the animosities toward Europe, the "Old World" which they pictured as beyond redemption, that historically were so familiar a part of the American outlook. The strong positive attitude toward Great Britain that had been an important part of the war effort turned into an equally strong negative reaction.

It was not until the 1930s, however, that the full extent of the disillusionment of American historians became apparent. The second phase of the revisionist movement was at its height from the time of the publication of Walter Millis' popular *Road to War* in 1935 to the issuance of Charles C. Tansill's scholarly *America Goes to War* three years later. Among the themes which the revisionists persistently stressed was that the United States' participation in the war had been an unqualified disaster, resulting from the pressures of self-interested bankers and businessmen, the propaganda activities of the British, and President Wilson's misconception of America's messianic role in the world.

For the most part, however, the revisionists had a purpose that went beyond trying to establish the historical record. To describe the United States' engagement in World War I as a catastrophe was for them essentially a means of demonstrating that America must not be drawn into the contemporary crises in Europe and Asia, that 1917 must not be repeated in the 1930s. The widespread conviction that the United States should insulate itself from foreign developments made for all kinds of strange ideological partnerships. Beard, for example, the formidable exponent of progressive scholarship and political liberalism, contended that the United States should remain free from involvement abroad and devote itself to perfecting democracy at home. Bemis, the scientific historian and ardent anti-New Dealer, while opposed to Beard's ideas of domestic reform, overwhelmingly endorsed his views on foreign policy.[29]

IV

In 1933 A. Whitney Griswold received his Ph.D. degree from Yale. At his insistence he had been permitted to combine American history with American and English literature in his graduate program and had been awarded the first Ph.D. degree ever given by Yale in History and the Arts and Letters, which was probably also the first advanced degree in American studies accorded in the United States. Following his graduation he became an instructor in history at Yale and worked in close association with Bemis, who regarded him as a young historian of brilliant promise. In 1935 he became a research assistant at the Yale Institute of International Studies, which was under the directorship of Nicholas John Spykman, one of the best known political scientists of his time. The institute sponsored Griswold's work on *The Far Eastern Policy of the United States.*[30]

Griswold's views about foreign affairs developed gradually from the early 1930s to the end of 1938, when *The Far Eastern Policy of the United States* was published. While still a graduate student at Yale he was an ardent advocate of the League of Nations, convinced that if the League did not succeed, western civilization was "absolutely, inexorably, doomed to destruction."[31] But presumably because of the growing pessimism affecting American intellectuals, he quickly lost faith in the concept of international cooperation. As time went by Griswold increasingly rejected the term "isolationist" because, as he stated in the 1940s, it became "so riddled with the most negative connotations."[32] Nevertheless, using the words internationalist and isolationist, interventionist and noninterventionist in the elastic and largely relative sense originally intended, it is clear that Griswold soon ranged himself on the isolationist, noninterventionist side.

Unlike Dennett, Griswold's noninterventionism was linked with a profound political liberalism. Basically he believed that as the result of a unique national experience, the United States was the only country qualified to develop a democratic society that would satisfy its own people and serve as a model for the rest of the world. With the advent of the Roosevelt administration Griswold became completely committed to the New Deal and correspondingly certain that the United States should insulate itself from international affairs so that the reforms which had been started could be completed. In a memorandum written in late 1935 he stated that he regarded it as "inconceivable" that a situation should arise whereby the national interests of the United States would be served by war. He was convinced that in foreign relations the United States should concentrate upon creating a "Pax Americana" based upon a "bona fide economic Pan Americanism," within which it could live in security and "let the hurricanes roar in Europe and Asia." Stressing the vital importance of geographical factors, he maintained that, owing to its great natural assets, the United States was virtually self-sustaining and could readily be made safe from attack.[33]

Because of these views, Griswold increasingly questioned the foreign policy of the Roosevelt administration. In relation to developments in Europe, during the Ethiopian crisis he came out strongly against the president's attempt to strengthen the League's efforts to obtain a more flexible neutrality law.[34] Throughout the first half of 1937, when talk of war in Europe was widespread, Griswold published monthly articles in *Events* in which he expressed the fear that the administration might engage in a "crusade vs. Fascism" and declared that the preservation of democracy at home did not require the destruction of totalitarianism abroad. Moreover, in keeping with the writings of many other disillusioned liberals, Griswold charged that however abhorrent nazism might be, it was the product of the postwar policies of the British and French, who were currently no more interested in defending democracy than they had been in 1917. The conflict in Europe, he maintained, was not the result of ideological differences but of the game of power politics in which all the large European nations participated equally.[35]

In regard to events in Asia, Griswold bitterly criticized Stimson's intervention in the Manchurian crisis and supported Roosevelt and Hull's policy during their first years in office, believing that they were determined to effect a major retreat from the advanced position Stimson had taken. But as time went by he began to suspect that they had adopted a policy of *reculer pour mieux sauter* and appealed for a clarification of the administration's position. Declaring that the overriding interest of the United States in East Asia, as elsewhere, was to avoid involvement in war, he stated that officials in Washington should abandon what he regarded as their preoccupation with befriending China and concentrate on the establishment of friendly relations with Japan.[36]

One of Griswold's major concerns was that the European nations might be engaging in behind-the-scenes maneuvers to involve the United States in their controversies. Imbued with the idea that Great Britain, in particular, had dragged the United States into war in 1917 and fully sharing the prevalent intense hostility to the British, Griswold reacted sharply to the frequent rumors in the mid-1930s that Prime Minister Chamberlain was attempting to persuade the president to take steps toward resolving the European crisis. He was especially fearful that the British might seek to draw the United States into the European situation through the "back door" of Asia and, after the outbreak of the Sino-Japanese War, when there was talk of the British government's urging the United States to intervene, warned that in the past America had "often waltzed to British fiddles" in the Far East.[37]

Griswold began his research on American Far Eastern policy in 1935 when he joined the Yale Institute of International Studies, starting, as he himself said with disarming frankness, from scratch.[38] In strong contrast to Dennett, he turned to the past with an unshakable belief in the present-mindedness that the progressive historians were currently so actively championing. As he stated in the preface to the Chinese edition of *The Far Eastern Policy of the United States*, it was his "personal philosophy that historians should have the courage to attack the problems vital to their own generation and lifetime even at the risk of becoming involved in political controversy."[39] In a rough draft of an introduction written for the original American edition but never finished, he declared that his book was intended not as a diplomatic history but as an "essay on the foreign policy of the United States today." He had undertaken it because of the critical nature of the times and the urgent necessity to determine what the policy of the United States in the Far East should be. He had been "concerned with the past only for the light it" shed "on the present."[40]

As Griswold's focus on the contemporary situation led him to limit his research to a relatively recent period of history that even included current events, he was keenly aware that he had to proceed without the kind of documentation that a more traditional historian would have regarded as essential. In his draft introduction he wrote that he had been able to use some hitherto unpublished documents—presumably the valuable Rockhill papers to which he was the first to gain access—but that for much of the period he covered only the "barest" written record was as yet available. While he realized that a historian, who wanted the "whole truth" based on a wealth of archival and other primary materials, might well question the use of writing such a book at all, he had felt the international situation did not permit any delay. Under the circumstances, his "greatest debt" was to the scholars who had preceded him in this area of study, "certain of whose works" constituted "his principal sources."

There can be little doubt that the scholar to whom Griswold was most heavily indebted was Tyler Dennett. While he undoubtedly owed much to others, especially to Bemis, who provided constant encouragement as well as valuable guidance, Griswold clearly based his study on Dennett's interpretation of American Far Eastern policy.[41] In particular he adopted the formula that Dennett had advanced in the 1930s and elaborated its three essential elements—that American Far Eastern policy was continuous, that it had persistently followed certain fixed aims, and that it had revolved in a repetitive pattern of aggression and retreat.

Griswold attached immense importance to the idea of the continuity of American Far Eastern policy. An early outline for a history of United States policy in the Far East, which appears in his files clipped to detailed notes on one of Dennett's articles published in 1934, shows that originally Griswold accepted in toto Dennett's theory of continuity. It states that the formulation of American Far Eastern policy had been completed by 1870 and in the intervening decades, although "war and revolutions and dynastic overturns" had "altered the face of the earth," United States policy had remained the same.[42] But Griswold qualified his position subsequently and adopted the view that at the time of the Spanish-American War, when the United States was seized with an expansionist mood, American Far Eastern policy had entered a new phase. Thus, while he made 1898 his starting point in *The Far Eastern Policy of the United States,* he emphasized the concept of continuity as much as previously.[43]

Griswold adhered with equal conviction to the view that the aims of American Far Eastern policy were always static and that the conduct of policy vacillated between advance and retreat. In essence his argument was that in the nineteenth century America's interest in the Far East was purely commercial so that it had a single objective—the maintenance of the Open Door in China.[44] Under the influence of the expansionist spirit of the 1890s, however, John Hay, believing that the maintenance of the Open Door required the preservation of China's integrity, issued his circular of July 1900. But while Hay regarded the integrity of China as a means to an end, the circular had the effect of raising it to the status of an end in itself. As a result, every new administration assumed that it had a vital commitment in the Far East, which was to defend the principles of the Open Door and, in particular, the integrity of China. Each administration, therefore, embarked upon an extensive diplomatic campaign in support of these principles only to be compelled to recognize that neither represented anything of real importance to the United States. The proverbial dream of the China market never materialized and, as an end in itself, the integrity of China remained an illusion sustained only by tradition and sentiment. Diplomatic advances were consequently transformed into diplomatic retreats, and each administration in turn reverted to the position from which it had started. From 1903 to 1938, Griswold declared,

> ... the history of American diplomacy [revolved] in a series of cycles. ... One after another, with variations only in manner and emphasis, the Presidents and Secretaries of State who followed McKinley and Hay ... moved toward identical objectives with identical results.[45]

In contrast to Dennett, who only cited certain outstanding events in support of his formula, Griswold attempted to apply it concretely throughout *The Far Eastern Policy of the United States.* In doing so, however, he encountered many difficulties.

The theory that during the first four decades of the twentieth century the policy of the United States was dictated by a firm determination to defend the Open Door and the integrity of China proved tenuous. Even for the early period, 1900 to 1914, for which he had substantial primary sources, Griswold did not present a convincing case. He ignored many factors such as that the United States, as an emerging world power still uncertain of its role in the international community, was not likely to adhere steadfastly to any course. As later historians have shown, if at times officials in Washington sought to champion the Open Door and the integrity of China, for the most part they pursued a variety of objectives among which the most persistent seems to have been the establishment of conditions of international stability and peace that were expected to serve the interests of the United States as well as other nations.[46] In dealing with the events of the later years, 1914-38, Griswold was even less able to sustain his argument. For in connection with the conduct of foreign policy under Wilson, Hughes, and Stimson, he repeatedly asserted that the main purpose of the United States government had been to create a new international order, a purpose that governed its actions in the Far East as in all other parts of the world.[47] Griswold even entitled his chapter on Stimson "The Quest for Collective Security" to emphasize that in the Manchurian crisis the overriding issue for the secretary of state was the furtherance of the international peace system developed after World War I. In short, Griswold himself departed from his thesis amd demonstrated that from the time of Wilson on the American statesmen who were convinced internationalists, insofar as they supported the Open Door and the integrity of China, were primarily moved not by tradition and sympathy but by a determination to construct a world free of aggression and intervention, from which they could scarely have excluded the Chinese.

Griswold also failed to substantiate the cyclical theory of aggression and retrenchment. His contention that in the opening years of the century the United States followed a challenging and dangerous course in the Far East has not been supported by the research of others. In fact it has become increasingly evident that under the direction of Hay and Roosevelt the United States government consistently adhered to a cautious policy based on a realistic appraisal of the country's limited strength.[48] Similarly, in regard to the 1914-18 period Griswold, lacking documentary materials that might have thrown some light on the behind-the-scenes activities of the United States and other governments, often quite arbitrarily appraised actions as aggressive or renunciatory and, as a result, his judgments did not stand up under scrutiny.

A notable case in point was his treatment of the Washington Conference. Griswold persistently maintained that the Washington Conference was the most determined and belligerent of all the "diplomatic offensives" undertaken by the United States to compel respect for the Open Door and the integrity of China and that the American delegation in effect imposed a settlement on the Japanese who "from start to finish" were "unwilling" participants.[49] But the studies of other historians indicate that both the Americans and the Japanese wanted to reach an agreement and cooperated in setting up a treaty system that was designed more to limit armaments and establish friendly relations between the United States and Japan (which, in fact, prevailed throughout the next ten years) than to provide any insurance of the Open Door and the integrity of China.[50]

Part of the difficulty, not only in relation to the Washington Conference but also to other instances in which Griswold saw a sharp conflict between the United States and Japan that does not appear to have existed, lay in his arbitrary assessment of the actions of the Japanese as well as the United States government. Having only an elementary knowledge of Japanese foreign policy (as he himself was the first to admit), Griswold proceeded on the assumption that ever since the turn of the century, when Japan became a world power, the Japanese government and people had been united in a fixed determination to expand their political and economic interests in China at any cost. As a consequence, he virtually ruled out the possibility of situations arising in which Japan and the United States might want to adjust their differences on a give-and-take basis.[51]

It would seem, therefore, that Griswold's efforts to spell out Dennett's formula illustrated further that it was basically too simple an interpretation to provide an adequate explanation of a substantial period of history charged with extraordinarily complex events, and that its appeal for Griswold, as well as for Dennett, lay fundamentally in the support that it accorded to many of the contemporary isolationist assumptions. In other words, as suggested earlier, it seemed to lend the weight of history to the isolationist belief that the United States must remain aloof from the conflicts in Europe and Asia and that any involvement in the Far East, in particular, could only be, in Bemis' oft-quoted phrase, "a great aberration."

In one other important respect Griswold's concept of present-mindedness made him turn to the past for answers to the questions of the 1930s. As already indicated, he was especially concerned that Great Britain might attempt to involve the United States in the current crisis in Europe through the "back door" of Asia. His initial plan was, therefore, to write a book on "Anglo-American Diplomacy in the Far East, 1898-1935" in the hope that an understanding of the historical background would throw some light on the immediate question of whether the United States should cooperate with Great Britain in East Asia or follow an independent course. After a year's work he abandoned this project in favor of writing a more general history of American policy in the Far East. But he apparently incorporated much of his earlier research into *The Far Eastern Policy of the United States,* as one of the most persistent themes in that study is that Anglo-American cooperation in East Asia had been a misfortune. His main argument was that, due to a naive conception of international relations in general and British policy in particular, United States officials had repeatedly relied upon British support, which did not materialize as the British were concerned only to promote their own interests—interests that, more often than not, were in conflict with those of the United States.[52]

During the years that he devoted to the writing of *The Far Eastern Policy of the United States,* which was completed in midsummer of 1938, Griswold's commitment to the present, if anything, deepened as the international situation deteriorated. He never again undertook any historical research on America's relations with East Asia but, from the outbreak of the Sino-Japanese War to Pearl Harbor, published numerous articles about the current policy of the United States in the Far East.[53] In the first of these, written shortly after President Roosevelt's decision to attend the Brussels Conference, he called for a reappraisal of American Far Eastern policy.[54] Summarizing the historical record, as he was to present it in *The Far Eastern Policy of the United States,* Griswold expressed his great concern that the Roosevelt administration might be initiating a "campaign" on behalf of the Open Door and the integrity of China such as he sought to demonstrate each successive administration had embarked upon in the past. As the end of his work on *The Far Eastern Policy of the United States* approached, Griswold seems above all to have hoped that the publication of his study would contribute to preventing the United States from "jumping into" a war in the Far East.[55]

In retrospect it is evident that Griswold's book appeared at a time of particular uncertainty in the United States, when the tide of opinion was almost imperceptibly beginning to recede from the high point of isolationism. Following the Munich agreement Roosevelt, having decided that in the interests of American security foreign affairs must take precedence over domestic reforms, undertook to mobilize the nation behind a program designed to meet the international crisis. He therefore sought a new neutrality law which would extend the cash-and-carry provisions of the existing legislation to trade in arms and munitions. The result was a nine month struggle between isolationists and internationalists not only in Congress but throughout the country, culminating in November 1939 in the passage of a new law that accorded with the president's wishes.

Throughout this controversy it was recognized that the situation in the Far East constituted a special problem, as the cash-and-carry rule was bound to operate in favor of Japan. In the spring of 1939 various members of Congress, including Senator Pittman, introduced resolutions in the Senate and House that would have authorized the president to impose embargoes on trade with the Japanese. The dramatic events of the summer of 1939 ensued: on July 18 Senator Arthur H. Vandenberg presented his resolution proposing the termination of the Japanese-American commercial treaty of 1911; on July 26 the administration announced that the treaty would expire after the necessary six month interval. As one of the leading isolationists in Congress, Vandenberg was apparently motivated by a desire to pave the way for the negotiation of a new agreement that might improve relations between Japan and the United States. The administration, on its part, seems to have seized upon the Vandenberg proposal as a compromise solution that might appease the advocates of an embargo by partially meeting their demands.[56]

The treaty expired in January 1940, but the question of what to do next remained unanswered. On the one hand embargo resolutions were still pending in Congress; pressure groups were demanding embargoes; and, according to the polls, a large majority of the American people favored a ban on war materials to Japan. On the other hand, when Congress reopened at the beginning of the year, Senators Vandenberg and Borah urged the negotiation of a new treaty with Japan.[57]

It is evident that Griswold watched indications of an increasing American involvement in Europe and Asia with growing anxiety. He continued to believe that it was, in essence, the responsibility of the United States to stay out of war and to attend to its own development. In a paper on American naval policy delivered at a joint session of the American Historical Association and the American Military Institute in December 1939, in which he argued for a limited defensive navy, Griswold stated that no nation had "so much to lose or so little to gain" by waging a war as the United States.[58] With its "only conceivable enemies" engulfed in hostilities, with the protection accorded by its ocean barriers, with an abundance of everything that other nations fought for—raw materials, trade, *lebensraum*—the United States alone among nations was "in full possession of its destinies." The "foremost objective" of the American people was the "achievement of a sound and prosperous economy and an efficient self-government within their own borders"; it was this objective that the country should pursue.

Granted these views, Griswold still hoped that he could contribute to keeping the United States out of war in the Far East. He was particularly angered by the activities of the propagandists who, in his opinion, were attempting to incite a "mob crusade to save China."[59] As a consequence, as early as February 1939 he wrote Walter Lippmann suggesting that the United States and Japan might negotiate a settlement of their outstanding differences and outlining the terms he had in mind.[60] He repeated his proposal to Vandenberg in July after the senator had advanced his resolution proposing the termination of the commercial treaty.[61] In the winter of 1939, when it looked as though the efforts to pass an embargo might be renewed in Congress, Griswold wrote an article for *Asia* magazine urging the conclusion of a comprehensive Japanese-American agreement. The article, which was intended to start a public discussion, was circulated by the editors to some forty people, many of whose replies were published, ranging from Charles Beard's very positive reaction to Lin Yutang's outraged protest. In the February 1940 issue of *Asia* Griswold sought to rebut his critics by restating his position.[62]

Griswold's argument for a settlement between the United States and Japan was based on ideas he had long maintained. Fundamentally his contention was that the United States should accept the basic principle that a foreign policy must be founded not on "hazy emotionalism" but on a realistic appraisal of a country's needs. In accordance with this principle, it should recognize that its national interests in the Pacific were connected not with China but with Japan and should abandon its present policy which was tied as it had been throughout four decades to the illusory aims of the Open Door and the integrity of China. It should seek a rapproachement with Japan which, as the third largest naval power in the world, was a potential threat to the United States, especially in the period before Philippine independence.

The specific measures that Griswold suggested might be taken included the following: the negotiation of a trade treaty which would be extended to Manchukuo and the Japanese-controlled areas of China proper on condition that the Open Door be observed in those regions; a renewal of the nonaggression pledges of the Four Power Pact and of the nonfortification provisions of Article 19 of the Washington Naval Treaty, the latter to be reinforced by arrangements for a systematic inspection of the territories involved; settlement of the Alaskan fisheries dispute and reconsideration of the immigration problem; the issuance by the Japanese of a categorical renunciation of any political ambitions in regard to Latin America. In addition to these positive steps Griswold asserted that the United States should refrain, at least for the time being, from taking any action, whether pro or con, in regard to the recognition of Japan's "New Order" in East Asia. It was this point which, as much as any other, became the target of attacks from his critics. T. A. Bisson, a well-known Far Eastern specialist, in the main response representing the opposition's point of view remarked that a commercial treaty that included the Japanese occupied areas of China would in itself constitute "recognition of the 'New Order' with a vengeance."[63]

Events, however, cut short any further discussion of a treaty with Japan or, temporarily, even of an embargo. From the early spring of 1940 to the end of the year all thought on the part of the vast majority of Americans centered on Hitler's conquest of most of western Europe and his devastating attack on England. The president proceeded cautiously as he was uncertain how far the country was willing to go in intervening in the European war, which in practical terms meant aiding Great Britain as the first line of defense. In the late summer, however, he transacted the important destroyers-for-bases deal. In January 1940, as Great Britain, having withstood months of aerial bombardment, entered into a new but equally acute stage of its struggle for survival, Roosevelt took the crucial step of introducing his famous Lend-Lease bill into Congress.

The initial reaction of the American people to the German blitzkrieg was a feeling of near-panic that Hitler was about to launch an attack on the United States. Although the sense of fear diminished, the determination to withstand the Nazis grew until, by the time the president announced his Lend-Lease plan, 70 percent of the American people, according to the polls, supported unlimited aid to Great Britain even at the risk of war.[64]

Meanwhile the propaganda activities of both the interventionists and the noninterventionists intensified. In the early part of the summer William Allen White's Committee to Defend America by Aiding the Allies was formed and not only campaigned vigorously during the following months for all-out aid to Great Britain but in midwinter came close to endorsing United States entry into the war. In September the America First Committee was established and declared that it was unequivocally opposed to United States participation in the war and only favored aid to Great Britain on a restricted basis that would not interfere with America's own rearmament program or run the chance of involving the United States in the hostilities.[65]

Neither the White Committee nor America First paid much attention to the Far East, even after the conclusion of the Tripartite Pact and Japan's advance into northern Indochina. However, as the debate over Lend-Lease started, the White Committee began to veer toward advocating an embargo against all war materials to Japan and a naval agreement with the British which was to serve as a deterrent to a Japanese attack on Singapore and the Netherlands East Indies. At the same time America First announced that it was opposed to any action concerning Japan as the United States had "no conceivable stake in Asia" worth fighting for, nor any reason to quarrel with the Japanese.[66]

In the final stages of the isolationist-internationalist conflict, of which the controversy between the White Committee and America First was a part, most of the liberal intellectuals who, caught up in the disillusionment of the 1930s, had been highly critical of Roosevelt's foreign policy went over to the internationalist side after the beginning of the German blitzkrieg. A few, like Beard, held out to the end.[67] For Griswold the shift from nonintervention to intervention was far from easy.

In a long article entitled "Our Policy in the Far East," published in the August edition of *Harper's* and evidently written sometime after the start of the German invasion of western Europe, Griswold repeated his suggestion of a settlement with Japan.[68] Asserting that the Roosevelt administration, while committing itself to the allied cause in Europe, had alienated the Axis powers, the Soviet Union, and Japan simultaneously, he stated that it was high time for the United States to decide realistically what it could and could not do. Given the existing situation, he declared, it was more important than ever for the United States to stabilize its relations with the Japanese so that it could concentrate on the situation in Europe, where it had a far larger stake than in Asia. Recapitulating the historical record, Griswold returned to the thesis that the current policy of the United States in the Far East was designed to preserve the Open Door and the integrity of China and was simply an extension of the policy of futility it had maintained throughout the "past forty years."

As the European war continued, Griswold came to accept the view that it was of great importance to the security of the United States to keep Britain, especially the British navy, "out of German hands." Nevertheless he was opposed to Lend-Lease and to giving the British a "blank check of any kind, shape, or description." His objection, according to his own statement, was in part due to his deep-seated mistrust of the British and a feeling that the United States should not "endorse a restoration of British hegemony over all Europe or even the prolonged survival of the British imperial status quo." But it was even more the result of his strong belief that any American commitment to unlimited support of the British was essentially a commitment eventually to fight in the war, an idea he still rejected.[69]

As Griswold's correspondence of this period shows, his continued adherence to noninterventionism was based, as earlier, on the conviction that the first obligation of the United States, both to itself and to óther peoples, lay in the realization of its own promise. Immediately following the president's message presenting the Lend-Lease bill to Congress, in which Roosevelt tried to make clear the dangers of the international situation, Philip La Follette, one of the most prominent spokesmen of liberal isolationism, delivered a response in a national broadcast under the auspices of the America First Committee. Charging that the president was trying to frighten the American people into a war which, even granted all the horror of nazism, was not their war, he appealed to Roosevelt to renew the "sublime faith" in the country he had shown when he led it out of the depression and to return to the job of creating a nation such as had been envisioned by the men and women who founded it.[70] The following day Griswold wrote La Follette congratulating him on his speech as a "masterpiece" and stating that he himself had been a hundred percent behind the president until Roosevelt "abandoned the New Deal and launched forth into world politics."[71] A few weeks later, in a letter to a friend, Griswold suggested attempting to form a new national party to reaffirm the principles of the New Deal and combine them with a "foreign policy of non-intervention in Europe and Asia."[72]

At the same time Griswold felt the world situation was so "utterly chaotic" and so critical that it was hard to maintain any position with certainty. In the autumn he had promised to write a memorandum for the America First Committee, although he had consistently refused to join that organization, but in late January he said that he could not do so because events had moved with such rapidity that he was "frankly confused . . . as to exactly what course to believe in."[73] Ultimately, as Great Britain was hit by one disaster after another,

Griswold became convinced of the compelling necessity of providing the British with all possible assistance and consequently drew closer to the president's position.

In regard to the Far East, Griswold declared that he was so "perplexed as to the methods to pursue" that he was "not inclined to urge any particular policy on anyone."[74] Nevertheless, in the short period left before Pearl Harbor he published two more articles on American Far Eastern policy, one in the May issue of the *Annals* of the American Academy of Political and Social Science, the other in the autumn number of the *Virginia Quarterly Review*.[75] In these he stated that, in view of Japan's partnership in the Triple Alliance and its announced territorial ambitions, there was within the foreseeable future "no possibility whatever of a negotiated adjustment in American-Japanese relations" such as he had proposed earlier. On the other hand, Nazi Germany was a "far greater menace" to the security of the United States than Japan, therefore America's policy in the Far East should be totally subordinated to its policy in Europe, specifically to its efforts to strengthen British resistance. The objective of the United States in the Far East should be not an "undeclared war" but an "undeclared peace." In this respect Griswold also came closer to supporting the president, whom he believed held similar views.

Griswold's articles did not outlast the period in which they were written. But *The Far Eastern Policy of the United States* achieved an immediate success, which it has sustained to a remarkable degree over the years. As Robert Ferrell has remarked in a recent essay on "The Griswold Theory of Our Far Eastern Policy," although a growing monographic literature on American Far Eastern relations in the twentieth century has appeared and although the archives of most of the major governments involved have been opened for the period covered by Griswold and dozens of manuscript collections of private papers have been made available, "the ideas of Griswold continue on relatively unimpaired through university and college lectures and again in the pages of the texts and outside reading for undergraduates and graduates alike."[76]

V

In conclusion it should be said that it would indeed be lacking in appreciation not to recognize that the widespread approval of both Griswold's and Dennett's writings has been well-founded. Their books undoubtedly marked a major advance in the study of American policy in East Asia. Nevertheless it is felt that their overall interpretation of the Far Eastern policy of the United States has been accepted with too little question. Granted the crucial events of the interwar years and the extent of their emotional involvement, it was not only human but perhaps inevitable for them to see a meaning in the past that had a strong message for the present. However, as I have tried to make clear throughout this paper, I believe that, in fact, their interpretation was better able to convey such a message than to provide a genuine understanding of the complexities of the history of American policy in the Far East.

Seen in a historiographical context, it is evident that in their approach to the writing of history Dennett and Griswold were far apart. Trained at a time when the scientific tradition still predominated in historical scholarship, Dennett was a scientific historian par excellence. In contrast Griswold, who undertook his graduate studies some ten years later, when the views of men such as Becker and Beard prevailed, was preeminently a progressive historian who also drew upon the findings of the political scientists of his day. Yet in the last analysis their ideas about the writing of history did not prove as decisive a factor for either Dennett or Griswold as their reactions to contemporary events.

* * *

The following is a list of Dennett's and Griswold's writings used in connection with this paper.

I. TYLER DENNETT

a.   Dennett Papers: Dennett's papers are in the possession of his family at Hague, New York. They consist largely of personal letters from Dennett (mostly dated from 1936), records of his trips abroad, speeches, miscellaneous memoranda, and some documentary and other materials collected for his books.

b.   Books:
The Democratic Movement in Asia. Association Press, 1918.
A Better World. George H. Doran, 1920.
Americans in Eastern Asia. Macmillan, 1922.
Roosevelt and the Russo-Japanese War. Doubleday, Page, 1925.

c.   Articles, essays, and speeches:
Articles on the Far East in *The World Outlook* of May, August, September, November 1915; April, July, September 1916.
"How Old is American Policy in the Far East?" *Pacific Review*, 1921.
"American Good Offices in Asia," *American Journal of International Law*, January 1922.
"Seward's Far Eastern Policy," *American Historical Review*, October 1922.
"Early American Policy in Korea," *Political Science Quarterly*, March 1923.
"American Policy in the Far East, *Current History*, July 1923.
Introduction to M. J. Bau's *The Open Door Doctrine*. Macmillan, 1923.
"American Choices in the Far East in 1882," *American Historical Review*, October 1924.
"Open Door Policy as Intervention," *Annals* of the American Academy of Political and Social Science, July 1933.
Articles on the Far East in every issue of *Current History* from October 1932 to July 1934.
"The Open Door," in Joseph Barnes, ed., *Empire in the East*. Doubleday, Doran, 1934.
Speeches during the years Dennett was president of Williams College (1934-37).

"Prejudices and Convictions," *Vital Speeches*, September 23, 1935.

"Mahan's 'The Problem of Asia,'" *Foreign Affairs,* April 1935.

"Why Bother About Japan?" *Current History*, February 1936.

"Alternative American Policies in the Far East," *Foreign Affairs,* April 1938.

"Japan's 'Monroe Doctrine' Appraised," *Annals* of the American Academy of Political and Social Science, May 1941.

"Security in the Pacific and the Far East: A Memorandum on Certain American Immediate Postwar Responsibilities," American Council, Institute of Pacific Relations, Mont Tremblant Conference, Data Paper, 1942.

II. A. WHITNEY GRISWOLD

a.   Griswold Papers: The Griswold papers are in the Yale University Library. They contain Griswold's personal correspondence (far more voluminous than that in the Dennett files), lecture notes, drafts of articles, memoranda, etc. One extremely interesting item is the first draft of *The Far Eastern Policy of the United States*, which is interspersed with voluminous comments by the senior members of the Yale Institute of International Studies to whom it was submitted for publication. The Yale Library also has Griswold's Ph.D. dissertation, "The American Gospel of Success."

b.   Books:
The Far Eastern Policy of the United States. Harcourt, Brace, 1938.

c.   Articles and essays:
Articles in *Events* of January, May, June, July, August, September 1937.

"Conflicts in Our Far Eastern Policy," *Yale Review*, Winter 1937.

"Facing Facts About a New Japanese-American Treaty," *Asia,* November 1939.

"The Influence of History Upon Sea Power," *American Military Institute Journal*, Spring 1940.

"Should Japan Be Embargoed?" *Asia,* February 1940.

"Our Policy in the Far East," *Harper's*, August 1940.

"European Factors in Far Eastern Diplomacy," *Foreign Affairs*, January 1941.

"Paving the Way for Hitler," *Atlantic,* March 1941.

"An Undeclared Peace?" *Annals* of the American Academy of Political and Social Science, May 1941.

"Perspective on Far Eastern Policy," *Virginia Quarterly Review*, Autumn 1941.

"The Future in American Foreign Relations," in Allan Nevins and Louis M. Hacker, eds., *The United States and Its Place in World Affairs, 1918-1943*. D. C. Heath, 1943.

"Headstone to History," *Far Eastern Survey*, August 23, 1944.

CHANGES IN JAPAN'S INTERNATIONAL POSITION AND THE RESPONSE OF JAPANESE INTELLECTUALS: TRENDS IN JAPANESE STUDIES OF JAPAN'S FOREIGN RELATIONS, 1931-1941

Mitani Taichirō

Translated by G. Cameron Hurst

This paper deals with the scholarly works and other writings on contemporary events published by influential Japanese specialists in international relations during the period from the outbreak of the Manchurian crisis to the beginning of the Pacific War. The term "specialists in international relations" should be interpreted in a very broad sense as including a wide range of disciplines. Moreover, while some of the books and articles are academic studies, others are limited to expressions of political opinion. It was felt that by exploring a wide range of publications it might be possible to throw some light upon the response of Japanese intellectuals, especially those who were members of the academic community, to the changes in Japan's international position in the decade from 1931 to 1941.

The most important problem for those who specialized in international relations was, of course, the question of China. Academic research on this question passed through two distinct phases. From the clash at Mukden to the Marco Polo Bridge Incident interest centered primarily on the causes of the Manchurian crisis, its effects upon Japan's foreign relations, and the legitimacy of the newly created state of Manchukuo. After the outbreak of hostilities in 1937 a wider concern developed that included first the "north China question," then all of China, and ultimately the "New Order in East Asia" which, it was thought, would be established as a result of the Sino-Japanese War.

The first part of this paper deals with studies of the Manchurian Incident and its aftermath, up to 1937. I have attempted to analyze the different approaches used by scholars in different disciplines and to explore the extent to which their writings influenced later thinking. The second part focuses on works related to the changes that took place following the outbreak of the Sino-Japanese War as Japan's involvement on the continent gradually deepened and extended not only over most of China but even into Southeast Asia.

It must be recognized, however, that any analysis of the writings on foreign policy in the 1931-41 period involves certain hazards. One difficulty is that, as they are concerned with contemporary events, they inevitably suffer from a lack of primary sources, which for the most part were not available at the time. While this unquestionably limits their academic value, the important point for our purposes is not *what* sources of information a given author used but *how* he used them.

Another problem arises from the restrictions that were placed upon academic freedoms, particularly on the freedom of expression, which affected all scholars in the years before the war. For example, in his *Nihon gaikōshi* (A Diplomatic History of Japan), Kiyosawa Kiyoshi, a representative liberal, said:

> In attempting to describe the Manchurian Incident and subsequent developments . . . there exists no calm atmosphere in which to write history simply as history. . . . It is extremely difficult to present fairly both Chinese and Japanese claims. How much more impossible it is to analyze and criticize freely! . . . Under such circumstances the most an author can do is to set forth the very best "facts" within the limits permissible![1]

In analyzing studies produced under such conditions, it is essential to remain constantly alert to any reflections of the author's opinion, which may appear in even the most factual presentations, and to try to sense where complex implications were intended in what may seem to be a simple statement.

I

Among those who reacted most strongly to the Manchurian question as it developed soon after the Manchurian Incident were those scholars who were experts in international law. They had been proceeding on the assumption that there existed a world order centered in the League of Nations and based on the treaty system devised at the Versailles and Washington conferences. As a consequence they were genuinely shocked by the Manchurian Incident and the subsequent creation of Manchukuo, events that obviously constituted a fundamental challenge to such a world order. The basic problem that confronted this particular group of experts was how to deal with the Manchurian crisis within the generally accepted framework of international law. Eventually most of them took the position that the Mukden Incident, the ensuing actions of the Japanese military, and the recognition of Manchukuo did not violate the existing international legal order as embodied in the League covenant, the Nine Power Treaty, and the Kellogg-Briand Pact. For example, Tachi Sakutarō, a professor of international law at Tokyo Imperial University, was of the opinion that the encounters between Japanese and Chinese troops after the Mukden Incident did not constitute "war" in the legal sense, as no declaration of war, no ultimatum, and no expressed intention to begin hostilities had been made by either Japan or China. (The latter did not adopt such measures out of fear that Japan would expand its military action.) Japan had, therefore, not violated the first article of the Kellogg-Briand Pact which renounced the use of "war as an instrument of national policy."[2]

Tachi further viewed the actions of the Japanese military in Manchuria as, in international legal terms, an exercise of the right of self-defense against an imminent violation of Japan's interests. In other words, he did not interpret the fighting in Manchuria as an attempt to settle a dispute between countries and consequently concluded that it was not a breach of Article 2 of the Kellogg-Briand Pact prohibiting the settlement of international disputes by nonpeaceful means, nor of Article 12 of the League covenant forbidding resort to force without having exhausted all peaceful measures.[3] He also argued that as Japan had acted in self-defense, it was absolved of any international responsibility for the developments that ensued, specifically the creation of Manchukuo. Moreover, he contended that Manchukuo had come into being as the result of a "spontaneous independence movement" among the people of the area and that recognition of Manchukuo therefore did not violate the pledge in Article 1 of the Nine Power Treaty to respect the independence and integrity of China and provide it with the opportunity to effect its political stability.[4] Tachi never departed from these views and continued to emphasize in particular that the right of self-defense took precedence over all other international obligations.[5]

Tachi's attempt to rationalize the fait accompli in Manchuria is characteristic of the reaction of most Japanese scholars of international law in the years before the war. For example, Shinobu Junpei in his *Man-Mō tokushu ken'ekiron* (A Treatise on Special Interests in Manchuria and Mongolia), which was greatly influenced by C. Walter Young's *Japan's Jurisdiction and International Legal Position in Manchuria* (3 vols., 1931), tried to clarify the historical and legal character of these "special interests." In doing so he rejected the view that they were unlimited and stressed the necessity of defining their legal basis as clearly as possible. But at the same time he asserted that since nothing but an appeal to the right of self-defense could guarantee its interests in Manchuria, Japan had been justified in claiming that its actions were based on that right and were therefore legitimate.[6]

Another professor at Tokyo Imperial University, Kamikawa Hikomatsu, a diplomatic historian, said that Manchuria was an "international buffer area" (*kokusai chūkan chiiki*) and claimed that Japan should receive a mandate from the League of Nations to control it.[7] Thus he too attempted to create a legal fiction in an effort to reconcile the Japanese fait accompli in Manchuria with the existing international legal order.

In contrast, Yokota Kisaburō, Tachi's successor at Tokyo Imperial University, was one of those who opposed the general trend among scholars of international law. Arguing from the standpoint of Kelsen's theory of pure legalism (*reine Rechtslehre*),[8] he denied their rationalizations of Japan's actions and questioned whether it could properly be claimed that the acts of the Japanese military in Manchuria were measures of "self-defense." He maintained that any such claim was decidedly doubtful if, after the clash at Mukden, the Chinese forces did not in fact constitute a threat and the Japanese army decided to begin hostilities and occupy Manchuria merely because the Chinese railway guards in the vicinity of Mukden outnumbered the Japanese.[9] Immediately after the Mukden Incident Yokota favored the intervention undertaken by the League, believing that the Manchurian crisis was a "threat of war" as envisaged in Article 11 of the covenant. In the succeeding weeks he thought that the Council of the League acted quite appropriately when it urged both Japan and China to end the hostilities and asked Japan to withdraw its troops from the occupied areas in order "to safeguard the peace of nations." He believed that Japan should comply with the League's requests and open negotiations with China and that, even if such negotiations failed, Japan should not again resort to the use of arms. As time went by Yokota felt increasingly that the continued expansion of Japan's military operations, in disregard of the League's protests, violated the Kellogg-Briand Pact, the Nine Power Treaty, and the League covenant and would ultimately destroy the very basis of the existing international order. The creation of Manchukuo and its subsequent recognition by Japan seemed to him further violations of international law.

While Yokota thus raised questions, the restrictions upon freedom of speech that prevailed at the time did not permit him to make any direct replies. He supplied some indirect answers, however, by postulating the legal principle that when a region or subdivision attempts to secede from a state, any action by another state in support of the secession would be intervention in the internal affairs of the first state and therefore a violation of general international law. Further, he asserted that even when secession took place under these circumstances, as long as it was likely that the seceded area would be restored to the original state should the third party cease its assistance, it would be a violation of international law for any nation to recognize the seceded area. Again, he argued that this type of action was an intervention in internal affairs. In addition he pointed out that both instances would constitute a breach of Article 10 of the covenant, which required its signatories to respect the territorial integrity and political independence of all members of the League.[10]

Yokota's position regarding the Manchurian question was also reflected in his evaluation of the Stimson Doctrine, which declared that the United States would not recognize any situation, treaty, or agreement created in violation of the Kellogg-Briand Pact. Yokota stressed the importance of the doctrine, for he believed, first, that it would supplement and strengthen the Kellogg-Briand Pact and, second, that a refusal to recognize any situation brought about by nonpeaceful means would encourage the upholding of the principles of international law. He therefore welcomed the trend toward codification of the doctrine into international law through such measures as its incorporation in League resolutions.[11] Yokota's endorsement of the Stimson Doctrine, with its strong emphasis upon the maintenance of the existing international legal order, also derived from pure legalism, upon which he based his interpretation of international law. His position was an exceptional one, however, and as the Manchurian crisis continued to expand, he became more and more isolated. In a review of *Jikyoku kokusaihōron* (International Law and the Current Situation) by his teacher Tachi Sakutarō, Yokota frankly pointed out that "scholars of foreign relations and international law who had praised the League of Nations and generally supported internationalism made a complete about-face when pressure was applied to limit freedom of speech after the Manchurian Incident, and not a few of them began to preach nationalism and criticize the League."[12]

Faith in the unity and predominance of the international legal order began to crumble after the Manchurian Incident, and it became fashionable to attach greater legal importance to national rights and interests. In the process a "*Grossraum* international law" evolved, based upon theories such as Carl Schmitt's *konkrete Ordnung.*

The Manchurian issue was also one of the main subjects in the writings of a number of political scientists who were deeply concerned with the China question. In his study of the Chinese revolution Yoshino Sakuzō consistently displayed a genuine understanding of and sympathy for Chinese nationalism. A year before the Manchurian Incident, in the conclusion of his *Tai-Shi mondai* (The China Question), Yoshino urged a reevaluation of Japan's policy toward China, stating:

> Our four hundred million neighbors, who in just seventeen or eighteen years since the revolution have made such progress in developing the great Chinese nation, can surely not be called incompetent. . . . Has not previous Japanese policy wholly ignored China's capacity to grow and to shape its own future? . . . We must return to the point from which we started and entirely reconstruct our view of China.[13]

The Manchurian Incident ran completely counter to the policy that Yoshino had been advocating, and he immediately expressed publicly his opposition to the actions of the Japanese military, saying that they could in no way be dismissed as acts of self-defense, since their purpose was to attain for Japan rights that were in dispute and to expand its security perimeter. He made it quite plain that in his judgment a course such as that which the military was pursuing could only be called imperialism.[14] He further voiced his regret at the lack of free criticism of the Manchurian Incident in Japan and deplored in particular the readiness of the press and certain factions in the proletarian parties to applaud the dispatch of troops to China.[15] But Yoshino was never able to develop his ideas further, for he soon became fatally ill and died.

About the time of Yoshino's death Rōyama Masamichi, a professor of public administration at Tokyo Imperial University, made his debut as a scholar of foreign relations and, as if succeeding to Yoshino's position, began to publish articles concerning the Manchurian question. Rōyama's basic thesis was that Japan had a "special position" in Manchuria which other nations must recognize.[16] He did not believe that this "special position" was merely a matter of Japan's economic interests in Manchuria being larger than those of other countries, nor did he think that it could be understood purely in terms of international law as C. Walter Young had analyzed it.[17] In the first place, Rōyama said, given the level of development of Manchurian society, international law could be applied only to certain aspects of the region.[18] Secondly, the foreign relations of Manchuria were governed not by legal considerations but by the concrete conditions existing in the area. The relationship between Japan and Manchuria was so close that Manchuria had to be regarded as an inseparable part of Japan's problem of national defense and national survival, as had been indicated in the official statement issued at the time of the conclusion of the Japan-Manchukuo Protocol.[19] Such a relationship could not be determined by general international law and treaties, which in any event constituted only a segment of international relations. It was in fact precisely the gap between law and reality that had created the Manchurian issue, and the solution lay not in interpreting the law in its present form but in changing it.[20]

Although he stressed the concept of Japan's "special position" in Manchuria, Rōyama was careful to qualify this idea. Writing in 1933 he warned against the narrow-minded isolationist-oriented nationalism that had developed in Japan since the Manchurian Incident and expressed the fear that relations with other countries would be sacrificed if Japan overplayed its "special position" in Manchuria. He was convinced that, even though Japan was currently in a nationalistic phase, it should not abandon internationalism and that, irrespective of all talk about Japan's "special position" in Manchuria, neither its "special position" nor Manchukuo itself could survive without international recognition. He contended that the Manchurian problem ought to be settled in cooperation with the League[21] and argued, in opposition to the popular demand for a Japan-Manchukuo economic bloc, that Japan could not sever its ties with the world economy.[22] Furthermore, by emphasizing the uniqueness of the Manchurian question, Rōyama made a distinction between Japan's policy toward Manchuria and toward China and, with all the power at his command, urged that Japan's "special position" be restricted to Manchuria.[23]

Yet despite his insistence upon internationalism, Rōyama was aware that the fires of nationalism that had been lit by the Manchurian Incident and Japan's withdrawal from the League could not be wholly extinguished. A solution somewhere between universal internationalism and nationalism had to be found,[24] and Rōyama sought it in what he called "regionalism." He tried to find a stronghold for Japan within the framework of a peace system that, in contrast to the League of Nations, would be established on a regional rather than a worldwide basis. Even after Japan withdrew from the League, he felt it should preserve a relationship with that body and consequently advocated the formation of a "Far Eastern regional organization of the League of Nations."[25] Kamikawa Hikomatsu similarly claimed that "even though Japan has withdrawn from the League of Nations in Geneva, it has certainly not abandoned the principles of the League," and he suggested that Japan "apply League principles to the Far Eastern area and create a Far Eastern League of Nations."[26] It is worth noting that Royama's and Kamikawa's "regionalism," originally intended to serve as an intermediary between universal internationalism and nationalism, was reinforced by the "geopolitik" imported from Nazi Germany and eventually developed into a new political ideology to justify Japanese advances on the continent after the Marco Polo Bridge Incident.

Rōyama, it will be recalled, also considered Chinese nationalism an important factor limiting Japan's "special position" in Manchuria. Looking at the situation in China in the light of Japan's historical experience as a non-Western nation, he seems to have been genuinely sympathetic toward the demands of Chinese nationalists for control of Manchuria. "If we say the Manchuria-Mongolia region is a lifeline and a strategic area for the Japanese," he declared, "the Chinese today can use the same argument."[27] And as for the anti-Japanese policy of the Chinese government, he asked:

Is this sort of policy peculiar to the Chinese government today? I hardly think so. I think it is a development of the "Asian revolt against the West" which originated in the *sonnō jōi* [revere the emperor, expel the barbarian] movement at the time of the Meiji Restoration in Japan. Sun Yat-sen's plan for creating a nation can be seen as mixing traditional Chinese thought with the ideas of Yoshida Shōin and the strategy of Lenin. Thus, when we try to decide how to deal with the strategies of the Chinese politicians today, we must look back at the history of our own country.[28]

Rōyama fully recognized the cultural identity of Manchuria and China.[29] It was partly because of this identity that he felt that, if the special relations between Japan and Manchuria were to be established on a firm basis, it would be necessary to counteract the appeal of Chinese nationalism by creating a regionalism that would transcend any nationalism. This regionalism he defined in political rather than cultural terms, in the belief that if Manchuria were to be effectively divided from China, it must be through the establishment there of an "efficient and just government, one with no corruption."[30] To effect such a government he favored an oligarchy or a dictatorship rather than a democracy. In short, he believed that in Manchuria political *results* were more important than political *process*, and therefore he did not hesitate to advocate that Japan intervene and assume responsibility for leadership in the area. Rōyama's concept of regionalism thus suggested a means of deflecting the mounting nationalistic spirit in Japan, checking the expansive nationalism of China, and, after the outbreak of the Sino-Japanese War, establishing Japan's "New Order."[31]

There were others besides Rōyama who urged after the Manchurian Incident that Japanese foreign policy be directed toward the creation of a new international framework based upon "regionalism." One was Kajima Morinosuke, who became a diplomatic historian after a career in the Foreign Ministry. To Kajima the "origins" of the Manchurian Incident were to be found in the Washington Conference. In his opinion "the greatest threat to peace in East Asia at the present moment is neither the nationalist movement in China nor the problem of Japan's exercise of its right of self-defense. It lies rather in the unsound peace system fashioned at the Washington Conference out of visionary, idealistic assumptions."[32] Kajima therefore stressed that the most important objective for so-called "peace advocates" should be the revision of the Washington system. He charged in particular that the policy of noninterference in China, the heart of the Nine Power Treaty, was untenable, being based upon the false premise that the Chinese people possessed the ability for democratic self-rule.[33]

In addressing himself to the question of how the Washington system should be revised, Kajima took much the same position as Rōyama and Kamikawa. On the one hand he believed in nationalism and a diplomacy based on national alliances; but on the other hand he did not want to scrap the legacy of internationalism left from the era of the First World War.[34] Therefore, he too formulated what he termed a "new peace system," to be organized in accordance with the principle of regionalism. Kajima found the theoretical basis for his ideas in the pan-Europeanism of Codenhove-Kalergi, which he applied to Asia as "pan-Asianism."[35] Pointing to the recognition of the Monroe Doctrine in Article 21 of the League of Nations covenant as a precedent, he proposed a regional organization of the League. Within the "new peace system" that was to emerge out of this organization, Japan was by common agreement to be the "stabilizing power" charged with the maintenance of peace in East Asia.[36] This amounted to a confirmation of Japan's "special position" vis-à-vis Manchuria and China. Thus Kajima, like Rōyama and Kamikawa, attempted to deal with the Manchurian problem within the context of international law by proposing a regional system that would allow for Japan's "special position" in East Asia.

Another writer, Yanaihara Tadao, a professor of colonial policy at Tokyo Imperial University, took an entirely different approach. Roundly attacking Japanese activities in Manchuria, he criticized Japan's entire colonial policy in terms of the theories of imperialism advanced by J. A. Hobson and R. Hilferding.[37] In a series of lectures given at the university upon his return from a trip to Manchuria in 1932,[38] he openly expressed his dissent from the government's policy in Manchuria. "What I have to offer in these lectures is neither data nor statistics," he declared. "It is simply the spirit of criticism, because the greatest danger of blindness lies in a lack of criticism."[39] Yanaihara's criterion for judging Japan's colonial policy in general and its Manchurian policy in particular was political and economic "rationality." He questioned whether in political terms Japan's policy would not run counter to the inevitable rise of Chinese nationalism and whether in economic terms it was not opposed to the theory of capitalism. In sum, Yanaihara attempted to undertake a "scholarly inquiry into and criticism of" Japan's course in Manchuria as related to Chinese nationalism and the principles of capitalism.[40]

Yanaihara concluded that Japan's "special position" in Manchuria was political in the sense that Japan demanded privileges that infringed upon China's sovereignty and prevented the free exercise of authority by the Chinese government. As a result, the threat to Japan's interests in Manchuria arose not from the economic competition of the powers but rather from the political opposition of the Chinese, which was in itself an expression of Chinese nationalism.

Yanaihara rejected the official interpretation that Manchukuo was "an expression of the desires of the people in the northeast" whose interests were quite different from those of China proper.[41] On the contrary, he argued that Manchurian interests were in reality inseparable from the rest of China and that the development of Chinese nationalism in the region was in the long run inevitable. He tacitly suggested that even the Mukden government had better served the interests of China, including Manchuria, than the new government of Manchukuo, a "hothouse of graft" that ran counter to the rising tide of nationalism. "Neither Chang Tso-lin nor Chang Hsueh-liang," he wrote, "could check or resist the current of modern nationalism, and they had no alternative but to ride with the current in order to protect their own position."[42] Certain of their policies, which on the surface might seem opposed to Chinese nationalism, actually served to strengthen it. For example, the expansion of armaments, in addition to providing employment, was the first step toward local industrialization, which provided an economic basis for nationalism and, furthermore, strengthened the Chinese in their struggle against the Japanese.[43] Likewise the inflation policy, which aimed at providing funds to support the military program, strengthened the Mukden forces to resist the Japanese invaders.[44] In addition, the fact that more than 110,000 people had chosen to link their fate with Chang Hsueh-liang's regime by fleeing Manchukuo, Yanaihara charged, raised doubts as to the spontaneity of the independence movement that had led to the establishment of Manchukuo.[45]

Calling upon Japan to reverse its policies in the region and support Chinese nationalism, Yanaihara declared that "the foundation of Japan's China policy must lie in aiding in the creation of a modern, unified Chinese nation."[46] To him this was a political rather than a moral issue for, in his own words, "without the unification of China, Japan will not prosper, and as long as there is anti-Japanese sentiment in China, there will be no good fortune for Japan."[47] Consequently, Japan's policy toward Manchuria was merely a politically irrational attempt to stem the inevitable growth and eventual triumph of Chinese nationalism.

In economic terms, Yanaihara's criticism of Japan's course in Manchuria derived from a rational consideration of the principles of capitalism. He was opposed to dealing with overpopulation in Japan by encouraging emigration to Manchuria[48] on the grounds that socio-economic conditions in Manchuria made it unsuitable for Japanese migration. Japanese farmers were used to a higher standard of living than the Manchurians, and unless they could lower their production costs through mechanization, their prices would not be competitive. Large areas of Manchuria were without railroads, and in these regions the industrial conditions for mechanization simply did not exist. Mechanization was also a necessary prerequisite for Japanese industrial laborers in Manchuria; but even if this were carried out, Yanaihara doubted that the replacement of Manchurian and Chinese labor by Japanese with a higher standard of living would lower production costs. Yanaihara therefore placed great importance upon the role of the Chinese labor force in both agriculture and industry in Manchuria and believed it impossible for Japanese immigrants to compete successfully with them.

Yanaihara also criticized on economic grounds the idea of a Japanese-Manchurian economic bloc that aimed at economic self-sufficiency. He pointed out that such a policy was unworkable as a foreign trading venture since Manchukuo accounted for only 7 percent of Japan's exports and 8 percent of its imports. Obviously Japan depended upon areas of the world other than Manchuria both as markets for its exports and as sources of raw materials. No matter how much Manchuria were to develop economically, he was of the opinion that a completely self-sufficient Japanese-Manchurian economic bloc was probably impossible. He took sharp issue additionally with the military's argument that in the event of an economic blockade during wartime Manchuria could be an adequate source of supply for raw materials essential to military production. Rather, under such circumstances an economic bloc would impose a heavy burden on Japan's finances.[49] Thus he concluded that Japan could not afford to sacrifice its relations with the rest of the world, and with the Chinese in particular, because of its exaggerated concern over Manchuria.[50]

Finally, Yanaihara criticized the economic rationality of a controlled Manchurian economy as the nucleus of a Japanese-Manchurian economic bloc.[51] For a society at Manchuria's low level of economic development, he contended, the formation of monopoly enterprises in heavy industries, such as mining and railroads, was not feasible and a merging of Japanese and Manchurian enterprises, which were economically and technologically dissimilar, would either result in a sacrifice on Manchuria's part for Japan's benefit or force Japan to lower its production for Manchuria's sake. In either case, he maintained, such a union would not bring about an increase in productivity (or what he called "rationalization") in the way that trusts did in highly developed capitalist societies. Moreover, Manchukuo was in principle an "independent country"; its industry would not necessarily supplement Japan's but might very well be parallel and competitive. In fact, military needs might actually demand parallel and potentially competitive industries in Manchuria, even though they violated the concept of an integrated economic bloc.

Yanaihara argued further that from a purely economic standpoint the idea of a planned economy had many irrational aspects. It was intended to benefit the military, but military and economic considerations were not necessarily compatible. For example, in deciding where immigrants should settle and railroads should be built, military and economic considerations frequently conflicted. At the conclusion of his critique he warned: "We must consider whether a Manchurian policy that makes Japan's economic survival contingent on Manchuria will not, in the end, lead to Japan's economic destruction."[52]

How then did Yanaihara view the China situation after the creation of Manchukuo? He had already criticized Japan's Manchuria policy as running counter to the inevitable rise of nationalism and capitalism in China and believed further that it was a "socially inevitable fact" that Nanking, supported by the Chekiang financial cliques that were the "nucleus of Chinese capitalism," would promote capitalism in China and bring about the creation of a modern, unified nation. Therefore, in dealing with the Nanking government Japan should recognize

> ... that China is a country on the road to national unification. Only a China policy based upon recognition of this fact will be scientifically correct. In the long run only a policy that supports the national unification of the Chinese people will be beneficial to Japan and China as well as promote peace in the Far East. If Japan pursues a policy running counter to the inevitable unification and capitalistic development of China, the consequences will be conflict, bloodshed, and great suffering for the peoples of China, Japan, and other parts of the Far East for many generations to come.[53]

Yanaihara's critical essays and lectures on the China War aroused the displeasure of the government. As a consequence, he was forced to resign from the university at the end of 1937 and was silenced.[54] Nevertheless, although the Kuomintang did not create the modern Chinese nation he had predicted, Yanaihara's prophecies of Japan's self-destruction were amply substantiated by subsequent events.

II

As the hostilities spread across China after the outbreak of the China War, the fait accompli in Manchuria was gradually accepted as an unchangeable fact even in academic circles. Yanaihara, Yokota, and others who had regarded the Manchurian problem as part of the larger China problem and had tried to deal with it in a spirit of internationalism and with due recognition of rising Chinese nationalism lost ground and were forced into silence by political pressures threatening their positions in the university.[55] But that was not all. Those who, in an effort to soften the collision between the post-World War I peace system and Japanese national policy, had interpreted the Manchurian Incident as an atypical event—the group that had been a majority in the academic world—now became a minority. For the majority, Manchuria was no longer an exception but rather the first step in an expansionist policy that was to include all of China and eventually the entire region of East Asia, including Southeast Asia. Most academic writing on Japanese foreign relations after 1937 supported the concept of a "New Order" and attempted to bolster it with convincing arguments. Let us first examine this tendency more concretely as it was manifested in the field of diplomatic history.

One writer who, in order to preserve the legacy of internationalism in Japan, continued to argue that Manchuria was an exception was the diplomatic historian Kiyosawa Kiyoshi. In Kiyosawa's view, expressed in a book published in 1942,[56] it was the military that had altered the course of Japanese foreign policy after the Manchurian Incident, and within the limits of freedom of expression permissible at the time, he criticized what he perceived to be the military's tendency to make Japan into an enemy of the international legal order. "Since the Manchurian Incident, and particularly since the China Incident," he claimed, "there has been no Japanese foreign policy."[57] By foreign policy he meant "Shidehara diplomacy," which had as its frame of reference the League covenant and the Washington treaties. He believed that as the domestic and international political conditions that had made Shidehara diplomacy possible disappeared, Japanese foreign policy had become subordinate to military affairs.

In criticizing the foreign ministers who succeeded Shidehara, Kiyosawa did so only indirectly. For example, he wrote that Tanaka's foreign policy, the antithesis of Shidehara diplomacy, lacked "a proper understanding of Chinese nationalism."[58] He declared that it was a "historical tragedy" that Uchida Yasuya, who had been foreign minister when Japan joined the League and who had signed the Washington treaties, was unfortunate enough to be foreign minister when Japan withdrew from the League.[59] The favorable response to the diplomatic appointments of Foreign Minister Matsuoka Yōsuke, who had swept the Anglo-American group out of the Foreign Ministry in 1940, Kiyosawa satirized as "reflecting the current trend of thought which applauds decisive action regardless of its content."[60]

Kiyosawa expressed his sympathy for Shidehara's foreign policy in a more direct manner in his evaluation of the Washington Conference, which Shidehara had attended as Japan's ambassador plenipotentiary, and of the London Conference during which Shidehara had been foreign minister. Kiyosawa regarded the agreement on naval armaments and the Four Power Treaty concluded at the Washington Conference as having been "diplomatic victories" for Japan.[61] He wrote:

Japan has been guaranteed by international agreement at least sufficient military power for its defense. Expert opinion holds that a successful attack upon Japan would require a naval strength twice that of Japan's. Japan has, however, achieved a 10:6 ratio vis-à-vis the United States and Great Britain and has been promised that those countries will not expand their fortified naval bases in the western Pacific.[62]

The Nine Power Treaty, Kiyosawa stated, may have been a victory for American diplomacy in the sense that it embodied the Open Door policy, but "whether or not this treaty will achieve the results desired by the United States depends on Japan's good will."[63] The real power on the Chinese continent, he believed, was Japan, not the United States, and although Japan had had to accept a Far Eastern order designed by the United States, what Japan had conceded was "not absolutely essential" to it.[64] He felt that Japan could extend its power within the framework of the Washington system.

Kiyosawa also approved of the results of the London Naval Conference, which was in a sense an extension of the Washington Conference. According to him, fixing Japan's ratio of auxiliary ships at 70 percent of America's had been "a compromise that ought to be recognized as the best possible under the conditions of the time."[65]

Although Kiyosawa supported the Washington system and the Shidehara diplomacy based on it, he nevertheless considered it extremely unfortunate that the conference had not dealt with the Manchurian problem. He blamed the United States for this, writing that "America was overly concerned with preserving the status quo and was unprepared to cope with the reality of China and Japan's development. Subsequent events are probably a good indication that the treaty was not based upon reality."[66] A principal cause of the Manchurian Incident, he charged, was America's "overly idealistic view of China's capability," an idealism that had been embodied in the Nine Power Treaty, as in the Paris Pact, and had encouraged the Chinese to assert national rights that were without "firm underpinnings."[67]

Kiyosawa also criticized American foreign policy as "legalistic"[68] in refusing to acknowledge the new situation that existed in Manchuria after the Manchurian Incident. Because of this legalistic attitude, he asserted, America was trying to force upon East Asia an international legal order based upon the principles of the Open Door policy and, in consequence, had committed "errors" of the type symbolized by Hull's rejection of Nomura's proposed modus vivendi in November 1941. Thus, while he did not argue for the acceptance of *every* fait accompli beginning with the Manchurian Incident, Kiyosawa advocated international recognition of the existing state of affairs in Manchuria. He therefore praised the report of the Lytton Commission for acknowledging the "special conditions" in Manchuria and criticized Japanese public opinion for failing to pay reasonable attention to the report and hindering resolution of the Manchurian problem.[69]

Although Kiyosawa was unusually outspoken in his criticism of Japanese foreign policy, his criticism of America's Far Eastern policy was echoed by many of his colleagues during the 1937-41 period. One example is Takagi Yasaka, a professor of American politics and foreign policy at Tokyo Imperial University, who traced the historical development of the Open Door policy in his *Beikoku tōyō seisaku no shiteki kōsatsu* (A Historical Analysis of American Far Eastern Policy).[70] The Open Door policy, Takagi maintained, had been formulated at the end of the nineteenth century in an effort to prevent the break-up of China and was not applicable to conditions in China after 1937 when Western imperialism was being liquidated.[71]

On the other hand, while Kiyosawa criticized the "legalism" of American policy, he placed high value upon the "realism" of British foreign policy. He contended that because Britain had a better appreciation of Japan's strength, it did not go along with the Stimson Doctrine but was more willing to accept Japan's policy in Manchuria.[72] This realistic estimate of Japan's strength also explained why Britain felt the Far Eastern problem had to be resolved jointly by Japan, Britain, and the United States, Britain's role being to enforce "mutual restraint" on the part of America, the League, and Japan.[73] This suggested to him that had the negotiations been conducted mainly between Japan and Great Britain instead of Japan and the United States, the results would perhaps have been different.[74]

Throughout his writing Kiyosawa argued that Britain's balance of power policy in Europe should serve as a model for Japan's policy in China. In the diary he kept during the war he anticipated Japan's defeat and wrote:

> ... it would have been wise for Japan to have adopted toward the Asian mainland a balance of power policy, somewhat like Britain's European policy, to deal with the collision that was bound to occur among the powers there. Japan's greatest mistake was to try to achieve hegemony over the continent.[75]

This statement makes it clear that Kiyosawa also favored "Shidehara diplomacy" because it was a balance of power policy. The aim of Japanese policy, he believed, should be to prevent the United States and Great Britain from cooperating against Japan. He claimed this was a feasible goal, and as long as the United States and Great Britain could be kept from cooperating in the region, peace would be maintained in the Far East.[76]

Japan's abandonment of the Washington and London treaties brought about the very cooperation he had feared. As Kiyosawa saw the situation, when in 1936 Japan withdrew from the London Naval Conference and the terminated Washington Treaty, its "relations with Britain and America changed abruptly: faced with a Japanese offensive, Anglo-American cooperation became a reality."[77] Anglo-Japanese relations were also damaged by Italy's adherence in 1937 to the Anti-Comintern Pact, which Japan and Nazi Germany had concluded the previous year. The pact had decreased the need for Japan to keep watch over the Russian situation and allowed it to proceed with a policy of stepped-up political and military pressure on China, particularly in north China. Such a policy was a "diplomatic prelude" to the spread of hostilities to central and south China and to a further increase in Anglo-Japanese antagonism.[78] The Japanese army's occupation of the British concession in Tientsin and the subsequent anti-British movement in Japan in 1940 were outstanding examples of this growing antagonism. Finally, linking the wars in China and Europe through an alliance with the Axis powers ensured Anglo-American cooperation against Japan.[79] Japan's abandonment of the Washington system and establishment of a "New Order" guaranteed by the Axis alliance was the worst policy Japan could have adopted, for it brought both Britain and the United States into conflict with Japan. Whereas mutual restraint and balance among the three countries might have preserved peace in the Far East,[80] Japanese foreign policy after Shidehara, Kiyosawa charged, had shattered that balance. Not regarding China's role in a solution to the Far Eastern situation as important as that of the United States and Great Britain, Kiyosawa's criticism of the New Order in East Asia was leveled not against its opposition to Chinese nationalism but against its opposition to the United States and, in particular, Great Britain.

Marxist Shinobu Seizaburō had a decidedly different interpretation of the China question. He concentrated his criticism on Western imperialism. In his *Kindai Nihon gaikōshi* (A Diplomatic History of Modern Japan) Shinobu focused on the relationship between the Anglo-American ruling order and Japan's foreign policy. He wrote that the Washington Conference system was a device for maintaining Anglo-American control of the western Pacific and the Far East and tried to show how extensively past Japanese policy had been subordinated to that of America and Britain.[81] Being a good Marxist, he found economic reasons for this subordinate relationship. He believed that Japan's reliance upon the United States and Great Britain for close to 50 percent of its import-export trade and much of its investment—particularly investment on the mainland—had resulted in its cooperation with, if not dependence upon those two countries in its foreign policy. While Japan had been striving since the Manchurian Incident to destroy the Washington system—i.e., the Anglo-American ruling order—it was nevertheless difficult to stop cooperating with Great Britain and the United States because the Japanese economy could not escape its dependence upon them.[82]

Thus, in the long run the only way to demolish the Washington system was for Japan to become economically self-sufficient and independent of the United States and Britain. In the conclusion of his *Kindai Nihon gaikōshi* Shinobu suggested that Japan might accomplish this goal by means of a "national defense state," to be developed through the China War, and by the creation of an East Asia Coprosperity Sphere that would provide its economic basis. He thought the Axis alliance and the Sino-Japanese Treaty of 1940, plus the Soviet-Japanese Neutrality Pact of 1941 marked a new stage in the development of Japan's foreign policy. As a Marxist, Shinobu particularly welcomed the pact with the Soviet Union, since it completely denied the Washington system that to him was a bulwark of Anglo-American imperialism.[83] Thus his equation of anti-imperialism with an anti-Anglo-American posture led him to favor a pro-Russian stance and cooperation with Germany and Italy in order to buttress the national defense state and the East Asia Coprosperity Sphere.

As previously discussed, Kamikawa Hikomatsu had urged either Japanese control over Manchuria in the form of a League mandate or a Far Eastern League led by Japan, in order to legitimize in terms of the League covenant Japan's actions subsequent to the Manchurian Incident. When the New Order in East Asia was proclaimed after the China War broke out, he hailed it as marking the breakdown of the "old order in East Asia" defined by the Nine Power Pact. Such "imperialistic special treaties" as the Nine Power Pact, he declared, were fundamentally incompatible with the League covenant, whereas the New Order in East Asia had expanded the covenant.[84] For him, the New Order in East Asia seems to have been a re-edition of the idea of a Far Eastern League. He talked of an "Asian Monroe Doctrine" resembling the American model and of "East Asian cooperation" similar to pan-Americanism as the "guiding principles of the New Order in East Asia."[85] From several articles he wrote on the Monroe Doctrine, it is clear that his notions of the New Order and the Far Eastern League were based on what he believed was the international situation in the Americas.

The New Order in East Asia also won the support of a number of political scientists. One was Rōyama Masamichi, whose support for "regionalism" as the basis of a Far Eastern international order we have already discussed. In the period after 1937, as one fait accompli followed another, his theory of regionalism, intended originally as a compromise between Japanese nationalism and the existing world legal order, ended up essentially as Japanese nationalism and was used to deny that order. Thus, after 1938 his "regionalism" was no longer local and particular but worldwide and universal. He developed the view that an organic synthesis of nature and culture on the earth divided the world naturally into a number of balanced regions, an idea that led him to envision a "New World Order" to replace the international legal system built up after World War I.[86] This was to include a "New Order in Europe" revolving around Germany and Italy and a "New Order in East Asia" revolving around Japan.[87] The New Order both in Europe and in East Asia was to be of "revolutionary significance" in that it would involve the "dissolution" of independent national states and their incorporation into the overall regional unit.[88] Rōyama believed that the goal of the China War should be the establishment of the New Order in East Asia as a link in the construction of a New World Order. He felt therefore that the China War was "basically different from a war with limited and partial goals such as envisaged by the League covenant and the Kellogg-Briand Pact." It was rather a "holy war" with "moral and idealistic goals"—an ideological war in which there could be no compromise.[89]

Rōyama argued that there were two obstacles to the establishment of the New Order in the Far East that had to be crushed by Japanese military force. One was Chinese nationalism; the other was Western imperialism, which utilized and thus cooperated with Chinese nationalism. Rōyama held that in the Far East nationalism could not contribute to the creation of internal and international order as it had done historically in the West.[90] The success of nationalism in non-Western Japan, he contended, was a unique development that had grown out of a number of special historical circumstances,[91] but it was no longer a principle that could save Asia. In order for the Chinese people to survive, they would have to seek a regional alliance that went beyond national boundaries. Since it was Chinese nationalism that was obstructing such a regional alliance, it was necessary that the China War be fought. Thus the final goal of the China War was the "conquest" of nationalism.[92]

Needless to say, the logic for this "conquest" of nationalism was "regionalism," and the logic of this "regionalism" was "inherent in the process of Japan's nationalistic expansion on the Asian continent." It was "not like original Western European imperialism, but was regionalism for the sake of defense and development."[93] Therefore its aims "should not be regarded as the construction of a colonial economy, but rather as the establishment of a regional structure for the cooperative destiny of the peoples of East Asia."[94] To Rōyama this was essentially the same as Germany's aim in central Europe, Italy's attitude toward the Mediterranean coastal area, and the United States' policy toward the American continent.[95] Japan's Asian policy arose from its regional unity with the Asian mainland and was not imperialism.

The "nationalism" that Rōyama felt had to be "conquered" was nationalism in a political and military sense, without reference to cultural content. According to him, in contrast to "Western civilization" there existed in the Orient a number of parallel cultural spheres but no single "Oriental civilization."[96] Even Japan and China had few points of cultural identity. In this idea he followed the works of Tsuda Sōkichi and others who stressed the cultural dissimilarities between China and Japan.[97] Consequently Rōyama emphasized that in a cooperative regional community in East Asia there would have to be respect for the racial and cultural differences of the individual members.[98] Although political and military unification was important for a New Order in East Asia, he did not regard cultural and philosophic unity as essential.[99] His "East Asia Cooperative Community" was essentially a political, military, and economic structure, not a framework for creating a common culture.

Concerning the second obstacle that the Japanese army had to crush before the New Order in the Far East could be established—Western imperialism —Rōyama wrote:

> Our enemy is not only the Chiang regime. It is also the semi-colonial policy of the West, in particular of the British and the French, which the regime has skillfully utilized and cooperated with in the name of national survival and reconstruction. The essential thing about the China Incident is this: its goals cannot be accomplished without crushing the world order that the British and French have built up over the past one hundred years.[100]

Rōyama placed great importance on the distinction between the New Order Japan should build and the old imperialism and criticized Japanese policy toward the continent for causing the people of Asia "to regard Japan in the same manner they regard the Western imperialists. In some cases, they see Japan as an invader who will rob them of their freedom and independence."[101] He felt that Japanese arrogance as well as foreign policy had brought about this reaction. Japan, he said, had not demonstrated a willingness to accept the national demands of Asian peoples, a willingness that would have distinguished Japanese policy from Western imperialism.

These ideas seem to have influenced the significance Rōyama attached to the war in China. If he had viewed that conflict simply as an expression of Japanese imperialistic expansion, it would have been difficult for him to see it as having "moralistic and idealistic goals." For that very reason he had to regard it as a war between Japan and Great Britain and/or Japan and the United States. Such an interpretation was by no means peculiar to Rōyama. It was generally accepted among intellectuals who had some doubts about Japan's policy toward the mainland; as a consequence they enjoyed a feeling of release from moral responsibility only after war broke out against America and Britain.[102]

Rōyama considered Americanism to be a threat to the New Order in East Asia. While agreeing with Arnold Toynbee when he likened America to the Roman empire, Rōyama differed with him in thinking that the only way to struggle against such an America was through "self-contained regionalism." Thus he wrote:

> A time will come when the struggle between Japan and China will have to be settled on a worldwide or a Pacific basis. At that time, what principle shall Japan employ to deal with the threat of universal empire that will come from across the Pacific? Is there any way other than through self-contained regionalism?[103]

Here again we can see Rōyama's belief in the inevitability of war with the United States.

As the struggle in China expanded, a small group of sinologists of Marxist persuasion expressed doubts concerning Japan's attempt to establish a New Order in East Asia, pointing to the rapid growth of a different "new order" in the form of the anti-Japanese national united front that dated from the outbreak of the China War. Ozaki Hotsumi and Hosokawa Karoku are representative of this group.

"The present war is being fought by China as a nation," Ozaki wrote. "The war has shown that China can attain a degree of national unity sufficient to carry on the fighting. This is quite different from anything in its past experience."[104] Ozaki acknowledged that there was always the danger of a split between the Kuomintang and the Chinese Communist Party. But even in that event, he maintained, the popular desire for a united front could not be so easily shattered. The trend toward unification in China was "an indisputable fact, something quite difficult to crush with cannons and bombs." Hence, "Japan's China policy must be ready to deal with the unification of China, whether desirable or not."[105]

From these premises Ozaki argued that Japan's New Order in East Asia had first of all to promote and facilitate the unity of the Chinese people and, secondly, to make possible the destruction of the "semi-feudal" and "semi-colonial" features of Chinese society, one of the aims of the anti-Japanese national united front as well. Consequently, the New Order could not be simply an expansion and strengthening of the "New China" created by the Japanese in the areas occupied by the Japanese army, nor could it be brought into being by "forceful, one-sided measures" on Japan's part.[106] Even that corollary of the New Order, the "East Asia Cooperative Community," could not, in Ozaki's opinion, be achieved without China's positive participation.[107] In actuality, the concept of an East Asia Cooperative Community was clearly denied by the anti-Japanese united front. In the face of this reality, declared Ozaki, "it should be fully recognized that the possibility of an East Asia Cooperative Community is pitifully small."[108]

Hosokawa likewise focused upon the fact that the war in China had given rise to "a national consciousness of unprecedented scope on the part of the Chinese people."[109] He criticized the theory of an East Asia Cooperative Community as lacking "a true understanding of revolutionary conditions on the mainland."[110] Furthermore, he expressed strong support for Sun Yat-sen's idea of a Greater Asia built around a union of China and Japan on a basis of both independence and equality. Hosokawa claimed that this proposed union, in which a revolutionary China would be assisted by economic and technical aid from Japan, was still worthy of serious consideration.[111]

Both Ozaki and Hosokawa argued that the New Order would be promoted by Japanese support for the Chinese revolution. They were thus concerned with the nature of the forces that had given rise to the revolution and the drive toward national unification. Ozaki saw the Kuomintang as possessing only limited revolutionary potential and without sufficient power to overcome the stagnation in Chinese society and bring about political independence. In his view it was a large military clique that had absorbed all the regional military cliques,[112] a concentrated manifestation of the semi-feudal, semi-colonial aspects of Chinese society, and "a form of bureaucracy."[113] He disagreed with Yanaihara's expectation that unification and capitalistic industrialization would be brought about under Kuomintang leadership[114] and argued that its weakness had spurred Japan's continental expansion.[115]

Hosokawa further contended that the Kuomintang's connection with the United States and Great Britain was an obstacle to revolutionary change in that it obstructed the elimination of semi-feudal and semi-colonial elements in Chinese society. He pointed out that the "Nanking government's national unification policy created the conditions that opened the door for Anglo-American imperialistic penetration into China."[116] However, he agreed with Ozaki that the expanded influence of the Communist Party after the outbreak of the China War had produced signs of change within the Kuomintang.[117]

The two Marxists both regarded the Chinese Communist movement with approval and had a clearer conception than most writers of the role the Communists were playing in the China War and of their possible contribution to the construction of a postwar "new order" in China. To Ozaki the destruction of the Chinese economy by the war, and with it the possibility of economic development along capitalist lines, would enable the Communist Party, whose influence had expanded as national unification had advanced, to lay the foundations "for noncapitalist advancement in the Chinese economy."[118] By "noncapitalist advancement" Ozaki probably meant socialism, which he believed to be an alternative road to economic development.[119]

Hosokawa, for his part, believed that it had been the Chinese Communists who had provided the impetus for the "unprecedented advance in China's national unification" that began with the China War.[120] He wrote that the Chinese Communists "have utilized the outbreak of the Manchurian Incident more skillfully than has the Nanking government. They have mobilized all the people of the nation and converted the government, which had betrayed the Three People's Principles, to their own policy."[121]

Earlier we discussed the reaction of international legal scholars to the Manchurian Incident and pointed out that their faith in the existence of a universal international order had been greatly shaken. It may be well, therefore, to examine briefly the manner in which universalism in international law was rejected and the theory of regionalism advanced to support the development of the East Asia Coprosperity Sphere.

As soon as the Japanese government in November 1940 proclaimed the establishment of the "Greater East Asia Coprosperity Sphere," a number of Japanese intellectuals responded by devising a "Greater East Asia international law" that defined both the internal and external relations of the new sphere. One important model utilized was the international law of the new European order as preached by Nazi legal scholars, in particular Carl Schmitt's theory of a broad European international law (*das Volkerrecht des europeischen Grossraum*) centering around Germany. Another was the international legal order on the American continents as embodied in the Monroe Doctrine. Because both of these were based on the principle of "regionalism" as opposed to a universal international legal order, they were seen as forerunners of the Greater East Asia International Law. The Monroe Doctrine was used to justify Japanese actions in China not only after the Manchurian Incident but even after the outbreak of the Pacific War. This approach to the Monroe Doctrine was clearly stated by Matsushita Masatoshi, for example, in his *Beishū kōiki kokusaihō no kiso rinen* (Basic Ideals of American Regional International Law), published in 1942, where he wrote that he had analyzed the Monroe Doctrine in such a way "as to be able to defend the Greater East Asia international law."[122]

The writings of Carl Schmitt, who also took the Monroe Doctrine as a precedent to support his own theories, came to have great influence upon Japanese scholars of international law as political and military ties between Japan and Germany increased. Yasui Kaoru, a professor of international law at Tokyo Imperial University, is representative of the writers influenced by Schmitt. Yasui and others applied Schmitt's theory to the Japanese situation in two ways. First, because it took international law not as an abstract, universal framework of rules but as a concrete order (*konkrete Ordnung*) that existed among peoples and nations,[123] it served as a valuable prop to the Greater East Asia Coprosperity Sphere. Schmitt divided law into three parts—*Norm, Dezision*, and *konkrete Ordnung*—among which he considered the last to be of central importance.[124] For Japanese scholars of international law the idea of *konkrete Ordnung* played a cardinal role in their assault on a universal international law.

Secondly, the concept of *konkrete Ordnung* was used to support Japan's claim to be the "leading nation" in a system of Greater East Asia international law. Schmitt described international law as that law which existed among nations and peoples who occupied specific areas which he called *Grossraum*.[125] For example, the Monroe Doctrine was international law for the *Grossraum* of the American continents, and the same concept could naturally be applied to Europe or the Far East. Moreover, he expected a "leading nation" (*Reich*) to guarantee order in each *Grossraum*[126] and, like the United States in the Americas and Germany in Europe, to prevent intrusions from outside the *Grossraum*. Consequently, a *Grossraum* could not exist without a *Reich*, which preceded and determined the *Grossraum*. Unfortunately for those who wrote on international law in Japan, however, the Greater East Asia Coprosperity Sphere was only a political program and did not fully satisfy Schmitt's definition of a *konkrete Ordnung*. Thus, while the concept of concrete order was used to buttress arguments for a Greater East Asia international law, that law was in reality undermined by the fact that such an order did not exist in Asia.

III

I should like to conclude this study by pointing to two of the major themes that recur in many of the Japanese foreign policy studies written in the

1931-41 period. International law, as embodied in the Versailles Treaty system in Europe and the Washington Treaty system in the Far East, was attacked as a device for shoring up and concealing American and British domination. Universal internationalism was divested of its authority by exposing it as the ideology that masked this intent. Consequently, anti-internationalism came to be synonymous with anti-Anglo-Americanism and at times, among Marxists, with anti-imperialism.

Secondly, "regionalism" came to replace universal internationalism. Originating in an effort to justify the Manchurian Incident, regionalism at first relied on the notion that Japan had a special but clearly defined position on the continent. But as the Japanese army pushed farther and farther into China and Southeast Asia, this more limited idea grew into the grandiose concept of a "Greater East Asia Coprosperity Sphere." Regionalism was contrasted with European imperialism as the basis for a new world order in which the "New Order in the Far East" was to be one link. Since the purpose of the China War was to establish the "New Order in East Asia," these writers concluded that it was directed not against China but against the "old order," represented by Chinese nationalism and the Nine Power Treaty that protected Anglo-American imperialism. Taking this approach, it was a simple step to justify the expansion of the China War into the Pacific War, a war against the United States and Great Britain.

THE STRUCTURE OF JAPANESE-AMERICAN RELATIONS IN THE 1930s

Mushakōji Kinhide

Translated by Shumpei Okamoto

I

This paper attempts to set up a theoretical model by which to examine the basic structure of Japanese-American relations in the 1930s (see Diagram I). It is hoped that the model will assist us in correlating and analyzing those factors essential to an understanding of how decision makers in both countries perceived relations between them and the ways in which they tried to guide those relations. Such a model is based upon two premises: First, that Japanese and American images of one another had a pervasive effect upon each country's basic policy orientation and influenced its evaluation of the other's capabilities and intentions, evaluations that guided the formulation of policies and the pursuit of interests and objectives. Second, that inasmuch as Japanese-American relations constituted only part of a broader international setting, their relations were inevitably affected by other factors. Thus, factors intrinsic to Japanese-American relations as well as outside factors determined the patterns of policy decisions of each country vis-à-vis the other.

Reviewing in the light of this theoretical model the papers contained in the present volume and the opinions expressed in the course of the conference, the basic structure of Japanese-American relations in the 1930s might be summarized as follows (see Diagram II):

1. *Mutual Images Held by Japan and the United States.* It should first be pointed out that for neither Japan nor the United States was the other nation its primary focus of interest. United States concern was directed primarily toward Europe; East Asia, particularly Japan, drew only limited attention from the general public as well as the leaders of the United States. Similarly, Japan's

primary interest was in China and only secondarily in the United States. It is true that Japan watched the United States with growing anxiety, but largely because of its conviction that the United States was blocking the execution of Japan's China policy. Furthermore, the shift in emphasis came about only in the late 1930s; until then Japan was concerned primarily with Britain and only secondarily with the United States.

This lack of attention on the part of both Japan and the United States naturally created an unfavorable atmosphere for Japanese-American relations. Furthermore, it weakened the position in both countries of those people—such as the members of the United States embassy in Tokyo and the "Europe-America faction" in the Japanese Foreign Ministry—who were interested in maintaining and promoting friendly relations between the two nations. As a consequence, neither country made vigorous efforts to collect information about the other, thus precluding any possibility that their distorted mutual images might have been corrected. This situation was at least partially to blame for the mutual distrust felt by Japan and the United States, a distrust that produced on both sides the conviction that the other sought constant aggrandizement. More importantly, however, these distorted images resulted in a fundamental misunderstanding of the other nation's policy objectives. Japan, for example, regarded United States espousal of a world peace structure based on the "Washington Conference system" as an attempt on the part of a "have" nation to apply pressure against a "have-not." On the other hand, the United States viewed Japan's countermeasure, the creation of the "New Order in East Asia," as an effort to change the existing world order by military force. These images further deteriorated as the result of several other factors. United States immigration policy, for example, conditioned the Japanese people to regard as hypocritical American devotion to internationalism and humanitarianism.

Another serious problem in U.S.-Japanese relations was that both countries miscalculated the other's capabilities. Leaders in the United States, recalling that Japan had backed down when Woodrow Wilson threatened to invoke economic sanctions at the time of the Siberian intervention, consistently advocated the necessity of a tough policy. Treasury Secretary Morgenthau, for instance, believed that Japan would capitulate in a week if economic sanctions were applied. Similarly, on the Japanese side Matsuoka Yōsuke, who spent ten years as a student in the United States, is said to have been firmly convinced that a forceful posture was essential in negotiating with the United States. Furthermore, the Japanese public harbored the view that the American national character was such that the United States was unlikely to endure a protracted war. As we shall see later, neither country possessed a leadership able to correct and eliminate the causes of these mutual miscalculations.

2. *Policy Objectives.* United States policy objectives can be summarized as follows: (1) to maintain the peace structure, the collective security system founded upon such international agreements as the Washington Conference treaties, the League covenant, and the Kellogg-Briand Pact; (2) to block any action designed to alter the existing order by military force; (3) to uphold the principle of the Open Door, especially in China.

Such objectives posed two questions: First, would not a policy that insisted on maintaining the existing structure be too rigid to permit an effective response by countries faced with the fluid and changing situation in the Far East, particularly with the rising Nationalist and Communist movements in China? Secondly, was the American position—that any change in the existing order should be allowed only by peaceful means, not by military force—feasible at all? Was peaceful change of the existing order possible?

Japan answered that the American policy was impracticable, for it would not allow Japan to take measures necessary to protect its rights and interests in China. Only military force, Japan believed, would achieve this objective. In addition, Japanese policy aimed, first, to eradicate Anglo-American influences in China and, second, to maintain the status quo in the region under Japanese hegemony by the establishment of a "New Order in East Asia." Japan defended (and explained) this policy by calling it an "East Asian Monroe Doctrine." Its Japanese advocates argued that, just as the United States claimed the right to intervene in the affairs of Caribbean countries in the name of the Monroe Doctrine, Japan should be able to intervene militarily in Manchuria and China proper. Clearly such policy objectives were unacceptable to the United States, for their attainment would mean alteration of the existing order by military force. Furthermore, the essential regionalism of Japan's policy was unacceptable to the United States, which viewed the peace structure as a global system.

The disagreement in policy objectives between Japan and the United States was most sharply revealed in their China policies. The United States sought to advance the modernization of China under the principle of the Open Door and with American aid. In Japan, however, with the exception of a few people such as the "Europe-America faction" in the Foreign Ministry, who entertained a more international outlook, most leaders insisted that China's modernization should be carried out only under Japanese hegemony.

3. *Conflicting Interests.* The people of the United States, influenced partly by the traditional image of China created by missionaries, held a more friendly attitude toward China than toward Japan. The paternalistic and protective policy that this attitude created was in harmony with those American economic interests that sought development of the China market. In actuality, the China market was significant for American foreign policy only in the sense that it promised vast future possibilities. Trade with Japan, on the other hand, was considerably greater than with China. But despite its limited economic interests in China, the United States pursued its Open Door policy in order to keep open its options for the future.

In contrast to the primarily economic interests of the United States, from the time of the Russo-Japanese War Japan had viewed its interests on the mainland essentially in terms of military necessity, regarding Japanese hegemony over the continent as essential to its national security. Japan naturally came to regard Russia, both under the czar and under the communists, as its primary hypothetical enemy. Predominantly economic interests in China led to American policies based upon the principle of the Open Door. Concentration on national security resulted in a Japanese program aiming at control of the continent. The Pacific War, it may be said, represented a clash between the "principle" and the "program." The clash developed into a military conflict when Japan embarked on its southward march, seeking in such places as French Indochina the resources necessary to carry out its program on the continent. With this fatal decision, Japan not only violated the American principle, but also disrupted the balance of power in the Pacific upon which the peace structure was based.

4. *The Influence of Europe.* Aside from the factors discussed above, we must keep in mind that the European situation too had an effect on Japanese-American relations in the 1930s. First of all, since Europe was the main concern of American policymakers, it can be said that Japan's conclusion of the Tripartite Pact with Germany and Italy in 1940 occasioned an irreversible deterioration in Japanese-American relations. With Japan's adherence to the pact, pro-Chinese organizations in the United States began to obtain a more favorable response to their endeavors to arouse public opinion against Japan. On the other hand, the Tripartite Pact caused the European situation to loom significantly in Japan's policymaking. Japanese military leaders, conscious of Japan's military inferiority vis-à-vis the United States, were dazzled by the remarkable results of the German blitzkrieg and came to hope that the presumed German victory in Europe would offset Japan's military inferiority in the Pacific and provide Japan with an opportunity to prevail over the United States.

Great Britain too had an important impact on Japanese-American relations. As Stanley Hornbeck's appraisal of the Washington Conference reveals, the United States, desiring to strengthen its position on the China issue, endeavored successfully to terminate the alliance between Japan and Britain. Thereafter, throughout the 1930s the United States opposed any British attempt to play the role of an intermediary between Japan and the United States and further sought an alliance with Britain so that the two nations might act in concert vis-à-vis Japan. Japan, for its part, worked to alienate Britain from the United States. Up to the beginning of the pre-Pearl Harbor negotiations in Washington, Japan regarded Britain rather than the United States as its hypothetical enemy and endeavored not to involve the United States in any conflict with Britain. Britain's posture toward Japan also gradually hardened and, from the mid-1930s onward, influenced the United States to adopt a more intransigent policy toward Japan. Japan's alliance with Germany and Italy may be deemed its response to the increasing cooperation between Britain and the United States. The upshot was that Japanese-American relations worsened decisively.

Thus there is no doubt that Japanese-American relations in the 1930s were greatly influenced by the European situation, particularly by the confrontation between Britain and the German-Italian Axis.

5. *The Inevitability of War.* These complex factors intensified the sense of isolation that had troubled Japan since the time of the Siberian intervention. Japanese military leaders in particular were increasingly gripped by what might be termed a "tunnel perception"—a conviction that war with the United States was in the end inevitable. This fatalistic view eventually permeated not only the leadership but also the general public in Japan and led Japan to make the final decision for war not through a consideration of rational alternatives but out of an exclusive concern with how and when the inevitable war should begin. In the United States too, along with the notion of the "yellow peril," the feeling that war with Japan was inevitable to some extent beclouded any calm consideration

of interest and principle. This pessimism and the increasing pressure from Britain and China made it impossible for American policymakers to evaluate and respond properly to the efforts of that tiny minority in Japan who endeavored to avert war.

The above examination of the factors that produced the deterioration in Japanese-American relations during the 1930s leads us to formulate several hypotheses concerning the general conditions that bring about tensions between nations:

1) Communication between nations deteriorates in proportion to the discrepancy that exists in the scope and direction of their interests, causing distorted mutual images and a greater probability of further conflict.

2) When two nations pursue conflicting policy objectives, the more one stresses an apparent gap between the other's intentions and its actual ability to carry them out, the greater will be the tendency to adopt a hard-line posture toward the other.

3) When a conflict in interests arises between a superior and an inferior power, the former will tend to appeal to universal principles, whereas the latter will tend to pursue a particularistic and regional program. The superior power, moreover, will define the status quo on a formal and territorial basis, the inferior in terms of substance and equal opportunity.

4) Two nations with conflicting interests do not limit their disagreement to themselves. Rather, they seek advantageous alliances with other nations, thereby expanding the conflict. As other nations in confrontation with one another for different reasons join them, the conflict between two nations will tend to develop into a confrontation between two alliances.

These are some of the general hypotheses that may be drawn from an examination of Japanese-American relations in the 1930s. In the course of the conference the American participants, as might be expected of "revisionist" historians, showed particular interest in an "if" question: What factors in Japanese-American relations might have been changed and the war with the United States thereby have been averted? In attempting to answer this question, we must examine in further detail various elements in the decision making processes of each country. Adopting a structure-function approach let us analyze the defects in the decision making processes of Japan and the United States that caused these two subsystems to fail to function properly in the international arena, that is, to maintain peace in Asia.

II

We have thus far identified certain factors that seem to have made war between Japan and the United States inevitable. Given different conditions, then, how might war have been averted? Speaking in abstract and theoretical terms, we may say that war might not have come had there existed in their respective decision making processes some mechanism that might have corrected those factors. In other words, the Pacific War could have been averted had their governmental structures been equipped to perform three functions: (1) image adjusting, (2) policy adjusting, and (3) interest adjusting (see Diagram III).

1. *Image Adjusting Function.* In both countries public opinion had little impact upon decision making. In Japan the mass media was thoroughly controlled by the government. Consequently, the government manipulated public opinion rather than being influenced by public opinion. In the United States as well, public opinion traditionally had little impact on presidential foreign policy discussions. Furthermore, even had American public opinion affected foreign policy decision making, the primary concern of the American public was directed at European politics. Asian affairs were left to an extremely small number of nongovernmental linkage-groups whose monopoly of information on the Far East and manipulation of public opinion had a dysfunctional effect on relations between the United States and Japan. Groups such as the American Committee for Non-Participation in Japanese Aggression struggled to mobilize public opinion either on behalf of China or in support of the international peace structure. They functioned, however, as skids, lest policies the United States government was then promoting should be reversed, and they neither influenced nor restricted significantly President Roosevelt's policy formulation. On the other hand, after the Manchurian Incident pro-Japanese groups in the United States lost their ability to promote the Japanese cause persuasively and found it virtually impossible to create a public opinion friendly to Japan. Had the anti-militarist linkage-groups in Japan continued their activities vigorously, an improvement in the American image of Japan might not have been totally impossible. In actuality no such possibility existed, as evidenced by the acquiescent stand taken by the League of Nations Association of Japan following Japan's withdrawal from the League. The impairment of the image adjusting function in Japan is also evident in the support given by Japanese intellectuals to the idea of a "New Order in East Asia," the "Asian Monroe Doctrine." Thus, with respect to the general state of public opinion and the activities of nongovernmental organizations, we must conclude that: (1) conditions giving public opinion significant influence in decision making were lacking, particularly in Japan; (2) in the United States objective factors that might have created a friendly image of Japan were absent. This being the case, even had public interest in the United States not been so Europe-oriented, the adjustment of images between Japan and the United States would still in the end have been impossible.

Some business leaders and organizations in both countries attempted to correct these distorted images. It is particularly noteworthy that both Japanese and American businessmen shared the conviction that no fundamental conflict existed between the economic interests of the two nations. Japanese hopes for American capital investment in Manchuria seem to indicate that the possibility of image adjustment in the economic sphere was greater than in the realm of political and military events. Their efforts, however, were marred by several misunderstandings. For instance, Japanese business leaders remained optimistic even after their American colleagues lost interest in Manchurian investment. In one overture to American business, the Japanese leaders employed a mission headed by General John F. O'Ryan, who had little influence in American business circles. Thomas W. Lamont's despair following the conclusion of the Tripartite Pact testifies to the disappearance of any possibility of adjusting economic images in the face of heightened political and military hostilities.

Under the circumstances, although a slight possibility of economic image adjustment remained, particularly if better communications had existed between business leaders in both countries, it should not be overestimated.

2. *Policy Adjusting Function.* In examining the actual policy adjusting function in Japanese-American relations during the 1930s, we face two fundamental questions. The hard-line policies adopted by the United States ranging from nonrecognition of Manchukuo to economic sanctions seem to have been formulated as if no other alternatives were available to American policymakers. Why? On the other hand, from the Manchurian Incident to the Pacific War Japan pursued an expansionist policy as if there were no possibility of policy adjustment. Why?

A comparison of the decision making processes in the two countries reveals that the American system had few structural restrictions and allowed more scope for informal and personal leadership. The Japanese system, on the other hand, worked under many structural limitations, and policymaking was often influenced by the necessity of balancing opinions among factions. In the United States policy was formulated by choice from among conflicting opinions. In Japan policy was formulated by a consensus of differing positions or by the force of a faction that represented the overwhelming majority of policymakers. In other words, the former was an open system based on an exchange of opinion and information, whereas the latter was a closed system that rigidly restricted the free exchange of opinion. Given this contrast in policymaking processes, different factors restricted the policy adjusting function in the two countries. In order to facilitate our examination of those factors, we may summarize the influences of the various organs involved in policymaking as follows: On the American side the president and the State Department (particularly its Far Eastern Division) were most influential, followed by the Treasury and Commerce departments, especially Treasury Secretary Henry Morgenthau. This distribution of influence emerged from the frequently-mentioned fact that policy toward Japan was accorded only peripheral importance, and thus only those decision makers directly responsible for the problem paid serious attention to the issue. In the Japanese government, on the contrary, power relations among the various decision making organs were more clearly institutionalized. The army and navy were paramount while the Foreign Ministry played only a secondary role because the two services possessed a veto power over the policymaking process by virtue of their right of supreme command and the active duty requirement for service ministers.

Given the decision making process in each country, any opinion or information that might have called for changes in policy was largely ignored, for neither system had the capability to explore such demands seriously and adjust its policy appropriately. A few examples will suffice to make this point clear. After the Manchurian Incident the U.S. army wanted to withdraw its troops from China, but its desire was overridden at State Department insistence. The navy too was prepared to reach a compromise with Japan and, more significantly, members of the American embassy in Tokyo recommended that Washington modify its policy toward Japan. Even had American leaders followed army and navy thinking vis-à-vis Japan, the overall situation might not have been greatly altered. Yet it is noteworthy that in contrast to the activities of the Japanese army and navy, at least some American military authorities disagreed with the hard-line policy toward Japan. But because of the decisive role of the president and the State Department, such a policy adjusting inclination on the part of the military had little effect. A similar but typical dilemma arose within the State Department, where disagreement between the embassy in Tokyo and the Far Eastern Division made it totally impossible for the former to bring about amendments of policy. This problem must also be related to Hornbeck's great personal influence within the department.

In Japan, on the other hand, the possibility for policy adjustment did exist. The Finance Ministry, concerned that Japan might be cut off from vital resources imported from areas under British and American control, strongly opposed the Tripartite Pact. The navy too was fully aware that Japan lacked the ability to fight a protracted war, and the "Europe-America faction" within the Foreign Ministry endeavored until the last moment to improve Japanese-American relations. The first possibility for policy adjustment was lost, however, when the budget-making power accorded the Finance Ministry under the constitution was undermined by the powerful service ministers. Worse yet, the personal influence of the finance minister within the councils of government declined continuously throughout the 1930s. Had navy leaders argued more adamently the impossibility of fighting a protracted war, the army might have been forced to back away from its advocacy of war. Had the decision for war been thus delayed in 1941, the development in Europe of a situation increasingly disadvantageous to Germany, upon whose victory the Japanese army counted so heavily, might have ruled out the decision entirely. But the navy failed to assert its position, and this hesitation, spurred on by the fierce rivalry between the navy and army and by the practice of consensus decision making, destroyed any possibility of policy adjustment. The ineffectualness of the Europe-America faction was also a dilemma characteristic of the Japanese decision making system: when confronting a dominant faction, the opinion of a dissenting minority fell on deaf ears.

Thus, in the United States the problem of Japan was not sufficiently important to involve the entire policymaking system and, as a consequence, decision makers with limited responsibilities wielded decisive influence. In Japan structural restrictions and other limitations arising from the characteristic practices of decision making, consensus building, and balancing among factions caused a paralysis of the policy adjusting function.

3. Interest Adjusting Function. By interest adjusting function I refer to the diplomatic function of adjusting interests between countries through negotiation. On this point Japan and the United States shared a basically similar problem: conflict of opinion among officials responsible for the conduct of foreign relations. In the United States serious disagreement developed between the Far Eastern Division under Hornbeck and the American embassy in Tokyo under Joseph C. Grew. Similarly, on the Japanese side clashes occurred between Foreign Minister Matsuoka Yōsuke and Ambassador Nomura Kichisaburō in Washington and between Matsuoka and Terasaki Tarō, chief of the Foreign Ministry's America Bureau. These personal clashes in both countries drastically lowered the efficiency of diplomatic negotiations between the two nations.

Examining the interest adjusting function from a somewhat different angle, several contrasts may be observed. One was that between Ambassadors Grew and Nomura in their respective roles as negotiators. While the former functioned as a faithful transmitter of information rather than as a skilled negotiator, the latter ignored his role as communicator and attempted primarily to be a negotiator. This difference in ambassadorial roles weakened, on the one hand, the United States' effectiveness in negotiation and, on the other, Japan's ability to make judgments. A second contrast was in the personnel with direct responsibility for the conduct of foreign policy. Whereas Japanese officials— starting with the foreign minister, who was replaced with almost every cabinet shift—were changed frequently, throughout the 1930s in the United States there was little alteration in the officials charged with responsibility for Far Eastern affairs. The outstanding example of this situation was Hornbeck. Entrenched in key positions in the Far Eastern Division, the "China hands," as they were often called, consistently espoused a rigid stand in negotiating with Japan. Meanwhile, the rapid turnover in personnel in the Japanese Foreign Ministry made it difficult for Japan to maintain a constant policy in its negotiations with the United States. In both cases the interest adjusting function was seriously impaired.

We have discussed some reasons, both structural and otherwise, for the failure of image, policy, and interest adjusting functions in Japan and the United States (summarized in Table I). Although conditions in the two nations differed, once a situation arose in which those three functions failed to perform effectively, a vicious cycle was set in motion: mutual images and policy objectives clashed with increasing severity and the possibility of adjustment decreased as the years passed.

These observations enable us to formulate the following general hypotheses: (1) When two nations with conflicting interests lack sufficient information about one another, any monopoly of information by linkage-groups tends to increase tensions between them. (2) The policy adjusting function may be impeded by excessive institutional restrictions on the one hand, or by excessive freedom of action by some decision maker on the other. Consequently, a decision making system must permit an optimum balance between institutionalization and independence of action. (3) Communicating and negotiating capacities are inversely proportional to one another. Consequently a negotiator must maintain a careful balance between the two capacities in order to discharge his interest adjusting function. (4) At each level of the image, policy, and interest adjusting functions, greater obstacles are met in the course of negotiations between countries with dissimilar decision making systems than in those between similar systems.

These are some of the lessons a student of political science may find in Japanese-American relations in the 1930s.

III

In summarizing the various structural and functional problems encountered in the decision making process in Japan and the United States during the 1930s, we have attempted to reexamine the basic characteristics of Japanese-

American relations during the decade, based upon the papers and scholarly opinions presented at the Conference on Japanese-American Relations. This short essay is merely preliminary in two aspects in particular: First, of the many valuable ideas presented in the course of the conference, I have been compelled to disregard those not directly relevant to the model adopted here. Secondly, the model itself represents a mere approximation of the aggregate of views expressed at the conference and hence can be no more than a theoretical basis for further exploration. Japanese-American relations in the 1930s are a tragic episode of developing tensions between two nations that, in the long run, shared many essential common interests and could enjoy prosperity only through coexistence. To learn more from the tragedy, the circumstances must be further explored. Should this short essay serve as a starting point for such exploration, its objective will have been achieved.

DIAGRAM I

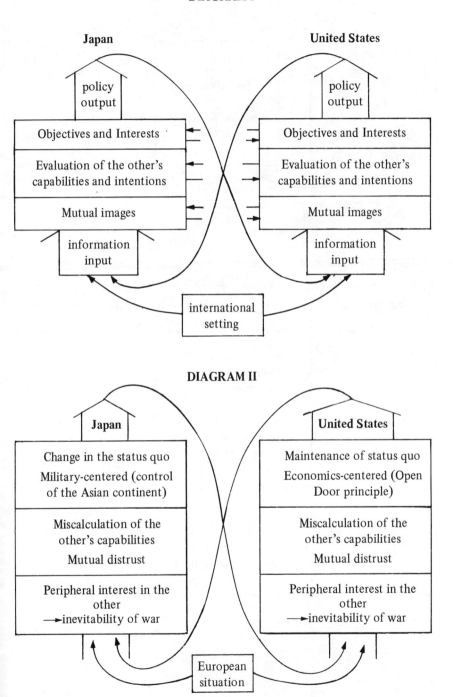

Japan   United States

policy output   policy output

Objectives and Interests   Objectives and Interests

Evaluation of the other's capabilities and intentions   Evaluation of the other's capabilities and intentions

Mutual images   Mutual images

information input   information input

international setting

DIAGRAM II

Japan   United States

Change in the status quo Military-centered (control of the Asian continent)   Maintenance of status quo Economics-centered (Open Door principle)

Miscalculation of the other's capabilities Mutual distrust   Miscalculation of the other's capabilities Mutual distrust

Peripheral interest in the other →inevitability of war   Peripheral interest in the other →inevitability of war

European situation

DIAGRAM III

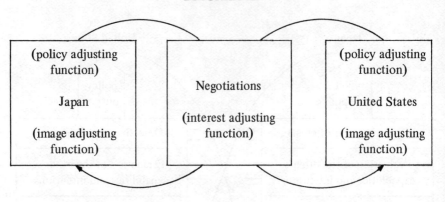

TABLE I

	Japan	United States
Image adjusting function	Public opinion control, malfunctioning of linkage-groups	Lack of interest, dysfunctioning of linkage-groups
Policy adjusting function	Institutional restrictions (independence of supreme command, factionalism)	Restrictions due to personalities of decision makers (excessive concentration of power in a small minority)
Interest adjusting function	Excessive turnover of personnel in charge Lack of communication	Entrenched personnel in charge Lack of negotiating capability

NOTES

A note on abbreviations:

FR = U.S., Department of State, *Foreign Relations of the United States: Diplomatic Papers.* Succeeding information in the notes indicates the year covered by the documents, volume, and facts concerning publication.

FR, Japan, 1931-1941 = U.S., Department of State, *Papers Relating to the Foreign Relations of the United States: Japan, 1931-1941* (2 vols., 1943), a special volume in the above series.

GS = *Gendaishi shiryō* (Source Materials on Contemporary History) (Tokyo: Misuzu Shobō, 1962-71). Succeeding information indicates volume number in series, individual volume title, and volume number under individual title.

Hoover, Roosevelt, and the Japanese

1. Herbert Hoover, *The Memoirs of Herbert Hoover, II: The Cabinet and the Presidency, 1920-1933* (New York, 1952), pp. 364-65.

2. Stimson to Wilson, September 23, 1931, in *FR, 1931* (Washington D.C., 1946), 3:49.

3. *Ibid.,* p. 248.

4. Quoted in Richard N. Current, "The Stimson Doctrine and the Hoover Doctrine," *American Historical Review,* 59 (1954):519.

5. Henry L. Stimson and McGeorge Bundy, *On Active Service in Peace and War* (New York, 1948), p. 233.

6. Stimson Diary, October 8, 1931, quoted in Current, "Stimson Doctrine," pp. 516-17.

7. Hoover, pp. 366-67.

8. See Stimson Diary, November 14, 1931, quoted in Stimson and Bundy, p. 244; also Current, "Stimson Doctrine," p. 520.

9. For the text of the Hoover cabinet memorandum see William Starr Myers, *The Foreign Policies of Herbert Hoover, 1929-1933* (New York, 1940), pp. 156-59.

10. Ray Lyman Wilbur and Arthur Mastick Hyde, eds., *The Hoover Policies* (New York, 1937), pp. 601-02.

11. Hoover, p. 373.

12. Stimson and Bundy, p. 235.

13. *Ibid.,* pp. 235-36.

14. *FR, Japan, 1931-1941* (Washington D.C., 1943), 1:178-79.

15. Stimson Diary, January 26, 1932, quoted in Stimson and Bundy, pp. 243-44.

16. *Ibid.,* p. 244.

17. *Ibid.,* p. 245.

18. Henry L. Stimson, *Far Eastern Crisis: Recollections and Observations* (New York, 1939), p. 157.

19. Stimson Diary, February 24, 1932, quoted in Stimson and Bundy, pp. 248-49; Current, "Stimson Doctrine," p. 530.

20. Stimson and Bundy, p. 249.

21. *FR, Japan, 1931-1941*, 2:83-87.

22. *FR, 1932* (Washington D.C., 1948), 4:76-77.

23. Stimson and Bundy, p. 258.

24. *Ibid.*, p. 259.

25. Wilbur and Hyde, p. 585.

26. See Patrick J. Hurley to Hoover, January 19, 1933, in Myers, pp. 164-65; also p. 169.

27. Quoted in E. H. Carr, *The Twenty Years' Crisis* (London, 1956), p. 35.

28. Grew to Stimson, February 23, 1933, *FR, 1933* (Washington D.C., 1949), 3:195.

29. Hugh R. Wilson, *Diplomat Between Wars* (New York, 1941), pp. 280-81.

30. See Elliott Roosevelt, ed., *F.D.R.: His Personal Letters, 1928-1945* (New York, 1949), 1:320-21.

31. *FR, Japan, 1931-1941*, 1:109.

32. Ales Hrdlicka to Roosevelt, February 25, 1933, President's Personal File 5101, Roosevelt Library, Hyde Park, N.Y. (hereafter cited as PPF).

33. Grew's report of May 11, 1933, President's Secretary's File: Diplomatic Correspondence, Japan, Box 13, Roosevelt Library (hereafter cited as PSF).

34. Dodd to Roosevelt, October 28, 1933, and Roosevelt to Dodd, November 13, 1933, PPF 1043; Roosevelt to George K. Briggs, February 26, 1934, PPF 402.

35. *The New York Times*, April 21, 1934.

36. Hull to Roosevelt, September 18, 1934, PSF: State Department, Box 32; Grew to Hull, December 27, 1934, PSF: Diplomatic Correspondence, Japan, Box 13.

37. Grew to Hull, December 27, 1934, PSF: Diplomatic Correspondence, Japan, Box 13.

38. Hornbeck Memorandum, May 9, 1933, PSF: China, 1933-1936, Box 3; Hornbeck Memorandum, February 2, 1934, PSF: Diplomatic Correspondence, Japan, Box 13.

39. Memorandum, April 26, 1934, PSF: Diplomatic Correspondence, Japan, Box 13.

40. Saitō to Hull, May 16, 1934, and Memorandum of Hull-Saitō conversations, May 19, 1934, PSF: Diplomatic Correspondence, Japan, Box 13.

41. Hornbeck Memorandum, May 16, 1933, *FR, 1933*, 3:328-29; Hull to Wilson, March 31, 1933, *ibid.*, pp. 239, 265.

42. Bullitt to Roosevelt, February 5, 1934, PSF: Diplomatic Correspondence, Japan, Box 13.

43. Hrdlicka to Roosevelt, February 25, 1933, PPF 5101.

44. Roosevelt to Malcolm E. Peabody, August 14, 1933, PPF 732; Elliott Roosevelt, 1:545-46.

45. Hornbeck Memorandum, May 9, 1933, PSF: China, 1933-1936, Box 3.

46. Memorandum of January 3, 1935, PSF: Diplomatic Correspondence, Japan, Box 13.

47. Harold L. Ickes, *The Secret Diary of Harold L. Ickes, II: The Inside Struggle, 1936-1939* (New York, 1954), p. 51; Memorandum, State Department to British Embassy, June 1, 1937, *FR, 1937* (Washington D.C., 1954) 1:103-05.

48. PSF: Great Britain, 1937.

49. Hamilton Memorandum, July 10, 1937, *FR, 1937*, 3:134.

50. Grew to Hull, July 14, 1937, *ibid.*, p. 166.

51. *Ibid.*, 1:699-700.

52. Hull Memorandum, August 20, 1937, *ibid.*, 4:5; Nelson T. Johnson to Hull, August 23, 1937, *ibid.*, 3:460-61.

53. Cordell Hull, *The Memoirs of Cordell Hull* (New York, 1948), 1:544-45.

54. Ickes, 2:213.

55. U.S., Department of State, *Peace and War: United States Foreign Policy, 1931-1941* (Washington D.C., 1943), pp. 383-87.

56. Dorothy Borg, *The United States and the Far Eastern Crisis of 1933-1938* (Cambridge, Mass., 1964), pp. 381-86. This is a superb account of the quarantine speech.

57. *FR, Japan, 1931-1941*, 1:394.

58. *FR, 1937,* 3:596; Borg, *Far Eastern Crisis*, pp. 401-02.

59. Memorandum in PSF: State Department, 1937, Box 32.

60. Roosevelt to Lloyd C. Griscom, October 22, 1937, PPF 4949.

61. Grew to Hull, October 7, 1937, *FR, 1937,* 3:586.

62. Bullitt to Hull, November 8, 1937, *ibid.,* pp. 666-67, 672, and 4:170, 172; Davis to Hull, October 29, 1937, *ibid.,* pp. 119-20.

63. Nancy H. Hooker, ed., *The Moffat Papers: Selections from the Diplomatic Journals of Jay Pierrepont Moffat, 1919-1943* (Cambridge, Mass., 1956), p. 166.

64. *Ibid.,* pp. 168-70.

65. Davis to Hull, November 17, 1937, *FR, 1937,* 4:199-200.

66. Davis to Hull, November 10, 1937, *ibid.,* pp. 175-76; Hull to Davis, November 12, 1937, *ibid.,* pp. 180-81.

67. Roosevelt to William Phillips, November 12, 1937, PSF: State Department, 1937, Box 32.

68. Stimson to Roosevelt, November 15, 1937; Roosevelt to Hull, November 22, 1937; Roosevelt to Stimson, November 24, 1937, PPF 20.

69. Elliott Roosevelt, 2 (New York, 1950):741-42.

70. Chihiro Hosoya, "Miscalculations in Deterrent Policy: Japanese-U.S. Relations, 1938-1941," *Journal of Peace Research* (Oslo), no. 2 (1968), p. 113.

71. George Marvin to Roosevelt, November 20, 1938, PPF 3518; Roy Howard to Roosevelt, December 22, 1938, PPF 68.

72. Roosevelt to Hull, January 28, 1938, *FR, 1938,* 4 (Washington D.C., 1955):250.

73. Fisher to Roosevelt, August 20, 1937, PPF 431; Carlson to Miss LeHand, November 15, 1938, PPF 4951.

74. *FR, 1938,* 3 (Washington D.C., 1954):425-27.

75. Hosoya, "Miscalculations," pp. 98-100.

76. McAdoo to Roosevelt, July 27, 1939, and Roosevelt to McAdoo, August 3, 1939, PPF 308; Byrd to Roosevelt, July 31, 1939, and Roosevelt to Byrd, August 2, 1939, PPF 201; Roger S. Greene to Roosevelt, July 21, 1939, PPF 5826; Carlson to Miss LeHand, January 4, 1940, PPF 4951.

77. Knox to Roosevelt, January 23, 1940, PSF: Frank Knox, Box 28.

78. Grew to Roosevelt, November 6, 1939, PSF: Diplomatic Correspondence, Japan, Box 13; Grew to Hull, December 18, 1939, *FR, 1939,* 3 (Washington D.C., 1955):622.

79. Sayre Memorandum, May 1, 1940, PSF: Diplomatic Correspondence, Japan, Box 13.

80. Bullitt to Roosevelt, August 8, 1938, PSF: France, 1933-1939, Box 5; Carlson to Miss LeHand, November 29, 1939 and January 1, 1939, PPF 4951.

81. *FR, 1938,* 3:321-22, 325, 376-77.

82. *Ibid.,* 4:104-05.

83. Sayre to Roosevelt, May 16, 1940, PSF: Diplomatic Correspondence, Japan, Box 13; Roosevelt to John F. O'Ryan, November 30, 1940, PPF 1948.

84. Quoted in Hosoya, "Miscalculations," p. 106.

85. *Ibid.*

86. Enoch Walter Earle to Roosevelt, October 2, 1940, PPF 6952.

87. Ickes to Roosevelt, October 17, 1940, PSF: Harold L. Ickes, 1940-1945.

88. Stimson and Bundy, p. 385.

89. Memorandum to Secretary of the Navy, November 4, 1940, PSF: Navy Department, 1940, Box 22; Herbert Feis, *The Road to Pearl Harbor: The Coming of the War Between the United States and Japan* (Princeton, 1950), p. 124.

90. Samuel I. Rosenman, comp. and ed., *The Public Papers and Addresses of Franklin D. Roosevelt, IX: War–and Aid to the Democracies, 1940* (New York, 1941), p. 587; State Department Memorandum to Roosevelt, December 1940, PSF: Diplomatic Correspondence, Japan, Box 13.

91. Hull, *Memoirs,* 1:915; Robert E. Sherwood, *Roosevelt and Hopkins: An Intimate History* (New York, 1948), p. 259.

92. Roosevelt to Grew, January 21, 1941, PSF: Diplomatic Correspondence, Japan, Box 13.

93. Quoted in U.S., Department of State, *The Department of State Bulletin,* 4 (January 18, 1941):86.

94. Hull to Roosevelt, March 14, 1941, PSF: State Department, 1941, Box 34.

95. State Department Memorandum to Roosevelt, February 13, 1941, *ibid.*

96. Memorandum of conversations between Roosevelt and Nomura, February 14, 1941, PSF: Diplomatic Correspondence, Japan, Box 13; *FR, Japan, 1931-1941,* 2:387-89.

97. Memorandum of conversations between Hull and Nomura, April 16, 1941, PSF: Diplomatic Correspondence, Japan, Box 13. Nomura's report of this conversation was so limited that not until September did the Japanese government recognize the significance of Hull's four principles. See Robert J. C. Butow, "The Hull-Nomura Conversations: A Fundamental Misconception," *American Historical Review,* 65 (1960):822-36.

98. Ickes to Roosevelt, June 23 and 25, 1941; Roosevelt to Ickes, June 23 and July 1, 1941, PSF: Harold L. Ickes, 1940-1942, Box 23.

99. Feis, pp. 215-16.

100. Marshall to Roosevelt, July 15, 1941, PSF: Diplomatic Correspondence, Japan, Box 13.

101. *FR, 1941* (Washington D.C., 1956), 4:835-40.

102. Memorandum of the Welles-Nomura conversations, July 24, 1941, PSF: Diplomatic Correspondence, Japan, Box 13.

103. Feis, p. 238.

104. Sherwood, p. 316.

105. Memorandum of Roosevelt-Nomura conversations, August 17, 1941, PSF: Diplomatic Correspondence, Japan, Box 13.

106. Penciled memorandum, Hull to Roosevelt, September 28, 1941, and Roosevelt to Hull, September 28, 1941, *ibid.*

107. Harry B. Hawes to Roosevelt, August 19, 1941, PPF 3947.

108. Feis, p. 277.

109. *Ibid.*, pp. 299, 300.

110. Samuel I. Rosenman, comp. and ed., *The Public Papers and Addresses of Franklin D. Roosevelt, X: The Call to Battle Stations, 1941* (New York, 1950), pp. 500-02, 512-13.

111. Quoted in Hosoya, "Miscalculations," p. 111.

112. *FR, 1941*, 4:673.

113. Hosoya, "Miscalculations," p. 112.

Cabinet, Emperor, and Senior Statesmen

1. Kuno Osamu and Tsurumi Shunsuke, *Gendai Nihon no shisō* (Contemporary Japanese Thought) (Tokyo, 1956), p. 132.

2. Shigemitsu Mamoru, *Shōwa no dōran* (Upheavals in Shōwa Japan) (Tokyo, 1952), 1:148.

3. Kitano Kei, *Ningen Saionji-kō* (Biography of Prince Saionji) (Tokyo, 1941), pp. 287-93.

4. Saionji Kimmochi was born into a Kyoto courtier family in 1849. After serving as governor general for pacification during the fighting that accompanied the Meiji Restoration, he studied in Paris from 1870 until 1880. Upon returning to Japan he became head of the *Tōyō jiyū shinbun*, a newspaper that supported the popular rights movement, but was obliged to resign from this position by the direct order of the Meiji emperor. Accompanying Itō Hirobumi on his constitutional study mission to Europe, Saionji became intimate with Itō and joined him in founding the Seiyūkai. In 1903 he succeeded Itō as the party's second president. Saionji's studies in France and his association with Japanese liberals such as Nakae Chōmin predisposed him to liberal political views. He envisioned Japan's development into an enlightened nation in response to general international trends and the progress of civilization and advocated constitutional government internally and the adoption of a cooperative policy in foreign affairs.

Saionji participated in the planning for publication of *Sekai no Nihon* (Japan in the World), a journal edited by Takekoshi Yosaburō. "Japan in the world" was an expression that Saionji used frequently. Japan, he believed, must maintain international good will, nurture the capability of its people, and hand in hand with the great nations of the West majestically advance the causes of peace, civilization, and economic prosperity. He rejected as vainglory Japan's fancying itself the hegemon of the Far East or the lord of Asia.

During the period following the Russo-Japanese War the Chōshū army clique, with Yamagata Aritomo as its "shogun," not only strengthened Japan's military control in Korea and Manchuria but, by concentrating leadership of the army in its hands, attempted also to assume direction of internal political affairs. The army's plans to take over Manchuria, however, only intensified discord between Japan and the United States at a time when relations between the two countries were already strained by the immigration problem. Military expansion, moreover, brought financial difficulties, increased taxes, and social unrest.

In the last decades of the Meiji era Saionji, alternating with Katsura Tarō of the Yamagata line of the bureaucracy, formed two cabinets. He did not do so, however, in his capacity as president of the Seiyūkai but as a senior statesman of the Meiji government. Only Hara Takashi and one or two others from the Seiyūkai were admitted into his cabinets. When the movement to "defend the constitution" overthrew the third Katsura cabinet during the Taishō political change of 1913, Saionji retired from public life. After accepting the policy demands of the Seiyūkai, Yamamoto Gonnohyōe, a senior officer of the "Satsuma navy," formed an administration.

The Saionji cabinets of the Itō bureaucratic line, while working carefully to maintain harmony with Britain and the United States, sought also to advance the cause of Japanese imperialism. Makino Nobuaki was education minister in the first Saionji cabinet, minister of agriculture and commerce in the second, and foreign minister in the Yamamoto administration. From the first Saionji cabinet through the Yamamoto cabinet, Saitō Makoto held the post of navy minister. Sakatani Yoshirō was finance minister during Saionji's first term; Yamamoto Tatsuo and Takahashi Korekiyo, finance ministers in the second Saionji and Yamamoto cabinets, later joined the Saitō cabinet as home minister and finance minister, respectively.

Makino Nobuaki was born in 1861, the second son of Ōkubo Toshimichi of Satsuma, who had been active in the Meiji Restoration. After studying in the United States from 1872 to 1874, Makino entered the Foreign Ministry and earned recognition for a memorandum on reform of the local government system that he submitted to Itō Hirobumi when the latter visited England during his constitutional study mission. Subsequently Makino held a variety of posts—including appointments as provincial governor, vice minister of education, and ambassador to Austria—before entering Saionji's first cabinet. During his term as foreign minister three Japanese were killed in the Nanking incident of September 1913 and Political Affairs Bureau chief Abe Moritarō was assassinated by zealots critical of the government's "weak foreign policy." About the same time the state of California passed its anti-Japanese law and Makino undertook to arrange an agreement that would guarantee the future status of Japanese in the United States. Although he successfully opened negotiations with the U.S.

government, his successor as foreign minister, Katō Takaaki, did not pursue them further. In contrast to Katō, who devoted himself to strengthening the alliance between Japan and Great Britain, Makino gave greater consideration to relations with the United States.

Saitō Makoto was born in 1858 in Iwate prefecture. He joined the Japanese navy soon after its formation as a modern military service and, gaining recognition for his ability, received the encouragement and support of Admiral Yamamoto. It has been said that whenever a new administrative office was created by the navy, Saitō was the first to be assigned to it. In 1884 he became the first naval attaché assigned to the Japanese embassy in the United States. From 1898 to 1906 he served as vice navy minister under Yamamoto, was navy minister from 1906 to 1913, and became governor general of Korea after World War I.

5. Kobayashi Tatsuo, ed., *Suiusō nikki* (Green Rain Villa Diary) (Tokyo, 1966), pp. 333-35.

6. Harada Kumao, *Saionji-kō to seikyoku* (Prince Saionji and the Political Situation), 1 (Tokyo, 1950):20-21.

7. *Ibid.*

8. Ko Sakatani Shishaku Kinen Jigyōkai (Committee to Commemorate the Late Viscount Sakatani), ed., *Sakatani Yoshirō den* (Biography of Sakatani Yoshirō) (Tokyo, 1951).

9. Harada, 1:17-18.

10. Imai Seiichi, "Shidehara gaikō ni okeru seisaku kettei" (The Policymaking Process in Shidehara Diplomacy), in Nihon Seiji Gakkai (Japan Political Science Association), ed., *Nenpō Seijigaku: Taigai seisaku no kettei katei* (Annual Report of the Japan Political Science Association: Foreign Policy Decision Making) (Tokyo, 1959), p. 104.

11. Yoshizawa Kenkichi, *Gaikō rokujū nen* (Sixty Years of Diplomacy) (Tokyo, 1958), p. 145.

12. Lord Keeper of the Privy Seal Makino to Saionji's personal secretary Harada Kumao, in Harada, 2 (Tokyo, 1951):201.

13. Gaimushō (Foreign Ministry), ed., *Nihon gaikō nenpyō narabi ni shuyō monjo* (Chronology and Major Documents of Japanese Foreign Policy), 2 (Tokyo, 1955):211-21.

14. *Ibid.*, pp. 206-10.

15. Shigemitsu Mamoru, *Gaikō kaisō roku* (Diplomatic Memoirs) (Tokyo, 1953), pp. 169-71; Harada, 3 (Tokyo, 1951):112, 204.

16. *Ibid.*, 2:396-97; Kikkawa Manabu, *Arashi to tatakau tesshō Araki* (Biography of General Araki Sadao) (Tokyo, 1955), p. 262 and *passim*.

17. Harada, 4 (Tokyo, 1951):16-19. The three points are not precisely known, but an army plan entitled "Teikoku kokusaku" (National Policy of the Empire) presented to the Five Ministers Conference on October 2, 1933 is contained in *GS 8: Nitchū sensō 1* (Sino-Japanese War 1) (Tokyo, 1964), pp. 11-13. Concerning disarmament policy the plan said: "We will strive to find a solution to the disarmament problem without jeopardizing Japan's national security, which is based on its particular geographical requirements. We will also, in seeking revision of the Washington and London treaties, try to come to an understanding with the countries concerned that will provide us with a favorable settlement. At the same time, Japan's national security must be guaranteed, to the point of disrupting the conference if necessary."

18. Sanbō Honbu, Daini Ka (Army General Staff, Second Section), "Kaigun gunshuku seigen mondai ni kan suru keii" (Problems Posed by the Reduction of Naval Armaments), in *GS 12: Nitchū sensō 4* (Sino-Japanese War 4) (Tokyo, 1965), pp. 3-9.

19. Prime Minister Okada escaped unharmed in the assault of the young officers, Lord Keeper of the Privy Seal Saitō was killed, and Grand Chamberlain Suzuki gravely wounded. Subsequently, Imperial Household Minister Yuasa was shifted to the post of lord keeper of the privy seal and replaced by Matsudaira Tsuneo, former ambassador to the United States and Britain.

20. Konoe Fumimaro, *Konoe-kō seidan roku* (Memoirs) (Tokyo, 1936), pp. 231-41.

21. Konoe Fumimaro, "Genrō, jūshin, to yo" (The Genrō, the Senior Statesmen, and I), in *Kaizō* (Reconstruction), December 1949, pp. 32-36.

22. Shōwa Dōjinkai (Shōwa Comrades Association), ed., *Shōwa Kenkyū-kai* (The Shōwa Research Association) (Tokyo, 1968), pp. 84-85.

23. Yabe Teiji, *Konoe Fumimaro*, 1 (Tokyo, 1951):283-90.

24. Kikkawa, p. 275; *GS 8*, p. 11. The "Teikoku kokusaku" presented by the army on October 2, 1933 stated: "The United States is driven by a desire to dominate the Far East and will unceasingly oppose Japan's policy in Manchuria. We will therefore prepare to resist any interference with our actions there." In an earlier draft, dated September 22, the second sentence read: "If a situation arises in which it appears that the United States is seeking to take advantage of possible hostilities between Russia and Japan to place military pressure on us, we will not hesitate to fight."

25. Konoe Fumimaro, "Kono-goro omou koto" (Things I Have Been Pondering), July 1936, in *Konoe-kō seidan roku*, pp. 39-42.

26. Ishii Itarō, *Gaikō-kan no isshō* (The Life of a Diplomat) (Tokyo, 1950), p. 271.

27. *Ibid.*, pp. 280-83.

28. Kazami Akira, *Konoe naikaku* (The Konoe Cabinets) (Tokyo, 1951), p. 47.

29. Hattori Takushirō, *Dai Tōa sensō zenshi* (A Complete History of the Greater East Asia War), 1 (Tokyo, 1953):246.

30. Ishii, *Gaikō-kan no isshō*, pp. 299-301.

31. Yabe, 1:525.

32. *Shōwa Kenkyūkai*, p. 113; Asahi Jānaru Henshūbu (Asahi Journal Editorial Staff), ed., *Shōwashi no shunkan* (Major Events in Shōwa History), 1 (Tokyo, 1966):274.

33. Ogata Taketora, *Ichi gunjin no shōgai* (The Life of an Admiral) (Tokyo, 1955), pp. 39-43. The date given for this is August 21, 1939, but according to a letter from Arita Hachirō to Ogata it was actually August 1938.

34. Konoe Fumimaro, *Heiwa e no doryoku* (My Struggle for Peace) (Tokyo, 1946), pp. 112-17.

35. *Ibid.*, p. 118.

36. Gaimushō, *Nihon gaikō nenpyō*, 2:431.

37. Hattori, 1:248.

38. For the Imperial Conference, see *ibid.*, pp. 63-71. For the meeting of the Privy Council, see Fukai Eigo, *Sūmitsuin jūyōkiji oboegaki* (Notes on Important Deliberations of the Privy Council) (Tokyo, 1953), pp. 69-92. Fukai has recorded the following impressions of the Privy Council session: "If Japan had concluded an alliance with Germany and Italy on the one hand and had made some kind of compromise with the United States on the other, I believe it could have secured a powerful position in the Far East without undue risk. But I could scarcely accept the argument that the way to prevent war with the United States was to place unremitting pressure on it. I could not help feeling that Foreign Minister Matsuoka's talk about preventing war was simply a pretext for the purpose of concluding the Tripartite Pact. . . . Although Prime Minister Konoe spoke tersely and did not go into details, he was not at all his usual unruffled self. He appeared quite grave and seemed aware that Japan stood at a great turning point in its history."

39. Tsunoda Jun, "Nihon no tai-Bei kaisen" (The Outbreak of War with the United States), in Nihon Kokusai Seiji Gakkai, Taiheiyō Sensō Gen'in

Kenkyūbu (Japan International Politics Association, Study Group on the Origins of the Pacific War), ed., *Taiheiyō sensō e no michi* (Road to the Pacific War), 7 (Tokyo, 1963):171-72.

40. Konoe, *Heiwa e no doryoku*, pp. 25-26.

41. *GS 3: Zoruge jiken 3* (The Sorge Case 3) (Tokyo, 1962), p. 532.

42. *Ibid.*, pp. 536-37.

43. Ishii, *Gaikō-kan no isshō*, pp. 280-85.

44. Tsunoda, pp. 293-305.

45. The meeting was attended by all the former prime ministers with the exception of the aged Kiyoura Keigo—Wakatsuki, Okada, Hirota, Hayashi, Konoe, Hiranuma, Abe, and Yonai—as well as by Privy Council President Hara Yoshimichi.

46. Harada, 1:21-22.

The Role of the Department of State

1. Hornbeck to Carlton Savage, March 27, 1962, Hornbeck Papers, Hoover Institution, Stanford University. As indicated, the prefatory quotation is from Hornbeck to Sumner Welles, May 18, 1940, Hornbeck Papers. Hornbeck was writing in response to questions raised by Welles' son Benjamin, a student of Samuel Flagg Bemis at Yale.

2. Typed sheet bearing Hornbeck name, no date, marked "file War Japan and U.S.," "Pearl Harbor" box, Hornbeck Papers.

3. The biographical data is found in Hornbeck's Draft Autobiography, undated, incomplete, and without page numbers, but apparently written in 1962, Hornbeck Papers; also "Biographical Material" file, Hornbeck Papers; *Who's Who in America*, 1950-51 edition, pp. 1293-94.

4. Draft Autobiography, section "1910-31," Hornbeck Papers. Hornbeck adds, parenthetically, "I wonder what Pres. Pusey is thinking and saying in connection with the migration from Harvard to Washington that has been taking place since January 1961!"

5. *Register of the Department of State*, January 1, 1931 (Washington D.C., 1931), p. 7. I am indebted to Mr. John Carter Vincent of Cambridge, Mass., a later division chief, for information on the usual allocation of responsibilities within the division during this period.

6. Graham H. Stuart, *The Department of State: A History of Its Organization, Procedure, and Personnel* (New York, 1949), pp. 326-27; see also Katherine E. Crane, *Mr. Carr of State: Forty-Seven Years in the Department of State* (New York, 1960), pp. 314-15.

7. Others also held the title of a second (or third) assistant chief from time to time, most notably Stuart J. Fuller, a former businessman who served as the division's (and the department's) chief specialist in problems pertaining to narcotics control; Fuller was not otherwise involved in FE policy matters. By 1941 Maxwell Hamilton had four assistant chiefs, a sudden increase.

8. Hornbeck to Wilbur J. Carr, June 30, 1930, Hornbeck Papers.

9. For biographical material on Hamilton, see the *Register of the Department of State*, October 1, 1942, p. 159. I am told that Hamilton's father was also a clergyman but have been unable to confirm this report.

10. Interview with Alger Hiss, New York City, December 8, 1969. Hiss served as special assistant to Hornbeck once the latter became political adviser.

11. Interview with John Carter Vincent, Cambridge, Mass., May 23, 1969. Vincent served as a junior officer in FE from 1935 to 1939 between China assignments.

12. Interview with Alger Hiss.

13. For biographical material on Ballantine, see the *Register of the Department of State*, October 1, 1942, p. 93.

14. Interview with Alger Hiss.

15. Draft Autobiography, "1937-40." The other three newly appointed advisers were James Dunn (Western Europe), Laurence Duggan (Latin America), and Wallace Murray (Near East).

16. See James R. Newcomer, "Cordell Hull and Role Perception," unpublished seminar paper, Department of Political Science, Stanford University, July 15, 1969.

17. Cordell Hull, *The Memoirs of Cordell Hull* (New York, 1948), 1:894-95, and 2:988-89, 1095.

18. *Ibid.*, 2:1031.

19. Herbert Feis, *The Road to Pearl Harbor: The Coming of the War Between the United States and Japan* (Princeton, 1950), pp. 173-74. Another participant in these talks was a junior Japanese language officer, Max W. Schmidt, of whom Feis writes (p. 174): "Schmidt was the youngest and most

tireless in trying to find words for policies; and like Hamilton, a believer in a chance of a just compromise if it were really wanted." By 1942 Schmidt had changed his name to Max W. Bishop (see the Department's *Register* for that year).

20. Elting E. Morison, *Turmoil and Tradition: A Study of the Life and Times of Henry L. Stimson* (New York, 1964), pp. 238, 233.

21. Quoted in Richard N. Current, "Henry L. Stimson," in Norman A. Graebner, ed., *An Uncertain Tradition: American Secretaries of State in the Twentieth Century* (New York, 1961), p. 182.

22. Quoted in William L. Neumann, *America Encounters Japan, from Perry to MacArthur* (New York, 1965), p. 264.

23. Current, "Stimson," pp. 170, 172. Hoover's words are recorded by Castle.

24. Hull, *Memoirs*, 1:536.

25. John Morton Blum, *From the Morgenthau Diaries: Years of Crisis, 1928-1938* (Boston, 1959), p. 519.

26. Dorothy Borg, *The United States and the Far Eastern Crisis of 1933-1938* (Cambridge, Mass., 1964), pp. 96-97.

27. Current, "Stimson," p. 171.

28. Draft Autobiography, "Manchurian Crisis."

29. *Ibid.*, "1910-31." General Frank McCoy was an old friend of Stimson who, at the secretary's suggestion, was appointed unofficial American representative to the Lytton Commission.

30. *Ibid.*

31. Hull, *Memoirs*, 1:202.

32. Crane, pp. 324-25.

33. *Ibid.* See also William Phillips, *Ventures in Diplomacy* (Boston, 1952), p. 185.

34. Hull, *Memoirs*, 1:202, 508-09.

35. *Ibid.*, 2:1229.

36. *Ibid.*, 1:671.

37. Interview with John Carter Vincent.

38. Stanley K. Hornbeck, *Contemporary Politics in the Far East* (New York, 1916; 8th impression, New York, 1928).

39. *Ibid.*, p. 357.

40. *Ibid.,* pp. 387, 381.

41. *Ibid.* pp. 390, 398-99.

42. *Ibid.*, pp. 402-03.

43. *Ibid.*, pp. ix, 347. See also Stanley K. Hornbeck, "Trade, Concessions, Investments—Conflict and Policy in the Far East," *Proceedings of the Academy of Political Science*, 17, no. 3 (1917):91-92.

44. *Ibid.,* p. 98.

45. Stanley K. Hornbeck, "Principles and Policies in Regard to China," *Foreign Affairs*, 1, no. 2 (December 15, 1922):124ff.

46. *Ibid.* Also Stanley K. Hornbeck, " 'Has the United States a Chinese Policy?' " *Foreign Affairs*, 5, no. 4 (July 1927):617-32.

47. Hornbeck, "Principles and Policies," pp. 121, 123.

48. *Ibid.*, p. 125.

49. Hornbeck, " 'Has the United States a Chinese Policy?' " p. 631.

50. Hornbeck, "Principles and Policies," p. 135.

51. Hornbeck, " 'Has the United States a Chinese Policy?' " p. 619.

52. Hornbeck, "Principles and Policies," p. 128.

53. Hornbeck, " 'Has the United States a Chinese Policy?' " p. 629.

54. Stanley K. Hornbeck, *China To-day: Political* (Boston, 1927), p. 481.

55. Morison, *Turmoil and Tradition,* p. 314.

56. Armin Rappaport, *Henry L. Stimson and Japan, 1931-33* (Chicago, 1963), p. 38. Rappaport's account is somewhat at odds with both the Morison biography and the Hornbeck papers at a number of junctures.

57. See, for instance, Drew Pearson and Constantine Brown, *The Diplomatic Game* (London, 1935), pp. 284-85. Hornbeck claims that such reports had "no basis in fact. True, Mr. Castle and I did not see in the same light all angles and all details of the problem; and the same was true regarding the Secretary and me. But, never were Mr. Castle and I nor the Secretary and I at odds." Draft Autobiography, "1910-31."

58. Rappaport, pp. 89-90.

59. Morison, *Turmoil and Tradition*, pp. 316-17.

60. *Ibid.*; also Rappaport, pp. 90-91.

61. Morison, *Turmoil and Tradition*, pp. 317-18; Rappaport, p. 94.

62. Draft Autobiography, "Manchurian Crisis." Hornbeck adds McCoy to those listed in the Bundy-Stimson memoirs and notes that "Mr. Castle 'believes' that he also was there."

63. *Ibid.*, "1933-37."

64. American Society of International Law, *Proceedings*, 26th Annual Meeting, Washington D.C., April 28-30, 1932 (Washington D.C., 1932), pp. 70-71.

65. Borg, *Far Eastern Crisis*, pp. 35-36, 45.

66. Draft Autobiography, "1933-37."

67. Borg, *Far Eastern Crisis*, pp. 78-79.

68. *Ibid.*, p. 79.

69. Draft Autobiography, "1933-37."

70. Borg, *Far Eastern Crisis*, pp. 79-80.

71. *Ibid.*, pp. 80-81.

72. . Hornbeck to Hull, May 16, 1934, State Department files 711.93/324, National Archives, Washington D.C.

73. *FR, 1934* (Washington D.C., 1950), 3:388-90.

74. *Ibid.*, p. 392.

75. Borg, *Far Eastern Crisis*, p. 243.

76. Ickes diary, quoted in *ibid.*, p. 244.

77. *Ibid.*

78. *FR, 1937* (Washington D.C., 1954), 3:954.

79. Borg, *Far Eastern Crisis*, p. 246.

80. *FR, 1937*, 3:973.

81. Borg, *Far Eastern Crisis*, p. 253. See also Waldo H. Heinrichs, Jr., *American Ambassador: Joseph C. Grew and the Development of the United States Diplomatic Tradition* (Boston, 1966), p. 235. Heinrichs sees Grew's approval of the FE "Contras" as evidence of the ambassador's disillusionment after the downfall of the Hirota cabinet in January. "Grew's central argument was that Japan could not be trusted to live up to contractual obligations. . . . For once he and Hornbeck were in complete accord."

82. Draft Autobiography, "1937-40."

83. *FR, 1935* (Washington D.C., 1953), 3:855-57.

84. John Morton Blum, *From the Morgenthau Diaries: Years of Urgency, 1938-1941* (Boston, 1965), p. 127.

85. Feis, p. 93. I am indebted to the research of P. Ellis Tinois, Harvard 1969, for material relating to the "embargo incident."

86. *FR, 1940* (Washington D.C., 1955), 4:576.

87. *Ibid.*, p. 583.

88. *Ibid.*, pp. 583-85.

89. Hornbeck to Sumner Welles, June 25, 1940, "Welles" box, Hornbeck Papers.

90. Blum, *Years of Urgency*, pp. 350-51.

91. *FR, 1940*, 4:586-87.

92. U.S., Congress, Senate, Internal Security Subcommittee of the Committee on the Judiciary, *Morgenthau Diary (China)*, 89th Congress, lst session (Washington D.C., 1965), 1:351-52.

93. Feis, p. 92.

94. Blum, *Years of Urgency*, p. 353.

95. Interview with John K. Emmerson, Stanford, California, January 29, 1969. Emmerson was the Foreign Service officer in question.

96. Nancy H. Hooker, ed., *The Moffat Papers: Selections from the Diplomatic Journals of Jay Pierrepont Moffat, 1919-1943* (Cambridge, Mass., 1956), p. 334. After talking to Hull, Moffat wrote that Hornbeck "is almost alone in advocating measures that almost certainly would bring us into war." *Ibid.*, p. 331.

97. Hornbeck to Sumner Welles, July 23, 1941, "Welles" box, Hornbeck Papers. Hornbeck makes this statement to indicate "one fundamental point of departure as between my reasoning and the reasoning which appears to underlie certain attitudes and positions which appear to prevail in certain other quarters." Notes Welles, "most helpful."

98. See, for instance, Hornbeck's one-page unaddressed memorandum of October 16, 1941 in which he cites the Hoover-Stimson failure. "Welles" box, Hornbeck Papers.

99. Hornbeck to Cordell Hull, September 25, 1941, *ibid.* Hornbeck was arguing here against both a Roosevelt-Konoe meeting and "any agreement between the U.S. and Japan."

100. Hornbeck to Sumner Welles, July 3, 1941, *ibid.*

101. Hornbeck to Sumner Welles, August 18, 1941, *ibid.* The annotated memorandum of July 16 is attached.

102. Draft Autobiography, "1941." Hornbeck claims substantial responsibility for the rejection of Konoe's proposal; he pushed Hull and Hull pushed Roosevelt. See also Heinrichs, *Grew*, pp. 339-50; and Feis, pp. 259-60.

103. Heinrichs, *Grew*, p. 349. Grew's reaction: "Appeasement. Is that what the Department thinks I have been advocating?" For a most cogent and lucid analysis of the views that divided the Stimsonian "idealists"—notably Hornbeck—from the Grew-Moffat "realists," see *ibid.*, pp. 267-70.

104. Draft Autobiography, "1941."

105. Conversation with Carlton Savage, Washington D.C., January 1969. Savage was an assistant to the assistant secretary of state in 1941.

106. Blum, *Years of Urgency*, p. 380.

107. *Ibid.*, p. 384.

108. Heinrichs, *Grew*, pp. 356-57.

109. Quoted in Roberta Wohlstetter, *Pearl Harbor: Warning and Decision* (Stanford, 1962), p. 264.

110. *Ibid.*, pp. 264-65.

111. Draft Autobiography, "1941."

112. Typed sheet bearing Hornbeck name, no date, marked "file War Japan and U.S.," "Pearl Harbor" box, Hornbeck Papers. This sheet bears three questions and answers: the first is quoted here, and the third is cited at the beginning of this essay and in note 2, above. The second question and answer: "Did I dissent from certain views expressed by Mr. Grew? The answer is: Yes, over the years, and in some particulars; and so did others of us here, on various occasions and in varying degrees."

113. Interview with Alger Hiss.

114. Hornbeck, "Trade, Concessions, Investments," p. 94.

115. Interview with Alger Hiss. See also Heinrichs, *Grew*, pp. 267-70.

116. Hornbeck to Welles, January 31, 1940, "Welles" box, Hornbeck Papers.

117. *Ibid.*

118. Draft Autobiography, "1941." His conclusion: "The views, the reasoning and the purposes of Washington and Tokyo differed so completely that there was no possibility of there being achieved a 'meeting of minds.'"

The Role of the United States Embassy in Tokyo

1. Joseph C. Grew, *Turbulent Era: A Diplomatic Record of Forty Years, 1904-1945* (Boston, 1952), 2:1230.

2. *Ibid.*, p. 1227.

3. Joseph C. Grew, *Ten Years in Japan* (New York, 1944), p. 304.

4. Grew diary, April 16, 1939, Grew Papers, Harvard University Library, Cambridge, Mass.

5. For details see Nihon Kokusai Seiji Gakkai, Taiheiyō Sensō Gen'in Kenkyūbu (Japan International Politics Association, Study Group on the Origins of the Pacific War), ed., *Taiheiyō sensō e no michi* (Road to the Pacific War), 3 (Tokyo, 1962):73ff (hereafter cited as *TSM*).

6. Cordell Hull, *The Memoirs of Cordell Hull* (New York, 1948), 1:279.

7. Grew to Hull, April 18, 1934, *FR, 1934* (Washington D.C., 1950), 3:112.

8. Grew to Hornbeck, June 29, 1934, Grew Papers.

9. Grew to Hull, April 26, 1934, *FR, 1934*, 3:140-41.

10. Grew to Hornbeck, June 29, 1934, Grew Papers.

11. Hull to Grew, April 26, 1934, *FR, 1934*, 3:139.

12. Grew to Hornbeck, June 29, 1934, Grew Papers.

13. Grew to Hull, April 20, 1934, *FR, 1934*, 3:117-21.

14. Phillips to Grew, April 24, 1934, *ibid.*, pp. 129-30.

15. Grew diary, April 25, 1934.

16. Grew to Hull, April 26, 1934, *FR, 1934*, 3:140-41.

17. Grew to Hornbeck, April 28, 1934, Grew Papers.

18. Dorothy Borg, *The United States and the Far Eastern Crisis of 1933-1938* (Cambridge, Mass., 1964), pp. 79-80.

19. Grew, *Ten Years in Japan*, p. 133.

20. Grew diary, April 24, 1934.

21. *Ibid.*, February 8, 1934.

22. *Ibid.*, April 9, 1934.

23. Grew to Hull, May 4, 1934, *FR, 1934*, 2:162; Grew, *Ten Years in Japan*, p. 133.

24. Honjō Shigeru, *Honjō nikki* (Honjō Diary) (Tokyo, 1967), p. 176.

25. Hirota Kōki Denki Kankōkai (Committee to Publish a Biography of Hirota Kōki), ed., *Hirota Kōki* (Tokyo, 1966), pp. 110-17.

26. Grew diary, April 26, 1934.

27. *Hirota Kōki*, pp. 133-41.

28. Hull, *Memoirs*, 1:270.

29. Hornbeck's marginal comment, May 1934, *FR, 1934*, 3:162, fn. 96.

30. Grew to Hull, May 1, 1934, *ibid.*, p. 152.

31. Waldo H. Heinrichs, Jr., *American Ambassador: Joseph C. Grew and the Development of the United States Diplomatic Tradition* (Boston, 1966), p. 218.

32. Grew, *Ten Years in Japan*, p. 207.

33. Hornbeck memorandum, July 14, 1937, *FR, 1937* (Washington D.C., 1954), 3:167-70.

34. Peck to Hull, July 9, 1937, *ibid.*, p. 129.

35. Hamilton memorandum, July 12, 1937, *ibid.*, pp. 143-44; Peck to Hull, July 12, 1937, *ibid.*, p. 147.

36. Myer memorandum, July 15, 1937, *ibid.*, p. 172; Grew to Hull, July 14, 1937, *FR, Japan, 1931-1941* (Washington D.C., 1943), 1:322-23.

37. Hata Ikuhiko, "Rokōkyō jiken" (The Marco Polo Bridge Incident), in *TSM*, 4 (Tokyo, 1963):5ff.

38. Grew, *Ten Years in Japan*, p. 212; *FR, Japan, 1931-1941*, 1:327-28.

39. Grew to Hull, July 14, 1937, *FR, 1937*, 3:164-66.

40. Hornbeck memorandum, July 12, 1937, *ibid.*, p. 144.

41. Hull to Grew, October 16, 1937, Grew Papers.

42. Grew diary, October 30, 1937.

43. Hull to Grew, October 16, 1937, Grew Papers.

44. Grew, *Turbulent Era*, 2:1094.

45. *Ibid.*, pp. 1094-95.

46. *GS 9: Nitchū sensō 2* (Sino-Japanese War 2) (Tokyo, 1964), p. 55.

47. Grew diary, November 1, 1937.

48. *Ibid.*, November 6, 1937.

49. *Ibid.*, November 5, 1937.

50. *Ibid*, November 15, 1937.

51. *Ibid.*, November 18, 1937.

52. *Ibid.*, November 20, 1937.

53. *Ibid.*, December 14, 1937. `For some details on the *Panay* crisis, see Manny T. Koginos, *The Panay Incident: Prelude to War* (Lafayette, Ind., 1967).

54. This paragraph is based on the *Asahi shinbun* of December 13 (evening), 14 (morning and evening), 15 (morning), and 16 (morning and evening).

55. Grew, *Ten Years in Japan*, p. 240.

56. *Asahi shinbun*, December 27 and 28, 1937.

57. *Ibid.*, December 14, 1937.

58. See the essays in this volume by Itō Takashi, Kakegawa Tomiko, and Mitani Taichirō.

59. Grew memorandum, April 1939, Grew Papers.

60. Grew, *Ten Years in Japan*, p. 281.

61. Grew diary, April 16, 1939.

62. Grew, *Turbulent Era*, 2:1211.

63. Grew diary, January 31 and April 10, 1939.

64. Hull to Grew, October 24, 1939, *FR, 1939* (Washington D.C., 1955), 3:590; Hull to Grew, October 7, 1939, *ibid.*, p. 584.

65. Okabe Saburō, "Chū-Nichi Beikoku taishi no shosetsu ni mukuyu" (Replying to the Views Expressed by the American Ambassador to Japan), *Gaikō jihō* (Revue Diplomatique), 92, no. 5 (December 1, 1939):82-98.

66. "Beikoku no kyokutō seisaku to Nichi-Bei kankei" (America's East Asian Policy and Japanese-American Relations), a report given by an anonymous member before the Japan Association for International Affairs and mimeographed for private distribution, April 1940.

67. Heinrichs, *Grew*, p. 346.

68. *Ibid.*, p. 357.

69. Letter from John K. Emmerson to the author, April 30, 1969.

The Role of the Foreign Ministry

1. Hirota Kōki Denki Kankōkai (Committee to Publish a Biography of Hirota Kōki), ed., *Hirota Kōki* (Tokyo, 1966), pp. 641-42.

2. Kawai Eijirō, "Gaikō no kakushin" (Renovation in Diplomacy), *Chūō kōron* (Central Review), 52, no. 13 (December 1937):31.

3. Harada Kumao, *Saionji-kō to seikyoku* (Prince Saionji and the Political Situation), 7 (Tokyo, 1952):334-35.

4. Gaimushō (Foreign Ministry), "Jōyaku no teiketsu hijun oyobi kōfu ni kansuru chōsho" (Report on the Conclusion, Ratification, and Publication of Treaties), December 1928, Foreign Ministry Archives.

5. Hasegawa Shin'ichi, "Zaigai gaikōkan hyōbanki" (Japanese Diplomats Abroad), *Kaizō* (Reconstruction), 17, no. 9 (September 1935):99.

6. Uchida Yasuya Denki Kankōkai (Committee to Publish a Biography of Uchida Yasuya), ed., *Uchida Yasuya* (Tokyo, 1968), pp. 334-38.

7. Two letters from Shiratori to Arita and one letter from Arita to Shiratori, November 1935, Foreign Ministry Archives.

8. Harada, 6 (Tokyo, 1951):229.

9. *GS 10: Nitchū sensō 3* (Sino-Japanese War 3) (Tokyo, 1964), p. 353.

10. Akamatsu Sukeyuki, *Shōwa jūsan nen no kokusai jōsei* (The International Situation in 1938) (Tokyo, 1940), p. 170.

11. Hirakawa Michio, "Gaimu kanryō o tsuku" (A Critique of the Foreign Ministry Bureaucracy), *Kaizō*, 21, no. 11 (November 1939):94.

12. *GS 10*, pp. 333-34.

Japan's Foreign Ministry and Its Embassy in Washington

1. See my "Twenty-Five Years after Pearl Harbor: A New Look at Japan's Decision for War," in Grant K. Goodman, comp., *Imperial Japan and Asia: A Reassessment* (New York, 1967), pp. 52-64.

2. Nomura Kichisaburō, *Beikoku ni tsukai shite* (My Mission to the United States) (Tokyo, 1948), p. 18.

3. *Ibid.*, pp. 19-25.

4. Ikawa Tadao, "Hōi no misshi" (Secret Emissary in a Sacred Gown), *Keizai hihan* (Economic Criticism), January 1952, p. 91.

5. *Ibid.* Some of these telegrams are in Nihon Kokusai Seiji Gakkai, Taiheiyō Sensō Gen'in Kenkyūbu (Japan International Politics Association, Study Group on the Origins of the Pacific War), ed., *Taiheiyō sensō e no michi: Bekkan shiryō hen* (Road to the Pacific War: Supplementary Volume of Documents) (Tokyo, 1963), pp. 403-08 (hereafter cited as *TSM*).

6. Matsuoka in Osaka to Nomura, March 17, 1941, Foreign Ministry Archives.

7. *FR, 1941*, 4 (Washington D.C., 1956):135-39.

8. The Draft Understanding was interpreted by high officials in the State Department as "a tentative basis for a possible counter-draft to the Japanese draft of April 9, 1941" and was regarded by Hull as "a basis for starting conversations." *Ibid.*, p. 159. See also Cordell Hull, *The Memoirs of Cordell Hull*, 2 (New York, 1948):995.

9. Ōhashi Chūichi, *Taiheiyō sensō yuraiki* (The Origins of the Pacific War) (Tokyo, 1952), pp. 112-17.

10. In particular the telegram sent by Colonel Iwakuro was instrumental in generating a mistaken impression of the Draft Understanding among Japanese leaders. See *TSM*, 7 (Tokyo, 1963):162-63.

11. Konoe Fumimaro, *Heiwa e no doryoku* (My Struggle for Peace) (Tokyo, 1946), pp. 43-45.

12. Kido Kōichi, *Kido Kōichi nikki* (Diary of Kido Kōichi), 2 (Tokyo, 1966):870.

13. Hosoya Chihiro, "Matsuoka Yōsuke," in Hayashi Shigeru, ed., *Jinbutsu Nihon no rekishi* (Prominent Figures in Japanese History), 14 (Tokyo, 1966):179-82.

14. *TSM: Bekkan shiryō hen*, p. 340.

15. Gaimushō (Foreign Ministry), ed., "Gaikō shiryō: Nichi-Bei kōshō keii no bu" (Diplomatic Documents: Details of the U.S.-Japanese Negotiations), 1946, p. 25, Foreign Ministry Archives (hereafter cited as Gaimushō, "Keii");

Ikawa, "Hōi no misshi," *Keizai hihan*, March 1952, pp. 59-60; *FR, 1941*, 4:113-14.

16. *FR, Japan, 1931-1941* (Washington D.C., 1943) 2:143-44.

17. Matsuoka received the telegram from Nomura on April 3 in Rome. Gaimushō, "Keii," p. 25.

18. *Ibid.*, pp. 24-25.

19. Gaimushō, ed., "Gaikō shiryō: Nichi-Bei kōshō kiroku no bu" (Diplomatic Documents: Records of the U.S.-Japanese Negotiations), 1946, pp. 1-2, Foreign Ministry Archives (hereafter cited as Gaimushō, "Kiroku").

20. Sanbō Honbu (Army General Staff), ed., *Sugiyama memo* (Liaison Conference Records of Chief of Staff Sugiyama), 1 (Tokyo, 1967):199-200.

21. *Ibid.*, pp. 203-04; Gaimushō, "Kiroku," pp. 35-37.

22. Hull, *Memoirs*, 2:997.

23. Nomura to Matsuoka, May 8, 1941, in Gaimushō, "Kiroku," pp. 40-44.

24. *FR, Japan, 1931-1941*, 2:420-25.

25. Gaimushō, "Kiroku," pp. 58-59.

26. Grew to Hull, May 16, 1941, *FR, 1941*, 4:194-95.

27. Nomura to Matsuoka, May 13, 1941, in Gaimushō, "Kiroku," p. 59; Matsuoka to Nomura, May 15, 1941, *ibid.*, p. 60.

28. Nomura to Matsuoka, May 8, 1941, *ibid.*, p. 44.

29. *FR, Japan, 1931-1941*, 2:428-30.

30. *Ibid.*, pp. 446-51.

31. Gaimushō, "Keii," pp. 102-04.

32. *FR, Japan, 1931-1941*, 2:454-55.

33. *FR, 1941*, 4:256-59.

34. *FR, Japan, 1931-1941*, 2:473-76; Hull, *Memoirs*, 2:1010.

35. *Ibid.*, pp. 486-92.

36. *Sugiyama memo*, pp. 265-73.

37. Matsuoka to Nomura, July 14, 1941, in Gaimushō, "Kiroku," pp. 100-02; Matsuoka to Nomura, July 15, 1941, *ibid.*, pp. 102-09.

38. *TSM: Bekkan shiryō hen*, pp. 475-78; Gaimushō, "Keii," pp. 144-51.

39. *FR, Japan, 1931-1941*, 2:597-600.

40. Toyoda to Nomura, September 4, 1941, in Gaimushō, "Kiroku," pp. 244-47.

41. *FR, Japan, 1931-1941*, 2:597, fn. 97. Nomura's proposal was withdrawn on September 10; Gaimushō, "Keii," p. 188.

42. Toyoda to Nomura, September 25, 1941, Foreign Ministry Archives.

43. Tōgō Shigenori, *Jidai no ichimen* (Cause of Japan) (Tokyo, 1952), p. 198.

44. Nomura to Toyoda, October 3, 1941, in Gaimushō, "Kiroku," pp. 341-43; Tōgō, pp. 183-84, 198.

45. *Sugiyama memo*, pp. 372-80.

46. On November 5 an Imperial Conference had set December 1 as the deadline for reaching an agreement; thereafter an attack on the United States might be launched at any moment. *Ibid.*, pp. 406-31.

47. Nomura to Tōgō, November 18, 1941, in Gaimushō, "Kiroku," pp. 455-56; *FR, Japan, 1931-1941*, 2:744-50.

48. Tōgō to Nomura, November 20, 1941, in Gaimushō, "Kiroku," p. 467.

49. Tōgō, pp. 266-68.

50. Toyoda to Nomura, September 4, 1941, in Gaimushō, "Kiroku," pp. 244-47; *FR, Japan, 1931-1941*, 2:608-09.

51. *FR, 1941*, 4:483-89.

52. Paul W. Schroeder, *The Axis Alliance and Japanese-American Relations, 1941* (Ithaca, 1958), p. 62.

53. *Ibid.*, pp. 60-61.

54. For the September 25 proposal, see Gaimushō, "Kiroku," pp. 302-14; *FR, Japan, 1931-1941*, 2:637-40.

55. Schroeder, pp. 68-69.

56. Nomura to Tōgō, November 16, 1941, Foreign Ministry Archives. Ballantine's memorandum on the discussion states: "We assume if the Japanese Government entered into an agreement with us the Tripartite Pact would automatically become a dead letter." *FR, Japan, 1931-1941*, 2:731-34.

57. Hull, *Memoirs*, 2:1008-09.

58. Among others, such important documents as the following may be cited: "Fundamentals of National Policy," August 7, 1936; and "Main Principles for Coping with the Changing World Situation," July 27, 1940.

59. Kawashima Takeyoshi asserts in his *Nihonjin no hō ishiki* (The Japanese Approach to Law) (Tokyo, 1967), pp. 113-14, that the Japanese tend to draw up contracts in a simplified manner, referring only to essential points. While the uncertainty of such contracts, he says, causes feelings of insecurity in Westerners, it tends to produce a sense of security in Japanese.

60. Concerning the assumption that memories of the Siberian Expedition affected the attitude toward Japan of some American officials, see Chihiro Hosoya, "Miscalculations in Deterrent Policy: Japanese-U.S. Relations, 1938-1941," *Journal of Peace Research* (Oslo), no. 2, (1968), pp. 111-12.

61. Prime Minister Konoe to President Roosevelt, August 27, 1941, in *FR, Japan, 1931-1941*, 2:572-73.

62. Roosevelt to Konoe, September 3, 1941, *ibid.*, pp. 591-92.

63. Following the Imperial Conference of September 6 Konoe met secretly with Ambassador Grew to convey his deeply felt desire for a reconciliation between Japan and the United States. Grew reported on the meeting as follows: "Prince Konoye ... conclusively and wholeheartedly agree[s] with the four principles enunciated by the Secretary of State as a basis for the rehabilitation of relations between the United States and Japan.
   "... [H]e likewise recognizes that only he can cause the desired rehabilitation to come about ... [and] is therefore determined to spare no effort ... to crown his present endeavors with success.
   "... He admitted that there are certain elements within the armed forces who do not approve his policies, but he voiced the conviction that since he had the full support of the responsible chiefs of the Army and Navy it would be possible for him to put down and control any opposition which might develop among these elements.
   "... Prince Konoye feels confident that all problems and questions at issue can be disposed of to our mutual satisfaction during the meeting with the President, and he ended our conversation with the statement that he is determined to bring to a successful conclusion the proposed reconstruction of relations with the United States regardless of cost or personal risk." *FR, Japan, 1931-1941*, 2:604-06.

64. On the problem of cultural differences affecting negotiating patterns in the diplomacy of Japan and the United States, see Mushakōji Kinhide, *Kokusai seiji to Nihon* (International Politics and Japan) (Tokyo, 1967), pp. 155-75.

The Role of the War Department and the Army

1. Lt. Col. J. G. McIlroy, Military Attaché, Tokyo, Report No. 6958, January 12, 1933, Military Information Division File No. 2657-H-377, Modern Military Records Division, Record Group 165, National Archives, Washington D.C. (hereafter cited as MID).

2. For a fuller discussion of the United States army between the world wars, see Russell F. Weigley, *History of the United States Army* (New York, 1967), chap. 17. The social composition of the American officer corps is analyzed in Morris Janowitz, *The Professional Soldier: A Social and Political Portrait* (Glencoe, Ill., 1960), especially chap. 5. For the concept of military professionalism in the American officer corps, see Samuel P. Huntington, *The Soldier and the State: The Theory and Politics of Civil-Military Relations* (Cambridge, Mass., 1957), especially chaps. 8-11.

3. These observations are drawn mainly from a reading of reports of the military attachés in Tokyo and General Staff comments upon them. See especially "Report on Sino-Japanese Operations in the Vicinity of Shanghai, 28 January, 1932-7 March, 1932, Prepared by the Intelligence Office, Fourth Marines, Marine Corps Expeditionary Forces," MID File No. 2657-H-377/183; Military Attaché, Tokyo, Report No. 6272, May 19, 1932, MID File No. 2657-H-399; Military Attaché, Tokyo, Report No. 6430, September 10, 1932, MID File No. 2023-825/13; "The Sino-Japanese Clash, Shanghai, January-March, 1932, Special Report Prepared in the Far Eastern Section, Military Intelligence Division, War Department General Staff, 3 June 1932," MID File No. 2657-H-377/183a; Military Attaché, Tokyo, Report No. 6513, October 31, 1932, MID File No. 2657-H-377/221; Military Attaché, Tokyo, Report No. 7319, May 2, 1934, MID File No. 2657-H-440/1; Military Attaché, Tokyo, Report No. 7533, November 13, 1934, MID File No. 2657-H-448/2; Memorandum for the Chief of Staff from Col. F. H. Lincoln, Assistant Chief of Staff, G-2, "The Japanese Situation," July 11, 1936, MID File No. 2657-H-439/25B; Military Attaché, Tokyo, Report No. 8601, January 13, 1937, MID File No. 2023-825/22; Military Attaché, Tokyo, Report No. 9404, May 27, 1938, MID File No. 2657-H-474/1.

4. Quoted in Forrest C. Pogue, *George C. Marshall: Ordeal and Hope, 1939-1942* (New York, 1966) p. 178; Mark Skinner Watson, *Chief of Staff: Prewar Plans and Preparations (United States Army in World War II: The War Department)* (Washington D.C., 1950), p. 121.

5. William L. Langer and S. Everett Gleason, *The Challenge to Isolation, 1937-1940* (New York, 1952), pp. 40-41; Watson, pp. 89-91.

6. Huntington, p. 342.

7. Quoted in Henry F. Pringle, *Theodore Roosevelt: A Biography* (New York, 1956), p. 287.

8. John A. S. Grenville and George Berkeley Young, *Politics, Strategy, and American Diplomacy: Studies in Foreign Policy, 1873-1917* (New Haven, 1966), pp. 313-17; Louis Morton, *Strategy and Command: The First Two Years (United States Army in World War II: The War in the Pacific)* (Washington D.C., 1962), pp. 21-23.

9. Grenville and Young, pp. 312-14; Morton, *Strategy and Command*, pp. 23-24.

10. Grenville and Young, pp. 317-19; Morton, *Strategy and Command*, p. 24.

11. Dudley W. Knox, *The Eclipse of American Sea Power* (New York, 1922), views the problem from the perspective of the 1920s. See also Morton, *Strategy and Command*, pp. 25-27; Harold and Margaret Sprout, *Toward a New Order of Sea Power* (2d ed., Princeton, 1946).

12. Dana George Mead, "United States Peacetime Strategic Planning, 1920-1941: The Color Plans to the Victory Program," Ph.D. dissertation, M.I.T., 1967, pp. 274-84; Morton, *Strategy and Command*, pp. 27-31.

13. Army Strategical Plan Orange, 1928, Modern Military Records Division, Record Group 94, National Archives.

14. Michael D. Reagan, "The Far Eastern Crisis of 1931-1932: Stimson, Hoover and the Armed Services," in Harold Stein, ed., *American Civil-Military Decisions: A Book of Case Studies* (University, Ala., 1963), pp. 29-37. For more general comments on the military's isolation from foreign policymaking in the 1930s, see Stein's introduction, pp. 6, 18, 24-25.

15. *FR, Japan, 1931-1941* (Washington D.C., 1943), 1:83-87; Elting E. Morison, *Turmoil and Tradition: A Study of the Life and Times of Henry L. Stimson* (Boston, 1960), pp. 395-98; Armin Rappaport, *Henry L. Stimson and Japan, 1931-1933* (Chicago, 1963).

16. Army and Navy Joint Defense Plan for Philippine Islands Coastal Frontier (Revision, 1932), Record Group 94.

17. Philippine Department, First Phase Plan-Orange, 1934, AG No. 198x, Record Group 94.

18. G-3 Estimate of the Situation, Philippine Department, First Phase Plan-Orange, 1934, AG No. 171, Record Group 94.

19. G-3 Annex to Philippine Department Plan, First Phase-Orange, 1936, AG No. 203x, Record Group 94.

20. Craig to Major General L. R. Holbrook, Commanding Philippine Department, April 7, 1937, carbon copy inserted into Philippine Department Plan, First Phase-Orange, 1936, AG No. 200x, Record Group 94.

21. Philippine Department, First Phase Plan-Orange, 1933, AG No. 199x, Record Group 94.

22. Morton, *Strategy and Command*, p. 35; Watson, p. 415.

23. Louis Morton, *The Fall of the Philippines (United States Army in World War II: The War in the Pacific)* (Washington D.C., 1953), p. 4; Morton, *Strategy and Command,* p. 36.

24. *Ibid.,* pp. 36-37. On a related issue, the army's reluctance to press even for as much equipment as it might have been able to obtain, see Watson, pp. 37-38.

25. Morton, *Strategy and Command,* p. 38; Watson, p. 415.

26. Morton, *Strategy and Command,* pp. 31-33.

27. Concentration Plan of Army Strategical Plan Orange, 1938, AG No. 228, Record Group 94; Morton, *Strategy and Command,* pp. 39-42; Watson, pp. 415-16.

28. Louis Morton, "Army and Marines on the China Station: A Study in Military and Political Rivalry," *Pacific Historical Review,* 29 (1960):51-73. Just as it is Professor Morton who has recounted in detail the story of the army's China garrison, so it is he who everywhere has broken ground in opening the history of the army in the Pacific before and during World War II, as a perusal of these notes indicates.

29. On MacArthur's ideas about the nature of armies, see Frederick Martin Stern, *The Citizen Army: Key to Defense in the Atomic Age* (New York, 1957), pp. 151, 356-57; Frank C. Waldrop, ed., *MacArthur on War* (New York, 1942), especially pp. 91-92. On his assuming command of the Philippine Commonwealth defense forces, see Douglas MacArthur, *Reminiscences* (New York, 1964), pp. 102-04; Morton, *Fall of the Philippines,* pp. 8-12; Pogue, pp. 175-76; Watson, p. 426.

30. MacArthur, pp. 104-08; Morton, *Fall of the Philippines,* pp. 12-13; Louis Morton, "The Philippine Army, 1935-39; Eisenhower's Memorandum to Quezon," *Military Affairs,* 12 (Summer 1948):103-07; Watson, pp. 420-21.

31. Pogue, pp. 16-17; Watson, pp. 98-99; Weigley, *History of the Army,* pp. 423-25. The army draft in question was one of the early essays leading to the Rainbow plans.

32. U.S., Congress, Joint Committee on the Investigation of the Pearl Harbor Attack, *Hearings,* 79th Congress, 1st session (Washington D.C., 1946), part 33; Maurice Matloff and Edwin M. Snell, *Strategic Planning for Coalition Warfare, 1941-1942 (United States Army in World War II: The War Department)* (Washington D.C., 1953), pp. 32-96; Watson, pp. 97-100, 103-04.

33. Pogue, pp. 139-65; Weigley, *History of the Army,* pp. 430-36.

34. Pogue, pp. 22-32, 42.

35. *Ibid.,* pp. 176-81; Watson, pp. 5-7, 414-17.

36. William L. Langer and S. Everett Gleason, *The Undeclared War, 1940-1941* (New York, 1953), pp. 176-80; Pogue, pp. 124-25; Watson, pp. 115-18. The memorandum in question is not to be confused with an earlier memorandum by General Strong, dated June 17; Watson, pp. 109-10.

37. Langer and Gleason, *Undeclared War,* pp. 221-23; Pogue, pp. 126-27; Watson, pp. 118-21.

38. Pogue, p. 127; Watson, pp. 121-23. The Joint Planning Committee believed that if the statement which included this dictum received the approval both of the Joint Board and of Undersecretary of State Sumner Welles, it might receive the formal concurrence of the Standing Liaison Committee. Such a formal action, some of the military planners hoped, might in turn elevate the importance of the Standing Liaison Committee as an instrument of cooperation between the armed services and the State Department. But formal action never occurred. Secretary of State Hull believed his department should remain apart from any association with issues that might be construed to be of a technical military nature. Hull did agree, however, to meet henceforth with the war and navy secretaries every Tuesday, and these meetings contributed something to advance coordination among the three departments beyond what the Standing Liaison Committee had accomplished. Watson, p. 123, gives the army's view of the matter.

39. Langer and Gleason, *Undeclared War,* pp. 40-43; Pogue, pp. 168-70, 173-74, 177-78; Watson, pp. 414, 417-25, 431-32; Roberta Wohlstetter, *Pearl Harbor: Warning and Decision* (Stanford, 1962), pp. 80-89, 152-60.

40. Watson, pp. 423-25.

41. MacArthur, pp. 108-09; Morton, *Fall of the Philippines,* pp. 15-19; Pogue, pp. 181-83; Watson, pp. 434-38.

42. Hanson W. Baldwin, *Battles Lost and Won: Great Campaigns of World War II* (New York, 1966), pp. 115-19, 123-24; MacArthur, pp. 109-14; Morton, *Fall of the Philippines,* pp. 19-30, 67-71; Watson, pp. 425-26, 431-33. Revision of Rainbow 5 in November 1941 authorized MacArthur's changes in the defense plan for the Philippines.

43. Baldwin, p. 116; Morton, *Fall of the Philippines,* pp. 31-50; Watson, pp. 437-39; Wohlstetter, pp. 246-52. For "the hungry table," see Pogue, chap. 3.

44. Baldwin, pp. 116-18; Wesley Frank Craven and James Lea Cate, eds., *The Army Air Forces in World War II, I: Plans and Early Operations, January 1939 to August 1942* (Chicago, 1948), pp. 33-71; Alfred T. Hurley, *Billy Mitchell: Crusader for Air Power* (New York, 1964), pp. 86-89; Langer and Gleason, *Undeclared War,* p. 845; Pogue, pp. 185-89; Watson, p. 440; Wohlstetter, p. 251-52.

45. Craven and Cate, pp. 176-93; Morton, *Fall of the Philippines,* pp. 37-45; Pogue, pp. 186, 189; Watson, pp. 100-01, 443-44, 449.

46. Pogue, pp. 186-88.

47. Baldwin, pp. 117-18, 420-21; Pogue, pp. 201-03; Watson, pp. 442, 450.

48. Morton, *Fall of the Philippines,* pp. 36-37, 67; Pogue, pp. 188-89; Watson, pp. 440-49.

49. Pogue, p. 187.

50. Baldwin, pp. 116, 122-24; Watson, pp. 448-49.

51. Langer and Gleason, *Undeclared War,* pp. 843-48; Pogue, pp. 194-96; Watson, pp. 411, 446-52, 503-04.

52. Wohlstetter, pp. 75n, 172-73.

53. Report of Brig. Gen. W. D. Conner, Commanding General, U.S. Army Forces in China, of visit to Japan, September 1, 1925, p. 26, Office of the Adjutant General Project Files, 1917-1925, Countries Files, Box No. 267, Record Group 94.

54. *Ibid.*

55. Report of Capts. C. L. Bolte and David D. Barrett on Japanese maneuvers, November 25, 1933, Office of the Adjutant General, Central Files, 1926-39, Countries Files, Box No. 499, Record Group 94.

56. Report of Capt. Edgar P. Sorenson on Japanese Army Air Corps, August 16, 1934, *ibid.*

57. For correspondence relating to the care with which military attachés for Japan were selected, see File 210.681 Japan, October 4, 1932, Office of the Adjutant General Central Files, 1926-39, Countries Files, Box No. 498, Record Group 94.

58. Quoted in MacArthur, p. 104. For examples of base commanders' concern over Japanese spies, see Maj. Gen. Edwin B. Winans, Commanding Eighth Army Corps, Fort Sam Houston, Texas, to the Adjutant General, April 21, 1933, Office of the Adjutant General Central Files, 1926-39, Box No. 499, Record Group 94; Col. Cortlandt Parker, 7th F.A., Commanding, Fort Ethan Allen, Vt., to the Adjutant General, July 13, 1936, *ibid.*

59. Capt. John Wecherling, Asst. Military Attaché, Tokyo, Report No. 8533, November 24, 1936, MID File No. 2657-H-411/10.

60. Huntington, p. 343.

The Role of the Japanese Army

1. Bōeichō Senshi Shitsu (Defense Agency, Military History Office), ed., *Senshi sōsho: Daihon'ei rikugunbu 1* (Military History Series: Imperial Headquarters, Army 1) (Tokyo, 1967), p. 244. The exact contents of this "Imperial National Defense Policy" are not known. However, a footnote on p. 251 indicates that one of the editors of the volume, Shimanuki Takeji, was an Imperial Headquarters staff officer at the time of the 1936 revision of the Imperial National Defense Policy. His statement would therefore seem to be quite reliable.

2. *Ibid.*, p. 252.

3. *Ibid.*, p. 416.

4. "Sekai jōsei no suii ni tomonau jikyoku shori yōkō" (Main Principles for Coping with the Changing World Situation), Imperial Headquarters, Army and Navy Divisions, decision of July 27, 1940, in Nihon Kokusai Seiji Gakkai, Taiheiyō Sensō Gen'in Kenkyūbu (Japan International Politics Association, Study Group on the Origins of the Pacific War), ed., *Taiheiyō sensō e no michi: Bekkan shiryō hen* (Road to the Pacific War: Supplementary Volume of Documents) (Tokyo, 1963), pp. 322-23 (hereafter cited as *TSM*).

5. See table in Bōeichō Senshi Shitsu, *Daihon'ei rikugunbu 1.*

6. I have discussed this point in my article, "Sensō shidōsha no seishin kōzō" (The Mentality of Japanese Wartime Leaders), in Hashikawa Bunsō and Matsumoto Sannosuke, eds., *Kindai Nihon seiji shisōshi* (History of Modern Japanese Political Thought) 2 (Tokyo, 1970):386-98.

7. "Sakusen yōmurei kōryō" (Principal Rules of Strategy).

8. On Major Meckel's influence on the Japanese army, see Shukuri Shigeichi, *Nihon rikugunshi kenkyū: Mekkeru shōsa* (History of the Japanese Army: Major Meckel) (Tokyo, 1944). See also Ernst L. Presseisen, *Before Aggression: Europeans Prepare the Japanese Army* (Tucson, 1965).

9. Bōeichō Senshi Shitsu, ed., *Senshi sōsho: Hitō kōryaku sakusen* (Military History Series: Philippine Operations) (Tokyo, 1967), p. 27.

10. For the army and navy administrative areas, see the November 20, 1941 Liaison Conference decision, "Nanpō senryōchi gyōsei jitchi yōryō" (Guidelines for the Administration of the Southern Occupied Areas), in *TSM: Bekkan shiryō hen*, p. 587.

The Role of the United States Navy

1. Robert Greenhalgh Albion, "Makers of Naval Policy, 1798-1947" (Washington D.C., 1950), microfilm of unpublished manuscript, Harvard University Library, p. 474. On the navy in the twenties, see Gerald E. Wheeler, *Prelude to Pearl Harbor: The United States Navy and the Far East, 1921-1931* (Columbia, Mo., n.d.).

2. Albion, p. 488.

3. Samuel P. Huntington, *The Soldier and the State: The Theory and Politics of Civil-Military Relations* (Cambridge, Mass., 1957), pp. 248-51, 301-03; Rear Admiral Julius Augustus Furer, *Administration of the Navy Department in World War II* (Washington D.C., 1959), p. 112.

4. Thomas W. Ray, "The Bureaus Go On Forever," *United States Naval Institute Proceedings,* 94 (January 1968):56.

5. Transcripts of Admirals Alan Goodrich Kirk and Walter Stratton Anderson, Columbia University Oral History Collection, New York; Roberta Wohlstetter, *Pearl Harbor: Warning and Decision* (Stanford, 1962), p. 313.

6. J. W. Thomason to Admiral H. E. Yarnell, March 20, 1939, Yarnell Papers, Library of Congress, Washington D.C.; Clark G. Reynolds, *The Fast Carriers: The Forging of an Air Navy* (New York, 1968), p. 165.

7. Albion, p. 163; Captain Francis S. Craven, "Painful Development of a Professional Navy," *United States Naval Institute Proceedings,* 92 (May 1966):82.

8. Albion, pp. 341, 349, 358; transcripts of Eugene Wilson and Admirals James Fife, Richard L. Conolly, and Thomas Charles Hart, Columbia Oral History Collection; Ernest J. King and Walter Muir Whitehill, *Fleet Admiral King: A Naval Record* (New York, 1952), pp. 291-92.

9. Captain Dudley Knox, "National Strategy," lecture delivered at Naval War College, December 1934, War Plans Division Files, Operational Archives, Naval History Division, Washington D.C. (hereafter cited as Naval History Archives).

10. Yarnell to Rear Admiral A. W. Johnson, July 7, 1937, Yarnell Papers, Library of Congress.

11. Memorandum for the Commander in Chief, Asiatic Fleet, no author, no date (probably early 1937), Yarnell Papers, Library of Congress.

12. Joint Army-Navy Board No. 305, Serial 499, Records of the Joint Army-Navy Boards, 1918-1938, Record Group 225, National Archives, Washington D.C.

13. Draft letter from Hart to Chief of Naval Operations (not sent), May 24, 1941, General Board 405, General Board Studies, Naval History Archives.

14. Admiral W. V. Pratt, Senior Member Present, Joint Army-Navy Board, to Secretary of War, October 23, 1931, Joint Board No. 305, Serial 499, Joint Board Records.

15. Yarnell to Chief of Naval Operations, February 11, 1937, Yarnell Papers, Library of Congress.

16. Taylor to his brother, January 27, 1932, Admiral Montgomery M. Taylor Papers, Library of Congress.

17. Upham to the Secretary of the Navy, September 30, 1936, File A14, Secret and Confidential file of the Office of Chief of Naval Operations (Secret Correspondence, 1927-1940), microreel 3, Record Group 38, National Archives.

18. Conolly transcript.

19. Draft memorandum, Pratt to Admiral Harold R. Stark, January 28, 1941, Admiral William V. Pratt Papers, Naval History Archives. See also memorandum, Pratt to Secretary of the Navy, May 29, 1941, *ibid.*

20. Transcript of Admiral John Jennings Ballentine, Columbia Oral History Collection.

21. Yarnell to Admiral A. J. Hepburn, September 27, 1937, Yarnell Papers, Library of Congress.

22. Yarnell to Admiral C. P. Snyder, January 10, 1939, *ibid.*

23. Ballentine transcript.

24. Richardson to Chief of Naval Operations, October 22, 1940, in U.S., Congress, Joint Committee on the Investigation of the Pearl Harbor Attack, *Hearings*, 79th Congress, 1st session (Washington D.C., 1946), part 14, p. 968.

25. Albion, p. 202.

26. "Preparation for Disarmament Conference," July 7, 1931, General Board Hearings, 1931, 2:31, Naval History Archives.

27. Captain R. E. Ingersoll, "The Naval Battle of the Future," lecture delivered at Army War College, March 28, 1938, and Commander P. N. L. Bellinger, "Naval Aviation," lecture delivered at Army War College, February 13, 1934, War Plans Division Files; Wilson transcript; Reynolds, p. 20

28. "Facilities for an Enlarged Aviation Program," August 10, 1934, General Board Hearings, 1934, 1:103-29

29. Testimony by Pratt, May 27, 1930, General Board Hearings, 1930, 1:176ff; "Characteristics of the Aircraft Carrier," August 20, 1934, General Board Hearings, 1934, 1:155.

30. King and Whitehill, pp. 285-88.

31. Conolly transcript; "Design of Future Aircraft Carriers," July 24, 1931, General Board Hearings, 1931, 2:548.

32. *Ibid.*, p. 555.

33. "Facilities for an Enlarged Aviation Program," August 10, 1934, General Board Hearings, 1934, 1:93.

34. Charles McVay to Admiral Pratt, April 11, 1931, Pratt Papers; "Outline of Action," February 21, 1932, Correspondence January-March 1932, Taylor Papers.

35. Taylor to his brother, February 24, 1932, Taylor Papers.

36. Pratt draft memorandum for Admiral Stark, January 28, 1941, Pratt Papers.

37. Taylor to his brother, June 14, 1933, Taylor Papers.

38. Armin Rappaport, *Henry L. Stimson and Japan, 1931-1933* (Chicago, 1963) pp. 160-62; Michael D. Reagan, "The Far Eastern Crisis of 1931-1932: Stimson, Hoover and the Armed Services," in Harold Stein, ed., *American Civil-Military Decisions: A Book of Case Studies* (University, Ala., 1963), pp. 29-37.

39. Diary of Admiral William D. Leahy, May 20, 1932, William D. Leahy Papers, Library of Congress.

40. Roosevelt to Malcolm Peabody, August 19, 1933, in Edgar B. Nixon, ed., *Franklin D. Roosevelt and Foreign Affairs* (Cambridge, Mass., 1969), 1:370.

41. Transcript of Admiral Emory Scott Land, Columbia Oral History Collection; Albion, p. 498.

42. Swanson to Roosevelt, November 28, 1934, File EF37, Confidential Correspondence of the Office of the Secretary of the Navy, 1927-1939, Record Group 80, National Archives.

43. Commander-in-Chief Asiatic Fleet to Chief of Naval Operations, January 31 and June 16, 1933, File A16/ND16, Secret Correspondence of the Office of the Secretary of the Navy, 1927-1939, *ibid.*

44. Chief of Naval Operations to Commander-in-Chief of U.S. Fleet, December 10, 1934, and Memorandum, Director of War Plans Division to Assistant Chief of Staff, War Plans, January 29, 1935, A16-3, Chief of Naval Operations Secret Correspondence, 1927-1940, microreel 8.

45. Louis Morton, *Strategy and Command: The First Two Years (United States Army in World War II: The War in the Pacific)* (Washington D.C., 1962), p. 36.

46. Joint Board 305, Serial No. 573 and Joint Board 325, Serial Nos. 533 and 570, Joint Board Records; Morton, *Strategy and Command*, pp. 36-39.

47. Swanson to President, April 22, 1935, File A16/QH (Pacific), Chief of Naval Operations Secret Correspondence, 1927-1940, microreel 7; memorandum for Secretary of the Navy by Roosevelt, May 3, 1935, File A16/QH (Pacific), Secretary of Navy Secret Correspondence, 1927-1939.

48. Greenslade, "Policy Regarding Naval Bases in the Pacific," May 21, 1935, File 438-1, General Board Studies.

49. Report No. 89 (Naval Attaché in Tokyo), March 22, 1934, President's Secretary's File: London Naval Conference, Roosevelt Library, Hyde Park, N.Y. (hereafter cited as PSF).

50. Memorandum by Commander R. E. Schuirmann, June 18, 1935, Memorandum, Schuirmann to Chief of Naval Operations, April 30, 1935, and Memorandum by Rear Admiral J. W. Greenslade, July 8, 1935, Miscellaneous Correspondence Relating to Naval Limitation and Naval Conversations, 1934-1935, File 438-1, General Board Studies; Report by Admiral R. H. Leigh on Participation at the London Naval Conversations, June 18-July 19, 1934, File 438-1, *ibid.*; General Board to Secretary of the Navy, October 1, 1934, Chief of Naval Operations Secret Correspondence, 1927-1940, microreel 12.

51. Memorandum by "W.D.B.," July 22, 1935, Miscellaneous Correspondence Relating to Naval Limitation and Naval Conversations, 1934-1935, File 438-1, General Board Studies.

52. J. P. Moffat diary, September 26 and October 3, 1934, J. P. Moffat Papers, Harvard University Library, Cambridge, Mass.

53. Leahy diary, August 13, 1936.

54. Dorothy Borg, *The United States and the Far Eastern Crisis of 1933-1938* (Cambridge, Mass., 1964), p. 333.

55. "Strategy in the Pacific," lecture by Captain H. E. Yarnell at Army General Staff College, September 8, 1919, File 425, General Board Studies; Albion, p. 173.

56. Yarnell to Vice Admiral John D. McDonald, January 9, 1938, Official and Personal Correspondence, 1930-1939, Admiral H. E. Yarnell Papers, Naval History Archives.

57. Yarnell to Leahy, October 15, 1937, *ibid.*

58. Leahy diary, August 24, 1937.

59. Leahy to the President, November 8, 1937, enclosing copy of Yarnell to Leahy, October 15, 1937, and Roosevelt to Leahy, November 10, 1937, PSF: Navy (unindexed).

60. Franklin D. Roosevelt, "Shall We Trust Japan?" *Asia* 23 (July 1923):476.

61. Captain Leland Lovette to Yarnell, no date (September 1937), Chinese Situation in 1937 and Related Material, Yarnell Papers, Naval History Archives; H. E. Overesch to Yarnell, April 11, 1939, Yarnell Papers, Library of Congress.

62. Navy Department to Department of State, received December 20, 1937, *FR, 1937* (Washington D.C., 1954), 4:513; Hallett Abend to Yarnell, December 20, 1937, Yarnell Papers, Library of Congress.

63. Leahy to Yarnell, December 30, 1937, *ibid.*

64. Borg, *Far Eastern Crisis*, pp. 496-97.

65. Leahy diary, December 13, 1937.

66. Memorandum for Chief of Naval Operations by Ingersoll (including Diary, December 31, 1937-January 13, 1938, memoranda of conversations with British officials, and agreed Record of Conversations, January 13, 1938), Papers of Admiral Royal E. Ingersoll, Naval History Archives. See also Captain Tracy B. Kittredge, "Historical Monograph: U.S.-British Cooperation, 1940-1945," vol. 1,

section 1, Naval History Archives; Samuel Eliot Morison, *The Rising Sun in the Pacific, 1931-April 1942 (History of United States Naval Operations in World War II*, vol. 3) (Boston, 1948), p. 49.

67. Major-General S. Woodburn Kirby, *The War Against Japan, I: The Loss of Singapore* (London, 1957), p. 17; Ingersoll testimony, *Pearl Harbor Attack Hearings*, part 9, p. 4274.

68. Kittredge, vol. 1, section 1.

69. Louis Morton, "War Plan Orange: Evolution of a Strategy," *World Politics*, 11 (January 1959):245-49.

70. Leahy diary, December 14, 1937.

71. President to Secretary of the Navy, July 2, 1935, PSF: Navy.

72. Naval attaché reports, Record Group 38.

73. *New York Times,* February 20, 1938.

74. Commander R. S. Wentworth, "The Islands of the Mid-Pacific: Staff Presentation," Naval War College, January 20, 1939, War Plans Division Files; Leahy to Secretary of State, July 23, 1937, File A21/5, Chief of Naval Operations Secret Correspondence, 1927-1940, microreel 12.

75. Leahy diary, August 2, 1937, February 18 and April 18, 1938; R. Walton Moore to President, January 27, 1938, and Memorandum by the President, April 13, 1938, PSF: State Department; R. Walton Moore to the President, October 21, 1937, PSF: Great Britain, 1937-1939; King and Whitehill, pp. 238-40; Francis X. Holbrook, "United States National Defense and Trans-Pacific Commercial Air Routes 1933-1941," Ph.D. dissertation, Fordham University, 1969.

76. Commander-in-Chief, United States Fleet to Chief of Naval Operations, May 11, 1938, File A16/EG53, Chief of Naval Operations Secret Correspondence, 1927-1940, microreel 3; "Studies of Strategic Areas: The Singapore-Torres Strait Line," Naval War College, 1935-1936, War Plans Division Files.

77. U.S., Congress, House, Hepburn Report, 76th Congress, 1st session, House Document no. 65.

78. Maurice Matloff and Edwin M. Snell, *Strategic Planning for Coalition Warfare, 1941-1942 (United States Army in World War II: The War Department)* (Washington D.C., 1953), p. 5.

79. *Ibid.*, pp. 5-10; Kittredge, vol. 1, sections 1 and 2.

80. Matloff and Snell, pp. 9-10; Kittredge, vol. 1, section 3, part C, chap. 12.

81. Stark to Admiral C. C. Bloch, August 29, 1939, Admiral C. C. Bloch Papers, Library of Congress.

82. Leahy diary, March 5 and April 6, 1939.

83. Yarnell to Chief of Naval Operations, February 11, 1937, Yarnell Papers, Library of Congress; Memorandum by Rear Admiral R. K. Turner for Chief of Naval Operations, December 3, 1940, File A16/QH (Pacific), Chief of Naval Operations Secret Correspondence, 1927-1940, microreel 7; Memorandum by G. J. Meyers to Director, War Plans Division, April 17, 1935, File A16/QH (Pacific), Secretary of Navy Secret Correspondence, 1927-1939.

84. Extract from letter, Admiral Thomas Hart to Chief of Naval Operations, April 12, 1940, General Board 405, Serial No. 1953, General Board Studies.

85. Memorandum by M. L. Deyo, January 27, 1938, Yarnell Papers, Library of Congress; "Studies of Strategic Areas: East Indian Area," 1938-1939, Naval War College Studies, War Plans Division Files.

86. Digest of conference held May 1, 1940 in office of Chief of Naval Operations, May 2, 1940, File A16/FF1, Chief of Naval Operations Secret Correspondence, 1927-1940, microreel 4.

87. Thomas Wilds, "How Japan Fortified the Mandated Islands," *United States Naval Institute Proceedings*, 81 (April 1955):401.

88. Naval attaché reports, Record Group 38.

89. Leahy diary, April 11 and 15, June 12, 1939; Kirby, pp. 19-21; Kittredge, vol. 1, section 1.

90. Marginal notes by Knox on Memorandum for Secretary of the Navy by Admiral Stark, November 4, 1940, PSF: Navy.

91. Stark to Admiral C. C. Bloch, November 20, 1939, Bloch Papers.

92. Chairman of the General Board to the Secretary of the Navy, April 11, 1940, File A1-3, Chief of Naval Operations Correspondence, 1940-1941, Naval History Archives.

93. Naval attaché reports, Record Group 38.

94. T. S. Wilkinson to Alan Kirk, March 18, 1938, Admiral Alan Kirk Papers, Naval History Archives.

95. Memorandum by Admiral Leahy, July 7, 1938, PSF: Navy.

96. Lt. Richard W. Leopold, "Fleet Organization, 1919-1941," 1945, Naval History Archives.

97. Samuel Eliot Morison, *The Battle of the Atlantic, September 1939-May 1943 (History of United States Naval Operations in World War II*, vol. 1) (Boston, 1948), p. 14.

98. Stark to Admiral C. C. Bloch, September 4, 1939, Bloch Papers.

99. Stark to Bloch, November 13, 1939, *ibid.*

100. Extract of Stark to Admiral H. E. Kimmel, November 25, 1941, *Pearl Harbor Attack Hearings*, part 5, p. 2104.

101. William L. Langer and S. Everett Gleason, *The Undeclared War, 1940-1941* (New York, 1953), pp. 33-44.

102. Kittredge, vol. 1, section 2, part B.

103. Memorandum for the Chief of Naval Operations by Admiral J. O. Richardson, October 9, 1940, *Pearl Harbor Attack Hearings*, part 14, p. 962.

104. Morton, *Strategy and Command*, p. 76.

105. Commander-in-Chief, U.S. Fleet, to Commander-in-Chief, Asiatic Fleet, October 16, 1940, and enclosures, *Pearl Harbor Attack Hearings*, part 14, pp. 1006-12.

106. Memorandum for Secretary of the Navy by Richardson, September 12, 1940, and Richardson to Chief of Naval Operations, October 22, 1940, *Pearl Harbor Attack Hearings*, part 14, pp. 954-59, 963-70.

107. Richardson's letter of October 22, 1940 (*ibid.*), a strong statement of his views, was written at Bremerton, Washington. The Stark group began work on the "Plan Dog" memorandum about October 25 (Stark to Richardson, November 12, 1940, *ibid.*, p. 971). The date given for the memorandum is often November 12, but this was the date of a revision of the original after consultation with the army (Morton, *Strategy and Command*, p. 81, fn. 27). A copy of the original is in PSF: Navy.

108. Albion, pp. 175, 951.

109. "The Strategic Employment of the Fleet: Staff Presentation," November 22, 1939, Naval War College Studies, War Plans Division Files.

110. Albion, p. 951.

111. Memorandum for the Secretary of the Navy by Admiral Stark, November 4, 1940, PSF: Navy.

112. *Ibid.*

113. Stark to Admiral Thomas Hart, November 12, 1940, *Pearl Harbor Attack Hearings*, part 14, p. 973.

114. Kittredge, vol. 1, section 3, part C, chap. 12; Morton, *Strategy and Command*, pp. 83-84.

115. Memorandum, "The Importance of Singapore to the Defense of the British Isles and the British Empire and to the Interests of the United States," December 4, 1940, PSF: State Department; Memorandum by S. K. Hornbeck to Stark, December 5, 1940, File EF13-13, Chief of Naval Operations Correspondence, 1940-1941.

116. Letter from Dooman to the author, July 18, 1965.

117. Morison, *Rising Sun*, p. 56.

118. J. R. M. Butler, *Grand Strategy, II: September 1939-June 1941* (London, 1957), pp. 489-90.

119. Morison, *Rising Sun*, p. 50, fn. 3; Kittredge, vol. 1, section 4, part B.

120. Morison, *Rising Sun*, p. 52.

121. *Ibid.*, p. 57.

122. Diary of H. L. Stimson, April 23-June 20, 1941, Stimson Papers, Yale University Library, New Haven, Conn.; Memorandum of Conversation with the President by Admiral H. E. Kimmel, June 9, 1941, File A3-2, Chief of Naval Operations Correspondence, 1940-1941.

123. *Pearl Harbor Attack Hearings*, part 11, table 1, p. 5505.

124. Kirby, pp. 84-85.

125. Chief of Naval Operations to Chief of Staff, U.S. Army, May 22, 1941, File A15-3(10), Chief of Naval Operations Correspondence, 1940-1941; Memorandum of Conversation with the President by Admiral H. E. Kimmel, June 9, 1941, File A3-2, *ibid.*

126. Langer and Gleason, *Undeclared War,* p. 649.

The Japanese Navy and the United States

Note: In preparing this paper I am greatly indebted to Messrs. Tomioka Sadatoshi of the Shiryō Chōsakai (Documentary Research Society), Tokyo; Inaba Masao, Suekuni Masao, and Nomura Minoru of the Bōeichō Senshi Shitsu (Military History Office, Defense Agency); Toyoda Kumao of the Ministry of Justice; and Tsunoda Jun of the National Diet Library.

1. Throughout this paper the term "naval policy" is used in the dual sense in which the Japanese navy employed it: (1) the management of the military-professional affairs of the navy itself; and (2) national policy which the navy urged on the government. In view of the peculiar nature of Japan's policymaking mechanism during the 1930s, I have chosen to stress the latter aspect.

2. Interesting statistics are given in Matsushita Yoshio, *Nihon gunbatsu no kōbō* (The Rise and Fall of Japanese Military Cliques), 3 (Tokyo, 1967): 79-81; Kaigun Heigakkō (Naval Academy), ed., *Kaigun heigakkō enkaku* (A History of the Naval Academy) (reprinted with new appendices, Tokyo, 1968), lists its graduates in the order of their class standings.

3. Tomioka Sadatoshi, *Kaisen to shūsen* (The Making and Losing of the War) (Tokyo, 1968), pp. 26-29, 151-52; Rear Admiral Takagi Sōkichi's recollections, "Ā Etajima" (The Naval Academy and the Combined Fleet), *The Mainichi Graphic* (Tokyo), August 1, 1969, pp. 92, 94, 133; records of interviews with former naval officers, manuscript and mimeographed materials in the War Crimes Section, Ministry of Justice (hereafter cited as Justice Ministry interview records).

4. Takagi Sōkichi, *Taiheiyō sensō kaisenshi* (A History of Naval Battles of the Pacific War) (rev. ed., Tokyo, 1959), p. xi; Takagi Sōkichi, *Taiheiyō sensō to riku-kaigun no kōsō* (The Pacific War and Army-Navy Rivalry) (Tokyo, 1967), pp. 27, 112-13, 227-78; Takagi Sōkichi, *Yamamoto Isoroku to Yonai Mitsumasa* (Yamamoto Isoroku and Yonai Mitsumasa) (new ed., Tokyo, 1967), p. 45.

5. Toyoda Soemu, *Saigo no teikoku kaigun* (The Last of the Imperial Navy) (Tokyo, 1950), pp. 25-26, 55-56. See also Admiral Hasegawa Kiyoshi's testimony in Nakamura Kikuo, ed., *Shōwa kaigun hishi* (Secret History of the Navy during the Shōwa Era) (Tokyo, 1969), p. 309.

6. The best overall treatment of the London Naval Conference is Kobayashi Tatsuo, "Kaigun gunshuku jōyaku, 1921-36" (The Naval Limitation Treaties, 1921-36), in Nihon Kokusai Seiji Gakkai, Taiheiyō Sensō Gen'in Kenkyūbu (Japan International Politics Association, Study Group on the Origins of the Pacific War), ed., *Taiheiyō sensō e no michi* (Road to the Pacific War) 1 (Tokyo, 1963):3-160 (hereafter cited as *TSM*). The domestic political aspects of the conference are thoroughly treated in Itō Takashi, *Shōwa shoki seijishi kenkyū* (The Political History of the Early Shōwa Era) (Tokyo, 1969), especially

chap. 2. For strategic aspects, see Ikeda Kiyoshi, "Rondon kaigun jōyaku to tōsuiken mondai" (The London Naval Treaty and the Question of the Right of Supreme Command), *Hōgaku zasshi* (Jurisprudence), 15, no. 2 (October 1968):149-84.

7. For a detailed treatment of the Washington Conference, see Sadao Asada, "Japan and the United States, 1915-25," Ph.D. dissertation, Yale University, 1963, especially chap. 5.

8. Miyata Mitsuo, *Gensui Katō Tomosaburō den* (Biography of Fleet Admiral Katō Tomosaburō) (Tokyo, 1928); Arai Tatsuo, *Katō Tomosaburō* (Tokyo, 1959).

9. Harada Kumao, *Saionji-kō to seikyoku* (Prince Saionji and the Political Situation) (reprinted, Tokyo, 1967), 3:147.

10. Hori accompanied Katō Tomosaburō to the Washington Conference, and Nomura served as his faithful aide at the conference. Okada used to say, "I consider myself a disciple of Admiral Katō Tomosaburō." Okada Keisuke, *Okada Keisuke kaikoroku* (Memoirs of Okada Keisuke) (Tokyo, 1950), p. 52.

11. Itō Kinjirō, *Ikiteiru kaishō Katō Kanji* (The Living Admiral Katō Kanji) (Tokyo, 1942), p. 166; Toyoda, p. 25; Nakamura, *Shōwa kaigun hishi*, p. 219.

12. *GS 10: Nitchū sensō 3* (Sino-Japanese War 3) (Tokyo, 1964), pp. 175-76, 339; Harada, 7:269; Rear Admiral Takagi's testimony in Andō Yoshio, ed., *Shōwa keizaishi e no shōgen* (Testimonies for an Economic History of the Shōwa Era), 2 (Tokyo, 1966):275.

13. In 1923 the Royal Naval College ceased to admit Japanese architect officers.

14. Katō Kanji Taishō Denki Hensankai (Committee to Compile a Biography of Admiral Katō Kanji), *Katō Kanji taishō den* (Biography of Admiral Katō Kanji) (Tokyo, 1941), pp. 714-27.

15. This account is based on the directory of former naval officers who served abroad, Military History Office, Defense Agency.

16. For example, Captain Kojima Hideo, naval attaché in Germany from 1936 to 1938, became so completely enthralled by Hitler as to proclaim the fuhrer's resemblance to "an Oriental sage," the special affinity of his ideology to Japanese thought, and his "genuine love for Japan." Kojima penned these extravagant words on the eve of the conclusion of the Nazi-Soviet pact of 1939. See "Saikin no Doitsu jijō" (Recent Conditions in Germany), *Yūshū*, 26 (August 1939):24-30.

17. Ogata Taketora, *Ichi gunjin no shōgai* (The Life of an Admiral) (Tokyo, 1955), pp. 73, 178, 256-57.

18. Ishikawa Shingo, *Shinjuwan made no keii* (The Circumstances Leading to Pearl Harbor) (Tokyo, 1960), pp. 113-23.

19. *Kaigun heigakkō enkaku*, appendix; Bōeichō Senshi Shitsu (Defense Agency, Military History Office), ed., *Senshi sōsho: Kaigun gunsenbi 1* (Military History Series: Naval Armaments and Preparations for War 1) (Tokyo, 1969), pp. 638-43.

20. Takagi, *Riku-kaigun no kōsō*, p. 200; Andō, *Shōwa keizaishi*, 2:269-70.

21. Harada, 2:197-99 and *passim*.

22. Memorandum by Rear Admiral Hori, *TSM: Bekkan shiryōhen* (Supplementary Volume of Documents) (Tokyo, 1963), pp. 65-66.

23. *Katō Kanji taishō den*, pp. 770-72; Harada, 3:114-15, 173-74.

24. Justice Ministry interview records.

25. Honjō Shigeru, *Honjō nikki* (Honjō Diary) (Tokyo, 1967), p. 163.

26. "Gunreibu kaisei no keii" (Circumstances Surrounding the Revision of the Rules of the Navy General Staff), record of Commander Takagi's interviews with Takahashi and Inoue on January 1934 and February 1935, respectively, and Navy General Staff, "Gunreibu enkaku no gaiyō" (Outline History of the Navy General Staff), October 25, 1933 (draft of lecture to be given in the imperial presence), Military History Office; Inoue Shigemi, "Omide no ki" (My Reminiscences), manuscript memoirs, a copy in my possession (hereafter cited as Inoue Memoirs).

27. As originally presented, Takahashi's demands would have given the chief of the Navy General Staff jurisdiction over the organization of squadrons, their missions and activities, education, training, and exercises, and personnel appointments. Of these, only the authority over personnel administration was retained by the navy minister. See memorandum on "Regulations Concerning the Mutual Jurisdiction of the Navy Ministry and the Navy General Staff," no date, Military History Office; Ōsumi Taishō Denki Kankōkai (Committee to Publish a Biography of Admiral Ōsumi), ed., *Danshaku Ōsumi Mineo den* (Biography of Baron Ōsumi Mineo) (Tokyo, 1943), pp. 586-89.

28. Inoue Memoirs.

29. Cited in Takagi, *Yamamoto to Yonai*.

30. Other victims of the "Ōsumi purge" were Admirals Yamanashi Katsunoshin and Taniguchi Naomi, Vice Admirals Sakonji Seizō, Terashima Takeshi, Shimomura Shōsuke, and Banno Tsuneyoshi, to name the most prominent of them. Inoue barely escaped a similar fate.

31. Specifically, "staff officer A" was charged with: "(1) matters relating to war guidance and national policy as they bear on naval affairs; (2) matters relating to the guidance of the international situation; and (3) matters relating to treaties as they bear on naval affairs."

32. Takagi, *Riku-kaigun no kōsō*, pp. 189-207.

33. *GS 8: Nitchū sensō 1* (Sino-Japanese War 1) (Tokyo, 1964), pp. 351-53.

34. Ishikawa, *passim*.

35. Notably, Tsunoda Jun, "Nihon no tai-Bei kaisen" (The Outbreak of War with the United States), in *TSM*, 7:84. Two other committees were simultaneously set up: the Second Committee charged with "war preparations" and the Third Committee charged with "information and public opinion guidance."

36. During this period the chief of the First Section of the Naval Affairs Bureau was Captain Takada Toshitane (who had served in Germany), and "staff officer A" was Captain Ōno Takeji (replaced by Captain Onoda Sutejirō in November 1941). In addition, Commanders Shiba Katsuo (formerly stationed in Berlin), Fujii Shigeru (an outspoken Axis sympathizer), and Onoda (known as a "hard-liner") served as secretaries of the First Committee.

37. Justice Ministry interview records, and my own interviews with former navy officers.

38. Apparently Katō had absorbed this philosophy from his immediate predecessor as president of the Navy War College, Rear Admiral Satō Tetsutarō, the leading exponent of Mahan's doctrine in Japan. That Mahan's books continued to be generally used at the Navy War College is clear from the fact that abridged translations of them were printed or mimeographed in great numbers during the 1930s. In 1932 the Suikōsha (the Japanese counterpart of the Navy League) published a translation of Mahan's *Naval Strategy Compared and Contrasted with the Principles and Practice of Military Operations on Land.*

39. Katō's "spiritualism" and right-wing Japanism may also have been affected by his view that the First World War represented "the bankruptcy of materialistic Western civilization" as well as by his shocked reaction to the Russian revolution, which he had witnessed during his expedition to Vladivostok in 1918. *Katō Kanji taishō den*, pp. 680, 746-60, 780-93, 809-14, 816-34, 924-29.

40. *Ibid.*, pp. 846-67, 918-19.

41. Bōeichō Senshi Shitsu, ed., *Senshi sōsho: Daihon'ei rikugunbu 1* (Military History Series: Imperial Headquarters, Army 1) (Tokyo, 1967), pp. 130-62, 217-37, 244-58; Tsunoda Jun, *Manshū mondai to kokubō hōshin* (The Manchurian Question and National Defense Policy) (Tokyo, 1967), pp. 658-715. For a short summary, see Hata Ikuhiko, "Meijiki ikō ni okeru Nichi-Bei Taiheiyō senryaku no hensen" (The Changing Pacific Strategies of Japan and the United States since the Meiji Era), in *Kokusai seiji: Nihon gaikōshi no shomondai 3* (International Relations: Problems in Japanese Diplomatic History 3), no. 37 (1968), pp. 96-115.

42. Mori Shōzō, *Senpū nijūnen* (Twenty Turbulent Years) (reprinted, Tokyo, 1967), pp. 658-715.

43. It was for this reason that Admirals Katō Kanji and Suetsugu had so adamantly insisted on retaining Japan's submarine tonnage of 78,497 at the time of the London Naval Conference.

44. Navy General Staff memorandum (strictly confidential), no date (1930), apparently prepared by Admiral Katō Kanji, Military History Office; Justice Ministry interview records; Ikeda Kiyoshi, *Nihon no kaigun* (The Japanese Navy) (Tokyo, 1967), 2:11-12, 137-38; Toyoda, p. 188; Nakamura, *Shōwa kaigun hishi*, p. 219.

45. Bōeichō Senshi Shitsu, ed., *Senshi sōsho: Hawai sakusen* (Military History Series: Hawaii Operations) (Tokyo, 1967), pp. 6, 38-39; *ibid., Kaigun gunsenbi 1*, pp. 130-32.

46. *Ibid., Daihon'ei rikugunbu 1*, pp. 393-94; *Daihon'ei rikugunbu 2* (Tokyo, 1968), pp. 690-92; staff studies, Military History Office.

47. Bōeichō Senshi Shitsu, *Hawai sakusen*, p. 37.

48. Yamamoto used to recommend to his subordinates Carl Sandburg's biography of Lincoln (in the English original) as the best introduction to the American national character. See Sorimachi Eiichi, *Ningen Yamamoto Isoroku* (The Life of Yamamoto Isoroku) (Tokyo, 1964), pp. 450-51. See also Takagi, *Yamamoto to Yonai*.

49. Bōeichō Senshi Shitsu, *Hawai sakusen*, pp. 7, 73-75.

50. "On New Armaments Plans," submitted to the navy minister, January 30, 1941, full text printed in *ibid.*, pp. 42-48; see also Inoue Memoirs.

51. "Study of Strategy and Tactics in Operations Against the United States," Military History Office.

52. For the full text of this study, see Bōeichō Senshi Shitsu, *Hawai sakusen*, Appendix 3, pp. 513-33; see also pp. 39-41.

53. The farthest conservative leaders would go was the formula of a "main fleet encounter under air cover"—that is, they conceived of naval aviation as something distinctly auxiliary to the battleship. See Bōeichō Senshi Shitsu, *Kaigun gunsenbi 1*, pp. 174, 198-99, 452, 581.

In late 1941 Captain Miyo Kazunari was one of the few members of the Operations Division of the Navy General Staff who had been closely connected with naval aviation. From the division and section chiefs on down, he later recalled, the overwhelming majority adhered to the old precept of "huge battleships and big guns" in the months immediately preceding Pearl Harbor and underestimated the role of aircraft. Justice Ministry interview records.

54. Memorandum by Rear Admiral Hori, *TSM: Bekkan shiryōhen*, pp. 64-65.

55. These included building each category of ships to treaty limits, construction of ships not covered by the treaty, renovation of the existing fleet, and an enlarged naval air force. New cruisers of 8,500 tons carrying 6-inch guns (the maximum caliber allowed for that category under the treaty) were so designed that they could be instantly reequipped with 8-inch guns upon termination of the treaty.

56. *TSM: Bekkan shiryōhen*, pp. 38-39; diary of Okada Keisuke, in *GS 7: Manshū jihen* (The Manchurian Incident) (Tokyo, 1964), pp. 6-7; Okada Taishō Kiroku Hensankai (Committee to Compile a Biography of Admiral Okada), ed., *Okada Keisuke* (Tokyo, 1956), pp. 65, 92-94; staff studies, Military History Office.

57. *TSM: Bekkan shiryōhen*, pp. 55-56; *Okada Keisuke*, pp. 147, 154-65, 187-88.

58. Abe to Prime Minister Hamaguchi, October 7, 1930, confidential no. 943, Military History Office; Suetsugu to Katō Kanji, September 17 and 27, Papers of Katō Kanji (copies in the possession of Professor Itō Takashi, who kindly loaned them to the author); Harada, 1:197, 200-01, 207-12.

59. The "first supplemental building program" consisted of thirty-two new warships including four *Mogami*-class cruisers, twenty-seven other vessels outside treaty restrictions, and doubling the size of the naval air force.

60. Naval Attaché Captain Shimomura Shōsuke to Vice Chief of Navy General Staff, nos. 57, 84, and 85, June 10 and August 20, 1932; and Shimomura to Navy Ministry, no. 67, July 14, 1932, Kōbun Bikō files, Naval Records, Military History Office. Kido Kōichi, *Kido Kōichi nikki* (Diary of Kido Kōichi) (Tokyo, 1966), 1:198.

61. Chief of Navy General Staff to Navy Minister, confidential no. 154, May 6, 1933, and Navy Ministry memorandum, strictly confidential no. 1, October 3, 1933, Papers of Saitō Makoto, National Diet Library. Navy minister's oral statement at Five Ministers Conference, September 21, 1933, and navy minister's draft statement at cabinet meeting, October 6, 1933, Saitō Papers and Foreign Ministry Archives. *GS 12: Nitchū sensō 4* (Sino-Japanese War 4) (Tokyo, 1965), p. 35.

62. Ishikawa memorandum on policy for the forthcoming naval conference, October 21, 1933, and draft of Suetsugu speech at the Supreme War Council, June 8, 1934, Katō Papers.

63. Draft of speech delivered by Katō at conference of senior naval leaders, July 16, 1934, Katō Papers.

64. Memorandum by Captain Yamashita Tomohiko *et al.*, no date (1934), Katō Papers; "Gunshuku mondai ni tsuite" (On Naval Limitation), *Yūshū*, 21, no. 10 (October 1934):6-7.

65. Harada, 3:155, 198-99 (entries of October 14 and December 13, 1933).

66. Navy minister's oral statement at Five Ministers Conference, October 16, 1933, and "Kaigun shūseian" (Navy amendment to Foreign Policy of the Empire), Foreign Ministry Archives.

67. *GS 12: Nitchū sensō 4*, pp. 16-18, 25-26, 28-29, 30-36.

68. Okada stated his philosophy of naval limitation succinctly when he wrote: "It is not a question of 'don'ts' such as 'don't fight a war with America and Britain.' It would be different if we could make adequate preparations for such a war, but this is clearly out of the question, given the inferiority of Japan's national power. This being the case, it is far wiser not to strain ourselves by entering into a naval race." Okada, *Kaikoroku*, pp. 42-43.

69. Kido, 1:328, 330, 346-47 (entries of May 17 and 23, July 16, 1934); Harada, 4:16-19, 22-23 (entry of July 20, 1934); Honjō, pp. 191, 192 (entry of July 19, 1934) (italics added).

70. Minutes of Five Ministers Conference, July 24, 1934, Foreign Ministry Archives; Harada, 4:20, 24, 27-28; Honjō, p. 192.

71. In June Katō had appealed to the fleet commanders that the best way to carry through the navy's demands would be to get him installed as prime minister. He and Admiral Suetsugu did not hesitate to divulge to their cronies in the fleets the secret deliberations of the Supreme War Council, but Katō finally overstepped the bounds when he instigated the joint memorial to Prince Fushimi. This irritated the prince, who had repented of his recent faux pas in

acting in a similar manner toward the emperor. He severely reprimanded Suetsugu for having transmitted such an improper memorial and Katō for his blatantly political machinations. Suetsugu to Katō, July 7, 1934, Katō Papers; Harada, 3:321-22 (entry of June 4, 1934), and 4:33-36 (entry of August 6, 1934); Kido, 1:350 (entry of August 2, 1934); *Katō Kanji taishō den*, pp. 903-04.

72. Draft speech by Suetsugu to Supreme War Council, June 8, 1934, and by Katō to conference of senior naval leaders, July 16, 1934, Katō Papers; Harada, 4:19-22 (entry of July 20, 1934).

73. *Ibid.*, pp. 44-48 (entry of August 29, 1934); Kido, 1:350 (entry of August 2, 1934); *Okada Keisuke*, p. 260; *GS 12: Nitchū sensō 4*, pp. 40-43.

74. Memorandum by navy minister, December 13, 1933, and revised draft of January 22, 1934, Foreign Ministry Archives; Honjō, pp. 194, 198 (entries of September 8 and November 2, 1934); *GS 12: Nitchū sensō 4*, pp. 4-9; Harada, 4:21.

75. *Ibid.*, pp. 20, 27, 44-45; Finance Ministry memorandum, no date (1934), sent to former Prime Minister Saitō Makoto with rider by the head of the Budget Bureau, Saitō Papers. For the background of right-wing "radical" movements within the navy, see *GS 4: Kokkashugi undō 1* (Nationalist Movements 1) (Tokyo, 1963), pp. 43-57, 65-82.

76. Honjō, pp. 193, 196; *GS 12: Nitchū sensō 4*, pp. 28-29, 33, 60-61. In connection with the abrogation of the Washington Naval Treaty, the problem of its Article 19 (which provided for maintaining the status quo in the fortification of the Pacific islands) deserves at least a passing mention. While the Japanese army wanted to retain this provision, the navy saw less value in it. In fact, the navy held that the restrictions placed on Taiwan and the Bonins were "most disadvantageous" to Japan, "if only from the viewpoint of our southward policy." Taiwan, of course, was to serve as a springboard for any program of "southward advance." Documents and memoranda at the Military History Office and Foreign Ministry Archives; see also *GS 12: Nitchū sensō 4*, pp. 5, 22, 31, 35, 37, 60.

77. Ishikawa memorandum, October 21, 1933, Katō Papers; Fukui Shizuo, *Nihon no gunkan* (Japanese Warships) (Tokyo, 1956), pp. 72-76; Bōeichō Senshi Shitsu, *Kaigun gunsenbi 1*, pp. 466, 482-89.

78. The great confidence which Japanese naval planners had in this strategy was based on certain recent advances in naval technology. By the mid-1930s the Japanese navy had clearly outstripped the other powers in developing large submarines with high speed and a long cruising range. In naval aviation, medium attack planes with an extended flying radius now emerged as an important factor and in 1937 were included in the annual plan of operations directed against the Philippines. Above all, the planners pinned their hopes on

"heavy torpedo ships" of 5,500 tons, each carrying forty oxygen torpedoes (type 9-3), and midget submarines. These ships were to be used at the outset of the fleet encounter to throw the enemy squadron into confusion, whereupon the mammoth battleships would administer the coup de grace. This scenario of victory at sea, however, left some officers unimpressed. Bōeichō Senshi Shitsu, *Daihon'ei rikugunbu 1*, p. 417; Fukui, pp. 94, 121; Justice Ministry interview records. See also Bōeichō Senshi Shitsu, *Kaigun gunsenbi 1*, pp. 83, 163, 178, 187.

79. *GS 12: Nitchū sensō 4*, pp. 83-85; Takagi, *Yamamoto to Yonai*, pp. 46-49.

80. Naval Affairs Bureau memorandum, February 8, 1936; staff studies by First Section, Naval Affairs Bureau, April and August 1935; also Reports of the Research Committee on Arms Limitation, vols. 5 and 6 (1935), Military History Office; Justice Ministry interview records.

81. Sometime in 1934 or 1935 Captain Yamaguchi, the naval attaché in Washington, sent to the Navy General Staff a copy of what was purported to be the war plan of the United States navy, which had allegedly been stolen from the office safe of the secretary of the navy. Captain Yamaguchi also obtained the operational work sheets drawn up by the students of the U.S. Naval War College. Staff studies, Military History Office; Justice Ministry interview records.

82. Bōeichō Senshi Shitsu, *Daihon'ei rikugunbu 1*, pp. 415-16; Ishikawa, pp. 107-13, 121-22; Justice Ministry interview records.

83. *GS 8: Nitchū sensō 1*, pp. 356-62.

84. *TSM: Bekkan shiryōhen*, pp. 216-23; *TSM*, 6:434; Harada, 5:44, 96-97.

85. Staff studies, Military History Office. For Pratt's position, see Armin Rappaport, *Henry L. Stimson and Japan, 1931-1933* (Chicago, 1966), pp. 212, 216.

86. Hirota Kōki Denki Kankōkai (Committee to Publish a Biography of Hirota Kōki), ed., *Hirota Kōki* (Tokyo, 1966), pp. 212-16; James B. Crowley, *Japan's Quest for Autonomy: National Security and Foreign Policy, 1930-1938* (Princeton, 1966), pp. 278-300.

87. *GS 8: Nitchū sensō 1*, pp. 209, 217-19, 221, 222-26, 231-33.

88. Tsunoda Jun, ed., *Ishiwara Kanji shiryō: Kokubō ronsaku* (Writings of Ishiwara Kanji: National Defense) (Tokyo, 1967), p. 440; *GS 9: Nitchū sensō 2* (Tokyo, 1964), pp. 5, 8-9.

89. Tomioka Sadatoshi, "Taiheiyō sensō zenshi" (A History of the Events Leading to the Pacific War), 1:48-50, Shiryō Chōsakai (Documentary

Research Society, Tokyo), mimeographed; Hata Ikuhiko, *Nitchū sensōshi* (History of the Sino-Japanese War) (Tokyo, 1961).

90. Inoue Memoirs.

91. Ogata, *Ichi gunjin*, pp. 19, 36-38.

92. The middle-echelon officers attributed this state of affairs to Yonai's "incompetency." They circulated various insidious rumors apparently intended to slander him, rumors based on either gross misunderstanding or distortion of the navy minister's statements at Five Ministers Conferences. Captain Takagi became so alarmed that he solicited the help of Baron Harada—and through him of several naval genro—to facilitate "ventilation" between the higher echelons and section chiefs. Harada, 7:34-35, 37, 39, 41-42.

93. *GS 10: Nitchū sensō 3*, pp. 153-54, 156, 160, 177, 183-84; Justice Ministry interview records.

94. Navy General Staff memorandum, "Why Our Feelings toward Britain Have Aggravated," September 1, 1938, and draft explanation to the navy vice minister, First Section, Naval Affairs Bureau, August 20, 1938, in *GS 10: Nitchū sensō 3*, pp. 174-76, 339-43 (italics added).

95. Harada, 7:267-69.

96. *GS 10: Nitchū sensō 3*, pp. 191-328, *passim*; Justice Ministry interview records.

97. Ogata, *Ichi gunjin*, pp. 40-43, 54, 58; Inoue Memoirs.

98. Taped interviews with Inoue, Military History Office.

99. *Documents on German Foreign Policy, 1918-1945*, series D, 6 (London, 1956):623-24, 737, 858; Harada, 8:37-38.

100. Harada, 7:249 and 8:30; Ogata, *Ichi gunjin*, p. 60; Takagi's testimony in Nakamura, p. 202.

101. Navy memorandum, October 20, 1939, Papers of Konoe Fumimaro (photocopies at Military History Office).

102. Okada, *Kaikoroku*, p. 197; Inoue Memoirs.

103. Yabe Teiji, *Konoe Fumimaro*, 2 (Tokyo, 1952):161-62.

104. Tomioka, "Taiheiyō sensō zenshi," 2:45-48; questions presented by the Navy General Staff to the government, September 16, 1940, in Kihon Kokusaku Kankei (Fundamental National Policy) collection, vol. 2, Papers of the Navy Minister, Military History Office (hereafter cited as KKK Papers);

Hosoya Chihiro, "Sangoku dōmei to Nisso chūritsu jōyaku, 1939-41" (The Tripartite Pact and the Japanese-Soviet Neutrality Treaty, 1939-41), in *TSM*, 5:159-331.

105. Staff studies, Military History Office.

106. Justice Ministry interview records; Harada, 8:189, 198; Toyoda, p. 51; Shigemitsu Mamoru, *Shōwa no dōran* (Upheavals in Shōwa Japan) 1 (Tokyo, 1952):259; memorandum by Navy General Staff, Intelligence Division, September 7, 1940, KKK Papers; Nomura Naokuni's testimony in Nakamura, pp. 28-31, 41-42; *TSM: Bekkan shiryōhen*, p. 388.

107. Hata Ikuhiko, "Futsuin shinchū to gun no nanshin seisaku, 1940-41" (The March into French Indochina and the Military's Southward Advance Policy, 1940-41), in *TSM*, 6:156-59; Tsunoda, "Nihon no tai-Bei kaisen," pp. 18-20.

108. Several drafts of the "Main Principles," memoranda concerning the Liaison Conference of July 27, 1940 and the cabinet meeting of July 20, 1940, Documentary Research Society; *TSM: Bekkan shiryōhen*, pp. 315-18, 322-24.

109. *GS 10: Nitchū sensō 3*, pp. 361-71, 497-501, 504-07; Tsunoda, "Nihon no tai-Bei kaisen," p. 47.

110. This was an intermediate stage between peacetime and wartime footing and consisted of advance preparations to mobilize 60 percent of naval vessels. *Ibid.*, pp. 46-53.

111. *Ibid.*, pp. 80, 85; *TSM: Bekkan shiryōhen*, p. 333, 353-54.

112. Takagi, *Yamamoto to Yonai*, p. 73.

113. Tsunoda, "Nihon no tai-Bei kaisen," pp. 202-04.

114. Taped interviews with Shiba Katsuo, Military History Office; Justice Ministry interview records.

115. Staff studies, Military History Office.

116. *TSM: Bekkan shiryōhen*, pp. 427-40; Justice Ministry interview records (italics added).

117. Ishikawa, pp. 294-97; Justice Ministry interview records.

118. Daihon'ei, Rikugunbu, Sensō Shidōhan (Imperial Headquarters, Army, War Guidance Office), "Kimitsu sensō nisshi" (Secret War Diary), entry of June 11, 1941; *TSM: Bekkan shiryōhen*, pp. 441-43, 468-69, 474, 481; Tsunoda, "Nihon no tai-Bei kaisen," p. 207.

119. Justice Ministry interview records; staff studies, Military History Office.

120. Tsunoda, "Nihon no tai-Bei kaisen," p. 241.

121. Justice Ministry interview records; Tomioka, "Taiheiyō sensō zenshi," 3:57, and *Kaisen to shūsen*, p. 59; Hattori Takushirō, *Dai Tōa sensō zenshi* (A Complete History of the Greater East Asia War) 1 (Tokyo, 1953): 142.

122. *TSM: Bekkan shiryōhen*, pp. 415-16.

123. Yabe, 2:361; Fukudome Shigeru, *Shikan: Shinjuwan kōgeki* (The Attack on Pearl Harbor: A Historical Interpretation) (Tokyo, 1955), pp. 136-37; *TSM: Bekkan shiryōhen*, pp. 508-12.

124. The Japanese navy was ill-equipped to deal realistically with the crucial problem of convoy protection, partly because its vital sea communications had never been seriously threatened in previous engagements during the Russo-Japanese War, the First World War, or the China War.

125. *TSM: Bekkan shiryōhen*, p. 512; Tsunoda, "Nihon no tai-Bei kaisen," pp. 322-37.

126. Bōeichō Senshi Shitsu, *Hawai sakusen*, pp. 7, 79, 82-85, 90, 105-10; Fukudome, pp. 144-59.

127. *TSM: Bekkan shiryōhen*, pp. 531-33; Sanbō Honbu (Army General Staff), ed., *Sugiyama memo* (Liaison Conference Records of Chief of Staff Sugiyama), 1 (Tokyo, 1967):116-18; Yabe, 2:379-81, 386-91, 394; Toyoda, p. 62; Itō Masanori, *Rengō kantai no saigo* (The Death of the Combined Fleet) (reprinted, Tokyo, 1969), pp. 255-56.

128. There is reason to suspect the army deliberately fostered this fear in the higher echelons of the navy. According to Vice Admiral Fukudome, then head of the Operations Division of the Navy General Staff, warnings of such a coup d'état came from the army leaders. Fukudome, pp. 128-29; Tomioka, *Kaisen to shūsen*, p. 57; Nakamura, pp. 92-93; Justice Ministry interview records; my own interviews with Rear Admiral Tomioka in December 1968 and January 1969.

129. Toyoda, p. 65.

130. Shimada memoranda of November 1 and 29, 1941, KKK Papers; manuscript memoirs of Navy Vice Minister Sawamoto Yorio.

131. *TSM: Bekkan shiryōhen*, pp. 560-61, 585; Tomioka, *Kaisen to shūsen*, pp. 53-56.

132. Bōeichō Senshi Shitsu, *Hawai sakusen*, pp. 94, 96; Tomioka, "Taiheiyō sensō zenshi," 4:2-5, 9-11.

133. *Ibid.*, pp. 5, 93-94; Tomioka, *Kaisen to shūsen*, pp. 55, 58. For the organization and research activities of the Institute, see Total War Research Institute file in "Teikoku no taigai seisaku kankei ikken" (Papers Relating to the Empire's Foreign Policy), Foreign Ministry Archives.

134. Testimony of Obata Tadayoshi, vice president of the Cabinet Planning Board, in Andō, 2:121, 287-88; Ishikawa, pp. 338-41; Justice Ministry interview records.

135. Satō Kenryō, *Tōjō Hideki to Taiheiyō sensō* (Tōjō Hideki and the Pacific War) (Tokyo, 1960), pp. 250-51; Naval Ordnance Bureau memorandum to the chief of the Navy General Staff, October 31, 1941, KKK Papers; Justice Ministry interview records.

136. *Ibid.*; Nakamura, pp. 143-52.

137. Attaché reports were gathered and analyzed by the Intelligence Division of the Navy General Staff. There was some dissatisfaction over the fact that its head and the information it supplied were not fully taken into account in the navy's policymaking process. Division heads Nomura Naokuni (1936-38) and Oka Takasumi (1939-40) were pro-German and their successor Maeda Minoru was a "war advocate." Nakamura, pp. 116-17, 143-45, 152-53; Bōeichō Senshi Shitsu, *Hawai sakusen*, pp. 292-93; Justice Ministry interview records; my own interviews with former naval officers.

For the cloak-and-dagger aspects of naval intelligence, see David Kahn, *The Codebreakers* (New York, 1966), chaps. 1 and 2. The Japanese edition of the book corrects some of its factual mistakes; see *Angō sensō*, translated by Hata Ikuhiko and Sekino Hideo (Tokyo, 1968).

138. Ishikawa, pp. 114-20; Justice Ministry interview records.

139. Secret War Journals, entries of February 17, 23, and 25, March 20, June 23, August 15, October 6 and 15, November 1, 1941; Bōeichō Senshi Shitsu, *Daihon'ei rikugunbu 2*, pp. 409-21.

140. Harada, 5:96 (entry of June 20, 1936).

141. Taped interview with Miyo Kazunari, Military History Office.

142. Cited in Takagi, *Yamamoto to Yonai*, p. 68.

143. Sanematsu Yuzuru, *Yonai Mitsumasa* (Tokyo, 1966), p. 169.

144. Ugaki Matome, *Sensō roku* (War Diary) (Tokyo, 1968), p. 31.

145. Tsunoda Jun, "Nihon kaigun sandai no rekishi" (Three Generations of the Japanese Navy), *Jiyū* (Liberty), January 1969, pp. 90-125.

The Role of the Commerce and Treasury Departments

1. See Joseph Brandes, *Herbert Hoover and Economic Diplomacy* (Pittsburgh, 1962), and Julius Klein, *Frontiers of Trade* (New York, 1927), both of which are essential background reading for this paper.

2. W.H. Rastall to Julean Arnold, August 6, 1931, File No. 020: Japan, Records of the Bureau of Foreign and Domestic Commerce, Record Group 151, National Archives, Washington D.C.

3. Roper to FDR, August 24, 1936, President's Secretary's File 17, Roosevelt Library, Hyde Park, N.Y. (hereafter cited as PSF).

4. "World Trade," *Foreign Commerce Weekly*, 2 (February 15, 1941):267-68, 301.

5. Copies of the Press Memo and Alexander Dye's letter of reply, dated July 28, 1938, are in Record Group 151.

6. Hull to Grew, November 20, 1938, State Department files 693.001/399, National Archives, Washington D.C. Hull's public statements were equally explicit on this point: "There can be no serious hostilities anywhere in the world which will not one way or another affect interests or rights or obligations of this country." "Statement by the Secretary of State," July 16, 1937, *FR, Japan: 1931-1941* (Washington D.C., 1943), 1:325-26.

7. Moser's comments from *Shanghai Evening News*, November 18, 1930, clipping enclosed in Julean Arnold to Moser, November 21, 1940, Record Group 151:211.1 China.

8. Halleck A. Butts to Director, Bureau of Foreign and Domestic Commerce (hereafter BFDC), August 4, 1931, Record Group 151:020 Japan; W.H. Rastall to Butts, September 10, 1931, *ibid.*; BFDC to Butts, May 4, 1933, *ibid.*, 200 Japan.

9. Roper to T. M. Rodgers, September 15, 1934, Records of the Department of Commerce, Record Group 40, National Archives, Washington D.C.

10. Herbert Feis, *The Road to Pearl Harbor: The Coming of the War Between the United States and Japan* (Princeton, 1950), p. 73; Dorothy Borg, *The United States and the Far Eastern Crisis of 1933-1938* (Cambridge, Mass., 1964), p. 128.

11. Allan Seymour Everest, *Morgenthau, the New Deal and Silver: A Study of Pressure Politics* (New York, 1950), pp. 101-24. Everest concludes:

"Recent writers have charged that American policy in the Orient was chiefly notable for the sending of scrap iron and oil to Japan at the same time that Russia was sending gasoline and planes to China. . . . A summary of silver purchases alone suffices to prove the exaggeration of this statement. . . . From 1934 through 1941 the United States purchased over half a billion ounces of Chinese silver, for which she paid some $260,000,000." Everest's conclusion, too, is somewhat overdrawn and misleading, especially in not considering pre-1936 agreement purchases in a separate category or in estimating the effects of speculation, smuggling, and hoarding.

12. Henry J. Morgenthau, Jr., diary entries, April 15, July 18 and 21, and October 29, 1935, Roosevelt Library. The Morgenthau "diary" is really a composite of dictated entries by Morgenthau, stenographic records of conferences in his office, memoranda from Treasury and other executive branches, and some letters to and from the Treasury or Morgenthau personally. No distinction will usually be attempted in these notes, although special memoranda will be cited to aid the reader in following the development of policy.

13. Morgenthau diary, August 14, 1935.

14. Lloyd C. Gardner, *Economic Aspects of New Deal Diplomacy* (Madison, Wis., 1964), pp. 59-61; Memorandum, Pierson to Members of the Advisory Committee, Morgenthau diary, October 15, 1937; *FR, 1937* (Washington D.C., 1957), 4:593-619.

15. Pierson to Hornbeck, March 9, 1938, State Department files 811.516/ Export-Import Bank/149.

16. Julean Arnold to William L. Cooper, December 23, 1930; C. K. Moser to Lamont, December 26, 1930; Ray Hall to Herbert M. Bratter, January 2, 1931; Cooper to Arnold, January 30, 1931; and Hall to C. O. Yoakum, March 25, 1931, Record Group 151:640. See also Herbert M. Bratter, "The Silver Episode II," *Journal of Political Economy,* 46 (September 1938):802-37.

17. On the intricacies of silver and a Chinese "gold exchange standard," see the testimony of Edwin W. Kemmerer, March 25, 1932, in U.S., Congress, House, Committee on Coinage, Weights and Measures, *Hearings: The Effect of Low Silver*, 72nd Congress, 1st session (Washington D.C., 1932), pp. 235-85. Moser's statement is from a letter, dated April 9, 1931, Record Group 151:492.

18. Akira Iriye, *After Imperialism: The Search for a New Order in the Far East, 1921-1931* (Cambridge, Mass., 1965), pp. 278-85. See also Julean Arnold to W.L. Cooper, December 23, 1930, Record Group 151:640.

19. Editorial, January 9, 1931, reprinted in U.S., Congress, Senate, Subcommittee of the Committee on Foreign Relations, *Hearings: Commercial Relations with China*, 71st Congress, 3rd session (Washington D.C., 1931), pp. 538-39. These hearings contain one of the best collections of silver-oriented speeches and articles available anywhere for this period.

20. Lloyd Griscom to John Hay, September 26, 1904, State Department files, Japan Dispatches. See also Charles A. Conant, "Putting China on the Gold Standard," *North American Review*, 177 (November 1903):691-704.

21. The origins of the first China Consortium are discussed in great detail in Charles Vevier, *The United States and China, 1906-1913: A Study in Finance and Diplomacy* (New Brunswick, N.J., 1955). The story is brought down through the 1920s in Frederick V. Field, *American Participation in the China Consortium* (Chicago, 1931).

22. Borg, *Far Eastern Crisis,* pp. 62-63, 68; John Morton Blum, *From the Morgenthau Diaries: Years of Crisis, 1928-1938* (Boston, 1959), pp. 53-54.

23. *Ibid.* On State Department reactions to Soong's European activities, see *FR, 1933* (Washington D.C., 1949), 3:497-508.

24. "Memorandum of a Conversation with the Japanese Ambassador," August 10, 1933, *ibid.*, p. 508.

25. Borg, *Far Eastern Crisis*, pp. 92-99. Dr. Borg's discussion of 1934 conversations between Hull and the Japanese ambassador opens our angle of vision on Japanese-American relations in the entire decade.

26. Morgenthau diary, February 26, 1934.

27. Rogers to Morgenthau, May 17, 1934, State Department files 033.1100 Rogers, James Harvey/37.

28. Hornbeck to Hull, May 18, 1934, *ibid.*, 893.51/5894; Hornbeck to Herbert Feis, May 19, 1934, *ibid.*, 033.1100 Rogers, James Harvey/39.

29. This paragraph is based upon documents in *FR, 1934* (Washington D.C., 1950), 3:388-421. Hornbeck's memorandum of his telephone conversation with Lamont on June 18, 1934, however, was not printed in that volume. See State Department files 893.51/5103.

30. Rogers to Morgenthau, July 6, 1934, *ibid.*, 033.110 Rogers, James Harvey/76; Rogers to Roper, September 12, 1934, Record Group 40; Morgenthau diary, September 10, 1934; Morgenthau to FDR, September 5, 1934, Official File 21, Roosevelt Library. See also Morgenthau to Hull, December 9, 1934, State Department files 893.515/369.

31. Morgenthau diary, November 27 and December 19, 1934.

32. FDR to Morgenthau, December 6, 1934, Official File 150, Roosevelt Library. The Treasury Memorandum, undated, is in PSF: Treasury. The episode is discussed in Everest, p. 108, and Blum, *Years of Crisis*, pp. 205-08.

33. Hornbeck memorandum, "Chinese Legation's Notes of February 5," February 19, 1935, State Department files 893.515/402.

34. Hornbeck to Hull, December 16, 1934, *ibid.*, 893.515/372; Memorandum of a Conversation, December 28, 1934, *ibid.*, 893.515/379; Hornbeck memorandum, "Silver Question and T. V. Soong," January 9, 1935, *ibid.*, 893.515/388.

35. Morgenthau diary, January 6, 1935. A most interesting dissent to this thesis was offered by a third secretary of the American legation in China, O. Edmund Clubb, whose memorandum, "Significant Current Developments Affecting Silver and Gold in China," January 18, 1935, offered evidence to support the president's views as expressed the previous December and concluded that the Chinese government sought foreign loans as a way of easing the need for reform at home. It is enclosed in Clarence E. Gauss to Secretary of State, January 18, 1935, State Department files 893.515/407. The Far Eastern Division's reader marked it as being of special interest.

36. Morgenthau diary, January 6, 1935.

37. Memorandum of a Conversation, December 28, 1934, State Department files 893.515/379.

38. *FR, 1935* (Washington D.C., 1953), 3:536-38; Morgenthau diary, February 14, 1935; Memorandum, February 19, 1935, State Department files 893.515/402.

39. Memorandum of a Conversation with the British Ambassador, February 25, 1935, *ibid.,* 983.515/421; *FR, 1935*, 3:547-50; Grew to Hull, March 4, 1935 and Hull to Grew, March 5, 1935, State Department files 893.515/432; Memorandum of a Conversation, March 4, 1935, *ibid.*, 893.515/446.

40. Raymond Atherton to Secretary of State, March 5, 1935, *ibid.*, 893.515/463; *FR, 1935*, 3:567-68.

41. Memorandum of a Conversation with the British Ambassador, February 25, 1935, State Department files 893.515/421; *FR, 1935*, 3:547-50; Grew to Hull, March 4, 1935 and Hull to Grew, March 5, 1935, State Department files 893.515/432; Memorandum of a Conversation, March 4, 1935, *ibid.*, 893.515/446.

42. Raymond Atherton to Secretary of State, March 5, 1935, *ibid.*, 893.515/463; *FR, 1935*, 3:567-68.

43. Memorandum of a Conversation with the Japanese Ambassador, April 3, 1935, State Department files 893.515/510; Nelson T. Johnson to Secretary of State, May 1, 1935, *FR, 1935*, 3:577; Morgenthau to FDR, June 14, 1935, PSF

3; Herbert Feis to Cordell Hull, June 15, 1935, State Department files 893.515/652; Morgenthau diary, April 15 and July 18, 1935.

44. Blum, *Years of Crisis*, pp. 208-10. But see also the fuller explanation of Chiang's supposed plan in the cable from the treasury attaché, Morgenthau diary, July 26, 1935.

45. See fn. 12 above.

46. Morgenthau diary, October 29, 1935; Blum, *Years of Crisis*, pp. 209-15. See also Hornbeck memorandum, October 30, 1935, State Department files 893.515/801.

47. Morgenthau diary, November 2, 5, and 6, 1935; Blum, *Years of Crisis*, pp. 212-17; Memorandum of a Telephone Conversation, November 5, 1935, State Department files 893.515/850.

48. Morgenthau diary, November 9 and 13, 1935; J. Lossing Buck to Morgenthau, November 9, 1935, State Department files 893.515/848; Borg, *Far Eastern Crisis*, p. 134.

49. Undated [1936] memorandum to Morgenthau, Papers of Harry Dexter White, Firestone Library, Princeton University, Princeton, N.J.

50. Atherton to SS, November 18, 1935, State Department files 893.51/6062; Memorandum of a Conversation with the British Ambassador, November 19, 1935, *ibid.*, 893.515/897; Morgenthau diary, November 20 and 22, 1935.

51. *Ibid.*, July 8, 1937. See also Arthur N. Young, *China and the Helping Hand, 1937-1945* (Cambridge, Mass., 1963), pp. 33-34.

52. Buck to Morgenthau, September 29, 1936, PSF 38.

53. Wayne C. Taylor to Morgenthau, Morgenthau diary, February 19, 1937.

54. Morgenthau to FDR, September 21, 1937, PSF 38; Harold L. Ickes, *The Secret Diary of Harold L. Ickes, II: The Inside Struggle, 1936-1939* (New York, 1954), pp. 51-54.

55. This paragraph is drawn from several letters: R. E. Harrison to Robert Alter, April 17, 1934; Julean Arnold to Roper, January 26, 1935; W. Rodney Long to Walter Sanders, October 12, 1935; E. P. Thomas to C. K. Moser, October 28, 1935; and Boettiger to Roper, February 13, 1937, Record Group 151:640 China, Boxer Indemnity; Memorandum of a Conversation with C. J. Carroll, January 6, 1935, State Department files 893.51/6071; Hornbeck to Hull, Feis to Hull, January 11, 1936, *ibid.*, 893.51/6070; Hornbeck memorandum, March 26, 1936, *FR, 1936* (Washington D.C., 1954), 4:469-72.

56. Memorandum of a conversation with Thomas Lamont, December 29, 1936, *ibid.*, pp. 502-04; J. P. Morgan and Company to SS, January 22, 1937,

State Department files 893.51/6280; W. E. Dodd to Hull, January 4, 1937, *ibid.*, 893.51/ 6277; Atherton to Hull, February 10, 1937, *FR,1937*, 4:568-69.

57. Roper to Boettiger, February 24, 1937, Record Group 151:640.

58. Chang Kia-ngau to Pierson, December 21, 1936, and Pierson to Chang, March 1, 1937, State Department files 893.51/6304; Pierson to R.C. MacKay, March 19, 1937, *ibid.*, 033.1190 Pierson, Warren Lee/1.

59. Gauss to Hull, May 4, 1937, *ibid.*, 033.1190 Pierson, Warren Lee/20; *FR, 1937*, 4:585-86; National Foreign Trade Convention, *Official Report, 1937*, pp. 258-60.

60. F. P. Lockhart to SS, May 7, 1937, State Department files 793.94/8642; A. C. Calder to Julean Arnold, May 10, 1937, Record Group 151:640.

61. Johnson to Hull, April 16, 1937, *FR, 1937*, 4:581-82; Johnson to Hull, May 12, 1937, *ibid.*, pp. 595-98.

62. Johnson to Hull, April 26, 1937, *ibid.*, pp. 584-85.

63. Robert Bingham to Hull, June 21, 1937, *ibid.*, pp. 605-07; American Chamber of Commerce to Hull, June 29, 1937, State Department files 893.51/6408; Borg, *Far Eastern Crisis*, pp. 269-75.

64. Los Angeles *Herald*, June 21, 1937, clipping in Record Group 151:640.

65. Morgenthau diary, June 30, 1937; Kung to Jesse Jones, July 12, 1937, *FR, 1937*, 4:612-13.

66. Roper to E. Draper, August 12, 1937, Record Group 40.

67. Pierson to Marvin H. McIntyre, July 17, 1937, Official File 971, Roosevelt Library.

68. Munoz and Co. to Commerce Department, January 11, 1938, Record Group 151:211.1 Japan.

69. Frank S. Williams to Alexander Dye, January 26, 1937, *ibid.*

70. Arnold to C. K. Moser, November 22, 1937, *ibid.*, 492.1.

71. Roper to Frank Nebeker, October 12, 1937, Record Group 40.

72. Roper to FDR, November 26, 1937, PSF 22.

73. Roper to Dye, April 19, 1938, Record Group 40; Louis Domeratzky to Assistant Director, BFDC, April 20, 1938, *ibid.*; A. R. Sowell to Dye, April 28, 1938, *ibid.*; Roper to FDR, September 1, 1938, PSF 22.

74. Blum, *Years of Crisis*, pp. 159-73; Morgenthau diary, September 7, 1937; George Haas to Morgenthau, *ibid.*, September 4, 1937.

75. *Ibid.*

76. Feis to Hull, September 7, 1937, State Department files 893.51/6460; Morgenthau to FDR, October 7 and 26, 1937, PSF 7; Borg, *Far Eastern Crisis*, chap. 13; FDR to Stimson, November 24, 1937, H. L. Stimson Papers, Yale University Library, New Haven, Conn.

77. Blum, *Years of Crisis*, pp. 484-90; Herman Oliphant to Morgenthau, December 15, 1937, PSF 7.

78. Morgenthau diary, December 17, 1937.

79. *Ibid.*, December 18, 1937.

80. *Ibid.*, June 1, 1938; Haas to Morgenthau, *ibid.*, June 6, 1938.

81. N. T. Johnson to Hull, July 1, 1938, State Department files 893.51/6638; Hull to Joseph P. Kennedy, July 13, 1938, *FR, 1938*, 3 (Washington D.C., 1954):536-37; Young, p. 74; FDR to Acting Secretary of the Treasury, August 16, 1938, PSF 25; Blum, *Years of Crisis*, pp. 508-10; Morgenthau diary, July 12, 1938.

82. *Ibid.*, September 22, 1938.

83. Morgenthau to FDR, October 17, 1938, PSF 38; Blum, *Years of Crisis*, pp. 526-28; Morgenthau diary, October 15, November 11 and 29, 1938.

84. *FR, 1938*, 3:569-77.

85. Memorandum to Morgenthau, George C. Marshall, and Frank Knox, October 2, 1940, Stimson Papers.

86. *FR, 1940* (Washington D.C., 1955), 4:645-68; U.S., Congress, Senate, Internal Security Subcommittee of the Committee on the Judiciary, *Morgenthau Diary (China)*, 89th Congress, 1st session (Washington D.C., 1965), 1:146-55; FDR to Morgenthau, June 1, 1940, PSF 3; John Morton Blum, *From the Morgenthau Diaries: Years of Urgency, 1938-1941* (Boston, 1965), pp. 346-48. Two points of view on the currency stabilization loan question are Young, pp. 166-205, and Ross Y. Koen, *The China Lobby in American Politics* (New York, 1960), chap. 1.

87. Memorandum for the president drafted by Harry Dexter White, July 1, 1940, *Morgenthau Diary (China)*, 1:175-76; July 9, 1940, *ibid.*; White to Morgenthau with enclosures, July 15, 1940, *ibid.*, pp. 176-81; Blum, *Years of Urgency*, pp. 346-50; Morgenthau to FDR, August 16, 1940, PSF 4.

88. September 19, 1940, *Morgenthau Diary (China)*, 1:208-09. The portion of the conversation at the end where Morgenthau talks about his bluff is not published; see Morgenthau diary, September 19, 1940.

89. Feis, p. 124.

90. September 23, 1940, *Morgenthau Diary (China)*, 1:225.

91. Blum, *Years of Urgency*, pp. 370-71.

92. See Young, pp. 193-94. Young regards the White proposals with deep suspicion, although he does not openly attack White's loyalty. This question is really beyond the present paper, but a copy of the first memorandum, dated only "May, 1941," in the White Papers can be consulted for further internal evidence on these points. I am persuaded, however, that it represented a position then being taken by a few officers in the State Department, most notably Maxwell Hamilton, whose loyalty was beyond question. If the proposal itself, therefore, was not especially subversive to Hamilton, who in fact regarded it as one of the most constructive ideas and programs he had seen for avoiding war with Japan, the researcher is left with the feeling that White's loyalty is of no importance and other questions about the fate of the two memoranda are of far greater significance. See William L. Neumann, *America Encounters Japan: From Perry to MacArthur* (New York, 1965), pp. 274-75. The details of the White Memorandum of May-June are used for this paragraph.

93. For the November memorandum, see *FR, 1941* (Washington D.C., 1956), 4:606-13.

94. *Ibid*.

95. Morgenthau to FDR, November 18, 1941, and FDR to Hull, November 21, 1941 (with Hull's note), PSF 13.

96. Diary of Henry L. Stimson, October 6, 1941, Stimson Papers.

97. Blum, *Years of Urgency*, pp. 389-90. Blum's treatment of the White memorandum (*ibid.*, pp. 385-87) is unsatisfactory, largely because he attempts to explain everything logically. He assumes that the memorandum and Hull's drafts could both gain Morgenthau's approval since each "contained Japan and protected China." One has to stretch these words beyond a normal breaking point to make them fit two entirely different approaches.

The Role of the Finance Ministry

1. Wakatsuki Reijirō, *Kofūan kaikoroku* (Memoirs Written at Kofūan) (Tokyo, 1950), p. 377.

2. *Ōsaka Asahi Shinbun*, July 21, 1928.

3. Recollections of Hoshino Naoki, Finance Ministry Archives.

4. *Ibid*. On the issue of attracting American capital for investment in Manchuria, see the essay by Chō Yukio, pp. 377-410.

5. Tsushima Juichi, *Takahashi Korekiyo no omoide* (Reminiscing About Takahashi Korekiyo).

6. Recollections of Kaya Okinori, Finance Ministry Archives.

7. *Ibid*.

8. Recollections of Aoki Kazuo, Finance Ministry Archives.

9. Imamura Takeo, *Ikeda Seihin den* (Biography of Ikeda Seihin) (Tokyo, 1962), p. 328.

10. Ishiwata Sōtarō Denki Hensankai (Committee to Compile a Biography of Ishiwata Sōtarō), ed., *Ishiwata Sōtarō* (Tokyo, 1954), pp. 263-81.

11. Recollections of Hoshino Naoki.

12. Yabe Teiji, *Konoe Fumimaro* (Tokyo, 1952), 2:132.

13. Recollections of Hirose Hōsaku, Finance Ministry Archives.

14. *Ibid*.

15. Recollections of Sakomizu Hisatsune, Finance Ministry Archives.

16. Recollections of Ōno Ryūta, *ibid*.

17. Recollections of Kaya Okinori.

The Role of the United States Congress and Political Parties

1. Kirk H. Porter and Donald Bruce Johnson, comps., *National Party Platforms, 1840-1956* (Urbana, 1956), pp. 331-51; William E. Leuchtenburg, *Franklin D. Roosevelt and the New Deal, 1932-1940* (New York, 1963), pp.

1-17; Walter Johnson, *1600 Pennsylvania Avenue: Presidents and the People, 1929-1959* (Boston, 1960), pp. 36-48.

2. Porter and Johnson, pp. 360-70; Leuchtenburg, pp. 175-96; Johnson, *1600 Pennsylvania Avenue*, pp. 89-92; interview with Alfred M. Landon, Topeka, Kan., July 27, 1966.

3. Porter and Johnson, pp. 381-94; Donald Bruce Johnson, *The Republican Party and Wendell Willkie* (Urbana, 1960), pp. 1-108; Johnson, *1600 Pennsylvania Avenue*, pp. 135-37.

4. *Ibid.*; Johnson, *Wendell Willkie*, pp. 109-65; Robert E. Sherwood, *Roosevelt and Hopkins: An Intimate History* (New York, 1948), pp.169-201.

5. Eleanor E. Dennison, *The Senate Foreign Relations Committee* (Stanford, 1942); Robert A. Dahl, *Congress and Foreign Policy* (New York, 1950); James A. Robinson, *Congress and Foreign Policy-Making* (Homewood, Ill., 1962).

6. Marian C. McKenna, *Borah* (Ann Arbor, 1961); Claudius O. Johnson, *Borah of Idaho* (New York, 1936).

7. Fred L. Israel, *Nevada's Key Pittman* (Lincoln, Neb., 1963); Wayne S. Cole, "Senator Key Pittman and American Neutrality Policies, 1933-1940," *Mississippi Valley Historical Review*, 46 (March 1960):644-62.

8. Tom Connally, *My Name Is Tom Connally* (New York, 1954); *Newsweek*, 16 (November 25, 1940):16-17; printed order in the Senate of the United States, July 31, 1941, Senate Foreign Relations Committee files, 77th Congress, Record Group 46, National Archives, Washington D.C.

9. Among others who served on the Senate Foreign Relations Committee during all or part of those years were Nathan L. Bachman of Tennessee, Alben W. Barkley of Kentucky, Hugo L. Black of Alabama, Robert J. Bulkley of Ohio, Dennis Chavez of New Mexico, Bronson Cutting of New Mexico, F. Ryan Duffy of Wisconsin, Simeon D. Fess of Ohio, Guy M. Gillette of Iowa, Joseph F. Guffey of Pennsylvania, Pat Harrison of Mississippi, J. Hamilton Lewis of Illinois, James E. Murray of Montana, James P. Pope of Idaho, David A. Reed of Pennsylvania, Arthur R. Robinson of Indiana, Lewis B. Schwellenbach of Washington, Elbert D. Thomas of Utah, Frederick Van Nuys of Indiana, and Wallace H. White of Maine. Dennison, pp. 192-95.

10. Wayne S. Cole, *Senator Gerald P. Nye and American Foreign Relations* (Minneapolis, 1962).

11. George W. Norris to John M. Leyda, December 12, 1931, George W. Norris Papers, Manuscript Division, Library of Congress, Washington D.C.; Memorandum of Conversation between Senator Shipstead and Mr. Hornbeck,

February 3, 1932, State Department files 793.94/3949, National Archives, Washington D.C.

12. *FR, 1932* (Washington D.C., 1948), 3:453; Armin Rappaport, *Henry L. Stimson and Japan, 1931-1933* (Chicago, 1963), pp. 140-44; Robert H. Ferrell, *American Diplomacy in the Great Depression: Hoover-Stimson Foreign Policy, 1929-1933* (New Haven, 1957), pp. 151-93.

13. William E. Borah to Mrs. Horace E. Goodwin, March 10, 1932, William E. Borah Papers, Manuscript Division, Library of Congress; Memorandum of Conversation by Joseph C. Green, February 14, 1933, State Department files 811.113/229; Dorothy Detzer, *Appointment on the Hill* (New York, 1948), pp. 138-50; Herbert Hoover, *The Memoirs of Herbert Hoover, II: The Cabinet and the Presidency, 1920-1933* (New York, 1952), pp. 362-79; Henry L. Stimson and McGeorge Bundy, *On Active Service in Peace and War* (New York, 1948), pp. 226-63.

14. Robert A. Divine, *The Illusion of Neutrality* (Chicago, 1962), pp. 41-56; Cole, "Pittman and Neutrality Policies," p. 653.

15. Borah to Stimson, August 25, 1932, and Borah to George W. Anderson, August 30, 1932, Borah Papers; Stimson to Borah, September 8, 1932, State Department files 861.01/1786.

16. *Congressional Record*, 74th Congress, 2nd session (1936), pp. 6801-02; *ibid.*, 75th Congress, 3rd session (1938), pp. 5840-50; Borah to Theodore B. Mitzner, April 4, 1938, Borah Papers.

17. Frank Knox to Major General Hugh A. Drum, March 13, 1933, and Knox to Cordell Hull, December 15, 1937, Frank Knox Papers, Manuscript Division, Library of Congress; William Gibbs McAdoo to Franklin D. Roosevelt, January 24, 1939, Cordell Hull Papers, Manuscript Division, Library of Congress; McAdoo to Roosevelt, September 19 and October 3, 1939, William Gibbs McAdoo Papers, Manuscript Division, Library of Congress; McAdoo to Roosevelt, August 22, 1940, President's Personal File 308, Roosevelt Library, Hyde Park, N.Y. (hereafter cited as PPF); Key Pittman, "Preparedness for Defense," *Vital Speeches of the Day*, 5 (April 15, 1939):404-06.

18. Norris to Paul K. Brandt, February 3, 1938, Norris to Arthur W. Peterson, February 3, 1938, and clipping from El Monte, Calif. newspaper datelined May 31, 1941, Norris Papers.

19. Hiram W. Johnson to Hiram W. Johnson, Jr., January 29, 1938, Hiram W. Johnson Papers, Bancroft Library, Berkeley, Calif.

20. Divine, *Illusion of Neutrality*; Cole, *Nye and American Foreign Relations*, pp. 97-123.

21. *Ibid.*, pp. 114-19; Divine, *Illusion of Neutrality*, pp. 162-99.

22. Elliott Roosevelt, ed., *F.D.R.: His Personal Letters, 1928-1945*, 2 (New York, 1950):873; Cordell Hull, *The Memoirs of Cordell Hull* (New York, 1948), 1:556-58.

23. *New York Times*, July 30, 1937, p. 1; Key Pittman, "Neutrality," *Vital Speeches of the Day*, 3 (September 1, 1937):700-02; *New York Times*, May 23, 1938, p. 8.

24. Norris to John W. Towle, December 12, 1938, and Norris to Harry J. Johnson, March 20, 1939, Norris Papers; Borah to Harold Graham, December 30, 1938, Borah Papers.

25. *New York Times*, August 15, 1937, p. 1; *Congressional Record*, 75th Congress, 1st session (1937), Appendix, pp. 2187, 2257-58.

26. *Ibid.*, pp. 8585-86.

27. Charles L. McNary to Doris Weber, October 13, 1939, Charles L. McNary Papers, Manuscript Division, Library of Congress.

28. Alfred M. Landon to William Hard, October 11, 1937, and Landon to William R. Castle, October 30, 1937, Alfred M. Landon Papers, Kansas State Historical Society, Topeka, Kan.

29. Frank Knox to George Messersmith, October 6, 1937, Knox Papers.

30. *New York Times*, October 7, 1937, p. 1.

31. *New York Journal-American*, October 8, 1937; *New York Times*, October 8, 1937, p. 2.

32. Telegram from Johnson to Raymond Moley, October 11, 1937, Johnson Papers.

33. Borah to Clark M. Eichelberger, November 5, 1937, Borah Papers.

34. Hull, *Memoirs*, 1:552; *FR, 1937* (Washington D.C., 1954), 4:85-86; *New York Times*, November 21, 1937, p. 38.

35. Knox to Hull, December 15, 1937, Hull Papers.

36. *New York Times*, December 14, 1937, p. 23.

37. Borah to William V. Allen, December 17, 1937, Borah Papers.

38. *Ivanhoe Times* (Minn.), December 23, 1937.

39. Manny T. Koginos, *The Panay Incident: Prelude to War* (Lafayette, Ind., 1967), pp. 80-83.

40. *Ibid.*, pp. 92-96; Roosevelt to William B. Bankhead, January 6, 1938, Official File 3084, Roosevelt Library; Knox to Mrs. Knox, December 19, 1937, Knox Papers; telegram from Landon to Roosevelt, December 20, 1937, Landon Papers; *New York Times*, August 23, 1938, p. 20; Norris to Leland H. Evans, March 17, 1939, Norris Papers.

41. Koginos, pp. 96-97.

42. G. H. Brown to Tom Connally, June 24, 1936, State Department files 611.946/318; J. E. McDonald to Tom Connally, November 28, 1939, *ibid.*, 711.942/371; George Sealy to Marvin McIntyre, May 22, 1939, PPF 6692; James A. White to William D. Felder, Jr., December 18, 1939, Foreign Relations Committee files, 76th Congress.

43. Earl Constantine to George W. Norris, December 30, 1937, Norris Papers.

44. John Taber to William Gibbs McAdoo, November 2, 1934, McAdoo Papers; George W. Norris to H. J. Gramlich, January 13, 1934, Norris Papers; Gerald P. Nye to Anne Harrington, February 20, 1939, Gerald P. Nye Papers, Chevy Chase, Md.

45. *New York Times*, August 15, 1931, p. 14; Borah to Orris Dorman, September 23, 1932, and Borah to O. O. Haga, September 17, 1932, Borah Papers.

46. Pittman to Norman H. Davis, March 30, 1931, and telegram from Pittman to Bernard M. Baruch, August 19, 1931, Key Pittman Papers, Manuscript Division, Library of Congress; William Phillips to Roosevelt, December 10, 1934, Cordell Hull to Roosevelt, February 7, 1935, telegram from Peck to Hull, February 2, 1935, Hull to Roosevelt, April 30, 1935, Memorandum of Conversation between Secretary Hull and the Chinese Minister, Jr. Sao-ke Alfred Sze, April 25, 1935, President's Secretary's File: China, 1933-37, Roosevelt Library; Pittman to Henry Morgenthau, Jr., January 10, 1940, Foreign Relations Committee files, 76th Congress.

47. Stanley J. Nichols to Pittman, November 29, 1937, Foreign Relations Committee files, 75th Congress; Cordell Hull to Tom Connally, April 18, 1935, State Department files 611.946/149; Walter F. George to Roosevelt, September 24, 1935, and Hull to George, October 19, 1935, *ibid.*, 611.9417/51; Roger L. Wensley to Eugene J. Keogh, May 8, 1937, House Foreign Affairs Committee files, 75th Congress, Record Group 233, National Archives, Washington D.C.

48. Norris to Edwin M. Borchard, January 4, 1938, and Earl Constantine to Norris, December 30, 1937, Norris Papers; Pittman to Homer L. Williams,

June 13, 1938, Foreign Relations Committee files, 75th Congress; Borah to Samuel E. Newman, October 7, 1937, Borah Papers.

49. Arthur Capper to Hull, January 27, 1939, Arthur Capper Papers, Kansas State Historical Society, Topeka, Kan.; Sam D. McReynolds to Hull, January 31, 1939, and enclosed print of H.R. 3419, State Department files 894.24/589; Nye to Clarence E. Parr, May 8, 1939, Nye Papers.

50. Donald J. Friedman, *The Road from Isolation: The Campaign of the American Committee for Non-Participation in Japanese Aggression, 1938-1941* (Cambridge, Mass., 1968), pp. 31-32; Harry B. Price to Pittman, March 28, 1939, Hull Papers, print of S.J. Res. 123, 76th Congress, 1st session, April 27, 1939 and July 11, 1939, in Papers Supporting Senate Bills and Resolutions, National Archives.

51. *Ibid.*; print of S.J. Res. 143, 76th Congress, 1st session, June 1, 1939, and Hull to Pittman, July 21, 1939, in Papers Supporting Senate Bills and Resolutions; Theodore Francis Green to Robert T. Paine, July 21, 1939, Theodore Francis Green Papers, Manuscript Division, Library of Congress.

52. Cordell Hull to Key Pittman, July 21, 1939, and attached print of S. Res. 166; A. H. Vandenberg to Hull, August 7, 1939; memorandum of telephone conversation between Hull and Stanley K. Hornbeck, August 19, 1939; Sumner Welles to Vandenberg, August 22, 1939; Vandenberg to Welles, August 24, 1939; and memorandum of M.M.H. on "American Policy in the Far East: Lippmann-Vandenberg Controversy," February 9, 1940, State Department files 711.942/174, 232, 271, 573.

53. Price to Pittman, October 30 and November 1, 1939; telegram from Price to Pittman, November 7, 1939; James A. White to William D. Felder, Jr., December 18, 1939; Henry L. Stimson to Pittman, January 22, 1940; telegram from Pittman to Vincent Sheean, January 24, 1940; and Pittman to Raymond Leslie Buell, February 1, 1940, Senate Foreign Relations Committee files. Lewis B. Schwellenbach to Theodore Granik, April 30, 1940, and enclosed copy of article on "Shall We Declare an Embargo Against Japan?" Lewis B. Schwellenbach Papers, Manuscript Division, Library of Congress.

54. Pittman to Pauline Chandler, May 25, 1940, and Price to Pittman, June 18, 1940, Senate Foreign Relations Committee files; Friedman, pp. 32-36; Herbert Feis, *The Road to Pearl Harbor: The Coming of the War Between the United States and Japan* (Princeton, 1950), pp. 72-74.

55. *Ibid.*, pp. 74-75, 236-49; Elliott Roosevelt, 2:1077; *Chicago Tribune*, July 27, 1941, p. 3.

56. *Ibid.*, August 28, 1941, p. 7; *Fargo Forum* (North Dakota), November 21, 1941.

57. *Pittsburgh Press*, December 8, 1841; *Pittsburgh Sun Telegraph*, December 8, 1941. John B. Gordon to Nye, December 9, 1941; Nye to Gordon, January 7, 1942; and undated account of Pittsburgh meeting in Nye's handwriting, Nye Papers. M. E. Armbruster to Page Hufty, December 11, 1941, and James L. Fallon to Gordon, February 6, 1941, America First Committee Papers, Hoover Library, Stanford, Calif.; *Congressional Record*, 77th Congress, 2nd session (1942), p. 8574; interview with Gerald P. Nye, July 20, 1959.

The Role of the Diet and Political Parties

1. Emergency ordinances and independent ordinances were reserved to the imperial prerogative. Formation of the Imperial Household, governmental organizations, the House of Peers, and colonial areas were all outside the sphere of Diet legislative authority. The budgetary power of the Diet was limited by the right of the government to consent to any decrease in expenditures or exclusion of continuing expenditures arising from the legal obligations of the government, to enact the preceding year's budget if the pending one failed to pass, and to take emergency financial measures.

2. There were only five standing committees in the House of Peers (Screening, Budget, Discipline, Petition, and Accounts) and four in the House of Representatives (Budget, Accounts, Discipline, and Petition). After the 65th Diet session (December 26, 1933-March 26, 1934) a Representation Committee was added in the lower house.

3. Even with regard to the selection of both houses of the Diet and their powers and sessions, the Imperial Diet was an exceedingly imperfect organ of popular representation. While the House of Representatives was selected by popular vote, the House of Peers was composed of members of the imperial family, certain members of the nobility, and persons nominated by the emperor. Except that the right of prior consideration of the budget rested with the House of Representatives, both houses of the Diet had equal authority. The emperor had the authority to convoke, adjourn, prorogue, close, and dissolve the Diet. Besides regular and annual sessions, special sessions could be convened at the request of the government. The Meiji constitution set the length of sessions at three months, and while there were occasional extensions, Diet activity was generally circumscribed by the short sessions. Furthermore, deliberation on the budget was fixed by Diet law to a three week period in the House of Representatives. After 1927 a similar restriction was placed upon budgetary deliberations in the House of Peers.

4. Mitarai Tatsuo, *Minami Jirō* (Tokyo, 1957), p. 200.

5. *Ibid.*

6. Nakano Masao, *Hashimoto taisa no shuki* (Memoirs of Colonel Hashimoto) (Tokyo, 1963), pp. 33, 45.

7. *Ibid.*, p. 151.

8. Harada Kumao, *Saionji-kō to seikyoku* (Prince Saionji and the Political Situation), 2 (Tokyo, 1951):116; Shiraki Masayuki, *Nihon seitōshi: Shōwahen* (A History of Political Parties in Japan: Shōwa Era) (Tokyo, 1949), pp. 92-94.

9. Nihon Kokusai Seiji Gakkai, Taiheiyō Sensō Gen'in Kenkyūbu (Japan International Politics Association, Study Group on the Origins of the Pacific War), ed., *Taiheiyō sensō e no michi: Bekkan shiryōhen* (Road to the Pacific War: Supplementary Volume of Documents) (Tokyo, 1963), p. 163.

10. Shūgiin-Sangiin (House of Representatives and House of Councillors), comp., *Gikai seido shichijūnenshi: Kenseishi gaikan* (A Seventy-Year History of the Parliamentary System: A General View of Japanese Constitutional History) (Tokyo, 1963), p. 364.

11. Shiraki, p. 112.

12. *Ibid.*, p. 113.

13. The number of party members serving as cabinet ministers during the period is indicated in the following table:

Cabinet	Total Number of Cabinet Ministers[a]	Number of Party Members
Katō Takaaki (1st) June 11, 1924- August 2, 1925	11 (12)	7 (8)[b]: 4 Kenseikai, 2 (3)[b] Seiyūkai, 1 Kakushin Kurabu
Katō Takaaki (2nd) August 2, 1925- January 30, 1926	12	8 Kenseikai
Wakatsuki Reijirō (1st) January 30, 1926- April 20, 1927	12	8 (7)[c] Kenseikai
Tanaka Giichi April 20, 1927- July 2, 1929	11[d]	8 (7)[e] Seiyūkai
Hamaguchi Osachi July 2, 1929- April 14, 1931	13	10 Minseitō
Wakatsuki Reijirō (2nd) April 14, 1931- December 13, 1931	13	10 Minseitō

Inukai Tsuyoshi December 13, 1931- May 26, 1932	13	10 Seiyūkai
Saitō Makoto May 26, 1932- July 8, 1934	13	5: 3 Seiyūkai, 2 Minseitō
Okada Keisuke July 8, 1934- March 9, 1936	13	5: 3 Seiyūkai,[f] 2 Minseitō
Hirota Kōki March 9, 1936- February 2, 1937	13	4: 2 Seiyūkai, 2 Minseitō
Hayashi Senjūrō February 10, 1937- June 4, 1937	10[g]	1 Shōwakai
Konoe Fumimaro (1st) June 4, 1937- January 5, 1939	13 (14)[h]	2: 1 Seiyūkai, 1 Minseitō
Hiranuma Kiichirō January 5, 1939- August 30, 1939	15[i]	2: 1 Seiyūkai, 1 Minseitō
Abe Nobuyuki August 30, 1939- January 16, 1940	14	2 (3)[j]: 1 Seiyūkai, 1 Minseitō, 1 Independent[j]
Yonai Mitsumasa January 16, 1940- July 22, 1940	14	4: 2 Seiyūkai, 2 Minseitō

[a]The total number of cabinet ministers includes the prime minister. Ministers holding more than one portfolio are counted as one in the table.

The first Katō cabinet included the following eleven ministers: prime minister, foreign minister, home minister, finance minister, army minister, navy minister, minister of justice, minister of education, minister of agriculture and commerce, minister of communications, and minister of railways. Subsequent changes in these positions are indicated in the footnotes below. Increases or decreases in the number of cabinet ministers are indicated by figures in parentheses.

[b]The increase is due to the elimination of the Ministry of Agriculture and Commerce and the establishment of two new ministries—Agriculture and Forestry, and Commerce and Industry.

[c]The decrease is due to the appointment of House of Peers member Inoue Kyōshirō (affiliated with the Kenkyūkai group in that body) as minister of railways.

[d]Prime Minister Tanaka concurrently held the portfolio of foreign minister and the newly-created position of colonial affairs minister.

[e]The decrease is due to the appointment of Shōda Kazue (a member of the Kenkyūkai group in the House of Peers) as minister of education.

[f]Includes those expelled from the Seiyūkai who first became independents and then joined the Shōwakai.

[g]Prime Minister Hayashi was concurrently minister of education; Minister of Commerce and Industry Godō Takuo was concurrently minister of railways; Finance Minister Yūki Toyotarō was concurrently colonial affairs minister.

[h]The increase is due to the creation of the Ministry of Welfare.

[i]Includes ministers without portfolio.

[j]The increase is due to the appointment of Akita Kiyoshi, an independent, as minister of welfare.

14. Shiraki, pp. 165-66.

15. *Ibid.*, p. 169.

16. Later, Prime Minister Okada Keisuke stated that the primary objective of the Cabinet Deliberative Council was to act as a "roadblock against the army" (Matsumura Kenzō, *Machida Chūji ō den* [Biography of the Venerable Machida Chūji] [Tokyo, 1950], p. 286), but this personal goal was completely betrayed.

17. The Cabinet Deliberative Council in August 1934 was conceived first as the National Policy Deliberative Council. Prime Minister Okada stated that its functions would be "limited to financial, economic, and educational problems and would not touch upon national defense or diplomatic questions at all." In response to a question by the emperor he said, "I do not intend to have the council deal with questions of national defense or diplomacy." Harada, 4:48, 51.

18. Matsumura, p. 346.

19. For the contents of this document, see Shūgiin-Sangiin, comp., *Gikai seido shichijūnenshi: Teikoku gikaishi* (A Seventy-Year History of the Parliamentary System: The Imperial Diet) (Tokyo, 1962), pp. 382-83.

20. *Ibid.*, p. 385.

21. Shūgiin-Sangiin, *Kenseishi gaikan*, p. 400.

22. Abe Shinnosuke, *Gendai sesō dokuhon* (On Contemporary Society) (Tokyo, 1937), p. 54.

23. *Ibid.*, p. 4.

24. When the Seiyūkai proposed that the Minseitō cosponsor a bill on agricultural policy, the Minseitō refused, fearing that the Seiyūkai might be trying to use such a joint action as a device to overthrow the cabinet.

25. Baba Tsunego, *Tachiagaru seijika* (Rising Politicians) (Tokyo, 1937), p. 62.

26. Abe, p. 5.

27. Iwabuchi Tatsuo, *Gendai Nihon seiji ron* (On Contemporary Japanese Politics) (Tokyo, 1941), pp. 301-02.

28. *Ibid.*, p. 466.

The Role of U.S. Business

1. U.S., Bureau of the Census, *Statistical Abstract of the United States, 1934*, p. 429; Mitsubishi Economic Research Bureau, *Japanese Trade and Industry* (London, 1936), p. 592; W. W. Lockwood, *Trade and Trade Rivalry Between the United States and Japan* (New York, 1936), p. 24; W. W. Lockwood, "American-Japanese Trade: Its Structure and Significance," *The Annals* of the American Academy of Political and Social Science, 215 (May 1941):86-87.

2. Mitsubishi, p. 594; National Foreign Trade Convention, *Official Report, 1934*, p. 268; U.S., Congress, Senate, Committee on Finance, *Reciprocal Trade Agreements, Hearings*, 73rd Congress, 2nd session, pp. 310ff, 332; U.S. Tariff Commission, *Recent Developments in the Foreign Trade of Japan* (Washington D.C., 1936).

3. Cordell Hull, *The Memoirs of Cordell Hull* (New York, 1948), 1:352-77.

4. *FR, 1934* (Washington D.C., 1950), 3:802.

5. *Reciprocal Trade Agreements, Hearings, passim,* especially pp. 187, 269, 333, 334.

6. *FR, 1935* (Washington D.C., 1953), 3:945, 948.

7. Lockwood, *Trade and Trade Rivalry*, p. 55; National Foreign Trade Convention, *Official Report, 1936*, pp. 314ff; *FR, 1935*, 3:947-49, 951-54, 957-1048; *FR, 1936* (Washington D.C., 1954), 4:880; Roosevelt press conference, April 12, 1935, in Edgar B. Nixon, ed., *Franklin D. Roosevelt and Foreign Affairs* (Cambridge, Mass., 1969), 2:476, 477; Secretaries of Commerce, State, Agriculture, and Labor to Roosevelt, October 28, 1935, *ibid.*, 3:38-40.

8. Mitsubishi, p. 594; National Foreign Trade Convention, *Official Report, 1935*, p. 217.

9. *FR, 1936*, 4:876, 883, 868-92; National Foreign Trade Convention, *Official Report, 1936*, p. 316; *Business Week*, May 30, 1936, p. 36.

10. Dorothy Borg, *The United States and the Far Eastern Crisis of 1933-1938* (Cambridge, Mass., 1964), p. 591; *FR, 1936*, 4:878-79; Nixon, 3:308.

11. *FR, 1936*, 4:936; *FR, 1937* (Washington D.C., 1954), 4:785, 787 (agreement dated January 22, 1937); National City Bank, *Monthly Letter*, May 1937, pp. 73-74.

12. U.S., Congress, House, Committee on Ways and Means, *Extending Reciprocal Foreign Trade Agreement Act, Hearings*, 75th Congress, lst session, pp. 539, 540.

13. *Business Week*, October 9, 1937, p. 54; December 4, 1937; January 8, 1938, pp. 24, 26.

14. *Ibid.* May 28, 1938, p. 39, reported that two buyers for American department stores found that rising costs in Japan, far more than American boycotts, were affecting their buying schedules.

15. U.S., Congress, House, Committee on Ways and Means, *Extension of Reciprocal Trade Agreements Act, Hearings*, 76th Congress, 3rd session.

16. *FR, 1935*, 3:1072, 1074, 1077; *FR, 1936*, 4:942-46; *FR, 1937*, 4:748ff, 764ff, 771; Harold L. Ickes, *The Secret Diary of Harold L. Ickes, II: The Inside Struggle, 1936-1939* (New York, 1954), pp. 296-97; Sumner Welles, *Seven Decisions that Shaped History* (New York, 1950), p. 77.

17. *Textile World*, 71 (March 5, 1932):60.

18. *Business Week*, January 8, 1938, pp. 24, 26; Thomas W. Lamont to Nelson T. Johnson, February 28, 1938, Box 184, Folder 14, Thomas W. Lamont Papers, Baker Library, Harvard University.

19. *New York Times*, July 27, 1941.

20. Compare Tables 1 and 2 in the text.

21. For example, *FR, 1936,* 4:848.

22. *Statistical Abstract of the United States, 1934*, pp. 424, 428; *ibid., 1938*, pp. 460, 464; *ibid., 1943,* pp. 534, 538.

23. Lockwood, "American-Japanese Trade," p. 90.

24. National Foreign Trade Convention, *Official Report, 1930*, pp. 34, 107; *ibid., 1931*, pp. 34, 37; *ibid., 1932,* p. 26.

25. Wallace M. Alexander, San Francisco Chamber of Commerce, at National Foreign Trade Convention, in *Official Report, 1932*, pp. 17-18.

26. *Ibid.,* pp. 23, 41, 47.

27. *Ibid., 1934,* pp. 247, 268, 269, 252.

28. *Ibid.,* p. xv.

29. *Ibid., 1935,* p. xviii.

30. Lockwood, *Trade and Trade Rivalry*, pp. 41-42; *Business Week,* April 11, 1936.

31. *Business Week*, May 30, 1936, p. 36; National Foreign Trade Convention, *Official Report, 1936*, p. xix.

32. Borg, *Far Eastern Crisis*, p. 340; *Business Week*, September 18, 1937, pp. 17, 18.

33. *FR, 1937,* 4:536, 540, 541, 543.

34. *Commercial and Financial Chronicle*, October 2, 1937, p. 2134; see also *ibid.,* October 9, 1937, p. 2291, and October 16, 1937, p. 2450.

35. *Business Week*, October 9, 1937, p. 55, October 16, 1937, p. 76, and October 23, 1937, p. 63; *Wall Street Journal*, October 6, 1937; *Journal of Commerce*, October 8, 1937; Borg, *Far Eastern Crisis*, p. 391.

36. *Commercial and Financial Chronicle*, October 9, 1937, p. 2291; October 16, 1937, p. 2450; December 8, 1937, p. 3876.

37. Robinson Newcomb, "American Economic Action Affecting the Orient," *The Annals* of the American Academy of Political and Social Science, 215 (May 1941):133-39; *FR, Japan, 1931-1941* (Washington D.C., 1943), 2:201-73; *FR, 1940* (Washington D.C., 1955), 4:568; Hull, *Memoirs*, 1:901, 915, and 2:1041; Harold L. Ickes, *The Secret Diary of Harold L. Ickes, III: The Lowering Clouds, 1939-1941* (New York, 1954), pp. 591-92; *Business Week*, January 4, 1941, p. 42.

38. *Commercial and Financial Chronicle*, June 18, 1938, p. 3855.

39. *Business Week*, May 14, 1938, pp. 42, 53; June 4, 1938, p. 43; June 11, 1938, p. 37; July 9, 1938, pp. 17-18; September 17, 1938, p. 57; October 22, 1938, p. 46; December 3, 1938, p. 15.

40. Statement printed in U.S., Congress, Senate, Committee on Foreign Relations, *Neutrality, Peace Legislation and Our Foreign Policy, Hearings*, 76th Congress, 1st session, pp. 631-36; *Business Week*, June 24, 1938, p. 15.

41. *Commercial and Financial Chronicle*, July 29, 1939, p. 625; *Business Week*, August 5, 1939, p. 12; *Wall Street Journal*, July 27, 1939 (this editorial was clearly written before its authors knew of the actual cancellation).

42. *Business Week*, January 20, 1940, p. 52; *Wall Street Journal*, January 27, 1940.

43. *Fortune*, 22 (September 1940):72-73, 114.

44. *Business Week*, July 13, 1940, p. 45.

45. *Wall Street Journal*, July 6, 1940 (the *Journal* did criticize the "preemptory manner" in which the controls were imposed); National Foreign Trade Convention, *Official Report, 1940*, pp. xix-xx (the meetings were held July 29-30, 1940); *Business Week*, October 19, 1940, p. 67.

46. *Commercial and Financial Chronicle*, October 5, 1940, p. 1952.

47. Herbert Feis, *The Road to Pearl Harbor: The Coming of the War Between the United States and Japan* (Princeton, 1950), p. 101; National Foreign Trade Convention, *Official Report, 1941*, p. xvi.

48. *Ibid.*, pp. xix, xxi.

49. U.S., Department of State, *Press Releases*, 18, no. 433 (January 15, 1938).

50. Summary of loans: Thomas W. Lamont to Takahashi (Japanese minister of finance), March 30, 1932, Box 188, Folder 22, Lamont Papers. For U.S. government estimate: U.S., Department of Commerce, Bureau of Foreign and Domestic Commerce (hereafter BFDC), *A New Estimate of American Investments Abroad* (*Trade Information Bulletin*, No. 767) (Washington D.C., 1931), p. 20.

51. Lamont, "Memorandum for Mr. Walter Lippmann," October 1, 1931, Box 187, Folder 10, Lamont Papers.

52. Lamont, "Memorandum for Mr. K. Suzuki," October 17, 1931, *ibid.*, Folder 11.

53. Lamont to Wirt W. Hallam, January 26, 1932, Box 184, Folder 5, Lamont Papers: see BFDC, *American Investments Abroad*, pp. 20-21, on defaults.

54. Lamont to Sonoda, March 10, 1932, and Lamont to Takahashi, March 30, 1932, Box 188, Folder 22, Lamont Papers; Lamont to Nelson T. Johnson, April 8, 1932, Box 184, Folder 5, Lamont Papers.

55. Lamont to Sonoda, March 10, 1932.

56. See correspondence in Box 188, Folder 22, Lamont Papers, especially Lamont, "Memorandum for Partners Alone," April 15, 1932.

57. Lamont to Johnson, November 3, 1933, Box 184, Folder 9, Lamont Papers; Borg, *Far Eastern Crisis*, pp. 64-65.

58. Lamont to Johnson, November 3, 1933.

59. Lamont, "Memorandum for Partners," December 19, 1933, Box 187, Folder 23, Lamont Papers; data in *ibid.*, Folders 24-25, relate to a dinner party Lamont had at his home for Ambassador Saitō.

60. *FR, 1920* (Washington D.C., 1935), 1:576; Frederick V. Field, *American Participation in the China Consortiums* (Chicago, 1931); Thomas W. Lamont, *Across World Frontiers* (New York, 1951), pp. 230, 227, 263; *FR, 1937*, 4:572.

61. *FR, 1934*, 3:391ff; Lamont to Stanley K. Hornbeck, October 11, 1934, Box 187, Folder 29, Lamont Papers.

62. Lamont to Hornbeck, June 11, 1934, Box 184, Folder 9, Lamont Papers.

63. Lamont to Li Ming (chairman of the board, Bank of China, Shanghai), December 21, 1934, *ibid.*, Folder 11. Later Lamont would write, "America's silver purchase policy has, to my mind, been perfectly intolerable and inexcusable . . . it is a sorry chapter in our history." Lamont to Johnson, May 19, 1936, *ibid.*, Folder 12.

64. Borg, *Far Eastern Crisis*, p. 264.

65. Lamont to Fukai, September 13, 1935, Box 187, Folder 32, Lamont Papers.

66. Lamont to Johnson, May 19, 1936, Box 184, Folder 12, Lamont Papers.

67. *FR, 1936*, 4:470-71, 472, 474; Hornbeck to Lamont, April 2, 1937, Box 184, Folder 13, Lamont Papers; *FR, 1937*, 4:571-73.

68. National City Bank, *Monthly Letter*, March 1938, p. 33; Lamont to Johnson, June 29, 1937, Box 184, Folder 14, Lamont Papers; Lamont to Hornbeck, December 11, 1944, *ibid.*, Folder 21, gives added details.

69. Lamont to Saitō, September 7, 1937, Box 188, Folder 4, Lamont Papers; see also other letters in Folders 4, 5, and 6.

70. J. S. Morgan to E. J. M. Dickson, September 30, 1937, *ibid.*, Folder 5. This letter was written by Thomas W. Lamont.

71. Lamont to Johnson, February 26, 1938, Box 184, Folder 14, Lamont Papers.

72. *Ibid.*; statement by Lamont, September 8, 1938, *ibid.*, Folder 15.

73. *FR, 1939* (Washington D.C., 1955), 3:722ff, especially pp. 733-35.

74. *New York Times*, July 14, 1940.

75. *Business Week*, October 26, 1940, p. 62. It is not clear where *Business Week* got its $500 million figure, which seems high.

76. A copy of the speech is in Box 141, Folder 4, Lamont Papers.

77. Lamont, "Memorandum for R. C. L[effingwell]," November 6, 1940, *ibid.*, Folder 3.

78. Grew to Lamont, November 13, 1940; Matsuoka to Lamont, December 27, 1940; and Lamont to Hornbeck, February 4, 1941, *ibid.*, Folder 5. Konoe to Lamont, December 27, 1940, Box 188, Folder 11, Lamont Papers; Draft of Lamont to Matsuoka, no date [early 1941], *ibid.*, Folder 12.

79. Basil Rauch, *Roosevelt from Munich to Pearl Harbor* (New York, 1950), p. 377. On April 9 Bishop Walsh and Father Drought presented Hull with a draft of an accord with Japan. The plan proposed: (1) U.S. recognition of Manchukuo, (2) revision of U.S. China policy, (3) an end to U.S. restrictions on exports to Japan, (4) credit for financing Japanese exports, and (5) assistance to Japan in obtaining raw materials from the Dutch East Indies (*ibid.*, p. 378). Matsuoka was not interested even in this (*ibid.*, p. 380).

80. Lamont, "Memorandum," June 16, 1941, Box 188, Folder 12, Lamont Papers; Hornbeck to Lamont, June 25, 1941, and Lamont to Hornbeck, June 30, 1941, Box 209, Folder 32, Lamont Papers.

81. National City Bank, *Monthly Letter*, August 1941, p. 85; Lamont, "Memorandum for Walter Lippmann," November 13, 1941, Box 188, Folder 13, Lamont Papers.

82. I have not been able to ascertain whether Lewis Strauss agreed with the Walsh-Drought proposals (see fn. 79 above). If he did, then when Lamont spoke for "businessmen," he was not speaking for Strauss. In any case, the Walsh-Drought mission did not alter American foreign policy.

83. *FR, 1931* (Washington D.C., 1946), 3:124; *FR, 1932* (Washington D.C., 1948), 4:241, 718; *FR, 1933* (Washington D.C., 1949), 3:486.

84. National City Bank, *Monthly Letter*, November 1934, p. 170; January 1935, pp. 6ff; May 1935, pp. 74ff; September 1935, pp. 135ff; December 1935, p. 183; January 1936, pp. 5ff; May 1936, pp. 36ff. *FR, 1935*, 3:552, 559.

85. *FR, 1939*, 3:377.

86. National City Bank, *Monthly Letter*, February 1937, p. 22.

87. *Ibid.*, September 1937, p. 114; *FR, 1939*, 3:377-78.

88. *Ibid.*, pp. 380-81, 398, 400. It seems clear that the bank would have preferred to cooperate with the Japanese and accepted U.S. policy begrudgingly. *Ibid.*, pp. 401, 404-05. There is no information concerning bank policies in 1940.

89. *New York Times*, July 6, 1941; July 31, 1941; July 27, 1941. National City Bank, *Monthly Letter*, August 1941, p. 85.

90. *FR, 1933*, 3:486.

91. B. Kopf to Riecks and Hesser, March 28, 1935, Accession 390, Box 85, Ford Archives, Dearborn, Mich.

92. Data from C. T. Alexander, Manufacturing Staff, Ford International, Dearborn, Mich.

93. *FR, 1935*, 3:1051.

94. Mira Wilkins and Frank Ernest Hill, *American Business Abroad: Ford On Six Continents* (Detroit, 1964), p. 255; Kopf to Crawford, November 2, 1937, and Crawford to Kopf, February 24, 1938, Accession 390, Box 85, Ford Archives.

95. Kopf to Crawford, September 1, 1938 and January 27, 1939, plus other correspondence in *ibid.*; Wilkins and Hill, p. 256; *Business Week*, June 4, 1938; U.S., Department of Commerce, Bureau of the Census, *Foreign Commerce and Navigation of the United States*, 1936-1940. These figures do not indicate whether the exports were going to occupied or unoccupied China.

96. *Ibid.*; E. M. Vorhees, "Political and Economic Conditions in China and Japan," November 22, 1938, Box 184, Folder 15, Lamont Papers.

97. Confidential interviews with U.S. businessmen in Japan, 1965.

98. *Business Week*, September 16, 1938.

99. U.S., Department of Commerce, Bureau of Foreign and Domestic Commerce, *American Direct Investments in Foreign Countries—1940 (Economic Series*, No. 20) (Washington D.C., 1942), p. 18.

100. *FR, 1937*, 4:525; Borg, *Far Eastern Crisis,* pp. 325, 329, 334; Ickes, *Inside Struggle*, p. 209.

101. Vorhees, "Political and Economic Conditions in China and Japan"; Johnson to Lamont, March 26, 1940, and A. M. A[nderson], "Memorandum for Mr. T. W. Lamont," April 15, 1940, Box 184, Folder 17, Lamont Papers.

102. *FR, 1935*, 3:754, 717; Table 4 in the text indicates U.S. exports of refined oil to Japan.

103. *FR, 1933,* 3:733; *FR, 1935,* 3:733-34; Mitsubishi, p. 216.

104. *FR, 1933*, 3:741-42; *FR, Japan, 1931-1941*, 1:141-43 (copy of the law).

105. *FR, 1934*, 3:756 (communication from Stanvac-Tokyo to Stanvac-N.Y., November 8, 1934).

106. *Ibid.*, p. 724. A. G. May of Stanvac wrote to the State Department indicating that the company, if requested, would submit bids on crude oil (August 8, 1934).

107. *Ibid.*, pp. 722, 728.

108. *Ibid.*, pp. 723, 729.

109. *Ibid.*, pp. 738-40.

110. *Ibid.*, pp. 702, 701, 706.

111. *FR, Japan, 1931-1941*, 1:130; *FR, 1934*, 3:718, 724-25.

112. *Ibid.*, p. 733.

113. *Ibid.,* pp. 817, 782.

114. *Ibid.,* pp. 747, 752, 757, 771, 775.

115. *FR, 1935*, 3:883, 931; *FR, 1937*, 4:725; *FR, 1935*, 3:896-97, 926-28, 931, 935-39; *FR, 1936*, 4:786-91, 797-803; *FR, 1937*, 4:725-26.

116. Rayner testimony, U.S., Congress, Senate, Special Committee Investigating Petroleum Resources, *American Petroleum Interests in Foreign Countries, Hearings*, 79th Congress, 1st session, p. 26.

117. *FR, 1935*, 3:935, 936; see also *FR, 1936*, 4:797; and *FR, 1937*, 4:726.

118. *FR, 1935*, 3:885-87, 893-94, 906-09, 915, 925, 928, 933; *FR, Japan, 1931-1941*, 2:146ff; *FR, 1937*, 4:734 (on Texaco's earlier pullout).

119. *FR, 1935*, 3:911.

120. *Ibid.*, pp. 903-04; *FR, 1936*, 4:793. In 1936 Standard Oil of California and Texaco were arranging joint marketing ventures; see Standard Oil of California, *Annual Report, 1936*.

121. *FR, 1938*, 4:221, 227, 337, 18.

122. *Ibid.*, pp. 23ff, 30, 42, 44, 47.

123. On the difficulties, see *ibid.*, pp. 109-10, 371, 374, 383, 400, 436, 467-68, 472, 513, 580; *FR, 1939*, 3:350, 352, 357-58, 360-61, 394, 460; *FR, 1940*, 4:556, 862, 884, 885-86, 888, 894-95. *Business Week*, May 14, 1938, p. 53; June 4, 1938, p. 43; June 11, 1938, p. 37; January 27, 1940, p. 58. *American Investments–1940*, p. 18.

124. According to British officials, when the United States put restrictions on aviation gasoline and lubricant exports, some American companies thought that the British government was responsible "in order to benefit through the sale of these same products to the Japanese from other sources." The British ambassador was anxious to deny complicity, since the British depended on the U.S. oil companies to aid in the British war effort. *FR, 1940*, 4:591-92.

125. *FR, Japan, 1931-1941*, 2:265; see also Hull, *Memoirs*, 2:983; and Ickes, *Lowering Clouds*, pp. 96, 132, 299, 322, 543-47, 550-60, 564-68, 588, 591. *FR, 1940*, 4:576, 591; *FR, 1941*, 4:839, 848-50.

126. Ickes, *Inside Struggle*, p. 49; Ickes, *Lowering Clouds*, p. 297; *FR, 1941*, 5:281 and 4:876; National Planning Association, *Stanvac in Indonesia* (Washington D.C., 1957), pp. 3, 25.

127. U.S., Congress, Senate, Internal Security Subcommittee of the Committee on the Judiciary, *Morgenthau Diary (China)*, 89th Congress, 1st session (Washington D.C., 1965), 1:182-85, 193-95, 232; Feis, p. 89.

128. *FR, 1941*, 4:863.

129. Lockwood, *Trade and Trade Rivalry*, p. 9.

Importing American Capital into Manchuria

1. Horikoshi Teizō, ed., *Keizai Dantai Rengōkai zenshi* (Early History of the Federation of Economic Organizations) (Tokyo, 1962), pp. 335-39.

2. See the Federation's bulletin, *Keizai renmei* (Economic Federation), 9, no. 2 (April 1939).

3. In addition to General O'Ryan and Hannah M. Syroboiarsky, secretary and translator, Warren S. Hunsberger, secretary, Simon N. Whitney, in charge of economic research, and Donald W. Smith, a staff member of the U.S. embassy, the guest list included: Akashi Teruo, Aoki Kamatarō, Ayukawa Gisuke, Ayusawa Iwao, Fujiyama Aiichirō, Gō Seinosuke, Haraguchi Hatsutarō, Hatsuta Yoshiaki, Hoshina Shinji, Ichinomiya Reitarō, Izaka Takashi, Kabayama Aisuke, Kadono Jūkurō, Kashiwagi Hideshige, Matsumoto Kenjirō, Miyoshi Shigemichi, Mori Kōzō, Morimura Ichizaemon, Nagai Matsuzō, Nanjō Kaneo, Ōtomo Nabio, Sawada Setsuzō, Shimada Katsunosuke, Takashima Seiichi, Tsushima Juichi, Yamamuro Sōbun, Yasuma Norikatsu, and Yūki Toyotarō. For brief biographies of the more important Japanese guests, see Appendix II.

4. In focusing my study on this totally vain endeavor of Japanese business leaders, I was interested not in determining quantitatively how successful or unsuccessful they were, but rather in ascertaining their attitudes as war approached. A well known thesis holds that finance capitalism and imperialist war are inseparable. Yet if the actual process that leads to war is examined carefully, doubts arise as to the direct causal connection between capitalist interests and behavior and war.

It may be possible to terminate an imperialist war by "transforming a war into revolution" (as, for example, when defeat has rendered the state authorities virtually powerless and brought the government to the verge of collapse). But to avoid or reduce the possibility of such a war, it is necessary to compel the state to adopt policies that will avert or moderate the crisis. This objective may be achieved through the formation of a united front of various political groups within the country, including liberal capitalists, against militaristic forces. During the 1930s terrorist acts, abortive coups d'état, and growing acceptance of the actions of the military destroyed both parliamentary democracy and freedom of political activity in Japan. Consequently, efforts to terminate or prevent the escalation of war in China (and the accompanying tension with the United States) could not take the form of open political struggle in the Diet and appeals to public opinion. Sporadic protests from individual Diet members were heroic but ineffectual. Only covert political maneuver remained as a tactic, and such efforts were feeble and, in the end, failed.

Under certain conditions there is clearly a close interrelationship between business aspirations for markets to absorb ever-greater exports of commodities and capital, and a militaristic desire to exert political control over foreign lands. They are not, however, identical. The correlation between capital and war cannot be fully explained from the logic of capital alone. The influence of military forces on capital movements must also be examined. One of the objectives of this essay is to explore the logic of capital manifested in the process of an expanding war.

Mira Wilkins has pointed to the establishment of the Manchurian oil monopoly as evidence of Manchukuo's hostility toward American capital. It should be pointed out that, like the Japanese petroleum law, Manchukuo's oil policy was similar to those of several European countries with meager oil resources—for example, the 1918 French oil industry law and the 1928 Spanish oil monopoly law. Furthermore, surplus supplies of oil encouraged American, British, and Dutch oil companies, which had a virtual monopoly of crude oil supplies to Manchuria, to reach a compromise with the Manchukuo authorities. Unfortunately, exacerbation of the political conflict in the 1930s left no room for such a "compromise." See Iguchi Tōsuke, "Sekiyu sangyō ni taisuru kenryoku no kainyū" (State Intervention in the Petroleum Industry), part 2, chap. 8 of *Sekiyu: Gendai Nihon sangyō hattatsushi 2* (Oil: A History of the Industrial Development of Modern Japan 2) (Tokyo, 1963), pp. 245-69; and "Nichi-Man ryōkoku no sekiyu seisaku to sono hamon" (Japan-Manchukuo Oil Policies and Their Impact), in Tōyō Keizai Shinpōsha (Oriental Economist), ed., *Nihon keizai nenpō* (Economic Yearbook of Japan), 19 (1935), sec. 9, pp. 269-90.

5. See C. F. Remer, *Foreign Investment in China* (New York, 1933), pp. 282-87, 335; for the Japanese translation, see C. F. Remā, *Rekkoku no taishi tōshi*, translated by Tōa Keizai Chōsa Kyoku (East Asia Economic Research Bureau, South Manchuria Railway), 3 vols. (Tokyo, 1934). See also Higuchi Hiroshi, *Nihon no tai-Shi tōshi kenkyū*, (A Study of Japanese Investment in China) (Tokyo, 1939); Imura Shigeo, *Gaikoku no tai-Shi tōshi to kakyō sōkin* (Foreign Investment in China and Overseas Chinese Remittances) (Tokyo, 1940); Tōa Kenkyūjo (East Asia Research Institute), ed., *Rekkoku tai-Shi tōshi to Shina kokusai shūshi* (The Investment of the Powers in China and China's Balance of Payments) (Tokyo, 1941); Tōa Kenkyūjo, ed., *Shogaikoku no tai-Shi tōshi* (Foreign Investment in China), 3 vols. (Tokyo, 1942-43).

6. Inoue Kaoru-kō Denki Hensankai (Committee to Compile a Biography of Inoue Kaoru), ed., *Segai Inoue-kō den* (Biography of Inoue Kaoru), 5 (Tokyo, 1968):103.

7. Andō Hikotarō, ed., *Mantetsu* (The South Manchuria Railway Company) (Tokyo, 1965), pp. 19-26.

8. Kurushima Hidesaburō, "Anshan seitetsujo tōji no omoide: Nichi-Bei gōben Manshū tankō seitetsu kaisha no yume kieru" (My Days at the Anshan

Iron Works: The Dream of a Joint Japanese-American Venture in Manchurian Coal and Iron Manufacturing Evaporates), in Nihon Kōgyō Kurabu Gojūnenshi Hensan Iinkai (Committee to Compile a Fifty-Year History of the Japan Industrialists Club), ed., *Zaikai kaisōroku* (Reminiscences of Financial Leaders), 1 (Tokyo, 1967):425-32. Kurushima's article also contains the detailed notes of Tamura Yōzō, the first head of the New York office of the South Manchuria Railway Company, who was present at several meetings between Elbert H. Gary, president of U.S. Steel, and Inoue Kyōshirō, president of the Anshan Iron Works. According to Tamura, Gary told Inoue that the consent of Kuhara Fusanosuke, president of Kuhara Mines, was necessary before the joint steel manufacturing enterprise could be undertaken. He also noted that "according to reliable sources, this idea for a joint Japanese-American venture originated with the management of the South Manchuria Railway Company, and prior to Inoue's departure for the United States it had the approval of the Hara cabinet." *Ibid.*, pp. 431-32.

9. Details on investment in Manchuria are from Nihon Kōgyō Ginkō Rinji Shiryō Shitsu (Industrial Bank of Japan, Special Historical Documents Section), ed., *Nihon Kōgyō Ginkō gojūnenshi* (A Fifty-Year History of the Industrial Bank of Japan) (Tokyo, 1957); and Manshikai (Manchurian Historical Association), ed., *Manshū kaihatsu yonjūnenshi* (A Forty-Year History of Manchurian Development), 2 vols. (Tokyo, 1964).

10. Takahashi Korekiyo, *Zuisōroku* (Random Thoughts) (Tokyo, 1936), pp. 412-13.

11. *GS 7: Manshū jihen* (The Manchurian Incident) (Tokyo, 1964), pp. 165-71.

12. *Ibid.*, pp. 172-79.

13. "Summary of the Discussion: A Report from the Chief of the Military Affairs Bureau to Vice Chief of Staff Itagaki Seishirō," in *GS 8: Nitchū sensō 1* (Sino-Japanese War 1) (Tokyo, 1964), pp. 801-02.

14. "Policies Regarding Implementation of the Five Year Plan for Major Industries: A Draft Proposal," in *ibid.*, pp. 733-51.

15. *Ibid.*, pp. 771-72.

16. Nihon Keizai Shinbunsha (East Asian Economic Newspaper Society), ed., *Watakushi no rirekisho* (My Career) (Tokyo, 1965), pp. 325-26.

17. Harada Kumao, *Saionji-kō to seikyoku* (Prince Saionji and the Political Situation) (reprinted, Tokyo, 1967), 7:86.

18. There are numerous examples of conflicts over monetary policies in Manchuria and China between business leaders and Finance Ministry bureaucrats on the one hand and army officers on the other. For example, after Finance Minister Takahashi Korekiyo recommended to the Budget Committee of the House of Representatives on January 27, 1933 that Manchukuo adopt a silver standard rather than a gold standard as in Japan, Kwantung Army Chief of Staff Koiso Kuniaki on February 1 protested this position in a telegram to Vice Army Minister Yanagawa Heisuke. Meanwhile, the Kwantung Army hurriedly sponsored the drafting of a monetary reform plan for Manchuria, drawn up by the army's adviser Suzumoto Boku, a former president of the Bank of Korea. When both the Manchukuo government and the Central Bank of Manchukuo voiced strong opposition to the army's actions, the Finance Ministry dispatched to Manchuria Aoki Kazuo, head of its Foreign Exchange Control Division, and Araki Eikichi, director of the Examination Division of the Bank of Japan. In the end the military's reform plan was rejected.

Following official recognition of Wang Ching-wei's regime in November 1940, the question arose of what currency should be used in central China. In opposition to Kodama Kenji, president of the Central China Development Company, who urged adoption of the Chinese fapi, the Japanese local army stationed at Nanking demanded that the use of military currency be continued, a policy clearly contrary to official recognition of the new government. Eventually the commander of the China Expeditionary Forces, General Nishio Toshizō, acquiesced in the Finance Ministry's judgment and a Central Savings Bank was established. Nevertheless, the paymaster's department of the local army attempted to restrict the quantity of notes issued by the Savings Bank and to designate certain areas in which military currency was to be used. When Aoki Kazuo, who was in charge of organizing the Savings Bank, complained to the Army Ministry about interference by the local army, the responsible section chief in the paymaster's department was transferred to a post as instructor at the Army Paymaster's School. Thereupon a staff officer of the local army threatened Aoki for having violated the army's right of supreme command over military personnel. The matter was finally settled when the local chief of staff, General Itagaki Seishirō, apologized for his subordinate's conduct. See Aoki Kazuo, "Manshū jihen oyobi Shina jihen to genchi heisei mondai no kaiko" (Reminiscences of the Manchurian Incident, the China Affair, and Questions of the Local Monetary System), in *Seizan zuisō* (Random Thoughts) (Tokyo, 1959), pp. 168-88.

Another outstanding example of conflict between the military and economic viewpoints was in 1935, when military opposition blocked implementation of the proposal for Japanese-British cooperation in Chinese monetary reform brought to Japan by the British special envoy, Sir Frederick Leith-Ross. The fundamental idea of the plan had been approved by Finance Minister Takahashi and Fukai Eigo, the president of the Bank of Japan.

On November 8 the military attaché in China, Major General Isogai Rensuke, issued a statement on behalf of the local army flatly opposing the Chinese monetary reform of November 3. The following day the army central command concurred in an unofficial statement that "our imperial nation firmly rejects the reform." The Foreign Ministry's subsequent expression of agreement merely gave diplomatic endorsement to the military's position. See Tsushima Juichi, *Hōtō zuisō, dai kyūshū: Takahashi Korekiyo ō no koto* (Random Thoughts 9: Memories of the Venerable Takahashi Korekiyo) (Tokyo, 1962); Aritake Shūji, *Shōwa keizai sokumenshi* (Sidelights on the Economic History of the Shōwa Era) (Tokyo, 1952); and "Shina ni okeru gin kyōkō to Nichi-Ei-Bei no kōsō" (The Silver Crisis in China and Conflict among Japan, Britain, and the United States), in *Economic Yearbook of Japan*, 23 (1936):1-54.

19. Asahi Shinbun Hōtei Kishadan (Asahi Shinbun Court Reporters), *Tōkyō saiban* (The Tokyo Trials), 4 (Tokyo, 1948):127, 132. See in particular Defense Attorney George C. Williams' interrogation of Hoshino, January 31, 1947, Defense Document No. 606A1, in Nitta Mitsuo, ed. *Kyokutō kokusai gunji saiban sokkiroku* (Stenographic Records of the International Military Tribunal for the Far East), 6 (Tokyo, 1968):706; and Obata Tadayoshi's affidavit, Defense Document No. 2592, in *ibid.*, p. 708.

20. Because the efforts of the senior statesmen, cabinet ministers, and business leaders to bring about an early termination of the war in China and to promote better relations between Japan and the United States were largely conducted behind the scenes, official documents provide little information on their activities. It is necessary, therefore, to turn to such memoirs as the Saionji-Harada "diary" and Imamura Takeo's *Ikeda Seihin den* (Biography of Ikeda Seihin) (Tokyo, 1962). In addition, the records of the International Military Tribunal for the Far East contain evidence of the struggle between the military and liberal forces that advocated cooperation with the Anglo-American powers.

Up to about 1936 the attitude in Japanese business circles was expressed in Finance Minister Takahashi's policy of defending the "lifeline of public finance." Takahashi's policy was carried on by Ikeda Seihin, head of the Mitsui zaibatsu and the undisputed leader of Japan's financial world. He enjoyed the trust of the senior statesmen and wielded considerable influence in political circles. As president of the Bank of Japan under the Hayashi cabinet, Ikeda took the position that national defense should be promoted in the context of the changing international situation and without destroying "the foundations of the existing economic structure." Harada, 5:254.

After May 1938, as minister of finance and minister of commerce and industry in the reshuffled first Konoe cabinet, Ikeda frequently came into conflict with the military when he urged policies to bring about an early solution to the war in China, opposed the army's advocacy of closer ties with Germany, and endeavored to maintain cooperation with Britain and the United States. See Ikeda Seihin, "Ashiato" (Footprints), in *Keizai ōrai* (Economic World), March 1950, pp. 30-38.

21. This section is based on *Nihon Kōgyō Ginkō gojūnenshi* and *Manshū kaihatsu yonjūnenshi*.

The Activities of the Japan Economic Federation

1. On the Japan Economic Federation the basic source is Horikoshi Teizō, ed., *Keizai Dantai Rengōkai zenshi* (Early History of the Federation of Economic Organizations) (Tokyo, 1962). My paper has drawn a good deal from this work. See also the paper by Chō Yukio, "An Inquiry into the Problem of Importing American Capital into Manchuria: A Note on Japanese-American Relations, 1931-1941," in the present volume.

2. Horikoshi, p. 93.

3. *Ibid.*, pp. 9-10, 26.

4. *Ibid.*, pp. 35-38. In 1940, however, with the tightening of governmental controls, the Conference of Strategic Industries Control Groups (Jūyō Sangyō Tōsei Dantai Konwakai) was established.

5. *Ibid.*, pp. 100-01.

6. *Ibid.*, p. 87.

7. *Ibid.*, pp. 94-95.

8. On the Yōkakai, see Nihon Kōgyō Kurabu Gojūnenshi Hensan Iinkai (Committee to Compile a Fifty-Year History of the Japan Industrialists Club), ed., *Zaikai kaisōroku* (Reminiscences of Financial Leaders), 1 (Tokyo, 1967):21-22.

9. Nihon Sen'i Sangyōshi Kankō Iinkai (Committee to Publish a History of the Japanese Textile Industry), ed., *Nihon sen'i sangyōshi: Kakuronhen* (A History of the Japanese Textile Industry: Collected Essays) (Tokyo, 1958), p. 61.

10. See Nichibō Shashi Hensan Iinkai (Committee to Compile a History of the Nihon Spinning Company), ed., *Nichibō shichijūgonenshi* (A Seventy-Five-Year History of the Nihon Spinning Company) (Osaka, 1966), p. 218.

11. Toyota Jidōsha Kōgyō Shashi Henshū Iinkai (Committee to Compile a History of the Toyota Automobile Company), ed., *Toyota Jidōsha sanjūnenshi* (A Thirty-Year History of the Toyota Automobile Company) (Toyota, 1967), pp. 24-82.

12. See Nissan Jidōsha Kabushiki Kaisha Somubu Chōsaka (Nissan Automobile Company, General Affairs Division, Research Section), ed., *Nissan Jidōsha sanjūnenshi* (A Thirty-Year History of the Nissan Automobile Company) (Yokohama, 1965), p. 76.

13. See Iguchi Tōsuke, *Sekiyu: Gendai Nihon sangyō hattatsushi 2* (Oil: A History of the Industrial Development of Modern Japan 2) (Tokyo, 1963), pp. 245-56.

14. The list of those present at this inaugural meeting indicates the importance that the Japanese government and financial circles attached to the council. The meeting was hosted by Fujiyama Raita (adviser), Izaka Takashi (director), and other officers of the Japan Economic Federation. The council members were: Richard M. Andrews, president, Andrews & George Co., Inc.; John Libby Curtis, Tokyo branch manager, National City Bank of New York; John C. Goold, Yokohama branch manager, Standard-Vacuum Oil Co.; Benjamin Kopf, manager, Ford Motor Company of Japan, Ltd.; F. C. Thompson, Yokohama branch manager, Dollar Steamship Lines; Ōtani Noboru, vice president, Nihon Yūsen; Kadono Jūkurō, vice president, Ōkura Gumi; Kashiwagi Hideshige, director, Yokohama Specie Bank; Tajima Shigeji, director, Mitsui Bussan; and Kushida Manzō, chairman, Mitsubishi Bank.

Among those invited as special guests were: American Ambassador Joseph Clark Grew, Consul General Arthur Garrels, and Commercial Attaché Frank S. Williams; from the Japanese Foreign Ministry, Vice Minister Shigemitsu Mamoru, International Trade Bureau Chief Kurusu Saburō, and America Bureau Chief Horinouchi Kensuke; and from the Ministry of Commerce and Industry, Minister Matsumoto Jōji, Vice Minister Yoshino Shinji, and Trade Bureau Chief Terao Susumu.

15. *Keizai renmei* (Economic Federation), 4, no. 3 (1934):1-3.

16. Horikoshi, p. 217.

17. The other members of the mission were Harold M. Bixby, John S. Campbell, John B. Chevalier, Philip K. Condict, Walter F. Dillingham, J. Harold Dollar, Frederick V. Field, Guy Holman, G. Ellsworth Huggins, Louis C. Jones, Sidney W. Minor, Hosea B. Phillips, C. F. Remer, Leighton W. Rogers, Julian Street, and Thomas Y. Wickham. *Keizai renmei*, 5, no. 2 (1935):133-34. [For brief biographies of these individuals, see *American Trade Prospects in the Orient: Report of the American Economic Mission to the Far East* (New York, 1935), pp. xlvii-liii. -ED.]

18. Horikoshi, p. 220. The council's activities after the outbreak of the Sino-Japanese War included: organizing in December 1938-January 1939 a conference on currency and trade controls in north China; advocacy of the establishment of a court of arbitration to settle commercial issues between Japan and the United States (May 1939); and discussions in September and November of possible renewal of the commercial treaty with the United States. In addition, it gave a reception for Boyce C. Hart, vice president of the National City Bank of New York and head of its Far Eastern section, and hosted a talk by Ambassador Grew in October 1939. *Ibid.*, pp. 332-34.

During this period the Japan Economic Federation focused its efforts to reduce tensions between Japan and the United States upon the External Relations Committee (Taigai Iinkai); see Chō paper in the present volume.

19. *Keizai renmei*, 5, no. 2 (1935):137.

20. Yokohama Shōkin Ginkō, Tōdoriseki Chōsaka (Yokohama Specie Bank, President's Office, Research Section), "Nihon kara mita Beikoku no

tai-Ka bōeki" (America's China Trade as Viewed from Japan). *ibid.*, no. 1, p. 97.

21. Fujiyama Raita, "Waga bōeki to kyōchō no seishin" (Japan's Trade and the Spirit of Cooperation), *ibid.*, 4, no. 2 (1934):9.

22. *Ibid.*, 5, no. 2 (1935):143.

23. The Forbes Mission report was published under the title *American Trade Prospects in the Orient* (see fn. 17 above). In addition, Forbes' journals and papers are available in the Forbes Collection, Houghton Library, Harvard University, Cambridge, Mass. -ED.

24. *Keizai renmei*, 7, no. 2 (1937):88.

25. Hayashi's report, mentioned above, also included an interesting statement by R. A. May, vice president of the New York General Motors Export Company. May argued that Japan's expanding trade was fundamentally weak because its promotional policies were "devious," because it kept the price of goods abnormally low and uneconomical, and because newly-acquired territories and spheres of influence were not necessarily economically advantageous. There is no doubt that up until about 1936 economic expansion into Manchuria served as an outlet for idle capital in Japan and that raw materials from Manchuria benefited Japanese domestic industry. But after 1936, as domestic production expanded and heavy industries were established in Manchuria, the balance was upset and the wisdom of continued investment in Manchuria came into question. See Nihon Kōgyō Ginkō Rinji Shiryō Shitsu (Industrial Bank of Japan, Special Historical Documents Section), ed., *Nihon Kōgyō Ginkō gojūnenshi* (A Fifty-Year History of the Industrial Bank of Japan) (Tokyo, 1957), pp. 290-92.

26. Horikoshi, p. 332.

27. Many views critical of such a conclusion were expressed. For example, on October 29, 1932 the *Tōyō keizai shinpō* (Oriental Economist), an important financial journal, published an editorial entitled "Points to Consider in Policy Toward Manchuria" which warned that the simplistic view that "arms are almighty" was mistaken and extremely dangerous. "It cannot be denied that the expansion of the Manchurian problem since last September is due to the might of the military. But this sort of military expansion should not be prolonged forever. . . . Japan, which claims that by watching carefully over and developing Manchuria eternal peace in the Far East may be secured, should without a moment's delay cast aside the idea that arms are almighty and adhere to the precepts of Mencius.
 ". . . The development of Manchuria should be for the good of the people of Manchuria; one should not think of using Manchuria for the benefit of Japan. . . . Only in a situation in which stability is established in Manchuria, when its industries are developed and the lives of its people fulfilled will Japan reap benefits from Manchuria. Even supposing some Japanese immigrants are transplanted to Manchuria, it will not amount to much. It is all too clear that

this will not solve Japan's population problem when one looks at the results of governing Taiwan and Korea, which after all belong to Japan. Now and then there are people who daydream of Japanese-Manchurian economic planning, as if one could forcibly steer Manchuria's economy to Japan's advantage. These efforts will in the end be useless. It is best to develop Manchuria from Manchuria's viewpoint and in the direction that will be most profitable to it. This will enrich Manchuria the most and, as a matter of course, bring benefits to Japan as well."

The Role of Private Groups in the United States

1. Interorganization Council on Disarmament Papers, Swarthmore College Peace Collection, Swarthmore, Pa. (hereafter cited as ICD Papers); Papers of the Emergency Peace Committee, Swarthmore College Peace Collection. These indicate that the Emergency Peace Committee (not to be confused with the later Emergency Peace Campaign) was constituted in April 1931 "to coordinate, develop and concentrate left-wing peace opinion on issues of immediate importance to world peace." The labels "left" and "right" as used within the peace movement, sometimes replaced by "radical" and "conservative," tend to be confusing. Robert Ferrell, in *Peace in Their Time* (New Haven, 1952), suggested that "crusading zeal, rather than a difference of ultimate objective, distinguished the radical from the more conservative groups" and noted a greater sense of urgency among the radicals. Although Ferrell wrote with reference to the 1920s, his distinctions appear valid for 1931 and 1932 as well.

2. Minutes of the Executive Committee, September 29, 1931 and October 14, 1931, ICD Papers; Minutes, October 14, 1931, Papers of the Emergency Peace Committee. A delegation from the Emergency Peace Committee had already called on Stimson. See State Department files 793.94/2085, National Archives, Washington D.C.

3. Minutes of the Executive Committee, October 26, 1931, ICD Papers.

4. Minutes of the Executive Committee, November 9, 1931, ICD Papers.

5. Minutes of the Executive Committee, November 23, 1931, ICD Papers.

6. Minutes of the Executive Committee, December 21, 1931, ICD Papers; for evidence of the position of the League of Nations Association, note roles of Philip Nash and Clark M. Eichelberger, respectively national director and midwest director of the League of Nations Association, at ICD meetings on October 14, 1931, October 26, 1931, and December 29, 1931. Also see the editorial in the association's *League of Nations Chronicle*, November 1931; Minutes, January 25, 1932, Papers of the Emergency Peace Committee.

7. Memorandum of conversation between Dorothy Detzer and Maxwell Hamilton, Division of Far Eastern Affairs, September 22, 1931, State Depart-

ment files 793.94/1910; Detzer to President Hoover, September 22, 1931, *ibid.*, 793.94/1948; Minutes of National Board Meeting, December 12-13, 1931, Women's International League for Peace and Freedom—U.S. files, Swarthmore College Peace Collection (hereafter cited as WILPF-US files); Detzer to Mrs. Hull, November 10, 1931, *ibid.*

8. Olmsted to Balch, December 31, 1931, *ibid.*

9. Minutes of National Board Meeting, January 15-16, 1932, *ibid.*; Balch and Hull to President Hoover, January 18, 1932, State Department files 793.93/P.C. 46.

10. Detzer to Balch, January 28, 1932, WILPF-US files.

11. Detzer to Balch, February 16, 1932, *ibid.*

12. Libby to Rogers, November 16, 1931, State Department files 500.A15 A 4 Personnel/137 1/2; November 26, 1931 (cable from Paris), *ibid.*, 793.94 P.C./39; memorandum of conversation between Libby and Rogers, December 4, 1931, with enclosure, *ibid.* 500.A15 A 4/637; Report of Executive Secretary to Annual Meeting, October 20, 1931, National Council for the Prevention of War files, Swarthmore College Peace Collection (hereafter cited as NCPW files); press release, November 30, 1931, *ibid.*; Libby to staff, December 9, 1931, *ibid.*; Libby, mimeographed letter, December 23, 1931, *ibid.*

13. Statement by Frederick J. Libby, January 30, 1932, *ibid.*

14. *Ibid.*

15. Eleanor Tupper and George E. McReynolds, *Japan in American Public Opinion* (New York, 1937), pp. 313-37; John W. Masland, "Group Interests in American Relations with Japan," Ph.D. dissertation, Princeton University, 1938; Stimson to Hugh Wilson, February 26, 1932, *FR, 1932* (Washington D.C., 1948), 3:453. For Eichelberger's views at this time, see Eichelberger to Libby, February 1, 1932, NCPW files.

16. Masland; Robert A. Divine, *The Illusion of Neutrality* (Chicago, 1962), p. 20.

17. Masland; Libby to Staff, February 21, 1932, NCPW files; NCPW press release, March 10, 1932, NCPW files.

18. Newton to President Hoover, February 15, 1932, State Department files 793.94/4800; Newton to Rogers, February 26, 1932, *ibid.*, 793.94/4801; Minutes, February 26, 1932, Papers of the Emergency Peace Committee; memorandum of conversation between Allen Klots and Emily Balch, Tucker P. Smith, and Ray Newton, March 2, 1932, with enclosures, State Department files 793.94/4802.

19. Sayre to Smith, March 12, 1932, Papers of the Emergency Peace Committee; Minutes, January 9, 1933, *ibid.*

20. Minutes of National Board Meeting, March 4, April 14-16, 1932, and Mrs. Hull to Detzer, March 15, 1932, WILPF-US files; Balch to Edith Pye, February 11, 1933, Emily Balch Papers, WILPF-US files.

21. "To Our Friends in China," June 27, 1933, Balch Papers.

22. Memorandum of conversation between W. W. Yen, minister to the United States, and George Blakeslee (on temporary duty with the Department of State), December 28, 1931, State Department files 793.94/4151. On Carter's activities, see also Nelson T. Johnson to Stimson, September 30, 1931, *ibid.*, 793.94/1944; and memorandum of conversation between Carter and Blakeslee, December 8, 1931, *ibid.*, 793.94/3228. For examples of the methods of missionaries and their organizations, see A. L. Warnshuis, International Missionary Council, to Stanley Hornbeck, chief, Division of Far Eastern Affairs, October 8, 1931, and February 6, 16, 19, 1932, *ibid.*, 793.94/2129, 4673, 4674, 4675; President Hoover to Stimson, October 9, 1931, with enclosures, especially telegram from W. W. Lockwood, Far Eastern secretary of the International YMCA, *ibid.*, 793.94/2031; Prentiss Gilbert to Stimson, November 20, 1931, with enclosures by Eugene Barnett, YMCA, *ibid.*, 793.94/3033; Wh. McCance, Foreign Missions Conference of North America, to President Hoover, June 14, 1932, with enclosure, *ibid.*, 793.94/5342. See also Paul A. Varg, *Missionaries, Chinese and Diplomats: The American Protestant Missionary Movement in China, 1890-1952* (Princeton, 1958), pp. 251ff.

23. *New York Times*, September 23, 1931, pp. 1, 11; September 24, 1931, pp. 1, 10; December 9, 1931, p. 20. Reports to the Fourteenth Annual National Convention of the American Legion, September 12-15, 1932; *New York Times*, September 16, 1932, pp. 1, 15; Masland.

24. C. Van H. Engert, Legation, Shanghai, to Stimson, April 17, 1932, enclosing memorandum prepared by Henry W. Kinney, employed by South Manchuria Railway. Jay Pierrepont Moffat of the Department of State was also very much impressed with the influence of "pacifist groups" in January 1932 but by April felt that events in the Far East had diminished their influence. See Nancy H. Hooker, ed., *The Moffat Papers: Selections from the Diplomatic Journals of Jay Pierrepont Moffat, 1919-1943* (Cambridge, Mass., 1956), pp. 56-57, 65.

25. National Peace Conference Papers, Swarthmore College Peace Collection (hereafter cited as NPC Papers); Masland; Elton Atwater, *Organized Efforts in the United States Toward Peace* (1936), pp. 38-39, reprints the National Peace Conference policy statement adopted June 3, 1935 and lists the thirty-four organizations that participated in 1936; Eichelberger to Libby, November 3, 1934, NCPW files; for the position of the American Legion, see *New York Times,* October 6, 1933, pp. 1, 5, September 24, 1936, p. 1, and September 25, 1936, pp. 1, 10.

26. Atwater, p. 38.

27. *Peace Action*, 1 (November 1934, December 1934-January 1935). For further indications of Libby's thoughts on Japanese-American relations, see Minutes of Executive Board Meeting, January 16, 1935, at which he announced that a contribution earmarked for the promotion of better relations with Japan had been entered in the books under the heading "Campaign Against Big Navy," NCPW files. See Report of the Policy Committee, February 20, 1935, for the "Peace in the Pacific" program, NCPW files. For an indication of the concern with which the Department of State greeted Libby's campaign, see memorandum prepared by Maxwell Hamilton, Division of Far Eastern Affairs, for Undersecretary William A. Phillips and Secretary Cordell Hull, April 3, 1935, State Department files 811.43 National Council for Prevention of War/16.

28. *Peace Action*, 1 (December 1934-January 1935).

29. *Ibid.*, 1 (May 1935), quoted and discussed in Divine, *Illusion of Neutrality*, p. 93.

30. Detzer to Balch, February 5, 1932, February 18, 1932, February 5, 1934, WILPF-US files.

31. Detzer to Balch, February 5, 1934, *ibid.*; Report of the Executive Secretary, July 31, 1934, *ibid.*

32. Divine, *Illusion of Neutrality*, pp. 95, 135-36; Dorothy Borg, *The United States and the Far Eastern Crisis of 1933-1938* (Cambridge, Mass., 1964), pp. 341-45; Eichelberger to Libby, September 17, 1935, October 15, 1936, and March 2, 1937, NCPW files. For evidence of continued efforts to unite the peace movement on vital issues, see draft reports of the National Peace Conference Committee on the Far East (also called the Committee on American Far Eastern Policy), 1936-37, NPC Papers.

33. Borg, *Far Eastern Crisis*, pp. 324-26, 344-49. Borg's sources apparently underestimate the extent of support for invoking the neutrality law. Libby to Branch Offices, August 31, 1937, NCPW files. The public announcement of the conference's internal dissension came in a press release, September 9, 1937, NPC Papers. For an indication of the relative unimportance of the Far East per se, see Eichelberger to Libby, August 27, 1937, NCPW files. The following sentence is illustrative: "Yes, I feel differently on the Far East, but there are so many other phases of the program to cooperate on and so much else to do that we will not let the dissension on neutrality and the Far East interfere with the other big tasks we are undertaking together."

34. Borg, *Far Eastern Crisis*, pp. 324-27, 346-49; NCPW, WILPF, et al. to President Roosevelt, September 8, 1937, State Department files 793.94/10068; see also Eugene Barnett, YMCA, to Libby, October 25, 1937, NCPW files.

35. Borg, *Far Eastern Crisis*, pp. 343-44.

36. *New York Times*, September 24, 1937, pp. 1, 15, and September 3, 1937, p. 3; Masland.

37. NCPW press release, August 18, 1937, NCPW files; Libby broadcast, NBC, September 24, 1937, enclosure in Libby to Cordell Hull, October 16, 1937, State Department files 793.94112/114.

38. Masland; telegram from Eichelberger to Hull, September 4, 1937, State Department files 793.94111/47; NCPW, WILPF, et al. press release, October 7, 1937, enclosure in Libby to Hull, October 16, 1937, *ibid.*, 793.94112/114, and press release dated October 2, 1937, NCPW files; Borg, *Far Eastern Crisis*, p. 387; George H. Blakeslee, World Peace Foundation, to Hull, with enclosure, October 23, 1937, State Department files 711.00 Pres. Speech, October 5, 1937/129; Blakeslee to Roosevelt, with enclosure, October 23, 1937, *ibid*, 793.94/10996; Villard to Raymond L. Buell, October 11, 1937, Oswald Garrison Villard Papers, Harvard University, Cambridge, Mass.; Minutes of National Board Meeting, October 23-24, 1937, WILPF-US files; Mercedes Randall, *Improper Bostonian: Emily Greene Balch* (New York, 1964), pp. 333-35; Balch to Miss Stevenson, April 19, 1938, Balch Papers; Olmsted to Balch, April 14, 1938, and Balch to Olmsted, undated (April 1938), WILPF-US files.

39. Borg, *Far Eastern Crisis*, p. 379; Masland; memorandum of conversation between Waldron of the Washington Committee for Aid to China and Myers of the Division of Far Eastern Affairs, December 15, 1937, State Department files 893.48/1383; Horace Trudell, Washington Committee for Aid to China, to Senator Key Pittman, March 24, 1938, May 9, 1938, Senate Foreign Relations Committee files 75A-F9-1 (China-Japan), National Archives, Washington D.C., (hereafter cited as SFRC files); Robert Norton, Committee for a Boycott Against Japanese Aggression, to Pittman, June 3, 1938, *ibid.*, 75A-F9-1 (Japanese-Embargo), stationery indicates that William Loeb, Jr. served as chairman and among the sponsors were Villard, John Dewey, Freda Kirchwey and Maxwell Stewart of the *Nation*, Arthur Lovejoy, and Nathaniel Peffer. The organization may have been an outgrowth of the American Committee for Peace and Security in the Pacific in which Loeb played an important role. See Loeb to William Allen White, November 4, 1937, Box 194, William Allen White Papers, Library of Congress, Washington D.C. Donald J. Friedman, *The Road from Isolation: The Campaign of the American Committee for Non-Participation in Japanese Aggression, 1938-1941* (Cambridge, Mass., 1968), is a monograph on the Price Committee. The papers of Stop Arming Japan! are deposited with the Harriet Welling Papers, University of Chicago, Chicago, Ill. Other groups with similar names and purposes appeared and disappeared over the years.

40. Masland; Varg, *Missionaries, Chinese and Diplomats*, p. 259; Borg, *Far Eastern Crisis*, pp. 352-53; press release, American Board of Commissioners for Foreign Missions, September 14, 1937, NCPW files; Florence Tyler, Foreign

Missions Conference of North America, to Max Weis, World Peaceways, November 5, 1937, to inform Weis that "we did not see our way clear to joining the group of organizations which are pressing for the invocation of the Neutrality Act because we strongly feel that it is not neutral," NCPW files. Of missionaries to Japan, Masland wrote: "No less loyal to the people whom they serve, they have been unable to give credit to the government of the country. . . . While some of them have attempted to justify Japan's Asiatic policy, the number has been small. . . . They condemn . . . provocative attitudes by the American government which assist in the strengthening of the militarists." See also James R. McGovern, "American Christian Missions to Japan, 1918-1941" (Ph.D. dissertation, Princeton University, 1957), for indications of the unhappy relationship between missionaries and the Japanese government. This may be contrasted with the Chiangs, as Methodists, encouraging missionaries.

41. Masland; see letters in State Department files 894.24 for 1938; SFRC files 76A-F9 (Churches, Missions, Missionaries); see also Price Committee files, Littauer Center, Harvard University.

42. Friedman, pp. 1-5. Friedman's discussion of the founding of the organization appears to be based on his correspondence with Harry Price and does not mention the relationship between the committee and the Chinese government. For evidence of this relationship, see Helen M. Loomis to H. Price, June 28, 1938; H. Price to Loomis, August 10, 1938; Roger S. Greene to H. Price, August 17, 1938 and September 7, 1938; H. Price to P. C. Chang, September 15, 1938; Earl Leaf to H. Price, March 27, 1939; and F. Price to H. Price, March 30, 1939, Price Committee files. For evidence that arrangements of which Price may not have been completely aware continued, see correspondence between Price and Mrs. George Fitch, especially Mrs. Fitch to Price, December 15, 1939 and January 5, 1940, and H. Price to Mrs. Fitch, December 30, 1939 and January 6, 1940; see also Greene to Price, January 10, 1940, Price Committee files. Before returning to China Frank Price also established the China Information Service, which distributed Chinese propaganda hostile to Japan and critical of American policy; Varg, *Missionaries, Chinese and Diplomats*, p. 260.

43. Greene to Price, August 17, 1938, September 7, 1938; H. Price to P. C. Chang, September 15, 1938, Price Committee files. See also memorandum by Joseph C. Greene, Division of Controls, October 31, 1939, State Department files 894.24/728. In May 1941 Greene was still arranging to return money the Chinese ambassador had contributed through his American nurse. See Greene to Katherine Greene, May 3, 1941 and May 19, 1941, Papers of Roger S. Greene, in possession of Mrs. Roger S. Greene, Worcester, Mass. (now at Houghton Library, Harvard University).

44. Friedman, pp. 12, 15, 19-20; Frederick V. Field to H. Price, September 28, 1938, January 7, 1939, January 11, 1939; H. Price to Greene, November 26, 1938, March 16, 1939; Greene to Price, August 26, 1939; Mrs. Edward C. Carter to Price, November 10, 1938 (this letter indicates that Carter

accompanied Price during his initial call on Stimson and also called Price's attention to Greene's influence with Roosevelt and Stimson); and Edward C. Carter to Price, December 21, 1938, Price Committee files.

45. Friedman, pp. 1-27 *passim.*

46. *Ibid.*, pp. 7-8; for copies, see State Department files 894.24/326.

47. Consul General, Shanghai, to Secretary of State, November 23, 1938, *ibid.*, 894.24/530.

48. H. Price to Greene, October 11, 1938, Greene to Price, October 18, 1938 and December 21, 1938, Price Committee files; Friedman, p. 19; Mrs. Fitch to H. Price, December 15, 1939 and January 5, 1940, Price to Mrs. Fitch, December 30, 1939, *ibid.*

49. H. Price to Hornbeck, December 12, 1938, State Department files 894.24/604; Friedman, p. 18.

50. Divine, *Illusion of Neutrality*, pp. 231-36.

51. *Ibid.*, p. 239.

52. *Ibid.*, pp. 242-45; Hu Shih to Pittman, April 10, 1939, SFRC files 76A-F9 (Neutrality, China-Japan).

53. Price to Hull, Welles, April 4, 1939, with copy of earlier letter to Pittman, State Department files 811.04418/375.

54. Divine, *Illusion of Neutrality*, p. 245; Friedman, p. 31; Mrs. H. Price to Pittman, May 8, 1939, and Pittman to Mrs. Price, May 15, 1939, SFRC files 76A-F9 (Japanese Aggression-Opposing) (Harry Price's Organization). See also Mrs. Price to Roosevelt and to Hull, with enclosures, May 5, 1939, State Department files 894.24/657.

55. Undated memorandum, probably July 1939, Papers of Harriet Welling, University of Chicago; Price to William Allen White, September 15, 1939, enclosing minutes of National Board meeting, August 30, 1939, Box 224, White Papers. Greene was also troubled by the failure of the Department of State to help; see Greene to Price, July 25, 1939, Price Committee files.

56. Herbert Feis, *The Road to Pearl Harbor: The Coming of the War Between the United States and Japan* (Princeton, 1950), pp. 21-23; Robert A. Divine, *The Reluctant Belligerent: American Entry into World War II* (New York, 1965), pp. 80-81. For evidence of earlier discussion focused on the need to terminate commercial clauses to appease cotton textile producers in order to save the trade agreements program, see memorandum prepared by Ballantine and Jones, Division of Far Eastern Affairs, April 3, 1939, State Department files 711.942/171.

57. Greene to Price, August 5, 1939, Price Committee files.

58. Price to Greene, August 15, 1939; copy of testimony of Geraldine Fitch before the House Committee on Foreign Affairs, July 19, 1939, *ibid*.

59. S. Shepard Jones, Director, World Peace Foundation, to Hull, February 21, 1939, State Department files 894.24/617; telegram, American League for Peace and Democracy to Senate Foreign Relations Committee, June 10, 1938, SFRC files 75A-F9-1 (Japanese Embargo); Henry F. Ward, National Chairman, American League for Peace and Democracy, to Welles, March 18, 1939, State Department files 860 F.00/704; William Loeb to William Allen White, November 30, 1938, Box 210, White Papers; Mary E. Wooley, Honorary Chairman, American Boycott Against Aggressor Nations, to White, June 14, 1939, Box 221, *ibid*.

60. Divine, *Illusion of Neutrality*, pp. 248, 254; mimeographed letters, Libby to Friends, January 25 and February 3, 1939, and Libby to NCPW Branch Offices et al., July 13, 1939, NCPW files; Detzer to Balch, August 7, 1939, WILPF-US files. For evidence of tension between the United States and International branches of the Women's International League, see Balch to Stevenson, April 19, 1938, Balch Papers; Minutes, Annual Meeting, April 29-May 1, 1938, WILPF-US files. It should be noted that although the U.S. branch protested against Roosevelt's quarantine speech, the Czech, Swedish, and Austrian branches praised him; see State Department files 711.00 Pres. Speech, October 5, 1937/189, 225, 229. For evidence of growing dissatisfaction within WILPF-US, see "Report to Mrs. Hull, Dorothy Detzer and the National Board of the W.I.L.P.F. RE: Massachusetts State Branch," prepared by Eleanor Eaton, WILPF-US files. However, the dissidents were apparently resigning, increasing the influence of Miss Detzer's supporters. Mrs. Libby became increasingly prominent in League affairs in 1939. The National Council for the Prevention of War had also been troubled by staff resignations and the withdrawal of affiliated organizations; see minutes of Executive Board meetings for the first half of 1938, NCPW files.

61. That such sentiment existed before the organization of the Price Committee is evident in the fact that in June 1938 the Department of State received 1,369 letters, postcards, and telegrams favoring an embargo. This figure does not include petitions. See memorandum by Office of Arms and Munitions Control, August 5, 1938, State Department files 894.24/288.

62. Divine, *Illusion of Neutrality*, pp. 288-301.

63. *Ibid.*, pp. 303-05; Friedman, *passim*.

64. Price to Maxwell Hamilton, Division of Far Eastern Affairs, September 15, 1939, State Department files 894.24/715; Price to William Allen White, September 15, 1939, Box 224, White Papers; Greene to Stimson, September 18, 1939, Greene to Price, September 23, 1939, and Greene to Grew, September 13,

1939, Price Committee files; *New World*, 11 (September 1939); Price to Pittman, October 30, 1939, SFRC files 76A-F9 (Japanese Aggression).

65. Greene to White, November 6, 1939, Box 226, White Papers; Memorandum, November 9, 1939, telegram from Pittman to Stimson, November 9, 1939, and Stimson to Pittman, SFRC 76A-F9 (Japanese Aggression).

66. Price to Greene, January 20, 1940, Price Committee files.

67. Greene to Evans Carlson, January 28, 1940, *ibid*.

68. Price to Greene, February 19, 1940, *ibid*.

69. Price to Stimson, April 25, 1940, *ibid*.

70. Friedman, pp. 33-36; Feis, p. 72; Greene to President Roosevelt (via General Watson), May 17, 1940, State Department files 894.24/952, and May 21, 1940, *ibid*., 894.24/944; Price to Maxwell Hamilton, June 19, 1940, with enclosed memorandum dated June 17, 1940, *ibid*., 894.24/960.

71. Minutes of meeting of the National Board, January 20-21, 1940, WILPF-US files; *Peace Action*, 6 (February 1940); minutes of Executive Board meeting, February 21, 1940 and April 22, 1940, NCPW files.

72. Greene to Price, May 15, 1940, Price Committee files. See Greene to Price, May 7, 1940, for evidence that Greene had become Eichelberger's consultant on the Far East; Price to Greene, June 15, 1940; and Greene to Price, June 16, 1940, August 22, 1940, Price Committee files; Friedman, pp. 75-81.

73. Feis, pp. 88-94; Greene to Price, August 22, 1940, Price Committee files.

74. Walter Johnson, *The Battle Against Isolation* (Chicago, 1944) is a history of the White Committee. The mimeographed statement of the committee's program, July 3, 1940, and July letter to local chapters in Committee to Defend America by Aiding the Allies Boxes, White Papers (hereafter cited as CDAAA Boxes).

75. Minutes of the Executive Committee, September 8, 1940, notes on Advisory Committee Meeting, September 9, 1940, and outline of policy dated September 9, 1940, White Committee files, Princeton University, Princeton, N.J.; Greene to President Roosevelt, September 18, 1940, with enclosure, written on White Committee letterhead, Price Committee files.

76. Wayne Cole, *America First: The Battle Against Intervention, 1940-1941* (Madison, Wis., 1953), especially pp. 189-93.

77. Eichelberger to White, October 1, 1940, enclosing draft memorandum of response to Tripartite Alliance, CDAAA Boxes; White to Arthur

Lovejoy, October 8, 1940, Box 243, White Papers; Hartley to White, October 7, 1940, CDAAA Boxes.

78. Johnson, *Battle Against Isolation*, p. 133; White to Hartley, October 11, 1940, Box 243, White Papers; Eichelberger to Chapter Chairmen, October 15, 1940, White Committee files.

79. William Allen White News Service, October 28, 1940, White Committee files; for evidence that Greene was the author, see Daily Report of National Office, October 28, 1940, CDAAA Boxes.

80. Daily Reports of National Office, November 20 and 23, 1940, CDAAA Boxes; telegram from Greene to McKee, November 24, 1940, White Committee files. See also McKee to Eichelberger, November 17, 1940, *ibid*.

81. Greene to Yarnell, February 27, 1941, and Yarnell to Greene, March 3, 1941, White Committee files.

82. Greene to Hartley, February 26, 1941, minutes of National Policy Board meeting, March 15, 1941, and Greene to E. Guy Talbott, March 22, 1941, White Committee files; Greene to White, March 20, 1941, Box 252, White Papers.

83. Hartley to Greene, March 26, 1941; Greene to Hartley, March 28, 1941; Eichelberger to local chapters, April 18, 1941; Price to Greene, May 24, 1941; Minutes of the Executive Committee, June 6, 1941; and press release, June 9, 1941, White Committee files.

84. Greene to Yarnell, June 12, 1941; Hartley to Greene, June 19, 1941; and Blaisdell to Greene, June 19, 1941, White Committee files.

85. *FR, Japan, 1931-1941* (Washington D.C., 1943), 2:527-28; press release, July 26, 1941, White Committee files. Roosevelt had reached the decision to "freeze" Japanese assets by July 24; see Feis, pp. 227-39.

86. Greene to T. L. Power, July 30, 1941; Washington Office Information Letters, No. 29 (August 1, 1941), No. 30 (August 8, 1941), White Committee files.

87. Greene to T. L. Power, August 20, 1941; Headquarters Letter, Eichelberger to Chapter Representatives, No. 2 (August 16, 1941); and Greene to Price, September 2, 1941, White Committee files.

88. Cole, *America First*, p. 192; Balch to Greene, enclosing copy of letter to Harold Ickes, Secretary of Commerce, June 1941, White Committee files; "Interview between Sumner Welles, Under-Secretary of State, and Dorothy Detzer, September 27, 1941: Confidential Memorandum to the National Board," Resolutions of National Board Meeting, October 18-19, 1941, WILPF-US files.

89. *Peace Action*, 7 (October 1941).

90. *New York Times*, June 8, 1940, p. 10; Report to the Twenty-Second Annual National Convention of the American Legion, 1940; Armstrong to Libby, September 17, 1940, Norman Thomas to Libby, November 28, 1940, Armstrong to Libby, December 8, 1940, and Mildred Scott Olmsted to Libby, December 26, 1940, NCPW files; *New York Times*, January 12, 1941, p. 14, January 13, 1941, p. 10; Armstrong to A. Whitney Griswold, with Statement on Japanese-American Relations, May 31, 1941, Papers of A. Whitney Griswold, Yale University, New Haven, Conn. (compliments of Dorothy Borg).

91. Armstrong to Libby, September 15, 1941, with enclosure, Libby to Armstrong, September 19, 1941, and Armstrong to Dear Friend (mimeographed), October 4, 1941, NCPW files; memorandum of conversation between Langdon, Division of Far Eastern Affairs, and Armstrong, September 30, 1941, State Department files 740.0011 Pacific War/553. Shaw had previously distinguished himself in the temperance movement in Japan; see McGovern, "Missions to Japan."

92. Armstrong to Libby, October 9, 1941 and October 18, 1941, Libby to Shaw, November 8, 1941, Shaw and Armstrong to Hull, November 14, 1941 (copy), and Shaw to Armstrong, November 26, 1941, with enclosure, NCPW files; memorandum of conversation between Mackay, Division of Far Eastern Affairs, and Armstrong, Jones, and Rev. O. G. Robinson, November 22, 1941, State Department files 711.94/2544.

93. Progress Bulletin No. 23, April 16, 1941, White Committee files; Mrs. Fitch to William Allen White, August 5, 1941, Box 257, White Papers. For evidence of the White Committee's problems with Mrs. Fitch, see Hartley to Power, August 18, 1941, and Power to Hartley, August 19, 1941, CDAAA Boxes. Greene was always generous, despite his earlier experiences with her; see Greene to Power, August 20, 1941, *ibid.*; Headquarters Letter, Eichelberger to Chapter Representatives, No. 3 (August 23, 1941), White Committee files; Price to Hull, September 26, 1941, State Department files 711.94/2366; Price to Hull, Hamilton, October 29, 1941, *ibid.*, 711.93/480.

94. Statement of Policy, September 16, 1941; Power to Greene, September 17, 1941; Greene to Power, September 19, 1941 and October 1, 1941, White Committee files.

95. Greene to Hornbeck, enclosing copy of letter from Randolph to President Roosevelt, September 23, 1941, State Department files 711.94/2342; memorandum by Emmett Corrigan to Executive Committee, October 17, 1941, White Committee files.

96. Hartley to Power, November 26, 1941, and Swope to Power, November 25, 1941, White Committee files. See also telegram, Price to Power, November 25, 1941, attempting to broaden commitment to China; Headquarters

Letter, Eichelberger to Chapter Representatives, No. 14, November 22, 1941; and press release, November 28, 1941, *ibid*.

97. On Fight for Freedom, see Mark L. Chadwin, *The Hawks of World War II* (Chapel Hill, N.C., 1968). Chadwin notes the group's disregard for Japan prior to November 1941 and attributes this to an inability to see Asians as a threat to American security. They viewed Japan's actions as those of a German satellite creating diversions. The Hull-Nomura negotiations led to some interest and action on the Far East, but not before late November 1941 (*ibid.* pp. 253-54, 257).

The Role of Liberal Nongovernmental Organizations in Japan

1. Shibusawa Seien Kinen Zaidan Ryūmonsha (Shibusawa Memorial Foundation), ed., *Shibusawa Eiichi denki shiryō* (Biographical Materials on Shibusawa Eiichi), 35 (Tokyo, 1961):151.

2. *Ibid.*, p. 534.

3. Ko Sakatani Shishaku Kinen Jigyōkai (Committee to Commemorate the Late Viscount Sakatani), ed., *Sakatani Yoshirō den* (Biography of Sakatani Yoshirō) (Tokyo, 1951), p. 593.

4. *Ibid.*, pp. 528-29.

5. *Ibid.*, p. 603.

6. The Hepburn Chair for the study and teaching of the United States was established at Tokyo Imperial University in 1917 through the contribution of A. Barton Hepburn, a banker and cousin of the medical missionary James Curtis Hepburn, who undertook the romanization of the Japanese language. A. B. Hepburn was greatly disturbed by the tension in Japanese-American relations and asked Shibusawa to act as intermediary. Saitō Makoto, "Takagi Yasaka sensei no Amerika kenkyū" (American Studies by Professor Takagi), in *Gendai Amerika no naisei to gaikō* (The Current Domestic and Foreign Policy of the United States) (Tokyo, 1959), p. 371.

7. Letter from John B. Clark, Carnegie Foundation for International Peace, to Sakatani Yoshirō, dated February 27, 1917, Sakatani Papers.

8. *Shibusawa Eiichi denki shiryō*, 35:318.

9. *Ibid.*, p. 549.

10. *Ibid.*, pp. 548-56.

11. *Ibid.*, pp. 579.

12. *Ibid.*, p. 585. This plan did not materialize immediately, but in 1938 the president of the America-Japan Society, Kabayama Aisuke, succeeded in persuading Maeda Tamon to open up a Japan Center in New York. Kokusai Bunka Kaikan (International House of Japan), ed., *Kabayama Aisuke* (Tokyo, 1955), pp. 15-16.

13. Yamakawa Tadao, "Nihon Kokusai Kyōkai no nijūnen" (A Twenty-Year History of the International Association of Japan), *Kokusai chishiki* (International Knowledge), July 1940, p. 79.

14. *Ibid.*

15. The Fukushima prefectural association was formed on February 28, 1934 with a membership of approximately one hundred. Its president was the chief of the Education Department of the prefectural government. Two of the four executive directors were section chiefs of the prefectural government, one was a mayor, and the fourth was president of the prefectural chamber of commerce. The six directors included a deputy mayor, a branch manager of the Bank of Japan, two hospital directors, one principal of a normal school, and one company president.

16. *Shibusawa Eiichi denki shiryō*, 36:419.

17. *Ibid.*, 37:356-57.

18. Yamagata Seiichi, "Kokuren fukyū undō no gojūnen" (Fifty Years of Publicity Work for the United Nations), *Kokuren* (The United Nations), March 1969, p. 43.

19. *Ibid.*, January 1969, p. 35.

20. *Shibusawa Eiichi denki shiryō*, 37:492.

21. *Ibid.*, p. 485.

22. *Ibid.*, pp. 528-34.

23. *Ibid.*, pp. 482-85.

24. Dōshisha Daigaku Jinbun Kagaku Kenkyūjo (Doshisha University, Social Science Research Institute), *Senjika teikō no kenkyū* (Studies of Wartime Resistance) (Tokyo, 1969), 2:140.

25. *Ibid.*, pp. 141-42.

26. *Ibid.*

27. *Ibid.*, pp. 138-39.

28. *Shibusawa Eiichi denki shiryō*, 35:151.

29. Rikugunshō (Army Ministry), ed., *Waga Man-Mō hatten no rekishi to rekkoku kanshō no kaiko*, (History of Japanese Expansion in Manchuria and Mongolia and Reflections on the Intervention of the Powers) (Tokyo, 1931), p. 38.

30. Yamaura Kan'ichi, *Mori Kaku* (Tokyo, 1941), pp. 21, 755.

31. *Sakatani Yoshirō den*, p. 594.

32. Matsushita Yoshio, *Mizuno Hironori* (Tokyo, 1950), pp. 54-55.

33. Yamagata, "Kokuren fukyū undō no gojūnen," *Kokuren*, February 1969, pp. 47-48.

34. "Kantō gen" (Lead Article), *Kokusai chishiki*, November 1931.

35. *Shibusawa Eiichi denki shiryō*, 35:391-92.

36. Letter from Sakatani Yoshirō to James T. Shotwell, director, Division of History and Economics, Carnegie Endowment for International Peace, July 16, 1926, Sakatani Papers.

37. *Sakatani Yoshirō den*, pp. 586-87.

38. *Asahi shinbun*, June 22, August 31, September 1 and 2, 1932.

39. *Shibusawa Eiichi denki shiryō*, 35:203-05.

40. *Ibid.*, p. 363.

41. *Ibid.*, p. 255.

42. *Ibid.*, 37:629.

43. Copy of *Japan Advertiser* in *ibid.*, p. 633.

44. *Ibid.*, p. 515.

45. Yanaihara Tadao, "Nitobe hakase o omou" (Thoughts on Doctor Nitobe), *Chūō kōron* (Central Review), October 1935, p. 194.

46. *Shibusawa Eiichi denki shiryō*, 35:607-09.

47. *Ibid.*

48. *Sakatani Yoshirō den*, p. 592.

49. *Ibid.*, p. 593; *Shibusawa Eiichi denki shiryō*, 36:94-107.

50. *Sakatani Yoshirō den*, pp. 589-91.

51. *Shibusawa Eiichi denki shiryō*, 37:515-16.

52. J. B. Condliffe, ed., *Problems of the Pacific, 1929* (Chicago, 1930), p.155.

53. *Ibid.*, p. 173.

54. *Ibid.*, p. 178-79.

55. *Ibid.*, p. 214.

56. *Ibid.*, p. 242.

57. *Ibid.*, p. 207.

58. *Ibid.*, p. 209.

59. *Sakatani Yoshirō den*, p. 538.

60. *Kokusai chishiki*, December 1, 1931, p. 4.

61. *Ibid.*, April 1, 1932, pp. 113-14.

62. Dōshisha Daigaku Kenkyūjo, 2:164.

63. *Tomo* (Friends), November 5, 1931.

64. Dōshisha Daigaku Kenkyūjo, 2:165-66.

65. *Ibid.*, p. 67.

66. Memorandum by Nitobe Inazō on the incident in Matsuyama, given to Takagi Yasaka.

67. Teikoku Zaigō Gunjinkai Honbu (Imperial Reservists Association Headquarters), *Ehime kenka ni okeru Nitobe hakase no kōen ni tsuite* (On the Lectures Given by Doctor Nitobe in Ehime Prefecture), March 1, 1932, pp. 26-32.

68. Nitobe Inazō memorandum.

69. Yanaihara Tadao, the liberal Mukyōkai professor, denied that any compromise was involved and deplored the fact that the report made Nitobe's speeches in the United States subject to mistrust and misunderstanding. Yanaihara, "Nitobe hakase o omou," p. 195.

70. *Ibid.*

71. Takagi Yasaka, "Nitobe Inazō no heiwa shisō to jissen" (The Thoughts on Peace and the Activities of Nitobe Inazō), *Kokoro* (Heart), August 1, 1963, p. 60.

72. Rōyama Masamichi et al., *Manshū mondai kaiketsu an* (A Plan for the Settlement of Manchurian Problems), June 16, 1932, pp. 73-74.

73. *Ibid.*, pp. 55-57.

74. Lead article, *Kokusai chishiki*, December 1, 1932.

75. Bruno Lasker, *Problems of the Pacific, 1931* (Chicago, 1932), p. 233.

76. *Ibid., 1933* (Chicago, 1934), pp. 12-13.

77. *Ibid.*

78. *Ibid.*, p. 444.

79. *Ibid.*

80. *Ibid.*, pp. 446-50.

81. Statement to the writer by Takagi Yasaka, September 23, 1968.

82. Ishii Kikujirō, "Kokusai Renmei to Nihon" (The League of Nations and Japan), *Kokusai chishiki*, December 1, 1932, p. 5.

83. Yamakawa, "Nihon Kokusai Kyōkai," p. 84.

84. Hayashi Kiroku, "Kokusai Renmei o ikani mirubeki ka" (How Should We Regard the League of Nations?), *Kokusai chishiki*, December 1, 1932; Tagawa Daikichirō, "Renmei o ijisuru kokoro" (The Spirit of Support for the League), *ibid.*

85. Sakatani Yoshirō, "Nihon no Kokusai Renmei dattai o ikani miru ka" (How Should We Regard Japan's Withdrawal from the League?), *Kokusai chishiki*, April 1, 1932, p. 8.

86. "Honkyōkai no teikan kaisei ni tsuite" (On Changing the Articles of Incorporation of the Association), *Kokusai chishiki*, June 1, 1933, pp. 1-3.

87. *Tomo*, March 5, 1933.

88. Yamakawa, "Nihon Kokusai Kyōkai," p. 84.

89. "Honkyōkai no teikan kaisei ni tsuite."

90. Matsushita, *Mizuno Hironori*, p. 214.

91. Henri Barbusse was a French poet, novelist, and journalist who after World War I turned to writing antiwar socialist novels. He started the so-called Clarté movement, named after his war novel *Clarté*, and appealed to intellectuals throughout the world to join forces against war. He became a member of the communist party and participated actively in antiwar movements. The Nobel Prize-winning novelist Romain Rolland, who also joined in the antiwar movement after the rise of international fascism, cooperated closely with Barbusse.

92. Katō Kanjū, "Shōwa shonen no rōdō undō" (Labor Movements in the Early Shōwa Era), in Andō Yoshio, ed., *Shōwa keizaishi e no shōgen* (Testimonies for an Economic History of the Shōwa Era) (Tokyo, 1965), pp. 169-70.

93. *Ibid.*, p. 167.

94. Kiyosawa Kiyoshi, "Uchida gaishō ni tou" (Question to Foreign Minister Uchida), *Chūō kōron*, March 1933, p. 196.

95. Tagawa, "Renmei o ijisuru kokoro," p. 25.

96. Dōshisha Daigaku Kenkyūjo, 2:171.

97. *Ibid.*, p. 68.

98. Yamakawa, "Nihon Kokusai Kyōkai," pp. 85-86. Ishii Kikujirō, "Taiheiyō Mondai Chōsakai tono gappei ni tsuite" (On the Merger with the Institute of Pacific Relations), *Kokusai chishiki*, December 1, 1935, pp. 79-80.

99. W. L. Holland and Kate L. Mitchell, eds., *Problems of the Pacific, 1936* (London, 1937), p. 96.

100. *Ibid.*, p. 98.

101. Yamakawa Tadao, "Dairokkai Taiheiyō Kaigi ni tsuite" (The Sixth Conference of the Institute of Pacific Relations), *Kokusai chishiki*, November 1, 1936, p. 18.

102. *Ibid.*, p. 96.

103. *Ibid.*, p. 193.

104. *Ibid.*, p. 195.

105. Tagawa Daikichirō, "Nichi-Doku-I to Ei-Futsu-Bei" (Japan, Germany, and Italy against Britain, France, and America), *Kokusai chishiki*, October 1, 1935, pp. 51-54.

106. *Sakatani Yoshirō den*, p. 610; Ishii Kikujirō, *Gaikō zuisō* (Essays on Diplomacy) (Tokyo, 1967), p. 362.

107. Yamagata, "Kokuren fukyū undō no gojūnen," *Kokuren*, August 1969, pp. 44-45.

108. "Jijihyōron" (Commentary), *Kokusai chishiki*, January 1, 1939, p. 81; *ibid.*, February 1, 1939, p. 89.

109. *Ibid.*

110. Joseph C. Grew, *Ten Years in Japan* (New York, 1944), p. 295.

111. *Ibid.*, p. 297.

112. *Ibid.*, p. 295.

113. Fukumenshi (Anonymous), "Guryū Bei taishi ni kotau" (In Answer to American Ambassador Grew), *Kokusai chishiki*, December 1, 1939, pp. 1-11.

114. Commentary, *Kokusai chishiki*, November 1, 1939, p. 81.

115. Kajima Morinosuke, "Nichi-Doku-I dōmei" (The Tripartite Pact), *Kokusai chishiki*, November 1, 1940, pp. 7-8.

116. Record of Privy Council meeting, in Gaimushō (Foreign Ministry), ed., *Nihon gaikō hyakunen shōshi* (A Short One Hundred-Year History of Japanese Diplomacy) (Tokyo, 1954), p. 157.

117. Statement to the writer by Matsumoto Shigeharu, May 7, 1969.

118. For the Shōwa Kenkyūkai, see Chalmers Johnson, *An Instance of Treason: Ozaki Hotsumi and the Sorge Spy Ring* (Stanford, 1964), pp. 114-39; and Shōwa Dōjinkai (Shōwa Comrades Association), ed., *Shōwa Kenkyūkai* (Shōwa Research Association) (Tokyo, 1968).

119. Statement to the writer by Takagi Yasaka, September 23, 1968.

120. Matsumoto Shigeharu, "Takagi sensei no gakugai katsudō" (Professor Takagi's Extra-Academic Activities), in *Gendai Amerika no naisei to gaikō*, p. 388.

121. Takagi Yasaka, *Toward International Understanding* (Tokyo, 1954), p. 65.

122. *Ibid.*, p. 69.

123. *Ibid.*, p. 70.

124. *Ibid.*, pp. 72-73.

125. In July 1932, after the defection of national socialist elements, the social democrats of the two labor parties, the Shakai Minshūtō and the Zenkoku Rōnō Taishūtō, formed the Shakai Taishūtō. Similarly, two trade union federations, the Nippon Rōdō Sōdōmei and the Zenkoku Rōdō Kumiai Dōmei, which had previously supported the two labor parties, united to set up the Nippon Rōdō Kurabu. When neither of the two new organizations proved willing to take a strong stand on questions of war and fascism, dissident unions under the leadership of Katō Kanjū and Suzuki Mosaburō formed the Nihon Rōdō Kumiai Zenkoku Hyōgikai. This group tried but failed to influence the Shakai Taishūtō to adopt an anti-fascist popular front policy, whereupon it joined with a number of other trade unions and popular front supporters to form a new labor party, the Nihon Musantō. The war in north China brought about strong repressive measures on the part of the government, and some four hundred popular front leaders were arrested. On the Japanese proletarian movement, see Evelyn S. Colbert, *The Left Wing in Japanese Politics* (New York, 1952).

126. Dōshisha Daigaku Kenkyūjo, 2:221.

127. *Ibid.*, pp. 227-30.

128. *Ibid.*, 1:32.

129. Japan Yearly Meeting of the Religious Society of Friends, *Kirisuto Yūkai shichijūnenshi* (A Seventy-Year History of the Religious Society of Friends), pp. 43-44.

130. Dōshisha Daigaku Kenkyūjo, 1:170-71.

131. Grew, *Ten Years in Japan*, p. 356.

The Role of Right-Wing Organizations in Japan

1. See Maruyama Masao, "Chōkokkashugi no ronri to shinri" (Theory and Psychology of Ultranationalism), in *Gendai seiji no shisō to kodō* (Thought and Behavior in Modern Japanese Politics) (Tokyo, 1964), pp. 11-28; and "Senzen ni okeru Nihon no uyoku undō" (The Right-Wing Movement in Prewar Japan), *ibid.*, pp. 187-99. English translations may be found, respectively, in Masao Maruyama, *Thought and Behaviour in Modern Japanese Politics*, edited by Ivan Morris (London, 1963), pp. 1-24; and in Maruyama's introduction to I. I. Morris, *Nationalism and the Right Wing in Japan* (London, 1960), pp. xvii-xxvii.

2. I have discussed this approach in my *Shōwa shoki seijishi kenkyū* (The Political History of the Early Shōwa Era) (Tokyo, 1969).

3. Naimushō Keihokyoku (Ministry of Home Affairs, Police Bureau), comp., *Shakai undō no jōkyō* (The Current State of Social Movements), 1934, p. 323 (hereafter cited as Police Bureau Report).

4. The special higher police, instituted in 1911 in the wake of the 1910 High Treason Case, was at first attached to the Peace Preservation Section of the Police Bureau, Ministry of Home Affairs. Following the 1928 roundup of communists, the organization was expanded and began to harass leftist movements generally and the Communist Party in particular. Only after the May 15, 1932 Incident did the higher police begin a surveillance of right-wing groups, which they had until then regarded as comrades-in-arms. Indeed, even after the incident the police remained friendly with many right-wing groups. The first discussion of the right wing in the Police Bureau Report appears in the 1932 volume. See my bibliographical introduction to Nihon Kindai Shiryō Kenkyūkai (Study Group on Modern Japanese Historical Materials), ed., *Taishō kōki Keihokyoku kankō shakai undō shiryō* (Materials on Social Movements Published by the Police Bureau during the Latter Half of the Taishō Era) (Tokyo, 1968).

5. The following account is from Police Bureau Report, 1932, pp. 809-11.

6. Among the organizations active during the Meiji Era were the Genyōsha (Dark Ocean Society, founded in 1880), Nihon Kōdōkai (Society to Spread the Way of Japan, 1887), and Kokuryūkai (Amur River Society, 1901). During World War I and after were founded the Daimin Kurabu (Great People's Club, April 1913), Rōsōkai (Society of Young and Old, October 1918), Jūō Kurabu (Acting at Will Club, June 1919), Yūzonsha (Society of Those Who Yet Remain, August 1919), Dai Nihon Kokusuikai (Great Japan National Essence Society, October 1919), Dai Nihon Sekkabōshidan (Great Japan Anti-Communist Corps, November 1922), Rikken Yōseikai (Society for the Cultivation of Constitutional Justice, November 1923), Kōchisha (Society to Carry Out Heaven's Way, February 1924), Kokuhonsha (National Foundation Society, March 1924), Dai Nihon Seigidan (Great Japan Justice Corps, February 1925), Kenkokukai (National Founding Society, February 1926), Aikokusha (Patriotic Society, August 1928), as well as such student groups as the Waseda University Ushiō-no-kai (Rising Tide Society, December 1923) and the Tokyo Imperial University Shichi-shōsha (Seven Lives Society, 1925).

7. The Police Bureau lists the following organizations as having been founded during this period of radicalization: the Dai Nihon Seisantō (Great Japan Production Party), Jinmukai (Jinmu Society), Shin Nihon Kokumin Dōmei (New Japan National League), Nihon Kokka Shakaitō (Japan National Socialist Party), Dai Nihon Seinen Dōmei (Great Japan Youth League), Jinmu Seinentai (Jinmu Youth Band), and Kokka Shakaishugi Seinen Dōmei (National Socialist Youth League).

8. For a detailed analysis of this issue, see my *Shōwa shoki seijishi kenkyū*.

9. The concern of the entire nation was aroused over the racial issue. In the course of its struggle to modernize, Japan on several occasions suffered humiliation at the hands of the Western powers. The most notable example was the Triple Intervention in 1895. Such bitter experience led Yamagata Aritomo to warn in August 1914 of the danger that the Western powers would together attack the yellow race as soon as the war in Europe came to an end. There was a deep feeling in Japan that such a war would be quite different from a war between Western nations and that a defeated Japan would be reduced to the status of colonial India or semi-colonial China. American and Australian exclusion of Japanese immigrants after World War I was a profound blow to Japanese pride, and insult was added to injury when the Paris Peace Conference rejected the racial equality clause Japan had proposed.

10. According to the Police Bureau the right wing gained popularity during the controversy over the London naval talks and the Manchurian Incident. Okamoto Seiichi wrote: "The incident in Manchuria literally transformed Japan. Surging nationalism determined a fixed direction for collective action and provided a solid ground for the nationalistic reformism known as 'Nipponism,' which opposed both Western democracy and Soviet communism. . . . We have never at any other time experienced such a clear-cut change as this. It was as if a force developing deep underground had risen to the surface just at that moment to cut a great cleavage in history." Okamoto Seiichi, *Funaguchi Manju den* (Biography of Funaguchi Manju) (Tokyo, 1942), pp. 111-12.

Recently Tsukui Tatsuo, a well-known right-wing leader, told me that the right wing had no financial problems after the Manchurian Incident because wealthy individuals were eager to contribute to nationalist causes.

11. The most detailed study of the March Incident is Seki Haruhiro, "Tairiku gaikō no kiki to sangatsu jiken" (Crisis in Japan's Continental Diplomacy and the March Incident), in Shinohara Hajime and Mitani Taichirō, eds., *Kindai Nihon no seiji shidō* (Political Leadership in Modern Japan) (Tokyo, 1965), pp. 433-90. For a concise discussion of the October Incident, see Takahashi Masae, *Shōwa no gunbatsu* (Shōwa Military Cliques) (Tokyo, 1969).

12. For detailed discussions of this incident, see Takahashi Masae, *Ni-ni-roku jiken* (The February 26 Incident) (Tokyo, 1965); and the novelist Matsumoto Seichō's *Shōwashi hakkutsu* (Delving into Shōwa History), vols. 7- (Tokyo, 1968-).

13. Police Bureau Report, 1932, pp. 894-95.

14. *Ibid.,* 1933, p. 825.

15. This pamphlet, entitled "Kokubō no hongi to sono kyōka no teishō" (The Essence of National Defense and Proposals to Strengthen It), was published

on October 10, 1934 by the Press Office of the Army Ministry as a sequel to "Yakushin Nihon to rekkyō no jūatsu" (Japan's Rapid Development and Pressures from Foreign Powers) issued in July. Numerous copies were distributed to army divisional and regimental headquarters, reservists associations, chambers of commerce and industry, school principals, local government officials, newspaper publishers, and press agencies throughout Japan. Although it "merely reiterated ideas that are widespread today and contained nothing particularly noteworthy," it gave vent to a strong feeling within the army that economic reforms were necessary in order to strengthen national defense and meet the current crisis. In the view of the Police Bureau, "the great majority of right-wing groups" had accepted this statement as their guideline and looked to the army for close cooperation in their activities. They distributed the pamphlet to their members and encouraged them to study it seriously. Except for a small number of critics, the bureau observed, "the general public seemed to support the army's arguments positively." See *ibid.*, 1934, p. 505.

16. *Ibid.*, p. 599.

17. The following account is based upon *ibid.*, 1935, pp. 355-56.

18. *Ibid.*

19. *Ibid.*, p. 817.

20. *Ibid.*, p. 818.

21. *Ibid.*, 1936, p. 170.

22. *Ibid.*, 1937, pp. 262-63.

23. *Ibid.*, p. 488.

24. *Ibid.*, pp. 258-59.

25. I have been studying this episode in detail and will soon publish the results of my research.

26. *Ibid.*, 1938, p. 262.

27. *Ibid.*, 1939, pp. 215-16.

28. *Ibid.*, 1940, pp. 734-35.

29. *Ibid.*, 1941, p. 542.

30. *Ibid.*

31. Shihōshō Keijikyoku (Justice Ministry, Criminal Affairs Bureau), *Kokkashugi dantai no dōkō ni kansuru chōsa* (Report on an Investigation of

Trends in the Activities of Nationalist Organizations), special supplementary issue of *Shisō shiryō panfuretto* (Materials on Thought Studies), 6 (1940):2.

32. Police Bureau Report, 1937, pp. 445-46.

33. *Ibid.*, 1938, p. 425.

34. *Ibid.*, pp. 455-56.

35. *Kokkashugi dantai*, pp. 2-3.

36. Police Bureau Report, 1939, p. 379.

37. *Ibid.*, 1940, p. 581.

38. *Ibid.*, 1941, pp. 543-44.

U.S. Press Coverage of Japan, 1931-1941

1. For a review of the relevant literature, see Ernest R. May, "An American Tradition in Foreign Policy: The Role of Public Opinion," in William H. Nelson, ed., *Theory and Practice in American Politics* (Chicago, 1964), pp. 101-22.

2. See Kent Cooper, *Barriers Down* (New York, 1942).

3. Harry Emerson Wildes, *The Press and Social Currents in Japan* (Philadelphia, 1927), pp. 181-82.

4. *Ibid.*, p. 180.

5. *Ibid.*, p. 177.

6. Cooper, p. 193.

7. *Ibid.*, p. 214.

8. *Fortune*, 7 (May 1933):94. The figures are given in an editorial note to Stephen Vincent Benet, "The United Press," *ibid.*, pp. 67ff.

9. Frank B. Noyes, quoted in Sir Roderick Jones, *A Life in Reuters* (London, 1951), p. 382.

10. Miles Vaughn, *Covering the Far East* (New York, 1936), pp. 1-62.

11. *Ibid.*, p. 241.

12. James R. Young, *Behind the Rising Sun* (New York, 1941).

13. Wildes, pp. 308-09; Howard M. Norton to Hugh R. Law, no date, in Hugh R. Law, "News Control and the Reporter's Outlook: American Correspondents in Japan During the 1930's," B.A. thesis, Harvard University, 1969, pp. 69-72; Young, *Behind the Rising Sun*, p. 279; Hugh Byas, *Government by Assassination* (New York, 1942).

14. *Who's Who in America, 1941-42* (New York, 1942); Wilfrid Fleisher, *Volcanic Isle* (Garden City, N.Y., 1941) and *Our Enemy Japan* (Garden City, N.Y., 1942).

15. Vaughn, pp. 124, 207, 209, 214; Young, *Behind the Rising Sun*, pp. 10-11.

16. Wildes, pp. 308-09; Eugene Lyons, ed., *We Cover the World, by Sixteen Foreign Correspondents* (New York, 1937).

17. Vaughn, p. 286.

18. *New York Times*, September 19, 1931, p. 1.

19. Wildes, pp. 199-202; Vaughn, pp. 262, 286.

20. *Washington Post,* September 21, 1931, p. 2; *San Francisco Examiner*, September 22, 1931, p. 1; *New York Times*, September 23, 1931, p. 8.

21. Vaughn, pp. 127-28, 239; *New York Times*, September 13, 1931, p. 13; *Chicago Tribune*, September 25, 1931, p. 4.

22. *Los Angeles Times*, September 23, 1931, p. 8; September 26, 1931, p. 1; January 9, 1932, p. 1; January 10, 1932, p. 1; January 14, 1932, p. 3; January 26, 1932, p. 1.

23. *Washington Post*, December 15, 1931, p. 5; *New York Times*, January 2, 1931, p. 2.

24. Vaughn, p. 262.

25. Wildes, pp. 201, 218-19.

26. *Literary Digest,* 111 (December 26, 1931):9, *ibid.,* 112 (January 16, 1932):11.

27. *Ibid.*, February 13, 1932, p. 6; March 5, 1932, pp. 8-9.

28. Law, p. 72.

29. *Ibid.*, p. 69.

30. Chalmers Johnson, *An Instance of Treason: Ozaki Hotsumi and the Sorge Spy Ring* (Stanford, 1964), p. 96.

31. Cooper, p. 254. Cooper and Jones, *A Life in Reuters,* are the principal sources for details on the AP-Reuters breach.

32. Relman Morin, *Circuit of Conquest* (New York, 1943), pp. 137-39. This book, Relman Morin, *East Wind Rising: A Long View of the Pacific Crisis* (New York, 1960), *Who's Who in America, 1968-1969* (New York, 1969), and Law are the principal sources on Morin.

33. Vaughn, p. 393; *Who's Who in America, 1941-42.*

34. Byas, p. 17.

35. Grew diary, April 4, 1933, Grew Papers, Harvard University Library, Cambridge, Mass.

36. W. J. Abbot of the *Monitor* was a signer of a 1932 petition to the president urging economic sanctions against Japan on account of the Manchurian affair. *Literary Digest,* 112 (March 5, 1932): 7.

37. William Henry Chamberlin, *The Confessions of an Individualist* (New York, 1940), pp. 200-03.

38. Johnson, *Instance of Treason,* pp. 107-08.

39. *Who's Who in America, 1968-69;* Young, *Behind the Rising Sun,* p. 214; Vaughn, p. 214.

40. Chamberlin, pp. 205-06.

41. Fleisher, *Volcanic Isle,* p. 264.

42. *Ibid.*

43. *Ibid.,* p. 279.

44. *Ibid.,* p. 281.

45. Johnson, *Instance of Treason,* p. 8, citing Kobayashi Gorō, *Tokkō keisatsu hiroku* (Secret Record of the Special Higher Police) (Tokyo, 1952); Young, *Behind the Rising Sun.*

46. Chamberlin, after his years in the Soviet Union, regarded conditions in Japan as relatively free. Even he, however, noted that Japanese were unwilling to talk with him in certain public places. Chamberlin, p. 206.

47. Grew diary, September 27, 1938, November 4, 1939; Cabot Coville to Hugh Law, no date, in Law, pp. 73-74.

48. Chamberlin, p. 203; Morin, *East Wind Rising*, p. 297.

49. *Chicago Tribune*, July 13, 1937, pp. 1, 6; July 14, 1937, p. 1; July 18, 1937, p. 16; July 19, 1937, p. 2.

50. *Washington Post*, July 14, 1937, p. 1; *Chicago Tribune*, July 17, 1937, p. 1, and July 19, 1937, p. 1.

51. See, for example, Hallett Abend, *My Life in China, 1926-1941* (New York, 1943), pp. 270-75.

52. *Chicago Tribune*, September 20, 1937, p. 1; September 21, 1937, p. 1; September 22, 1937, p. 1; September 24, 1937, pp. 1, 2; September 25, 1937, p. 6.

53. *Washington Post*, December 15, 1937, p. 1.

54. *Chicago Tribune*, December 9, 1937, p. 4; *Washington Post*, December 13, 1937, p. 1; *Chicago Tribune*, December 14, 1937, p. 1.

55. *New York Times*, December 13, 1937, p. 1; *New York Herald Tribune*, December 12, 1937, p. 1; *Washington Post*, December 14, 1937, p. 1.

56. *Chicago Tribune*, December 14, 1937, p. 1; *Washington Post*, December 17, 1937, p. 1, and December 18, 1937, p. 3.

57. *Ibid.*, December 23, 1937, p. 1.

58. Morin, *Circuit of Conquest*, pp. 3-12; Joseph Newman, *Goodbye Japan* (New York, 1942), pp. 151, 241, 253, 261; Otto D. Tolischus, *Tokyo Record* (New York, 1943), p. 64.

59. Newman, pp. 258-61; Young, *Behind the Rising Sun*, p. 163.

60. Newman, p. 139.

61. *Ibid.*, pp. 257-61; Fleisher, *Volcanic Isle*, pp. 313-18.

62. *Ibid.*, pp. 280-87; Newman, pp. 146-51; Tolischus, pp. 88-89.

63. Morin, *Circuit of Conquest*, pp. 60-65; Fleisher, *Volcanic Isle*, pp. 307-09; Newman, pp. 167, 253-54; Young, *Behind the Rising Sun*, pp. 284ff; Tolischus, p. 1.

64. *Washington Post*, August 26, 1941, p. 3; *New York Herald Tribune*, September 3, 1941, p. 1; *Washington Post*, September 6, 1941, p. 1; *Los Angeles Times*, September 10, 1941, p. 1; *Washington Post*, September 10, 1941, p. 9.

65. *New York Herald Tribune*, September 15, 1941, p. 1; *New York Times*, September 21, 1941, p. 3, September 27, 1941, p. 1, and September 28, 1941, p. 7; *New York Herald Tribune*, October 12, 1941, p. 3.

66. Newman, p. 141.

67. *New York Times*, August 16, 1941, p. 1, and August 18, 1941, p. 1; *Los Angeles Times*, August 30, 1941, p. 1; *Chicago Tribune*, September 1, 1941, p. 1; *Washington Post*, September 1, 1941, p. 5.

68. *New York Times*, September 2, 1941, p. 1; September 7, 1941, p. 5; September 14, 1941, p. 5.

69. *New York Herald Tribune*, September 15, 1941, p. 1, and September 20, 1941, p. 1; *Washington Post*, October 16, 1941, p. 1.

70. *Ibid.*, September 12, 1941, p. 1, and August 29, 1941, p. 3.

71. *New York Herald Tribune*, July 27, 1941, p. 8.

72. *Washington Post*, August 28, 1941, p. 15.

73. *Ibid.*, September 12, 1941, p. 5.

74. *Ibid.*, September 3, 1941, p. 11; *PM*, July 27, 1941, quoted in William L. Langer and S. Everett Gleason, *The Undeclared War, 1940-1941* (New York, 1953), p. 652.

75. *Washington Post*, August 28, 1941, p. 15.

76. Roberta Wohlstetter, *Pearl Harbor: Warning and Decision* (Stanford, 1962), pp. 130-31, praises American newspapermen for having shown better judgment than U.S. intelligence evaluators.

77. Vaughn, p. 210.

78. Norton to Law, no date, in Law, p. 71.

79. See Langer and Gleason, *Undeclared War*, pp. 639-40.

The Press and Public Opinion in Japan, 1931-1941

1. A. Whitney Griswold, *The Far Eastern Policy of the United States* (New Haven, 1962), p. 373.

2. Hanihara assumed responsibility and resigned from his post. He never again served in an official position. Kiyosawa Kiyoshi, *Nihon gaikōshi* (A Diplomatic History of Japan), 2 (Tokyo, 1942):431.

3. The Tokyo *Asahi* played a leading role in promoting democratic movements in Japan during the 1910s. Its open criticism of the Satsuma-Chōshū oligarchy and its campaign for the "protection of constitutional government" led to the fall of the Katsura cabinet. Such activities gave the Tokyo *Asahi* a reputation as one of the more liberal Japanese papers.

4. One movie theater owner, however, refused to join the boycott. On July 1, while other theaters were empty, his house thrived. The other owners were soon forced to rescind their boycott and on July 12 again started showing American movies. Tokyo *Asahi*, July 12, 1924.

5. The Tokyo *Asahi* pointed to the *New York World*, the *New York Times*, and the *New York Herald Tribune* as papers that "maintain a fair and broad-minded stand . . . representing the majority opinion of the American people who cherish freedom and equality," and sent them a telegram asking them to arouse public opinion against the immigration law. Tokyo *Asahi*, April 20, 1924.

6. Imai Seiichi, *Taishō demokurashii* (Taisho Democracy), vol. 23 of *Nihon no rekishi* (History of Japan) (Tokyo, 1966), pp. 474-76.

7. The Hearst press in particular reported on the "Yellow Peril" in sensational terms, contributing to the surge of mass sentiment against Orientals. For example, on September 28, 1915 the *New York American* reported with a banner headline "Japan's Plan to Invade and Conquer U.S.A." See also W. A. Swanberg, *Citizen Hearst* (New York, 1961). In contrast to the term "yellow peril," the Japanese mass media coined the term *beika* (American peril).

8. Broadcasting was often suspended without warning by government order. The first overseas broadcast suspended by the government was reported in the Tokyo *Asahi* on May 21, 1932, which stated that a talk by a reporter for the *New York Cosmopolitan* entitled "Historic Moment for Japan," scheduled to be broadcast to the United States on that date, had been canceled. On January 19, 1932 the Tokyo *Asahi* reported that governmental authorities had cut into the broadcasting as many as seven times on a single evening.

9. The first Japanese daily, the Yokohama *Mainichi shinbun,* was published in 1870. As early as 1875 the government promulgated a press code that restricted freedom of speech and criticism and gave the government the power to suspend objectionable newspapers.

10. For a more detailed discussion of the *kokutai* ideology, see Masao Maruyama, "The Ideology and Dynamics of Japanese Fascism," in *Thought and Behaviour in Modern Japanese Politics*, edited by Ivan Morris (London, 1963), pp. 25-83.

11. The Tokyo *Asahi* held a commanding position in the Japanese press not only because of its great influence but also because it set the basic pattern for newspaper writing. Because it was widely regarded as a "liberal"

paper, I have analyzed its editorials to assess the nature of "liberalism" in Japan. Other newspapers tended on the whole to be more emotional and aggressive.

12. Johnson reportedly had said: "It is clear that Japan began the war with China. The machine-like precision of the Japanese troops is good evidence that Japan had been preparing for an opportunity to attack China for many years. I cannot understand why our State Department remains silent at this time of grave crisis. What action is the League taking? What has happened to the sacred Kellogg Pact?"

13. The Research Office of the Army Ministry attacked Yokota for giving "perfect propaganda material to the Chinese." *GS 11: Zoku-Manshū jihen* (The Manchurian Incident 2) (Tokyo, 1965), p. 537.

14. Maruyama, "Ideology and Dynamics of Japanese Fascism," pp. 57-65.

15. Maruyama Masao, *Gendai seiji no shisō to kōdō* (Thought and Behavior in Modern Japanese Politics) (Tokyo, 1964), pp. 174-77.

16. Kiyosawa Kiyoshi, "Matsuoka zenken ni atau" (To Plenipotentiary Matsuoka), *Chūō kōron* (Central Review), May 1933, pp. 162-73.

17. Kiyosawa, *Nihon gaikōshi*, 2:482.

18. See Yokota Kisaburō, "Gunshuku no kiso jōken" (Essential Conditions for Arms Reduction), *Kaizō* (Reconstruction), January 1935, pp. 52-63.

19. Kiyosawa, *Nihon gaikōshi*, 2:491.

20. Nakayama Ryūji, *Atagoyama jisseisō* (A Ten-Year History of NHK), vol. 1; Nihon Hōsōkyōkai (NHK), ed., *Hōsō* (Broadcasting), 9, no. 4:51.

21. Tokyo *Asahi*, March 15, 1932.

22. Tosaka Jun, *Tosaka Jun zenshū* (Complete Works of Tosaka Jun), 5 (Tokyo, 1967):157-62.

23. For the background of the establishment of the Dōmei Tsūshinsha, see Tsūshinshashi Kankōkai (Committee to Publish a History of News Agencies), ed., *Tsūshinshashi* (A History of News Agencies) (Tokyo, 1958); and Furuno Inosuke, ed., *Iwanaga Yūkichi kun* (Tokyo, 1941).

24. Uchikawa Yoshimi and Kōuchi Saburō, "Nihon fashizumu keiseiki no masu media tōsei" (Control of the Mass Media during the Formative Years of Japanese Fascism), *Shisō* (Thought), November 1961, p. 27.

25. Naimushō Keihokyoku Toshoka (Ministry of Home Affairs, Police Bureau, Publications Section), *Shuppan keisatsuhō* (Police Report on Publications), no. 107.

26. Uchikawa and Kōuchi, p. 37.

27. In February 1939 Prince Saionji Kimmochi lamented that "recent newspapers are of such low quality and so disregarding of international courtesy and morality that they are just like the talk of a drunkard. They are harming our nation's prestige." Harada Kumao, *Saionji-kō to seikyoku* (Prince Saionji and the Political Situation) (Tokyo, 1967), 7:282.

28. Tokyo *Asahi*, December 10, 1941.

29. See Ikeuchi Hajime, "Taiheiyō sensō chū no senji ryūgen" (Rumors during the Pacific War), *Shakaigaku hyōron* (Sociological Review), no. 6 (1951), pp. 30-42.

Tyler Dennett and A. Whitney Griswold

1. Of the many historiographical studies, John Higham's *History* (Englewood Cliffs, N.J., 1965) is especially useful. Among other books published within the past decade are: W. Stull Holt, *Historical Scholarship in the United States and Other Essays* (Seattle, 1967); Robert Allen Skotheim, *American Intellectual Histories and Historians* (Princeton, 1966); Harvey Wish, *The American Historian* (New York, 1960). Charles E. Neu was kind enough to let me read an advance copy of his essay on "Progressive History and American Foreign Policy," which is the first effort to survey the field of diplomatic history. Professor Neu read a shorter paper on the same subject at the American Historical Association's annual meeting in December 1968, which was followed by a commentary by Waldo H. Heinrichs, Jr. As Professor Heinrichs pointed out, the generalizations that apply to historians who specialize in American history do not, by any means, always apply to those who specialize in American diplomatic history, which makes research in this area more difficult.

The subject matter discussed in the present paper also formed the basis of a session at the annual meeting of the Association for Asian Studies, April 1966. The papers read there were subsequently published in Dorothy Borg, comp., *Historians and American Far Eastern Policy* (New York, 1966).

2. W. Stull Holt, *Historical Scholarship in the United States, 1876-1901: As Revealed in the Correspondence of Herbert B. Adams* (Baltimore, 1938). Among those who attended Adams' seminar were Frederick Jackson Turner and Woodrow Wilson.

3. Among Hart's many publications were *The Foundations of American Foreign Policy* (New York, 1901) and *National Ideals Historically Traced, 1607-1907* (New York and London, 1907). In 1911 Hart published *The Obvious Orient*, a book based upon an eight-month trip to the Far East. Moore, an outstanding authority on international law, was also a diplomatic historian whose best known works were *American Diplomacy* (New York and London, 1905), *Four Phases of American Development* (Baltimore, 1912), and *The Principles of American Diplomacy* (New York and London, 1918). Moore's

Collected Papers (7 vols., New Haven, 1944) have many short pieces on American foreign policy. Unlike Hart and Moore, Latané and Coolidge were primarily specialists in diplomatic history. Latané's *America as a World Power, 1897-1907* (New York and London, 1907) and *From Isolation to Leadership* (Garden City, N.Y., 1918) were his most widely read volumes. Coolidge's writings were relatively limited, his main publication being *The United States as a World Power* (New York, 1908). While both Latané's and Coolidge's books were generally acknowledged to lie somewhere between journalistic reports and intensive scholarly studies, they admittedly exercised an unusual influence on the views of contemporary historians. See W. Stull Holt's biography of Latané in the *Dictionary of American Biography*, 21:483; and Harold Jefferson Coolidge and Robert Howard Lord, *Archibald Cary Coolidge* (Boston and New York, 1932).

4. Foster also wrote *A Century of American Diplomacy* (Boston and New York, 1900) and *Diplomatic Memoirs* (Boston and New York, 1909). In 1895 he served as special adviser to the Chinese commission to negotiate the peace settlement following the Sino-Japanese War.

5. It was Dennett's custom when on a trip to keep a daily record of his interviews and other experiences, which he sent home to his family. Members of his family have generously permitted me to read the records covering his journey to the Far East in 1916-17 and to Europe in 1918-19, which are still in their possession.

Dennett wrote many articles in 1915 and 1916 for *The World Outlook*, a magazine which was founded in 1915 by the Board of Foreign Missions of the Methodist Episcopal Church and later became *The Christian Herald*. In its initial number *The World Outlook* stated editorially that it was the task of missionaries to help bring about fundamental conditions of worldwide democracy and "hasten the golden age of the Federation of the World."

6. "Outline of Proposed Source Book for the History of American Relations with China," and letters from John Van Antwerp MacMurray, July 12 and August 9, 1921, Dennett Papers, Hague, N.Y.

7. Tyler Dennett, *Americans in Eastern Asia* (New York, 1922), p. ix.

8. Tyler Dennett, "The Open Door Policy as Intervention," *The Annals* of the American Academy of Political and Social Science, July 1933, p. 81.

9. Dennett, *Americans in Eastern Asia*, pp. viii, 663, 674-76.

10. Tyler Dennett, "Seward's Far Eastern Policy," *American Historical Review*, October 1922, p. 45.

11. The main themes of *Americans in Eastern Asia* are summarized in the preface and in chaps. 33 and 34.

12. *Ibid.*, pp. viii-ix.

13. Dennett seems to have been persuaded by some of the members of the Johns Hopkins faculty to obtain his Ph.D. degree although he was at the time over forty. Frank J. Goodnow, then president of Hopkins, and W. W. Willoughby, sometimes called the "dean" of political scientists in the United States, may have had a special interest in Dennett's work as they both served as advisers to the Chinese government. There were apparently few course requirements, and Dennett attended only Latané's seminar on United States history and Goodnow's course on international law. His dissertation was submitted to Latané and Willoughby. A letter from Latané in the Dennett papers is an enthusiastic endorsement. Dennett lectured at several universities and was professor of international relations at Princeton from 1931 to 1934. The lecture notes in his papers appear to be for the course given at Princeton. (Letters from Tyler Dennett's sister, Mrs. Bruce Mudgett, June 7, 17, 19, 1968; letter from Miss Lilly Lavarello, secretary of the History Department, Johns Hopkins University, September 5, 1968.)

14. Tyler Dennett, *Roosevelt and the Russo-Japanese War* (New York, 1925), p. 4.

15. Most historians doubt that Roosevelt ever delivered such a warning. For Dennett's own statements, see *ibid.*, pp. 2, 30, 92, 317, 332, 335. For comments, see, for example, Howard K. Beale, *Theodore Roosevelt and the Rise of America to World Power* (Baltimore, 1956), p. 501, fn. 362; and Raymond A. Esthus, *Theodore Roosevelt and Japan* (Seattle, 1966), p. 58.

16. Dennett, *Russo-Japanese War*, pp. 330, 332.

17. "Memorandum on Policy of Cooperation of the Foreign Powers in the Far East"; also "Memorandum on 'Open Door' Policy" and "Memorandum on History of American Cooperation with Japan," Dennett Papers. These memoranda are brief. The quotation from *Americans in Eastern Asia* is on p. ix.

18. Tyler Dennett, "American Policy in the Far East," *Current History*, July 1923, p. 600.

19. "America's Supreme Folly in the East," Dennett Papers. This article was accepted by *Asia* magazine but by some oversight was not immediately published. Dennett served as chief of the Division of Publication in the State Department from 1924 to 1929 and as the department's historical adviser for two years thereafter and did not want the article published during this period because of his official connections. He recalled the manuscript in 1926 but not because of any change of mind as to its substance. Letter from L. D. Froelick, editor of *Asia* magazine, June 4, 1926, Dennett Papers.

Dennett's thinking at this time may have been partly influenced by Latané. Contrary to many historians in the interwar period, Latané remained strongly pro-British and pro-League of Nations. In the concluding passage of *America as a World Power* he had asserted that an Anglo-Saxon union would "constitute the highest guarantee of the political stability and moral progress of the world." He elaborated this thesis in *From Isolation to Leadership*, which was reprinted in 1922, and in some of his articles of the early 1920s. (See, for example, "American Foreign Policy," published in three parts in *World's Work*, April-May 1921.) Moreover, it had been a popular thesis among historians during the war, and Latané himself borrowed heavily from George Louis Beer's *The English Speaking Peoples* (New York, 1917).

Latané was a confirmed Wilsonian internationalist. W. Stull Holt states in a brief biography that during the discouraging years from 1919 to 1930 Latané addressed "hundreds of meetings in favor of the League of Nations." He, however, believed in international cooperation supported by the use of force. (See, for example, *From Isolation to Leadership*, pp. 57-58; Holt's biography of Latané in *Dictionary of American Biography*, 21:483; and *John Holladay Latané, '92, Ph.D. 1895*, reprinted from *The Johns Hopkins Alumni Magazine*, 21 [November 1932], consisting of the tributes of friends written in memoriam.)

20. In addition to articles cited in fn. 21, Dennett published articles in *Current History* monthly from October 1932 to July 1934.

21. The most important of the 1933-34 articles are "The Open Door Policy as Intervention" in *The Annals* of the American Academy of Political and Social Science, July 1933, pp. 78-83; and "The Open Door," in Joseph Barnes, ed., *Empire in the East* (Garden City, N.Y., 1934), pp. 269-97. See also "Japan's Diplomatic Isolation," *Current History*, February 1933, pp. 635-41.

22. "The Open Door" in *Empire in the East* is a good example of the constant confusion of aims.

23. In a letter written in November 1939 Dennett stated, "I am an isolationist." A month earlier he told Harold Sprout that he had "somewhat reluctantly . . . reached an almost completely isolationist point of view." Letter to Richard A. Newhall, November 4, 1939; letter to Harold Sprout, October 11, 1939, Dennett Papers.

Originally a strong element in Dennett's noninterventionism was his repudiation in the early 1930s of all forms of international cooperation. In a speech given at the opening session of the Williamstown Institute of Human Relations on August 23, 1935 he asserted that the principle underlying the League of Nations covenant, that "every war or threat of war is a matter of international concern," was a "vicious notion." *Vital Speeches of the Day, 1935*, p. 837.

Dennett's intense reaction against the concept of international cooperation was partly based on the belief that he had been wrong earlier in supposing that it was possible for large numbers of people, such as comprise a nation, to act collectively on a high level of Christian morality. He therefore thought that, while Americans as individuals could not help condemning Germany, Italy, and

Japan, the United States as a nation should tolerate their actions and strictly refrain from any interference in their affairs. As he frequently said, he had a kind of "mystical faith" that a cosmic force existed which destroyed that which was in itself destructive and that, consequently, nations that violated fundamental ethical laws were inviting their own punishment. Speech tu Williamstown Institute of Human Relations; interview in Boston *Sunday Post*, October 17, 1937, p. A-3; letter to Herbert Brookes, July 9, 1940, Dennett Papers.

After the mid-1930s Dennett's isolationism, as explained in the text, was closely tied to his hostility to the New Deal and Roosevelt. By this time Dennett's political views had traveled across the spectrum, for in the days when he went to Union Theological Seminary he was regarded as a champion of liberal, even radical ideas.

24. Carl L. Becker, *Everyman His Own Historian: Essays on History and Politics* (New York, 1935); Burleigh Taylor Wilkins, *Carl Becker: A Biographical Study in American Intellectual History* (Cambridge, Mass., 1961), pp. 201, 203, 205.

25. Higham, *History*, pp. 124-28; Richard Hofstadter, *The Progressive Historians* (New York, 1968), pp. 304-15.

26. At the time his textbook was published, Bemis wrote Dennett stating that he thought the volume had "much in common . . . with many of your ideas." Dennett Papers.

27. Frederick S. Dunn, "The Present Course of International Relations Research," *World Politics*, October 1949, pp. 80-95; William T. R. Fox, "Interwar International Relations Research: The American Experience," *ibid.*, pp. 67-79; Robert Endicott Osgood, *Ideals and Self-Interest in America's Foreign Relations* (Chicago, 1953), pp. 391-97. See also Grayson Kirk, *The Study of International Relations in American Colleges and Universities* (New York, 1947).

28. Richard W. Leopold, "The Problem of American Intervention, 1917: An Historical Retrospect," *World Politics*, April 1950; and Ernest R. May, "Emergence to World Power," in John Higham, ed., *The Reconstruction of American History* (New York, 1962). These are among the most useful guides to the literature of revisionism. Of the recent books Warren I. Cohen's *The American Revisionists* (Chicago, 1967) is an unusually helpful study.

29. See Bemis' laudatory review of Beard's *The Open Door at Home* in the *American Historical Review*, April 1935, pp. 541-43.

30. Edgar S. Furniss, *The Graduate School at Yale* (New Haven, 1965), p. 117; Edgar S. Furniss, *Alfred Whitney Griswold, 1906-1963, In Memoriam* (1964); George Wilson Pierson, *Yale: College and University, 1871-1937* (New Haven, 1955), pp. 271, 284, 311, 392-93. There are a number of letters from Bemis in the Griswold Papers at Yale University, in which

Bemis indicated his great expectations for Griswold's future. See especially his letter of November 2, 1937.

31. Letter, April 8, 1931, Griswold Papers.

32. A. Whitney Griswold, "The Future in American Relations," in Allan Nevins and Louis M. Hacker, eds., *The United States and Its Place in World Affairs, 1918-1943* (Boston, 1943), p. 585.

33. Memorandum on "The United States in the Far East," October 27, 1935, Griswold Papers. The reference to a "Pax Americana" is taken from a letter to Herbert Feis, October 27, 1936.

34. Letter to *New York Herald Tribune* on Ethiopian crisis, December 30, 1935; letter to Senator Arthur H. Vandenberg supporting his stand on the neutrality legislation, December 30, 1935, Griswold Papers.

35. See especially articles published in the issues for May, June, and July.

36. "America's Far Eastern Policy," *Events*, September 1937; memorandum on "The United States in the Far East," October 27, 1935, Griswold Papers; "Conflicts in Our Far Eastern Policy," *Yale Review*, December 1937.

37. "America in World Politics," *Events*, May 1937, p. 326; "An Uncertain Diplomacy," *ibid.*, July 1937, p. 6; "America's Far Eastern Policy," *ibid.*, September 1937, p. 176.

38. Robert H. Ferrell, "The Griswold Theory of Our Far Eastern Policy," in Borg, *Historians and American Far Eastern Policy*, p. 14.

39. Preface to Chinese edition, with letter to D. T. Lieu, July 2, 1940, Griswold Papers.

40. There are three separate papers in the Griswold files marked either "Introduction" or "Preface"; they contain many erasures, notations, etc. The published volume has neither an introduction nor a preface.

41. Letters from Bemis to Griswold, especially letter of November 2, 1937, Griswold Papers.

42. Memorandum on "The United States in the Far East."

43. *The Far Eastern Policy of the United States* was originally published by Harcourt, Brace. It was reissued in January 1962 by Yale University Press and has been through seven printings since. The pagination, however, remains as in the original edition.

44. Griswold made a partial summary of his conclusions in the final chapter of *Far Eastern Policy*, pp. 466-73.

45. *Ibid.*, p. 87.

46. See Paul A. Varg's discussion of the aims of American Far Eastern policy for the 1897-1912 period in *The Making of a Myth* (East Lansing, 1968), chap. 1. Marilyn Blatt Young gives a good picture of the many factors that motivated Hay's policy throughout *The Rhetoric of Empire* (Cambridge, Mass., 1968). Two influential books on Theodore Roosevelt are John Morton Blum's *The Republican Roosevelt* (Cambridge, Mass., 1954), and Howard K. Beale's *Theodore Roosevelt and the Rise of America to World Power* (Baltimore, 1956). Blum deals with Roosevelt's foreign policy in chap. 8, stressing the president's efforts to develop the United States as a world power that would play a major role in the maintenance of stability and peace. The same theme runs throughout Beale's volume. In *An Uncertain Friendship: Theodore Roosevelt and Japan, 1906-1909* (Cambridge, Mass., 1967), Charles E. Neu, while fundamentally in agreement with Blum and Beale, adds a new dimension by emphasizing Roosevelt's preoccupation with domestic problems and its effect upon his foreign policy (see especially chaps. 1 and 13).

47. See, for example, pp. 197, 221, 269, 272-73, 316, 380, 393-94, 433, 465.

48. Of the more recent studies, see Marilyn Blatt Young, "American Expansion, 1870-1900: The Far East," in Barton J. Bernstein, ed., *Towards a New Past: Dissenting Essays in American History* (New York, 1968), pp. 191-92; Charles E. Neu, "Theodore Roosevelt and American Involvement in the Far East, 1901-1909," *Pacific Historical Review*, November 1966, pp. 433-99; Varg, *Making of a Myth*, pp. 22, 28-29, 31-32, 129-30, 173. Neu's article was specifically written to refute Griswold's cyclical theory as applied to Theodore Roosevelt's policy.

49. *Far Eastern Policy*, p. 298. Chaps. 7 and 8 are on the Washington Conference. Especially good examples of Griswold's interpretation are to be found on pp. 270, 321-24, 331-32.

50. The theme of the efforts of Japan, the United States, and Great Britain to cooperate on the basis of the Washington Conference agreements and the eventual breakdown of those efforts runs through Akira Iriye's *After Imperialism: The Search for a New Order in the Far East, 1921-1931* (Cambridge, Mass., 1965). Ernest R. May, whose lectures for the Albert Shaw Lectures on Diplomatic History were devoted to the Washington Conference, concluded that for a variety of reasons Japan and the United States were determined to reach an understanding at the Washington Conference.

51. *Far Eastern Policy*, pp. 400-06.

52. Memorandum, "Anglo-American Diplomacy in the Far East: 1898-1935," "Memorandum on Research Project," and letter to Tyler Dennett, March 20, 1936, Griswold Papers. The first of these memoranda consists of an outline

in which the final section is headed by the question, "Was the United States the 'Ally or Agent' of the British in the Far East?"

53. In 1948 Griswold published a book on a very different subject— *Farming and Democracy*—which he had begun even before the war. After he became president of Yale University in 1950, he published *Essays on Education* (New Haven, 1954), *In the University Tradition* (New Haven, 1957), and *Liberal Education and the Democratic Ideal* (New Haven, 1959).

54. "Conflicts in Our Far Eastern Diplomacy," *Yale Review*, Winter 1938, pp. 366-80.

55. Letter dated December 27, 1937, Griswold Papers.

56. T. A. Bisson, *America's Far Eastern Policy* (New York, 1945), pp. 83-87; Robert A. Divine, *The Illusion of Neutrality* (Chicago, 1962), pp. 244-46; William C. Johnstone, *The United States and Japan's New Order* (New York, 1941), p. 279.

57. Bisson, *America's Far Eastern Policy*, p. 99, and Johnstone, *Japan's New Order*, pp. 277-78, have data on polls and public opinion. For material on organized propaganda groups, see the essays by Wayne S. Cole and Warren I. Cohen in the present volume; also Donald J. Friedman, *The Road from Isolation: The Campaign of the American Committee for Non-Participation in Japanese Aggression, 1938-1941* (Cambridge, Mass., 1968), pp. 31-44; and Walter Johnson, *The Battle Against Isolation* (Chicago, 1944), pp. 31-62. The information on Borah and Vandenberg comes from Marian C. McKenna, *Borah* (Ann Arbor, 1961), p. 267.

58. "The Influence of History upon Sea Power," *American Military Institute Journal*, Spring 1940, pp. 1-7. The Griswold Papers contain an early draft of this article with long passages that were not used.

59. Quotation from letter cited in fn. 61 below.

60. Two letters to Lippmann, one dated February 5, 1939, the other undated but evidently written a few weeks later, Griswold Papers.

61. Griswold Papers, draft of a letter which does not have a name or date, but it seems evident from the contents that it was written to Vandenberg right after the senator presented his resolution concerning abrogation of the treaty. Griswold had earlier written to Vandenberg under similar circumstances; see fn. 34 above.

62. A. Whitney Griswold, "Facing Facts About a New Japanese-American Treaty," *Asia*, November 1939, pp. 615-19; "Should Japan Be Embargoed?" *Asia*, February 1940, pp. 92-96. The editorial policy of *Asia* was similar to the views expressed by Griswold; see R. J. W., "The Peace Must

Begin in the Orient," *Asia*, November 1939, p. 619. For some of the letters replying to Griswold's article, see the December issue of *Asia*, pp. 682-86.

63. T. A. Bisson, "Facing Facts about a Far Eastern Peace Settlement," *Asia*, January 1940, p. 42.

64. Robert A. Divine, *The Reluctant Belligerent: American Entry into World War II* (New York, 1968), p. 91.

65. For the William Allen White Committee, see Johnson, *Battle Against Isolation*, especially chap. 8, which deals with the events of the winter of 1940-41 and White's resignation on the grounds that the committee was taking too strong a stand. For the America First Committee, see Wayne S. Cole, *America First: The Battle Against Intervention, 1940-1941* (Madison, Wis., 1953), chap. 3.

66. See Cohen, "The Role of Private Groups," pp. 447-50; also Johnson, *Battle Against Isolation*, p. 136, and *William Allen White's America* (New York, 1947), p. 542; Cole, *America First*, pp. 190-93.

67. The position of Beard and the few noted historians who held out to the end is discussed in Cohen's *American Revisionists*, chap. 8. See also Bernard C. Borning, *The Political and Social Thought of Charles A. Beard* (Seattle, 1962), pp. 236-46, and Hofstadter's *Progressive Historians*, pp. 318-34.

68. *Harper's*, August 1940, pp. 259-67.

69. Letter to R. Douglas Stuart, January 16, 1941, Griswold Papers.

70. "The Doctrine of Fear," *Vital Speeches of the Day*, January 6, 1941.

71. Letter to La Follette, January 7, 1941, Griswold Papers.

72. Letter to Jonathan Bingham, January 31, 1941, *ibid*.

73. Letter to R. Douglas Stuart, January 16, 1941, *ibid*. Stuart was a student at Yale Law School, where he and a number of fellow students became greatly concerned with the problem of keeping the United States out of war and in the spring of 1940 met informally to consider what they could do about it. Subsequently Stuart assumed much of the initiative in forming America First. Cole, *America First*, p. 10.

74. Letter to O. K. Armstrong, June 4, 1941, Griswold Papers. For Armstrong's activities at this time, see Cohen, "The Role of Private Groups," pp. 452-53.

75. "An Undeclared Peace?" *The Annals* of the American Academy of Political and Social Science, May 1941, pp. 179-81; "Perspective on Far Eastern Policy," *Virginia Quarterly Review*, Autumn 1941, pp. 539-61.

76. Ferrell, "The Griswold Theory," pp. 15-16.

Japanese Studies of Japan's Foreign Relations

1. Kiyosawa Kiyoshi, *Nihon gaikōshi* (A Diplomatic History of Japan), 2 (Tokyo, 1942):443.

2. Tachi Sakutarō, *Jikyoku kokusaihōron* (International Law and the Current Situation) (Tokyo, 1934), pp. 5, 19.

3. *Ibid.*, pp. 14, 21.

4. *Ibid.*, pp. 35, 251-52.

5. *Ibid.*, pp. 253-54.

6. Shinobu Junpei, *Man-Mō tokushu ken'ekiron* (A Treatise on Special Interests in Manchuria and Mongolia) (Tokyo, 1932), pp. 512, 519-23, 540.

7. Kamikawa Hikomatsu, "Manshū i'nin tōchiron (Mandate in Manchuria), in *Kokka Gakkai zasshi* (Journal of the Association of Political and Social Science), 46, no. 4 (April 1932):97, 100, 111.

8. *Reine Rechtslehre* postulates a hierarchical legal order in which one form of law takes precedence over another, with international law transcending all others. Thus, national sovereignty is bound and restricted by international law. *Reine Rechtslehre* further assumes that laws can and should be interpreted objectively and through a process of strict, logical deduction from a given law. Among Japanese scholars Yokota was said to have been the most insistent on a strict application of Kelsen's theory to actual situations.

9. Yokota Kisaburō, "Manshū jihen to kokusaihō" (The Manchurian Incident and International Law), in *Kokusaihō gaikō zasshi* (Journal of International Law and Diplomacy), 31, no. 4 (April 1932):46-47, 49-52. Japan's representative at the League, Yoshizawa Kenkichi, had pointed out that Chinese troops numbered 220,000 compared with only 10,000 Japanese railway guards and that in the Mukden area where the incident occurred there were 25,000 Chinese troops to only 500 Japanese. Under such circumstances, he stated, it was necessary to occupy several cities in order to protect the lives and property of the several hundred thousand Japanese residents of Manchuria.

10. Yokota Kisaburō, "Manshū jihen to Kokusai Renmei" (The Manchurian Incident and the League of Nations), *Teidai shinbun* (Tokyo Imperial University Newspaper), October 5, 1931.

11. Yokota Kisaburō, "Manshū jihen to Hūbāshugi" (The Manchurian Incident and the Hoover Doctrine), *Kokusaihō gaikō zasshi*, 32, no. 1 (January 1933):47, 76, 81.

12. Yokota Kisaburō, "Shōkai: Tachi Sakutarō 'Jikyoku kokusaihō-ron' " (Review of Tachi Sakutarō's *International Law and the Current Situation*), *ibid.*, 33, no. 8 (October 1934):93.

13. Yoshino Sakuzō, *Tai-Shi mondai* (The China Question) (Tokyo, 1930), p. 153.

14. Yoshino Sakuzō, "Minzoku to kaikyū to sensō" (Nation, Class, and War), *Chūō kōron* (Central Review), no. 528 (January 1932), pp. 28, 31.

15. *Ibid.*, p. 33.

16. Rōyama Masamichi, "Manshū jihen to Kokusai Renmei" (The Manchurian Incident and the League of Nations), July 1932, in *Sekai no henkyoku to Nihon no sekai seisaku* (The Changing World Situation and Japanese Foreign Policy) (Tokyo, 1938), p. 22.

17. Rōyama Masamichi, *Nichi-Man kankei no kenkyū* (Japanese-Manchurian Relations) (Tokyo, 1933), p. 218.

18. *Ibid.*, p. 219.

19. *Ibid.*, pp. 192-93.

20. *Ibid.*, p. 225.

21. Rōyama pointed out that through the Council decision of December 10, 1931 the League had in a measure recognized the exceptional character of the situation in Manchuria. He argued that if Japan stressed that a settlement therefore did not establish a legal precedent, eventually the League members and the United States would probably recognize Manchukuo. Rōyama, "Manshū jihen," pp. 22-25, 28.

22. He said that the Japanese-Machurian economic bloc then being considered was fundamentally different from the economic blocs formed around continental powers like the Soviet Union and the United States and claimed that a noncontinental power like Japan should not develop such a bloc. "Sekai no sai'ninshiki to chiikiteki kokusai renmei" (A Revised Perception of the World and a Regional League of Nations), in *Sekai no henkyoku*, p. 101

23. Rōyama, "Manshū jihen," p. 26.

24. Rōyama Masamichi, "Kokubō to gaikō to no renkan" (National Defense and Diplomacy), November 1933, in *Sekai no henkyoku*, p. 156.

25. Rōyama, "Sekai no sai'ninshiki," p. 102.

26. Kamikawa Hikomatsu, "Ajia rengō ka kyokutō renmei ka" (A United Asia or a Far Eastern League?), *Kokka Gakkai zasshi*, 47, no. 4 (April 1933):90.

27. From about 1933 on Rōyama came to feel that not only were universal international law and treaties important as a basis for foreign policy, but political and geographical conditions as well. Toward that end he stressed the necessity of learning the geopolitik method of thought. See "Sekai seisaku to waga gaikō gensoku" (World Politics and the Fundamental Principles of Japanese Diplomacy), March 1935, in *Sekai no henkyoku*, pp. 318-19.

28. Rōyama, *Nichi-Man kankei*, p. 248.

29. *Ibid.*, p. 249.

30. Rōyama Masamichi, "Manshū jikyoku ni taisuru kansatsu" (Observations on the Current Situation in Manchuria), *Shintenchi* (New World), February 1932, quoted in Tachibana Shiraki, "Dokusai ka minshu ka" (Dictatorship or Democracy?), in *Tachibana Shiraki chosakushū* (Collected Works of Tachibana Shiraki), 2 (Tokyo, 1966):76.

31. *Ibid.*, pp. 75, 79.

32. Kajima Morinosuke, "Shin heiwa shugi" (A New Peace Doctrine), April 1935, in *Gendai no gaikō* (Contemporary Diplomacy) (Tokyo, 1937), p. 4.

33. *Ibid.*, p. 5.

34. Kajima Morinosuke, "Shin heiwa kikō no teishō" (A Proposal for a New Peace Structure), April 1935, in *ibid.*, pp. 14, 16.

35. Kajima Morinosuke, "Taiheiyō tenbō" (A View over the Pacific), January 1935, in *ibid.*, pp. 22-23.

36. Kajima Morinosuke, "Renmei no kaiso to han-Yōroppa mondai" (Reorganization of the League and Pan-Europeanism), 1936, in *ibid.*, pp. 37, 52.

37. In writing his *Teikoku shugika no Taiwan* (Taiwan under Imperialism) (Tokyo, 1929) and *Nanyō guntō no kenkyū* (A Study of the South Sea Islands) (Tokyo, 1935), Yanaihara was heavily influenced by J. A. Hobson's *Imperialism: A Study* (1902, 3d ed. 1938), and after the war he published a Japanese translation of the book. He was also greatly impressed with R. Hilferding's approach to imperialism as expressed in *Das Finanzkapital* (1910).

38. These lectures were subsequently published under the title *Manshū mondai* (The Manchurian Problem) (Tokyo, 1934).

39. In August 1932 Yanaihara was on a train from Changchun to Harbin which was attacked by Chang Hsueh-liang's troops and the inhabitants of the area. Yanaihara himself narrowly escaped, and the experience strongly impressed upon him the fact that the Manchurian question was fundamentally a Chinese problem. In 1937 Yanaihara lost his position at the university due to

right-wing and governmental pressure, but according to his notes published in a private journal, the trip brought his scholarship and faith together and decided his opposition to Japan's Manchuria policy. Yanaihara Tadao, *Watakushi no ayunde kita michi* (The Path I Have Trodden) (Tokyo, 1958), p. 100.

40. Yanaihara Tadao, *Manshū mondai* (The Manchurian Problem) (1934), reprinted in *Yanaihara Tadao zenshū* (The Complete Works of Yanaihara Tadao), 2 (Tokyo, 1963):487.

41. *Ibid.*, p. 603.

42. *Ibid.*, p. 542.

43. *Ibid.*, pp. 546-47.

44. *Ibid.*, p. 547.

45. *Ibid.*, p. 541.

46. *Ibid.*, p. 548.

47. *Ibid.*, p. 518.

48. *Ibid.*, pp. 569-71.

49. *Ibid.*, pp. 588-89.

50. *Ibid.*, p. 588.

51. *Ibid.*, pp. 583, 632.

52. *Ibid.*, pp. 597-99.

53. Yanaihara Tadao, "Tai-Shi mondai no shozai" (The Central Issue in the China Question), *Chūō kōron*, no. 591 (February 1937), pp. 10, 17.

54. In his articles and lectures he made a number of indirect statements to the effect that the China War was against "national ideals" and called for the downfall of the kind of nation that was trying to accomplish such goals. Yanaihara's stand brought a good deal of criticism and a number of attacks upon him.

55. Yanaihara lost his position at the university due to right-wing and government pressure. The Monbushō (Ministry of Education) prevented Yokota's receipt of a doctorate approved by the university's faculty council.

56. Kiyosawa, *Nihon gaikōshi*, vol. 2. Although this work was published in 1942 after the Pacific War had begun, the major portion was published in his

preparatory *Gaikōshi* (Diplomatic History) (Tokyo, 1941), so I have included it in my study.

57. *Ibid.*, p. 576.

58. *Ibid.*, p. 426.

59. *Ibid.*, p. 492.

60. *Ibid.*, p. 558.

61. *Ibid.*, pp. 408, 416.

62. *Ibid.*, p. 407.

63. *Ibid.*, p. 412.

64. *Ibid.*, p. 419.

65. *Ibid.*, p. 438.

66. *Ibid.*, p. 418.

67. *Ibid.*, pp. 419-20.

68. *Ibid.*, p. 465.

69. *Ibid.*, p. 481.

70. This work was published in 1942. It was based on a series of special lectures given at the Law Faculty of Tokyo Imperial University "at the time when negotiations between Japan and the United States had reached the final stage. Right after their completion the Pacific War broke out." Takagi Yasaka, *Beikoku Tōyō seisaku no shiteki kōsatsu* (A Historical Analysis of America's Far Eastern Policy) (Tokyo, 1942), p. 1.

Takagi's critical view of United States Far Eastern policy was in accord with the opinions expressed by such American isolationists as Charles A. Beard and A. Whitney Griswold, of whom Takagi in fact thought highly.

71. *Ibid.*, p. 110.

72. According to Kiyosawa this was because "a nation like Great Britain, with enormous interests in China, would not allow recklessness in legal questions as would the United States." Kiyosawa, *Nihon gaikōshi*, 2:468.

73. *Ibid.*, p. 470.

74. *Ibid.*, p. 622.

75. Kiyosawa Kiyoshi, *Ankoku nikki* (Diary of the Dark Days) (Tokyo, 1965), entry of March 17, 1944, p. 63.

76. Kiyosawa, *Nihon gaikōshi*, 2:407-08.

77. *Ibid.*, p. 501.

78. *Ibid.*, p. 509.

79. He wrote in his diary: "Japan should not have driven Britain from the Asian stage. With Britain there, the two countries could have checked America in East Asia. America would have been no threat. . . . The anti-British movement was the worst possible example of amateur diplomacy." Kiyosawa, *Ankoku nikki*, entry of November 8, 1943, p. 39.

80. Kiyosawa, *Nihon gaikōshi*, 2:470.

81. Shinobu Seizaburō, *Kindai Nihon gaikōshi* (A Diplomatic History of Modern Japan) (Tokyo, 1942), p. 2.

82. *Ibid.*, pp. 276-79.

83. *Ibid.*, p. 280.

84. Kamikawa Hikomatsu, "Tōa ni okeru kyūtaisei to shintaisei" (The Old Order and the New Order in East Asia), *Kokusaihō gaikō zasshi*, 39, no. 4 (April 1940):40, 44.

85. *Ibid.*, pp. 42, 43.

86. Rōyama Masamichi, *Tōa to sekai* (East Asia and the World) (Tokyo, 1941), p. 32.

87. *Ibid.*, p. 3.

88. *Ibid.*, p. 280.

89. *Ibid.*, p. 4.

90. *Ibid.*, p. 10.

91. *Ibid.*, p. 14.

92. *Ibid.*, p. 16.

93. *Ibid.*, pp. 16-17.

94. *Ibid.*, p. 19.

95. *Ibid.*, p. 23.

96. *Ibid.*, p. 229.

97. In his *Shina shisō to Nihon* (Chinese Thought and Japan) (Tokyo, 1938) Tsuda sought, through a comparative study of political and moral thought, religion, and literature, to clarify the cultural dissimilarities between the two countries and disprove the idea of an "Oriental civilization."

98. Rōyama, *Tōa to sekai*, p. 235.

99. *Ibid.*, p. 10.

100. *Ibid.*, p. 113.

101. *Ibid.*, p. 197.

102. For them, the China War acquired new significance on December 8, 1941. See Itō Sei, "Jūnigatsu yōka no kiroku" (Records of December 8), in Shōwa Sensō Bungaku Zenshū Henshū Iinkai (Committee to Compile a Complete Collection of the Wartime Literature of the Shōwa Era), ed., *Shōwa sensō bungaku zenshū 4: Taiheiyō kaisen jūnigatsu yōka* (A Complete Collection of the Wartime Literature of the Shōwa Era 4: The Outbreak of the Pacific War, December 8) (Tokyo, 1964), pp. 213-19.

103. Rōyama, *Tōa to sekai*, p. 355.

104. Ozaki Hotsumi, *Gendai Shina hihan* (Critique of Modern China) (Tokyo, 1938), p. 158.

105. *Ibid.*, pp. 169, 182, 183.

106. Ozaki Hotsumi, *Gendai Shina ron* (On Modern China) (Tokyo, 1939), pp. 211-12.

107. Ozaki Hotsumi, " 'Tōa kyōdōtai' no rinen to sono seiritsu no kyakkanteki kiso" (The Idea of an "East Asian Cooperative Community" and the Objective Basis for its Establishment), 1939, in *Gendai Shina ron* (new ed., Tokyo, 1964), p. 200.

108. *Ibid.*, p. 203.

109. Hosokawa Karoku, *Ajia minzoku seisakuron* (On Asian Racial Policies) (Tokyo, 1940), p. 33.

110. *Ibid.*, p. 41.

111. *Ibid.*, pp. 5-6.

112. Ozaki, *Gendai Shina hihan*, p. 13.

113. Ozaki, *Gendai Shina ron* (1939), p. 65.

114. Ozaki, *Gendai Shina hihan*, p. 138.

115. *Ibid.*, p. 50.

116. Hosokawa, *Ajia minzoku seisakuron*, p. 209.

117. Ozaki, *Gendai Shina ron* (1939), pp. 194-95; Hosokawa, *Ajia minzoku seisakuron*, p. 211.

118. Ozaki, *Gendai Shina hihan*, pp. 382-83.

119. *Ibid.*, p. 138.

120. Hosokawa Karoku, *Shokuminshi* (A History of Colonization) (Tokyo, 1941), p. 545.

121. Hosokawa, *Ajia minzoku seisakuron*, p. 211.

122. Matsushita gave two reasons for studying the Monroe Doctrine from the standpoint of the Greater East Asia International Law. One was the fact that both were opposed to universal international law; the other, that the Monroe Doctrine might serve as a precedent in the "ideological struggle" for the Greater East Asia International Law.

123. Yasui Kaoru, *Ōshū kōiki kokusaihō no kiso rinen* (Basic Concepts of European Regional International Law) (Tokyo, 1942), p. 39.

124. Carl Schmitt, *Über die drei Arten des rechtswissenschaftlichen Denkens* (On the Three Types of Jurisprudential Thinking) (1934).

125. Yasui, pp. 64-65.

126. *Ibid.*, p. 77.

Advisory Council on Foreign Relations	臨時外交調査委員会	Rinji Gaikō Chōsa Iinkai
Agriculture and Commerce, Ministry of	農商務省	Nōshōmushō
Agriculture and Forestry, Ministry of	農林省	Nōrinshō
Aikoku Kakushin Renmei	愛国革新聯盟	Patriotic Renovation League
Aikoku Kinrōtō	愛国勤労党	Patriotic Labor Party
Aikoku Nōmin Dantai Kyōgikai	愛国農民団体協議会	Patriotic Farmers Association Council
Aikoku Rōdōkumiai Zenkoku Konwakai	愛国労働組合全国懇話会	National Council of Patriotic Labor Unions
Aikoku Rōdō Nōmin Dōshikai	愛国労働農民同志会	Patriotic Labor Farmer Comrades Society
Aikoku Seiji Dōmei	愛国政治同盟	Patriotic Political Alliance
Aikokusha	愛国社	Patriotic Society
Aikoku Undō Itchi Kyōgikai	愛国運動一致協議会	Council for a Union of Patriotic Movements
Aikyōjuku	愛郷塾	Institute for Rural Patriotism
All-Party Committee to Renovate the Diet	議会振粛各派委員会	Gikai Shinshuku Kakuha Iinkai
America-Japan Society	日米協会	Nichi-Bei Kyōkai
Anshan Iron Works	鞍山製鉄所	Anzan Seitetsusho
Antung Cement	安東セメント	Antō Semento
Antung Light Metals	安東軽金属	Antō Keikinzoku
Army Academy	陸軍士官学校	Rikugun Shikan Gakkō
Army General Staff	参謀本部	Sanbō Honbu
Committee to Study Preparations for War against the United States	対米戦備研究委員会	Tai-Bei Senbi Kenkyū Iinkai
Operations Division	作戦部	Sakusenbu
Operations Section	作戦課	Sakusenka
Army Ministry	陸軍省	Rikugunshō
Military Affairs Bureau	軍務局	Gunmu Kyoku
Military Affairs Section	軍務課	Gunmuka
Press Office	新聞班	Shinbunhan
Research Office	調査班	Chōsahan
Army Paymaster's School	陸軍経理学校	Rikugun Keiri Gakkō
Army War College	陸軍大学校	Rikugun Daigakkō
Asahi shinbun	朝日新聞	
Asama-maru incident (January 1940)	浅間丸事件	Asama-maru jiken
Asameshikai	朝飯会	Breakfast Club
Asia Development Board	興亜院	Kōain

Asian Students Association	亜細亜学生会	Ajia Gakuseikai
Association for the Renovation of the Foreign Ministry	外務省革新同志会	Gaimushō Kakushin Dōshikai
"The Attitude To Be Adopted by the Imperial Navy under Present Circumstances" (June 1941)	現情勢ニ於テ帝国海軍ノ執ルベキ態度	"Genjōsei ni oite teikoku kaigur no torubeki taido"
Automobile Industry Law	自動車製造事業法	Jidōsha seizō jigyō hō
Banchōkai	番町会	Banchō Club
Bank of Japan Examination Division	日本銀行考査部	Nihon Ginkō Kōsabu
"Basic Principles of National Policy" (June 1936)	国策大綱	"Kokusaku taikō"
beika	米禍	American peril
Beikoku tōyō seisaku no shiteki kōsatsu	米国東洋政策の史的考察	A Historical Analysis of American Far Eastern Policy (by Takagi Yasaka)
Beishū kōiki kokusaihō no kiso rinen	米洲広域国際法の基礎理念	Basic Ideals of American Region International Law (by Matsushita Masatoshi)
betsudō-tai	別動隊	detached column
Blood Brotherhood Incident (1932)	血盟団事件	ketsumeidan jiken
Board of Field Marshals and Admirals of the Fleet	元帥府	Gensuifu
Bōeichō Senshishitsu	防衛庁戦史室	Military History Office (Nationa Defense Agency)
Bōkyō Gokokudan	防共護国団	Anti-Communist National Defense Corps
Bungei shunjū	文芸春秋	
bunka seiji	文化政治	enlightened administration
bunmei no seiji	文明の政治	enlightened administration
Cabinet Advisory Group	内閣参議制	Naikaku Sangisei
Cabinet Deliberative Council	内閣審議会	Naikaku Shingikai
Cabinet Information Bureau	内閣情報局	Naikaku Jōhō Kyoku
Cabinet Information Committee	内閣情報委員会	Naikaku Jōhō Iinkai
Cabinet Information Division	内閣情報部	Naikaku Jōhōbu
"Cabinet Plan" (August 1941)	内閣案	"Naikaku an"
Cabinet Planning Board	企画院	Kikakuin
Cabinet Research Bureau	内閣調査局	Naikaku Chōsa Kyoku
Central Bank of Manchukuo	満州中央銀行	Manshū Chūō Ginkō
Central Bank of the Industrial Association	産業組合中央金庫	Sangyō Kumiai Chūō Kinko
Central China Development Company	中支那振興会社	Naka Shina Shinkō Kaisha
Central Korean Association	中央朝鮮協会	Chūō Chōsen Kyōkai
Chalai Coal Mine	札賚炭鉱	Satsurai Tankō
Changkufeng Incident (1938)	張鼓峯事件	Chōkohō jiken

Cherry Blossom Society	櫻会	Sakurakai
Chikujō kenpō seigi	逐条憲法精義	Commentary on the Constitution (by Minobe Tatsukichi)
China Expeditionary Forces	支那派遣軍	Shina Hakengun
Central China Expeditionary Forces	中支那方面派遣軍	Naka Shina Hōmen Hakengun
China Incident (1937)	支那事変	Shina jihen
Chinchou Pulp	錦州 パルプ	Kinshū Parupu
Chūgai shōgyō	中外商業	
Chūō kōron	中央公論	Central Review
Closed Institutions Liquidation Commission	閉鎖機関整理委員会	Heisa Kikan Seiri Iinkai
Colonial Affairs, Ministry of	拓務省	Takumushō
Combined Fleet	連合艦隊	Rengōkantai
Commerce and Industry, Ministry of	商工省	Shōkōshō
Trade Bureau	貿易局	Bōeki Kyoku
Communications, Ministry of	通信省	Teishinshō
Telegraph and Telephone Bureau	電務局	Denmu Kyoku
Conference of Strategic Industries Control Groups	重要産業統制団体懇話会	Jūyō Sangyō Tōsei Dantai Konwakai
Daidō Kurabu	大同倶楽部	Great Unity Club
Daiichi Bank	第一銀行	Daiichi Ginkō
Daiichi Hikaeshitsu	第一控室	First Chamber Faction
Diamin Kurabu	大民 クラブ	Great People's Club
Dai Nihon Gokokugun	大日本護国軍	Great Japan Defense Corps
Dai Nihon Kokusuikai	大日本国粋会	Great Japan National Essence Society
Dai Nihon Seigidan	大日本正義団	Great Japan Justice Corps
Dai Nihon Seinen Dōmei	大日本青年同盟	Great Japan Youth League
Dai Nihon Seisantō	大日本生産党	Great Japan Production Party
Dai Nihon Sekiseikai	大日本赤誠会	Great Japan True-Hearted Society
Dai Nihon Sekkabōshidan	大日本赤化防止団	Great Japan Anti-Communist Corps
Dairen Shipbuilding Company	大連船渠鉄工	Dairen Senkyo Tekkō
Deliberative Council on Diet Organization	議会制度審議会	Gikai Seido Shingikai
Dōmei Tsūshinsha	同盟通信社	Dōmei News Agency
Domestic Policy Council	内政会議	Naisei Kaigi
Dōwa Automobile Industries	同和自動車工業	Dōwa Jidōsha Kōgyō
East Asia Common Culture Academy	東亜同文書院	Tōa Dōbun Shoin
East Asia Common Culture Association	東亜同文会	Tōa Dōbunkai
East Asia Cooperative Community	東亜協同体	Tōa Kyōdōtai

East Asia League 東亜連盟 Tōa Renmei

Eastern Manchuria Industries 東満州産業 Higashi Manshū Sangyō

Education, Ministry of 文部省 Monbushō

   Religious Bureau 宗教局 Shūkyō Kyoku

"The Essence of National Defense and Proposals to Strengthen It" (October 1934) 国防の本義と其強化の提唱 "Kokubō no hongi to sono kyōka no teishō"

"Evaluation of Conditions In Late Autumn 1931 and Some Remedial Policies" 昭和六年秋末における情勢判断同対策 "Shōwa rokunen akimatsu ni okeru jōsei handan dō taisaku"

"An Evaluation of the Situation" (by Itagaki Seishirō, 1932) 情勢判断 "Jōsei handan"

February 26 Incident (1936) 二二六事件 ni-ni-roku jiken

Federation of Japanese Chambers of Commerce 全国商業会議所 Zenkoku Shōgyō Kaigisho

Fellowship for the Limitation of Armaments 軍備縮少同志会 Gunbi Shukushō Dōshikai

Finance Ministry 大蔵省 Ōkurashō

   Finance Section 金融課 Kin'yūka

   Foreign Exchange Bureau 為替局 Kawase Kyoku

   Foreign Exchange Control Division 外国為替管理部 Gaikoku Kawase Kanribu

First/Second/Third Committee 第一,第二,第三委員会 Daiichi/Daini/Daisan Iinkai

First Movement for Constitutional Government 第一次護憲運動 daiichiji goken undō

First Submarine Squadron 第一潜水戦隊 Daiichi Sensui Sentai

Five Ministers Conference 五相会議 Goshō Kaigi

Five Year Plan for the Industrialization of Manchuria (June 1936) 満州国産業五ヶ年計画 Manshūkoku sangyō gokanen keikaku

Foreign Ministry 外務省 Gaimushō

   America Bureau 亜米利加局 Amerika Kyoku

   Asia Bureau 亜細亜局 Ajiya Kyoku

   Cultural Affairs Division 文化事業部 Bunka Jigyōbu

   East Asia Bureau 東亜局 Tōa Kyoku

   Europe-America Bureau 欧米局 Ō-Bei Kyoku

   Europe-Asia Bureau 欧亜局 Ō-A Kyoku

   International Trade Bureau 通商局 Tsūshō Kyoku

   Political Affairs Bureau 政務局 Seimu Kyoku

   Public Information Division 情報部 Jōhōbu

   Research Division 調査部 Chōsabu

   Secretariat 官房 Kanbō

   South Seas Bureau 南洋局 Nanyō Kyoku

   Treaties Bureau 条約局 Jōyaku Kyoku

Four Ministers Conference 四相会議 Yonshō Kaigi

Four Year Plan for the Expansion of the Industrial Capacity of Japan (January 1931) 生産力拡充四ヶ年計画 Seisanryoku kakujū yonkanen keikaku

Friends for Peace in the Far East 極東平和の友の会 Kyokutō Heiwa no Tomo no Kai

Fuchow Mining Company 復州鉱業 Fukushū Kōgyō

Fuhsin Coal Mine 阜新炭鉱 Fushin Tankō

"Fundamentals of National Policy" (August 1936) 国策の基準 "Kokusaku no kijun"

Fushun Cement Company 撫順セメント Bujun Semento

Fushun Coal Mine 撫川順炭鉱 Bujun Tankō

Gaikō jihō 外交時報 Revue Diplomatique

Gakushūin 学習院 Peers School

gekokujō 下剋上 rule from below

Gendai kensei hyōron 現代憲政評論 Critique of Modern Constitutional Government (by Minobe Tatsukichi)

General National Mobilization Law (1938) 国家総動員法 Kokka sōdōin hō

"General Outline of a Program for the Economic Construction of Japan, Manchukuo, and China" (November 1940) 日満支経済建設要綱 "Nichi-Man-Shi keizai kensetsu yōkō"

"General Outline of a Program for the Economic Construction of Manchukuo" (1933, 1936) 満州経済建設要綱 "Manshū keizai kensetsu yōkō"

"General Plan for the Establishment of Heavy Industries in Manchuria" (October 1937) 満州重工業確立要綱 "Manshū jūkōgyō kakuritsu yōkō"

Genyōsha 玄洋社 Dark Ocean Society

Gikai seiji no kentō 議会政治の検討 Examination of Parliamentary Government (by Minobe Tatsukichi)

Go-ka-jō Seigan Kisei Dōmeikai 五ヶ条請願期成同盟会 Alliance to Achieve Our Five Demands

grand chamberlain 侍従長 jijūchō

Greater East Asia Coprosperity Sphere 大東亜共栄圏 Dai Tōa Kyōeiken

Greater Japan Association for Service to the State through Industry 大日本産業報国会 Dai Nihon Sangyō Hōkokukai

Hachigatsukai 八月会 August Society

Hao-kang Coal Mine 鶴岡炭鉱 Haokang Tankō

Harbin Cement ハルピン・セメント Harupin Semento

Heaven-Sent Soldiers Unit Incident (July 1933) 神兵隊事件 shinpeitai jiken

Hōchi 報知

Home Affairs, Ministry of 内務省 Naimushō

　　Peace Preservation Section 保安課 Hoanka

Police Bureau	警保局	Keiho Kyoku
Publications Section	図書課	Toshoka
Hoshigaoka Kondankai	星ヶ岡懇談会	Hoshigaoka Forum
House of Peers	貴族院	Kizokuin
Accounts Committee	決算委員会	Kessan Iinkai
Budget Committee	予算委員会	Yosan Iinkai
Discipline Committee	懲罰委員会	Chōbatsu Iinkai
Petition Committee	請願委員会	Seigan Iinkai
Screening Committee	資格審査委員会	Shikaku Shinsa Iinkai
House of Representatives	衆議院	Shugiin
Accounts Committee	決算委員会	Kessan Iinkai
Budget Committee	予算委員会	Yosan Iinkai
Discipline Committee	懲罰委員会	Chōbatsu Iinkai
Petition Committee	請願委員会	Seigan Iinkai
Representation Committee	建議委員会	Kengi Iinkai
Imperial Conference	御前会議	Gozen Kaigi
Imperial Education Association	帝国教育会	Teikoku Kyōikukai
Imperial Headquarters-Cabinet Liaison Conference	大本営・政府連絡会議	Daihon'ei-Seifu Renraku Kaigi
"Imperial National Defense Policy" (1907)	帝国国防方針	"Teikoku kokubō hōshin"
Imperial Reservists Association	帝国在郷軍人会	Teikoku Zaigō Gunjinkai
Imperial Rule Assistance Association	大政翼賛会	Taisei Yokusankai
Imperial Rule Assistance Diet	翼賛議会	Yokusan Gikai
Imperial Way	皇道	kōdō
Industrial Bank of Manchukuo	満州興業銀行	Manshū Kōgyō Ginkō
inspector general of military education	教育総監	kyōiku sōkan
International Association of Japan	日本国際協会	Nihon Kokusai Kyōkai
International Education Association	国際教育協会	Kokusai Kyōiku Kyōkai
International Press Association	国際新聞協会	Kokusai Shinbun Kyōkai
International Service Bureau	国際通信局	Kokusai Tsūshin Kyoku
Interparty Council	各派交渉会	Kakuha Kōshōkai
ishin seitō kessei junbikai	維新政党結成準備会	
Japan Broadcasting Association	日本放送協会	Nihon Hōsōkyōkai (NHK)
Japan-China Academic Society	日華学会	Nikka Gakkai
Japan Christian Association	日本基督教団	Nihon Kirisuto Kyōdan
Japan Christian League	日本基督教連盟	Nihon Kirisutokyō Renmei
Japan Communist Party	日本共産党	Nihon Kyōsantō
Japan Economic Federation	日本経済連盟会	Nihon Keizai Renmeikai
Administrative Section	総務課	Sōmuka
Business Section	事業課	Jigyōka

Editorial Division	編集部	Henshūbu
Executive Office for External Relations	対外事務局	Taigai Jimukyoku
External Relations Committee	対外委員会	Taigai Iinkai
Research Section	調査課	Chōsaka
Japan Industrialists Club	日本工業倶楽部	Nihon Kōgyō Kurabu
Japan League of Peace Movements	平和運動日本連盟	Heiwa Undō Nihon Renmei
Japan-Manchuria Flour Mill	日満製粉	Nichi-Man Seifun
Japan-Manchuria Magnesium Company	日満マグネシウム	Nichi-Man Maguneshūmu
Japan-Manchuria Pulp Manufacturing	日満パルプ製造	Nichi-Man Parupu Seizō
Japan-Manchuria Steel Tubing	日満鋼管	Nichi-Man Kōkan
Japan Peace Society	大日本平和協会	Dai Nihon Heiwa Kyōkai
"Japan's Rapid Development and Pressures from Foreign Powers" (July 1934)	躍進日本と列強の重圧	"Yakushin Nihon to rekkyō no jūatsu"
Japan Trade Association	日本貿易協会	Nihon Bōeki Kyōkai
Japanese-American Relations Committee	日米関係委員会	Nichi-Bei Kankei Iinkai
Japanese-American Trade Council	日米通商評議会	Nichi-Bei Tsūshō Hyōgikai
Japanese Bar Association	日本弁護士協会	Nihon Bengoshi Kyōkai
Japanese-British Trade Committee	日英通商委員会	Nichi-Ei Tsūshō Iinkai
Japanese Immigrants Association	日本移民協会	Nihon Imin Kyōkai
Jiji shinpō	時事新報	
Jikishin Dōjō	直心道場	Pure Heart Seminary
Jikyoku kokusaihōron	時局国際法論	International Law and the Current Situation (by Tachi Sakutarō)
Jikyoku Kyōgikai	時局協議会	Society for the Discussion of Current Affairs
Jinmukai	神武会	Jinmu Society
Jinmu Seinentai	神武青年隊	Jinmu Youth Band
jōmu rijikai	常務理事会	executive board
jōnin iinkai	常任委員会	standing committee
Junsei Ishin Kyōdō Seinentai	純正維新共同青年隊	Pure Restoration Youth Corps
junsei Nipponshugi	純正日本主義	pure Nipponist
Junsei Nipponshugi Seinen Undō Zenkoku Kyōgikai	純正日本主義青年運動全国協議会	Nationwide Council of Pure Nipponist Youth Movements
Jūō Kurabu	縦横倶楽部	Acting at Will Club
jūshin	重臣	senior statesmen
Justice Ministry	司法省	Shihōshō
Criminal Affairs Bureau	刑事局	Keiji Kyoku
Kaizō	改造	Reconstruction
Kakumeisō	鶴鳴荘	Society of the Cry of the Crane
Kakushin Kurabu	革新倶楽部	Reform Club

Kamakura-maru 鎌倉丸

Kang-te Mining 康徳鉱業 Kōtoku Kōgyō

Keizai Dantai Rengōkai zenshi 経済団体連合会前史 Early History of the Federation of Economic Organizations

Keizai renmei 経済連盟 Economic Federation

kengi 建議 representations

Kenkokukai 建国会 National Founding Society

Kenpei 憲兵 military police

Kenpō satsuyō 憲法撮要 Essentials of the Constitution (by Minobe Tatsukichi)

Kenseikai 憲政会 Constitutional Association

ketsugi 決議 resolutions

Kindai Nihon gaikōshi 近代日本外交史 A Diplomatic History of Modern Japan (by Shinobu Seizaburō)

Kinrō Nihontō 勤労日本党 Laboring Japan Party

Kirin Synthetic Oil 吉林人造石油 Kitsurin Jinzō Sekiyu

Kōa Dōshikai 興亜同志会 Asian Development Comrades Society

Kōain 興亜院 Asia Development Board

kō buin 甲部員 staff officer A

Kōchisha 行地社 Society to Carry Out Heaven's Way

Kōdōha 皇道派 Imperial Way faction

Kōdōkai 皇道会 Imperial Way Society

kōdo kokubō kokka 高度国防国家 advanced national defense state

Kōfūjuku 皇風塾 Imperial Way Institute

kōgi kokubō 広義国防 broad national defense

"Kokka no risō" 国家の理想 The Ideal of a Nation (by Yanaihara Tadao)

Kokka Shakaishugi Seinen Dōmei 国家社会主義青年同盟 National Socialist Youth League

Kokkashugi dantai no dōkō ni kansuru chōsa 国家主義団体の動向に関する調査 Report on an Investigation of Trends in the Activities of Nationalist Organizations

Kokka to shūkyō 国家と宗教 State and Religion (by Tagawa Daikichirō)

Kōkoku Jichikai 興国自治会 Autonomous Council for Reviving the Nation

Kōkoku Nōmin Dōmei 皇国農民同盟 Imperial Farmers Alliance

Kokuhonsha 国本社 National Foundation Society

Kokumin Dōmei 国民同盟 Nationalist League

Kokumin Kyōkai 国民協会 Nationalist Association

Kokumin Kyōryoku Kaigi 国民協力会議 Council for National Cooperation

Kokumin Nihontō 国民日本党 Japan Nationalist Party

Kokumin Seishin Sōdōin Chūō Renmei 国民精神総動員中央聯盟 Alliance to Mobilize the National Spirit

Kokumin shinbun 国民新聞

Kokumintō (Rikken Kokumintō)	国民党（立憲国民党）	Constitutional Nationalist Party
kokumu	国務	affairs of state
Kokunan Dakai Rengō Kyōgikai	国難打開聯合協議会	Joint Council to Solve the National Crisis
Kokuryūkai	黒龍会	Amur River Society
Kokusai chishiki	国際知識	International Knowledge
kokusai chūkan chiiki	国際中間地域	international buffer area
Kokusai Hankyō Renmei	国際反共聯盟	International Anti-Communist League
Kokusai Tsūshinsha	国際通信社	International News Agency
Kokushikan	国士館	
Kokusui Taishūtō	国粋大衆党	National Essence Mass Party
kokutai	国体	national polity
kokutai meichō mondai	国体明徴問題	issue of the clarification of national polity
Kokutai Meichō Tassei Renmei	国体明徴達成聯盟	League for the Clarification of National Polity
Kokutai Yōgo Rengōkai	国体擁護聯合会	Joint Association to Defend the National Polity
K'uan-ch'eng-tzu	寛城子	
Kuomintang	国民党	Nationalist Party
Kwantung Army	関東軍	Kantōgun
Kyokoku Itchi Renmei	挙国一致聯盟	National Unity League
Kyōwa Industries	協和工業	Kyōwa Kōgyō
Kyūdō	求道	Search for the Way
kyūtaisei-teki	旧体制的	old school
Law for Protection against and Surveillance of the Holders of Dangerous Thoughts (1936)	思想犯保護観察法	Shisōhan hogo kansatsu hō
League of Nations Association of Japan	日本国際連盟協会	Nihon Kokusai Renmei Kyōkai
lord keeper of the privy seal	内大臣	naidaijin
Lungyen Iron Ore Mine	龍烟鉄鉱	Ryūen Tekkō
"Main Principles for Coping with the Changing World Situation" (July 1940)	世界情勢の推移に伴う時局処理要綱	"Sekai jōsei no suii ni tomonau jikyoku shori yōkō"
Mainichi shinbun	毎日新聞	
Manchukuo Investment Securities Company	満州投資証券	Manshū Tōshi Shōken
Manchukuo News Agency	満州国通信社	Manshūkoku Tsūshinsha
Manchuria Aircraft Manufacturing	満州飛行機製造	Manshū Hikōki Seizō
Manchuria Arsenal	満州工廠	Manshū Kōshō
Manchuria Automobile Manufacturing	満州自動車製造	Manshū Jidōsha Seizō
Manchuria Aviation	満州航空	Manshū Kōkū
Manchuria Bean Stalk Pulp Company	満州豆稈パルプ	Manshū Tōkan Parupu

Manchuria Bearing Industries	満州 ベアリング製造	Manshū Bearingu Seizō
Manchuria Cast Steel Works	満州 鋳鋼所	Manshū Chūkōsho
Manchuria Cement	満州 セメント	Manshū Semento
Manchuria Chemical Industries Company	満州 化学工業	Manshū Kagaku Kōgyō
Manchuria Coal Liquefaction Research Institute	満州石炭液化研究所	Manshū Sekitan Ekika Kenkyūsho
Manchuria Coal Mine	満州炭鉱	Manshū Tankō
Manchuria Colonial Development Company	満州拓殖公社	Manshū Takushoku Kōsha
Manchuria Communications Machinery	満州通信機	Manshū Tsūshinki
Manchuria Electric Chemicals Industries	満州電気化学工業	Manshū Denki Kagaku Kōgyō
Manchuria Electric Industries Company	満州電業	Manshū Dengyō
Manchuria Foundry	満州鋳物	Manshū Imono
Manchuria Gold Mining Company	満州採金	Manshū Saikin
Manchuria Heavy Industries Development Corporation	満州重工業開発株式会社	Manshū Jūkōgyō Kaihatsu Kabushiki Kaisha
Manchuria Heavy Machinery	満州重機	Manshū Jūki
Manchuria Hitachi Manufacturing	満州日立製作所	Manshū Hitachi Seisakusho
Manchuria Iron Works	満州製鉄	Manshū Seitetsu
Manchuria Kubota Cast Steel Tubing	満州久保田鋳鋼管	Manshū Kubota Chūkōkan
Manchuria Lead Mining Company	満州鉛鉱	Manshū Enkō
Manchuria Light Metals Manufacturing Company	満州軽金属製造	Manshū Keikinzoku Seizō
Manchuria Mining	満州鉱山	Manshū Kōzan
Manchuria Mining Development Company	満州鉱業開発	Manshū Kōgyō Kaihatsu
Manchuria Mitsubishi Machinery	満州三菱機器	Manshū Mitsubishi Kiki
Manchuria Oils and Fats	満州油脂	Manshū Yushi
Manchuria Onoda Cement	満州小野田セメント	Manshū Onoda Semento
Manchuria Petroleum Company	満州石油	Manshū Sekiyu
Manchuria Powder Industries	満州火薬工業	Manshū Kayaku Kōgyō
Manchuria Pulp Manufacturing	満州パルプ工業	Manshū Parupu Kōgyō
Manchuria Salt Industry	満州塩業	Manshū Engyō
Manchuria Soda Company	満州曹達	Manshū Sōda
Manchuria Soybean Chemical Industries	満州大豆化学工業	Manshū Daizu Kagaku Kōgyō

Manchuria Special Paper Manufacturing Company	満州特殊製紙	Manshū Tokushu Seishi
Manchuria Sugar Manufacturing	満州製糖	Manshū Seitō
Manchuria Sumitomo Steel Tubing	満州住友鋼管	Manshū Sumitomo Kōkan
Manchuria Synthetic Fuels	満州合成燃料	Manshū Gōsei Nenryō
Manchuria Telegraph and Telephone Company	満州電信電話	Manshū Denshin Denwa
Manchuria Vehicle	満州車輛	Manshū Sharyō
Manchuria-Yalu River Hydroelectric Power Plant	満州鴨緑江水電	Manshū Ōryokkō Suiden
Manchurian Incident (September 1931)	満州事変	Manshū jihen
Man-Mō tokushu ken'ekiron	満蒙特殊権益論	A Treatise on Special Interests in Manchuria and Mongolia (by Shinobu Junpei)
March Incident (1931)	三月事件	sangatsu jiken
Marco Polo Bridge Incident (July 7, 1937)	蘆溝橋事件	rokōkyō jiken
Matsukata Nisso Oil Company	松方日ソ石油	Matsukata Nisso Sekiyu
May 15 Incident (1932)	五一五事件	go-ichi-go jiken
Meirinkai	明倫会	Society of Enlightened Ethics
Metropolitan Police Board	警視庁	Keishichō
Minseitō (Rikken Minseitō)	民政党（立憲民政党）	Constitutional Democratic Party
Minzoku to heiwa	民族と平和	The Nation and Peace (by Yanaihara Tadao)
Mishan Coal Mine	密山炭鉱	Mishan Tankō
Mitsubishi Gōshi	三菱合資	Mitsubishi Combine
Mitsubishi Oil Company	三菱石油	Mitsubishi Sekiyu
Mitsui Bussan	三井物産	Mitsui Trading Company
Mitsui Gōmei	三井合名	Mitsui Combine
Mukden Arsenal	奉天造兵所	Hōten Zōheisho
Mukden Manufacturing	奉天製作所	Hōten Seisakusho
Mukyōkai	無教会	Non-Church Movement
National Federation of Industrial Organizations	全国産業団体連合会	Zenkoku Sangyō Dantai Rengōkai
National Policy Deliberative Council	国策審議会	Kokusaku Shingikai
"National Policy of the Empire" (October 1934)	帝国国策	"Teikoku kokusaku"
National Society for Learning	国民学術協会	Kokumin Gakujutsu Kyōkai
Naval Academy	海軍兵学校	Kaigun Heigakkō
Naval Aviation Headquarters	航空本部	Kōkū Honbu
Technical Division	技術部	Gijutsubu
Navy General Staff	軍令部	Gunreibu
Intelligence Division	情報部	Jōhōbu
Naval Ordnance Bureau	兵備局	Heibi Kyoku

Operations Division	作戦部	Sakusenbu
Operations Section	作戦課	Sakusenka
Section Chiefs Conference	課長会議	Kachō Kaigi
Navy Ministry	海軍省	Kaigunshō
Bureau Chiefs Conference	局長会議	Kyokuchō Kaigi
Information Division	軍事普及部	Gunji Fukyūbu
Mobilization Section	動員課	Dōinka
Naval Affairs Bureau	軍務局	Gunmu Kyoku
Naval Ordnance Bureau	兵備局	Heibi Kyoku
Research Section	調査課	Chōsaka
Secretariat	官房	Kanbō
Navy War College	海軍大学校	Kaigun Daigakkō
New Order in East Asia	東亜新秩序	Tōa Shinchitsujo
Nichi-Doku-I Gunji Dōmei Yōsei Zenkoku Seinen Renmei	日独伊軍事同盟要請全国青年聯盟	Nationwide Youth League to Demand a Military Alliance with Germany and Italy
Nigatsukai	二月会	February Society
Nihon Denpō Tsūshinsha	日本電報通信社	Japan Telegraph News Agency
Nihon Gaikō Kyōkai	日本外交協会	Japan Council on Foreign Affai
Nihon gaikōshi	日本外交史	A Diplomatic History of Japan (by Kiyosawa Kiyoshi)
Nihon Industrial Company	日本産業株式会社	Nihon Sangyō Kabushiki Kaish (Nissan)
Nihon kaizō hōan taikō	日本改造法案大綱	General Outline of Measures fo the Reconstruction of Japan (by Kita Ikki)
Nihon Kakushintō	日本革新党	Japan Reform Party
Nihon kenpō no kihonshugi	日本憲法の基本主義	Basic Principles of the Japanese Constitution (by Minobe Tatsukichi)
Nihon Kōdōkai	日本弘道会	Society to Spread the Way of Heaven
Nihon Kokka Shakaishugi Gakumei	日本国家社会主義学盟	Japan National Socialist Studen League
Nihon Kokka Shakaitō	日本国家社会党	Japan National Socialist Party
Nihon Musantō	日本無産党	Japan Proletarian Party
Nihon Rōdō Kumiai Zenkoku Hyōgikai	日本労働組合全国評議会	National Council of Japanese Labor Unions
Nihon Yūsen (NYK)	日本郵船	
Nippon Kokumintō	日本国民党	Japan Nationalist Party
Nippon Rōdō Kurabu	日本労働倶楽部	Japan Labor Club
Nippon Rōdō Sōdōmei	日本労働総同盟	Japan General Federation of Labor
Nipponshugi Bunka Dōmei	日本主義文化同盟	Alliance for a Nipponist Culture
Nipponshugi Seinen Kaigi	日本主義青年会議	Nipponist Youth Council
Nirokukai	二六会	Twenty-Sixth Day Club
Nishichikai	二七会	Twenty-Seventh Day Club

Nissan Automobile Company	日産自動車株式会社	Nissan Jidōsha Kabushiki Kaisha
Nomonhan Incident (1939)	ノモンハン事件	Nomonhan jiken
North China Transportation Company	華北交通	Kahoku Kotsū
November 20 Incident (1934)	十一月二十日事件	jūichigatsu hatsuka jiken
October Incident (1931)	十月事件	jūgatsu jiken
ōdō	王道	kingly rule
"Outline for Foreign Policy" (1939)	対外施策方針要綱	"Taigai shisaku hōshin yōkō"
"Outline of Disciplinary Policy for the Diet" (July 1932)	議会振肅要綱	"Gikai shinshuku yōkō"
"Outline of Policy toward America" (1939)	対米外交施策案	"Tai-Bei gaikō shisaku an"
Overseas Japanese Newspaper Association	海外邦字新聞協会	Kaigai Hōji Shinbun Kyōkai
Peace Preservation Law (1925)	治安維持法	Chian iji hō
Pen-chi-lu Special Steel	本溪湖特殊鋼	Honkeiko Tokushukō
Pen-chi Region Coal Mine	溪域炭鉱	Keiiki Tankō
Petroleum Industry Law (March 1934)	石油業法	Sekiyugyō hō
Petroleum Monopoly Law (Manchukuo, November 1934)	石油専売法	Sekiyu senbai hō
"Plan for the Settlement of Manchurian Problems" (March 1932)	満州問題解決案	"Manshū mondai kaiketsuan"
"Policies for Adjusting to New Japan-China Relations" (November 1938)	日支新関係調整方針	"Nisshi shin kankei chōsei hōshin"
Popular Front Incident	人民戦線事件	jinmin sensen jiken
Popular Rights Movement	自由民権運動	jiyū minken undō
Privy Council	枢密院	Sūmitsuin
Railways, Ministry of	鉄道省	Tetsudōshō
"Regulations Concerning the Mutual Jurisdiction of the Navy Ministry and the Navy General Staff"	省・部事務互渉規定	"Shō-Bu jimu goshō kitei"
Renmei jihō	連盟事報	Current News of the League
Research Committee on Diet Organization	議院制度調査会	Giin Seido Chōsakai
"Resolution on the National Polity" (March 1935)	国体ニ関スル決議	"Kokutai ni kansuru ketsugi"
right of supreme command	統帥権	tōsuiken
Rikken Yōseikai	立憲養正会	Society for the Cultivation of Constitutional Justice
rikugun yōnen gakkō	陸軍幼年学校	military preparatory schools
Rōdō Nōmintō	労働農民党	Labor-Farmer Party
Rōsōkai	老壮会	Society of Young and Old
"Rules of the Navy General Staff"	軍令部条例	"Gunreibu jōrei"

Saitama Young Patriotic Volunteers	救国埼玉青年挺身隊	Kyūkoku Saitama Seinen Teishintai
sakubun shugi	作文主義	emphasis on literary style
San-ka-jō Seigan Kisei Dōmeikai	三ヶ条請願期成同盟会	Alliance to Achieve Our Three Demands
sanseikan	参政官	
sanyokan	参与官	
sayoku	左翼	left wing
Second Movement for Constitutional Government	第二次護憲運動	dainiji goken undō
Seiji Kakushin Kyōgikai	政治革新協議会	Political Reform Council
Seikyō Ishin Renmei	政教維新聯盟	League for Restoration of Political Education
Seinen Ajia Renmei	青年亜細亜聯盟	Asian Youth League
Seisen Kantetsu Dōmei	聖戦貫徹同盟	Alliance for Total Victory in the Holy War
Seiyūkai (Rikken Seiyūkai)	政友会(立憲政友会)	Friends of Constitutional Justice Association
Sekai no Nihon	世界の日本	Japan in the World
Sekai to warera	世界と我等	The World and Ourselves
Shakai Minshūtō	社会民衆党	Social Mass Party
Shakai Taishūtō	社会大衆党	Social Mass Party
Shakai undō no jōkyō	社会運動の状況	The Current State of Social Movements
Shichishōsha	七生社	Seven Lives Society
Shinbun Rengōsha	新聞連合社	Associated Press
Shin Nihon Kokumin Dōmei	新日本国民同盟	New Japan National League
shin taisei undō	新体制運動	new political structure moveme
Shintōsha	振東社	Society to Arouse the East
Shiryō Chōsakai	史料調査会	Documentary Research Society
Shisō shiryō panfuretto	思想資料パンフレット	Materials on Thought Studies
shitsugi	質疑	questions
shitsumon	質問	interpellations
Shinzanjuku	紫山塾	Purple Mountain Institute
shōgyō kaigisho	商業会議所	chamber of commerce
shōkō kaigisho	商工会議所	chamber of commerce and industry
Shōtoku Mining	昭徳鉱業	Shōtoku Kōgyō
Shōwakai	昭和会	Shōwa Society
Shōwa Kenkyūkai	昭和研究会	Shōwa Research Society
Shōwa Steel Works	昭和製鋼所	Shōwa Seikōsho
Sian Coal Mine	西安炭鉱	Seian Tankō
"The Significance of Japan's Continental Policy from the Viewpoint of Cultural History"	大陸政策の文化史的意義	"Tairiku seisaku no bunkashi teki igi" (by Shiratori Toshio

South Manchuria Railway Company	南満州鉄道株式会社	Minami Manshū Tetsudō Kabushiki Kaisha
State Affairs, Ministry of (Manchukuo)	国務院	Kokumuin
General Affairs Bureau	総務庁	Sōmuchō
"Study of Strategy and Tactics in Operations against the United States" (November 1936)	対米作戦用兵ニ関スル研究	"Tai-Bei sakusen yōhei ni kansuru kenkyū"
Suikōsha	水交社	Navy League
Supreme War Council	軍事参議官会議	Gunji Sangikan Kaigi
Tactical Plan	用兵綱領	Yōhei kōryō
Tai-Bei Seisaku Shingi Iinkai	対米政業審議委員会	Committee to Deliberate Policies toward the United States
Tai-Ei Dōshikai	対英同志会	Anti-British Comrades Society
taikan kyohō shugi	大艦巨砲主義	principle of huge battleships and big guns
Taisei Yokusankai Junka Yūshi Kondankai	大政翼賛会純化有志懇談会	Volunteers Council to Purify the the IRAA
Tai-Shi mondai	対支問題	The China Question (by Yoshino Sakuzō)
Tai-So Dōshikai	対ソ同志会	Anti-Soviet Comrades Society
Talien Coal Mine	塔連炭鉱	Tōren Tankō
Ta-t'ung Coal Mine	大同炭鉱	Daidō Tankō
Ta-t'ung Colliery	大同洋炭	Daidō Yōtan
Tenkōkai	天行会	Society for Heavenly Action
Textile Federation	紡績連合会	Bōseki Rengōkai
Three Ministry Officials Conference	三省事務当局会議	Sanshō Jimutōkyoku Kaigi
Tōa Kensetsu Kokumin Renmei	東亜建設国民連盟	National Alliance for the Reconstruction of East Asia
Tōhōkai	東方会	Eastern Society
Tokkō	特高	thought police
Tokyo Chamber of Commerce	東京商業会議所	Tōkyō Shōgyō Kaigisho
Tokyo College of Foreign Languages	東京外国語学校	Tōkyō Gaikokugo Gakkō
Tokyo Institute of Politics and Economics	東京政治経済研究所	Tōkyō Seiji Keizai Kenkyūjo
Tōkyō nichi-nichi shinbun	東京日日新聞	
Tōseiha	統制派	Control faction
Total War Research Institute	総力戦研究所	Sōryokusen Kenkyūjo
Tōtenjuku	統天塾	Institute for Controlling Heaven's Way
Tōyō jiyū shinbun	東洋自由新聞	
Tōyō keizai shinpō	東洋経済新報	Oriental Economist
Tōyō Synthetic Fiber	東洋人織	Tōyō Jinsen
Toyoda Automatic Loom Manufacturing Company	豊田自動織機製作所	Toyoda Jidōshokki Seisakusho

Ushiō-no-kai	潮の会	Rising Tide Society
uyoku	右翼	right wing
Welfare, Ministry of	厚生省	Kōseishō
Women's Peace Association	婦人平和協会	Fujin Heiwa Kyōkai
World Christian League	基督教世界連盟	Kirisutokyō Sekai Renmei
yaji	弥次	supporter
Yamashita Shipping Company	山下汽船	Yamashita Kisen
Ying-k'ou	営口	
yōgeki sakusen	邀撃作戦	strategy of interceptive operations
Yōkakai	八日会	Eighth Day Club
Yokohama Specie Bank	横浜正金銀行	Yokohama Shōkin Ginkō
Yūzonsha	猶存社	Society of Those Who Yet Remain
Zenkoku Rōdō Kumiai Dōmei	全国労働組合同盟	National Labor Union Federation
Zenkoku Rōnō Taishūtō	全国労農大衆党	National Labor-Farmer Mass Party
Zen Nihon Aikokusha Kyōdōtōsō Kyōgikai	全日本愛国者共同闘争協議会	All-Japan Patriots Joint Struggle Council
zentaishugi	全体主義	totalitarianism

GLOSSARY OF PERSONAL NAMES

Abe Isamu	阿部 勇	Chō Yukio	長 幸男
Abe Isoo	安部 磯雄	Dan Takuma	団 琢磨
Abe Moritarō	阿部 守太郎	Date Gen'ichirō	伊達 源一郎
Abe Nobuyuki	阿部 信行	Debuchi Katsuji	出淵 勝次
Abe Shinnosuke	阿部 真之助	Doihara Kenji	土肥原 賢二
Abo Kiyokazu	安保 清種	Ebara Soroku	江原 素六
Adachi Kenzō	安達 謙蔵	Etō Genkurō	江藤 源九郎
Aizawa Saburō	相沢 三郎	Fujii Hitoshi	藤井 斉
Akao Bin	赤尾 敏	Fujii Shigeru	藤井 茂
Akashi Teruo	明石 照男	Fujimura Nobuo	藤村 信男
Akita Kiyoshi	秋田 清	Fujisawa Takeyoshi	藤沢 武義
Akiyama Teisuke	秋山 定輔	Fujiwara Akira	藤原 彰
Amano Tatsuo	天野 辰夫	Fujiyama Aiichirō	藤山 愛一郎
Amaya Kikuo	雨谷 菊夫	Fujiyama Raita	藤山 雷太
Amō (Amau) Eiji	天羽 英二	Fukai Eigo	深井 英五
Anami Korechika	阿南 惟幾	Fukudome Shigeru	福留 繁
Anesaki Masaharu	姉崎 正治	Fukui Kikusaburō	福井 菊三郎
Aoki Kamatarō	青木 鎌太郎	Funatsu Shin'ichirō	船津 辰一郎
Aoki Kazuo	青木 一男	Fushimi Hiroyasu (Prince)	伏見宮 博恭
Aoki Morio	青木 盛夫	Gō Seinosuke	郷 誠之助
Arahata Kanson	荒畑 寒村	Godō Takuo	伍堂 卓雄
Araki Eikichi	新木 栄吉	Gotō Fumio	後藤 文夫
Araki Sadao	荒木 貞夫	Gotō Ryūnosuke	後藤 隆之助
Arima Ryōkitsu	有馬 良橘	Gotō Shinpei	後藤 新平
Arima Yoriyasu	有馬 頼寧	Hamada Kunimatsu	浜田 国松
Arisawa Hiromi	有沢 広巳	Hamaguchi Osachi (Yūkō)	浜口 雄幸
Arita Hachirō	有田 八郎	Hanihara Masanao	埴原 正直
Ariyoshi Akira	有吉 明	Hara Takashi (Kei)	原 敬
Asada Sadao	麻田 貞雄	Hara Yoshimichi	原 嘉道
Ashida Hitoshi	芦田 均	Harada Kumao	原田 熊雄
Asō Hisashi	麻生 久	Harada Tasuku	原田 助
Ayukawa Gisuke (Yoshisuke)	鮎川 義介	Haraguchi Hatsutarō	原口 初太郎
Ayusawa Iwao	鮎沢 巌	Hasegawa Nyozekan	長谷川 如是閑
Baba Eiichi	馬場 鍈一	Hashimoto Kingorō	橋本 欣五郎
Baba Tsunego	馬場 恒吾	Hata Hikosaburō	秦 彦三郎
Banno Tsuneyoshi	坂野 常善	Hata Shunroku	畑 俊六
Chang Hsueh-liang	張 学良	Hatakeyama Toshiyuki	畠山 敏行
Chang Tso-lin	張 作霖	Hatoyama Ichirō	鳩山 一郎
Chiang Kai-shek (Chieh-shih)	蒋 介石	Hatsuta Yoshiaki	八田 嘉明
Chichiba Keitarō	千々波 敬太郎	Hattori Takushirō	服部 卓四郎
Ch'in Te-ch'un	秦 徳純	Hayashi Kaoru	林 馨

761

Hayashi Kiroku	林 毅陸
Hayashi Senjūrō	林 銑十郎
Higashikuni Naruhiko (Prince)	東久邇宮稔彦
Hioki Eki	日置 益
Hiraide Hideo	平出 英夫
Hirakawa Masatoshi	平川 正寿
Hiranuma Kiichirō	平沼 騏一郎
Hirohito (Emperor)	裕仁
Hirose Hōsaku	広瀬 豊作
Hirota Kōki	広田 弘毅
Ho Ying-ch'in	何應欽
Homma Ken'ichirō	本間 憲一郎
Honjō Shigeru	本庄 繁
Honryō Shinjirō	本領 信次郎
Hori Teikichi	堀 悌吉
Horinouchi Kensuke	堀内 謙介
Horiuchi Kanjō	堀内 干城
Hoshina Shinji	星名 信二
Hoshina Zenshirō	保科 善四郎
Hoshino Naoki	星野 直樹
Hosokawa Karoku	細川 嘉六
Hosoya Chihiro	細谷 千博
Ichijō Sanetaka	一条 実孝
Ichiki Kitokurō	一木 喜徳郎
Ichimura Kesazō	市村 今朝蔵
Ichinomiya Reitarō	一宮 鈴太郎
Ida Iwakusu	井田 磐楠
Ikawa Tadao	井川 忠雄
Ikeda Hiroshi	池田 弘
Ikeda Seihin	池田 成彬
Imai Seiichi	今井 清一
Imamaki Yoshio	今牧 嘉雄
Imamura Hitoshi	今村 均
Inaba Masao	稲葉 正夫
Inahara Katsuji	稲原 勝治
Inoue Hideko	井上 秀子
Inoue Junnosuke	井上 準之助
Inoue Kaoru	井上 馨
Inoue Kiyosumi	井上 清純
Inoue Kyōshirō	井上 匡四郎
Inoue Nisshō	井上 日召
Inoue Shigemi	井上 成美
Inukai Tsuyoshi (Ki)	犬養 毅
Irie Tanenori	入江 種矩

Ishibashi Tanzan	石橋 湛山
Ishii Itarō	石射 猪太郎
Ishii Kikujirō	石井 菊次郎
Ishii Kō	石井 康
Ishikawa Shingo	石川 信吾
Ishiwara Kanji	石原 莞爾
Ishiwata Sōtarō	石渡 荘太郎
Isogai Rensuke	磯谷 廉介
Itagaki Seishirō	板垣 征四郎
Itō Hirobumi	伊藤 博文
Itō Masanori	伊藤 正徳
Itō Miyoji	伊東 巳代治
Itō Nobufumi	伊藤 述史
Itō Takashi	伊藤 隆
Iwabuchi Tatsuo	岩淵 辰雄
Iwakuro Hideo	岩畔 豪雄
Iwamura Seiichi	岩村 清一
Iwanaga Yūkichi	岩永 裕吉
Iwasaki Koyata	岩崎 小弥太
Iwata Ainosuke	岩田 愛之助
Izaka Takashi	井坂 孝
Kabayama Aisuke	樺山 愛輔
Kadono Jūkurō	門野 重九郎
Kagawa Toyohiko	賀川 豊彦
Kai Fumihiko	甲斐 文比古
Kaji Ryūichi	嘉治 隆一
Kajima Morinosuke	鹿島 守之助
Kakegawa Tomiko	掛川 トミ子
Kamei Kan'ichirō	亀井 貫一郎
Kami Shigenori	神 重徳
Kamikawa Hikomatsu	神川 彦松
Kanaya Hanzō	金谷 範三
Kaneko Kentarō	金子 堅太郎
Kan'in Kotohito (Prince)	閑院宮載仁
Kasai Jūji	笠井 重治
Kashiwagi Gien	柏木 義円
Kashiwagi Hideshige	柏木 秀茂
Katō Kanji	加藤 寛治
Katō Kanjū	加藤 勘十
Katō Taiichi	加藤 鐲一
Katō Takaaki (Kōmei)	加藤 高明
Katō Tomosaburō	加藤 友三郎
Katsura Tarō	桂 太郎
Kawada Isao	河田 烈

Kawagoe Shigeru	川越 茂	Maeda Torao	前田 虎雄
Kawai Misao	河合 操	Maeda Yonezō	前田 米蔵
Kawai Tatsuo	河相 達夫	Makino Nobuaki (Shinken)	牧野 伸顕
Kawakami Isamu	川上 勇	Makino Ryōzō	牧野 良三
Kawakami Jōtarō	河上 丈太郎	Matsuda Genji	松田 源治
Kaya Okinori	賀屋 興宣	Matsudaira Kōtō	松平 康東
Kayano Nagatomo	萱野 長知	Matsudaira Tsuneo	松平 恒雄
Kido Kōichi	木戸 幸一	Matsui Iwane	松井 石根
Kikuchi Takeo	菊地 武夫	Matsukata Kōjirō	松方 幸次郎
Kishi Michizō	岸 道三	Matsukata Saburō	松方 三郎
Kishi Nobusuke	岸 信介	Matsuki Yoshikatsu	松木 良勝
Kita Ikki	北 一輝	Matsumiya Jun	松宮 順
Kiyosawa Kiyoshi	清沢 洌	Matsumoto Jōji	松本 烝治
Kiyoura Keigo	清浦 奎吾	Matsumoto Kenjirō	松本 健次郎
Kobayashi Ichizō	小林 一三	Matsumoto Shigeharu	松本 重治
Kobayashi Jun'ichirō	小林 順一郎	Matsumoto Tadao	松本 忠雄
Kobayashi Seizō	小林 躋造	Matsuoka Komakichi	松岡 駒吉
Kobayashi Shōichirō	小林 正一郎	Matsuoka Yōsuke	松岡 洋右
Kodama Kenji	児玉 謙次	Matsushima Shikao	松島 鹿夫
Koga Mineichi	古賀 峯一	Matsushita Masatoshi	松下 正寿
Koike Chōzō	小池 張造	Mazaki Jinzaburō	真崎 甚三郎
Koiso Kuniaki	小磯 国昭	Miki Kiyoshi	三木 清
Koizumi Shinzō	小泉 信三	Mimurodo Yukimitsu	三室戸 敬光
Kojima Hideo	小島 秀雄	Minami Jirō	南 次郎
Komura Jutarō	小村 寿太郎	Minobe Ryōkichi	美濃部 亮吉
Kondō Nobutake	近藤 信竹	Minobe Tatsukichi	美濃部 達吉
Konoe Atsumaro	近衛 篤麿	Minoda Kyōki	蓑田 胸喜
Konoe Fumimaro	近衛 文麿	Misawa Shigeo	三沢 潤生
Kubo Hisaji	久保 久治	Mitani Taichirō	三谷 太一郎
Kuhara Fusanosuke	久原 房之助	Mitsuchi Chūzō	三土 忠造
Kunieda Kanji	邦枝 完二	Miyake Haruteru	三宅 晴輝
Kuno Osamu	久野 収	Miyaoka Tsunejirō	宮岡 恒次郎
Kuratomi Yūzaburō	倉富 勇三郎	Miyazaki Ryūsuke	宮崎 竜介
Kurihara Tadashi	栗原 正	Miyo Kazunari	三代 一就
Kurihara Yasuhide	栗原 安秀	Miyoshi Shigemichi	三好 重道
Kurusu Saburō	来栖 三郎	Mizuno Hironori	水野 広徳
Kushida Manzō	串田 万蔵	Mizuno Rentarō	水野 錬太郎
Kuwashima Kazue	桑島 主計	Mochizuki Keisuke	望月 圭介
Kuzū Yoshihisa	葛生 能久	Mori Kaku	森 恪
Li Hung-chang	李 鴻章	Mori Kōzō	森 広蔵
Mabuchi Itsuo	馬淵 逸雄	Morimoto Keizō	森本 慶三
Machida Chūji	町田 忠治	Morimura Ichizaemon	森村 市左衛門
Maeda Minoru	前田 稔	Morishima Gorō	守島 伍郎
Maeda Tamon	前田 多門	Mushakōji Kinhide	武者小路 公秀

Nagai Matsuzō	永井 松三	Ōmori Issei	大森 一声
Nagai Ryūtarō	永井 柳太郎	Ōno Ryūta	大野 龍太
Nagano Osami	永野 修身	Ōno Takeji	大野 竹二
Nagata Tetsuzan	永田 鉄山	Onoda Sutejirō	小野田 捨二郎
Naitō Hisahiro	内藤 久寛	Ōshima Hiroshi	大島 浩
Nakae Chōmin	中江 兆民	Ōsumi Mineo	大角 岑生
Nakagawa Tōru	中川 融	Ōta Kōzō	太田 耕造
Nakajima Chikuhei	中島 知久平	Ōtani Noboru	大谷 登
Nakajima Kumakichi	中島 久万吉	Ōtomo Nabio	大友 七備雄
Nakajima Shōzō	中島 省三	Ōuchi Hyōe	大内 兵衛
Nakajima Tetsuzō	中島 鉄蔵	Ōyama Iwao	大山 巌
Nakamura Hideichirō	中村 秀一郎	Ozaki Hotsumi	尾崎 秀実
Nakamura Shintarō	中村 震太郎	Ozaki Yukio	尾崎 行雄
Nakano Seigō	中野 正剛	Rōyama Masamichi	蠟山 政道
Nakatani Takeyo	中谷 武世	Ryū Shintarō	笠 信太郎
Nakayama Ryūji	中山 竜次	Saburi Sadao	佐分利 貞男
Nakazawa Benjirō	中沢 弁次郎	Sagōya Tomeo	佐郷屋 留雄
Nanjō Kaneo	南条 金雄	Saigō Takahide	西郷 隆秀
Ninomiya Saburō	二宮 三郎	Saionji Kimmochi	西園寺 公望
Nishida Kitarō	西田 幾多郎	Saionji Kinkazu	西園寺 公一
Nishida Mitsugu	西田 税	Saitō Hiroshi	斎藤 博
Nishihara Kamezō	西原 亀三	Saitō Makoto	斎藤 実
Nishio Suehiro	西尾 末広	Saitō Sōichi	斎藤 惣一
Nishio Toshizō	西尾 寿造	Saitō Takao	斎藤 隆夫
Nishiyama Tsutomu	西山 勉	Sakatani Yoshirō	阪谷 芳郎
Nitobe Inazō	新渡戸 稲造	Sakomizu Hisatsune	迫水 久常
Nomura Kichisaburō	野村 吉三郎	Sakonji Seizō	左近司 政三
Nomura Minoru	野村 実	Sanekawa Tokijirō	実川 時次郎
Nomura Naokuni	野村 直邦	Sasaki Mosaku	佐々木 茂索
Obama Toshie	小汀 利得	Sassa Hiroo	佐々 弘雄
Obata Tadayoshi	小畑 忠良	Satō Naotake	佐藤 尚武
Obata Toshishirō	小畑 敏四郎	Satō Tetsutarō	佐藤 鉄太郎
Ogata Sadako	緒方 貞子	Sawada Setsuzō	沢田 節蔵
Ogata Taketora	緒方 竹虎	Sawamoto Yorio	沢本 頼雄
Ōgi Kazuto	扇 一登	Sawayanagi Masatarō	沢柳 政太郎
Ōguchi Kiroku	大口 喜六	Shiba Katsuo	柴 勝男
Ogura Masatsune	小倉 正恒	Shiba Kinpei	芝 均平
Oikawa Koshirō	及川 古志郎	Shibayama Kaneshirō	柴山 兼四郎
Oka Takasumi	岡 敬純	Shibusawa Eiichi	渋沢 栄一
Okabe Saburō	岡部 三郎	Shidehara Kijūrō	幣原 喜重郎
Okada Keisuke	岡田 啓介	Shigemitsu Mamoru	重光 葵
Ōkawa Shūmei	大川 周明	Shimada Katsunosuke	島田 勝之助
Ōkubo Toshimichi	大久保 利通	Shimada Saburō	島田 三郎
Ōkuma Shigenobu	大隈 重信	Shimada Shigetarō	嶋田 繁太郎

Shimanaka Yūsaku 嶋中雄作

Shimomura Shōsuke 下村正助

Shimonaka Yasaburō 下中弥三郎

Shimura Gentarō 志村源太郎

Shinobu Junpei 信夫淳平

Shinobu Seizaburō 信夫清三郎

Shiratori Toshio 白鳥敏夫

Shōda Kazue 勝田主計

Soeda Juichi 添田寿一

Suehiro Izutarō 末弘巌太郎

Suekuni Masao 末国正雄

Suetsugu Nobumasa 末次信正

Sugimura Yōtarō 杉村陽太郎

Sugiyama Gen 杉山元

Suma Yakichirō 須磨弥吉郎

Sun Yat-sen (I-hsien) 孫逸仙

Sung Che-yuan 宋哲元

Suzuki Bunji 鈴木文治

Suzuki Bunshirō 鈴木文史朗

Suzuki Kantarō 鈴木貫太郎

Suzuki Kisaburō 鈴木喜三郎

Suzuki Mosaburō 鈴木茂三郎

Suzuki Teiichi 鈴木貞一

Suzumoto Boku 鈴本穆

Tachi Sakutarō 立作太郎

Tagawa Daikichirō 田川大吉郎

Taira Teizō 平貞蔵

Tajima Shigeji 田島繁二

Takada Toshitane 高田利種

Takagi Sōkichi 高木惣吉

Takagi Yasaka 高木八尺

Takahashi Gen'ichirō 高橋元一郎

Takahashi Korekiyo 高橋是清

Takahashi Masao 高橋正雄

Takahashi Sankichi 高橋三吉

Takamine Jōkichi 高峰譲吉

Takarabe Takeshi 財部彪

Takase Shin'ichi 高瀬真一

Takashima Seiichi 高島誠一

Takayanagi Kenzō 高柳賢三

Takekoshi Yosaburō 竹越与三郎

Tamura Yōzō 田村羊三

Tanabe Sōei 田辺宗英

Tanaka Giichi 田中義一

Tani Masayuki 谷正之

Taniguchi Naomi 谷口尚真

Tatekawa Yoshitsugu 建川美次

Terada Inejirō 寺田稲次郎

Terao Susumu 寺尾進

Terasaki Tarō 寺崎太郎

Terashima Takeshi 寺島健

Terauchi Hisaichi 寺内寿一

Terauchi Masatake 寺内正毅

Tōgō Heihachirō 東郷平八郎

Tōgō Shigenori 東郷茂徳

Tōhata Seiichi 東畑精一

Tōjō Hideki 東条英機

Tokonami Takejirō 床次竹二郎

Tokutomi Sohō 徳富蘇峰

Tomioka Sadatoshi 富岡定俊

Tomita Tsunejirō 富田常次郎

Tōyama Hidezō 頭山秀三

Tōyama Mitsuru 頭山満

Toyoda Kumao 豊田隈雄

Toyoda Soemu 豊田副武

Toyoda Teijirō 豊田貞次郎

Tsuchida Yutaka 土田豊

Tsuda Sōkichi 津田左右吉

Tsuji Masanobu 辻政信

Tsukui Tatsuo 津久井竜雄

Tsumura Jūsha 津村重舎

Tsunoda Jun 角田順

Tsurumi Yūsuke 鶴見祐輔

Tsushima Juichi 津島寿一

Uchida Shinya 内田信也

Uchida Yasuya 内田康哉

Uchimura Kanzō 内村鑑三

Ueda Kenkichi 植田謙吉

Ueda Teijirō 上田貞次郎

Uehara Etsujirō 植原悦二郎

Uehara Yūsaku 上原勇作

Ugaki Kazushige 宇垣一成

Ugaki Matome 宇垣纏

Umezu Yoshijirō 梅津美治郎

Uramatsu Samitarō 浦松佐美太郎

Ushiba Nobuhiko 牛場信彦

Ushiba Tomohiko 牛場友彦

Ushiroku Jun 後宮淳

Usui Katsumi	臼井 勝美	Yamazaki Tatsunosuke	山崎 達之輔
Wada Toyoji	和田 豊治	Yanagawa Heisuke	柳川 平助
Wakasugi Kaname	若杉 要	Yanagida Kunio	柳田 国男
Wakatsuki Reijirō	若槻 礼次郎	Yanaihara Tadao	矢内原 忠雄
Wakimura Yoshitarō	脇村 義太郎	Yasui Kaoru	安井 郁
Wang Ching-wei	汪 精衛	Yasui Tatsuya	安井 達弥
Watanabe Chifuyu	渡辺 千冬	Yasuma Norikatsu	安間 徳勝
Watanabe Sahei	渡辺 佐平	Yokoi Tadao	横井 忠雄
Watsuji Tetsurō	和辻 哲郎	Yokota Kisaburō	横田 喜三郎
Yamagata Aritomo	山県 有朋	Yokoyama Ichirō	横山 一郎
Yamaguchi Tamon	山口 多聞	Yonai Mitsumasa	米内 光政
Yamakawa Tadao	山川 端夫	Yoshida Masuzō	吉田 益三
Yamamoto Gonnohyōe (Gonbei)	山本 権兵衛	Yoshida Shigeru	吉田 茂
Yamamoto Hidesuke	山本 英輔	Yoshida Zengo	吉田 善吾
Yamamoto Isoroku	山本 五十六	Yoshino Sakuzō	吉野 作造
Yamamoto Kamejirō	山元 亀次郎	Yoshino Shinji	吉野 信次
Yamamoto Tatsuo	山本 達雄	Yoshioka Yayoi	吉岡 弥生
Yamamoto Teijirō	山本 悌二郎	Yoshizawa Kenkichi	芳沢 謙吉
Yamamura Katsurō	山村 勝郎	Yoshizawa Seijirō	吉沢 清次郎
Yamamuro Sōbun	山室 宗文	Yuan Shih-k'ai	袁 世凱
Yamanashi Katsunoshin	山梨 勝之進	Yuasa Kurahei	湯浅 倉平
Yamashita Kamesaburō	山下 亀三郎	Yūki Toyotarō	結城 豊太郎

CONTRIBUTORS

ASADA SADAO was graduated from Carleton College (B.A. 1958) and Yale University (Ph.D. 1963). He is professor of international history in the Political Science Department, Faculty of Law, Doshisha University. He has contributed articles on American diplomatic history and U.S.-Japanese relations to the *American Historical Review, Doshisha American Studies, Kokusai seiji* (International Relations), and various Japanese publications.

MICHAEL K. BLAKER was graduated from the University of Southern California (B.A. 1962, M.A. 1967) in international relations and is currently a Ph.D. candidate at Columbia University, where he is completing a dissertation on Japanese international negotiating behavior before World War II. His essay on the Advisory Council on Foreign Relations is included in *Columbia Essays in International Affairs, Volume VII: The Deans' Papers, 1971* (1973). He was an instructor in Japanese at Manhattanville College (1969-70) and bibliographer of the Japan Documentation Center of the East Asian Institute, Columbia University (1970-71). As administrative assistant for the Kawaguchi Conference, he co-edited with Dale K. A. Finlayson the "Proceedings" of the conference.

DOROTHY BORG, a senior research associate of the East Asian Institute, Columbia University, is a graduate of Wellesley College (A.B. 1923) and Columbia University (M.A. 1931, Ph.D. 1946) and was previously a research associate of the Institute of Pacific Relations (1938-59) and the East Asian Research Center, Harvard University (1959-61). Her publications include *American Policy and the Chinese Revolution, 1925-1928* (1947), *The United States and the Far Eastern Crisis of 1933-1938* (1964), and, as compiler, *Historians and American Far Eastern Policy* (1966).

CHŌ YUKIO, professor at Tokyo University of Foreign Studies, is a graduate of the Economics Department, Tokyo University (1948). A specialist on monetary and banking policy and the history of Japanese economic thought, he is the author of *Nihon keizai shisōshi kenkyū: burujoa-demokurashii no hatten to zaisei kinyū seisaku* (A History of Japanese Economic Thought: The Development of Bourgeois Democracy and Financial and Monetary Policy) (1963), *Doru kiki* (Dollar Crisis) (1965), and *En no shōrai* (The Future of the Yen) (1970); and editor of *Jitsugyō no shisō* (Business Thought) (1964) and *Kindai Nihon keizai shisōshi* (A History of Economic Thought in Modern Japan) (2 vols., 1969).

WARREN I. COHEN, professor of history at Michigan State University, graduated from Columbia College in 1955, received an M.A. from the Fletcher School of Law and Diplomacy in 1956, and, after three years as a line officer with the U.S. Navy, Pacific Fleet, received a Ph.D. from the University of Washington in 1962. His writings include *The American Revisionists: The Lessons of Intervention in World War I* (1967) and *America's Response to China* (1971).

WAYNE S. COLE, professor of history at the University of Maryland, graduated from Iowa State Teachers College in 1946 and received his doctorate from the

University of Wisconsin in 1951. His writings include *America First: The Battle against Intervention, 1940-1941* (1953); *Senator Gerald P. Nye and American Foreign Relations* (1962); *An Interpretive History of American Foreign Relations* (1968); "Senator Key Pittman and American Neutrality Policies, 1933-1940," *Mississippi Valley Historical Review* (March 1960); and "American Entry into World War II: A Historiographical Appraisal," *Mississippi Valley Historical Review* (March 1957).

TERUKO CRAIG received a B.A. from Manhattanville College in 1952, has taught Japanese in the Far Eastern Languages Department of Harvard University, and is now working on a book on childhood in Japan.

DALE K. A. FINLAYSON graduated from Vassar College in 1963 and received her M.A. in Chinese history from Columbia University in 1971. As administrative secretary for the Kawaguchi Conference, she co-edited with Michael K. Blaker the "Proceedings" of the conference and has overseen the production of this volume as publications assistant at the East Asian Institute (1970-72). She now does free-lance editing in East Asian studies from her home in Edinburgh, Scotland.

FUJIWARA AKIRA, professor in the Faculty of Sociology, Hitotsubashi University, is a graduate of the Faculty of Literature, Tokyo University (1949). A specialist on the political history of modern Japan, he is the author of *Gunjishi* (History of the Japanese Military) (1965), *Nihon teikokushugi* (Japanese Imperialism) (1968), and *Taiheiyō sensō* (The Pacific War) (1970).

LLOYD C. GARDNER, professor of history and chairman of the Department of History, Rutgers College, was graduated from Ohio Wesleyan University in 1956 and received his M.A. (1957) and Ph.D. (1960) degrees from the University of Wisconsin. He is the author of *Economic Aspects of New Deal Diplomacy* (1964) and *Architects of Illusion: Men and Ideas in American Foreign Relations, 1941-1949* (1970) and is co-author, with Walter LaFeber and Thomas McCormick, of *History of American Foreign Policy* (forthcoming).

NORMAN A. GRAEBNER is Edward R. Stettinius professor of modern American history at the University of Virginia. He received his B.S. degree from Milwaukee State Teachers College (1939), his M.A. from the University of Oklahoma (1940), and his Ph.D. from the University of Chicago (1949). Among his writings are *Empire on the Pacific* (1955), *Cold War Diplomacy* (1962), and *Ideas and Diplomacy* (1964). He is co-author of *A History of the United States* (2 vols., 1970), *A History of the American People* (1970), and *Recent United States History* (1972) and is editor of *An Uncertain Tradition: American Secretaries of State in the Twentieth Century* (1961) and *Manifest Destiny* (1968).

EDGAR C. HARRELL, chief of the Economic Analysis Division at the Agency for International Development's Mission to Thailand, received his B.S. from Dickinson College in 1955 and his Ph.D. in economics from Columbia University in 1972. His writings include "Japan and Southeast Asia in the 1970s" (discussion paper for the Council on Foreign Relations, 1970) and "Japanese Economic Assistance–Past Trends and Projections" (presented at AID Mission Directors Conference, 1972).

WALDO H. HEINRICHS, JR. is professor of American diplomatic history at the University of Illinois, Urbana-Champaign. A graduate of Harvard (B.A. 1949, Ph.D. 1960), he is the author of *American Ambassador: Joseph C. Grew and the Development of the United States Diplomatic Tradition* (1966) and "Bureaucracy and Professionalism in the Development of American Career Diplomacy," in *Twentieth Century American Foreign Policy*, edited by John Braeman, Robert H. Bremner, and David Brody (1971).

HOSOYA CHIHIRO, professor in the Faculty of Law, Hitotsubashi University, is a graduate of the Faculty of Law, Tokyo University (1945) and received his Doctor of Law from Kyoto University in 1961. A specialist on diplomatic history and international relations, his writings include *Shiberia shuppei no shiteki kenkyū* (A Historical Study of the Siberian Expedition) (1955), *Roshia kakumei to Nihon* (The Russian Revolution and Japan) (1972), and as co-author, *Sangoku dōmei Nisso chūritsu jōyaku* (The Tripartite Pact and the Japanese-Soviet Neutrality Pact), Vol. 5 of *Taiheiyō sensō e no michi* (The Road to the Pacific War) (1962).

G. CAMERON HURST, assistant professor of history and East Asian studies at the University of Kansas, received his A.B. degree from Stanford in 1963 and his Ph.D. from Columbia University in 1972. His translations include "Politics and Man in the Contemporary World," in Masao Maruyama, *Thought and Behaviour in Modern Japanese Politics*, edited by Ivan I. Morris (1969) and a forthcoming edition (co-translated with David Dilworth) of Fukuzawa Yukichi's *Bunmeiron no gairyaku* (Outline Theory of Civilization). He is the author of "The Reign of Go-Sanjō and the Revival of Imperial Power," *Monumenta Nipponica* (Spring 1972), and two articles—"The Structure of the Heian Court: Some Thoughts on the Nature of 'Familial Authority' in Heian Japan" and "The Development of the *Insei*: A Problem in Japanese History and Historiography"—will appear in *Medieval Japan: Essays in Institutional History*, edited by John W. Hall (forthcoming).

IMAI SEIICHI, professor in the Faculty of Liberal Arts and Sciences, Yokohama City University, and a specialist on the political history of modern Japan, is a graduate of Tokyo University Faculty of Law (1945). He is the author of *Taishō demokurashii* (Taishō Democracy) (1966) and co-author of *Shōwashi* (A History of the Shōwa Era) (1959) and *Shōwashi no shunkan* (Decisive Moments in Shōwa History) (1966).

AKIRA IRIYE is professor of American diplomatic history at the University of Chicago. A graduate of Haverford College (A.B. 1957) and Harvard University (Ph.D. 1961), he is the author of *After Imperialism: The Search for a New Order in the Far East* (1965), *Across the Pacific: An Inner History of American-East Asian Relations* (1967), and *Pacific Estrangement: Japanese and American*

Expansion (1972), and editor of *U.S. Policy in China* (1968). In Japanese his works include *Bei-Chū kankei no imēji* (Sino-American Relations: A Study in Images) (1966) and *Nihon no gaikō* (Japanese Diplomacy) (1966).

MITSUKO IRIYE received her Ph.D. in comparative literature from Harvard University in 1969. She is co-author, with William H. McNeill, of *Modern Asia and Africa* (1971) and is currently writing a study of Nagai Kafū's early years.

ITŌ TAKASHI, a graduate of the Faculty of Literature, Tokyo University (1958), and the Cultural Science Research Division, Tokyo University Graduate School (1961), is associate professor of Japanese history in the Faculty of Literature, Tokyo University. A specialist on the political history of modern Japan, he is the author of *Shōwa shoki seijishi kenkyū* (A Study of the Political History of the Early Shōwa Period: The London Naval Conference Controversy) (1969) and co-editor of *Kido Kōichi nikki* (The Diary of Kido Kōichi) (2 vols., 1966), *Kido Kōichi kankei bunsho* (Kido Kōichi Papers) (1966), *Ni-ni-roku jiken hiroku* (Confidential Records of the February 26 Incident) (1971-72), and *Gendaishi o tsukuru hitobito* (Makers of Modern History) (1971-72).

KAKEGAWA TOMIKO, lecturer in the International Relations Department of Tsudajuku University, is a graduate of the English Literature Department of Tsudajuku (1954) and of the Sociology Research Division, Tokyo University Graduate School (1962). A specialist in the history of mass communications, she is the author of "Amerika no shōzasshi 'The Masses' to sono keiseisha tachi" (A Little American Magazine, *The Masses*, and Its Creators), *Tōkyō Daigaku Shinbun Kenkyūjo kiyō* (Tokyo University Newspaper Research Institute Bulletin) (1967), and "Tennō kikan setsu jiken" (The Emperor-Organ Theory Incident), in *Kindai Nihon seiji shisōshi* (A History of Modern Japanese Political Thought), edited by Hashikawa Bunsō and Matsumoto Sannosuke, Vol. 2 (1970).

RICHARD W. LEOPOLD, William Smith Mason professor of American history at Northwestern University, received his B.A. from Princeton University in 1933 and his Ph.D. from Harvard University in 1938. He is author of *The Growth of American Foreign Policy: A History* (1962), *Elihu Root and the Conservative Tradition* (1954), and *Robert Dale Owen: A Biography* (1940). He is co-editor, with Arthur S. Link and Stanley Cohen, of and contributor to *Problems in American History* (1952, 4th ed. 1972) and has contributed to *Change and Continuity in Twentieth-Century America*, edited by John Braeman et al. (1964), and *Interpreting American History: Conversations with Historians*, edited by John A. Garraty (1970). His other writings deal with the American presidency, sectionalism in American foreign policy, World War I, the *Foreign Relations* series, and the role of the federal government and presidential libraries in research by students of American foreign policy.

ERNEST R. MAY, professor of history and director of the Institute of Politics at Harvard University, received a Ph.D. from the University of California (Los Angeles) in 1951, served as a naval officer first at sea and then as a historian for the Joint Chiefs of Staff, and joined the Harvard faculty in 1954. His writings include *The World War and American Isolation, 1914-1917* (1959), *Imperial Democracy: The Emergence of the United States as a Great Power* (1961), and *American Imperialism: A Speculative Essay* (1968); he is co-editor, with James C. Thomson, Jr., of *American-East Asian Relations: A Survey* (1972). He has been since 1960 chairman of the Harvard History Department's Committee on American-Far Eastern Policy Studies and since 1970 chairman of the American Historical Association's Committee on American-East Asian Relations.

MISAWA SHIGEO, professor of economics at Saitama University, is a graduate of the Tokyo University Faculty of Law (1951). A specialist on political theory and the political process, he is the author of "Seisaku kettei katei no gaikan" (A Study of the Decision-Making Process), *Nenpō seijigaku 1967* (Political Science Annual, 1967) and "Furuton Iinkai hōkokusho ni miru Eikoku kōmuin seido kaikaku no mondaiten" (Some Problems in the Reform of the British Civil Service as Reflected in the Fulton Committee Report), *Saitama Daigaku shakai kagaku ronshū* (Saitama University Social Science Review) (1969), co-editor of *Shiryō sengo nijūnenshi I: seiji* (Sources for a Twenty-Year History of Postwar Japan, I: Politics) (1966), and translator into Japanese of R. T. McKenzie, *British Political Parties* (2 vols., 1965).

MITANI TAICHIRŌ, associate professor in the Tokyo University Faculty of Law, from which he graduated in 1960, is a specialist on the political history of Japan. He is the author of *Nihon seitō seiji no keisei: Hara Takashi no seiji shidō no tenkai* (The Establishment of Party Politics in Japan: The Development of Hara Takashi's Political Leadership) (1967) and editor of *Yoshino Sakuzō*, Vol. 48 of *Nihon no meicho* (Great Books of Japan) (1972).

MUSHAKŌJI KINHIDE, a graduate of Gakushūin University (1952), is a professor at Sophia University and director of its International Relations Research Institute. A specialist on international politics, he is the author of *Gendai Furansu no seiji ishiki* (Political Consciousness in Contemporary France) (1960), *Kokusai seiji to Nihon* (International Politics and Japan) (1967), *Heiwa kenkyū nyūmon* (Introduction to the Study of Peace) (1970), *Takyokuka jidai no Nihon gaikō* (Japanese Diplomacy in an Age of Multi-Polarization) (1971), and *Kōdō kagaku to kokusai seiji* (Behavioral Science and International Politics) (1972).

NAKAMURA HIDEICHIRŌ, professor at Senshū University Economics Department, is a graduate of the Economics Department of Keio University (1947). A specialist on economic policy and industrial organization theory, he is the author of *Chūken kigyōron* (Medium Industries) (1964), *Daikibo jidai no owari* (End of the Era of Big Industry) (1970) and *Bentyā bijinesu* (Venture Business) (1971), and co-author of *Nihon sangyō to kasen taisei* (Japanese Industry and Oligopoly) (1966).

NINOMIYA SABURŌ, a graduate of Tokyo University (1953), is a research analyst in foreign affairs in the Research and Legislative Reference Department of the National Diet Library.

OGATA SADAKO received her B.A. from the University of the Sacred Heart (1951), her M.A. from Georgetown University (1953), and her Ph.D. from the University of California at Berkeley (1963). A specialist on international relations, she is lecturer at International Christian University and the author of *Defiance in Manchuria: The Making of Japanese Foreign Policy, 1931-1932* (1964).

SHUMPEI OKAMOTO, associate professor of history at Temple University, is a graduate of Aoyama Gakuin University (1954), Anderson College (B.A. 1959), and Columbia University (M.I.A. 1962, Ph.D. 1969). He is the author of *The Japanese Oligarchy and the Russo-Japanese War* (1970).

JAMES C. THOMSON, JR., lecturer on history and curator of the Nieman Fellowships for Journalism at Harvard University, was graduated from Yale University in 1953, was a Yale-Clare Scholar at Cambridge University (B.A. 1955, M.A. 1959), and received his Ph.D. from Harvard in 1961. From 1960 to 1966 he served as an East Asian policy specialist successively on the staff of a congressman, in the Department of State, and at the White House. His writings include *While China Faced West: American Reformers in Nationalist China, 1928-1937* (1969) and "How Could Vietnam Happen?" in *Who We Are: An Atlantic Chronicle of the United States and Vietnam*, edited by R. Manning and M. Janeway (1969); he is co-editor, with Ernest R. May, of *American-East Asian Relations: A Survey* (1972).

USUI KATSUMI, professor in the Faculty of Literature at Kyushu University, is a graduate of the Faculty of Literature, Kyoto University (1948). A specialist on modern Japanese history, he is the author of *Nitchū sensō* (The Second Sino-Japanese War) (1967), *Nitchū gaikōshi: hokubatsu no jidai* (A History of Sino-Japanese Diplomatic Relations: The Northern Expedition Period) (1971), and *Nihon to Chūgoku—Taishō jidai* (Japan and China during the Taishō Period) (1972), and editor of *Nihon gaikō nenpyō narabi ni shuyō bunsho* (Chronology and Major Documents of Japanese Foreign Relations) (1955).

H. PAUL VARLEY, associate professor of Japanese history at Columbia University, received his B.A. from Lehigh University (1952) and his M.A. (1961) and Ph.D. (1964) from Columbia University. He is the author of *The Ōnin War* (1967), *A Syllabus of Japanese Civilization* (1968), *The Samurai* (1970), *Imperial Restoration in Medieval Japan* (1971), and *Japanese Culture: A Short History* (1973).

RUSSELL F. WEIGLEY, professor of history at Temple University, received his B.A. from Albright College in 1952 and his Ph.D. from the University of Pennsylvania in 1956. His writings include *Quartermaster General of the Union Army: A Biography of M. C. Meigs* (1959), *Towards an American Army: Military Thought from Washington to Marshall* (1962), *History of the United States Army* (1967), *The Partisan War: The South Carolina Campaign of 1780-1782* (1970), and *The American Way of War: A History of United States Military Policy and Strategy* (1973). He edited *The American Military: Readings in the History of the Military in American Society* (1969).

MIRA WILKINS received her A.B. from Radcliffe College in 1953 and her Ph.D. from Cambridge University in 1957. She has taught at Columbia University, Union College, Smith College, and the University of Massachusetts (Amherst). She is the author of *The Emergence of Multinational Enterprise: American Business Abroad from the Colonial Era to 1914* (1970), "American Radiator Company in Europe," *Business History Review* (Autumn 1969), and "The Businessman Abroad," *The Annals* of the American Academy of Political and Social Science (November 1966); co-author of *American Business Abroad: Ford on Six Continents* (1964); and research associate on *Ford: Decline and Rebirth*, by Allan Nevins and Frank Ernest Hill (1963), and *Timber and Men: The Weyerhaeuser Story*, by Ralph Hidy, Frank Ernest Hill, and Allan Nevins (1963). She is presently a member of the editorial advisory board of *Business History Review*.

YAMAMURA KATSURŌ is a graduate of Tokyo University Faculty of Law (1948). A professor in the Economics Department at Kanazawa University, he is a specialist on Japanese financial history and policy. He is the author of "Zaisei kikan" (Financial Organs) in *Shōwa zaiseishi* (Financial History of the Shōwa Era), Vol. 2 (1956), and "Kaikei seido" (The Accounting System) in *Shōwa zaiseishi*, Vol. 17 (1959).

STUDIES OF THE EAST ASIAN INSTITUTE

The Ladder of Success in Imperial China, by Ping-ti Ho. New York: Columbia University Press, 1962.

The Chinese Inflation, 1937-1949, by Shun-hsin Chou. New York: Columbia University Press, 1963.

Reformer in Modern China: Chang Chien, 1853-1926, by Samuel Chu. New York: Columbia University Press, 1965.

Research in Japanese Sources: A Guide, by Herschel Webb with the assistance of Marleigh Ryan. New York: Columbia University Press, 1965.

Society and Education in Japan, by Herbert Passin. New York: Bureau of Publications, Teachers College, Columbia University, 1965.

Agricultural Production and Economic Development in Japan, 1873-1922, by James I. Nakamura. Princeton: Princeton University Press, 1966.

Japan's First Modern Novel: Ukigumo of Futabatei Shimei, by Marleigh Ryan. New York: Columbia University Press, 1967.

The Korean Communist Movement, 1918-1948, by Dae-Sook Suh. Princeton: Princeton University Press, 1967.

The First Vietnam Crisis, by Melvin Gurtov. New York: Columbia University Press, 1967.

Cadres, Bureaucracy, and Political Power in Communist China, by A. Doak Barnett. New York: Columbia University Press, 1967.

The Japanese Imperial Institution in the Tokugawa Period, by Herschel Webb. New York: Columbia University Press, 1968.

Higher Education and Business Recruitment in Japan, by Koya Azumi. New York: Teachers College Press, Columbia University, 1969.

The Communists and Chinese Peasant Rebellions: A Study in the Rewriting of Chinese History, by James P. Harrison, Jr. New York: Atheneum, 1969.

How the Conservatives Rule Japan, by Nathaniel B. Thayer. Princeton: Princeton University Press, 1969.

Aspects of Chinese Education, edited by C. T. Hu. New York: Teachers College Press, Columbia University, 1969.

Documents of Korean Communism, 1918-1948, by Dae-Sook Suh. Princeton: Princeton University Press, 1970.

Japanese Education: A Bibliography of Materials in the English Language, by Herbert Passin. New York: Teachers College Press, Columbia University, 1970.

Economic Development and the Labor Market in Japan, by Koji Taira. New York: Columbia University Press, 1970.

The Japanese Oligarchy and the Russo-Japanese War, by Shumpei Okamoto. New York: Columbia University Press, 1970.

Imperial Restoration in Medieval Japan, by H. Paul Varley. New York: Columbia University Press, 1971.

Japan's Postwar Defense Policy, 1947-1968, by Martin E. Weinstein. New York: Columbia University Press, 1971.

Election Campaigning Japanese Style, by Gerald L. Curtis. New York: Columbia University Press, 1971.

China and Russia: The "Great Game," by O. Edmund Clubb. New York: Columbia University Press, 1971.

Money and Monetary Policy in Communist China, by Katharine Huang Hsiao. New York: Columbia University Press, 1971.

The District Magistrate in Late Imperial China, by John R. Watt. New York: Columbia University Press, 1972.

Law and Policy in China's Foreign Relations: A Study of Attitudes and Practice, by James C. Hsiung. New York: Columbia University Press, 1972.

Pearl Harbor as History: Japanese-American Relations, 1931-1941, edited by Dorothy Borg and Shumpei Okamoto, with the assistance of Dale K. A. Finlayson. New York: Columbia University Press, 1973.

Japanese Culture: A Short History, by H. Paul Varley. New York: Praeger, 1973.

Doctors in Politics: The Political Life of the Japan Medical Association, by William E. Steslicke. New York: Praeger, 1973.

Japan's Foreign Policy, 1868-1941: A Research Guide, edited by James William Morley. New York: Columbia University Press, 1973.

The Japan Teachers Union: A Radical Interest Group in Japanese Politics, by Donald Ray Thurston. Princeton: Princeton University Press, 1973.

Palace and Politics in Prewar Japan, by David Anson Titus. New York: Columbia University Press, 1973.

The Idea of China: Aspects of Geographic Myth and Theory, by Andrew March. Devon, England: David and Charles, 1974.